The History of Accounting

GARLAND REFERENCE LIBRARY OF THE HUMANITIES (VOL. 1573)

The History of Accounting
An International Encyclopedia

Edited by
Michael Chatfield
Richard Vangermeersch

GARLAND PUBLISHING, INC.
New York & London
1996

Library of Congress Cataloging-in-Publication Data

The History of accounting : an international encyclopedia / edited by Michael
    Chatfield, Richard Vangermeersch.
            p.   cm. — (Garland reference library of the humanities ; vol.
    1573)
        Includes bibliographical references and index.
        ISBN 0-8153-0809-4 (hardcover : alk. paper)
        1. Accounting—History.   I. Chatfield, Michael.
    II. Vangermeersch, Richard G. J.   III. Series.
        HF5605.H573   1996
        657'.09—dc20   95-20710
                                                                        CIP

Cover illustration copyright Tony Stone Images.
Cover design by Lawrence Wolfson Design, New York.

Figures appearing on pages 417, 418, and 419 are reprinted, courtesy of the author, from Hanns-Martin
W. Schoenfeld, *Cost Terminology and Cost Theory: A Study of Its Development and Present State in Central Europe,* Center for International Education and Research in Accounting (Urbana, Ill., 1974), pp. 62,
96, 98, 101, 103.

Printed on acid-free, 250-year-life paper
Manufactured in the United States of America

Contents

Introduction

This is the first encyclopedia to focus on the history of accounting and accounting thought. There are, however, a significant number of other types of encyclopedias and handbooks in the field of accounting. Beach and Thorne, for instance, edited the third edition of *The American Business and Accounting Encyclopedia* in 1901. Williams and Doris edited the 1956 four-volume *Encyclopedia of Accounting Systems*. Ronald Press, starting in 1923, published the *Accountants' Handbook* through seven editions. These are just some of the examples in the field of accounting. Hence, there is a well-established tradition of the encyclopedia-type format in accounting.

A rich literature has also been developed in the history of accounting and accounting thought, much more than is realized by accountants, accounting students, and accounting professors. Three examples of such works are Brown's *A History of Accounting and Accountants* (1905), Littleton's *Accounting Evolution to 1900* (1933), and Previts and Merino's *A History of Accounting in America* (1979). Deinzer's *Development of Accounting Thought* (1965) and Chatfield's *A History of Accounting Thought* (1974) are examples of works on the history of accounting thought. The academic base for this encyclopedia has been well laid out by many scholars.

This encyclopedia has as its underpinnings the prior works of its two editors. Michael Chatfield's *A History of Accounting Thought* has been translated into Japanese, Korean, and Chinese. Furthermore, Chatfield edited *Contemporary Studies in the Evolution of Accounting Thought* in 1968 and *The English View of Accountants' Duties and Responsibilities* in 1978, and has published a significant number of articles about the history of accounting.

Richard Vangermeersch developed two tracks of interest in the field of accounting history. One is the reporting of financial data in annual reports, best typified by his 1979 book, *Financial Reporting Techniques in 20 Industrial Companies since 1861*. The second is the search for lost ideas in the field of cost/management accounting, best typified by his 1988 book, *Alexander Hamilton Church: A Man of Ideas for All Seasons* and his July 1983 *Management Accounting* article, with Henry R. Schwarzbach, "Why We Should Account for the Fourth Cost of Manufacturing." Vangermeersch has further detailed reasons for the study of our accounting heritage: developing support for proposals for change with the use of past writings; enlarging the pantheon of accounting heroes; and pointing out timeless topics of a controversial nature.

There is also a strong institutional base for accounting history. Perhaps the most significant was the founding in 1973 of The Academy of Accounting Historians. The Academy has greatly increased the number of articles, notes, and monographs in accounting history through the *Accounting Historians Journal*, the *Accounting Historians Notebook*, its working paper series, its monograph series, its classic reprint series, and its conference proceedings. Six international congresses on the history of accounting have been held—Brussels, 1970; Atlanta, 1976; London, 1980; Pisa, 1984; Sydney, 1988; and Kyoto, 1992. There are accounting history societies in a number of countries, among them Italy, Japan, Australia, and New Zealand. The Accounting Hall of Fame was founded in 1950 at The Ohio State University. A significant number of "new" journals have been added to the publication outlets for accounting history: *Abacus*; *Accounting*; *Accounting Business Research*; *Accounting Organizations and Society*; *Auditing and Accountability*; *Critical Perspectives on Accounting*; *International Journal of Accounting Education & Research*; *Research in Accounting Regulation*. The publication of *The History of Accounting: An International Encyclopedia* follows by only two years the 500th anniversary celebrations in 1994 of Luca Pacioli's treatise on accounting. There were five major celebrations. They took place in Edinburgh, sponsored by the Institute of Chartered Accountants of Scotland; in Venice, sponsored by the European Accounting Association; and in Sansepolcro, Italy, the birthplace of Pacioli, three celebrations were held. The first celebration in Sansepolcro was sponsored by an Italian consortium of the Piero della Francesca di Sansepolcro Foundation, the Municipality of Sansepolcro, the Department of Mathematics at the University of Florence, the Province of Arezzo, the Region Toscana, and the Italian Ministries of Treasury and Scientific Research. The other two Sansepolcro celebrations were sponsored by the Pacioli Society, which was founded by two accounting professors from Seattle University, David E. Tinius and William L. Weis.

Pacioli, while sometimes labeled the "Father of Accounting," is probably more aptly described as the key promoter of accounting. Luca Pacioli belonged to the Franciscan Order and was a renowned professor of mathematics at various Italian universities. He included an accounting treatise "Particulars of Reckonings and their Recording" as part of his encyclopedia of mathematics *Summa De Arithmetica, Geometria, Proportioni, et Proportionalita*. Pacioli utilized the "Method of Venice" as the basis for his accounting treatise. Venice was then a key trading network. Pacioli did have some business experience which, undoubtedly, led him to see the great significance of the double entry system of accounting. Because of the encyclopedic nature of Pacioli's book, different writers in *The History of Accounting: An International Encyclopedia* will refer to the accounting treatise in it with varying titles. Some will use the full title of Pacioli's book. Others will refer to the title of the specific treatise on accounting.

The editors intend this encyclopedia to be used by a variety of readers. It is a single-volume reference work for junior and senior accounting majors, M.S. and M.B.A. majors in accounting, Ph.D. students in accounting, and accounting professors. It is also useful for scholars in other academic areas, and for researchers in both public accounting firms and in large corporations.

Accounting students can use this encyclopedia as a source for short essays and for an historical background in class discussions. M.S. and M.B.A. accounting majors can find it useful as an historical background to their studies. Limited bibliographies provide sufficient information for most written assignments. Ph.D. students, as well, would find the text useful and the bibliographies helpful for further research. Accounting researchers in public accounting and in larger corporations should find this encyclopedia very helpful in developing a paragraph or two on the history of a particular problem area. Accounting professors will be able to obtain a better perspective on research topics as well as use the encyclopedia as a guide for further research.

The editors went through several steps in the process of developing this encyclopedia. The members of The Academy of Accounting Historians were surveyed in late 1990 regarding their thoughts about the topics to be covered in the encyclopedia. Over 120 responses were forthcoming. The editors searched the *Accounting Historians Journal*, the *Accounting Historians Notebook*, and their extensive libraries for further ideas on topics for inclusion. The editors spent a week with this data and with the index to each of Chatfield's books on the history of accounting thought to develop a tentative list of entries in June of 1991. That list was tightened to avoid redundancies and then was increased to cover topics that were more important than originally thought.

The editors are confident that this encyclopedia fills a significant need in the literature of accounting. They have devoted four years to this effort and have learned much about the history of accounting and accounting thought in the process. They hope that you will have this same experience.

Michael Chatfield
Richard Vangermeersch

Acknowledgments

The first acknowledgment is to Lois Pazienza, secretary of the Accounting Department of the University of Rhode Island. Lois has worked with Richard Vangermeersch on a number of long projects in accounting history and this project was, by far, the longest and largest. Pazienza means "patience" in Italian. She needed all of that for this four-year project. We would also like to acknowledge the contributors for their outstanding efforts.

List of Entries

Contributors

Michael Chatfield holds B.A. and M.B.A. degrees from the University of Washington, a D.B.A. from the University of Oregon, and is a certified public accountant. He is the author of three previous books on accounting history and coauthor of a cost accounting textbook. He is a professor of accounting at Southern Oregon State College.

Richard Vangermeersch has a B.S. degree from Bryant College, a Liberal Arts Certificate and an M.S. from the University of Rhode Island, and a Ph.D. from the University of Florida. He is both a certified public accountant and a certified management accountant. He is the author and the editor of a number of previous books on accounting history and is a professor of accounting at the University of Rhode Island.

The other contributors to the encyclopedia are thanked for their efforts by the editors.

Ajay Adhikari
Assistant Professor of Accounting
American University

Rick Antle
Professor of Accounting
Yale University

Tito Antoni
Emeritus Professor of Accounting
University of Pisa

C. Edward Arrington
U. J. LeGrange Research Fellow
Louisiana State University

Stanley Baiman
Professor of Accounting
Wharton School
University of Pennsylvania

Vahé Baladouni
Professor of Accounting
University of New Orleans

Lu Ann G. Bean
Assistant Professor of Accounting
Pittsburg State University

Victoria Beard
Assistant Professor of Accounting
University of North Dakota

Maureen H. Berry
Associate Professor of Accounting
University of Illinois

Robert Bloom
Professor of Accounting
John Carroll University

Edmund J. Boyle
Associate Professor of Accounting
University of Rhode Island

Peter Boys
Faculty of Social Science
University of Kent at Canterbury

Carl W. Brewer
Assistant Professor of Accounting
Sam Houston State University

Peter Brownell
Arthur Andersen Professor
University of Melbourne

Dale A. Buckmaster
Professor of Accounting
University of Delaware

Homer H. Burkett
Associate Professor of Accounting
University of Mississippi

Thomas J. Burns
Professor of Accounting
Ohio State University

Kees Camfferman
Professor of Accounting in the Department
of Economics
Vrije Universiteit
Amsterdam

John D. Cathcart
Archivist
Bentley College

R. J. Chambers
Emeritus Professor of Accounting
University of Sydney

Nadine Chandar
Ph.D. Student
Case Western Reserve University

Gyan Chandra
C. Rollin Niswonger Professor of Accountancy
Miami University

Michael Chatfield
Professor of Accounting
Southern Oregon State College

Robert Chatov
Associate Professor of Accounting and Law
State University of New York
Buffalo

Frank L. Clarke
Professor of Accounting
University of Newcastle

Edward N. Coffman
Professor of Accounting
Virginia Commonwealth University

W. W. Cooper
Nadya Kozmetsky Scott Centennial Fellow
University of Texas
Austin

Allen T. Craswell
Professor of Acounting
University of Sydney

Srikant M. Datar
Associate Professor of Accounting
Stanford University

Harry Z. Davis
Professor of Accounting
Baruch College
City University of New York

Graeme W. Dean
Associate Professor of Accounting
University of Sydney

Jean-Guy Degos
Professor of Accounting
Centre de Recherches et D'études en Gestion
University of Bordeaux

Joel B. Dirlam
Emeritus Professor of Economics
University of Rhode Island

Mortimer A. Dittenhofer
Professor of Accounting
Florida International University

Patricia C. Douglas
Doctoral Student in Accounting
Virginia Commonwealth University

Timothy S. Doupnik
Professor of Accounting
University of South Carolina

Angela M. Downey
Lecturer in Accounting
University of Lethbridge

Pamela J. Duke
Ph.D. Candidate
Georgia State University

John H. Engstrom
Professor of Accounting
Northern Illinois University

Marc J. Epstein
Visiting Professor of Accounting
Harvard University

William L. Ferrara
David M. Beights Professor in Accounting
Stetson University

Kent T. Fields
Associate Professor of Accounting
Auburn University

Eric G. Flamholtz
Professor of Accounting
University of California
Los Angeles

Richard K. Fleischman
KPMG Peat Marwick Accounting Professor in
International Business
John Carroll University

Dale L. Flesher
Arthur Andersen and Company Alumnus Lecturer in Accountancy
University of Mississippi

Tonya K. Flesher
Professor of Accounting
University of Mississippi

David A. R. Forrester
Lecturer in Accounting
University of Strathclyde

Anne Fortin
Professor of Accounting
Université du Quèbec à Montréal

George Foster
Paul L. and Phylis Wattis Professor of
Management
Stanford University

John Freear
Professor of Accounting
University of New Hampshire

Giuseppe Galassi
Professor of Concern Economics and Accounting
University of Parma

S. Paul Garner
Dean Emeritus of College of Commerce and
Business Administration
University of Alabama

Marshall A. Geiger
Associate Professor of Accounting
University of Rhode Island

Robert W. Gibson
Associate Professor of Accounting
Deakin University

Leonard Goodman
Deloitte and Touche Accounting Faculty Fellow
Rutgers University
New Brunswick

Julia Grant
Assistant Professor of Accounting
Case Western Reserve University

O. Finley Graves
Associate Professor of Accounting
University of Mississippi

David O. Green
Professor of Accounting
Baruch College
City University of New York

Guo Daoyang
Professor of Accounting
Zhongnan University of Finance and Economics

Mary E. Harston
Assistant Professor of Accounting
St. Mary's University

Leon E. Hay
Ralph L. McQueen Distinguished Professor of
Accounting
University of Arkansas

Laurie Henry
Assistant Professor
Old Dominion University

Esteban Hernández-Esteve
Subdirector
Bank of Spain

Mark Higgins
Associate Professor of Accounting
University of Rhode Island

Yoshihiro Hirabayashi
Professor of Accounting
Osaka City University

Karen L. Hooks
Professor of Accounting
University of South Florida

James O. Horrigan
Professor of Accounting
University of New Hampshire

Hugh P. Hughes
Associate Professor of Accounting
Georgia State University

Yuji Ijiri
Robert M. Trueblood University Professor
of Accounting and Economics
Carnegie Mellon University

Kozo Iwanabe
Professor of Accounting
Saitama University

Alicia Jaruga
Head of the Department of Accounting
University of Lodz

Roxanne T. Johnson
Assistant Professor of Accounting
University of Scranton

Robert Jordan
Assistant Professor of Accounting
University of Wisconsin—Superior

Roger Hugh Juchau
Foundation Professor
Accounting and Marketing
University of Western Sydney

Valery V. Kovalev
Professor of Accounting
St. Petersburg Institute of Commerce
and Economics

Robert M. Kozub
Associate Professor of Accounting
University of Wisconsin—Milwaukee

Harold Q. Langenderfer
KPMG Peat Marwick Professor of Professional
Accounting
University of North Carolina

Thomas A. Lee
Culverhouse Chair Professor of Accounting
University of Alabama

Hekinus Manao
Ph.D. Student
Case Western Reserve University

R. Penny Marquette
Professor of Accounting
University of Akron

Jimmy W. Martin
Professor of Accounting
University of Montevallo

Richard V. Mattessich
Emeritus Professor of Accounting
University of British Columbia

Robert K. Mautz
Retired Professor of Accounting
University of Michigan

Kevin H. McBeth
Assistant Professor of Accounting
Weber State University

Gary A. McGill
Assistant Professor of Accounting
University of Florida

Peter L. McMickle
Professor of Accounting
Memphis State University

C. J. McNair
Associate Professor of Accounting
Babson College

Barbara D. Merino
O. J. Curry Professor of Accounting
Regents Professor
University of North Texas

Paul J. Miranti Jr.
Associate Professor of Accounting
Rutgers University
New Brunswick

Maurice Moonitz
Emeritus Professor of Accounting
University of California
Berkeley

Kenneth S. Most
Professor of Accounting
Florida International University

George J. Murphy
Professor of Accounting
University of Saskatchewan

Roger R. Nelson
Vice Chairman
Management Consulting
Ernst and Young

Christopher Nobes
Coopers Deloitte Professor of Accounting
University of Reading

Hiroshi Okano
Associate Professor of Accounting
Osaka City University

Joseph R. Oliver
Professor of Accounting
Southwest Texas State University

Paul Pacter
Professor of Accounting in Residence at
Stamford Campus
University of Connecticut

Jacob B. Paperman
Professor of Accounting
California State University
Fullerton

Felix Pomeranz
Professor of Accounting
Florida International University

Boris Popoff
Associate Professor of Accounting
University of Otago

Grover L. Porter
Professor of Accounting
University of Alabama
Huntsville

Jeffrey W. Power
Assistant Professor of Accounting
University of Rhode Island

Frank R. Rayburn
Alumni and Friends Professor of Accounting
University of Alabama, Birmingham

Alan J. Richardson
Associate Professor of Accounting
Queens Univeristy

Alfred R. Roberts
Professor of Accounting
Georgia State University

Elizabeth Roberts
Professor of Accounting
University of Melbourne

Rodney K. Rogers
Ph.D. Candidate
Case Western Reserve University

John A. Ruane
Director of Media Relations
Arthur Andersen and Company

Richard Ruggles
Emeritus Professor of Economics
Yale University

Stanley C. W. Salvary
Professor of Accounting
Canisius College

William D. Samson
Professor of Accounting
University of Alabama

Robert E. Schlosser
Professor of Accounting
Rutgers University; Newark Graduate School

Dieter Schneider
Professor of Accounting
Ruhr-Universität Bochum

Hanns-Martin Schoenfeld
H. T. Scovill Professor of Accounting
University of Illinois

Henry R. Schwarzbach
Professor of Accounting
University of Rhode Island

Wilbert H. Schwotzer
Associate Professor of Accounting
Georgia State University

Adrianne E. Slaymaker
Visiting Professor of Accounting
University of Windsor

Jaroslav V. Sokolov
Professor of Accounting
St. Petersburg Institute of Commerce and
Economics

A. A. Sommer
Former Commissioner of the Securities and
Exchange Commission and Former Member of
the Financial Accounting Standards Advisory
Committee

John B. Sperry
Professor of Accounting
Virginia Commonwealth University

Henry Francis Stabler
Professor of Accounting
Georgia State University

George J. Staubus
Michael N. Chevkovich Professor of Accounting
University of California, Berkeley

Howard F. Stettler
Emeritus Professor of Accounting
University of Kansas

Ross E. Stewart
Associate Professor of Accounting
Seattle Pacific University

Joyce A. Strawser
Assistant Professor of Accounting
Baruch College
City University of New York

Sudarwan
Ph.D. Student
Case Western Reserve University

Edward P. Swanson
KPMG Peat Marwick Professor of Accounting
Texas A & M University

Anne Jeannette Sylvestre
Associate Professor of Accounting
University of South Alabama

Anna Szychta
Professor of Accounting
University of Lodz

J. Bruce Tabb
Professor of Accounting
University of Auckland

Deborah W. Thomas
Assistant Professor of Accounting
University of Arkansas

James E. Thomashower
Executive Director
National Association of State Boards of
Accountancy Inc.

Joel E. Thompson
Associate Professor of Accounting
Northern Michigan University

Anthony Maxwell Tinker
Professor of Accounting
Baruch College
City University of New York

Rasoul Tondkar
Associate Professor of Accounting
Virginia Commonwealth University

Roger R. Trask
Chief Historian
U.S. General Accounting Office

Atsuo Tsuji
Emeritus Professor of Accounting
Osaka City University

James J. Tucker III
Associate Professor of Accounting
Widener University

Thomas N. Tyson
Associate Professor of Accounting
St. John Fisher College

A. van Seventer
Emeritus Professor of Accounting
Stanford University

Richard Vangermeersch
Professor of Accounting
University of Rhode Island

Curtis C. Verschoor
Professor of Accounting
DePaul University

Frans Volmer
Professor of Accounting
Rijksuniversiteit Limburg

Xiao Wei
Ph.D. Candidate
Department of Accounting
The People's University of China

Murray C. Wells
Director
Graduate School of Business
University of Sydney

Paul F. Williams
Professor of Accounting
North Carolina State University

Carel M. Wolk
Associate Professor of Accounting
University of Tennessee
Martin

Charles W. Wootton
Associate Professor of Accounting
Eastern Illinois University

Arthur R. Wyatt
Professor of Accounting
University of Illinois

Basil S. Yamey
Emeritus Professor of Accounting
London School of Economics

Stephen J. Young
Ph.D. Candidate
Case Western Reserve University

Edward W. Younkins
M.B.A. Director and Chairman of Business and
Administration
Wheeling Jesuit College

Stephen A. Zeff
Herbert S. Autrey Professor of Accounting
Rice University

Vernon K. Zimmerman
I.B.E. Distinguished Professor of Accounting
University of Illinois

The History of Accounting

A

A Statement of Basic Accounting Theory (ASOBAT)

The fifth statement by the American Accounting Association (AAA) on the development of accounting principles, standards, and theory was published in 1966 by an AAA committee chaired by Charles T. Zlatkovich. This statement marked a significant change from its predecessors in that the committee broadened the scope of accounting to an information system for the entity, whether it be profit or nonprofit oriented. The committee also included an internal-management focus as well as an external user focus. The committee stressed four basic standards, which have become well used in the literature: relevance, verifiability, freedom from bias, and quantifiability. It also stressed the importance of communication.

The report recommended the use of multi-column statements to show historical cost and current cost results. It also considered the use of a statistical range for the reporting of accounting information. ASOBAT is an example of a timely and a timeless piece of accounting literature.

Richard Vangermeersch

See also American Accounting Association; Definitions of Accounting; Generally Accepted Accounting Principles; Historical Cost

Academy of Accounting Historians

The Academy of Accounting Historians was formed in 1973 to serve as an autonomous, service-oriented organization to assist academicians and practitioners throughout the world to further their study in the many aspects of the evolution of accounting thought and practice. In addition to holding annual meetings, the academy holds meetings of trustees, officers, and other key personnel to transact the affairs of the organization. The academy has an organizational structure consisting of a number of committees and publication outlets to assist in accomplishing its objectives. Its publications include *Accounting Historians Journal*, *Accounting Historians Notebook*, and a monograph series.

The academy has two research centers. The Accounting History Research Center is located on the campus of Georgia State University, and the Tax History Research Center is located on the campus of the University of Mississippi. The primary purposes of the centers are to promote research in accounting history and tax history, respectively. The academy has an extensive videotape library on the Mississippi campus. The academy has established several awards, including the Richard G. Vangermeersch Manuscript Award and the Hourglass Award, to recognize significant contributions to the literature of accounting history.

Membership in the academy is open to persons in all countries who are interested in accounting history. As of 1994, the membership (individuals and institutional affiliates) totals approximately 875 representing more than 34 different countries.

Edward N. Coffman

Bibliography

Coffman, E.N., A.R. Roberts, and G.J. Previts. "A History of the Academy of Accounting Historians, 1973–1988," *Accounting Historians Journal*, December 1989, pp. 155–206.

See also AMERICAN ACCOUNTING ASSOCIATION; ARCHIVES AND SPECIAL COLLECTIONS IN ACCOUNTING; BRIEF, RICHARD P.; GARNER, S. PAUL; JOHNSON, H. THOMAS; PREVITS, GARY JOHN; SPACEK, LEONARD; STONE, WILLIARD E.; WELLS, MURRAY CHARLES

Accounting and the Accountant: Portrayals

As one of the classical information-generating systems, accounting can be traced to the first known civilizations of Mesopotamia, Egypt, and Central America. From these earliest times to the present—a time span of about 6,000 years—accounting has served societies in various and increasingly complex capacities. The list of informational needs that accounting has served in the past and can serve in the future is a long one. Suffice it to say that it has served for a wide range of control objectives; determining as well as planning profits; cost-benefit analyses; and the formulation of major financial and economic policy decisions in a variety of contexts and within a diversity of institutions.

The earliest performer of the accounting function was the *scribe*. With his ability to read and write, the scribe rendered indispensable services to many classes of society. In ancient Egypt, boys before the age of puberty were recruited with promises of a good future and sent to schools in the temple or palace for instruction in writing and calculating. Along with technical skills, they were also taught the importance of accuracy and honesty. Upon completion of the program of study, each was pronounced "scribe" and appointed as apprentice to some experienced official. Scribes were known, above all, for their service in public administration and commerce. Without scribes, centralized governments would hardly have been possible. In commerce, it was the duty of the scribe to put business transactions in writing and to see that the parties to agreements complied with the legal provisions.

With the advent of capitalism around A.D. 1000, both accounting and the accountant went through a major transformation. By the 1400s a new accounting methodology, known as the double entry method, was developed and later refined and elaborated. This method, which is to this day the dominant accounting method, has helped accountants to deal intelligently with the economic events of the capitalist era. The method has served as a conceptual framework for analyzing business transactions and distinguishing between capital and income. Over its long existence, the double entry method has drawn the attention and admiration of many intellectuals. In his *Wilhelm Meister* (1824), Goethe calls this method one of the "finest inventions of the human intellect." A political economist, Werner Sombart, stated that "double entry bookkeeping is born of the same spirit as the system of Galileo and Newton" and that "[it] discloses to us the cosmos of the economic world." Finally, Arthur Cayley, one of the founders of modern matrix algebra, called the double entry method "in fact, like Euclid's theory of ratios, an absolutely perfect one."

Aside from the view of orderliness and rationality, the double entry method is also seen as a metaphor for good and evil. From Shakespeare to Defoe, Agatha Christie, James Joyce, and others, there is no dearth of examples. Here it should suffice to mention two of them. In his *Robinson Crusoe* (1719), Daniel Defoe writes: ". . . I began to comfort my self as well as I could, and to set the good against the evil, that I might have something to distinguish my case from worse, and I stated it very impartially, like debtor and creditor, the comforts I enjoyed against the miseries I suffered." Some two-and-a-half centuries later, we read in B.S. Johnson's amusing novel, *Christie Malry's Own Double Entry* (1973): "Perhaps every bad must have its corresponding good. An extension might be called Moral Double Entry."

The double entry method of accounting should not, however, be equated with the discipline of accounting. Despite its critical role, the double entry method is only one of the many methods available to the accountant. Moreover, the accounting discipline is not a mere aggregate or collection of methods and techniques. As a discipline, accounting possesses a generalized and systematic body of knowledge together with well-developed methods and techniques of application.

Since the turn of the twentieth century, accounting and accountants have rapidly risen to professional status. The recognition of this status is based on three fundamental attributes: (1) a high degree of generalized and systematic knowledge; (2) primary orientation to public interest rather than to individual self-interest; and (3) control of behavior through a code of ethics. As early as 1932, *Fortune* magazine acknowledged that accounting had attained professional status: "Today," as stated in the magazine, "it is no overstatement to say that there are preeminently three professions upon whose ethics as well as upon whose skill modern society depends: law, medicine, and certified public accounting." It must perhaps be emphasized that professional status is proffered upon those who have undergone a rigorous university education and conform to a standard of professional qualifications governing admission.

Like so many other professionals, accountants, too, are often reminded of their humble beginnings. The most popular of the images of the early accountant is that of a thin, calculating individual seated in isolation on a high stool, wearing green eyeshades, and bent over a massive ledger. But what of his personality? The great English essayist, Charles Lamb, depicts an accountant of the early nineteenth century as follows: "With Tipp [the accountant] form was everything. His life was formal. His actions seemed ruled with a ruler." Elsewhere, he writes: "The striking of the annual balance in the company's books (which, perhaps, differed from the balance of last year in the sum of 25 l. 1 s. 6 d.) occupied his days and nights for a month previous." And a little later he notes: ". . . to a genuine accountant . . . the fractional farthing is as dear to his heart as the thousands which stand before it."

Such uncomplimentary lines are followed on occasion by downright derogatory remarks. This particular one by F.B. Modell is from the *New Yorker* (1962). Aggressive-looking young woman to studious-looking young man at a cocktail party: "You certainly have a wonderful way of expressing yourself for a certified public accountant."

While old images of the accountant still persist, today's accountant emerges with a distinctly different portent. Far from being yesteryear's technician engaged merely in repetitive or routine tasks, the modern accountant is an articulate, diplomatic, and independent professional. He brings into his work not only a sophisticated technical body of knowledge, but also a creative mind in the solution of problems. He is people oriented and sensitive to the consequences that flow from the solutions of problems.

Some of the challenges that face the professional accountant are of societywide interest, such as generating information that can be useful in evaluating social problems and public problems of considerable intricacy. A growing social consciousness in the United States continues to bring out the potential of accounting in assisting in the solution to such problems as corporate social performance, urban problems, pollution and crime control, public programs, human resources, and economic development.

The challenges of accounting practice precipitate, in turn, new challenges for the academician-scholar. The accounting academician undertakes the required research to push the frontiers of accounting knowledge forward. Research activity in accounting spreads far and wide. Some research activities are, however, of greater critical importance to the field than others. The most challenging research problems are those that deal with the creation of new perspectives that may at times be partial modifications of older views and, at other times, the complete displacement of the familiar and "safe" vantage points.

The type of research problem connected with the growth of accounting knowledge is that which raises searching questions about the workings of our continually changing environment. This type of problem is critical to the real progress of the field. To penetrate and illuminate the "twilight zones" of accounting knowledge is the primary motivation of basic research in accounting. To the extent that the general public holds to the stereotypical view of the accountant working with a quill pen on a high stool at a countinghouse desk, accountants and accounting are limited in meeting these tests.

Vahé Baladouni

Bibliography

"Accountant in Fiction," News and Views, *CPA Journal*, June 1981, p. 6. (Excerpt from *Accountancy*, February 1981).

Beard, V. "Accounting in Literature: Faulkner's *The Hamlet*," *Woman CPA*, July 1987, pp. 24–25, 29.

———. "Popular Culture and Professional Identity: Accountants in the Movies," *Accounting, Organizations, and Society*, vol. 19, no. 3, 1994, pp. 303–318.

Boys, P.G. "Novel Image of Accountants," *Accountant's Magazine*, July 1982, pp. 254–261.

———. "Taking a Look at the Books," *Man-*

agement Accounting (Eng.), December 1981, pp. 22–23.

Cayley, A. *The Principles of Book-keeping by Double Entry,* Cambridge University Press, 1894.

"Certified Public Accountants," *Fortune,* June 1932, pp. 63–66, 101–102.

Givens, H.R. "'Novel' Accountant," *Massachusetts CPA Review,* April–May 1966, pp. 215–219.

MacDonald, W., ed. *The Works of Charles Lamb,* vol. 1. London: J.M. Dent and Company, 1903.

Modell, F.B. "You certainly have a way of expressing yourself for a Certified Public Accountant," *New Yorker,* May 19, 1962, p. 48.

Parkinson, J.M. "Daniel Defoe: Accomptant," *Accounting History,* December 1986, pp. 33–49.

Smith, L.M. "Novel Approach," *New Accountant,* December 1991, pp. 10–12, 34.

Sombart, W. *Der Moderne Kapitalismus.* Leipzig: Duncker and Humbolt, 1902.

See also DOUBLE ENTRY BOOKKEEPING: ORIGINS; EGYPT; PROFESSIONAL ACCOUNTING BODIES; SCRIBES; SOCIAL RESPONSIBILITIES OF ACCOUNTANTS; SOMBART, WERNER

Accounting Education in the United States

Education is a malleable social construct characterized by change, uncertainty, and controversy. It is a series of well-intentioned compromises between academics and practitioners, students and administrators, business and government. A complete education includes both an understanding of where we have come from and an ability to evaluate alternative paths to where we are going.

Brief History

In colonial America, an apprenticeship in a local merchant's "compting house" was considered appropriate training for a career in commerce and bookkeeping. Later, as the United States was expanding both economically and geographically and as the corporate form of business gained legal stature following the *Dartmouth College v. Woodward* decision (1819), apprenticeships were no longer adequate to support the growing record-keeping demands of large-scale private and public enterprises, such as railroads. Independent teachers began offering classes in practical accounting, not only teaching the rules of bookkeeping in classrooms far removed from any business setting but frequently teaching from texts they had developed themselves. These teachers included James Bennett, Thomas Turner, John Caldwell Colt, Thomas Jones, George Comer, E.K. Losier, and Benjamin Franklin Foster. In the 1850s, private accounting teachers followed the migration westward. E.G. Folsom's mercantile college in Cleveland, under H.B. Bryant and H.D. Stratton, eventually grew into a chain of over 50 commercial business colleges, teaching the rules of bookkeeping to, among others, John D. Rockefeller.

Unregulated, proprietary business colleges continued to expand into the 1900s under educators such as Silas Sadler Packard and George Soulé. At the same time, accountants began seeking professional recognition through both state CPA legislation and efforts to establish accounting programs at universities. In 1883 the Wharton School at the University of Pennsylvania introduced the first sustained accounting course at the college level, followed by the University of Chicago, Dartmouth and New York University. Henry Rand Hatfield became the first full-time accounting professor in 1904 at the University of California at Berkeley. By 1915, 37 more universities had opened schools of commerce or business. These early efforts laid the foundation for accounting in higher education as we know it today.

Entrance into the college curriculum was not without its problems. Suitable textbooks were scarce, accounting professors had to be recruited from practice or from more established departments of economics, and curriculum quality varied widely among schools. Furthermore, many practicing accountants questioned the rationale behind substituting university coursework for on-the-job experience.

The AAA

In 1916, to deal with these growing concerns, the American Association of University Instructors in Accounting (AAUIA) was founded. Specifically excluding teachers in proprietary business schools, the AAUIA sought to raise academic accounting standards, to regularize the collegiate accounting curriculum, and to build respect for accounting educators. The first 20 years of association, however, saw only moderate progress toward these goals. By 1934 only nine college programs had accounting courses extending beyond the first two years, and academics and practitioners were still in disagreement over which group should develop the 120-hour accounting curriculum and who should set the guidelines for accrediting accounting programs in higher education. In 1936, the AAUIA changed its name to the American Accounting Association (AAA) and modified its mission to emphasize accounting research over strictly pedagogical concerns. The AAA remains today the largest organization of accounting educators in the world, active both in theoretical research and in accounting education.

Who Benefits from Accounting Education?

The history of accounting education is a history of unanswered questions and practical compromises. Who, for example, should be considered the primary beneficiary of accounting education: the individual student, the public accounting firms that hire them, colleges, faculty, textbook publishers, regulatory agencies, for-profit businesses, investors, or society in general? The answer matters. It makes a difference in the curriculum, in funding, in instructional pedagogy and in the direction accounting education will take in the future.

Several ideologies compete for attention when trying to answer this question. Human-capital theory, for example, emphasizes the role of education in developing human capital to support economic growth and development. Part of the U.S. educational debate since the 1880s when urbanization, immigration, and industrialization forced schools to take on broader social functions, human-capital theory and American pragmatism provided the foundation both for the turn-of-the-century introduction of vocational education in high schools and the entrance of accounting into the university curriculum. In a parallel vein, social-engineering theorists posit education as a powerful instrument of government in maintaining the social order.

If the student, rather than society, is identified as the primary beneficiary of education, which is more valuable for that individual: a classical liberal education in arts, humanities, and science or a conventional business school curriculum? Which undergraduate route will produce the best practitioner: a well-educated individual conversant in social and economic theory, problem solving and critical thinking or

a technically proficient, procedure-wise undergraduate accounting major ready to enter the workforce upon graduation? Combining the best of liberal and professional education into a single accounting program is the goal of the new 150-hour requirement.

150-Hour Requirement

The most appropriate structure for accounting education has yet to be settled upon. In 1959, the American Institute of Certified Public Accountants (AICPA) recommended a bachelor's degree in accounting as the minimum educational requirement for CPAs; now, however, a 120-hour degree is considered insufficient in light of the complexities of the global economy. A master's degree in accountancy, on the other hand, provides extra training that many firms are not ready to pay for, and M.B.A. programs prepare managers rather than accountants. Law and medical schools are frequently cited as models of excellence in professional education, yet true professional schools of accountancy, established at several universities in the 1970s as sites for advanced applied-accounting research, are too much of a commitment for most universities to support. The 150-hour requirement represents the latest compromise in setting the formal structure of professional accounting education.

Curriculum and Standards

Historically, a number of institutional stakeholders have shared, sometimes uneasily, responsibility for setting curriculum and maintaining accounting education standards. The AICPA, representing practitioners, has had a powerful, if indirect, voice in curricular matters based on its administration of the semiannual uniform CPA examination. Complaints that the CPA examination drives the college accounting curriculum are as old as the examination itself. The American Assembly of Collegiate Schools of Business (AACSB), founded in 1916, accredits both graduate and undergraduate business faculty and curriculum, thereby influencing all aspects of accounting education. The AAA has tended to defer to the AICPA and the AACSB on accreditation matters, but, periodically, concern that accounting become a service discipline for business schools stimulates the move for separate accreditation of accounting programs. Both public accounting firms and private businesses exert influence on the college accounting curriculum through their hiring patterns and their financial support of university programs. The Securities and Exchange Commission (SEC), the Internal Revenue Service (IRS), and the Financial Accounting Standards Board (FASB), of course, need only change regulations to have these changes reflected in college textbooks. And, finally, while the faculty have the ultimate power to select the textbooks from which they teach, the choices are often similar enough to make form, not content, a driving factor in that selection.

Curriculum Content

Responding to these diverse interest groups, accounting programs have increased considerably the technical content of their courses since the days when colonial apprentices were taught "casting accounts." Such additions include auditing, external reporting, cost and managerial accounting, taxes, not-for-profits, information systems, international accounting, business law, and ethics. But as technical content increased, nontechnical areas of the curriculum, such as history and critical thought, were often left out, and in 1959, two reports, by Frank C. Pierson and by Robert Aaron Gordon and James Edward Howell, severely criticized the quality of business education and suggested that accounting be regarded primarily as a managerial-support tool. Three risks, then, are associated with a poorly balanced accounting curriculum: failure to attract the brightest students, not being accepted as a legitimate academic field, and the threat that accounting will lose its leadership role and be reduced to a tool of management. Although professional associations and academic publications have long acknowledged these risks and have offered an open forum for curricular reform, changes have been slow in coming.

Philosophies of Teaching

The problem of how to teach accounting is another continuing educational dilemma. On the one hand, supported by the Progressive Education movement and John Dewey's emphasis on experiential learning, the case study and the problem format, which aim at duplicating practice, have long dominated the American accounting classroom. Likewise, internships and an experience requirement for the CPA certificate have been strongly supported by practitioners. One pedagogical alternative, however, places theory development at the forefront of the university's educational mission. Accounting students, for example, should graduate with a good working knowledge of various foundational theories currently being used worldwide to establish accounting principles. Only in this way, it is argued, can students effectively question, and thereby improve, current practice. This more radical approach to accounting education emphasizes the role of imagination, creative thinking, and conceptual skills over the more routinely acquired practical accounting techniques.

Assessment

The issue of how to assess academic progress is equally problematic. Since Edward L. Thorndike first introduced the concept of education as a scientific profession in the early 1900s, accounting educators have supported rigorous factual testing as the preferred method of determining academic success. Present-day educational reformers question whether the profession, and the student, will benefit more by the current system of limiting access through rigorous undergraduate major requirements or by encouraging diversity among students and letting the demands of the profession select the fittest.

Professors and Practitioners

Since the fifteenth century when Luca Pacioli gained notoriety for bringing double entry bookkeeping out of the monasteries into the hands of the merchants, there has been a perceived communication gap between accounting educators and accounting practitioners. Reinforcing this distinction between the work of academics and practitioners, in 1967 both the AAA and the AACSB supported the doctoral degree as a requirement for university accounting faculty, in effect mandating a strong research component to the work of accounting professors. In 1979, the AAA Schism Committee noted that academic research was not being directed toward improving practice. Later efforts, such as the introduction in 1987 of *Accounting Horizons*, a journal published by the AAA to be readable by and interesting to both educators and accounting practitioners, and the 1988 Committee on the Relationship between Practitioner and Academic Communities, have continued the work to bridge the gap between professors and practitioners.

Accounting Education Research

The academic accounting community has been slow to recognize the importance of research in accounting education. Although *Accounting Review* included a short section on education from its first issue in 1926 until 1986 and the AAA's Accounting Education Series documents a history of concern over educational reform, only since the early 1980s have national journals dedicated exclusively to accounting-education research appeared on library shelves: *Journal of Accounting Education, Issues in Accounting Education* and *Accounting Educators' Journal.*

Reform

In 1986, the Bedford Committee on the Future Structure, Content, and Scope of Accounting Education recommended a major reorganization of accounting education. In 1989, in *Perspectives on Education: Capabilities for Success in the Accounting Profession,* the Big Eight public accounting firms expressed similar concerns over the quality of accounting students. To help implement the needed improvements in accounting education, they funded the Accounting Education Change Commission (AECC) to challenge colleges and universities, through a program of grants, to rethink all aspects of curriculum, course design, teaching techniques, and educational philosophy. Through the coordinated efforts of practitioners and academics, fundamental changes in accounting education are being developed and tested so that accountants are prepared for an active leadership role in the global economy of the twenty-first century.

Victoria Beard

Bibliography

Anderson, W.T., E.K. St. Pierre, and R.L. Benke Jr. *Essays on Accounting Education.* Harrisonburg, VA: Center for Research in Accounting Education, 1987.

Flesher, D.L. *The Third Quarter Century of the American Accounting Association, 1966–1991.* Sarasota, FL: American Accounting Association, 1991.

Gordon, R.A., and J.E. Howell. *Higher Education for Business.* New York: Columbia University Press, 1959.

Pierson, F.C., et al. *Education of American Businessmen: A Study of University-College Programs in Business Administration.* New York: McGraw-Hill, 1959.

Previts, G.J., and B.D. Merino. *A History of Accounting in America: An Historical Interpretation of the Cultural Significance of Accounting.* New York: John Wiley & Sons, 1979.

Zeff, S.Z. *American Accounting Association: Its First Fifty Years, 1916–1966.* Sarasota, FL: American Accounting Association, 1966. Reprint, 1991.

See also AMERICAN ACCOUNTING ASSOCIATION; AMERICAN INSTITUTE OF CERTIFIED PUBLIC ACCOUNTANTS; BENTLEY, HARRY CLARK; BIG EIGHT ACCOUNTING FIRMS; CERTIFIED PUBLIC ACCOUNTANT EXAMINATION: THE EARLY YEARS (1896–1930); CHARTERED ACCOUNTANTS EXAMINATIONS IN ENGLAND AND WALES; COLONIAL AMERICA, ACCOUNTING IN; COMPUTING TECHNOLOGY IN THE WEST: THE IMPACT ON THE PROFESSION OF ACCOUNTING; DEBIT AND CREDIT; GARNER, S. PAUL; GRAHAM, WILLARD J.; HASKINS, CHARLES WALDO; HATFIELD, HENRY RAND; JONES, THOMAS; LITTLETON, A.C.; MONTGOMERY, ROBERT HIESTER; PACIOLI, LUCA; PATON, WILLIAM ANDREW; PERSONIFICATION OF ACCOUNTS; SELLS, ELIJAH WATT; SOULÉ, GEORGE; SPRAGUE, CHARLES EZRA; STERRETT, JOSEPH EDMUND; TRUEBLOOD, ROBERT MARTIN; WILDMAN, JOHN RAYMOND

Accounting Hall of Fame

The Accounting Hall of Fame was established in 1950 at Ohio State University for the purpose of honoring accountants who have made or are making significant contributions to accounting in the twentieth century. Criteria for nomination and election to the Hall of Fame include: recognition as an authority in a particular field of accounting; significant service to professional accounting organizations; contributions to accounting research and literature; and public service.

Through 1992, 52 American and foreign accountants have been elected to the Hall of Fame (Table 1); no selections were made for the years 1962 and 1969 through 1973. Twenty-five members have been chiefly involved in public accounting, twenty members were university professors, five were government officials, including three chief accountants for the Securities and Exchange Commission (SEC) and one comptroller general of the United States, and two members were prominent in industry. Four members are non-U.S. citizens. A biographical sketch of

TABLE 1

Accounting Hall of Fame Membership

Year of Entry	Member	Year of Entry	Member	Year of Entry	Member
1950	George O. May*	1957	Roy B. Kester*	1975	Leonard P. Spacek
	Robert H. Montgomery*		Hermann C. Miller*	1976	John W. Queenan
	William A. Paton*	1958	Harry A. Finney*	1977	Howard I. Ross*+
1951	Arthur L. Dickinson*		Arthur B. Foye*	1978	Robert K. Mautz
	Henry R. Hatfield*		Donald P. Perry*	1979	Maurice Moonitz
1952	Elijah W. Sells*	1959	Marquis G. Eaton*	1980	Marshall S. Armstrong
	Victor H. Stempf*	1960	Maurice H. Stans	1981	Elmer B. Staats
1953	Arthur E. Andersen*	1961	Eric L. Kohler*	1982	Herbert E. Miller
	Thomas C. Andrews	1963	Andrew Barr	1983	Sidney Davidson
	Charles E. Sprague*		Lloyd Morey*	1984	Henry A. Benson+
	Joseph E. Sterrett*	1964	Paul F. Grady*	1985	Oscar S. Gellein
1954	Carman G. Blough*		Perry E. Mason*	1986	Robert N. Anthony
	Samuel J. Broad*	1965	James L. Peirce	1987	Philip L. Defliese
	Thomas H. Sanders*	1968	George D. Bailey*	1988	Norton M. Bedford
	Hiram T. Scovill*		John L. Carey*	1989	Yuji Ijiri+
1955	Percival F. Brundage*		William W. Werntz*	1990	Charles T. Horngren
1956	Ananias C. Littleton*	1974	Robert M. Trueblood*	1991	Raymond J. Chambers+
				1992	David Solomons

*Deceased
+Non-U.S. citizen

Program for the Ohio State University Accounting Hall of Fame and Alumni Breakfast, Washington D.C., August 1992.

each member inducted through 1992 is provided in *The Accounting Hall of Fame: Profiles of Fifty Members* by T.J. Burns and E.N. Coffman.

Hall of Fame members are nominated and elected by a multinational Board of Nominations consisting of 45 eminent accountants who equally represent the three major areas of accounting practice: public accounting, industry and government, and education. Each member of the board serves a fixed term.

Nominations and election to the Hall of Fame by the board are made annually by mail in two steps. Individual board members are asked to nominate a living or deceased accountant for possible election to the Hall of Fame. Nominations from outside the board are referred to board members. From these preliminary nominations, a ballot is prepared containing the names alphabetically listed of not more than four candidates who were nominated most frequently. The board members then cast their votes for one of the four nominees. The single candidate receiving the

most votes on the ballot is entered into the Hall. Members of the Ohio State University faculty are not eligible for election to the Hall of Fame.

Evidence of election to the Hall of Fame takes three forms. A certificate bearing the seal of Ohio State University and signed by the president of the university and a representative of the Board of Nominations is presented to each person elected (or the person's representative when the person elected is deceased). The names of the elected persons are inscribed on a scroll, and a photographic portrait of each person elected and the citation attesting to the election are permanently displayed, together with the scroll, in the corridors of Hagerty Hall on the Ohio State University campus.

Thomas J. Burns
Edward N. Coffman

Bibliography

Burns, T.J., and E.N. Coffman. *The Accounting Hall of Fame: Profiles of Fifty Mem-*

A

No.	Year	Title
1	1962	New Depreciation Guidelines and Rules
2	1962	Accounting for the "Investment Credit"
3	1963	The Statement of Source and Application of Funds
4	1964	Accounting for the "Investment Credit"
5	1964	Financial Reporting of Leases in Financial Statements of Lessee
6	1965	Status of Accounting Research Bulletins
7	1966	Accounting for Leases in Financial Statements of Lessors
8	1966	Accounting for Cost of Pension Plans
9	1966	Reporting the Results of Operations
10	1966	Omnibus Opinion—1966
11	1967	Accounting for Income Taxes
12	1967	Omnibus Opinion—1967
13	1969	Amending Paragraph 6 of APB Opinion No. 9, Application to Commercial Banks
14	1969	Accounting for Convertible Debt and Debt Issued with Stock Purchase Warrants
15	1969	Earnings per Share
16	1970	Business Combinations
17	1970	Intangible Assets
18	1971	The Equity Method of Accounting for Investments in Common Stock
19	1971	Reporting Changes in Financial Position
20	1971	Accounting Changes
21	1971	Interest on Receivables and Payables
22	1972	Disclosure of Accounting Policies
23	1972	Accounting for Income Taxes—Special Areas
24	1972	Accounting for Income Taxes—Investments in Common Stock Accounted for by the Equity Method
25	1972	Accounting for Stock Issued to Employees
26	1972	Early Extinguishment of Debt
27	1972	Accounting for Lease Transactions by Manufacturer or Dealer Lessors
28	1973	Interim Financial Reporting
29	1973	Accounting for Nonmonetary Transactions
30	1973	Reporting the Results of Operations . . .
31	1973	Disclosure of Lease Commitments by Lessees

bers. Columbus: College of Business, Ohio State University, 1992.

See also ANDERSEN, ARTHUR E.; CHAMBERS, RAYMOND JOHN; CHIEF ACCOUNTANTS OF THE SECURITIES AND EXCHANGE COMMISSION; DAVIDSON, SIDNEY; DICKINSON, ARTHUR LOWES; GRADY, PAUL; HATFIELD, HENRY RAND; HORNGREN, CHARLES T.; IJIRI, YUJI; KOHLER, ERIC LOUIS; LITTLETON, A.C.; MAUTZ, ROBERT K.; MAY, GEORGE OLIVER; MONTGOMERY, ROBERT HIESTER; MOONITZ, MAURICE; PATON, WILLIAM ANDREW; SANDERS, THOMAS HENRY; SELLS, ELIJAH WATT; SOLOMONS, DAVID; SPACEK, LEONARD; SPRAGUE, CHARLES EZRA; STERRETT, JOSEPH EDMUND; TRUEBLOOD, ROBERT MARTIN

Accounting Principles Board (1959–1973)
The Accounting Principles Board (APB) replaced the Committee of Accounting Procedure (CAP) of the American Institute of Certified Public Accountants (AICPA). Alvin R. Jennings, then president of the AICPA, in 1957 was the prime mover in the establishment of the APB, after substantial criticism about financial reporting by critics like Leonard Spacek of Arthur Andersen and Company. These critics stressed that the CAP issued Accounting Research Bul-

No.	Year	Title
1	1962	Untitled. Dealt with the reaction of the accounting community to ARS No. 1 "The Basic Postulates of Accounting" by Maurice Moonitz and ARS No. 3 "A Tentative Set of Broad Accounting Principles for Business Enterprises" by Robert T. Sprouse and Maurice Moonitz
2	1967	Disclosure of Supplemental Financial Information by Diversified Companies
3	1969	Financial Statements Restated for General Price-Level Changes
4	1970	Basic Concepts and Accounting Principles Underlying Financial Statements of Business Enterprises

letins in a manner of putting out "brushfires," based on expediency rather than logical response to pressing problems. Jennings admitted to the failure in accounting to educate the public about the limitations of accounting. However, he was of the opinion that the failure of accounting research was the key reason for this criticism. Jennings called for "pure research" in accounting by an independent research foundation. Ultimately, the AICPA upgraded its own research staff to do the work and, in effect, substituted the APB for the CAP in 1959.

APB opinions, called APBs, were to be issued in accordance with the general guidelines promulgated in Accounting Research Studies (ARSs), done by the research staff of the AICPA. APBs were also to be based on a specific ARS dedicated to a problem area. Perhaps the clearest delineation of these problem areas was made in 1959 by Carman G. Blough, the then long-term director of research for the AICPA. He considered these areas to be: (1) price-level changes; (2) point of realization; (3) use of retained earnings; (4) regulatory accounting and generally accepted accounting principles (GAAP); (5) accounting alternatives; (6) deferred compensation; (7) leases; (8) pension plans; (9) research and development costs; (10) accounting for mergers; (11) earnings of subsidiaries on books of parent; (12) loss of productivity of capital assets; (13) upward revaluation of assets; (14) nonprofit organizations; (15) dividends; (16) deferred credits; (17) valuation on reorganizations; and (18) tax allocation. Ultimately, the private-sector setting of generally accepted accounting principles has to be judged as to whether the accounting bodies, the APB and its successor, the Financial Accounting Standards Board (FASB), have performed adequately to solve problem areas raised by Blough and others.

As superseded APB opinions are dropped from the current printing of extant generally accepted accounting principles, these opinions are, in effect, lost to most researchers. This fact necessitates that each APB opinion be mentioned in this entry. The dropping of superseded opinions is a space-saver but does add to the difficulties of developing background material for an understanding of what is currently GAAP. Lists of APBs and APB Statements are included in this entry.

Three of the first APBs, No. 2, No. 4, and No. 6, are inextricably linked in a struggle for the power to determine GAAP. The issue in No. 2 was the determination of GAAP for the 1962 investment credit. The APB, then composed of 20 members with each of the Big Eight accounting firms represented by its managing partners, voted 14–6 for the deferral approach. Four of the Big Eight members were in opposition, representing a similar split in letters received by the APB. When the Securities and Exchange Commission (SEC) decided in Accounting Series Release No. 96 to allow either the deferral or the flow-through approaches, the APB backed down in APB No. 4. While proclaiming its authority to create GAAP, the APB held that a satisfactory degree of acceptability for APB No. 2 did not exist anymore. This weakening of public-sector setting of GAAP was countered in APB No. 6, which announced that the Council of the AICPA required that APB opinions and Accounting Research Bulletins be followed. It also showed the importance of a consensus of the Big Eight accounting firms in arriving at APB opinions. This controversy also so politically sensitized the issue that Congress in 1972 ruled that the "flow-through" method was to be allowed for the reinstated provision for the investment credit.

No.	Year	Author(s)	Title
1	1961	Maurice Moonitz	The Basic Postulates of Accounting
2	1961	Perry Mason	"Cash Flow" Analysis and The Funds Statement
3	1962	Robert T. Sprouse Maurice Moonitz	A Tentative Set of Broad Accounting Principles for Business Enterprises
4	1962	John H. Myers	Reporting of Leases in Financial Statements
5	1963	Arthur R. Wyatt	A Critical Study of Accounting for Business Combinations
6	1963	Staff of Accounting Research Division of the AICPA	Reporting the Financial Effects of Price-Level Changes
7	1965	Paul Grady	Inventory of Generally Accepted Accounting Principles for Business Enterprises
8	1965	Ernest L. Hicks	Accounting for the Cost of Pension Plans
9	1966	Homer A. Black	Interperiod Allocation of Corporate Income Taxes
10	1968	George R. Catlett Norman O. Olson	Accounting for Goodwill
11	1969	Robert E. Field	Financial Reporting in the Extraction Industries
12	1972	Leonard Lorensen	Reporting Foreign Operations of U.S. Companies in U.S. Dollars
13	1973	Horace G. Barden	The Accounting Basis of Inventories
14	1973	Oscar S. Gellein Maurice S. Newman	Accounting for Research and Development Expenditures
15	1973	Beatrice Melcher	Stockholders' Equity

However, there were some significant successes early on for the APB. One of these was the recommendation in APB No. 3 that companies issue a statement of source and application of funds, followed eight years later by requiring it in APB No. 19. Another example of success was greater uniformity in accounting for leases in APBs No. 5, No. 7, No. 27, and No. 31. APB No. 8 on pensions probably had the most significant positive impact on society of any accounting standard ever issued. On these topics, the APB had the benefit of an ARS No. 2 on the funds statement, No. 4 on leases, and No. 8 on pensions. While the APB opinions were not necessarily the same as the recommendation of the ARSs, these studies were well referenced in the APBs. A list of ARSs are included in this entry.

The APB was successful, although without a related ARS, in getting unanimous agreement on the tightening of accounting for extraordinary items in APB No. 9. This opinion also brought the topic of earnings per share into a formal part of financial accounting after many years of being "outside the fold." While unanimity was gone (15 votes for to 3 votes against), APB No. 15 further defined the procedures to arrive at earnings per share. APB No.

30 again tightened the accounting for what is called extraordinary items.

The starting anew of contentious issues on the APB occurred with APB No. 11, "Accounting for Income Taxes." The APB, down to 18 members and with the top technical partners replacing the managing partners of the Big Eight, split 12–6 on this opinion. A two-thirds vote was needed to pass an opinion. The controversy continued into APBs No. 23 and No. 24, with the same level of dispute on accounting for earnings of subsidiaries and investees. APB No. 14 on convertible debt received a 14–4 vote, with the dissenters stating that APB No. 14 belied economic reality. Perhaps the most contentious issue ever faced by the three private-sector rules body (CAP, APB, and FASB) was the accounting for mergers issue, which culminated in APBs No. 16 and No. 17.

The late 1960s brought a recurrence of "merger mania" in the "go-go years." With this came the accounting issues of: (1) valuation—purchase, pool, or part purchase/part pool—of the merger; (2) the bugaboo of goodwill; (3) the continuation of retained earnings; and (4) the size of the buyer compared to the seller. The Big Eight were badly split. Accounting for mergers became "headline news." The only way the

APB could arrive at a two-thirds vote was to split the topic into two opinions—APB No. 16, "Business Combinations," and No. 17, "Intangible Assets." The two sets of dissenters to No. 16 were quite critical. One set believed that it was not a sound or logical solution of the problem. The second set stated that the real abuse was pooling itself. One of the dissenters to No. 17 believed that goodwill should never be shown as an asset in the balance sheet. The wound to the APB was so deep that its days were numbered. One reason was that ARS No. 5 and ARS No. 10 both favored a size test and an immediate write-off of goodwill, respectively. Another reason was a significant split (12–6 vote) on APB No. 20, "Accounting Changes," in which dissenters found no supportable rationale but found that accounting requirements were becoming disciplinary tools rather than rational standards.

Even though undergoing external and internal pressure, the APB did some highly regarded and trailblazing work until its demise in 1973. Such opinions as No. 18 on the equity method, No. 21 on interest, No. 22 on disclosure, No. 26 on early extinguishment of debt, No. 28 on interim financial reporting, and No. 29 on accounting for nonmonetary transactions were well received at the time and continue as GAAP. Opinion No. 25 on accounting for stock options was controversial at passage—fifteen (of whom six assented with qualification) in favor and three against—and remains so today, as accounting and society grapple with this thorny issue of executive compensation.

There were four other APBs: No. 1 on depreciation; No. 10 and No. 12 on various minor matters (labeled "omnibus opinions"); and No. 13 on a specific issue related to banking. When one examines Blough's 18-point agenda, one does note significant efforts, if not successes, in a number of points: (3) use of retained earnings; (7) leases; (8) pension plans; (10) accounting for mergers; (11) earnings of subsidiaries on books of parent; and (18) tax allocation. Groundwork had been laid for subsequent work by the FASB on: (1) price-level changes; (2) point of realization; and (9) research and development costs.

The ARSs are reviewed separately in this encyclopedia. The APB also issued four statements. Both Statements No. 1 and No. 2 were very short and inconsequential. This was not true for the other two. Statement No. 3 on general price-level changes followed by six years ARS No. 6 on the same topic. Statement No. 3 detailed a systematic response to this complex issue and received at least a two-thirds vote of the APB but was not an opinion. Statement No. 4 was conceptual in nature and was a follow-up of the conceptual ARSs No. 1, No. 3, and No. 7. Statement No. 4 is one of the most literate pieces in the theory of accounting. Unfortunately, it has been effectively lost to researchers, as the FASB has replaced it with its own statements of financial concepts.

The barrage of criticism over accounting for mergers led to the forming of the Wheat Study Group (named after its chairman, Francis M. Wheat). This group recommended the replacement of the APB with another private body but one independent from the AICPA. The APB was replaced by the FASB in 1973. The APB has been underrated as a rule-making body, especially since much of its output is no longer printed in the list of current GAAP. It is a major error in research to ignore this literature, which should be read as preparatory to doing research in accounting.

Richard Vangermeersch

Bibliography

American Institute of Certified Public Accountants, Accounting Principles Board, "Basic Concepts and Accounting Principles underlying Financial Statements of Business Enterprise." APB Statement No. 4. New York: 1970.

Blough, C.G. "Challenges to the Accounting Profession in the United States," *Journal of Accountancy*, December 1959, pp.37–42.

Davidson, S., and G.D. Anderson. "The Development of Accounting and Auditing Standards," *Journal of Accountancy*, May 1987, pp. 110–127.

Jennings, A.R. "Present-Day Challenges in Financial Reporting," *Journal of Accountancy*, January 1958, pp. 28–34.

Zeff, S.A. *Forging Accounting Principles in Five Countries: A History and an Analysis of Trends*. Champaign, IL: Stipes, 1972.

———. "Some Junctures in the Evolution of the Process of Establishing Accounting Principles in the U.S.A., 1917–1972," *Accounting Review*, July 1984, pp. 447–468.

See also ACCOUNTING RESEARCH BULLETINS; ACCOUNTING RESEARCH STUDIES; AMERICAN INSTITUTE OF CERTIFIED PUBLIC ACCOUNTANTS; BIG EIGHT ACCOUNTING FIRMS; CHIEF ACCOUNTANTS OF THE SECURITIES AND EXCHANGE COMMISSION; COMPOUND INTEREST; CONCEPTUAL FRAMEWORK; DAVIDSON, SIDNEY; DEFERRED INCOME TAX ACCOUNTING; DEFINITIONS OF ACCOUNTING; FINANCIAL ACCOUNTING STANDARDS BOARD; GENERALLY ACCEPTED ACCOUNTING PRINCIPLES; GOODWILL; INCOME STATEMENT/INCOME ACCOUNT; INFLATION ACCOUNTING; INTANGIBLE ASSETS; MATCHING; MOONITZ, MAURICE; POOLING OF INTERESTS; SPACEK, LEONARD; WHEAT COMMITTEE

Accounting Research Bulletins

Accounting Research Bulletins (ARBs) of the Committee on Accounting Procedure (CAP), were publications of the American Institute of Accountants (AIA) that delineated the AIA version of generally accepted accounting principles. The committee, founded in 1936, issued ARB No. 1 in September 1939 and ended with ARB No. 51 in August 1959. Of the 51 ARBs, eight dealt with accounting terminology issues. The ARBs are listed on pages 16–17, as are Accounting Terminology Bulletins, on page 18. The CAP was replaced by the Accounting Principles Board (APB) in 1959.

There was a long gestation period before ARB No. 1 was issued. In 1917, the AIA, with the approval of the Federal Reserve Board and the Federal Trade Commission, published *Uniform Accounting*, which dealt more with auditing than accounting principles. This publication was revised in 1929. By 1930, the AIA, under the leadership of George Oliver May, began working with the Committee on Stock List of the New York Stock Exchange. In 1932 May sent a letter to the Committee on Stock List enumerating five broad principles of accounting as discussed in ARB No. 1. These five principles were: (1) unrealized profit not taken to the income statement; (2) capital surplus not to be used for items belonging on the income statement; (3) earned surplus of a subsidiary prior to acquisition does not result in a credit to the parent's earned surplus; (4) dividends on treasury stock are not income; and (5) notes receivable from officers are reported separately from other receivables. In 1936, the American Accounting Association issued a report that delineated 20 very general principles of accounting. Carman G. Blough, first chief accountant of the Securities and Exchange Commission (SEC), was critical in a 1937 speech of the accounting profession's lack of agreed-upon principles. In 1938, the SEC issued Accounting Securities Release No. 4, "Administrative Policy on Financial Statements," which announced that accounting principles used in filings must have substantial authoritative support. By 1939, the AIA appointed Thomas Henry Sanders to the part-time post of director and coordinator of research.

ARB No. 1 adopted the five principles delineated in May's 1932 letter plus a sixth one on the accounting for donated capital stock, all of which had been approved by the membership of the AIA. The CAP consisted then of 22 voting members and required a two-thirds majority to issue an ARB. The number of dissenters would be noted. The CAP included such leading practitioners as May, A.H. Carter, Walter A. Staub, and Victor H. Stempf. There were three academicians on it: Roy B. Kester, A.C. Littleton, and William Andrew Paton. In ARB No. 5 in 1940, the four dissenters were permitted to have summaries of their views published in the ARB. In December 1939, the CAP included a notes section to ARB No. 4 that "it is felt, however, that the burden of justifying departure from accepted procedures must be assumed by those who adopt other treatment."

There are five ARBs that have significant application into the 1990s. ARB No. 3 in 1939 delineated the accounting principles for a quasi reorganization. Fair and conservative values were to be used in the process of eliminating the deficit, but accountants were warned about the future effects of understatements. ARB No. 5 in 1940 stated that appreciation, to be recorded in abnormal situations, should be followed by depreciation based on the new valuation. The reasoning was that "a corporation should not at the same time claim larger property values . . . and provide for the amortization of only smaller property sums." ARB No. 29 in 1947 promulgated the basic rules for inventory accounting. The two dissenters and the one assentor with qualifications attacked the determination of the ceiling of market, which is not realizable value, and the floor of market, which is net realizable value less normal profit margin. ARB No. 30 in 1947 defined the terms "current assets," "current liabilities," and "working

No.	Year Issued	Title
1	1939	General Introduction and Rules Formerly Adopted
2	1939	Unamortized Discount and Redemption Premium on Bonds Refunded
3	1939	Quasi-Reorganization or Corporate Readjustment—Amplification of Institute Rule No. 2 of 1934
4	1939	Foreign Operations and Foreign Exchange
5	1940	Depreciation on Appreciation
6	1940	Comparative Statements
7	1940	Reports of Committee on Terminology
8	1941	Combined Statement of Income and Earned Surplus
9	1941	Report of Committee on Terminology
10	1941	Real and Personal Property Taxes
11	1941	Corporate Accounting for Ordinary Stock Dividends
12	1941	Report of Committee on Terminology
13	1942	Accounting for Special Reserves Arising Out of the War
14	1942	Accounting for United States Treasury Tax Notes
15	1942	The Renegotiation of War Contracts
16	1942	Report of Committee on Terminology
17	1942	Post-War Refund of Excess-Profits Tax
18	1942	Unamortized Discount and Redemption Premium on Bonds Refunded (Supplement)
19	1942	Accounting Under Cost-Plus-Fixed-Fee Contracts
20	1943	Report of Committee on Terminology
21	1943	Renegotiation of War Contracts (Supplement)
22	1944	Report of Committee on Terminology
23	1944	Accounting for Income Taxes
24	1944	Accounting for Intangible Assets
25	1945	Accounting for Terminated War Contracts
26	1946	Accounting for the Use of Special War Reserves
27	1946	Emergency Facilities
28	1947	Accounting Treatment of General Purpose Contingency Reserves
29	1947	Inventory Pricing
30	1947	Current Assets and Current Liabilities—Working Capital
31	1947	Inventory Reserves
32	1947	Income and Earned Surplus
33	1947	Depreciation and High Costs
34	1948	Recommendation of Committee on Terminology—Use of Term "Reserve"
35	1948	Presentation of Income and Earned Surplus
36	1948	Pension Plans—Accounting for Annuity Costs Based on Past Services
37	1948	Accounting for Compensation in the Form of Stock Options
38	1949	Disclosure of Long-Term Leases in Financial Statements of Lessees
39	1949	Recommendation of Subcommittee on Terminology—Discontinuance of the Use of the Term "Surplus"
40	1950	Business Combinations
41	1951	Presentation of Income and Earned Surplus (Supplement to Bulletin No. 35)
13	1951	Limitation of Scope of Special War Reserves (Addendum)
26	1951	Limitation of Scope of Special War Reserves (Addendum)
42	1952	Emergency Facilities—Depreciation, Amortization, and Income Taxes
11	1952	Accounting for Stock Dividends and Stock Split-Ups (Revised)
37	1953	Accounting for Compensation Involved in Stock Option and Stock Purchase Plans (Revised)
43	1953	Restatement and Revision of Accounting Research Bulletins

No.	Year Issued	Title
44	1954	Declining-balance Depreciation
44	1959	Declining-balance Depreciation (Revised)
45	1955	Long-term Construction-type Contracts
46	1956	Discontinuance of Dating Earned Surplus
47	1956	Accounting for Costs of Pension Plans
48	1957	Business Combinations
49	1958	Earnings per Share
50	1958	Contingencies
51	1959	Consolidated Financial Statements

capital." ARB No. 51 in 1959 stated the requirement of more than 50 percent ownership of the outstanding voting shares for consolidation to occur. It is interesting to note that no one dissented from ARB No. 51, but nine of the 21 asserted with qualification for such reasons as: (1) there are other measures of the existence of a consolidated entity than 50 percent ownership and (2) ARB No. 51 encouraged the further nonconsolidation of certain subsidiaries.

There are five classics in the 51 ARBs. They are: No. 28, "Accounting Treatment of General Purpose Contingency Reserves" (1947); No. 32, "Income and Earned Surplus" (1947); No. 33, "Depreciation and High Costs" (1947); No. 34, "Use of Term 'Reserve'" (1948); and No. 39, "Discontinuance of the Use of the Term 'Surplus'" (1949). The term "classics" is used because of the insightful and excellent texts of these ARBs. For instance, this quote from ARB No. 28: "In reaching this conclusion, consideration has been given to the declining use of general-purpose contingency reserves as charges to income and to the general recognition that their use may either arbitrarily reduce income or be the means of shifting income from one year to another." It was recommended to establish an appropriation of surplus (retained earnings) and that current charges be components of net income.

The text of ARB No. 32 also warned against income equalization and described what is labeled today the "tentativeness" principle. It gives a most informative "debate" between the proponents of the "all-inclusive" concept and the "current operating performance" concept. The proponents of the first concept "assert that, over a period of years, charges resulting from extraordinary events tend to exceed the credits, and their omission has the effect of indicating a greater earning performance than the corporation actually has exhibited." The proponents of the second concept "point out that, while some users of financial reports are able to ana-

lyze a statement and eliminate from it those unusual and extraordinary items that tend to distort it for their purposes, many users are not trained to do so." This text remains the most lucid description of the role of accountants in determining net income.

In ARB No. 33, AIA Director of Research Blough and his staff did substantial investigation on which to base the promulgation. The CAP was cautious and favored basing depreciation on the historical cost of fixed assets, not their replacement costs. In an October 1948 supplement to ARB No. 33, the CAP stated: "Should inflation proceed so far that original dollar costs lose their practical significance, it might become necessary to restate all assets in terms of depreciated currency, as has been done in some countries." Four of the 21 members dissented from the amendments to ARB No. 33.

Two terms, "reserve" and "surplus," are still used by many laymen and, occasionally, even by accountants. In ARB No. 34, the CAP discussed the four current uses of the term "reserves" and recommended its use only for "the indication of an amount of unidentified or unsegregated assets held or retained for a specific purpose." In ARB No. 39, the CAP found that "the term 'surplus' has a connotation of excess, overplus, residue or 'that which remains when use or need is satisfied' (Webster), whereas no such meaning is intended where the term is used in accounting." The CAP recommended that the term be dropped in accounting.

There were 10 ARBs dealing with World War II wartime and Korean conflict eras. Some of these were excluded from ARB No. 43, "Restatement and Revision of Accounting Research Bulletins," in 1953. ARB No. 43 did include some updating and corrections of the previous ARBs. ARB No. 43 and the eight subsequent ARBs remain generally accepted accounting principles, unless superseded by a Financial

Accounting Standards Board or an Accounting Principles Board opinion.

Many ARBs were brief attempts to solve accounting issues later addressed in a much more formal and lengthy manner. Such ARBs were: No. 11, stock dividends (1941, 1948, and 1952); No. 23, income taxes (1944); No. 24, intangible assets (1944); No. 36 and No. 47, pension plans (1948); No. 37, stock options (1948 and 1953); No. 38, leases (1938); No. 40, business combinations (1950); No. 49, earnings per share (1958); and No. 50, contingencies (1958). It is fairly evident that the CAP did not have the logistical support to do the level of effort needed to attain what critics like Leonard Spacek of Arthur Andersen and Company were demanding in public forums.

The formal movement that led to the demise of the CAP was started in 1957 by Alvin R. Jennings, then the president of the American Institute of Certified Public Accountants (AICPA). Jennings called for accounting research to be the key for setting new accounting principles. He felt there might be a need for five to six full-time researchers of outstanding ability to be affiliated with the research body that would make this effort. Jennings felt that there had been too much emphasis on speedy solutions to problems. Within two years, in 1959, the CAP was replaced by the APB.

The CAP and its ARBs traded off renowned part-time members who met infrequently and a small, but highly talented, research staff for in-depth responses to complex problems. The CAP and its ARBs may have been a little late being born, but they died at the right time.

Richard Vangermeersch

Bibliography

American Accounting Association, "A Tentative Statement of Accounting Principles affecting Corporate Reports," *Accounting Review*, June 1936, pp. 187–191.

American Institute of Certified Public Accountants, *Accounting Research and Terminology Bulletins, Final Edition.* New York: AICPA, 1961.

Anonymous, "The Accounting Procedure Committee," *Journal of Accountancy*, September 1959, pp. 29–30.

Jennings, A.R. "Present-Day Challenges in Financial Reporting," *Journal of Accountancy*, January 1958, pp. 28–34.

Spacek, L. "Professional Accountants and Their Public Responsibility." In *A Search for Fairness in Financial Reporting to the Public.* Chicago: Arthur Andersen & Co., 1969.

Zeff, S.A. *Forging Accounting Principles in Five Countries: A History and an Analysis of Trends.* Champaign, IL: Stipes, 1972.

See also ACCOUNTING PRINCIPLES BOARD; AMERICAN ACCOUNTING ASSOCIATION; AMERICAN INSTITUTE OF CERTIFIED PUBLIC ACCOUNTANTS; CHIEF ACCOUNTANTS OF THE SECURITIES AND EXCHANGE COMMISSION; CONCEPTUAL FRAMEWORK; CONSOLIDATED FINANCIAL STATEMENTS; FINANCIAL ACCOUNTING STANDARDS BOARD; GENERALLY ACCEPTED ACCOUNTING PRINCIPLES; GOODWILL; HOXSEY, J.M.B.; INCOME STATEMENT/INCOME ACCOUNT; INFLATION ACCOUNTING; INTANGIBLE ASSETS; INVENTORY VALUATION; JONES, EDWARD THOMAS; LAST IN, FIRST OUT (LIFO); LIABILITIES; LITTLETON, A.C.; MANIPULATION OF INCOME; MAY, GEORGE OLIVER; NEW YORK STOCK EXCHANGE; PATON, WILLIAM ANDREW; POOLING OF INTERESTS; RETAINED EARNINGS; SANDERS, THOMAS HENRY; SECURITIES AND EXCHANGE COMMISSION; SPACEK, LEONARD; STOCK DIVIDENDS; TREASURY STOCK; *UNIFORM ACCOUNTING*

Accounting Research Studies

Accounting Research Studies (ARSs) are monographs issued from 1961 through 1973 on various financial-accounting topics that reported studies conducted by experts from academics and from practice. The experts were assisted by a project advisory committee and by the director and the research staff of the Accounting Research Division of the American Institute of

Certified Public Accountants (AICPA). After detailing the work done and giving pro and con arguments, the writer(s) of the monograph would offer conclusions. Comments could be made by the members of the project advisory committee and the director of accounting research, who made the decision to publish the study.

These research studies were an outgrowth of the increased interest in the late 1950s in accounting research as a basis for generally accepted accounting principles and for accounting rules and procedures. The call for this research came in 1957 from Alvin R. Jennings, then president of the AICPA, and was followed by the Special Committee on Accounting Research, chaired by Weldon Powell. The recommendation of the committee led to the formation of the Accounting Principles Board (APB) and of the Accounting Research Division of the AICPA in 1959. ARSs that were well received were to be the basis of APB decisions (APBs). There was a clear delineation of the research backlog in an 18-point agenda offered by the former director of research, Carman G. Blough. The committee also recommended that the accounting-research program start with an immediate study of basic postulates and principles.

Fifteen ARSs were issued from 1961 through 1973, all written by outstanding academicians and practitioners. ARSs differ from the discussion memorandums of the Financial Accounting Standards Board (FASB) in that conclusions were drawn by the writer(s) of ARSs. Many of the conclusions were controversial, and most were tightly reasoned. Controversy was not to be avoided, as ARSs were viewed as somewhat experimental in nature. The drawing of conclusions made ARSs more interesting reading than FASB discussion memorandums.

ARS No. 1, *The Basic Postulates of Accounting* (1961), was written by a leading academic, Maurice Moonitz, who was then the director of accounting research for the AICPA. Moonitz relied on deductive reasoning to arrive at five accounting postulates for the environment: (1) quantification, (2) exchange, (3) entities, (4) time period, and (5) unit of measure. There were four propositions for the field of accounting: (1) financial statements, (2) market prices, (3) entities, and (4) tentativeness. Moonitz then discussed five imperatives: (1) continuity, (2) objectivity, (3) consistency, (4) stable unit, and (5) disclosure. He ended the work by stating a close association to accounting of "wealth" and "entities." Moonitz noted a theory of valuation had not been stated. ARS No. 1 thus laid the groundwork for ARS No. 3, *A Tentative Set of Broad Principles for Business Enterprises.*

ARS No. 2, *Cash Flow Analyses and the Funds Statement* (1961), was written by Perry Mason, a noted academic. The director of research, Maurice Moonitz, noted the ferment of the times, which had led to a conflict between "cash-flow accounting" and "accrual accounting." Mason called for the "funds statement," for caution in the use of "cash flow," and for the "all financial resources" approach to be used. He carefully listed his research approach to the stated problems and developed his presentation of the proposed solution. Mason's efforts led to APBs No. 3, "The Statement of Sources and Application of Funds" (1963), and No. 19, "Reporting Changes in Financial Position" (1971), which closely followed this ARS.

ARS No. 3, *A Tentative Set of Broad Accounting Principles for Business Enterprises* (1962), was written by Robert T. Sprouse, a noted academic and subsequent member of the FASB, and Moonitz. This companion study to ARS No. 1 attained controversy. The writers stressed the importance of "capital" and wanted a revitalization of the balance sheet. They questioned the reliance on sales as the only test for realization and argued that objectivity was not solely dependent on sales. They wrote, "Even in the absence of a significant event, the accounts (plant and equipment) could be restated at periodic intervals, perhaps every five years." They espoused what was later to be labeled the balance sheet approach. The comments by the members of the advisory committees for ARS No. 1 and No. 3 mirrored the controversy about this study. These nine comments are perhaps best summarized by Carman G. Blough's comment, "Shades of the 1920s!" This strongly negative response to ARS No. 3 marked the end of the deductive approach by the APB to establishing accounting principles. ARS No. 3, however, remains an important work to read and study, as the issues discussed have not gone away.

ARS No. 4, *Reporting of Leases in Financial Statements* (1962), was written by John H. Myers, a professor at Northwestern University. He did a masterful job in laying the groundwork for his solution, which was the capitalization of the value of the property rights on the books of the lessee. Myers's exposition was well done but was rejected in APB No. 5, "Financial Reporting of Leases in Financial Statements of Lessee," which followed the "in substance a purchase of property" approach. ARS No. 4 remains excellent background reading for the topic of accounting for leases.

ARS No. 5, *A Critical Study of Accounting for Business Combinations* (1963), was written by Arthur R. Wyatt, then at the University of Illinois. Wyatt later became a partner at Arthur Andersen and Company, a member of the FASB, and chairman of the International Accounting Standards Committee. Wyatt prepared an excellent history of the "accounting for merger" issue and called for a limiting of the "pooling of interest" method, as most mergers were exchanges. However, he also counseled against the goodwill account, an important outgrowth of the "purchase" method. Moonitz, still director of accounting research, included a six-page "position paper" by Robert C. Holsen that argued for the continuation of the pooling approach. Wyatt's recommendations in ARS No. 5 may not have been followed in ARB No. 16, "Business Combinations" (1970), and No. 17, "Intangible Assets" (1970), but his arguments were certainly referenced. ARS No. 5 remains an extremely readable look at a timeless problem.

ARS No. 6, *Reporting the Financial Effects of Price-Level Changes* (1963), was written by the staff of the Accounting Research Division. This study delineated the long-held view of the AICPA that the "purchasing power of the dollar" approach, measured by a general price-level index, was to be utilized in a supplementary manner with or without the replacement-cost approach. There also was a measurement of the "purchase power gains or losses on monetary items." The staff did a fine job developing its conclusions, which were the basis for APB Statement No. 3, *Financial Statements Restated for General Price-Level Changes* (1969), and then Financial Accounting Statement (FAS) No. 33, "Financial Reporting and Changing Prices" (1979), on inflation accounting. ARS No. 6 provides a well-developed approach to accounting for inflation.

ARS No. 7, *Inventory of Generally Accepted Accounting Principles for Business Enterprises* (1965), was written by Paul Grady, a leading accounting practitioner and former director of accounting research. The study was in response to the criticisms of ARS No. 3 and followed the more cautious approaches of (1) Thomas Henry Sanders, Henry Rand Hatfield, and Underhill Moore (1938) and (2) William Andrew Paton and A.C. Littleton (1940). The study favored the inductive approach and delineated a somewhat different base of "10 concepts" from ARS No. 1's "14 postulates." The most significant inclusion was "conservatism"; the most significant exclusion was "market prices." Grady then carefully placed generally accepted accounting principles into a series of objectives, with emphasis on the auditing function. He included the then-current pronouncements for each topic covered.

ARS No. 8, *Accounting for the Cost of Pension Plans* (1965), was written by Ernest L. Hicks, a practitioner. It is a most significant ARS as it was put into effect in 1966 by APB No. 8, "Accounting for the Cost of Pension Plans," which changed U.S. accounting for pensions for the better. Hicks carefully developed the importance of an approach to pension accounting that was based on the accrual basis. The topics covered by Hicks remain the base for subsequent opinions on pensions, FAS No. 35, "Accounting and Reporting by Defined Benefit Pension Plans" (1980), No. 36, "Disclosure of Pension Information" (1980), and No. 87, "Employer's Accounting for Pensions" (1985).

ARS No. 9, *Interperiod Allocation of Corporate Income Taxes* (1966), was written by Homer A. Black, a respected academic. It was based on the belief that since the allocation issue had been settled in the affirmative, the only issue was "a little allocation versus a lot of allocation." Black developed very carefully the reasoning for various approaches to the topic and then made his recommendation for the comprehensive method based on a combination of the liability and the deferred method. Strong objections were raised by two members of the project advisory committee, Sidney Davidson and Richard C. Gerstenberg. However, ARS No. 9 became the general basis of APB No. 11, "Accounting for Income Taxes" (1967). Since the topic of deferred taxes remains a most controversial one, ARS No. 9 remains an important source for accountants.

ARS No. 10, *Accounting for Goodwill* (1968), was written by George R. Catlett and Norman O. Olson. The study was premised on the demise of the "pooling of interest" method, as recommended in ARS No. 5. Hence, goodwill would become much more significant. They concluded that goodwill should be immediately written off to stockholders' equity. There were seven comments from the advisory committee, only two of which were favorable. The approach of ARS No. 10 was rejected in APB No. 17, but since goodwill is still a vital topic in financial accounting, ARS No. 10 remains a vital piece of accounting literature.

ARS No. 11, *Financial Reporting in the Extractive Industries* (1969), was written by Robert E. Field from Price Waterhouse and Company. He presented an excellent detailed description of the industry and developed 19 recommendations, like the cost-center approach and the write off of unsuccessful exploration and development expenditures. While FAS No. 19, "Financial Accounting and Reporting by Oil and Gas Producing Companies" (1977) adopted the successful-efforts approach, the FASB in FAS No. 25, "Suspension of Certain Accounting Requirements for Oil and Gas Producing Companies" (1979) reinstituted the full-cost approach as an alternative to the successful-efforts approach.

ARS No. 12, *Reporting Foreign Operations of U.S. Companies in U.S. Dollars* (1972), was written by Leonard Lorensen of the AICPA. Significant changes in the foreign-exchange environment called for a change in the old "ad hoc" methods. Lorensen's temporal approach was developed and presented as a solution, in which the cash, receivables, and payables of foreign subsidiaries are translated at the current rate. The other asset and liability accounts are translated according to their accounting basis—past or current. Lorensen carefully distinguished that approach from the models of the (1) current-noncurrent; (2) monetary-nonmonetary; and (3) current rate. The director of accounting research was supportive of this deductive effort, as was the FASB in FAS No. 8. While FAS No. 52, "Foreign Currency Translation" (1981) updated FAS No. 8, there still remain two instances—a highly inflationary country and when the foreign subsidiary's functional currency is the reporting currency—when the temporal approach is used.

The last three ARSs were issued in 1973, just as the APB was replaced by the FASB. As such, these studies never were given the attention the others received. They are:

ARS No. 13, *The Accounting Basis of Inventories*, by Horace G. Barden from Ernst and Ernst.

ARS No. 14, *Accounting for Research and Development Expenditures*, by Oscar S. Gellein and Maurice S. Newman from Haskins and Sells.

ARS No. 15, *Stockholders' Equity*, by Betrice Melcher of the AICPA Accounting Research Division Staff.

Barden made a good case for the use of "lower of cost or net realizable value" rather than the "cost or market, whichever is lower" approach. Gellein and Newman made a strong case for the sometime capitalization of research and development cost. Melcher developed an approach that would more realistically recognize the true costs to the company of stock options.

The ARSs were successful in exploring controversial topics and engendering much discussion. Most of Blough's 18-point agenda of 1959 were the subjects of ARSs. Some, like ARSs No. 2, No. 8, No. 9, and No. 12, were the basis for APBs and FASs. Perhaps the goal of a scientifically and deductively based set of postulates, principles, and rules was never attainable. Each one of the ARSs stands up well as readings for current accounting issues. They should be required background reading for those interested in given topics.

Richard Vangermeersch

Bibliography

Barden, H.G. "Excerpts—Accounting Research Study No. 13: *The Accounting Basis of Inventories*," *Journal of Accountancy*, July 1973, pp. 69–74.

Black, H.A. "Excerpts from Accounting Research Study No. 9: *Interperiod Allocation of Corporate Income Taxes*," *Journal of Accountancy*, July 1966, pp. 63–68.

Blough, C.G. "Challenges to the Accounting Profession in the United States," *Journal of Accountancy*, December 1959, pp. 37–42.

Catlett, G.R., and N.O. Olson. "Excerpts from Accounting Research Study No. 10: *Accounting for Goodwill*," *Journal of Accountancy*, November 1968, pp. 64–67.

Gellein, O.S., and M.S. Newman. "Accounting for Research and Development Expenditures," *Journal of Accountancy*, August 1973, pp. 72–74.

Hicks, E.L. "Summary of ARS No. 8: *Accounting for the Cost of Pension Plans*," *Journal of Accountancy*, May 1965, pp. 55–65.

Jennings, A.R. "Present-Day Challenges in Financial Reporting," *Journal of Accountancy*, January 1958, pp. 28–34.

Lorensen, L. "Temporal Principle of Translation," *Journal of Accountancy*, August 1972, pp. 48–54.

Paton, W.A., and A.C. Littleton. *An Introduction to Corporate Accounting Standards*. American Accounting Association Monograph No. 3. New York: American Accounting Association, 1940.

Powell, W. "The Challenge to Research," *Journal of Accountancy*, February 1960, pp. 34–41.

Sanders, T.H., H.R. Hatfield, and U. Moore. *A Statement of Accounting Principles*. New York: American Institute of Accountants, 1938.

Sapienza, S.R. "Examination of Accounting Research Study No. 5: Standards for Pooling," *Accounting Review*, July 1964, pp. 582–590.

Sprouse, R.T. "Historical Cost and Current Assets: Traditional and Treacherous," *Accounting Review*, October 1963, pp. 687–695.

Tierney, C. "Price-Level Adjustments: Problem in Perspective," *Journal of Accountancy*, November 1963, pp. 56–60.

See also ACCOUNTING PRINCIPLES BOARD; AMERICAN INSTITUTE OF CERTIFIED PUBLIC ACCOUNTANTS; *AN INTRODUCTION TO CORPORATE ACCOUNTING STANDARDS;* CHIEF ACCOUNTANTS OF THE SECURITIES AND EXCHANGE COMMISSION; CONCEPTUAL FRAMEWORK; DAVIDSON, SIDNEY; DEFERRED INCOME TAX ACCOUNTING; FINANCIAL ACCOUNTING STANDARDS BOARD; FOREIGN CURRENCY TRANSLATION; FUNDS FLOW STATEMENT; GENERALLY ACCEPTED ACCOUNTING PRINCIPLES; GOODWILL; GRADY, PAUL; HISTORICAL COST; INFLATION ACCOUNTING; LIABILITIES; MATCHING; MOONITZ, MAURICE; POOLING OF INTERESTS; POSTULATES OF ACCOUNTING; SANDERS, HATFIELD, AND MOORE; SWEENEY, HENRY WHITCOMB

Accounting Series Release No. 190

Issued by the Securities and Exchange Commission (SEC) on March 23, 1976, as a response to the inflationary period of the early and mid-1970s, Accounting Series Release (ASR) No. 190 adopted a "current replacement cost" approach for inventory and for buildings and equipment, as well as for yearly cost of sales and for depreciation. ASR No. 190 followed quite closely the views of the then-chief accountant of the SEC, John C. Burton, who strongly opposed the "general price level" approach favored by the Financial Accounting Standards Board (FASB) in the early 1970s.

ASR No. 190 was utilized by larger registrants. The SEC traded off precision of this "supplementary to the statements" calculation for what it felt to be important information to investors. The SEC permitted a range of figures as well as a single figure. It did not take into account the effect of inflation on other assets or on liabilities. The SEC tried to discourage users from recalculating net income into "true income." Buildings and equipment were to be stated at "the estimated current cost of replacing (new) the productive capacity." The SEC required the use of the same useful lives for these assets as used in the historical cost approach, as well as the straight-line method of depreciation. Companies would be allowed to "describe what consideration, if any, was given in responding to the related effects on direct labor costs, repairs and maintenance, utility and other indirect costs as a result of the assumed replacement of productive capacity." ASR No. 190 was dropped by the SEC in late 1979 when the FASB passed FAS No. 33, "Financial Reporting and Changing Prices." This FAS required supplementary disclosure on both the "current cost without technology adjustments" and the "general price level" approaches, as well as the purchasing power gains or loss on net monetary items. It also required the supplementary disclosure of income from continuing operations for both approaches. FAS No. 33 was later repealed by FAS No. 82, "Financial Reporting and Changing Prices: Elimination of Certain Disclosures," dealing with the "general price level" figures, in 1984 and by FAS No. 89, "Financial Reporting and Changing Prices," dealing with the current cost figures, in 1986.

ASR No. 190 represents one more noble effort at accounting for inflation in countries experiencing a sudden increase in inflation but not for an extended period of time. It should be studied along with the Sandilands Report, the 1975 report of the Inflation Accounting Committee of the United Kingdom and Ireland, and

FAS No. 33 during the next round of severe inflation in the United States.

Richard Vangermeersch

Bibliography

Bierman, H. Jr., and R.E. Dukes. "Limitations of Replacement Cost," *Quarterly Review of Economics and Business*, Spring 1979, pp. 131–140.

Burton, J.C. "Financial Reporting in an Age of Inflation," Statements in Quotes section, *Journal of Accountancy*, February 1975, pp. 68–71.

"Corporations Doubt Usefulness of Replacement-Cost Data, Survey Shows," *Management Accounting*, August 1976, pp. 5–6.

Johnson, L.T., and P.W. Bell. "Current Replacement Costs: A Qualified Opinion," *Journal of Accountancy*, November 1976, p. 63–76.

"Replacement-Cost Disclosure," *Management Accounting*, September 1978, pp. 58–59.

U.S. Securities and Exchange Commission. "Release No. 190," *Accounting Series Releases: Compilation of Releases to 195 as in Effect August 1976*. Washington: GPO, 1976.

See also CHIEF ACCOUNTANTS OF THE SECURITIES AND EXCHANGE COMMISSION; COMPARABILITY; FINANCIAL ACCOUNTING STANDARDS BOARD; HISTORICAL COST; INFLATION ACCOUNTING; PHILIPS INDUSTRIES (N.V.); SANDILANDS REPORT; SECURITIES AND EXCHANGE COMMISSION; SWEENEY, HENRY WHITCOMB

Accretion Concept of Income

In place of the assumption that income is earned entirely at the moment of sale, G. Edward Philips proposed an accretion concept of income, under which some portion of profit would be considered earned during each phase of a company's operating cycle. The proportional performance method of accounting for service contracts, and the percentage of completion method of accounting for long-term construction contracts are techniques for recognizing profits ratably as successive tasks are performed. Accretion income also results from natural growth (crops, timber), reproduction (livestock), and aging processes (liquor, lumber, tobacco). Natural growth in agriculture is equivalent to value added in manufacturing. Failure to record livestock births and other natural increases understates assets and income.

In contrast to long-term construction profits, recognition of income from natural growth requires estimates of future market prices as well as future costs in preparing the product for sale. Mining companies sometimes recognize accretion income by valuing ending inventories at their current selling prices. In animal husbandry, the valuation process is simplified because the product has a market price at each stage of growth. If eventual sale is not reasonably certain, or if the future selling price or additional costs are not predictable, accretion income should probably not be recorded.

Michael Chatfield

Bibliography

Philips, G.E. "The Accretion Concept of Income," *Accounting Review*, January 1963, pp. 14–25.

See also REALIZATION

Accrual Accounting

When Renaissance merchants felt the need to summarize the results of their trading judgments, income calculation replaced accountability as the major bookkeeping problem and the double entry system evolved. According to A.C. Littleton, "it must be concluded that income determination by matching cost and revenue has, for 500 years, been the central feature of double entry." The unique aspect of this new system, and the one that distinguished it from earlier attempts to measure income, was the integration of real and nominal accounts, which allowed the results of many transactions to be expressed as the balance of a single profit and loss account. Double entry provided the mechanism to replace subjective assessments of income with a quantitative, uniform calculation that made gross profit essentially the difference between buying and selling prices.

But this income finding potential was scarcely used before the seventeenth century. Because of the sporadic nature of venture trading, and the fact that different ventures had very different profit margins, merchants preferred to open a separate account for each consignment of goods and leave it open until everything was sold. At that time, the venture account was ruled and its balance transferred to profit and loss, which at longer intervals was closed to capital. In each case profit was considered earned when the venture was liquidated.

The lack of periodic balancing and closing, and the mixing of business and personal affairs in the ledger, are evidence of a disinterest in calculating total income. Venture accounting was dominated by the need for comprehensive records for owners' reference. Accruals and deferrals were handled inconsistently. Bad debts were sometimes written off to profit and loss but often were transferred to a special asset account such as "desperate debtors." This treatment overstated income but maintained a record of all debts owed the firm, regardless of quality. Rents and interest were sometimes anticipated by accruals but were more commonly recorded in full when payment came due. In inventory accounting also the intention was not to find the correct transfer to cost of goods sold, but to segregate the results of trading in different goods, mainly for accounting control. Both textbooks and surviving records show separate inventory accounts for different types of goods, and often these had quantity columns next to the money columns so that perpetual inventory records could be maintained. Not until the nineteenth century did it become common for a ledger to contain only a single inventory account.

The main technical improvement between the sixteenth and nineteenth centuries was the more frequent use in later accounts of double entry's summarizing ability. James Winjum concluded that "double entry brought the concept of capital into the accounting records." But the eighteenth century merchant still valued it chiefly for its ability to bring order to his accounts. Most problems we associate with profit finding and asset valuation concerned him hardly at all. Without the paraphernalia of accruals, matching, or periodic balancing, his venture accounts measured the results of particular operations, while paging through the ledger gave him some idea of overall activity. But he developed neither a clear concept of income nor systematic procedures for judging the success or failure of his business over a period of time.

When trading developed into a fairly continuous process involving permanent capital investments, it became more useful to view the business as a going concern. Operating continuity and the advent of the corporation required periodic reckonings as a prelude to dividend payments. Attempts to measure the income earned during a particular time period led naturally to a system of accruals and deferrals. It was now the use of goods and services, not merely their purchase, that created expense, and sales rather than cash collections which signaled that income had been earned.

Michael Chatfield

Bibliography

Littleton, A.C. *Accounting Evolution to 1900.* New York: American Institute Publishing Company, 1933. Reprint. New York: Russell and Russell, 1966.

Winjum, J. "Accounting in its Age of Stagnation," *Accounting Review*, October 1970, pp. 743–761.

Yamey, B.S., H.C. Edey, and H.W. Thomson. *Accounting in England and Scotland, 1543–1800.* London: Sweet and Maxwell, 1963.

See also BAD DEBTS; CASH FLOW ACCOUNTING; CLOSING ENTRIES AND PROCEDURES; CONTINUITY; DIVIDENDS; DOUBLE ENTRY BOOKKEEPING: ORIGINS; INCOME STATEMENT/INCOME ACCOUNT; LITTLETON, A.C.; MATCHING; OBJECTIVITY; PERIODICITY; PERPETUAL INVENTORY; POSITIVE ACCOUNTING; REALIZATION

Activity Based Costing

Activity based costing (ABC) is a method of cost analysis and product costing that was popularized during the 1980s by Robin Cooper, H. Thomas Johnson, and Robert S. Kaplan. Although their efforts were not an extension of prior work, activity based costing has its roots in the writings of Eric Louis Kohler, who wrote on activity accounting, and George J. Staubus, who described a system of activity costing. Additionally, Johnson (1992) relates how General Electric (GE) accountants used a form of activity cost analysis in the early 1960s. GE may have been the first to use the term "activity" as an object that causes costs.

In the 1930s, while he was controller of the Tennessee Valley Authority (TVA), Kohler developed a responsibility accounting system in which managers in charge of the various "activities" of the TVA were held accountable for the cost of those activities. He dubbed his system "activity accounting." The system was for a governmental unit or a regulated company;

however, Kohler believed it could be extended to business organizations.

Staubus's activity costing framework was presented in his monograph, *Activity Costing and Input-Output Accounting*, published in 1971. The system had five fundamental ideas. The first was the activity focus. Accountants need to provide managers decision-useful information on the cost of carrying out activities. Second, the object of costing should be the output of an activity. Staubus claimed that the value of cost accounting depends on identifying objects of costing that are of interest to managers. Third was the definition of cost as an economic sacrifice, an outflow of wealth. Fourth, the cost of an activity was the cost of using resources both from outsiders and from internal services. The use of an internal service was termed a "synthetic resource." The final idea was the cost-benefit test for cost accounting. Staubus's work was more of an "idea" monograph rather than a guide for implementation. It was not followed by additional literature on how to apply the system in practice. However, it was read by many accounting scholars and could have indirectly influenced later developments in cost accounting.

During the 1980s, managers and accountants alike began to question the usefulness of traditional cost-accounting systems to provide information to managers. A major area of concern was the treatment of overhead in the traditional model. Johnson and Kaplan's 1987 book, *Relevance Lost: The Rise and Fall of Management Accounting*, along with articles written by these authors, brought the problem to the forefront. A major criticism of the traditional model was that overhead was grouped in one or a small number of cost pools and allocated to products according to some measure of production volume (usually direct labor hours or cost). This imprecise tracing of overhead to products could result in distorted product costs and poor decision making. Activity based costing was proposed as a costing system that would provide better information for managers.

The major tenet of activity based costing is that there are certain activities that cause (drive) all costs. Thus, a firm first determines its cost drivers. It then traces costs to the activities. Then the costs of activities are assigned to products based upon their use of activities. Robin Cooper (1990) suggested that activities (cost drivers) can be one of four types: (1) unit, where costs are driven by individual units; (2) batch, where costs are driven by batches regardless of the units in a batch; (3) product, where costs, such as design engineering, are driven by the product and not the production of individual batches or units of the product; and (4) facility-sustaining costs that cannot be associated with individual products but rather the overall facility.

ABC supports the notion that products or services do not directly consume resources; rather they use up activities. ABC is a research-based allocation system in which the organization is first carefully analyzed to determine cost drivers. This initial phase provides a better understanding of the cause-and-effect relationships between the factors of production and individual products.

One could say that ABC is a market-driven technique. As overhead became a proportionally larger part of manufacturing costs, there became a market for a better system. ABC, however, is not a radical departure from conventional systems. It merely takes a more careful look at the factors causing overhead and allocates overhead to products based upon use of those factors. ABC still gives product costs that may not be appropriate for some management decisions, and criticism of the system has started to appear.

Henry R. Schwarzbach

Bibliography

Aiyathurai, G., W.W. Cooper, and K.K. Sinha. "Note On Activity Accounting," *Accounting Horizons*, December 1991, pp. 60–68.

Cooper, R. "Cost Classification in Unit-Based and Activity-Based Manufacturing Cost Systems," *Journal of Cost Management*, Fall 1990, pp. 4–14.

Cooper, R., and R.S. Kaplan. *The Design of Cost Management Systems: Text, Cases, and Readings.* Englewood Cliffs, NJ: Prentice-Hall, 1991.

Johnson, H.T. "Activity-Based Information: A Blueprint for World-Class Management Accounting," *Management Accounting*, June 1988, pp. 23–30.

———. *Relevance Regained: From Top-Down Control to Bottom-Up Empowerment.* New York: Free Press, 1992.

Johnson, H.T., and R.S. Kaplan. *Relevance Lost: The Rise and Fall of Management Accounting.* Boston: Harvard Business School Press, 1987.

Kohler, E.L. "Notes on Activity Accounting," *International Journal of Accounting,*

Education, and Research, Spring 1967, pp. 58–60.

Piper, J.A., and P. Walley. "ABC Relevance Not Found," *Management Accounting* (England), March 1991, pp. 42–44.

Schwarzbach, H.R., and R.G. Vangermeersch. "Why We Should Account for the Fourth Cost of Manufacturing," *Management Accounting*, July 1983, pp. 24–29.

Staubus, G.J. *Activity Costing and Input-Output Accounting*. Homewood, IL: Irwin, 1971.

———. "Activity Costing: Twenty Years On," *Management Accounting Research* (England), 1990, vol. 1, No. 1, pp. 249–264.

See also BREAK-EVEN CHART; COMMON COSTS; COST AND/OR MANAGEMENT ACCOUNTING; DIRECT COSTING; INSTITUTE OF MANAGEMENT ACCOUNTANTS; INVENTORY VALUATION; JOHNSON AND KAPLAN'S *RELEVANCE LOST: THE RISE AND FALL OF MANAGEMENT ACCOUNTING;* JOHNSON, H. THOMAS; KOHLER, ERIC LOUIS; STANDARD COSTING

Advertising by Accountants

Have accountants changed their philosophy about advertising in order to meet a change in the environment in which accounting functions? A possible side issue is the effect of advertising (in this case, nonadvertising) on the making of a profession.

The first restriction on advertising by accountants in the United States was adopted by the American Association of Public Accountants (AAPA) in 1894. The AAPA had little prestige or power, and this rule lacked an effective enforcement vehicle. Thus, it was largely ignored.

Previously, in the nineteenth century, Norman E. Webster (1954) noted accountants advertised. He describes a circular referring to planning and remodeling books for business firms, preparation and adjustment of partnership accounts, and periodic auditing and verification of statements.

During the same period, British accountants were wrestling with the issue of advertising. In 1881 the Institute of Chartered Accountants in England began a movement to eliminate accountants "touting" for business, although as Robert Hiester Montgomery (1939) noted, it was nearly 20 years before the practice died out.

Meanwhile, in America, accountants were advertising unfettered by any prohibition. The *Journal of Accountancy* was motivated to publicize what it considered "particularly offensive" advertisements. In 1919 it printed an editorial by the chairman of the professional ethics committee of the American Institute of Accountants (AIA). The editorial followed by a year a recommendation by the ethics committee for the establishment of a standing committee with power to censor advertising by AIA members.

Subsequently, in 1920 the Council of the AIA added Rule Nine to the rules of conduct: "For a period not exceeding two years after notice by the committee on ethics publicity, no member or associate shall be permitted to distribute circulars or other instruments of publicity without the consent and approval of said committee."

Rule Ten, effective in 1922, prohibited advertising by a member through the mail, in public print, or by any other written word. Excluded was a card which could indicate only the name, title and address without further qualifying words. The size of the card was specified.

Neither Rule Nine nor subsequent Rule Ten worked. By 1958 the first era of advertising by the accounting profession ended when the American Institute of Certified Public Accountants (AICPA) banned all advertising, including "cards." The AICPA had ensured that accounting was safely on its way to becoming a respected profession.

The second era of advertising by accountants began in 1977 with the case of *Bates v. the State Bar of Arizona* (97 S.Ct. 2691), in which two Arizona attorneys were successful in having the Arizona Bar Association's restrictions on advertising ruled unconstitutional as violating the First Amendment to the U.S. Constitution. The AICPA reacted, after polling its membership, by amending Rule 502 of the Code of Professional Ethics in 1978 to allow advertising that is not "false, misleading, or deceptive."

In response to the question, have accountants changed their philosophy about advertising? the answer is, "yes." Between the 1930s and the late 1970s, accountants were virtually unchallenged in their roles as auditors, tax consultants, and bookkeepers. Federal laws passed in 1933, 1934, and 1940 required financial-statement certification by public accountants. The 1939 Internal Revenue Code was a complex law to which accountants rightfully responded with vigor. The examination for certification of accountants, aside from becoming uniform for all, became substantially more rigorous. The supply of accountants tended to be constrained by an entry examination and experience requirements, while demand increased. In short, there were no pretenders to the accountants' throne, and advertising was very likely unnecessary. The power of the federal government to "regulate trade" is vast. Since the 1960s, forces in support of expanded competitive environments and freedoms have gained considerable power. Consider the number of "rights" acts passed or proposed by Congress since 1954. Advertising by accountants existed before 1922 (and for a while afterward) because it was necessary. It may well be necessary again.

Accountancy wanted to be a profession. That aspiration realized, there is no real reason for banning the marketing of services. But does a prohibition on advertising help make a profession? The perception of the users of professional services with regard to advertising will be the principal determinant of the impact of advertising on the "professional image." The advertising phenomenon seems to have been accepted by users of all the other professions without loss of credibility.

Anne Jeannette Sylvestre

Bibliography

Montgomery, R.H. *Fifty Years of Accountancy*. New York: Ronald Press, 1939.

Webster, N.E. *The American Association of Public Accountants: Its First Twenty Years*. New York: AIA, 1954.

Woods, T., and A.J. Sylvestre. "The History of Advertising by Accountants," *Accounting Historians Journal*, Fall 1985, pp. 59–72.

See also AMERICAN INSTITUTE OF CERTIFIED PUBLIC ACCOUNTANTS; BIG EIGHT ACCOUNTING FIRMS; ETHICS, PROFESSIONAL; INSTITUTE OF CHARTERED ACCOUNTANTS IN ENGLAND AND WALES; MONTGOMERY, ROBERT HIESTER

Agency Theory

When one person (the principal) hires another (the agent) to perform some service, the principal and agent must agree upon a contractual relationship to govern their exchange. Agency theory is the study of the efficiency properties of alternative contractual relationships. A contractual relationship includes: the allocation of decision rights among the individuals (i.e., who has the responsibility for making which decisions), the specification of what information is to be reported to whom, and the specification of the relationship between the information that is collected and the compensation paid to the agent. Because accounting and auditing are concerned with the collection and dissemination of information on which contracts and decisions are based, the agency paradigm has been used in accounting and auditing research to study the efficiency properties of different managerial-accounting, financial-accounting, and auditing procedures.

At its simplest, the agency paradigm is based on a hypothesis of how individuals behave in small group, as opposed to competitive market settings. As part of its model of individual behavior, the agency paradigm takes as given that people have different preferences and act in their own best interest, even to the point of acting opportunistically. In an agency analysis, each individual's actions are endogenously derived and based solely on his own self-interest. Further, each individual chooses his own actions based on the expectation that every other individual will act solely in their own self-interest. Any solution to an agency problem must therefore be an equilibrium solution. There are actually three branches of agency research in accounting: principal-agent, "transaction cost economics," and the positive-theory. A major difference between them is whether individuals are assumed to be unboundedly rational (as in the principal-agent branch) or not (as the "transaction cost economics" and positive-theory branches).

In an agency analysis, the contractual relationship is designed to maximize the efficiency of the exchange between the principal and the agent. Efficiency is typically made up of three parts: productive (i.e., incentive) efficiency, or maximizing the total output available to be allocated among the contracting parties; risk-sharing efficiency, or properly allocating the risk inherent in using a stochastic production function; and wealth-redistribution efficiency, or, from the principal's point of view, minimizing the rents that the agent can earn on the basis of any private information that he may have. An agent earns rents on his private information when the principal is forced to pay the agent more than the latter's outside opportunity wage. An agency problem exists when distortions in production, risk sharing, or rent extraction remain even with the agreed-upon contractual relationship.

The agency model provides accounting research with a formal, well-specified and internally consistent economic framework for analyzing the demand for and efficiency effects of accounting procedures. An early precursor of agency research in accounting was the stewardship literature (see Ijiri 1975, 1971; and Rosenfield 1974). While the stewardship literature recognized that accounting and auditing information is used to help govern relationships between individuals with conflicting interests, it failed to specify an explicit equilibrium concept that describes how information is used to resolve the conflicting interests. The agency model provides such an equilibrium concept and hence can be used to formally analyze the demand for and usefulness of accounting procedures and information in settings of multiple individuals with conflicting interests.

Among the papers that have had the most impact on the direction of agency research in accounting are: Holmstrom (1979, 1982), Jensen and Meckling (1976), and Watts and Zimmerman (1978). The Holmstrom papers formally described and analyzed the agency relationship and some of the potential sources of agency problems. The papers established necessary and sufficient conditions under which costless information has strictly positive value in mitigating agency problems. The theoretical accounting and auditing literature has applied the Holmstrom-type analysis to evaluate the efficiency effects of accounting and auditing procedures. Jensen and Meckling (1976) laid out a similar agency relationship between managers, shareholders and bondholders, while Watts and Zimmerman (1978) adapted it to a financial-accounting context. The latter two papers, while less formal, applied agency analysis to more general contexts and broader issues. These latter two papers have served as the basis for most of the empirical agency research in financial accounting.

In managerial-accounting research, the agency model has been used to study the design of a firm's management-control system as a means of mitigating agency problems. Some specific topics analyzed include: budgets (Demski and Feltham 1978), costly conditional variance investigation systems (Baiman and Demski 1980), cost-allocation systems (Rajan 1992), and the design of responsibility centers (Melumad, Mookherjee, and Reichelstein [forthcoming]).

One decision right often allocated to management is the choice of financial-accounting methods and disclosure policy. Thus, in financial accounting, the agency model has been used to study management's choice of financial-reporting methods and disclosure policies (Healy 1985; Hagerman and Zmijewski 1979; and Dye 1988) as well as the effect of mandated changes in financial-accounting policies on other management decisions (Watts and Zimmerman 1978).

From an agency perspective, auditing is an additional mechanism for influencing management's incentives. However, the agency model recognizes that the auditor is also an economic agent and therefore subject to the same incentive difficulties as the manager. Thus, the agency model has been used to study the contractual relationship between the principal and the auditor and its effect on the incentives of management (Antle 1982; and Baiman, Evans and Noel 1987).

In summary, a major contribution of the agency model to accounting and auditing research has been its analysis of the role of accounting and auditing procedures within the context of models in which a demand for those procedures can be endogenously derived. The demand for those procedures is to mitigate efficiency problems within firms made up of self-interested individuals. Previous to the agency model, such inquiries were done within the context of models in which the demand for accounting and auditing procedures had to be exogenously assumed.

However, the agency model has thus far focused little attention on the cost of accounting procedures and the cost of incorporating their outputs in contracts. Hence, it has been difficult to empirically test agency findings. One may not find the predicted procedures either because the cost of implementing them outweighs the benefits or because the model is not descriptive. Thus, extending the agency model to better incorporate contracting costs will improve the analysis and our understanding of the role of accounting and auditing.

Stanley Baiman

Bibliography

Antle, R. "The Auditor as an Economic Agent," *Journal of Accounting Research*, Part II, Autumn 1982, pp. 503–527.

Baiman, S., and J. Demski. "Economically Optimal Performance Evaluation and Control Systems," *Journal of Accounting Research*, Supplement 1980, pp. 184–220.

Baiman, S., J. Evans, and J. Noel. "Optimal Contracts with a Utility-Maximizing Auditor," *Journal of Accounting Research,* Autumn 1987, pp. 217–244.

Demski, J., and G. Feltham. "Economic Incentives in Budgetary Control Systems," *Accounting Review,* April 1978, pp. 336–359.

Dye, R.A. "Earnings Management in an Overlapping Generations Model," *Journal of Accounting Research*, Autumn 1988, pp. 195–235.

Hagerman, R.L., and M.E. Zmijewski. "Some Economic Determinants of Accounting Policy Choice," *Journal of Accounting and Economics*, August 1979, pp. 141–161.

Healy, P. "The Impact of Bonus Schemes on the Selection of Accounting Principles," *Journal of Accounting and Economics,* April 1985, pp. 81–108.

Holmstrom, B. "Moral Hazard and Observability," *Bell Journal of Economics,* Spring 1979, pp. 74–91.

———. "Moral Hazard in Teams," *Bell Journal of Economics*, Autumn 1982, pp. 324–340.

Ijiri, Y. "A Defense for Historical Cost." In *Asset Valuation and Income Determination*, edited by R.R. Sterling, pp. 1–14. Lawrence, KS: University of Kansas Press, 1971.

———. *Theory of Accounting Measurement.* Studies in Accounting Research. Sarasota, FL: American Accounting Association, 1975.

Jensen, M.C., and W.H. Meckling. "Theory of the Firm: Managerial Behavior, Agency Costs, and Ownership Structure," *Journal of Financial Economics*, October 1976, pp. 305–360.

Melumad, N., D. Mookherjee, and S. Reichelstein. "A Theory of Responsibility Centers," *Journal of Accounting and Economics* (forthcoming).

Rajan, M. "Cost Allocation in Multiagent Settings," *Accounting Review*, July 1992, pp. 527–545.

Rosenfield, P. "Stewardship." In *Objectives of Financial Statements*, vol. 2: Selected Papers, pp. 123–140. New York: AICPA, 1974.

Watts, R., and J. Zimmerman. "Towards a Positive Theory of the Determination of Accounting Standards," *Accounting Review*, January 1978, pp. 112–134.

A

See also DEMSKI, JOEL S.; EFFICIENT MARKET HYPOTHESIS; EXTERNAL AUDITING; IJIRI, YUJI; MANIPULATION OF INCOME; POSITIVE ACCOUNTING; STEWARDSHIP

Agricultural Accounting

Agricultural accounting traces back to early rural societies when tallies were made of crops and livestock. In the time of medieval Britain, the nobility (often absentee landlords) had accounts prepared to monitor certain farming activities of their stewards. Receipts and expenditures constituted the usual formal records.

The seventeenth-century farm accounts of Robert Loder from 1610–1620 are frequently quoted as a key starting point for tracing the history of more formal accounting in agriculture. Accounting developments in eighteenth-century Britain were spurred by the agricultural revolution, a period when the keeping of accounts was widely advocated. It was known that by the end of the eighteenth century there were farmers whose accounts included the capitalization of their farms and contained data for cost calculations and financial summaries.

Farmers had, by the middle of the nineteenth century, access to a number of pamphlets, farm-accounting stationery, and texts to guide the preparation of accounts. These were accompanied by frequent homilies on such themes as "no one is ever ruined who keeps good accounts"! Illustrations of account keeping can be found in Alexander Trotter, *Method of Farm Book-keeping* (1825), and Inness Munro, *A Guide to Farm Book-keeping* (1821). By the turn of the century, literature in agricultural accounting had developed a strong basis as shown in the *Accountants' Index* (1920). Much farm accounting was still wedded to a merchant system of bookkeeping, and some writers tendered anecdotal evidence that accounting had little of practical value to offer to farming. Yet the accumulated wisdom on farm accounting led to formal entries on the subject in the *Encyclopaedia of Accounting* (1903) and the *Cyclopedia of American Agriculture* (1909), the latter stressing the performance measurement attributes of accounting especially for determining departmental profit. In Australia, Francis Vigar's pioneering work on pastoral accounts led to two editions of his book *Station Book-keeping*, the last one in 1901.

The period between World Wars I and II witnessed the growth of farm accounting in Britain and the United States. The growth was largely stimulated by the impact of tax legislation on farm incomes, the growth of agricultural-accounting firms and the research of agricultural economists that generated data for analysing farm financial results and enterprise costs. In Britain, the milk and sugar-beet industries gained from such research, and in the United States, university agricultural economists generated valuable research for the livestock industry. For example, the Bureau of Business Research of University of Texas produced research on ranch accounting, *A System of Accounting Procedures for Livestock Ranches* (1930). The growth of farm accounting was attributed to the needs of farmers to deal with taxation, to handle increased competition, and to know which farm products performed best.

The period from World War II through to the 1960s saw strong growth in farm-accounting activity. Leading practitioners, while emphasizing the importance of accurate financial recording, also exhorted the strengths of comparative analysis. Gross margin analysis emerged during this period as a preferred technique for analysis since it enabled enterprises and products to be compared without the drudgery of cost accounting. Accompanying comparative analysis was the movement for uniform account codes and terminology standardization.

The information value of farm accounts, especially for internal-management purposes, came under stronger focus from the late 1950s onward. Successive editions of widely read texts reflected the growing importance of accounts to improve decision making on the farm. For example, C.A. Mallyon claimed that his book, *The Principles and Practice of Farm Management Accounting* (1961), was the first in Australia to show how accounts assist profitable

decision making and claimed that literature in the Southern Hemisphere was nonexistent in the area of modern farm-management accounting. In Britain, S.U.P. Cornwell, who wrote *Management Accounting for Agriculture* (1957), claimed that his book was the first in Britain to apply management accounting to the problems of agriculture.

A constant concern in this period was the pervasive effect of taxation on farm-accounting practice where profit was not a measure of business return but an income result conditioned by tax rules. Of particular concern was accounting-policy choice where tax-liability effects dominated financial-result determination. Taxation, to many writers, has distorted livestock values, confused capital and revenue, created unrealistic depreciation schedules, and mismatched revenues and expenses. The persistent challenge to practitioners was to convince the farmer that information for decision making is as critical as information for taxation reports.

In terms of knowledge and practice development, the 1980s were a golden period for those practitioners seeking more guidance in applying conventional accounting principles to agriculture and to improve their reporting and audit activities. Accounting firms and professional bodies released reports and guides to extend and deepen professional knowledge. Arthur Andersen and Company produced a study, *The Management Difference: Future Information Needs of Commercial Farmers and Ranchers* (1982), to offer fresh perspectives on accounting's information role. The Canadian Institute of Chartered Accountants' *Accounting and Financial Reporting by Agricultural Producers* (1986) and the American Institute of Certified Public Accountants' *Audits of Agricultural Producers and Agricultural Cooperatives* (1987) produced guidelines for applying conventional principles to a wide range of agricultural activity and have increased the scope for financial reporting and auditing in agriculture. In particular, the AICPA made a valuable contribution in delineating the audit issues for agricultural asset categories: field and row crops, orchards and vineyards, intermediate-life plants, breeding and production animals, animals held for sale, and land-development costs.

Paralleling these guidelines have been professional publications and technical bulletins to address specific accounting and reporting issues in agriculture. The New Zealand Society of Accountants has released a number of publications addressing horticultural, forestry, and bloodstock matters. A more comprehensive review of financial accounting matters is provided in Roger Hugh Juchau, Murray Clark, and Jack Radford, *Agricultural Accounting: Perspectives and Issues* (1989), where the challenges and research matters in accounting for agricultural production have been discussed by various authors and authorities. Challenges posed for agricultural accounting by conceptual-framework developments are to be explored in a discussion paper published by the Australian Accounting Research Foundation, *Accounting for Self-Generating and Regenerating Assets* (1995).

Agriculture will continue to challenge the professional accountant. Such traditional challenges as dealing with short and long production cycles that are difficult to accelerate, slow, or redirect; resolving information-provision objectives of taxation or decision making; handling live, variable and imprecise data; making cost allocations—intra- and interperiod and intra- and interenterprise—will persist and will be extended by the continuing changes in technologies and the advent of new biological production systems. Agriculture encompasses diverse production, cultural, and distribution activities. New forms of agriculture will emerge to cater to future food, fiber, energy, and aesthetic needs. The conventional reporting framework of accounting will be tested as it deals with events and transactions emerging from new modes of agriculture and associated economic relationships.

Roger Hugh Juchau

Bibliography

Adams, A., L. Hagan, D. Roberts, and J. Staunton. *Accounting for Self-Generating and Regenerating Assets.* Caulfield: Australian Accounting Research Foundation, 1995.

American Institute of Certified Public Accountants. *Audits of Agricultural Producers and Agricultural Cooperatives.* New York: AICPA, 1987.

Canadian Institute of Chartered Accountants. *Accounting and Financial Reporting by Agricultural Producers.* Toronto: CICA, 1986.

Cornwell, S.U.P. *Management Accounting for Agriculture.* London: Gee, 1957.

Freear, J. "Robert Loder, Jacobean Management Accountant," *Abacus,* September 1970, pp. 28–38.

Juchau, R., M. Clark, and J. Radford. *Agricultural Accounting: Perspectives and Issues.* Lincoln, New Zealand: Lincoln University, 1989.

Mallyon, C.A. *The Principles and Practices of Farm Management Accounting.* Sydney: Law Book Company, 1961.

McMurray, K., and P. McNall. *Farm Accounting: Principles and Problems.* Chicago: A.W. Shaw, 1926.

Sturrock, F. *Farm Accounting and Management.* 7th ed. London: Pitman, 1982.

Woodbridge, F.W. *System of Accounting Procedure for Livestock Ranchers.* University of Texas Bulletin No. 3040. Research Monograph No. 5. Austin, TX: Bureau of Business Research, University of Texas, 1930.

See also "Charge and Discharge" Statement; Cost and/or Management Accounting; Distribution Costs; Germany; Manorial Accounting; Medieval Accounting; Poland; Tally Stick

Alberti del Giudice

Between 1300 and 1345, the most powerful Florentine merchant-banking houses were the Bardi, the Peruzzi, and the Acciaiuoli. In the 1340s, all three failed due to overextension of credit and defaults on loans to monarchs. The Alberti del Giudice banking house was then chosen to collect the papal revenues and became important until it split into several rival firms because of family quarrels. Like the Peruzzi accounts, surviving Alberti records contain elements of double entry bookkeeping but no complete system. Not all transactions are recorded twice, there is no trace of the expense or income summary accounts that would have permitted a check on the equality of debits and credits, and profits were calculated without balancing the books. The most extensive Alberti accounts are in the *libro segreto,* secret book, containing data on partners' capital from 1302 to 1339, together with 12 financial statements prepared at irregular intervals to determine income. As in many Florentine companies, from one to five years passed between such settlements, at which time the books were closed, assets and liabilities were inventoried, and the partnership agreement was renewed or extended. In the meantime, partners could not withdraw from the firm and no new partner could join.

Michael Chatfield

Bibliography

De Roover, R. "The Development of Accounting prior to Luca Pacioli according to the Account-Books of Medieval Merchants." In *Studies in the History of Accounting*, edited by A.C. Littleton and B.S. Yamey, pp. 114–174. Homewood, IL: Irwin, 1956.

———. "The Story of the Alberti Company of Florence, 1302–1348, as Revealed in its Account Books," *Business History Review*, vol. 32, Spring 1958, pp. 14–59.

See also BARDI; BRANCH ACCOUNTING; CLOSING ENTRIES AND PROCEDURES; DOUBLE ENTRY BOOKKEEPING: ORIGINS; PARTNERSHIP ACCOUNTING; PERUZZI

American Accounting Association

What is now known as the American Accounting Association (AAA) was founded in 1916. The original name was the American Association of University Instructors in Accounting. John Raymond Wildman of New York University was the moving force behind the establishment of the organization and was its first president. The organizational meeting was held on December 28, 1916, at a meeting of the American Economic Association at Columbus, Ohio.

The AAA's first formal publication consisted of the papers and proceedings of the annual meetings, which began with the 1916 meeting. In March 1926, what was to become the organization's premiere journal, the *Accounting Review*, was first published under the editorship of William Andrew Paton. This was a major undertaking for an organization that had fewer than 600 members. This membership base changed very little until 1938 when membership reached 936. The 1946 membership was 1,570, while in 1947 it nearly doubled to 2,963. By 1951, there were over 4,000 members.

In 1936, the name of the organization was changed to the American Accounting Association. It was in 1936 that the AAA issued its first major principles statement, which was entitled "A Tentative Statement of Accounting Principles Underlying Corporate Financial Statements." This statement was revised in 1941, 1948, and 1957. Other major publications included the monograph series, which began in 1937 under the direction of research directors William A. Paton and A.C. Littleton. The third monograph in the series, which appeared in 1940 under the authorship of Paton and Littleton, was entitled *An Introduction to Corporate Accounting Standards* and was the best selling in the series. In essence, the AAA changed in the late 1930s from an organization for teachers to a major research organization.

Regionalization

Although the AAA was founded in 1916, regional meetings were not held until 1949 when the Southeastern Region group held its first meeting in Atlanta, Georgia. By the early 1990s, there were seven regional groups within the AAA. The influence of the Southeastern Region meetings were instrumental in this overall regionalization of the AAA. Regionalization, in turn, led to changes in organizational structure. In 1952, following the early success of the Southeastern Regional group, the AAA Executive Committee established a subcommittee on regional meetings.

To this day, the regional organizations have as their objective the facilitation of wider membership participation in the activities of the AAA. This participation is accomplished through an annual meeting that is more economically accessible than the annual meeting of the association.

Recent History

The AAA celebrated its 50th anniversary in 1966 in Miami, Florida, with Herbert E. Miller as the 50th president. In many ways, that 1966 meeting marked the beginning of a new era for the organization. In that year, the AAA hired a full-time executive secretary (Paul Gerhardt) and opened a permanent office in Evanston, Illinois. Gerhardt was also responsible for the association's move to Sarasota, Florida, in 1971.

AAA Leadership

The 10-member Executive Committee is the primary governing body of the AAA. Although the presidents have been important, they have not been as important as the Executive Committees, of which they are a part. In a sense, people become president because of their past contributions to the AAA, and as president they have to be willing to allow others to make contributions.

The democratization of AAA began with the setting up of Council in 1978. The establishment of Council was a move to assure that there would be broad membership involvement in the governance of the organization. A 1977–1978 committee dealing with the roles of regions and sections recommended an advisory council composed of section and regional leaders. That recommendation was approved in 1978, and the Advisory Council met for the first time at the 1978 meeting in Denver, Colorado. Initially a purely advisory group, Council became an official part of the governing structure with a 1980 bylaws amendment. Council, composed of 30 members, is made up of representatives from all of the regions and sections, plus four members at large. Although Council provides an advisory role to the Executive Committee, its most important function is the electing of four members to the seven-person Nominating Committee.

Membership Trends

The membership of the AAA has stayed stable or declined over the past 25 years, but the composition of that membership has changed. In 1966, there were 10,762 members, of which 70 percent were practitioners. Only 3,475 were academicians. By 1990, the membership had declined to 9,303, of which 6,948, or 75 percent, were academicians. Foreign membership increased throughout the period. In 1991, there were 1,855 foreign members. Overall, 20 percent of the membership reside outside the United States.

Special-Interest Sections

One of the more controversial subjects during the recent history was whether special-interest sections should be allowed to form. There was fear among members of the various Executive Committees that the formation of interest groups would result in a splintering of the organization.

Ultimately, Gary John Previts, S. Paul Garner, and Alfred R. Roberts were responsible, albeit indirectly, for the AAA moving to an acceptance of sections. Previts, Garner, and Roberts, along with five others on the initial Chartering Committee, established the Academy of Accounting Historians in 1973. Part of the motivation for establishing a new organization for historians was the fact that the AAA had ignored various committee reports over the years that recommended more association involvement in accounting history.

The splintering off of the historians might not have been so alarming to the Executive Committee had not D. Larry Crumbley, then at the University of Florida, noted the ease with which the academy had been formed. Crumbley had been voicing displeasure over the fact that tax professors were not having a large enough voice in the AAA and were not given sufficient time on the annual program. Inspired by the academy activities of Previts, Garner, and Roberts, Crumbley copied the academy's bylaws and used them to incorporate the American Taxation Association (ATA) in 1974. The ATA grew quickly, as did the Academy of Accounting Historians. Fearing that the AAA would lose these members, and perhaps others in specialized disciplines, the Executive Committee addressed the issue of sections.

A proposal that had been presented at the two preceding meetings to allow sections was again made in March 1975. The vote passed. Formal guidelines were approved later in the year. The formation of sections was an event waiting to happen. Individuals throughout the United States quickly began securing the necessary 100 signatures to form a variety of sections. At the 1976 annual meeting in Atlanta, six sections held their first meetings. These first sections were the Auditing Section, the International Accounting Section, the Public Sector Section (later renamed the Government and Nonprofit Section), the Management Advisory Service Section (later renamed the Information Systems/Management Advisory Services Section), the Community/Junior College Section (later renamed the Two-Year College Section), and the Administrators of Accounting Programs Group. In later years, other sections were formed, including the Accounting, Behavior, and Organizations Section, the Management Accounting Section, the Public Interest Section, and the Gender Section. In addition, the American Taxation Association returned to the fold as a section in 1978.

Despite the fears of the Executive Committee, the establishment of sections has not splintered the association. As of 1994, the AAA was stronger than ever, probably because of the membership benefits offered by the sections. Indeed, it is possible that a failure to establish sections could have been detrimental to the organization in that the sections would have been formed anyway, but outside the AAA structure (as did occur with accounting history and taxation). Ultimately, the movement toward sections led to a change in the governing structure of AAA in that the Council was formed in 1978 to permit the sections and regions to have a voice in the activities of the AAA. In summary, what was feared would cause a breakup of the AAA led to greater democratization of the group.

The most recent quarter century of the AAA has been one of pluralism as individuals, sections, and regions have all grown and developed. The growth in sectional and regional activities has resulted in an array of programs taking place under the umbrella of the AAA. In 1966, the AAA published one journal and no newsletters; in 1992, it published eight journals and 12 newsletters. Specialized conferences were nonexistent in 1966. By 1992 there were ten association-wide conferences held on either an annual or biannual basis, plus others sponsored by the sections.

Activities surrounding the annual meeting, long a highlight of member activities, have also grown. In 1966 the meeting was only two days in length. The 1992 meeting lasted three days and was preceded by a day of continuing-education activities, and still another day of committee meetings.

Increased activities have meant increased costs, and budget deficits, as total membership declined or stayed constant into the 1990s due to the loss of practitioner members, and in 1991 the AAA increased dues to relieve the budget problem. In 1965, contributions to the AAA amounted to about $1,000. In 1990, the figure was close to $1 million. Given that increase in monetary support, the declining number of practitioner members can be overlooked.

Dale L. Flesher

Bibliography

Arens, A.A. "Presidential Address: Celebration, Evaluation, and Rededication," *Accounting Horizons*, December 1990, pp. 88–96.

Flesher, D.L. *The Third Quarter Century of the American Accounting Association, 1966–1991.* Sarasota, FL: American Accounting Association, 1991.

Zeff, S.A. *American Accounting Association: Its First Fifty Years, 1916–1966.* Sarasota, FL: American Accounting Association, 1966.

See also A STATEMENT OF BASIC ACCOUNTING THEORY; ACADEMY OF ACCOUNTING HISTORIANS; ACCOUNTING EDUCATION IN THE UNITED STATES; ACCOUNTING RESEARCH BULLETINS; *AN INTRODUCTION TO CORPORATE ACCOUNTING STANDARDS;* BEAVER, WILLIAM; CONCEPTUAL FRAMEWORK; DEFINITIONS OF ACCOUNTING; GARNER, S. PAUL; GENERALLY ACCEPTED ACCOUNTING PRINCIPLES; HATFIELD, HENRY RAND; HISTORICAL COST; HORNGREN, CHARLES T.; IJIRI, YUJI; KOHLER, ERIC LOUIS; LITTLETON, A.C.; MATCHING; MAUTZ, ROBERT K.; McKINSEY, JAMES O.; MOONITZ, MAURICE; PAID IN CAPITAL; PATON, WILLIAM ANDREW; PREVITS, GARY JOHN; SECURITIES AND EXCHANGE COMMISSION; SELLS, ELIJAH WATT; SOLOMONS, DAVID; THOMAS'S *THE ALLOCATION PROBLEM IN FINANCIAL ACCOUNTING THEORY;* TREADWAY COMMISSION; WELLS, MURRAY CHARLES; WILDMAN, JOHN RAYMOND; ZEFF, STEPHEN A.

American Institute of Certified Public Accountants

The American Institute of Certified Public Accountants (AICPA) traces its origins back to a predecessor organization, the American Association of Public Accountants (AAPA), which was incorporated in New York during January 1887. This pioneering body primarily represented an elite circle of Northeastern practitioners who sought to emulate the model of professionalism developed earlier in Britain by the Institute of Chartered Accountants. The AAPA's founding had in fact been encouraged by a British chartered accountant, Edwin Guthrie of the firm of Thomas, Wade, and Guthrie of London. Like many of his British professional associates with practice responsibilities in the United States, Guthrie was eager to identify reliable local accountants who might serve as correspondents for his firm.

Two issues permeated the subsequent drives of the AAPA and its successors to craft a viable system of professionalism for American accountancy. These were the needs: (1) to define institutional relationships between practitioners and the society they served, and (2) to form organizational structures that were effective in coordinating the activities of the diverse elements within the professional community. Institutions represented both formal and informal rules that were broadly acceptable to practitioners and thus provided a basis for maintaining order within the profession. They were also critical in creating links with external groups whose actions might affect the profession's interest. Organizational structures, on the other hand, represented formal social entities that were formed to channel the collective action of practitioners toward some common purpose. Institutional relationships played a vital role within organizations. Institutions defined the limits as to the policies and activities that could be undertaken in governing particular organizations.

The definition of institutions and organizations for the new profession, however, was difficult. Although they sought to follow the chartered accountants' example, the American accountants had to take into consideration the special circumstances unique to this country that impinged on professional development. In this century-long voyage of discovery, the national representative association experienced four metamorphoses. During the first phase, covering the period 1887–1905, a highly centralized national association sought to define formal boundaries for a community of competent practitioners. The second phase, lasting from 1905 to 1916, saw a transformation of the national organization into a federation that incorporated many state societies. Besides beginning the standardization of several aspects of professional life, this second epoch witnessed the broadening recognition among business and government leaders of the usefulness of accountants' specialized knowledge. During the third stage, spanning the period 1916–1936, the national organization reverted back to a tighter and more centralized organizational structure. The experience of this period culminated in two other fundamental changes. First, the profession's attestation services were formally accepted by the newly formed Securities and Exchange Commission (SEC) in its national framework for corporate governance. Secondly, the national association's leadership recognized that self-regulating professionalism depended both on the preservation of practitioners' unity and on the effective application of their expertise by accountants protecting the investing public. The achievements of the last, or contemporary, phase, which involved primarily the refinements of the technical and ethical dimensions of practice, were built up from the firm foundations laid down over the course of a century's professional experience.

First Phase—The Independent AAPA (1887–1905)

The first phase of professional development coincided with a takeoff in demand for accountants' services beginning late in the nineteenth century. One impetus to professional growth was the desire of leading American bankers to include financial statements certified by respected accounting firms in the prospectuses for the security issues that they floated in London and other European financial centers. Railroad refinancing and initial public offering of shares in many giant industrial enterprises such as the United States Steel Company, the nation's first billion-dollar corporation, reached a crescendo during the period 1898–1904. The practice of certifying statements was especially important in bolstering confidence of distant investors who had little direct knowledge of the enterprises that were seeking capital infusions.

Initially, the AAPA was slow in formalizing a program for accounting professionalization. This, however, changed during the early 1890s, because of the initiative taken by a rival accounting organization, the New York Institute of Accounts (NYIA), to establish its own exclusive badge of professional competency. The NYIA was a generalist body that attracted bookkeepers, businessmen interested in accounting, and a sprinkling of independent practitioners. It was from among this latter segment of its membership that a plan emerged to establish a qualifying examination for "certified accountants." Frustrated by their inability to win many engagements from local underwriters, these NYIA members believed that a distinctly "American" certification would enhance their prestige and help in their competition with the highly esteemed British chartered accountants.

The AAPA responded to the NYIA's drive to establish a certifying test in accountancy in two ways. First, it successfully complained to the New York State Board of Regents, which controlled professional licensing and collegiate curriculums, that the NYIA's sponsorship of certifying examinations had exceeded the powers granted in its state charter. Secondly, the AAPA further countered in 1892, by organizing its "College of Accounts" for certifying the competency of entry-level practitioners. It was hoped that its new collegiate degree represented a first step in extending the AAPA's overall authority in determining who was sufficiently competent and morally fit to be admitted to the profession. Although the College of Accounts conducted classes for one year (1894), it was abandoned when the Board of Regents decided that the curriculum was insufficient to warrant the granting of any degree.

In 1895 both the AAPA and the NYIA again sought to gain state recognition through the promotion of plans to secure licensing, along lines similar to those already followed in the older professions of law and medicine. Following the example of the chartered accountants, the AAPA wanted the state to grant it full power for certifying practitioners through its own examination. The NYIA, on the other hand, sought a state-controlled licensing system that would also require practitioners to be either American citizens or intending to become naturalized. This latter stipulation represented a crude effort to undermine the prestige of chartered accountants—most of whom understandably were reluctant to give up their British citizenship.

A licensing bill akin to the one sponsored by the NYIA was eventually ratified by the New York State legislature on April 17, 1896. The NYIA's success was partially due to the fact that its bill more closely followed the pattern of state control already in place for other professional groups. The NYIA's success also derived from the strong political influence of one of its leaders, Charles Waldo Haskins, a founder of the firm of Haskins and Sells. Haskins had married into the politically influential Havemeyer family. His wife's uncle, William F. Havemeyer, had been a mayor of New York City and had led the drive to oust the Tweed Ring from power during the 1870s. Through this connection, Haskins enjoyed cordial relations with many members of the Regents Board and with its secretary Melvil Dewey (inventor of the library filing system).

The primary achievement of this first epoch in professional development was that a viable model for state licensing was defined. Although the licensing did not restrict practice to licensees, it did provide recognition of special status through demonstrated competency. Subsequently, however, licensing did not remain the exclusive domain of the state. Accounting's national representative association later became more intimately involved with the various state boards in the process of designing and grading a uniform certifying examination.

Second Phase—The Federated AAPA (1905–1916)

Although the implementation of the new CPA licensing soon heightened tensions within the profession—particularly over determining which practitioners might be grandfathered in through a waiver of the qualifying examination—leaders of the rival groups recognized a need for harmony. This appreciation was reflected in the growing cooperation of Haskins, who had established the New York State Society of Certified Public Accountants (NYSSCPA) in 1897, and Arthur Lowes Dickinson, a British chartered accountant with the firm of Price Waterhouse and Company who was a leader of the AAPA. Although Haskins did not live to see the full blooming of this connection (he died in 1903), it eventually led to the merger in 1905 of the AAPA with a new body, the Federation of State Societies of Public Accountants in the United States of America, which had been founded three years earlier by George Wilkinson, a chartered accountant practicing in Chicago. The new federated body, which retained the AAPA name, incorporated both the national association and one society to represent each state with CPA licensing.

One achievement of the federated AAPA was its success assisting local practitioners in many states to organize and to secure licensing legislation. The AAPA provided monetary assistance and helped to lobby state legislatures. It also drafted a model CPA bill that sought to standardize national CPA licensing requirements. The success of these efforts was reflected by the fact that by 1913, accountants in 31 states had been able to win passage of some form of professional-licensing legislation in accounting.

The federated AAPA was also effective in gaining public recognition of the usefulness of the accountants' special skills through voluntary service to the government. In 1905, for example, three leading firms—Haskins and Sells, Price Waterhouse and Company, and Deloitte, Plender, Griffiths—helped to restore confidence in New York's leading insurance companies through their audits of their financial statements after the damaging revelations of the special state investigatory (Armstrong) commission into the industry's financial practices. A special AAPA committee also provided counsel on the development of accounting systems for many new independent executive agencies created during the administration of President Theodore Roosevelt. Another AAPA committee sought unsuccessfully to dissuade the Interstate Commerce Commission (ICC) in 1906 from standardizing railroad accounting through the application of rigidly uniform methodologies. Still other committees assisted the Federal Trade Commission (FTC) in 1914 in preparing uniform costing systems for many types of small businesses and in advising the Internal Revenue Service (IRS) about many aspects of accounting that were relevant to the federal income tax law passed in 1913.

The federated AAPA also worked to standardize practice. One factor in this development was the publication of the *Journal of Accountancy,* which was taken over from the Illinois Society of CPAs in 1905. This periodical provided useful information about technical matters in accounting and taxation as well as the progress of professional affairs. Additionally, the goals of the profession were defined and communicated through the agendas of specialized committees as well as through periodic meetings and conventions.

Yet in spite of the solid achievements of this era, not all were happy with the direction of developments in accounting, and this led eventually to another momentous reorganization of the national representative body. Some leaders were restive over the unevenness of licensing standards in particular jurisdictions and also the inability of the federated association to exercise strong powers to cure these deficiencies. Some states, for example, did not mandate any educational prerequisites; in others, the quality of certifying examinations was low; and in a few, the licensing process was susceptible to political pressure.

In addition to these concerns about professional governance, accountants were divided because of the ways in which their knowledge was being used in practice. This translated into different perceptions as to the priorities that should be given to various types of programs that the national association sponsored. The perspective of the elite practitioners was conditioned by their service to the nation's largest businesses. What was most highly prized was their ability to propose useful measurement methods to better reflect the underlying economic realities stemming from the technological and managerial innovations that propelled forward their clients' businesses. Elite status was also associated with a capacity for proposing useful accounting estimates to deal with the

many contingent developments affecting the operations of large business entities. Local practitioners, on the other hand, were usually much less specialized in their practices and concentrated on providing routine services to relatively small and uncomplex businesses. Given the dichotomy in the nature of practice, it is understandable why the elite wanted the association to invest its resources in providing more research support in the form of greater library facilities and more technical publications. The locals, contrarily, believed that more emphasis should be placed on promoting the benefits of practitioner services among small businesses.

The elite also believed that the association was too distracted by the concerns of members who were not in practice. Few of the elite practitioners were interested in the curriculum surveys and drives to win greater acceptance for collegiate accounting training that educator members favored. Nor was there much enthusiasm among elite practitioners, who were primarily concerned with the problems of financial and tax accounting, with the cost-accounting problems that were so central in the professional lives of industrial accountants.

These concerns eventually boiled over in 1916 and led to another reordering of the national representative body. The old nuclear AAPA abandoned the federation, redesignating itself as the American Institute of Accountants (AIA) and maintaining headquarters in New York City. The AIA's bylaws enhanced the powers of its central Executive Committee. The state societies also were detached and no longer maintained formal connection with the national association. Moreover, the transformation redefined who could enjoy full membership. Accounting educators, who were reduced to the status of associate members, formed their own representative group in 1916, the American Association of University Instructors in Accounting (AAUIA) (later renamed the American Accounting Association). The industrial accountants, who also had been marginalized, established their own representative body, the National Association of Cost Accountants (now the Institute of Management Accountants).

Third Phase—The Independent AIA (1916–1936)

The AIA soon initiated a drive to raise professional standards and to provide support to the type of research-driven practice in which the elite accounting firms excelled. In 1917, admission to the AIA was made contingent on passage of its own rigorous examination. This test was also offered to the nation's licensing boards and, by 1921, 36 had adopted it. Eventually, the uniform certifying examination would be accepted by all the licensing authorities in the United States. In addition, research capabilities were greatly augmented by the formation of a professional library in 1918 located at the AIA's New York City headquarters and the beginnings of its technical bibliographic service, the *Accountants' Index*, in 1920.

The AIA also continued to garner prestige for the profession through the valuable national service rendered both by its committees and by prominent leaders during World War I. The AIA assisted the War Department by evaluating professional qualifications of accountants applying for defense-service posts. AIA committees created standard accounting systems for military bases and assisted the War Industries Board (WIB) in the development of contracts and analyses for cost-plus contracts for defense suppliers. Leading members also played critical roles during the emergency. Robert Hiester Montgomery of Lybrand, Ross Brothers and Montgomery, served as the Army representative to the WIB; Joseph Edmund Sterrett of Price Waterhouse and Company served as vice chairman of the Advisory Tax Board; and George Oliver May of Price Waterhouse served as an adviser to the War Finance Board.

But in spite of these solid achievements, the AIA experienced a disruptive revolt in 1921. Two events precipitated this crisis, which divided the profession for over a decade. First, the AIA promulgated ethical rules that prohibited both advertising and direct client solicitation. This action persuaded many local accountants that the elite intended to use professional reform as a subterfuge for driving them out of practice. Second, through 1922, the AIA unsuccessfully lobbied the U.S. Congress for a federal charter. This latter action, taken in conjunction with the recent efforts to improve the quality of certifying examinations, was interpreted by many local practitioners as a first step in a drive sponsored by the elite to substitute membership in the AIA for state-granted CPA licenses as the primary badge of professional competency. Consequently, many local practitioners were drawn to a rival organization, the American Society of Certified Public Accountants (ASCPA) founded in December 1921 by Durand Springer of Michigan. Some measure of

the depth of these concerns can be gauged by comparing the size of the memberships of the rival associations. By 1936, the ASCPA had recruited a membership of 2,135, compared to the 2,239 members of the AIA.

The circumstances that eventually reversed this polarizing trend did not emerge until well into the 1930s. During the prosperous 1920s, the public was little concerned about the issues that had divided practitioners and, instead, generally exhibited a growing deference toward a professional group that had been such a strong contributor to the nation's progress. A laissez-faire attitude was in vogue. As long as the economy and financial markets continued to prosper, few individuals were concerned about the problems of either professional or corporate governance.

Nevertheless, there were some critics who harbored misgivings about how effectively accountancy was serving the public. Foremost among these concerns was the belief that the failure to begin the formal standardization of financial accounting potentially subjected investors to dangers from incomplete, misleading, or false information about corporate finance.

One group concerned about financial reporting were retail brokerage concerns, whose success depended on how well they directed their clients to safe and profitable investments. They generally embraced the notion that the analysis of financial information provided a strong support for making successful investment decisions. But their desire to mandate great disclosure among companies trading on the New York Stock Exchange (NYSE) was opposed by other elements in the Exchange's membership—most notably, the floor traders who speculated for their own accounts. The floor traders' opposition was rooted in the belief that more rigorous financial-reporting requirements would raise compliance costs and, thus, induce many registrants to abandon the NYSE for markets with laxer rules. It was this latter perspective that guided policy at the NYSE prior to the Crash of 1929.

Criticism of financial reporting also emanated from academe. Eric Louis Kohler, for example, an accounting educator at Northwestern University who later became a partner at Arthur Andersen and Company, reproached the AIA in editorials appearing in *Accounting Review* (the official publication of the AAUIA) for its failure to standardize financial accounting. Additionally, Professor William Z. Ripley, an economist at Harvard University, took public companies to task for the general unevenness of their financial-reporting quality in a series of articles appearing in the *Atlantic Monthly* in 1926, which was reissued the following year as a book entitled *Main Street and Wall Street*. In 1926 Ripley chaired a special committee sponsored by the Social Science Research Council (SSRC) to investigate the broader social implications of the growing holdings of corporate financial assets by the investing public. Ripley was joined on this committee by May, who had been particularly disturbed by the unfavorable implications about the role of accountants in *Main Street and Wall Street*. The urgency of the committee's inquiry into more effective ways for governing corporate financial affairs was soon heightened by the stock market crash in 1929, which heralded the beginning of a decade-long depression. The chief outcome of the committee's deliberations was its sponsorship of the research of Adolf A. Berle Jr. and Gardiner C. Means, which was later published under the title *The Modern Corporation and Private Property* (1932). Although this latter work is best remembered for its findings about the uneven distribution of wealth in America and its implications for sustaining national prosperity, the authors also stressed the need for more reliable information for investors to assure probity in the financial markets.

The circumstance, however, that ultimately transformed the AIA was the encroachment of the federal government on what previously had been considered the exclusive prerogatives of the profession. Although the AIA and the NYSE tried in 1933 to implement the Berle and Means recommendations, these actions came too late and seemed insufficient. The New Deal administration of President Franklin D. Roosevelt had, through the Securities Act of 1933, increased substantially federal oversight powers over the flotation of new stock and bond issues. Later, under the Securities Act of 1934, federal regulation mandated continuous financial disclosure for all public companies and also focused primary responsibility for financial-market governance in the SEC.

What caused the most chagrin to accountancy's leaders were the specific powers these acts granted government in evaluating the professional work of independent practitioners. The SEC, for example, could issue stop orders, which effectively prevented the registration of new securities issues in cases where accounting or disclosure were deemed insufficient. Moreover, by 1935, SEC Commissioner James M. Landis and Chief Accountant Carman G. Blough, irritated by the poor quality of reports submitted by many registrants, began threatening to exercise the agency's inherent powers to promulgate accounting and auditing rules.

These mounting pressures, which threatened to undermine the autonomy of public accountants, soon induced the AIA's leaders to try to build political power by reunifying the fractured practitioner community. Division in the profession had confused external groups about the proper focus of authority within accountancy. This ambiguity and the demoralized condition of the financial markets encouraged those who believed that a more active federal intervention represented the best means for regulating the nation's financial markets and for assuring effective corporate governance. It was difficult for practitioners to rebut this view as long as they failed to speak with one voice about these matters.

AIA leaders, such as Robert Hiester Montgomery and Federick H. Hurdman, recognized the need to reach a reconciliation with the ASCPA so as to present a unified front to countervail the SEC's encroachment. In 1935 the general acceptance of this view among the membership was evidenced by Montgomery's election to the AIA's presidency on a platform of reconciliation. The following year, the two rival associations merged, while retaining the AIA name. In addition to ending the disruptive split, the reorganized AIA also began to work more closely with the state CPA societies to promote broader professional cohesion nationwide.

The success of the AIA's strategy was soon reflected in the acceptance by government of the association's efforts to standardize accounting and auditing. The SEC agreed to recognize the AIA's authority in these matters as long as their results were deemed to be effective in protecting the public interest. In 1939 the AIA's Committee on Accounting Procedure began issuing its Accounting Research Bulletins as a means for standardizing financial accounting. That same year, after the revelations of the McKesson and Robbins audit failure, the AIA also sponsored the publication of "Extensions of Auditing Procedures." This document became the nucleus of a second body of authoritative guidance, entitled "Statements on Auditing Procedure," that were issued by the AIA's Committee on Auditing Procedure, formed in 1940.

A

As the decade of the 1930s closed, the AIA had succeeded in establishing a viable structure for integrating the activities of its members into what historian Louis Galambos has termed America's "triocracy." The key elements of this new form of governance crystallized somewhat later for accountants than it had for other business and professional groups. Under this system, Congress, federal bureaucracies, and professional associations representing business or professional interests functioned as key players in defining public policy over particular aspects of the nation's economic life. The line of demarcation separating the scope of these competing elements, however, was ultimately determined by public opinion, which was expressed through congressional action. During periods of economic stability, private groups generally exercised their greatest influence. At these junctures, the public was most likely to be persuaded that private groups were most capable of protecting the public interest. During crises, on the other hand, private groups often seemed less effective in maintaining order. This led to public outcries for governmental intervention to afford relief.

Fourth Phase—The Contemporary Profession
The imperatives of the new triocratic order put in place during the New Deal era provided strong incentives for the extension and refinement of institutional relationships by the AIA, which changed its name to the American Institute of Certified Public Accountants (AICPA) in 1959. Five dimensions of professional ordering were particularly crucial in the AICPA's contemporary program of professionalization: financial accounting, auditing and related attestation services, ethics, education, and practice governance.

Although financial-accounting standardization was pursued with vigor, it became one of the most controversial aspects of professionalism. Three separate bodies served at various times as sources of authoritative guidance for these matters. The first two, the Committee on Accounting Procedure (1936–1959) and the Accounting Principles Board (APB 1959–1973), were committees of the national association. Although they were responsible for broadening greatly the body of promulgated generally accepted accounting principles (GAAP), the efforts of these two pioneering bodies evoked several criticisms. First, some believed that the research support was insufficient for the important missions of these committees. The Committee on Accounting Procedure had been assisted by a part-time research staff led by Professor Thomas Henry Sanders and W. Arnold Hosmer of the Harvard University Graduate School of Business Administration. Later, the APB engaged Professor Maurice Moonitz of the University of California to head its research staff. This latter unit intended to release Accounting Research Studies, which analyzed underlying theoretical issues and were to serve as guides for the accounting matters that had been placed on the APB's agenda. Unfortunately, too often the APB completed its standardization activities prior to the completion of the related research study.

A second criticism was that the committees had been dominated by practitioners whose busy schedules only allowed them to work part-time on standards setting. Moreover, these committees did not provide for any direct participation in deciding about standards by either representatives of statement issuers or users. A few also believed that the judgment of practitioners was biased, to the extent that they were unwilling to promulgate rigid standards that would adversely affect the statements of important clients.

Third, many were disturbed that financial accounting had been standardized without any consideration for first defining the underlying theoretical concepts that supported this body of knowledge. Instead, practitioner committees debated particular issues until a consensus was formed. To critics, the process of arriving at truth in this field seemed more rooted in politics than in science. One result of this approach was the incorporation within GAAP of many alternative methodologies for measuring the effects of particular classes of economic events. This flexibility, some feared, would erode the usefulness of corporate financial statements for the purpose of comparative analysis.

These criticisms, in conjunction with a rising wave of costly litigation from audit failures during the 1960s and 1970s, eventually led to two momentous reforms. An AICPA committee chaired by attorney Francis M. Wheat recommended in 1972 that accounting standardization be transferred from the AICPA to an independent body supported by CPA associations, the securities market organizations, and representative associations for statement issuers and user groups. This led to the establishment of the Financial Accounting Foundation (FAF), whose primary subsidiary, the Financial Accounting

Standards Board (FASB), became the third authoritative source of guidance in financial accounting in 1973. The FASB was endowed with a large research staff and a seven-member full-time board. To assure a wider sampling of opinion, three of the voting board members had to be drawn from backgrounds other than public accounting.

The second transformation in financial accounting emanated the following year from yet another AICPA committee chaired by Robert Martin Trueblood of Touche Ross and Company. The Trueblood committee was concerned with identifying the types of information that financial statements should endeavor to communicate to user groups. Its findings were laid out in *Objectives of Financial Statements* (1973). This work inspired the subsequent conceptual-framework studies undertaken by the FASB to define the underlying theoretical grounding for financial accounting.

Other steps were taken that modified the structure of accounting standardization during this period. In 1984, the FAF also established the Governmental Accounting Standards Board (GASB), which sought to standardize accounting practices for state and local governmental entities. The AICPA, on the other hand, continued to remain active in financial-accounting research through the activities of its Accounting Standards Executive Committee (AcSEC) formed in 1972. This latter body focused on many accounting problems that ordinarily would not have been included on the FASB's full agenda. The AcSEC issued Statements of Position (SOPs) on these matters, which Statement on Financial Accounting Standards (SFAS) No. 32 indicated represented "preferable accounting principles" in applying APB No. 20, "Accounting Changes."

Auditing guidance was also a fertile field for the AICPA during the contemporary era. In 1948, the institute began issuing audit guides for specialized industries with unusual reporting or auditing problems. By 1975, 13 such guides had been issued for businesses as diverse as construction, savings and loan associations, and hospitals and health-care organizations. All but three of these guides were also recognized under SFAS No. 32 as sources of preferable accounting principles in complying with APB No. 20.

In 1972, the philosophy underlying auditing guidance changed. A new committee, the Auditing Standards Executive Committee (AudSEC), started to concentrate on promulgating broad standards that defined the minimal performance expected of auditors rather than concentrating on specific practice procedures as had been the case earlier with the Statements on Auditing Procedure (SAPs). Moreover, all existing SAPs were codified in a new Statement on Auditing Standards (SASs). Although AudSEC functioned only until 1978, it was responsible for issuing an additional 25 SASs.

A new sensitivity to the factors that differentiate local and national firm practice led in 1977 to the establishment of a Division of Firms within the AICPA and creation of two new authoritative bodies for standardizing practice. The Division of Firms had two components: the SEC Practice Section (SECPS) for firms whose clients were primarily public companies, and the Private Companies Practice Section (PCPS) to serve CPA firms whose predominant clientele were non public companies. Paralleling this development was the approval by the AICPA Council on May 10, 1978 of the formation of the Auditing Standards Board (ASB), which replaced AudSEC. The ASB, however, conceived its mission as one directed toward providing guidance in auditing—a service thought most relevant for public companies. Guidance for other services such as reviews and compilation of nonpublic companies became the responsibility of a newly formed Accounting and Review Services Committee (ARSC) whose formation was approved by the AICPA Council on September 17, 1977.

Other aspects of practice were also the subject of standardization drives, including tax practice (1964), management advisory services (1969), continuing professional education (1971), accountants' services on prospective financial statements (1985), and attestation engagements (1986). As in the case of auditing, these new pronouncements also sought to define the minimum levels of performance expected of practitioners for these specialized engagements.

The development of professional ethics, on the other hand, was influenced by two factors. As early as 1940, the SEC had pressured the AIA to promulgate rules dealing with practitioner independence. What was essential was that the public retain high confidence in the objectivity of auditors. The rules that were eventually promulgated sought to prevent damaging conflicts of interests as well as the perception of such conflicts, which might undermine investors' confidence in accountants' independence.

A

The second development with respect to ethics came about from actions taken by the FTC to eliminate restraints of trade in the markets for professional services. In 1988, the AICPA's Council voted to enter into an agreement with the FTC to modify particular rules concerning advertising, contingent fees, and commissions. The AICPA agreed to lift its ban against accepting commissions or contingent fees except in cases where they related to an accountant's performance of audit, review, compilation, and prospective financial-information engagements. The AICPA also agreed that members would be required to make disclosures to clients in cases where fees or commissions were accepted in recommending the products or services of others. Lastly, the earlier prohibition on advertising was also essentially eliminated.

Educational reform represented another important dimension of the AICPA's program of professionalization during this period. Earlier, steps had been taken to strengthen collegiate education in accounting. Various committees surveyed university curricula and sought to make useful suggestions about how the content of studies might be best structured in preparing prospective practitioners. During the late 1920s, the AIA had also formed an Office of Placements at the behest of F.W. Nissley, a partner at Arthur Young and Company, to encourage firms to engage college graduates. But by 1940, only one state, New York, required candidates for the CPA examination to complete four years of college.

The AICPA again became deeply involved in defining collegiate accounting curricula because of the sharply critical reports issued by both the Ford and Carnegie foundations in 1959 on the overall quality of business education. The AICPA became involved in this controversy by sponsoring research that sought to identify the typical matters in which practitioners should receive training while in college. This effort was guided by a committee chaired by Elmer G. Beamer, a partner at Haskins and Sells. The product of this effort were the recommendations contained in the publication *Horizons for a Profession: The Common Body of Knowledge of Certified Public Accountants* (1967), by Robert H. Roy, dean of the Engineering School at Johns Hopkins University, and Professor James H. MacNeill, chairman of the Accounting Department at Fordham University's Graduate School of Business Administration. In addition, the Beamer Committee endorsed the recommendation made in the *Horizons* study that the normal term of collegiate education in accounting be extended to 150 credit hours. This was to be mandated as a prerequisite for all applicants for admission to the AICPA beginning in the year 2000.

Lastly, the AICPA played a leading role in the reformulation of the institutional setting for practice oversight and review. This new round of reform took cognizance of the need for effective practice management in the performance of professional services. Consequently, steps were taken to define minimal standards for practice quality as well as the establishment of a review capability for determining how well firms were adhering to these strictures. Practice-quality standards were first promulgated by the AICPA in 1977. Adherence to these standards was also made mandatory for CPA firms to remain members in good standing within either of the two aforementioned sections of the Divisions of Forms. This was to be evidenced by the successful completion of periodic peer reviews of section members' practices. Moreover, the review process was to be evaluated annually by a new four-member body, the Public Oversight Board (POB), whose first chairman was attorney John J. McCloy.

In these and other ways, the AICPA has been able to establish new organizational structures and institutional arrangements to strengthen the ability of accountants to serve their clients and to protect the public. On these foundations the profession's representative association looks forward to the challenges of the next millennium.

Paul J. Miranti Jr.
Leonard Goodman

Bibliography

Berle, A.A. Jr., and G.C. Means. *The Modern Corporation and Private Property*. New York: Commerce Clearing House, 1932.

Carey, J.L. *The Rise of the Accounting Profession*. 2 vols. New York: AICPA, 1969–1970.

Edwards, J.D. *History of Public Accounting in the United States*. East Lansing: Bureau of Business and Economic Research, Michigan State University, 1960. Reprint. University, AL: University of Alabama Press, 1978.

———, and P.J. Miranti Jr. "The AICPA: A

Professional Institution in a Dynamic Society," *Journal of Accountancy*, May 1987, pp. 22–38.

Galambos, L. *America at Middle Age: A New History of the United States in the Twentieth Century*. New York: McGraw-Hill, 1982.

Miranti, P.J. Jr. *Accountancy Comes of Age: The Development of an American Profession, 1886–1940*. Chapel Hill: University of North Carolina Press, 1990.

———. "Associationalism, Statism, and Professional Regulation: Public Accountants and the Reform of the Financial Markets, 1896–1940," *Business History Review*, Autumn 1986, pp. 438–468.

———. "Professionalism and Nativism: The Competition for Professional Licensing Legislation in New York during the 1890s," *Social Science Quarterly*, June 1988, pp. 361–380.

———. "Robert H. Montgomery: A Leader of the Profession," *CPA Journal*, August 1986, pp. 106–108.

McCraw, T.K. *Prophets of Regulation: Charles Francis Adams, Louis D. Brandeis, James M. Landis, Alfred E. Kahn*. Cambridge: Harvard University Press, 1984.

Olson, W.E. *The Accounting Profession: The Years of Trial, 1969–1980*. New York: AICPA, 1980.

Previts, G.J., and B.D. Merino. *A History of Accounting in America: An Historical Interpretation of the Cultural Significance of Accounting*. New York: John Wiley & Sons, 1979.

Previts, G.J., ed. *The Development of SEC Accounting*. Reading, MA: Addison-Wesley, 1981.

Ripley, W.Z. *Main Street and Wall Street*. Boston: Little, Brown & Co., 1927.

Roy, R.H., and J.H. MacNeill. *Horizons for a Profession: The Common Body of Knowledge for Certified Public Accountants*. New York: AICPA, 1967.

See also ACCOUNTING EDUCATION IN THE UNITED STATES; ACCOUNTING PRINCIPLES BOARD; ACCOUNTING RESEARCH BULLETINS; ACCOUNTING RESEARCH STUDIES; ADVERTISING BY ACCOUNTANTS; AUDIT COMMITTEES; AUDITOR'S REPORT; BERLE AND MEANS; BIG EIGHT ACCOUNTING FIRMS; CERTIFIED PUBLIC ACCOUNTANT; CERTIFIED PUBLIC ACCOUNTANT EXAMINATION: THE EARLY YEARS (1896–1930); CHIEF ACCOUNTANTS OF THE SECURITIES AND EXCHANGE COMMISSION; COMPARABILITY; CONCEPTUAL FRAMEWORK; CONGRESSES ON ACCOUNTING, INTERNATIONAL; CONGRESSIONAL VIEWS; CONTINUING PROFESSIONAL EDUCATION; DEFINITIONS OF ACCOUNTING; DICKINSON, ARTHUR LOWES; ETHICS, PROFESSIONAL; EXTERNAL AUDITING; FINANCIAL ACCOUNTING STANDARDS BOARD; GENERALLY ACCEPTED ACCOUNTING PRINCIPLES; GRADY, PAUL; HASKINS, CHARLES WALDO; HOXSEY, J.M.B.; INDEPENDENCE OF EXTERNAL AUDITORS; INFLATION ACCOUNTING; INSTITUTE OF MANAGEMENT ACCOUNTANTS; INTERNAL CONTROL; KOHLER, ERIC LOUIS; LAST IN, FIRST OUT (LIFO); LEGAL LIABILITY OF AUDITORS; MANAGEMENT ADVISORY SERVICES BY CPAs; MAUTZ, ROBERT K.; MAY, GEORGE OLIVER; McKESSON AND ROBBINS CASE; MONTGOMERY, ROBERT HIESTER; MOONITZ, MAURICE; NATURAL BUSINESS YEAR; NEW YORK STOCK EXCHANGE; OBJECTIVITY; OPERATIONAL (VALUE-FOR-MONEY) AUDITING; PREVITS, GARY JOHN; PUBLIC OVERSIGHT BOARD; QUASI-REORGANIZATION; REALIZATION; RETAINED EARNINGS; RIPLEY, WILLIAM Z.; SANDERS, THOMAS HENRY; SECURITIES AND EXCHANGE COMMISSION; SELLS, ELIJAH WATT; SPACEK, LEONARD; STATE REGULATION OF THE ACCOUNTANCY PROFESSION (U.S.); STATISTICAL SAMPLING; STERRETT, JOSEPH EDMUND; STUDY GROUP ON BUSINESS INCOME'S *FIVE MONOGRAPHS ON BUSINESS INCOME;* TREADWAY COMMISSION; TRUEBLOOD, ROBERT MARTIN; *ULTRAMARES CORPORATION V. TOUCHE, NIVEN AND COMPANY; UNIFORM ACCOUNTING;* UNIFORMITY; UNITED STATES STEEL CORPORATION; WHEAT COMMITTEE.

A

An Introduction to Corporate Accounting Standards

William Andrew Paton and A.C. Littleton's *An Introduction to Corporate Accounting Standards* (1940) was the first codification of accounting principles to be developed deductively rather than as a series of generalizations from practice. Doctrines such as conservatism and the lower of cost or market rule were either not supported or not even discussed. Paton and Littleton rigorously distinguished between accounting principles and methods and were the first to explore their interactions.

Paton and Littleton's core argument was that "earning power—not cost price, not replacement price, not sale or liquidation price—is the significant basis of enterprise value." The accountant's primary task was income determination via the matching of related costs and revenues. This made asset valuation less important than the conversion of balance sheet items to expense. Assets were discussed in the chapter on "Costs" and were considered residuals, unexpired costs. "Inventories and plant are not 'values,' but cost accumulations in suspense, as it were, awaiting their destiny." Acquisition prices of assets were suitable initial valuations. Paton and Littleton scarcely considered the question of subsequent valuation. Value was assumed to equal cost because asset conversion, not asset valuation, was the issue. In this way the authors avoided the problem of which costs were to be matched with revenues.

Michael Chatfield

Bibliography

Paton, W.A., and A.C. Littleton. *An Introduction to Corporate Accounting Standards*. American Accounting Association Monograph No. 3. New York: American Accounting Association, 1940.

Storey, R.K. *The Search for Accounting Principles: Today's Problems in Perspective*. New York: AICPA, 1964.

See also ACCOUNTING RESEARCH STUDIES; AMERICAN ACCOUNTING ASSOCIATION; ENTITY THEORY; GENERALLY ACCEPTED ACCOUNTING PRINCIPLES; INCOME-DETERMINATION THEORY; LITTLETON, A.C.; MATCHING; PATON, WILLIAM ANDREW; POSTULATES OF ACCOUNTING; SCHRADER, WILLIAM JOSEPH

Andersen, Arthur E. (1885–1947)

Arthur E. Andersen was stern, erect, somewhat ascetic, exceedingly proper—and an unrepentant maverick.

After learning the accounting business in a corporate environment and then as a lowly paid novice in a public accounting firm, he began teaching at Northwestern University, where he had earned his degree as a night student. His first problem was that there was no text from which to teach. So he wrote his own, *Complete Accounting Course*, which became the basis for early accounting education, not only at Northwestern but elsewhere as well.

A restless man with a burning desire to "make a difference," Andersen left the groves of academe in 1913 to found a small Midwestern accounting firm that is today a $6 billion worldwide enterprise. Along the way, he grappled continually with the conservative accounting establishment, ignored tradition, and, in the process, turned the genteel accounting profession upside down.

Andersen was a visionary, a lateral thinker who stated at the outset his determination to build "a different kind of accounting firm"—one that would respond to need rather than tradition, that placed economic reality above academic theory in enhancing the quality of financial statements, and that would not only help clients comply with laws and regulations but also help them manage their businesses more effectively.

Although his firm was small by any measure, Andersen's personal stature was such that he was able to exert great—and usually unwanted—influence on his profession. In the 1910s, the practice was to hire bookkeepers, teachers, even farmers to serve on a part-time basis as accounting firm staff during the busy year-end season. Andersen would have none of it. He insisted on college graduates who not only knew numbers but also "knew how to think." And he hired them on a full-time basis. The elders of the profession declared that he would bankrupt not only himself but them as well with such an approach. Eventually, of course, they, too, hired full-time staffs and, later still, college graduates. And no one went bankrupt.

In that era, many business executives viewed an audit as a necessary evil. Some often hid material facts from their accountants, and they certainly did not share Andersen's view that proper accounting could help managers manage more effectively. But Andersen persevered. He hired bright young men who could "dig behind the figures to understand their underlying significance to a business." And he demonstrated to his clients that he could, in fact, help them manage better.

He created the accounting profession's first program of industry specialization, because he felt that his people needed to understand the peculiarities of their clients' businesses if they were to "do more than tick and tie the numbers." Drawing on his own experience as a professional, he insisted that learning is a lifetime commitment, and he created the first common training program in the profession—bringing people from all offices to Chicago for common training in technical, industry, and business topics to help them serve clients better. That, in turn, attracted new clients, and the business began to grow—and to expand from Chicago into other cities: Milwaukee, New York, Kansas City and so on. By the mid-1990s, the firm had 318 offices in 72 countries.

Andersen found the accounting profession was as reluctant as some of his clients to accept his "maverick" ideas. He fought a lonely but ultimately successful battle to replace accounting theory with "common-sense accounting." Later, as the profession expanded exponentially in the years following Andersen's untimely death in 1947, his ideas became the cornerstone for accounting standards and auditing principles.

Andersen had significant impact on the accounting profession. This was an enormous achievement for a man who started his life in public accounting as a $25-a-week assistant and ended it as perhaps the best-known and most-respected American accountant. The organization bearing his name has grown to become a leader in professional services worldwide.

John A. Ruane

Bibliography

Arthur Andersen & Co. *Behind the Figures: Addresses and Articles by Arthur Andersen, 1913–1941.* Chicago: Arthur Andersen & Co., 1970.
Arthur Andersen Worldwide Organization. *Vision of Grandeur.* Chicago: Arthur Andersen & Co., 1988.
Burns, T.J., and E.N. Coffman. *The Accounting Hall of Fame: Profiles of Fifty Members.* Columbus: College of Business, Ohio State University, 1992.

See also ACCOUNTING HALL OF FAME; BIG EIGHT ACCOUNTING FIRMS; INSTITUTE OF MANAGEMENT ACCOUNTANTS; MANAGEMENT ADVISORY SERVICES BY CPAS; PREVITS, GARY JOHN; SPACEK, LEONARD

Antoni, Tito (1915–)

Tito Antoni has been one of the most visible and versatile Italian professors of accounting history of his generation. He was the chief organizer of the Fourth International Congress on the History of Accounting in Pisa, Italy, in 1984. His ability to deal with central accounting history issues in a scientific way is reflected in his diverse contributions to the advancement of accounting history. Over the years, Antoni's activity has culminated in a number of scholarly works in the history of accounting, which can be classified into three groups: a) studies of extant commercial and monetary documents of the eleventh and twelfth centuries, for instance, "The Pisan Document of Philadelphia," in the *Accounting Historians Journal*, Spring 1977; b) studies of extant account books of Italian merchants of the fourteenth century, for instance, "Il Bilancio di Una Compagnia Mercantile del Trecento," *Rivista del Diritto Commerciale (Review of Commercial Law)* (1946); and c) examination and analysis of great accounting schools of thought of different times to stress the accounting evolution and revolution through the centuries, for instance, "Tre Precursori Nella Storia della Ragioneria: Leonardo Fibonacci, Luca Pacioli, Fabio Besta," *Rivista Italiana di Ragioneria e di Economia Aziendale (Italian Review of Accounting and Concern Economics)* (1974).

Antoni's output reflects his excitement for research and the pleasure he gets from its challenge. He generates his own personal force for crystallizing and disseminating accounting history ideas. His writing on a variety of subjects has been highly instrumental in the development of accounting history and has received favorable recognition. As such, he occupies an important place in the study of accounting history.

Giuseppe Galassi

Bibliography

Antoni, T. "The Pisan Document of Philadelphia," *Accounting Historians Journal*, Spring 1977, pp. 17–24.

See also LEONARDO OF PISA

Arabic Numerals

The Arabic numeration system originated in India. The modern system of Arabic numbers, including the zero, was used in the Muslim world beginning in the ninth century. They appear in European manuscripts dating from 976 and 1143. In *Liber Abaci* (1202), Leonardo of

Pisa demonstrated the superiority of Arabic numbers by presenting accounts in which Roman numerals in the text were contrasted with Arabic figures in columns at the right. Within a generation Arabic numbers were widely used by Italian merchants. Double entry bookkeeping appeared no later than the thirteenth century, but Roman numerals were nearly always used in accounting records until the sixteenth century. The widespread adoption of Arabic numerals was therefore not a precondition for the development of double entry bookkeeping. However, the additive qualities of Arabic numbers gave an advantage to the bilateral form of account, in which receipts and payments were placed in two columns side by side. G.E.M. de Ste. Croix argues that this columnar separation may have given rise to the notion of debit and credit and thereby facilitated the emergence of double entry bookkeeping.

Michael Chatfield

Bibliography

De Ste. Croix, G.E.M. "Greek and Roman Accounting." In *Studies in the History of Accounting*, edited by A.C. Littleton and B.S. Yamey, pp. 14–74. Homewood, IL: Irwin, 1956.

Williams, J.J. "A New Perspective on the Evolution of Double Entry Bookkeeping," *Accounting Historians Journal*, Spring 1978, pp. 29–39.

See also ARITHMETIC AND ACCOUNTING; DEBIT AND CREDIT; DOUBLE ENTRY BOOKKEEPING: ORIGINS; INDIA; LEONARDO OF PISA; ROMAN NUMERALS; SPAIN

Archives and Special Collections in Accounting

An archive is an organized body of records pertaining to an organization or institution. An archivist is one in charge of archives and, hence, a custodian of archives. Special collections are specific groupings of materials that are focused on particular topics of importance to an archivist. The role of the archivist is to collect, organize, preserve, and make the material accessible to scholars. Archives can be found in libraries, businesses, governmental units, religious bodies, museums—almost any organization.

Scholars interested in the history of accounting have a multitude of archival sources available to them. The 1991 edition of the *Directory of Special Libraries and Information Centers* listed 174 special libraries in accounting, including many located in large offices of international public accounting firms, and nearly 1,000 special libraries in the related fields of business, commerce, and management. A search done by the Archives Committee of the Academy of Accounting Historians in the late 1970s found 55 business archives, which are listed in the Fall 1984 issue of *Accounting Historians Notebook*.

There are many untapped sources available to scholars of the history of accounting and accounting thought. Richard H. Homberger (1970) defines these sources as "original accounting records and related materials; books that deal with accounting matters related to past periods; bibliographies of such books, and books on the history of bookkeeping and accounting; and periodicals, to the extent that they present past accounting matters or articles on the history of accounting."

Homberger briefly describes manuscript holdings in many libraries, including the Kress Manuscript Collection at Harvard University; the Montgomery Collection at the Rare Book and Manuscript Library in the Butler Library at Columbia University; the Bancroft Library at the University of California at Berkeley; the Robert E. Gross Collection at UCLA; the University of Pennsylvania; the Archivio Salvati in Pisa, Italy; the state archives of Florence, Italy; the Datini Archives in Prato, Italy; the British Library of Political and Economic Science in London; the Stadsarchief in Antwerp, Belgium; the Nederlandsche Economish-Historisch Archief at The Hague; the Archives of the University of Melbourne, Australia; and the Historical Materials Museum at Shiga National University in Japan. Homberger also describes special book collections, such as the Kress Collection at Harvard; the Harry Clark Bentley Collection of the Rare Books Collection of the Boston Public Library; the Montgomery Collection at Columbia; the Herwood Collection now at the University of Baltimore; the American Institute of Certified Public Accountants (AICPA) library in New York; the University of California Rare Books Division at Berkeley; the Antiquarian Collection of the Institute of Chartered Accountants of Scotland in Edinburgh; the collection of the Institute of Chartered Accountants in England and Wales in London; the Economic History Library in

Amsterdam, Netherlands; Bibliothèque Royale of Brussels, Belgium; the Biblioteca Nacional in Madrid, Spain; the Commerzbibliothek in Hamburg, Germany; and in Buenos Aires, Argentina, the Colegio de Graduados en Ciencias Economicas.

Members of the Academy of Accounting Historians were queried about archives they had used or had known. Vahé Baladouni of the University of New Orleans has made significant use of the accounting records of the East India Company at the India Office Library and Records of the British Library in London. There are over 50 major, self-contained subject areas, each of which is divided further into several subsections. Victoria Beard of the University of North Dakota has done research at the North Dakota Institute for Regional Studies, which has records of North Dakota bonanza farms and land companies from the 1870s to the 1950s and is in Fargo. Richard K. Fleischman of John Carroll University related his experiences at the Royal Commission on Historical Manuscripts in London, which has compiled an extensive database on existing business archives in the United Kingdom. Lou Goldberg of the University of Melbourne said the Australian Society of Certified Practicing Accountants has some good archival material relating to it and its antecedent bodies. Fernando Gutierrez-Hidalgo mentioned the Archives of the Royal Tobacco Factory at the Archivo Historico de Tabacalera in Sevilla, Spain. Roxanne T. Johnson of the University of Scranton noted the Hagley Museum and Library, which is located at the site of the original E.I. DuPont de Nemours and Company gunpowder works in Wilmington, Delaware. The cornerstone of the manuscript collection, the DuPont Company records, date back to the early nineteenth century. Alicia Jaruga of the University of Lodz detailed nine archives in Poland, including the Wojewodzkie Archiwum Panstwowe we Wroclawiu, which has agricultural accounts from the sixteenth century and accounts of factories. Susumu Katsuyama of Nihon University in Tokyo wrote about the library collection at his school. Dieter Schneider of Ruhr-Universität Bochum mentioned the Institut der Wirtschaftsprüfer in Deutschland in Düsseldorf, Germany, with more than 30,000 volumes on the subjects of accounting and auditing. Luigi Serra of the Istituto Tecnico Commerciale described the Montecassino Archives in Cassino, Italy, which has artifacts of accounting records for the famous Benedictine Abbey back to 1066 A.D.

In addition to some of the above resources, Richard Vangermeersch reported finding valuable archival material at the New York office of United States Steel Company, the Charles Schwab Collection at the Hagley Museum and Library, the Annual Report Room at the Baker Library at Harvard, and the archives of the Renold Company, now housed at the University of Manchester in England.

Another aspect of the archives topic is the role accounting historians can and should play in the development of archives in the field as well as corporate archives in general. Wendy Chandley and Peter Boys (1991) have described a project to save accounting and other records of public accounting firms in England. Accounting and business historians, professional organizations, businesses, and archivists need to develop some operating guidelines for preservation of archival material, as well as a detailed list of archives and special collections relevant to scholars in accounting.

Richard Vangermeersch
John D. Cathcart

Bibliography

"Business Archives with Potential," *Accounting Historians Notebook*, Fall 1984, pp. 28–29.

Chandley, W., and P. Boys. "Hidden Assets and Secret Reserves: An Exciting Project Is Currently Under Way to Survey Firm's Archive Material," *Accountancy*, June 1991, p. 106.

Compton, C.A. "Profiting from the Past," *World*, vol. 24, No. 1, 1990, pp. 30–33.

Homberger, R.H. "Appendix: Sources of Accounting History." In *Committee Reports* (supplement to vol. 45 of *Accounting Review*), pp. 56–64. Evanston, IL: American Accounting Association, 1970.

Riggs, J.B. *A Guide to the Manuscripts in the Eleutherian Mills Historical Library.* Wilmington, DE: Eleutherian Mills Historical Library, 1970.

See also ACADEMY OF ACCOUNTING HISTORIANS; BENTLEY, HARRY CLARK; EAST INDIA COMPANY; MONTGOMERY, ROBERT HIESTER; RESEARCH METHODS IN ACCOUNTING HISTORY; SCOTLAND: EARLY WRITERS IN DOUBLE ENTRY ACCOUNTING; UNITED STATES STEEL CORPORATION

Arithmetic and Accounting

Every ancient society had arithmetic, but none developed a simple way of making calculations. A basic reason for the backwardness of Greco-Roman accounting can be found in their system of numerical notation. These were inferior partly because of the large variety of symbols used for numbers (the Greeks had 28), and partly because the Greeks and Romans never learned to express a number's value merely by the position of each of its digits in relation to the others. This lack of position value meant that there was little incentive to arrange numbers in columns, since they could not be added down digit by digit to arrive at a total. Without a columnar separation of receipts and payments, it was relatively difficult to cumulate and summarize accounting data.

The modern system of Arabic numerals was used in the Muslim world beginning in the ninth century. Arabic numbers appear in a Spanish manuscript dating from 976. In *Liber Abaci* (1202), Leonardo of Pisa demonstrated by comparison the superiority of Arabic numbers for account keeping, and within a generation they were widely used by Italian merchants. Double entry bookkeeping appeared no later than the thirteenth century. But double entry accounts were at first written in narrative form, and Roman numerals predominated in accounting records until the sixteenth century. Widespread adoption of Arabic numerals was therefore not a precondition for the development of double entry bookkeeping. But without Arabic numbers, the bilateral form of account, in which debits and credits were placed in two columns side by side, would have had less advantage over the alternative form of entry in which debits and credits were placed one below the other, or put in different parts of the account book. The adoption of Arabic numerals also facilitated classification of data in ledger accounts.

Michael Chatfield

Bibliography

De Ste. Croix, G.E.M. "Greek and Roman Accounting." In *Studies in the History of Accounting*, edited by A.C. Littleton and B.S. Yamey, pp. 14–74. Homewood, IL: Irwin, 1956.

Swetz, Frank J. *Capitalism and Arithmetic: The New Math of the Fifteenth Century.* La Salle, IL: New Court, 1987.

Williams, J.J. "A New Perspective on the Evolution of Double Entry Bookkeeping," *Accounting Historians Journal*, Spring 1978, pp. 29–39.

See also ARABIC NUMERALS; DEBIT AND CREDIT; DOUBLE ENTRY BOOKKEEPING: ORIGINS; GREECE; LEDGER; LEONARDO OF PISA; MEDIEVAL ACCOUNTING; ROMAN NUMERALS; ROME (509 B.C.–A.D. 476); STEVIN, SIMON

Audit Committees

Although the board of directors of some publicly held U.S. corporations have designated a standing audit committee of their members since the late 1930s, greater appreciation of audit committees and their importance began to take place in the 1970s. Subsequently, actions by government regulators or the threat of regulations have been significant factors motivating private-sector initiatives to strengthen corporate governance, including audit committee responsibilities for matters of internal control, financial reporting, and auditing. Likewise, increased awareness of the legal liability of officers and directors has also underscored the significance of audit committee activities.

Audit committees provide the focus and means for fuller collaboration among the full board, senior management, and both internal and external auditors. Audit committees have been appointed in the nonprofit/public sector but are most prominent in large publicly held corporations. Increased expectations from board committees designated as oversight committees reflect the concerns of shareholders, other stakeholders, and the general public for exercise of greater accountability over corporate actions of all types.

Early Historical Development of Audit Committees

As early as 1940, the Securities and Exchange Commission (SEC) endorsed the concept of audit committees composed of nonofficer board members that had been suggested earlier by the New York Stock Exchange (NYSE). The American Institute of Certified Public Accountants (AICPA) was also an active proponent of the concept, and issued a policy statement in 1967 recommending establishment of audit committees consisting of outside directors. Robert K. Mautz and F.L. Neumann, in a study financed by the Touche Ross Foundation, recommended in 1970 further utilization of the audit committee. In a follow-up study in 1977, these researchers noted an increasing interest in audit committees.

The SEC reaffirmed its support of audit committees in 1974 and required proxy-statement disclosure of the existence and composition of such standing committees in all publicly held corporations where they were in place. At this same time, an NYSE white paper recommended to listed corporations that they form audit committees. In 1977, the NYSE enacted a formal requirement that corporations should appoint an audit committee consisting entirely of outside directors as a condition of continued listing. In later years, the American Stock Exchange and NASDAQ enacted similar audit committee requirements.

The legal profession endorsed the concept of audit committees in publicly held corporations as early as the 1978 edition of the *Corporate Director's Handbook* issued by the American Bar Association (ABA). At the same time, a committee of the ABA developed recommendations for the operation of oversight committees such as audit committees in a report titled *The Oversight Committees of the Board of Directors*. As of 1994, audit committees were mandated by the corporation law of only one state, Connecticut.

Regulatory Direction by the SEC

During the late 1970s and early 1980s, the SEC continued to be the most important spokesperson that articulated the responsibilities of audit committees and supported their establishment. The SEC introduced several proposals for more extensive disclosures concerning the independence of audit committee members and the functions they performed. The SEC has also encouraged management reporting of internal-control activities, including those of the audit committee. However, because private-sector initiatives were in process to achieve similar objectives, none of these was implemented.

The SEC proposed in July 1988 that a management report on internal controls and financial reporting be made by each publicly held corporation. This initiative differed from earlier proposals in that its focus was directed to the entire internal-control environment rather than just accounting controls. As of 1994, the SEC had taken no subsequent actions with regard to the proposal.

The Treadway Commission

As a response to the interest in financial reporting and auditing expressed by the SEC and by its congressional oversight committees, five professional accounting organizations in 1985 formed and funded the National Commission on Fraudulent Financial Reporting, also known as the Treadway Commission after its chairperson, James C. Treadway Jr., a former commissioner of the SEC. (Similar commissions have been constituted in other countries. In Canada it is the MacDonald Commission; in Britain, the Cadbury Committee.)

The importance the Treadway Commission accorded to audit committees was reflected in its 1987 final report: 11 of the 19 specific recommendations for implementation by corporations involved audit committees of the board. This reflected Treadway's assessment of the critical importance of audit committees in preventing or detecting fraudulent financial reporting. The 11 recommendations were designed to clarify the oversight processes to be followed by audit committees and also to emphasize the importance of their mission in the areas of internal controls, financial reporting, and auditing, both internal and external.

Professional Pronouncements

In response to some of the recommendations made in the Treadway report, the AICPA and the Institute of Internal Auditors (IIA), which were both sponsoring organizations of the Treadway effort, issued professional guidance dealing specifically with audit committees. The Auditing Standards Board of the AICPA issued in 1988 its Statement on Auditing Standards No. 61, titled "Communication with Audit Committees." This statement requires an external auditor to be sure that significant matters affecting annual audits where a report is furnished to the SEC are communicated directly to the audit committee. The internal-auditing profession's response to the various Treadway Commission recommendations was issued in June 1989 by the Internal Auditing Standards Board. It is the Statement on Internal Auditing Standards No. 7, titled "Communication with the Board of Directors."

Bank Legislation Mandates Independent Audit Committees

The FDIC Improvement Act of 1991 (FDICIA) decrees specific requirements for the existence, composition, and functions to be performed by audit committees in banks and savings institutions having more than $150 million in assets. Although this law affects only depository institutions insured by the federal government, it is viewed by many observers as a forerunner of practices that may be required in the future in other regulated industries, such as insurance, utilities, telecommunications, and transportation.

Under the statute, each audit committee member must be independent of management, and the implementing regulations define specific proscribed relationships. In large depository institutions (those with assets above $500 million), audit committee members must have access to independent legal counsel, must have banking or financial expertise, and cannot be a large customer of the institution. In addition to their oversight responsibilities for financial reporting and auditing functions, the FDICIA assigns specific responsibilities to audit committees. Included are the need to review management's reports required by the FDICIA evaluating the effectiveness of the institution's internal controls over financial reporting and the degree of its compliance with specified laws and regulations.

Appropriate Audit Committee Functions
Independence of management and the organization is viewed as the primary condition for audit committees to perform effectively their oversight functions. The Treadway Commission's "Good Practice Guidelines for the Audit Committee" contain generalized statements of appropriate practices. The most authoritative listing of functions and powers of audit committees is contained in the *Principles of Corporate Governance,* published in 1992 by the American Law Institute (ALI). The ALI is an organization of prominent practicing attorneys, judges, and law school deans; its primary objective is "clarification and simplification of the law and its better adaptation to social needs."

Summary
The contributions of audit committees to the processes of effective corporate governance of both publicly held and nonprofit organizations in the areas of internal control, auditing, and financial reporting are expected to continue to increase in the future.

Curtis C. Verschoor

Bibliography
Abdolmohammadi, M.J., and E.S. Levy. "Audit Committee Member's Perceptions of Their Responsibility," *Internal Auditing,* Summer 1992, pp. 53–63.

"AICPA Executive Committee Statement on Audit Committees of Boards of Directors," *Journal of Accountancy,* September 1967, p. 10.

American Law Institute. *Principles of Corporate Governance: Analysis and Recommendations.* Philadelphia: American Law Institute, 1994.

Apostolov, B., and R. Jeffords. *Working With the Audit Committee.* Almonte Springs, FL: Institute of Internal Auditors, 1992.

Bull, I. "Board of Directors Acceptance of Treadway Responsibilities," *Journal of Accountancy,* February 1991, pp. 67–74.

Mautz, R.K., and F.L. Neumann. *Corporate Audit Committees.* Urbana, IL: Bureau of Economic and Business Research, University of Illinois, 1970.

———. *Corporate Audit Committees: Policies and Practices.* Cleveland: Ernst & Ernst, 1977.

Metz, M.S. "Inside the Audit Committee," *Internal Auditor,* October 1993, pp. 42–47.

National Commission on Fraudulent Financial Reporting. *Report of the National Commission on Fraudulent Financial Reporting* [The Treadway Report]. Washington, DC: National Commission on Fraudulent Financial Reporting, 1987.

Verschoor, C.C. "Benchmarking the Audit Committee," *Journal of Accountancy,* September 1993, pp. 59–64.

———, and J.P. Liotta. "Communication with Audit Committees," *Internal Auditor,* April 1990, pp. 42–47.

See also AMERICAN INSTITUTE OF CERTIFIED PUBLIC ACCOUNTANTS; EXTERNAL AUDITING; INSTITUTE OF INTERNAL AUDITORS; INTERNAL AUDITING; INTERNAL CONTROL; MAUTZ, ROBERT K.; NEW YORK STOCK EXCHANGE; SECURITIES AND EXCHANGE COMMISSION; TREADWAY COMMISSION

Auditing, External
See EXTERNAL AUDITING

Auditor's Report
Expansion of stock ownership in the United States in the early twentieth century meant that people were receiving statements with auditor's

reports. Misunderstandings arose over the meaning of the auditor's reports because many readers believed that the report was a guarantee.

In an attempt to standardize financial statements, the American Institute of Accountants (AIA), now the American Institute of Certified Public Accountants or AICPA, prepared *A Memorandum on Balance-Sheet Audits* at the request of the Federal Trade Commission. The commission approved the memorandum and sent it to the Federal Reserve Board. The board published it in the *Federal Reserve Bulletin* of April 1917 and distributed it to interested parties as a pamphlet, first in 1917 with the title *Uniform Accounting,* and again in 1918 with the new title, *Approved Methods for the Preparation of the Balance-Sheet Statements*. The report was commonly called a certificate and patterned after the English certificate.

Following World War I, a period of business expansion, speculation, and inflation resulted in misleading financial-reporting practices. Accountants lacked authoritative support to combat such deceptive practices, but auditors began to object and make qualifications in their reports, prefaced by the words "subject to."

In May 1929, the pamphlet *Approved Methods for the Preparation of the Balance-Sheet Statements* was revised by a committee of the AIA. The revision was published by the Federal Reserve Board under the title *Verification of Financial Statements* (1929). It suggested that companies provide not only a balance sheet but also a statement of profit and loss in detail. Before this change, the profit and loss account was usually shown as one figure on the balance sheet without support. The auditor's report now applied to both financial statements. The opening phrase became "we have examined the accounts" rather than "we have audited the books and accounts."

As a result of the stock market crash of 1929, conferences began between the Committee on Stock List of the New York Stock Exchange (NYSE) and a special AIA committee on cooperation with stock exchanges. The NYSE committee was responsible for reviewing applications from corporations for trading privileges. The AIA committee's six members were senior partners of firms with the largest numbers of clients listed on the Exchange, and its chairman was George Oliver May. Correspondence between these two groups continued from 1932 to 1934 and contained suggestions for preparation of financial statements, the auditor's responsibilities and the auditor's report.

In January 1933, the NYSE began requiring annual audits by independent public accountants, and their report had to be in a form satisfactory to the Exchange. The AIA committee suggested such a report, and the makeup of the committee's membership contributed to the suggested report's general acceptance. Although the auditor's report and procedures applied only to listed corporations, they established that a lower degree of performance was inadequate. The suggested auditor's report became recognized as the first standard report.

The correspondence between the NYSE committee and the AIA committee was published in 1934 in *Audits of Corporate Accounts*, and its recommendations became available to a wider audience. It said the auditor should make an examination as described in *Verification of Financial Statements.* The auditor's written communication should be referred to as a report rather than a certificate. The auditor's report should be addressed to the directors of the company or to the stockholders if the appointment is made by them. Separate paragraphs should be used for the scope and the opinion.

The scope paragraph was: "We have made an examination of the balance sheet and the statement of income and surplus. In connection therewith, we examined or tested accounting records of the company and other supporting evidence and obtained information and explanations from officers and employees of the company; we also made a general review of the accounting methods and of the operating and income accounts for the year, but we did not make a detailed audit of the transactions." Any special forms of confirmation should be referred to in the second sentence. An effort should be made to limit use of the word "verify."

The opinion paragraph was: "In our opinion, based upon such examination, the accompanying balance sheet and related statement of income and surplus fairly present, in accordance with accepted principles of accounting consistently maintained by the company during the year under review, its position at ——, and the results of its operations for the year." Any material change in accounting principles or their application should be indicated. Words such as "certify" and "correct" were eliminated from the opinion paragraph.

The McKesson and Robbins fraud was revealed in December 1938. The Securities and Exchange Commission (SEC) investigated this matter and issued a report in December 1940. The report recommended an extension of auditing procedures to include confirmation of receivables and observation of inventories and an amendment of the auditor's report to include, in addition to the description of the scope of the audit, clear certification that the audit performed was or was not adequate for the purpose of expressing an independent opinion. If any generally accepted procedures were omitted, these omissions were to be stated and labeled as exceptions. Before the SEC report was issued, however, the AIA had taken action.

In October 1939, the AIA's Committee on Auditing Procedure issued Statement on Auditing Procedure (SAP) No. 1, "Extensions of Auditing Procedure." Members of the institute approved these extensions at the 1939 annual meeting. A new form of report was recommended in SAP No. 1. The scope paragraph contained reference to review of the internal-control system but did not contain reference to obtaining information from officers and employees. The explanation for this omission was that serious misconceptions had resulted about the degree of reliance on such information. According to SAP No. 1, the auditor should decide whether to rely on information without disclosure of the source. The opinion paragraph included reference to generally accepted accounting principles for the first time. The phrase "based upon such examination" was excluded because it was obvious that the auditor cannot express an opinion without completion of the work referred to in the scope paragraph. "Fairly present" was turned into "present fairly" after much discussion by the committee, which then failed to include this discussion in its report.

The SEC determined that the language of the scope paragraph was inadequate and issued in February 1941 Accounting Series Release (ASR) No. 21, "Amendment of Rules 2-02 and 3-07 of Regulation S-X," to require reference to the generally accepted auditing standards. The AIA objected because generally accepted auditing standards had not been prescribed. In February 1941, SAP No. 5 was issued; in March 1941, SAP No. 6. Both were entitled "The Revised SEC Rules on 'Accountants' Certificates.'" After deliberations by the SEC and the AIA committee on auditing procedure, the following assertion was added to the scope paragraph:

"Our examination was made in accordance with generally accepted auditing standards applicable in the circumstances and included all procedures which we considered necessary."

Nine generally accepted auditing standards were prescribed after approval at the 1948 annual meeting of the AIA of a special report of the Committee on Auditing Procedure, *Auditing Standards—Their Generally Accepted Significance and Scope*. This action led to SAP No. 24, "Revision in Short-Form Accountant's Report or Certificate," issued in October 1948. SAP No. 24 amended the scope paragraph to read: "We have examined the balance sheet of X Company as of ———, and the related statements of income and surplus for the year then ended. Our examination was made in accordance with generally accepted auditing standards, and accordingly included such tests of the accounting records and such other auditing procedures as we considered necessary in the circumstances." The committee believed reference to internal control in the scope paragraph was no longer needed since the newly adopted standards required a study of the internal-control system.

In 1974, the AICPA created the Commission on Auditors' Responsibilities to identify and deal with issues about the auditor's role and responsibilities. The commission had to deal with the standard report because it recognized that the report is almost the only formal means used both to educate and inform users about the audit function.

The commission responded to research that described the standard report as a symbol. One criticism was that while some of its intended messages were explicit, other messages had to be inferred. Another criticism concerned the use of technical terminology without the clarifying language that could adequately limit readers' interpretations.

The commission recommended deleting the reference to consistency and the addition of new messages. Reference to consistency was removed because the commission believed auditors should not originate financial information; disclosure of changes in accounting principles was to originate with management according to accounting standards. New messages pertained to the basic financial statements, other financial information, and internal-accounting controls.

The new messages pertaining to the basic financial statements were (1) the financial statements are the representations of management, and (2) there should be a description of the nature of the audit function. Back in 1933, the first standard report had contained a message about the nature of the audit function, and the new message recommended by the commission was similar to the old 1933 message.

The new messages pertaining to other financial information dealt with the subject matter of Statement on Auditing Standards (SAS) No. 8, "Other Information in Documents Containing Audited Financial Statements," and SAS No. 13, "Reports on a Limited Review of Interim Financial Information." The commission believed that explicit reporting should apply to other financial information, but during this same time frame the AICPA's Auditing Standards Executive Committee (AudSEC) adopted a different approach and gave official recognition to the concepts of "exception reporting" and "expanded standard report."

In formulating SAS Nos. 8 and 13 in 1975 and 1976, AudSEC made an important distinction between basic financial statements and other financial information. Only the basic financial statements were necessary for the presentation of an entity's financial position and the results of its operations and its cash flows in conformity with generally accepted accounting principles. The standard report applied solely to the basic financial statements. The basic financial statements might warrant use of the standard report even though the other information either is inconsistent with the basic financial statements or, for interim financial information, does not conform to applicable guidelines or was not reviewed. In these circumstances, an expanded standard report, but a standard report nevertheless, should be used. Exception reporting requires an additional explanatory paragraph, but only if necessary in the circumstances to inform users of problems with other financial information. The expanded standard report, therefore, contains three paragraphs, two of which cover the basic financial statements.

In 1987, the Auditing Standards Board of the AICPA issued 10 exposure drafts dealing with errors, illegal acts, auditor communications, auditing client estimates, internal control, continued existence, and analytical procedures. The exposure drafts dealing with auditor communications included significant revision of the standard report.

Three paragraphs and new messages were proposed in the exposure draft. The three paragraphs were introductory, scope, and opinion paragraphs. The new messages were (1) the financial statements are the representations of management, and (2) the auditor's responsibilities and the nature and limitations of the audit function should be described. The first message was given in the introductory paragraph, and the second message was given in the scope paragraph. The opinion paragraph stated: "In our opinion, the financial statements referred to above are, in all material respects, fairly presented in conformity with generally accepted accounting principles." "Present fairly" was changed back to the 1939 version of "fairly present," and there was no reference to consistency in the opinion paragraph. In the sense of the expanded standard report initially recommended by AudSEC in 1975, but without the connotation of exception reporting, the ASB recommended that early-warning information should be added if necessary in the circumstances to inform users of forthcoming financial difficulties.

SAS No. 58, "Reports on Audited Financial Statements," was issued in April 1988. The new standard report was similar to the exposure draft's standard report. The expanded standard report, however, would not contain the early-warning information recommended in the exposure draft but would inform users of inconsistency, uncertainties, going-concern problems, and emphasis of a matter, if necessary in the circumstances. The guidance provided by the ASB to inform users conforms with the belief expressed by the Commission on Auditors' Responsibilities that the auditor should not originate financial information, report financial information in the report, or interpret the significance of financial information presented for past performance or future prospects.

Tonya K. Flesher
Homer H. Burkett
Dale L. Flesher

Bibliography

Carmichael, D.R. *The Auditor's Reporting Obligation: The Meaning and Implementation of the Fourth Standard of Reporting.* New York: AICPA, 1972.

Cochran, G. "The Auditor's Report: Its Evolution in the U.S.A.," *Accountant*, November 4, 1950, pp. 448–460.

Commission on Auditors' Responsibilities. *Report, Conclusions, and Recommenda-*

tions. New York: Commission on Auditors' Responsibilities, 1978.

Elliott, R.K., and P.D. Jacobson. "The Auditor's Standard Report: The Last Word or in Need of Change? (Weighing the Pros and Cons of Proposed Changes)," *Journal of Accountancy*, February 1987, pp. 72–78.

Geiger, M.A. "SAS No. 58: Did the ASB Really Listen?" *Journal of Accountancy*, December 1988, pp. 55–57.

Roth, J.L. "Breaking the Tablets: A New Look at the Old Opinion," *Journal of Accountancy*, July 1968, pp. 63–67.

See also AMERICAN INSTITUTE OF CERTIFIED PUBLIC ACCOUNTANTS; *CARPENTER V. HALL;* EXTERNAL AUDITING; GENERALLY ACCEPTED ACCOUNTING PRINCIPLES; *HERZFELD V. LAVENTHOL, KREKSTEIN, HORWATH AND HORWATH;* HOXSEY, J.M.B.; INTERNAL CONTROL; LAW AND ACCOUNTING; MAY, GEORGE OLIVER; MCKESSON AND ROBBINS CASE; NEW YORK STOCK EXCHANGE; SECURITIES AND EXCHANGE COMMISSION; *ULTRAMARES CORPORATION V. TOUCHE, NIVEN AND COMPANY;* UNIFORM ACCOUNTING

Australia

The knowledge of, and skill in, the Italian method of double entry bookkeeping probably arrived in Australia with the First Fleet in 1788. It also is believed that the military paymasters in this distant British gaol (jail) used a form of "charge and discharge" accounting. For half a century, all official accounts were operated as a branch of the British Treasury. In the absence of financial institutions, the Government Commissariat (or storehouse) issued notes that substituted for a monetary system. The pattern of isolated settlements from which the pioneers radiated out into the country led to six separate colonies. This also meant the creation of local accounting bodies, beginning in Adelaide in 1885. Following federation and the creation of the Commonwealth of Australia, these local organizations merged into national bodies but still retained strong state influences.

Victoria in 1896 was the first place in the British Commonwealth to require the presentation of annual audited accounts to company annual meetings. In due course, the other states followed. Yet, while there has been this emphasis on disclosure, there remained a dominant view that the determination of accounting numbers was a professional discretion.

Australians have made their mark in developing and publishing theoretical material. Sir Alexander Fitzgerald, in the 1930s, independently developed ideas on terminology that appeared almost simultaneously in the United States. Later, Professor R.J. Chambers in the early 1960s developed a form of exit-price accounting, Continuously Contemporary Accounting (CoCoA), independently of similar ideas developed by Robert Sterling in the United States. Chambers has been honored with a gold medal of the American Institute of Certified Public Accountants (AICPA), and with the Outstanding Accounting Educators Award of the American Accounting Association (AAA). Two expatriate Australians, Ray Ball and Phillip Brown, wrote what is acknowledged as the most widely cited reference in the last 20 years. Their study, *An Empirical Evaluation of Accounting Income Numbers* (1968), was honored with the first AAA Seminal Contribution to Accounting Literature Award.

While Australia led the world in 1976 by issuing a provisional standard for the application of current cost accounting, it was the only major English-speaking country to fail to achieve, even on a temporary basis, any widespread application of fundamentally different methods of accounting to reflect changing prices. Nevertheless, there has never been a blind adherence to historical cost, and revaluation of assets by directors has long been a widespread and accepted practice.

The Australian Society of Certified Practicing Accountants (ASCPA) is the largest professional accounting organization, with over 62,000 members, including many in commerce, industry, and government and a dominant representation among small practitioners. The Institute of Chartered Accountants in Australia (ICAA) has 21,000 members, including the partners of the local affiliates of the major international audit firms. Historically, the ASCPA has had its power base in Victoria, while the ICAA has been dominant in New South Wales. There has always been a degree of overlapping membership of over 5,000 in the two bodies, but attempts to merge have failed due to opposition in the smaller-population states. It is believed some younger members opposed the merger because of their experience with and attitudes to the alternative professional entry programs for the CPA qualification of the ASCPA or the Professional Year of the ICAA.

While the ICAA has traditionally emphasized the role of the accountant in public practice, in the 1990s for the first time, it permitted candidates to proceed with the professional year while employed with an accredited industrial or commercial enterprise. This reflects the reality that about one-third of the ICAA members are not involved in public practice.

The professional qualifications of both bodies are recognized in the statutory control of auditors, liquidators, and tax agents. Their professional designations have legal protection against use by nonmembers. However, there is no general restriction or regulation on the practice of accounting, whatever other form of qualification may be claimed by the individual concerned.

The Australian profession reflects the Australian paradox of conformity with rules combined with a fierce individual independence. For many years, accounting and audit practice was influenced strongly by English example. These traditional links were consistent with the origins of accounting in the United Kingdom, with an emphasis on audit, and the development of the joint-stock company. In the 1950s, standards reflecting U.S. practice were adopted almost verbatim, reflecting a new emphasis on the managerial functions of accounting that developed in the hothouse of the U.S. manufacturing industry.

In 1969 the ASCPA and the ICAA jointly sponsored the Australian Accounting Research Foundation (AARF) to assist in developing professional standards. The AARF services the Australian Accounting Standards Board (AASB), which issues mandatory standards for corporate entities. The ASCPA and the ICAA continue to issue similar Australian accounting standards. Members of these bodies are bound to make their best effort to secure compliance with these standards by other entities.

Until the 1970s, accounting education occurred largely through preparation for examinations conducted by the professional bodies. University education in accounting commenced at the University of Melbourne in 1929, and the adoption of the undergraduate-degree entry was matched by the existence of full account-

ing programs in every university in Australia. The development in the early 1990s of a unified system of higher education has seen the merger of the previous college sector into the large universities. The college sector, with its origins in the earlier technical institutes and colleges, had played a major role in accounting education during the previous 50 years.

In the 1960s, the academic community created the Accounting Association of Australia and New Zealand, which provides opportunities for academic dialogue and has developed as a lobbying vehicle for the interests of the academics and accounting education. It has a membership in the mid 1990s of about 1,000.

In public esteem, the accounting profession ranks close behind the traditional professions of law and medicine. However, accountants who are prominent in tax practice do not enjoy the same protection of legal privilege over their advice to clients as do legal practitioners working in the same field.

The Australian periodical literature includes the *Australian Accountant*, journal of the ASCPA, and *Charter*, the ICAA journal. In academic fields, the Sydney-based *Abacus* and the journal of the Accounting Association of Australia and New Zealand, *Accounting and Finance*, have achieved worldwide recognition. Other research-oriented journals include *Accounting History*, *Australian Accounting Review*, *OUT Accounting Research Journal*, and *Accounting Forum*, each of which is developing its own specialist niche in the marketplace.

Robert W. Gibson

Bibliography

Gibson, R.W. "Development of Corporate Accounting in Australia," *Accounting Historians Journal*, Fall 1979, pp. 23–38.
———, and R. Arnold. "The Development of Auditing Standards in Australia," *Accounting Historians Journal*, Spring 1981, pp. 51–65.

See also BALL AND BROWN'S "AN EMPIRICAL EVALUATION OF ACCOUNTING INCOME NUMBERS"; CHAMBERS, RAYMOND JOHN; EDWARDS AND BELL: REPLACEMENT-COST ACCOUNTING; HISTORICAL COST; STERLING, ROBERT R.; WELLS, MURRAY CHARLES

B

Babbage, Charles (1792–1871)

The English mathematician and scientist Charles Babbage demonstrated the world's first practical mechanical calculator, his "difference engine," in 1822. His computer, or "analytical engine," was never built during his lifetime, but has since been constructed and proved workable. It had all the essential components of a modern computer, including a punch-card input system, a binary calculating system, and external memory storage.

Like Adam Smith, Babbage was fascinated by the economies that could be achieved through division of labor, and he considered that all advanced civilizations had become so by rationalizing production in this way. *On the Economy of Machinery and Manufactures* (1832) was probably the first work in English on the scientific management of factories. Using as his illustration the manufacture of pins, Babbage broke production down into seven basic steps, for each of which he calculated the time and cost of making one pound of pins, the labor cost per day, and "the price of making each part of a single pin, in millionths of a penny." Though he was not concerned with cost accounting as such, Babbage emphasized the need for cost analysis and control. He understood that the unit cost of manufacturing a product changes with the number of items produced, and he showed the effect of such changes on total machine costs. Babbage considered wear and tear of machinery a legitimate cost of production and proposed that depreciation be calculated and reported.

Michael Chatfield

Bibliography

Babbage, C. *On the Economy of Machinery and Manufactures*. London: Charles Knight, 1832. Reprint. New York: Augustus M. Kelly, 1963.

Bernstein, J. *The Analytical Engine*. New York: Random House, 1963.

Hyman, A. *Charles Babbage: Pioneer of the Computer*. Oxford: Oxford University Press, 1982.

Morrison, P., and E. Morrison, ed. *Charles Babbage and His Calculating Engines*. New York: Dover Publications, 1961.

Moseley, M. *Irascible Genius: A Life of Charles Babbage, Inventor*. London: Hutchinson, 1964.

See also CHURCH, ALEXANDER HAMILTON; COMPUTING TECHNOLOGY IN THE WEST: THE IMPACT ON THE PROFESSION OF ACCOUNTING; COST AND/OR MANAGEMENT ACCOUNTING; DEPRECIATION; SMITH, ADAM; STANDARD COSTING

Babylonia

From obscure beginnings more than 7,000 years ago, the Chaldean-Babylonian, Assyrian, and Sumerian civilizations produced what may have been the first organized government in the world, several of the oldest written languages, and the oldest surviving business records. Periodic flooding made the valley between the Tigris and Euphrates Rivers a particularly rich farming area. Various types of service businesses and small industries were established in the towns, and an extensive trade grew up within and outside the Mesopotamian Valley. There were at least two banking firms, and notations exist of "money current with the merchant" comprising standard measures of gold and silver. The principle of credit was understood. It was common practice for drafts drawn on one place to be payable in another. The cities of Babylon and Ninevah were known as the "queens of commerce," and Babylonian became the language of business and politics throughout the Near East. Record keeping is thought to have begun about 2000 B.C., though the oldest surviving commercial documents date from 2500 B.C.

By all descriptions, the Babylonians were obsessive bookkeepers, with a passion for organization. They lived in a densely populated river valley whose fertility depended on an intricate system of irrigation canals. Sumeria was a theocracy whose early rulers were considered "bailiffs of the gods" and in this capacity possessed most of the lands and herds. Both they and their subjects had to render detailed stewardship accounts to their supernatural masters. Formal legal codes provided even stronger incentives for recording business events. The best known is the Code of Hammurabi, king of the first dynasty of Babylonia (2285–2242 B.C.). It required that an agent selling goods for a merchant give the merchant a sealed memorandum quoting prices; if this was not done, a contested agreement was legally unenforceable. It was customary for every business transaction, even the smallest, to be put in writing and signed by the contracting parties and witnesses. Such was the national temperament that it seems doubtful whether many transactions or commodity movements of any kind went unrecorded.

Michael Chatfield

Bibliography

Garbutt, D. "The Significance of Ancient Mesopotamia in Accounting History," *Accounting Historians Journal*, Spring 1984, pp. 83–101.

Jones, T.B. "Bookkeeping in Ancient Sumer," *Archaeology*, vol. 9, Spring 1956, pp. 16–21.

Keister, O.R. "Commercial Record-Keeping in Ancient Mesopotamia," *Accounting Review*, April 1964, pp. 371–376.

See also CREDIT; EGYPT; EXTERNAL AUDITING; SCRIBES; STEWARDSHIP

Bad Debts

Today's methods of accounting for bad debts have been used for hundreds of years. The Medici Bank (1397–1494) operated branches throughout Western Europe. Every year, on March 24, books of the branch offices were closed and copies of their balance sheets were sent to the home office in Florence. These listed separately the balance of each customer's account, resulting in balance sheets that sometimes included more than 200 line items. Since bad debts were the chief threat to a Renaissance banker's solvency, audit by the general manager and his assistants consisted of examining these statements to prevent the granting of excess credit and to pick out doubtful or past-due accounts. The Medici policy was to make provision for bad debts before profits were distributed. Allowances for doubtful accounts were established just as they are today. Branch managers were severely reprimanded if it was later discovered that these reserves were inadequate because of misleading reports about the solvency of debtors.

Between the fifteenth and nineteenth centuries, the main goal of asset accounting was the maintenance of comprehensive ledger records for the owner's reference. It was common practice to list every debtor's receivables separately in the general ledger. A merchant could then review his credit dealings simply by scanning his ledger accounts. Two treatments of bad debts were recommended by textbook authors and widely used in practice. Debts considered to be worthless were written off directly to the profit and loss account, though this was often done belatedly. Debts considered doubtful but possibly collectable were often segregated in a special asset account called by such names as "bad and desperate debtors." This treatment overstated current income but maintained a record of all debts owed the firm, regardless of quality. It also reduced the number of receivables accounts in the ledger, thereby saving space and making the ledger easier to balance and close. But the "desperate debtors" were still carried at full value until they were judged to be worthless and written off. The account title alone warned of their diminished collectability.

After 1850, pressures for consistency in bad debt accounting came from three sources: the companies acts, the courts, and the accounting profession. The Companies Acts of 1855–1856 contained a model balance sheet, which included a space for "debts considered doubtful and bad." This suggests that preferred practice, if not common practice, favored making provision for doubtful accounts.

Nineteenth century legal attitudes toward bad debts were ambiguous. While corporate managers had wide discretion to ignore uncollectable accounts or write them off, courts would intervene to correct blatant abuses. A British trading company's balance sheet of February 1864 contained debts due from the Confederate States of America, as well as cotton owned by the company but still in the blockaded Southern states. According to the balance sheet, there were ample profits to cover the dividend proposed for payment in May 1864. The court ruled that there was no fraud, because there was no attempt to conceal the status of these doubtful assets. However, when directors of another corporation declared a dividend on the basis of a balance sheet that contained receivables known by them to be uncollectable, the court declared that the corporation had acted illegally, and it held the directors liable for the entire amount of the dividend. The legal view seems to have been that provision should be made for bad debts before stockholders were entitled to cash dividends. On the other hand, courts were generally unwilling to question the judgment of corporate directors who acted in good faith.

In contrast, professional auditors believed that bad debts should be written off immediately and that reserves should be established to protect against future losses. Methods for estimating uncollectable accounts were described in the periodical accounting literature as early as 1880. The account analysis portion of a British audit program of the 1880s has a modern sound. The auditor examined securities, assayed notes for genuineness and collectability, aged accounts receivable and estimated bad debts, and confirmed by mail all outstanding accounts receivable. Still, as A.C. Littleton said, if auditors had the power to criticize, corporate directors had the power of final judgment. In 1882 English auditor F.W. Pixley called the omission of bad debt allowances and depreciation reserves "the most frequent errors in the accounts of public companies."

American capital markets during the late nineteenth century were mainly local and regional rather than national, and businesses financed themselves more often by bank borrowing than by issuing stock. Bankers wanted assurance that a debtor could repay his loan at maturity. They judged that the best indicators of future liquidity were to be found in the relationship between current assets and current liabilities. A safe margin of working capital and a two-to-one current ratio became the standards for credit granting. This made it natural for bankers to anticipate potential losses but not gains, to favor the writedown of inventories to their lower of cost or market price, and to encourage the use of depreciation reserves and bad debt allowances.

But it was the income tax laws that did most to standardize the accounting treatment of bad debts. The Revenue Act of 1913, which established the permanent American personal income tax, specified that bad debt write-offs were deductible expenses in calculating taxable income. The Revenue Act of 1921 permitted the use of bad debt allowances, which encouraged taxpayers to anticipate bad debt losses and deduct them before they occurred. The widespread adoption of allowances for doubtful accounts and statistical estimation methods owes much more to passage of the Sixteenth Amendment than to the development of accounting theory or practice.

Michael Chatfield

Bibliography

Littleton, A.C. *Accounting Evolution to 1900*. New York: American Institute Publishing, 1933. Reprint. New York: Russell and Russell, 1966.

Yamey, B.S. "Some Seventeenth and Eighteenth Century Double-Entry Ledgers," *Accounting Review*, October 1959, pp. 534–536.

———. "Some Topics in the History of Financial Accounting in England, 1500–1900." In *Studies in Accounting Theory*, edited by W.T. Baxter and S. Davidson, pp. 14–43. Homewood, IL: Irwin, 1962.

See also ACCRUAL ACCOUNTING; BALANCE SHEET; COMPANIES ACTS; CONTINUITY; DIVIDENDS; FINANCIAL-STATEMENT ANALYSIS; LIQUIDITY: ACCOUNTING MEASUREMENT; MEDICI ACCOUNTS; PEELE, JAMES; PIXLEY, FRANCIS WILLIAM; RETAINED EARNINGS APPROPRIATIONS; SIXTEENTH AMENDMENT

Badoer, Jachomo

Jachomo Badoer was a Venetian merchant who traded in Constantinople between 1436 and 1440. His double entry ledger was the only commercial document written in Constantinople that survived, in its entirety, the Turkish conquest of that city in 1453. As such it is a unique source of information on the commerce, currencies, and marketing practices of the Levant during the first half of the fifteenth century. Badoer was a bookkeeping innovator, but his ledger also portrays the state of the accounting art at that time.

Badoer maintained only one ledger, and no unified journal, though he kept a series of memorandum books in which he recorded various types of payments and receipts. His ledger was written in the Venetian double entry style, with debits and credits side by side on the open folio. Bills of exchange, consignment accounts, barter transactions, and payments for marine insurance are included in his accounts. He established separate accounts for each client and each consignment of goods, calculating profits and losses individually. His profit and loss account also included profits on money exchange and on discounts granted by creditors, suppliers, and agents. Badoer's ledger contains one of the oldest known compound entries.

Michael Chatfield

Bibliography

Martinelli, A. *The Origination and Evolution of Double Entry Bookkeeping to 1440.* Ph.D. diss., North Texas State University, 1974. Ann Arbor, MI: University Microfilms, pp. 887–900.

Peragallo, E. "Development of the Compound Entry in the Fifteenth Century Ledger of Jachomo Badoer, A Venetian Merchant," *Accounting Review*, January 1983, pp. 98–104.

———. "Jachomo Badoer, Renaissance Man of Commerce, and His Ledger," *Accounting and Business Research*, vol. 10, no. 37A, 1980, pp. 93–101.

———. "The Ledger of Jachomo Badoer: Constantinople September 2, 1436, to February 26, 1440," *Accounting Review*, October 1977, pp. 881–892.

See also BARTER; COMPOUND ENTRIES; DEBIT AND CREDIT; LEDGER

Balance Account

The balance account was a summary ledger account to which were posted all asset, liability, and capital balances after expenses and revenues had been closed to capital. A balance account served the same purposes as today's post–closing trial balance. It tested the accuracy of ledger closings and was used to collect open account balances for transfer to a new ledger. When a ledger was full, the bookkeeper could simply post each individual account balance to a new book. Or, preferably, he could collect all open account balances in a balance account, check the equality of debits and credits, and post all the opening balances in the new ledger from a single source.

Andrea Barbarigo's 1435 ledger contains the oldest surviving balance account. During the next 150 years the balance account became a standard bookkeeping procedure, and it remained so until the late nineteenth century. Eventually the balance account evolved into a balance sheet, but there is no evidence in early account books or texts that any balance account was meant to be reproduced outside the ledger. Like the profit and loss account, its function was as a clearing and transfer medium.

Michael Chatfield

Bibliography

Littleton, A.C. *Accounting Evolution to 1900.* New York: American Institute Publishing, 1933. Reprint. New York: Russell and Russell, 1966.

Yamey, B.S. "Closing the Ledger," *Accounting and Business Research*, Winter 1970, pp. 71–77. Reprinted in B.S. Yamey, *Essays on the History of Accounting.* New York: Arno Press, 1978.

See also BALANCE SHEET; BARBARIGO, ANDREA; CAPITAL ACCOUNT; CLOSING ENTRIES AND PROCEDURES; DEBIT AND CREDIT; FAROLFI COMPANY LEDGER; FLORI, LUDOVICO; LEDGER; TRIAL BALANCE; YMPYN, JAN

Balance Sheet

Because it elaborates the accounting equation, the balance sheet is the logical end product of double entry bookkeeping. The oldest surviving double entry balance sheets were made by fourteenth century Florentine banks. The Medici Bank was founded in 1397 and lasted nearly a hundred years, establishing branches throughout Western Europe. The Medici used double entry technique for essentially modern purposes—management and control, audit, even income tax calculation. Every year on March 24, books of the branches were closed and copies of their balance sheets were sent to the home office in Florence. These listed separately the balance of each customer's account. Thus some Medici balance sheets contained more than 200 items, and since bad debts were the chief threat to a Renaissance banker's solvency, audit by the general manager and his assistants consisted of examining these statements to prevent the granting of excess credit and to pick out doubtful or past due accounts.

In "Particularis de Computis et Scripturis," Luca Pacioli made no provision for financial statements. Since business in his day was typically a series of disconnected ventures, there was little interest in unfinished operations and few of the modern reasons for periodic reckonings. Owners were usually in personal contact with their affairs, operations could easily be observed, and profits were not hard to estimate. Most financial information was taken directly from the ledger accounts. Balance sheets were normally prepared only at the end of a major project, such as a trading voyage, or after all the pages in a ledger had been filled.

In 1586 Don Angelo Pietra, a Benedictine monk, published *Indrizzo Degli Economi*, the first printed book on accounting for nonprofit organizations. Pietra thought monastery accounts could best be reviewed by examination of detached financial statements. Though statements had been used in practice for more than 200 years, this was the first time an author had mentioned them. Pietra was also the first writer to consider an enterprise as separate and distinct from its owners, and his advocacy of a balance sheet, income statement, and detailed statement of monastery capital resulted from his desire to account for all changes in the entity's financial status, not just changes in owner's equity. In 1636 Ludovico Flori, a Jesuit of Palermo, published *Trattato del Modo di Tenere il Libro Doppio Domestico* on monastery accounting, elaborating Pietra's ideas. Flori also stressed the importance of financial statements and was the first author to mention the placing of transactions in their proper fiscal periods. He used a trial balance not only to prove the ledger's correctness but to facilitate its closing.

Authors of commercial bookkeeping textbooks came to financial statements by way of the balance account. This was a single account that listed all the debit and credit balances in the ledger. It not only tested the accuracy of ledger closing, but collected asset and equity balances into a summary convenient for transfer to a new ledger. Its emergence as a standard bookkeeping procedure also increased awareness of the interrelationship between real and nominal accounts. For example, Johann Gottlieb in 1546 calculated profit in the balance sheet as the sum of changes in assets, liabilities, and beginning of period capital. But there is no evidence in early texts that the balance account was meant to be reproduced outside the ledger. Like the profit and loss account, its main use was as a clearing and transfer medium.

How did the balance account evolve into a balance sheet? There were a number of causes. During the Middle Ages, Italian city states and German municipalities levied property taxes which required the preparation of financial statements. A French government ordinance, the Code Savary of 1673, required merchants to prepare an "inventory" every two years "of all their fixed and movable properties and of their debts receivable and payable." The intention was to aid possible bankruptcy proceedings by preserving an overview of each firm up to the latest statement date. From the earliest Florentine *Balancio* in the fourteenth century, partnership profits had been calculated as the difference between the net assets of two successive accounting periods. The admission or withdrawal of partners legally dissolved such businesses and required a new calculation of partners' capitals. Merely closing partnership books might not suffice, for then only the bookkeeping partner would preserve a record of the situation at that moment. The need for asset revaluations at the time of ownership changes also called for a separate schedule of resources and debts.

Above all, as companies grew larger, more people had an interest in their operations, and separate statements were needed because direct access to the ledger became impossible for all who wanted information. Following the appearance of joint stock companies in the seventeenth century, demands for separate statements became urgent as creditors and shareholders sought data about their investments.

Early financial statements were made either by copying the accounts as they appeared in the ledger or by working from trial balance figures to produce columnar reports. In his

1635 text, *The Merchant's Mirrour*, Richard Dafforne illustrated a six-column statement in which the first pair of columns showed a trial balance of totals; the middle pair, a trial balance of balances; and the right hand columns, a balance sheet containing the remaining assets and equities. Later writers added profit and loss columns and entered inventory counts to adjust beginning figures, creating what we would call a worksheet. In time these unwieldy columnar statements dropped out of textbooks, to be replaced by "account" and "report" form balance sheets showing final figures but not their derivation.

Throughout this period, the balance sheet was by far the most important financial statement and often the only one prepared. Users wanted information about assets and capital; revenues and expenses were considered incidental. Simon Stevin's *Hypomnemata Mathematica* (1605–1608) broke this pattern by stressing the equal importance of nominal accounts. In presenting his most famous illustrative example, Stevin explained that the "estate" (balance sheet) of Derrick Roose was so called because it included only such accounts as "make up the estate on a certain day" and excluded other accounts that "indicate increase or decrease of capital." His balance sheet was typical for its time, with assets opposite liabilities, and income shown as the net change in capital during an accounting period:

TABLE 1

The Estate of Derrick Roose
made up on the last day of December 1600

Estate of Capital debit		*Estate of Capital credit*	
	£ s d		£ s d
(list of liabilities)	51- 8-0	(list of assets)	3191-17-1
Balance debit, to close the statement	3140- 9-1		
Total	3191-17-1	Total	3191-17-1
The remainder (Capital) at year end is			3140- 9-1
At the beginning of the year it was			2153- 3-8
Increase during the year			987- 5-5

But Stevin did not stop there. "In order to make certain that the account is correct, I collect all remainders of accounts increasing or decreasing capital," and including all remainders of accounts omitted from the balance sheet

"because they do not represent actual things." But this "Proof of the Estate" was more than the traditional test of ledger equality. It not only confirmed the profit figure shown in the balance sheet but described how it was earned, enumerating the expenses and revenues that caused the net capital change represented by income:

TABLE 2

Proof of the Estate

Estate of Capital debit		*Estate of Capital credit*	
	£ s d		£ s d
Trading expenses	57-7-0	Profit on cloves	75-4-7
Household expenses	107-10-1	Profit on nuts	109-7-2
Total	164-17-0	Profit on pepper	18-19-0
		Profit on ginger	41- 8-4
Profit, agreeing with the above statement	987- 5-5	Profit and Loss (prior credit bals.)	907-3-4
	1152- 2-5		1152- 2-5

Modern balance sheet formats were influenced by the English companies acts. During the eighteenth century, British bookkeeping began to be adapted to corporate needs. Its purpose was no longer simply to aid businessmen but also to inform investor decisions and, in a broader sense, to help allocate resources and maintain a money market in an economy that was becoming industrialized. The collapse of the South Sea Company speculations, accompanied by large invesxtor losses, led to the Bubble Act of 1720, which for more than a hundred years restricted the formation of new corporations. It was not until 1844 that the Joint Stock Companies Act again made the corporate form available for general use.

In framing the companies acts, Parliament was probably more influenced by the English tradition of responsibility accounting than by Italian double entry bookkeeping. Incorporation was granted as a privilege in return for which joint stock companies incurred specific public duties. Promoters and company officers were considered stewards placed in charge of investors' capital; as such, they had a duty to publicize their use of these assets. Acting on this premise, the British pioneered legislation to protect investors. The Companies Act of 1844 required the distribution to stockholders of audited balance sheets. The

Companies Acts of 1855–1856 abandoned earlier audit and reporting requirements but included a model balance sheet that reflected the English view of corporate disclosure responsibility.

Like the charge and discharge statement, this model report grouped related items into subtotals and placed obligations and their discharge opposite each other. These were improvements in themselves, representing an interpretive arrangement of data in place of the earlier random sequence of ledger balances. Since management's initial responsibility was created by the sale of stock, the top section of the 1856 model balance sheet contrasted permanent capital from stock sales and the permanent assets bought with the proceeds. The distinction made by classical English economists between fixed and circulating capital may have persuaded legislators to separate current from long-term assets and liabilities. The last two items of stewardship were the reserve for contingencies and retained earnings available for dividends; contrasted to these were the cash and operating assets that funded them:

TABLE 3

BALANCE SHEET of the _____ Co.
           made up to _____ 1856

Capital and Liabilities	Property and Assets
I. Capital from stock sales	III. Property
a. Shares outstanding	a. Immovable
b. Price per share	b. Movable
II. Debts and Liabilities	IV. Debts owing to the firm
a. Long-term liabilities	
b. Short-term debts	a. Notes Receivable
	b. Accounts Receivable
	c. Bad debts
VI. Reserve for Contingencies	V. Cash and Investments
VII. Profit available for div'ds.	
_____	_____
_____	_____
Contingent Liabilities	

This model format, with assets on the right, equities on the left, and permanent capital at the top, was almost a complete reversal of the modern American balance sheet. It was also a departure from classical Italian practice, and several different explanations have been given for this. Some point to Simon Stevin's influence on English textbook presentations. Also, the balance account showed such a reversed order after an old ledger had been closed but before the new one had been opened. And several early English corporations produced balance sheets in this format. Earlier British legislation was another influence on these model statements. English accounting texts written between 1821 and 1858 showed balance sheets with assets on the left, but after 1858 this order was reversed. The assets-on-the-right arrangement was recommended by the Companies Act of 1862. The Regulation of Railways Act of 1868 not only made it mandatory but also required a horizontal division of the data in terms of "opposites."

In America as in England, the balance sheet was the primary financial statement—but for different reasons. The British balance sheet developed as a report to stockholders on management's stewardship of contributed funds. Nineteenth century American corporations had no comparable history of large losses from stock speculation and were not as closely regulated, nor was incorporation considered a privilege that created reciprocal disclosure obligations. American corporations were usually small and drew most of their capital from short-term bank loans rather than sales of stock. For this reason their balance sheets were directed mainly toward bankers, whose conventional wisdom was that a borrower's ability to repay maturing loans was related more to the conversion of inventory into cash than to earning power. This emphasis on liquidity caused current assets and liabilities to be placed at the top of the American balance sheet. And it is likely that the absence of government regulation encouraged statement formats that simply followed the ledger balances, placing assets on the left, equities on the right.

The bankers' "liquidity doctrine" was severely tested during the inventory depression of 1920–1921, when American wholesale prices fell 40 percent, causing a billion dollar inventory price shrinkage. Current sales from inventories then had to be made much below historical cost, reducing cash inflows and making loan repayments difficult. As credit dried up, bankers saw the limitations of a loan policy based solely on liquidity, and corporate borrowers realized their vulnerability during recessions if they depended for financing on short-term bank loans. They accordingly sought funds from sources less sensitive to changes in their current cash position. During the 1920s, mass marketing of stock issues became a popular way to finance corporate expansion, since the resulting equity increase put no immediate pressure on working capital.

When stock sales became the chief external source of funds, and stockholders the primary readers of financial statements, the income statement became the more meaningful report. Of course the shift in emphasis from balance sheet to income statement had causes other than the changed method of corporate financing. These included long run institutional and technological changes, such as the growth of railroads and the regulation of quasi-public corporations. Income taxation shifted attention to revenues and expenses, as did the rapid development of cost accounting. Even long-term creditors found earning power more significant than tests of solvency. It began to be argued that determining net asset values at the balance sheet date was not only of secondary importance but was impossible to accomplish. Later the same would be said of income measurement.

Michael Chatfield

Bibliography

Baladouni, V. "An Early Attempt at Balance Sheet Classification and Financial Reporting," *Accounting Historians Journal*, June 1990, pp. 27–45.

De Roover, R. *The Rise and Decline of the Medici Bank, 1397–1494.* Cambridge: Harvard University Press, 1963. Reprint. New York: W.W. Norton, 1966.

Edey, H.C., and P. Panitpakdi. "British Company Accounting and the Law, 1844–1900." In *Studies in the History of Accounting*, edited by A.C. Littleton and B.S. Yamey, pp. 356–379. Homewood, IL: Irwin, 1956.

Howard, S.E. "Public Rules for Private Accounting in France, 1673 and 1807," *Accounting Review*, June 1932, pp. 91–102.

Littleton, A.C. *Accounting Evolution to 1900.* New York: American Institute Publishing, 1933. Reprint. New York: Russell and Russell, 1966.

Littleton, A.C., and V.K. Zimmerman. *Accounting Theory: Continuity and Change.* Englewood Cliffs, NJ: Prentice-Hall, 1962.

Moyer, C.A. "Trends in Presentation of Financial Statements and Reports." Chap. 15 in *Handbook of Modern Accounting Theory*, edited by M. Backer. Englewood Cliffs, NJ: Prentice-Hall, 1955.

Peragallo, E. *Origin and Evolution of Double Entry Bookkeeping: A Study of Italian Practice from the Fourteenth Century.* New York: American Institute Publishing, 1938. Reprint. Osaka: Nihon Shoseki, 1974.

Takatera, S. "Early Experiences of the British Balance Sheet," *Kyoto University Economic Review*, October 1967, pp. 34–47. Reprinted in *Historical Studies of Double-Entry Bookkeeping*, edited by O. Kojima, pp. 299–305. Kyoto: Diagakudo Shoten, 1975.

Ten Have, O. "Simon Stevin of Bruges" In *Studies in the History of Accounting*, edited by A.C. Littleton and B.S. Yamey. Homewood, IL: Irwin, 1956.

Walker, R.G. "Asset Classification and Asset Valuation," *Accounting and Business Research*, 1974, pp. 286–296.

See also BAD DEBTS; BALANCE ACCOUNT; BRANCH ACCOUNTING; "CHARGE AND DISCHARGE" STATEMENT; CLOSING ENTRIES AND PROCEDURES; COMPANIES ACTS; DAFFORNE, RICHARD; FINANCIAL-STATEMENT ANALYSIS; FLORI, LUDOVICO; FRANCE; INCOME STATEMENT/INCOME ACCOUNT; LEDGER; LIABILITIES; LIQUIDITY: ACCOUNTING MEASUREMENT; MEDICI ACCOUNTS; PACIOLI, LUCA; PIETRA, ANGELO; SOUTH SEA BUBBLE; STEVIN, SIMON; TRIAL BALANCE

Ball and Brown's "An Empirical Evaluation of Accounting Income Numbers"

This seminal work examined the association of security returns and accounting earnings. Ball and Brown (1968) is a major antecedent of what became known as the positive-accounting approach. Brown (1989) explained the motivation for the 1968 work. While criticisms of traditional accounting practices since the 1920s had been legion, little in the way of substantive change in accounting practices had occurred, and it was this survival feature of historical cost accounting that needed to be explained.

Ball and Brown sought to test the null hypothesis that accounting income numbers are "not useful" to share-market investors, against the specific alternative hypothesis that they are. They regarded the "completely analytical approach to usefulness," said to be the approach of many critics of historical cost accounting, as insufficient since it ignores a significant source of knowledge of the world, namely, "the extent to which the predictions of the [chosen] model conform to observed behavior." Ball and Brown acknowledged that existing income measures can be defined as the result of the application of a set of procedures "{X_1, X_2...} to a set of events {Y_1, Y_2, ...}" with no other definitive substantive meaning at all, and cautioned that it is dangerous to conclude, in the absence of further testing, that "a lack of substantive meaning implies a lack of utility."

Based on developments in capital-markets theory and access to large samples of security prices, Ball and Brown focused on the behavior of security prices to test their hypothesis about the usefulness of annual earnings numbers. They assumed market efficiency and investigated monthly security-return behavior of firms in the 12-month period up to, and including, the month that annual earnings were announced for 261 firms listed on the New York Stock Exchange for fiscal years 1957–1965.

Relying on the reasoning that market participants forecast what an entity's earnings numbers are likely to be, these assessments should be reflected in its current share price. Release of accounting income numbers thus affords an opportunity for the market to compare the forecast with the actual figures. Their empirical testing required an estimating device for market earnings forecasts, and Ball and Brown used the classical naive model, which predicts that earnings per share (EPS) this year will be no different from EPS last year, to identify good and bad EPS news. Results showed that while most of the price change takes place prior to the earnings release, reported accounting information is relied upon by the market as there exists a positive association between unexpected earnings and excess returns. A 10 percent to 15 percent price-response rate occurred in the release month. Hence, their conclusion was that historical cost accounting data are "useful." Brown (1989) listed several reasons why the paper had such an impact, a major one being that it appeared when there was an increasing perception of the need for more empirical, finance-oriented research in accounting.

Ball and Brown noted some limitations: The subpopulation did not include young firms, those that had failed, those that did not have a fiscal year ending on December 31, and those that were not represented on Compustat, the Center for Research in Security Prices (CRSP) tapes, and

the *Wall Street Journal*. These and other limitations have been commented upon by others—for example, Watts and Zimmerman (1986) and Brown (1989). Still the most apposite criticism is that of Chambers (1974), on stock market prices and accounting research in general, that the products of accounting enter into many more deliberative or bargaining situations than those of the public market in ordinary shares. This is especially true, given Ball and Brown's aim to test the usefulness of annual earnings numbers.

The Ball and Brown article heralded a perceived shift toward empirical finance-based accounting research examining the relationship of accounting and security-price behavior. That such an emphasis dominated accounting research in the 1970s and 1980s was largely attributable to Ball and Brown.

Frank L. Clarke
Graeme W. Dean

Bibliography

Ball, R., and P. Brown. "An Empirical Evaluation of Accounting Income Numbers," *Journal of Accounting Research*, Autumn 1968, pp. 159–178.
Brown, P. "Ball and Brown [1968]," *Journal of Accounting Research*, Supplement, 1989, pp. 202–217.
Chambers, R.J. "Stock Market Prices and Accounting Research," *Abacus*, June 1974, pp. 39–54.
Watts, R., and J. Zimmerman. *Positive Accounting Theory*. Englewood Cliffs, NJ: Prentice-Hall, 1986.
Zeff, S.A., and S. Davidson. "Two Decades of the *Journal of Accounting Research*," *Journal of Accounting Research*, Spring 1984, pp. 225–297.

See also BEAVER, WILLIAM; CANNING, JOHN BENNETT; CHAMBERS, RAYMOND JOHN; EDWARDS, JAMES DON; EFFICIENT MARKET HYPOTHESIS; EXTERNAL AUDITING; FINANCIAL-STATEMENT ANALYSIS; HISTORICAL COST; INCOME STATEMENT/INCOME ACCOUNT; POSITIVE ACCOUNTING; STERLING, ROBERT R.

Bankruptcy Acts

Beginning with the first Bankruptcy Act in 1542, the English government intervened directly to protect creditors against fraud. Recurring business crises during the nineteenth century resulted in a series of new statutes and a continued demand for men trained in bookkeeping and asset appraisal. The Victorians chose to regard insolvency as a moral shortcoming. There was often a presumption of asset concealment, and the examination of debtor's accounts introduced an element of extreme skepticism not normally found in stewardship audits. In bankruptcy investigations, court-appointed accountants were involved as third parties interested not only in creditor protection but in the administration of the bankrupt's affairs. The resulting tradition of examination and reporting by impartial experts added a new dimension to the verification process.

H.A. Shannon estimated that just over 30 percent of all English corporations formed between 1856 and 1883 ended in insolvency, and that a majority of these were liquidated within six years of their inception. Business depressions followed one another with machinelike regularity. The British government responded to these crises, with their attendant upsurge in business failures, by passing a series of bankruptcy acts. It is likely that no other laws enacted during the nineteenth century, not even the companies acts, provided so much work for accountants. The stewardship provisions of these statutes varied, but all required the appointment of administrators to take control of the bankrupt's property, both in his interest and to protect his creditors from asset concealment and conversion.

The Bankruptcy Act of 1825 authorized the appointment of commissioners in bankruptcy to manage the properties of insolvent debtors. The Bankruptcy Act of 1831 created a court of bankruptcy and gave the lord chancellor authority to select not more than 30 official assignees, "being merchants, bankers, accountants, or traders." This was the first governmental recognition of English accountants, who were particularly fitted for these jobs because the reasons for insolvency were sought by tracing back through the debtor's accounts to the time when he was solvent. The Bankruptcy Act of 1849 created a specific role for accountants by requiring every bankrupt to deliver his account books to an official assignee and help him prepare a summary of financial condition. The bankrupt also had to file such balance sheets and accounts as the court directed and swear to their truth. Passing the final hearing in bankruptcy court depended on a favorable report by the official assignee regarding the accuracy of the accounts. It became usual for the debtor

awaiting discharge to employ a public accountant to make sure that his statement of affairs and deficiency statement would pass inspection. This was also prudent because creditors opposed to a bankruptcy settlement sometimes hired accountants of their own to investigate the statements filed by a debtor with the court.

The Bankruptcy Act of 1861 abolished the position of official assignee and placed the debtor's property in the hands of assignees chosen by the creditors. The latter usually preferred outright liquidation to bankruptcy proceedings, and they now had the power to make compositions and distribute the bankrupt's assets as they pleased, without court intervention. Under the Bankruptcy Act of 1869, accountants were hired not only to appraise and manage the property of bankrupts but actually to liquidate insolvent businesses on behalf of the creditors. So many men began calling themselves accountants to obtain this employment that within a few years after the 1869 act the number of accountants had doubled. As H.W. Robinson put it, the British accounting profession "was born through bankruptcies, fed on failures and frauds, grew on liquidations and graduated through audits."

Michael Chatfield

Bibliography

Littleton, A.C. *Accounting Evolution to 1900*. New York: American Institute Publishing, 1933. Reprint. New York: Russell and Russell, 1966.

Robinson, H.W. *A History of Accountants in Ireland*. Dublin: Institute of Chartered Accountants in Ireland, 1964.

Shannon, H.A. "The First Five Thousand Limited Companies and their Duration," *Economic History*, vol. 2, 1932.

See also "CHARGE AND DISCHARGE" STATEMENT; STEWARDSHIP

Barbarigo, Andrea (d. 1449)

Andrea Barbarigo was a Venetian import merchant. His account books (1431–1449) provide the earliest Venetian example of mature venture bookkeeping. Luca Pacioli's "Particularis de Computis et Scripturis" (1494) described an accounting system essentially like Barbarigo's. Journal and ledger are integrated. Ledger accounts are cross referenced, and opposite each journal entry are page references to ledger postings. Debits and credits are identified by the words "per" and "a" respectively. Money values are placed in a crude column at the right. Barbarigo entered in the same cotton account all shipments from a particular agent even if they were spread over several years. For more frequent imports, such as English cloth, he opened new accounts for each lot received and left them open until the entire lot was sold. Since his business was not continuous in the modern sense, and different voyages had very different chances of success, he determined profits separately for each such venture and seldom had reason to balance or close his books. He prepared trial balances in 1431, 1435, and 1440, then let the accounts run until his death in 1449. His son Nicolo kept a ledger from 1456 to 1482 but struck a balance only once, in 1482 when the ledger was full.

Michael Chatfield

Bibliography

De Roover, R. "Andrea Barbarigo's Trial Balance," *Accounting Review*, January 1946, pp. 98–99.
Lane, F.C. *Andrea Barbarigo, Merchant of Venice, 1418–1449*. Studies in Historical and Political Science, vol. 62, no. 1, pp. 153–181. Baltimore: Johns Hopkins University, 1944.

See also BALANCE ACCOUNT; CLOSING ENTRIES AND PROCEDURES; DEBIT AND CREDIT; JOURNAL; LEDGER; PACIOLI, LUCA; TRIAL BALANCE

BarChris Case

See ESCOTT V. BARCHRIS CONSTRUCTION COMPANY

Bardi

Between 1300 and 1345, the most powerful Florentine merchant-banking houses were the Bardi, the Peruzzi, and the Acciaiuoli. The Bardi was the largest of these "pillars of Christendom," but only fragments of its accounting records survive. These suggest that the Bardi kept fairly advanced double entry records but did not employ a complete double entry bookkeeping system. In the 1340s all three companies failed due to overextension of credit and defaults on loans to monarchs.

Michael Chatfield

Bibliography

Martinelli, A. *The Origination and Evolution of Double Entry Bookkeeping to 1440.* Ph.D. diss., North Texas State University, 1974. Ann Arbor, MI: University Microfilms.
Peragallo, E. *Origin and Evolution of Double Entry Bookkeeping, A Study of Italian Practice from the Fourteenth Century.* New York: American Institute Publishing, 1938. Reprint. Osaka: Nihon Shoseki, 1974.

See also ALBERTI DEL GIUDICE; BRANCH ACCOUNTING; DOUBLE ENTRY BOOKKEEPING: ORIGINS; MEDICI ACCOUNTS; PERUZZI

Barter

Barter, the exchange of one commodity for another, is the oldest form of commerce. In his treatise on accounting, "Particularis de Computis et Scripturis" (1494), Luca Pacioli described entries for barter transactions, which he preferred to value at market prices, and many other authors of bookkeeping texts mentioned barter in passing. But in the ancient world, barter was the normal method of exchange. It probably inhibited accounting development. The options of a largely illiterate society that lacks a medium of exchange will always be limited. Pre-Hellenistic cultures never had coined money—that is, lumps of metal stamped to identify their purity and weight and intended for use as currency. Their accounting described commodity movements, treating measures of gold and silver not as units of value but merely as articles of trade. The inability to express merchandise values in terms of a single substance made cumulation and summation very difficult, and an integrated accounting system virtually impossible.

Men who understood the monetary concept could do better than this, even if they lacked money itself. In many ways, the economy of colonial America was more backward than that of ancient Egypt. Commerce was more localized, the inland transportation system was less developed, much of the land was less fertile, and agricultural methods were only marginally better. The British would not let the colonists coin money, which was extremely scarce, and until the 1820s trade was conducted largely without it. As a substitute for cash they evolved a system of "bookkeeping barter"—barter with a time lag. For example, a dairyman might deliver milk on credit to a tailor each day and be paid with a new suit at year end. This required literacy and the ability of both parties to keep books in terms of an identical medium of exchange. In other respects, the accounting system could be as primitive as some found in the ancient world. It needed just a record, or at most a balance, never a summary of all accounts. Ledgers consisted mainly of charges and credits to men's names. No attempt was made to isolate income, success being measured in terms of asset increases. Though known, double entry bookkeeping was rarely used.

Michael Chatfield

Bibliography

Baxter, W.T. "Accounting in Colonial America." In *Studies in the History of Accounting*, edited by A.C. Littleton and B.S. Yamey, pp. 272–287. Homewood, IL: Irwin, 1956.
Stone, W.E. "Barter: Development of Accounting Theory and Practice," *Accounting Historians Journal*, Fall 1985, pp. 95–108.

See also BADOER, JACHOMO; COLONIAL AMERICA, ACCOUNTING IN; CREDIT; GREECE; LEDGER; MONEY; PACIOLI, LUCA; PEELE, JAMES; SINGLE ENTRY BOOKKEEPING

Base Stock Method

A firm that adopted the base stock method specified a portion of its inventory as the minimum amount needed for the business to operate as a going concern. This minimum inventory quantity was considered a permanent investment and changes in its value were ignored. Inventory quantities above this base stock were treated as temporary investments that could be valued at acquisition cost, lower of cost or market, or even at current market prices. Inventory sales were assumed to come from purchases in excess of the base stock. However, if sales depleted ending base stock inventory, the goods sold were considered to be temporarily borrowed from the base stock and had to be repurchased. Because any base stock deficiency had to be replenished at current prices, sales from the base stock and repurchased base stocks were normally credited to inventory or charged to cost of goods sold at current market prices.

The precise origins of the base stock method are obscure, tax avoidance being a private matter. Apparently, the base stock method originated in Britain during the late nineteenth century. It was used mainly in the metals trades and the textile industry. It was attractive to income taxpayers because of its tendency to match current cost with current revenues while suppressing changes in base stock inventory values. The result was that inventory price changes tended not to be reflected in current income, and profit fluctuations between years were minimized.

A committee appointed by England's Ministry of Reconstruction evaluated the base stock method in 1918. The result was that firms already using the method were permitted to continue doing so, but no others were allowed to adopt it. This decision effectively stopped the growth of the base stock method in Britain.

In 1903 American Smelting and Refining Company became the first American firm to adopt the base stock method. The National Lead Company followed in 1913. But the base stock method was never widely used in America. In 1919 the Treasury Department prohibited its use for tax purposes. Finally, in 1930, in the Kansas City Structural Steel Company decision, the Supreme Court ruled unanimously that the base stock method was unacceptable for income tax purposes. A 1938 survey by the National Industrial Conference Board found that of 826 firms polled, only 4 percent used the base stock method.

While the base stock method was disallowed for tax reporting, the reasons for its use did not disappear, because inventory prices continued to fluctuate. An alternative was sought. The base stock method and the LIFO (last in, first out) method produce similar results. The difference was that both the quantity and the value of the base stock depended on managerial judgment and were therefore subject to manipulation. In contrast, LIFO is based on an objective rule: The last items purchased are the first sold. The base stock era ended with the acceptance of LIFO by the accounting profession and by Congress in the Revenue Act of 1938.

Michael Chatfield

Bibliography

Davis, H.Z. "History of LIFO," *Accounting Historians Journal*, Spring 1982, pp. 1–23.
Devine, C.T. *Inventory Valuation and Peri-*

odic Income. New York: Ronald Press, 1942. Reprint. New York: Arno Press, 1980.

See also CONSERVATISM; INCOME TAXATION IN THE UNITED STATES; INFLATION ACCOUNTING; INVENTORY VALUATION; LAST IN, FIRST OUT (LIFO); MANIPULATION OF INCOME; MATCHING; SANDILANDS REPORT; UNITED STATES STEEL CORPORATION

Beaver, William (1940–)

William Beaver has been the most consistent contributor of important capital-market research papers since that field emerged in the 1960s as a major research area. With a B.B.A. from the University of Notre Dame in 1962, he entered the University of Chicago M.B.A./Ph.D. program at a time when students and faculty were producing seminal works in economics and finance. His teachers and colleagues included Raymond J. Ball, Philip R. Brown, Joel S. Demski, Nicholas Dopuch, Eugene F. Fama, Michael C. Jensen, Merton H. Miller, Richard Roll and Myron Scholes. Beaver flourished in this exciting intellectual environment. His early research on financial ratios as predictors of failures helped spawn a large literature on the analysis of financial distress. His subsequent research on how variability in stock returns and trading volume increased at the time of earnings announcements was influential in promoting the capital market-accounting information school of thought. Beaver used the notion of market efficiency (that prices fully reflect all available information) to bring cohesion to his subsequent studies in this area. Beaver's numerous speeches and presentations in the 1970s on market efficiency consistently drew large audiences—and lively, sometimes hostile, responses.

Beaver consistently examines the implications of his research for the accounting profession. For example, he has long argued that, in efficient capital markets, the existence of disclosure is more important than the location of disclosure (above or below the "bottom line" income number) regarding security-price determination. He advanced that viewpoint while a member of the Securities and Exchange Commission (SEC) Advisory Committee on Corporate Disclosure (1976–1977) and in many interactions with the Financial Accounting Standards Board, including the 1980s debate over accounting for changing prices.

Beaver was a pivotal leader of the major changes in doctoral-level accounting education that occurred in the mid- to late 1960s, including more substantive training in related disciplines such as economics, econometrics, and finance, and the use of state-of-the-art analytical or empirical research methodologies to probe structured hypotheses. He has chaired many doctoral dissertations that launched his students into successful academic careers in accounting. At Stanford University, where he has taught since 1969, students actively seek him out for his knowledge, perspective, willingness to give timely, detailed feedback, and seemingly endless enthusiasm for conducting empirical research and working with doctoral students in a true coauthor role. Beaver's resume contains numerous publications with students in the Stanford doctoral program (Roland E. (Pete) Dukes, James G. Manegold, Dale C. Morse, Roger Clarke, William F. Wright, Richard A. Lambert, Andrew A. Christie, Wayne R. Landsman, Stephen G. Ryan, and Mary Barth). A common focus in his work with all of them—work that stretches over 20 years—is modeling the association between financial information and capital market variables.

He is the author of one book, *Financial Reporting: An Accounting Revolution*; coauthor of a monograph in 1983 for the Financial Accounting Standards Board, *Incremental Information Content of Statement 33 Disclosures*; and author or coauthor of over 50 articles.

Beaver has received numerous awards for research from the American Accounting Association (AAA) and the American Institute of Certified Public Accountants (AICPA), including three AAA/AICPA Notable Contribution to Accounting Literature Awards in 1969, 1979, and 1983 and the AAA Seminal Contribution in Accounting Literature in 1989. He received the Distinguished Teaching Award from Stanford in 1985, the Faculty Excellence Award of the California Society of CPAs in 1978, and the AAA Outstanding Educator Award in 1990. He was president of the American Accounting Association in 1988.

George Foster

Bibliography
Beaver, W. *Financial Reporting: An Accounting Revolution*. 2d ed. Englewood Cliffs, NJ: Prentice-Hall, 1989.

B

———. "The Information Content of Annual Earnings Announcements." In *Empirical Research in Accounting: Selected Studies*. Supplement to *Journal of Accounting Research*, 1968, pp. 67–92.

Beaver, W., C. Eger, S. Ryan, and M. Wolfson. "Financial Reporting and the Structure of Bank Share Prices," *Journal of Accounting Research*, Autumn 1989, pp. 157–178.

Beaver, W., R. Lambert, and D. Morse. "The Information Content of Security Prices," *Journal of Accounting and Economics*, March 1980, pp. 3–28.

———, and W.R. Landsman. *Incremental Information Content of Statement 33 Disclosures*. Stamford, CT: Financial Accounting Standards Board, 1983.

See also AMERICAN ACCOUNTING ASSOCIATION; BALL AND BROWN'S "AN EMPIRICAL EVALUATION OF ACCOUNTING INCOME NUMBERS"; DAVIDSON, SIDNEY; DEMSKI, JOEL S.; FINANCIAL-STATEMENT ANALYSIS; LIQUIDITY: ACCOUNTING MEASUREMENT; POSITIVE ACCOUNTING

Bentley, Harry Clark (1877–1967)

A linchpin between the business schools of the late nineteenth century and the accounting program in business colleges of the early to midtwentieth century, Harry Clark Bentley was a student at a business school founded by the father of George Eastman of Eastman Kodak fame; a president of a business school; an early graduate of probably the first university program in accounting; a certified public accountant (CPA); a practicing accountant; an early-twentieth-century writer in accounting theory and practice; a professor of accounting; the founder of the highly successful business college, Bentley College of Accounting and Finance; and an accounting bibliographer and bibliophile of note.

Bentley attended New York University (NYU) from 1901 through 1903. Classes were held from 8 to 10 p.m. Monday through Friday so students could work during the day. NYU's degree program was started in 1900 by Charles Waldo Haskins, the first dean of NYU's School of Commerce, Accounts, and Finance and partner of the Haskins and Sells accounting firm. The staff included such leading names as Charles Ezra Sprague, author of

The Philosophy of Accounts (1908); William Lafrentz, president of the American Audit Company; Frederick Cleveland, an early editor of the *Journal of Accountancy*; and Edward Sherwood Mead, a leading political economist.

Bentley contributed two early-twentieth-century books and many articles on accounting theory and practice. *Corporate Finance and Accounting* (1908, 1911) and *The Science of Accounts* (1911) were pioneering efforts. Bentley strove to match the information needs of the business with its accounting system. He warned against the presence of the goodwill account, the portrayal of a deficit as an asset, and writing up the value of land. Bentley urged accounting uniformity in terminology and in statements in a seven-part series, titled "Standardization of Accounting Forms and Methods," in the *Journal of Accountancy* (1912). He changed gears by stressing cost-accounting issues from an educator's viewpoint in a two-part series in 1913 in the *Journal of Accountancy*, titled "A Problem in the Distribution of Expense Burden: A Paper for Accounting Students."

His next two books were classics dealing with the CPA exam. The first of these, published in 1914, was *C.P.A. Auditing Questions to January 1, 1914*. At the time, there was no uniform CPA exam. The book presents 705 questions chosen from 18 states from 1896 through 1913. *Massachusetts Certified Public Accountant Examination Questions: With Answers* (1927) is a classic, as Bentley's answers are incisive.

Bentley's chief contribution to the history of accounting was the two-volume work he coauthored with Ruth S. Leonard, *Bibliography of Works on Accounting by American Authors*. Volume One, covering the years 1796–1900, was published in 1934. Volume Two, covering 1901–1934, followed in 1935. Bentley financed and supervised the work over a five-year period, and Leonard, a librarian, did voluminous research at the Library of Congress, the U.S. Copyright Office, the library of the American Institute of Accountants, public libraries, private libraries, subscription and society libraries, business and technical libraries, and such university libraries as Harvard, Yale, Columbia, New York, Princeton, Johns Hopkins, Pennsylvania, Illinois, Northwestern, Chicago, and Catholic University of America.

Bentley considered William Mitchell, with a book published in 1796, the pioneer American accounting author. Bentley's inclusion of only accounting and bookkeeping books copyrighted and published in the United States and written by authors then residing in the United States excluded mathematics books with a brief coverage of bookkeeping. While his list has been updated by later researchers, it marked a milestone in interest in American accounting books. The two-volume bibliography is listed as a primary-work bibliography in Theodore Besterman's *A World Bibliography of Bibliographies* (1965). Bentley owned many of the eighteenth- and nineteenth-century books listed in the first volume. He donated them to the Boston Public Library in 1948.

Bentley is a good example of accounting educators at the turn of the twentieth century. He had an impressive list of publications in accounting theory and practice. However, Bentley should be best remembered for his pioneering work on the two-volume bibliography of early works on bookkeeping and accounting by American authors.

Richard Vangermeersch
John D. Cathcart

Bibliography

Bentley, H.C., and R.S. Leonard. *Bibliography of Works on Accounting by American Authors*. 2 vols. Boston: Harry Clark Bentley, 1934–1935.

Lockwood, J. "Early University Education in Accounting," *Accounting Review*, June 1938, pp. 131–144.

Sheldahl, T.K. "America's Earliest Recorded Text in Accounting: Sarjeant's 1789 Book," *Accounting Historians Journal*, Fall 1985, pp. 1–42.

Vangermeersch, R., and J.D. Cathcart. "Harry Clark Bentley, 1877–1967." In *Biographies of Notable Accountants*. 2d ed., pp. 4–6. Edited by Abdel M. Agami. New York: Random House, 1989.

See also Accounting Education in the United States; Archives and Special Collections in Accounting; Certified Public Accountant Examination: The Early Years (1896–1930); Goodwill; Haskins, Charles Waldo; Sprague, Charles Ezra; Treasury Stock; Uniform Accounting Systems; Uniformity

Berle and Means

Lawyer Adolph A. Berle Jr. and economist Gardiner C. Means produced the first authoritative, scholarly analysis of the modern corporation, its position in society, and its relation to stockholders. *The Modern Corporation and Private Property* (1932) has been called a blueprint for the Securities Acts of 1933–1934. Certainly it expressed the philosophy underlying them and increased the pressure for legislation to protect investors.

Berle and Means's thesis was that the modern corporation had revolutionized the American economy and that solutions to the problems it had created required equally radical changes in public policy. They pointed out that in 1930 the 200 largest nonbanking corporations controlled nearly half of the nonbanking corporate wealth of the nation and almost one-fourth of the total national wealth. Half of the anthracite coal was mined by four companies; one-fourth of the steel industry was in the hands of two companies; aluminum and nickel production were virtual monopolies. Three corporate groups controlled more than half of the electric power industry; two companies made nearly two-thirds of the cars; three controlled 70 percent of cigarette manufacturing; one company made half of the agricultural machinery. Berle and Means calculated that in 1932, 65 percent of American manufacturing assets were owned by about 600 corporations, which meant that the 2,000 active directors of those corporations virtually controlled American economic life. If the current rate of industrial concentration continued, by 1950, 70 percent of the nation's corporate activity would be conducted by just 200 businesses.

Oligopoly was no longer the exception but rather the norm and the trend. The competitive "trading market" described by Adam Smith had been replaced by an "administered market" dominated by a few large corporations. These corporations, by bringing so much of the nation's economic life within their administrative control, had decisively altered the nature of the economy. As fixed markups replaced competitive prices, markets no longer had the same tendency toward equilibrium. In the classical trading market, an excess of supply over demand caused a fall in *prices* until demand caught up, whereas an excess supply in an administered market was apt to cause a fall in *production* while prices were maintained. This in fact tended to happen during the 1930s.

Large corporations had also become much too powerful in relation to the individual employees, customers, and investors with whom they dealt. The diffusion of stock ownership gave management almost complete control over corporate finances and the distribution of accounting information to investors. The mass of "owners" were effectively disenfranchised; their only options were to hold their stock or sell it at the market price. Corporate managers were not primarily interested in paying dividends to stockholders. Their companies were becoming social institutions, influencing cultural values, contending for political as well as economic power.

In such circumstances, much depended on responsible business leadership. But the business community, wrote Berle and Means, was still characterized by "seizure of power without recognition of responsibility—ambition without courage." Corporate managers recognized few obligations to their communities, their customers, or their workers. They deliberately misled stockholders by withholding financial information and by misusing accounting alternatives. They also lacked cohesion, quarreling among themselves. The managerial class might in time mature and build a "technocracy," a "collectivism without communism." In the meantime, the federal government had to create the socioeconomic environment appropriate to an advanced industrial society. This should include programs of unemployment, sickness, and retirement insurance. The banking system must be centralized, the stock market reorganized, and the marketing of securities brought under federal control. There must be immediate government spending programs to stimulate demand. The antitrust laws should be revised to permit further corporate consolidation and even monopoly, which after all was a fact of American life. But the public welfare required federal regulation of all such concentrated industries.

Michael Chatfield

Bibliography

Berle, A.A. Jr., and Means, G.C. *The Modern Corporation and Private Property*. New York: Commerce Clearing House, 1932.

See also AMERICAN INSTITUTE OF CERTIFIED PUBLIC ACCOUNTANTS; RIPLEY, WILLIAM Z.; SECURITIES AND EXCHANGE COMMISSION

Big Eight Accounting Firms

For over half a century, the term "the Big Eight" was used to refer to the eight largest public accounting firms in the United States. In 1932, *Fortune* magazine published an article, "Certified Public Accountants," that reviewed the development of the "newest profession" in the United States—public accounting. Although the names of several of the firms listed by *Fortune* were subsequently altered through merger activity, those that were industry leaders in 1932 continued to dominate the auditing of major corporations and to shape the direction of the profession in this country for the next 60 years.

When the Big Eight firms began their ascent to prominence, accounting was a stable, conservative, and slow-growing industry. Competition was minimal. Accounting and auditing provided the major source of billings. However, all of this changed.

Individual Big Eight accounting firms experienced a growth in annual U.S. revenues from approximately $1 million in the 1920s to over $1 billion by the 1980s. During this period, the major sources of revenues shifted from traditional accounting and auditing services to more profitable areas such as tax and management consulting. Competition between the firms increased dramatically. By the 1980s, the Big Eight were large, dynamic, international firms with total worldwide billings approaching $25 billion.

The following firms composed "The Big Eight" accounting firms in the 1980s: Arthur Andersen and Company; Arthur Young and Company; Coopers and Lybrand; Deloitte Haskins and Sells; Ernst and Whinney; KPMG Peat Marwick; Price Waterhouse; and Touche Ross and Company. In 1989 the merger of Ernst and Whinney and Arthur Young to form Ernst and Young was quickly followed by a merger of Deloitte Haskins and Sells and Touche Ross to form Deloitte and Touche. Thus, references to "the Big Eight" suddenly became obsolete, and a new era of "the Big Six" accounting firms began.

Early Beginnings

It was in England and Scotland that many of the Big Eight firms had their early beginnings. In 1845 William Welch Deloitte opened an accounting office in London, and there he and his firm played a prominent role in the early history of accounting in England. Four years later, Samuel Lowell Price opened a small accounting firm in London. He was later joined in the partnership by William Holyland and Edwin Waterhouse. In 1890 this firm, now known as Price Waterhouse and Company, opened its first office in the United States. William Cooper opened an accounting firm in London in 1854. Over the next few years, he was joined by three of his brothers, and the firm became known as Cooper Brothers and Company. Although Cooper Brothers quickly expanded across Europe, it did not open an office in the United States until 1926. A predecessor firm of Ernst and Whinney—Whinney Murray and Company— also began in London and had three founders of the Institute of Accountants in London among its partners.

The firm of Marwick, Mitchell, Peat and Company—becoming Peat, Marwick, Mitchell and Company, then KPMG Peat Marwick— had its roots in Scotland. All three of its founders—William Barclay Peat, James Marwick, and R. Roger Mitchell—were born and educated there, before Peat moved to London in 1870, Marwick to the United States in 1894, and Mitchell there as well, in the 1890s. Another firm with a Scottish background, Touche, Niven and Company—later Touche Ross and Company—was founded in 1900. Its founders—George A. Touch (later changed to Touche) and John B. Niven—were born in Edinburgh, where they both apprenticed for the same firm before moving to the United States. The firm of Arthur Young and Company was founded by a Scottish immigrant of 1890, in 1894 in Chicago.

It was also during the late 1800s that two major American accounting firms were founded that later merged with British firms. In 1895 Charles Waldo Haskins and Elijah Watt Sells, who had met while working for a joint commission of Congress, opened an accounting firm in New York City under the name of Haskins and Sells. Then, in 1898, four partners in the firm of Heins, Lybrand and Company—William M. Lybrand, Adam A. Ross, T. Edward Ross, and Robert Hiester Montgomery—decided to open a firm in Philadelphia, and called it Lybrand, Ross Brothers and Montgomery.

Growth and Change

Until the turn of the century, services provided by most accounting firms were limited to bookkeeping and an occasional bankruptcy or liquidation. As American industry expanded, major changes correspondingly took place in the accounting firms. One important change was an increased emphasis on audit services. The 1900s saw a continuation of a corporate-merger pattern that began around 1895. Accounting firms were engaged to examine the books and financial statements of the merging companies. These companies were often geographically diverse. In order to meet this need, Big Eight firms began to open offices across the United States.

The turn of the century witnessed the creation of another major firm. In June 1903, Alwin C. Ernst and Theodore C. Ernst formed the accounting partnership of Ernst and Ernst in Cleveland, Ohio, in 1903. Sixteen years later, Ernst and Ernst decided it needed an overseas representative and established a working relationship with Whinney, Smith and Whinney of London. This association continued until 1979 when the two firms merged as Ernst and Whinney.

In 1913 an event occurred that would forever change the accounting profession. The states ratified the Sixteenth Amendment to the Constitution, and a federal income tax was created. With the entrance of the United States into World War I, the low tax rates of 1913 (and the complexities of the tax code) quickly increased, expanding the demand for tax services. Most Big Eight firms developed a tax service area to assist their clients in coping with the new tax law. Over the next 60 years, this service area expanded in importance.

Also in 1913, Arthur E. Andersen and Clarence M. DeLany purchased the net assets of the Audit Company of Illinois. On December 1, 1913, the partnership that was to become Arthur Andersen and Company began business in a small office in Chicago under the name of Andersen, DeLany and Company.

Although the Depression in the United States drastically reduced billings of most accounting firms, it provided the foundation for a period of growth and increased responsibility for the profession. After the stock market crash in 1929 and subsequent investigations into its failure, Congress passed laws requiring many corporations to file financial statements with the newly established Securities and Exchange Commission. At the same time, the New York Stock Exchange began requiring companies to file audited statements and to expand the scope of required audits. These events greatly increased the potential market for auditing services, especially for large national auditing firms.

Enactment of these laws resulted in increased prestige and opportunity for accounting firms but also expanded their responsibility to shareholders and to the general public. Not only did accountants have a social responsibility to the public, they now often had a legal liability as well.

Both world wars expanded the client-auditor relationship. The two entities had traditionally kept each other at arm's length. However, government imposition of regulations for cost determination and bidding procedures for defense contracts during the wars resulted in accounting firms becoming actively involved in the day-to-day operations of many of their clients' businesses, serving as advisors regarding efficiency, systems, and management services. This closeness gave corporations a new view of and respect for the Big Eight firms and made them more receptive to the management services these firms offered.

The Big Eight firms had offered management services prior to World War II, but it was only after the war that they established separate divisions or departments for these services. The creation of management-services departments was not without its critics. Individuals within and outside the accounting profession questioned the ability of public accountants to maintain independence and objectivity while auditing the clients for whom they also provided management consulting. This criticism continues today.

The end of World War II resulted in a period of growth and international expansion for both corporate America and the Big Eight accounting firms. As corporations grew, both nationally and internationally, larger accounting firms were needed to perform the auditing and management services that these corporations demanded.

Although much of their growth was achieved internally, the Big Eight firms have a long tradition of growth through merger. World War II caused a temporary halt to this practice. With the end of the war, however, the merger pattern began again. In 1947, Touche, Niven and Company merged with Allen R. Smart and Company and George Bailey and Company to form Touche, Niven, Bailey and Smart. Then in 1950, Peat, Marwick, Mitchell and Company merged with Barrow, Wade, Guthrie and Company, one of the first accounting firms founded in the United States. In 1957, the international firm of Coopers and Lybrand was created from combining Cooper Brothers and Company, Lybrand, Ross Brothers and Montgomery, and several other firms.

The decade of the 1970s was a period of challenge for the Big Eight. Competition had not previously been a major factor in the profession. Firms were prevented from actively soliciting clients or advertising services. However, in the late 1970s this changed. After successful court cases involving other professions and an implied suit by the Justice Department, the American Institute of Certified Public Accountants (AICPA) modified its Code of Ethics to allow advertising and solicitation. In response, some Big Eight firms began aggressively seeking clients, often drastically cutting audit fees. As a result, the audit area became less profitable, causing many firms to expand the more lucrative management-services area. For some Big Eight firms, such as Arthur Andersen and Company, management consulting became their largest source of revenue.

During the 1970s, questions were raised about some of the practices of the Big Eight firms and their possible dominance of the accounting profession. The major challenge to the Big Eight was put forth in *The Accounting Establishment*, a study prepared by the staff of the Subcommittee on Reports, Accounting, and Management of the Committee on Government Operations of the United States Senate. The report was critical of the Big Eight, alleging that it controlled the AICPA and its committees, greatly influenced the Financial Accounting Standards Board (FASB), dominated auditing of large corporations, and dominated the practice of accounting in the United States and probably throughout the world. In rebuttal, the major accounting firms asserted that large international firms were necessary to audit large industrial clients, and that the accounting profession, with "eight" major competitors, was in fact more competitive than many other industries.

The 1980s witnessed a major change in the composition of the workforce at major accounting firms. Historically, most Big Eight firms had not hired women and minorities for their professional staffs. But during the 1960s and 1970s, these hiring practices began to change. By the late 1980s, Big Eight firms were hiring nearly an equal number of men and women. However, the number of women and minorities at the manager and partner level remained small.

The decade of the 1980s was a period of significant merger activity for major accounting firms, and often the mergers were between the large firms themselves. In 1986, the Big Eight firm Peat, Marwick, Mitchell and Company merged with the international firm of KMG Main Hurdman to create the largest accounting firm in the world, KPMG Peat Marwick. Three years later, the Big Eight firm Ernst and Whinney agreed to merge with another Big Eight firm, Arthur Young and Company, to form Ernst and Young. This merger was followed by the merger of two other Big Eight firms—Deloitte Haskins and Sells and Touche Ross and Company—to create Deloitte and Touche. The reason given for these mergers, which resulted in "the Big Six," was a need to achieve the critical mass necessary to remain competitive.

The Future

Historically, the Big Eight firms adapted well to political, social, and economic changes. They grew from small local partnerships to large international firms. Whereas they once offered only accounting and auditing services, they now offer dozens of different services to thousands of clients throughout the world. They have seen the accounting marketplace change from one where competition among firms was prohibited to one where competition is often fierce.

The Big Six firms will face future challenges as important as any previously faced by the Big Eight. For example, their hiring and promotion practices will have to reflect the changing workforce. They will also have to resolve the increased problem of litigation that has caused several large accounting firms to file for bankruptcy. Finally, the Big Six will have to respond to the increased responsibility placed upon them by both the courts and the public.

Charles W. Wootton
Carel M. Wolk

Bibliography

"Architects of the U.S. Balance Sheet," *Fortune*, June 1932, pp. 64–66, 101–102.
"Certified Public Accountants," *Fortune*, June 1932, pp. 63, 95–98.
Deloitte and Company, 1845–1956. London: Deloitte, Plender, Griffiths, 1958.
DeMond, C.W. *Price Waterhouse and Company in America*. New York: Comet Press, 1951.
The Early History of Coopers and Lybrand. New York: Garland, 1984.
Edwards, J.D. *History of Public Accounting in the United States*. East Lansing: Bureau of Business and Economic Research, Michigan State University, 1960. Reprint. University, AL: University of Alabama Press, 1978.
Ernst and Ernst: A History of the Firm. Cleveland: Ernst & Ernst, 1960.
The First Fifty Years, 1913–1963. Chicago: Arthur Andersen & Co., 1963.
Haskins and Sells: Our First Seventy-Five Years. New York: Garland, 1984.
Swanson, T. *Touche Ross: A Biography*. New York: Touche Ross & Co., 1972.
U.S. Congress. Senate. Committee on Government Operations. Subcommittee on Reports, Accounting, and Management. 95th Cong. 1st Sess. 1977. *The Accounting Establishment: A Staff Study*, 1977. Washington, DC: GPO, 1977.
Wise, T.A. *Peat, Marwick, Mitchell and Company: Eighty-Five Years*. New York: Peat, Marwick, Mitchell, 1982.
Young, A. "The Starting of the Firm," *Arthur Young Journal*, Spring/Summer 1969, pp. 16–19.

See also ACCOUNTING EDUCATION IN THE UNITED STATES; ACCOUNTING PRINCIPLES BOARD; ADVERTISING BY ACCOUNTANTS; AMERICAN INSTITUTE OF CERTIFIED PUBLIC ACCOUNTANTS; ANDERSEN, ARTHUR E.; CHIEF ACCOUNTANTS OF THE SECURITIES AND EXCHANGE COMMISSION; CONGRESSIONAL VIEWS; DICKINSON, ARTHUR LOWES; EXTERNAL AUDITING; FINANCIAL ACCOUNTING STANDARDS BOARD; GRADY, PAUL; HASKINS, CHARLES WALDO; INDEPENDENCE OF EXTERNAL AUDITORS; KRAAYENHOF, JACOB; LEGAL LIABILITY OF AUDITORS; MANAGEMENT ADVISORY SERVICES BY CPAs; MAUTZ, ROBERT K.; MAY, GEORGE OLIVER; McKESSON AND ROBBINS CASE; MONTGOMERY, ROBERT HIESTER; NATURAL BUSINESS YEAR; NEW YORK STOCK EXCHANGE; SCOTLAND: EARLY WRITERS IN DOUBLE ENTRY ACCOUNTING; SECURITIES AND EXCHANGE COMMISSION; SELLS, ELIJAH WATT; SIXTEENTH AMENDMENT; SOCIAL RESPONSIBILITIES OF ACCOUNTANTS; SPACEK, LEONARD; STANDARD COSTING; STERRETT, JOSEPH EDMUND; TREADWAY COMMISSION; TRUEBLOOD, ROBERT MARTIN; *UNIFORM ACCOUNTING*; *UNITED STATES OF AMERICA V. CARL SIMON*; UNITED STATES STEEL CORPO-

B

Big Six Accounting Firms
See BIG EIGHT ACCOUNTING FIRMS

Blotter
See MEMORANDUM BOOK

Branch Accounting

The Florentine practice of branch accounting played an important part in the development of double entry bookkeeping. Like their Venetian counterparts, Florentine merchants were basically opportunists. It was natural for a rich trader who wished to settle debts without transferring bullion to add banking to his activities. Florence had 80 banks in 1338 and over a hundred by the end of the century. The distinctive feature of Florentine business organization came to be large merchant-banking partnerships that, like holding companies, controlled a network of foreign branches and subpartnerships. An articulated Florentine double entry system was a response to the need for accounting records, not just for the trader's private use as in Genoa or Venice, but for submission to others. When merchant-bankers set up permanent foreign branches, the physical separation of owners and managers required indirect supervision and the periodic reporting of summarized accounting data to the home office.

Between 1300 and 1345, the most powerful Florentine merchant-banking houses were the Bardi, the Peruzzi, and the Acciaiuoli. The Bardi was the largest of these three "Pillars of Christendom," but only fragments of its records survive. In 1336 the Peruzzi, the second largest, had 15 branches in Western Europe and the Levant and a staff of 90 agents. The Peruzzi accounts stand partway between single and double entry. They included a great many poorly integrated journals. Though income and expense accounts were used, no arithmetic proof of equality was made, and profits were found, not by closing the ledger but by inventorying assets and deducting them from total liabilities and capital.

In the 1340s, all three companies failed due to overextension of credit and defaults on loans to monarchs. The firm of Alberti del Giudice of Florence was then chosen to collect the papal revenues and became important until it split into several rival firms because of family quarrels. The Alberti books also contain elements of double entry but no complete system. Not all transactions are recorded twice, there is no trace of the expense or profit and loss accounts that would have permitted complete arithmetic check, and again, profits were calculated without balancing the ledger.

Francesco de Marco Datini (1335–1410) made in his own lifetime the transition from a local business using single entry bookkeeping to large-scale branch operations employing a complete double entry system. He was retailer, importer, banker, commission agent, and manufacturer, seeing in diversification a hedge against the risks that had bankrupted others who grew too quickly. He expanded by opening more than 20 branches, establishing bookkeeping control over his foreign agents, who he ruled with an iron hand. The Datini ledgers run continuously from 1366 to 1410. After 1390 a fully developed double entry system, complete with balance sheets, was used in his foreign branches and at his main office in Florence.

The Medici Bank was founded in 1397 and lasted nearly a hundred years, though it operated only in Western Europe and never attained the size of the Bardi or the Peruzzi. The Medici accounts are significant because of their use of double entry technique for essentially modern purposes—management and control, audit, even income tax calculation. Every year on March 24, books of the branch offices were closed, and copies of their balance sheets were sent to Florence. These listed separately the balance of each customer's account, resulting in balance sheets that sometimes included more than 200 line items. Since bad debts were the chief threat to a Renaissance banker's solvency, audit by the general manager and his assistants consisted of examining these statements to prevent the granting of excess credit and to pick out doubtful or past-due accounts. A thorough check also required the presence of branch managers. They were called to Florence once a year if they resided in Italy and at least once every other year if they lived abroad. The weakness of this internal audit system was that, while balance sheets were checked, branches were not regularly visited by traveling auditors. The bank incurred huge losses because of uncontrolled and insubordinate branch managers and a general lack of coordination. Even its power as papal banker to obtain the excommunication of anyone failing to pay church revenues could not save the Medici Bank, and it failed in 1494.

Michael Chatfield

Bibliography

Brun, R. "Fourteenth Century Merchant of Italy: Francesco Datini of Prato," *Journal of Economic Business History*, May 1930, pp. 452–466.

De Roover, R. "The Development of Accounting prior to Luca Pacioli according to the Account-books of Medieval Merchants." In *Studies in the History of Accounting*, edited by A.C. Littleton and B.S. Yamey, pp. 114–174. Homewood, IL: Irwin, 1956.

———. *The Rise and Fall of the Medici Bank, 1397–1494*. Cambridge: Harvard University Press, 1963. Reprint. New York: W.W. Norton, 1966.

———. "The Story of the Alberti Company of Florence, 1302–1348, as Revealed in its Account Books," *Business History Review*, Spring 1958, pp. 14–59.

Peragallo, E. *Origin and Evolution of Double Entry Bookkeeping: A Study of Italian Practice from the Fourteenth Century.* New York: American Institute Publishing, 1938. Reprint. Osaka: Nihon Shoseki, 1974.

See also ALBERTI DEL GIUDICE; BALANCE SHEET; BARDI; CLOSING ENTRIES AND PROCEDURES; CREDIT; DATINI, FRANCESCO DE MARCO; DOUBLE ENTRY BOOKKEEPING: ORIGINS; EAST INDIA COMPANY; FAROLFI COMPANY LEDGER; INCOME STATEMENT/INCOME ACCOUNT; MEDICI ACCOUNTS; MEDIEVAL ACCOUNTING; PERUZZI

Brazil: Inflation Accounting

Brazil has experimented with inflation accounting since 1951. During the period 1964–1990, the primary financial statements in annual reports were inflation-adjusted, and inflation-adjusted income was used as the basis for corporate taxation. The evolution of inflation accounting in Brazil can be divided into three periods: prior to 1964, 1964–1976, and post-1976.

Prior to 1964

The indexation of financial-statement items was introduced into Brazilian accounting practice in 1951 when a law was passed allowing a one-time revaluation of fixed assets (with the counterpart going to a special reserve in equity) via a set of index coefficients supplied by government. The purpose was to provide business enterprises with some relief from a special tax on profits exceeding some percentage return on equity. Few companies availed themselves of the opportunity to revalue their fixed assets for two reasons: Only original cost could be depreciated for tax purposes, and a 10 percent tax was levied on the amount of the revaluation. Due to continued high inflation, a second, voluntary revaluation of fixed assets was allowed by law in 1956.

Regular indexation of fixed assets was introduced by law in 1958. Index coefficients fixed biannually by the National Economic Council were used, thus making indexation possible only at the end of every two years. The law in 1958 introduced the term "monetary correction" to describe the indexation of fixed assets.

The Period 1964–1976

In April 1964, the Brazilian military hierarchy took over in a bloodless coup d'etat. A major cause of the collapse of civilian government was its inability to bring inflation under control. Major economic goals of the new government were to reduce existing economic distortions caused by inflation and to reduce the inflation rate without causing a severe economic recession. It became apparent that to achieve the latter goal, inflation would have to be allowed to continue in the short run. To mitigate some of the distortions caused by inflation, while implicitly allowing inflation to continue, the new government devised the most extensive system of indexation in the world. Monetary correction was extended to government and corporate borrowing, housing finance, savings accounts, wages, and corporate income taxation. The system attempted to ensure a certain real rate of interest to creditors and a certain real wage to workers, and also to ensure that companies paid taxes only on real profits.

A law passed July 17, 1964, created indexed treasury bonds (ORTNs) and made the monetary correction of fixed assets mandatory. A 5 percent tax was imposed on the revaluation amount, but companies were able to avoid this tax by purchasing the new ORTNs in an amount equal to 10 percent of the revaluation amount. In either case, companies were re-

B

quired to help finance the public debt. The new law also introduced tax depreciation of the indexed amount of fixed assets.

In 1968 an amount needed to "maintain working capital" was allowed as a deduction in calculating taxable income. Working capital was defined as current assets plus long-term receivables less all liabilities. This appears to have been an attempt to measure the inflationary profits associated with carrying inventory at historical cost and, at the same time, to reflect the purchasing power gain or loss on monetary items. A provision for the maintenance of working capital was calculated by multiplying beginning working capital by the change in the general price index. For reporting purposes, the provision (debit) could be shown either in income or as a reduction of retained earnings. The credit was carried as a reserve in owners' equity.

Gains from a negative-working-capital position were not included in income. This asymmetry was corrected in 1974 when Brazilian law recognized for the first time that inflation can be the source of gains as well as losses.

The major improvements in Brazilian inflation accounting during the period 1964–1976 were that depreciation expense was allowed to be calculated on the inflation-adjusted cost of fixed assets, and the provision for working-capital maintenance was allowed as a deduction from both tax and accounting income. The major theoretical limitation of the system was the use of beginning working capital in the calculation of working-capital maintenance, ignoring any changes during the year. An important practical limitation involved the time lag in recording monetary correction. Because indices were published on an ex post annual basis, fixed assets were not indexed until from one to two years after their purchase.

The System of Monetary Correction since 1976

A new corporation law (Law No. 6404) was passed in 1976. A major objective of the new law was to stimulate investment in corporate equities. To achieve this objective, the law required firms to pay dividends—either in an amount stated in the corporate charter, or, if no provision in the corporate charter existed, one-half of net profit after reduction of amounts sent to legal reserves. Because the law required firms to pay dividends, the law was obliged to define income in such a way that firms did not run the risk of decapitalization. The elimination

of inflationary profits became all the more necessary as firms became subject to the double jeopardy of income taxation and obligatory dividend distribution. Accordingly, the corporation law also prescribed new procedures for the monetary correction of financial statements.

The general rules of the new system of monetary correction were outlined in the new corporation law; the method of implementation was specified in the tax law of 1977 (Decree Law 1598). The corporation law required the indexation of: (1) permanent assets (fixed assets, investments, and deferred charges), and (2) owners' equity accounts. The correction amounts were added directly to the related account, with no separation of original cost and the correction amount. The counterparts were accumulated in a "monetary correction account" taken to income. The tax law of 1977 required the use of the index used to adjust treasury bonds (ORTN index), thereby eliminating the previous time-lag problem.

The theory underlying this system is that owners' equity is protected from inflation-induced erosion only to the extent that there are "permanent" assets whose values are free to fluctuate in response to economic conditions (i.e., are nonmonetary in nature). If owners' equity exceeds permanent assets, a portion of equity is not protected and a loss results. Theoretically, this system was imperfect in that inventory (a nonmonetary asset) was not subject to monetary correction. This limitation was accepted for practical reasons and was based on the assumption that inventory turns over rapidly enough to make the difference between adjusted and unadjusted inventory insignificant.

Under the assumptions that ending inventory is acquired at year end and the first in, first out inventory method (FIFO) is used, it has been shown that the system of monetary correction produces the same income figure as traditional methods of "general purchasing power" accounting (for example, as defined by Accounting Principles Board (APB) Statement No. 3) "Financial Statements Restated for General Price-Level Changes" (1969). In effect, monetary correction reflects the "general price level" adjustment of all revenues and expenses (other than cost of goods sold), as well as the purchasing power gain or loss on monetary items, through a much simpler mechanical process.

The practical ability of the system of monetary correction to protect firms from inflation was severely constrained through the tax law's choice of the ORTN index. The ORTN index was the index used for most index-linked financial instruments. In an attempt to reduce the inflation feedback caused by indexation—that is, indexation itself contributes to inflation—the government did not allow the ORTN index to increase at the same rate as the wholesale price index (WPI). For example, in 1980, when the WPI increased 121 percent, ORTN was prefixed at a rate of only 51 percent. By the end of 1980, ORTN reflected only 44 percent of the cumulative increase in the WPI since 1965. The indexation of financial statements was never accused of contributing to inflation feedback. It is unfortunate that the tax law required use of the only index that did not effectively measure the rate of inflation.

In 1985 the indexation of financial statements was effectively discontinued as the government froze the value of the ORTN index. Indexation resumed in 1986 under a new index, Obrigação de Tesouro Nacional or National Treasury Obligation (OTN), but, in a comprehensive program to combat inflation, the indexation of financial statements was abolished early in 1989. However, the system was again reinstated several months later, with the novelty of daily rather than monthly correction due to the extremely high rates of inflation being experienced. Since then, several different indexes have been used, with the IPCA (Broad Consumer Price Index) introduced on January 1, 1992.

Timothy S. Doupnik

Bibliography

Doupnik, T.S. "The Brazilian System of Monetary Correction," *Advances in International Accounting*, 1987, pp. 111–135.
———. "The Evolution of Financial Statement Indexation in Brazil," *Accounting Historians Journal*, Spring 1986, pp. 1–18.
Martins, E. *Analise da Correcao Monetaria das Demonstracoes Financeiras*. Sao Paulo: Editora Atlas, 1980.

See also Fisher, Irving; Historical Cost; Inflation Accounting; Money; Tax-Ordained Accounting

Break-Even Chart

A break-even chart is "any one of several types of charts on which the *break-even* point is shown" (Kohler). This essay will concentrate on the concepts, controversy, and implications relative to the early history, more recent history, and subsequent developments and projections concerning the future of the break-even chart and its analytical implications.

Early History

While there is some dispute about the origin of the break-even chart (see Barton 1956, Chapin 1955, and Villers 1955), perhaps the earliest published examples were provided by Henry Hess in 1903 in "Manufacturing: Capital, Costs, Profits, and Dividends" in *Engineering Magazine*.

In the article, Hess superbly blended words and graphics to explain the break-even chart. For example: "Volume of business is more or less proportional to the number of people employed, and, if a commodity is being produced, to the output per productive worker's hour." And: "All those items that are to be provided to put the plant in readiness" are fixed costs. And: "total variable costs per productive hour are the remaining cost elements . . . that may be reduced to a ratio with the productive hours."

Hess prepared a detailed hypothetical illustration of the cost structure of a company and then plotted it in a form easily recognizable as a break-even chart. The volume, or "X" axis, was plotted in terms of both workers and tons of output. The revenue function was based on an assumed average selling price.

In his illustration, Hess included fixed and variable elements of capital, which he added to a second break-even chart in order to graphically portray "total profits as a percent of capital employed." Describing this early reference to return on investment, he wrote: "Whether profits are good or poor will depend on their ratio to the capital required to produce them."

Hess's second break-even chart included two other items: (1) a line in the form of a rectangular hyperbola that plotted the selling price per hour or pound to balance costs at various output levels, and (2) a line that plotted the "percent dividends on capital employed." He wrote about the need for dividends to be less than income in order to "reserve a sinking fund," which, when it reached a certain level, put the firm in a position to pay all income out as dividends. In this case, Hess became an early contributor to the literature on dividend policy.

Other aspects of Hess's 1903 article involved a possible double counting of some items as both fixed costs and fixed capital, a sentence that implied the concept of the "relevant range," and a detailed description of the flexible-budget concept.

"Forecasting is quite useful," Hess wrote, "but far more important is it to make sure that results agree materially with such forecasts and to find the causes for whatever divergences there may be. . . . Very often are discrepancies attributed to the influence of a fluctuating output. . . . With lines as here laid down . . . the influence of fluctuation is considered and eliminated as a disturbing factor in costs."

Hess then plotted illustrations of planned versus actual costs for two specific costs over various volume levels. He suggested that the plotted costs be for four-week periods rather than a month in order to avoid the influence of varying work days per month. His conviction was that one could readily locate the items responsible for divergences if various sub-items of cost were plotted.

Hess's contribution was impressive: The comprehensive analytical approach to planning and control he developed is still embodied in most managerial-accounting texts of the 1990s. In fact, some of his analytics, charts, and thoughts go beyond them.

More Recent History

After a period of some 50 years of further discussion and application of the break-even chart and its related conceptual foundations, as described in the articles of A.D. Barton, Ned Chapin and Raymond Villers, came the comparison between "marginal analysis of economics" and "the new cost accounting" based on the conceptual foundation of break-even analysis. James Earley (1955), discussing this literature, wrote of the historical emphasis in accounting on inventory valuation, income measurement and control, concluding that "cost accounting obliterates the distinctions needed for 'marginal' costing and tends to lead management toward 'full cost' bases for decision making."

Speaking of the new form of accounting as "management accounting," which concentrates on planning and decision making, Earley said it "implied basing decisions on their estimated effects on marginal balances and contribution margins rather than upon 'full-cost' calculations. It involves consistent references to variable costs and 'specific' fixed costs where these are relevant—and neglect of those costs unaf-

fected by decisions." A primary source Earley used were the research studies of the Institute of Management Accountants (formerly the National Association of Accountants), especially studies 16, "The Variations of Costs with Volume" (1949), 17, "The Analysis of Cost-Volume-Profit Relationships" (1949), and 18, "Volume Factors in Budgets in the Control of Costs" (1950).

All of the above implicitly involves the controversy concerning direct costing versus absorption costing that simmered in the 1950s and 1960s. Under direct costing, the whole fabric of break-even ideology was built into regular, recurring accounting reports and became the foundation of modern managerial accounting with its emphasis on cost-volume-profit relationships. Earley anticipated this by his conclusion that "cost-accounting principles appear to be fast incorporating the wisdom of economists. Far from constituting an impediment to profit maximization via marginal principles, the new accounting is providing techniques by which these estimable principles can at last be properly applied to modern business." Even Joel Dean (1948) anticipated this in "Cost Structures of Enterprises and Break-Even Charts" when he concluded: "Thus conceived, the break-even analysis no longer concentrates on the break-even point or on a single static profit function. Instead it provides a flexible set of projections of costs and revenue under expected future conditions and under alternative management programs. Profit prediction under these multiple conditions becomes then a tool for profit making."

Subsequent Developments and Projections

During the 1980s, an objection to modern managerial accounting based upon cost-volume-profit or break-even analysis arose in the form of activity-based costing, or ABC (see the writings of Robin Cooper and Robert S. Kaplan). ABC emphasizes the need for a total average cost per unit for a variety of product emphasis and pricing decisions because modern manufacturing has become more diverse and complex. ABC also pays little or no attention to the fixity or variability of costs.

An alternative to ABC is the theory of constraints, or TOC (see the writings of Eliyahu Goldratt). Interestingly TOC is a variation of linear programming as applied to cost-volume-profit analysis which is considered in most managerial accounting texts today.

Both ABC and TOC are the subject of debate, reminiscent of the old controversy concerning direct versus absorption costing. Intertwined in this debate is the subject of "target costing," which has been emphasized heavily in Japan as a part of a new approach to management accounting (see the writings of Toshiro Hiromoto, Yasuhiro Monden and Michiharu Sakurai).

Target costing emphasizes a market-driven allowable standard cost which doesn't seem to need much of a differentiation between fixed and variable costs. On the other hand, ABC, TOC and cost-volume-profit analysis emphasize an engineering-driven standard cost.

How the debate or conflict between ABC, TOC and target costing and the current rich tradition of management accounting based upon cost-volume-profit or break-even analysis will be resolved is difficult to predict, but the break-even ideology will most likely survive as a significant part of management accounting.

William L. Ferrara

Bibliography

Barton, A.D. "The Break-Even Chart," *Australian Accountant*, September 1956, pp. 375–388.

Chapin, N. "The Development of the Break-Even Chart: A Bibliographical Note," *Journal of Business*, April 1955, pp. 148–149.

Dean, J. "Cost Structures of Enterprises and Break-Even Charts," *American Economic Review*, May 1948, pp. 153–164.

Earley, J.S. "Recent Developments in Cost Accounting and the 'Marginal Analysis,'" *Journal of Political Economy*, June 1955, pp. 227–242.

Hess, H. "Manufacturing: Capital, Costs, Profits, and Dividends," *Engineering Magazine*, December 1903, pp. 367–379.

Kohler, E.L. *A Dictionary for Accountants*. 4th Ed. Englewood Cliffs, NJ: Prentice-Hall, 1970.

Villers, R. "Communications: The Origin of the Break-Even Chart," *Journal of Business*, October 1955, pp. 296–297.

See also ACTIVITY BASED COSTING; BUDGETING; COMMON COSTS; COST AND/OR MANAGEMENT ACCOUNTING; DIRECT COSTING; GERMANY; INSTITUTE OF MANAGEMENT ACCOUNTANTS; MANAGEMENT ACCOUNTING

Brief, Richard P. (1933–)

B

A scholar in accounting history and a professor of business statistics at New York University, Richard P. Brief received his Ph.D. in 1964 from Columbia University. Brief was president of the Academy of Accounting Historians in 1980 and 1981 and a recipient of its Hourglass Award in 1983. Since 1976 he has been an advisory editor in accounting history for Arno Press and Garland Publishing, which have reprinted classics and published new works in accounting history. Brief advised on 11 different series through 1993 for a total of 351 books. He has edited 8 of these and written one new work, *Nineteenth Century Capital Accounting and Business Investment* (1976). His 1993 edited book, *The Continuing Debate Over Depreciation, Capital and Income*, contains much of his published research.

Brief's historical works have some consistent themes. Accounting is subject to much uncertainty, and this uncertainty really has not been effectively handled. With his background in business statistics, he has brought a different frame of reference to the field of accounting. His immersion into the nineteenth-century accounting literature of Great Britain and the United States led to a study, "Nineteenth Century Accounting Error" (1965), of depreciation of railroads, which was based on the cost of replacing the original fixed assets, and of industrial companies, which was based on some variant of valuation. He concluded in both cases that uncertainty (error) was quite likely and unpredictable. His research (1967) yielded an 1890 paper by O.G. Ladelle in *The Accountant* that gave a strong rationale for associating the problems of depreciation with the allocation of joint costs. Brief (1975) added nineteenth-century legal literature on profits, capital, and dividends to his arguments in the examination of uncertainty of accounting rules set by legislation, of audit scope and the audit certificate of estimates and forecasts, and, finally, of profit. He found the term "profit" to be "vague and loosely used and without definition."

In an example of better coping with the uncertainty of the annual profit figure, Brief and others (1980) designed a set of cumulative financial statements. This approach shows accounting history in a financial-management mode, dealing with recasted statements. It allowed for a comparison for cumulative income and cumulative cash flows over a period of 53 years.

Brief (1982) rigorously analyzed the writings of J.R. Hicks on accounting to give a much more holistic picture of this writer, who is generally, and loosely, quoted as being in favor of price-level adjustments but who, on closer look, shows the opposite viewpoint.

Brief was chosen to write an article for the American Institute of Certified Public Accountants (AICPA) Centennial issue (May 1987) of the *Journal of Accountancy*. In it he discussed the extreme variations noted in accounting statements in annual reports at the turn of the twentieth century.

Richard Vangermeersch

Bibliography

Brief, R.P. "The Accountant's Responsibility in Historical Perspective," *Accounting Review*, April 1975, pp. 285–297.

———. "Corporate Financial Reporting at the Turn of the Century," *Journal of Accountancy*, May 1987, pp. 142–157.

———. "Hicks on Accounting," *Accounting Historians Journal*, Spring 1982, pp. 91–101.

———. "A Late Nineteenth Century Contribution to the Theory of Depreciation," *Journal of Accounting Research*, Spring 1967, pp. 27–38.

———. "Nineteenth Century Accounting Error," *Journal of Accounting Research*, Spring 1965, pp. 12–31.

———. *Nineteenth Century Capital Accounting and Business Investment*. New York: Arno Press, 1976.

Brief, R.P., B. Merino, and I. Weiss. "Cumulative Financial Statements," *Accounting Review*, July 1980, pp. 480–490.

See also ACADEMY OF ACCOUNTING HISTORIANS; CAPITAL MAINTENANCE; CONSERVATISM; DEPRECIATION; DIVIDENDS; DOUBLE ACCOUNT METHOD; LADELLE, O.G.; RAILROAD ACCOUNTING (U.S.)

Briloff, Abraham J. (1920–)

Since 1989, Distinguished Professor Emeritus of the City University of New York, Abraham J. Briloff has been described by those interested in financial reporting as the most famous accountant in the world because of the exposure of his views in his books and in *Barron's*. Renowned for numerous in-depth investigations of audit failures and a prescience that, for example, led him to forecast the savings and loan fiasco several years before the scandal broke, Briloff directs his appeals to the large accounting firms and the American Institute of Certified Public Accountants to rededicate themselves to their public mandate. Few in accounting are able to match his oratory and writings in terms of their scholarship, humor, witticisms, and use of religious and mythological allusion.

Briloff's erudition and accessible style have earned him access to public forums not normally available to accountants. His articles in the national press, especially *Barron's*, challenging the veracity of corporate financial reports has incurred the litigious wrath of several corporate executives. None has prevailed to date. The high level of public interest in his writings led one Stanford University scholar to undertake a study of the "Briloff effect" on stock prices. Briloff has testified on numerous occasions before congressional committees and provided expert testimony before several U.S. courts. His books are best sellers, notably *Unaccountable Accounting* (1972) and *More Debits Than Credits* (1976).

Briloff has been one of the most controversial figures in accounting for nearly 20 years. He is a champion of small accounting practitioners in their competitive skirmishes with large firms. In the eyes of many, he is the *bête noire* of the accounting establishment. His notoriety among the large firms reached such a pitch that, in the 1980s, he—together with persons, events, and educational institutions affiliated with him—was ostracized by these powerful institutions.

The intense reactions to Briloff cannot be explained merely in terms of Briloff's eristic "style." They require an understanding of the professional and social context in which Briloff operates. Briloff comes from an earlier age when accounting more closely resembled a guild craft than an industry. This craft lineage is reflected in Briloff's rhetoric: appeals to accountants to honor their professional "duty," "honesty," "truth," "responsibility," "integrity," and "fairness," and such admonishments that the profession has "desecrated" its covenant to society.

Like the professions, guilds, and crafts of earlier times, accounting is undergoing an enormous upheaval. By fits and starts, it is transforming into an international system of commodity production. Institutionally, this is expressed in a growing divide between small accounting practitioners—bearers of the traditional professional code—and large, multinational firms, with their extensive systems of work specialization and product differentiation. Historically, the transformation from traditional (handicraft) work methods, to highly specialized, large-scale production, rarely passes without difficulty. Cotton production, medicine, farming, silk production, the law, and many other forms of production have experienced considerable social conflict in their transformation into capitalist commodity production as instanced by the Luddite destruction of machines and the current struggles to privatize the British national health system.

In this context, Briloff stands as a formidable spokesperson for the ancient régime—nostalgic for the morality and integrity of the Old Order, and challenging the rise of capitalist accounting, with its transformed (more specialized) work methods, reskilling, cost cutting, competition, devalued educational experience, lowballing, and "fee grubbing." While some might see a historical inexorability to the expanding commodification of accounting—thereby consigning Briloff to the role of a Canute—this underrates his (and his colleagues') capacity to socialize accounting and turn it toward the public interest. Briloff stands for "the social" in the contradiction between the private accumulation propensities of large accounting firms and their social role as public institutions. He is a model for all in the profession who want to make a difference.

Anthony Maxwell Tinker

Bibliography

Briloff, A. "Accountancy and Society: A Covenant Desecrated," *Critical Perspectives on Accounting*, March 1990, pp. 5–30.
———. *More Debits Than Credits.* New York: Harper & Row, 1976.
———. *The Truth about Corporate Accounting.* New York: Harper & Row, 1972.
———. *Unaccountable Accounting.* New York: Harper & Row, 1972.
Tinker, T., C. Lehman, and M. Neimark. "Falling Down the Hole in the Middle of the Road: Political Quietism in Corporate Social Reporting," *Accounting, Auditing, and Accountability Journal*, vol. 4, no. 2, 1991, pp. 28–54.

See also SOCIAL RESPONSIBILITIES OF ACCOUNTANTS

Brown, F. Donaldson (1885–1965)

The pioneering managerial accountant in the 20th century, F. Donaldson Brown had no formal education in accounting, finance, or economics. He received a bachelor's degree in systems engineering from Virginia Polytechnic Institute at the age of 17. He joined the DuPont Powder Company's sales department in 1909 and was promoted to assistant department manager in 1912. While in this position, Brown created what is known today as the "return on investment" formula. This achievement brought him to the notice of Coleman DuPont, who promoted him to the position of junior assistant treasurer.

After General Motors neared collapse, the DuPonts, who owned a major stake, took operating control of the company. Brown was installed as the vice president of Finance at GM on January 1, 1921. In 1924 he became chair of the General Sales Committee and a member of the Executive Committee at General Motors. While at GM, he created the extremely powerful Finance Department, a department that continues to dominate the company today.

While at DuPont in 1912, Brown came up with the idea of return on investment (ROI). This was a revolutionary discovery and helped the management at DuPont and later General Motors efficiently process the information provided by their far-flung corporate empires. The concept of capital turnover as an important factor in profitability was the addition that made ROI so useful. It is so useful that the concept is still widely used in corporations and taught in business schools.

Critics of ROI contend that it drives managers to emphasize short-term results at the expense of long-term profitability. It appears that Brown in 1924 appreciated this problem and suggested that "It is apparent that the object of management is not necessarily the highest attainable rate of return on capital, but rather the highest return consistent with attainable volume, care being exercised to assure profit with each increment of volume will at least equal the economic cost of additional capital required."

To control General Motor's complex operating system, a solution to transfer pricing between the divisions had to be developed. Again Brown rose to the task, forcing interdivisional pricing that was competitive with outside suppliers. He well understood in a 1927 speech and subsequent article the behavioral importance of the role of transfer pricing. "The question of pricing product from one division to another is of great importance. Unless a true competitive situation is preserved, as to prices, there is no basis upon which the performance of the divisions can be measured." In addition to ROI and transfer pricing, he brought the concept of standards from DuPont to General Motors and popularized their usage. He developed a sophisticated and innovative pricing policy for GM based in long-term standard volumes and costs. He was instrumental in creating the Manager's Securities Company at General Motors. This wholly owned subsidiary purchased GM stock and offered it to top executives at present prices as operating goals were met. The program was immensely successful and enabled GM's top managers to share in the company's successes in the 1920s. In spirit and in design, the Manager's Securities Company was the forerunner for many modern incentive-compensation schemes for executives.

Brown created a great deal for the accounting profession. He was a pioneer in understanding and evaluating the operations of large and diversified organizations. Without his contributions, the management of such enterprises as DuPont and General Motors could not have evaluated the performance of their operating divisions. Although his ideas have been extensively analyzed and embellished, he remains the creator of many of them. His contributions remain current in investment policy (ROI), transfer pricing, standard setting, and executive compensation.

Stephen J. Young

Bibliography

Brown, F.D. "Centralized Control with Decentralized Responsibilities," *Annual Convention Series*, No. 57, pp. 3–24. New York: American Management Association, 1927.
———. "Pricing Policy in Relation to Financial Control," *Management and Administration*, February 1924, pp. 195–198, and March 1924, pp. 283–286.
Chandler, A.D. *The Visible Hand: The Managerial Revolution in American Business.* Cambridge, MA: Belknap Press, 1977.
Johnson, H.T. "Management Accounting in an Early Multidivisional Organization: General Motors in the 1920s," *Business History Review*, Winter 1978, pp. 36–63.
Johnson, H.T., and R.S. Kaplan. *Relevance Lost: The Rise and Fall of Management Accounting.* Boston: Harvard Business School Press, 1987.
Sloan, A.P. Jr. *My Years with General Motors.* New York: Doubleday, 1963.

See also JOHNSON AND KAPLAN'S *RELEVANCE LOST: THE RISE AND FALL OF MANAGEMENT ACCOUNTING;* JOHNSON, H. THOMAS; MANAGEMENT ACCOUNTING; RETURN ON INVESTMENT; STANDARD COSTING; TRANSFER PRICES

Brushaber v. Union Pacific Railroad Company

Following ratification of the Sixteenth Amendment to the U.S. Constitution in February 1913, the Revenue Act of 1913, including a 15-page income tax section, became law on October 3. When opponents of income taxation appealed to the courts, citing the due process clause of the Fifth Amendment because the tax law permitted exemptions and graduated rates, the income tax was upheld by the U.S. Supreme Court in *Brushaber v. Union Pacific Railroad Company* (1916).

Michael Chatfield

Bibliography

Brushaber v. Union Pacific Railroad Company, 240 U.S. 1 (1916).

See also INCOME TAXATION IN THE UNITED STATES; SIXTEENTH AMENDMENT

Budgeting

The word "budget" is from the Old French *bourgette*, meaning "small bag" or "pouch." Its use is thought to have originated in the seventeenth-century British Parliament where the chancellor of the exchequer opened his "budget" of documents and accounts to present the annual financial statements to Parliament. These statements included an account of the previous year's government expenditures, an estimate of the coming year's expenditures, and recommendations for levying the taxes necessary to cover the proposed expenditures. The term "budget" came to mean not just the bag containing the documents but the documents themselves.

Uses of Budgeting in Government

A government's budget is now generally understood to be the forecast of the expenditure the government expects to meet in the next financial year and the revenue it will raise, after allowing for the costs of borrowings. Additionally, in many places, it has become a vehicle for review of, and debate relating to, a country's entire economic situation and national objectives.

Government budgeting began in Britain in the late seventeenth century with the enactment of the 1689 Bill of Rights. This bill restricted the king's power to levy taxes by providing that taxes could only be charged with the consent of Parliament. Parliamentary control of expenditure was gradually extended from the authorization of Crown expenditure to the details and purposes of spending programs. By the 1820s, the British government's annual statement of finances included comprehensive details of revenues and expenditures and a projected surplus or deficit.

In the United States, budgeting developed much later. The Treasury Department was established in 1789, and in 1800 a law was passed that directed the secretary of the treasury to present an annual financial report to Congress. The Treasury Department, however, did not comply with this law. Instead, federal government agencies prepared their own, individual, financial estimates, and these were simply combined by the Treasury Department and presented to Congress without revision or comment.

In the late nineteenth century, the U.S. Senate delegated appropriating authority to several of its standing committees. Several attempts to introduce federal budgeting and financial management in the early 1900s failed, although, by 1920, some 44 individual states had passed laws related to budgets. Federal activities expanded during and after the war, and a national Budgeting and Accounting Act was adopted in 1921. This act required the president to provide Congress with the budgeted federal revenues and expenditures for the coming year. At the same time, a centralized Bureau of the Budget was created. It was not until the mid-1940s that the federal budget included identification of the major goals and program objectives, a systematic analysis of supplies and needs for both military and nonmilitary purposes, and an extended time horizon that included long-range projects.

With the introduction and use of performance budgeting in the U.S. Defense Department in the 1950s, and its application to programs in the 1960s, the Planning-Programming-Budgeting System (PPBS) was developed. President Lyndon B. Johnson called for the adoption of this system throughout the federal government in 1965. Unfortunately, the results of PPBS have been mixed. While it continued essentially unchanged in the Defense Department, it was abandoned by all other departments in the 1970s.

In the early 1970s, a new type of budgeting—zero-based budgeting (ZBB)—was gaining adherents in private enterprises. ZBB requires that each organizational unit prepare incremental decision packages for each activity that assess the costs and benefits of each. These packages are ranked against all other activities competing for resources. After the ranking, management decides on a cutoff point, and all activities above this point are approved. During the 1970s, a number of organizations implemented ZBB, or some modified form. Governor Jimmy Carter (prior to his U.S. presidency, 1976–1980) was instrumental in introducing ZBB to government in the state of Georgia in 1973. In that fiscal year, ZBB was used to develop the entire executive budget recommendations for the State of Georgia. However, as a system of government budgeting, it was a failure; the volume of effort and the time involved were prohibitive.

Uses of Budgeting in Business

Budgeting in business organizations has a different focus than government budgeting. While governments can, in theory, decide on the programs they wish to undertake, and raise finance accordingly, most businesses must forecast revenues first, and then appraise the costs of their operations within the limitations of the revenue forecast.

The first business budgets concentrated on controlling costs with little or no attempt to measure effectiveness. However, in the early twentieth century, industrial developments required careful factory planning, and the use of budgets burgeoned. Systematic budgeting in manufacturing organizations developed from two sources: industrial engineering and cost accounting. Industrial engineers applied scientific methods to calculate production standards, and these could then be used to estimate future operations and performance standards. Cost-accounting techniques were applied to establish standard costs and to estimate future expected costs in a budgetary form.

That era also saw the emergence of the earliest comprehensive texts on budgeting and managerial accounting. Notable among these was McKinsey (1924), whose career, prior to the establishment of the consulting firm bearing his name, included a distinguished, if lesser-known, period as a professor of accounting at the University of Chicago. A perusal of his book reveals astonishing survival of the test of time, particularly its coverage of organizational and, in parts, even behavioral issues. The modern-day counterpart of this work is Welsch (1957), which, more than 30 years later, surfaced in its fifth edition. The book is unique because of the depth of its technical and procedural analysis and for the conceptual foundations it lays for the design of budgeting systems.

Budgeting has become an essential facet of management control systems and can be viewed as a formalized system in an organization for realizing management's responsibilities for planning, coordination and control. The budgeting process involves the development and application of the broad strategic objectives of an organization, the detailed organizational goals, a broad, long-term financial plan, and the short-run financial plan or annual budget (often broken down into a number of separate parts, by division, product, process, or project).

The Impact of Budgeting on People and Organizations: The Research Evidence

Argyris (1952) was probably the first person to study some of the behavioral effects resulting from the way budgets are used in organizations. The results of his study showed that the style of use could cause dysfunctional behavior in subordinates, regardless of the degree of technical refinement of the budgetary system. Other studies of the impact of budgets on the people in organizations followed, such as Stedry (1960), Becker and Green (1962), Lowe and Shaw (1968), Hofstede (1967), and Schiff and Lewin (1970). This research, while clearly signaling great interest on the part of academics in the behavioral effects of budgets, lacked a coherent theme and constituted a very difficult to integrate set of ideas and theories.

Notwithstanding this handicap, Caplan (1971) wrote the first text that integrated the technical and behavioral issues in budgeting and was designed for use in the classroom. The book is notable for its strong theoretical and conceptual focus, which still provides the student of managerial accounting with an accessible reference source on the matter of the human interface with budgeting.

The start of the 1970s saw a significant uplift in the rigor and scholarship in all accounting research, and management accounting was no exception. Hopwood (1972) started a long line of inquiry into the effects of budgets on human behavior, with his study that showed that the use by a superior of a budget-constrained style of evaluation gave rise to significant levels of job-related tension, had adverse effects on peer and superior relations, and was clearly implicated in manipulative behavior on the part of subordinates.

In a systematic replication of Hopwood's study, Otley (1978) was unable to confirm any of Hopwood's results, finding, instead, evidence contradictory to that of Hopwood. Fueled by a rapidly maturing debate in organizational behavior, contingency theory was squarely embraced by management-accounting researchers in a bid to resolve the Hopwood-Otley conflict. Within the framework of contingency theory, the basic premise was that Hopwood and Otley were both "right" and that their differing results could be attributed to one or more situational, or contingency, variables that differed between their studies.

A long line of studies, beginning around 1980 and continuing into the 1990s, has uncovered a substantial array of variables that govern the effects of reliance on budgets on behavioral outcomes, including managerial performance. Examples of these variables are:

Budgetary participation (Brownell 1982). Provided managers are given the opportunity to participate in budget setting, the adverse behavioral consequences of a heavy reliance on budgets by superiors in their evaluation of subordinates can be ameliorated.

Task uncertainty (Hirst 1983). Heavy reliance on budgets and accounting information in performance evaluation should be confined to situations in which the tasks undertaken by organizations are well understood and can be analyzed into cause-effect relations.

Environmental uncertainty (Govindarajan 1984). Reliance on financial controls, such as budgets, is problematic where the influence of factors beyond the organization's control cannot be separated from those within its control. High environmental uncertainty characterizes such a setting.

Strategy (Govindarajan and Gupta 1985). Organizations (or organizational subunits) whose strategic focus is on high-growth, innovative activities should rely less on budgets as forms of control than those focusing on mature, established activities.

Culture (Harrison 1992). Because budgeting can reinforce the hierarchical structural arrangements within the organization, national cultures that depend on clear status and rank distinctions find more comfort with budgeting as a form of control than those nations whose culture de-emphasizes these distinctions.

This research constitutes what can be argued to be the only (certainly the most important) "critical mass" of research in managerial accounting. Increasingly sophisticated theoretical bases, the use of improved empirical methods, and, above all, a shared belief in the need to better understand when budgets work and when they don't have all contributed to this state of affairs.

Peter Brownell
Elizabeth Roberts

Bibliography

Argyris, C. *The Impact of Budgets on People.* Ithaca, NY: Controllership Foundation, 1952.

Becker, S.W., and D. Green Jr. "Budgeting and Employee Behavior," *Journal of Business*, October 1962, pp. 392–402.

Brownell, P. "The Role of Accounting Data in Performance Evaluation, Budgetary Participation, and Organizational Effectiveness," *Journal of Accounting Research*, Spring 1982, pp. 12–27.

Caplan, E.H. *Management Accounting and Behavioral Science.* Reading, MA: Addison-Wesley, 1971.

Chatfield, M. *A History of Accounting Thought.* Hinsdale, IL: Dryden Press, 1974.

Govindarajan, V. "Appropriateness of Accounting Data in Performance Evaluation: An Empirical Examination of Environmental Uncertainty as an Intervening Variable," *Accounting, Organizations, and Society*, vol. 9, no. 2, 1984, pp. 125–135.

Govindarajan, V., and A.K. Gupta. "Linking Control Systems to Business Unit Strategy: Impact on Performance," *Accounting, Organizations, and Society*, vol. 10, no. 1, 1985, pp. 51–66.

Harrison, Graeme L. "The Cross-Cultural Generalizability of the Relation between Participation, Budget Emphasis, and Job Related Attitudes," *Accounting, Organizations, and Society*, vol. 17, no. 1, 1992, pp. 1–16.

Hirst, M.K. "Reliance on Accounting Performance Measures, Task Uncertainty, and Dysfunctional Behavior: Some Extensions," *Journal of Accounting Research*, Autumn 1983, pp. 596–605.

Hofstede, G.H. *The Game of Budget Control.* Assen, Netherlands: Van Gorcum, 1967.

Hopwood, A.G. "An Empirical Study of the Role of Accounting Data in Performance Evaluation." In *Empirical Research Accounting: Selected Studies* (Supplement to vol. 10 *Journal of Accounting Research*, 1972), pp. 156–182.

Lowe, E.A., and R.W. Shaw. "An Analysis of Managerial Biasing: Evidence from a Company's Budgeting Process," *The Journal of Management Studies*, October 1968, pp. 304–315.

McKinsey, J.O. *Managerial Accounting.* Chicago: University of Chicago Press, 1924.

Otley, D.T. "Budget Use and Managerial Performance," *Journal of Accounting Research*, Spring 1978, pp. 122–149.

Pyhrr, P.A. *Zero-Based Budgeting.* New York: John Wiley & Sons, 1973.

Schiff, M., and A.Y. Lewin. "The Impact of People on Budgets," *Accounting Review*, April 1970, pp. 259–268.

Stedry, A.C. *Budget Control and Cost Behavior.* Englewood Cliffs, NJ: Prentice-Hall, 1960.

Welsch, G.A. *Budgeting: Profit Planning and Control.* Englewood Cliffs, NJ: Prentice-Hall, 1957.

Welsch, G.A., R.W. Hilton, and P.N. Gordon. *Budgeting: Profit Planning and Control.* 5th ed. Englewood Cliffs, NJ: Prentice-Hall, 1988.

See also BREAK-EVEN CHART; CONTROL ACCOUNTS; CONTROL: CLASSICAL MODEL; COST AND/OR MANAGEMENT ACCOUNTING; ENGINEERING AND ACCOUNTING; FEDERAL GOVERNMENT ACCOUNTING (U.S.); GANTT, HENRY LAURENCE; HARRISON, G. CHARTER; HOPWOOD, ANTHONY G.; MANAGEMENT ACCOUNTING; MCKINSEY, JAMES O.; MUNICIPAL ACCOUNTING REFORM; STANDARD COSTING; TAYLOR, FREDERICK WINSLOW

C

Canada

Canada is a federation of 10 provinces and two territories. Under the Constitution, the provinces are responsible for education, professional training, and certification, while responsibility for economic affairs, including the regulation of financial reporting, is shared between the federal and provincial governments. This division of powers, coupled with the diverse geography, cultures, and economies of the country, has resulted in great regional differences in the development of the profession.

The Development of the Profession and Accounting Regulation

The first accounting firms developed in the commercial centers of Toronto and Montreal in the 1840s. Initially, much of their revenue was derived from bankruptcies, but auditing work expanded as the economy stabilized and the joint stock company became more common. In 1879 associations were formed in Montreal and Toronto. Although each association used the "chartered accountant" designation, they differed in entrance requirements and operated as rivals. In 1902 the Association of Accountants of Montreal (later renamed the Ordre des Comptables Agréé du Québec) sponsored the federal incorporation of the Dominion Association of Chartered Accountants.

In 1908 representatives of the Toronto Institute and the Dominion Association met at the annual convention of the American Association of Public Accountants. Under the chairmanship of Harry L. Price, president of the Society of Incorporated Accountants and Auditors of England, a reconciliation was reached. In 1910 the Dominion Association was restructured as a federation of provincial Institutes of Chartered Accountants and was charged with securing incorporation of institutes in provinces where none existed, securing uniform provincial legislation, securing uniformity of standards of entry and training, arranging for reciprocity of membership, and considering the question of ethics. The provincial institutes retained control over education, certification, and discipline.

The Canadian Accountants' Association (later renamed the Certified General Accountants' Association of Canada) was formed in 1908 under the sponsorship of John Leslie, assistant comptroller of the Canadian Pacific Railways. This group was composed of accountants in business and government. Their interests differed from the focus of the Institutes of Chartered Accountants on public accounting. In addition, the association provided a mechanism for professional advancement without the hardship of an apprenticeship with a public accountant, which was required by the Institute of Chartered Accountants.

In 1913 the Canadian Accountants' Association received a federal charter as the General Accountants' Association. The application was opposed by the Institute of Chartered Accountants. In return for the withdrawal of their opposition, the Canadian Accountants' Association had changed its name in order to avoid the initials CAA and gave assurances that it was concerned solely with the standards of competence of management accountants.

In Quebec the Institute of Accountants and Auditors formed in 1912. This group was composed of Francophone accountants. Their organization competed with the primarily Anglophone Chartered Accountant Institute. In particular, they blocked attempts by the chartered accountants in Quebec to gain a monopoly on practice in Quebec by arguing that the group would be incapable of servicing the Francophone business community.

After World War I, the question of the division of labor in accounting returned to the fore. The Income Tax Act of 1917 created the need for businesses to keep accounting records and to file tax returns. In many cases, this was the first time companies had assembled complete accounting records. The act also required a bureaucracy to process and audit tax returns. The war created a massive increase in employment by the state. Many people who went into accounting after the war were involved in payroll accounting for the armed services or in the administration of cost-plus contracts.

The war had created a new kind of accounting and accountant. In England and the United States, this was marked by the creation of associations of "cost" or "management" accountants in 1919. In Canada, the Dominion Association of Chartered Accountants created the Canadian Society of Cost Accountants (later renamed the Society of Management Accountants of Canada). The first board of the society consisted of the presidents of the provincial Institutes of Chartered Accountants and of the Dominion Association.

The Canadian Society of Cost Accountants was not intended to be a professional body. It would not offer training or tests of competence or use a designation. The domain defined for the society by the Dominion Association of Chartered Accountants, however, did not meet the aspirations of its members. By 1927 the society was offering "certificates of efficiency," and in 1939 it voted to authorize the use of a designation. The change in emphasis of the society was not unanimously supported. Some of those who preferred to focus on management issues rather than the training of cost accountants left the association in 1939 to form the Controllers' Institute of Canada (later renamed the Financial Executives Institute).

World War II marked another turning point for the Canadian profession. In the postwar boom, accounting associations began competing for students and for practice rights. Under the Constitution, education and the regulation of the professions is a provincial responsibility. This meant that if an accounting association was going to maintain its place in the profession, it would need a strong provincial presence. The chartered accountants' groups had begun as provincial associations

and were well entrenched. Other accounting groups had to build from the top down—using a federally incorporated body (for example, the Society of Management Accountants of Canada and the Certified General Accountants' Association of Canada) or a single provincial body (for example, the Certified Public Accountants' Association of Ontario) as the basis for growth.

The creation of provincial associations by various accounting associations can be understood, in part, by their desire to control the education of their members and to provide a designation certifying their competence. Another motive for seeking provincial incorporation was to establish a formal presence in provinces contemplating the regulation of public accounting. This factor is important for understanding the pattern of mergers that resulted in the current structure of accounting associations in Canada.

Access to various accounting roles has been regulated by specific statutes since at least 1897 when the Ontario Municipal Act was revised to require that municipal auditors be Fellows of the Institute of Chartered Accountants of Ontario or some other group of expert accountants. The first act to regulate public accountancy, as broadly conceived, was enacted in Quebec in 1946. The history of the Quebec profession leading to this act illustrates many of the pressures to "rationalize" the profession.

In 1916 the primarily Anglophone Chartered Accountant Institute, in concert with the Francophone Institute of Accountants and Auditors, approached the premier with legislation to close the profession. The premier suggested that the matter be deferred until after the war. In 1918 they returned to press their case but again were rebuffed. In 1919 they succeeded in getting a bill before the legislature, but it was voted down. In general the legislature was suspicious of the motives of an Anglophone organization seeking to control entry to a profession that would have to serve both Anglophone and Francophone communities.

In 1945–1946 the Chartered Accountants Bill, with minor amendments, gained the support of the major accounting associations and the government. Legislation closing the profession was enacted in 1946. Under this law, all existing public accountants in Quebec were merged into the Quebec Institute of Chartered Accountants. The act gave the new institute expanded disciplinary powers and formalized the link between the universities and the profession in the education of accountants.

Since the introduction of regulation of the right to practice in 1946, there have been continued but unsuccessful attempts to "rationalize" the profession. In Ontario in 1962 the Chartered Accountants and Certified Public Accountants merged as a prelude to revising accounting regulation in Ontario. As the Ontario CPA Association provided all services for the other provinces, the Ontario merger was followed by mergers across the country. Throughout the 1960s, there were attempts to merge the provincial Societies of Management Accountants and the provincial Certified General Accountants Associations. During the 1970s there were attempts to merge the Chartered Accountants, Certified General Accountants and Society of Management Accountants. As of the mid-1990s, these three groups were represented federally and in all 10 provinces, and were vibrant, growing organizations.

Accounting Education and Research

The first formal accounting education in Canada became available in the late 1840s when Egerton Ryerson imported texts on bookkeeping from the Irish school system for use in the public education system. By the 1860s proprietary business schools began offering accounting training and Canadian texts were produced by W.C. Eddis, S.G. Beatty, W.R. Orr, D. Hoskins, J.W. Johnson, R. Miller, and others. Accounting associations initially did not offer education programs but recommended proprietary courses to their members. The authors of these early accounting texts were usually members of the associations. The first university program in accounting was offered by the University of Saskatchewan. This program was approved in 1913, but the onset of the war delayed the first classes until 1917. The first degree in accountancy was issued in 1923.

In 1920 the Institute of Chartered Accountants of Ontario changed the pattern of education for accountants by contracting with Queen's University to develop a correspondence program for its students. In conjunction with this program, influential textbooks were written by R.G.H. Smails and W.G. Leonard. This model was followed by chartered accountants and industrial accountants in other provinces. In 1970 the Chartered Accountants in each province began requiring an undergraduate degree of candidates for the chartered accountant designation. In 1984 the Institute of Chartered Accountants of Ontario sponsored the

development of a professional School of Accountancy at the University of Waterloo. The shift of accounting education into professional schools of accountancy seems likely to continue.

Both practitioners and academics have made significant contributions to Canadian accounting research. The research department of the accounting firm of Clarkson Gordon, for example, produced important books on analytical auditing by R. Skinner, D. Leslie and R. Anderson, while H. Ross of Touche Ross and Company wrote on financial-statement presentation. In 1961 the Canadian Institute of Chartered Accountants began its Research Studies series. In the public sector, the Comprehensive Auditing Foundation, formed in 1980, has contributed to the development of "value for money" auditing. The growing research emphasis of accounting academics was marked by the formation in 1976 of the Canadian Academic Accounting Association, which replaced the Canadian Region of the American Accounting Association formed in 1967.

Financial Reporting

Canadian financial reporting has been influenced by both the United States and Great Britain. Prior to 1900, financial-reporting requirements followed the example of English companies acts quite closely. There were also numerous specific disclosure requirements in acts relating to industries such as banks, railways, and municipalities. After 1900 the Institute of Chartered Accountants of Ontario began actively developing and promoting standards of financial reporting. These standards are reflected in the Ontario Companies Act of 1907 and were copied by the Canadian Companies Act of 1917. This pattern of innovation is also reflected in the Canadian Companies Act of 1964, which was modeled on the Ontario Companies Act of 1953. The Ontario act, in turn, implemented the disclosure standards suggested in the Canadian Institute of Chartered Accountants Bulletin No. 1, issued in 1946, which was written by the Committee on Accounting and Auditing of the Institute of Chartered Accountants of Ontario.

Since the 1930s, Canadian financial-reporting practice has also been influenced by developments in the United States. This influence reflects the growing economic ties between these countries in this period, specifically the increase in U.S.-based companies operating subsidiaries in Canada and the development of in-

C

ternational accounting firms. In addition, the standard-setting activities of the U.S. accounting profession and the Securities and Exchange Commission were recognized as directly relevant to the Canadian context.

While the influence of the United States and Great Britain on Canadian financial reporting has been significant, there are important differences. First, Canada has had fewer financial scandals; hence, financial-reporting reform has occurred more deliberately and less in reaction to crises. Second, the profession has more authority to develop accounting standards independently of government intervention.

The Canadian Institute of Chartered Accountants began issuing bulletins on accounting practice in 1946. In 1968 these bulletins (then numbering 26) were replaced with a loose-leaf binder known as the *Canadian Institute of Chartered Accountants' Handbook*. In 1972 the Canadian Securities Administrators issued National Policy Statement No. 27, which required all financial statements filed with Canadian securities commissions to conform to generally accepted accounting principles as reflected in the handbook. The following year, the Institute of Chartered Accountants of Ontario required its members to qualify any financial statement that did not conform to the handbook. Finally, in 1975, the Canada Business Corporations Act required that all companies incorporated under the act conform with the generally accepted accounting principles and generally accepted auditing standards codified in the handbook. This series of changes, reinforced by subsequent provincial companies acts, delegated standard setting for financial reporting to the Canadian Institute of Chartered Accountants without any formal oversight mechanism.

Conclusion
The development of the Canadian accounting profession reflects the institutional heritage of its colonial ties with Great Britain and the economic influence of the United States. In coming to grips with its own economic and cultural history, however, the profession has developed unique institutional arrangements that have allowed it to make international contributions in education and financial reporting.

Alan J. Richardson

Bibliography
Allan, J.N. *History of the Society of Management Accountants of Canada.* Hamilton: The Society of Management Accountants of Canada, 1982.

Creighton, P. *A Sum of Yesterdays: Being a History of the First One Hundred Years of the Institute of Chartered Accountants of Ontario.* Toronto: Institute of Chartered Accountants of Ontario, 1984.

Murphy, G. "A Chronology of the Development of Corporate Financial Reporting in Canada," *Accounting Historians Journal,* Spring 1986, pp. 31–63.

Richardson, A.J. "Accounting Competence: Canadian Experiences." In *International Handbook of Accounting Education and Certification,* edited by K. Anyane-Ntow, pp. 263–278. Oxford: Pergamon, 1992.

———. "An Interpretative Chronology of the Development of Accounting Associations in Canada, 1879–1979." In *Anthology of Canadian Accounting History,* edited by G. Murphy, pp. 551–628. New York: Garland, 1993.

Skinner, R. "Research Contributions to Canadian Standards: A Retrospective," *Research in Accounting Regulation,* 1989, pp. 197–217.

Stuart, R.C. *The First Seventy-Five Years: A History of the Certified General Accountants' Association of Canada.* Vancouver: The Certified General Accountants' Association of Canada, 1988.

See also OPERATIONAL (VALUE-FOR-MONEY) AUDITING

Canning, John Bennett (1884–1962)
John Bennett Canning was professor of economics and head of the Division of Accountancy at Stanford University. His only book, *The Economics of Accountancy* (1929), was the first systematic attempt to restate accounting concepts in economic terms. Canning's original intention was to make the work of accountants intelligible to economists. But because economics was the more rigorously defined discipline, his book mainly benefited accountants. Canning's method was to examine closely, and define precisely, the nature of assets, liabilities, capital, and income. His concepts of asset valuation and income measurement were far ahead of their time and seem startlingly modern today.

Canning began *The Economics of Accountancy* by considering the nature of assets, asserting that "one who seeks an answer by searching the texts on accounting for formal definitions will first be surprised that many, perhaps most, of the writers offer none at all." Examining accounting practice to derive a definition from the methods in use, he showed that accountants excluded much which economists would call assets and income. He concluded that accounting practice was legally rather than economically oriented; that while accountants practiced asset valuation, they had no theory of value.

After giving comprehensive definitions of assets, liabilities, and capital, Canning proposed a theory of asset valuation transplanted from economics. The proper valuation of any asset should be based on the expected receipts from its use. "An inventory valuation, as such, can have no significance except as an index of funds to be produced." This kind of "direct valuation" was appropriate for assets whose future cash inflows could be reasonably forecast. It would be best to have direct valuations of all assets, but "indirect valuation" must be applied when no estimate can be made of an asset's future earnings. In either case, increases in asset values produce income, which should be recognized in the accounts as soon as reliable estimates of future conversion value can be made.

Following this line of reasoning, Canning argued that income is realized when three conditions have been met: (1) the receipt of money within a year has become highly probable, (2) the amount to be received is known or can be accurately estimated, and (3) the expenses incurred or to be incurred in producing the revenues are known or can be estimated.

Michael Chatfield

Bibliography

Canning, J.B. *The Economics of Accountancy.* New York: Ronald Press, 1929.
Smith, W.R. "John Bennett Canning," *Accounting Historians Journal,* January 1974, pp. 29–31.

See also BALL AND BROWN'S "AN EMPIRICAL EVALUATION OF ACCOUNTING INCOME NUMBERS"; CONCEPTUAL FRAMEWORK; FISHER, IRVING; MACNEAL, KENNETH

Capital Account

Several early writers on double entry bookkeeping emphasized the new system's ability to provide automatic capital balances. The capital account was seen as a ready reference to a businessman's financial status and was associated with wealth changes. Frequent mention was made in early accounting texts of the employment of capital in business activities, and a few authors saw that capital was wealth employed to reproduce itself. Henry Rand Hatfield claimed that the word "capital" was introduced into the English language in James Peele's bookkeeping text *The Pathe Waye to Perfectness* (1569) and that accountants understood the concept of capital long before economists discovered it.

Many accounting textbooks illustrated the process of determining the capital account balance by inventorying a merchant's assets and debts prior to opening his books. Authors described in detail the transfer of profit and loss account balances to capital when the ledger was closed. They understood that profits increased the owner's original capital contribution and that the profit and loss account was a temporary haven for capital changes. Capital was also seen as a balancing figure that permitted arithmetic proof of the equality of debits and credits in the ledger. Finally, the capital account was useful in explaining the logic of double entry bookkeeping. Luca Pacioli's transaction analysis in *Summa de Arithmetica* (1494) focused on proprietorship changes.

But these were counsels of perfection. Most fifteenth century merchants kept single entry records that amounted to little more than lists of payments and receipts. Even double entry accounts could be very crude. Many were hybrids, containing elements of double entry bookkeeping but no complete system. Among the oldest surviving double entry records are those of Rinerio and Baldo Fini (1296–1305). They included receivables and payables, expenses, and operating results, but no capital account. The oldest known Venetian accounts are contained in two ledgers of Donaldo Soranzo and Brothers, merchants. The first of these (1410–1417) also employed a partial double entry system, in which every debit had a credit, and merchandise accounts were closed to profit and loss, but profit and loss accounts were never combined or closed to capital.

Those merchants who adopted double entry and those who did not had similar motives for keeping accounts. At a minimum, they had to keep track of credit dealings, inventory balances, and partners' capitals. The result was a sliding scale of care within the double entry system, in which the accounts of customers, suppliers, and partners were kept current and accurate, but no great effort was made to verify total operating results. James Winjum wrote that "double entry brought the concept of capital into the accounting records." But until the nineteenth century most businessmen still valued it chiefly for its ability to bring order to their accounts.

Accounting theory began with attempts to answer questions about the nature of capital. The English classical economists, who were contemporary with the first accounting theorists, emphasized the distinction between a stock of wealth (capital) and its flow (income). At this same time, corporate accountants were given the tasks of calculating the amount of retained earnings available for dividends and of making sure that invested capital was maintained intact while fixed asset balances were being converted to expense. For these and other reasons, the capital account became associated with ownership rather than being simply a residual balance. The accounting equation was rediscovered, and a more strategic view was taken of the bookkeeping process, giving less importance to the exchange of values between accounts and more to the effect of transactions on capital.

In 1718 Alexander Malcolm touched on the essence of proprietary theory when he distinguished between the totality of a merchant's capital and its constituent parts. He saw that while some transactions merely shifted assets from one account to another, others raised or lowered total capital, changing the proprietor's wealth at the same time that they altered net assets.

James Fulton, a bookkeeper with the Board of Revenue in Bengal, wrote in *British-Indian Book-keeping* (1800) that owner's equity is the collective expression of all other accounts, which "form merely the particulars of it: and the grand aim of double entry is, to ascertain the true state of the stock (capital) account." He also perceived that the balance of capital is not only the difference between assets and liabilities but is also the owner's original investment plus and minus operating changes since the company's inception. To illustrate this, Fulton prepared a forerunner retained earnings statement that showed the effect of all transactions on capital and reconciled the capital account balance with net changes in asset and liability accounts.

The exposition of proprietary theory was completed by Frederic William Cronhelm in *Double Entry by Single* (1818). Taking Fulton's book as a point of departure, Cronhelm emphasized the equivalence of total capital with its constituent parts and argued that the purpose of bookkeeping "is to show the owner at all times the value of his total capital, and of every part of it." In Cronhelm's algebraic approach to transaction analysis, the capital account became a mathematical equilibrating device, by inference a credit item opposite assets. Transactions affected the accounting equation by increasing or decreasing assets, liabilities, or capital. Cronhelm envisioned a series of asset conversions during a firm's operating cycle, with income entering the capital account as a net increase in proprietorship. Expense and revenue accounts, including profit and loss, were created to avoid the inconvenience of recording every change in wealth directly to capital. Cronhelm treated them as subdivisions of owner's equity.

Considering accounting a branch of mathematics, Charles Ezra Sprague in 1880 visualized operating results in terms of an algebraic equation ("assets equal liabilities plus proprietorship") that must always be kept in balance. The proprietary theory was presented in complete form by Sprague in *The Philosophy of Accounts* (1907), and also in Hatfield's *Modern Accounting* (1909). Neither of them added anything to the system described by earlier writers. But they expressed a doctrine whose time had come and whose underlying assumptions quickly dominated American textbook presentations. The proprietor is the center of accounting interest. Accounting records are kept and statements prepared from his viewpoint and are intended to measure and analyze his net worth. Assets represent things owned by the proprietor or benefits accruing to him. Liabilities are his debts. The capital account shows the firm's value to its owner. As Werner Sombart put it in *Der Moderne Kapitalismus*, capital had finally become "wealth for profit controlled by double entry bookkeeping."

Michael Chatfield

Bibliography

Hatfield, H.R. "The Early Use of 'Capital,'" *Quarterly Journal of Economics*, November 1934, pp. 162–163.

Littleton, A.C. *Accounting Evolution to 1900*. New York: American Institute Publishing, 1933. Reprint. New York: Russell and Russell, 1966.

Winjum, J.O. *The Role of Accounting in the Economic Development of England, 1500–1750.* Urbana, IL: Center for International Education and Research in Accounting, 1972.

See also BALANCE ACCOUNT; CASH BASIS ACCOUNTING; CLOSING ENTRIES AND PROCEDURES; CRONHELM, FREDERIC WILLIAM; DIVIDENDS; DONALDO SORANZO AND BROTHERS; DOUBLE ENTRY BOOKKEEPING: ORIGINS; FINI, RINERIO; HATFIELD, HENRY RAND; INCOME-DETERMINATION THEORY; INCOME STATEMENT/INCOME ACCOUNT; KEMPTEN, VALENTIN MENNHER VON; MANZONI, DOMENICO; PEELE, JAMES; PROPRIETARY THEORY; PROPRIETORSHIP; SINGLE ENTRY BOOKKEEPING; SOMBART, WERNER; SPRAGUE, CHARLES EZRA; TRIAL BALANCE

Capital Maintenance

Between the fifteenth and the eighteenth centuries most businesses were small, trading tended to be sporadic, and profits were calculated separately for individual voyages or commodities. In contrast, as A.C. Littleton put it, corporations were "the catalyst in whose presence the permanent investment of capital assets was united with the mechanism for measuring income." The corporation gave legal validity to the idea of business continuity and radically changed accounting technique. Whereas bookkeeping for a completed venture was entirely historical, for a going concern it became a problem of viewing segments in a stream of continuous activity. Not only were results much more tentative, but the whole emphasis of record keeping shifted toward the future.

With business continuity came a need for capital maintenance. A corporation cannot rationally claim to have indefinite life while dissipating its invested capital. Both limited liability and the economic need for permanent investments required that paid in capital be kept in the business. The existence of large permanent assets made capital maintenance an economic necessity. A corporation had to keep its capital intact to ensure real continuity of existence and to preserve its economic power so that investors, employees, customers, and all others who depended on it would not lose because of its diminished wealth and earning ability. The statutory recognition of limited liability created

a legal obligation to preserve capital intact. The law denied corporate creditors recourse to a stockholder's personal assets, but it compensated them by protecting their claims against corporate assets.

To make sure that invested capital was maintained intact, a series of court decisions, reinforced by statutes in England and the United States, required that dividends could be declared only from current and accumulated income. By the year 1700, English common law included two restrictions on dividend distributions. A "capital impairment rule" specified that no dividend should be paid that left the value of the remaining assets below the firm's contribute capital. A "profits test" limited dividends to the total of current and retained earnings. The profits test was codified in the Companies Act of 1862. One or the other of these rules still governs dividend distributions in many American states.

As a result, as Basil S. Yamey said, "what had often been incidental, became central." Calculating the amount of profit available for dividends became the corporate accountant's most important task. It required that a sharp distinction be made between assets and expenses and that revenues be associated with the costs of producing a particular period's income.

But for many years the law did not specify the components of profit and capital in sufficient detail to make its capital maintenance rules effective. Except where fraud was involved, the courts were reluctant lawgivers. The business community was expected to develop its own standards. Court decisions were ambiguous on the treatment of unrealized appreciation of fixed assets and on the distinction between capital and revenue expenditures. Case law on asset valuation was sparse, sometimes contradictory, and it was often hard to tell how broadly a particular decision applied.

The rule that dividend payments could not reduce capital below the amount paid in by stockholders was weakened by two English court decisions. In *Lee v. Neuchatel Asphalte Company* (1889), the Court of Appeals ruled that in calculating profits from which dividends were to be paid, a firm could ignore declines in the value of depletable assets. This decision was reinforced by *re Kingston Cotton Mills* (1896), in which the court held that depreciation in the value of fixed assets did not affect a company's ability to declare dividends.

Corporate managers of the early 1800s had great freedom in their choice of accounting methods. They could in each company very largely make the rules by which assets were valued and income was measured. Financial overstatement reflected the mood of entrepreneurs in a rapidly industrializing and expanding economy. And overstatement worked to a corporation's short run advantage. Firms trying to raise capital by selling stocks and bonds to the public had every incentive to inflate asset and income figures. High reported profits encouraged investment, increased the market values of securities, and raised executive salaries to the extent that these were tied to earnings.

The accounting methods in use also led to overstatement. Manufacturers commonly accounted for depreciable assets as if they were unsold merchandise. Plant and equipment were revalued at the end of each accounting period, increases as well as decreases in value being charged directly to profit and loss. In contrast, most railroads, utilities, and other public service corporations used some type of replacement accounting. Original investments in assets were capitalized and never depreciated. Asset replacements and maintenance charges were expensed. Since capital investments created no charge to expense until they were replaced, this method made railroads seem an attractive investment by maximizing reported income during the early years of their life cycle when they most needed capital.

Richard P. Brief has demonstrated that reported profits during the nineteenth century were materially higher than they would have been if today's accounting methods had been in use. That is, if periodic depreciation had been taken, if asset appreciation had not been credited to income, and if a more consistent distinction had been made between capital and revenue expenditures, earnings and dividends would have been substantially lower.

An accounting policy of systematic understatement seemed a natural antidote to management's known tendency to overstate. Its early advocates were creditors who wished to protect paid in capital against excessive dividend payments. Acceptance of this policy depended largely on stockholder attitudes. Accounting methods that favored short term speculators often continued until investors became willing to forego high current dividends to assure larger ones in the future. For example, after 1850 a tendency to understate profits began to replace the deliberate overstatement that had characterized the speculative inception of the railroads.

The emerging accounting profession had its own reasons to prefer financial understatement. As Robert Henry Parker said, it had grown up in an environment of "bankruptcies, failures, frauds, and disputes" that filled accountants with "a vivid sense of disaster." Business depressions occurred about every 10 years in Victorian England. The accounting response was to provide for all foreseeable future contingencies, even if such contingencies were not precisely definable or measurable. By 1880 English auditors had made the writedown of obsolete or damaged goods to lower of cost or market prices a standard procedure. Auditors also verified that dividends had not reduced legal capital. Textbooks and journal articles of the 1880s began to take the view that assets should be valued at historical cost less depreciation due to wear and tear, with all other fluctuations in value being ignored.

During this period the pitfalls of optimism were demonstrated by a succession of bankruptcies and fraud trials. Auditors were repeatedly named as defendants in lawsuits brought by investors who claimed that financial statements overstated net income or capital. But almost never was an accounting firm sued on the grounds that audited statements were too conservative. Accountants therefore had reason to believe that a conservative resolution of doubtful issues would shield them from legal liability. To avoid the legal risks that might result from paying dividends out of capital, they tended to go to the opposite extreme by deliberately understating asset values and profits. Judicial rulings on capital maintenance gave conservatism legal backing at one of the most formative stages in the development of asset valuation and income measurement concepts.

The accounting literature of the time and other evidence suggest that conservatism was widely ineffective in preventing managerial manipulation. Company directors simply had too much latitude in their stewardship of invested capital. In effect the corporate manager had it both ways. By overstating assets and income, and paying dividends from capital, he could favorably impress potential investors. If on the other hand he chose to understate, he could create secret reserves, shift profits from year to year, and present an attractive appearance of stability, while distorting analyses of managerial effectiveness and future earnings potential.

Before the twentieth century, capital maintenance was exclusively a financial concept. That is, legal capital was to be preserved by distributing to stockholders an amount that left the corporation as well off in dollar terms at the end of the period as it had been at the beginning. Between 1900 and 1910, William Morse Cole, Arthur Lowes Dickinson, and others expanded this concept to include the maintenance of physical capital. In the physical capital, or operating maintenance approach, capital is maintained only if a company retains sufficient profits to replace its existing assets or has the ability to produce a constant supply of goods and services. In measuring physical capital maintenance, revenues are matched with the current costs of productive assets. Instead of being included in income, holding gains and losses are considered adjustments to stockholders' equity.

In *Stabilized Accounting* (1936), Henry Whitcomb Sweeney advocated a physical concept of capital maintenance. Sweeney favored not only general price level adjustments and the calculation of purchasing power gains and losses, but replacement cost valuations of inventories and plant assets, to measure capital changes in productivity terms. Sweeney's work had little immediate impact because inflation was not a problem during the 1930s.

A 30 percent increase in the consumer price index between 1945 and 1948 produced the first popular interest in price level adjustments and replacement cost accounting. Inflation on this scale impaired stockholders' equity and encouraged the creation of secret reserves and the whole paraphernalia of conservatism. Price level changes also put the balance sheet and income statement in conflict, forcing the accountant constantly to choose between them. They provoked criticisms of unrealistic statement figures in audited reports. But initially the accounting profession rejected radical alternatives to historical cost in favor of solutions that it hoped would ease inflationary pressures without upsetting orthodox valuation theory.

But for management the problem was entirely different and far more critical. The doctrine that value equaled cost was unhelpful to companies faced with the need to replace assets bought in the 1920s and 1930s at prices that had more than doubled. Depreciation on such assets did not begin to cover replacement costs at 1947 levels. This led to sales prices too low to recover the real costs of using equipment. Depreciation based on understated asset values also inflated reported income, creating demands for higher wages, dividends, and tax payments at a time when cash was urgently needed for asset replacement. It is estimated that almost half of the $17 billion reported as profits by American companies in 1947 was the result of inflation rather than operations.

Such exceptional conditions forced major companies to go beyond existing accounting rules. In the first quarter of 1947, United States Steel Corporation deducted 30 percent ($26.3 million) more than normal depreciation charges from income, calling it "wear and exhaustion of facilities" based on price level indices and engineering estimates of plant replacement costs. In the same year, E.I. DuPont de Nemours and Company wrote off in advance of use that part of new plant construction costs which it deemed excessive because of prevailing high prices. Also in 1947, Chrysler Corporation began charging depreciation on historical cost at an accelerated rate, on the grounds that it had made new asset purchases at prices that were only justified by exceptional sales possibilities predicted for the next few years.

U.S. Steel's auditors took exception to its supplementary depreciation charges because they ultimately would have totaled more than the historical costs of the assets. DuPont also received a qualified auditor's opinion because it had written off a large part of its new assets' cost before their use, violating the matching concept. The Securities and Exchange Commission (SEC) issued a bulletin rejecting the use of replacement costs, and of course neither method was allowed for tax purposes. Finding no institutional support, both companies abandoned their procedures in 1948. But the "Chrysler formula," though its effect was similar, was theoretically respectable, being limited to historical cost and based on amortization over a period of economic usefulness. It led eventually to the accelerated depreciation provisions of the 1954 tax code.

Last in, First out (LIFO) and accelerated depreciation may be seen either as limited counterinflationary measures or as palliatives whose effect was to delay any real solution to the capital maintenance problem during the moderate inflation of the 1950s. Both reinforced an older tradition of balance sheet conservatism, so much so that taxpayers were not allowed to use LIFO together with lower of cost or market inventory valuations. Both gave precedence to management's need for cash retention and asset replacement, even at the expense of the accountant's desire for more precise asset valuations. Neither was designed to cope with an environment in which constant price increases were a normal business expectation. Nor was either effectively used for this purpose. Both became devices for deferring income taxes in the guise of making partial price level adjustments.

In 1938–1939 the tax code had been revised to permit LIFO inventory valuations in certain industries that were subject to cyclical changes in the prices of raw materials. The intention was to avoid taxing unearned income. As Maurice Moonitz said, LIFO was compensation for the lack of an income averaging provision in the tax codes of the 1930s. When instead of cyclical ups and downs, the postwar years brought continual price rises, LIFO no longer served its original purpose. Its new rationale was as a substitute for price level changes, but the real motive for its widespread use continued to be its ability to postpone tax payments in periods of rising prices.

Accelerated depreciation was more defensible theoretically and had been advocated by Henry Rand Hatfield and William Andrew Paton during the 1920s. If assets are future economic benefits, one goal of depreciation policy should be to recover enough dollars each period to equal capital consumption in original dollars. When prices rise, straight line depreciation on historical cost fails to do this; accelerated depreciation tends to more closely approximate the asset's loss of economic value. Though it may not compensate for inflationary pressures throughout the asset's useful life, fast depreciation can promote internal financing by improving company liquidity. It also provides a tax incentive for replacing productive assets. Finally, it does for plant and equipment what LIFO does for inventories, transferring the bulk of asset costs to the income statement before inflation can make major inroads on their book value.

In 1979 the Financial Accounting Standards Board (FASB) issued Statement on Financial Accounting Standards No. 33, "Financial Reporting and Changing Prices," which required certain large corporations to report supplemental information about the current cost and price level adjusted values of their assets. Statement No. 33 specified that purchasing power gains and losses on monetary items and changes in current costs net of inflation should be excluded from income. The statement also included a discussion of financial and physical capital maintenance, but the Board expressed no preference, though the exposure draft that preceded Statement No. 33 had favored financial capital maintenance. Five years later, the Statement No. 33 requirements were allowed to lapse, bringing to an end FASB attempts to mandate capital maintenance in the United States.

Michael Chatfield

Bibliography

Brief, R.P. "Nineteenth Century Accounting Error," *Journal of Accounting Research*, Spring 1965, pp. 12–31.

Gellein, O.S. "Capital Maintenance: A Neglected Notion," *Accounting Historians Journal*, Fall 1987, pp. 59–69.

Gynther, R.S. "Capital Maintenance, Price Changes, and Profit Determination," *Accounting Review*, December 1970, pp. 712–730.

Kehl, D. *Corporate Dividends*. New York: Ronald Press, 1941. Reprint. New York: Arno Press, 1976.

Sterling, R.R., and K.W. Lemke. *Maintenance of Capital*. Houston: Scholars Book, 1982.

Wilcox, E. "Fluctuating Price Levels in Relation to Accounts." In *Handbook of Modern Accounting Theory*, edited by M. Backer, pp. 320–338. Englewood Cliffs, NJ: Prentice-Hall, 1955.

Yamey, B.S. "The Case Law Relating to Company Dividends." In *Studies in Accounting Theory*, edited by W.T. Baxter and S. Davidson, pp. 428–442. Homewood, IL: Irwin, 1962.

See also BRIEF, RICHARD P.; COLE, WILLIAM MORSE; COMPANIES ACTS; CONSERVATISM; CONTINUITY; CORPORATIONS: EVOLUTION; DEPRECIATION; DICKINSON, ARTHUR LOWES; DIVIDENDS; DOUBLE ACCOUNT METHOD; FIXED ASSETS; HATFIELD, HENRY RAND; HISTORICAL COST; INFLATION ACCOUNTING; *KINGSTON COTTON MILLS COMPANY;* LAST IN, FIRST OUT (LIFO); *LEE V. NEUCHATEL ASPHALTE COMPANY;* LEGAL LIABILITY OF AUDITORS; LIMITED LIABILITY; MANIPULATION OF INCOME; PAID IN CAPITAL; PATON, WILLIAM ANDREW; PIXLEY, FRANCIS WILLIAM;

RAILROAD ACCOUNTING (U.S.); RETAINED EARNINGS APPROPRIATIONS; SECURITIES AND EXCHANGE COMMISSION; STEWARDSHIP; SWEENEY, HENRY WHITCOMB; UNITED STATES STEEL CORPORATION

Capital Stock

The issuance of corporate stock eventually fulfilled two imperatives of large-scale business organization: transferable ownership rights, and limited liability for investors.

Italian *commenda* partnerships were direct ancestors of the limited liability corporation. During the Renaissance, investors evaded church usury laws, which held that money was barren, by entrusting their cash to overseas traders for a share in the profits of joint ventures. Besides combining venture capital and trading ability, the partnership contract *en commendite* established the precedent that while trading partners were fully liable for partnership debts, a nonparticipating investor might get a share of profits while risking only the amount of his investment.

Influenced by Italian practice, many European commercial codes made a distinction between the liability of active and silent partners, holding the latter responsible only to the extent of their contribution. The French Code Savary of 1673 provided specifically for limited partnerships in the Italian manner. But in England, the concept of partnership rested on the agency relationship, in which each partner could bind the others and all were jointly and severally liable for debts. This made corporations hard to establish in the nation that first required them on a large scale.

The discovery of America and the opening of sea routes to China and India turned investors' attention to overseas trading. The earliest British "Companies of Adventurers" formed to carry on this trade were partnerships, but as with the Italian *commendas*, certain partners wished to trade actively while others merely wanted to invest. In a high-risk environment, some form of limited liability was needed if investor and adventurer were to collaborate effectively.

The first joint-stock companies were partnerships with a few corporate features. They generally had limited life and imposed unlimited liability for company debts, but in many cases they issued transferable shares. Their purposes ranged from trade to colonization and included military expeditions and voyages of discovery. Parliament preferred them to competitive businesses because they were easier to regulate and tax. They were granted monopoly rights partly as compensation for the large initial investments such ventures required. The Russia Company (lumber), the Virginia Company (tobacco), the East India Company (spices), and the Hudson's Bay Company (furs) were four of the best known. In chartering companies such as the Bank of England, whose activities touched vital national interests, the government allowed shareholders individual immunity from the bankruptcy laws if the firm failed. The effect was to make them liable for company debts only up to the amount unpaid on their shares.

The East India Company, chartered by Queen Elizabeth in 1600, evolved in just 60 years from a series of speculative voyages with terminable stocks to a continuing corporation with permanently invested capital. Between 1600 and 1617 the company sponsored 113 voyages, each financed with newly subscribed capital and treated as a separate venture. This made liquidation necessary after each voyage so that investors who wished to drop out might do so and new "adventurers" might be admitted. It also meant the stock was not readily negotiable, since there was no way to enter a venture in progress except by buying unissued stock or a fraction of a share held by an existing investor. At the end of each voyage, assets as well as earnings were subject to "divisions" among the shareholders. Profit was easily measured by the individual stockholder: He gained to the extent that he got back more than he had paid in.

But ships, trading posts, and other long-lived assets tended to carry over from one venture to the next, until finally the company's accounts became a jumble of successive voyages. As unliquidated balances or "remains" of earlier voyages were merged with later ones, it became necessary for the company's accountants to juggle the assets and profits of many ventures in various stages of completion. Also, during the seventeenth century trading abroad developed into a fairly continuous process requiring permanent capital. It became more useful to view the business as a going concern.

In 1613 the East India Company stopped issuing stocks for each venture and began selling four year subscriptions, with one-fourth of the stock price to be paid each year and used to finance that year's voyages. A new charter in 1657 established the principle of permanently

C

invested capital and extended the right to transfer individual shares before liquidation. Stock was to be priced by the company, first at the end of seven years, then every three years thereafter. Any shareholder could at any time sell his stock at these prices. This not only simplified the problem of transferring shares but made it easier for the company to attract capital. In 1661, following the logic of permanently invested capital, the company's governor announced that future distributions would consist of "dividends" paid from profit rather than the familiar "divisions" of profits and assets.

Early in the seventeenth century, certain English corporations extended a type of limited liability to their investors as an inducement to buy shares. The "par value doctrine" did not protect stockholders' personal assets from company creditors but merely guaranteed subscribers to fully paid shares that the corporation would not call on them for further capital contributions.

Today's par value shares are issued with a nominal price printed on each stock certificate. This par value may have no relationship to the stock's original sale price or subsequent market value. Its purpose is to establish the contingent liability of stockholders if the corporation becomes insolvent or bankrupt. If stock is issued at or above par value and the corporation later incurs liabilities it cannot repay, stockholders may lose their entire investment but cannot lose more. But if stock is issued below par value and the corporation cannot subsequently repay its debts, the creditors can force original purchasers of the stock to pay into the corporation the amount of discount on their shares. In that case, stockholders may lose their original investment plus an amount equal to the discount at which they purchased the stock. This contingent liability is due to the corporation's creditors, not to the corporation. It becomes an actual liability only if the amount of discount is needed to pay creditors when the corporation is liquidated.

Michael Chatfield

Bibliography
Littleton, A.C. *Accounting Evolution to 1900.* New York: American Institute Publishing, 1933. Reprint. New York: Russell and Russell, 1966.

See also COMMENDA CONTRACTS; CORPORATIONS: EVOLUTION; DIVIDENDS; EAST INDIA COMPANY; LIMITED LIABILITY; PAR VALUE DOCTRINE; PARTNERSHIP ACCOUNTING; SAVARY, JACQUES

Carpenter v. Hall

Ernest M. Hall, president of Western Equities (Westec), inflated the price of his company's shares by making speculative purchases and sales of Westec securities and by choosing accounting methods that maximized current income. Westec's common stock rose from a low of $2.00 per share in 1964 to a high of $67.125 per share on April 12, 1965. During this period Westec's management acquired 14 companies, mainly by exchanging Westec stock for shares of the acquired firms. However, in July and August 1966, Westec share prices declined, and several proposed acquisitions fell through.

On August 25, 1966, the Securities and Exchange Commission suspended trading in Westec securities when it became known that Hall had placed orders for about 160,000 shares of Westec common stock without making adequate payment arrangements. Western Equities became bankrupt. Hall and other Westec officers were convicted on a number of criminal counts, including improper security transactions.

Westec's trustee in bankruptcy charged that the company's reported earnings in 1964 and 1965 were inflated partly because the pooling of interests method was improperly applied to six corporations acquired by Westec. The audit report was held open until March 26, 1965, the date when three of the six companies were acquired, so that the prior year's earnings of all six companies could be included in Westec's 1964 consolidated income. The effect of retroactively pooling these three companies was to increase 1964 income by 23 percent. Accounting Principles Board Opinion No. 16 later forbade this practice.

The Westec case suggests that when accounting methods are chosen to achieve a certain effect—in this case, to recognize revenues as soon as possible and defer expenses as long as possible—auditors may be held liable for certifying to misleading financial statements, even if the methods chosen are "generally accepted" accounting alternatives.

Michael Chatfield

Bibliography
Briloff, A. "Dirty Pooling," *Accounting Review*, October 1967, pp. 489–496.

Carpenter v. Hall, 311 F. Supp. 1099 (S. D. Texas 1970).

Ernst and Ernst v. United States District Court for the Southern District of Texas, 439 F. 2d 1288 (C.A. 5 Texas 1971).

Fiflis, T., and H. Kripke. *Accounting for Business Lawyers*. St. Paul: West, 1971, pp. 423–427.

See also AUDITOR'S REPORT; *ESCOTT V. BARCHRIS CONSTRUCTION CORPORATION*

Cash Basis Accounting

Modern financial accounting grew out of an earlier tradition of recording cash receipts and payments. Pre-double entry bookkeeping was primarily concerned with resources rather than profits. Medieval stewards kept accounts not for the entity's sake, but for their own, to control assets for which they were responsible. There was no clear distinction between capital and income, no cost accounting to build up asset values by components, and no tradition of precise income measurement to impose a discipline on asset valuation and amortization. The accounting systems in use did not favor data accumulation and did not look to the future.

In contrast, double entry bookkeeping began with the need of Italian merchant-bankers for debt records. The vital interests of these men lay in the future, and they emphasized this in their words of accountability ("shall give, shall have"). But the development of double entry did not end cash basis accounting. Luca Pacioli's *Summa de Arithmetica* (1494) illustrated a cash basis double entry system. In his time and for hundreds of years afterward, most businesses kept single entry records that amounted to little more than lists of receipts and payments. Even double entry accounts could be quite crude. Because of the sporadic nature of venture trading, and the fact that different ventures had very different profit margins, merchants preferred to open a separate account for each consignment of goods and leave it open until everything was sold. At that time, the venture account was ruled and its balance transferred to profit and loss, which at longer intervals was closed to capital. In each case, profit was considered earned when the venture was liquidated. Accruals and deferrals were unnecessary.

The main technical improvement between the sixteenth and nineteenth centuries was the more frequent use in later accounts of double entry's summarizing ability. James Winjum concluded that "double entry brought the concept of capital into the accounting records." But the eighteenth century merchant still valued it chiefly for its ability to bring order to his accounts. Most problems we associate with profit finding and asset valuation concerned him hardly at all. Without the paraphernalia of accruals, matching, or periodic balancing, his venture accounts measured the results of particular operations, while paging through the ledger gave him some idea of overall activity. But he developed neither a clear concept of income nor systematic procedures for judging the success or failure of his business over a period of time.

Operating continuity and the advent of the corporation required periodic reckonings as a prelude to dividend payments. Attempts to measure the income earned during a particular time period led naturally to a system of accruals and deferrals. It was now the use of goods and services, not merely their purchase, that created expense, and sales rather than cash collections which signaled that income had been earned.

Michael Chatfield

Bibliography

Jack, S.M. "An Historical Defence of Single Entry Book-keeping," *Abacus*, December 1966, pp. 137–158.

Littleton, A.C. *Accounting Evolution to 1900*. New York: American Institute Publishing, 1933. Reprint. New York: Russell and Russell, 1966.

Winjum, J. "Accounting in its Age of Stagnation," *Accounting Review*, October 1970, pp. 743–761.

See also CASH FLOW ACCOUNTING; CONTINUITY; CORPORATIONS: EVOLUTION; DIVIDENDS; DOUBLE ENTRY BOOKKEEPING: ORIGINS; LEDGER; MANORIAL ACCOUNTING; MEDIEVAL ACCOUNTING; PACIOLI, LUCA; REALIZATION; SINGLE ENTRY BOOKKEEPING

Cash Flow Accounting

Cash flow accounting (CFA) is a term used by accountants and others to describe a system of external reporting designed to disclose the reporting entity's financial performance in cash terms. CFA is based on a presentation of related cash inflows and outflows describing the operating, financing, and investing activities of the reporting entity. The basic CFA reporting model is OCF+FCF-ICF-TCF-DCF=ΔC; where OCF is the net cash flow from trading operations; FCF is the net cash flow from external funding sources; ICF is the net cash flow relating to capital expenditures; TCF is the net cash flow for payment of tax liabilities; DCF is the cash outflow for dividends; and ΔC is the reconciling periodic change in net cash resources. Alternative models can be presented using these basic elements, and depending on the sign attributable to each element.

CFA, as defined above, is a relatively new phenomenon in the history of financial accounting. It gradually appeared in this form in the accounting literature of the late 1960s and early 1970s and has since become a significant part of both accounting theory and practice. However, in its most basic form of a simple matching of total cash inflows and outflows, CFA can be argued to be one of the oldest forms of accounting and reporting in monetary terms.

CFA was the main system of accounting for business activity prior to the nineteenth century (as, for example, in accounts charge and discharge). However, the accounting accruals and allocation procedures that resulted from the costing revolution of the nineteenth and early twentieth centuries caused CFA to be relegated to the role of the basis for a more complex accounting for periodic income and financial position. In this respect, CFA should be distinguished from funds-flow accounting and reporting that originated in the early twentieth century as a means of describing in accrual and allocation terms the periodic change in the financial position of the reporting entity.

Little explicit interest in an external reporting of CFA data appears to have been expressed by accountants of the twentieth century until the late 1960s. The reason for this general failure to appreciate the reporting potential of CFA is likely the custom and habit of accounting reporters, users, and auditors to rely totally on the conventional income-orientated reporting system. This is not to say that there was no interest in reporting in CFA terms prior to the late 1960s. John W. Coughlan (1960, 1962, 1964) in the United States, and Harold C. Edey (1963, 1970) in Great Britain, both presented arguments in the early 1960s for a reporting of forecast cash flows. Their ideas, however, appear to have been ignored at that time.

But, in the late 1960s and early 1970s, two British academics, G.H. Lawson (1969, 1971) and Thomas A. Lee (1971, 1972), separately began to develop normative accounting arguments and reporting prescriptions for a full CFA system of external financial statements. Their research initially was concerned with a perceived need for entities to report multiperiod forecast cash flows relating to their operating, financing, and investing activities, and to also disclose the realized cash flows from these activities. Their proposals were aimed at enabling report users to assess entity financial performance in accounting terms that avoided the manipulatory effects of accounting accruals and allocations.

Both Lawson and Lee prescribed a cashflow reporting in terms compatible with the structure outlined and defined above. In particular, they argued that such a CFA system of reporting is relevant to a variety of investment and other decisions, assessment of management's financial stewardship, monitoring of the reporting entity's liquidity and financial condition, and avoidance of the subjectivity in financial reporting caused by periodic cost allocations.

The initial response was muted. CFA appeared to be of interest mainly to accounting academics in Great Britain, Australia, and New Zealand as part of the "golden age" of normative accounting theory of the 1960s and 1970s. It was ignored in the United States. The main reason for the relatively low-key response may have been that it was part of a larger debate in the 1970s and 1980s on the need for a reporting alternative to the much criticized historical-cost system. CFA ideas tended to get swamped by a larger literature on alternative current-value accounting systems.

Nevertheless, during the repeated corporate liquidity crises in the United States, Great Britain and elsewhere during the 1970s and 1980s, three important developments took place that solidified CFA's place as a means of improving external reporting. First, CFA ideas appeared more widely in the accounting literature, including most accounting-theory texts, by the late 1980s. Second, a significant research effort emerged to test the utility and predictability of CFA-based data. Third, accounting policy-makers and standard-setters such as the American Institute of Certified Public Accountants (AICPA) and the Financial Accounting Standards Board (FASB) initiated studies to propose a feasible reporting of CFA information.

However, this enlarged support was accompanied in the 1980s by criticisms of the CFA arguments presented in the 1970s. Critics such as B.A. Rutherford (1982) and Don A. Egginton (1984) in Great Britain and George J. Staubus (1989) in the United States articulated previously spoken doubts about CFA's prescribed relevance for entity performance assessment, and reliability with respect to the avoidance of accounting allocations. In response, Lawson and Lee extended their original CFA ideas. Lee (1981b, 1985) presented an amended CFA system, incorporating income and financial-position statements by using net realizable values as the valuation basis and reporting both realized and unrealized cash flows. Lawson (1985) argued for the reporting of the entity's market capitalization as evidence of the value of its past capital expenditure.

Despite their apparent lack of interest in the non-U.S. normative arguments for CFA reporting, U.S. accounting researchers led the way in the 1980s research effort to test the utility of CFA data. This effort was concerned with three specific areas. The first was whether CFA data provided additional information to that contained in the conventional reporting set, and as impounded in stock market prices. The second area related to the reaction of the stock market to CFA disclosures. The third area assessed the predictive ability of CFA data with respect to business failure. No specific or consistent conclusions were reached regarding the utility of CFA, and more needs to be done to develop research models that adequately reflect the use of CFA in practice. In particular, such research has tended to concentrate on the utility of data about operating cash flow.

In both the United States and Great Britain, the late 1980s and early 1990s saw the introduction of specific standards requiring the reporting of statements of realized cash flow as replacements for the allocation-based funds statements introduced in the 1960s and 1970s. It is clear that accounting policymakers became aware in the 1980s of the need to inform report users of both entity profitability and liquidity.

Besides Lawson and Lee, contributors to the history of ideas for CFA reporting include, in the United States, Loyd C. Heath (1978, the need to move away from conventional funds reporting), and Yuji Ijiri (1978, the development of a historic cost-based cash recovery rate as a substitute for the entity's internal rate of return); and, in Great Britain, A.J. Arnold and R.I. Wearing (1988, variations on the Lawson and Lee arguments), and A.W. Stark (1992, relating CFA data to entity performance assessment). The two biblio-graphical citations to this entry provide a history of CFA ideas to 1980 (Lee) and extending to 1990 (Arnold and Wearing).

Thomas A. Lee

Bibliography

Arnold, A.J., and R.T. Wearing. *A Report on Cash-Flow Statements/Accounting.* London: Institute of Chartered Accountants in England and Wales and Institute of Chartered Accountants of Scotland, 1991.

Arnold, A.J., and R.T. Wearing. "Cash Flows, Exit Prices and British Airways," *Journal of Business Finance and Accounting* (Eng.), Autumn 1988, pp. 311–334.

Coughlan, J.W. "Accounting and Capital Budgeting," *Business Quarterly*, Fall 1962, pp. 39–48.

———. "Contrast Between Financial-Statement and Discounted-Cash-Flow Methods of Comparing Projects," *NAA Bulletin*, June 1960, pp. 5–17.

———. "Funds and Income," *NAA Bulletin*, September 1964, pp. 23–34.

Edey, H.C. "Accounting Principles and Business Reality," *Accountancy* (Eng.), November 1963, pp. 998–1002; December 1963, pp. 1083–1088.

———. "The Nature of Profit," *Accounting and Business Research* (Eng.), Winter 1970, pp. 50–55.

Egginton, D.A. "In Defense of Profit Measurement: Some Limitations of Cash Flow and Value Added on Performance Measures of External Reporting," *Accounting and Business Research* (Eng.), Spring 1984, pp. 99–111.

Heath, Loyd C. *Financial Reporting and the Evaluation of Solvency.* Accounting Research Monograph No. 3. New York: American Institute of Certified Public Accountants, 1978.

Ijiri, Y. "Cash-flow Accounting and Its Structure," *Journal of Accounting, Auditing and Finance* (Eng.), Summer 1978, pp. 331–348.

Lawson, G.H. "Cash-flow Accounting," *Accountant* (Eng.), October 28, 1971, pp. 586–589; November 4, 1971, pp. 620–622.

———. "Profit Maximization Via Financial Management," *Management Decision* (Eng.), Winter 1969, pp. 6–12.

———. "The Measurement of Corporate Performance on a Cash Flow Basis: A Reply to Mr. Egginton," *Accounting and Business Research* (Eng.), Spring 1985, pp. 99–108.

Lee, T.A. "A Case for Cash Flow Reporting," *Journal of Business Finance* (Eng.), Summer 1972, pp. 27–36.

———. "Cash Flow Accounting and Corporate Financial Reporting." In *British Essays in Accounting Research*, edited by A. Hopwood and M. Bromwich, pp. 63–78. London: Pitman, 1981a.

———. "Cash Flow Accounting, Profit and Performance Measurement: A Response to a Challenge," *Accounting and Business Research* (Eng.), Spring 1985, pp. 93–97.

———. "Cash Flow Accounting's Recent History: A Kuhnian Interpretation of a Changing Accounting Emphasis," pp. 19–37 in T.A. Lee, editor, *Cash Flow Reporting: A Recent History of an Accounting Practice*. New York: Garland, 1993.

———. "Goodwill—an Example of Will-o'-the-Wisp Accounting," *Accounting and Business Research* (Eng.), Autumn 1971, pp. 318–328.

———. "Reporting Cash Flows and Net Realizable Values," *Accounting and Business Research*," Spring 1981b, pp. 163–170.

Rutherford, B.A. "The Interpretation of Cash Flow Reports and the Other Allocation Problem," *Abacus* (Australia), June 1982, pp. 40–49.

Stark, A.W. "Problems in Measuring the Cash Recovery Rate and Measurement Error in Estimates of the Firm IRR," Working Paper 92/02. Colchester: University of Essex, 1992.

Staubus, G.J. "Cash Flow Accounting and Liquidity: Cash Flow Potential and Performance," *Accounting and Business Research* (Eng.), Spring 1989, pp. 161–169.

See also ACCRUAL ACCOUNTING; CASH BASIS ACCOUNTING; EFFICIENT MARKET HYPOTHESIS; FINANCIAL-STATEMENT ANALYSIS; FUNDS FLOW STATEMENT; HISTORICAL COST; IJIRI, YUJI; LIQUIDITY: ACCOUNTING MEASUREMENT; MAUTZ, ROBERT K.; OBJECTIVITY; STEWARDSHIP

Center for International Education and Research in Accounting

In 1962 the University of Illinois Board of Trustees established the Center for International Education and Research in Accounting as a part of the Department of Accountancy of the University of Illinois at Urbana-Champaign. Believed to have been the first international accounting center, the center was established to recognize institutionally the increasing international educational involvement of the Department of Accountancy. This international involvement had been growing, particularly at the graduate level, for more than a generation. In addition, the department had become increasingly involved with seminars and programs designed specifically for international visitors and students. Substantial financial support from two interested alumni made possible the original commitment to establish the center.

The center has sponsored a number of special programs for key personnel in the controller's office of the Agency for International Development. Its staff has been also involved in two major foreign educational contracts. With the assistance of the government of Tunisia and the Agency for International Development, the center assisted the University of Tunisia in the 1970s in designing and establishing the first business school in Tunis. Direct specific assistance of this program for seven years resulted in a thriving M.B.A. program. In the late 1980s, the center assisted the Midwest University Consortium of International Affairs with funding of the World Bank in conducting a program to train approximately 100 Bangladesh business professors either by arranging for a graduate degree program in business or devising special programs at selected universities to update the skills of the professors. This program continued until 1990.

The center also embarked on a publishing program that includes a quarterly journal, the *International Journal of Accounting*, and a monograph series of 11 titles by 1993. The journal was the first scholarly publication in the field of international accounting. In addition, the center has sponsored more than 30 international seminars in accounting and has published the proceedings of a number of them. These various publications have assisted the exchange of views between accounting and related disciplines and have provided the opportunity for discussions between international academicians and practitioners in accounting in a dynamic environment. An individual program of research and teaching is the usual method by which a visiting staff member is related to the ongoing programs of the center and the university. More than 300 international professors from leading universities have visited the center as visiting scholars.

Vernon K. Zimmerman

See also ZIMMERMAN, VERNON K.

Certified Management Accountant (CMA) Examination

The CMA examination was established in 1972 by the National Association of Accountants (NAA, which became the Institute of Management Accountants in 1991). It is important to differentiate between the Institute of Management Accounting established by the NAA in 1972 to administer the CMA program and the current Institute of Management Accountants. They are separate bodies. The Institute of Management Accounting established in 1972 was renamed the Institute of Certified Management Accountants (ICMA) in 1986.

The CMA examination had its start from the recommendations of the NAA's Committee on Long Range Objectives in 1968, chaired by I. Wayne Keller. Robert Beyer, a managing partner of Touche Ross and Company (now Deloitte and Touche), was instrumental in ironing out details of the program. In 1972 Touche Ross established the Robert Beyer Medal awards (gold, silver, and bronze) for the top three finalists on the CMA examinations. Herbert C. Knortz, senior vice president and comptroller of International Telephone and Telegraph Corporation, was the first chairman of the IMA in 1972. The nine-member board included such noted academics as R. Lee Brummet from the University of North Carolina and David Solomons from the Wharton School of the University of Pennsylvania. Professor James Bulloch from the University of Michigan was appointed director of the IMA (1972–1986) in 1972 and served about 20 years in that capacity. The Certificate in Management Accounting Examination was changed to the Certified Management Accountant Examination in 1983. Some other administrative milestones are: (1) the 1,000th certificate awarded in 1978, (2) the first CMA review manual in 1978, (3) the 5,000th CMA

awarded in 1985, (4) the first foreign examination site in 1987, (5) the Corporate Sponsor program in 1990, and (6) the 10,000th CMA awarded in 1991.

The CMA exam was given yearly from 1972 through 1976, and then twice a year starting in 1977. The examination had a five-part format for its first 32 sittings until December 1990. The five parts were: (1) economics and business finance; (2) organization and behavior, including ethical considerations; (3) public reporting standards, auditing, and taxes; (4) internal reporting and analysis; and (5) decision analysis, including modeling and information systems. Major changes were made in December 1990. The exam was streamlined to four parts to be taken over a two-day, rather than the former two-and-a-half-day, period. The four parts, with ethical issues appearing in any part, are: (1) economics, finance, and management; (2) financial accounting and reporting; (3) managerial reporting, analysis, and behavioral issues; and (4) decision analysis and information systems. Credit for Part 2 is given to those who successfully pass the Certified Public Accountant (CPA) examination.

While the CMA exam is not designed to compete with the CPA exam, comparisons between the two are important. The ICMA has not adopted the 150 credit hours to sit for the CMA exam, as many CPA jurisdictions have. The CMA exam will become a non-disclosed one in 1997, following the non-disclosure of the CPA exam in 1996. The CMA examination relies much more on cases and much less on objective-type questions than does the CPA examination. There is a more predictable pattern of questions on the CMA examination. There has been a fairly stable pass rate of 40 to 50 percent on all the parts under both formats through the years. About 15 to 20 percent of candidates sitting for all parts will pass all the parts in one sitting. Candidates with advanced degrees perform much better than candidates with a bachelor's degree. After an understandably slow start and a long plateau period in the 1980s, the CMA examination has attracted significantly more candidates into the 1990s.

Richard Vangermeersch

Bibliography
"Board of Regents Named to Administer Institute of Management Accounting," *Management Accounting*, April 1972, pp. 11–12, 64.

Bulloch, J. "Institute Achieves Solid Progress during First Year," *Management Accounting*, July 1973, pp. 60–61.

"CMA and CPA Examinations: The Difference," *Management Accounting*, February 1989, p. 54.

"The CMA Is Twenty Years Old," *Management Accounting*, April 1992, pp. 23–27.

Harris, J.K., and J.L. Krogstad. "Assessing Progress of the CMA Program," *Management Accounting*, February 1977, pp. 17–23.

Hastings, J.E. Jr., A.P. Ameiss, and C.R. Huehl. "CMA Review: The Monsanto Experience," *Management Accounting*, February 1976, pp. 57–60.

Madden, D.L. "The CMA Examination: A Step Toward Professionalism," *Management Accounting*, October 1974, pp. 17–20.

"Report and Recommendations of the Long-Range Objectives Committee of the National Association of Accountants," *Management Accounting*, August 1968, Section 3, pp. 1–35.

Siers, H.L., and R.B. Sweeney. "Ethics and the CMA," *Management Accounting*, April 1992, pp. 47–50.

See also CERTIFIED PUBLIC ACCOUNTANT EXAMINATION: THE EARLY YEARS (1896–1930); CHARTERED INSTITUTE OF MANAGEMENT ACCOUNTANTS; COST AND/OR MANAGEMENT ACCOUNTING; INSTITUTE OF MANAGEMENT ACCOUNTANTS; SOLOMONS, DAVID

Certified Public Accountant

Certified Public Accountant is the professional title chosen in 1894 by a joint committee of 14 members from the Institute of Accounts, the American Association of Public Accountants (AAPA)—now the American Institute of Certified Public Accountants (AICPA)—and public accountants belonging to neither organization. This title had been chosen by the Institute of Accounts and became the focal point for an 1895 bill in the New York Senate. The bill was rejected but was resubmitted in 1896 and became law on April 17, 1896. It provided for the issuance of a certificate conferring the title "Certified Public Accountant" upon qualified persons and prohibited the use of that title by others. Pennsylvania adopted similar legislation in

1899, followed by Maryland in 1900, California in 1901, Illinois and Washington in 1903, New Jersey in 1904, and Florida and Michigan in 1905.

Even though there were prestigious British public accounting branches established in the United States in the 1880s and early 1890s, the use of the designation "Chartered Accountant" was discouraged in the United States. Among those against its use was British accountant Edwin Guthrie, who founded the firm of Barrow, Wade, Guthrie and Company, Public Accountants, in New York in 1883. When Guthrie, who sent James T. Anyon to the United States in 1886 to be partner in charge, visited the United States that year, he urged the development of what became the AAPA in 1887 and strongly advised the use of some designation other than "Chartered Accountant." That designation would, he felt, cause confusion with the chartered accountants sent from England and Scotland to do audits of major U.S. corporations for clients in Great Britain.

Richard Vangermeersch

Bibliography

Brown, R. *A History of Accounting and Accountants*. Edinburgh: T.C. & E.C. Jack, 1905.

Carey, J.L. *The Rise of the Accounting Profession*, vol. 1, *From Technician to Professional, 1896–1936*. New York: AICPA, 1969.

See also AMERICAN INSTITUTE OF CERTIFIED PUBLIC ACCOUNTANTS; HASKINS, CHARLES WALDO; INSTITUTE OF CHARTERED ACCOUNTANTS IN ENGLAND AND WALES; PACKARD, SILAS SADLER; SPRAGUE, CHARLES EZRA; STATE REGULATION OF THE ACCOUNTANCY PROFESSION (U.S.)

Certified Public Accountant (CPA) Examination: The Early Years (1896–1930)

The First Exam

In New York during the 1880s, two rival groups of accountants sought to establish themselves as being the most skilled professionals. The Institute of Accounts, founded in 1882, sought to demonstrate to the business community the competence of its membership by examining the members' accounting knowledge. Upon passing this test, thereby demonstrating practical and technical accounting knowledge, the member was issued a certificate and became a "Fellow."

The rival New York group, the American Association of Public Accountants (AAPA), sought to distinguish its members by issuing a university degree in accounting. Since all university education in the state of New York is supervised by the University Board of Regents, the AAPA proposed in 1892 that it be allowed to operate a "College of Accounts," which would be under the jurisdiction of the Board of Regents. Thus, accounting degrees issued by the AAPA would attest to the degree-holding members' knowledge of accounting. The board initially rejected this novel program but indicated its willingness to supervise an examination of accounting knowledge for those seeking to practice in public accounting. The AAPA pursued the idea of a college of accounting and degree granting by quickly counterproposing the "New York School of Accounts," which the AAPA would operate and guarantee its financial success. The Board of Regents approved, and the AAPA hired a dean and faculty and recruited students. However, only seven students enrolled, and the school was dissolved in 1894. The primary cause of the failure was that students did not perceive any professional advantage in securing a degree.

Both the Institute of Accounts and the AAPA sought to establish the professional advantage for their memberships by legal recognition and licensing restrictions of nonmembers. This required state legislation, with which both organizations were actively involved in drafting, proposing, and lobbying. In 1896 the New York legislature passed a compromise version of the proposals put forth by these accounting organizations. Some of both groups' ideas can be seen in the law enacted. The law restricted the use of a new title "Certified Public Accountant" ("certified" no doubt came from the Institute of Accounts). This title could be acquired only by those licensed by the University Board of Regents of the State of New York (the AAPA approach). By using the Board of Regents as the licensing agency, there was an implicit idea that licensing would require an examination of accounting knowledge. The designation "CPA" behind an accountant's name was equated with a university-degree designation; thus, for accountants, the vast majority of whom had no university education, the CPA designation was thought of as the "CPA degree" during the early years.

The first CPA exam was given by the state of New York in December 1896. A copy of this exam can be found in Edwards (1978). Much of the current examination can be directly traced to this earliest exam. For example, "75" was specified as the pass rate. The exam was given in half-day sections over a two-day period. In writing the first exam, the Board of Regents tested "theory," "practice," and "auditing"—the same sections administered today. "Commercial law" was added later and was part of the New York exam by January 1906. Perhaps the most noteworthy tradition established by the 1896 CPA exam was the rigor: No candidate passed either the 1896 or the 1897 exam. Six candidates did pass in 1898. Over the 10-year period 1898–1907, only 164 candidates of the approximately 450 who sat for the New York CPA exam passed, for a very modern 36 percent pass (64 percent failure) rate. This low pass rate was attributed to alleged lack of education and preparation on the part of candidates rather than to any grading problems or tricky exam questioning. Thus early on, the CPA exam became known for its rigor, and the CPA designation undoubtedly was enhanced because of this. Noteworthy also, the Board of Regents did "grandfather" (waive the examination requirement for licensing) reputable accountants who had been practicing before 1890; thus, all 126 CPA certificates issued in New York during the first two years were via waiver.

The Spread of CPA Licensing

Other states quickly followed New York's lead and passed similar legislation for licensing CPAs and restricting the use of the title to those who had passed an examination (modeled closely after New York's laws) and had met experience and character requirements. These early states were Pennsylvania (1899), Maryland (1900), California (1901), Washington (1903), Illinois (1903), New Jersey (1904), Florida (1905), and Michigan (1905). While following closely the New York pattern, these states had no equivalent of a University Board of Regents. Instead these states formed Boards of Examiners to write and grade CPA examinations and to approve credentials of applicants. These boards generally consisted of three to five members, typically with as many as three accountants and two lawyers. Illinois differed slightly by making the testing and grading of the CPA exam a responsibility of the faculty at the University of

Illinois. In addition to copying the New York CPA statutes, states followed the New York exam, both its content and level of rigor.

The CPA movement spread rapidly; states that had passed CPA license legislation grew to 19 by 1909, 33 by 1914 and 40 by 1916. While following the form of the New York CPA license closely, there were differences in requirements. Many of the new states were much less restrictive in their licensing. Experience requirements and waiver procedures varied from state to state; even worse, the CPA exam varied from state to state in difficulty of questions and rigor of grading. States with high pass rates were condemned by CPAs in several states, particularly those from New York, where the standards were increasing. For example, on the 1913 New York exam only six out of 134 (4.5 percent) passed all parts. To remedy the low pass rate, which was attributed to poor preparation by candidates, New York increased the experience requirement to sit for the exam from two to five years. The problem of uneven qualification became worse as more states adopted CPA legislation and as the newer states tended to be less restrictive and had higher pass rates on their CPA exams. In reaction, the more restrictive states limited reciprocal licensing of those CPAs from other states.

The Uniform CPA Exam

The lack of reciprocity in state licensing was too costly to the profession not to be resolved. Fortunately, the problem had a relatively easy solution: a nationwide CPA examination. The cooperation between Missouri and Kansas, which used the joint efforts of both states' Board of Examiners to write and administer one test in 1916, showed the advantages of state cooperation. At this time, the American Institute of Accountants—formerly the AAPA and later the American Institute of Certified Public Accountants (AICPA)—wanted its members to have passed its admission exam; it was suggested that the institute might also offer states the same exam for the purpose of the CPA license, thus avoiding the duplicate testing of its members. Three states (New Hampshire, Kansas, and Oregon) agreed to use the test prepared by the institute's Board of Examiners. This test was given in June 1917. In addition to writing the test, the American Institute of Accountants also helped in the supervising and grading, thereby ensuring uniformity state to state. Thus the "uni-

form" CPA exam tradition commenced. Also, the practice of offering the exam twice a year began with the exam offered in November 1917, when nine states used the uniform examination for their candidates. The exam was next offered in May 1918, thus beginning the practice that has continued of offering the CPA exam in May and November. By 1925, 34 states had adopted the uniform CPA examination. Interestingly, some of the first CPA states were among the last to adopt the uniform examination: among the laggards were New York, Maryland, and Ohio, which continued giving their own state exams into the 1940s.

Comparison between the uniform CPA exam and the state CPA exams as to level of difficulty is uncertain given the wide variation from state to state. The combined pass rate on the two 1917 uniform exams was 82 percent, compared to the overall 69.2 percent pass rate on state exams. However, the high pass rate was fleeting. It declined to 49 percent on the exams taken from May 1917 to May 1919 and to 25 percent on the three exams that followed, in November 1919, May 1918, and November 1918. The November 1920 uniform exam was passed by only 110 out of 820 candidates, a 13 percent pass rate.

From the mid to late 1920s, the pass rate declined in a sawtooth pattern. On the November 1924 exam, 30 percent of the candidates passed the entire exam and 24 percent "conditioned." By November 1929, the percentage of candidates passing the exam had fallen to 9 percent, with 13 percent passing conditionally. Needless to say, the Great Depression may have started with the CPA exam pass rate a decade before the Wall Street plunge in stock prices.

Conclusion

In the 1990s, the CPA exam is undergoing several changes. With the May 1992 examination, matching questions were utilized for the first time in decades; the utilization of a variety of objective-question types was to continue. In May 1994, there were more changes. The auditing exam was lengthened from three and one-half hours to four and one-half hours so professional responsibilities could be included as part of the coverage. The business law exam was shortened to three hours. The tradition of testing theory and practice separately, with practice a two-part exam, ended. Instead, financial-accounting theory and practice were combined into one exam, with a second exam to test theory and practice in cost-managerial, governmental-nonprofit and tax accounting. The May 1994 exam also permitted the use of calculators for the first time. Beginning in 1996, CPA examinations and answers will no longer be publicized. Instead only certain exams will be released, with most exams remaining confidential (nondisclosed).

Even with the changes in format, the modern CPA exam is similar in many ways to those given 50, 75, or even 100 years ago. Much of the wisdom of the New York Board of Regents in establishing the first CPA exam continues. Vestiges, legacies, and traditions started at the turn of the century are evident even as innovations and new knowledge are incorporated.

William D. Samson
Kent T. Fields

Bibliography

Carey, J.L. *The Rise of the Accounting Profession*. 2 vols. New York: AICPA, 1969–1970.

"Editorial," *Journal of Accountancy*, March 1909, pp. 390–393.

"Editorial," *Journal of Accountancy*, February 1918, p. 121.

Edwards, J.D. *History of Public Accounting in the United States*. East Lansing: Bureau of Business and Economic Research, Michigan State University, 1960. Reprint. University, AL: University of Alabama Press, 1978.

"Preparing for the CPA Exam," *Journal of Accountancy*, June 1930, p. 445.

Previts, G.J., and B.D. Merino. *A History of Accounting in America: An Historical Interpretation of the Cultural Significance of Accounting*. New York: John Wiley & Sons, 1979.

Richardson, A.P. "Schools and Schools," *Journal of Accountancy*, March 1921, p. 187.

See also ACCOUNTING EDUCATION IN THE UNITED STATES; AMERICAN INSTITUTE OF CERTIFIED PUBLIC ACCOUNTANTS; BENTLEY, HARRY CLARK; CERTIFIED MANAGEMENT ACCOUNTANT (CMA) EXAMINATION; CHARTERED ACCOUNTANTS EXAMINATIONS IN ENGLAND AND WALES; HASKINS, CHARLES WALDO; SPRAGUE, CHARLES EZRA; STATE REGULATION OF THE ACCOUNTANCY PROFESSION (U.S.); ZEFF, STEPHEN A.

Chambers, Raymond John (1917–)

C

Raymond John Chambers is widely acknowledged as one of the leading academic contributors to the profession of accounting. Chambers's research has promoted accounting as a university discipline. His objective has been to improve the practice of accounting, exposing the unsystematic practices of conventional accounting and the unserviceability of its product. Strengthening the necessary relationship between practice, research, and education has been the dominant and consistent theme in Chambers's work since the 1940s. His research output has been voluminous—numbering over 230 articles and nine major books. His seminal work, *Accounting, Evaluation, and Economic Behavior* (1966), propounded a comprehensive theoretical foundation for a style of accounting, continuously contemporary accounting (CoCoA), that would mitigate error and eliminate many of the flaws and infelicities in accounting practice. In 1986 a five-volume collection of his major articles was published by Garland Publishing. Chambers was the founder of the accounting journal *Abacus*.

CoCoA was first presented at length in *Accounting, Evaluation, and Economic Behavior* in 1966. It is consistent with a large body of economics literature on money, prices, price levels and price structures, the tenets of measurement theory, and the common-sense rules of financial calculation. Accordingly, a business entity's wealth is measured as the amount of unencumbered current general purchasing power it commands; income for a period is the increase in its wealth; and loss, the decrease. Wealth is calculated as the aggregate of the face values of its cash and other liquid assets plus the cash equivalent of its physical assets, less the contractual amount of its liabilities. The cash equivalent of a physical asset is taken to be best indicated by its current selling price. In many respects, CoCoA has similarities to historical cost accounting: The double entry principle is consistently applied, cash and credit transactions are accounted in exactly the same way, and the matching principle is used systematically. Income for a period under CoCoA has three components: net revenues, which comprise all receipts less all payments made in the course of business; the price-variation adjustment, which is the net amount of all changes in the cash equivalents of physical assets; and the capital-maintenance adjustment, which is the amount necessary to restate wealth at the period's commencement in terms of the general purchasing power of the currency at the end of the period. It is a scale adjustment to account for the price variation in the general purchasing-power dimension of the monetary unit of measure.

Concern with explicating his ideas to wary audiences resulted in Chambers employing novel devices to explain and instruct. One of particular and enduring significance was recourse in the 1960s to mathematical notation as a means of explaining how his system of accounting would simultaneously accommodate changes in specific prices and changes in the general level of prices. Chambers's notation has become an integral part of many professional, governmental, and educational analyses and reports into what has been coined "accounting for inflation."

His response upon receipt of the American Accounting Association's Outstanding Educator Award in 1991 provides an insight into what motivates his research. He explained that "economics . . . presupposes the rational and knowledgeable pursuit of ends in a volatile world, where up-to-date and reliable information would be essential." Clearly, accounting had a role to play in indicating contemporary shifts in the solvency of firms, in their rates of return, and in their financial capacity for growth or adaptation. But observations of practice and his experience as a teacher suggested the products of accounting were not useful for that purpose. Most of the products of accounting (except cash, receivables, and payables) were the outcome of "self-contradictory rules, unrealistic presumptions, and unsupported dogma." At his 1991 induction to Ohio State University's Accounting Hall of Fame, he provided an explanation for this parlous state of affairs in accounting. He noted, as printed in the *Accounting Historians Journal*, that practice demands versatility, patience, and comprehension to match the exigencies of diverse clients with the performance of a socially necessary task. Scholars and teachers in most disciplines, on the other hand, serve no immediate clients. Ideally, they are the monitors of practice in general, discriminators between what is generally serviceable and what is merely expedient. "In accounting it is still otherwise. Teachers and researchers on a large scale confuse the generally serviceable with the merely expedient."

Throughout his works, the connection between observation and prescription is clearly and unashamedly expressed. So is the connection between research, education, and practice. The general background of the relevant factors affecting accounting, business, and management after World War II puts Chambers's contributions in perspective. This period covering Chambers's writings witnessed substantial business growth worldwide, merger and amalgamation, multinational corporate expansion, increasing use of novel modes of organization, and invention of idiosyncratic and complex methods of financing. Interspersed were large, often unexpected, corporate failures, dilemmas involving takeovers, and instances (exposed by the press, academics, or government inquiries) of the use of permissible, but questionable, accounting and auditing practices. Calls for government regulation of the accounting profession were met by pleas to allow greater professional self-regulation. It was claimed practices would become more systematic, initially based on principles, and then translated into standards. Standards have proliferated, but the failures and the use of questionable accounting and auditing practices continued. The unserviceability of accounting remained a perennially unanswered complaint.

Chambers's ideas were drawn freely from the literatures of other fields of inquiry, including economics, law, measurement, communication, and information theory. An unusual feature, at least in accounting, is that his theory, CoCoA, represents the convergence of ideas from these cognate disciplines.

Critics of CoCoA are legion. Nonetheless, the basic propositions remain unrefuted. To date there have been ad hoc, albeit increasing, movements to some form of "market-price based" system of accounting—for example, the calls for "marked to market" accounting.

Chambers's impact on the development of accounting thought is without question. Reference to his work appears in most university and college accounting programs. His name either heads or ranks highly in virtually every listing of contributions to the international accounting-journal literature in the post-World War II period.

Frank L. Clarke
Graeme W. Dean

Bibliography
Brown, R.S. "Raymond John Chambers: Biography," *Abacus*, December 1982

(festschrift issue), pp. 99–105.

Chambers, R.J. *Accounting Evaluation and Economic Behavior.* Englewood Cliffs, NJ: Prentice-Hall, 1966.

———. "Continuously Contemporary Accounting: Misunderstandings and Misrepresentations," *Abacus*, December 1976, pp. 137–151.

———. "Response: 1991 Accounting Hall of Fame Induction," *Accounting Historians Journal*, June 1992, pp. 83–85.

———. "Historical Cost-Tale of a False Creed, "*Accounting Horizons*, March 1994, pp. 76–89.

Chambers, R.J., and G.W. Dean. *Chambers on Accounting.* 5 vols. New York: Garland, 1986.

Gaffikin, M.J. *Accounting Methodology and the Work of Professor Chambers.* New York: Garland, 1990.

"1991 Outstanding Accounting Educator Award," *Accounting Education News*, November 1991, pp. 1, 4–5.

See also ACCOUNTING HALL OF FAME; AMERICAN ACCOUNTING ASSOCIATION; AUSTRALIA; BALL AND BROWN'S "AN EMPIRICAL EVALUATION OF ACCOUNTING INCOME NUMBERS"; CONCEPTUAL FRAMEWORK; DEFINITIONS OF ACCOUNTING; EDWARDS AND BELL: REPLACEMENT-COST ACCOUNTING; HISTORICAL COST; INCOME-DETERMINATION THEORY; INFLATION ACCOUNTING; INVENTORY VALUATION; MATCHING; NORMATIVE ACCOUNTING; THOMAS'S *THE ALLOCATION PROBLEM IN FINANCIAL ACCOUNTING THEORY;* WELLS, MURRAY CHARLES

"Charge and Discharge" Statement

The "charge and discharge" statement took various forms and acquired different significances in its widespread, long, and interesting history. Consider first those times and systems earlier than Italian double entry in which the statement found roots. This suggests its influence on the frequencies, terms, content, and form of today's accounting. Finally, it is possible to point to the better-developed Cameralist accounting of Central Europe.

Innumerable and beautifully penned statements can be found in the archives of states and estates, of enterprises and trusts where there was stewardship and accountability, notably in the English Exchequer, Italian religious *azienda,* and German princely camera. Different delegations, accountabilities, and controls were needed for feudal and bureaucratic hierarchies from those appropriate to traders and bankers. Some see double entry bookkeeping as an adaptation using Italianate terms of a prior single entry system. The charge-discharge system is not, however, a single entry account of classified period receipts and payments without prime entry bookings and with no associated ledger for nominal, real, or personal accounts. Its essence lies in its adaptability, its focus on period and personal accountability, and in the vouched evidence required of stewards.

Most balances in charge-discharge were netted in a single outstanding figure of "rests." Heritable wealth was seldom the subject of booking, until joint stock utilities purchased land. Capital-revenue distinctions were then solved ingeniously by the double account method.

Accounting systems developed through interaction as single memoranda, journal, and ledger adapted to the multiple recordings that were required on estates with variegated operations, for each of which period performance and results were required. The profits and losses on aperiodic ventures were displaced for managerial and tax purposes by the gross and net revenues and results of a specific stewardship, or fund, for defined periods. Input data also changed when traders' personal debts owed and owing were displaced by the ordered dues recorded in rentals or assessment lists and payrolls. Different also were the vouched data inputs and the special periodic "rests" or balances carried forward.

Charge-discharge statements also document changes over the centuries to a market and cash economy. Gradually, records of commodity yields and consumptions became less important than cash flows for the enjoyments, crusades, or campaigns of absentee landlords. Charges and discharges were recorded commonly in a copy "counter-roll"; but this check was less effective than the control of all "actuals" by their prior "dues." Even today, cash flows remain subservient in all bureaucracies to a distinct system of authorization: Orders precede ordered movement or payment.

The concept of charge and discharge is pervasive. Ships' cargoes have to be loaded before they can be discharged. The law, too, interprets (largely as metaphor) any duties transferred as an "onus," a charge and responsibility with implications that fulfillment, requital, or equilibration is required. "Balancing" in equating and discharging charges comes as naturally as when a banker uses scales for coin or offsets entries on the opposed pages of each account.

Charge and discharge entries were originally listed on vellum rolls, sewn at the top. Subtotaling of grouped items helped in a "totting," or reckoning, from the head to the foot of each account. In distant imitation, it is found that intricate and vertical statement formats have more than technical advantages over traders' memoranda and opposed postings. An example is given of how personal and other headings could be adopted in classifying charges summarized from Thomas Richard's *The Gentlemans Auditor: or a New and Easie Method for Keeping Accompts, of Gentlemens Estates* (1707):

A SHORT VIEW OF YE LORD'S REVENUES AND THE DISPOSAL THEREOF FOR ONE WHOLE YEAR TO LADY DAY, 1707:

CHARGE	£	]Subtotals
by schedules of Rents		
augmentations	£	]
by surplus with bailiff	£	]
		and *TOTAL CHARGE*
DISCHARGE by taxes, etc. in A/cs		
of Bailiff X	£	
Bailiff Y	£	Subtotal
expenses by cashiers		
by Lord himself	£	
Butler	£	
Groom etc	£	
Cashier's salary	£	Subtotal
by Supers returned	£	
and Money at interest	£	Subtotal
		TOTAL DISCHARGE
RESTS in Cashier's hands [= net]		£699.14.02

All entries required some voucher or sworn evidence. Initial recordings were in the varied books appropriate to the activities and geographical dispersion of the estate. Actuals in cash or kind were recorded, but the chief charges were for obligations or dues. These might have diverse origins. Yet the textbooks and records preserved show that officials remained committed to the exaction or disbursement of unchanging sums and to modify precedents only through approved new plans or budgets. Taxes or rents formally budgeted became dues for which officials could be "charged" until exonerated. Similarly, they could be required to discharge themselves for loans or sums received. That stewards should account only for actual receipts (or cash flows) was resisted by landlords who demanded a "full charge" in which stewards were responsible for all rents due but could be granted allowances every few years for uncollectable debts. Less commonly, interest was chargeable between accountings.

In addition to natural agricultural years, there were shorter timespans so that managers accounted for monthly, weekly, or daily (diet) routines and consumptions. Seasons determined the timing of work, and often of the ensuing accounting, although yields were most often calculated each year or annual "crop." After early medieval harvests, stewards submitted to audit in the form of oral presentations supported by vouchers or tallies; subsequently, "charge and discharge" statements were drafted, sometimes with money values *en face* and commodity quantities or "stocks" listed *en dorse*.

The single "rest" due from the steward comprehended controllable and not heritable items, but there is evidence that the balance was seldom settled at audit. In England the "Winchester Form" of statement showed acquittances and loss of rent among the receipts. All arrears were taken as settled before the audit. From 1260, however, a "Westminster or Common Form" showed authorized deductions as discharges and not as reductions in the steward's charge: Rests due began to appear as working capital rather than as a simple debt.

There is also evidence that "rests" often remained outstanding until the steward's retirement or death. The English Exchequer ground slowly but exceeding small. Delays in accounting or in settlement were less risky because recourse could be had beyond the steward or officeholder to his guarantors or sureties. Guarantees, credit, and trust permitted late accounting and postponed settlement until the final reckoning.

The format for "charge and discharge" statements evolved, but they were not negotiable by the managers. Heinrich A. Lange in 1776 asserted in his book *Ausfühtiche Abhandlung von Rechrungswesen* that German stewards must *account as their lord directs*, neither entering nor removing any rubric (class) of their own. At this time there was, however, experiment and change. Rests were being classified into real assets and debts due—classified according to maturity. Traders' unclassified balances, moreover, were being structured and complemented by special statements of property brought forward, plus period revenues, less "the exact application" thereof. Such corporate "sources and applications of funds" statements can be found from 1791. More generally, one can trace relations between the civil *State*, landed *estates*, and the *statements*, or *"Staetsproefs,"* by which stewards were controlled, according to Simon Stevin, a Dutch writer in accounting, as well as many other fields, in the late 1500s and early 1600s.

"Cargo y discargo" or "cargo y data" (dues and actuals?) was extensively and ingeniously used in Spain. Records were kept first on unbound "pliegos horodado o de pliegos sueltos" (perforated and detached sheets). The stages by which "double entry" was preferred (except for the treasury of the first Bourbon kings) are now well documented, but with an emphasis on technique rather than institutionalized accountability, as noted by Esteban Hernández-Esteve (1992), an expert in the history of Spanish accounting.

Generally, charge-discharge accounting attracts ignorant criticism. In Central Europe, however, the developments and adaptability of state and estate accounting from "the camera" have been much studied and appreciated. Interactions between period planning for the state's purse and for the firm's budget are clear from two centuries ago. Much rationality has gone into the calculation of charges leviable on a province or person, and ingenuity should be sought in the perfection of systems and controls. For these, little is derived from double entry, and much is owed to the accountabilities and dues required from those in any position of trust.

David A.R. Forrester

Bibliography

Baxter, W.T. "The Account Charge and Discharge," *Accounting Historians Journal,* Spring 1980, pp. 69–71.

Filios, V. "The Cameralistic Method," *Journal of Business Finance and Accounting,* Autumn 1983, pp. 443–450.

Forrester, D.A.R. "Rational Administration, Finance, and Control," *Critical Perspectives on Accounting,* Spring 1990, pp. 285–311.

———. "Whether Malcolm's Is Best or Old Charge and Discharge," *Accounting Historians Journal,* Fall 1978, pp. 51–61.

Hernández-Esteve, E. "Problematica General de una Historia de la Contabilidad en España." Paper presented at workshop on accounting history, Madrid, Spain, September 1992.

Jack, S.M. "An Historical Defence of Single Entry Book-keeping," *Abacus,* December 1966, pp. 137–158.

Jones, R.H. "Accounting in English Local Government from the Middle Ages to c. 1835," *Accounting and Business Research,* Summer 1985, pp. 197–209.

Schneider, D. *Allgemeine Betriebswirtschaftslehre.* Munich: Oldenbourg, 1981.

See also AGRICULTURAL ACCOUNTING; BALANCE SHEET; BANKRUPTCY ACTS; EXTERNAL AUDITING; FUNDS FLOW STATEMENT; MANORIAL ACCOUNTING; MEDIEVAL ACCOUNTING; PIPE ROLL; SCOTLAND: EARLY WRITERS IN DOUBLE ENTRY ACCOUNTING; SCRIBES; SINGLE ENTRY BOOKKEEPING; STEWARDSHIP; TRUSTEE ACCOUNTS

Chart of Accounts

European commercial codes first made financial statements compulsory and then specified the types of account books to be kept and the accounting methods to be used. Jacques Savary was the principal author of a 1673 French government ordinance that required every merchant and banker to keep written records of his transactions in a book signed by a public official, and to prepare semiannual inventories "of all their fixed and movable properties and of all their debts receivable and payable." The Code Savary was meant to reveal a merchant's ability to pay his debts from his existing assets in case he went bankrupt and thereby to facilitate a fair sharing of his resources among creditors. If a merchant did not keep authenticated accounting records, his bankruptcy was considered fraudulent and he was subject to the death penalty. The bankruptcy provisions of this 1673 ordinance were incorporated into the Napoleonic Code of 1807.

Several early accounting writers attempted to classify ledger accounts in a logical order. In *Instructie van het Italiaans Boekhouden* (Amsterdam 1693), Abraham de Graef divided accounts into three groups: (1) accounts of the merchant as a person: capital, profit and loss, insurance, equity reserves, housekeeping, interest; (2) accounts of other persons, such as creditors, debtors, and participants in trade ventures; and (3) merchandise accounts: goods on hand and on ships, cash available for merchandise purchases, and so on. The Frenchman Edmond Degrange Sr. based his Five Account System in 1795 on the theory that cash, merchandise, receivables, payables, and profit and loss function as subsidiaries to capital, and that by debiting and crediting them and their subdivisions the merchant was in effect debiting and crediting himself.

The English Companies Acts of 1855–1856 included an extremely progressive model balance sheet. Assets and liabilities were classified by type, bad debts were provided for, depreciation was shown for both plant assets and inventories, and retained earnings was divided into portions reserved for contingencies and available for dividends. But this statement format was permissive, not mandatory. And after 1900 the companies acts concentrated on improving financial statement quality by requiring specific disclosures, not by regulating accounting methods.

In a textbook published in 1864, the Belgian H. Godefroid suggested the use of titles, chapters, and sections for classifying cost and financial accounts. Godefroid's methodology became popular in Europe, and his followers added numbers to his classification categories. By the end of the nineteenth century the decimal chart of accounts, based primarily on balance sheet categories but including a section of revenues and expenses, was widely used as a teaching device and in actual accounting systems.

Eugen Schmalenbach was the most important German influence on the development of an international chart of accounts. Schmalenbach favored "dynamic accounting" based on the income statement in preference to "static accounting" based on the balance sheet. Accordingly, the legally mandated German chart of accounts derived from his classifications allotted more categories to income statement accounts than to balance sheet accounts. The sequence of accounts in Schmalenbach's chart followed the cycle of manufacturing activity: First capital is raised and invested in fixed and current assets; then materials are purchased and processed to create products that are sold; and finally all accounting elements are assembled prior to closing the ledger.

Probably the most influential charts of accounts were contained in uniform accounting plans developed by the French government. In 1942 the Vichy government sponsored but did not mandate an accounting plan partially derived from the "Goering Plan" adopted in Germany in 1937. The 1942 plan contained two charts of accounts: a ten-category chart for manufacturers, including cost accounts, and a simplified seven-category plan for other businesses.

After World War II, the French government nationalized many large industrial and financial corporations. A uniform accounting plan offered a way to standardize the different accounting methods of these nationalized enterprises. The 1947 *Plan Comptable Général*, the first plan sanctioned by government decree, was the real beginning of accounting uniformity in France. Besides a chart of accounts, the 1947 plan included definitions of cost and financial accounting terms, uniform rules for asset valuation and depreciation, standardized cost accounting procedures, and model financial statements. The chart of accounts had 10 numbered account categories, and the order of appearance of accounts on the balance sheet was the same as in the chart. Provisions of the 1947 plan were legally binding on nationalized companies and on firms in which the French government had a financial interest. It was considered that uniform accounts made such businesses easier to manage and control. It also improved the quality of data collected for national accounting purposes. The 1957 revision of the *Plan Comptable Général* has become the model for accounting laws in present and former French colonies and in other countries such as Greece and Turkey.

Among American manufacturers, the codification of accounting methods began with attempts to establish industrywide cost standards. As early as 1889, the National Association of Stove Manufacturers introduced a standard "formula" for costing the industry's products. The printing industry and many others followed suit. According to the National Association of Cost Accountants Research Department, 69 such uniform systems existed in 1920. Though these may have helped to rationalize production, their usual purpose was to reduce competition by fostering price-fixing agreements based on cost estimates. Enforcement of the antitrust laws discouraged this type of uniform costing. In later years, a number of industrial trade associations persuaded their members to report operating results according to uniform charts of accounts. Averages compiled from the resulting figures gave individual manufacturers a standard of comparison by which to judge their relative efficiency.

In 1869 Massachusetts passed the first American statutes regulating railroads, and in 1876 the railway commissioners of Massachusetts required that railroads keep accounts. By 1906 the Interstate Commerce Commission (ICC) had caused a uniform system of railroad accounts to be adopted throughout the United States, though its enforcement was ineffective. The 1906 Hepburn Act authorized the ICC to prescribe uniform railroad accounting methods. The ICC complied in 1907 by publishing "Classification of Operating Expenses," and in 1914 a complete "Accounting Classification for Steam Railroads."

To date those nations that regulate accounting practice through uniform charts of accounts have shown little interest in theory. On the other hand, American accountants of the early twentieth century, with no legal code or chart of accounts to guide them, tended more than others to judge accounting procedures by reference to general principles.

The first important effort to codify accounting principles was made in 1932 by the American Institute of Accountants Special Committee on Cooperation with Stock Exchanges, chaired by George Oliver May, an expert on railroad accounting. The New York Stock Exchange had expressed concern about the wide variety of accounting and reporting methods used by companies whose securities it listed. On the institute's side there was uncertainty about the precise wording of the audit certificate and the responsibility it imposed on CPAs. The committee was appointed to formulate improved accounting standards that might then be enforced through the Stock Exchange's listing requirements.

In May's view, the committee had two specific tasks: to educate the public as to why a variety of accounting methods was necessary, and to suggest ways to curtail that variety and gradually make the better methods universal:

> In considering ways of improving the existing situation two alternatives suggest themselves. The first is the selection by competent authority out of the body of acceptable accounting methods in vogue today a detailed set of rules which would become binding on all corporations of a given class. This procedure has been applied broadly to the railroads and other regulated utilities, though even such classifications as, for instance, that prescribed by the Interstate Commerce Commission allow some choice of method to corporations governed thereby. The arguments against any attempt to apply this alternative to industrial corporations generally are, however, overwhelming.

> The more practicable alternative would be to leave every corporation free to choose its own methods of accounting within the very broad limits to which reference has been made, but require disclosure of the methods employed and consistency in their application from year to year. . . .

Ironically therefore, the American decision to develop accounting practices from generally accepted principles resulted in part from the profession's bad experiences with the rigid chart of accounts mandated for use by the railroads.

Michael Chatfield

Bibliography

Audits of Corporate Accounts, Correspondence with New York Stock Exchange. New York: American Institute of Accountants, 1934.

Fortin, A. "The 1947 French Accounting Plan: Origins and Influence on Subsequent Practice," *Accounting Historians Journal*, December 1991, pp. 1–23.

Howard, S.E. "Public Rules for Private Accounting in France, 1673 and 1807," *Accounting Review*, June 1932, pp. 91–102.

Most, K.S. *Accounting Theory.* 2nd ed. Columbus, OH: Grid, 1982.

———. *Uniform Cost Accounting.* London: Gee, 1961.

Schmalenbach, E. *Dynamic Accounting,* translated by G.W. Murphy and K.S. Most. London: Gee, 1959.

See also COMPANIES ACTS; COMPARABILITY; FRANCE; GERMANY; INSTITUTE OF MANAGEMENT ACCOUNTANTS; JONES, EDWARD THOMAS; MAY, GEORGE OLIVER; RAILROAD ACCOUNTING (U.S.); RUSSIA; SAVARY, JACQUES;

SCHMALENBACH, EUGEN; TRIAL BALANCE;
UNIFORM ACCOUNTING SYSTEMS;
UNIFORMITY

Chartered Accountants Examinations in England and Wales

The Institute of Chartered Accountants in England and Wales (ICAEW) was granted a Royal Charter in 1880. It held its first examinations in London in 1882 and has been conducting professional examinations ever since (Freear, 1982). For many years, the ICAEW conducted accounting education and training in England and Wales independently of the universities, and mostly by way of its examinations. These comprised a preliminary examination, an intermediate examination, and a final examination. High-school leaving certificates gradually replaced the preliminary examination for those entering the five-year training period known as articles of clerkship. By passing university qualifying examinations, usually after a further two years at high school, candidates could reduce the length of training to four years. The possession of a university baccalaureate degree further reduced the training to about three years. The ICAEW examinations have focused on licensing individuals to practice as chartered accountants and thus have sought to measure professional competence. In the early days, the emphasis was on the needs of public practice. The ICAEW, while retaining its public practice emphasis, has evolved over the years into more of a generalist accounting body.

The pass rate in the final examinations has varied from highs of over 70 percent in the very early years to 50 percent in more recent years, with occasional dips to around 30 percent. The numbers taking the final examinations have increased from 50 in the first examination to about 9,000 in the 1980s and 1990s. The ICAEW continued to hold examinations during both world wars, although the number of candidates was low. For the most part, the ICAEW has held examinations twice a year. Until the 1960s, candidates had to pass the whole final examination at one sitting. Thereafter, it became possible to retake, on one occasion only, a single failed paper rather than the whole examination.

The ICAEW's first final examination in 1882 comprised six papers (13 hours of examinations) over three days, with a strong emphasis on legal issues: bookkeeping, partnership

and executorship accounts (a three-hour paper), auditing, the rights and duties of liquidators, trustees, and receivers, bankruptcy and company law, and mercantile law and the law of arbitration and awards (all two-hour papers). That structure remained in place until 1922. Pressure for change had been building for several years, but World War I delayed action. Among others, A.E. Cutforth, who would later become president of the ICAEW, had pressed for change. Writing in 1913 in the *Accountant*, he observed that the profession must move with the times and that professional accountants must equip themselves to undertake the "altered duties and responsibilities" that altered conditions imposed upon them.

In 1922 the ICAEW changed the final examination to include more cost accounting and to introduce a limited elective structure in which the candidate had to choose one from three papers in economics, actuarial science, and banking, currency, and foreign exchanges. The separate paper on the rights and duties of liquidators, trustees, and receivers was dropped, and all papers except bankruptcy law and actuarial science (both two hours), became three-hour papers. Total examining time increased to 19 or 20 hours, according to the elective chosen. The 1922 changes did not remain unchanged for long. The paper on mercantile law reverted to two hours in 1924, and in 1930 the ICAEW dropped the actuarial-science option.

Frederic Rudolf Mackley de Paula proposed in 1928 a five-year process: six months at university learning "preclinical" skills, followed by a year of practical training, followed by a further year of university to merge theory and practice. There would be a further 18 months of practical training and a final university year, with the ICAEW final examination at the end. The candidate would receive a university diploma and membership in the ICAEW.

A lively correspondence ensued, notably in the journal *Accountant*. Examples of such correspondence are (1) leader article, March 9, 1929 (pp. 285–286); (2) E.L. Tanner, "The Institute Examinations: Criticisms and Suggestions," June 22, 1929, pp. 791–794; (3) L.H. Jones, "Notes," January 19, 1929, pp. 85–90; and (4) Correspondence on January 25, 1930, p. 130; March 31, 1930, p. 693; June 7, 1930, p. 725; June 21, 1930, pp. 795–796; and January 31, 1931, p. 138. Several ideas emerged that the ICAEW eventually adopted, such as the division of the final into two parts. In 1934 the

ICAEW removed the elective element from the final and added a two-and-a-half-hour paper on general financial knowledge that included cost accounting, taxation, and foreign exchanges. In addition, there were three financial-accounting papers and an auditing paper, each three hours long, and three law papers, each two hours long, giving a total of 20 1/2 hours of examinations.

The 1947 restructuring, unlike that of 1934, did not follow a prolonged and public debate in the professional press, although de Paula remained an activist for change, and the McNair Committee on the relationship between the universities and the profession reported in 1944. In many ways, the 1947 changes were more evolutionary than revolutionary and reflected the considerable changes in the economic environment. The number of papers fell from eight to seven, but all were of three-hour duration, a total of 21 hours of examinations. This enabled the ICAEW to reduce the three 1934 law papers to two, to examine taxation in a separate paper, and to incorporate general financial knowledge and cost accounting in one paper. Auditing remained a separate paper, but the three accounting papers in the 1934 examinations became two. In 1957, cost accounting became cost and management accounting, and auditing became auditing including investigations, but otherwise the 1947 structure remained in place until 1965.

Although the examination structure remained stable between 1947 and 1965, the ICAEW faced considerable pressure for change. In 1949, the Carr-Saunders Committee, appointed by the minister of education in 1946, issued its report. Its recommendations included the increased availability of part-time day tuition in colleges and greater standardization among the examination syllabi of the various professional accountancy bodies. The ICAEW (1951) greeted the report with hostility, finding the Carr-Saunders recommendations "wholly inappropriate" and arguing that they would undermine the ICAEW's entire system of training. The ICAEW argued also that commercial and technical institutions were unsuited to the major tuition work needed to prepare candidates. It could not envisage "any scheme, outside the universities" that it could recommend to members as a basis for granting exemption from the intermediate examination. The ICAEW went on to defend its approach to training as providing a sound technical knowl-

edge of the principles underlying the work of the profession; a working knowledge of the law; practical experience of the application of the principles and the law; understanding of the ethics of the profession; and "the widest possible education in a broader sense than the strictly vocational training."

The ICAEW appointed its own committee, the Parker Committee, in 1958. Parker reported in 1961 that the ICAEW should make no changes to the "fundamental character" of the ICAEW qualification, but it must adapt the "means and terms of entry into membership" to "changed and changing conditions." Parker proposed that the final examination be divided into two parts, that the syllabus be amended, and that the number of papers be increased to nine. After discussion and debate, the ICAEW implemented the new structure in 1965. The first part of the final contained four three-hour papers: accounting, taxation, and two law papers. The second part contained two accounting papers (one of which included cost and management accounting), auditing, a second taxation paper, and a general paper that included the elements of economics. The new finals required 27 hours of examinations, normally taken in two sittings, although the ICAEW allowed candidates to take both parts together.

In 1970 an attempt to amalgamate the major professional accounting bodies in Great Britain failed. The failure led the ICAEW to publish draft revisions to the examination syllabus and to invite comment. An article in *Accountancy* in November 1970 pointed out that ICAEW examinations must increasingly reflect the needs of the 80 percent of those who qualify "who will spend the majority of their working lives in an industrial environment."

In 1972 the ICAEW introduced proposals further to revise its examination structure. The new structure became effective in 1975. A foundation examination replaced the intermediate examination, and Professional Examination I (PE I) and Professional Examination II (PE II) replaced the two-part final examination. The change was more than a change in name. For the first time, there was a clear indication that the examinations would be cumulative, that the examinations could test candidates in the PE II on topics that had been covered in PE I or even in the foundation examination. It was no longer possible to take both final examinations at the same sitting. PE I consisted of four three-hour papers: financial accounting, taxation, law, and a paper in auditing, systems and data processing. PE II comprised five three-hour papers: financial accounting, taxation, auditing, management accounting, and elements of financial decisions. Again, the total number of hours for the two examinations was 27.

Meanwhile, the Long Range Enquiry into Education and Training for the Accountancy Profession had begun its work under Professor David Solomons. Its report, written by Solomons and T.M. Berridge, was published in 1974 as *Prospectus for a Profession*. In the context of the findings published in that report, another review of the ICAEW examinations appeared in 1979, to take effect in 1981. PE I became a 5-hour examination consisting of five three-hour papers, thus increasing the total time for both examinations to 30 hours. The five papers were: financial accounting, accounting techniques (including basic cost and management accounting), law, auditing, systems and data processing, and taxation. PE II consisted also of five three-hour papers: financial accounting, financial management, management accounting, auditing, and advanced taxation.

Effective for the 1988 examinations, the ICAEW reduced the number of papers from ten to nine, and the total number of hours back to 27. In PE I were five courses: auditing, financial accounting, law, management accounting and financial management, and taxation. The paper on management accounting and financial management replaced the one on accounting techniques that had contained some financial and some cost accounting. PE II comprised four courses: auditing, financial accounting, management accounting and financial management (previously two separate papers), and taxation.

In 1993–1994, the ICAEW introduced a new examination structure as explained in *Examinations Conduct and Syllabuses (1992/93)*. There was a foundation examination (with four papers), and a five-paper Intermediate examination reappeared, comprising auditing and information systems, financial reporting, financial planning and control, business finance and decisions, and taxation. The final examination consisted of four papers. One was a "multidisciplinary case study paper," in which candidates must demonstrate that they can integrate the "knowledge and skills which they have acquired from their other studies and training across all subjects." In addition, there was a paper on auditing and financial accounting

combined, a taxation paper, and a business planning and evaluation paper. This last emphasized strategic planning, decision making, financing decisions and valuation principles, with a section on written communications. The total number of examining hours, taking the intermediate and final together, remained at 27.

Throughout their history, the ICAEW examinations have included bookkeeping and accounts, auditing and law. Until 1922, they were almost the only components. Taxation first had its own paper in 1947, reflecting the increased taxation needed to pay for the costs of World War II. Economics has acquired a more managerial and financial flavor and appears in several different papers. Systems and data processing, cost and management accounting, financial management, and strategic planning have become much more significant, at the expense of law and bookkeeping. Auditing has remained a prominent part of the syllabus. The examinations contained an integrative case study for the first time in 1994. The total number of examination hours has increased from a low of 13 in 1882 to a high of 30 hours in 1981 (in two sittings), but has settled back to 27 hours.

Environmental and governmental pressures, including statute and case law, have been major influences, especially in auditing and taxation. Other influences have been less easy to identify. At various times over the past century or so, key individuals and groups have perceived change and its impact on the present and future role of the accountant, and have urged corresponding changes in the examination structures and syllabi. The ICAEW has recognized that most of its members do not remain in public practice and that it must continue to be rapid and flexible in its anticipation of, and response to, change.

John Freear

Bibliography

Carr-Saunders Report: Report of the Special Committee on Education for Commerce. London: H.M.S.O, 1949.

Cutforth, A.E. "The Organization of an Accountant's Department," *Accountant*, May 10, 1913, pp. 729–735.

de Paula, F.R.M. "The Future of the Accountancy Profession," *Accountant*, May 8, 1943, pp. 239–242.

———. Letter to the Editor, the *Accountant*, December 1, 1928, pp. 711–712.

Freear, John. "Institute Examinations behind Barbed Wire, 1939–45," *Accounting and Business Research*, 1979/80, no. 37A, pp. 143–157.

———. "The Final Examination of the Institute of Chartered Accountants in England and Wales, 1882–1981," *Accounting Historians Journal*, Spring 1982, pp. 53–89.

ICAEW. *Education and Training for Membership*. London: Institute of Chartered Accountants in England and Wales, 1951.

ICAEW. *Examinations Conduct and Syllabuses, 1992–93*. London: Institute of Chartered Accountants in England and Wales, 1992.

Jones, L.H. "Notes on Economics," *Accountant*, June 22, 1929, pp. 85–90.

McNair Report: Report of the Joint Committee Representing the Universities and the Accountancy Profession. London: Institute of Chartered Accountants in England and Wales, 1944.

Parker Report: Report of the Committee on Education and Training. London: Institute of Chartered Accountants in England and Wales, 1961.

Solomons, D., and T.M. Berridge. *Prospectus for a Profession*. London: Gee, 1974.

Spicer, E.E. "The Articled Clerk in Relation to Education," *Accountant*, March 26, 1927, pp. 465–469.

Tanner, E.L. "The Institute Examinations: Criticisms and Suggestions," *Accountant*, June 22, 1929, pp. 791–794.

See also ACCOUNTING EDUCATION IN THE UNITED STATES; CERTIFIED PUBLIC ACCOUNTANT; CERTIFIED PUBLIC ACCOUNTANT EXAMINATION: THE EARLY YEARS (1896–1930); DE PAULA, FREDERIC RUDOLF MACKLEY; INSTITUTE OF CHARTERED ACCOUNTANTS IN ENGLAND AND WALES; SOLOMONS, DAVID

Chartered Institute of Management Accountants

The Chartered Institute of Management Accountants (CIMA) was founded in 1919 in Great Britain on the realization that the traditional methods of accountancy were unable to provide the range of information required in order to plan and manage modern business. This realization resulted, in part, from the interest shown by the British government during World War I in introducing cost accounting into munitions factories. Many early supporters of the CIMA were industrial managers or engineers who had become aware of the limitations of traditional accounting. The CIMA began life as the Institute of Cost Accountants, later becoming the Institute of Cost and Works Accountants. In 1972 it was renamed the Institute of Cost and Management Accountants. It was incorporated by Royal Charter in 1975 and became the Chartered Institute of Management Accountants in 1986.

The CIMA's objectives are the promotion and development of management-accounting methods and techniques. It has developed a set of structured, voluntary guidelines for post-qualification professional development. The CIMA seeks to influence legislation affecting the accounting profession, organizes conferences, and formulates measures of professional competence through its training requirements and programs. It maintains a library and offers research grants to further the study of management accounting. It supports two professorial chairs, organizes conferences, and publishes a monthly professional journal, *Management Accounting*.

The CIMA has maintained entry requirements that are broadly similar to the other five major accountancy bodies in Great Britain, although its professional examinations focus more on management accounting. Until recently, its members were not licensed to practice as public accountants. By 1993, however, almost 1,000 members had registered as members in practice. The great majority of its members works in commerce, industry, or finance, although central and local government, the health service, and education employ increasing numbers. More than half the professionally qualified accountants employed by the British government are CIMA members. Throughout its history, the CIMA has concentrated on equipping students with the advanced skills necessary to become financial directors and controllers of corporations. It has long emphasized the importance of the global dimension, as illustrated by its founder membership of the Fédération des Experts Comptables Européens and the International Federation of Accountants.

A new examination structure took effect in 1993. It contains 16 three-hour papers, a total of 48 hours of examinations. Cost and management accounting represent 24 percent of the total; financial accounting, 17 percent; law, taxation, and economics, 25 percent; quantitative methods and information-technology management, 16 percent; financial management, 6 percent; and management, corporate strategy, and marketing, 12 percent. The examination is divided into four stages, each with four papers. Students with a baccalaureate degree may be exempted from most of the first stage. The CIMA's official syllabus stresses the cumulative nature of the examining process: "In preparing for the examination, students should always remember that the syllabi of papers contained in earlier stages will be reexamined in related papers in later stages." The percentage pass rate in 1992 was 38.8 percent overall, and 33.3 percent in the final, stage-four examination. Admission to CIMA membership requires a minimum of three years' prescribed practical experience of management accounting in an industrial setting for associate status and a further three years' approved experience in a "senior and responsible" position for fellows.

In December 1992, the CIMA had 33,664 members, a gain in membership of almost 60 percent since 1982. As a further indication of growth, the number of student members increased from 40,599 in 1982 to 55,882 in 1992, a 38 percent increase. The median age of the student body in 1992 was 25 to 29 years, and 27 percent held a bachelor's degree. The percentage of overseas members dropped only slightly, from 26 percent to 24 percent, over the 1982–1992 period, although overseas students have decreased from 45 percent to 38 percent of the student body over the same period. Nevertheless, there are members and students in more than 100 countries, and the CIMA holds examinations in 40 regular centers outside Great Britain. It actively encourages the growth of the profession in developing countries. The most significant change has been in the representation of women. In 1982 less than 2 percent of the members were women, but that had increased to 9 percent by 1992. Women are likely to be more strongly represented in the future since women students represented 31 percent of the total in 1992 compared to only 14 percent in 1982.

John Freear

Bibliography

CIMA. *Annual Report, 1992*. London: Chartered Institute of Management Accountants, 1992.
CIMA. *The Chartered Institute of Management Accountants*. A brochure published by the Chartered Institute of Management Accountants. London: n.d.
CIMA. "Professional Development for Management Accountants," *Management Accounting* (England), October 1990, pp. 28–33.
CIMA. *Syllabus, with Effect from the 1993 Examinations*. London: Chartered Institute of Management Accountants, 1992.
Thanks for his generous help from Mr. Martin M.P. Nimmo, director, member and corporate affairs, Chartered Institute of Management Accountants.

See also CERTIFIED MANAGEMENT ACCOUNTANT (CMA) EXAMINATION; COST AND/OR MANAGEMENT ACCOUNTING; INSTITUTE OF MANAGEMENT ACCOUNTANTS

Chief Accountants of the Securities and Exchange Commission

Carman G. Blough (1895–1981) served as first chief accountant of the Securities and Exchange Commission (SEC) from December 1935 to May 1938. He became a certified public accountant in 1922, the same year in which he received his master's degree from the University of Wisconsin. He was on the faculty of the University of North Dakota prior to being appointed to the Wisconsin Tax Commission. He pursued graduate studies at Harvard University and held other academic appointments before joining the SEC staff in 1935. Accounting Series Releases (ASR) No. 1 through No. 8 are attributable to Blough, most notably ASR No. 4, issued April 25, 1938. This release created the doctrine of substantial authoritative support as a basis for relating the role of the private-sector public accounting profession to the SEC's authority over accounting practices of publicly held companies. Blough was also instrumental in the early establishment of SEC procedures related to accounting matters. After leaving the SEC in 1938, Blough worked for Arthur Andersen and Company before returning to government employment during World War II in 1942–1944. He also served for 16 years as research director for the American Institute of Certified Public Accountants (AICPA), starting in 1944.

William Welling Werntz (1908–1964) was educated at Yale University, receiving an undergraduate degree in 1929 and a law degree in 1931. His perspective was thus influenced by the relationship between law and accounting. He taught accounting and finance at Yale from 1929 to 1935, and his later academic career included appointments at George Washington University and the University of Pennsylvania. He joined the SEC staff in 1935 and was named chief accountant in May 1938. He held this post throughout World War II and left in April 1947. Income determination was an important issue for Werntz, who focused on investors' needs. As a result of the McKesson and Robbins case and other auditing questions that arose during his tenure, Werntz was instrumental in influencing the accounting profession's auditing standards.

Earle King (d. 1984) received a certificate from Eastman Business School, subsequently working as a cost accountant over a 10-year period. Although not a CPA, he worked for Arthur Andersen and Company as a field auditor prior to joining the SEC staff in 1934. He was assistant chief accountant to both Blough and Werntz; in that position, he collaborated on many of the ASRs and was thus well acquainted with established precedents. He was appointed chief accountant in April 1947 and served until November 1956. He addressed the issue of income-determination effects of accounting for depreciation in the inflationary postwar years and encouraged the institution of accelerated depreciation as an alternative to current-value revisions. He was also instrumental in establishing the all-inclusive concept of income measurement, in opposition to the current-operating concept of the AICPA's Committee on Accounting Procedure.

Andrew Barr (1901–) received his bachelor's and master's degrees from the University of Illinois. He became a certified public accountant in 1924 and worked for two years in public accounting before joining the faculty at Yale in 1926, teaching and studying economics. After 12 years in academia, he was recruited by Blough to the SEC, where he remained until retirement, with the exception of service as a field-grade officer in World War II. He was appointed chief accountant in November 1956 and held the position until January 1972, the longest tenure in that office to date. During his years on the staff, he was heavily involved in the McKesson and Robbins case and related hearings that led to audit-confirmation procedures

for current assets. During his term as chief accountant, he devised disclosures for nonconsolidated subsidiaries as a result of working on such cases as the Atlantic Research Corporation. Other important contributions he made included the articulation of the independence standard for auditors and the decision to support both deferral and flow-through methods for reporting the investment tax credit.

John C. Burton (1932–) graduated from Haverford College (1954), employed with Arthur Young and Company from 1956–1960, and undertook graduate work leading in 1962 to his Ph.D. at Columbia University, where he has taught both before and since his tenure at the SEC and with New York City. He was appointed chief accountant in April 1972 and served until September 1976, when he became New York City deputy mayor for finance. He was the first chief accountant to be appointed from outside the SEC staff. He assisted in establishing formal acknowledgment of the authority of the Financial Accounting Standards Board (FASB) in ASR No. 150 in 1973 and played a major role in laying the groundwork for establishment of the SEC Practice Section and peer review. He was also instrumental in establishing inflation reporting in ASR No. 190 in 1976.

A. Clarence Sampson (1929–) graduated from the University of Maryland in 1953 and joined the staff of the SEC in 1959 after two years on the staff of Arthur Young and Company and two years in industry practice. He served as acting chief accountant from September 1976 until he was appointed chief accountant in August 1978. He left the office in December 1987 and was appointed to the FASB in 1988. During his term as chief accountant, the passage of the Federal Energy Act and the oil embargo led to a focus on accounting for natural resources and the resulting proposal for reserve-recognition accounting (RRA). When studies of RRA were inconclusive, the final outcome was the authorization of the two alternative methods, full costs and successful efforts, in contrast to the FASB's early standard that singularly employed successful-efforts accounting. Sampson also laid the groundwork for dealing with the expectations gap facing the auditor, and played a role in changing the two-paragraph report of apparent guarantee to the three-paragraph report allowing more qualifying language.

Edmund Coulson (1945–) graduated from the University of Maryland and spent six years

C

in public practice prior to joining the SEC staff in 1975. A certified public accountant, he served as deputy chief accountant prior to being appointed to the office of chief accountant in January 1988. He resigned in January 1991 and entered partnership in New York with Ernst and Young's national practice office. Coulson advanced to the chief accountancy just after the Treadway Commission report was issued in October 1987. He worked with the profession to address the expectations gap related to auditing. He also addressed the issue of auditor independence and the SEC's role in the determination of such independence, particularly in relation to the changing scope of services offered by large firms.

George H. Diacont (1941–) served as acting chief accountant from March 1991 to January 1992, when he became the chief accountant to the Division of Enforcement.

Walter Schuetze (1932–) graduated from the University of Texas, Austin, in 1957 and was a partner at KPMG Peat Marwick and a charter member of the FASB (1973–1976). He rejoined Peat Marwick in 1976. He also served on the AICPA Accounting Standards Executive Committee and the Financial Accounting Standards Advisory Council prior to being appointed chief accountant in January 1992. He has focused on the issue of requiring current-value measurement and other disclosure practices, particularly for financial institutions in the wake of concerns over failures in that industry in the late 1980s and early 1990s.

Julia Grant

Bibliography

Burns, T.J., and E.N. Coffman. *The Accounting Hall of Fame: Profiles of Fifty Members.* Columbus: College of Business, Ohio State University, 1992.

"A Journal Roundtable Discussion: Frank Talk from Former SEC Chief Accountant," *Journal of Accountancy,* December 1988, pp. 76–82.

See also ACCOUNTING HALL OF FAME; ACCOUNTING PRINCIPLES BOARD; ACCOUNTING RESEARCH BULLETINS; ACCOUNTING RESEARCH STUDIES; ACCOUNTING SERIES RELEASE NO. 190; AMERICAN INSTITUTE OF CERTIFIED PUBLIC ACCOUNTANTS; BIG EIGHT ACCOUNTING FIRMS; COMPARABILITY; HISTORICAL COST; INDEPENDENCE OF EXTERNAL AUDITORS; INFLATION ACCOUNTING; MANAGEMENT ADVISORY SERVICES BY CPAS; MCKESSON AND ROBBINS CASE; SECURITIES AND EXCHANGE COMMISSION; TREADWAY COMMISSION

China

China was once a leader in the field of accounting. The history of accounting in China spans about 10,000 years from the origin of accounting to the development of a Chinese style of single entry and double entry bookkeeping.

In about 7000 B.C. in Xian, there was a fairly complicated system of calculation. During this primitive period in China, Chinese bookkeepers engraved accounts on bones and wood boards. This represented an early form of single entry bookkeeping. There were advances made in bookkeeping during the Shang Dynasty (1650–1100 B.C.) and the Zhou Dynasty (1100–256 B.C.). Confucius (551–479 B.C.) started his working career as a frontline official responsible for stores accounting.

The Chinese government adopted the "receipts/payments record-keeping" method and the equation receipts – payments = surplus was used to balance accounts. This process was called *sanzhufa* (the "three-column accounting" method). During the Zhou Dynasty, a quite complete financial and accounting organization was established. The grand treasurer (*dafu*) was the highest-ranking officer in the treasury. The auditor of the national treasury was labeled *zaifu*. The chief accountant (*sikuai*) was the highest-ranking accounting officer and had three subordinate cashiers in charge of receipts, payments, and surplus for the Imperial Court. In tune with the financial and accounting principle of "planning expenditures in the light of revenues," the court of the Zhou Dynasty devoted a great deal of attention to budgeting and to accounting reports. Every year the court decided its budgeted expenditures according to its budgeted revenues. It controlled its expenditures by the estimate of revenues so to achieve a balanced budget. There were 10-day reports, monthly reports, yearly reports, and final reports for each three-year period. These final reports would be submitted to the king. This system was called the *shangji* (grand calculation) system. The King of Zhou and the *zaifu* made decisions for rewards or punishments based on the general final report (the *shouji*). This reporting process, which developed further through the years, was probably without peer in the procedural areas of internal control, budgeting, and auditing (Chatfield 1974).

The Qin Dynasty (221–207 B.C.) and the Han Dynasty (207–A.D. 220) marked the developmental stage of feudal society in China. It was necessary to develop an accounting system from the central government to the local governments. The explanation of commerce during these dynasties called for the development of commercial accounting. Fundamental methods for the calculation of gain or loss in commerce and simple methods of calculating costs of hand-crafted goods were developed. For example, in the wine-processing industry, the costs for raw materials, fuel, and labor were computed separately and also used as the basis for review.

During the prosperous Tang Dynasty (A.D. 618–906), both governmental and commercial accounting made dramatic progress. A department of accounting was established as one of the administrative departments of the national administration. An independent auditing department, the *Bibu*, was established and played an important role in the management of the financial and accounting aspects of the imperial court. Internal-control systems were further perfected. During the Tang Dynasty, a system of cross-checks was established between the accounting department, the cashier, the national treasury, the tax department, auditing, and economic regulators. Instead of the principle of "planning expenditures in the light of revenues," Tang Dynasty financier Yang Yan initiated "controlling expenditures in the light of revenues," in which all expenditures were first budgeted and then all revenues were projected. It was then necessary for the Imperial Court to develop a general budget. During the Song Dynasty (A.D. 960–1279), the accounting department would record and check all accounts based on the balanced budget. Two kinds of accounting equations were popularly employed—the "four-column balance" formula (beginning balance + receipts = payments + ending balance) and the "four-column difference" formula (receipts – payments = ending balance – beginning balance). The four-column method then formed the core of Chinese accounting methodology.

At the end of the Ming Dynasty (A.D. 1368–1644) and the beginning of the Qing Dynasty (A.D. 1644–1912), innovations in commercial bookkeeping began to occur in light of the slow emergence of capitalism. A Chinese version of double entry bookkeeping—the Longmen account—was developed from the four-foot account. The Longmen account adopted a dual approach to account for gains and loss, whereas the four-foot account focused on the concept of assets – liabilities = capital. While the principles were similar to Western bookkeeping, the failure of the capitalistic economic system to develop fully caused China's double entry bookkeeping to be only partially developed. Hence, Western double entry bookkeeping had to be imported at the beginning of the twentieth century.

In 1905 Cai Xiyong wrote an accounting manual that started the spread of Western double entry bookkeeping to China. By 1907 this method was tried by some banks. During the Republic of China (A.D. 1912–1949), Chinese accountants Pan Xulun, Xie Lin, Xu Yongzuo, Yong Jiayuan, An Shaoyun, and Zhao Xiyu made efforts to introduce Western accounting adapted to China. These accountants did reform Chinese accounting and hence helped establish the field of accounting in China.

After the founding of the People's Republic of China in 1949, accounting entered into a new historical stage, characterized by organizational, legislative, philosophical, and theoretical reform. To meet the challenge of globalization, accounting will play an even more significant role in the economy of the twenty-first century.

Guo Daoyang

Bibliography

Chatfield, M. *A History of Accounting Thought*. Hinsdale, IL: Dryden Press, 1974.

Guo, Daoyang. *Accounting History of China*. Vol. 1. Beijing: China Finance and Economic Press, 1982.

———. "Confucius and Accounting," *Accounting Historians Notebook*, Spring 1988, pp. 8–10.

———. "The Historical Contributions of Chinese Accounting (or R – P = E – B)," *Accounting Historians Notebook*, Fall 1989, pp. 6–10.

———. *An Outline History of Accounting Development*. Beijing: Central University of Broadcast and Television Press, 1984.

See also GUO, DAOYANG

C

Church, Alexander Hamilton (1866–1936)

A plant engineer, an accountant, an editor of an engineering magazine, an accounting writer, a management writer, a management consultant, an industrial economist, and an industrial engineer, Alexander Hamilton Church was associated with some of the greatest names in the history of management thought and practice. He worked with J. Slater Lewis, a pioneer writer in management, and with Hans Renold, who was credited with bringing Frederick Winslow Taylor's scientific management to England. Church and L.P. Alford later led the movement to articulate principles of management, which were contrary to standard shop methods of the Taylor school. Church considered himself to be a disciple of Charles Babbage, a nineteenth-century writer on the effects of machinery on the economy and the founder of data processing.

Church was born in England into the British branch of the family of Philip Schuyler, famed American Revolutionary War general. Church's grandmother was Angelica Schuyler, and there is some evidence that Church's father was the illegitimate son of Alexander Hamilton, who was married to another daughter of General Schuyler. Church came to the United States in 1910.

Church was a writer who presented ideas that were holistic solutions to everyday problems. One set of these ideas dealt with machinery. He felt that the "machine-hour rate" method was far superior to other methods of accounting for overhead in a highly capital-intensive firm. Church considered direct-labor approaches to overhead to be disastrous, especially in light of shrinking direct laborers and increasing overhead.

A second set of ideas dealt with time and waste. Church held that machines must not be idle and that accounting should immediately highlight idle machines and, hence, idle capacity. He also stressed that accountants have to be as vitally involved in the issues of waste, spoilage, scrap, and by-product as they are in accounting for utilization of machinery. Accounting, itself, has to be concerned with efficiencies in time, number, and weight, as well as dollars.

A third set of ideas centered on the principle of management. Church believed that each business is different and that local needs must be met within the framework of overall principles. He held that scientific management is a body of principles and not a system. The principles may be applied in a great variety of ways,

so long as the principles are kept. These principles are to be articulated and placed in a logically rigorous system. The control system for an organization is as needed as, and similar in function to, the nervous system of a person.

A fourth set of ideas dealt with distribution costs and expansion policies. Church wrote that expansion to meet new business must be planned and, perhaps, expansion efforts should be focused on wastes. In his view, selling costs and office costs are to be analyzed in many different ways, including unit costs. He maintained that a customer on the books should be a permanent asset to the business. Church was wary of installing specialized machinery without practical assurance that it can be kept working to its full capacity.

Church's best books were *The Proper Distribution of Expense Burden* (1908); *Production Factors in Cost Accounting and Works Management* (1910); *The Science and Practice of Management* (1914); *Manufacturing Costs and Accounts* (1917); and *The Making of an Executive* (1923). In addition to these books, he wrote several others and many journal articles.

Church was well respected in his day, and his writings received good coverage. Because of his failure to develop a school of supporters as did Frederick Taylor, Church became somewhat of a lost figure in accounting and in management. However, he was included in 1956 in Urwick and Wolf's list of pioneers in the history of management. Church was reintroduced into the management literature by Litterer (1961) and Jelinek (1980). Although Garner (1954) gave much coverage to Church, his work in accounting was revived by Schwarzbach and Vangermeersch (1983) in their work on accounting for a highly capital-intensive company. The most significant coverage to Church from the point of view of publicity was given by Johnson and Kaplan (1987) in their classic, *Relevance Lost: The Rise and Fall of Management Accounting*. Church was considered to be the linchpin between the efficiency era and the management accounting needed today in a world in which data-collection techniques are both available and relatively inexpensive compared to the early 1900s.

Richard Vangermeersch

Bibliography

Garner, S.P. *Evolution of Cost Accounting to 1925.* University, AL: University of Alabama Press, 1954.

Jelinek, M. "Toward Systematic Management: Alexander Hamilton Church," *Business History Review*, Spring 1980, pp. 63–79.

Johnson, H.T., and R.S. Kaplan. *Relevance Lost: The Rise and Fall of Management Accounting*. Boston: Harvard Business School Press, 1987.

Litterer, J.A. "Alexander Hamilton Church and the Development of Modern Management," *Business History Review*, Winter 1961, pp. 211–225.

Schwarzbach, H.R., and R. Vangermeersch. "Why We Should Account for the 4th Cost of Manufacturing," *Management Accounting*, July 1983, pp. 24–29.

Scorgie, M.E. "Alexander Hamilton Church: His Family and Early Life." Paper presented at the Sixth World Congress of Accounting Historians, Kyoto, Japan, 1992.

Urwick, L.F., and W.B. Wolf. *The Golden Book of Management*. New York: American Management Associations, 1956, 1984.

Vangermeersch, R. "Alexander Hamilton Church, 1866–1936." In *Biographies of Notable Accountants*, edited by H.R. Givens, pp. 1–3. New York: Random House, 1987.

———. *Alexander Hamilton Church: A Man of Ideas for All Seasons*. New York: Garland, 1988.

See also BABBAGE, CHARLES; COMMON COSTS; COST AND/OR MANAGEMENT ACCOUNTING; DISTRIBUTION COSTS; ENGINEERING AND ACCOUNTING; GARNER, S. PAUL; IMPUTED INTEREST ON CAPITAL; INVENTORY VALUATION; JOHNSON AND KAPLAN'S *RELEVANCE LOST: THE RISE AND FALL OF MANAGEMENT ACCOUNTING*; LEWIS, J. SLATER; MANAGEMENT ACCOUNTING; STANDARD COSTING; TAYLOR, FREDERICK WINSLOW; WELLS, MURRAY CHARLES; WHITMORE, JOHN

City of Glasgow Bank

The British Companies Act of 1855 offered businesses the right to incorporate with limited liability for company managers and directors. The 1856 Companies Act abandoned earlier audit and disclosure requirements. The prevailing attitude was that accounting disclosure was a personal matter best settled by agreement between shareholders and company directors. But despite its policy of noninterference with commercial corporations, Parliament had always been willing to regulate companies whose failure might disrupt the whole economy. The 1855–1856 acts had excluded banks and insurance companies from the privilege of limited liability, and when this right was granted them in 1862, it was on condition that they publish semiannual balance sheets and file copies with the Board of Trade. By the 1880s, statutory regulation was an accepted fact of life for nearly all public service corporations.

Contributing to this change in regulatory policy was the failure in 1878 of the incorporated City of Glasgow Bank. By overvaluing assets, undervaluing liabilities, and misdescribing balance sheet items, the bank's directors had for years hidden its insolvency while continuing to pay dividends. An immediate response to this fraud was a clause in the Companies Act of 1879 requiring annual audits of financial institutions in exchange for the privilege of incorporation with limited liability. The bank's failure also directed attention to public accountants when leading Glasgow practitioners helped liquidate the bank while others testified for the prosecution or the defense.

Michael Chatfield

Bibliography
Edey, H.C., and P. Panitpakdi. "British Company Accounting and the Law, 1844–1900." In *Studies in the History of Accounting*, edited by A.C. Littleton and B.S. Yamey, pp. 356–379. Homewood, IL: Irwin, 1956.

Tyson, R.E. "The Failure of the City of Glasgow Bank and the Rise of Independent Auditing," *Accountant's Magazine*, April 1974, pp. 126–131.

See also COMPANIES ACTS; FRAUD AND AUDITING; LIMITED LIABILITY; SCOTLAND: EARLY WRITERS IN DOUBLE ENTRY ACCOUNTING

Clark, John Maurice (1884–1963)

Born in Northampton, Massachusetts, the son of John Bates Clark and Myra Almeda Smith, John Maurice Clark received a bachelor's degree from Amherst College in 1905 and then went on to earn a doctorate in economics from Columbia University in 1910. Although he initially taught at Colorado College, Amherst, and the University of Chicago, Clark returned to Columbia in 1923, to occupy for the subsequent three decades of his career the professorship that had been previously held by his father.

Clark, a theoretical economist, first set out to explain the factors that contributed to the great efficiency of the giant, capital-intensive industrial organizations that had radically transformed the American economy since the last quarter of the nineteenth century. This interest represented an extension of his father's earlier studies of the economics of industrial concentration. Like his father, Clark believed that the functioning of giant enterprises could not be adequately explained through the use of the traditional tools of classical economic analysis. What he believed was lacking was a clear understanding about how cost-volume relationships varied in businesses burdened with high fixed overheads. Clark thought that the nature of these functions could be discovered through inductive research methodologies. In pursuing this objective, the economist developed two related lines of inquiry. First, he sought to classify cost categories that were relevant in informing particular business decision processes. Second, he demonstrated how crucial precise cost information was for formulating effective regulatory policy for monopolistic and oligopolistic firms.

Clark's thinking about the relationship between costs and decision making was extensively laid out in his first book, *Studies in the Economics of Overhead Costs* (1923). In this work, he emphasized the dynamic elements that drove cost levels over the spectrum of output. Central to his discussion was the analysis of how firms with high fixed costs could, by increasing their volume of output, reduce sharply their average costs of manufacture and thus greatly enhance their efficiency. He also showed how fixed costs could take on the character of variable costs through the extension of time and output ranges. Clark's sensitivity to the complexities of analyzing the activities of business enterprises of great scale and scope was reflected in his elaboration of an array of what today remain fundamental cost categories such as fixed, variable, differential, sunk, joint, direct, and indirect. By extending the conceptual horizons of cost accounting, Clark did much to enhance the usefulness of its information for business decision making.

His book, however, was not limited to a narrow exposition of theoretical issues. Instead, he illustrated the relevance of particular cost concepts through analyses of contemporary problems affecting transportation, public utilities, labor, and other aspects of economic life. Such an understanding, he believed, was important because it provided a precise gauge of the true costs to society of idle or underutilized capacity. He also thought that knowledge of costs was vital to government officials in their drives to structure more equitable contracts for allocating the benefits and burdens of regulated industries.

Clark's second study, *Social Control of Business* (1926), also incorporated an extensive discussion of accounting issues but in the context of national economic governance. In this wide-ranging work he reviewed the institutional relationships that society depended on to control business. Greatest emphasis was placed on explaining the economic and legal factors that impinged on the oversight of monopolistic and oligopolistic firms. Accounting was presented as a vital mechanism for monitoring whether these powerful entities conducted their activities within the bounds established by prevailing public policies. In addition, the study evaluated the underlying technical problems encountered in defining accounting measures that both provided useful economic information and also satisfied the legal and administrative imperatives set down by regulatory legislation. One such problem involved the frustrations encountered in allocating the joint costs of regulated industries either to determine the relative burdens to be imposed on particular consumer segments or to define economically relevant bases for calculating rates. Besides the study of economic institutions and cost accounting, Clark's later scholarship addressed the problems of business cycles and economic decision making, the economic consequences of war, and the preservation of peace.

Paul J. Miranti Jr.

Bibliography

Clark, J.M. *Social Control of Business*. Chicago: University of Chicago Press, 1926.
———. *Studies in the Economics of Overhead Costs*. Chicago: University of Chicago Press, 1923.
Dorfman, J. *The Economic Mind in American Civilization*. Vol. 5. New York: Viking, 1959.

Gruchy, A.G. *Modern Economic Thought: The American Contribution.* New York: Prentice-Hall, 1947. Reprint. New York: A.M. Kelley, 1967.

Hickman, C.A. *J.M. Clark.* New York: Columbia University Press, 1975.

Seligman, B.B. *Main Currents in Modern Economics.* New York: Free Press of Glencoe, 1962.

See also COMMON COSTS; COST AND/OR MANAGEMENT ACCOUNTING; DIRECT COSTING; JOHNSON AND KAPLAN'S *RELEVANCE LOST: THE RISE AND FALL OF MANAGEMENT ACCOUNTING;* MANAGEMENT ACCOUNTING; SOCIAL RESPONSIBILITIES OF ACCOUNTANTS

Closing Entries and Procedures

Historically there have been two motives for closing account books—one relating to bookkeeping procedure and the other to operating results. Today's accounting systems are designed to produce financial statements as their end products. Before the nineteenth century, the bookkeeping objectives accomplished by the closing process were more important. The old ledger was balanced and proved correct, nominal account balances were closed through profit and loss to capital, and the new ledger was opened. Businessmen were usually in personal contact with their affairs, operations could easily be observed, and profits were not hard to estimate. Most financial information was taken directly from the ledger accounts. Statements were normally prepared only at the end of a major project, such as a trading voyage, or after all the pages in a ledger had been filled. Accounting periods were usually unnecessary. The pace of operations guided the accounting process.

Chapters 27 to 34 of Luca Pacioli's "Particularis de Computis et Scripturis" deal mainly with the process of closing and balancing the books. Under the Venetian system, when a venture was concluded, the accounts relating to it were ruled and their balances transferred to profit and loss, which at longer intervals was balanced and closed to the capital account. Another peculiarity was that these closing entries originated in the ledger rather than being posted from the journal.

Though he never mentioned financial statements or periodic income finding, Pacioli recommended annual balancing. He also assumed that a new ledger would be opened each time such a balance was struck, even if the old book was not full. The piecemeal nature of venture trading made the main purpose of annual balancing the detection of errors, not statement preparation. Before the old ledger was closed, its correctness had to be proved. This Pacioli did in two steps—by comparison and then by taking a trial balance. He carefully explained the technique of comparing journal and ledger entries by "calling over" the accounts. The journal was given to an assistant, while the proprietor took the ledger. The assistant read each journal entry aloud and checked it off, while the owner located and ticked off the corresponding ledger entries. If all accounts were correct and no unticked items remained in either book when this calling over was finished, the old ledger could be closed and the new one opened. All asset and liability balances were ruled and their balances transferred to the new book. Expense and revenue accounts were closed to profit and loss, and its balance to capital, which was then ruled and its balance carried forward. This process had to be completed in one day and no new entries were to be made in the meantime.

Pacioli's accounting cycle ended with the trial balance (*summa summarium*). The bookkeeper listed all debit amounts from the old ledger on the left side of a sheet of paper and all credit amounts on the right. If their two "grand totals" were equal, the old ledger was finally considered correct. If they failed to balance, "that would indicate a mistake in your Ledger, which mistake you will have to look for diligently with the industry and intelligence God gave you and with the help of what you have learned."

Andrea Barbarigo was a sedentary merchant whose account books (1431–1449) afford the earliest Venetian example of mature venture bookkeeping. Pacioli described an accounting system essentially like Barbarigo's. Since his business was not continuous in the modern sense, and different voyages had very different chances of success, Barbarigo determined profits separately for each such venture and rarely had reason to close his books. He drew up trial balances in 1431, 1435, and 1440, then let the accounts run until his death in 1449. His son Nicolo kept a ledger from 1456 to 1482 but struck a formal balance only once, in 1482 when the ledger was full.

Alvise Casanova's bookkeeping text *Specchio Lucidissimo* (Venice, 1559) was also mainly a copy of Pacioli's. Casanova was the first author to omit the memorandum book and use only a journal and ledger. But his main contribution was a more systematic ledger closing procedure. He introduced the practice of journalizing not only closing entries but also transfers of open account balances to new ledgers. His venture accounts were closed, not as was usual at the completion of each voyage, but only at year end. All open balances were then transferred to a balance account, after which the ledger was closed and the contents of the balance account were posted to a new ledger.

Like Pacioli, Simon Stevin (1548–1620) was a man of general learning and wide interests who believed in finding practical applications for his ideas. Stevin helped bridge the gap between Renaissance and modern closing procedures. He not only insisted on annual balancing, but contrary to the usual practice of authors, his summary listing of assets and liabilities was made outside the ledger. He recommended that the owner draw up a *staet*, or sheet, listing all assets and liabilities. Periodic income could then be found by comparing net assets with corresponding figures produced at the previous closing. Double entry bookkeeping came to sixteenth century Britain by way of the Low Countries, and Stevin was a major influence on English accountants.

The commercial life of Tudor England was much like that of Renaissance Venice, and the British were fortunate that the Venetian style of double entry, with its venture accounts and irregular balancing, set the pattern for Italian bookkeeping throughout Europe. English businesses were small, trading tended to be sporadic, and profits were calculated separately for individual voyages or commodities. Most firms kept single entry records that amounted to little more than lists of payments and receipts. But even double entry systems could be very crude. Most were hybrids, using some dual entries but without profit and loss or capital accounts. The typical sixteenth century ledger was a single book containing all a firm's accounts, with little attempt at classification. When one ledger page was filled, the balance was simply transferred forward to the next empty page, with the result that cash and other commonly used accounts reappeared at intervals throughout the ledger. Even a century later, many books contained only receivables and payables, and the same customer's account might handle both. Business and personal affairs were mixed together. Not

until the eighteenth century was there a general awareness of double entry's ability to summarize as well as record.

Those merchants who used double entry and those who did not had similar motives for keeping accounts. At a minimum, they had to keep track of credit dealings, inventories, and partners' capital. The authors of bookkeeping texts stressed that double entry's main advantage was its ability to make such records orderly and complete. That is, little data was provided that could not be got by simpler means, but ledger balances afforded a classified record of past transactions for ready reference. And the descriptive style of journal and ledger entries made it easy for merchants to review particular transactions in detail. Though there was often a desire to calculate profits, automatic profit finding was never built into surviving sixteenth century English account books and does not seem to have been a dominant motive for adopting double entry. Nor were historical accounting results typically used in choosing among alternatives or in allocating resources. The opportunistic nature of trading made past operations an uncertain guide to the future, and most merchants apparently did not rely on venture accounts for decisionmaking data—experience was considered less important than fresh news.

Under such conditions, the closing process furnished an arithmetic check and, by clearing the ledger of nominal accounts, facilitated the opening of new books. It might incidentally provide the owner with financial statements. While texts often mentioned statements, the greater importance in practice of narrow bookkeeping goals is shown by (1) the irregularity and infrequency of balancing, (2) the failure to correct errors, (3) the limited use made of the profit and loss account, and (4) the variety of asset valuation methods employed.

The striking difference between the seventeenth century and modern bookkeeping technique was the failure to balance and close the books regularly. The closing process was tied to random events: the end of a voyage, the filling of a ledger, the sale of a business, the dissolving of a partnership, a merchant's bankruptcy or death. There was no concept of periodic reckoning. Many early texts recommended closing ledgers only when they were full, and most authors who demonstrated annual balancing implied that it was optional.

The infrequency of balancing made it a difficult process, and the great test of "accountantship" was the ability to get a correct trial balance. Yet in many cases no attempt was made to correct books that were out of balance. With no responsibility to outsiders, merchants could please themselves, and close contact with their affairs may also have reduced the need for periodic checks on ledger accuracy. The result was a sliding scale of care within the double entry system, in which the accounts of customers, suppliers, and partners were kept current and accurate, but no great effort was made to verify total operating results.

The lack of accrual accounting and periodic balancing, and the mixing of personal and business affairs in the ledger, are all evidences of a disinterest in calculating total income. Venture account balances showed the profitability of particular goods and voyages. Total profit was usually thought of as the change in value of all a merchant's possessions from all causes between two balancing dates, or "rests." Its determination was not a task in itself, but a by-product of the closing process. Profit and loss tended to become simply a clearing account. Realized and unrealized income and losses, business and personal items, capital and revenue expenditures, venture accounts, capital contributions and drawings, asset revaluations—all were cleared through or entered directly to the profit and loss account. It also became a receptacle for items that did not seem to belong anywhere else and a contra entry for debits which appeared to have no credit entries, and vice versa. Even if the resulting net profit figure had been considered important, it could not have revealed a firm's comparative progress or isolated the business reasons for capital changes.

The main technical increment between the sixteenth and nineteenth centuries was the more frequent use in later accounts of double entry's summarizing ability. James Winjum considered that "double entry brought the concept of capital into the accouting records." But the eighteenth century merchant still valued double entry chiefly for its ability to bring order to his accounts. Most problems we associate with profit finding and asset valuation concerned him hardly at all. Without the paraphernalia of accruals, matching, or periodic reckonings, his inventory accounts measured the results of particular operations, while paging through the ledger gave him some idea of overall activity. But he developed neither a clear concept of income nor systematic proce-

dures for judging the success or failure of his business over a period of time. Public investment in firms was rare, a tradition of accountability to outsiders was lacking, and financial statements were of minor importance. It was the industrial revolution, not the bookkeeping innovations preceding it, that drew out accountancy's analytical potential. The adoption of standardized periodic closing procedures by a majority of businesses came only after 1850, with the manufacturing corporation, the income tax, and the emerging accounting profession as major stimulants.

Michael Chatfield

Bibliography

Geijsbeek, J.B. *Ancient Double-Entry Bookkeeping: Lucas Pacioli's Treatise.* Denver: University of Colorado, 1914. Reprint. Houston: Scholars Book, 1974, and Osaka: Nihon Shoseki, 1975.

Solomons, D. "The Maner and Fourme How to Keepe a Perfect Reconyng," *Lloyds Bank Review*, no. 43, 1957, pp. 34–46.

Winjum, J.O. "Accounting in its Age of Stagnation," *Accounting Review*, October 1970, pp. 743–771.

———. *The Role of Accounting in the Economic Development of England, 1500–1750.* Urbana, IL: Center for International Education and Research in Accounting, University of Illinois, 1972.

Yamey, B.S. "Closing the Ledger," *Accounting and Business Research*, Winter 1970, pp. 71–77.

———. "The Functional Development of Double-Entry Bookkeeping." *Accountant*, November 2, 1940, pp. 332–342.

———. "Some Topics in the History of Financial Accounting in England, 1500–1900." In *Studies in Accounting Theory*, edited by W.T. Baxter and S. Davidson, pp. 14–43. Homewood, IL: Irwin, 1962.

See also ACCRUAL ACCOUNTING; ALBERTI DEL GIUDICE; BALANCE ACCOUNT; BALANCE SHEET; BARBARIGO, ANDREA; BRANCH ACCOUNTING; CAPITAL ACCOUNT; DOUBLE ENTRY BOOKKEEPING: ORIGINS; FLORI, LUDOVICO; JOURNAL; LEDGER; MANZONI, DOMENICO; PACIOLI, LUCA; PEELE, JAMES; PERIODICITY; PIETRA, ANGELO; SAVARY, JACQUES; STEVIN, SIMON; *SUMMA SUMMARIUM;* TRIAL BALANCE; YMPYN, JAN

Cohen Commission: Commission on Auditors' Responsibilities

The Cohen Commission (1974–1978) was formed in October 1974 by the American Institute of Certified Public Accountants (AICPA) in the aftermath of the Equity Funding debacle, which became public knowledge in the spring of 1973 (AICPA 1975). The committee was chaired by Manuel F. Cohen, a former commissioner of the Securities and Exchange Commission (SEC).

The commission's charge was to arrive at conclusions and make recommendations pertaining to the responsibilities of independent auditors. The greatest concern was whether a gap existed between the public's expectations of an audit and what an audit actually accomplishes. Should a gap exist, then the disparity between expectation and accomplishment would have to be resolved.

Research conducted or sponsored by the commission was used in developing its conclusions and recommendations. The research projects consisted of background papers, conferences and interviews, analyses of major legal cases alleging audit failures, and surveys.

The commission concluded that (1) a gap did exist; (2) the gap was traceable to the failure of the auditing profession to react and evolve to keep abreast of the changing environment; and (3) users' expectations (in most cases) are reasonable, but there is some misunderstanding of the auditor's role and the nature of audit services. The following is a brief distillation of the Committee's conclusions and recommendations:

1. *The Role of the Independent Auditor*—Management has the direct responsibility for the integrity of the financial statements; whereas, the auditor has the responsibility to audit the financial statements and express an opinion on them.

2. *The Selection of Accounting Principles*—The auditor should neither accept management's selection of an accounting principle because its use is not denied, nor accept management's rejection of a principle because it is not required. Instead, the auditor should evaluate the overall effect of management's judgment in the presentation of the financial statements.

3. *Reporting of Uncertainties*—Uncertainties should not be discussed as part of the audit report but should be disclosed in a separate note to the financial statements, similar to the note on accounting policies.

4. *Responsibility for Detecting Fraud*—The auditor has a duty to search for fraud and is expected to detect those frauds which are detectable with the exercise of professional skill and care.

5. *Corporate Conduct*—The auditor has the responsibility to review information and representations of management and its counsel to determine the adequacy of the quality and completeness of disclosures pertaining to any illegal and questionable acts of management.

6. *Boundaries of the Auditing Function*—The audit function should not include separate evaluations of the degree to which corporate activities are efficient, economic, or effective.

7. *Communication with Users*—The audit report should be revised to reflect the technical elements of the audit function in a more precise and less ambiguous manner, and the consistency requirement should be eliminated.

8. *Competence*—To ensure adequate education, training, and development of competent auditors, emphasis was placed on the development of professional schools of accounting and involvement of accounting educators, who are not CPAs, in the ongoing activities of the state society and institute activities.

9. *Independence*—The acceptance of an audit engagement expecting to offset lower revenues with higher fees to be charged in the future is deemed a threat to the auditor's independence. Likewise, the acceptance of gifts or favors from clients controverts the maintenance of an attitude of independence.

10. *Auditing Standards*—Outside groups should be involved in the standard setting process. A statement on the role of the auditor should be incorporated in the auditing standards; this statement should be revised periodically to reflect the changing conditions.

11. *Audit Quality Control*—To improve and ensure high quality of audit performance, the institution of independent peer reviews of accounting firms, issuance of the findings of the peer reviews, and the establishment of independent oversight groups to supervise the peer reviews were recommended

Stanley C. W. Salvary

Bibliography

American Institute of Certified Public Accountants. *Report of the Special Com-*

mittee on Equity Funding. New York: AICPA, 1975.

Commission on Auditors' Responsibilities. *Statement of Issues: Scope and Organization of the Study of Auditors' Responsibilities.* New York: AICPA, 1975.

———. *Report, Conclusions, and Recommendations.* New York: AICPA, 1978.

See also FRAUD AND AUDITING; INDEPENDENCE OF EXTERNAL AUDITORS

Cole, William Morse (1866–1960)

Corporations have published funds flow statements since 1862 in Britain and since 1863 in the United States. By 1903 at least four variants existed: reports summarizing changes in cash and cash equivalents, in current assets, in working capital, and in all financial activities. But there was no agreement about which type of statement was superior or what form it should take.

In four textbooks published between 1908 and 1921, the American accountant William Morse Cole illustrated a "where-got, where-gone" statement designed to summarize changes in all balance sheet accounts. Cole reasoned that net increases in asset balances indicated that expenditures had been made to acquire property, whereas decreases in liability accounts showed that debts had been paid. Similarly, net increases in assets indicated something taken from asset accounts during the year and spent elsewhere, while liability increases suggested that the firm had acquired resources by borrowing. Cole labeled increases in liabilities and decreases in assets "Where-got (*or* Receipts *or* Credits)," and listed asset increases and liability decreases as "Where-gone (*or* Expenditures *or* Debits)." By comparing beginning and ending balance sheet items, Cole hoped to show the effects of internal transactions and especially to portray shifts in liquidity. But in cumulating *net* changes in balance sheet accounts, he failed to isolate the sources of liquidity changes and thereby to reveal the ultimate effects of receipts and expenditures. He also tacitly assumed that every balance sheet change increases or decreases the total amount of a firm's resources.

Michael Chatfield

Bibliography

Cole, W.M. *Accounts, Their Construction and Interpretation.* Boston: Houghton Mifflin, 1908 and 1915.

———. *Accounting and Auditing.* New York: Cree Publishing Co., 1910.

———. *The Fundamentals of Accounting.* Boston: Houghton Mifflin, 1921.

Kafer, K., and V.K. Zimmerman. "Notes on the Evolution of the Statement of Sources and Application of Funds," *International Journal of Accounting,* Spring 1967, pp. 89–121.

Rosen, L.S., and D.T. DeCoster. "Funds Statements: A Historical Perspective," *Accounting Review,* January 1969, pp. 124–136.

See also CAPITAL MAINTENANCE; FUNDS FLOW STATEMENT; IMPUTED INTEREST ON CAPITAL; LIQUIDITY: ACCOUNTING MEASUREMENT

Collector v. Hubbard

See *SPRINGER V. UNITED STATES*

College and University Accounting

Accounting and financial reporting for colleges and universities evolved primarily through the efforts of college business officers. The emphasis has been primarily on control—the need for the chief business officer to keep track of and report, in a stewardship fashion, the college and university transactions in accord with the many restrictions and categories. For many years, the primary standard-setters, the American Institute of Certified Public Accountants (AICPA) and the Financial Accounting Standards Board (FASB), paid little attention to college and university accounting; recently, however, college and university accounting and reporting have been at the center of controversy regarding jurisdiction of standard-setting between the FASB and the Governmental Accounting Standard Board (GASB).

Detailed histories can be found in various editions of *College and University Business Administration,* published first by the American Council on Education and later by the National Association of College and University Business Officers (NACUBO). The very first publication was *Standard Forms for Financial Reports,* issued in 1910 by the Carnegie Foundation for the Advancement of Teaching. In 1935 the National Committee on Standard Reports for Institutions of Higher Education issued a report, *Financial Reports for Colleges and Universities*, which was considered the definitive work at that time. Beginning in 1935, the American Council on Education was responsible for issuing 21 bulletins over a period of five years.

In 1952 the first edition of *College and University Business Administration* was published by the American Council on Education. This volume contained illustrative financial statements, basic accounting principles, sections on budgetary accounting and on auditing, and an appendix with accounting terminology. The book was revised in 1968.

In 1974 a third edition of *College and University Business Administration: Administrative Service* was published by the NACUBO. This edition was the result of the efforts of the NACUBO, the AICPA, and the National Center for Higher Education Management Systems. The AICPA issued *Audits of Colleges and Universities* in 1973 and Statement of Position 74-8, "Financial Accounting and Reporting by Colleges and Universities," in 1974. At that time, the NACUBO and AICPA documents were very similar and considered the standard for reporting. The NACUBO document is maintained in looseleaf form, with periodic changes and supplements. However, these standards were not under Rule 203 of the AICPA—that is, the principles did not carry the same weight as principles passed by the Accounting Principles Board and the then-new FASB. In 1979 the FASB passed Statement No. 32, which declared that accounting and reporting standards in several AICPA Audit Guides and Statements of Position, including those for colleges and universities, were considered preferable until the FASB issued standards. The standards contained in the 1973 and 1974 publications, with a few exceptions, remain preferable practice as of this writing. Fund accounting is used, distinctions are made between restricted and unrestricted resources, accrual accounting is practiced (although expenditures, not expenses, are reported), plant funds are used for fixed assets and long-term debt, and endowments, life income funds, and annuities are reported separately as of 1994.

In 1978 the FASB issued a research report by Robert N. Anthony, *Financial Accounting in Nonbusiness Organizations*, which raised many issues for governmental and nongovernmental not-for-profit organizations, including colleges and universities, and which launched a process of inquiry into the jurisdiction of standard-setting. In 1984 the GASB was created to set accounting and reporting principles for state and local governmental units. In 1986 the AICPA gave the GASB Rule 203 authority; from that year, GASB pronouncements were fully authoritative.

Once the GASB was created, the possibility existed that different standards would be passed for colleges and universities that are government related and for those that are not. Subsequent policy statements tended to do just that. For example, FASB Statement No. 93, "Recognition of Depreciation by Not-for-Profit Organizations" (1987), required private institutions, such as the University of Chicago, to record depreciation. GASB Statement No. 8, "Applicability of FASB Statement No. 93, Recognition of Depreciation by Not-for-Profit Organizations, to Certain State and Local Government Entities" (1988), permitted public colleges and universities, such as the University of Illinois, to ignore FASB Statement No. 93.

Statement on Auditing Standards No. 69, issued in 1991, generally reaffirmed the existing standard-setting jurisdiction, ensuring that accounting and reporting principles would differ in the future, depending upon whether the college or university is public or private. As the 1990s progressed, the FASB was moving toward a common display for all nongovernmental, not-for-profit organizations, including colleges and universities, that would present resources in categories of "unrestricted," "temporarily restricted," and "restricted."

The GASB has a project specifically concerned with accounting and reporting for colleges and universities and in 1988 it issued a report on a user needs study by John H. Engstrom from Northern Illinois University. In 1991 the GASB issued Statement No. 15, "Governmental College and University Accounting and Financial Reporting Models," indicating that public colleges and universities could use either the "governmental" model used for state and local governmental units or the "AICPA Model," as shown in the AICPA Audit Guide. Most will likely use the "AICPA model."

A number of texts have been written on college and university accounting including those by Lloyd Morey, *University and College Accounting* (1930), Gail A. Mills, *Accounting Manual for Colleges* (1937), Edward V. Miles, Jr., *Manual of Teachers College Accounting* (1940), Clarence Scheps, *Accounting for Colleges and Universities* (1949), and Scheps and E.E. Davidson (1970, 2nd ed., 1978, 3rd ed.).

The history of college and university accounting reflects a need for control by college and university business officers, for accountability to the public and sponsoring governments and agencies by college administrators and boards, and for information useful to resource providers and policymakers. A tension exists between the need for common information reported by all of higher education and the inherent differences between institutions in the private and public sectors. Determination of reporting standards has passed from college business officers to public standard-setters. Only time will tell whether user needs will be better met by this change.

John H. Engstrom

Bibliography
American Council on Education. *College and University Business Administration.* Washington, DC: American Council on Education, 1952.
———. *College and University Business Administration.* Rev. ed. Washington, DC: American Council on Education, 1968.
American Institute of Certified Public Accountants. *Audits of Colleges and Universities.* Audit Guide. New York: AICPA, 1973, 1975.
———. "Financial Accounting and Reporting by Colleges and Universities." Statement of Position 74-8. New York: AICPA, 1974.
———. "The Meaning of 'Presents Fairly in Conformity with Generally Accepted Accounting Principles' in the Independent Auditor's Report." Statement on Auditing Standards No. 69. New York: AICPA, 1991.
Anthony, R.N. *Financial Accounting in Nonbusiness Organizations: An Exploratory Study of Conceptual Issues.* FASB Research Report. Norwalk, CT: FASB, 1978.
Carnegie Foundation for the Advancement of Teaching. *Standard Forms for Financial Reports.* New York: Carnegie Foundation, 1910.
Engstrom, J.H. *Information Needs of College and University Financial Decision Makers.* GASB Research Report. Norwalk, CT: GASB, 1988.
Miles, E.V. Jr. *Manual of Teachers College Accounting.* Washington, DC: American Council on Education, 1940.
Morey, L. *University and College Accounting.* New York: John Wiley & Sons, 1930.
National Association of College and University Business Officers. *College and University Business Administration: Administrative Service.* 3d ed. Washington, DC: NACUBO, 1974.
National Committee on Standard Reports for Institutions of Higher Education. *Financial Reports for Colleges and Universities.* Chicago: University of Chicago Press, 1935.

See also FINANCIAL ACCOUNTING STANDARDS BOARD

C

Colonial America, Accounting in

Accounting has been a significant factor in America from the beginning, starting with the accountant placed with Columbus's crew by Ferdinand and Isabella. Some of the early colonies—for example, Jamestown in 1607, Plymouth in 1620, and Massachusetts Bay in 1629—were settled by undertakings of joint stock companies. Accounting disputes were numerous between the settlers of Plymouth and the English shareholders until the final settlement of accounts in 1641. Municipal accounting was much better developed. For instance, London stockholders in 1645 created the post of auditor general in their Massachusetts Bay Colony.

The economy of the English colonies was primarily agrarian. In New England, where the main trade items were timber and fish, about 90 percent of the settlers lived on small farms and hence had a minimum need for accounting records. The operation of Southern plantations, which supplied tobacco and were much larger than New England farms, called for more formal accounting record-keeping as witnessed by the account books of Presidents Washington and Jefferson. Since the mother country wanted the colonies to buy finished goods made in England, manufacturing in the colonies was discouraged. However, there was a merchant class that depended on accounting records to handle business events. Alexander Hamilton, perhaps the most significant financial figure in U.S. history, was a successful countinghouse clerk in St. Croix before coming to America in 1773.

Although accounts were kept in English currency, there were almost none of these coins in circulation. While some Spanish coins circulated, most accounts were settled by barter—hence, the term "barter-bookkeeping"—or by exchange of drafts or by an occasional cash payment. Each of the colonies eventually issued paper currency, causing inflation and exchange problems.

Education about bookkeeping and accounting was conducted by experts giving lectures and later running their own schools. John Morton was hired by the Plymouth Colony in 1671 to teach the young how to "read an write and cast up accounts" as noted in the *Three Centuries of Accounting in Massachusetts*. McMickle and Jensen (1988) credit Andrew Bradford's *The Secretary's Guide, or Young Man's Companion,* published in 1737, as the first American book to include a section on bookkeeping. Mair's book, published in Edinburgh, in its 1763 edition included a section on the produce and commerce of the Tobacco Colonies. This book appears to have been the standard text of the late colonial period.

Richard Vangermeersch

Bibliography

Baxter, W.T. "Accounting in Colonial America." In *Studies in the History of Accounting*, edited by A.C. Littleton and B.S. Yamey, pp. 272–287. Homewood, IL: Irwin, 1956.

Gambino, A.J., and J.R. Palmer. *Management Accounting in Colonial America*. New York: National Association of Accountants, 1976.

Holmes, W., L.H. Kistler, and L.S. Corsini. *Three Centuries of Accounting in Massachusetts*. New York: Arno Press, 1978.

Mair, John. *Book-keeping Methodized*. 7th ed. Edinburgh: Sands, Kincaid and Bell, Donaldson, 1763.

McMickle, P.L., and P.H. Jensen. *The Birth of American Accountancy*. New York: Garland, 1988.

Scott, W.R. *The Constitution and Finance of English, Scottish, and Irish Joint-Stock Companies to 1720*. Vol. 2, *Companies for Foreign Trade, Colonization, Fishing, and Mining*. London: Cambridge University Press, 1910.

Shenkir, W.B., G.A. Welsh, and J.A. Bear Jr. "Thomas Jefferson: Management Accountant," *Journal of Accountancy,* April 1972, pp. 33–47.

See also ACCOUNTING EDUCATION IN THE UNITED STATES; BARTER; FEDERAL GOVERNMENT ACCOUNTING (U.S.); MONEY; SINGLE ENTRY BOOKKEEPING; STONE, WILLIARD E.

Commander Theory

Australian accountant Louis Goldberg viewed the corporation as a fictitious person substituting for actual decision makers. He agreed with William J. Vatter that emphasis on ownership rights handicapped the proprietary and entity theories. But he also criticized Vatter's fund theory for failing to account for changes in the size and composition of asset groupings and for ignoring personal motivations. Goldberg considered that stockholders, whose very numbers typically prevent them from controlling company policy, are seldom the driving force in modern corporations. He suggested that the most strategic view of corporate activities is that of the top executives or "commanders" who make the decisions and run the business from day to day. Rather than focusing on the special interests of one ownership group or another, accountants should judge how effectively managers have used corporate resources.

The commander theory treats financial statements as reports on stewardship. The balance sheet is a statement of accountability for the resources placed in management's care. The income statement expresses the results of managerial activities and shows how resources have been used to achieve these results. The cash flow statement shows how managers have obtained resources and what they have done with them.

This theory of the firm fails to specify the recipients of accounting information. Nor does it consider the external political and social influences on decision makers. It is true that managers direct company operations, but the corporation must also interact with its environment. Because it focuses entirely on power and decision making within the firm, the commander theory does not offer a comprehensive description of business activities or a basis for evaluating the whole spectrum of accounting concepts and methods.

Michael Chatfield

Bibliography

Goldberg, L. *An Inquiry into the Nature of Accounting*. American Accounting Association Monograph No. 7. Sarasota,

FL: American Accounting Association, 1965.

See also STEWARDSHIP; VATTER, WILLIAM JOSEPH

Commenda Contracts

Seaborne trading through consignment agents and single-venture partnerships was of primary importance in developing the Venetian and Genoese styles of double entry bookkeeping. An investing partner, or *commendator*, trusted his goods to a traveling merchant (*tractador*), who risked the sea voyage, did the actual trading, and on his return made a detailed accounting. In twelfth-century Genoa, such partnership contracts took two main forms: the *commenda*, financed entirely by the investing partner, who got three-fourths of the profits, and the *societas maris*, in which the traveling partner usually invested a third of the capital and shared profits equally.

Michael Chatfield

Bibliography

De Roover, F.E. "Partnership Accounts in Twelfth Century Genoa." In *Studies in the History of Accounting*, edited by A.C. Littleton and B.S. Yamey, pp. 86–90. Homewood, IL: Irwin, 1956.

Littleton, A.C. *Accounting Evolution to 1900*. New York: American Institute Publishing, 1933. Reprint. New York: Russell and Russell, 1966.

See also LIMITED LIABILITY; PAR VALUE DOCTRINE; PARTNERSHIP ACCOUNTING; SAVARY, JACQUES

Common Costs

The issue of how to treat common costs such as rent, interest, and central administration costs came to prominence in Great Britain and the United States toward the end of the nineteenth century. The issue arose when prices became very competitive and manufacturers were perceived to be underpricing and thereby threatening their industry. The stove, footwear, ceramics, railway, and tin-mining industries were among the first to discuss the problem openly. They campaigned vigorously during the 1880s to ensure that manufacturers understood the importance of covering their overheads. However, it was the American mechanical engineers who actively promoted systems for the treatment of overhead costs within their costing systems. Alexander Hamilton Church was the most notable advocate for the allocation of common costs. Interest was also stimulated by the "scientific management" movement usually associated with Frederick Winslow Taylor. Murray C. Wells in 1978 reported that E.L. Burton, Holden A. Evans, Morrell W. Gaines, and Henry Laurence Gantt were prominent in offering solutions for dealing with common costs in the United States while J. Slater Lewis, Emile Garke and J.M. Fells, H.R. Towne and G.P. Norton were also active in Great Britain.

The difference between fixed and variable costs had been recognized early in the nineteenth century. However, costing systems in general, and the treatment of overhead costs in particular, received little attention until the last quarter of that century. Several authors have suggested that this was because, early in the nineteenth century, profits on manufactured goods and in other industries such as mining were high enough to absorb all the costs of the enterprise and because overheads were relatively small. It was the advent of the large, centrally managed manufacturing concerns and the capital-intensive industries such as the railways that brought the issues to the fore. Even then, it was not the large capital investments introduced by the industrial revolution that brought about an awareness of the need to account for overhead costs; it was competition. And it was no coincidence that the issue came to prominence following the economic downturn of the 1880s. It was the effects of that depression that led industry associations to become involved, and, in both the general literature and the proceedings of trade associations of the time, the importance of allocating overheads arose in the context of pricing. There are frequent references to "the correct apportionment" or "an equitable basis" for the allocation of common costs, especially manufacturing overheads, to products.

While Britain was the first nation to benefit from the industrial revolution, the natural tendency of British managers and owners to treat the accounts as secret inhibited discussion of costing methods. Nevertheless, some prominent manufacturers are cited, by L. Urwick and E.F.L. Brech (1946) including Wedgewood (ceramics), Boulton and Watt (steam engines) and

Cowan (roads and bridges), although descriptions of systems in use are scant and often vague about the details. In contrast, the American mechanical engineers appeared to have no such inhibitions. Between 1880 and 1910, the proceedings of their society meetings are replete with references to, and examples of, costing methods. Many famous names are among the contributors, including Taylor, Andrew Carnegie, F.A. Halsey, and, of course, Church (there is even reference to "Herr A Messerschmidt of Essen, Germany").

The most commonly advocated allocation base was direct labor hours, but the effects of the industrial revolution were soon apparent in the growing support for machine hours as the most appropriate base. One of Church's main contributions was the notion of a "supplementary rate" designed to allocate the "undistributed balance of shop charges due to idleness of production centers." The nature and components of common costs were also the subject of much debate. Engineers, generally, favored the allocation of all costs. Several, like Sterling H. Bunnell in 1911, advocated different bases for the allocation of "shop costs" and "office costs." Others, like L. Whittem Hawkins in 1910, included all indirect costs under the generic heading of "oncosts."

By 1914 the interest of engineers in costing methods appears to have waned. Discussion shifted to professional groups of accountants, and the emphasis changed from pricing and efficiency to the valuation of inventories. The accountants added nothing new. By the time discussion of the "correct," "best," or "most equitable" method of overhead allocation appeared in the accounting literature, all of the issues, including the treatment of interest, depreciation, the use of a "supplementary rate," variance analysis, and even the use of standard costing, had already been debated by the engineers. Little changed over the next 50 years despite sporadic attention to such topics as variable costing, relevant costing, and, more recently, activity-based costing. Even now, costing systems in use bear a close resemblance to those developed 100 years ago. Only the technology has changed; the system in use is fundamentally the same.

Murray C. Wells

Bibliography

Battersby, T. *The Perfect Double Entry Book-Keeper (Abridged) and the Perfect Prime Cost and Profit Demonstrator for Iron and Brass Founders, Machinists, Engineers, Shipbuilders, Manufacturers, Etc.* Manchester and London: John Heywood, 1878.

Bunnell, S.H. "Expense Burden: Its Incidence and Distribution," *Transactions of the American Society of Mechanical Engineers*, vol. 33, 1911, pp. 538–539.

Church, A.H. "The Proper Distribution of Expense Burden," *Engineering Magazine*, July–December 1901, July, pp. 508–517, August, pp. 725–734, September, pp. 804–812, October, pp. 31–40, November, pp. 231–240, and December, pp. 367–376 respectively.

Hawkins, L.W. *Cost Accounting: An Explanation of Principles and a Guide to Practice.* Chicago: LaSalle Ext. University, 1910.

Norton, G. *Textile Manufacturers Bookkeeping for the Counting House, Mill, and Warehouse.* London: Hamilton, Adams, 1889.

Urwick, L., and E.F.L. Brech. *The Making of Scientific Management*; vol. 2, *Management in British Industry.* London: Management Publications Trust, 1946.

Wells, M.C. *A Bibliography of Cost Accounting: Its Origins and Development to 1914.* Champaign, IL: Center for International Education and Research in Accounting, University of Illinois, 1978.

See also ACTIVITY BASED COSTING; BREAK-EVEN CHART; CHURCH, ALEXANDER HAMILTON; CLARK, JOHN MAURICE; COST AND/OR MANAGEMENT ACCOUNTING; DIRECT COSTING; ENGINEERING AND ACCOUNTING; GANTT, HENRY LAURENCE; GARCKE AND FELLS; HARRISON, G. CHARTER; INVENTORY VALUATION; JOHNSON AND KAPLAN'S *RELEVANCE LOST: THE RISE AND FALL OF MANAGEMENT ACCOUNTING*; JUST-IN-TIME MANUFACTURING; LADELLE, O.G.; LEWIS, J. SLATER; MANAGEMENT ACCOUNTING; METCALFE, HENRY; NICHOLSON, J. LEE; SANDERS, THOMAS HENRY; STANDARD COSTING; TAYLOR, FREDERICK WINSLOW; THOMAS'S *THE ALLOCATION PROBLEM IN FINANCIAL ACCOUNTING THEORY*; WELLS, MURRAY CHARLES

Companies Acts

The British companies acts were intended to regulate the formation of corporations and to permit continuing supervision of their directors' handling of company affairs. To achieve these goals, a reporting obligation was imposed in exchange for the right to incorporate with limited liability. Between 1844 and 1900, the acts tried principally to establish minimum auditing and reporting standards. Since 1900 they have concentrated on improving financial statement quality by raising standards of disclosure.

Incorporation by registration, but with unlimited liability, was first permitted by the Joint Stock Companies Act of 1844. This act was soon amended and reissued as the Companies Clauses Consolidation Act of 1845. It required that account books be kept and periodically balanced and that directors prepare and sign a "full and fair" annual balance sheet, which would then be examined by one or more of the stockholders. It was hoped that these shareholders would be able, through their knowledge of conditions obtained by audit, to learn what the company's directors were doing, to make them justify their actions, and to influence their subsequent behavior. The 1845 act authorized such investor-auditors to inspect the company's books and to question officers and employees. Their main task was to evaluate the balance sheet and report to the assembled stockholders whether it displayed a "true and correct View of the State of the Company's Affairs." Directors were to send printed copies of the balance sheet, together with the auditor's report, to stockholders 10 days before their general meeting and were to file an identical balance sheet with the registrar of joint stock companies.

Though ambitious in intent, this first effort at audit legislation was weak procedurally and far ahead of its time in the sense that means to implement it did not yet exist. Moreover, audit attention was fixed on the traditional issues of company solvency and managerial integrity, ignoring questions of profit measurement and dividend policy, which most stockholders would have found more relevant. The acts provided for the appointment of auditors but were silent as to their qualifications, tenure, remuneration, and specific duties. No attempt was made to specify the form or contents of the statutory balance sheet or the asset valuation methods to be used. This lack of precision would have been less damaging had there been a coherent body of doctrine to give substance to the phrase "true and correct." But the 1844–1845 acts were needed precisely be-

cause there was no professional control over accounting practice. The same factors that made accounting regulation necessary made it inadequate.

The acts assumed that stockholders themselves would form a committee, check the books, and report back to their colleagues. And at midcentury one could actually find teams of investors making periodic visits to corporations in which they held shares, ticking off ledger balances against their printed balance sheets, and seeing that each cash payment was covered by a voucher. This was nothing but the traditional stewardship audit in modern dress, with shareholders taking the part of manorial lords, and company directors cast in the role of medieval bailiffs. James Hutton called audits under the 1845 act a "complete farce," and certainly directors found it easy to file misleading or simply uninformative financial statements. Parliament had neglected to provide enforcement machinery, and the registrar of companies had no authority to reject balance sheets submitted to him. The law did not require the date of the statutory balance sheet to be related to the date of the stockholder's meeting, and some corporations filed identical statements year after year. In other cases, meetings were called with minimum notice, or shareholders friendly to management were appointed as auditors. It soon became evident that only an examination by professionals could provide the meaningful check of directors intended by the law. The 1844–1845 statutes provided for the employment of skilled accountants as "assistants" to the stockholder-auditors. Finally these assistants took over the whole audit examination.

The Companies Acts of 1855–1856 introduced corporate registration with limited liability. It would have been logical to remedy the defects of the 1845 act and protect against abuses of the new law by strengthening the mandatory audit requirements. Instead, Parliament eliminated the compulsory bookkeeping, reporting, and auditing clauses of the earlier act, leaving the accounting methods of most commercial corporations completely unregulated. This abandonment of statutory requirements may actually have increased the auditor's importance, but it weakened the idea that incorporation was a privilege that implied an obligation of financial disclosure. Only after 1900 was there a gradual return to the kind of regulation Parliament had approved in 1844, but worked out with greater precision and attention to detail, as the development of auditing skills caught up with the intention of the original law.

In place of statutory requirements, the 1855–1856 acts included a model balance sheet and model articles of association (corporate bylaws). These were permissive. Any registered company that chose to adopt its own articles could ignore the model set, which was compulsory only for firms that did not bother to register articles of their own. The model balance sheet was extremely progressive. Assets and liabilities were classified by type, bad debts were provided for, depreciation was shown for both plant assets and inventories, and retained earnings was divided into portions reserved for contingencies and available for dividends. The model articles included nearly all the audit and accounting provisions of the 1845 act plus others even more advanced. Books were to be kept in double entry form. No dividend was to be paid that reduced capital. An income statement was not required, but different sources of revenue were to be distinguished. By specifying that auditors no longer had to be shareholders in the company, the model articles made it easier to employ outside professionals. As additional protection the new law provided that, even if no auditor was appointed, a petition by 20 percent of the stockholders required the Board of Trade to name an inspector who would investigate the company's affairs.

The Companies Act of 1862 reproduced the model balance sheet and articles of association with only a few important changes. The auditor's examination was described in more detail, and for the first time a model audit certificate was illustrated. The 1862 act soon became known as "the accountant's friend." By stating explicitly that dividends could be paid only from accumulated income, it made the services of skilled accountants absolutely necessary. The 1862 act also created the position of official liquidator for the purpose of winding up insolvent companies, and this job was usually given to a professional accountant. This act completed the conceptual framework of English company law. Though there have since been many procedural additions and refinements, its basic provisions have changed very little during the last 130 years.

In 1895 the Davey Committee recommended that annual audits be made compulsory for all registered companies, and this proposal was incorporated into the Companies Act of 1900. This in effect restored the main statutory

requirements of the 1844 act, because by requiring an audit the law inferred an obligation to prepare annual balance sheets. The 1900 act also specified that at the first stockholder's meeting of a new corporation there be submitted a summary of receipts and payments incurred since the date of incorporation, including details of organizational expenses, contracts entered into, and stock issued, all of which was to be certified as correct by the auditor. But there was still no prescribed form of balance sheet and no requirement that professional auditors be appointed.

The Companies Act of 1907 required that publicly held corporations file annual audited balance sheets with the registrar of companies. These were to disclose the amount of capital on which interest had been paid, the rate of such interest, commissions paid on stock or debentures, and discounts on debentures. The auditor's certificate and report were combined into one document, which had to be attached to the balance sheet or referred to therein. The auditor's report was reworded to state explicitly that the law required an examination that went beyond mere comparisons of ledger balances with balance sheet figures. To strengthen auditor tenure and independence, two weeks' notice of intention to change auditors had to be given the management, the stockholders, and the retiring auditor.

The Companies Act of 1929 included major changes in accounting and auditing regulations. For the first time, an annual income statement had to be submitted to stockholders, though it did not have to be filed with the registrar of companies and was not specifically covered by the auditor's report. Current and fixed assets had to be segregated on the balance sheet, and corporations were required to state how they had valued fixed assets. Authorized and issued capital stock were to be shown separately, as were organizational expenses, goodwill, patents, and trademarks. Disclosure had to be made of loans to directors and officers, of loans made for purchase of the firm's own shares for the benefit of employees, and of discounts on shares issued. Corporations could no longer file out-of-date balance sheets with the registrar. Prospectuses of new stock issues were to be accompanied by an auditor's report on past profits of the company whose securities were to be issued, as well as past profits of any business that was to be acquired from the proceeds of the sale. While not requiring consolidated balance sheets, the 1929 act defined holding companies and required disclosure of the treatment of subsidiary income. The holding company's balance sheet was to describe investments in and loans to and from subsidiaries.

The Cohen Committee on Company Law Amendment recommended in its 1945 report that only members of a recognized professional body be allowed to serve as corporate auditors, and a clause to this effect was included in the Companies Act of 1947, later consolidated into the Companies Act of 1948. The committee further recommended, and the 1947–1948 acts provided, that the auditor's report should state whether in his opinion the company had kept proper account books, whether he had obtained all data necessary for his audit, and whether the balance sheet and income statement were in agreement with the books and gave a "full and fair" view of the company's financial status and operating results. Consolidated financial statements were required for the first time. The principle of independence was reinforced by giving the auditor tenure from one stockholder's meeting to the next, and the right to attend meetings and defend himself before the stockholders if he received notice that he would not be reappointed.

The Companies Act of 1967, following the report of the Jenkins Committee, set additional disclosure requirements. It became mandatory for all companies incorporated with limited liability to file accounts with the registrar of companies. Like the American Institute of Certified Public Accountants' Accounting Principles Board Opinion No. 9 (1966), the 1967 Companies Act required the all-inclusive income statement. Balance sheets now had to show: (1) the basis for inventory valuation; (2) totals of fixed assets acquired, disposed of, or destroyed during the year; (3) capital expenditures authorized by directors but not yet contracted for; (4) total amounts of quoted and unquoted investments; (5) a subdivision of land into freehold, long leasehold, and short leasehold categories; (6) the total of loans, other than bank loans or overdrafts, that were not repayable within five years, including terms of repayment and interest rates; (7) the name of each subsidiary of a holding company, with details of the nature of the stock investment; (8) or, in the case of subsidiaries, the name and country of incorporation of its ultimate holding company.

In the United States, financial reporting requirements and auditing standards have mainly been established by the accounting profession. In Britain the profession was directed by statute, through a series of laws that mandated detailed audit regulations and enforced minimum disclosure requirements.

Michael Chatfield

Bibliography

Edey, H.C., and P. Panitpakdi. "British Company Accounting and the Law, 1844–1900." In *Studies in the History of Accounting*, edited by A.C. Littleton and B.S. Yamey, pp. 356–379. Homewood, IL: Irwin, 1956.

Edwards, J.R., ed. *British Company Legislation and Company Accounts, 1844–1976.* New York: Arno Press, 1980.

———, ed. *Legal Regulation of British Company Accounts, 1836–1900.* New York: Garland, 1986.

Hein, L.W. "The Auditor and the British Companies Acts," *Accounting Review*, July 1963, pp. 508–520.

———. *The British Companies Acts and the Practice of Accountancy, 1844–1962.* New York: Arno Press, 1978.

Littleton, A.C. *Accounting Evolution to 1900.* New York: American Institute Publishing, 1933. Reprint. New York: Russell and Russell, 1966.

Stewart, I. "The Ethics of Disclosure in Company Financial Reporting in the United Kingdom, 1925–1970," *Accounting Historians Journal*, June 1991, pp. 35–54.

See also BAD DEBTS; BALANCE SHEET; CAPITAL ACCOUNT; CAPITAL MAINTENANCE; CITY OF GLASGOW BANK; CONSERVATISM; CORPORATIONS: EVOLUTION; DIVIDENDS; EXTERNAL AUDITING; LIMITED LIABILITY; MANORIAL ACCOUNTING; PIXLEY, FRANCIS WILLIAM; REGULATION OF RAILWAYS ACT (BRITAIN, 1868); RETAINED EARNINGS APPROPRIATIONS; SCOTLAND: EARLY WRITERS IN DOUBLE ENTRY ACCOUNTING; TRUSTEE ACCOUNTS

Comparability

For centuries after the introduction of double entry bookkeeping, commerce was typically a series of disconnected ventures, with income calculated piecemeal. Even firms organized for longer periods tended to be small, owners were usually in personal contact with their business affairs and kept accounts almost solely for their own use. The opportunistic nature of trading made past operations an uncertain guide to the future, and many merchants apparently did not use their venture accounts to choose among alternatives or allocate resources. More often the purpose of bookkeeping was to segregate the results of trading in particular commodities. In the absence of reporting to outsiders, there was little incentive to restrict the variety of accounting methods in use. The modern reasons for accounting consistency and comparability hardly existed.

The corporation gave legal validity to the notion of business continuity. The larger scale of corporate activities encouraged routinization, consistency, and bookkeeping economy. The need to inform investors made periodic reporting more important than the reference use of the ledger. The need for audited financial statements encouraged the professionalization of accountancy both in England and America. The need to stabilize capital markets and protect stockholders eventually involved governments in corporate reporting.

Corporate continuity tended to shorten and regularize accounting periods. The life of a business now eclipsed not only specific ventures but even the life spans of its owners. Periodic accounting reports were useful in pricing company shares. They were sometimes required by legal and tax authorities. The calculation of profits for a particular time interval became a major determinant of dividend payments. Often stockholders were absentee owners who had little direct contact with company affairs. The periodic profit figure became an index of managerial effectiveness in the minds of many who lacked the time to study operations in detail.

The calendar year proved to be a convenient corporate reporting period. It was usually long enough to encompass one or more complete cycles of business activity, yet short enough to give investors fairly current information. Useful comparisons could be made when financial statements covered the same time span and appeared on the same date each year. As record keeping became more standardized, there was a tendency for corporations to prepare statements at progressively shorter intervals until they arrived at an annual reporting basis. By 1800, at least in England, the usual practice was to close the books either at

year end or on the anniversary of the firm's inception.

Once statement preparation became the main purpose of bookkeeping, ledger figures began to be refined to more closely approximate current market prices. But there was a considerable time lag between adoption of annual reporting and acceptance of comparability, consistency, and other doctrines needed to answer questions it has raised. For example, it was not until the late nineteenth century and the widespread use of financial statements that standardized inventory pricing and fixed asset valuation methods began to develop. Before then there had existed a great variety of acceptable valuation methods with little or no tendency toward uniformity. The need to compare published accounting results strengthened arguments in favor of historical cost accounting and realization at sale.

The English Companies Acts of 1855–1856 included a model balance sheet that was intended to standardize account terminology and formats. Before 1900 the commercial laws of several European countries went further than the companies acts by requiring corporate directors to furnish stockholders with income statements as well as balance sheets. In France and Germany, the forerunners of uniform accounting codes even specified the types of account books to be kept and in some cases the accounting methods to be used.

In contrast, the amount of financial data reported by American corporations was left almost entirely to the discretion of management. They presented whatever information they wished and arranged it as they pleased. Some firms issued reports irregularly or long after the end of their fiscal year. Many others told their stockholders nothing at all. Since there was no tradition of accompanying published reports with an independent auditor's certificate, even the meager information given was colored by management's viewpoint. Certain industries were notoriously secretive. The smaller closely held corporations were among the worst in this respect, but so were many of the largest monopolistic "trusts." Companies heavily dependent on outside sources of capital, and those whose securities were listed on the stock exchanges, often published detailed accounting reports. But very few corporate managements considered financial disclosure a good policy.

Corporate charters were often silent on the question of management's financial reporting responsibility. By 1900 corporation acts in about half the states provided for some kind of report to stockholders, but they seldom specified its contents or required that it be mailed to shareholders who failed to attend the company's annual meeting. Accountants might deplore the results of this system, but without a strong professional organization or a body of doctrine they were in no position to challenge their clients' preference for secrecy. They repeatedly tried and failed to obtain federal disclosure legislation. Public opinion, which supported detailed regulation of railroads and banks, seemed generally indifferent to legislation affecting industrial corporations. Nor were accountants able to improve standards of practice. The choice of accounting methods was left entirely to management.

The dominant role of industrial corporations after 1900, and the rapid increase in the number of their stockholders, produced for the first time a widespread feeling that corporate secrecy was antisocial and that the general public as well as individual investors required the protection of financial publicity. American corporations gradually improved their reporting practices. By 1930 balance sheets had become more standardized, a brief income statement was typically included in annual reports to stockholders, and certification by independent auditors was the rule rather than the exception. United States Steel Corporation and a few other enlightened companies became voluntary proponents of a full disclosure policy. But most industrial managers did not consider financial reporting a matter of great importance, and there were still major corporations that published no accounting reports of any kind. Throughout this period, company managements had almost complete control over the selection of financial information distributed to the public. The reporting provisions of most state corporation acts had not changed since the nineteenth century, and federal law remained silent on the question.

Between 1920 and 1927, the Investment Bankers Association of America issued a series of bulletins in which they proposed minimum standards of disclosure for use in prospectuses and other statements involving securities. The association wished not only to standardize the information given investors, but also to protect legitimate investment bankers from growing public resentment against sales of fraudulent stocks, and thereby to forestall securities regulation by the state and federal governments. They suggested the use of consolidated financial statements, summaries of earnings by years, and standard methods of reporting inventories, working capital, and depreciation. Few of these recommendations were ever put into effect by investment bankers or corporations. Partly this lack of support reflected the old attitude that the reputation of the investment banker was the stockholder's best protection. In other cases, investment bankers relied on nondisclosure to hide weaknesses in the securities they offered for sale.

The major influence for improved disclosure during this period was the New York Stock Exchange. The Exchange had a long history of opposition to corporate secrecy. As early as 1866 it had tried to collect financial statements from listed companies. By 1900 all corporations applying for listing had to agree to publish annual balance sheets and income statements, though this rule was not always enforced. In 1910 the Exchange abolished its Unlisted Department, which traded stocks of companies that were not required to furnish the Committee on Stock List with accounting data. Beginning in 1922 it collected information on the financial condition of each of its member firms of stockbrokers and required that all listed corporations file with it copies of their financial statements. By 1926, 90 percent of all industrial companies listed on the Exchange were audited annually, and each listed company was required to publish a report containing its financial statements and submit it to stockholders at least 15 days before the annual meeting. Holding companies had to prepare either consolidated statements or statements for the parent and each majority-owned subsidiary. In addition, listed companies were asked to publish semiannual or quarterly income statements. In 1930 the Exchange began its famous correspondence with the American Institute of Accountants (AIA), intended to settle problems of audit scope and responsibility and to establish approved methods of financial reporting.

The first nationwide society of American accountants was founded in 1887, but not until 30 years later did the profession seriously attempt to standardize reporting practices. Prepared by the AIA and sponsored by the Federal Trade Commission and the Federal Reserve Board, *Uniform Accounting* (1917), as its title suggests, was intended to improve financial reporting by promoting accounting uniformity.

However, its proposals had little immediate effect on published reports, mainly because bankers, afraid of antagonizing their clients, would not insist on audited statements from loan applicants. In addition, many businessmen felt that the model financial statements in *Uniform Accounting* required too much disclosure and might be used to their detriment by competitors.

Discussions and correspondence between the AIA and the New York Stock Exchange, aimed at improving reporting standards, began in 1930 and continued for more than three years. Instead of trying to formulate uniform procedures to be followed by every company, the AIA's Committee on Cooperation with Stock Exchanges, headed by George Oliver May, proposed that corporations be free to choose their own accounting methods within a framework of "accepted accounting principles," provided they disclosed such methods and used them consistently from year to year. In October 1933 these recommendations were approved by the New York Stock Exchange, which earlier in the year had announced that corporations requesting permission to list their stocks on the Exchange must produce financial statements certified by independent public accountants and must then file similar audited statements annually. No longer was management to be the sole arbiter of the contents of financial statements.

It is doubtful whether collaboration between the AIA and the Stock Exchange could have enforced reporting consistency throughout American industry. Investors were not corporately aware of their interests. Managers had shown a preference for selective disclosure based on a wide choice of accounting options. The AIA at that time had only a few thousand members and very limited resources with which to combat the nation's largest corporations. Accountants had never achieved effective control over the contents of published reports. Not much had been done to develop technical accounting standards, and those that existed had no support in law. There was no agreed-on conceptual framework within which specific problems could be solved, and lacking this, practitioners could not easily reach a consensus on controversial issues. In any case, within six months the AIA's program was preempted by the federal government. The election of Franklin D. Roosevelt and passage of the Securities Acts of 1933–1934 resulted in financial reporting practices being subjected to a degree of control that would have seemed impossible a few years earlier.

The government's task was not only to upgrade the quality of published reports, but also to make the results of a technical accounting process intelligible to ordinary people and to convince investors that such reports were worth relying on in judging the value of securities. These goals were based on the assumptions that the public's willingness to invest depended partly on a study of, and confidence in, financial statements, that this confidence had been shaken by the 1929 stock market crash and its aftermath, and that the national interest required that it be restored.

Their advocates compared the securities acts with the English companies acts, but the American laws proposed to regulate the accounting methods used by corporations as well as their published reports. Section 13(b) of the Securities and Exchange Commission Act of 1934 authorized the Securities and Exchange Commission (SEC) not only to specify the form and content of financial statements submitted to it, but even to dictate the accounting procedures to be used by corporations that were subject to SEC jurisdiction.

> The Commission may prescribe. . . the form or forms in which the required information shall be set forth, the items or details to be shown in the balance sheet and the earnings statement, and the methods to be followed in the preparation of reports, in the appraisal or valuation of assets and liabilities, in the determination of depreciation and depletion, in the differentiation of reoccurring and nonreoccurring income. . . .

At this pivotal moment in accounting development, Congress had in effect given a government agency the power to introduce a uniform system of corporate accounts. One can only speculate what might have happened had the SEC made full use of this power. SEC Accounting Series Releases (ASRs) have permitted fewer alternative methods than have Accounting Principles Board (APB) or Financial Accounting Standards Board (FASB) pronouncements. Accounting principles have hardly ever been invoked to justify SEC rulings. The SEC bulletins on replacement cost accounting (ASR No. 190, 1976) and oil and gas accounting (ASR No. 253, 1978) dispensed with the principles of historical cost and objectivity in order to disclose specific information. If Section 13(b) had been implemented, accounting today would presumably be far more a matter of legal interpretation and far less a matter of "individual judgment in the circumstances."

However, after an uneasy four year period of reflection, the SEC in 1938 decided not to enforce Section 13(b). Carman G. Blough, the first chief accountant of the SEC, stated that ". . . the policy of the Securities and Exchange Commission was to encourage the accountants to develop uniformity of procedure themselves, in which case we would follow. . . . Only as a last resort would the Commission feel the necessity to step in. . . ."

Why was Section 13(b) held in abeyance? First, because the SEC did not have, and expected never to have, sufficient resources to supervise directly the accounting practices of the nation's publicly owned corporations. Also, because efforts at self-regulation by the New York Stock Exchange and the AIA had been successful enough so that their continuation seemed a feasible alternative to direct government control. The SEC standardized the formats of the 10K and other reports submitted to it, but generally refrained from detailed regulation of financial statements distributed to the public. Within somewhat narrower limits than before, corporate managers still had their choice of accounting methods. Certification of published reports remained in the hands of the accounting profession, which was encouraged by the SEC to develop auditing standards and accounting principles.

In trying to narrow the areas of difference in reporting on similar events, the SEC had the advantage of being able to quickly impose minimum standards on all its registrants. Few hesitated to discard an accounting procedure that had been rejected by the Commission. But in reacting against the financial abuses of the 1920s, the SEC emphasized objectivity, consistency, and historical cost valuation—concepts many accountants of the postwar era would wish to modify or supersede entirely. It chose to promote uniformity by encouraging the old accounting bias toward conservatism, with its implications of understatement and concealment. Registrants were discouraged from giving investors price level adjusted data, estimates of future earnings, or appraisals of almost any kind. The final result of SEC rule making was

to enforce a situation of mutual dependence between the SEC and the accounting profession on the one hand, and between accountants and their corporate clients on the other. Regardless of differences in philosophy or actual influence, each was now compelled to deal with the others on terms prescribed by law.

Efforts to standardize financial reporting soon produced a body of doctrine. In 1936 the AIA revised *Verification of Financial Statements* (1929) to emphasize reporting to stockholders rather than creditors. The SEC and the AIA, taking a case-by-case approach, developed a series of accounting and reporting guidelines that dramatically raised the average quality of corporate financial statements. Beginning in 1966, the American Institute of Certified Public Accountants (AICPA) required disclosure of all material departures by audited statements from procedures specified in Accounting Research Bulletins and Accounting Principles Board Opinions. Instead of resulting in conflicting sources of authority, SEC and AICPA pronouncements generally reinforced each other. Both rule making bodies agreed that stockholders of large corporations were now the principal group to which financial statements should be directed.

The financial statements published today by American corporations are among the most detailed and comprehensive in the world. The latest disclosure laws in several countries consciously imitate American practice. Since World War II there has been a constant tendency to add to the amount of background data being reported. Footnotes, supplementary schedules, and historical summaries proliferate, and items such as backlog and segment operating results are increasingly included. The formerly sharp dividing line between secretive and progressive corporations has all but disappeared.

Still, it is possible to note similarities in the events and attitudes of the early 1900s, the 1930s, and the present. Then as now, the government was concerned about the quality of published reports but reluctant to interfere directly. Then as now, investors complained that financial statements did not provide the data they needed to evaluate management's direction of the firm or to compare the earnings prospects of different companies. Then as now, the accounting profession's response to these problems, being developed pragmatically, always seemed to be a step behind the latest corporate developments.

C

A perennial problem results from management's wide choice of accounting options. The existence of alternative methods that produce different results makes it possible to create an appearance of earnings and growth without actually improving performance. Because the SEC and the AICPA have not specified accounting procedures in enough detail to make the reports of different companies comparable, mere footnote disclosure of the methods used by each firm is usually of little help to the ordinary investor. There is evident need to eliminate alternatives that prevent comparability, to simplify and standardize terminology and account classifications, and to define rigorously the accounting concepts on which reporting practices are based.

Michael Chatfield

Bibliography

Barr, A. "Accountants and the Securities and Exchange Commission," *Journal of Accountancy*, April 1962, pp. 31–37.

Benston, G.J. "The Value of the SEC's Accounting Disclosure Requirements," *Accounting Review*, July 1969, pp. 515–532.

Brundage, P.F. "Influence of Government Regulation on Development of Today's Accounting Practice," *Journal of Accountancy*, November 1950, pp. 384–391.

Clare, R.S. "Evolution of Corporate Reports," *Journal of Accountancy*, January 1945, pp. 39–51.

Hawkins, D.F. "The Development of Modern Financial Reporting Practices among American Manufacturing Corporations," *Business History Review*, Autumn 1963, pp. 135–168.

McLaren, N. *Annual Reports to Stockholders*. New York: Ronald Press, 1947.

Parrish, M.E. *Securities Regulation and the New Deal*. New Haven: Yale University Press, 1970.

"Uniform Accounting," *Journal of Accountancy*, June 1917, pp. 401–433.

See also ACCOUNTING SERIES RELEASE NO. 190; AMERICAN INSTITUTE OF CERTIFIED PUBLIC ACCOUNTANTS; CHART OF ACCOUNTS; CHIEF ACCOUNTANTS OF THE SECURITIES AND EXCHANGE COMMISSION; CONSERVATISM; CONTINUITY; CORPORATIONS: EVOLUTION; GENERALLY ACCEPTED ACCOUNTING PRINCIPLES; HISTORICAL COST; MAY, GEORGE OLIVER; NEW YORK STOCK EXCHANGE; OBJECTIVITY; POSTULATES OF ACCOUNTING; SECURITIES AND EXCHANGE COMMISSION; *UNIFORM ACCOUNTING;* UNIFORM ACCOUNTING SYSTEMS; UNIFORMITY; UNITED STATES STEEL CORPORATION

Compound Entries

Professor Federigo Melis discovered a compound entry in a Pisan journal of 1399 and concluded that such entries were a regular feature of Tuscan bookkeeping by the second half of the fourteenth century. The Venetian Jachomo Badoer included a compound entry in his 1436–1440 ledger. It seems likely that the use of compound entries had become fairly common in Italian practice by the sixteenth century.

In contrast, most sixteenth-century bookkeeping textbooks illustrated only simple journal entries, with one debit and one credit. Early authors usually preferred to divide complex transactions into two or more simple entries. But this was evidently a teaching device, not the result of ignorance. Basil S. Yamey shows that compound entries were understood but not used by Luca Pacioli (1494) and Domenico Manzoni (1540). Compound entries were demonstrated in the earliest published German bookkeeping text by Heinrich Schreiber, *Ayn New Kunstlich Buech* (1518). The first English textbook to illustrate compound entries was John Weddington's *A Breffe Instruction* (1567). In Holland, Simon Stevin gave an early and widely imitated exposition of compound entries in *Hyponmemata Mathematica* (1608). These textbook illustrations of compound entries are important, because they reflect a transition from the need to provide basic double entry instruction, to a concern for bookkeeping efficiency and a desire to minimize clerical work.

Michael Chatfield

Bibliography

Peragallo, E. "Development of the Compound Entry in the Fifteenth Century Ledger of Jachomo Badoer, A Venetian Merchant," *Accounting Review*, January 1983, pp. 98–104.

Yamey, B.S. "Compound Journal Entries in Early Treatises on Bookkeeping," *Accounting Review*, April 1979, pp. 323–329.

See also Badoer, Jachomo; Flori, Ludovico; Schreiber, Heinrich; Stevin, Simon; Yamey, Basil Selig

Compound Interest

Compound interest was understood by the Babylonians of 1600–1800 B.C. European mathematics texts, beginning with Leonardo of Pisa's *Liber Abaci* (1202), included compound interest problems. A compound interest table in manuscript form was prepared for the Bardi banking house about 1340. Luca Pacioli's *Summa de Arithmetica* (1494) demonstrated calculations for simple and compound interest. Compound interest tables were first published by the mathematicians Jan Trenchant (Lyons, 1558) and Simon Stevin (Antwerp, 1582).

The operations of British life insurance companies during the seventeenth and eighteenth centuries gave rise to actuarial science as mortality tables were combined with compound interest allowances to compute the value of life annuities and later to make statistically based calculations of life insurance premiums. Cost forecasts made by eighteenth-century English industrialists sometimes included compound interest calculations. The earliest known bond yield table was published by New York banker Joseph M. Price in 1843. Compound interest and annuity factors were employed in mine valuations and railroad rate calculations during the second half of the nineteenth century.

The discounted cash flow techniques used today in capital budgeting analysis are rooted in compound interest calculations because of the need to discount the projected receipts and payments from investment proposals back to their present value.

Michael Chatfield

Bibliography

Parker, R.H. *Management Accounting: An Historical Perspective.* New York: Augustus M. Kelly, 1969.

See also Accounting Principles Board; Babylonia; Discounted Cash Flow; Fisher, Irving; Germany; Income-Determination Theory; Leonardo of Pisa; Money; Peele, James; Sprague, Charles Ezra; Stevin, Simon

Computing Technology in the West: The Impact on the Profession of Accounting

C

When Luca Pacioli in 1494 described bookkeeping as then practiced in Venice, the tools of the accountant's trade were quills, ink, and paper. These tools were supplied by other tradesmen. Innovations in accounting tools, including computer aids, are still supplied mostly by nonaccountants. It now appears that the profession of accounting has been grievously injured by the widespread inattention and lack of involvement of accountants in the development of computing technology.

The Advent of the Calculating Machine

It was not until the late 1800s that workable mechanical calculators began to be manufactured in the United States and Europe. J.A.V. Turck, looking back on the 1890s from the perspective of 1921, noted: "It was strongly evident that the efforts of book-keepers and counting-house clerks to prevent these machines entering their department were inspired by the fear that it would displace their services and interfere with their chance of a livelihood."

Interestingly, one of the very first American calculating machines to be invented continued to be sold worldwide, virtually unchanged, for the better part of a century. The comptometer was the 1886 invention of 24-year-old Dorr E. Felt. All the power to drive the machine was provided by pushing the keys, and it could only add and successfully carry results to the next-higher decimal level. However, a talented comptometer operator could perform various manipulations to also achieve subtraction, multiplication, division, square root, cube root, and foreign-exchange conversion.

The other basic type of adding machine calculator was called a "recorder." The most successful recorders were produced by the American Arithmometer Company renamed in 1905, on behalf of the inventor, the Burroughs Adding Machine Company. In 1908 the company offered 58 different models. Special wide-carriage versions were commonly referred to as "bookkeeping machines." Burroughs's basic design with various improvements was used for the manufacture of at least a million calculators between 1891 and 1940. Competitors included Baldwin, Brunsviga, Monroe, National, Dalton, McCaskey, Wales, Victor, and Corona.

The first cash register was invented in 1878 by James Ritty. It used a large dial to keep track of sales. In 1882 Ritty sold his business to Jacob

H. Eckert, who formed the National Manufacturing Company. The next owner was John H. Patterson, who changed the company's name to the National Cash Register Company (NCR). By 1910 NCR was selling more than 100,000 registers a year. The cash register quickly became one of the most important accounting-control devices over sales. In many firms, the cash register was the principal source of accounting information regarding company receipts.

The Invention of the Punched-Card Sorter and Tabulator

During this same period, a more expensive accounting tool, called the tabulating machine, was being introduced into organizations with large data-processing needs. Herman Hollerith had been a special agent in the U.S. Census Office for the 1880 census. In 1882 he left the Census Office and joined Massachusetts Institute of Technology as an instructor in mechanical engineering. He applied for a patent in 1884 for a tabulating machine that stored data on a continuous paper roll with holes punched in it. However, the paper roll was inadequate for summarizing data. To solve this fundamental problem, he had the idea of using punched cards. He later said that he was inspired by a ticket-punch technique called the "punch photograph" then used by some train conductors to record on the ticket the physical description of the purchaser, such as color of eyes and hair. Hollerith was also familiar with the jacquard loom invented a century before that used punched cards to guide the weaving.

In 1884 Hollerith became an assistant examiner in the U.S. Patent Office. There he gained valuable knowledge that he ultimately used to secure 32 patents. In 1885 he went to work for a maker of train brakes, which became a second major interest in his life. He continued to develop his tabulating system and was able to arrange an experiment of his machines with the Baltimore Department of Health. The health departments of New Jersey and New York City were the next to acquire his system. In 1888 the U.S. Surgeon General's Office of the War Department installed his system. In 1890, after competitive tests, the U.S. Census Office awarded him an important contract. Hollerith tabulators were also used in the 1890s for the census of Canada, Norway, France, Germany, and Austria. In 1896 he formed a corporation named the Tabulating Machine Company.

The Growth of Machine Accounting

By 1907 Hollerith's tabulating machines had gained acceptance in the accounting departments of many large businesses and they had been used for the large Russian census and the U.S. census of 1900. The Tabulating Machine Company's product line consisted of (1) a vertical sorter around the size and height of a man, (2) a horizontal adding tabulator, (3) a manually operated gang punch, and (4) a manually operated card punch with numeric keyboard. The company would claim, "The Electric Tabulating System is now in successful operation for: Auditing freight accounts; Computing shop costs; Sales accounting and analysis; Distribution of expenditures and Special requirements demanding analysis of a considerable volume of detail," as noted by Geoffrey D. Austrian (1982).

Hollerith did not get the contract for the 1910 U.S. census. Instead, the Census Office decided to build its own machines. To do this, they hired away some of Hollerith's experienced employees and contracted with an inventive Russian immigrant named James Powers. Powers negotiated an agreement that stipulated that he was to retain the patent rights to any machines he developed. He later formed, in 1911, the Powers Accounting Machine Company, which would become a major rival to the Tabulating Machine Company.

That same year, Hollerith decided to sell the Tabulating Machine Company to financier Charles R. Flint, who merged the company with three other firms to form the Computing-Tabulating-Recording Company (CTR). The new company's product line was computing scales, tabulators, and recording time clocks. On May 1, 1914, a new general manager was hired, Thomas J. Watson, who had previously been second-in-command to Patterson at NCR. For a while, the Powers company moved ahead of CTR with machines with greater capacities and the Powers Company was first to offer a printing tabulator. However, Watson responded with improvements and his superior sales force, following along the lines of NCR, brought in the larger market share.

In 1917 CTR introduced a new product called a "verifier," which was to become a mainstay well into the 1970s. The verifier was an important control device over the accuracy of the card-punch operator. A deck of punched cards would be fed into the verifier, and the verifier operator would reduplicate the keystrokes of the punch operator. When a keystroke difference was detected, the verifier would lock up and any needed correction could be made.

In 1924 Watson decided to give CTR's image a boost by changing the name to International Business Machines (IBM). IBM introduced a new type of punched card in 1928 in response to requests from accountants for a card with a greater storage capacity. The new card incorporated three major changes: rectangular holes instead of round; a larger, 80-column format; and two new rows along the top of the card, called the X and Y rows. IBM referred to negative numbers with the accounting term "credit"; positive numbers were "debits." A punch in the X row meant that the number was a credit. Remington Rand, which the year before had acquired the Powers Accounting Machine Company, responded to IBM improvements with its own new card design whereby 90 columns of round holes were divided into upper and lower data sets of six rows each.

The 1930s and 1940s brought many improvements to IBM's tabulating equipment. By the end of 1935, IBM had over 80 percent of the tabulating-equipment market and was selling about 3 billion blank punch cards a year. World War II marked the end of an era for computing. Until that time, computing had been principally for the benefit of accountants. IBM referred to its mainstay tabulating machine operation as the Electric Accounting Machine Division. Accountants bought the machines, ran the machines, and used the output of the machines. All of that was about to change.

The Birth of the Electronic Computer

During the decades around World War II, there were many projects, most conceived by mathematicians, to develop machines capable of performing large scale calculations. In 1948 IBM identified 19 significant computer projects then underway outside of their company.

For example, IBM built the large ASCC (Automatic Sequence Controlled Calculator), which was installed at Harvard University in 1944 and later dubbed the Harvard Mark I. That work influenced John Mauchly, who, with J. Presper Eckert, was developing a secret calculator called ENIAC for the military at the Moore School of Electrical Engineering at University of Pennsylvania, Philadelphia. The first significant effort in America to develop a

"computer" with electronic stored programs was the Electrical Discrete Variable Automatic Computer (EDVAC), which was to be the successor to the Moore School's Electronic Numerical Integrator and Computer (ENIAC). This work influenced the development of EDSAC, which was one of two British computers, both operational in 1949, that are generally considered rivals for the title of "world's first working, stored-program computer." The other was the Manchester Mark I. The Electronic Delay Storage Automatic Calculator (EDSAC) had been financed in part by the large British bakery firm of J. Lyons and Company. Later, in 1951, it constructed its own version, called LEO I, which was the world's first commercial computer placed in operation. Lyons used it in part to compute tax tables and process payroll.

ENIAC team leaders Mauchly and Eckert had left the Moore School in 1946 to form a commercial venture called the Electronic Control Company. They negotiated a study into the specifications for a proposed computer with the Census Bureau and the National Bureau of Standards. The name of the computer was UNIVAC (Universal Automatic Computer). A major feature of the UNIVAC was that it was to use magnetic tape storage.

Financial problems soon beset the company. After first offering the company to IBM, the owners sold it in February 1950 to Remington Rand. Remington Rand delivered the first UNIVAC to the Census Bureau in March 1951. IBM's most direct response to Remington Rand's UNIVAC was the Type 702. The 702 was soon replaced by the Type 705 Electronic Data Processing Machine, which used the newly invented core memory. By the middle of 1956, IBM had 87 Type 702 and 705 machines in operation and 190 on order, compared to 41 in operation and 40 on order for all other American computer makers. By the late 1950s, other computer companies included: RCA, General Electric, Bendix, Hughes, Burroughs, National Cash Register, and Teleregister. However, IBM had about two-thirds of the computer marketplace, and over the next several decades all of these competitors would fall to the wayside.

The Loss of Accounting Jobs

As the accounting profession entered the mid-1960s, some accountants began to realize what had happened to them in the last decade. They

C

had lost control of machine accounting. In fact, machine accounting no longer existed. It had been replaced by "data processing," and many accounting jobs had been filled by non-accountants who were knowledgeable about computers. The National Machine Accountants Association officially recognized what had happened. In 1962 it changed its name to the Data Processing Managers Association. Accounting academics have always responded most to the expectations of public accounting. Because public accounting was blind to what was happening, the accounting professors were blind, and they did not incorporate serious computing skills into the college accounting curriculum. So the accounting academics passively allowed new departments of computer science and information systems to arise and fill the void left by the accounting profession's inaction.

The Rise of the Minicomputer

IBM continued throughout the 1960s as the leading computer company in the world. In 1964 it introduced the System/360, which was the first line of computers intended to be both business and scientific. The System/360 family included models spanning all levels of computing, which, for the first time, used identical software and peripheral devices. By 1969 more than 18,000 System/360 systems had been installed in the United States alone.

In that period, General Electric sold out to Honeywell, and RCA quit the computer business and sold its division to Sperry Rand UNIVAC. Xerox entered the business and purchased Scientific Data Systems but gave up on computers by the early 1980s.

By the 1970s, a small computer maker named Digital Equipment Corporation (DEC) had earned a big market for its line of "mini" computers. In April 1965, DEC introduced an integrated circuit minicomputer, the PDP-8, at an amazing sales price of $18,000. DEC's success with the PDP-8 brought other companies into the minicomputer marketplace. By 1971 there were around 75 minicomputer makers. In 1975 DEC completed development of an upgrade of the PDP line named the VAX-11. VAX stood for "virtual address extension." Demand for the virtual memory VAX helped propel DEC to a sales level in 1977 in excess of $1 billion.

IBM's minicomputer response was the System/3 series, models 1 through 7. Later model numbers were 32, 34, 38, and 36 (in order of introduction). The first System/3 was available in July 1969. In order to reduce its impact on the System/360 line, the new computer used the RPG programming language, which was weak in comparison to the 360's COBOL and FORTRAN languages.

The Revolution of Personal Computers

In 1971 Intel developed the four-bit computer-on-a-chip, the Intel 4004, to supply a request by the Japanese firm ETI for use in a hand-held calculator. In 1973 Intel brought out an eight-bit computer chip, the 8008, which was used in the first nationally marketed personal computer, the Scelbi Computer Consulting 8–H.

The personal computer revolution was really energized by the Altair 8800, manufactured by Micro Instrumentation and Telemetry Systems (MITS). The first model Apple computer, introduced in 1976, was soon upgraded to the Apple II, which generated sales of $800,000 for Apple Computer Company in 1977. That year also saw the introduction of the Commodore PET and the Radio Shack TRS-80. Soon many other companies entered the market.

Some of Apple's early success was a function of Visicalc, the mother of all spreadsheet software programs, which was first marketed in October 1979 and originally available only on the Apple II. It was a program that would change forever the profession of accounting. In fact, the first commercial customer for Visicalc was the CPA firm of Laventhol and Horwath.

By 1981, 12,000 copies of Visicalc were being sold each month. That year Mitch Kapor was hired to develop two Visicalc utilities, Visiplot and Visitrend. He used the proceeds of that effort to cofound Lotus Development Corporation, which in 1982 introduced a competing spreadsheet called Lotus 1-2-3. Because it was more powerful than Visicalc and was the first spreadsheet to run on IBM's new PC (personal computer), Lotus 1-2-3 quickly became the leading spreadsheet product—a market position it held for the next seven years.

IBM had been paying attention to the growth of the personal-computer industry. It decided to put together a machine that mostly used currently available, nonspecialized parts and software. The CPU chip was provided by Intel and the operating system by Microsoft. The computer that would cause the personal-computer market to explode was formally announced in August 1981 and was shipping by October. More than 13,000 IBM PCs were sold before the first one was shipped.

However, Apple was not standing still. Cofounder Steve Jobs had been impressed with what he had seen on a visit to Xerox's Palo Alto Research Center. Apple improved upon Xerox's ideas in a new type of easy-to-use computer called the Lisa, introduced in January 1983. The Lisa inspired the computer for the "rest of us," the Apple Macintosh. The Macintosh, introduced in 1984 and based on a chip set from Motorola, changed the way all computers in the future would present themselves to the user.

By the late 1980s, IBM was selling less than 15 percent of the Intel-based personal computers. Apple had been smarter in developing a proprietary Macintosh system, which, almost 10 years after its introduction, could still only be purchased from Apple. However, Apple was not so clever at holding on to its easy-to-use graphical user interface (GUI). The Macintosh computer needed software, and Microsoft was the leading software maker. Microsoft privately threatened to quit making Macintosh software unless Apple would license to it certain aspects of the Macintosh GUI, which Apple quietly did. Microsoft used the Macintosh interface in an inexpensive software program for use on Intel-based computers. The program, called Windows, became arguably the most successful computer software package in history.

The immediate future of commercial computing is in developing workable client-server networks for data retrieval and transaction processing. Although the basic computer component will become inexpensive, designing, developing, assembling, and maintaining systems will provide the mainstay of the future profitability of the computing industry.

Conclusion

The accounting profession has been grievously injured, possibly beyond repair, by its lack of an ongoing, organized response to the evolution of computing technology. A most significant and permanent loss to the accounting profession was the rise in the 1950s and early 1960s of a new profession, data processing. Accountants should have continued to provide the data-processing service just as they always had. There should have been no need for a new profession. But a leadership void and a lack of a clear-cut professional identity resulted in business having to look elsewhere for the valuable services that it needed.

Accounting in the United States is defined by a common body of knowledge expressed in the CPA exam and offered in the college curriculum. The officers of the American Institute of Certified Public Accountants (AICPA) and the college academics did not consider advanced data-processing skills to be part of the paradigm of accounting as they then perceived it. However, this was not an explicit determination. It happened more by default without any direct consideration. Interestingly, as recently as 1989, the leadership of the AICPA quietly squashed a major national effort to have an accounting system specialization for the CPA certificate.

With the widespread introduction of computer spreadsheets, clients can now perform much of the analysis work they previously hired accounting firms to do. Write-up services that many CPA firms performed for their clients have declined drastically as these clients obtained their own affordable, computerized accounting systems. Auditing fees are declining because of competition and the greater ease of conducting an audit due to computerization of accounting systems and audit tools. Clients can now purchase inexpensive tax planning and preparation software for use on their personal computers. An entire tax library is now available on a handful of compact disks. If accountants had retained the data-processing function, their professional services in this area would be in much greater demand. As it is, the profession is currently in the mid-1990s facing a general cash flow decline with a corresponding need to find new services to sell. Because of technological advances, the next ten years will be a telling decade for both computer manufacturers and accountants.

Peter L. McMickle

Bibliography

Austrian, G.D. *Herman Hollerith: Forgotten Giant of Information Processing.* New York: Columbia University Press, 1982.

Bashe, C.J., et al. *IBM's Early Computers.* Cambridge: MIT Press, 1986.

Computerworld, June 22, 1992 (special twenty-fifth anniversary edition).

Harmon, M. *Stretching Man's Mind: A History of Data Processing.* New York: Mason/Charter, 1975.

Lavington, S.H. *Early British Computers.* Bedford, MA: Digital Press, 1980.

Metropolis, N., J. Howlett, and G.C. Rota, eds. *A History of Computing in the Twentieth Century.* New York: Academic Press, 1976.

Slater, R. *Portraits in Silicon*. Cambridge: MIT Press, 1987.

Turck, J.A.V. *Origin of Modern Calculating Machines*. Chicago: Western Society of Engineers, 1921.

Watson, T.J. Jr., and P. Petre. *Father, Son and Company: My Life at IBM and Beyond*. New York: Bantam, 1990.

See also ACCOUNTING EDUCATION IN THE UNITED STATES; BABBAGE, CHARLES; DEBIT AND CREDIT; EXTERNAL AUDITING; FRAUD AND AUDITING; INTERNAL CONTROL; JOHNSON AND KAPLAN'S *RELEVANCE LOST: THE RISE AND FALL OF MANAGEMENT ACCOUNTING;* JOURNAL; LEDGER; MANAGEMENT ADVISORY SERVICES BY CPAS; SPACEK, LEONARD; TRUEBLOOD, ROBERT MARTIN

Conceptual Framework

The term "conceptual framework" is defined as a basic structure underlying the formation of ideas. Natural, or physical, scientists categorize species within an environment framework, such as the physical universe. Social scientists are not so fortunate; for the most part, they must attempt categorization of phenomena associated with human behavior. The difficulty with proposing a specific conceptual framework for accounting lies in the requirement that all known and unknown elements be placed within the concepts embodied as the whole structure, or framework. It is assumed that accountancy, as a subset of economics, is a social science that portrays human behavior.

According to scientific logic, a conceptual framework can be established by a deductive or an inductive process. The deductive process flows from a general premise to specific logical conclusions. The inductive process takes particular facts to form a general logical conclusion. Of the two methods, deductive reasoning is most prevalent in the physical sciences. Inductive logic is dominant for the exploration of human behavior in the social sciences.

In 1776 Adam Smith generalized human behavior in the marketplace to initiate the discussion of a basic framework for macroeconomics in *The Wealth of Nations*. Smith portrayed humans collectively reacting in a rational manner in the production, exchange, and consumption of goods and services. He defined "capital" and "stock," a preliminary basis for the elements of the balance sheet; and

"gross revenue" and "net revenue," a basis for income measurement.

Economists in the late nineteenth and early twentieth centuries expanded Smith's discussion of individuals and enterprises interacting within the economy. The economists of that period and their major work who have received the most recognition in accounting literature are Alfred Marshall in *Principles of Economics* (1890), Irving Fisher in *The Nature of Capital and Income* (1925), and J.R. Hicks in *Value and Capital* (1939). Of particular interest to the establishment of a conceptual framework for accounting is these authors' discussion of the interrelationship between the elements of the financial economy: wealth, capital, and earnings.

Accountants joined the economists' conceptual discussion on the interrelationship between the elements of financial statements in that period, most notably Charles Ezra Sprague (1908), William Andrew Paton (1922), and John Bennett Canning (1929). These three authors employed the economists' inductive logic, which describes human behavior as an interaction of "actors" in the environment.

Sprague described wealth as proprietorship. Canning defined assets, liabilities, and proprietorship in economic terms. Paton described accounting as a discipline whose major function is to classify, measure, and report values so that owners and their representatives may wisely use capital. In combination, these authors suggested that the function of accounting should be classifying, valuing, and reporting reality within an economic framework.

Although accountants and economists of the period generally agreed on the concepts of assets and liabilities, two schools of thought appeared for the measurement of earnings. Canning provided the best summary of the two schools, contrasting accountants' "earned income," measured in tangible terms of visible revenues and expenses, with economists' "realized income," approximated in theoretical terms by changes in wealth. The first school of thought, the revenue-expense approach, determines income as the difference between revenues and expenses. The second school of thought, the asset-liability approach, determines income as the difference in "net assets" from the beginning to the end of the period.

The first formal reference to concepts within the context of a "conceptual framework" appeared in 1952 in the Introduction to the report of American Institute of Accountants

(AIA) Study Group on Business Income, *Changing Concepts of Business Income*. There the Study Group focused on the conflicting approaches to income measurement, stating "Income may be measured in a variety of ways. It may be *conceived* in terms of a particular currency without regard to changes in value of that currency. . . . it may be *expressed* . . . in terms of any given currency or even in a conceptual unit," the monetary unit designed primarily for use as a medium of exchange, and secondarily as an "accounting symbol." The Study Group accepted the revenue-expense approach in its three postulates: (1) monetary, (2) permanence, and (3) realization.

In 1961 a second set of basic accounting postulates was proposed in Maurice Moonitz's Accounting Research Study No. 1, *Basic Postulates of Accounting*, published by the American Institute of Certified Public Accountants (AICPA). This larger set of postulates also accepted the revenue-expense approach to "provide a basis on which to formulate numerous generalizations." Moonitz grouped his postulates into three classes. The first five refer to the economic environment: (1) quantification, (2) exchange, (3) economic entities, (4) time period, and (5) unit of measure. These were followed by four accounting-specific postulates: (1) financial statements, (2) market prices, (3) accounting entities, and (4) tentativeness. The third set of postulates related to accounting "imperatives": (1) continuity, (2) objectivity, (3) consistency, (4) stable unit, and (5) disclosure.

Richard V. Mattessich in 1964 proposed a "metatheory" of accounting to provide a "hull" for accounting in *Accounting and Analytical Methods: Measurement and Projection of Income and Wealth in the Micro-and-Macro Economy*. Mattessich stated that the purpose of accounting is the quantitative description and projection of wealth aggregates. He added time to unify the revenue-expense and asset-liability schools of income measurement in a mathematically ordered array of elements. He defined the environment as composed of ten "basic assumptions" and eight "empirical assumptions."

Mattessich's 18 assumptions augmented prior works by adding concepts for revenue recognition and allocation of costs (matching of expenses) to the framework. The assumptions are: (1) monetary values, (2) time intervals, (3) structure, (4) duality, (5) aggregation, (6) economic objects, (7) inequity of monetary claims, (8) economic agents, (9) entities, (10) economic transactions, (11) valuation, (12) realization, (13) classification, (14) data input, (15) duration, (16) extension, (17) materiality, and (18) allocation.

The works of Yuji Ijiri (1967, 1975) continued the discussion on income measurement. Like the frameworks proposed by his predecessors, Ijiri believed that accountants can use the economic definition of control of services for classification. He used the term "value" to discuss income measurement. Value is measured by numbers representing "utility" and "disutility," benefit and sacrifice (1967).

For Ijiri, an exchange on an open market qualifies for the measurement process; especially when one element of the exchange is money (1975). However, Ijiri found valuation to be ambiguous and difficult. Ijiri considered that money satisfies two criteria of valuation: valuation by exchange and relative value between two elements. However, if money is unstable over time, there exist multiple expressions for the value of an element, he concluded.

Ijiri (1967) extracted a set of axioms and rules from conventional accounting in a way that assures them to be both necessary and sufficient to explain most of the principles and practices in accounting. While noting that some accounting principles and practices are "mutually inconsistent," Ijiri believed that his set satisfactorily explained conventional accounting in the same manner that Euclidean geometry is described by a set of axioms and theorems.

Departing from the economic approach, R.J. Chambers (1966) used a systems approach to define a conceptual framework for accounting. In *Accounting, Evaluation and Economic Behavior*, he developed a series of "arguments" to describe accounting. Chambers began his arguments with a set of statements in which the individual dominates, describing "individual thought and action." The second set of arguments outlined individual choices, or "ends and means." Chambers's third set of arguments described the "environment of action" with which the individual interacts. Following the asset-liability approach, Chambers's money-calculation arguments were based on "the dimension of the monetary unit at a point of time as its annual purchasing power." His financial-position arguments introduced the concept of financial capital maintenance. With a stable monetary unit, financial capital is maintained using the traditional historical-cost concept. Inflation requires restatement in "constant dollars." The sixth set of Chambers's arguments were based on a time element in positive and negative measures (debits and credits). His concluding set of arguments pertained to the objectives of information. Focusing on the individual's requirements for information, he introduced the characteristics of relevance, neutrality, reliability, objectivity, and correspondence, as qualities of information.

Following Chambers, the Study Group on the Objectives of Financial Statements of the AICPA focused on the individual as a user of accounting information. The Trueblood Report issued by the Study Group in 1973 formally defined the user at the outset, stating: "The objective of financial statements is to provide information useful for making economic decisions. . . . An objective of financial statements is to serve primarily those users who have limited authority, ability, or resources to obtain information and who rely on financial statements as their principle source of information about an enterprise's economic activities." Departing from economics-based methodologies, the 1973 Study Group adopted a political model. Thus, the 1973 Study Group defined the characters that interacted in the accounting environment. The FASB focused on the six necessary elements of the political approach: (1) origin of the issue; (2) need to identify pressures and sanctions; (3) "preferred" solution; (4) complexity of the network developed to gather information; (5) continuance of the political differences beyond the policy statement stage; and (6) execution dependent on institutional mechanisms (Most and Winters, 1977). The Financial Accounting Standards Board (FASB) adopted the political approach for its conceptual framework.

Reflecting this approach, the first of the FASB's six Statements of Financial Accounting Concepts (SFAC), which was published in 1978, began: "Financial reporting is not an end in itself but is intended to provide information that is useful in making business and economic decisions. . . . Financial reporting should provide information that is useful to present and potential investors and creditors and other users in making rational investment, credit, and similar decisions. . . . Financial accounting is not designed to measure directly the value of a business enterprise, but the information it provides may be helpful to those who wish to estimate its value."

The FASB's ongoing Conceptual Framework Project has also embodied a majority of the concepts established by previous authors. The third (superseded by the sixth) Statement reflected the basic definitions of assets and liabilities enumerated by Canning. The conflict between the revenue-expense and asset-liability approach to income measurement discussed in prior works is also evident in the six SFACs. The FASB's ambiguous choice of a definition for comprehensive income in the fourth and sixth Statements illustrated the board's attempt to integrate the two approaches to income measurement as follows:

Comprehensive income of a business enterprise results from (a) exchange transactions and other transfers between the enterprise and other entities that are not its owners, (b) the enterprise's productive efforts, and (c) price changes, casualties, and other effects of interactions between the enterprise and the economic, legal, social, political, and physical environment of which it is part.

Comprehensive income comprises two related but distinguishable types of components. It consists of not only its basic components—revenues, expenses, gains, and losses—but also various intermediate components that result from combining the basic components. Revenues, expenses, gains, and losses can be combined in various ways to obtain several measures of enterprise performance with varying degrees of inclusiveness. . . . Those intermediate components are, in effect, subtotals of comprehensive income and often of one another in the sense that they can be combined with each other or with the basic components to obtain other intermediate measures of comprehensive income.

The systems approach taken by the FASB required conceptual definition of the characteristics of information used by the characters. Differing from Chambers's "arguments," the FASB provided a hierarchy of characteristics, or qualities in its second Statement. The primary qualities were relevance, and reliability and neutrality (where reliability includes verifiability and representational faithfulness). The secondary qualities were comparability and consistency.

In summary, a conceptual framework of accounting has been proposed by numerous authors in the twentieth century. Earlier frameworks were inductively derived from an economic environment; later ones have employed a systems approach to describe the "users" and the characteristics of information necessary to the users. Each framework reflects the logical approach taken. All the works basically agree on the concepts of assets and liabilities. They also agree that definitive income management only occurs with a stable measuring unit.

Lacking a stable measuring unit, many question whether any framework of accounting can answer all known and unknown questions on income measurement, and financial and physical capital maintenance. The American Accounting Association's Committee on Accounting and Auditing Measurement best described in 1991 this dilemma, stating: "Caught between the rock of imperfect and incomplete markets and the hard place of the irrelevance of past costs for decision-making and as an indicator of current values, it is not surprising that accountants have argued about their relative merits for decades without reaching agreement."

Adrianne E. Slaymaker

Bibliography

American Institute of Accountants. *Changing Concepts of Business Income.* Report of the Study Group on Business Income. New York: Macmillan, 1952.

American Institute of Certified Public Accountants. *Objectives of Financial Statements.* Report of the Study Group on Objectives of Financial Statements [The Trueblood Report]. New York: AICPA, 1973.

Canning, J.B. *Economics of Accountancy.* New York: Ronald Press, 1929.

Chambers, R.J. *Accounting, Evaluation and Economic Behavior.* Englewood Cliffs, NJ: Prentice-Hall, 1966.

———. "Blueprint for a Theory of Accounting," *Accounting Research*, January 1955, pp. 17–25.

Financial Accounting Standards Board. *Elements of Financial Statements*, Statement of Financial Accounting Concepts No. 6. Stamford, CT: FASB, 1985.

———. *Elements of Financial Statements of Business Enterprises.* Statement of Financial Accounting Concepts No. 3. Stamford, CT: FASB 1980.

———. "Objectives of Financial Reporting by Business Enterprises." Statement of Financial Accounting Concepts No. 1. Stamford, CT: FASB, 1978.

———. *Objectives of Financial Reporting by Nonbusiness Organizations.* Statement of Financial Accounting Concepts No. 4. Stamford, CT: FASB, 1980.

———. "Qualitative Characteristics of Accounting Information." Statement of Financial Accounting Concepts No. 2. Stamford, CT: FASB, 1980.

———. *Recognition and Measurement in Financial Statements of Business Enterprises.* Statement of Financial Accounting Concepts No. 5. Stamford, CT: FASB, 1984.

Ijiri, Y. *The Foundations of Accounting Measurement.* Englewood Cliffs, NJ: Prentice-Hall, 1967.

———. *Theory of Accounting Measurement.* Studies in Accounting Research No. 10. Sarasota, FL: American Accounting Association, 1975.

Koeppen, D.R. "Using the FASB's Conceptual Framework: Fitting the Pieces Together," *Accounting Horizons*, June 1988, pp. 18–26.

Mattessich, R. *Accounting and Analytical Methods: Measurement and Projection of Income and Wealth in the Micro-and-Macro Economy.* Homewood, IL: Irwin, 1964.

Moonitz, M. *The Basic Postulates of Accounting.* Accounting Research Study No. 1. New York: AICPA, 1961.

———. "Basic Postulates of Accounting," *Journal of Accountancy*, November 1961, pp. 71–72.

Most, K.S., and A.L. Winters. "Focus on Standard Setting: From Trueblood to the FASB," *Journal of Accountancy*, February 1977, pp. 67–75.

Paton, W.A. *Accounting Theory: With Special Reference to the Corporate Enterprise.* New York: Ronald Press, 1922.

Scott, DR. "The Basics for Accounting Principles," *Accounting Review*, December 1941, pp. 341–349.

Sprague, C.E. *The Philosophy of Accounts.* New York: Author, 1908.

See also ACCOUNTING PRINCIPLES BOARD; ACCOUNTING RESEARCH BULLETINS; AC-

C

COUNTING RESEARCH STUDIES; AMERICAN ACCOUNTING ASSOCIATION; AMERICAN INSTITUTE OF CERTIFIED PUBLIC ACCOUNTANTS; CANNING, JOHN BENNETT; CHAMBERS, RAYMOND JOHN; DEFERRED INCOME TAX ACCOUNTING; DEFINITIONS OF ACCOUNTING; FINANCIAL ACCOUNTING STANDARDS BOARD; FISHER, IRVING; GENERALLY ACCEPTED ACCOUNTING PRINCIPLES; GILMAN, STEPHEN; HATFIELD, HENRY RAND; IJIRI, YUJI; LIABILITIES; MATCHING; MATERIALITY; MATTESSICH, RICHARD; MOONITZ, MAURICE; MOST, KENNETH S.; NORMATIVE ACCOUNTING; PATON, WILLIAM ANDREW; POSTULATES OF ACCOUNTING; SCHRADER, WILLIAM JOSEPH; SMITH, ADAM; SOLOMONS, DAVID; SPRAGUE, CHARLES EZRA; STERLING, ROBERT R.; STUDY GROUP ON BUSINESS INCOME'S *FIVE MONOGRAPHS ON BUSINESS INCOME;* TRUEBLOOD, ROBERT MARTIN

Congresses on Accounting, International

The International Congresses on Accounting began in St. Louis, Missouri, in 1904; the 14th assembly was held in Washington, D.C., in October 1992. The primary purpose of the meetings is to provide a forum for the exchange of accounting theory and methods among practitioners from various nations. Additional European international conferences convened from 1889 through the 1960s in Paris, Brussels, and Edinburgh. The latter do not seem to have achieved the same recognition as the Congresses originating in 1904 and conducted at various locations throughout the world.

Presentation content at the International Congresses has evolved from a mere listing of diverse accounting practices to discourses promoting the international harmonization of accounting and auditing standards in order to meet the challenges of a modern global economy. In recent years, the conferences have offered several plenary sessions on general international issues, followed by technical and group discussion sessions on specific topics. National accounting institutes send official representatives to present summary reports at the technical sessions.

Lack of international coordination precluded consistency in both the timing and the subject matter of early conferences. The occurrence of successive sessions was erratic until after World War II and ceased entirely from 1938 until the Sixth Congress in London in

1952. With World War II threatening, delegates attended the Fifth Congress (1938), in Berlin, under strained conditions.

Although North Americans and Europeans have dominated assemblies, attendance from Asian and South American countries has increased. The first session conducted outside Europe and the United States was in Sydney, Australia, in 1972. Since that time, conferences have also taken place in Mexico (1982) and Japan (1987).

The underlying objective of the first conference at St. Louis was not to provide a medium for the exchange of international perspectives but to unify divergent interests of the nascent accounting profession in the United States into one cohesive national organization, the American Association of Public Accountants (AAPA). The international atmosphere served only to convey status to a fledgling profession attempting to achieve recognition in the United States.

Although assemblies before World War II lacked continuity, they presented a medium for topics of interest of the period and reflected the different accounting methods of individual nations. Subjects included comparisons of accounting legislation, accounting education, and accountants' responsibilities. Discourses also entailed inflation accounting, taxation, managerial (industrial) accounting and consolidated financial statements. Unfortunately, dialogue among members of different national accounting organizations usually ceased with the closing ceremonies. Delegates made little effort to strive toward achieving common objectives for accounting practice and rarely pursued discussion of shared values between conferences.

After World War II, interests in integrating accounting concepts at the international level began to emerge. At the first conference after the war, the Sixth Congress (1952), in London, the president, H.G. Howitt, suggested that accounting might make an international contribution to resolving world economic problems that were at the root of recent wars. However, conference members failed to propose measures that would coordinate the accounting profession at an international level.

The Eighth Congress (1962), in New York, reflected a growing interest in assuming an international perspective regarding accounting and auditing practice. Members suggested establishing a permanent structure to investigate and resolve international financial-reporting issues through harmonization of accounting objectives. The legalistic approaches to accounting, found in many nations, and the inherent lack of agreement on accepted accounting practices within most nations deterred the harmonization process and precluded acceptance of explicitly defined international rules.

Not until the 10th Congress (1972), in Sydney, did efforts of leading accounting representatives result in a proposal to establish an international body that would determine international accounting standards. The formation of the International Accounting Standards Committee (IASC) in 1973 was an outgrowth of the 1972 Congress and was perhaps the most significant contribution of these Congresses to date.

The Sydney conference also generated the formation in 1972 of the International Coordination Committee for the Accountancy Profession (ICCAP), which was the predecessor to the current sponsoring organization of the Congresses, the International Federation of Accountants (IFAC). The IFAC was established in 1977, just prior to the 11th Congress that year, in Munich, and assumed the roles of conducting future Congresses and representing the accounting profession at an international level on all matters except setting accounting standards.

International professional issues continued to be the major concern of the IFAC and pervaded the 14th International Congress in Washington, D.C., in 1992. The theme of the conference, "The Accountant's Role in a Global Economy," reflected the IFAC's promotion of a unified worldwide accounting profession that understands accelerated business globalization, changing capital markets and a demanding public.

A significant benefit of the Congresses is that the proceedings offer a first-hand narrative of accounting theory and practice as they evolve. However, conferences often have reflected the prejudice of the Congress organizers and at times have presented a microscopic rather than a comprehensive discussion of accounting theory and practice. An additional problem exists in that while Congresses have offered simultaneous interpretations of selected presentations in three or four major languages, many of the proceedings are published solely in the native language of the presenter. Translation is necessary for many researchers who utilize the proceedings in their studies. Copies of individual presentation papers and of many published proceedings can be obtained from the Library Services Division of the American Institute of Certified Public Accountants (AICPA) in New York.

A listing of all International Congresses, the major topic of each, and availability of reprinted published proceedings follows:

1904 First Congress—St. Louis—unification of the U.S. accounting profession—*Congress of Accountants, World Fair, St. Louis September 26–28th, 1904.* Reprinted (Rpt.) in Richard P. Brief, ed. *Development of Contemporary Accounting Thought Series.* New York: Arno Press, 1978.

1926 Second Congress—Amsterdam—accountants' responsibilities—*Het Internationaal Accountantscongres.* Amsterdam: J. Muusses, Purmerend, 1926. Rpt. in Richard P. Brief, ed. *Dimensions of Accounting Theory and Practice.* New York: Arno Press, 1980.

1929 Third Congress—New York—various subjects, including the development of public accounting in Europe—*International Congress on Accounting, 1930.* Rpt. in Richard P. Brief, ed. *Accountancy in Transition Series.* New York: Garland, 1982.

1933 Fourth Congress—London—various subjects, including the "science" of accounting and consolidated accounting—*Fourth International Congress on Accounting.* London: Gee, 1933. Rpt. in Richard P. Brief, ed. *Accountancy in Transition Series.* New York: Garland, 1982.

1938 Fifth Congress—Berlin—various subjects, many presented by German delegates—*The Fifth International Congress on Accounting.* Berlin: Kommissionsverlag Preussische Druckerei und Verlags Aktiengesellschaft, 1939. Rpt. in Richard P. Brief, ed. *Accounting Thought and Practice through the Years.* New York: Garland, 1986.

1952 Sixth Congress—London—managerial and inflation accounting—*The Sixth International Congress on Accounting.* London: Gee, 1952. Rpt. in Richard P. Brief, ed. New York: Garland, 1984.

1957 Seventh Congress—Amsterdam—external and internal auditing—*Proceedings of the International Congress of Accountants, Seventh, 1957.* Rpt. in Richard P. Brief, ed. *Foundations of Accounting Series No. 26.* New York: Garland, 1988.

1962 Eighth Congress—New York—the effects of a world economy on auditing and financial reporting.

1967 Ninth Congress—Paris—accounting for consolidated and government entities as well as the harmonization of accounting principles.

C

1972 10th Congress—Sydney—various subjects, including common goals of international accounting.

1977 11th Congress—Munich—establishment of the IFAC—harmonization of accounting and auditing practice.

1982 12th Congress—Mexico City—first conference conducted under the auspices of the IFAC—professional responsibilities of accountants in a changing world.

1987 13th Congress—Tokyo—first congress in Asia—international accounting and auditing standards.

1992 14th Congress—Washington, D.C.— the accountant's role in a global economy.

The predominant purpose of the Congresses probably will remain the exchange of ideas among diverse accounting communities. The conferences likely will continue to mirror the evolution of an integrated, international accounting profession and provide insight into the development of accounting within specific nations. The proceedings may prove particularly useful in analyzing accounting practices in Third World and former Eastern-bloc nations as their economies develop and their demand for complex financial systems increases. Increased understanding of emerging countries, obtained through Congress dialogue, may ease the entry of nations into the accounting harmonization effort.

Mary E. Harston

Bibliography

Barrett, G.R. "Preparing for October's XIV World Congress of Accountants," *Journal of Accountancy*, January 1992, pp. 41–44.

Choi, F.D.S., and G.G. Mueller. *International Accounting*. Englewood Cliffs, NJ: Prentice-Hall, 1984, pp. 501–502.

Howitt, H.G. "Opening Address by the President." In *The Sixth International Congress on Accounting*. London: Gee, 1952. Reprint. New York: Garland, 1984.

Mueller, G.G. "Some Thoughts about the International Congress of Accountants," *Accounting Review*, October 1961, pp. 548–554.

Murphy, M.E. "The Seven International Congresses of Accountants," *Accounting Review*, October 1961, pp. 555–563.

Previts, G.J., and B.D. Merino. *A History of Accounting in America: An Historical Interpretation of the Cultural Significance of Accounting*. New York. John Wiley & Sons, 1979.

Samuels, J.M., and A.G. Piper. *International Accounting: A Survey*. New York: St. Martin's Press, 1985.

See also AMERICAN INSTITUTE OF CERTIFIED PUBLIC ACCOUNTANTS; INTERNATIONAL ACCOUNTING STANDARDS COMMITTEE; KRAAYENHOF, JACOB; MONTGOMERY, ROBERT HIESTER; SCHMIDT, JULIUS AUGUST FRITZ

Congressional Views

Congressional views on private-sector accounting have (1) been responsive to accounting and financial reporting problems corresponding to sequential stages in U.S. economic development, focusing mainly on financial and securities issues; (2) been most invasive during times of financial crisis or scandal; and (3) not resulted, for the most part, in dramatic impacts upon the practice of accounting or upon accountant independence from the federal government.

In 1887, while the nation was in its first horizontal (business trust) merger movement, the first national accounting society, the American Association of Public Accountants (AAPA) was formed and Congress created the first independent regulatory commission, the Interstate Commerce Commission. These related events demonstrated industrialization's arrival in the United States. Gradually drawing away from the British accounting firms that had organized them as American branches, the early U.S. accounting firms combined English auditing and accounting practice with the methods of financial accounting and analysis pioneered by railroading people like Albert Fink and David McCallum.

Practitioner control over the profession was established early and followed the typical American pattern of creating state regulatory groups composed of practitioners who exercised their control over the profession through state authority delegations. The individual state societies moved toward establishing accounting, auditing and ethical standards, albeit without uniformity. Although the national societies did little in the way of standard-setting, they gradually assumed the role of representing the profession in dealings with the federal government. This established the persistent interactive pattern between the profession and the government that became the focus of significant congressional attention as the century progressed.

Government interest in record keeping and financial reporting increased along with its taxation function and extension of control over major economic areas like banking and transportation. The most significant interaction of the profession with government prior to the 1930s was with individual agencies or commissions, rather than with Congress. President Theodore Roosevelt appointed the Keep Commission in 1906 to examine U.S. government business and accounting methods, and accounting leaders were invited to confer with the commission. Prior to World War I, important members of the AAPA—which became the American Institute of Accountants (AIA) in 1916—and the American Institute of Certified Public Accountants (AICPA) in 1957—interacted with the Federal Trade Commission (FTC) and the Federal Reserve Board (FRB), as well as with the Treasury in connection with the Revenue Acts of 1909 and 1913. Added regulation in the form of the Federal Reserve, Clayton and Federal Trade Commission Acts in 1913 and 1914 created more emphasis on financial record keeping and increased the market for accounting information. Congressional proposals to regulate securities during the 1920s were stopped in committee because of private-sector opposition, mainly from the Investment Bankers Association (IBA) and the New York Stock Exchange (NYSE). Federal scrutiny of the accounting function, however, received its first intense examination in the wake of the financial-sector crisis of 1929–1932.

Some of the most important conclusions reached during the Senate Banking and Currency Committee hearings of 1932–1934 (popularly referred to as the Pecora hearings) on the role of the financial sector during the boom years of the 1920s revealed that nonuniform corporate financial reporting was determined by corporations themselves, that published information frequently was misleading and obscure—particularly among investment and holding companies—and that the accounting profession was unable to exercise sufficient influence over clients' choices of reporting conventions. Neither was the NYSE found to have significant influence. In addition, manipulation of legal devices and corporate financial-reporting techniques by executives, to the disadvantage of shareholders, was found to be widespread, as was stock market manipulation by major Wall Street firms.

Since these shortcomings involved accountants both directly and indirectly, it was inevitable that corrective measures, when enacted, would focus upon the accounting function, and possibly upon professional organization and self-regulation. Comprehensive congressional remedial legislation during the first months of the Franklin D. Roosevelt administration was foiled by inept draftsmanship of the intended statute. A new team, headed by Harvard Law School Professor Felix Frankfurter, with James M. Landis, Thomas Corcoran and Benjamin Cohen, wrote what was to become the Securities Act of 1933. They had time only to develop the provisions dealing with new securities issuance. Significant consequences arose from the partial treatment of the problem and from its permissive remedial provisions for shareholders. No new agency was created, and the radical legal treatment that provided for recision (entitling shareholders to return stocks for the purchase price when the prospectus was deficient) created enormous opposition.

It is difficult to overestimate the importance of the conflict over the revision of the Securities Act of 1933 by the Securities and Exchange Commission Act of 1934. The occurrences of 1933–1934 became the basis for congressional oversight; thereafter the fundamental structure of the government's relation to the accounting profession and to the financial-reporting function for publicly traded firms remained relatively constant.

When the 1934 act was being fought over in Congress, the administration realized that it would have to compromise. The recision aspect contained in Section 11 was removed. Accountants and other experts being sued under the act would no longer have to prove they had no knowledge of material information in registration statements that was either misleading or omitted. A new agency with enormous power was created, the Securities and Exchange Commission (SEC), at the insistence of Wall Street, to administer the two acts. It could specify the standards of financial reporting (Section 13). It could become involved in a wide range of corporate governance issues (Section 2). It could establish rules for the trading of issued stocks, and of the Stock Exchanges. It could conduct investigations, recommend prosecutions, and bring civil actions. In short, the basis for modern securities regulation was established.

The congressional mandate that the SEC should create rules for corporate financial reporting (1933 act Sections 19A, 19B; 1934 act Sections 13(a), 13(b)) was liberally interpreted by the agency to permit it to assign that function in January 1937 to the private sector, in the form of the AIA, which sought and welcomed the delegation. The AIA assigned the rule-making responsibility to its preexisting Committee on Accounting Procedures (CAP). Although the manifest impact was to keep rule making for financial reporting in the private sector, the more subtle, latent effect was to shift the attention of Congress from the SEC to the AIA when questionable matters of financial reporting emerged. This shielded the SEC, but made the profession potentially more vulnerable to congressional criticism.

No serious congressional challenge to the system established in 1937 for corporate financial reporting occurred for 40 years, however. Congress was relatively uninvolved in the substitution of the Accounting Principles Board (APB) in 1959 for the CAP. Not until the aftermath of the conglomerate merger movement (1964–1969) did a congressional body direct a searching investigation into private accounting operations and accounting's relation with the SEC. This was the investigation begun in 1977 by the Senate Subcommittee on Reports, Accounting, and Management, which became known as the Metcalf Committee hearings named after the chairman of the Subcommittee, Lee Metcalf (D, Montana). There was similar interest shown in the House by Congressman John E. Moss (D, California) at about the same time. The Metcalf hearings were preceded by the committee's staff study, *The Accounting Establishment,* which had been influenced by the publication of *Corporate Financial Reporting: Public or Private Control?* the year before. The staff study was a critical and controversial inquiry into the setting of accounting standards by the private sector. Criticism contained in the study included allegations with respect to the operation of the Big Eight accounting firms and their apparent domination of the AICPA, the poor performance of the SEC with respect to rule making, questionable accountant independence from clients, and the potential conflict of interest when an accounting firm performed both auditing and management advisory services (MAS) for one client.

The recommendations in the staff study were the most dramatic set of structural revisions ever recommended for accounting organizations and financial rule making by a congressional group. Of greatest significance was the proposed federal creation of financial standards, not through the SEC, which the study believed too compromised to do it effectively, but through either the U.S. General Accounting Office (GAO) or a group like the Cost Accounting Standards Board (CASB). Also recommended were: amending the securities laws to overturn *Hochfelder v. Ernst and Ernst,* so that aggrieved individuals could sue independent auditors, even though the auditor had not intended to deceive, manipulate or defraud; annual reports from the 15 largest accounting firms; divorcing auditing and accounting from MAS if possible, and encouragement of increased competition among the Big Eight. Those attacked in *The Accounting Establishment* defended themselves in the hearings, which began in 1977. The SEC, the AICPA, the Financial Accounting Standards Board (FASB), and a large group of other witnesses argued against the staff-study recommendations and stressed that the recently organized (1972) FASB ought to be given a chance to work. The final report of the committee was very mild, compared to the staff study. No structural changes were recommended. Instead, only a series of behavioral alterations, including firm peer reviews, were recommended. The SEC instituted Accounting Series Release (ASR) No. 250, requiring notice in a prospectus when accounting and auditing services were combined with MAS by one accounting firm, but it was rescinded in 1982.

Sparked largely by several spectacular audit failures—situations in which nationally important firms had received positive audit reports, only to fail shortly afterward and then be found to have been insolvent at the time of the audit—the Dingell hearings named after Congressman John D. Dingell (D, Michigan) began in the House in February 1985, taking up a series of unresolved issues left over from the Metcalf hearings. The Dingell Committee investigation continued over a longer period than the Metcalf hearings and managed to influence some alterations in private-sector rule-making structure and behavior. The AICPA's role in the FASB was reduced. The National Commission on Fraudulent Financial Reporting (called the Treadway Commission after its chairman,

James C. Treadway Jr.) was formed in 1985 and issued its report in 1987. It called for more intensive development of internal-control mechanisms within corporations and specified that auditors should assume more responsibility for the integrity and operation of those controls. The following year, the AICPA issued two Statements of Auditing Standards (SAS) providing new guidelines for the evaluation of the internal-control structure.

In 1986, Congressman Ron Wyden (D, Oregon), a member of the Dingell Committee, introduced a bill, called the Financial Fraud Detection and Disclosure Act, amending the 1934 act. It would require auditors finding irregularities in a client's operations to report them to corporate officials and, if not corrected within 90 days, to inform the SEC. The bill was not introduced in 1987, but was re-introduced thereafter, failing, however, to get out of committee. Rep. Wyden expected the bill to get to the House floor in the 1993 session. As of 1994, no action has yet occurred on this bill.

Congressional attention to accounting and auditing has focused upon the information content of audits and financial information. When serious incidents occur in the financial area, congressional oversight committees can be expected to begin investigations both of accounting groups and of SEC exercise of its authorities under the Securities Acts. Into the mid-1990s, no serious attempt had been made to alter the essentially private-sector control over financial reporting, and the accounting profession continued to resist added government regulation. Should the profession in the future feel forced to appeal to Congress for federal legislation for protection against growing common law liabilities, however, the price may be a reduction in accountant independence.

Robert Chatov

Bibliography

Chatov, R. "Corporate Codes of Conduct: Economic Determinants and Legal Implications for Auditors," *Journal of Accounting and Public Policy*, Spring 1993, pp. 3–35.

———. *Corporate Financial Reporting: Public or Private Control?* New York: The Free Press, 1975.

Dingell, J.D. "Who Audits the Auditors?" *New York Times*, March 13, 1985, sec. B, p. 3.

"Moss Report Says SEC Should Set Accounting/Auditing Rules; FASB's Armstrong Issues Strong Rebuttal," *Journal of Accountancy*, December 1976, pp. 26, 28.

National Commission on Fraudulent Financial Reporting. *Report of the National Commission on Fraudulent Financial Reporting* [The Treadway Report]. Washington, DC: National Commission on Fraudulent Financial Reporting, 1987.

U.S. Congress. House. Committee on Energy and Commerce. Subcommittee on Oversight and Investigations. *Consolidating the Administration and Enforcement of the Federal Securities Laws within the Securities and Exchange Commission.* April 1987. 100th Cong., 1st sess. Committee Print 100-G. Washington, DC: GPO, 1987.

U.S. Congress. House. Committee on Energy and Commerce. Subcommittee on Oversight and Investigations. *Effectiveness, Independence, and Regulation of Corporate Audits.* 99th Cong., 1st sess. February 20 and March 6, 1985, Serial No. 99–17. Washington, DC: GPO, 1985.

U.S. Congress. Senate. Committee on Government Operations. Subcommittee on Reports, Accounting, and Management. *Improving the Accountability of Publicly Owned Corporations and Their Auditors.* 95th Cong., 1st sess. 1977. Washington, DC: GPO, 1977.

U.S. Congress. Senate Committee on Government Operations. Senate, Subcommittee on Reports, Accounting, and Management. *The Accounting Establishment.: A Staff Study.* 95th Cong., 1st sess. Washington, DC: GPO, 1977.

See also AMERICAN INSTITUTE OF CERTIFIED PUBLIC ACCOUNTANTS; BIG EIGHT ACCOUNTING FIRMS; COST ACCOUNTING STANDARDS BOARD; DIVERSIFIED REPORTING; FEDERAL GOVERNMENT ACCOUNTING (U.S.); FINANCIAL ACCOUNTING STANDARDS BOARD; GENERAL ACCOUNTING OFFICE, U.S.; *HOCHFELDER V. ERNST AND ERNST;* INDEPENDENCE OF EXTERNAL AUDITORS; LAW AND ACCOUNTING; LEGAL LIABILITY OF AUDITORS; MANAGEMENT ADVISORY SERVICES BY CPAS; NEW YORK STOCK EXCHANGE; PUBLIC OVERSIGHT BOARD; SECURITIES AND EXCHANGE COMMISSION; TREADWAY COMMISSION; UNIFORMITY; U.S. INDUSTRIAL COMMISSION

Conservatism

Medieval stewardship accounting laid the foundations for the modern doctrine of conservatism. During the Middle Ages, concentration of land ownership among the nobility produced a system of administration by proxy. The manorial lord often depended for his living on the productivity of large estates and the efforts of hundreds of people whom he could not personally supervise. Day to day management was left to a hierarchy of officials and department heads. When the right to use land was delegated from an owner to his agent, the agent assumed a stewardship responsibility.

The lord's incentive for keeping accounts arose from his need to check on the integrity and reliability of these stewards, to prevent loss and theft, and generally to encourage efficiency. He wished to protect his property by controlling his servants. For the manorial steward facing audit, a conservative stance was a form of self-protection. A man entrusted with someone else's assets will not normally anticipate increases in their value, because in doing so he may become responsible for the result. Concealment of unrealized gains was the steward's natural response to the feudal stipulation that the lord must suffer no loss from fraud, negligence, or bad judgment. It was safer to understate.

In framing the companies acts, beginning in 1844, Parliament was strongly influenced by this English tradition of responsibility accounting. Promoters and company officers were considered stewards placed in charge of investors' capital. Incorporation was granted as a privilege, in return for which managers were required to publicize their handling of corporate affairs. The British balance sheet evolved as a formal report of management's stewardship of assets held in trust. Annual audits were seen as an instrument of stockholder control over the performance of duties that they had delegated to management. The asset valuation methods in use today are to some extent holdovers from a feudal tradition in which financial understatement was considered a practical necessity.

Mercantile Accounting

Double entry bookkeeping developed during the Italian Renaissance in response to the need of merchants and bankers for a complete, systematic record of their activities. Conservatism could not play the same role in this trading environment that it did in the master-servant re-lationship characteristic of feudalism. The typical fifteenth century merchant did not regularly report to anyone outside his business, and had after all no interest in deceiving himself. A policy of understatement gave way to one of concealment. In "Particularis de Computis et Scripturis" (1494), Pacioli described the ledger as a book the merchant should preferably keep himself, to preserve the secrecy of its contents.

Yet it was during this period that the methods associated with conservatism were first used systematically. Capital reserves were employed in the thirteenth century. The lower of cost or market rule was used in estate valuations as early as 1393. The Datini accounts of 1410 include lower of cost or market inventory valuations. Florentine bankers regularly wrote accounts receivable down to net realizable value.

Between the fifteenth and eighteenth centuries, conservatism was often an expedient but not yet a doctrine. Its operative technique, the lower of cost or market rule, was applied for a variety of reasons. Taxes levied on business property may sometimes have given merchants an incentive to reduce asset valuations. In other cases, such writedowns were substitutes for depreciation. Market prices were also recorded by merchants in situations where acquisition costs were unknown.

Probably the strongest motive for lower of cost or market writedowns was the desire to reduce assets and especially inventories to net realizable value. During accountancy's "age of stagnation" inventories were usually small, closings were irregular, and merchants commonly wished to know their profits on each type of goods in stock. Asset valuation was part of the process of pricing merchandise for sale. Pacioli, Jan Ympyn and other early writers considered cost the normal value for reporting assets but were ready to depart from it when estimates were needed. The particular situation rather than any fixed policy determined how such estimates were made. Assets were often written up when there were indications of a value increase, or written down when selling prices fell. In *Debtor and Creditor Made Easie* (1675), Stephen Monteage gave examples of livestock inventories in which earlier acquisition costs of sheep, horses, and bulls were revalued upward or downward according to prices paid for later purchases. Angelo Pietra, in *Indrizzo Degli Economi* (1586), advised that crops and manufactured goods should be recorded at an amount below current market price "so that the proceeds will not fall below this value in case of sale." The motive was clearly to make the accounts more responsible to economic forces.

Jacques Savary was the individual most responsible for promoting the lower of cost or market rule. In *The Complete Tradesman* (1675) he recommended current price valuations of inventory, unless it had begun to deteriorate or go out of style, in which case its book value should be reduced. Book value should also be lowered if replacement cost falls below acquisition price. Savary was the principal author of a 1673 French government ordinance that required merchants and bankers to keep accounts and prepare balance sheets every two years. The Code Savary recommended but did not require lower of cost or market valuations. In this case the purpose was to show the ability of assets to cover debts in case a merchant went bankrupt, to facilitate a fair sharing of his resources among creditors.

In 1794 the Prussian government enacted a law which required that balance sheets be prepared on a lower of cost or market basis. The law was dropped from the 1857 Prussian Code but was revived in 1873, after a business panic. The German Commercial Code of 1897 required lower of cost or market treatment for inventories and securities for which quoted market prices were available, with other assets to be valued at cost. This was in part a response to stock speculations during which promoters had valued assets at selling prices to entice potential investors. The intent of this law, and of the Code Savary of 1673, was to narrow the opportunities for fraud. It cannot be inferred that either statute deliberately promoted an accounting principle. But they gave legal sanction to conservatism and have often been cited as precedents by English and American scholars.

Several conclusions can be drawn about the interaction between conservatism and double entry bookkeeping. First, there are so many possible reasons for accounting understatement that it would be hard to imagine a society in which at least some were not operative. Second, conservative practices have been more favored and useful at certain times than at others. Conservatism has always been important when reporting to outsiders was a primary accounting task. It has sometimes been less significant when accounts were kept for personal inspection by the owner of a firm. Third, conservatism has become more important with the

standardization of accounting methods, and indeed is a means of achieving such standardization. A prime motive for conservatism in its modern setting is to provide guidelines for asset valuation in cases of uncertainty, thereby making estimates more consistent. But between the fifteenth and eighteenth centuries, there was little evident pressure for standardized asset valuations. The venture accounting that predominated did not typically describe continuous business operations, so there was less need for consistency and comparison. Most modern incentives for conservatism were lacking before the industrial revolution.

The English Industrial Corporation

The doctrine of conservatism developed mainly in response to demands by nineteenth century creditors and stockholders for reliable financial data. Corporate managers of the early 1800s had great freedom in their choice of accounting methods. They could in each company largely make the rules by which assets were valued and income was determined. Financial overstatement reflected the mood of entrepreneurs in a rapidly industrializing and expanding economy. And overstatement worked to a corporation's short run advantage. Firms trying to raise capital by selling stocks and bonds to the public had every incentive to inflate asset and income figures. High reported profits induced investment, increased the market value of securities, and raised executive salaries to the extent that these were tied to earnings.

The accounting methods in use also led to overstatement. Manufacturing companies commonly accounted for depreciable assets as if they were unsold merchandise. Plant and equipment were revalued at the end of each accounting period, increases as well as decreases in value being charged directly to profit and loss. In contrast, most railroads, utilities, and other public service corporations used some type of replacement accounting. Original investments in assets were capitalized and never depreciated. Asset replacements and maintenance charges were expensed. Since capital investments created no charge to expense until they were replaced, this method made railroads seem an attractive investment by maximizing reported profits during the early years of their life cycle when they most needed capital. George Oliver May believed that the construction of America's transcontinental railroads by private companies would probably have been impossible if cost based depreciation had been required. He added however that "it is no doubt true that as a result of accounting methods followed, large amounts of capital have been lost by investors."

Richard P. Brief has demonstrated that reported profits during the nineteenth century were materially higher than they would have been if today's accounting methods had been in use. That is, if periodic depreciation had been taken, if asset appreciation had not been credited to income, and if a more consistent distinction had been made between capital and revenue expenditures, earnings and dividends would have been substantially lower. Unconservative accounting methods produced a large, unstable accounting error which influenced resource allocation, prices and output levels, the business cycle, and economic growth in general.

An accounting policy of systematic understatement seemed a natural antidote to management's known tendency to overstate. Its first advocates were creditors who wished to safeguard legal capital against excessive dividend payments. Acceptance of this policy depended partly on stockholder attitudes. Accounting methods that favored short term speculators often continued until investors became willing to forgo high current dividends to assure larger ones in the future. For example, after 1850 a tendency to understate profits began to replace the deliberate overstatement that characterized the speculative inception of the railroads.

The emerging accounting profession had its own reasons to prefer financial understatement. As Robert Henry Parker said, it had grown up in an environment of "bankruptcies, failures, frauds, and disputes" that filled accountants with "a vivid sense of disaster." Business depressions occurred about every 10 years in Victorian England. The accounting response was to provide for all reasonable future contingencies, even if such contingencies were not precisely definable or measurable. By 1880 English auditors had made the writedown of obsolete or damaged goods to lower of cost or market prices a standard procedure. Textbooks and journal articles of the 1880s began to take the view that assets should be valued at historical cost less depreciation due to wear and tear, with all other fluctuations in value being ignored.

The accounting literature of the time and other evidence suggests that conservatism was widely ineffective in preventing managerial manipulation. Company directors simply had too much latitude in their stewardship of invested capital. In effect the corporate manager had it both ways. By overstating assets and income and paying dividends from capital, he could favorably impress potential investors. If on the other hand he chose to understate, he could create secret reserves, shift profits from year to year, and present an attractive appearance of stability, while distorting analyses of managerial effectiveness and future earnings potential.

Conservatism and the Law

By the year 1700, English law included two conservative accounting standards. A capital impairment rule specified that no dividend should be paid that left the value of the remaining assets below the firm's contributed capital. A profits test limited dividends to the total of current and retained earnings. The profits test was codified in the Companies Act of 1862. One or the other of these rules still governs dividend distributions in many American states.

But for many years the law did not specify the components of profit and capital in sufficient detail to make these rules effective. Except where fraud was involved, the courts were reluctant lawgivers. The business community was expected to develop its own standards. Court decisions were ambiguous on the treatment of unrealized appreciation of fixed assets and on the distinction between capital and revenue expenditures. Case law on asset valuation was sparse, sometimes contradictory, and it was often hard to tell how broadly a particular decision applied.

The rule that dividend payments could not reduce capital below the amount paid in by stockholders was weakened in *Lee v. Neuchatel Asphalte Company* (1889). An English Court of Appeals ruled that in calculating profits from which dividends were to be paid, the firm could ignore declines in the value of wasting assets. This decision was reinforced in *re Kingston Cotton Mills* (1896), in which the court held that depreciation in the value of fixed assets did not affect a company's ability to declare dividends. These decisions led accountants to distinguish sharply between the valuation of fixed and current assets and to emphasize the latter as being more important.

During this period the pitfalls of optimism were demonstrated in a succession of bankruptcies and fraud trials. Auditors were repeatedly named as defendants in lawsuits brought by investors who claimed that financial statements overstated net income or capital, but almost never was an accounting firm sued on the grounds that audited statements were too conservative. Accountants therefore had reason to believe that a conservative resolution of doubtful issues would shield them from legal liability. To avoid the legal risks that might result from paying dividends out of capital, they tended to go to the opposite extreme by deliberately understating asset values and profits. Judicial rulings on capital maintenance gave conservatism legal backing at one of the most formative stages in the development of asset valuation and income measurement concepts.

Conservatism in Accounting Theory

By 1900 conservatism was the dominant accounting convention, to which others were subordinated when they came in conflict. Not logically derived from conservatism, but governed and justified by reference to it, were several corollary doctrines. The going concern concept, which implied an obligation to maintain plant and equipment intact throughout the corporation's life, did not conflict with conservatism. It required only that provision be made for asset replacements before dividends were paid. Falling prices between 1870 and 1900 fostered conservatism by making asset replacement comparatively cheap and compatible with low balance sheet valuations. Business continuity had brought with it the idea that fixed assets should not be revalued unless such changes reflected the value of the going concern. It made historical cost valuations "both conservative and convenient." But these concepts, so similar to our own, were based on different reasoning. As Reed Story put it: "Valuation at cost or at cost or market was defended in terms of the historical nature of accounting or the need for conservatism rather than in terms of the need for objective evidence or the process of matching. Essentially, asset valuation and income determination were based on an incomplete application of the going concern convention tempered by conservatism."

The American Experience: Reporting to Creditors

In Britain the doctrine of conservatism emerged from a tradition of stewardship accounting and lower of cost or market writedowns. In the United States conservatism became even more entrenched, but for different reasons. American bankers were the most influential consumers of accounting data, and conservatism protected them against inflated collateral values.

Bankers wanted assurance that a borrower could repay his loan at maturity. They judged that the best indications of future liquidity were to be found in the relationship between current assets and current liabilities. A safe margin of working capital and a two-for-one current ratio became the standards for granting credit. It was only natural for bankers to anticipate losses but not gains, to favor the writedown of inventories to lower of cost or market price, and to encourage the use of bad debt allowances and depreciation reserves. But they went further. Assuming that businessmen had an optimistic bias, credit granters exerted a counterbias, including a tendency to disregard most plant assets and all intangibles that did not support short-term debt paying ability.

Businessmen applying for loans were encouraged to submit balance sheets in which liquidation prices were substituted for going concern valuations. Conservative accounting was considered a sign of conservative management. Understatement became almost laudable, a form of financial modesty. Corporations showed their strength and stability by writing down real property and goodwill to one dollar. Equity reserves often were reported as liabilities. Though it hardly exists today, this classic type of conservatism based on crude understatement continues to be denounced by the doctrine's critics.

Public accountants developed an audit examination that looked to the future, but with a strong conservative bias. Nominal accounts, long-term assets, and bookkeeping accuracy might be reviewed briefly, but the primary audit tasks were analysis of working capital and liquidity. Eldon Henriksen considers that this "balance sheet audit" influenced accounting theory by temporarily counteracting those forces that otherwise would have shifted accounting emphasis to the income statement much sooner.

Conservatism and Its Critics

In the 1920s American corporations began large-scale stock sales to the general public. When equity financing became the chief external source of funds, and stockholders the primary readers of financial statements, reporting emphasis shifted from the balance sheet to the income statement. This required an accounting adaptation to the realities of large scale corporate operations.

Stewardship is a prime bookkeeping motive when most firms are short lived ventures and the main accounting responsibility is for protecting assets. In this setting conservatism is natural and rational. A steward would be foolish to raise expectations that might not be borne out by subsequent events. No one is misled so long as ownership interests are not expected to be exchanged.

But the stewardship assumptions on which accounting had traditionally rested no longer reflected the real interests of corporate managers or investors. In a large continuing business the profitable use of resources is more important than their physical protection. The value of such a company depends mainly on its future earning power, not on the liquidation value of its assets. The need to write loan collateral down to net realizable value was no longer adequate justification for conservatism. Neither was the belief that accountants and their clients will get into less trouble if income is understated. The shift from stewardship accounting to reporting economic data for investment decisions seemed to make conservatism inappropriate.

Beginning in the late 1930s, Paton, Gilman, Hatfield, May, and others established the fashion of deriding conservatism which continues to this day. Their criticisms were highly patterned and may be summarized as follows:

(1) *Conservatism is inconsistent.* One cannot be consistently conservative. Asset understatement leads sooner or later to income overstatement. Writing down inventories when their market price falls below cost reduces current income but overstates income in the next period. Depreciating fixed assets too quickly, or charging capital acquisitions to expense, achieves a conservative asset position but reduces the depreciation base and inflates future profits. Balance sheet conservatism is less important than a proper matching of costs and revenues. Ultimately conservatism accomplished nothing except to shift income from one period to another. And it does this unpredictably. The distorting effects of conservatism on earnings cannot be depended on to offset each other in later years. This often makes it hard to tell whether a particular accounting method will be conservative or not. Conservatism in its modern corporate context becomes a problem of interpreting the future.

(2) *Conservatism is arbitrary.* Understatement is the least exact of sciences. Conservative policies and influences may be modest or extreme. They may vary in extent from year to year. Little is known about their cumulative effects, which resist quantification, except that they are apt to be capricious and unstable. It is typically impossible to reverse conservative procedures if the expected losses do not occur. Experience with conservative methods rarely leads to greater efficiency in their use or to improvement in the methods themselves.

(3) *Conservatism prevents full disclosure.* The judgments involved in asset writedowns are hard to communicate to readers of annual reports. Not knowing how conservative methods were applied, the average investor cannot easily make allowance for them in his own decision making. And understatement is inherently deceptive and unfair. Its usual effect is to delay the impact of market events on financial statements. An unscrupulous management can use conservative methods to shift financial disaster into the future. Given the widespread feeling that withholding information is antisocial, a conservative policy might make accounting firms more rather than less vulnerable to lawsuits.

(4) *Conservatism gives managers and accountants too much discretionary authority.* Accountants and managers decide when and where to be conservative, what information to withhold and what to reveal. This is justified on the grounds that they are best qualified to assess the risks and assumptions inherent in accounting measurements. But their selection process nearly always favors certain groups at the expense of others. It may give creditors an advantage over stockholders or favor actual against potential investors. Generally this discretionary power to withhold information aids corporate insiders as opposed to those who must rely on published reports. It sometimes forces or tempts accountants to make assessments that should be left to individual financial statement readers.

(5) *Conservatism conflicts with other accounting principles.* It violates the matching principle, by requiring that declining market values be taken up immediately as realized losses. It distorts the realization principle. All traditional conservative procedures tend to make periodic income initially too small, then too large in later years. Conservative financial statements are not comparable between years or between firms, because conservative methods

produce inconsistent results and because there can be no uniform standards for their implementation. Conservatism conflicts with the going concern concept, in which acquisition costs are reduced to make them equivalent to liquidation prices. Conservatism conflicts with the objectivity principle, by requiring accountants to make arbitrary and subjective judgments about asset values.

(6) *Conservatism prevents fairness in financial reporting.* A policy of systematic bias is incompatible with the goal of describing business events realistically. A major reason for promulgating accounting principles was to narrow the areas of difference in reporting on similar events. Conservatism prevents uniform treatment of similar events because asset writedowns and other conservative procedures are nearly always subjective. The use of conservative methods has increased rather than reduced the number of allowable accounting options, especially in the areas of inventory pricing and fixed asset valuation.

Conservatism Today

These criticisms may have reduced conservatism's influence on other accounting principles. Conservatism certainly became less defensible as an overall policy and less apt to be cited as justification for particular accounting actions. But the evolution of conservative doctrine has nullified most of these criticisms or made them less important. Conservatism does not in any major way cause the shortcomings of other accounting principles. Rather it is necessary precisely because of their shortcomings.

Today conservatism acts as a restraint on judgment in cases of accounting uncertainty. The dominant principles of historical-cost valuation, matching, and realization create many such uncertainties. Neither their permutations nor the "extent of their domain" has been specified in detail. This creates jurisdictional disputes as to which principle governs a particular business transaction. It notoriously leads to situations in which alternative accounting methods that give different results seem equally applicable. Quite apart from the principles problem, many business events involve estimates about the future. To other problems there is no single correct answer, and accountants must choose arbitrarily among alternative assumptions.

Such estimates and judgments will be more consistent if the accountant can define upper and lower limits within which the true value lies. They will be still more consistent if he reports each time a figure at one extreme of the possible range of values. Much experience suggests that, when the true value is not known, a low estimate is usually less risky than a high estimate.

The doctrine of conservatism holds that when accounting theory is ambiguous, or when there is reasonable support for alternative methods of different measurements, accountants should choose the option with the least favorable immediate effect on assets, income and capital. This does not require or condone a policy of understatement. Under conditions of uncertainty, and given accountants' historical experience with such conditions, conservatism becomes a form of probability analysis.

Because it functions mainly when other accounting principles are held in abeyance, conservatism may be said to override such concepts without violating them. The historical cost, matching, and realization principles are inherently conservative because they prevent the booking of unrealized asset increases prior to sale, while permitting provisions for probable losses. And they are flexible enough to allow for such exceptions as cost or market writedowns and deferred realization on installment sales. But they require other concepts to make them workable. Conservatism, consistency, materiality, and disclosure are needed to refine and as it were lubricate the dominant measurement conventions. The tendency of conservative methods to cut across accounting periods and equalize profits over the business cycle counteracts the tendency of matching and realization to compartmentalize operating results within the year. In general, conservatism functions as a moderating influence to be applied, not so much to specific assets, but to the matching process as a whole, particularly when balance sheet items are allocated to the income statement.

This is largely a matter of emphasis and timing. Where different acceptable valuation methods exist, the lower asset price and the higher liability amount tend to be recorded. Increases in asset values, and anticipated gains, are normally ignored until a transaction occurs, but declines in asset values, and anticipated losses, are immediately disclosed and are booked as soon as their amounts become reasonably determinable.

When applied in this conglomerate sense to all accounts and all financial statements, conservatism becomes less vulnerable to charges of inconsistency. Conservative income measurement can be a highly consistent process, if the balance sheet effects are ignored. Accelerated depreciation continues to have a conservative effect on both financial statements so long as fixed asset purchases are maintained at a moderate level. Neil Churchill has presented empirical evidence that corporations adopting conservative methods tend to do so pervasively—that is, firms which value inventory on a last in, first out basis will also use accelerated depreciation and other conservative procedures. Corporations that are consistently conservative in their choice of accounting methods also tend to exhibit conservative levels in their solvency ratios.

Summary

What does the historical record say in defense of conservatism? It is the oldest accounting principle. Its origins were social and psychological as well as economic. Conservative methods have been used by every society that has developed systematic bookkeeping. As a policy of caution it has close parallels in other professions. Conservatism affects every financial statement and all account categories. It interacts with and supports other accounting principles and is often capable of overriding them in conflict situations. And conservatism will remain important in the future, no matter what asset valuation methods are employed or how income is measured. Even the adoption of market price valuations will not eliminate areas of uncertainty in accounting. Nor can all such uncertainties be described statistically. Conservatism is to some degree inseparable from accounting judgment. Even those who repudiate the doctrine continue to follow out its implications. Finally, it is widely believed that being unconservative can be dangerous to a firm, its investors, and its accountants. In Gilbert Byrne's strong phrase, the principle of conservatism is thought to embody a "coercive and compelling force which carries a penalty for violation."

Michael Chatfield

Bibliography

Brief, R. *Nineteenth Century Capital Accounting and Business Investment*. Ph.D. diss., Columbia University, 1964. Reprint. New York: Arno Press, 1976.

Chen, R. "Social and Financial Stewardship," *Accounting Review*, July 1975, pp. 533–543.

Churchill, N.C. Discussion comments on papers on "The Behavioral Implications of Accounting Measurements." In *Research in Accounting Measurement.*, pp. 215–218. Palo Alto, CA: Stanford University, 1966.

Devine, C.T. "The Rule of Conservatism Reexamined," *Journal of Accounting Research*, Autumn 1963, pp. 127–138.

Dewhirst, J. "Dealing with Uncertainty," *Canadian Chartered Accountant*, August 1971, pp. 139–146.

Jack, S.M. "An Historical Defense of Single Entry Book-keeping," *Abacus*, December 1966, pp. 137–158.

Kehl, D. *Corporate Dividends*. New York: Ronald Press, 1941. Reprint. New York: Arno Press, 1976.

Littleton, A.C. "Genealogy for Cost or Market," *Accounting Review*, June 1941, pp. 161–167.

Parker, R.H. "Lower of Cost or Market in Britain in the United States: An Historical Survey," *Abacus*, December 1965, pp. 156–172.

Storey, R.K. "Revenue Realization, Going Concern, and Measurement of Income," *Accounting Review*, April 1969, pp. 232–238.

Vance, L.L. "The Authority of History in Inventory Valuation," *Accounting Review*, July 1943, pp. 219–227.

Weiner, J.L. "Balance Sheet Valuation in German Law," *Journal of Accountancy*, September 1929, p. 195–206.

Winjum, J. "Accounting in its Age of Stagnation," *Accounting Review*, October 1970, pp. 743–761.

See also BASE STOCK METHOD; BRIEF, RICHARD P.; CAPITAL MAINTENANCE; COMPANIES ACTS; COMPARABILITY; CONTINUITY; DATINI, FRANCESCO DE MARCO; DEPRECIATION; DIVIDENDS; FINANCIAL-STATEMENT ANALYSIS; GERMANY; GILMAN, STEPHEN; GOODWILL; HATFIELD, HENRY RAND; INVENTORY VALUATION; KINGSTON COTTON MILLS COMPANY; LAST IN, FIRST OUT (LIFO); LEE V. NEUCHATEL ASPHALTE COMPANY; LEGAL LIABILITY OF AUDITORS; LIQUIDITY: ACCOUNTING MEASUREMENT; MACNEAL, KENNETH; MANIPULATION OF INCOME; MANORIAL ACCOUNTING; MATCHING; MATERIALITY; MAY, GEORGE OLIVER; MEDIEVAL ACCOUNTING; MONTEAGE, STEPHEN; OBJECTIVITY; PACIOLI,

LUCA; PATON, WILLIAM ANDREW; PIETRA, ANGELO; PIXLEY, FRANCIS WILLIAM; RAILROAD ACCOUNTING (U.S.); REALIZATION; RETAINED EARNINGS APPROPRIATIONS; *REX V. KYLSANT;* SAVARY, JACQUES; STATE REGULATION OF THE ACCOUNTANCY PROFESSION (U.S.); STEWARDSHIP; TAX-ORDAINED ACCOUNTING; UNIFORMITY; YMPYN, JAN

Consignment Accounts

The Venetian and Genoese practice of trading through overseas agents played an important part in the development of double entry bookkeeping. The taxation to which strangers were subject in many trading ports could be avoided by employing a local merchant as consignment agent. Such consignees were expected to remit sales proceeds to owners, and needed accounting records that showed a running balance of sales, expenses, and indebtedness to their principals. Duality was implied in two parties being at interest in selling the same goods, and in the fact that both independently made entries for shipments, sales, and amounts due. Each party in effect recorded the same transactions from an opposite viewpoint. Consignment bookkeeping may also explain the emergence of specialized inventory accounts. Consignment agents needed an accurate record of the goods entrusted to them by different firms, with details of quantities received and sold.

Michael Chatfield

Bibliography

De Roover, R. "The Development of Accounting prior to Luca Pacioli according to the Account-Books of Medieval Merchants." In *Studies in the History of Accounting*, edited by A.C. Littleton and B.S. Yamey, pp. 114–174. Homewood, IL: Irwin, 1956.

See also DOUBLE ENTRY BOOKKEEPING: ORIGINS

Consistency

See COMPARABILITY

Consolidated Financial Statements

The evolution of consolidated financial statements largely parallels the evolution of big business in the United States. Although there are some examples of earlier presentation, combined or consolidated financial statements gained widespread use in the first decade of the twentieth century. The United States Steel Corporation, chartered in New Jersey in 1901, set a pattern by publishing consolidated statements from its inception.

Although the nation's first trust had been established in 1882 when John D. Rockefeller created the Standard Oil Trust, prior to 1890 intercorporate stockholding, except for special purposes, was generally prohibited by state statutes. After 1890 most states gradually liberalized their laws to permit a corporation to hold the stock of another corporation for any legitimate business purpose, including investment and control. Holding companies designed to control the operations of various operating units, rather than individual companies operating in isolation, became the business norm. The wave of business mergers in the liberalized climate at the turn of the century fundamentally altered the structure of American industry from 1898 to 1903. At the end of the Civil War, no single company dominated any industry, but by 1904 one or two giant firms—usually the result of mergers—controlled at least half of the output in 78 industries.

The absence of regulatory barriers to new accounting techniques and a social climate in which innovation was highly regarded contributed to the development of consolidated statements. Accountants, although not acting as a professional body, appear to have acted as change agents in the development of consolidated statements. The advantage of consolidated statements at that time appears to have been for internal rather than external purposes, although changes in investor composition and in the way securities were sold also made external reporting increasingly important.

Until the 1880s, when the large industrial combinations began to be formed, the principles of laissez-faire capitalism were accepted by the general public, and caveat emptor was the general rule. Securities were bought primarily based on the reputation of the investment banker offering them, not on the financial condition of the investee companies. Securities were usually sold in large blocks to sophisticated investors. An increase in the number of small individual investors in the capital markets made the assumption that both seller and buyer were of equal strength and capable of understanding the facts of the transaction increasingly dubious. The provision of information to investors became increasingly important.

During the 1920s, those outside the accounting profession began urging the use of consolidated statements. Between 1920 and 1927, the Investment Bankers Association of America encouraged the voluntary action of its membership to standardize the financial information presented to the public, and it issued at least six reports of recommended minimum standards for financial disclosures. In the case of holding companies, the bankers' group suggested that investors be provided with a consolidated balance sheet, a consolidated statement of earnings, and an income statement for the holding company. The New York Stock Exchange began requiring listed companies to provide either consolidated statements or parent-company statements accompanied by separate statements for each unconsolidated subsidiary. The Revenue Act of 1917 required consolidated returns of affiliated corporations, although legislation beginning in 1921 made such returns optional.

Today, consolidation practice is governed by the rules of the Securities and Exchange Commission (SEC) and by the relevant accounting standards. Article 4 of SEC Regulation S–X specifies the form and content of consolidated and combined financial statements and requires the consolidation of majority-owned subsidiaries only. Relevant accounting standards are Accounting Research Bulletin (ARB) No. 51, "Consolidated Financial Statements" (1959) of the Committee on Accounting Procedure, Accounting Principles Board (APB) Opinions No. 16, "Business Combinations" (1970), No. 17, "Intangible Assets" (1970), and No. 18 "The Equity Method of Accounting for Investments in Common Stock" (1971), and Statement on Financial Accounting Standards (SFAS) No. 94, "Consolidation of All Majority-Owned Subsidiaries" (1987), of the Financial Accounting Standards Board. These standards specify the consolidation of all subsidiaries in which more than 50 percent of the voting shares are held, except those held temporarily or those that are not controlled; criteria by which a pooling of interests is distinguished from a purchase; accounting for goodwill; and methods of accounting for investments in unconsolidated subsidiaries.

Edward N. Coffman
Patricia C. Douglas

Bibliography

Chatfield, M., ed. *Contemporary Studies in the Evolution of Accounting Thought*. Belmont, CA: Dickenson, 1968.

Childs, W.H. *Consolidated Financial Statements: Principles and Procedures*. Ithaca, NY: Cornell University Press, 1949.

Moonitz, M. *The Entity Theory of Consolidated Statements*. Sarasota, FL: American Accounting Association, 1944.

Nobes, C., and R. Parker. *Comparative International Accounting*. 3d ed. London: Prentice-Hall International, 1991.

O'Sullivan, J., and E.F. Keuchel. *American Economic History: From Abundance to Constraint*. 2d ed. New York: Markus Wiener, 1989.

See also ACCOUNTING RESEARCH BULLETINS; DICKINSON, ARTHUR LOWES; FOREIGN CURRENCY TRANSLATION; GOODWILL; MOONITZ, MAURICE; NEW YORK STOCK EXCHANGE; POOLING OF INTERESTS; UNITED STATES STEEL CORPORATION

Continental Vending Case
See UNITED STATES OF AMERICA V. CARL SIMON

Continuing Professional Education

Continuing professional education (CPE) is the education necessary after a person has fulfilled all the formal educational requirements for entrance to a particular profession. Most professional accountants are committed to the concept of lifelong learning because they are well aware that their services depend heavily on the current nature of their professional knowledge. The American Institute of Certified Public Accountants (AICPA) invested $50,000 in 1958 to fund a few seminars for its members; by 1992 the AICPA was grossing over $20 million in revenue from its Continuing Professional Education Division.

The Formal Period for CPE

April 1, 1958, marked the formal beginning of the AICPA's embarkation into the field of CPE. An ad hoc AICPA committee recommended "a much more ambitious program of staff training and continuing education than the present resources of the Institute's educational department can provide." The remainder of 1958 and the first three months of 1959 were spent in planning for the inaugural year of the new Professional Development (PD) division under a full-time director and a small support staff.

During the first year of operation, the PD division engaged in two primary activities: It disseminated information about the seminars that had been developed in previous years by the education division, and it began to plan for the future. The PD division decided that seminars would be offered to AICPA members through the state societies of certified public accountants (CPAs). The PD division would prepare the instructor and participant manuals as well as the promotional brochures. The state organizations were expected to engage the discussion leader, promote the program, arrange for the presentation site and take care of the other administrative details of running the seminar. The other programs under development, consisting of a two-week staff training course and a program entitled "Building an Accounting Practice," called a regional program, would be more directly under the control of the PD division. These arrangements worked well in the early years of the PD division, but as the state societies became more experienced in the continuing-education arena, they wanted to "cosponsor" all of the AICPA-developed programs like they were doing with seminars. A change to effect this arrangement was made shortly after 1971 when the AICPA made required continuing professional education a matter of policy.

Required CPE

The issue of requiring CPAs to spend a minimum amount of time in continuing-education programs was put into focus by Marvin L. Stone, who was the 1967–1968 president of the AICPA. In his column "From the President" in the November 1967 issue of *CPA*, he wrote: "CPAs are licensed in order to protect the public. Real protection, however, requires something beyond one-time evaluation and accreditation. The public is entitled to expect that a CPA remain continually aware of the latest developments in his field. The public does not receive what it is entitled to expect from a CPA who has permitted his knowledge to become a victim of galloping obsolescence."

The Iowa State Board of Accountancy was the first to heed Stone's suggestion. In the spring of 1969, it issued regulations requiring registrants to "furnish evidence of participation in continuing education for a minimum of 15 days within the previous three years." Following the Iowa board action, in 1969 the AICPA charged an ad hoc committee, chaired by Elmer G. Beamer, a partner in the large public accounting company Haskins and Sells (now Deloitte Touche) to examine the feasibility and desirability of making continuing education a formal requirement of the profession and to study ways of implementing such a requirement. After over 18 months of intensive research and study, as reported by Beamer (1972), the Committee on Education and Experience Requirements for CPAs concluded "that the individual states, as part of their legal responsibility for licensing and controlling the practice of public accounting, are at present the only instrument that can effectively impose and enforce a continuing education requirement."

Members of the ad hoc committee never dreamed that their 1971 recommendations would be so uniformly and quickly accepted. Twenty-three years after the committee report was accepted by the AICPA, all of the 54 CPA jurisdictions had effected a program of formal CPE.

The Expansion of CPE Activities

To cope with the ever-increasing demand for educational material, a long-range planning committee was formed in 1971 and charged with recommending structural changes essential to provide adequate CPE materials and services to AICPA members, as noted by Robert E. Schlosser, Bernard Z. Lee, and George A. Rabito (1987). The committee addressed many issues and concluded in 1973 that the name of the PD division be changed to the Continuing Professional Education Division and that the scope of involvement of members in the governance of the division be expanded so that materials and services could be expanded. The latter recommendation led to the expansion of the governance of the division from a board of managers consisting of five members to an executive committee of seven members and four subcommittees: marketing and distribution, educational material and exchange, curriculum, and planning.

National Curriculum Project

One of the major outcomes, apart from coping with the tremendous increase in CPE activity, from the above reorganization was the National Curriculum Project. Urged by participating state societies, the CPE division's curriculum subcommittee engaged a member of the profession as a consultant to direct and coordinate the professionwide effort to complete a national CPE curriculum. Such a project is never completed; the exposure draft of the curriculum issued in 1986, the final report (1987) stated: "The National Curriculum Project is designed to provide accounting professionals with assistance in program selection by providing a framework of specified knowledge and skill. It also supplies (program) developers with a guide to help them develop comprehensive continuing professional education programs." As William Shakespeare wrote in *The Tempest*, "What's past is prologue." Past practice ensures that formal programs of learning will continue to be an integral part of a CPA's professional life.

Robert E. Schlosser

Bibliography

Beamer, E.G. "Continuing Education: A Professional Requirement," *Journal of Accountancy*, January 1972, pp. 33–34.

"Iowa Board Adopts Continuing Education Requirement," *Journal of Accountancy*, May 1969, p. 18.

National Curriculum Task Force. American Institute of Certified Public Accountants, *National CPE Curriculum: A Pathway to Excellence*. New York: AICPA, 1987.

National Curriculum Task Force. *National Curriculum: A Pathway to Excellence*. Exposure Draft. New York: AICPA, 1986.

Schlosser, R.E., B.Z. Lee, and G.A. Rabito. "Continuing Professional Education, 1882–1987," *Journal of Accountancy*, May 1987, centennial issue, pp. 240–254.

See also AMERICAN INSTITUTE OF CERTIFIED PUBLIC ACCOUNTANTS; INSTITUTE OF CHARTERED ACCOUNTANTS IN ENGLAND AND WALES

Continuity

The legal doctrines underlying modern corporations derived from three much older ideas: (1) that each such firm is an independent, property-owning entity in its own right, (2) that therefore, the individuals comprising it have limited liability for corporate activities, and (3) that it has continuity of existence apart from the lives of its owners. Three leading institutions of the medieval world—the church, the town, and the craft guild—all were treated as separate entities with perpetual existence. Monastery property was never considered as belonging to individual monks or abbots, nor were they personally responsible for church obligations. Medieval municipalities were also viewed as entities apart from their inhabitants, and they often obtained articles of incorporation that legally recognized their separate status. Craft guilds offered mutual association for the protection of an occupational group. Like the church and town, they held property in their own names and created permanent offices through which many individuals passed.

Commerce in Elizabethan England, as in Luca Pacioli's Venice, typically took the form of desultory venture-speculations. In this environment, incorporation promoted business continuity. It was at first a privilege conferred only by Royal Charter and always for monopoly purposes. Trade guilds interested in dominating areas of commercial life had begun incorporating as early as 1394. Soon there were municipal corporations for activities such as firefighting and banking, and for almost 200 years such livery companies monopolized various public services.

The discovery of America and the opening of sea routes to China and India turned investors' attention to overseas trading. The first joint-stock companies were partnerships with a few corporate features. They generally had limited life and imposed unlimited liability for company debts, but they also in many cases issued transferable shares. Their purposes ranged from trade to colonization and included military expeditions and voyages of discovery. Parliament preferred them to competitive businesses because they were easier to regulate and tax. They were granted monopoly rights partly as compensation for the large initial investments such ventures required. The Russia Company (lumber), the Virginia Company (tobacco), the East India Company (spices), and the Hudson's Bay Company (furs) were four of the best known.

The East India Company, chartered by Queen Elizabeth in 1600, evolved in just 60 years from a system of speculative voyages with terminable stocks to a continuing corporation with permanently invested capital. Between 1600 and 1617, the company sponsored 113 voyages, each supplied with newly subscribed capital and treated as a separate venture. This made liquidation necessary after each voyage so that those who wished to drop out might do so and new "adventurers" might be admitted. It also meant the stock was not readily negotiable, since there was no way to enter a venture in progress other than by buying unissued stock or a fraction of a share held by a current stockholder. At the end of each voyage, assets as well as earnings were subject to "divisions" among the shareholders. Profit was easily measured by the individual investor: He gained to the extent that he got back more than he had paid in.

But ships, trading posts, and other long-lived resources carried over from one venture to the next, until the company's accounts became a jumble of successive voyages. As unliquidated balances or "remains" of earlier voyages were merged with later ones, it became necessary to juggle assets and profits of many distinct ventures in various stages of completion. Also, during the seventeenth century, trading abroad had developed into a fairly continuous process requiring permanent capital. It now became more useful to view the business as a going concern.

In 1613 the East India Company stopped issuing stocks for each venture and began selling four year subscriptions, with one-fourth of the stock price to be paid each year and used to finance that year's voyages. A new charter in 1657 established the principle of permanently invested capital and extended the right to transfer individual shares before liquidation. Stock was to be priced by the company, first at the end of seven years, then every three years thereafter. Any shareholder could at any time sell his stock at these prices. This not only simplified the problem of transferring shares but made it easier for the company to attract new capital. In 1661, following out the logic of permanently invested capital, the East India Company's governor announced that future distributions would consist of "dividends" paid from profits rather than the familiar "divisions" of assets and income.

It was continuity of operations, not limited liability or the corporation's separate entity status, that radically changed accounting technique. Whereas bookkeeping for a completed venture was entirely historical, for a going concern it became a problem of viewing segments in a stream of continuous activity. Not only were results much more tentative, but the whole emphasis of record keeping shifted toward the

future. Asset valuation now depended on a corporation's long run earning power. Continuity also brought with it the idea that assets should not be revalued unless such changes reflected the changing value of the going concern.

With business continuity came a need for capital maintenance. A corporation cannot rationally claim to have indefinite life while dissipating its invested capital. The presence of permanent assets made capital maintenance an economic necessity. The corporation had to keep its capital intact to assure real continuity of existence and to preserve its economic power so that investors, consumers, employees, and all others who depended on it would not lose because of its diminished wealth and earning ability.

To make sure that invested capital was maintained intact, a series of court decisions, reinforced by statutes in England and the United States, required that dividends could be declared only from current and accumulated income. As a result, as Basil S. Yamey said, "What had often been incidental, became central." Calculating the amount of profit available for dividends became the corporate accountant's most important task. The courts also ruled that provision for future operations must be made before stockholders were entitled to cash dividends, and specifically that profit finding indicated a need for bad debt writeoffs, depreciation allowances, and for equity reserves in general. This required that a sharp distinction be made between assets and expenses. It also meant that income measurement now depended on anticipating future events.

Continuity of operations shortened and regularized accounting periods. When the life of a business eclipsed not only specific ventures but even the life spans of its owners, it became impractical to wait until liquidation before preparing financial statements. Periodic accounting reports were useful in pricing company shares. They were sometimes required by legal and tax authorities. The calculation of profits for a particular time interval became a major determinant of dividend payments. Often stockholders were absentee owners who had little direct contact with company affairs. The periodic profit figure became an index of managerial effectiveness in the minds of many who lacked the time to study operations in detail.

Reporting convenience dictated the use of calendar intervals. Many expenses, such as wages, were paid weekly or monthly, and others, such as interest, had an annual connotation. The calendar year was usually long enough to encompass one or more complete cycles of business activity, yet short enough to give investors fairly current information. Useful comparisons could be made when statements covered the same time span and appeared on the same date each year. As record keeping became more standardized, there was a tendency for corporations to prepare statements at progressively shorter intervals until they arrived at an annual reporting basis. A fiscal year ending at the low point in operations—a natural business year—was used as early as the 1770s and reappeared at various times and places during the nineteenth century. But by 1800, in England at least, the usual practice was to close the books either at year end or on the anniversary of the firm's inception.

To make the continuity principle technically feasible, events of different accounting periods had to be sharply distinguished. The idea of estimating periodic income by matching cost and related revenues followed naturally. Profit estimates were refined by a system of accruals and deferrals that allowed the effects of transactions to be split between periods.

But the transition from venture to going concern made record keeping more subjective and left a wide area of accounting discretion to management. In apportioning costs between periods, accountants had to make estimates whose accuracy depended on the course of future events. Honest differences of opinion about inventory pricing and asset life spans could lead to large variations in reported profits. Or corporate managers could deliberately blur periodic results by shifting income from one period to another, overdepreciating assets, and charging capital goods to expense. There was also a considerable time lag between adoption of the period concept and acceptance of comparability, consistency, and other doctrines needed to answer questions it had raised.

And from the beginning there was a contradiction between the continuity assumption and the periodicity assumption that it made necessary. The one tells us to look at operations as a continuous flow; the other says to break the flow into comparable time segments. The root of the period problem is that, in assigning revenues and expenses to time periods, the accountant is doing something that is absolutely necessary but is at the same time quite arbitrary and artificial.

The English chartered accountant Lawrence Dicksee (1864–1932), more than any other man, established the continuity assumption as a meaningful accounting concept. Dicksee reasoned that the main goal of most firms is to continue in business and that asset valuation should reflect this fact. Even companies that did not take depreciation faced the certainty of asset revaluation when assets were sold or the firm changed hands. The point of sale was a moment of truth that revealed an asset's real value. So it was not simply current sale prices—liquidation prices—which mattered, but also these future sale prices. To anticipate them as nearly as possible, assets should be valued "as a going concern," meaning "at such value as they would stand in the books if proper depreciation had been provided for."

Dicksee's assumption of indefinite life for the corporation ruled out the use of liquidation prices in its balance sheet. If a business must maintain its fixed assets permanently, it seemed illogical to determine profits by annual appraisals based on current resale values. There being no intention to see such assets, fluctuations in their market prices could not be considered gains or losses. Long term assets should be valued at acquisition cost less depreciation. The justification for ignoring value changes not caused by "time and wear" was that asset realization was not contemplated. Such assets were bought to be used, not to be sold at a profit.

However, the logic of business continuity required that current assets be priced at net realizable value. Having been manufactured or purchased to be sold, they were sensitive to value changes, and any fall in price ought to be booked as a loss. By the same logic, asset appreciation should be credited to income, but Dicksee was not quite that bold. Since before the sale "there must always be a doubt as to whether any such realization has actually occurred, it is only prudent to postpone taking credit for the assumed profit until such time as it has actually been earned."

The American Henry Rand Hatfield agreed with Dicksee that "the proper value of assets is that which they have to the holding concern, and not that which they might have to other persons." Hatfield stated three general valuation rules: (1) inventory prices should be those of the going concern, (2) depreciation should always be taken, and (3) conservatism requires that changes in the market value of fixed assets be ignored. He reasoned that a firm would not buy any asset unless the value of its output was expected to equal or exceed its cost. Then, assuming the business lasted long enough to receive the asset's service benefits, liquidation prices were irrelevant. Hatfield attacked conservatism more directly than Dicksee had and particularly denounced the lower of cost or market rule. Writing in an era when inflation was already a problem, he was from the first less inclined than Dicksee to accept historical cost as an imperative. He argued for the use of replacement costs in the balance sheet and, in his 1927 text, advocated accelerated rather than straight line depreciation as corresponding better to economic realities.

Dicksee and Hatfield had thought through the continuity principle to its logical conclusions: that asset valuations depend on future events, and that increases as well as decreases in current asset values should be taken up as profit and loss. Both believed that if value to the going concern is the key to asset valuation, and if the selling price of fixed assets is irrelevant because they are not purchased to be sold, then conversely, the selling price of inventories should be on the balance sheet because they exist only to be sold. But as a practical matter, conservatism—both the accounting doctrine and the political instincts of accountants—prevented this. The realization rule was superimposed on the going concern concept because the latter was too radical and subjective in its implications for current asset writeups above cost. As Reed Storey put it, "The failure to carry the going concern assumption to its logical conclusion left a gap in accounting theory which was filled by the realization convention." The realization rule required only that all assets be valued at historical cost prior to sale. But its popularization meant that "asset valuation and income measurement were based on an incomplete application of the going concern convention tempered by conservatism."

Michael Chatfield

Bibliography
Brief, R., ed. *Dicksee's Contribution to Accounting Theory and Practice.* New York: Arno Press, 1980.
Hatfield, H.R. *Modern Accounting.* New York: Appleton-Century, 1909. Reprint. New York: Arno Press, 1976.
Littleton, A.C. *Accounting Evolution to 1900.* New York: American Institute Publishing, 1933. Reprint. New York:

Russell and Russell, 1966.
Storey, R.K. "Revenue Realization, Going Concern, and Measurement of Income," *Accounting Review*, April 1959, pp. 232–238.
Yamey, B.S. "Some Topics in the History of Financial Accounting in England, 1500–1900." In *Studies in Accounting Theory*, edited by W.T. Baxter and S. Davidson, pp. 14–43. Homewood, IL: Irwin, 1962.

C

See also ACCRUAL ACCOUNTING; BAD DEBTS; CAPITAL MAINTENANCE; CASH BASIS ACCOUNTING; COMPARABILITY; CONSERVATISM; CORPORATIONS: EVOLUTION; DEFERRED INCOME TAX ACCOUNTING; DEPRECIATION; DICKSEE, LAWRENCE; DIVIDENDS; EAST INDIA COMPANY; FIXED ASSETS; HATFIELD, HENRY RAND; HISTORICAL COST; INCOME-DETERMINATION THEORY; LIMITED LIABILITY; NATURAL BUSINESS YEAR; OBJECTIVITY; PERIODICITY; PIXLEY, FRANCIS WILLIAM; POSTULATES OF ACCOUNTING; REALIZATION; SEPARATE ENTITIES

Control Accounts

Modern control accounts summarize large numbers of receivables, payables, and inventory items, which are shown in detail in subsidiary ledgers. This is an old practice. Fifteenth century Italian ledgers sometimes included control accounts. But for the next 400 years, accounting's summarizing ability was considered less important than its ability to show the details of operations. Double entry bookkeeping was originally promoted as an aid to memory. Every merchant needed a record of his credit dealings and inventory balances. Authors of bookkeeping textbooks stressed that double entry's main advantage was its ability to make such records orderly and complete. That is, little data was provided that could not be got by simpler means, but ledger balances afforded a classified record of past operations for ready reference. A businessman could review his financial affairs simply by scanning his ledger accounts. The descriptive style of journal and ledger entries made it easy for him to review particular transactions in detail.

When financial statements were prepared, they also tended to enumerate rather than summarize. All the branches of the Medici Bank (1397–1494) prepared annual balance sheets and forwarded them to the home office in Florence. These balance sheets listed separately the amount owed by each customer, with the result that statements sometimes contained more than 200 line items. Since bad debts were the chief threat to a Renaissance banker's solvency, audit by the bank's general manager and his assistants involved examining each debtor's account to see that excess credit had not been granted and to pick out doubtful or past-due accounts.

In inventory accounting, the intention was to segregate the results of trading in particular commodities. Both textbooks and surviving accounting records show separate inventory accounts for different types of goods, and often these had quantity columns next to the money columns. Perpetual inventory records were maintained by recording purchases and sales directly in the inventory accounts. Not until the nineteenth century did it become common for a ledger to contain only one inventory control account.

The traditional purpose of accounting was the maintenance of comprehensive ledger accounts for owner's reference. Record keeping was emphasized rather than analysis, and description rather than tabulation. The important topics in modern accounting textbooks—asset valuation, income finding, financial statements—took up very little space in most accounting texts written before 1850. The eventual emergence of control accounts was a sign that accounting was finally becoming statistical rather than descriptive.

Michael Chatfield

Bibliography

Winjum, J.O. "Accounting in its Age of Stagnation," *Accounting Review*, October 1970, pp. 743–771.

Yamey, B.S. "The Functional Development of Double-Entry Bookkeeping," *Accountant*, November 2, 1940, pp. 332–342.

———. "Some Topics in the History of Financial Accounting in England, 1500–1900." In *Studies in Accounting Theory*, edited by W.T. Baxter and S. Davidson, pp. 14–43. Homewood, IL: Irwin, 1962.

See also DOUBLE ENTRY BOOKKEEPING: ORIGINS; INTERNAL AUDITING; MEDICI ACCOUNTS; NICHOLSON, J. LEE; PERPETUAL INVENTORY

Control: Classical Model

The classical model of control was attributed to Frederick Winslow Taylor and Henri Fayol, long after their deaths, by management and accounting writers. Taylor wrote in the first two decades of the twentieth century about his experiences in the United States in what became labeled "scientific management." Fayol was a French executive who first wrote about his management philosophy in 1916. This was translated into English as *General and Industrial Administration* in 1929. Many of Taylor's followers have questioned the harshness of treating workers attributed to Taylor. Lee D. Parker has said that in Taylor's model, "control of the individual was to be achieved by exception control, by enforced control, and by authority-based controls." To Fayol, who focused more on management than the individual and who developed 14 principles of management, control was necessary for implementing the principles of unity of command, unity of direction, and subordination of individual interest to general interest. Many accounting writers, like Parker and Edwin H. Caplan, have said that the classical model of control was relatively authoritarian, paternalistic, and mechanistic and paid little regard to the human dimension. Writers in management such as Lyndall F. Urwick in *Papers on the Science of Administration* (1937) and Harold Koontz in "A Preliminary Statement of Principles of Planning and Control" (1958) continued on this path. There have been many proponents of other views of control than the classical theory. Examples are behavioralists like May Parker Follett in *Creative Experience* (1924), Chris Argyris in *Personality and the Organization* (1957), Abraham Maslow in *Motivation and Personality* (1954), James G. March and Herbert A. Simon in *Organizations* (1958), and Douglas McGregor in *The Human Side of Enterprise* (1960); structuralists like Max Weber in the early 1900s; and the systems approach of Ludwig von Bertalanffy in "The Theory of Open Systems in Physics and Biology" (1950) and Talcott Parsons in *The Social System* (1951).

The classical control model also was evident in the approaches toward budgeting espoused by James O. McKinsey in "Accounting as an Administrative Aid" (1919), and DR Scott in *The Cultural Significance of Accounts* (1931) and the introduction of standard cost accounting in the 1920s. It gained steam as the topic of goal congruence became popular in the 1970s.

However, a serious attack in accounting occurred in the 1960s, led by Caplan's application of the behavioral assumptions of the "traditional" management accounting model of the firm to the behavioral assumptions of modern organization theory and Andrew C. Stedry's 1960 book, *Budget Control and Cost Behaviour*. David A. Drinkwater felt that the behavioral school in management was already dead by then, killed in 1957 by Malcolm McNair's analysis in the *Harvard Business Review*. Drinkwater predicted in 1973 that the structural school of management would become the crucial school and the financial plan would replace the budget as the key control mechanism.

While the classical model remains, in accounting at least, an important part of the teaching of control practices in the United States, European scholars such as Anthony G. Hopwood and G.H. Hofstede have added much depth to the topic of control. Hopwood's journal, *Accounting, Organizations, and Society*, has published works by both Americans and Europeans using social theories developed by Jacques Derrida, Michel Foucault, and Jurgen Habermas.

The continuation of the classical model of control in the teaching and practice of management accounting probably meets an important market test in the United States. As the academic field of management moves further from the classical model but U.S. management still has a felt need for it, it is from courses in management accounting that students learn about important control tools like budgets and standards. Beyond that, there may be a significant cultural difference between the United States and Europe on the topic of managerial control, which might also help explain the continuation of the classical model.

Richard Vangermeersch

Bibliography

Arrington, C.E., and J.R. Francis. "Letting the Chat Out of the Bag: Deconstruction, Privilege, and Accounting Research," *Accounting, Organizations, and Society*, vol. 14, nos. 1/2, 1989, pp. 1–28.

Caplan, E.H. "Behavioral Assumptions of Management Accounting." In *Accounting and Its Behavioral Implications*, edited by W.J. Bruns Jr. and D.T. DeCoster. New York: McGraw-Hill, 1969.

Drinkwater, D.A. "Management Theory and the Budgeting Process," *Management Accounting*, June 1973, pp. 15–17.

Gerth, H.H., and C. Wright Mills. *From Max Weber: Essays in Sociology*. New York: Oxford University Press, 1946.

Hopwood, A. *Accounting and Human Behaviour*. Englewood Cliffs, NJ: Prentice-Hall, 1974.

McNair, M.P. "Thinking Ahead," *Harvard Business Review*, March-April 1957, pp. 15–16, 20, 25–26, 28, 30, 32, 34, 39.

Parker, L.D. *Developing Control Concepts in the Twentieth Century*. New York: Garland, 1986.

Taylor, F.W. *The Principles of Scientific Management*. New York: Harper & Brothers, 1911.

von Bertalanffy, L. "The Theory of Open Systems in Physics and Biology," *Science*, January 13, 1950, pp. 23–29.

See also BUDGETING; EMERSON, HARRINGTON; HOPWOOD, ANTHONY G.; INTERNAL CONTROL; MANAGEMENT ACCOUNTING; MCKINSEY, JAMES O.; SCOTT, DR; STANDARD COSTING; TAYLOR, FREDERICK WINSLOW

Cooper, William Wager (1914–)

William Wager Cooper was born in Birmingham, Alabama, moved to Chattanooga, Tennessee, and then to Chicago. Entering the University of Chicago in 1934, he graduated in 1938 with a B.A. in economics, having experienced the excitement of Robert Maynard Hutchins's university, in company with others like Herbert A. Simon, Martin Bronfenbrenner, Milton Friedman, and Paul Samuelson.

Cooper's interest in accounting grew from a fortuitous meeting with Eric Louis Kohler, then a principal at Arthur Andersen and Company. Joint work began when Kohler asked Cooper to review the mathematics used for engineering calculations in a lawsuit involving an Andersen client. Further joint efforts followed when Kohler left Andersen in 1938 to become comptroller of the Tennessee Valley Authority (TVA) to help respond to a congressional investigation that, with prompting from the utility industry, was questioning the TVA's accounting practices. A centerpiece was the report that the TVA was required to prepare on its methods for allocating fixed and common costs—between electric power, flood control, navigation, and national defense. Cooper served as Kohler's research assistant in preparing the report. When the job was completed, Kohler asked Cooper to help him develop new types of audits for use in the TVA. One type, later called "performance audits," the two developed further in the "end-use audits" Kohler introduced as comptroller of the Marshall Plan.

Kohler encouraged Cooper to continue graduate work, which he did, starting in 1940 at Columbia, with Roy B. Kester in accounting and Harold Hotelling in mathematical economics and statistics. In 1942, with U.S. involvement in World War II, Cooper joined the Office of Statistical Standards in the U.S. Bureau of the Budget, where he was charged with responsibility for all government surveys involving uses of accounting statistics. Cooper frequently sought Kohler's help, subsequently collaborating with him on a 1945 article, "Cost, Prices, and Profits: Accounting in the War Program," which received the first American Institute of Accountants award in 1945 as "the most significant and valuable article on an accounting subject."

In 1944 Cooper returned to teach at the University of Chicago. In 1946 he joined Carnegie Institute of Technology (now Carnegie Mellon University), where he helped develop a new "management program" in place of the school's previous programs in industrial engineering and engineering economics. To provide a broader base, Cooper combined the courses in accounting and statistics into a new course, "Quantitative Controls in Management," which became a foundation for the program of the new Graduate School of Industrial Administration (GSIA) at Carnegie Mellon University—a program that had a major impact in redirecting management education in the United States and elsewhere (Gleeson and Schlossman 1992).

The innovative and supportive climate of the GSIA encouraged responses to new opportunities, as in the newly developing disciplines of operations research and management science. Cooper actively participated in the development of these professions and became the founding president of the Institute of Management Sciences. His interest in economics and accounting continued, and he became a Fellow of the Econometric Society in recognition of his contributions to econometrics. With Robert Martin Trueblood and others, including Kohler and W. Edwards Deming (Cooper's colleague at the Bureau of the Budget), he initiated early research on uses of statistics in accounting and auditing. In collaboration with Andrew C. Stedry and Neil Churchill, Cooper also initiated some of the earliest work in what is now called "behavioral research in accounting" (Birnberg and Schields 1989).

Collaborative efforts enabled Cooper to pursue a broad range of topics, with results reported in 15 books and some 400 authored and coauthored articles. The significance of his research has been recognized in numerous awards, including the American Accounting Association's (AAA) Outstanding Educator Award (1990), Distinguished Service to Auditing Award (1988), and Distinguished International Visiting Lecturer in Accounting (1986). Recognition has also been accorded by other disciplines, as in the award of the John von Neumann Theory Medal by the Institute of Management Sciences and the Operations Research Society of America (1982) "for fundamental contributions to the theory of operations research and management science." Cooper's coverage in accounting was broad, as recognized in the Notable Contributions to the Accounting Literature Award (1991) by the Government and Nonprofit Section of the AAA "for his work in Data Envelopment Analysis," and in his receipt of the Comptroller General Award (1986) "for contributions to the U.S. General Accounting Office." His work has also been accorded university recognition by honorary doctorates at Ohio State University (1970) and Carnegie Mellon University (1982).

In 1969 Cooper left the GSIA to become the founding dean of the School of Urban and Public Affairs (later renamed the H. John Heinz III School of Public Policy and Management) at Carnegie Mellon. In 1976 he left for Harvard, where he served on a committee that set new directions for the business school's doctoral programs. In 1980 Cooper joined the Graduate School of Business at the University of Texas at Austin, where he is professor of management, accounting, and management science and information systems. In 1990 he was inducted into the school's Hall of Fame "for distinguished contributions to the university and the business community" and appointed Nadya Kozmetsky Scott Fellow in the university's Innovation, Creativity, and Capital Institute.

He has been a long-time active member of the AAA. He began his services for the association as book review editor of *Accounting Review* (1940–1942), and he served as the founding editor (1979–1982) of *Auditing: A Journal* of *Practice and Theory*. He has served on many AAA committees, and as director of publications and member of the Executive Committee (1987–1989). He served on the AAA Committee on Accounting and Auditing Measurement and participated in its report in *Accounting Horizons*, September 1991.

Cooper's work has provided new analytical frameworks for use in accounting and facilitated contact with other disciplines, including psychology, economics, operations research, management science, and statistics. He also made many contributions to each of these disciplines while adapting their methods and concepts to uses in accounting. As an example, his path-breaking article "Breakeven Programming and Budgeting to Goals," written with A. Charnes and Yuji Ijiri in the first issue in the spring of 1963 of the *Journal of Accounting Research*, opened the way for uses of goal programming and network concepts in accounting and showed how double entry principles could be extended from financial to other (multidimensional) aspects of planning and budgeting. Conversely, it introduced the accounting concept of a "spread sheet" as an application of double entry principles for use with computers.

In his AAA Outstanding-Educator-Award speech and in a 1992 article with Stephen A. Zeff, Cooper expressed concern over the growing separation of research from the problems (and opportunities) of accounting practice. A 1993 paper he wrote with George Kozmetsky, that was delivered at a conference in Siena, Italy, in honor of Luca Pacioli, argued that the applied-science character of accounting research needs to be strengthened and, in analogy with the Pasteur Institute for Medical Research, it suggested that a Pacioli Institute for Research in Accounting could help to improve the balance between "pure science and applied science" approaches to research in accounting.

Yuji Ijiri

Bibliography

Birnberg, J.G., and J. Schields. "Three Decades of Behavioral Accounting Research: A Search for Order," *Behavioral Research in Accounting*, 1989, pp. 23–74.

Charnes, A., W.W. Cooper, and Y. Ijiri. "Breakeven Budgeting and Programming to Goals," *Journal of Accounting Research*, Spring 1963, pp. 16–43.

Cooper, W.W., and G. Kozmetsky. "Accounting Research and Practice, from Pacioli to Ijiri," *Economic Notes, Special Issue: Proceedings of Conference in Accounting and Economics Commemorating the Five Hundredth Anniversary of the First Publication on Double-Entry Bookkeeping by Luca Pacioli*, Siena, Italy, 1993.

Cooper, W.W., and S.A. Zeff. "Kinney's Design for Accounting Research," *Critical Perspectives on Accounting*, March 1992, pp. 87–92.

Gleeson, R., and S. Schlossman. "The Many Faces of the New Look: The University of Virginia, Carnegie Tech, and the Reform of American Management Education in the Post-War Era," part 2, *Selections* (the magazine of the Graduate Admissions Council), Spring 1992, pp. 1–24.

Ijiri, Y., and R.A. Watts. *Bill and Ruth Cooper and Their Friends*. Pittsburgh: Carnegie Mellon University Press, 1990.

Ijiri, Y., and A.B. Whinston. *Quantitative Planning and Control: Essays in Honor of William Wager Cooper on the Occasion of His Sixty-Fifth Birthday*. New York: Academic Press, 1979.

Kohler, E.L., and W.W. Cooper. "Cost, Prices and Profits: Accounting in the War Program," *Accounting Review*, July 1945, pp. 287–308.

See also AMERICAN ACCOUNTING ASSOCIATION; COST AND/OR MANAGEMENT ACCOUNTING; IJIRI, YUJI; KOHLER, ERIC LOUIS; TRUEBLOOD, ROBERT MARTIN; ZEFF, STEPHEN A.

Corporations: Evolution

The corporation was a concept well developed in the Roman Republic and the Roman Empire, with corporate bodies established for specific purposes and then municipalities. The concept was retained by the primitive Christian Church and through its monastic orders, with the first real impetus coming from the founding by St. Benedict of the monastery of Monte Cassino in 528. Municipalities in England gained charter status as feudalism waned. Merchant guilds were also developed about that time, and charters were granted to universities, the first being the University of Paris in 1210.

There were two great English companies of the fourteenth and fifteenth centuries—the Merchants of the Staple and the Merchant Adventurers. The first joint stock companies appeared in England in 1553, one of these a monopoly granted by Parliament for Russian trade. The joint stock concept arose about that time in France and Holland but was well developed by then in both Germany and Italy. The English companies were resubscribed for each venture for many years until a more permanent financial-capital policy was adopted in the seventeenth century. English companies were also chartered for colonial development, such as the London Company and the Plymouth Company to develop the territory of Virginia in 1606. By the 1690s, there was active trading of stock in London. Soon after, the South Sea Bubble burst in England in 1720, shortly after the Mississippi Bubble of John Law burst in France. The use of corporations for business purposes was rare for the next 50 years in England. The Joint Stock Companies Act of 1844 required registration of all joint stock companies. In the United States, the most significant event was the 1875 "liberal" incorporation statute in New Jersey, which ultimately, in 1892, permitted corporations to hold securities of other corporations, starting the first "trust movement."

Richard Vangermeersch

Bibliography

Abbott, C.C. *The Rise of the Business Corporation*. Ann Arbor, MI: Edwards Brothers, 1936.

Davis, J.P. *Corporations: A Study of the Origin and Development of Great Business Combinations and of the Relation to the Authority of the State*. New York: G. Putnam's Sons, 1905. Reprint. New York: Capricorn Books, 1961.

Jenkins, A. *The Stock Exchange Story*. London: William Heinemann, 1973.

See also CAPITAL MAINTENANCE; CAPITAL STOCK; CASH BASIS ACCOUNTING; COMPANIES ACTS; COMPARABILITY; CONTINUITY; EXTERNAL AUDITING; GOODWILL; LIMITED LIABILITY; MERCANTILISM; PAR VALUE DOCTRINE; PARTNERSHIP ACCOUNTING; PERIODICITY; ROME (509 B.C.–A.D. 476); SEPARATE ENTITIES; SOUTH SEA BUBBLE

Cost Accounting Standards Board (1970–1980; 1988–)

One of the provisions of the Defense Production Act of 1950 (DPA) prohibited government contractors from discriminating against the government by charging higher prices or imposing less favorable terms than those used in commercial business. When the DPA was undergoing its required biannual review by the Congress in 1968, Admiral Hyman G. Rickover, U.S. Navy, testified that this provision could not be enforced. Long a critic of accounting practices used in defense contracting, Rickover stated that the methods used for charging overhead, the approaches to pricing component parts, and the treatment of intercompany profits were not standardized and were almost impossible to reconstruct.

He argued that the variety of acceptable accounting practices and the inconsistency with which they were applied made it impossible for a government contracting officer to determine what costs were and whether the government was paying excessive profits. Rickover estimated that uniform cost-accounting standards would save the government over $2 billion per year.

When the hearings were concluded, the DPA was extended and, based primarily on Admiral Rickover's testimony, the comptroller general of the United States was required to work with the secretary of defense and the director of the Bureau of the Budget in conducting a feasibility study of the application of uniform cost-accounting standards to negotiated defense contracts of $100,000 or more.

Eighteen months later, January 19, 1970, the comptroller general issued the report on the feasibility study. The report concluded that it was feasible to establish and apply cost-accounting standards to provide a greater degree of uniformity and consistency in cost accounting as a basis for negotiating and administering procurement contracts.

When debate on the extension of the DPA was renewed in 1970, the proposal to establish a Cost Accounting Standards Board, championed by Admiral Rickover, also was supported by Senator William Proxmire of Wisconsin, the feasibility study, the Defense Department, the Bureau of the Budget, other government agencies, and the accounting profession.

Opposition came only from industry representatives who argued that imposition of cost-accounting standards could result in the withdrawal of some companies from government work. Additionally, they testified that uniform cost-accounting standards would not save the government the $2 billion per year that Rickover had estimated, that a single set of standards would be too rigid to be applied equitably to 24,000 defense contractors, and that such standards would not achieve the desired goal of comparability of cost data.

The Cost Accounting Standards Board (CASB) was established by Public Law 91–379, an amendment to the Defense Production Act of 1950. President Richard M. Nixon signed the enabling legislation on August 15, 1970.

The CASB was created as a part of the legislative branch of government. Unlike the Financial Accounting Standards Board (FASB), whose pronouncements have legal implications but are not law, cost-accounting standards promulgated by the CASB carry the full force of the law. The board was charged by statute to develop standards for use in the pricing, administration, and settlement of all negotiated defense contracts and subcontracts with the United States in excess of $100,000 (effective January 1, 1975, this threshold was increased by the CASB to $500,000).

The objectives of the CASB were sixfold: uniformity, consistency, allocability and allowability, fairness, materiality, and verifiability.

The first CASB was chaired by Elmer B. Staats, comptroller general of the United States, and had four other members: two from the accounting profession, one from industry, and one from an agency or department of the federal government. The board issued 19 cost-accounting standards: CAS 401–418 and CAS 420. The board's primary objectives of increasing uniformity of accounting practices among government contractors and consistency in the use of accounting practices over time by individual contractors were substantially achieved.

In the late 1970s, there was a strong move toward deregulation, and public interest in government procurement declined following cessation of the Vietnam War. In the face of vigorous opposition from the defense industry and with no one in power to champion its cause, the U.S. Congress did not appropriate funds for the CASB's fiscal 1981 budget, and the CASB went out of business on September 30, 1980.

After the death of the CASB, its standards, rules, and regulations were law and remained in effect. Procurement agencies, primarily the Defense Department, and their auditors continued to enforce the board's rules and regulations. New contracts had to comply with extant cost-accounting standards. However, no one federal agency was charged with the administration of cost-accounting standards. Disputes between contractors and the government had to be processed by administrative boards of appeal and, possibly, the courts. Contractors found this to be an expensive and time-consuming process.

By the late 1980s, defense procurement had increased significantly under the Reagan Administration, waste and/or excess profits in government procurement were well publicized, deregulation was being questioned, and voices in industry and government were strongly in support of a cost-accounting standard-setter. Action by the Defense Department in 1984 to assume responsibility for maintenance and promulgation of cost-accounting standards had renewed interest in the issue. There was widespread concern over the primary procurement agency (the Defense Department) also acting as the policymaker.

In 1986 the Senate Committee on Banking, Housing, and Urban Affairs instructed the Defense Department to stop exercising any of the functions previously accorded the CASB under Public Law 91–379. This action was a precursor to reestablishment of the Cost Accounting Standards Board.

The Office of Federal Procurement Policy Act Amendments of 1988 (Public Law 100–679) created a new Cost Accounting Standards Board as an independent unit of the executive branch of government—in the Office of Federal Procurement Policy (OFPP), a part of the Office of Management and Budget. The law broadened the scope of the CASB, mandating that its pronouncements apply to contracts with all U.S. government agencies.

It also stipulated that the administrator of the OFPP would chair the CASB and be authorized to appoint four members—two representatives of the federal government and two from the private sector.

On March 1, 1990, the Senate confirmed Allan V. Burman as administrator of the OFPP. He was replaced by Steven Kelman in 1993. The CASB was constituted and held its first meeting July 25, 1990. In its first years, the CASB devoted its attention to organizational issues, maintenance activities, jurisdictional items, a recodification project, identification of agenda items, and concepts. In a report of May 1994, the U.S. General Accounting Office noted little progress made by CASB in resolving important issues.

Frank R. Rayburn

Bibliography

Defense Production Act Amendments, *U.S. Statutes at Large* 84 (1970): 796.

Office of Federal Procurement Policy Act Amendments of 1988, *U.S. Statutes at Large* 102 (1988): 4055.

Rayburn, F.R. "The Cost Accounting Standards Board: Its Creation, Its Demise, and Its Reestablishment." In *The Costing Heritage: Studies in Honor of S. Paul Garner*, edited by O.F. Graves, pp. 99–121. Monograph No. 6. Harrisonburg, VA: Academy of Accounting Historians, 1991.

U.S. General Accounting Office. *Cost Accounting Standards Board: Little Progress Made in Resolving Important Issues*. Washington, DC: U.S. General Accounting Office, 1994.

See also Congressional Views; Cost and/or Management Accounting; General Accounting Office, U.S.; Imputed Interest on Capital; Mautz, Robert K.; Uniformity

Cost and/or Management Accounting

Cost and/or management accounting was defined by Eric Louis Kohler as "that branch of accounting dealing with the classification, recording, allocation, summarization, and reporting of current and prospective costs." This information on costs provides information about the total and unit costs of making and distributing a product or a service. Cost accounting is pertinent to industrial concerns, retailers, mines, farms, transporters, and service organizations, including not-for-profits and governmental bodies.

The gradual replacement of the highly regulated guild systems with a market-based economy led to the development of techniques for gathering cost information for manufacturers in, for instance, fourteenth-century Italian, English, Flemish, and German commerce. Even earlier, as witnessed in extant records kept by scribes on Genoese ships, shipping and distributing goods called for a control of costs by product and voyage. Examples of extant accounts are the Fugger accounts for silver and copper mines of Tyrol and Carinthia in Austria in the fifteenth century and the Medici accounts for silk and wool production in the fifteenth and sixteenth centuries. The Plantin accounts for a Flemish printer and publisher of the sixteenth century contain many elements of a modern job-order cost system. Two examples of authors of texts concerning factory accounting are the Englishmen John Collins in 1697 with *The Perfect Methods of Merchants Accompts* and Roger North in 1714 with the *Gentleman Accomptant*.

The take-off point for manufacturing occurred in the late 1700s with the industrial revolution. Robert Hamilton, a Scottish writer of that period, stressed in his *Introduction to Merchandise* (1788), the importance of determining gain or loss on each stage of manufacturing. He recommended a similar system for large farmers in their control of their fields. Anselme Payen, a French writer, described in 1817 in *Essai sur la tenus Livres d'un Manufacturies*, the accounting for both a job-order system and a process-cost system. The well-developed nature of French accounting in that period has been described by Marc Nikitin in a 1990 article on the Compagnie de Saint-Gobain. Frederic William Cronhelm, an Englishman, in 1818 in *Double Entry by Single Entry* introduced the concept of perpetual inventory and discussed the need of statistical controls outside the general ledger. The logistical orientation of cost accounting remains a salient control feature. It is also important to note the work in the 1830s of Charles Babbage, one of the earliest exponents of scientific management. The importance of the use of cost accounting in Britain during the industrial revolution has been shown in a 1991 article by Richard K. Fleischman, Lee D. Parker, and Wray Vamplew. A 1972 study by H. Thomas Johnson of the Lyman Mills in the United States in the 1850s illustrates the importance of the control aspects of cost accounting.

Perhaps the overriding reason, until recently, for the lack of knowledge of the strength of cost accounting in the industrial revolution was the secrecy of this data; only top management had full access to it. However, there was one type of business, the railroad, that was subject to demands for data by various parties. Dionysius Lardner in 1850 published a classic study of the importance of cost data for railroads. Such data is illustrated in Richard Vangermeersch's study of the Baltimore and Ohio Railroad, published in 1979.

The beginning of the modern era of cost accounting started in 1885 with the publication of Henry Metcalfe's *Cost of Manufacturers and the Administration of Workshops*. His emphasis on the use of a loose-leaf recording arrangement and of a card system for each transaction emphasized the control aspects of cost accounting. Two English writers, Emile Garcke and J.M. Fells, in 1887 in their *Factory Accounts* published their pioneer work which called for integration of the cost records with the general ledger. Another practicing English accountant, G.P. Norton, was in 1889 one of the first to treat comprehensively the cost problems of a firm using the process cost method in *Textile Manufacturers' Bookkeeping*. J. Slater Lewis in 1896 drew attention to accounting for manufacturing burden in *Commercial Organization of Factories*.

During this time period, the American Society of Mechanical Engineers (ASME) began its interest in cost accounting. Such engineers as Clarence M. Day, Frederick Winslow Taylor, C.E. Knoeppel, and Henry Laurence Gantt added a richness of thought and much detail to the field of cost accounting. These proponents of "scientific management" spurred interest in cost accounting. In fact, the field became theirs for about 30 years. Alexander Hamilton Church began his writings on manufacturing overhead at the turn of the twentieth century and did much to further the development of that cost element. One of the important and controversial components of such costs was the possible imputation of interest on invested capital. This viewpoint was stressed by J. Lee Nicholson in 1909 in *Factory Organization and Costs* and by Clinton H. Scovell as typified by his book, *Interest as a Cost*. Following the earlier lead of Harrington Emerson in 1908, G. Charter Harrison in 1918 began to develop the concept of standard costing. The work of J.P. Jordan and G.L. Harris in 1920 in their *Cost Accounting* perhaps typifies the thought process to that date. By 1920 cost accounting for direct materials and direct labor had reached its full development. While the topic of manufacturing overhead remained less well settled, such subtopics as (1) product costs vs. other costs, (2) idle time, (3) imputed interest, and (4) capacity had been at least well defined.

Both the National Association of Cost Accountants (NACA), located in New York City, and the Institute of Cost and Works Accountants, located in London, were founded in 1919. These organizations have done much to institutionalize the field of cost accounting. By the end of the 1920s, cost accounting was firmly in the hands of cost accountants, not industrial engineers. The decades of the 1920s, 1930s, and 1940s were dominated by the topics of budgeting, standard costs, uniformity by industry, concepts of capacity, distribution costs, and varying concepts of costs. Cost accounting was even extended into governmental accounting, as witnessed by Eric Louis Kohler's work at the Tennessee Valley Authority (TVA).

The concept of flexible budgeting greatly aided the development of the literature and practice of budgeting. The managerial functions of planning and control made their way into accounting mainly via the budgeting process. Standard costs were further developed in the 1930s by such NACA stalwarts as Eric A. Camman and Charles Reitell. The NACA took a strong stance in favor of uniform accounts for each industry for the statistical information that could result in lower costs. The National Recovery Administration in the early 1930s required that businesses could not sell below costs. The requirements of World War II regulations for costs in connection with war contracts broadened the base for the uniformity movement. The "normal," "practical," and "ideal" concepts of capacity for distributing overhead were developed and espoused in numerous publications in these decades. Distribution costs were well analyzed by such NACA experts as William B. Castenholz in "The Application of Selling and Administrative Expenses to Product" (1922), Howard Greer in "Development of Standards for the Control of Selling Activities" (1932), and J. Brook Heckert in *Distribution Costs* (1940). The varying concepts of costs, first expounded by the economist John Maurice Clark in his *Studies in the Economics of Overhead Costs* in 1923, were further extended by such NACA leaders as Wyman S. Fiske in "The Nature of Costs and its Uses" (1942), and Theodore Lang in "Concepts of Cost, Past and Present" (1947). These decades could well be labeled as the golden years of cost accounting.

The next four decades of the 1950s, 1960s, 1970s, and 1980s witnessed much turbulence in cost accounting. Perhaps the most significant development was the proposal for direct costing. Although first mentioned in 1936 in an article "What Did We Earn Last Month" by Jonathan Harris, direct costing became a hot topic in the 1950s with strong NACA support. While there was widespread acceptance, for internal uses, the failure of direct costing to win Internal Revenue Service approval or to become a generally accepted accounting principle led to a weakening of its support. By the late 1980s, with increased analysis of "fixed overhead," direct costing was replaced by activity-based costing.

In the 1960s, the term "management accounting" began replacing "cost accounting." While such writers as James O. McKinsey, William Joseph Vatter, and Billy Goetz had used the term before him, Charles T. Horngren brought "management accounting" to the forefront with his many texts dating from the early 1960s. The Certified Management Accountant exam program was started in 1972; the NACA's successor, the National Association of Accountants (NAA) issued Management Accounting Principles; and the NAA became the Institute of Management Accountants in 1991. By the 1990s, "cost accounting" seemed to have become a subtopic of "management accounting."

Clearly there has been an explosion in the literature of budgeting, to which findings from the behavioral sciences have added much. Outstanding contributions have been made by such writers as Edwin H. Caplan and Andrew C. Stedry, *Budget Control and Cost Behavior* (1960).

However, there were also areas of slippage. The topic of "distribution costs" faded to a relatively insignificant part of the literature of cost accounting—since the early 1970s, surprising in the light of vast expenditures for distribution costs. The topic of "standard costs" by the early 1970s became trivialized into an endless quest for variances and seemed to become the major casualty of the continuous improvement quest for "total quality management." The topic of "operations research," so skillfully entered into accounting (1967) by Abraham Charnes and W.W. Cooper, was somewhat spun-off into another field of knowledge, "management science."

The field of cost accounting has had a long and rich tradition, but it has focused all too long on the manufacturing of a product by a private-sector company. That focus has caused accountants, managers, and the general public to fail to utilize fully the field of cost accounting as it relates to distribution costs, administrative costs, and organizations providing services of all types. Even the replacement of "cost accounting" by "management accounting" may not materially change this. What may be needed is a constant effort of accounting scholars and practitioners to recast "cost accounting" into an accounting field such as that recommended in 1987 by Johnson and Robert S. Kaplan. This field was perhaps best described by an editorial in 1991 in *Management Accountant* (India): "The ground rules for cost and management accounting provide a very extensive area of management control and decision making and affect at every point of activity operations, whether it is related to manufacture or sales or pricing or designing or budgeting or inventory control."

S. Paul Garner
Richard Vangermeersch

Bibliography

Caplan, E.H. "Behavioral Assumptions of Management Accounting," edited by W.J. Burns Jr. and D.T. DeCoster in *Accounting and Its Behavioral Implications,* pp. 113–130. New York: McGraw Hill, 1969.

Charnes, A., and W.W. Cooper. "Some Network Characterizations for Mathematical Programming and Accounting Approaches to Planning and Control," *Accounting Review*, January 1967, pp. 24–52.

Fleischman, R.K., L.D. Parker, and W. Vamplew. "New Cost Accounting Perspectives on Technological Change in the British Industrial Revolution." In *The Costing Heritage: Studies in Honor of S. Paul Garner*, edited by O.F. Graves, pp. 11–24. Harrisonburg, VA: Academy of Accounting Historians, 1991.

Garner, S. Paul. *Evolution of Cost Accounting to 1925*. University, AL: University of Alabama Press, 1954. Reprint. New York: Garland, 1990.

———. "Highlights in the Development of Cost Accounting," *National Public Accountant*, March 1950, pp. 167–170, 186–187, 189–192.

Jackson, J.H. "A Quarter Century of Cost Accounting Progress," *NACA Bulletin*, June 1, 1947, pp. 1201–1209.

Johnson, H.T. "Early Cost Accounting for Internal Management Control: Lyman Mills in the 1850s," *Business History Review*, Winter 1972, pp. 466–474.

Johnson, H.T., and R.S. Kaplan. *Relevance Lost: The Rise and Fall of Management Accounting*. Boston: Harvard Business School Press, 1987.

Kohler, E.L. "Accounting for the TVA," *Accounting Forum*, June 1941, pp. 48–51, 61–62.

Lardner, D. *Railway Economy.* London: Taylor, Walton, and Maberly, 1850. Reprint. New York: Augustus M. Kelley, 1968.

Nikitin, M. "Setting-up an Industrial Accounting System at Saint-Gobain, 1820–1880," *Accounting Historians Journal*, December 1990, pp. 75–93.

Staubus, G.J. "The Dark Ages of Cost Accounting: The Role of Miscues in the Literature," *Accounting Historians Journal*, Fall 1987, pp. 1–18.

Vangermeersch, R. "Comments on Accounting Disclosures in the Baltimore and Ohio Annual Reports from 1828 through 1850." Working paper no. 38 in *Working Paper Series Volume 2*, edited by E.N. Coffman, pp. 318–337. Richmond, VA: Academy of Accounting Historians, 1979.

"The Way to Management Accountancy and Beyond," *Management Accountant* (India), September 1991, pp. 667–668.

Wells, M.C. "Some Influences on the Development of Cost Accounting," *Accounting Historians Journal*, Fall 1977, pp. 47–61.

See also ACTIVITY BASED COSTING; AGRICULTURAL ACCOUNTING; BABBAGE, CHARLES; BREAK-EVEN CHART; BUDGETING; CERTIFIED MANAGEMENT ACCOUNTANT (CMA) EXAMINATION; CHARTERED INSTITUTE OF MANAGEMENT ACCOUNTANTS; CHURCH, ALEXANDER HAMILTON; CLARK, JOHN MAURICE; COMMON COSTS; COOPER, WILLIAM WAGER; COST ACCOUNTING STANDARDS BOARD; CRONHELM, FREDERIC WILLIAM; DICKSEE, LAWRENCE; DIRECT COSTING; DISTRIBUTION COSTS; DODSON, JAMES; EMERSON, HARRINGTON; ENGINEERING AND ACCOUNTING; FUGGER COST ACCOUNTS; GANTT, HENRY LAURENCE; GARCKE AND FELLS; GARNER, S. PAUL; HAMILTON, ROBERT; HARRISON, G. CHARTER; HOPWOOD, ANTHONY G.; HORNGREN, CHARLES T.; INSTITUTE OF MANAGEMENT ACCOUNTANTS; JOHNSON AND KAPLAN'S *RELEVANCE LOST: THE RISE AND FALL OF MANAGEMENT ACCOUNTING*; KOHLER, ERIC LOUIS; LEWIS, J. SLATER; MANAGEMENT ACCOUNTING; MCKINSEY, JAMES O.; MEDICI ACCOUNTS; METCALFE, HENRY; MICROECONOMICS IN GERMANY; NICHOLSON, J. LEE; PAYEN, ANSELME; PERIODICITY; PERPETUAL INVENTORY; PLANTIN, CHRISTOPHER; RAILROAD ACCOUNTING (U.S.); STANDARD COSTING; TAYLOR, FREDERICK WINSLOW; UNIFORM ACCOUNTING SYSTEMS; UNIFORMITY; VATTER, WILLIAM JOSEPH; WHITMORE, JOHN

Cotrugli, Benedetto

Luca Pacioli's was the first *printed* treatise on double entry bookkeeping. In 1458, 36 years before Pacioli's *Summa de Arithmetica* appeared, Benedetto Cotrugli wrote *Delia Mercatura et del Mercante Perfetto* (Of Trading and the Perfect Trader), but it was not published until 1573. This work on business methods contained a short chapter describing double entry bookkeeping. Like Pacioli, Cotrugli wrote in Italian and used the same three account books. Though his system lacked an income summary account, closing entries going directly to capital, he recommended preparation of a trial balance. Pacioli had read this manuscript and even attributed the invention of double entry bookkeeping to Cotrugli. However, it is doubtful that Cotrugli invented any part of the system he described. He wrote at a time when business practices were more sophisticated than the textbooks, and Cotrugli, Pacioli, and their immediate successors only tried to set out bookkeeping mechanics as developed by merchants.

Michael Chatfield

See also DOUBLE ENTRY BOOKKEEPING: ORIGINS; PACIOLI, LUCA

Craig v. Anyon

An auditor's responsibility to his clients was the subject of *Craig v. Anyon* (1925). The CPA firm of Barrow, Wade, Guthrie and Co. had audited the accounts of Bache and Company, brokers, from 1913 to 1917 without discovering that over a five year period a Bache employee had embezzled more than a million dollars. A jury found the CPA firm guilty of negligence and assessed damages equal to the entire amount of Bache's loss. But the New York Appeals Court reduced the damages to $2,000, the amount of the auditor's fee, on the grounds of contributory negligence—Bache should not be allowed to recover for losses it could have prevented by establishing an effective internal control system. The *Craig* decision reinforced precedents established in earlier English cases: An auditor's legal liability to his client was extremely limited so long as he exercised "reasonable care" in performing his duties.

Michael Chatfield

See also LEGAL LIABILITY OF AUDITORS

Credit

A.C. Littleton included credit as one of seven preconditions for the development of systematic bookkeeping: "*Credit* (i.e., incompleted transactions), since there would be little impulse to make any record whatsoever if all exchanges were completed on the spot."

The Babylonians conducted credit transactions 4,000 years ago. It was common practice for drafts to be drawn in one city and payable in another. But commerce in the ancient world generally did not require sophisticated credit arrangements. Most pre-Christian societies were agricultural and largely self-sufficient. Ordinary people had little purchasing power, the supply of trade goods was small, and transportation facilities were often poor. Barter, the normal method of exchange, required no bookkeeping because transactions were settled immediately. There were credit dealings, but not of a kind that offered much incentive for systematic record keeping. Borrowing was more often for consumption than for production or trade. Loans tended to be secured by pledged valuables, and in such cases the creditor, like a modern pawnbroker, could be indifferent as to whether the money was ever repaid.

Double entry bookkeeping came into being with the rise of Mediterranean commerce during and just after the Crusades (1096–1291). Besides requiring ships and provisions, the crusaders brought back silks, spices, and other Eastern products, stimulating demand for such items and for the production of European exchange goods. New trade contacts gave impetus to a 300-year commercial expansion. Genoa and Venice quickly established themselves as intermediaries in trade relations between Europe and the Near East. The resulting accumulation of capital and the distances over which trading was carried on led naturally to branch operations, credit arrangements, and consignment transactions. Italians not only became the leading merchants of the Renaissance but nearly monopolized international banking. They regularly put trade competitors out of business and limited others, such as the English, to a local sphere of influence.

Their success resulted particularly from superior business organization. Besides inventing double entry bookkeeping, they devised the bill of exchange in draft form, experimented with marine insurance, and evolved a body of codified mercantile law that forms the basis of commercial law today. Money shortages were a perennial problem during the Middle Ages, and foreigners marveled at the Italians' ability to do business without cash. But the wide use of credit required written records of amounts owed and owing. The need to group all entries concerning the same person to form a running balance was probably the earliest motive for creating bilateral accounts with opposing debits and credits.

The oldest surviving double entry records are those of Florentine bankers who began by making dual entries for certain credit transactions. Even the Latin words from which debit and credit were derived (*debent dare*, shall give; *debent habere*, shall have) looked to the future and connoted settlement of receivable and payable balances. Bankers had several reasons to extend these rudimentary personal accounts into a complete double entry system that included tangible assets, expenses, and equities. Nominal accounts may have been added when early bankers added trading operations to finance and needed an accounting system that produced capital and income figures. Also, because of the difficulty and risk of transferring cash, much of the bank's business consisted of acting as an intermediary in settling debts. Merchants deposited money in order to make payments by means of bank transfers. The bank simply debited one client and credited another, but this tended toward an integration of accounts. All this suggests that credit was not only a precondition for double entry bookkeeping but a major contributor to its development.

Michael Chatfield

Bibliography

De Roover, R. "The Development of Accounting prior to Luca Pacioli according to the Account-Books of Medieval Merchants." In *Studies in the History of Accounting*, edited by A.C. Littleton and B.S. Yamey, pp. 114–174. Homewood, IL: Irwin, 1956.

Littleton, A.C. *Accounting Evolution to 1900*. New York: American Institute Publishing, 1933. Reprint. New York: Russell and Russell, 1966.

Lopez, R.S., and I.W. Raymond. *Medieval Trade in the Mediterranean World.* New York: Columbia University Press, 1955.

See also BABYLONIA; BARTER; BRANCH ACCOUNTING; DEBIT AND CREDIT; DOUBLE ENTRY BOOKKEEPING: ORIGINS; INCOME STATEMENT/INCOME ACCOUNT; LITTLETON, A.C.; MONEY

Critical Event Theory

In place of the assumption that income is earned at the moment of sale, John H. Myers proposed in a 1959 article that profits be recognized when a business owner or manager makes the most critical decision during the earnings process, or when his company performs the most critical task during its operating cycle. This critical event could occur during production of an item with an assured market price. The purchase of highly salable merchandise below normal cost might justify revenue recognition at the time of acquisition. Anticipated profits on a bank loan could be recognized when the loan was made, since the critical decision was whether or not to extend the loan. If receivables collections were doubtful, revenue recognition might be deferred until cash was received.

A manager's choice of critical events could be influenced by his perceptions of the relative importance of various production-sale functions. However, a critical events test would not radically alter current practice, because the critical event in most businesses is the sale. But it would substitute a general principle of revenue recognition for the existing series of rules that only cover particular situations.

Michael Chatfield

Bibliography

Myers, J.H. "The Critical Event and Recognition of Net Profit," *Accounting Review,* October 1959, pp. 528–532.

See also REALIZATION

Cronhelm, Frederic William

In *Double Entry by Single* (1818), the English accounting practitioner Frederic William Cronhelm gave the first complete exposition of proprietary theory and the first comprehensive description in English of a factory cost accounting system.

Taking James Fulton's *British-Indian Book-keeping* (1800) as his point of departure, Cronhelm emphasized the equivalence between total capital and its constituent parts. He argued that the purpose of bookkeeping "is to show the owner at all times the value of his whole capital, and of every part of it." In Cronhelm's algebraic approach to transaction analysis, the capital account became a mathematical equilibrating device, by inference a credit item opposite to assets. Transactions affected the accounting equation by increasing or decreasing assets, liabilities, or capital. Cronhelm envisioned a series of asset conversions during a firm's operating cycle, with income entering the capital account as a net increase in proprietorship. Expense and revenue accounts, including profit and loss, were created to avoid the inconvenience of recording every change in wealth directly to capital. Cronhelm treated them as branches of owner's equity.

Frenchman Anselme Payen (1817) and Cronhelm (1818) published the first comprehensive descriptions of factory accounting systems. Using as his example a woolen cloth manufacturer, Cronhelm set up memorandum books for raw materials, work in process, and finished goods, with labor costs subdivided by spinning, weaving, and finishing processes. Although they showed only quantities, not money values, Cronhelm's memorandum accounts were probably the earliest textbook examples of perpetual inventories. A raw materials account was debited for purchases and credited for wool put into process. A manufacturing account debited pounds of wool put into process and credited finished pieces of cloth. The finished goods account was debited for materials completed and credited for goods sold. An inventory control sheet drew quantities from these three materials books and extended them into money values, work in process being averaged at the "middle stage" of completion.

Cronhelm's system permitted the calculation of ending inventories and cost of goods sold but not the analysis of costs by processes or batches of goods. The absence of money values in the memorandum books also meant that manufacturing records were poorly coordinated with purchases and sales accounts. However, Cronhelm demonstrated how to transfer costs between ledger accounts, how to accumulate total costs in control accounts, how to isolate ending inventory balances, and how to link manufacturing balances to general ledger totals. S. Paul Garner judged that Payen and Cronhelm "were far superior to any who wrote for the next 50 years."

Michael Chatfield

Bibliography

Cronhelm, F.W. *Double Entry by Single.* London: Longman, Hurst, Rees, Orme, and Brown. 1818. Reprint. New York: Arno Press, 1978.

Garner, S.P. *Evolution of Cost Accounting to 1925.* University, AL: University of Alabama Press, 1954.

Littleton, A.C. *Accounting Evolution to 1900.* New York: American Institute Publishing, 1933. Reprint. New York: Russell and Russell, 1966.

See also CAPITAL ACCOUNT; COST AND/OR MANAGEMENT ACCOUNTING; GARNER, S. PAUL; PAYEN, ANSELME; PERPETUAL INVENTORY; PROPRIETARY THEORY; STANDARD COSTING

D

Dafforne, Richard

Richard Dafforne, London accountant and arithmetic teacher, had lived many years in Amsterdam and wrote a bookkeeping text to introduce Dutch accounting methods into England. *The Merchants' Mirrour* (1636) adopted Simon Stevin's method of platonic dialogue, posing "250 rare Questions with their Answers," but omitted such Dutch practices as special journals, subsidiary ledgers, and compound entries. However, Dafforne's was the first English text to describe a complete double entry system and the first to go into multiple editions. After the work of Dafforne and his immediate successors, it becomes hard to trace foreign influences on English bookkeeping manuals. Though they often lagged behind practice, later treatises were based essentially on the English experience.

Nearly all bookkeeping texts written before the nineteenth century consisted essentially of explanations as to which journal entries were appropriate to particular transactions. Since there were thousands of possible transactions, most authors resorted to lists of rules to be memorized as a basis for transaction analysis. Dafforne gave 30 "rules of aid" intended to cover every type of transaction. He put rules into verse to impress them on the student's memory.

Early financial statements were made either by copying the accounts as they appeared in the ledger or by organizing trial balance figures into columnar reports. Dafforne illustrated a six column statement in which the left pair of columns showed a trial balance of totals, the middle pair a trial balance of balances, and the two right hand columns a balance sheet containing the remaining assets and equities. Later writers added profit and loss columns and entered ending inventories to adjust beginning figures, creating what is today called a worksheet. In time these unwieldy columnar statements dropped out of textbooks, to be replaced by balance sheets that showed the final figures but not their derivation.

Michael Chatfield

Bibliography

Littleton, A.C. *Accounting Evolution to 1900*. American Institute Publishing, 1933. Reprint. New York: Russell and Russell, 1966.

Yamey, B.S., H.C. Edey, and H.W. Thomson. *Accounting in England and Scotland, 1543–1800*. London: Sweet and Maxwell, 1963.

See also BALANCE SHEET; DEBIT AND CREDIT; PEELE, JAMES; STEVIN, SIMON

Datini, Francesco de Marco (1335–1410)

Francesco de Marco Datini made in his own lifetime the transition from a local business using single entry bookkeeping to large scale branch operations employing a complete double entry system. He was retailer, importer, banker, commission agent, and manufacturer, seeing in diversification a hedge against the risks that had bankrupted others who grew too rapidly. He expanded by opening branch offices throughout Europe, using accounting records to review and control his operations. The Datini ledgers run continuously from 1366 to 1410. After 1390 a complete double entry system including balance sheets was used in most of his foreign branches and at his main office in Florence.

The major innovation in Datini's ledgers was the conversion from vertical to bilateral account form. Traditionally, the debit and credit sections of Florentine ledger accounts were placed one above the other instead of side by side as in Venice. This meant, for example, that when a debit was recorded at the top of a particular ledger page, a blank space had to be left below for the payment entry. Placement of debits and credits on the basis of page position was impossible, and the Florentine system never could have evolved into the "shorthand" ledger entries used today. After the introduction of bilateral accounts from Venice, no important changes occurred in Florentine bookkeeping technique, evidence that both systems were basically alike.

Michael Chatfield

Bibliography

Brun, R. "A Fourteenth Century Merchant of Italy: Francesco Datini of Prato," *Journal of Economic Business History*, May 1930, pp. 451–466.

De Roover, R. "The Development of Accounting prior to Luca Pacioli according to the Account-books of Medieval Merchants." In *Studies in the History of Accounting*, edited by A.C. Littleton and B.S. Yamey, pp. 114–174. Homewood, IL: Irwin, 1956.

Peragallo, E. *Origin and Evolution of Double Entry Bookkeeping: A Study of Italian Practice from the Fourteenth Century.* New York: American Institute Publishing, 1938. Reprint. Osaka: Nihon Shoseki, 1974.

See also BRANCH ACCOUNTING; CONSERVATISM; DEBIT AND CREDIT; DOUBLE ENTRY BOOKKEEPING: ORIGINS; SINGLE ENTRY BOOKKEEPING

Davidson, Sidney (1919–)

One of the rewards of teaching is that "you and your work live on in the work of your students." While evident at all levels, this may be especially true for university teaching, where the intensity of the impact is often quite strong.

Sidney Davidson epitomizes the opening homily. He has extended the influence of his mentor, whom the American Institute of Certified Public Accountants (AICPA) designated the Accounting Educator of the Century, William Andrew Paton of the University of Michigan, which conferred three degrees each on both Paton and Davidson. Davidson has also exerted his own influence on the profession over the years through his Ph.D. students, including Baruch Lev, Katherine Schipper, George Sorter, William Beaver, Joel S. Demski, George Benston, Frederick Neumann, Gary Biddle, Grant Clowery, and Robert Lipe.

Trained in the days of "working your way through" (no fellowships), Davidson began his teaching at Michigan, where he taught both economics and accounting as an instructor (1946–49) and also taught during various subsequent summers as a visiting professor. After Michigan, he taught at Johns Hopkins University (1949–1958) as assistant, associate, and then professor of accounting. He attained the CPA in Maryland in 1951, along with a medal for top performance.

In 1958 Davidson joined the faculty at the University of Chicago as a professor of accounting. In his 35-plus years there, he has served as the creator, grantee, and director of the Institute of Professional Accounting; Arthur Young Professor of Accounting, the first to be so designated and financially supported, in 1962; dean of the Graduate School of Business (1969–1974); Arthur Young Distinguished Service Professor of Accounting (1984–1989); and as of 1989, Ernst and Young Distinguished Service Professor of Accounting Emeritus. Davidson also taught as a visiting professor at the University of California at Berkeley (1950); often at Florida Atlantic University; the University of Hawaii (1960); and Hebrew University (1965 and 1969), among others.

A visiting professorship at the London School of Economics (1956–1957) led Davidson and the Institute of Professional Accounting to join with William T. Baxter and the London School of Economics in creating the *Journal of Accounting Research* in 1963.

Davidson has also influenced the profession through his writings—as of 1993, 28 books as author, editor, or contributor of a section, 55 articles, and nine book reviews—and active participation in professional organizations. In the American Accounting Association (AAA), Davidson's record of service dates back over 40 years, including president (1968–1969), director of research (1955–1956), and Membership Committee (1952–1955). In the AICPA he served as a member of the Accounting Principles Board (1965–1970), and the

Commission on the Study of the Common Body of Knowledge (1963–1966), as well as vice president (1986–1987). Other professional memberships include the Financial Executives Institute, the American Economic Association, and the Illinois Society of CPAs, which made him an honorary life member in 1984.

Davidson received the AAA's Outstanding Educator Award in 1976, the Illinois Society of CPAs Outstanding Educator Award in 1984, and Beta Alpha Psi's National Accountant of the Year Award in 1984, among others. He is a member of the Accounting Hall of Fame.

David O. Green

Bibliography

Baxter, W.T., and S. Davidson. *Studies in Accounting Theory.* Homewood, IL: Irwin, 1962.

Burns, T.J., and E.N. Coffman. *Accounting Hall of Fame: Profiles of Fifty Members.* Columbus, OH: College of Business, Ohio State University, 1992.

Davidson, S. "Accelerated Depreciation and the Allocation of Income Taxes," *Accounting Review*, April 1958, pp. 173–180.

———. "Day of Reckoning—Managerial Analyses and Accounting Theory," *Journal of Accounting Research*, Autumn 1963, pp. 117–126.

———. "Old Wine into New Bottles," *Accounting Review*, April 1963, pp. 278–284.

———. "Should Companies be Required to Publish Their Earnings Forecasts? Yes," *Institutional Investor*, April 1972, pp. 56–59.

———, and G.D. Anderson. "Development of Accounting and Auditing Standards," *Journal of Accountancy*, May 1987, pp. 110–114, 116–118, 122–124, 127.

See also ACCOUNTING HALL OF FAME; ACCOUNTING PRINCIPLES BOARD; ACCOUNTING RESEARCH STUDIES; AMERICAN INSTITUTE OF CERTIFIED PUBLIC ACCOUNTANTS; BEAVER, WILLIAM; DEMSKI, JOEL S.; PATON, WILLIAM ANDREW

Day Book

See MEMORANDUM BOOK

Debit and Credit

The terms "debit" and "credit" are, like the origins of double entry accounting, enshrouded in mystery. A.C. Littleton (1933), the noted accounting historian and theorist from the University of Illinois, associated "debit" with "give" and "credit" with "have." The idea of "give" (i.e., return to the proprietor or agent) was directly associated with debits and "have" (i.e., receive from the proprietor or agent) with credits. The debit side of an account was the "give" side and the credit side the "have" side.

Luca Pacioli, the author of the first printed treatise on accounting, "Particulars of Reckoning and Their Recording," did use the terms "debit" and "credit" early in his treatise, as noted in the English translation of Pacioli by the American John B. Geijsbeek (1914). Pacioli used the terms in his description of the opening of a ledger by a merchant. A long list of accounts were to be posted to the debit side of the asset accounts. Various liabilities and capital were to be posted to the credit side of liability and capital accounts. Pacioli, while using the terms "debit" and "credit," did not use them in his sample entries in his journal. Pacioli used // (two slanted lines) to separate the debit and credit parts of the entry. Domenico Manzoni in *Quaderno doppio col suo giornale secundo il costume di Venetia* (1540) and Jan Ympyn in *Niewe Instructie* (1543) both used // in their sample journal entries. The terms "debit" and "credit" were first used in journal entries in accounting texts in 1550 in French by Valetin Mennher von Kempten, a German mathematics teacher, in *Practique brifue pour cyfrer et tenir livres de compte* and in English by the English teacher and clerk James Peele in *The maner and fourme how to kepe a perfect reconying* (1553).

J.B. Geijsbeek considered debit to be derived from the Latin *debita* and *debeo*, which in business and from the standpoint of the proprietor means "owe" or "he owes to the proprietor" that which was loaned or given him by the proprietor. Credit is from the Latin word *credo*, or "trust or believe," as in business the creditors were "believers" in the integrity of the proprietor and, therefore, loaned or gave him something.

Debit and credit become the basis on which bookkeeping and accounting were taught from the mid-sixteenth century. Different authors developed different rules and used examples of many different types of journal entries so that students could be exposed to all possible transactions. For instance, London accountant Richard Dafforne in 1636 in *Merchants Mirrour* listed 30 rules; William Weston from England in *The Complete Merchants' Clerk* in 1754 utilized 45 rules; and John Mair, a Scottish teacher, in 1765 had six rules in *Bookkeeping Methodiz'd*. It was not until 1880, in a series of articles by American Charles Ezra Sprague in *The Book-Keeper,* that the accounting equation of A (Assets) = L (Liabilities) + P (Proprietorship) and the debit and credit rules for each account type come into being. Littleton credited Sprague and J.F. Schär of Germany as the two writers who adapted bookkeeping to the modern world.

Richard Vangermeersch

Bibliography

Geijsbeek, J.B. *Ancient Double-Entry Bookkeeping: Lucas Pacioli's Treatise*. Denver: Geijsbeek, 1914.

Littleton, A.C. *Accounting Evolution to 1900*. New York: American Institute Publishing, 1933. Reprint. New York: Russell and Russell, 1966.

Previts, G.J., and B.D. Merino. *A History of Accounting in America: An Historical Interpretation of the Cultural Significance of Accounting*. New York: John Wiley & Sons, 1979.

See also ACCOUNTING EDUCATION IN THE UNITED STATES; ARABIC NUMERALS; ARITHMETIC AND ACCOUNTING; BADOER, JACHOMO; BALANCE ACCOUNT; BARBARIGO, ANDREA; COMPUTING TECHNOLOGY IN THE WEST: THE IMPACT ON THE PROFESSION OF ACCOUNTING; CREDIT; DAFFORNE, RICHARD; DATINI, FRANCESCO DE MARCO; FINI, RINERIO; JONES, THOMAS; JOURNAL; LITTLETON, A.C.; MANZONI, DOMENICO; PACIOLI, LUCA; PEELE, JAMES; PERSONIFICATION OF ACCOUNTS; SPRAGUE, CHARLES EZRA

Deferred Income Tax Accounting

Deferred taxes result from differences between pretax accounting income calculated for external reporting purposes and taxable income calculated to determine taxes due. The transactions that cause such differences include revenues and gains or expenses and losses recognized at different times under the two methods. Although the total difference over time is the same, on a year-by-year basis the differences originate and reverse. The impact on the financial statements is called interperiod tax allocation. Examples of these timing or temporary differences include straight-line depreciation or immediate revenue recognition for accounting purposes and accelerated depreciation or installment revenue recognition for tax purposes.

When the differences between pretax accounting income and taxable income have been identified, the next step is to broaden the treatment to include the extent of interperiod tax allocation, whether partial or comprehensive. Partial allocation occurs when a firm recognizes nonrecurring differences between the two income amounts. Examples of nonrecurring items would be isolated asset purchases by a firm on a sporadic basis. Such asset purchases occur so irregularly that the reversal of existing timing differences is not offset by originating timing differences associated with other asset purchases. Accounting for the tax effects of both nonrecurring and recurring items constitutes comprehensive allocation. Recurring items would be, for example, regular asset purchases by a firm that result in additional timing differences due to new and probably higher cost-depreciation schedules that may not only offset but exceed existing timing reversals.

The decision concerning the method of interperiod tax allocation depends, in part, on the financial-statement focus of the prevailing rule-making body. When the income statement is emphasized, the matching principle becomes imperative to recognition, and the identification of the expense that most accurately reflects events of the period is imperative. If, however, the balance sheet is the most important statement, then accurate balance-sheet account balances become the primary focus. The financial-statement emphasis of the profession changed during the past century, and that change is reflected in changes in the methods of accounting for income taxes.

The treatment of interperiod tax allocation has been far from uniform. The three generally recognized methods for accomplishing interperiod tax allocation are the liability method, the deferred method, and the net-of-tax method. Homer A. Black, in Accounting Research Study (ARS) No. 9, *Interperiod Allocation of Corporate Income Taxes* (1966), found that all three methods were either directly or indirectly supported in the literature and by the American Institute of Certified Public Accountants (AICPA) and the Securities and Exchange Commission (SEC). Timing differences resulted in the need for interperiod tax allocation, and consequently deferred taxes, under two of the three methods, the liability method and the deferred method. The third method, the net-of-tax method, which resulted in the direct adjustment of the tax effect to the asset or liability accounts, was considered the least desirable of the three methods described.

From 1967 until 1987, Accounting Principles Board (APB) Opinion No. 11, "Accounting for Income Taxes," required the use of the deferred method of comprehensive interperiod tax allocation. Under the deferred method, the emphasis was placed on matching the tax expense and the revenues of the current period without regard to expected changes in the tax rate. The resultant impact on the balance sheet would be the recognition of deferred charges and/or deferred credits which were not assets or liabilities in the usual sense and would be classified as current or noncurrent depending on the classification of the related asset or liability. A significant problem developed because of the interaction between the deferred method and the comprehensive-allocation requirement. Recurring items essentially caused the balance in the deferred tax account to build up on the balance sheet—originating new deferred taxes were far greater than those reversing, nor were changes in income tax rates accommodated. The balance in the deferred tax account would, therefore, not decrease and would usually increase with asset expansion and/or the increase in new asset costs, resulting, in conjunction with increases in the tax rates, in virtually permanent deferrals of reversing differences. Eventually, the amounts in the deferred tax accounts would probably not relate to existing assets.

In response to continuing concerns within the profession over the ever increasing balances in the deferred tax accounts and the lack of theoretical justification for APB No. 11, the Financial Accounting Standards Board (FASB) added accounting for income taxes to its technical agenda in January 1982. The APB had delayed dealing with the issue as a whole since 1967, despite a great deal of pressure from various special-interest groups. Professional concerns over the issue were identified by Beresford, Best, Craig, and Weber in a research report, *Accounting for Income Taxes: A Review of Alternatives* (1983). The report focused on the alternatives evidenced in the prevailing literature and offered a thorough explanation of the issues, methods, degree, and history of the subject of accounting for income taxes.

Despite the information available, the complexity of the issue delayed the release of a statement, although the Discussion Memorandum "An Analysis of Issues Related to Accounting for Income Taxes" was issued in August 1983. After additional prolonged debate, numerous changes, and continued discord prompted by the Discussion Memorandum, the Exposure Draft "Accounting for Income Taxes" was issued in September 1986. After public hearings and comment letters, Statement on Financial Accounting Standards (SFAS) No. 96, "Accounting for Income Taxes," was issued in December 1987, effective for fiscal years beginning after December 15, 1988. It completely superseded APB No. 11 and the deferred method in determining deferred taxes.

The FASB retained comprehensive allocation but required the use of the liability method in recognizing temporary differences resulting from interperiod tax allocation. The liability method results in the recognition of an asset or liability for taxes prepaid or payable in the future because of the current difference between pretax accounting income and taxable income. The temporary differences between the tax bases and book bases of assets and liabilities produced future tax consequences resulting in taxable or deductible amounts consisting of one or more originating and/or reversing differences. Earlier recognition of expenses on the tax return or revenues on the financial statements resulted in future taxable amounts and a deferred tax liability. Earlier recognition of revenues on the tax return or expenses on the financial statements resulted in future deductible amounts and a deferred tax asset. In addition, a detailed schedule of the estimated year in which each originating and/or reversing difference would occur would be necessary to determine the existence of a deferred tax asset or deferred tax liability. Unlimited recognition of the deferred tax liability was allowed, and the FASB indicated that the account conformed to the definition of a liability as evidenced in Statement of Financial Accounting Concepts No. 6, "Elements of Financial Statements" (1985), in that it represented probable future sacrifices.

The recognition of the deferred tax asset was limited, however, based on the application of net operating loss carryback techniques to net deductible amounts to the extent that taxable income in current or past years existed. Application of carryforward techniques to net deductible amounts was limited to the extent that offsetting future taxable amounts existed. The FASB took the position, in conformance with tax law, that complete recognition of the asset would require assumptions about the future earnings capabilities of a firm, and that the tax consequences of these earnings, or events, should not be anticipated. In addition, the deferred tax liability or asset accounts would be adjusted as necessary to conform to enacted changes in the tax law resulting in changes in the tax rates. Graduated tax rates would be used unless average tax rates did not result in a material difference. The focus of the new statement indicated a shift in emphasis on the part of the FASB and the profession from the income statement to the balance sheet.

SFAS No. 96 was controversial from the beginning. In fact, most companies delayed adoption of it for a number of different reasons. Among the most obvious reasons for this delay, Klingler and Savage (1988) and Chaney and Jeter (1989) found that the costs of the implementation of SFAS No. 96 were exorbitant, and in some cases prohibitive, largely because of the need to schedule each originating and reversing difference. In addition, despite the FASB's assertions to the contrary, Kripke (1989) criticized SFAS No. 96 for violating the conceptual framework because of its statements with respect to the deferred tax liability. Further, Means (1989) attacked the limitation on recognition of the deferred tax asset as a violation of the going-concern assumption. All of these issues and the consequent uproar in the profession caused the FASB to delay the effective date of SFAS No. 96—with SFAS No. 100 (1988), for one year; with SFAS No. 103 (1989), for an additional two years; and with SFAS No. 108 (1991), for an additional year. The enactment difficulties, as well as the repeated delays by the FASB, caused a great deal of skepticism in the profession over the future of SFAS No. 96.

That skepticism was justified and was reflected in the release of another Exposure Draft, "Accounting for Income Taxes," issued in June 1991, and SFAS No. 109, "Accounting for Income Taxes," issued in February 1992 and effective for fiscal years beginning after December 15, 1992. While keeping the liability method and the recognition of the future tax consequences of temporary differences, the FASB significantly relaxed the most complicated and controversial aspects of SFAS No. 96: the limitations on deferred tax asset recognition and the detailed scheduling of future taxable and deductible amounts. The scheduling was no longer necessary because the application of net operating loss carryback/carryforward techniques to net deductible amounts was no longer a requirement. Rather, unlimited recognition of a deferred tax asset was authorized unless it was "more likely than not," or there was a greater than 50 percent likelihood, that the tax consequences would not be realized. In that case, a valuation allowance account was to be used to reduce the deferred tax asset to the amount that would "more likely than not" be realized. The Exposure Draft and SFAS No. 109 diverged on the issue of the tax rate to use when calculations involving graduated tax rates were necessary. Whereas the Exposure Draft required the use of the highest marginal tax rate for all calculations, SFAS No. 109 required the use of the average tax rate in effect when the deferred tax assets or liabilities were expected to be realized or settled. SFAS No. 109 seemed to resolve the most controversial aspects of SFAS No. 96 while retaining the components of the statement that addressed the significant issues associated with accounting for income taxes. As of 1994, SFAS No. 109 remained the current standard.

Roxanne T. Johnson

Bibliography

Beresford, D.R., L.C. Best, P.W. Craig, and J.V. Weber. *Accounting for Income Tax: A Review of Alternatives*. Stamford, CT: Financial Accounting Standards Board, 1983.

Chaney, P.K., and D.C. Jeter. "Accounting for Income Taxes: Simplicity? Usefulness?" *Accounting Horizons*, June 1989, pp. 6–13.

Johnson, R.T. "A History of Accounting for Income Taxes." In *Historical Perspectives of Selected Financial Accounting*, edited by E.N. Coffman, R.H. Tondkar, and G.J. Previts. Homewood, IL: Irwin, 1993, Ch. 7-2, pp. 271–285.

Klingler, J.P., and J.B. Savage. "Deciphering the New Accounting for Income Tax Rules," *Management Accounting*, August 1988, pp. 32–38.

Kripke, H. "Reflections on the FASB's Conceptual Framework for Accounting and on Auditing," *Journal of Accounting, Auditing, and Finance*, Winter 1989, pp. 3–66.

Means, K.M. "Accounting for Income Taxes: FAS 96—Unexpected Results," *Journal of Accounting, Auditing, and Finance*, Fall 1989, pp. 571–579.

Plunkett, L.M., and D.H. Turner. "Accounting for Income Taxes: The Last Fifty Years," *The Woman CPA*, October 1988, pp. 28–32, 37.

Rayburn, F.R. "A Chronological Review of the Authoritative Literature on Interperiod Tax Allocation, 1940–1985," *Accounting Historians Journal*, Fall 1986, pp. 89–108.

See also ACCOUNTING PRINCIPLES BOARD; ACCOUNTING RESEARCH STUDIES; CONCEPTUAL FRAMEWORK; CONTINUITY; DEPRECIATION; FINANCIAL ACCOUNTING STANDARDS BOARD; LIABILITIES; MATCHING; OBJECTIVITY

Definitions of Accounting

In 1941 the Committee on Terminology of the American Institute of Certified Public Accountants (AICPA), in Accounting Terminology Bulletin No. 1, defined accounting in terms of what accounting did—that is, record, classify, and summarize the transactions of an entity and interpret the results. In 1970 the 1941 definition was superseded by the Accounting Principles Board (APB) of the AICPA in its Statement No. 4, "Basic Concepts and Accounting Principles Underlying Financial Statements of Business Enterprises," which defined accounting in terms of what accounting ought to do—that is, provide information useful in making economic decisions. The difference in these two viewpoints, the difference between accounting being a history of the firm versus a provider of information useful for decision making, is a capsule indication of the conflict that has plagued financial accounting for most of the second half of the twentieth century.

The 1941 Committee on Terminology definition is not significantly different from that of William Andrew Paton, a noted U.S. accounting theorist, in *Accounting* (1924) and other contemporary writers on accounting, and it reflects the beliefs held at that time. The basis of these beliefs was the stewardship function of management, and, therefore, the function and purpose of accounting was to report on this stewardship. It is clear that in 1941 when the definition was formulated, a majority of accountants accepted this view of accounting. If

so, what propelled the departure from this definition? To answer this question requires an analysis of why a consensus was achieved in the first place.

The definition of accounting (or any subject) is not far removed from the theoretical basis underlying that subject. But a theoretical basis of accounting (other than the double entry mechanism) was nonexistent in the early part of the twentieth century. Though accounting was a well-understood ritual by its participants, the application of that ritual to the evolving modern business phenomenon was less understood, as was accounting's relationship to the emerging profession of public accounting. There was a vagueness as to accounting's role (as well as the new public accounting profession's role) in the increasingly complex socioeconomic environment. New phenomena—depreciation, for example—were encountered that created problems and increased the pressures on this relationship.

Though a need for a theoretical basis to resolve these problems was beginning to become evident, it was the stock market crash of 1929, the resultant Securities Acts of 1933 and 1934, and the role of the Securities and Exchange Commission (SEC) that hastened efforts to develop a theoretical foundation. The search was on for principles of accounting that had general acceptance; the anticipation was that such a conceptual foundation would aid in solving current and future problems. Given the tenor of the times, it is not surprising that the stewardship function and the transaction basis formed the core of the official definition that eventually was recognized and promulgated in 1941. (It is important to note that the search for accounting theory was conducted by two different groups: the AICPA, composed largely of practitioners, and the American Accounting Association (AAA), composed largely of academics.)

In a classic article in November 1937 in the *Journal of Accountancy* titled "To What Extent Can the Practice of Accounting be Reduced to Rules and Standards?" Gilbert Byrne, a public accounting practitioner, proposed that accounting and reporting be separated. He was almost alone among writers of his day in making this distinction.

The 1930s also witnessed the general acceptance of historical cost (prompted perhaps by the SEC) and the matching concepts by both practitioners and the academic accounting com-

D

munity. Thus, a consensus was reached on both a theory and a definition of accounting, but the seeds of discord had already been unknowingly sown.

Most of the academic community of the 1940s era accepted the transaction-based view of accounting and continued to do so. This is true of the Paton and A.C. Littleton collaboration *An Introduction to Corporate Accounting Standards* (1940) and Littleton's *Structure of Accounting Theory* (1953). Even those of the academic community who seemed to imply that accounting should report useful information (as the Paton and Littleton monograph also did) made such stipulation within the framework and limitations of transaction-based accounting.

But some in the academic community grew dissatisfied with the theoretical implications of cost-based accounting and its limitations—for example, arbitrary cost allocations. These academics were trained not only in accounting but also in areas such as economics and finance, and they sought to either incorporate these other disciplines within the existing accounting framework or, if need be, create a revolutionary new framework.

With R.J. Chambers's, a noted accounting theorist from Australia, "Blueprint for a Theory of Accounting" in 1955, there began to appear in the accounting literature a thread of argument and research in favor of recognizing that the purpose of financial accounting was to provide information useful in economic decision making. Around this time and into the early 1960s, accounting as an academic discipline began to evolve. This movement, adopting the empirical research paradigm, was given impetus by the new accounting academics and began to gather momentum.

AAA statements on accounting theory (principles) issued in 1936, 1941, and 1957 were all basically in agreement with the old (1941) definition of accounting. Then, in 1966 the AAA announced the radically different *A Statement of Basic Accounting Theory* (ASOBAT). ASOBAT not only defined accounting as a three-phase process that identifies, measures, and communicates economic information that permits informed decisions by users, but it also explicitly stated that "(t)here is no implication that accounting information is necessarily based only on transaction data." The revolution in accounting was becoming widespread.

ASOBAT was soon followed by APB Statement No. 4 in 1970 and the AICPA Study Group on Objectives of Financial Statement's *Objectives of Financial Statements* in 1973, which held the view that the basic objective of financial statements was to provide information that is useful in making economic decisions. It is worth noting that in the latter statement, Byrne's accounting-reporting dichotomy seems to have been implicitly recognized in that the publication focused on reporting—that is, financial statements. During this same period, the pressures of accounting problems on public accounting forced the separation of accounting from public accounting (auditing) as represented by the establishment in 1973 of the Financial Accounting Foundation and the Financial Accounting Standards Board (FASB). The AICPA was dropping out of the accounting-theory endeavor.

The FASB swiftly embarked on its own search for a theoretical basis of accounting in the form of the Conceptual Framework Project. The initial result was FASB Statement of Financial Accounting Concepts (SFAC) No. 1, "Objectives of Financial Reporting by Business Enterprises" (1978), which, like its recent predecessors, asserted that financial reporting should provide information useful in economic decision making and, in addition, be useful in determining present and future cash flows. At this point in time, the concept of usefulness had become well entrenched in authoritative literature.

Clearly, stewardship had been discarded as the primary purpose of accounting by the FASB, and, just as clearly, a view endorsing what accounting "ought to do" was being placed in its stead. This is so because orthodox accounting circa 1978 did not provide information explicitly useful in either making economic decisions or predicting future cash flows. Accounting stood at a point where the authoritative body, the FASB, had discarded the old and embraced the new.

But have accountants in general, academic and practitioner, accepted this change? In the main, the answer is no. Those who learned accounting as a transaction-based discipline seem reluctant to abandon a fundamental belief. Another reason may be the FASB has yet to be able to restructure accounting theory around its definition in such a way that the theory works in practice. Though the FASB has consistently sought to retool the balance sheet since SFAC

No. 1 and subsequent statements, the overall implementation of SFAC No. 1 and what it truly implies has, as of 1994, yet to occur.

Accounting is left with an authoritative definition very similar to a normative theory—that is, a definition of what ought to be, and, along with this, it faces all of the problems inherent in obtaining agreement on a theory of what ought to be. The difficulties regarding accounting-theory acceptance were examined by the AAA in 1977 in its *Statement on Accounting Theory and Theory Acceptance*. The statement's conclusion, which is open to debate, was that theory closure (agreement) cannot be dictated. Agreement is an emotional, not a rational, process. If that conclusion is valid for theory, then it seems reasonable to presume that the conclusion holds for a definition, especially one that is based on or implies a theory.

If agreement cannot be dictated, how might it be achieved, assuming that the FASB is concerned about closure? Time and attrition seem the most likely method. The FASB's conceptual framework (including SFAC No. 1) dominates the theoretical discussion of most textbooks on accounting; this tends to indicate that eventually new generations of accountants will come to accept the new definition and the theory it implies, especially if the old viewpoint is not presented. However, regardless of any theory or definition to the contrary, accounting still proceeds based on transactions and the limitations that this implies.

By incorporating the usefulness criteria in Concept Statement No. 1, the FASB has placed the seeds of revolution in a most visible field. But will the seeds germinate?

The definitions of accounting are inherently intertwined with what accounting is—that is, the definition evolved as accounting itself did (and still does). Perhaps the new definitions, resulting as they did from the revolutionary pressures in accounting, bear witness to a new phenomenon, the rise of a new discipline as different from accounting as sociology is from mathematics.

William Joseph Schrader, a professor of accounting at Pennsylvania State University, in "An Inductive Approach to Accounting Theory" in 1962 said that changing the focal point of accounting from transactions to some other activity can only be done by "changing the character of accounting." Given the new definition of accounting as the process of providing information useful in making economic decisions and predicting future cash flows, accountants are left with the ponderable difficulty of working to accomplish this without yet knowing just what the character of accounting will be.

Carl W. Brewer

Bibliography

American Accounting Association. *Accounting and Reporting Standards for Corporate Financial Statements and Preceding Statements and Supplements*. Evanston, IL: American Accounting Association, 1957.

———. Committee on Concepts and Standards for External Financial Reports. *Statement on Accounting Theory and Theory Acceptance*. Evanston, IL: American Accounting Association, 1977.

———. Committee to Prepare a Statement of Basic Accounting Theory. *A Statement of Basic Accounting Theory*. Evanston, IL: American Accounting Association, 1966.

American Institute of Certified Public Accountants, Accounting Principles Board. "Basic Concepts and Accounting Principles Underlying Financial Statements of Business Enterprises." APB Statement No. 4, 1970. In *APB Accounting Principles*. Vol. 2, *Original Pronouncements as of December 1, 1971*. New York: Commerce Clearing House, 1971.

———. Committee on Terminology, "Review and Resume." Accounting Terminology Bulletin No. 1, 1953. In *APB Accounting Principles*. Vol. 2, *Original Pronouncements as of December 1, 1971*. New York: Commerce Clearing House, 1971.

Beaver, W.H. *Financial Reporting: An Accounting Revolution*. Englewood Cliffs, NJ: Prentice-Hall, 1981.

Chambers, R.J. "Blueprint for a Theory of Accounting," *Accounting Research*, January 1955, pp. 17–25.

Financial Accounting Standards Board. "Objectives of Financial Reporting by Business Enterprises." Statement of Financial Accounting Concepts No. 1. Stamford, CT: FASB, 1978.

Flamholtz, E. "The Role of Academic Accounting Research: An Historical Perspective." In *Accounting Research: Bridging the Gap between Theory and Practice*, edited by E.G. Flamholtz and J.L. Arnold, pp. 9–26. Selected papers presented at the UCLA Accounting-Information Systems Research Program Conference, May 7, 1976. Los Angeles: Graduate School of Management, University of California, Los Angeles, 1976.

Ijiri, Y. *Theory of Accounting Measurement.* Studies in Accounting Research. Sarasota, FL: American Accounting Association, 1975.

Schrader, W.L. "An Inductive Approach to Accounting Theory," *Accounting Review*, October 1962, pp. 645–649.

See also *A Statement of Basic Accounting Theory;* ACCOUNTING PRINCIPLES BOARD; AMERICAN ACCOUNTING ASSOCIATION; AMERICAN INSTITUTE OF CERTIFIED PUBLIC ACCOUNTANTS; *An Introduction to Corporate Accounting Standards;* CHAMBERS, RAYMOND JOHN; CONCEPTUAL FRAMEWORK; FINANCIAL ACCOUNTING STANDARDS BOARD; HISTORICAL COST; LITTLETON, A.C.; MATCHING; NORMATIVE ACCOUNTING; PATON, WILLIAM ANDREW; SCHRADER, WILLIAM JOSEPH; SECURITIES AND EXCHANGE COMMISSION; STEWARDSHIP

Demski, Joel S. (1940–)

Prolific, creative accounting scholar and key proponent of the "economics of information" perspective on accounting, Joel S. Demski pioneered the use of formal deductive techniques in accounting theory. Hallmarks of his work are precisely specified models, formal definitions, and rigorous, mathematical proofs. Demski uses these methods to study a variety of topics, including information processing in financial markets, the value of information in competitive contexts, hierarchical incentive structures, the theory of cost measurement, the concept of income, and the process of setting accounting standards. His 1980 book, *Information Analysis*, provides an elementary introduction to his approach and methods.

Demski views accounting systems as social constructions, and he adopts the position of social scientist, rather than inventor or advocate. As an accounting scholar, he seeks to explain the choices made among alternative accounting methods and systems using the mathematical economists' description of human behavior as expected utility maximization. Because he sees the essence of accounting as information production, Demski considers choices among accounting systems as essentially choices among the information structures induced by them. In turn, information is viewed as valuable only to the extent that it improves decisions. Thus, another hallmark of Demski's work is the study of accounting choices as integral parts of some broader decision context. The representation of preferences by expected utility maximization is used to study both the accounting choices and the underlying choices, the improvement of which is the target of the accounting decisions.

An example is Demski's analysis of accounting standards. Accounting policymakers had sought to capture good accounting choices in a list of attributes such as relevance, timeliness, objectivity, and the like. Building on the work of the American statistician David Blackwell, who was interested in game theory and decision analysis, Demski noted that the only such criterion guaranteed to reflect the preferences of users of information is a measure of the amount of information, called fineness, contained in an accounting system. Fineness, however, is an incomplete relation. Some information systems convey different things, rather than more or less information about the same things. Therefore, no list of attributes specified independently of users' decision problems could capture their preferences over accounting systems. Further, given any two accounting systems not ordered by fineness, there exist users' decision problems in which each of the two systems is the preferred one.

Demski also applies these techniques to provide a framework for studying the performance-evaluation and control aspects of accounting. The efforts of William Joseph Vatter from the University of Chicago, Charles T. Horngren from Stanford University, and others provide a foundation for studying accounting in models of planning decisions like capital budgeting and cost-volume-profits contexts. Demski has been instrumental in extending models of accounting to include the control aspects budgeting, variance analysis, and divisional-performance measurement. In the models of control problems, two or more decision makers, modeled as expected utility maximizers, interact. If information about the various decision makers' actions is incomplete and their preferences diverge, an incentive problem results. This allows the study of accounting systems and methods that help mitigate these incentive problems.

Demski received early training in industrial engineering at the University of Michigan, where he also earned an M.B.A. with High Distinction in 1963. He earned his doctorate from the University of Chicago in 1967. Demski has served on the faculties of Columbia, Stanford and Yale Universities, holding the prestigious Paul E. Holden and Joan E. Horngren professorships at Stanford and the Milton Steinbach professorship at Yale. Demski's research twice won the American Institute of Certified Public Accountants (AICPA)-American Accounting Association (AAA) Notable Contributions to Accounting Research Award, and in 1986 he was given the Outstanding Educator Award by the American Accounting Association. In 1989, in recognition of his teaching at a New Haven high school, Demski received the Elm and Ivy Award for Town-Gown Relations from the New Haven Foundation. From 1975 to 1978, he directed the doctoral program at Stanford's Graduate School of Business.

Rick Antle

Bibiliography

Baiman, S., and J.S. Demski. "Economically Optimal Performance Evaluation and Control Systems," *Journal of Accounting Research,* Supplement, 1980, pp. 184–220.

Blackwell, D., and M.A. Girshick. *Theory of Games and Statistical Decisions.* New York: Wiley, 1954.

Demski, J.S. "The General Impossibility of Normative Accounting Standards," *Accounting Review,* October 1973, pp. 718–723.

———. *Information Analysis.* 2nd ed. Reading, MA: Addison-Wesley, 1980.

Demski, J.S., and G.A. Feltham. *Cost Determination: A Conceptual Approach.* Ames, IA: Iowa State University Press, 1976.

See also AGENCY THEORY; AMERICAN ACCOUNTING ASSOCIATION; BEAVER, WILLIAM; DAVIDSON, SIDNEY; HORNGREN, CHARLES T.; VATTER, WILLIAM JOSEPH

De Paula, Frederic Rudolf Mackley (1882–1954)

If the accounting profession is to remain a viable part of society, its members must include individuals who can recognize the need for and initiate positive change. These individuals must be dedicated, articulate, analytical, and be recognized by their peers. Frederic Rudolf Mackley De Paula was such a person.

De Paula practiced public accounting from 1909 until 1929, except for government service during World War I. After the war, he also joined the staff of the London School of Economics. In 1926 De Paula was awarded the Sir Ernest Cassel Chair of Accountancy and Business Methods.

In late 1929, De Paula departed academe and public practice for the position of controller of finance of Dunlop Rubber Company. He remained with Dunlop, except for a leave of absence to serve in the British War Office, until 1941. He then became a senior executive with Harding, Tilton and Hartley, from which he retired in 1945.

His professional service included directorships of a number of companies, and he served as an officer of both the British Institute of Management and the Federation of British Industries. He enjoyed widespread recognition as a reputable university teacher and practitioner, an effective speaker, a strategic thinker, and an effective industrial financial executive.

In addition to contributed articles to professional journals, he authored a classic, *Principles of Auditing,* in 1914. *Developments in Accounting*, a compendium of selected articles and talks, was published in 1948 and reprinted in 1978. It is evident that De Paula recognized the need to improve corporate reporting in the early 1940s and so testified before appropriate professional and legislative committees.

De Paula was a man ahead of his time. In his career, he (1) initiated asset and liability current and noncurrent disclosures in 1929 for Dunlop Rubber (as opposed to the traditional legalistic form then in vogue); (2) proposed the elimination of secret reserves; (3) correctly indicated, repeatedly, that excess conservatism is misleading; (4) focused on the need for precise, uniform terminology; (5) championed disclosure of fixed-asset historical cost and accumulated depreciation (although he advocated separate recording of obsolescence); (6) advocated market value for securities held for investment; (7) preferred precise delineation of income tax expense—that is, matching expense with revenue in the period in which revenue was earned; (8) recognized the need for consistency between periods; (9) pioneered presentation of consolidated financial statements; (10) initiated disclosure of declared stockholder dividends on the balance sheet; and (11) recognized that stockholders should receive information, not legal documentation.

De Paula relied upon his readings of accounting research published in the United States. This influenced his advocacy of the study of accounting at universities as opposed to existing practice, which relied upon practical experience. In England in the 1920s, such a recommendation was considered heretical.

Prior to the early 1940s, the balance sheet was considered the key financial statement. Based upon his writings and statements, it is fair to say that De Paula was at least partially responsible for making the income statement more important in Great Britain. He also wrote and spoke about segment disclosure, equity method, foreign-currency translations, and the need for formal, enunciated accounting principles (conceptual framework). De Paula deplored the lack of an authoritative rule-making body, and he likely would have been an avid supporter of the Financial Accounting Standards Board.

De Paula made invaluable contributions to accounting knowledge. Further, his work remains valid today. For example, Chapter 10 of *Developments in Accounting* opens with this sentence: "It may be said that the interpretation of accounts is the art of making figures speak and figures speak to those who understand the language."

John B. Sperry

Bibliography

De Paula, F.R.M. *Developments in Accounting.* London: Pitman, 1948. Reprint. New York: Arno Press, 1978.

De Paula, F.R.M., and F.C. De Paula. *Principles of Auditing: A Practical Manual for Students and Practitioners.* 14th ed. London: Pitman, 1970.

Zeff, S.A. "A Profile of F.R.M. De Paula," *Accounting Historians Journal,* 1974–1976, vol. 1 (1974), p. 31.

See also CHARTERED ACCOUNTANTS EXAMINATIONS IN ENGLAND AND WALES; INCOME STATEMENT/INCOME ACCOUNT

Depreciation

Conventional accounting defines depreciation as the process of allocating the cost of long-lived assets to the periods that benefit from their use, but depreciation as a cost allocation has been part of the accounting process for less than 100 years.

Pre-Nineteenth-Century Development

One of the first references to depreciation dates back to the Roman Empire during the reign of Augustus Caesar (27 B.C.–A.D. 14). Vitruvius, a Roman writer on architecture, described a process of valuing masonry "party-walls" that is perhaps the first suggestion of a straight-line depreciation concept. He suggested that one-eighteenth of the cost of the wall should be deducted for each year it had stood, based on the assumption that the wall had a life of 80 years.

Interestingly, Luca Pacioli, the man given credit as the first to describe modern double entry accounting in the late fifteenth century, did not describe a method of depreciation. However, by the sixteenth and seventeenth centuries, bookkeeping texts of accounts made some direct provision for recognizing changes in the value of long-lived assets. A.C. Littleton, a professor of accounting at the University of Illinois, in *Accounting Evolution to 1900* (1933), referred to these references as the "proprietor's" view of depreciation. At this time, there appears to have been two ways to look at the matter of depreciating assets and depreciation itself. Depreciating property was considered the unsold merchandise of a simple proprietor, and depreciation was related to the maintenance of long-lived assets.

Littleton also made reference to a bookkeeping text, *Debtor and Creditor Made Easie,* published in 1682 (2nd ed.) by Stephen Monteage, from England, in which a credit was made in a "horse" account, with the notation of "lost by their use." The idea of depreciation was beginning to find its way into the accounts of proprietors, but the asset accounting and related transactions were all found in one account. The depreciation factor was not separately recognized as a cost of operations resulting from the consumption of fixed assets but was considered a loss in asset value.

By the eighteenth century, depreciation was still being treated as a valuation process. In *Bookkeeping Methodiz'd,* published in 1757, John Mair, an accounting text writer from Scotland, illustrated the use of asset accounts in his instruction to pupils of the time. Besides the cost or value of the asset, entries for repairs or other expenses were entered into the debit side of the asset account. Any profits arising from the asset were entered on the credit side of the account. Long-lived assets were treated as mixed accounts much like the present-day treatment of supplies and inventory accounts. During this period, there is no record of depreciation as an expense.

Nineteenth-Century Development

During the early nineteenth century, depreciation continued to be recorded as a decline in value treated by the inventory method described above. However, as the nineteenth century progressed, the concept of depreciation emerged as a "cost of production." Manufacturers' schedules of the time accounted for the use of tools and machinery when computing the cost of manufacturing engines.

In an 1817 text, *Essai sur la tenus Livres d'un Manufacturies,* by Anselme Payen, a French accounting writer and industrialist, a cost computation for a glue factory contained an amount representing a decline in value of long-lived assets. A boiler account recorded depreciation as a cost of production. Depreciation was still carried in the asset account in the "inventory method," but instead of being charged to profit or loss, it was charged to a cost account. Similar treatment was accorded other assets used in the business.

As the nineteenth century progressed, many factors combined to alter the concept of depreciation. The industrial revolution gained momentum, and greater amounts of capital were invested in long-lived assets. In "The Development of Company Accounting Conventions" in 1961, B.S. Yamey, an English expert in the history of accounting, declared that the advent of general liability at this time gave rise to many of today's accounting conventions, including depreciation. Previously, a businessman who was closely and continuously involved with his own business operations was unlikely to be concerned with periodic calculations of his firm's profits.

As a consequence of the greater capital investment and the emergence of absentee owners, more sophisticated reporting techniques were needed to inform shareholders and to attract new investors. In his 1970 Ph.D. thesis and 1988 book, "The Evolution of Selected Annual Corporate Financial Reporting Practices in Canada," G.J. Murphy, a professor of accounting from Canada, summarized these new concerns: "Early depreciation theory evolved out of a concern for the inter-related concepts of capi-

tal maintenance, asset replacement and dividend distribution."

Perhaps nowhere did these interrelated concepts become as evident as in the railway industry, which expanded rapidly during this period. Stockholders had primary interest in the valuation of assets as these valuations affected income and related dividends. Management was concerned with the problems of asset valuation as it related to the maintenance of capital and competitive position. Articles of this period appearing in railroad journals, both in Britain and the United States, suggested that railroad managers needed to be concerned with carefully and periodically ascertaining the degree of wear and tear on their assets so that only bonafide net income would be apportioned to the shareholders. However, by charging repairs and replacements to expense, they considered depreciation provided for. It was thought at this time that if repairs and maintenance were undertaken properly, assets would be in as good condition at the end of the year as they were at the beginning, and wear and tear would be accounted for.

Twentieth-Century Development

Although railway as well as utility companies tended to feel that depreciation was looked after with proper repairs and replacements, other views on how to treat depreciation were beginning to appear by the late nineteenth and early twentieth century. The idea that a yearly deduction from the original cost of an asset should be made to allow for deterioration or wear and tear is found in the texts and journals of the early 1900s.

As the 1900s advanced, writers frequently discussed depreciation concepts. Due to the advancements being made in production technology and marketing processes, even larger investments in long-lived assets were required. Furthermore, an increase in the use of the corporate form of business required reports on stewardship. The governments of the time began to increase their control over the business environment, as well as enact tax legislation that focused on income measurement. This interest in income determination consequently focused attention on the depreciation practices of the time.

The modern-day components of depreciation, such as wear and tear, the passage of time, and obsolescence, began to be recognized in the early 1900s. By 1907 the Interstate Commerce

D

Commission, which controlled railway rate structures, revised its system of account classifications to include a provision for depreciation of equipment.

Although the accounting profession clearly recognized depreciation as a cost of doing business, those outside the profession did not formally recognize the concept until 1909. In that year, the courts of the United States ruled on the question of whether current consumers should pay for the costs of wasting assets as part of their rates for utility service. U.S. Supreme Court Justice William Henry Moody, in *Knoxville v. Knoxville Water Company* 212 US1, 53L Ed. 371 (1909), stated that plants begin to depreciate in value as soon as they are put into operation. Furthermore, he ruled, before a final determination of profit is made, a company is entitled to withhold enough income to provide for current repairs as well as the future replacement of assets when they reach the end of their lives. This case was also discussed in an editorial in the *Engineering Record* of February 20, 1909.

Perhaps as important to the development of the concept of depreciation as the court decisions that favored its recognition was the impact of income tax laws. In the United States in 1909, and in Canada in 1917, tax legislation recognized depreciation as a bonafide expense deduction in computing taxable income. This recognition began to shift the concern regarding depreciation from "why" to "how."

Logically, the recognition of depreciation in tax regulation and by the regulatory institutions should have led to a general acceptance of depreciation as a cost of production and to an agreement on acceptable practices. This was not the case. Practices of the railways and the regulated industries diverged concerning the systematic write-off of plant assets. Also, nonregulated businesses held the opinion that appreciation of assets looked after any depreciation effects.

At this time, an account title, "reserve for depreciation," was created that resulted in confusion regarding the concept of depreciation. Businesses, which finally accepted the practice of recognizing depreciation, implemented "secret reserves" that were actual funds set aside for asset replacement. The journals of the first and second decades of the 1900s are replete with articles on how to calculate the amount of monies needed for replacement using the sinking-fund method. However, businessmen gradually began to realize that they could usually receive a greater return on their replacement funds if they invested these monies in productive assets in their own businesses as opposed to outside funds. When the term "reserve" was removed from the account title, the idea that depreciation was a method to set aside funds for asset replacement faded.

The advent of higher taxes resulting from World War I further encouraged businesses to recognize depreciation as a legitimate cost of production. Whether depreciation was an allocation or valuation process was still debated. When the accounting emphasis was on the balance sheet, the focus of depreciation was on the valuation of the assets of a business. As the focus in accounting began to shift to the income statement, depreciation began to be recognized as a cost of operations. Assets began to be looked upon as services required to generate revenue, and the cost of these services needed to be allocated to the periods receiving their benefit. Accountants now viewed income as the end result of revenue recognition according to certain criteria coupled with the appropriate matching of expenses with those revenues.

In 1953 the Committee on Terminology of the American Institute of Certified Public Accountants (AICPA), in Accounting Terminology Bulletin No. 1, "Review and Résumé," defined depreciation as a system of accounting that was aimed at distributing the cost or other basic value of tangible capital assets, less salvage value (if any), over the estimated useful life of the unit (which may be a group of assets) in a systematic and rational manner. Depreciation was finally defined as a process of cost allocation, not a method of asset valuation.

However, the late 1960s and onward saw both accounting practitioners and academics questioning the assumptions and estimates that allocation theory required. Arthur L. Thomas polarized the accounting writers of the time when he suggested that accounting allocations were both arbitrary (decided at random) and incorrigible (incapable of verification).

In the 1990s, as in the 1960s, most accountants would agree that accounting allocations are problematic. However, allocation theory provides the income measurement that users depend on for decision making in today's business environment, and depreciation is fully accepted as a legitimate allocation.

Methods of Depreciation

With depreciation accepted as a legitimate allocation, twentieth-century accountants focused on the methods of allocation. Allocating the cost or other basic value of a long-lived asset, less its salvage or residual value, over its useful life in a rational and systematic manner involves decisions that require the prediction of future events. As accountants are not clairvoyant, these decisions require numerous estimates and predictions.

Based on the cost, revenue, and matching principles of conventional financial accounting, several depreciation methods are generally accepted. However, the method of depreciation used should reflect the economic reality of an asset's contribution to the revenue-producing process of the accounting period.

By the second and third decade of the century, accountants began to compare and contrast the merits of various depreciation methods. The most commonly accepted methods of depreciation in the 1990s can be characterized as straight line, accelerated, units of activity, group and corporate, retirement and replacement, and compound interest. The most often used are the straight-line method, which allocates cost evenly over time, and accelerated methods ("sum of the year's digits" and declining balance), which attempt to equalize the total annual charge for depreciation and maintenance.

Income tax legislation, which so greatly influenced the acceptance of depreciation in the early twentieth century, continued to influence the method of depreciation in the mid-1900s. In Canada, although quite briefly, and in the United States, income tax laws demanded that if an accelerated form of depreciation were used to calculate taxable income, it must also be used in the financial-statement presentation. Since 1940, the method of depreciation used to calculate taxable income (capital cost allowance) is unrelated to the method or methods used to calculate financial-statement net income as noted by Richard Vangermeersch from the University of Rhode Island. This difference is one of the major contributors to the deferred tax credits and debits that are seen on present-day balance sheets.

Accounting research in depreciation is, for the most part, aimed at generating new depreciation methods that more realistically reflect an asset's contribution to the revenue-generating process. Sophisticated probabilistic theory that attempts to take into account the expected values of depreciation estimates, game theory approaches that attempt to account for the interaction between assets in the revenue-producing stream, and current or market-based methods that abandon the historical cost-theory are just a few areas in which depreciation research has been focused since the early 1950s.

Angela M. Downey

Bibliography

Baxter, W.T. *Depreciation*. London: Sweet and Maxwell, 1971.

"Depreciation of Plant and Fair Rates for Public Service," *Engineering Record*, February 20, 1909, pp. 197–198.

Hatfield, H.R. "What They Say about Depreciation," *Accounting Review*, March 1936, p. 19.

Littleton, A.C. *Accounting Evolution to 1900*. New York: American Institute Publishing, 1933.

Murphy, G.J. *The Evolution of Selected Annual Corporate Financial Reporting Practices in Canada, 1900–1970*. New York: Garland, 1988.

Schroeder, R.G., L.D. McCullers, and M. Clark. *Accounting Theory: Text and Readings*. 4th ed. New York: John Wiley & Sons, 1991.

Thomas, A.L. *The Allocation Problem in Financial Accounting Theory*. Studies in Accounting Research No. 3. Sarasota, FL: American Accounting Association, 1969.

Vangermeersch, R. "A Historical Overview of Depreciation: U.S. Steel, 1902–1970," *Mississippi Valley Journal of Business and Economics*, Winter 1971–1972, pp. 56–74.

Yamey, B.S. "The Development of Company Accounting Conventions," *Accountant's Magazine (England)*, October 1961, pp. 753–763.

See also BABBAGE, CHARLES; BRIEF, RICHARD P.; CAPITAL MAINTENANCE; CONSERVATISM; CONTINUITY; DEFERRED INCOME TAX ACCOUNTING; DICKINSON, ARTHUR LOWES; DICKSEE, LAWRENCE; DOUBLE ACCOUNT METHOD; FIXED ASSETS; HISTORICAL COST; INCOME TAXATION IN THE UNITED STATES; LADELLE, O.G.; MAY, GEORGE OLIVER; MONTEAGE, STEPHEN; NEW YORK STOCK EX-

CHANGE; PAYEN, ANSELME; PHILIPS INDUS-
TRIES (N.V.); RAILROAD ACCOUNTING (U.S.);
RETAINED EARNINGS APPROPRIATIONS;
SINGLE ACCOUNT METHOD; STUDY GROUP
ON BUSINESS INCOME'S *FIVE MONOGRAPHS ON
BUSINESS INCOME;* THOMAS'S *THE ALLOCATION
PROBLEM IN FINANCIAL ACCOUNTING THEORY;*
UNITED STATES STEEL CORPORATION;
VITRUVIUS

Devine, Carl (1911–)

Carl Devine is perhaps the most formidable
intellectual in the history of accounting
thought. Written over four decades, Devine's
five-volume *Essays in Accounting Theory* is a
fascinating voyage through the history of ideas
in the twentieth century, ideas ranging from
mathematics to poetry, all situated in a rich
and uncontrived context of accounting and the
human sciences. This massive tome earned him
Outstanding Contribution to the Accounting
Literature Awards from both the American
Institute of Certified Public Accountants and
the American Accounting Association in 1985.
Devine also received the 1983 American Accounting Association's Outstanding Educator
Award.

Valedictorian, he received a B.S. with majors in mathematics and physical science from
Davis and Elkins College in 1935. He received
an M.B.A. degree in 1938 as well as the seventh
Ph.D. ever granted in business administration
from the University of Michigan in 1940. Important mentors for Devine as a student included William Andrew Paton, a leading accounting theorist, and A.P. Ushenko, a logician
in philosophy.

Like his intellect, his reading habits, and
his pen, Devine's professional life has been no-
madic. It includes professorial stints at 10
universities, with the longest tenures at the
University of Southern California, the University of California at Berkeley, and Florida State
University.

The eclectic style of Devine's writing be-
trays a consistent allegiance to American pragmatism, particularly the pragmatism of John
Dewey. Even more so than Dewey, Devine never
takes rigid, unequivocal stances. This sort of
pragmatic intellectual flexibility has never been
popular in accounting thought. It has been and
still is true that the academically *chic* approach
to accounting theory has been to rigidly and
often dogmatically argue for the *universal* pri-

ority of this or that accounting alternative, this
or that paradigm of theory and research, and
this or that singular goal or value as the moral
support for accounting. But Devine—the pragmatist, the organic intellectual, and the eclectic
student—dialectically tacks in and out of a variety of claims and counterclaims, showing how
situational aspects of experience demand that
accounting practice and accounting thought
remain malleable if they are to remain valuable
to humans with diverse and conflicting needs in
ever-changing economic situations.

Devine's pragmatism can be construed in
three thematic ways, one practical, one epistemological, and one moral. At a practical level,
accounting choices are seen as responses to situations in which uses for accounting—stewardship, control, prediction—vary with the ebb
and flow of interpersonal relations, economic
conditions, and broader moral, political, social,
and institutional settings. Preference for accounting alternatives is situationally and historically contingent for Devine, and he illustrates that contingency across a variety of quite
specific practical accounting concerns like inventory valuation, depreciation, and income
measurement. In this way, though with a much
less constructed vision, Devine is a precursor to
the contemporary views of agency theorists and
critical theorists who ground accounting choice
in political-economic experience.

At an epistemological level, Devine anticipated the post-Kuhnian insight into the poverty
of grounding the validity of knowledge claims
in a singular, overreaching commitment to this
or that paradigm or methodology. In the early
essays, there is a celebration of the possibilities
of science as a model for accounting. Indeed, the
level of sophistication that adheres to Devine's
three-decade-old understanding of science sur-
passes most of what one reads in contemporary
methodological papers in accounting. Through
appreciating the value of a credibly modest
positivism (perhaps an operationalism), Devine
holds fiercely to the pragmatists' interest in a
science of *experience.* This focus on experience
leads to some serious interest in gestalt psychology and various phenomenological philosophies. In a likewise pragmatic way, Devine wel-
comes epistemological paradigms that are not
"scientific"—the methods of science are ill
suited to handle the full range of consequences
of accounting for human experience. More,
rather than fewer, approaches to knowledge are
necessary if all of the consequences of account-

ing for human experience are to be subjects of academic inquiry.

Again like Dewey, Devine gives moral concerns at least as much importance as epistemological ones. Knowledge of things human is to be governed by an overriding fixation upon the consequences of knowledge for the human pursuit of the good and just life. Thus, a science indifferent to, or even antagonistic toward, questions of values ethics and virtues—however these might be construed—is a very partial, if not simply false, science: The human world and the world of accounting are saturated with moral terms and moral dimensions of experience. To deny these terms and dimensions a place at the intellectual table is to ignore an important part of accounting.

It would be wrong to conclude that Devine is simply an accounting disciple of Dewey. There are two major differences. First, Devine has more appreciation for order, stability, and equilibrium than does Dewey. That is why, for example, operationalist variants of pragmatic arguments are attractive to him. However, Devine never surrenders his situationalist perspective to the advocates of monolithic systems, grand theories, and universalized models. Second, Devine is less dogmatic than Dewey with respect to values and their place in education. Far from a moral relativist, Devine nonetheless understands that the traditional social-democratic, American values so dear to Dewey may or may not be the "best" moral posture in all situations (including the classroom).

This admittedly philosophical approach to Devine's work should not cause the reader to lose sight of Devine's own focus upon very specific, practical issues in accounting. Perhaps that is his unique talent: to be able to take the most mundane of accounting issues and overlay the most abstract ideas upon them in a richly synthetic and intelligible way. Most "philosophical" theorists in accounting cannot donate that sort of accounting specificity to their writings; most "practical" theorists falter on the shore of philosophical ideas, ideas about which they know little.

In 1994 Devine is actively engaged in the writing of volumes six and seven of *Essays in Accounting Theory*. A rough draft of volume six has been circulated to friends in 1993. In addition to the *Essays*, he has written numerous articles published in *Accounting Review* over five decades, as well as several books, mono-

graphs, and book chapters concerned with both managerial and financial-accounting issues. Scholars interested in the development of accounting thought in the second half of the twentieth century would do well to focus on systematic study of Carl Devine.

C. Edward Arrington

Bibliography

Anton, H.R., E.H. Caplan, and C.P. Stickney. "Review of *Essays in Accounting Theory*," *Accounting Review*, April 1987, pp. 312–315.

Arrington, E. "Review Essay: Reflections on a Renaissance Scholar: Carl Devine's *Essays in Accounting Theory*, Volume I-V," *Accounting Historians Journal*, Spring 1988, pp. 135–140.

Devine, C.T. *Essays in Accounting Theory,* Studies in Accounting Research No. 22, American Accounting Association, 5 volumes in 2 books. Sarasota, FL: American Accounting Association, 1985.

Ushenko, A.P. *Power and Events: An Essay on Dynamics in Philosophy*. Princeton, NJ: Princeton University Press, 1946. Reprint. New York: Greenwood Publishers, 1969.

See also AMERICAN ACCOUNTING ASSOCIATION; PATON, WILLIAM ANDREW; SOCIAL RESPONSIBILITIES OF ACCOUNTANTS; STEWARDSHIP

Dickinson, Arthur Lowes (1859–1935)

Arthur Lowes Dickinson was born in London, educated at Cambridge University, and began practice as a chartered accountant in 1887. In 1901 he was appointed managing partner of the American branch of Price Waterhouse and Company and remained in the United States until 1913. Dickinson became a U.S. citizen, qualified as a certified public accountant and helped organize the accounting profession in America. His writings dramatically raised the level of American accounting discourse. He argued for the exclusion from product costs of rent and interest expenditures, on the grounds that these were distributions of profit. He believed that, in addition to normal depreciation charges, a depreciation reserve should be established to provide for asset replacements. Dickinson invented the format of today's income statement. That format was revised and published by the Federal Reserve Board in *Uniform Accounting* (1917) and was updated in *Verification of Financial Statements* (1929).

Accounting Practice and Procedure (1914) was Dickinson's attempt to sum up "twenty-five years of practice on both sides of the Atlantic." It was a compendium of knowledge that ranged over the known world of accounting. Besides asset valuation and income measurement, Dickinson discussed uniformity in financial reporting, adequate disclosure, estimates of future earnings, interim statements, fluctuations in foreign exchange, depreciation, consolidated statements, the impact of English law and accounting methods on American practice, cost accounting, and the duties and responsibilities of auditors. His book remains a time capsule of early twentieth-century accounting thought.

Michael Chatfield

Bibliography

Dickinson, A.L. *Accounting Practice and Procedure*. New York: Ronald Press, 1914. Reprint. Houston: Scholars Book, 1975.

"Uniform Accounting," *Journal of Accountancy*, June 1917, pp. 401–433.

"Verification of Financial Statements," Washington, D.C.: U.S. Government Printing Office, 1929.

See also ACCOUNTING HALL OF FAME; AMERICAN INSTITUTE OF CERTIFIED PUBLIC ACCOUNTANTS; BIG EIGHT ACCOUNTING FIRMS; CAPITAL MAINTENANCE; CONSOLIDATED FINANCIAL STATEMENTS; DEPRECIATION; IMPUTED INTEREST ON CAPITAL; MACNEAL, KENNETH; PIXLEY, FRANCIS WILLIAM; SANDERS, THOMAS HENRY; TREASURY STOCK; *Uniform Accounting;* UNITED STATES STEEL CORPORATION

Dicksee, Lawrence (1864–1932)

Lawrence Dicksee was born in London and grew up in a modestly successful family of artists. In 1881, at age 17, he became an articled accounting clerk, and in 1886 he qualified by examination for membership in the Institute of Chartered Accountants in England and Wales. He then set up his own accounting practice in Cardiff, where he also lectured on bookkeeping at the local technical schools. In 1902 he was appointed to the chair of accounting at the University of Birmingham. In the same year he became a part time lecturer at the London School of Economics, where he continued to teach until his retirement in 1926.

Dicksee was among the most prolific accounting writers of his time, with an astonishing range of interests and expertise. The best known of his 17 books was *Auditing* (1892), which went through 19 British editions and was the model for Robert H. Montgomery's *Auditing Theory and Practice* (1912) in the United States. Dicksee was also the first accountant to write books on goodwill and depreciation. He published specialized works on foreign currency translation, auctioneer's accounts, solicitor's accounts, gas accounts, hotel accounts, mine accounting and management, and garage accounts. His book on business organization and office management anticipated the revolution in information processing by almost 50 years.

Dicksee's reputation today is based mainly on his theoretical writings. Unlike most of his contemporaries, he explored accounting problems in terms of what he called "first principles." He made one of the first systematic efforts to formulate a rational basis for asset valuation and income measurement.

Before considering Dicksee's proposals, one must understand accounting practice as he found it. In the late nineteenth century, most manufacturing firms still used the single account or inventory method of asset valuation, which priced fixed assets as if they were unsold merchandise. Assets were appraised or revalued at the end of each accounting period, and for most firms using this method, profit was the change in value of all assets from all causes. No distinction was made between capital and revenue expenditures, between current and long term assets, or between inflationary increases and real income.

English railroads and certain public utilities were required by law to value their assets by the double account method. Acquisition costs of long-lived assets were capitalized and never depreciated. Because such firms had to maintain fixed assets permanently, asset values were assumed to remain constant so long as the items were kept in good working order. This made it natural to capitalize asset betterments and additions, while charging replacements and repairs directly to expense. Since the timing of asset replacements was a managerial option, so logically was the depreciation charge. If taken at all, depreciation was seen not as an operating expense but as a holding back of revenue to replace lost asset value.

Dicksee's immediate target was the double account method, which he criticized for failing to require depreciation and for its assumption that capital consumption would not exceed the rate of asset replacement. He reasoned that the main goal of most firms is to continue in business, and that asset valuation should reflect this fact. Even companies that did not take depreciation faced the certainty of asset revaluation when assets were sold or the firm changed hands. So it was not simply the current prices of assets—liquidation prices—which mattered, but also these future prices. To anticipate them as nearly as possible, Dicksee believed assets had to be valued "as a going concern," meaning "at such value as they would stand in the books if proper depreciation had been provided for" (*Auditing*, 5th ed., 1902).

Dicksee's assumption of indefinite life for the corporation also ruled out the use of liquidation prices in the balance sheets of manufacturing companies. If a business maintained its fixed assets permanently, it seemed illogical to determine profits by annual appraisals based on resale values. Since there was no intention to sell such assets, fluctuations in their market prices could not be considered gains or losses. Long term assets should be valued at acquisition cost less depreciation. Dicksee's justification for ignoring value changes not caused by "time and wear" was that asset realization was not contemplated. Such assets were bought to be used, not sold at a profit.

However, the logic of business continuity required that current assets be priced at net realizable value. Because they were purchased or manufactured to be sold, they were sensitive to value changes, and any fall in price, reasoned Dicksee, ought to be booked as a loss. By the same logic, asset appreciations should be credited to income, but Dicksee was not quite that bold. Since before goods were sold "there must always be a doubt as to whether any such realization has actually occurred, it is only prudent to postpone taking credit for the assumed profit until such time as it has actually been earned" (*Advanced Accounting*, 1903).

At the turn of the century, these ideas were revolutionary. That they now seem orthodox is evidence of their general acceptance. Dicksee more than any other individual established the continuity principle as a meaningful accounting concept. In so doing, he helped shift accounting attention from the strictly historical view of valuation implied by liquidation pricing and conservatism to the view that asset values depend on future events. This in turn laid the groundwork for a synthesis of other accounting principles—historical cost, objectivity, matching, and realization—around the going concern concept.

Michael Chatfield

Bibliography

Brief, R., ed. *Dicksee's Contribution to Accounting Theory and Practice*. New York: Arno Press, 1980.

Kitchen, J. "Fixed Asset Values: Ideas on Depreciation 1892–1914," *Accounting and Business Research*, Autumn 1979, pp. 281–291.

———. "Lawrence Dicksee, Depreciation, and the Double Account System." In *Debits, Credits, Finance, and Profits*, edited by H. Edey and B.S. Yamey. London: Sweet and Maxwell, 1974.

Kitchen, J., and R.H. Parker. *Accounting Thought and Education: Six English Pioneers*. London: Institute of Chartered Accountants in England and Wales, 1980. Reprint. New York: Garland, 1984, pp. 51–63.

See also CONTINUITY; DEPRECIATION; DEVINE, CARL; FIXED ASSETS; GOODWILL; HISTORICAL COST; INSTITUTE OF CHARTERED ACCOUNTANTS IN ENGLAND AND WALES; MATCHING; MONTGOMERY, ROBERT HIESTER; OBJECTIVITY; PIXLEY, FRANCIS WILLIAM; REALIZATION; SINGLE ACCOUNT METHOD

Direct Costing

The primary objective of accounting is to provide information to investors, creditors, management, regulatory agencies, and others for decision making. Various accounting practices, based on the same accounting concepts and principles, have been developed to satisfy the multiple and changing needs of the users of accounting reports. "Direct" (variable) and "absorption" (full) costing are two such accounting practices. Controversy continues to exist as to which of these two costing methods is better for decision making and for reporting to the users of accounting information.

A Historical Perspective

In the early stages of accounting development, accountants utilized prime costs (direct materials and direct labor) as the only product costs. By the turn of the twentieth century, accountants determined product costs by charging all manufacturing costs—direct material, direct labor, and both direct and indirect manufacturing (factory) overheads—to the product. This is commonly understood as absorption costing. Thus, under absorption costing, the cost of inventory of a finished product includes portions of both variable and nonvariable manufacturing overheads, and the income of a firm fluctuates more as a function of production than the sale of a product. The method has been influenced by two objectives: (1) to provide information for product pricing, and (2) to provide information on cost of goods sold and inventory for financial reporting.

However, the product costs determined under absorption costing did not meet the needs of the "scientific managers." In acknowledging this weakness, supporters of absorption costing advocated the use of supplementary managerial tools such as flexible budgets and break-even analysis. Accountants recommended that the additional information be incorporated within the framework of accounting records so as to routinely provide reports for planning and control.

Direct costing is based on the "variable and nonvariable (fixed) costs" classification. Since fixed costs are constant in total, under direct costing, product cost includes direct material and direct labor costs plus *only* the variable portion of the manufacturing-overhead costs. Fixed factory-overhead costs are excluded and charged to the income statement as a period expense. In short, under direct costing only the variable manufacturing costs are considered as legitimate increases to inventory valuation. The income of a firm depends, as it should, on sales and not on production. The income statement produced by this method avoids the accounting anomaly of lower profit with higher sales sometimes created by mismatching of sales and production.

Financial accounting had its beginning early in civilization, developing with trade and industry. Accounting historians have traced the beginnings of cost accounting to the early part of the seventeenth century. Henry Metcalfe from the U.S., Emile Garcke and J.M. Fells from England, G.P. Norton from England, J. Slater Lewis from England, and later J. Lee Nicholson from the U.S., and John Maurice Clark from the U.S. were pioneers as they introduced new cost concepts in the literature such as variable and nonvariable costs, standard cost, cost centers, relevant costs, and the like. The development of cost accounting in this period was undoubtedly slow as cost accounting tried to adapt itself within the framework of financial accounting while attempting to maintain corporate confidentiality.

The rapid advancement of cost accounting at the beginning of the twentieth century was influenced by the growth of "scientific management" and a shift of emphasis from cost determination to cost control. Cost accounting was now integrated with general accounting, and standard costs were being initiated to measure performance. From 1920 through 1940, economic concepts of short-run time periods and the associated concepts of variable and nonvariable costs influenced the management decision-making process as accountants became aware of the various uses of cost information. Numerous articles appeared in the literature in the 1930s and thereafter extolling the virtues of the two costing methods. At first the authors found numerous disagreements. However, many of the disagreements were resolved in subsequent years. Direct costing for management use in decision making has long been accepted. Since the early 1960s, the controversy rested basically on the issue of using direct costing for external reporting. However, in the late 1980s the activity-based costing movement has raised some serious questions about direct costing.

Resolution of Disagreements

The statements of cost of goods manufactured and earnings prepared in the direct-costing format follow the management decision-making thought process. Hence, the user of this information is readily provided with data related to cost-volume-profit relationships for profit planning. This concept is based on the premise that accounting for direct costs also relates to the economic concept of marginal costs. The proponents of direct costing argue that product costs that represent marginal costs will enable management to make better decisions. The opponents argue that product prices are established on the basis of total costs and that the continued use of variable costing in pricing decisions will result in losses in the long run.

Noble (1952) noted a positive correlation between the degree of competition and the understanding and use of direct costing. "What is needed is a general recognition, in practice as well as in theory, of a short-run and long-run accounting concept in much the same way that this distinction exists in economics." The opposing parties resolved their differences when they realized that different costs are needed for different purposes and that costs were only part of the information necessary in the complex pricing decisions and differential-cost analyses.

Other arguments against direct costing in the early 1950s involved the difficulty of distinguishing different types of costs, particularly the breakdown of semivariable costs into the variable and nonvariable components. Practicing accountants were wary of the cost of maintaining two cost systems (one for internal and the other for external use), although they were not mutually exclusive. The use of computers has resolved some of these difficulties.

A 1961 National Association of Accountants (NAA) study, "Current Application of Direct Costing" of 50 companies reported management's generally favorable experience with direct costing. It also reported that while the supporters of direct costing favored its application to both internal and external reporting, others pleaded for the use of absorption costing for external reporting.

A Synthesis

The Internal Revenue Service and the Securities and Exchange Commission have refused to accept annual reports prepared under direct costing until the accounting profession considers the method to be a generally accepted accounting principle. The opponents of direct costing cite Accounting Research Bulletin No. 43, "Restatement and Revision of Accounting Research Bulletin" (1953), as the authority for their rejection of direct costing. "As applied to inventories, cost means in principle the sum of the applicable expenditures and charges directly or indirectly incurred in bringing an article to its existing condition and location." Many writers have indicated that this pronouncement was issued in 1947 before accountants were adequately acquainted with direct costing. They even wonder whether this situation requires the application of all indirect costs to the inventories. The 1961 NAA study noted that several participating firms published financial statements using direct costing and none received a qualified opinion from its auditors.

Horngren and Sorter (1962) advocated a new concept of "relevant costing" when they stated that direct costing may not be appropriate in all situations. "Under relevant costing, only one basic assumption is needed: Any cost is carried forward as an asset if, and only if, it has a favorable economic effect on expected future costs or future revenues." The test for asset recognition (i.e., inventorying a cost) under relevant costing is quite simple—a given cost should either avoid cost or generate revenue in the future.

Conclusion

Direct costing is considered to provide more useful information for managerial decision making. However, the use of absorption costing is deeply rooted in practice. Today's computerized accounting systems can easily generate direct-costing information for internal-management purposes and regroup the information under absorption costing for external financial reporting. Both systems, direct and absorption costing, are likely to continue in practice in the foreseeable future.

Gyan Chandra
Jacob B. Paperman

Bibliography

Chandra, G., and J.B. Paperman. "Direct Costing vs. Absorption Costing," *Accounting Historians Journal, 1974–76*, vol. 3, 1976, pp. 1–9.

Clark, J.M. *Studies in the Economics of Overhead Costs*. Chicago: University of Chicago Press, 1923.

Garcke, E., and J.M. Fells. *Factory Accounts: Their Principles and Practice*. London: Crosby, Lockwood & Son, 1887.

Harris, J. "What Did We Earn Last Month?" *NACA Bulletin*, January 15, 1936, pp. 501–526.

Horngren, C.T., and G.H. Sorter. "Asset Recognition and Economic Attributes: Relevant Costing Approach," *Accounting Review*, July 1962, pp. 391–399.

Lewis, J.S. *The Commercial Organisation of Factories*. London: E. & F.N. Spon., 1896.

Marple, R.P., ed. *National Association of Accountants on Direct Costing: Selected Papers*. New York: National Association of Accountants, 1965.

Metcalfe, H. *The Cost of Manufacturers and the Administration of Workshops*. New York: John Wiley & Sons, 1885.

Nicholson, J.L. *Cost Accounting Theory and Practices*. New York: Ronald Press, 1913.

Noble, P.L. "Differential Cost Accounting." Ph.D. diss., Ohio State University, 1952.

Norton, G.P. *Textile Manufacturers' Book-keeping for the Counting House, Mill and Warehouse*. London: Hamilton, Adams, 1889.

Weber, C. *The Evolution of Direct Costing*. Monograph No. 3. Champaign, IL: Center for International Education and Research in Accounting, University of Illinois, 1966.

See also ACTIVITY BASED COSTING; BREAK-EVEN CHART; CLARK, JOHN MAURICE; COMMON COSTS; COST AND/OR MANAGEMENT ACCOUNTING; GARCKE AND FELLS; HORNGREN, CHARLES T.; INSTITUTE OF MANAGEMENT ACCOUNTANTS; INVENTORY VALUATION; JOHNSON AND KAPLAN'S *Relevance Lost: The Rise and Fall of Management Accounting*; LEWIS, J. SLATER; METCALFE, HENRY; NICHOLSON, J. LEE; PERIODICITY

Directives of the European Community (Union)

See EUROPEAN COMMUNITY (UNION) ACCOUNTING: FOURTH AND SEVENTH ACCOUNTING DIRECTIVES

Discounted Cash Flow

A refined evaluation of investment decisions requires not only a forecast of cash inflows and outflows, but knowledge of compound interest and a calculation of the discounted value of money. Compound interest tables were first published by mathematicians Jan Trenchant (Lyons, 1558) and Simon Stevin (Antwerp, 1582). Stevin was also the first to apply the net present value approach to financial investments. He explained that the differences between the present values of two or more proposed loans, calculated at a given interest rate, showed how much more profitable one loan was than another. It was harder to set out the cash implications of capital budgeting decisions, where expected receipts and expenditures were less definitely known, and only toward the end of

the nineteenth century did engineers and economists attack this problem.

In the 1887 edition of *The Economic Theory of the Location of Railways*, American civil engineer A.M. Wellington anticipated the capital budgeting problem in its modern form and offered some tentative solutions. Railroad construction required massive cash outlays before any returns were received, and prior to committing itself to such projects, management had to judge whether there was sufficient need for a new line to assure a fair return on construction expenses. This primary question— whether to build a new line at all—should be decided systematically on the basis of estimated cost, probable receipts, the capital available for construction, and the expected return on investment. Wellington pointed out that the cost of capital increases with the amount invested and that rate of return is a better measure than gross receipts. He suggested analysis of the present value of cash inflows and outlays and reproduced the appropriate compound interest tables in his book. Emphasizing that forecasts into the distant future become progressively less precise, he concluded that while the tendency is for railway traffic to increase, it is usually inexpedient and even dangerous to anticipate such increases more than five years ahead in order to justify immediate capital outlays.

Alfred Marshall's *Principles of Economics* (1890) established a conceptual basis for capital budgeting. Marshall's premise was that returns on investment must exceed outlays by an amount which increases, at compound interest, in proportion to the time of waiting. The longer an investor has to wait, the richer his ultimate compensation should be. Changes in the general purchasing power of money are a complicating factor. An alert businessman will continue a particular type of speculation until he feels that the marginal gains resulting from further investments will no longer compensate him for his outlays.

The first reference to present value in American economic literature was in Irving Fisher's *The Rate of Interest* (1907). Fisher described four methods of choosing among investment alternatives and claimed that each gave the same result. Out of all suitable opportunities, an investor should select: (1) the one with the highest present value, calculated at the market rate of interest; (2) the one whose present value returns outweigh by the greatest margin its present value costs when both returns and costs are discounted at the market rate of interest; (3) the one whose rate of return over cost exceeds the interest rate by the greatest amount; and (4) where investment alternatives differ by continuous gradations, the one whose difference from its nearest rivals gives a rate of return over cost equal to the interest rate.

During the 1930s, John Maynard Keynes, Kenneth Boulding, Paul Samuelson, and other economists considered the question of return on capital. Refinements such as salvage value and sinking fund depreciation were added to capital budgeting calculations at this time. But the periodical accounting literature contained few references to investment decisions, nor was the subject well covered in American cost or financial accounting textbooks. Before World War II, the time value of money hardly ever seems to have been an important consideration in managerial decisions to expand or contract operations. During the war, capital expenditures tended to be justified on grounds other than expected monetary return; in the immediate postwar period, demand pressed on capacity and profits were attainable without careful selection among investment alternatives. Not until the early 1950s did business interest in capital budgeting become widespread.

In 1954 managerial economist Joel Dean studied the handling of investment proposals by 50 large, "well managed" companies. He found that "decisions are made on the basis of ill-defined standards and intuitive judgment." Managers did not rank proposals systematically, they could not defend their choices logically, and they did not understand the economic concepts involved. The most common decision criteria seemed to be the degree of necessity or postponability. While admitting the importance of interpretation and judgment in forecasting, Dean saw a need for an analytical framework that would help executives decide which proposals meant most to their firm's long run prosperity. He favored rate of return analysis based on discounted cash flows. His aim was to sum up all relevant data in one net present value figure, which would be applicable to all types of capital budgeting choices and would permit appraisal in terms of a single set of standards.

Studies made during the 1950s indicated that more businesses were adopting discounted cash flow procedures. But the rate of return and "payback period" methods based on financial accounting input data remained by far the most popular, though the accrual and realization methods used in financial accounting were not refined enough for capital budgeting. And it was typically accountants, as financial experts in residence, who were consulted on capital budgeting decisions, despite the fact that nearly all the writing on this subject had been done by nonaccountants. These contradictions are only partly explained by the accountant's preoccupation with historical and external reporting. They were also a result of his highly specialized education, which seldom included much economic theory or statistical inference. Widespread use of discounted cash flow methods by accountants was delayed until the 1960s. Only in 1971 did Accounting Principles Board Opinion No. 21 require financial accountants to make present value calculations.

Michael Chatfield

Bibliography

Dean, Joel. *Capital Budgeting*. New York: Columbia University Press, 1951.

Jones, T.W., and J.D. Smith. "An Historical Perspective of Net Present Value and Equivalent Annual Cost," *Accounting Historians Journal*, Spring 1982, pp. 103–110.

Parker, R.H. "Discounted Cash Flow in Historical Perspective," *Journal of Accounting Research*, Spring 1968, pp. 58–71.

See also COMPOUND INTEREST; FISHER, IRVING; MANAGEMENT ACCOUNTING; RETURN ON INVESTMENT; SANDILANDS REPORT; SPRAGUE, CHARLES EZRA; STEVIN, SIMON; STUDY GROUP ON BUSINESS INCOME'S *Five Monographs on Business Income*

Distribution Costs

"Distribution costs" is a term that has been unclear in accounting for a considerable time. It has been used for: (1) physical costs of transporting and storing physical products, (2) selling expenses, and (3) selling and administrative expenses or all costs between "gross profit" and "net profit before interest expense and income tax." Perhaps because of this lack of clarity, this topic, as well as administrative expenses, has received diminished coverage in accounting, as witnessed by a review of *The Accountants' Index* through the years.

TABLE 1 NUMBER OF ENTRIES

	Distribution Cost and Selling Expenses	Administration Expenses
1910–1919	2	0
1920–1929	76	11
1930–1934	84	4
1940–1949	57	7
1950–1959	77	14
1960–1969	55	17
1970–1979	30	8
1980–1989	26	8
	407	69

The third approach—selling and administrative expenses—is the broadest and allows accountants to be more helpful to firms than the other two more limited, and limiting, definitions.

With so little coverage in the current literature and with such a great need to control distribution costs, attention must be paid to the past. The following discussion focuses on 11 classics from the accounting literature on distribution costs.

William B. Castenholz, an early expert on distribution-cost accounting, spoke at the annual meeting of the National Association of Cost Accountants (NACA), now the Institute of Management Accountants on the topic in 1925. His speech and the responses he made to questions on it could have been given in 1995 and regarded as totally up-to-date. Castenholz argued for the broadest definition of distribution costs. Costs were either production or distribution. Since distribution costs are not allied to the gross profit shown on the monthly income statement, separate statistical studies are needed to arrive at another income statement based on a standardized distribution costing. His goal was to move to perfection one step at a time.

Howard Greer, who had the advantage of access to data from the Institute of American Meat Packers, published many excellent articles on distribution costs. Greer wrote in 1930 that cost accountants were coming forward to help those involved in distribution. He called for studies to find more useful bases for apportionment of these costs. Greer gave excellent examples of how allocation of distribution costs can lead to improper decisions, such as accepting small orders. He urged a leadership role for accountants on distribution costs.

The Association of National Advertisers in 1933, in conjunction with the NACA, published a detailed statistical analysis of distribution costs for 19 industries. A wide variation was found not only between industries but within industries. This was caused by the wide divergence of selling methods and by the early state of the art of distribution costing.

In a 1936 article, A.C. Nielsen, a well-recognized expert in the field of market research, stressed the accountant's role in insisting that decisions be based not on sales from the manufacturing plant but on consumer sales. Nielsen said manufacturers cannot accurately judge the effectiveness of promotions unless they focus on the consumer, and he described his research techniques for obtaining and analyzing this information. He said that information must be received on competitors' sales and promotional expenditures as well to determine market share, and that accountants can be very useful in demanding the pretesting of various promotional strategies.

Charles Reitell, one of the most interesting writers in management accounting, warned in 1938 against the use of flat-percent selling costs based on manufacturing costs. Since distribution costs were a greater and greater percent of total cost, he said, they warranted serious treatment. He discussed five large fields to analyze—territory, sales outlets, advertising, selling methods, and delivery methods—stressed that many variables must be considered. Reitell espoused the use of standard-costing techniques to determine profitability and said salesmen must be enticed to sell items that yield the highest net profit, not gross profit.

I. Wayne Keller of Armstrong Cork Company urged in 1949 that caution be used in deriving per-unit costs for various distribution activities. He considered distribution costs to be a quite different type of cost from production costs, especially nonstandardized items like creativity. Keller gave an interesting illustration of the difficulties of allocating sales costs to an order. He favored an approach that allocated distribution costs by the budget process to attain profit margins on a comparable base.

J. Brooks Heckert and Robert B. Miner, writing in 1953 perhaps the classic book on the topic, adopted a broad definition of distribution costs. Their book, like most textbooks on business of the 1920s through the 1950s, includes list after list, such as 12 distribution problems and types of analyses to be made. The authors provided a detailed chart of accounts, along with sample reporting forms and formats, and specified channels of distribution. They presented 43 items to be considered for what today would be called a marketing database, and they reviewed transportation costs, once a heavily covered topic in colleges of business. Their book is even more vital today than when it was written.

In their own fine book, written in 1955, Donald R. Longman and Michael Schiff adopted the broad definition of distribution costs, focusing on the list of expenses following the gross-profit figure. Their book included a punch-card system. The writers contrasted the take-off of marketing research in the post–World War II years with the then more slowly developing topic of distribution-cost analysis and predicted that it would catch up to market research. However, rather than catch up, the topic of distribution costs has almost disappeared.

The American Marketing Association in 1958 published a compilation of five presentations made at a seminar on sales research. At the seminar, it was reported that economists had found that distribution costs accounted for 60 percent of the consumer dollar. The presenters recommended that these costs be controlled so as to increase sales and thereby lower the cost per unit, noting that small savings would aggregate into a significant amount. They also said that unprofitable sales must be highlighted, that abnormal allocations were to be avoided, and that "marketing intelligence" allows not only control of costs but the creation of a changed environment for the product.

L. Gayle Rayburn, who has been instrumental in keeping the topic of distribution costs alive in accounting, wrote in 1970 about many of the same points that Castenholz raised in 1925, but her article gives the problems a broader historical and social setting.

Douglas M. Lambert and Howard M. Armitage in 1979 took a narrower definition of distribution costs. Focusing on an "integrated physical distribution" margin, they bemoaned the fact that accountants had not kept pace with developments in integrated physical distribution management. They also favored a "total cost analysis" approach over the minimization of one activity. Lambert and Armitage reported on the inadequacy of the academic training in distribution cost given to accountants and concluded that "the emphasis on the manufactur-

ing side has led to a distribution accounting myopia."

It is important to note three other contributors to the topic of accounting for distribution costs, as reported by Paul F. Anderson (1979). Alexander Hamilton Church is considered the first accounting writer on the topic. George E. Frazer wrote an early article. Wroe Alderson of the U.S. Commerce Department was very involved in the analysis of distribution costs by functional-cost groups.

There can be no evolution of ideas if past literature is lost, as has happened on this topic. In the 1990s, accounting for distribution costs is far behind what it was in the early 1950s.

Richard Vangermeersch

Bibliography

American Marketing Association. *Distribution Costs: A Key to Profits*. Chicago: American Marketing Association, 1958.

Anderson, P.F. "Distribution Cost Analysis Methodologies, 1901–1941," *Accounting Historians Journal*, Fall 1979, pp. 39–51.

Association of National Advertisers. *An Analysis of the Distribution Costs of 312 Manufacturers*. New York: Association of National Advertisers, 1933.

Castenholz, W.B. "Administrative and Selling Costs," *NACA Yearbook 1925*, pp. 83–106.

Greer, H.C. "Distribution Cost Analyses: Methods and Examples," *NACA Bulletin*, June 1, 1930, pp. 1305–1320.

Heckert, J.B. and R.B. Miner. *Distribution Costs*. 2nd ed. New York: Ronald Press, 1953.

Keller, I.W. "Relative Profit Margin Approach to Distribution Costing," *NACA Bulletin*, March 1, 1949, pp. 759–770.

Lambert, D.M., and H.M. Armitage. "Distribution Costs: The Challenge," *Management Accounting*, May 1979, pp. 33–45.

Longman, D.R., and M. Schiff. *Practical Distribution Costs Analysis*. Homewood, IL: Irwin, 1955.

Nielsen, A. C. "Continuous Marketing Research: A Vital Factor in Controlling Distribution Costs," *NACA Yearbook 1936*, pp. 220–255.

Rayburn, L.G. "Comparison of Distribution and Production Accounting," *California CPA Quarterly*, March 1970, pp. 18–21, 42.

Reitell, C. "Standard Costs in the Field of Distribution," *NACA Bulletin*, October 1, 1938, pp. 159–164.

Vangermeersch, R. "Renewing Our Heritage," *Management Accounting*, July 1987, pp. 47–49.

See also AGRICULTURAL ACCOUNTING; CHURCH, ALEXANDER HAMILTON; COST AND/ OR MANAGEMENT ACCOUNTING; INSTITUTE OF MANAGEMENT ACCOUNTANTS; PATON, WILLIAM ANDREW

Diversified Reporting

Diversified reporting covers accounting information made available to readers of annual reports about an enterprise that operates in different lines of business not necessarily related to each other. The term "conglomerate" is applied to a diversified enterprise that is, in effect, a grouping of unrelated businesses. Diversified enterprises were the result of the third wave of merger movements in the United States. The first movement, 1898–1902, led to a great increase in manufacturing concentration. The second movement, 1926–1929, led to a great increase in vertical control over the entire business process from raw materials through distribution. The third movement, post–World War II, led to the diversification movement.

Diversified firms, unlike vertically or horizontally integrated firms, present special problems for financial reporting. Although a vertically integrated enterprise may make a number of unlike products, they are successively transformed or consumed within the firm in the course of producing the final product from which revenues and profits are derived. Diversification involves, however, apart from relatively minor intersegment transactions, marketing unrelated products or services to external customers, with diverse origins for revenues and profits.

An accelerating trend toward diversification in the late 1950s and continuing in the 1960s caused creditors, investors, and antitrust authorities a multitude of problems. "Mushrooming growth" of conglomerate corporations in the 1960s gave rise to the impression that a new form of business organization had been created. The 100 largest U.S. industrial corporations were unquestionably more diversified in 1963 than they had been in 1930. And the "explosive" growth in the number of conglomerate mergers in the late 1960s resulted in a further sharp increase in the number of diversified firms.

There are a number of theories to explain or justify the diversification movement. Companies with high price-earnings ratios could realize substantial profits by merging with companies with a low price-earnings ratio, since the latter's earnings would be valued at a higher multiple. When a company moved into unrelated areas, this extension could lower the overall risk of its business. Diversification was also said to allow a firm to benefit from "synergism," a process that involved mutual increases in productivity originated by combining unrelated activities under the same management. Investors, however, could confidently appraise the value of a diversified firm's stock only if the data permitted comparisons with other, single-line firms, or with a similarly diversified company, if the extent and results of the diversification were known.

Although the Securities and Exchange Commission (SEC) in 1965 required that S–1 registration statements disclose nonspecified material information of important lines of business at the time of registration, neither the SEC regulations nor the then-current accounting standards required that the information be brought up to date in any ordered or uniform manner. The SEC had no clearly expressed standards with respect either to selection of lines of business or to the information that was to be provided. Unless investors and their advisers had the financial statements that would enable them to appraise the efficiencies and risks associated with maintenance of current profits in a firm's major markets, they could not make informed investment decisions. From a larger perspective, capital might, in the long run, tend to flow to less productive areas of the economy.

Also in 1964, the Antitrust Subcommittee of the Senate Judiciary Committee launched a three-year inquiry into economic concentration. Although the structure, behavior, and financial reporting of diversified firms was only one of the many aspects of economic concentration, at least three of the eight volumes of testimony on the topic were devoted to diversification. In March and April of 1965, a number of economists testified on the characteristics and consequences of the diversification movement. There was testimony relating to both anticompetitive potential and financial statements of diversified firms. At the congressional hearing Joel B.

Dirlam stressed the difficulties faced by analysts attempting to measure the economic impact of firms engaged in many different industries when basic financial data were not available, either to the investing public or—apart from special inquiries—even to government agencies.

Coming in the context of the Washington hearings on economic concentration, Dirlam's insistence on a statutory remedy attracted the attention of both lawyers and accountants. An investment analyst from the Dreyfus Corporation wrote to Senator Philip A. Hart (D. Michigan), Chairman of the Subcommittee on Antitrust and Monopoly, expressing agreement with Dirlam's proposal. Stockholders had to rely either on anecdotal information or merely mechanical extrapolation of financial data in evaluating the performance of diversified firms. More information was necessary to enable stockholders to appraise management and check on its efficiency. Invited to respond directly to Dirlam's proposal, the SEC at first took the position that improvement was not needed. Dirlam's proposal was probably impracticable, if not impossible, to enforce in many cases, wrote Manuel F. Cohen, chairman of the SEC.

Beginning in the summer of 1966, however, the SEC held meetings with financial analysts, accountants, and industry representatives to discuss the issue. In September 1966, Cohen testified that the SEC, under existing legislation, could require disclosure of necessary information. After another year lapsed, the professional associations of accountants organized research teams to determine what standards should be adopted. There were parallel activities by the Financial Executives Research Foundation and the New York Stock Exchange. As the research progressed, reports of the committees and articles by accountants proposing specific standards began to appear. To resolve differences, the National Association of Accountants (NAA), the American Institute of Certified Public Accountants (AICPA), and the Financial Executives Research Foundation set up a Task Force in 1974 to report to the Financial Accounting Standards Board (FASB). The SEC agreed, in effect, that it would, in revising its own regulations, take account of whatever the FASB issued.

After acknowledging in 1966 that some reforms were in order, the SEC had in July 1969 adopted a September 1968 proposal that registrants disclose sales and earnings by line of business. This was extended to Form 10–K in 1970. By 1974, not only S–ls but 10–Ks had to include information on revenues, contribution to pretax income, the importance of a single or few customers, and the nature and risk of foreign operations. Although the SEC required disclosure of lines of business that contributed at least 10 percent of gross revenues or income or loss before income taxes, no specific basis for selecting segments was adopted.

Each specific requirement for segment reporting in FAS No. 14, issued in December 1976, was accompanied by a careful explanation of its terms and presentation format. Moreover, in Appendix B, the FASB showed how the response to its 1974 Discussion Memorandum on segment reporting and the Exposure Draft were taken into account before promulgating the requirements in their final form. Some of the requirements inevitably allowed for managerial discretion and judgment; differences among organization and functions of firms would have made overly precise requirements unacceptable and unenforceable.

The Discussion Memorandum had brought out the importance of comparisons over time for "line of business" data for the same, or similar, firms. To be in accord with the purpose of FAS No. 14, the reporting firms should attempt, as far as they can do so, to achieve year-to-year consistency. A corollary of consistency is that there be a full explanation of changes in the components of lines of business groups or segments. If substantial, these changes will most certainly affect the weight an investment analyst gives to different segment variables—operating profits, assets, sales, and foreign operations. In short, if they are to carry out the intentions of FAS No. 14, the reporting firms should prepare, display, and explain the data so it will be of assistance to the users.

Selection of the reportable segments is the most important decision the reporting firm must make. Through its choice of segments, the reporting firm can assist, or hopelessly hinder, attempts by analysts to penetrate the detailed and widely varying business experiences not noticeable in consolidated statements. Yet this is a selection particularly difficult for a conglomerate to do with precise specification because each conglomerate is unique. The initial standard is that a "reportable" segment be significant to an enterprise as a whole.

Diversified reporting is an area in which adequate study and participation occurred before the establishment of rules. A recent study by Dirlam and Richard Vangermeersch (1992) indicates that management has perhaps too much latitude in the selection and reporting of business segments through the years. On the other hand, management may be stymied by the informal limit of 10 business segments established in FAS No. 14. Once again, in 1992, a rehearing of the general topic is being conducted by the FASB and remains on the agenda of the FASB in 1994.

Joel B. Dirlam
Richard Vangermeersch

Bibliography

Backer, M., and W.B. McFarland. *External Reporting for Segments of a Business.* New York: National Association of Accountants, 1968.

Dirlam, J.B., and R. Vangermeersch. "A Reexamination of Segment Reporting Since 1965," *Accounting Enquiries*, February 1992, pp. 294–308.

Financial Accounting Standards Board. "An Analysis of Issues Related to Financial Reporting for Segments of a Business Enterprise." FASB Discussion Memorandum. Stamford, CT: FASB, 1974.

Skousen, K.F. "Chronicle of Events Surrounding the Segment Reporting Issue," *Journal of Accounting Research*, Autumn 1970, pp. 293–299.

U.S. Congress. Senate. Judiciary Committee. Subcommittee on Antitrust and Monopoly. 88th Cong., 2nd Sess. 1964. Hearings before the Subcommittee on Antitrust and Monopoly. Part 1. "Overall and Conglomerate Aspects," C.D. Corwin testimony, pp. 36–56; G.C. Means Testimony, pp. 836. Washington, D.C.: GPO, 1964.

U.S. Congress. Senate. Judiciary Committee. Subcommittee on Antitrust and Monoppoly. 89th Cong., 1st sess. 1965. Hearings before the Subcommittee on Antitrust and Monopoly. Part 2. "Mergers and Other Factors Affecting Industry Concentration," J.B. Dirlam testimony, pp. 745–777; M.F. Cohen letter, p. 1069–1071. Washington, D.C.: GPO, 1965.

See also AMERICAN INSTITUTE OF CERTIFIED PUBLIC ACCOUNTANTS; CONGRESSIONAL VIEWS; INSTITUTE OF MANAGEMENT ACCOUNTANTS; NEW YORK STOCK EXCHANGE; SECURITIES AND EXCHANGE COMMISSION; UNITED STATES STEEL CORPORATION; VATTER, WILLIAM JOSEPH

Dividends

The East India Company, chartered by Queen Elizabeth in 1600, evolved in just 60 years from a series of speculative voyages with terminable stocks to a continuing corporation with permanently invested capital. Between 1600 and 1617, the company sponsored 113 voyages, each financed with newly subscribed capital and treated as a separate venture. This made liquidation necessary after each voyage so that investors who wished to drop out might do so and new "adventurers" might be admitted. It also meant the stock was not readily negotiable, since there was no way to enter a venture in progress except by buying unissued stock or a fraction of a share held by an existing investor. At the end of each voyage, assets as well as earnings were subject to "divisions" among the shareholders. Profit was easily measured by the individual stockholder: He gained to the extent that he got back more than he had paid in.

But ships, trading posts, and other long-lived assets tended to carry over from one venture to the next, until finally the company's accounts became a jumble of successive voyages. As unliquidated balances or "remains" of earlier voyages were merged with later ones, it became necessary for the company's accountants to juggle the assets and profits of many ventures in various stages of completion. Also, during the seventeenth century, trading abroad developed into a fairly continuous process requiring permanent capital. It now became more useful to view the business as a going concern.

In 1613 the East India Company stopped issuing stock for each venture and began selling four-year subscriptions, with one-fourth of the stock price to be paid each year and used to finance that year's voyages. A new charter in 1657 established the principle of permanently invested capital and extended the right to transfer individual shares before liquidation. Stock was to be priced by the company, first at the end of seven years, then every three years thereafter. Any shareholder could at any time sell his stock at these prices. This not only simplified the problem of transferring shares, but also made it easier for the company to attract capital. In 1661, following out the logic of permanently invested capital, the company's governor announced that future distributions would consist of "dividends" paid from profits rather than the familiar "divisions" of profits and assets.

With business continuity came a need for capital maintenance. A corporation cannot rationally claim to have indefinite life while dissipating its invested capital. By the year 1700, English common law included two restrictions on dividend distributions. A capital impairment rule specified that no dividend should be paid that left the value of the remaining assets below the firm's contributed capital. A profits test limited dividends to the total of current and retained earnings. The profits test was codified in the Companies Act of 1862. One or the other of these rules still governs dividend distributions in many American states.

For many years, the law did not specify the components of profit and capital in sufficient detail to make these rules effective. Except where fraud was involved, the courts were reluctant lawgivers. The business community was expected to develop its own standards. Court decisions were ambiguous on the treatment of unrealized appreciation of fixed assets and on the distinction between capital and revenue expenditures. Case law on asset valuation was sparse, sometimes contradictory, and it was often hard to tell how broadly a particular decision applied.

The rule that dividend payments could not reduce capital below the amount paid in by stockholders was weakened in *Lee v. Neuchatel Asphalte Company* (1889). The English Court of Appeals ruled that in calculating profits from which dividends were to be paid, the firm could ignore declines in the value of wasting assets. This decision was reinforced in *Re Kingston Cotton Mills Company* (1896), in which the court held that depreciation in the value of fixed assets did not affect a company's ability to declare dividends. These decisions led accountants to distinguish sharply between the valuation of fixed and current assets and to emphasize the latter as being more important.

To avoid the legal risks that resulted from paying dividends out of capital, accountants after 1850 tended to deliberately understate income. The lower of cost or market rule became more respectable, as did the valuation of fixed assets at historical cost. Judicial rulings on capital maintenance gave the doctrine of conservatism legal support at a formative stage in the development of asset valuation and income measurement concepts.

Michael Chatfield

Bibliography

Kehl, D. *Corporate Dividends*. New York: Ronald Press, 1941. Reprint. New York: Arno Press, 1976.

Littleton, A.C. *Accounting Evolution to 1900*. New York: American Institute Publishing, 1933. Reprint. New York: Russell and Russell, 1966.

Yamey, B.S. "The Case Law Relating to Company Dividends." In *Studies in Accounting Theory*, edited by W.T. Baxter and S. Davidson, pp. 428–442. Homewood, IL: Irwin, 1962.

See also ACCRUAL ACCOUNTING; BAD DEBTS; BRIEF, RICHARD P.; CAPITAL ACCOUNT; CAPITAL MAINTENANCE; CAPITAL STOCK; CASH BASIS ACCOUNTING; COMPANIES ACTS; CONSERVATISM; CONTINUITY; DOUBLE ACCOUNT METHOD; EAST INDIA COMPANY; *KINGSTON COTTON MILLS COMPANY*; *LEE V. NEUCHATEL ASPHALTE COMPANY*; *LEEDS ESTATE BUILDING AND INVESTMENT COMPANY V. SHEPARD*; LIMITED LIABILITY; MANIPULATION OF INCOME; OBJECTIVITY; PAID IN CAPITAL; PIXLEY, FRANCIS WILLIAM; REALIZATION; REGULATION OF RAILWAYS ACT (BRITAIN, 1868); RETAINED EARNINGS APPROPRIATIONS; SEPARATE ENTITIES; U.S. INDUSTRIAL COMMISSION

Dodson, James (1710–1757)

Cost finding techniques are as old as double entry bookkeeping, but systematic cost accounting hardly existed at the start of the industrial revolution. Yet to determine income, manufacturers had to calculate the cost not only of finished products but of goods at various stages of completion.

James Dodson, an English mathematician, teacher, and accountant, began *The Accountant, or the Method of Book-keeping* (1750) with a short discussion of bookkeeping theory. He then presented illustrative accounts for a landed estate and farm, a large merchant, partnerships, a banker, and, most significantly, a shoemaker who also kept a retail store. The shoemaker's accounts included transactions involved in buying and cutting leather, delivering soles and uppers to journeymen for shoemaking, and selling five styles of men's shoes, accounting separately for each. This required Dodson to demonstrate batch costing in the shoemaker's accounts, showing the flow of costs from one stage of production to the next, the increasing value of work in process, and, finally, the division of manufacturing costs among the different types of shoes.

Michael Chatfield

Bibliography
Bywater, M.F., and B.S. Yamey. *Historic Accounting Literature: A Companion Guide.* London: Scholar Press, 1982.
Garner, S.P. *Evolution of Cost Accounting to 1925.* University, AL: University of Alabama Press, 1954.

See also COST AND/OR MANAGEMENT ACCOUNTING

Domesday Book

The English authorities shared with earlier governments a need to regulate the levying and collecting of taxes. After his invasion of England in 1066, William the Conqueror took title to the whole country in the name of the Crown. In 1086 he had a survey made that included all real properties and the taxes due on them. The Domesday Book is remembered mainly as a census, but it also served as a register of land values on which Crown assessments could be based. The oldest surviving accounting record in English is the Pipe Roll, or "Great Roll of the Exchequer," compiled annually from property valuations in the Domesday Book and from statements of account by sheriffs and others bringing payments to the treasury.

Michael Chatfield

Bibliography
Maitland, F.W. *Domesday Book and Beyond.* New York: W.W. Norton, 1966, first article.

See also EXTERNAL AUDITING; MANORIAL ACCOUNTING; MEDIEVAL ACCOUNTING; PIPE ROLL; TAX-ORDAINED ACCOUNTING

Donaldo Soranzo and Brothers

The oldest surviving Venetian mercantile accounts are contained in two ledgers of Donaldo Soranzo and Brothers. The first of these (1410–1417) is fragmentary but employed a partial double entry system. A more complete double entry system was used in the second ledger (1406–1434), which was compiled for use as evidence in a lawsuit involving division of the Soranzo family estate.

Both ledgers grappled rather unsuccessfully with the problem of coordinating accounts of the home office and overseas ventures. The four Soranzo brothers imported cotton, one brother in Syria acting as commission agent both for the partnership and for other Venetian merchants. To complete their ledger, the Soranzos had to combine Venetian records with those kept in Syria. But the partner abroad failed to send in regular reports, and the Venetian partners failed to promptly consolidate all their records. There were too many books of original entry. The Soranzo accounts were kept in many poorly integrated journals; there was no unified basis for making ledger postings. Early fifteenth century journals were usually just chronological records of specific events, such as expenses, rent collections, and agent's reports. There was as yet no sense that the purpose of the journal was to serve as a foundation for the ledger.

Michael Chatfield

Bibliography
De Roover, R. "The Development of Accounting prior to Luca Pacioli according to the Account Books of Medieval Merchants." In *Studies in the History of Accounting*, edited by A.C. Littleton and B.S. Yamey, pp. 114–174. Homewood, IL: Irwin, 1956.
Martinelli, A. *The Origination and Evolution of Double Entry Bookkeeping to 1440.* Ph.D. diss., North Texas State University, 1974. Ann Arbor, MI: University Microfilms.

See also CAPITAL ACCOUNT; DOUBLE ENTRY BOOKKEEPING: ORIGINS; JOURNAL; LEDGER

Double Account Method

Railroads were the first businesses to confront the whole spectrum of asset valuation problems. Requiring much larger capital investments and more long-lived equipment than most nineteenth-century industries, they were compelled to account methodically for fixed assets. Corollary to this was concern for capital maintenance through depreciation. During the construction boom of the 1840s, many railroads paid large dividends out of capital, creating a windfall for short term speculators at the expense of creditors and long-term investors. In response to the resulting scandals, some lines adopted cost-based depreciation, but they usually abandoned it when accumulated depreciation turned out to be lower than asset replacement costs. The most common valuation method for railroads, utilities, and other public service corporations came to be some form of replacement accounting.

The Regulation of Railways Act of 1868 required British railroads to adopt the double account method, which divided the balance sheet into current asset and long-term asset categories. Long-term assets were considered permanent investments if they were maintained in good working order. Accordingly, long-term assets were capitalized at acquisition cost and never depreciated, while asset replacements and maintenance costs were charged to expense. After the line was built, only expenditures for additions and betterments were capitalized. There were many variants of replacement accounting. Some railroads charged all capital costs to expense if maintenance charges were thought to equal the physical depreciation of assets. Some formed a "depreciation fund" by setting aside for repairs an annual percentage above ordinary maintenance charges. Others ignored depreciation only if repairs were sufficient to make good equipment wear and tear.

Replacement accounting was simple and flexible in practice, and gave managers wide accounting discretion. It avoided the problem of forecasting the useful lives of fixed assets. And because capital investments created no charge to expense until they were repaired or replaced, replacement accounting made railroads seem an attractive investment by maximizing their reported income during their early years when they most needed capital. George Oliver May believed that America's transcontinental railroads could never have been built by private companies if periodic cost-based depreciation had been required. However, he added that "it is no doubt true that as a result of accounting methods followed, large amounts of capital have been lost by investors."

Replacement accounting created serious liquidity problems. Railroad asset valuation policies had two conflicting purposes: to attract investors with the prospect of large earnings and dividends while at the same time accumulating funds to replace equipment. Railroads that paid high dividends from inflated profits in their early years had to depend on future income to finance asset replacements. Also, it was assumed that repairs and maintenance would keep rolling stock in working order, but this did not always happen. Obsolescence as well as use decreased asset values. Because depreciation expense was not recognized until assets were replaced, there was an incentive to keep income high by not replacing worn out equipment. An ulterior motive for interweaving repairs, replacements, and depreciation was to facilitate internal financing by allowing managers to create secret reserves.

Richard P. Brief called the replacement method an inherently unstable offshoot of cash basis accounting. In an era of chronic business depressions, amounts spent on maintenance and charged to expense tended to fluctuate widely. Reporting inconsistency was the rule, within and between quasi-public corporations, and the variety of asset valuation methods used made comparison of published results very difficult. The resulting accounting "error" was often deliberately fostered by management. Stockholders were misled about actual income, future earnings potential, and managerial efficiency. They were not the only ones deceived by the tendency of replacement accounting to understate capital consumption charges. Half the railroad track mileage constructed in the United States before 1900 was ultimately placed in receivership.

Michael Chatfield

Bibliography

Brief, R. "The Origin and Evolution of Nineteenth Century Asset Accounting," *Business History Review*, Spring 1966, pp. 1–22.

Litherland, D.A. "Fixed Asset Replacement a Half Century Ago," *Accounting Review*, October 1951, pp. 475–480.

May, George O. *Twenty-Five Years of Accounting Responsibility, 1911–1936.* New York: American Institute Publishing Company, 1936, vol. 2, p. 341.

Pollins, H. "Aspects of Railway Accounting before 1868." In *Studies in the History of Accounting*, edited by A.C. Littleton and B.S. Yamey, pp. 332–355. Homewood, IL: Irwin, 1956.

See also BRIEF, RICHARD P.; CAPITAL MAINTENANCE; DEPRECIATION; DICKSEE,

LAWRENCE; DIVIDENDS; FIXED ASSETS; MAY, GEORGE OLIVER; RAILROAD ACCOUNTING (U.S.); REGULATION OF RAILWAYS ACT (BRITAIN, 1868); SINGLE ACCOUNT METHOD

Double Entry Bookkeeping: Origins

Uncertainty surrounds the exact date, place, and circumstances of the birth of double entry bookkeeping (DEB).

The evidence is nonexistent or tenuous for claims that DEB was first practiced in ancient Rome, India, Korea, or Spain or that it was invented by the Jews. It is generally agreed that DEB originated in Italy; for several centuries, it was known outside Italy as the Italian method or system. For many years, it was believed that the 1340 ledger of the city stewards (*Massari*) of the commune of Genoa was the earliest surviving example of DEB. However, in 1950 Federigo Melis, an accounting historian from Italy, showed that there were earlier mercantile examples in Tuscany, from around 1300.

DEB may have emerged independently in more than one Italian commercial center. Regional differences in terminology—for the ledger, for example—and in the format of the ledger suggest independent and possibly broadly simultaneous development. The Venetian ledger format (*alla veneziana*)—with debits and credits on adjacent pages—proved to be the most effective and displaced others; but its use was not confined to DEB.

The precise date and place of the birth of DEB remain conjectural. So, too, are the reasons for, or the driving forces behind, the emergence of DEB in Italy, presumably in the late thirteenth century. It is commonly supposed that the system must have developed to meet some unsatisfied needs in the business world. DEB has been seen as the response to the emerging needs of nascent capitalism; political economist Werner Sombart, as discussed by Basil S. Yamey (1964) and Kenneth S. Most (1972), and, after him, Melis wrote that capitalism and DEB were inextricably interrelated. The historical evidence for such views, however, is meager. The specific business needs that required DEB for their efficient satisfaction have not been identified. Many business firms, both large and small, operated without DEB long after it was available. Notable examples include the sixteenth-century Fugger "conglomerate" of Augsburg and the Dutch East India Company. DEB was not necessary—for partnership enterprise, corporate enterprise, banking, the replacement of traveling merchants by sedentary merchants using agents, the calculation of enterprise profits, or the acceptability of account books in law courts. Attempts to ascribe to DEB a significant, even crucial, role in the emergence and growth of capitalism endow it with properties it did not have, such as making people pursue profits acquisitively and enabling them to act rationally.

Raymond de Roover, a noted accounting and economic historian, in 1955 wrote that DEB was inherent in the two-sided nature of business transactions. It is plausible that DEB may have come about through the automatic extension to *all* transactions of the practice of making two entries for some transactions—for the payment of a debt by a merchant who kept a cash account as well as personal accounts, for example, or for transfers of amounts between a bank's customers. It is plausible, also, that the arithmetic check intrinsic to DEB may have contributed to its development, and *a fortiori* to its use once the system was available. But even this is not certain. Several of the surviving double entry ledgers of the early centuries do not balance—in defiance of the exhortations of the textbooks from Luca Pacioli onward, the discipline of DEB was frequently evaded.

Basil S. Yamey

Bibliography

De Roover, R. "New Perspectives of the History of Accounting," *Accounting Review*, July 1955, pp. 405–520.

Lee, G.A. "The Coming of Age of Double Entry: The Giovanni Farolfi Ledger of 1299–1300," *Accounting Historians Journal*, Fall 1977, pp. 79–95.

Martinelli, A. "The Ledger of Cristianus Lomellinus and Dominicus De Caribaldo, Stewards of the City of Genoa, 1340–41," *Abacus*, December 1983, pp. 83–118.

Melis, F. *Storia della Ragioneria*. Bologna: Cesare Zuffi, 1950.

Most, K.S. "Sombart's Propositions Revisited," *Accounting Review*, October 1972, pp. 722–734.

Yamey, B.S. "Accounting and Rise of Capitalism: Further Notes on a Theme by Sombart," *Journal of Accounting Research*, Autumn 1964, pp. 117–136.

———. "Notes on the Origin of Double-Entry Bookkeeping," *Accounting Review*, July 1947, pp. 263–272.

Yamey, B.S. and A. von Gebsattel. *Luca Pacioli: Exposition of Double Entry Bookkeeping, Venice, 1494.* Venice: Albruzzi Editore, 1994.

See also ACCOUNTING AND THE ACCOUNTANT: PORTRAYALS; ACCRUAL ACCOUNTING; ALBERTI DEL GIUDICE; ARABIC NUMERALS; ARITHMETIC AND ACCOUNTING; BARDI; BRANCH ACCOUNTING; CAPITAL ACCOUNT; CASH BASIS ACCOUNTING; CLOSING ENTRIES AND PROCEDURES; CONSIGNMENT ACCOUNTS; CONTROL ACCOUNTS; COTRUGLI, BENEDETTO; CREDIT; DATINI, FRANCESCO DE MARCO; DONALDO SORANZO AND BROTHERS; FAROLFI COMPANY LEDGER; FINI, RINERIO; FUGGER COST ACCOUNTS; JAPAN; MASSARI COMMUNE LEDGERS; MEDICI ACCOUNTS; PACIOLI, LUCA; PARTNERSHIP ACCOUNTING; PERIODICITY; PROPRIETORSHIP; ROME (509 B.C.–A.D. 476); SINGLE ENTRY BOOKKEEPING; SOMBART, WERNER

Doyle v. Mitchell Brothers Company

D

The Revenue Act of 1918 based the calculation of taxable income on the methods used in financial accounting practice. Every subsequent revenue act has contained a statement similar to the 1918 declaration that "approved standard methods of accounting will ordinarily be regarded as clearly reflecting income," which should be calculated "in accordance with the method of accounting regularly employed in keeping the books. . . ." Court decisions supported the accounting determination of taxable income. In *Doyle v. Mitchell Brothers Company* (1918), the U.S. Supreme Court held that deductions from revenues to arrive at gross profit are inherent and do not depend on specific provisions of the tax law.

Michael Chatfield

Bibliography
Doyle v. Mitchell Brothers Company, 247 U.S. 179 (1918).

See also INCOME TAXATION IN THE UNITED STATES

E

Earned Surplus
See RETAINED EARNINGS

East India Company
The original charter of the East India Company was granted by Queen Elizabeth on December 31, 1600. It incorporated 218 adventurers into "one body corporate" under the name of "the Governor and Company of Merchants of London trading into the East Indies." Incorporation rights included the right to corporate succession, with power to admit and expel members; to receive, hold, and grant property; to sue and be sued in the corporate name; and to use a common seal. This select, corporately organized group of merchants was given monopoly rights to trade in the seas east of the Cape of Good Hope and west of the Straits of Magellan. It essentially exported broadcloth and imported a wide range of commodities such as tobacco, sugar, Indian cotton textiles, raw silk, coffee, and tea.

Although the corporate enterprise known as the joint-stock company had its beginnings in the second half of the sixteenth century, it was not until the foundation of the East India Company that this type of organization assumed a definitive form and nomenclature. Before the emergence of the joint-stock company, and for a long time thereafter, the greater part of English trade was captured by the regulated companies. The regulated company, however, was no more a form of business organization or ownership than is a modern chamber of commerce or trade association. It did not itself engage in trading. Rather, it was an association of traders formed primarily for the control and proper conduct of a particular branch of over-

seas trade. Within its ranks were found the well-known forms of business ownership: the sole proprietorship and the partnership.

As overseas trade developed and expanded in the sixteenth and seventeenth centuries, voyages became longer and more risky. Frequent wars between the maritime nations—the Portuguese, the Dutch, and the English—for the domination of the seas, piracy, and the attacks of the Asiatic rulers against European adventurers necessitated the formation of a far more powerful business organization than those represented by the regulated company. This new, powerful form of business organization came to be known as the incorporated joint-stock company.

As in the case of many forms of organizations, the incorporated joint-stock company, too, evolved rather slowly. Permanent capital, so characteristic to this form of enterprise, became a feature of the East India Company only some 57 years after its foundation. During those years, the company traded on separate and short-term capital known as terminable stock. Some terminable stocks were issued for ventures of single voyages, and others for three or four voyages. When a venture was completed, the entire proceeds were divided among the shareholders on the basis of their individual investments. In some instances, part of the distribution was made in goods. The distribution of the proceeds was actually liquidation of capital stock as well as distribution of profit.

From this early period, there are, unfortunately, no surviving account books, such as journals or ledgers. However, an almost complete series of minutes and other documents, such as *The Lawes or Standing Orders of the East India Company* and *The Order and*

Method that the Accomptants General Shall Observe and Performe (1621), provide a fairly good picture not only of the general state of accounting affairs, but also of the account books in use. Unlike a well-integrated modern accounting department, the organization of the accounting function at the East India Company during this period extended over several of the operating departments. The accounting activity also suffered from the slow communication lines between the home office and the East Indies and the confusion resulting from keeping the ventures in various stages of completion separate from each other. Given this state of affairs, there were continual delays in financial reporting. In addition to these problems, the board of directors itself was not particularly open to the dissemination of financial information.

A new charter granted by Oliver Cromwell to the company on October 19, 1657, ended the practice of trade on terminable stock and introduced in its place the principle of capital permanency. The establishment of permanent capital necessitated the adoption of an accounting system that would permit the integration of economic data relating to capital and income. While venture accounting was satisfactory to the company's earlier business setting, the new environment, generated by the introduction of permanent capital, called for the adoption of what is known as double entry bookkeeping. Over the years, this system of accounting was found to be well suited for an enterprise whose operations were to continue indefinitely, thereby necessitating the preparation of periodic financial statements.

With the introduction of the double entry system of bookkeeping, the board of directors had at its disposal a systematic record of the company's multifarious transactions. The extant account books for the period 1664–1698 clearly suggest that accounting information was available for a variety of decisions. There is also evidence that such information was put to use. It must be mentioned, however, that the declaration of dividend did not have a firm basis in accounting. During the next decade or so (1698–1709), a struggle between the old company and a new East India Company for the control of trade affected the activities of the accounting department adversely. The regularity and standardization of accounting entries that characterized the earlier period was now conspicuously absent. However, the merger

between the new and the old companies in 1709—the first known case of merger in the history of corporate enterprise—led to the reorganization of the accounting system along lines of rigorous double entry bookkeeping. From that year until its demise in 1858, the merger company, known as the United East India Company, maintained an accounting system that must have given its decision makers increasingly better control over the daily activities.

Despite the implementation of an irreproachable double entry system, the company failed to produce reliable financial statements. A common complaint leveled against the accounting department was the lag in keeping the accounts current or, in the parlance of the time, "perfected to the present." But the main defect of the balance sheet, variously known as balance of accounts, stock valuation, stock per computation, stemmed from the fact that they were not based on historical data; they were merely estimations of assets and liabilities. The difference between the assets and the liabilities, which included the stockholders' investment, was shown as a balance figure "in favour of" or "against the Company." Calculations of income that were made for strictly internal purposes were also based on approximate methods.

Failure to produce reliable balance sheets was reflected in two historic confrontations between the stockholders and the board of directors. The first of these occurred in 1782. Serious questions about the credibility of the company's balance sheet led the stockholders to move and resolve "that a Committee of Thirteen Proprietors be appointed to examine into the General State of the Debts, Credits and Effects both in England and abroad, and to report the same with all convenient speed to a General Court of Proprietors." This inquiry eventually resulted in the preparation of the earliest known classified balance sheet with extensive supplementary notes. The second confrontation took place in the following year. Again, dissatisfied with the one-page balance sheet prepared in T-account form, the stockholders demanded and received a revised seven-page-long report and, in addition, unprecedented supplementary information running into several tens of printed pages. Both of these documents testified to a long-felt need for more informative reporting than was customary to provide. They represent the earliest manifestations of the concept of full disclosure, a subject that occupies an important place in modern accounting research.

Vahé Baladouni

Bibliography

Baladouni, V. "Accounting in the Early Days of the East India Company," *Accounting Historians Journal*, Fall 1983, pp. 63–80.

———. "An Early Attempt at Balance Sheet Classification and Financial Reporting," *Accounting Historians Notebook*, June 1990, pp. 27–45.

———. "East India Company's 1783 Balance of Accounts," *Abacus*, September 1986, pp. 59–64.

See also ARCHIVES AND SPECIAL COLLECTIONS IN ACCOUNTING; BRANCH ACCOUNTING; CAPITAL STOCK; CONTINUITY; DIVIDENDS; LIMITED LIABILITY; PERIODICITY

Edwards and Bell: Replacement-Cost Accounting

Economists and co-authors of the classic book, *The Theory and Measurement of Business Income* (1961), Edgar O. Edwards and Philip W. Bell, both from the United States, developed a system of accounting, referred to as replacement-cost accounting, that is based on current market prices rather than historical costs. Their accounting system reports assets and liabilities at the cost to replace them at the balance-sheet date. Revenues from operations are generally the same as under historical cost accounting, but expenses are based on replacement costs at the time they are incurred. The difference between revenues and replacement-cost expenses is referred to as "current operating profit." Total business income includes this amount plus "holding gains and losses," which consist of the change in replacement costs of assets and liabilities held during the year. The core of their theory is comprised of arguments for dichotomizing income into current operating profit and holding gains and losses.

Edwards and Bell maintained that a system of accounting based on historical costs produces essentially meaningless data for decision making. Historical costs would be valid only if general prices in the economy and specific prices of the items owned by the firm are stable and certainty exists about the occurrence of future events. Under conditions of changing prices and uncertainty, they argued for the superiority of replacement-cost accounting over both historical cost accounting and exit-value accounting. The latter system is based on market prices at which assets could be sold and liabilities could be settled (see R.J. Chambers). Edwards and Bell regarded exit values as useful in providing a short-run measure of firm performance, in the sense that assets would be sold and the business discontinued. They preferred replacement-cost accounting, however, arguing it provides a better long-run measure of firm performance.

Edwards and Bell argued that the profits of a firm are derived from two sources: (1) combining or transforming factors of production (labor, materials, overhead) into products whose sale value exceeds the current value of those factors, and (2) gains arising because the prices of assets held by the firm rise (or its liabilities fall). Historical cost, by combining the gains from these two sources, can impair managers' ability to evaluate the profitability of their production processes. In particular, gains from holding activities can conceal the existence of insufficient profits from adding value through production to warrant continuation (or expansion) of the production process. In contrast, current operating profit, by measuring whether profits would occur upon replacing assets, provides a measure of value added from continuing the existing production process over the long run. Further, price changes from assets and liabilities held during the period are reported separately as holding gains (losses) in the period they occur.

Edwards and Bell emphasized the usefulness of accounting data for the internal evaluation of business decisions by managers since "the bulk of accounting data" is never made available outside of the business firm. They argued, however, that their system of income measurement has sufficient flexibility to serve other purposes, including reports to owners, tax authorities, and government policymakers.

The Edwards and Bell book also includes an extensive discussion of accounting procedures that could be used to implement a replacement-cost system. They emphasized that an advantage of their system is that it can be implemented via end-of-period adjustments to accounting records that have been maintained according to existing practices. The consideration of issues encountered in practical application of their system illustrates their intention to bridge the gap between economists, who view income as an essentially subjective measure derived from expectations about future events, and accountants, who insist on measuring actual, and "unfortunately often historic" events. Their emphasis on income measurement, with a lesser emphasis on the balance sheet, also may appeal to practicing accountants.

Subsequent research by David F. Drake and Nicholas Dopuch (1965) and by Prem Prakash and Shyam Sunder (1979), has identified weaknesses in their analysis, including the difficulty of separately measuring profits from production decisions and holding decisions. Furthermore, in implementing replacement cost, substantial measurement error can result from the use of price indexes and technological change (including cost savings in the production process and improvements in existing products), as noted by Edward P. Swanson and Keith A. Shriver (1987) and Edward P. Swanson (1990).

The impact of Edwards and Bell on the practice of accounting is evident in the frequent practice of revaluing fixed assets in England, Australia, Ireland, Singapore, Hong Kong, and a few other countries. In addition, large U.S. companies were required to report supplemental replacement-cost (current cost) data on an experimental basis from 1976 to 1985. The usefulness of that experimental data remains unclear, but with greatly reduced rates of price change in the late 1980s, the Financial Accounting Standards Board (FASB) discontinued the experiment.

Edward P. Swanson

Bibliography

Drake, D.F., and N. Dopuch. "On the Case for Dichotomizing Income," *Journal of Accounting Research*, Autumn 1965, pp. 192–205.

Prakash, P., and S. Sunder. "The Case against Separation of Current Operating Profit and Holding Gain," *Accounting Review*, January 1979, pp. 1–22.

Revsine, L. *Replacement Cost Accounting.* Englewood Cliffs, NJ: Prentice-Hall, 1973.

Sutton, T.J. "The Proposed Introduction of Current Cost Accounting in the U.K.: Determinants of Corporate Preference," *Journal of Accounting and Economics*, April 1988, pp. 127–149.

Swanson, E.P. "Relative Measurement Errors in Valuing Plant and Equipment under Current Cost and Replacement Cost," *Accounting Review*, October 1990, pp. 911–924.

Swanson, E.P., and K.A. Shriver. "The Accounting-for-Changing-Prices Experiment: A Valid Test of Usefulness?" *Accounting Horizons*, September 1987, pp. 69–77.

See also AUSTRALIA; CHAMBERS, RAYMOND JOHN; HISTORICAL COST; INCOME-DETERMINATION THEORY; INFLATION ACCOUNTING; INVENTORY VALUATION; MATCHING; SWEENEY, HENRY WHITCOMB

Edwards, James Don (1926–)

J.M. Tull Professor of Accounting at the University of Georgia, James Don Edwards received his Ph.D. from the University of Texas. He is a past president of the American Accounting Association (1971) and a trustee of the Financial Accounting Standards Board (1972–1978). He also was a member of the Trueblood Committee on Objectives of Financial Statements (1971–1973).

Edwards in 1960 wrote *History of Public Accounting in the United States*, a comprehensive work that relies on original documentation to portray the development of the public accounting profession and that remains a valuable source for historical research. For instance, Edwards included an analysis of CPA certificates issued by each state.

In 1961 Edwards and Roland F. Salmonson coauthored a book analyzing the contributions of four pioneer writers in accounting: Eric Louis Kohler, A.C. Littleton, George Oliver May, and William Andrew Paton. This book provides an excellent view of both the writers and accounting in the synopses of the works of these men. Among other things, these synopses show: Kohler's concern for the language of accounting, Littleton's faith in historical cost, May's concerns for placing accounting into the overall economy, and Paton's quest for accounting based on current values.

Edwards edited the May 1987 AICPA Centennial Issue of the *Journal of Accountancy*. For his work on that issue, which showed him at his best in relating accounting history to accounting practitioners, he was awarded the Hourglass Award by the Academy of Accounting Historians in 1993. Also, in 1993, Edwards was awarded the Gold Medal for Meritorious Service from the American Institute of Certified Public Accountants. In 1994, he received an honorary doctorate in accounting from the University of Paris.

Richard Vangermeersch

Bibliography

Edwards, J.D. "Emergence of Public Accounting in the United States, 1748–1895," *Accounting Review*, January 1954, pp. 52–63.

———. *History of Public Accounting in the United States.* East Lansing: Bureau of Business and Economic Research, Michigan State University, 1960. Reprint. University, AL: University of Alabama Press, 1978.

———. "Public Accounting in the United States, 1896–1913," *Accounting Review*, April 1955, pp. 240–251.

———, ed. *Journal of Accountancy*, May 1987 (*1887–1987 AICPA Centennial Issue*).

Edwards, J.D., and R. Salmonson. *Contributions of Four Accounting Pioneers: Kohler, Littleton, May, and Paton.* East Lansing: Bureau of Business and Economic Research, Michigan State University, 1961.

"Edwards Receives AICPA Gold Medal Award for Meritorious Service," *Accounting Historians Notebook, Fall 1993*, p. 4.

See also ACADEMY OF ACCOUNTING HISTORIANS; AMERICAN ACCOUNTING ASSOCIATION; KOHLER, ERIC LOUIS; LITTLETON, A.C.; MAY, GEORGE OLIVER; PATON, WILLIAM ANDREW; TRUEBLOOD, ROBERT MARTIN

Efficient Market Hypothesis

Accountants have always assumed that financial statement analysis can improve investor performance in securities markets. Given this assumption, the problem becomes one of selecting appropriate accounting and reporting methods for particular firms, or of choosing comparable methods for different companies whose operations are similar. When inappropriate accounting methods are used, investors may be misled and resources may be misallocated in capital markets. Certain securities could become overpriced compared to others, and some corporations might be able to raise capital more cheaply than others, even if the only differences between them were their accounting and reporting procedures. If financial statements are resource allocation devices, the misuse of alternative accounting methods could cause an inefficient distribution of invested capital throughout the economy.

But much empirical evidence suggests that capital markets are capable of absorbing and adjusting for financial information regardless of how it is reported. The semistrong form of the efficient market hypothesis states that *all* publicly available information about a corporation will immediately be reflected in the market prices of its securities. If capital markets are efficient, no investment strategy based on financial statement analysis will allow an investor in publicly traded securities to earn an above average return on his portfolio, because the information in those financial statements has already been assimilated by the securities markets.

What implications has the efficient market hypothesis for accounting? It does not imply that financial statement disclosure is unimportant or that investors cannot use accounting data in assessing the risk of individual security investments. On the contrary, failure to disclose accounting information may result in speculative profits for insiders at the expense of other investors and the public. Moreover, accounting data are useful for internal reporting and for such noninvestment purposes as obtaining credit and reporting to tax and regulatory agencies. The efficient market hypothesis does suggest that the *manner* in which financial statement information is made public may not be as important as accountants have supposed. A contingent liability that is disclosed only in a footnote, or perhaps in a 10K report to the Securities and Exchange Commission, should be reflected in securities prices just as surely as if it was reported as a line item in the balance sheet. Also, efforts to reduce the number of accounting options and to refine financial statement disclosure may be less rewarding than accountants have thought, especially if the choice of options does not affect actual operating results. A change from first in, first out to last in, first out inventory valuation for reporting purposes only does not alter a corporation's economic condition and therefore should not permanently affect the price of its securities.

Michael Chatfield

Bibliography
Dyckman, T., and D. Morse. *Efficient Capital Markets and Accounting.* Englewood Cliffs, NJ: Prentice-Hall, 1986.

See also AGENCY THEORY; BALL AND BROWN'S "AN EMPIRICAL EVALUATION OF ACCOUNTING INCOME NUMBERS"; CASH FLOW ACCOUNTING; FINANCIAL-STATEMENT ANALYSIS; MANIPULATION OF INCOME; UNIFORMITY

Egypt

Government accounting in Babylonia and Egypt had a generally similar development, though the introduction of papyrus as a writing material made Egyptian records less cumbersome and permitted more extensive use of supporting documents. The oldest surviving Egyptian accounts date from about 2390 B.C. As in Babylonia, national cohesion depended on the organization of royal finance, whereby storehouses in each district received taxes paid in kind and forwarded the less perishable items to a central treasury. In such an empire, held together by record keeping, scribes were described by A.H. Woolf as the "pivots on which the whole machinery of the treasury and other departments turned." With minute care, the bookkeepers attached to each storehouse recorded all that was received and the details of its use. Nothing left the treasury without a written order. Additional security was provided by an elaborate internal control system that required that the records of one official agree with those of another. Accuracy was advisable, because accounts were audited by the storehouse superintendent, gross irregularities being punished even by mutilation or death.

The importance given such records contrasts curiously with their lack of sophistication. Egyptian bookkeeping seems to have developed rapidly and then virtually stagnated for several thousand years. Government receipt and disbursement records remained essentially columnar lists that cannot be considered accounts at all in the modern sense of data accumulation categories. It has been argued that better methods were not needed because the Egyptian economy changed so little after its initial period of development. The contrast between ancient and modern accounting can be expressed in terms of a complex but primitive Egyptian economic system that never progressed to a point where bookkeeping cumulation and summation would have been useful.

Michael Chatfield

Bibliography
Stevelinck, E. "Accounting in Ancient Times," *Accounting Historians Journal,* Spring 1985, pp. 1–15.
Woolf, A.H. *A Short History of Accountants and Accountancy.* London. Gee, 1912. Reprint. Osaka: Nihon Shoseki, 1974.

See also ACCOUNTING AND THE ACCOUNTANT: PORTRAYALS; BABYLONIA; EXTERNAL AUDITING; GREECE; INTERNAL CONTROL

Eisner v. Macomber

Many of the rules used today by American accountants to determine business income emerged from tax cases decided between 1913 and 1920. In *Towne v. Eisner* (1918) and *Eisner v. Macomber* (1920), the courts upheld the doctrine of realization at sale by ruling that common stock dividends were not taxable income to the recipient, because such dividends took nothing from the property of the corporation and added nothing to that of the investor. In his opinion on *Eisner v. Macomber*, U.S. Supreme Court Justice Charles Evans Hughes emphasized that income cannot arise without (1) an addition to the recipient's wealth, and (2) a "severance" of gain from capital. A man may grow rich by owning assets that increase in value, but he incurs no tax liability until he sells them. The *Eisner v. Macomber* decision became a precedent for later court tests of realization. Its thesis that income requires a separation from capital by way of an exchange transaction remains the basic rule in law and accounting.

Michael Chatfield

Bibliography
Eisner v. Macomber, 252 U.S. 189 (1920).

See also INCOME TAXATION IN THE UNITED STATES; OBJECTIVITY; REALIZATION; STOCK DIVIDENDS

Emerson, Harrington (1853–1931)

American efficiency engineer Harrington Emerson helped establish a technical basis for standard costing in a series of articles titled "Efficiency as a Basis for Operation and

Wages" (1908–1909). Emerson showed that cost figures collected after goods had been manufactured were not only delayed and obsolete, but also were wrong, mixing legitimate factory costs with avoidable losses that contributed nothing to the product and impeded efforts to eliminate waste and poor performance.

Like Frederick Winslow Taylor, Emerson preferred task control to accounting control by way of variance analysis. He wanted to improve efficiency by accomplishing tasks expressed as a standard quantity of work to be completed in a specified time. Emerson therefore gave priority to standard setting. While he vacillated between ideal and attainable standards, he favored using the hour as the "real standard unit of cost." A worker's hourly output and pay could be measured, and such small time intervals permitted accurate comparisons between task standards and accomplishments. Emerson did not consider it useful to make detailed comparisons between standard and actual costs, because they were affected by too many variable factors. In his system, the standard cost was primarily an index used to measure improvements in efficiency.

Michael Chatfield

Bibliography

Emerson, H. "Efficiency as a Basis for Operation and Wages," *Engineering Magazine,* July 1908–March 1909.

Okano, H. "Harrington Emerson's Standard Costing Reconsidered: His Critical Viewpoints on Cost Accounting." In *Business Review No. 2.* Osaka: Society of Business Research, Osaka City University, 1989.

Solomons, D. "The Historical Development of Costing." In *Studies in Costing,* edited by D. Solomons. London: Sweet and Maxwell, 1952.

See also CONTROL: CLASSICAL MODEL; COST AND/OR MANAGEMENT ACCOUNTING; ENGINEERING AND ACCOUNTING; JOHNSON AND KAPLAN'S *RELEVANCE LOST: THE RISE AND FALL OF MANAGEMENT ACCOUNTING;* MANAGEMENT ACCOUNTING; RAILROAD ACCOUNTING (U.S.); STANDARD COSTING; TAYLOR, FREDERICK WINSLOW

Engineering and Accounting

Engineering is a diverse profession, and generalizations about the contribution of engineers to accounting are inevitably oversimplifications. Nevertheless, some trends are easily discernible, and the records of proceedings of meetings of engineering societies and associations give a clear idea of which topics excited interest among members.

All branches of engineering contributed to the development of cost accounting, but in different ways. Civil engineers paid close attention to methods of estimating costs in order to quote accurately for new work. Mechanical engineers were concerned to trace costs of the specialist manufacturers that were common in the nineteenth century. Electrical engineers struggled with the problems of economies of scale. Foundrymen had to deal with waste and bad castings. The railways were concerned about the "cost of carriage" in the light of empty return journeys and variable loads on different sectors. All of these problems have a familiar modern ring to them. They remain issues of interest to accountants.

Job costing emerged from the need to calculate a price for unique items of manufacture for which there was no market price. Boulton and Watt were among the first to face the problem when they commenced the manufacture of steam engines in their Soho Foundry. They developed a system of detailed record keeping that enabled Watt to establish the price to be charged with great accuracy. Indeed, they went further and estimated the operating costs of their engines with such accuracy that they were able to lease out their engines on the basis of savings over the costs of operating the earlier Newcomen engines then in use in the Cornish tin mines and elsewhere, as reported by Sidney Pollard, professor of Economic History at the University of Sheffield, in 1965.

Costings systems were, however, not widely discussed in England, despite the rapid development of factories during the course of the industrial revolution. Rather, it was the American mechanical engineers who threw off the traditional cloak of secrecy that surrounded financial records in general and cost calculations in particular. Between 1880 and 1910, the proceedings of the meetings of the American Society of Mechanical Engineers and journals such as the *Engineering Magazine* and the *American Machinist* are replete with discussions on costing methods, estimating, overhead allocations, economies of scale and other topics normally associated with the accounting profession. Famous names also recur, such as Frederick Winslow Taylor, F.A. Halsey, Henry Laurence Gantt, Alexander Hamilton Church, Sterling Bunnell, Oberlin Smith, H.R. Towne, to name a few.

Most important, however, was the engineers' contribution to the development of overhead-allocation methods for "common costs." It was a matter of abiding interest to engineers and, at that time, of apparently little interest to accountants. References to allocation procedures were common in all branches of engineering during the period 1880 to 1910 but were rare in accounting journals. The most common allocation base advocated by engineers was direct wages. However, Church's advocacy of different allocation bases for different costs and his "supplementary rate" were widely discussed.

Engineers were quick to notice the arbitrary nature of cost allocations. In that respect, they preceded accountants by 50 years or more. Among accountants there was little discussion of the arbitrary nature of cost allocations until the direct-costing controversies of the 1950s, as noted by Brummett (1955). However, while some engineers were careful to differentiate between "actual" and "estimated" or "arbitrary" costs, not all engineers were as careful. H.L. Arnold (writing in 1898 under the nom de plume of Henry Roland) recognized that the costs were only "probable" but still maintained that the system yielded "absolutely correct information"; L.S. Randolph claimed that the costing system he used was "accurate"; and H. Diemer (1903) described the costs derived from a system he advocated as "accurate" and the records as "correct." In making these claims, the engineers (as did the accountants who followed them) failed to recognize the difference between a system that allocated all of the overhead costs "accurately"—there were no residual costs unallocated—and the arbitrary cost of production that resulted from the use of some broad allocation base such as direct wages.

Church stands out as an engineer who played a major role in popularizing costing methods. He was a prolific writer and a staunch advocate of allocation procedures that would enable the profit or loss to be established on every item of production. He proposed that the factory be divided into a series of "little shops" to which all costs could be allocated prior to their allocation to individual products. Even office and selling expenses were to be allocated on "a more or less arbitrary basis" in order to show when a product was failing to meet the market.

Arising out of the engineers' need for better cost information were a number of proposals for costing standards. Some of those proposals were tied to incentive schemes for employees, based on some predetermined standard of performance or a profit-sharing arrangement. In a paper delivered in 1885 to the American Society of Mechanical Engineers, Towne stated that "the basis or starting-point of the system is an accurate knowledge of the present cost of product." Better known, however, is Taylor's system based on predetermined physical standards of performance. It developed into the "scientific management" movement.

Scientific management generated a great deal of interest in the United States early in the twentieth century. It appears to have given some impetus to the development of better costing systems, although Taylor's publications make only passing reference to cost records. In 1911, a Navy engineer, Holden Evans, published a series of articles that were later produced as a book titled *Cost Keeping and Scientific Management*. In it he claimed that "scientific shop management and accurate cost keeping are inseparable."

Despite frequent claims that scientific-management systems required the allocation of overhead costs to products and/or departments, the contrary is true. Taylor's system required the careful identification of responsibilities, comparison of achievement with expectations (standards), and reporting by exception. Allocating costs for which a manager was not responsible was anathema to that system.

Engineers, especially U.S. mechanical engineers in the first decades of the twentieth century, had a profound effect on the development of cost accounting. They had a need to know the cost of manufactured goods, and they had a sound understanding of the record-keeping systems required to provide that information. They pioneered standard costs and variance analysis. The electrical engineers also understood clearly the relationship between costs and output, especially in relation to electricity generation, as witnessed by Hopkinson (1892) and then Lewis (1896), and produced graphs that bear a striking resemblance to more modern cost-volume-profit and break-even charts. Railway engineers were concerned about the recovery of fixed costs and the debilitating financial effects of one-way freight contracts. They understood marginal costs and the arbitrary nature of common cost allocations, as noted by Dionysius Lardner in 1850 and Marshall M. Kirkman in 1880.

Curiously, by 1915 engineers appear to have lost interest in costing. Accountants were, by that time, paying much more attention to costing systems, and papers on cost-accounting topics began to appear regularly in the accounting journals and in the proceedings of meetings of the fledgling accounting societies. The terms "cost accounts" and "costing" first appeared in *The Accountant* in 1892, but only became common after 1900. The proceedings of the American Society of Mechanical Engineers (ASME), by comparison, include a number of papers on costs and cost estimation from the early 1880s. Indeed, in 1885, Towne, a prominent member of the ASME, called for the formation of an "Economic Section" of the ASME to discuss such things as "Shop management and Shop accounting."

On the evidence of published papers, it would not be overstating the case to suggest that the pioneers of cost accounting, even as we know it today, were not accountants but engineers.

Murray C. Wells

Bibliography

Brummett, R.L. "Direct Costing: Should It Be a Controversial Issue?" *Accounting Review*, July 1955, pp. 439–443.

Bunnell, S.H. "Cost Keeping for Small Machine Shops," *American Machinist*, vol. 33, 1910, pp. 736–737.

Church, A.H. *The Proper Distribution of Expense Burden*. New York: Engineering Magazine Co., 1913.

Cowan, D. "Administration of Workshop, with Special Reference to Oncost; What It Should Include; Its Allocation and Recovery," *Transactions of the Institution of Engineers and Shipbuilders in Scotland*, vol. 43, 1899–1900, pp. 227–244.

Diemer, H. "Cost-Finding Methods of Moderate Sized Shops," *Engineering Magazine*, vol. 24, 1903, pp. 577–589.

Evans, A.H. *Cost Keeping and Scientific Management*. New York: McGraw-Hill, 1911.

Halsey, F.A. "An Accurate Cost Keeping System," *Transactions of the American Society of Mechanical Engineers*, vol. 19, 1897, pp. 397–400.

Hopkinson, J. "The Cost of Electricity Supply," *The Electrical World*, vol. 20, 1892, pp. 411–412.

Kirkman, M.M. *Railway Expenditures: Their Extent, Object, and Economy*. Chicago: Railway Age, 1880.

Lardner, D. *Railway Economy: A Treatise on the New Art of Transport*. London: Taylor Walton & Maberly, 1850.

Lewis, J.S. *The Commercial Organisation of Factories*. London: E. & F.N. Spon, 1896.

Pollard, S. *The Genesis of Modern Management: A Study of the Industrial Revolution in Great Britain*. Cambridge, MA: Harvard University Press, 1965.

Randolph, L.S. "Comments on 'Accurate Cost-keeping System' by H.M. Norris," *Transactions of the American Society of Engineers, 1897*, vol. 19, pp. 405–406.

Roland, H. (H.L.Arnold). "An Effective System for Finding and Keeping Shop Costs," *Engineering Magazine*, Vols. 15–16, 1898, pp. 610–620.

Taylor, F.W. *The Principles of Scientific Management*. New York: Harper & Brothers, 1911.

Towne, H.R. "The Engineer as an Economist," *Transactions of the American Society of Mechanical Engineers*, vol. 7, 1885, pp. 428–432.

Wells, M.C. *Accounting for Common Costs*. Champaign, IL: Center for International Education and Research in Accounting, University of Illinois, 1978.

———. *A Bibliography of Cost Accounting: Its Origins and Development to 1914*. Champaign, IL: Center for International Education and Research in Accounting, University of Illinois, 1978.

See also BUDGETING; CHURCH, ALEXANDER HAMILTON; COMMON COSTS; COST AND/OR MANAGEMENT ACCOUNTING; EMERSON, HARRINGTON; GANTT, HENRY LAURENCE; JOHNSON AND KAPLAN'S *RELEVANCE LOST: THE RISE AND FALL OF MANAGEMENT ACCOUNTING;* LEWIS, J. SLATER; MANAGEMENT ACCOUNTING; STANDARD COSTING; TAYLOR, FREDERICK WINSLOW; WELLS, MURRAY CHARLES

Enterprise Theory

The enterprise theory reflects the view of Peter Drucker and Waino Suojanen that a large corporation is a social institution influencing society as a whole, operating for the benefit of many interested parties, and having reporting obligations to each of the major groups affected by its actions. It follows that corporate financial statements should be prepared not only for stockholders and creditors but also for employees, customers, the government as a taxing body and regulatory agency, and the general public. Corporate income statements should measure wealth changes in value-added terms by calculating the market value of goods and services produced by the firm less the value of goods and services acquired from other companies. Claims against the total asset pool should be treated impartially. Dividends paid to stockholders, interest payments to creditors, wages paid employees, and tax payments would all be considered distributions of income. Because it implies a social commitment that takes precedence over a company's responsibility to its owners, the enterprise theory has been used to justify regulatory policies that have held corporations liable for product defects, advertising misrepresentation and environmental damage.

Michael Chatfield

Bibliography

Drucker, P.F. *Concept of the Corporation.* New York: John Day, 1946.

Suojanen, W.W. "Accounting Theory and the Large Corporation," *Accounting Review*, July 1954, pp. 391–398.

———. "Enterprise Theory and Corporate Balance Sheets," *Accounting Review*, January 1958, pp. 56–65.

See also SOCIAL RESPONSIBILITIES OF ACCOUNTANTS

Entity Theory

Proprietary theory envisioned few parties at interest, close contact by businessmen with their affairs, and data summarized for use by owners and creditors who were assumed to have specialized knowledge of the business. Whether assets were valued at historical costs or current prices was considered to be of secondary importance because these informed parties could make the necessary mental and mathematical adjustments.

But a corporation was legally distinct from its owners and managers, and corporate "proprietorship" typically involved a constantly changing group of shareholders. Assets could not realistically be thought of as belonging to these people because the law recognized prior claims of creditors and preferred stockholders in liquidation. Nor, because of limited liability, did investors personally owe the firm's debts. Corporate income distributions could not be made with the informality of proprietary withdrawals. Financial statements were now communication devices between management and outsiders who often had no access to the corporation's accounting records and little detailed knowledge of its operations.

A.C. Littleton considered medieval agency accounting a forerunner of the entity concept. Investors in joint ventures and the parties to consignment agreements were also considered to be independent of the accounting entities involved. References given by Leon Gomberg indicate that elements of the entity theory were described in textbooks as early as 1838. In *The Logic of Accounts* (1873), American E.G. Folsom explained transaction analysis in terms of abstract value exchanges instead of giving the usual examples of commodity movements or dealings between individuals. In 1882 a Dutch author, I.N. Brenkman, argued that the essence of double entry bookkeeping was not equilibrium between debits and credits but the keeping of a statistical record that allowed proper accounting for business assets. Five years later a German, Manfred Berliner, independently advanced similar views. Like Brenkman, he noted the separation of the modern company from its owners and concluded that bookkeeping was primarily concerned with recording value exchanges, not with the affairs of proprietors. Business assets were debts of the firm to its owners; liabilities were claims by the firm on its owners. Profit measured the value of the proprietor's services and was calculated as the increase in value of invested property.

William Andrew Paton is the best known American advocate of the entity concept. His *Accounting Theory* (1922) was one of the first attempts to adapt ownership doctrine to the realities of an economy dominated by large corporations. Though he took the writings of Charles Ezra Sprague and Henry Rand Hatfield as a starting point, Paton complained that bookkeeping texts were "saturated" with the proprietary viewpoint. While accounting technique had developed to meet corporate needs, theorists still assumed that disclosure of proprietor's capital was the main accounting task. Paton's writings take "the conception of the business enterprise as in all cases a distinct entity or personality." If the corporation is functionally separate from its owners and creditors then it, not they, should be the center of accounting attention. This implied a wider view of business operations than accountants had ever taken. Paton viewed capital as the sum of property active in the business, whether contributed by owners or creditors. So the right side of the balance sheet represented equities in assets, and the left side represented asset market values—not costs—because it is changes in asset values that largely determine corporate income. Assets and liabilities are those of the entity, which reports to its shareholders and creditors much as a trustee might account for his stewardship or resources entrusted to him. Because creditors and stockholders have similar status as equity holders, financial statements should be directed impartially to both groups.

Paton saw the worst effects of proprietary theory in its definition of expenses and revenues "as mere accessories of proprietorship." If it is assumed that net profit from all sources goes directly to the owner, then no distinction need be made between operating income and other gains and losses. This has "tended to shut the door to all discriminating analysis of the income sheet," making its classifications illogical. Whereas proprietary theory was mainly concerned with the balance sheet and took a legal view of capital, the entity theory emphasized corporate income and a more economic concept of profit measurement. Revenues and expenses were no longer simply increases or decreases in stockholders' equity. Revenues were compensation for services provided by the firm. Expenses measured the cost of services consumed in obtaining revenues. Profit accrued to the corporation, not to its owners or creditors. Its disposition was left to the entity. Interest payments, income taxes, and dividends were distributions of profit rather than expenses or proprietary withdrawals of capital. Retained earnings represented an undistributed allocation of income to stockholders.

Paton combined assets and expenses in one category of "services," which differed only in the timing of their matching with revenues. He considered assets deferred costs awaiting conversion to expense, rather than objects intended

for liquidation to satisfy creditors. Thus an asset's value was not directly related to its physical existence or to its acquisition cost or current market price. Rather it reflected the value of future service benefits to be received by the corporation. These ideas were the groundwork of Paton's contribution to the 1940 monograph, *An Introduction to Corporate Accounting Standards*, which may be called the high point of entity theory exposition.

Michael Chatfield

Bibliography

Littleton, A.C. *Accounting Evolution to 1900*. New York: American Institute Publishing, 1933. Reprint. New York: Russell and Russell, 1966.

Paton, W.A. *Accounting Theory*. New York: Ronald Press, 1922. Reprint. Chicago: Accounting Studies Press, 1962; Lawrence, KS: Scholars Book, 1973.

See also AN INTRODUCTION TO CORPORATE ACCOUNTING STANDARDS; HISTORICAL COST; LIMITED LIABILITY; PATON, WILLIAM ANDREW; POSTULATES OF ACCOUNTING; PROPRIETARY THEORY; VATTER, WILLIAM JOSEPH

Escott v. BarChris Construction Corporation

The introduction of automatic pinsetting machines in 1952 made bowling a popular sport, and during the 1950s "bowling centers" were built throughout the country. BarChris was engaged primarily in constructing bowling alleys, and its net sales increased from about $600,000 in 1956 to over $9.1 million in 1960. In that year, BarChris installed about 3 percent of all bowling lanes built in the United States.

BarChris's method of operation was to make a contract with a customer, receive a small down payment on the purchase price, and then build and equip the bowling alley. When the job was done, the customer remitted the balance of the contract price in notes that were payable in installments over a period of years. BarChris would construct and equip the interior of a bowling center and sell it to a factor, who would immediately pay BarChris the full contract price. The factor then leased the interior either to a BarChris customer or to a BarChris subsidiary, which would lease it to the customer.

Under either financing method, BarChris incurred large construction costs before receiving remuneration. As a result, BarChris was in constant need of cash to finance its operations, a need that grew as its construction activities expanded. In December 1959, BarChris sold 560,000 shares of common stock to the public at $3 per share. By early 1961, needing additional working capital, BarChris filed a registration statement with the Securities and Exchange Commission (SEC) to issue 15 year debenture bonds; in May 1961, BarChris received the cash from this bond sale.

By that time BarChris was having trouble collecting notes receivable from some of its customers. Though BarChris continued to build bowling centers, in 1961 and 1962 these difficulties increased, and it became evident that the bowling industry was overbuilt. Bowling alley operators began to fail, defaulting on their notes. On October 29, 1962, BarChris Construction Corporation filed for Title XI bankruptcy.

Sixty-five owners of BarChris's debenture bonds brought a class action suit against the company officials who signed the SEC registration statement, the underwriters who sold the debentures, and Peat, Marwick, Mitchell and Company, BarChris's auditors during 1958–1960. Plaintiffs charged that the registration statement filed by BarChris with the SEC, which included a prospectus and a consolidated balance sheet, contained material false statements and material omissions as defined by Section 11 of the Securities Act of 1933.

In 1968 a New York district court ruled that overstatement of current assets and understatement of current liabilities resulted in a material (16 percent) misstatement of BarChris's current ratio. The court also concluded that Peat, Marwick's S–1 review of the registration statement was inadequate. The purpose of an S–1 review is to determine whether there has been any material change in a company's financial condition between the date of its last audited financial statements and the date of the registration statement. The accountant in charge of BarChris's S–1 review was acting as a senior accountant for the first time. He was not yet certified, had no previous experience auditing firms in the bowling industry, yet spent only 20 1/2 hours on the job. Judge Edward Mclean ruled that the accountant had failed to take certain steps recommended in Peat, Marwick's program for an S–1 review. "He asked questions, he got answers which he considered satisfactory, and he did nothing to verify them."

BarChris was the first important case decided under Section 11 of the Securities Act of 1933, and it established at least three accounting precedents. For the first time, a court articulated the responsibilities of accountants in S–1 reviews. By expanding the scope of audit investigations of events subsequent to the date of certified financial statements, the *BarChris* decision extended the attest function. The court recognized that an S–1 review could not be a complete audit. But in preparing a registration statement, an accountant could not simply accept without confirmation reports prepared by others, or statements made by company officials.

Secondly, the court ruled that it was misleading to include profit from a sale in which the property had been leased back by the seller. BarChris sold bowling alleys to a factor, who leased them to a BarChris subsidiary, and the transactions were treated as sales in BarChris's consolidated income statement. The court judged that profits from sale-and-leaseback contracts should have been eliminated from BarChris's consolidated reports. Accounting Principles Board Opinion No. 5 in 1964 later mandated this by requiring that sales and leasebacks not be accounted for as independent transactions.

Finally, the *BarChris* decision is considered to have impaired the accountant's privity defense in common law. For many years after the decision in *Ultramares Corporation v. Touche, Niven and Company* (1931), auditors assumed that they could be held liable to their clients for negligence but to third parties only for gross negligence or fraud. The *BarChris*, Westec, (*Carpenter v. Hall* [1970]), and Yale Express (*Fischer v. Kletz* [1967]) cases involved as plaintiffs third parties who had no contractual relationship with the auditors. Negligence actions by third parties have since been successful in SEC hearings and in the courts.

Michael Chatfield

Bibliography

Davies, J.J. "Accountants' Third Party Liability: A History of Applied Sociological Jurisprudence," *Abacus*, December 1979, pp. 93–112.

Escott v. BarChris Construction Corporation, 283 F. Supp. 643 (S.D.N.Y. 1968).

Miller, R.L., and G.P. Brady. *CPA Liability: Meeting the Challenge.* New York: Ronald Press, 1986.

See also Carpenter v. Hall; Fischer v. Kletz; Law and Accounting; Legal Liability of Auditors; Regulation (Federal U.S.) and Accounting; Securities and Exchange Commission; *Ultramares Corporation v. Touche, Niven and Company*

Estate Accounting
See Manorial Accounting

Ethics, Professional

A primary goal of U.S. accountants in the late 1800s and early 1900s was the attainment of professional status. With aspirations modeled on the "older professions" of medicine and law, and the example of their British and Scottish counterparts, U.S. accountants sought to distinguish the "profession of accountancy" from other commercial activities. Essential to that goal was a code of conduct that would set the accountant apart from the laity and govern his professional conduct.

Two years before his inauguration as president of the American Association of Public Accountants (AAPA), Joseph Edmund Sterrett outlined the agenda for future debate and development of codes of professional ethics. His address to the 20th annual meeting of the AAPA in 1907 formulated a framework for ethical conduct that guided the profession for over half a century. Divided into responsibilities to clients, "professional brethren," and the public, his recommendations sound modern even at the close of the twentieth century: confidentiality, due professional care, tact combined with courageous honesty, not certifying misleading financial statements, impartiality, financial independence from clients, speaking well of one's professional colleagues, duties of a subsequent auditor, and duties to assistants. In addition to these positive aspects of professional practice, Sterrett called for banning a series of "unprofessional behaviors," including contingent fees, encroachment on the business of other accountants through solicitation, advertising, competitive bidding, fee splitting, commissions not earned through professional work, and practicing as a corporation. Although other writings make it clear that independence was considered the essence of ethical behavior, early codes did not specifically mention independence. Rather, the negative rules against advertising, competitive bidding, and contingent fees were intended to protect the auditor's independence of mind. Independence did not enter the language of the professional code until 1941 at the urging of the Securities and Exchange Commission (SEC).

Adherence to these standards was by no means the norm in the early 1900s, nor was there universal agreement on the necessity for written codes. Many practitioners opposed written codes, which they believed would reduce ethical issues to the lowest common denominator. Others felt that the rules created an unreasonable burden on practitioners. Throughout the first two decades of the 1900s, the vast majority of accountants solicited, advertised, and accepted commissions from stationers and other client vendors. It was also common for auditors to have financial interests in their clients' businesses and to hold management or director positions in those businesses.

The AAPA became the American Institute of Accountants (AIA) in 1916, responding in part to criticisms that the AAPA was powerless to enforce even its limited rules of ethics due to its membership structure. The AIA promptly established the first comprehensive "Code of Professional Ethics" in 1917. Consisting of eight rules, the code forbade practitioners from: (1) calling themselves members of the AIA unless all partners were members, (2) certifying financial statements that contained false or misleading statements or omissions, (3) allowing someone to practice in their name who was not a partner or employee, (4) engaging in fee splitting or kickbacks, (5) engaging in incompatible occupations, (6) issuing opinions on financial statements not properly examined, (7) lobbying on legislation without first notifying the AIA, and (8) engaging in solicitation or encroachment. Additional rules were added to the code, which continued to expand before and after the AIA merged with the American Society of Certified Public Accountants in 1959 to become the AICPA. Among the more significant expansions were prohibitions against: accepting contingent fees (1919); vouching for the accuracy of forecasts (1932); competitive bidding (1934); having a *substantial* financial interest in audit clients, violating client confidentiality (1941); committing acts discreditable to the profession (1962); and having *any* financial interest in an audit client (1964).

In 1965, Thomas Higgins, chairman of the AICPA Ethics Committee, told the annual meeting of the AICPA that its code of ethics was probably "the worst piece of literature in circulation," consisting entirely of negative prohibitions, as noted in his 1972 article. His speech began a process that led to the acceptance of a totally restructured code in March 1973. The new code began with a philosophical essay defining ethical concepts and discussing their role in a professional and cultural context, followed by a series of enforceable rules of conduct covering independence, competence and technical standards, responsibilities to clients, responsibility to colleagues, and other rules covering discreditable acts, solicitation, commissions, incompatible occupations, and form of practice and name. The rules were followed by interpretations. Perhaps the most revolutionary change in the 1973 code was Rule 203, which requires members to offer a qualified opinion on financial statements that contain any departure "from an accounting principle promulgated by a body designated by the Council." This rule effectively combines ethics enforcement, generally accepted accounting principles (GAAP) and generally accepted auditing standards (GAAS) into a unified structure. A similar rule proposed in the late 1960s failed to obtain the necessary two-thirds majority of the membership by six-tenths of one percent.

A series of audit failures followed by congressional investigations into the profession's ability to regulate itself led to a major self-examination of the profession and the code in the 1980s. The Anderson Commission on standards of professional conduct, formed in 1984, recommended formally in 1987 sweeping changes for the profession, but only minor changes in the code. The code was restructured into two interrelated sections—standards of professional conduct and rules of performance and behavior, which would be extended to all AICPA members, not only those in public practice.

Another evolutionary change affecting the code has been the expansion of professional services. Management advisory services (MAS) in particular have repeatedly raised the specter of lost independence. One of the earliest discussions of the relationship between independence and management advisory services (MAS) can be found in *The Philosophy of Auditing* by Robert K. Mautz of the University of Illinois and Hussein A. Sharaf of the University of Cairo. MAS was also studied by several AICPA committees, including the Anderson Committee (1987) and the Treadway Commission (1987) but, despite considerable criticism, most MAS services are not currently considered to auto-

matically undermine audit independence. To better control MAS activities, however, the AICPA issued the first in a series of Statements on Standards for Consulting Services (SSCS) in 1991, defining the CPA's responsibilities in consulting engagements. MAS activities have fallen under the scope of the AICPA Code since a 1977 revision brought all areas of public practice under the aegis of a single "Code of Professional Ethics."

As other branches of accounting have defined their professional roles, they, too, have developed codes of professional ethics. The National Association of Accountants (now the Institute of Management Accountants) adopted its first "Standards of Ethical Conduct for Management Accountants" in 1983, addressing issues of competence, confidentiality, integrity, objectivity, and resolution of ethical conflict. In 1988, the Institute of Internal Auditors (IIA) issued a revised code of ethics covering the activities of all members of the IIA and requiring them to comply with the "Standards for the Professional Practice of Internal Auditing." Unique codes of ethics have been adopted by the International Federation of Accountants Council (IFAC), the Government Finance Officers Association (GFOA) and other professional accounting groups.

A series of court cases brought by the U.S. Justice Department during the 1970s and 1980s had a major influence in changing the focus of professional codes. In *Goldfarb v. Virginia State Bar*, 421 US 773 (1975), the United States Supreme Court ruled that professional organizations were subject to antitrust regulations which forbade fee-setting. In *National Society of Professional Engineers v. US*, 435 US 679 (1978), the United States Supreme Court held that professional society ethics which prohibited competitive bidding were an unreasonable restraint of trade. These cases removed from accounting and other professions their long-assumed immunity from federal antitrust regulations. Physicians, lawyers, engineers, and accountants were forced to rewrite codes that forbade advertising, solicitation, competitive bidding, and contingent fees. In each case, the AICPA attempted to salvage what it could of these older rules while negotiating consent decrees with the Justice Department and the Federal Trade Commission. Nevertheless, the atmosphere in the 1990s will allow for far more open competition than the Code of Professional Ethics has permitted since the first rules were passed by the Ethics Committee of the AAPA in 1906.

R. Penny Marquette

Bibliography

Anderson, G.D. "Restructuring Professional Standards," *Journal of Accounting*, May 1987, pp. 77.

Anderson, G.D., and R.C. Ellyson. "Restructuring Professional Standards: The Anderson Report," *Journal of Accountancy*, September 1986, pp. 92, 94, 96–100, 102, 104.

Bialkin, K. "Government Antitrust Enforcement and the Rules of Conduct," *Journal of Accountancy*, May 1987, pp. 105–106, 108–109.

Briloff, A.J. "Old Myths and New Realities in Accountancy," *Accounting Review*, July 1966, pp. 484–495.

Carey, J.L. *The Rise of the Accounting Profession,* Vol. 1: *From Technician to Professional, 1896–1936*; Vol. 2: *To Responsibility and Authority, 1937–1969.* New York: AICPA, 1969–1970.

Elliott, R.K., and P.D. Jacobson. "The Treadway Report—Its Potential Impact," *Journal of Accountancy*, October 1987, pp. 23, 26, 28, 31, 32.

Higgins, T.G., and W.E. Olson. "Restating the Ethics Code: A Decision for the Times," *Journal of Accountancy*, March 1972, pp. 33–39.

Hurdman, F.H. "Ethics of the Accounting Profession," *Journal of Accountancy*, November 1941, pp. 412–420.

Mautz, R.K., and H.A. Sharaf. *The Philosophy of Auditing.* Sarasota, FL: American Accounting Association, 1961.

Merz, C.M., and D.F. Groebner. *Toward a Code of Ethics for Management Accountants.* New York: National Association of Accountants, 1981.

Olson, W.E. *The Accounting Profession: Years of Trial, 1969–1980.* New York. AICPA, 1982.

Sterrett, J.E. "Professional Ethics," *Journal of Accountancy*, October 1907, pp. 407–431.

See also ADVERTISING BY ACCOUNTANTS; AMERICAN INSTITUTE OF CERTIFIED PUBLIC ACCOUNTANTS; GENERALLY ACCEPTED ACCOUNTING PRINCIPLES; INDEPENDENCE OF EXTERNAL AUDITORS; INSTITUTE OF INTERNAL AUDITORS; INSTITUTE OF MANAGEMENT ACCOUNTANTS; INTERNAL AUDITING; MANAGEMENT ADVISORY SERVICES BY CPAs; SOCIAL RESPONSIBILITIES OF ACCOUNTANTS; STATE REGULATION OF THE ACCOUNTANCY PROFESSION (U.S.); STERRETT, JOSEPH EDMUND

European Community (Union) Accounting: Fourth and Seventh Accounting Directives

The European Economic Community (hereafter referred to as EC, for the European Community) was formally established on March 25, 1957, by the Treaty of Rome. This treaty, signed by Belgium, France, Germany, Italy, Luxembourg, and the Netherlands, was intended to promote full economic integration among the member countries, facilitating the free movement of persons, capital, and goods and services among member states. To ensure that the objectives of the Treaty of Rome were met, the EC Commission—the executive and administrative branch of the EC—was established. Since its formation in 1957, the United Kingdom, Denmark, Ireland, Greece, Spain, and Portugal have become EC member states, bringing the total number of signatories to 12. The EC was first titled in 1957 the European Economic Community (EEC). It formally became the EC in 1992 even though the designation EC was widely used since the late 1980s. In late 1993, the EC became the European Union (EU).

In order to achieve full economic integration among member countries, national import tariffs must be eliminated, national monetary and fiscal policies coordinated, and national accounting practices and company laws harmonized. The EC, as part of its efforts to harmonize the company laws of member countries, has issued a number of directives.

Directives are documents issued by the EC Commission after unanimous approval by the EC's Council of Ministers. Development of these directives follows a specific procedure. First, an accounting issue is identified. After preliminary work on it is completed, a "Draft Directive" (Exposure Draft) is issued by the EC Commission. After public hearings and other evaluations, the Draft Directive is revised and reissued. Once the EC Commission feels that the Draft Directive is in acceptable form, it is submitted to the EC Council of Ministers. After unanimous approval by the EC Council of Ministers, it becomes a directive binding on member states. The member states are required to incorporate directives into their national law within a specified time; however, in many cases, member states have exceeded the specified deadlines. The process is time consuming and, in some cases, has taken several years from the time that an issue has been identified to the time it is ratified.

As of 1994, the EC had issued 13 directives pertaining directly to accounting. Two in particular have had a significant influence on the company laws of the member states: the Fourth Directive, "Formats and Rules of Accounting"; and the Seventh Directive, "Consolidated Accounting."

The Fourth Directive, approved in July 1978, deals with the presentation and contents of annual reports and the valuation methods to be used in their preparation. This directive applies to all public and private companies in EC-member countries, with the exception of banks and insurance companies. It establishes the minimum requirements to be followed and provides some flexibility in meeting these requirements. The affected companies are required to issue annual reports that include a balance sheet, an income statement, and notes to the financial statements. The directive does not require a cash-flow statement or statement of changes in financial position to be presented as part of basic financial statements, although many member states have such a requirement of their own.

In relation to financial-statement presentation, companies have flexibility in the format of the financial statements. For instance, the balance sheet can be presented on a horizontal format, sometimes referred to as a T Account format, in which assets are presented on the left side, and liabilities and stockholders' equity are presented on the right side. This is similar to U.S. format except that items are presented in reverse order of liquidity. The balance sheet can also be presented on a vertical format (a narrative form that arrives at stockholders' equity by subtracting each classification of liabilities from its respective classification of assets). Similarly, some flexibility is provided in the presentation of the income statement. This directive also specifies certain accounting concepts, such as going concern, accrual accounting, consistency, and prudence, to be applied in the preparation of financial statements.

Under the Fourth Directive, which encourages the companies to provide additional information, the overriding requirement in the presentation of an annual report is to provide a "true and fair view" of a company's financial position and its results of operations, and it is generally presumed that this requirement will be met if a company complies with all of the requirements of the Fourth Directive. The incorporation of the concept of "true and fair view" reflects the British influence on the Fourth Directive. Member states were required to incorporate this directive into their national law by July 1980; however, many far exceeded that deadline. It is generally agreed that the Fourth Directive is the most important directive in harmonizing the accounting practices of member states.

The Seventh Directive of 1983 deals with consolidation of certain groups of companies. In complying with its requirements, it also stresses the basic requirements of the Fourth Directive— that is, the formats of accounts, presentation of financial statements, and notes to financial statements. The Seventh Directive emphasizes economic factors such as dominance and dependence among entities as the basis for identification of a group and for consolidation purposes. It requires that: (1) a parent company must provide consolidated financial statements that give a "true and fair view" of the financial position of the consolidated entity; (2) all subsidiaries must be included in consolidated statements unless the inclusion of certain subsidiaries would not give a "true and fair view"; (3) all intra-company items must be eliminated in the consolidation process; and (4) the equity method of accounting must be used for associated/affiliated companies. Additionally, the Seventh Directive allows: (1) either the purchase or the "pooling of interests" method of accounting to be used for the acquisition of new subsidiaries; and (2) goodwill resulting from the use of the purchase method of accounting to be written off against the retained earnings immediately or to be amortized over a number of years.

The incorporation of this directive into the national law of member states was scheduled by January 1, 1988; however, as with the Fourth Directive, many member states have exceeded the scheduled time and thus far by 1994 have not fully implemented this directive.

Rasoul Tondkar
Ajay Adhikari

Bibliography
Barker, P. "Just Take an Option from 7th Directive," *Accountancy*, July 1985, pp. 135–136.

Choi, F.D.S., ed. *Handbook of International Accounting*. New York: John Wiley & Sons, 1991.

Coopers & Lybrand. *Accounting Comparisons: UK/Europe-II*. London: Coopers & Lybrand, 1990.

Ernst & Whinney. *The Fourth Directive: Its Effects on the Annual Accounts of Companies in the European Economic Community*. London: Kluwer, 1979.

———. *The Impact of the Seventh Directive*. London: Financial Times Business Information, 1984.

Tondkar, R.H., E.N. Coffman, and J.B. Sperry. "The Role of the European Economic Community in the Harmonization of the Accounting Practices among Member Countries," *Collected Papers of the American Accounting Association's Southeastern Regional Meeting*, April 1986, pp. 262–265.

Vangermeersch, R. "The Route of the Seventh Directive: Slow, Steady, Studied, and Successful," *International Journal of Accounting Education and Research*, Spring 1985, pp. 103–118.

See also GOODWILL; POOLING OF INTERESTS

External Auditing

From the beginning, the nature and growth of external auditing were influenced by two factors: (1) the needs and expectations of the users of audited information, and (2) the technology available to meet their demands. In Egypt, Babylonia, and Persia, the first accountants in recorded history were government accountant-auditors. The ruler held national property in trust for the people; the accountant-auditor played a social role in protecting these national assets. The ancient auditor's basic objective was the prevention or detection of fraud affecting government property. Contrariwise, modern auditing facilitated the development of capital markets that met the demands growing out of the industrial revolution.

Many regard classical Athens as the locale that gave birth to both internal and external auditors. The *logistae*, the equivalents of internal auditors, audited the public treasurer's account. The *efthini*, elected by the public, audited managerial accounts in association with the *logistae*. Athenian auditors were particularly concerned with the accounts of people leaving any public position that involved management of the state's money.

While the Athenian precursors of external and internal auditors hold historic interest, U.S. practice has been influenced by more recent British precedents. The earliest surviving accounting record in English is the sheepskin Pipe Roll or "Great Roll of the Exchequer." The Pipe Roll was prepared annually from the Domesday Book, a census and record of real properties and the taxes assessed thereon; the information was based on a survey originally made in 1086 after William the Conqueror had taken title to all property in the name of the crown. The Pipe Roll covers 700 years; it relates to taxes and other levies due the king, the amounts of such taxes collected and remitted by the county sheriffs to the Court of the Exchequer, and the expenses incurred in collecting the taxes.

The Pipe Roll was maintained in the department of the Upper Exchequer and represented an accounting for all receipts and payments. The Upper Exchequer had authority to audit the Lower Exchequer, or Treasurer's Department. The latter received all monies and payments in kind, either directly or through the sheriffs, who were the king's representatives. In any case, checking and verification appear to have proceeded without involvement of external auditors.

Large feudal estates were normally managed by stewards. The lord depended on the keeping of accounts as a check on the honesty and performance of the steward. Two important aspects of the manorial system were reflected by the "charge and discharge" statement pertaining to the principal-agent relationship and the management use of accounting information—activities that resemble some modern audit objectives.

Similarly, acquisitions of goods from distant places gave rise to owner-agent arrangements. The agents were entrusted with goods or money to carry on trading activities on behalf of their principal, or groups of principals, associated in a trading venture. Venture results were examined by an expert selected by the participants in the ventures. It was soon realized that the incipient auditor's opinion had more value if he stood independent of the parties at interest.

Some present-day scholars feel that the British legal profession was primarily responsible for the emergence of auditing as a profession. This assertion is supported by two types of occurrences. Each of four nineteenth-century British depressions was followed by enactment of a new bankruptcy statute. The statutes placed additional responsibilities on accountants, such as verifying the correctness of a bankrupt's quarterly financial statements and serving either as trustees in bankruptcy or as assignees of creditors.

A more important stimulus to auditing was provided by the emergence of social control through statutory regulation of publicly owned corporations. The Joint Stock Companies Act of 1844 specified that companies had to keep detailed accounting records subject to independent verification by "auditors" who were to be appointed by shareholders. The detection of fraud was still the auditor's main goal, although he had now acquired some responsibility for detecting technical errors and errors of principle.

A surge of opposition to government regulation resulted in the elimination of the aforementioned accounting and reporting requirements from the Companies Acts of 1855–1856. The resulting company law remained essentially unchanged until 1900.

In the United States, by 1900 about half the state incorporation statutes provided for either periodic reports to stockholders or reports to be issued upon demand of minority stockholders. But the state laws did not mention auditor verification of financial statements. Consequently, auditing developed purely as a service activity available to those who sought such services.

Eventually, the auditor's functioning as an integral part of the entity being audited gave way to an externally based professional who provided auditing services to clients. Thus, the specialist in accounts and their auditing emerged as a *public* accountant. Accounting gained recognition as an essential tool of successful industrial management and as the source of information that could serve as the basis for more-rational credit and investment decisions. Auditing, as a companion activity, helped to assure reliability of the reported financial data used by all parties external to the business organizations whose affairs were of interest to them.

Essentially, before the turn of the century, audits represented detailed reviews; the concepts of planning, internal control, audit risk management, and cost-benefit measurement remained largely unrecognized. In time,

uniquely American modifications emerged: (1) Displacement of the detailed audit by one utilizing testing. The audit test, which grew out of practicality and expediency, was introduced during the last 10 years of the nineteenth century. The increasing size and activity of business enterprises gave further impetus to testing. (2) Emergence of the "balance-sheet audit," which reflected an increasingly analytical approach. Methods were adopted for the verification of transactions by securing evidence outside the records of the client, rather than by relying solely on verifying the internal recording of transactions and the related documentary support. (3) Recognition of the importance of internal check and control in generating reliable accounting records and as a basis to determining the extent of audit testing of supporting evidence. The idea seems to have made its first appearance in the 1905 American version of Lawrence Dicksee's *Auditing*, edited by Robert Hiester Montgomery. (4) The use of statistical techniques in setting sample sizes based on a quantification of the reliability and precision desired from the testing process.

In England, 1900 marked the end of the swing away from government regulation that had begun with the Companies Act of 1856. An annual audit became obligatory for all registered companies; by implication this imposed an obligation to prepare an annual balance sheet. Auditors were required to sign a certificate at the foot of the balance sheet stating whether all their requirements as auditors had been met and to make a report to shareholders on the accounts that had been examined and on every balance sheet laid before the general meeting during their tenure of office.

By 1932 there was a considerable time lag between England and the United States. The New York Stock Exchange had required listed companies to provide financial statements audited by qualified accountants. However, the Securities Act of 1933 and the Securities Act of 1934 mandated CPA audits of listed companies, regardless of stock exchange. Although the traditional role of the voluntarily hired auditor was to detect and report breaches of implicit or explicit contracts, the auditor's role intended by legislation was to monitor management disclosure of information assumed to be used in investor decisions.

While the Securities Act of 1933 was still under consideration, Congress was persuaded, largely through the testimony of George Oliver

May and Col. Arthur H. Carter, that financial statements relating to a proposed issue of securities should be audited and that the public accounting profession, rather than government auditors, should be designated to provide audits quickly and economically. Subsequent regulations of the Securities and Exchange Commission (SEC) provided only that the certifying accountant must be *independent*; there has been no regulatory reference to the *professional* qualifications of the certifying accountant. The liability provisions of the 1933 and 1934 Acts were of immediate consequence; auditors, now bearing the burden of proof, were to be held liable for any misstatements or omissions of material facts.

Accounting and auditing have achieved prominence through practitioners' ability to cope with the challenges of an increasingly complex business environment. Accounting information has been invaluable to business profitability on an internal basis by helping to identify inefficiency and by aiding in the control of widely dispersed operations. On a macro basis, communication of reliable information about profitability has contributed to the productivity of capital, and to economic well-being, by helping to channel capital to the most profitable opportunities.

The introduction of mandatory audit requirements, together with the value of audits to important user constituencies, contributed to a veritable population explosion in individual accountants and accounting firms. The merger activity that hit the accounting profession in 1988 was fueled by opportunities that may open with the removal of economic boundaries in Europe in the early 1990s.

The revenue volumes of the Big Six accounting firms reflect the concentration of audits of major U.S. companies with large firms. Similar results were noted in a study (Wootton, Tonge, and Wolk, 1990) that compared companies listed on the New York Stock Exchange for 1956 and 1989. In 1956 the Big Eight audited 78.51 percent of these listed companies, while the top four firms audited 50.27 percent. In 1989 the comparable figures were 96 percent and 68.94 percent, respectively. Until the early 1990s, many smaller firms seemed to shy away from the practice of auditing. However, published tabulations of auditor changes may presage a reversal; smaller firms may be reentering the audit market, armed with technological know-how.

For decades, members of the accounting profession ranked near the top of all professions in terms of public esteem. That esteem may have eroded; the accountants' image has been tarnished by the savings and loan debacle. Audit profitability and productivity seem to have deteriorated in this era of increased competition, while legislators, regulators, and journalists have questioned audit effectiveness. Improvements in audit effectiveness may mean doing more auditing, while enhanced audit productivity may suggest doing less. The resulting dilemma must be resolved; practitioners' application of available and accessible technology is likely to be helpful.

Although the profession has published a commendable code of ethics, some open questions merit discussion: (1) The audit firm is selected and paid by management. Although the formal opinion is rendered to the public in general (in the annual report of the corporation) the management letter, if, as, and when rendered, is usually directed to management and often to the controller or treasurer most involved in any weaknesses of internal control that might be reported therein. (2) It is not entirely clear to what degree auditors are responsible for detection of employee or management fraud. (3) Auditing procedures have changed from the verifying of mathematical accuracy (and the absolution of management) to sampling techniques and an opinion as to the fairness of the financial statements. Both the sampling techniques and the accountant's opinion are still subject to controversy. The sampling controversy centers on the use of statistical sampling; the technique has not been accepted or even understood by many auditors. Also, statistical sampling appears to be losing ground to renewed popularity of detailed reviews, made cost-effective by computer utilization. (4) There is general acceptance of the approach wherein the review of internal control is the starting point of the audit, and the results the basis for determining the extent of testing required. However, questions persist. Internal control is a *management* procedure for addressing risk. Accordingly, auditors must bring their own *independent* judgment to bear regarding risks of misstatement; they must design their own tests to ascertain whether management procedures did in fact address such risks. On reflection, when practical, many auditors would opt for unrestricted substantive tests.

E

On balance, the fundamental conditions underlying the practice of auditing continue to be positive. Internationalization of business will be fostered by freer markets abroad, as well as by computerized technology transfers across national borders. An upsurge in audit effectiveness and efficiency and the return of smaller firms to the audit market are foreseen.

Howard F. Stettler
Felix Pomeranz

Bibliography

Adelberg, A.H. "Auditing on the March: Ancient Times to the Twentieth Century," *Internal Auditor*, November/December 1975, pp. 35–47.

Becker, E.A. "The Evolution of Financial Auditing in the United States," *Baylor Business Studies*, May/June/July, 1980, pp. 37–54.

Brown, R.G. "Changing Audit Objectives and Techniques," *Accounting Review*, October 1962, pp. 696–703.

Falk, H. "A Comparison of Regulation Theories: The Case for Mandated Auditing in the United States," *Research in Accounting Regulation*, 1989, pp. 103–124.

Filios, V.P. "A Concise History of Auditing, 3000 B.C.–A.D. 1700," *Internal Auditor*, June 1984, pp. 48–49.

Moyer, C.A. "Early Developments in American Auditing," *Accounting Review*, January 1951, pp. 3–8.

Stone, W.E. "The Auditor's Changing Role in the United States," *Chartered Accountant in Australia*, June 1982, pp. 16–20.

Wootton, C., S.D. Tonge, and C.M. Wolk. "From the 'Big Eight' to the 'Bix Six' Accounting Firms," *Ohio CPA Journal*, Spring 1990, pp. 19–23.

See also AGENCY THEORY; AMERICAN INSTITUTE OF CERTIFIED PUBLIC ACCOUNTANTS; AUDIT COMMITTEES; AUDITOR'S REPORT; BABYLONIA; BIG EIGHT ACCOUNTING FIRMS; "CHARGE AND DISCHARGE" STATEMENT; COMPANIES ACTS; COMPUTING TECHNOLOGY IN THE WEST: THE IMPACT ON THE PROFESSION OF ACCOUNTING; CORPORATIONS: EVOLUTION; DOMESDAY BOOK; EGYPT; FRAUD AND AUDITING; GREECE; INDEPENDENCE OF EXTERNAL AUDITORS; INTERNAL AUDITING; INTERNAL CONTROL; *LEEDS ESTATE BUILDING AND INVESTMENT COMPANY V. SHEPARD;* LEGAL LIABILITY OF AUDITORS; MANORIAL ACCOUNTING; MAUTZ, ROBERT K.; MAY, GEORGE OLIVER; MCKESSON AND ROBBINS CASE; MEDIEVAL ACCOUNTING; MONTGOMERY, ROBERT HIESTER; NEW YORK STOCK EXCHANGE; PIPE ROLL; PIXLEY, FRANCIS WILLIAM; PROFFER SYSTEM; SECURITIES AND EXCHANGE COMMISSION; SNELL, CHARLES; STATISTICAL SAMPLING; TREADWAY COMMISSION; TRUSTEE ACCOUNTS; *UNIFORM ACCOUNTING;* U.S. INDUSTRIAL COMMISSION

F

Farolfi Company Ledger

Giovanni Farolfi and Company was a Florentine mercantile firm, dealing mainly in agricultural products, whose head office was at Nimes, France. The only surviving Farolfi ledger (1299–1300) was kept for the company branch at Salon in Provence. The Farolfi Company employed a comprehensive, articulated double entry system, suggesting that Florentine double entry was well developed by the year 1300. The ledger included real and nominal accounts, a home office (capital) account, and accounts for different kinds of merchandise. Ledger entries were cross-referenced to at least five other account books, and some were referenced to a profit and loss account. The ledger was regularly balanced and closed by means of a balance account. There were four accounts for prepaid rent, which was correctly treated as a deferred expense.

Michael Chatfield

Bibliography

Lee, G.A. "The Coming of Age of Double Entry: The Giovanni Farolfi Ledger of 1299–1300," *Accounting Historians Journal*, Fall 1977, pp. 79–96.

See also BALANCE ACCOUNT; BRANCH ACCOUNTING; CLOSING ENTRIES AND PROCEDURES; DOUBLE ENTRY BOOKKEEPING: ORIGINS; JOURNAL; LEDGER

Federal Government Accounting (U.S.)

The development of the U.S. government's accounting system covers a period of well over two centuries. The system had its origins in the accounting that was performed by the founding colonies and thus was influenced by the concepts of accounting that were brought from England and adapted to the needs and rigors of the fledgling governments.

The concept of appropriations in government can be traced to activity in 1688 of the British Parliament. However, this aspect of the financial structure was sporadically used. The use of the Exchequer, the national treasury, as an audit device demonstrates the fact that there was little accounting and that the accountability was discharged essentially through the proffering of original media of support of revenues and expenditures. This condition continued to exist in England until the enactment of the Exchequer and Audit Control Act in 1862. This act provided for officials and systems of accounts and reports.

The colonies and later the states experimented with financial-management systems that resulted in domination by the legislatures over the executive branch. The concept of money bills originating in the lower house of the legislature also originated in England and was strong in the colonies by the eighteenth century. In addition, the colonies developed a realistic separation of power; thus, there could be presumed to be accounts and reports that were the substance of preaudit and postaudit. The experiences of the colonies, later the states, represented the pattern on which the federal accounting system was to be based.

The Revolutionary War resulted in the development of an accounting system that would record the payment of troops and the purchase of materials. In July 1775, the Continental Congress provided for two joint treasurers and a paymaster system. In February 1776, a resolution was adopted establishing a committee to superintend the treasury and to (1) examine the accounts of the treasurers and to report to Congress, (2) consider ways and means of supplying gold and silver, (3) employ and instruct persons to audit accounts of paymasters, commissioners, and others entrusted with public money, and (4) superintend the emission of bills of credit.

In April 1776, the Congress established a Treasury Office of Accounts under supervision of the Board of Treasury, a Standing Committee of Congress, to "state, arrange and keep public accounts." Also, a procedure was developed for withdrawing money through the use of warrants. These warrants were certified and entered on the books of the treasury, and periodically commissioners, paymasters, and others had to produce their accounts and vouchers for settlement.

In March 1777, the Congress provided for the appointment of commissioners to examine claims against the United States. In April 1777, the commissioners were authorized to adjust the accounts of those to whom money had been advanced. In 1778 the Congress established, in the treasury, offices of a comptroller, auditor, treasurer, and six commissioners of accounts to function under the Treasury Board. As a result of complaints of mismanagement and incompetence, Congress in 1781 established the office of the superintendent of finance. Later that year, it abolished the Treasury Board and replaced the other old offices with a comptroller, a treasurer, a register, auditors, and clerks.

In 1789 as, in part, a reaction to the financial problems of the Revolutionary War and the failure of the Articles of Confederation, a new accounting system was adopted. The features of this new system were later adopted by the federal government under the U.S. Constitution.

The foundation of the present federal accounting system is Article 1, Section 9 of the Constitution. However, the Treasury Act of 1789 was required to carry out the constitutional provisions. The act created the Treasury Department, establishing its organization and its basic fiscal procedure. The act provided for four basic elements: (1) general direction and coordination of fiscal matters, (2) division of responsibility and activities relative to the receipt, custody, and disbursement of funds, (3) audit of financial transactions, and (4) monitoring of records and publishing reports. The organization included a secretary of the treasury, a comptroller, an auditor, a treasurer, a registrar, and an assistant to the secretary.

Congress, in the Act to Provide for the Prompt Settlement of Public Accounts of March 3, 1817, attempted to provide for the prompt settlement of public accounts. It eliminated the offices of the accountant and additional accountant in the War Department and of the accountant in the Navy Department and provided that claims that had been processed by their offices should be a responsibility of the Treasury Department. The act also established a second comptroller and four more auditors, making a total of five.

The act designated reporting responsibilities of the auditors and the comptrollers and provided that all accounts of public expenditures were to be settled within one year. The act also set the pattern of nineteenth-century financial administration, and its impact, with few exceptions, remained until 1894 when the Dockery Act was passed.

From 1817 to 1894, some changes were made in the federal accounting structure, but the modifications were mostly cosmetic and related to organization and areas of responsibilities. In 1830, for example, Congress created the office of the solicitor of the treasury; in 1836 a sixth auditor was added to the Treasury Department to handle postal accounts; in 1849 the office of commissioner of customs was established, with the commissioner functioning, in effect, as the third comptroller. In 1855 Congress created a Court of Claims to hear the increasing number of claims for alleged violations of contracts presented to the Treasury Department's second comptroller; in 1866 the Court of Claims was given jurisdiction over accounts from the Civil War, and judgments made by the court were made conclusive. In 1868 Congress passed legislation stating that government department heads were to be bound by comptrollers' decisions and could not change or modify balances certified to them. In 1870 it passed the Antideficiency Act, which resulted in the provisions of Section 3679 of the Revised Statutes, to prevent agencies from expending amounts in excess of congressional appropriations. And in 1882 it authorized the printing of decisions of the first comptroller of the treasury.

During the three decades following the Civil War, four major studies of the financial operations of the federal government were conducted. The goal of these studies, the first such efforts since the early 1800s, was to improve and modernize the fiscal functions of the government. Frederick C. Mosher (1979), a professor of government at the University of Virginia, reported that the first three were the Patterson Committee (1869–1871), the Boutwell Committee (1875–1876), and the Cockrell Committee (1887–1889). These committees were each authorized by the Congress, as was the fourth body, the Dockery-Cockrell Commission (1893–1895). It was by far the most productive of the four. The Dockery-Cockrell commission had the authority to engage consultants, and it hired three top accountants from the private sector, two of whom were Charles Waldo Haskins and Elijah Watt Sells, the founders of the firm of Haskins and Sells. The commission produced 29 reports emphasizing financial management, accounting, and auditing. Much legislation resulted from its efforts.

The Dockery Act of July 31, 1894, brought about these principal changes: (1) The office of comptroller of the treasury took the place of the several existing comptrollers; (2) the duties of the six auditors of the Treasury Department were redefined, their jurisdictions were established, and settlements made by them were given general finality; (3) a division of bookkeeping and warrants was established and assigned the official maintenance of appropriation accounts, which previously had been maintained in four decentralized offices; and (4) the secretary of the treasury was required to report to Congress an annual combined statement of all receipts and expenditures.

One of the most important results of this legislation was the centralization of the federal government's bookkeeping. Also transferred were the "personal ledgers" in which were recorded advances of funds and warrants.

In 1905 President Theodore Roosevelt appointed the Keep Committee, whose objective was to identify changes needed for placing the government on an economical and effective basis. Among the accomplishments of the committee, which operated from 1905 to 1909 and consisted of five members within the executive branch, were: (1) rendering of accounts that should be stated in a consolidated format instead of by appropriation or by account, (2) establishment of business-methods committees in each section of the Treasury Department, (3) development of cost accounting procedures for government agencies, (4) requiring government creditors to certify amounts due, and (5) instal-

lation of a double entry system of bookkeeping. The double entry system, long overdue, provided a more accurate method of accounting. Concurrently, other improvements were made in the handling of warrants and in the auditing of expenditures. Also, the forms used for ledgers and accounts were improved to show more information and to expedite their audit and reporting. The Keep Committee was composed of Charles H. Keep, Assistant Secretary of the Treasury; Lawrence O. Murray, Assistant Secretary of Commerce and Labor; James A. Garfield, Commissioner of the Bureau of Corporations; Gifford Pinchot, Chief of the Forest Service; and Frank H. Hitchcock, first Postmaster General (Kraines).

The Taft Commission on Economy and Efficiency was established in 1910 by Congress at the behest of President William Howard Taft to examine government procedures and to recommend more efficient and economical methods. Mosher listed these members of the Commission: Frederick A. Cleveland, Chairman and the Director of the New York Bureau of Municipal Research; Harvey S. Chase, a certified public accountant; Frank J. Goodnow, a political scientist; W.W. Warwick, a jurist; W.F. Willoughby, assistant director of the Census; and M.O. Chase, the auditor for the post office. The commission, which enlisted the participation of personnel within and outside the government, made the following recommendations related to the federal accounting system: (1) consolidation of the several Treasury Department auditing offices into a single auditing office; (2) institution of a national budget; and (3) institution of uniform accounting systems in administrative agencies.

The budget recommendation, although supported by President Taft, received insufficient congressional support. However, the third recommendation was implemented by President Taft's executive order in 1911, introducing into the federal government uniformity in classification of accounts and terminology, documents and forms, and systems and procedures. Unfortunately, when the commission terminated in 1913, so did the improvements recommended under its sponsorship.

World War I brought a large increase in the national public debt, a substantial growth in revenues and expenditures, and a large expansion in the administrative aspects of the national government. These growth factors pushed the federal government toward a budget system.

F

The result was the Budget and Accounting Act of 1921, which was probably the most important piece of legislation concerning the improvement of federal accounting and auditing. The act consisted of three separate parts that established the General Accounting Office (and the office of comptroller general), The Bureau of the Budget (in the Treasury Department), and the office of the comptroller of the treasury. It also abolished the offices of the six auditors in the Treasury Department.

The act gave the General Accounting Office numerous responsibilities, including (1) settlement of claims; (2) prescription of forms, systems, and procedures for appropriation and fund accounting; (3) investigation of matters relating to receipt, disbursement, and application of funds; and (4) inquiry of departments and agencies as to their financial transactions and business methods.

The powers and duties of the comptroller of the treasury, the assistant comptroller of the treasury and the six treasury auditors were assigned to the General Accounting Office, as were the duties of the division of bookkeeping and warrants, especially those relating to the maintenance of the personal ledgers. This latter transfer removed one of the links in the double entry bookkeeping system established in 1907. However, the basic federal accounting system was left in the Treasury Department as had been provided by the Dockery Act of 1894. No changes were made in the procedure of collecting and disbursing money. Also, the warrant system was unchanged except that the countersigning of warrants was assigned to the comptroller general.

President Herbert Hoover, under the authority of the provisions of the Economy Act of 1932, made a number of recommendations for changes in the functions of executive-branch agencies, but none became effective because the House of Representatives disapproved of them. However, Executive Order No. 6226, issued July 27, 1933, and Treasury Department Circular 494, also issued that year, did require that agencies apportion appropriations on a monthly basis and report monthly the obligations incurred.

Treasury Circular 494 defined the terms "obligation" and "encumbrance." However, there was still a lack of uniformity in application of the terms. This confusion also resulted in problems relative to the content of "unencumbered balances," "unexpended balances," and "unobligated balances."

During the period 1936–1937, several congressional and executive-branch studies were made. As a result of these studies changes were made in federal accounting procedures to: (1) centralize and consolidate record keeping and reporting, (2) fix on the executive the responsibility for fiscal management, (3) simplify the appropriation system, (4) provide budgetary control in the Treasury Department, (5) transfer to the Treasury Department (from the General Accounting Office) authority over administrative accounting, (6) transfer to the Treasury Department the prescribing of administrative forms and methods of accounting; and (7) establish a system of central-control accounts in the Treasury Department. The intent and, presumably, the result of these changes was the improvement of the organization of the government.

Executive Order 8512 in 1940 authorized the Treasury Department to: (1) prepare financial reports for the president and the Bureau of the Budget; (2) establish a system of summary accounts reflecting all financial transactions; (3) establish uniform standards for the valuation of assets, determination of liabilities, and treatment of revenues and expenditures, (4) establish uniform classifications of assets, liabilities, revenues, and expenditures, and (5) establish a uniform accounting terminology. Executive Order No. 9084 in 1942 provided for the concurrence of the comptroller general on the above items as related to terminology, classifications, principles, and standards. These orders spurred eforts to improve accounting and reporting. The improvements were intended to accomplish (1) the protection of funds, securities, and other assets; (2) economy and efficiency in government operations; (3) cooperation and participation of agencies; and (4) better service to the public and to the agencies served.

The Joint Accounting Improvement Program (JAIP), now the Joint Financial Management Improvement Program (JFMIP), was created in 1947 by the U.S. General Accounting Office (GAO), the Treasury Department, and the Bureau of the Budget to develop accounting systems suited to the managerial needs of the various federal departments through implementation of an integrated, governmentwide accounting pattern. The principal function of the current JFMIP is to serve as a coordinator, stimulator, and catalyst for the improvement of financial management practices throughout the government. Mosher reported that the Comptroller General of GAO would provide leadership with the support of the Secretary of the Treasury and the Director of the Budget.

The Budget and Accounting Procedures Act of 1950 was very important relative to current federal accounting procedures. The act was divided into three parts: Title I, covering budgeting and accounting; Title II, covering appropriations; and Title III, stipulating repeal and deletion of legislation that was no longer applicable. It authorized performance-based budgets, budgets related to programs and activities, and required financial information in terms of functions and activities. The act also directed agencies to achieve (1) consistency in accounting and budget classification, (2) synchronization between budget and accounting classification and organizational structure, and (3) support of budget justification by information on performance and program costs by units.

The Accounting and Auditing Act of 1950, a part of the Budget and Accounting Procedures Act of 1950, made the maintenance of accounting systems and the issuance of reports the responsibility of the executive branch. It stipulated that the Comptroller General's audits were to be directed at determining (1) the extent to which accounting and financial reporting fulfilled the purposes specified, (2) that financial transactions complied with laws and regulations, and (3) that adequate financial controls over operations were extended so as to afford an effective basis for account settlement.

The act made the comptroller general responsible for prescribing principles, standards, and related requirements for all agencies, and the head of each agency responsible for establishing and maintaining the systems of accounting and financial controls to accomplish (1) full disclosure; (2) adequate information for management; (3) effective control and accountability over assets, including internal audit; (4) reliable accounting results for budget execution; and (5) suitable integration with the Treasury Department. Title III of the Accounting and Auditing Act required that budgets be prepared on a performance basis emphasizing functions and activities and justified by work-load and unit-cost data. Also required was information reconciling expenditures with appropriations.

In 1956 Public Law 84–863 amended the 1950 acts as well as the Budget and Accounting Act of 1921 with provisions to (1) require budget information on program costs and accomplishments, (2) maintain accounts on an accrual basis, and (3) achieve simplified controls over the subdivision of appropriations and funds.

Federal accounting was also affected by the Supplemental Appropriation Act of 1955, which is known for its Section 1311 that established statutory criteria to define valid obligations. It provided eight forms of documentary evidence and required inventories at year end of unliquidated obligations and unobligated appropriation balances.

The last half of the twentieth century brought many peripheral improvements. The JFMIP became more active, with personnel assigned from each of the four supporting agencies in which the Chairman of the Civil Service Commission was added in 1966. However, it was not until the 1970s when one of the Big Eight accounting firms, Arthur Andersen and Company (1975), on a voluntary basis, produced an unofficial set of federal financial statements on an accrual-accounting basis. The Treasury Department subsequently provided such statements and continues with them in 1994.

Two important acts that had an impact on the federal accounting system were the Inspector General Act of 1978, which created in each agency an inspector general combining the auditing and investigating activities of the agency; and the Single Audit Act of 1984, which outlined the auditing of grants and contracts issued by the federal government.

The latter 1980s saw a series of improvements, including the development of a more definitive accounting text by the GAO and the provision of a standard set of general-ledger accounts by the Office of Management and Budget. The comptroller general, with the auditor general of Canada, set up a commission that developed a prototype national accounting and reporting format. Also, Congress passed a bill establishing, in the Office of Management and Budget, a federal financial manager to function as a comptroller. Concurrently, similar officials were established in each of the major departments and agencies. The bill also authorized the agencies' inspectors general to audit the financial aspects of agency operations or to have such audits performed by public accounting firms.

The first four years of the 1990s have placed accounting in the forefront of management changes in the federal government. The Chief Financial Officers (CFO) Act of 1990

F

required the establishment in the federal government of a foundation of basic financial manager practices that are common and considered vital in the private sector. The Federal Accounting Standards Advisory Board was established in 1990 by the Secretary of the Treasury, the Director of the Office of Management and Budget, and the Comptroller General. The nine-member Board was created to consider and recommend accounting principles for the federal government. The Government Performance and Results Act (GPRA) of 1993 required federal agencies over time to develop strategic plans, identify outcome goals, and measure and report on progress toward achieving these goals.

In a report in 1993 by Vice President Al Gore, strong commitments for change in federal government accounting were adopted. These commitments are: (1) The President should issue an annual financial report to the citizens; (2) Legislation should be enacted to allow funds for debt collection activities to come from revenue generated from collections, letting agencies keep a portion of any increased collection amounts for further improvements; (3) Issue all federal payments through Electronic Funds Transfer or Electronic Benefits Transfer; (4) Issue a comprehensive set of federal accounting standards within 18 months; (5) Allow agencies and departments to create "innovative capital funds" out of retained savings from operational funds as well as other sources; and (6) The President should instruct agency heads to implement, at their discretion, franchising for service functions.

Mortimer A. Dittenhofer

Bibliography

Arthur Andersen and Company. *Sound Financial Reporting in the Public Sector: A Prerequisite to Fiscal Responsibility.* Chicago: Arthur Andersen and Company, 1975.

Bolles, A.S. *The Financial History of the United States from 1774 to 1789.* 4th ed. New York: D. Appleton, 1884. Reprint. New York: Augustus M. Kelley, 1969.

Colleta, P.E. *The Presidency of William Howard Taft.* Lawrence, KS: University Press of Kansas, 1973.

Gore, Al, Vice President. *From Red Tape to Results: Creating a Government that Works Better and Costs Less: Improving Financial Management.* Accompanying Report of the National Performance Review. Washington, D.C.: U.S. GPO, 1993.

"If the U.S. Kept Books the Way a Business Does," *Business Week*, September 29, 1975, pp. 74–75, 79.

Kraines, O. "The President Versus Congress: The Keep Commission, 1905–1909, First Comprehensive Presidential Inquiry into Administration," *Western Political Quarterly*, March 1970, pp. 5–54.

Mansfield, H.C. Jr. *The Comptroller General: A Study in the Law and Practice of Financial Administration.* New Haven, CT: Yale University Press, 1939.

Maycock, R. "History of Government Accounting." Unpublished manuscript in the archives of the U.S. General Accounting Office, Washington, DC.

Mosher, F.C. *The GAO: The Quest for Accountability in American Government.* Boulder, CO: Westview Press, 1979.

Tierney, C.E. *Handbook of Federal Accounting Practices.* Reading, MA: Addison-Wesley, 1982.

See also BUDGETING; COLONIAL AMERICA, ACCOUNTING IN; CONGRESSIONAL VIEWS; GENERAL ACCOUNTING OFFICE, U.S.; HASKINS, CHARLES WALDO; SELLS, ELIJAH WATT; STERRETT, JOSEPH EDMUND

Financial Accounting Standards Board

The Financial Accounting Standards Board (FASB) is the body that establishes and improves standards of financial accounting and reporting in the United States. The FASB is an independent, nonprofit, private-sector organization, not a government agency. Its standards are authoritative because they are enforced by the Securities and Exchange Commission (SEC Financial Accounting Release No. 1, Section 101), the American Institute of Certified Public Accountants (Rule 203 of the AICPA Code of Professional Conduct), and CPA licensing statutes and regulations in all 50 states. The FASB was established in 1973. For nearly 40 years before then, accounting standards-setting in the United States was the responsibility of the AICPA—from 1936–1959 by its Committee on Accounting Procedure (CAP) and from 1959–1973 by its Accounting Principles Board (APB). Both were part-time volunteer committees with limited staff resources. Pronouncements of the CAP and APB continue in force today unless amended or replaced by the FASB.

The FASB operates under the oversight of the Financial Accounting Foundation (FAF), which is jointly sponsored by, but independent of, the following eight organizations: the American Accounting Association, the American Institute of Certified Public Accountants, the Association of Investment Management and Research, the Financial Executives Institute, the Institute of Management Accountants, the Securities Industry Association, the Government Finance Officers Association, and the National Association of State Auditors, Comptrollers, and Treasurers.

The FAF has 16 trustees, who oversee the work of the FASB, appoint its members, approve its budget, and raise funds for its operations. FAF trustees have no say in setting FASB standards, however. The FAF also oversees the work of the companion Governmental Accounting Standards Board (GASB), which establishes standards for financial accounting and reporting for units of state and local government.

The FASB has seven members, all of whom are compensated and serve full-time. In contrast, the FASB's predecessors—the CAP and the APB—had many more members (generally 15–21), none of whom were compensated, and all of whom were part-time. In accepting appointment, FASB members must sever all ties to their former firms or organizations, another major difference from its predecessors. There is no required number or percentage of particular backgrounds. Since the mid-1980s, there have tended to be three from public accounting, two from industry, an educator, and a financial-statement user from the private sector or government, another marked contrast with the predecessor bodies, which were composed mostly of CPAs in public accounting practice.

A vote of at least 5 to 2 is required to adopt an accounting standard. That "super-majority" voting requirement was imposed by the FAF trustees in 1990 to enhance general acceptance of FASB standards. The previous requirement of a simple majority had been criticized by some as insufficient evidence of a consensus solution to an accounting problem.

The FASB has a director of research and 40 professional staff members who conduct research and develop materials on agenda projects for the board.

The FASB was created after a blue-ribbon Study Group (commonly called the "Wheat Committee" for its chairman, Francis M. Wheat) concluded in 1972 that the APB suf-

fered from some important shortcomings. In its report, the committee made the following points:

(1) A part-time volunteer committee will always be perceived as lacking independence. Public confidence in accounting standards demands an independent board with a full and open decision-making process.

(2) The magnitude of the workload requires a full-time standards board. Progress of the part-time efforts was too slow.

(3) APB members were mostly auditors—CPAs in public accounting practice. The constituency for accounting standards is much broader than that, including preparers and users of financial statements, accounting educators, and government. The standards board must represent the entire constituency.

(4) Effective standards-setting requires a much larger full-time research and support staff than the AICPA could provide.

(5) All of the constituencies should share in the funding obligation, not just the auditing profession.

The FASB structure was designed to remedy each of those shortcomings.

The FASB has an advisory group—the Financial Accounting Standards Advisory Council (FASAC)—that serves as its "eyes and ears" to the world of accounting practice. The FASAC basically functions as an early-warning device for problems the board may need to consider, and as a mechanism for feedback from the FASB's various constituencies regarding the board's standards and processes. The FASAC has approximately 30 members broadly representative of preparers, auditors, and users of financial statements, academia, banking, law, and government.

In 1984 the FASB created the Emerging Issues Task Force (EITF), whose members are selected by various professional organizations because the EITF members are in a position to become aware of emerging accounting issues before they become widespread and before divergent accounting practices become entrenched. The composition of its 13 voting members are: 9 from CPA firms and 4 from industry. There is one observer each from the SEC and the FASB. The FASB's director of research chairs the Task Force, which meets approximately eight times per year.

EITF meetings are open to the public, and proceedings are published issue by issue. The EITF attempts to reach a consensus among its

F

members on the appropriate accounting practice for each emerging issue. If an EITF consensus is reached and published, the FASB usually will not get further involved with the issue. If the EITF cannot reach a consensus, the FASB will often put the matter on its own agenda. While an EITF consensus does not have the "force of law" of an FASB standard, EITF recommendations are almost always followed in practice.

The procedures followed by the FASB in establishing accounting standards are collectively referred to as "due process"—a phrase generally used to describe judicial and legislative proceedings. First and foremost, the FASB's procedures are a public process designed to ensure that the board has heard and considered all reasonable points of view before it makes its decisions. The Wheat Committee, which developed the procedures, wisely recognized that the key to public confidence in the FASB is a belief that the standard-setting process is fair and open.

The board may complete the process on narrower issues in less than a year, while major projects may demand three to five years. In no case, however, can the board issue a final pronouncement without first having solicited public comment.

Agenda items are called to the board's attention by the SEC, the EITF, the FASAC, committees of professional organizations such as the AICPA, and individual accountants, including especially auditors and accountants in industry. Factors such as urgency, pervasiveness, technical feasibility, practical consequences, and availability of resources all enter into the board's agenda decision, which is made at a public meeting.

For the major projects, the board appoints a Task Force of outside experts to assist in defining the scope of the problem, identifying additional research that may be needed, and reviewing drafts of one or more discussion documents that the board may issue to solicit public comment. Task Force meetings are announced, and observers are welcome.

For most major projects, an FASB Discussion Memorandum (DM) is the initial discussion document prepared by the FASB staff to solicit public comment. The DM defines the scope of the project and the issues involved. It analyzes relevant literature, including consideration of similar issues by accounting-standards bodies in other countries. It presents alternative solutions to the issues and the arguments and implications relative to each, and it requests written comments on the issues and alternatives. Generally, around six months are allowed for comments.

The DM is a neutral document intended to ensure that every reasonable alternative receives fair consideration. Only after the board has solicited and analyzed the views of its various constituencies does decision making begin.

After analyzing the written comments, the views expressed at the hearing, research findings, and drafts of other materials prepared by the staff, the board begins its deliberations on the issues at meetings that are open to public observation. Deliberations often include questions of senior staff involved with the project, particularly the director of research and the project manager. The goal of the deliberations is to reach agreement on proposed standards that the board will issue for public comment in a document known as an Exposure Draft. A simple-majority vote is required to issue an Exposure Draft.

Written comments on the Exposure Draft are solicited, generally for a period of from two to six months, occasionally longer for complex projects. Sometimes the board will arrange for field tests of its proposals in an Exposure Draft, to help assess the costs and difficulties of implementation. The comments are analyzed and board deliberations resume, leading ultimately to a final FASB pronouncement, known as a Statement of Financial Accounting Standards. Sometimes comments received on an Exposure Draft cause the board to make significant changes to the standards it had proposed. In those cases, the board may issue a revised Exposure Draft before proceeding to a final Statement.

FASB Statements usually contain four distinct sections: (1) the standards of financial accounting and reporting being promulgated; (2) the vote of the board members, including reasons expressed by any dissenting board members; (3) background and historical information on the project; and (4) the basis for conclusions, including the alternatives considered, the pros and cons of each, and the board's reasons for accepting some alternatives and rejecting others. Sometimes a fifth section, containing examples of how to apply the new standards in practice, is included.

The FASB has two other types of pronouncements that can be used to deal with narrow issues. One is an FASB Interpretation, which may be issued by the Board after limited exposure to the FASAC and others the board identifies. Interpretations may only elaborate on existing standards, not establish new ones.

The other type of pronouncement is a Technical Bulletin, which is issued by the FASB staff rather than by the board itself, though it must be discussed by the board at a public meeting and may not be issued if a majority of the board objects. Technical Bulletins are used only to clarify a point in an FASB Statement when the staff concludes it has a clear understanding of the board's intent.

The FASB is a good example of private-sector self-regulation in an area that government could just as easily have seized as its own responsibility. Indeed, federal securities laws give the SEC the power to establish standards for accounting and financial reporting for the 12,000 or so companies in the United States whose securities are publicly traded. But the SEC, while retaining the ultimate statutory authority, has opted instead to look to the FASB.

Only in a few instances has the SEC overruled the FASB. The most prominent case was in 1978, when the SEC agreed to accept either the successful-efforts method or the full-cost method of accounting for oil- and gas-producing activities even though the FASB just a year earlier had prohibited the full-cost method in FAS No. 19, "Financial Accounting and Reporting by Oil and Gas Producing Companies" (1977). The successful-efforts method immediately writes off the costs of unsuccessful exploration efforts ("dry holes"), whereas the full-cost method capitalizes and amortizes such costs. Fas No. 25, "Suspension of Certain Accounting Requirements for Oil and Gas Producing Companies" (1978), followed the SEC approach.

The SEC has sometimes issued guidelines in the absence of FASB standards—for example, with respect to financial-statement disclosures. For example, Rule 502 of SEC Regulation S-X requires detailed disclosures about cash, receivables, inventories, long-term contracts, long-lived assets and depreciation, payables, minority interests, and redeemable preferred stock, among many other balance sheet items, beyond FASB requirements. Similarly, Rule 503 requires disclosures about income statement items and Rule 504 requires supplemental financial statement schedules, all beyond FASB requirements. Regulation S-X delineates the main body of financial and non-financial data required to be filed with the SEC. A lesser number of examples may be found with respect to accounting standards for measuring assets, liabilities, and earnings.

On a number of occasions since the FASB's creation in 1973, Congress has raised the question of whether the SEC should continue to rely on a private-sector standard-setting body. Hearings and investigations conducted by Senators Harrison Williams (D-New Jersey) in 1974, Lee Metcalf (D-Montana) in 1976 and 1977, and Thomas Eagleton (D-Missouri) in 1976 and by Congressmen John E. Moss (D-California) in 1976, 1977, and 1978, and John Dingell (D-Michigan) from the mid-1980s until the mid-1990s generally tended to put pressure on the FASB to take a harder line in its standards or to tighten its procedures to ensure total independence. In the most significant effort of these senators and congressmen, Metcalf's Subcommittee on Reports, Accounting and Management of the Committee on Government Operations recommended that the Federal Government should directly establish financial accounting standards for publicly owned corporations in its 1977 report "The Accounting Establishment." Congress has never hesitated to pressure the FASB to ease off in response to lobbying by powerful constituent groups—on such matters as recognizing loan losses and securities losses, for example.

The FASB's mission extends to the not-for-profit arena, as well as to businesses. Though the lion's share of its work has focused on the latter, the board has issued several pronouncements in the not-for-profit area: FAS No. 93, "Recognition of Depreciation by Not-for-Profit Organizations" (1987); FAS No. 116, "Accounting for Contributions Received and Contributions Made" (1993); and FAS No. 117, "Financial Statements of Not-for-Profit Organizations" (1993).

Financial accounting and reporting by governmental units is the responsibility of the GASB, not FASB. That includes accounting standards used in the separate financial statements of government-owned hospitals, colleges, and utilities whose counterparts in the private sector are subject to FASB standards.

The FASB's mission also includes developing a conceptual framework of the objectives and underlying concepts of financial accounting and reporting. To that end, it has issued Statements of Financial Accounting Concepts on the objectives of financial reporting, qualitative characteristics of accounting information, elements of financial statements (defining assets, liabilities, revenues, expenses, gains, losses, income, and the like), and concepts for recognizing and measuring those elements in financial statements. The concepts statements are: No. 1, "Objectives of Financial Reporting by Business Enterprises" (1978); No. 2, "Qualitative Characteristics of Accounting Information" (1980); No. 3, "Elements of Financial Statements of Business Enterprises" (1980); No. 4, "Objectives of Financial Reporting by Nonbusiness Organizations" (1980); No. 5, "Recognition and Measurement in Financial Statements of Business Enterprises" (1984); and No. 6, "Elements of Financial Statements" (1985). The primary beneficiary of the concepts statements is the board itself, which relies on them to help it reach consistent answers in similar circumstances.

Accounting standards are regulations that constrain behavior. As with all kinds of regulation, most people would prefer less to more, and most people would prefer to continue doing what they had been doing rather than be forced to change. So, like other regulatory bodies, the FASB meets resistance to everything it proposes, often vocal resistance, sometimes political.

Because there is usually a range of alternative solutions to each accounting problem, and because accounting standards are human-made conventions rather than scientific "truths," there will always be many people who disagree with the board's answer. However, if they have confidence in the process by which the standards are developed, and if they believe that the board took every reasonable point of view into consideration, most people will accept, comply with, and generally support the board's decision. It is for that reason that the FASB's extensive due process is not overkill but rather is absolutely essential to progress in financial accounting and reporting.

Paul Pacter

Bibliography

American Institute of Certified Public Accountants. *Establishing Financial Accounting Standards.* Report of the Study (Group) on Establishment of Accounting Principles. [The Wheat Report]. New York: AICPA, 1972.

Financial Accounting Standards Board. *Rules of Procedure.* Amended and restated periodically. Norwalk, CT: FASB.

"Hill Supports CPAs before Moss Subcommittee," *Journal of Accountancy,* July 1976, p. 10.

"Metcalf Subcommittee Submits Questions to Accounting Bodies," *Journal of Accountancy,* July 1976, pp. 9–10.

Miller, P.B.W., R.J. Redding, and P.R. Bahnson. *The FASB: The People, The Process, and the Politics.* 3rd ed. Homewood, IL: Irwin, 1994.

"Moss Delays Hearings Pending AICPA Action," *Journal of Accountancy,* December 1977, p. 7.

"Moss Plans to Introduce Regulating Legislation," *Journal of Accountancy,* April 1978, pp. 7–8.

"Moss Subcommittee Releases SEC Report," *Journal of Accountancy,* July 1976, p. 10.

See also ACCOUNTING PRINCIPLES BOARD; ACCOUNTING RESEARCH BULLETINS; ACCOUNTING RESEARCH STUDIES; ACCOUNTING SERIES RELEASE NO. 190; AMERICAN ACCOUNTING ASSOCIATION; AMERICAN INSTITUTE OF CERTIFIED PUBLIC ACCOUNTANTS; BIG EIGHT ACCOUNTING FIRMS; COLLEGE AND UNIVERSITY ACCOUNTING; CONCEPTUAL FRAMEWORK; CONGRESSIONAL VIEWS; DEFINITIONS OF ACCOUNTING; GENERALLY ACCEPTED ACCOUNTING PRINCIPLES; MATCHING; MATERIALITY; POOLING OF INTERESTS; SECURITIES AND EXCHANGE COMMISSION; SOLOMONS, DAVID; SPACEK, LEONARD; SWEENEY, HENRY WHITCOMB; UNIFORMITY; WHEAT COMMITTEE

Financial-Statement Analysis

Analysis is an activity that presumably dates back to the origins of the financial statement. Individuals reading those first statements had to interpret them, one way or another, to draw out the information they desired. However, surprisingly little is known about how statements were analyzed in the early eras of accounting. The first examples of any kind of rigorous analysis appeared in the late nineteenth century, in the form of operating-expense ratios in analyses of railroads and liquidity ratios in general credit analyses. Prior to the appearance of these financial ratios, it can only be surmised that early analysts must have developed their own favorite ways of perceiving the information in financial statements.

The appearance of financial ratios as the first harbingers of formal systems of financial-statement analysis makes sense in retrospect. The raw information in financial statements must be retranslated in some form so that it can be compared with previous time periods and other entities. Ratios and percentages serve that need very well. Also, certain ways of thinking about firms, such as their profitability, efficiency, liquidity, and other attributes, are conceptualized in terms that are best measured by ratios. Consequently, much of the history of financial-statement analysis involves the development of its basic tool, the financial ratio.

At least five different schools of thought can be identified in the evolution of systematic financial-statement analysis since the late nineteenth century: (1) Empirical Pragmatists; (2) Ratio Statisticians; (3) Multivariate Modelers; (4) Distress Predictors; and (5) Capital Marketers. These schools are listed roughly in the order of their appearance in the history of financial-statement analysis, and they are all more or less still flourishing today.

The Empirical Pragmatists were professional analysts who promoted their favorite sets of financial ratios from their work in credit analysis (Brown, 1955, and Horrigan, 1968). Their primary interest was evaluations of the ability of firms to meet their short-term obligations, so many of their ratios involved working capital and various liabilities. The more successful spokesmen of this school managed to have their sets of ratios published by credit-management firms, the most famous of which survives to this day in the Dun and Bradstreet Series developed by the American Robert Foulke, a Dun and Bradstreet credit analyst and vice-president. The major contribution of these early Empirical Pragmatists was their description of the rich variety of measures that could be developed from the data in financial statements.

In the early part of the twentieth century, financial-statement analysts soon recognized that comparative criteria were needed to evaluate the levels of the financial ratios that they were using. A group of Ratio Statisticians developed quickly, inspired by the early work of the American Alexander Wall, the Secretary-Treasurer of the Robert Morris Associates, a professional organization of bankers. They concerned themselves with the nature of the statistical distributions of ratios and the question of whether ratio criteria should be developed for various categories of firms (Brown, 1955, and Horrigan, 1968). They usually concluded that average ratios could serve as useful comparative criteria and that firms ought to be stratified into groups, such as industries and size classes, before making any comparisons. In the modern era of financial-statement analysis, which began during the 1960s, the attention of the Ratio Statisticians shifted to other statistical attributes of ratios, such as collinearity and stationarity. They found generally that ratios were significantly correlated with each other and were correlated over time as well, which meant that the use of financial ratios required a careful awareness of their statistical properties. In light of the collinearity findings, the work of this school since the mid-1970s has shifted to analyses that identify groups of ratios that behave in similar patterns, through sophisticated statistical techniques such as factor analysis. Also, a renewed interest occurred in the early 1980s in the basic statistical distributions of financial ratios. Nonnormal distributions have been the dominant finding here, which means that the ratio data may have to be transformed or be used in a limited array of statistical techniques (Barnes, 1987). In general, the Ratio Statisticians continue to work today on all fronts, albeit with more sophisticated tools and comprehensive databanks at their disposal.

At roughly the same time as the Ratio Statisticians school in the early twentieth century, the Multivariate Modelers school was emerging. This school attempted to develop an integrated framework in which ratios were interrelated with each other and with some measure of overall firm performance. The overall measure was usually a "return on investment" ratio; and various individual ratios, especially profit margins and turnover ratios, were arrayed in a descending order to portray their contribution to the ultimate "return on investment" achievement. The major insight gained here was that the activities measured by ratios often involved trade-offs so not all ratios could be maximized simultaneously. The most notable early example of developments in this school were the works of James Bliss, the controller at the meat packing firm of Libby, McNeill and Libby. In the field of finance, especially in the 1970s, computer-simulation models were devised to show the relationship of the market value of common stock to various measures of firm characteristics. Many of the characteristics used in these allied efforts were financial-ratio measures. The basic contributions of the Mul-

F

tivariate Modelers were the hypotheses they developed about the relationships of ratios to some overall measure of achievement. Those hypotheses moved the field of financial-statement analysis away from the previous, somewhat simple-minded approach of just comparing ratios with some average ratio (Barnes, 1987). However, a commonly accepted field theory of financial-statement analysis has still not evolved by the mid-1990s from their efforts.

The Great Depression of the 1930s was the backdrop for the emergence of a new school of financial-statement analysis, the Distress Predictors (Brown, 1955, and Horrigan, 1968). Adherents of this school changed the focus from analysis of past results to prediction of future events. Their underlying philosophy was that financial-statement analysis derives its usefulness only through its ability to predict events of interest. The 1930 study of failing firms by Raymond F. Smith and Arthur H. Winakor, both researchers at the Bureau of Business Research at the University of Illinois, was the first effort in this school; virtually all of its efforts since have proven to be successful. Bankruptcy and other types of financial distress have been shown to be predictable through analyses of ratios measuring liquidity, capital structure, profitability, and other assorted characteristics. Since the mid-1970s this school has turned its attention to combining groups of ratios into single index predictors, the most notable example being Edward Altman's Z-score model. More than any other school, the Distress Predictors have done the most to incorporate the whole range of modern statistical tools in analyses of financial accounting data. However, despite their empirical successes, a field theory of financial distress had still not developed by the mid-1990s.

Finally, a new school of financial statement analysis, the Capital Marketers, has evolved since the 1960s, paralleling the allied developments of the efficient-market hypothesis and "capital asset pricing" model in finance. This school has postulated that the value of financial-statement analysis lies in its usefulness in explaining and predicting returns on securities and their related risk levels. Aside from some efforts to show that financial ratios can be used to predict market risk measures, this school has focused most of its efforts on the nature of accounting earnings and its relationships to security returns. The seminal work by University of Rochester Accounting Professor Ray Ball and University of Western Australia accounting professor Philip Brown in 1968, while they were graduate students at the University of Chicago, launched this school, and subsequent works by William Beaver, an accounting professor at Stanford University, and others extended its influence. Their findings are much too voluminous to summarize here, but they generally concur that unexpected earnings changes do affect the returns on securities. Therefore, any statement-analysis techniques that could predict unexpected earnings changes would presumably be useful. As of the mid-1990s, those techniques have not been uncovered yet. This school differs from the previous schools in one important respect: It is dominated almost entirely by academic researchers, whereas all of the previous schools were composed of a mixed group of practicing analysts and academics. As a result, it remains to be seen whether the Capital Marketers' efforts will find their way into the practical world of financial-statement analysis.

As for the future of financial-statement analysis, it will undoubtedly change along with its parent discipline, financial accounting. The increased emphases on cash-flow statements in the late 1980s and on current values, rather than historical costs, in the mid-1970s will probably change the types of measures used in statement analyses. Also, with the long anticipated advent of the information systems era almost upon us, deconstructed, nonaccounting measures will play a larger role in statement analysis. By the mid-1990s there is more emphasis on such firm characteristics as market shares, workforce and workplace quality, environmental impacts, and product quality, and less on the traditional measures of liquidity, capital structure, profitability, and similar items. But, at the same time, virtually every past development in the history of financial-statement analysis will continue to evolve and play some role in its future.

James O. Horrigan

Bibliography

Altman, E.I. *Corporate Financial Distress.* New York: John Wiley & Sons, 1983.

Ball, R., and P.R. Brown. "An Empirical Evaluation of Accounting Income Numbers," *Journal of Accounting Research*, Autumn 1968, pp. 159–178.

Barnes, P. "The Analysis and Use of Financial Ratios: A Review Article," *Journal of Business Finance and Accounting*, Winter 1987, pp. 449–461.

Beaver, W.H. *Financial Reporting: An Accounting Revolution.* 2d ed. Englewood Cliffs, NJ: Prentice-Hall, 1989.

Bliss, J.H. *Financial and Operating Ratios in Management.* New York: Ronald Press, 1923.

Brown, Sister I. "The Historical Development of the Use of Ratios in Financial Statement Analysis to 1933." Ph.D. diss., Catholic University of America, 1955.

Foulke, R.A. *The Genesis of the Fourteen Important Ratios.* New York: Dun & Bradstreet, 1955.

Horrigan, J.O. "A Short History of Financial Ratio History," *Accounting Review,* April 1968, pp. 284–294.

Smith, R.F., and A.H. Winakor. *A Test Analysis of Unsuccessful Companies.* Urbana, IL: Bureau of Business Research, University of Illinois, 1930.

Wall, A. "Study of Credit Barometrics," *Federal Reserve Bulletin,* March 1919, pp. 229–243.

See also BAD DEBTS; BALANCE SHEET; BALL AND BROWN'S "AN EMPIRICAL EVALUATION OF ACCOUNTING INCOME NUMBERS"; BEAVER, WILLIAM; CASH FLOW ACCOUNTING; CONSERVATISM; EFFICIENT MARKET HYPOTHESIS; HISTORICAL COST; INCOME STATEMENT/INCOME ACCOUNT; LIQUIDITY: ACCOUNTING MEASUREMENT; RAILROAD ACCOUNTING (U.S.)

Fini, Rinerio

Among the oldest surviving double entry accounts are those of Rinerio Fini de' Benzi and Brothers. The three Fini brothers were Florentine merchants who operated in France, particularly as traders and moneylenders at the fairs of Champagne. The Fini account book (1296–1305) included most elements of a complete double entry system. Each ledger entry was cross referenced to its corresponding debit or credit. The profit or loss from every transaction was calculated and transferred to a clearing account. Besides the receivables and payables found in earlier Florentine ledgers, nominal accounts appeared for the first time, in the form of interest expense and expenses for clothing and footwear. But apparently no attempt was made to balance or close the Fini ledger. The accounts continued from year to year with no arithmetic check, no transfers of nominal account balances to capital, and no overall calculations of income.

Michael Chatfield

F

Bibliography
Martinelli, A. *The Origination and Evolution of Double Entry Bookkeeping to 1440.* Ph.D. diss., North Texas State University, 1974. Ann Arbor, MI: University Microfilms.

See also CAPITAL ACCOUNT; DEBIT AND CREDIT; DOUBLE ENTRY BOOKKEEPING: ORIGINS; LEDGER

Fischer v. Kletz

Benjamin Eskow founded Yale Express System in 1938 and built it into a successful trucking business by offering shippers special services such as late pickups and weekend deliveries. In 1959 Yale Express acquired American Freight Forwarding for $250,000, and in 1963 it acquired Republic Carloading, another freight forwarder, for $13 million. Yale's financial problems began when its freight-forwarding segments adopted policies similar to those of its trucking business. Extensive services were made available to freight-forwarding customers, but those services were not warranted by the narrow profit margins available from freight forwarding.

After Yale's 1963 audit, its auditor, Peat, Marwick, Mitchell and Company, was hired by Yale's president to make special studies of the firm's past and current income and expenses. While performing these management services, Peat Marwick discovered that Yale's 1963 audited financial statements were materially misleading because of unrecorded liabilities and uncollectable receivables. However, Peat Marwick did not disclose these findings to the Securities and Exchange Commission (SEC) or the public until May 1965. Early in March 1965, Peat Marwick released its 1964 audit report for Yale Express, which included a revised $1.88 million loss for 1963 and a $2.8 million loss for 1964.

When efforts to raise new capital failed, Yale Express System filed for bankruptcy. Stockholders and creditors of Yale Express sued the company, two securities firms, and the auditors. The gist of the complaint against Peat Marwick was that (1) Peat Marwick failed to disclose material facts that were at variance with the 1963 audit report long after it became aware that the 1963 financial statements were false and misleading, and (2) Peat Marwick failed to correct Yale's management when the latter released unaudited interim financial statements that Peat Marwick knew to be overly optimistic as to Yale's 1964 earnings. The plaintiffs claimed that the errors in the 1963 statements were known to Peat Marwick before June 29, 1964, when Yale Express filed with the SEC a 10K report containing the certified statements. Peat Marwick denied knowing of the errors prior to the SEC filing.

Peat Marwick moved for dismissal of the charges, contending that an auditor has no legal or ethical duty to reveal information to persons other than his client if such information contradicts previously certified financial statements. In November 1966, the SEC filed a brief *amicus curiae* in opposition to Peat Marwick's motion to dismiss. The SEC argued that a public accountant has a "continuing duty" to disclose any material information that is at variance with the data in previously audited statements.

The trial judge refused to dismiss the complaint, and Peat Marwick eventually paid $650,000 in settlement of investor claims. In holding that a duty to correct existed, Judge Harold R. Tyler specified that "common law has long required that a person who has made a representation must correct that representation if it becomes false and he knows people are relying on it." He noted that Peat Marwick's dilemma arose from the dual responsibilities the firm assumed as auditors and management advisory consultants. However, Peat Marwick's duty to the investing public did not end once the financial statements were certified, but existed afterward and dominated the auditor's obligation to his client.

The 1967 *Fischer v. Kletz* decision caused the American Institute of Certified Public Accountants to issue Statement on Auditing Procedure No. 41 (1969), which requires auditors to disclose new information that makes previously issued financial statements misleading.

Michael Chatfield

Bibliography

Davies, J.J. "Accountants' Third Party Liability: A History of Applied Sociological Jurisprudence," *Abacus*, December 1979, pp. 93–112.

Fischer v. Kletz, 266 F. Supp. 180 (S.D.N.Y. 1967).

Miller, R.L., and G.P. Brady. *CPA Liability: Meeting the Challenge*. New York: Ronald Press, 1986.

See also AMERICAN INSTITUTE OF CERTIFIED PUBLIC ACCOUNTANTS; *ESCOTT V. BARCHRIS CONSTRUCTION CORPORATION*; LEGAL LIABILITY OF AUDITORS; SECURITIES AND EXCHANGE COMMISSION

Fisher, Irving (1867–1947)

Professor of political economy at Yale University (1898–1935) and author of 29 books on a wide range of matters of academic and public interest, Irving Fisher was widely and deeply respected among his peers. In a memorial to Fisher in the September 1947 issue of the *American Economic Review*, Paul H. Douglas, then a professor of economics at the University of Chicago and later a United States senator (D–Illinois, 1949–67), wrote "More than any other American economist he united a subtle and powerful mind with a passionate crusading spirit for human welfare, and backed up by an ample means he was equally tireless in promoting both."

In *The Nature of Capital and Income* (1906), his fourth book, he sought to "supply a link long missing between the ideas and usages underlying" business transactions and economic theory. Wealth, said Fisher, is use of material objects owned. The dated value of a quantity of wealth is the product of the quantity of wealth objects and the dated selling price of a unit quantity. That value is "purely objective." Capital may be used of a dated quantity of wealth instruments, and of the value of that quantity (capital-value). A dated stock was distinguished from a flow of wealth. Income was described as a flow of services of wealth through a period of time. Like capital, income (and outgo) may be used in two senses, of income-service, and of income-value, the product of the quantity of services (and disservices) and their several prices. This was the "philosophically correct" method of constructing income accounts.

The ratio of income-value to dated capital-value was called the value return, which, if the income is perpetual and uniform, is called the realized rate of interest on capital. If the expected income from a known capital is uniform and known with certainty, and the rate of interest is foreknown and constant, the capital-value of any item of property is the present worth (discounted value) of the future income. Where the stipulated (standard) conditions are not met, there may be many such values, depending on the assumptions made about the future. Capital-value in this sense is subjective.

The use of capital-value in two senses (since called ex post and ex ante) is confusing. Fisher did not proceed to show that both enter in distinctive ways into the processes of choice, the ex post value identifying the stake at risk, and the ex ante value(s) indicating the prospect(s) of employing that stake. Rather, he averred that ordinary business accounting is "nothing but a method of recording the items of income and their capitalization at different points of time. A merchant's balance sheet is a statement of the prospects of his business." This, of course, is at odds with the determination of a dated stake or capital, and with the general style of accounting in Fisher's day and since.

The confusion has been perpetuated, perhaps through the influence of John Bennett Canning's, a professor of economics at Stanford University, *The Economics of Accountancy* (1929), in the contentions of some that business accounts, which are held almost universally to be historical (ex post and, in principle, objective), should use, as dated values, prospective (ex ante and, in principle, subjective) valuations.

R.J. Chambers

Bibliography

Chambers, R.J. "Income and Capital: Fisher's Legacy," *Journal of Accounting Research*, Spring 1971, pp. 137–149.

Fisher, I. *The Nature of Capital and Income.* New York: Macmillan, 1906. Reprint. New York: Augustus M. Kelly, 1965.

Fisher, I.N. *My Father, Irving Fisher.* New York: Comet Press, 1956.

Schumpeter, J.B. "Irving Fisher's Econometrics," *Econometrica*, July 1948, pp. 219–231.

Westerfield, R.B., and P.H. Douglas. "Memorials: Irving Fisher," *American Economic Review*, September 1947, pp. 656–663.

See also Brazil: Inflation Accounting; Canning, John Bennett; Compound Interest; Conceptual Framework; Discounted Cash Flow; National-Income Accounting; Return on Investment; Schmidt, Julius August Fritz

Fixed Assets

The "inventory" technique was a traditional method of valuing fixed assets. John Mellis described it in *Briefe Instruction* (1588), as did Stephen Monteage in *Debtor and Creditor Made Easie* (1675) and John Mair in the fifth edition of *Bookkeeping Methodiz'd* (1757). In the late nineteenth century most manufacturers and retailers still used this inventory or single account method of asset valuation. While it had many variations in practice, assets had to be appraised or at least revalued at the end of each accounting period. Typically the new value was debited and the old one credited to the asset account; in this way the "inventory" portion was carried forward and any shrinkage in value reduced profit. Depreciation in these terms was wholly a valuation concept, and for the majority of firms using this method, profit was the change in value of net assets from all causes between two successive accounting periods. No distinction was made between capital and revenue expenditures, between current and fixed assets, between depreciation and appreciation, or between inflationary increases and real income.

English railroads and certain public utilities were required by law to value their assets by the double account or replacement method. Acquisition costs of long-lived assets were capitalized and never depreciated. Because such firms had to maintain their fixed assets permanently, asset values were assumed to remain constant so long as the assets themselves were kept in good working order. This made it natural to capitalize asset betterments and additions, while charging replacements and repairs directly to expense. Since the timing of asset replacements was a managerial option, so logically was the depreciation charge. If taken at all, depreciation was seen not as an operating expense but as a holding back of revenue to replace lost asset value.

The first effective critic of these traditional valuation methods was the English chartered accountant Lawrence Dicksee (1864–1932). Dicksee's immediate target was the double account method, which he criticized for failing to require depreciation and for its assumption that capital consumption would not exceed the rate of asset replacement. He reasoned that the main goal of most firms is to continue in business and that asset valuation should reflect this fact. Even companies that did not take depreciation faced the certainty of asset revaluation when assets were sold or when the firm changed hands. The point of sale was a moment of truth that revealed an asset's real value. So it was not simply current sale prices—liquidation prices—which mattered, but also these *future* sale prices. To anticipate them as nearly as possible, Dicksee believed assets should be valued "as a going concern," meaning "at such value as they would stand in the books if proper depreciation had been provided for" (*Auditing*, 5th ed., pp. 180–181).

Dicksee's assumption of indefinite life for the corporation also ruled out the use of appraisal prices in the balance sheets of manufacturing companies. If a business had to maintain its fixed assets permanently, it seemed illogical to determine profits by annual appraisals based on current resale prices. There being no intention to sell such assets, fluctuations in their market prices could not be considered gains or losses. Long-term assets should be valued at acquisition cost less depreciation. Dicksee's justification for ignoring value changes not caused by "time and wear" was that asset realization was not contemplated. Fixed assets were bought to be used, not sold at a profit.

At the turn of the century these ideas were revolutionary. That they now seem orthodox is evidence of their general acceptance. Dicksee more than any other man established the continuity principle as a meaningful accounting concept. In doing so he helped shift accounting attention from the strictly historical view of valuation implied by appraisal pricing to the view that asset values depend on future events. This in turn laid the groundwork for a synthesis of other accounting principles—historical cost, objectivity, matching, and realization—around the going concern concept.

Michael Chatfield

Bibliography

Brief, R., ed. *Dicksee's Contribution to Accounting Theory and Practice.* New York: Arno Press, 1980.

Edwards, J.F., ed. *Reporting Fixed Assets in Nineteenth Century Company Accounts.* New York: Garland, 1986.

Kitchen, J. "Fixed Asset Values: Ideas on Depreciation 1892–1914," *Accounting and Business Research*, Autumn 1979, pp. 281–291.

———. "Lawrence Dicksee, Depreciation, and the Double Account System." In *Debits, Credits, Finance, and Profits*, edited by H. Edey and B.S. Yamey. London: Sweet and Maxwell, 1975.

Litherland, D.A. "Fixed Asset Replacement a Half Century Ago," *Accounting Review*, October 1951, pp. 475–480.

See also CAPITAL MAINTENANCE; CONTINUITY; DEPRECIATION; DICKSEE, LAWRENCE; DOUBLE ACCOUNT METHOD; HISTORICAL COST; MATCHING; MONTEAGE, STEPHEN; OBJECTIVITY; REALIZATION; SINGLE ACCOUNT METHOD

Flint v. Stone Tracy Company

While awaiting ratification of the Sixteenth Amendment to the U.S. Constitution, Congress in 1909 passed a bill creating a corporate income tax disguised as a "special excise tax" of 1 percent on net income above $5,000, to be paid "on the privilege of using the corporate form to do business." The act's constitutionality was upheld by the U.S. Supreme Court in *Flint v. Stone Tracy Company* (1911), setting the stage for Congress to enact a federal income tax on individuals as well as corporations.

Michael Chatfield

Bibliography

Flint v. Stone Tracy Co., 220 U.S. 107, 3 AFTR 2834, 31 sect. 342. (1911).

See also INCOME TAXATION IN THE UNITED STATES; SIXTEENTH AMENDMENT

Flori, Ludovico (1579–1647)

In 1633 Ludovico Flori, a Jesuit of Palermo, published the second printed textbook on monastery accounting. *Trattato del Modo di Tenere il Libro Doppio Domestico* derived its basic accounting procedures and much of its exposition from the Benedictine Don Angelo Pietra's *Indrizzo Degli Economi* (1586). Both authors described a system surprisingly like modern accounting. Both believed that monastery accounts could best be viewed, not by inspecting the ledger as a merchant would, but by examining detached financial statements. Flori was the first writer to insist that transactions be placed in their proper fiscal periods. This required making a sharp distinction between current year income and profits and losses of prior periods, which were to be closed directly to capital. Flori accounted separately for long-term and current assets; described and illustrated compound journal entries; and discussed the advantages of forecasting revenues and expenses. Suspense accounts appear for the first time in his text. Like Pietra, Flori favored annual ledger closing, but Flori used a balance account, not just to prove the ledger's correctness, but to facilitate its closing and reopening. Edward Peragallo and Federigo Melis consider Flori's the best exposition of Italian bookkeeping prior to 1800.

Michael Chatfield

Bibliography

Bywater, M.F., and B.S. Yamey. *Historic Accounting Literature: A Companion Guide.* London: Scholars Press, 1982.

Peragallo, E. *Origin and Evolution of Double Entry Bookkeeping: A Study of Italian Practice from the Fourteenth Century.* New York. American Institute Publishing, 1938. Reprint. Osaka: Nihon Shoseki, 1974.

See also BALANCE ACCOUNT; BALANCE SHEET; CLOSING ENTRIES AND PROCEDURES; COMPOUND ENTRIES; ITALY, AFTER PACIOLI; PERIODICITY; PIETRA, ANGELO; TRANSFER PRICES

Foreign Currency Translation (1931–1981)

The operating environment of multinational firms frequently necessitates their participation in financial activities denominated in foreign currencies. For consolidation of foreign and domestic divisions, the accounting elements measured in such foreign currencies must be translated into the reporting currency of the parent organization. Translation is accomplished through the utilization of an exchange rate between the local currency and the parent currency. This may be the historical rate of exchange at the transaction date, the current rate at the balance sheet date, or a weighted average rate covering the time period under consideration. The determination of the appropriate rate to be used in the translation of financial statements was the basis of the difficulties surrounding accounting for foreign operations.

The first official pronouncement on accounting for foreign operations was Bulletin No. 92, "Foreign Exchange Losses," issued by the American Institute of Accountants (AIA) on December 5, 1931. It was prompted by numerous, severe exchange-rate fluctuations and advocated the current-noncurrent method of translation. Under this method, current assets and liabilities are translated at the current rate of exchange, and noncurrent assets and liabilities are translated at the historical rates.

Questions regarding the proper treatment of exchange-rate gains resulted in the issuance of Bulletin No. 117 by the Special Committee on Accounting Procedure of the AIA. Zeff (1972) reported that this Special Committee was the forerunner for the 1936 Committee on Accounting Procedure on January 11, 1934. Titled "Memorandum on Accounting for Foreign Exchange Gains," it advised that translation gains were to be deferred when the revaluation of the foreign currency giving rise to the gain might reverse. However, it required that translation losses be realized currently regardless of any possibility of a recovery in the value of the foreign currency.

Reinforcing the conservatism expressed in Bulletin No. 117, Accounting Research Bulletin (ARB) No. 4, "Foreign Operations and Foreign Exchange," issued by the Committee on Accounting Procedure (CAP) in 1939, cautioned against the consolidation of foreign subsidiaries because of the risk involved in the realization of foreign earnings. Instead, it advised disclosure of the foreign subsidiaries' earnings and proposed four possible procedures, but it did not indicate which procedure was preferable.

Accounting Series Release (ASR) No. 11, "Consolidation of Foreign Subsidiaries of Domestic Corporations," was issued by the Securities and Exchange Commission (SEC) in 1940 in response to the question of consolidating foreign subsidiaries whose operations and assets were endangered by war conditions or affected in terms of restricted foreign currencies. Registrants were advised to carefully consider the effect of inclusion on the readers of their financial statements. It pointed out that if omission of these subsidiaries from the consolidated financial statements prevented the domestic corporation from making a clear and fair presentation of its financial condition and the results of its operations, then inclusion was desirable with ample disclosure of the foreign-exchange restrictions and war conditions.

Foreign Operations and Foreign Exchanges, published in 1941 by the Research Department of the AIA, emphasized that care should be taken to determine whether foreign earnings could be made available in the United States before such earnings were consolidated with those of domestic companies. It concluded that there could be instances where it would no longer be appropriate to even translate separate foreign financial statements into U.S. dollars. In that event, the only course would be to present them in their respective foreign currencies.

Accounting Problems Arising from Devaluation of Foreign Currencies was issued by the Research Department of the AIA in 1949. Its purpose was to comment on foreign-exchange problems arising from the devaluation of currencies in 25 countries. This statement recommended various translation procedures.

Chapter 12 of ARB No. 43, "Restatement and Revision of Accounting Bulletins," incorporated in 1953 many of the Research Department's previous recommendations, including use of the current-noncurrent method of translation.

A study conducted by Samuel R. Hepworth, an accounting professor at the University of Michigan, in 1956, titled *Reporting Foreign Operations,* first proposed the monetary-nonmonetary method of translation. Hepworth suggested that balance-sheet accounts other than stockholders' equity accounts should be divided into those of a financial nature and those of a physical nature. Financial items would be translated using the current rate, and physical items would be translated using the historical rate.

The National Association of Accountants published in 1960 a research report titled *Management Accounting Problems in Foreign Operations.* This report criticized the current-noncurrent method of translation and supported the monetary-nonmonetary method.

Accounting Principles Board (APB) Opinion No. 6, "Status of Accounting Research Bulletins," modified in 1965 the previous recommendations of the standard-setting bodies and officially supported the monetary-nonmonetary method as an alternative to the current-noncurrent method.

A survey conducted in 1972 by the American Institute of Certified Public Accountants (AICPA) revealed that, among firms disclosing their methods of reporting, 19 percent followed the monetary-nonmonetary method, 42 percent followed the current-noncurrent method, and 39 percent used the current rate for all accounts except property (Pakkala, 1975). In the same year, Accounting Research Study (ARS) No. 12, *Reporting Foreign Operation of U.S. Companies in Dollars,* was issued. It criticized the current-noncurrent method of translation and pro-

posed the temporal method as a substitute. Under the temporal method, cash, receivables, and payables (both current and noncurrent) are translated at current rates. The translation rates of other assets and liabilities depend upon their characteristics. Exchange gains and losses are recorded as current income items. Also in 1972, APB Opinion No. 22, "Disclosure of Accounting Policies," included the accounting method chosen for the translation of foreign currencies in its requirements for financial-statement disclosure.

APB Opinion No. 30, "Reporting the Results of Operations," required in 1973 that all gains and losses from the translation of foreign currencies be treated as ordinary rather than extraordinary items. Also in 1973, the Financial Accounting Standards Board (FASB) issued Financial Accounting Statement (FAS) No. 1, "Disclosure of Foreign Currency Translation Information," which required more complete and extensive disclosure of translation information, including translation policies, the aggregate amount of exchange adjustments originating in the period, and the aggregate amount of exchange adjustments included in the determination of income for the period. It did not supersede, alter, or amend any method previously promulgated, and it disclaimed any intention of implying that one method was more acceptable than any other. FAS No. 1 was adopted by the board by a unanimous vote.

In April 1973, the FASB, recognizing the lack of definitive accounting procedures in this area, placed a project on the technical agenda titled "Accounting for Foreign Currency Translation."

The FASB Discussion Memorandum, "An Analysis of Issues Related to Accounting for Foreign Currency Translation," was issued in February 1974. The Discussion Memorandum addressed 26 issues. These included: a consideration of the nature of the exchange adjustment resulting from foreign currency risk, when such exchange adjustments should be recorded, the appropriate unit of measure for financial-statement purposes, which assets and liabilities should be adjusted for changes in exchange rates, how revenue and expense accounts should be translated, when a translation adjustment should be recorded, and which currency should be the reporting currency. The FASB staff also prepared a "Financial Statement Model on Accounting for Foreign Currency Translation" to aid practitioners in identifying possible implementation problems related to adopting a particular method or combination of methods from among the alternatives available. The resulting Exposure Draft was issued December 31, 1974.

FAS No. 8, "Accounting for the Translation of Foreign Currency Transactions and Foreign Currency Financial Statements," was issued in 1975. It specified the use of the temporal method for translating foreign currencies and required immediate recognition of gains and losses with no deferrals or other smoothing techniques permitted.

In May 1978, the FASB requested comments on FAS Nos. 1–12. Of the 205 letters received, 86 addressed FAS No. 8. All but two letters expressed dissatisfaction. Respondents from industry were unanimously critical of the standard and called for major changes in the foreign currency reporting practices.

In January 1979, after considering a staff analysis of the comment letters, the board added a reconsideration of FAS No. 8 to its agenda. The Task Force included representatives from academia, the financial community, government, industry, public accounting, and international professional accounting organizations.

In August 1980, the FASB issued an Exposure Draft titled "Foreign Currency Translation." It had a three-month comment period, and more than 360 letters were received. The board conducted a public hearing on the Exposure Draft, and 47 organizations and individuals presented their views at the four-day hearing.

During January and June 1981, foreign currency translation was addressed at four additional public board meetings and one public Task Force meeting. The board's consideration of the issues resulted in modifications of the Exposure Draft that the board believed were significant. A revised Exposure Draft was issued on June 30, 1981. It had a 90-day comment period, and more than 260 letters were received. In October and November, foreign currency translation was addressed at two public board meetings and one public Task Force meeting. Consideration of the written comments resulted in further modifications. Finally, in December 1981, FAS No. 52, "Foreign Currency Translation," was issued. It was approved by the board in a 4-to-3 decision. A compromise solution, it bases the translation rate on the functional currency of the firm, thus permitting use of either the temporal or current-rate method of translation and immediate recognition or deferral of gains and losses as appropriate. It remains in effect in 1994.

Pamela J. Duke

Bibliography

Gray, D. "SFAS 52 in Perspective: Background of Accounting for Foreign Currency Translation in Financial Reports of United States Multinational Corporations," Working Paper No. 59, *Working Papers Series vol. 3, No. 41–60*, pp. 260–284, edited by A.C. Bishop and D. Richards, pp. 260–284. Harrisonburg, VA: Academy of Accounting Historians, 1984.

Hepworth, S.R. *Reporting Foreign Operations*. Michigan Business Studies, vol. 12, No. 5. Ann Arbor, MI: School of Business Administration, University of Michigan, 1956.

Lorensen, L. *Reporting Foreign Operations of U.S. Companies in U.S. Dollars*. Accounting Research Study No. 12. New York: American Institute of Certified Public Accountants, 1972.

National Association of Accountants. *Management Problems in Foreign Operations*. Research Report No. 36. New York: National Association of Accountants, 1960.

Pakkala, A.L. "Foreign Exchange Accounting of Multinational Corporations," *Financial Analysts Journal*, March/April 1975, pp. 32–34, 36, 38–41, 76.

Zeff, Stephen A. *Forging Accounting Principles in Five Countries: A History and an Analysis of Trends*. Champaign, IL: Stipes, 1972.

See also ACCOUNTING PRINCIPLES BOARD; ACCOUNTING RESEARCH STUDIES; CONSOLIDATED FINANCIAL STATEMENTS; FINANCIAL ACCOUNTING STANDARDS BOARD; SECURITIES AND EXCHANGE COMMISSION

France

Before the 1900s, a great number of French authors wrote on the keeping of accounts (financial or cost accounts) and on their classification. Some of the most notable contributors are Jacques Savary, *Le Parfait Négociant* (1675): Matthew de la Porte, *Le Guide des Négociants et Teneurs de Livres* (1685); Edmond Degrange Sr., *La Tenue des Livres*

Rendue Facile (1795); Anselme Payen, *Essai sur la Tenue des Livres d'un Manufacturier* (1817); and Eugène Léautey and Adolphe Guilbault, *La Science des Comptes Mise à la Portée de Tous* (1889).

In fact, until the 1900s, French accounting developed relatively freely, bounded only by the provisions of the 1673 ordinance known as the Code Savary, which were taken up and extended in the 1807 Napoleonic Code of Commerce, and by the 1867 Company Law. The Code Savary was promulgated by Louis XIV under the influence of Jean-Baptiste Colbert, who held the posts of superintendent of commerce and controller of finance, among others. Colbert sought to increase the central control of the state through strengthening and enlarging the role of local administrative officials and ensuring the systematic flow of information from the provinces. The regulation of private-enterprise accounting was adopted within this context and reflected a preoccupation with greater order in the governing of affairs, including business. The Code Savary called for the keeping of a *livre journal* (journal), giving instructions on how to make proper entries, asked for the periodic establishment of *l'inventaire* (inventory), and allowed the presentation of books in courts in cases involving succession, *communauté*, dissolution of partnerships, and business failure.

Later, the 1867 Company Law influenced accounting through its concern with the distribution of fictitious dividends. The law had an impact on accounting concepts and procedures, mainly for the balance sheet, through the jurisprudence that was established as a consequence of its application. Finally, in this pre-1900s era, an attempt was made at the first congress of French accountants, in 1880, to obtain a consensus on the normalization of balance sheets, but it failed due to a general lack of interest in accounting normalization at the time.

The next important step in the development of French accounting was the passage of the income tax law in 1917. The law was passed at a time when there was no organized and generally accepted body of accounting principles, and its provisions gradually filled this void. In the 1930s, following the period of economic difficulties experienced throughout the world, decrees were passed to require consistency from year to year in financial-statement presentation and valuation rules, and to strengthen the auditing profession. The purpose of these decrees was to increase the credibility of financial statements and give shareholders and creditors greater protection.

During World War II, the policy of economic *dirigisme* (state intervention) common to both the German occupiers and the Vichy administration led to the drafting of the 1942 Uniform Accounting Plan and to the establishment of the Order of Expert Accountants and Chartered Accountants. Both institutions were to be tools for monitoring and controlling industries. After the war, a Committee for the Rationalization of Accounting was set up by the Ministry of Finances and Economic Affairs. Its mandate was to design an accounting plan that could be broadly applied in every sector of the economy, thus forming the basis of a system of national accounts.

The accounting plan drafted by the committee was published in 1947. It included a chart of accounts (in which financial, cost, and statistical accounts were presented separately and spread among 10 classes) and related definitions, rules for valuation and use of accounts, model financial statements, and a section on cost accounting. The work was called the *Plan Comptable Général*, although its conceptual framework was based upon the characteristics of industrial firms. The plan nevertheless was generally well received by public firms and partially state-owned companies, in the agricultural sector, in private commercial and industrial firms, in the insurance and banking sectors, and in accounting for state and local communities. The Higher Council of Accounting (renamed the National Council of Accounting (CNC) in 1957), which was created in 1947, implemented the plan. During the 1950s, the council made the first revision of the 1947 plan, which was approved in 1957. A 1962 decree required the 1957 plan to be used in the private economic sector. The 1957 plan thus became legally binding in 90 lines of business for which adaptations of the plan were developed by professional committees under the direction of the trade associations concerned.

With changing economic conditions in France, the passing of new laws, the rapid development of information-processing techniques, and the internationalization of trade and capital markets, the 1957 plan needed revision. The need to improve the possibilities for financial and economic analysis offered by the plan's financial statements played an important role in drafting the revised plan's conceptual framework. In the revised plan (1975), the classification criteria adopted in the 1947 and 1957 plans were changed, and a number of innovations were introduced. The classification of balance-sheet elements according to their degree of liquidity/maturity was replaced by a classification of assets and debts according to their economic function in the firm. The impact of tax regulations on accounting income and on the balance sheet was to be shown separately in accounts such as regulated provisions. The preparation of a statement of changes in financial position was made mandatory as a result of banks' and financial analysts' requests for information about cash flows. In the income statement, components of production were shown separately, and computation of value added was required to meet national accountants' information needs.

In fact, the 1975 plan could not be adopted as such, since it had to be harmonized with the requirements of the European Economic Community's Fourth Directive, on company financial statements, which was adopted in 1978. The Fourth Directive had both positive and negative impacts on French accounting. Among the positive results were the introduction of the "true and fair view" concept used in English-speaking countries, the new importance granted to notes to financial statements, the breakdown of income taxes between current and noncurrent income, and the requirement to provide information on deferred income taxes. Among the negative impacts of the Fourth Directive were the abandonment of the requirement for the preparation of a statement of changes in financial position, the partial abandonment of the functional classification in the balance sheet, and the abandonment of the computation of value added in the income statement.

To retain as many as possible of the innovations of the 1975 plan, a compromise solution involved providing, in addition to the basic set of financial statements (true to the Fourth Directive's provisions), a more elaborate, optional set of documents with the same basic structure as the European Economic Community's (later the European Community and in 1993 the European Union) Fourth Directive statements. A third, much shorter, set of statements was adopted for small firms.

The revised plan was approved by the Ministry of Economy and Finances in June 1979. A final version of the plan, very similar to the 1979 draft, was approved in April 1982, and went into effect with the passage of the accounting law on April 30, 1983. The objective of this accounting law was to harmonize the accounts of French companies with those of other European Economic Community companies by incorporating the provisions of the Fourth Directive into the national legislation.

France had a great impact on accounting in many foreign countries through the 1957 accounting plan. The plan of the African, Madagascar, and Mauritius Organization (OCAM plan), the Tunisian plan and the Algerian plan are all examples of the international influence of French accounting. These plans were drafted in the 1960s, and their preparation gave the CNC and French national accountants the opportunity to incorporate some of the emerging ideas that would later be included in the 1975 plan. In fact, the OCAM Plan constituted a step in the evolution made between the 1957 Plan and the 1975 Plan.

Anne Fortin

Bibliography

Code de Commerce. Collection: Petits Codes Dalloz. Paris: Dalloz, edited yearly.

Conseil National de la Comptabilité. *Plan Comptable Général*. Paris: Imprimerie Nationale, 1982.

Fortin, A. "The 1947 French Accounting Plan: Origins and Influence on Subsequent Practice," *Accounting Historians Journal*, December 1991, pp. 1–25.

———. "French Accounting Thought from 1970 to 1982 as Reflected in the Evolution of the *Plan Comptable Général*." In *Advances in International Accounting*, pp. 65–105.

Fourastié, J. *La comptabilité*. 14th ed. Collection: Que sais-je? Paris: Presses Universitaires de France, 1979.

Holzer, H.P., and W. Rogers. "The Origins and Developments of French Costing Systems (as Reflected in Published Literature)," *Accounting Historians Journal*, December 1990, pp. 95–112.

Howard, S.E. "Public Rules for Private Accounting in France, 1673 and 1807," *Accounting Review*, June 1932, pp. 91–102.

Miller, P. "On the Interrelations between Accounting and the State," *Accounting, Organizations and Society*, vol. 15, no. 4, 1990, pp. 315–338.

Most, K.S. "The French Accounting Experiment," *International Journal of Accounting*, Fall 1971, pp. 15–27.

Vlaemminck, J.H. *Histoire et doctrines de la comptabilité*. Brussels: Éditions du Treurenberg, 1956.

See also BALANCE SHEET; CHART OF ACCOUNTS; DIRECTIVES OF THE EUROPEAN COMMUNITY (UNION); LIMITED LIABILITY; PAR VALUE DOCTRINE; PARTNERSHIP ACCOUNTING; PAYEN, ANSELME; SAVARY, JACQUES; TAX-ORDAINED ACCOUNTING; UNIFORMITY

Fraud and Auditing

Fraud exists in unexpected places and has become a worldwide phenomenon. Fraud may be more common than many have thought: 12 percent of respondents to a British survey, published in 1988, said that their company had suffered a loss due to fraud in the last three years. Perhaps not very logically, half the respondents felt that their controls against fraud were good, although in need of some improvement. Given what seems to be a persistent laissez-faire attitude toward fraud, opportunities for thievery will continue to offer temptations, especially to those whose actions are not subject to checks and balances via separation of duties.

Fraud comprehends both employee and management fraud. Embezzlement and fiduciary frauds can be defined as the conversion to one's own use or benefit of money or property of another over which one has custody, or with which one has been entrusted, or over which one exercises fiduciary control. Management fraud can be defined as an intentional misrepresentation of a material nature, involving upper-level employees, that is being disguised by fraudulent financial reporting. Management fraud may involve both an initial abstraction of assets and a consequent "cooking" of the books.

Auditors stand as a thin line of defense against both management and employee fraud. Historically, the detection of fraud was the auditor's prime objective. However, twentieth-century practitioners, especially those who make rules on behalf of the profession, acknowledge that the prime objective of an audit has evolved from fraud detection into the expression of an opinion on the fairness of the financial statements. Unfortunately for the profession, many financial-statement users continue to cling to the possibly archaic notion that auditors are responsible for fraud detection. The divergent perceptions on fraud constitute a special expectation gap with ominous implications, because many lawmakers share the public's broad view of the auditor's responsibility for fraud detection.

Court decisions pertaining to auditors' responsibilities for fraud detection have tended to be ambivalen

t. Individual state courts balance policies in the public interest to determine the party to whom auditors owe a duty; however, there is no uniform interpretation of the public interest and no uniform rule governing auditor's duty of care to foreseeable third parties.

Statement on Auditing Standards (SAS) No. 53, "The Auditor's Responsibility to Detect Errors and Irregularities" (1987), issued by the Audit Standards Board of the American Institute of Certified Public Accountants, aimed at a compromise with respect to fraud detection. It states that auditors should design the audit to provide reasonable assurance of detecting errors and irregularities material to the financial statements. Further, auditors are expected to exercise due care in planning, performing, and evaluating the results of an audit. *Montgomery's Auditing* (1990) advises auditors to maintain an attitude of professional skepticism throughout the audit, especially when gathering and evaluating evidence, including management's answers to audit inquiries. When warning signals are detected, the auditor is enjoined to reconsider his testing plan to assure that sufficient competent evidence will be obtained to support a conclusion that the financial statements are free of material misstatements.

As to internal auditors, Statement on Internal Auditing Standards No. 3, "Detection, Investigation, and Reporting of Fraud" (1985), issued by the Institute of Internal Auditors, recommends that they have sufficient knowledge of fraud to be able to identify indicators pointing to fraud that might have been committed. If significant control weaknesses are detected, additional tests should be performed, including tests directed toward identification of further indicators of fraud.

Companies that wish to limit the exposure to fraud usually pursue two approaches: (1) managing the risk of fraud, predicated on the theory that, to some extent at least, unfavorable possibilities can be anticipated and their effects shifted, controlled, or otherwise mitigated; and (2) engaging auditors concerned, among other things, with the prevention and detection of material fraud. In addition, management should create companywide awareness of the need for security. If such awareness permeates all levels of the organization, employees will observe common-sense precautions likely to frustrate potential perpetrators.

Criminologists have set out a simple model related to control over theft. In order for an embezzlement to take place, there must be (1) an item worth stealing, (2) a potential perpetrator willing to steal, and (3) an opportunity for the crime to take place. The prevention/detection implications are readily apparent: Modern technology can help to draw a series of rings around each part of the equation, thereby isolating the perpetrator from the asset and from the opportunity and knowledge for access.

Consequently, management's initial, mundane task involves identification, inventory, and valuations of the resources to be protected. The next step, identification of potential perpetrators, affords further, albeit limited, opportunities for isolating the elements in the equation. Unfortunately, many will steal, as long as they can rationalize their behavior to their own satisfaction. Thus, control must focus on restricting perpetrators' opportunities for illegal access. In many circumstances, management will achieve quick payback for its investment in security by introducing well-defined and traditional control mechanisms, such as the separation of functions involved in a particular process to preclude one individual's absolute control.

Advances in technology, reflected in control techniques and in audit applications, may ultimately assist the "white hats" in preventing or detecting fraud. Negative aspects of technology are mirrored in new types and sizes of transactions and have been accompanied by new exposures, including computer viruses. "Fraud proofing" may be particularly difficult when two or more organizations are involved, such as in electronic data interchange.

The audit-related benefits of technology have included the development of new or improved controls, the emergence of public online databases, and the creation of powerful interactive software. For example, controls using logic may strengthen physical protection over assets and safeguard computer access; biometric security techniques allow computer users to be identified by voice, fingerprint, hand geometry, or retinal patterns. Some logical controls can determine who is seeking access to files, from where access is sought, and what the accessing individual is authorized to do with respect to specific information.

Public online databases have come to epitomize the information age. The databases help users, including auditors, to gain a better understanding of the economic climate within which the client operates and of the client's business and industry.

Moreover, databases help users to gain perspective about the backgrounds of client executives, to find and consider their uttered or published comments, and to search for any prior legal difficulties the executives, or the auditee organization, may have experienced; legal and related databases include judgments in state and federal courts, administrative decisions, and information from federal agencies. In addition, the online databases facilitate audits of individual accounts, usually by enhancing the quantity, quality, and independent nature of evidence available to an auditor.

Typically, audits commence with an appraisal of the control environment. A quick assessment of that environment can be made by looking at four surrogate measures: (1) management's attitude toward internal control; contempt for internal control should be viewed as a bright red flag; (2) attitude toward audit adjustments; failure to respond positively to recommendations for adjustments sends a strong warning signal; (3) attitude toward perks; if management views the shareholders' money as its own, the risks of not discovering a fraud and expressing an incorrect opinion are greatly increased; (4) attitude toward criminal behavior; tolerant attitudes toward wrongdoers can indicate moral corrosion.

Poor business and economic conditions increase the risk of management fraud. As pointed out, an auditor can update himself about conditions in the client's business and industry by reference to the online databases. Of course, the risk of management fraud is not always related to business conditions outside the client's organization.

Since management fraud is within the realm of possibility, the auditor should give particular attention to functions or areas in which such fraud might be perpetrated. The first such area involves physical protection over whatever may be worth stealing (including information), or over the hardware, software, and data needed to assure the continuity of business operations. Assuming that most companies are automated—and given dishonest managers' penchants for concealing conversion of assets or results of bad decisions by manipulating the books—access to computers, programs, and data represents the second focal point for control. The third, and potentially most dangerous, area for auditors involves management representations and the auditors' penchant for undue reliance on those representations in lieu of gathering objective evidence. Research has shown that auditors are most likely to discover indication of fraud in the course of analytical reviews and behaviorally oriented interviews.

The answer to the problem of excessive reliance on management representations lies in *de novo* verification of management's assertions on the basis of independently developed evidence. For example, this concept could be applied to the valuation assertion in the case of receivables and inventories. Finally, auditors should conduct a rigorous and unrelenting search for all symptoms of possible fraud or for surrogate evidence of fraud; discovery sampling may prove useful in this respect.

On a long-term basis, the coalescing of the audit and security functions represents an encouraging trend. For example, internal auditors may assess the adequacy of resources devoted to security, and security officers may provide guidance relative to special investigations conducted primarily by internal auditors. Indeed, an entirely new profession, that of the forensic accountant/auditor has emerged. This new field shows explosive growth especially in regard to security reviews, special investigations, and litigation-support engagements. In 1988, the formation of the Association of Certified Fraud Examiners (ACFE), has been followed by licensing programs, requirements for continuing professional education, and ethics pronouncements. Generally accepted forensic auditing standards cannot be far behind and may emerge from ACFE'S research programs.

Felix Pomeranz

Bibliography

Audit Commission for Local Authorities in England and Wales. *Survey of Computer Fraud and Abuse: Third Triennial Survey.* London: Her Majesty's Stationery Office, 1988.

Defliese, P.L., H.R. Jaenicke, V.M. O'Reilly, and M.B. Hirsch. *Montgomery's Auditing.* 11th ed. New York: John Wiley & Sons, 1990.

Lambert, J.C., and T.D. Hubbard. "Internal Auditors' Changing Responsibilities for Fraud Detection," *Internal Auditor,* June 1989, pp. 13–16.

Pomeranz, F. *The Successful Audit: New Ways to Reduce Risk Exposure and Increase Efficiency.* Homewood, IL: Irwin, 1992.

Sawyer, L.B. *Sawyer's Internal Auditing.* 3d ed. Altamonte Springs, FL: Institute of Internal Auditors, 1988.

See also AMERICAN INSTITUTE OF CERTIFIED PUBLIC ACCOUNTANTS; CITY OF GLASGOW BANK; COHEN COMMISSION: COMMISSION ON AUDITORS' RESPONSIBILITIES; COMPUTING TECHNOLOGY IN THE WEST: THE IMPACT ON THE PROFESSION OF ACCOUNTING; EXTERNAL AUDITING; *HOCHFELDER V. ERNST AND ERNST;* INDEPENDENCE OF EXTERNAL AUDITORS; INTERNAL AUDITING; INTERNAL CONTROL; LAW AND ACCOUNTING; LEDGER; LEGAL LIABILITY OF AUDITORS; MCKESSON AND ROBBINS CASE; SECURITIES AND EXCHANGE COMMISSION; TREADWAY COMMISSION; *ULTRAMARES CORPORATION V. TOUCHE, NIVEN AND COMPANY*

Fugger Cost Accounts

Between the Renaissance and the late eighteenth century, cost accounting technique developed hardly at all. Most bookkeeping texts taught double entry procedures for merchants and ignored manufacturing. However, a few cases of preindustrial cost finding stand out as exceptions to a generally low level of practice. Among other ventures, the Fugger family operated silver and copper mines and smelters in the Tyrol and Carinthia districts of Austria. As early as 1577, materials and labor costs were collected in a "mine and factory" account, which also included inventories of assets and rental income and expense. Transportation and other costs were summarized. Smelter accounts were charged with operating costs and credited with shipments. Total production costs were calculated, and profits on the sales of various types of ore were determined.

Michael Chatfield

Bibliography

Garner, S.P. *Evolution of Cost Accounting to 1925*. University, AL: University of Alabama Press, 1954.

See also Cost and/or Management Accounting; Double Entry Bookkeeping: Origins; Germany

Funds Flow Statement

Funds flow statement is defined by Eric Louis Kohler as "a statement of funds received and expended; a statement of sources and applications of funds in which elements of net income and working capital contributing to an understanding of the whole of financial operations during the reporting period replace totals of these items." This statement had a long, but checkered, past in accounting until its replacement in the United States by the cash flow statement in 1987.

There has been a general feeling among writers of accounting history that the funds statement was first developed by William Morse Cole, an early accounting theorist in the United States, in his text, *Accounts: Their Construction and Interpretation* (1908). Cole analyzed the changes in beginning and ending balance sheets to arrive at a "Where got, Where gone" statement whose two columns balanced. Cole assumed that an income statement was not given. He was of the opinion that it had only been in the five years preceding his book that some railroads had utilized the funds flow statement, which had been practically unknown to that point. Cole utilized the "all resources" approach to the statement, as all changes in balance-sheet accounts were displayed. His approach did not focus on changes in working capital or in cash.

Much earlier, however, the Baltimore and Ohio had published in its 1834 report a statement of its treasurer that detailed cash paid by expenditure type and ending balance of cash and balanced that total with a schedule of beginning balance of cash plus receipts by source. The format of that statement is somewhat reminiscent of the old "charge and discharge" statements in which the accountant listed for what he was responsible on one side and what he did with this responsibility on the other side. There were other examples of such reporting by different enterprises in both the 1800s and the early 1900s. In its annual report in 1902, its first full year of operations, United States Steel Corporation issued a summary of financial operations for all properties.

This statement detailed "resources and payments made" with an ending balance of the increases in current assets for the year. In its 1903 report, U.S. Steel balanced the "resources and payments made" with the "increase in working capital" accounts, although they were not so labeled. However, there is no doubt that U.S. Steel was an early trailblazer with few followers until much later.

The topic of the funds statement became an issue when problems that required it as a solution began to appear on the certified public accountant (CPA) exams of various states, such as the January 1912 New York exam, as noted by L.S. Rosen and Don T. DeCoster (1969). Paul-Joseph Esquerré, another early theorist in accounting in the United States, in 1914 presented a solution to that question that was similar to Cole's approach. Esquerré utilized "resources applied to." Seymour Walton, the editor of the Student's Department of the *Journal of Accounting*, expressed a different viewpoint, stating that the importance of liquidity called for a working capital format for the funds statement.

In a May 1925 article, Esquerré attacked the solution to a problem on the May 1921 exam, given by the American Institute of Accountants, on the statement of resource offered in the *Journal of Accountancy*. This solution followed the lines of a "funds provided and funds applied" (including an increase in working capital) format. A key, if unlabeled, figure in funds provided was "funds provided by operation"—net profits plus depreciation and provision for bad debts. Esquerré said the solution did not clearly indicate whether the "cash" or the "working capital" format was being used, led to the impression that depreciation created funds, and was not understandable to laymen. He then offered his first three-part statement of resources and application: (1) increase in corporate wealth, (2) decrease in corporate wealth, and (3) net increase of wealth through reinvestment of profits.

In a classic response to Esquerré, H.A. Finney wrote an article in the next issue defending the original solution. Finney was an associate of Walton, and author of a leading textbook in accounting. Finney first stressed the mechanistic, or worksheet, solution to the problem. He had stated in his 1923 text that "students do not easily comprehend mere verbal statements of accounting procedure, and it is doubtful whether it is possible to over illustrate a text on accounting." Finney stressed the working capital approach, rather than the cash approach. He also defended the adding-back of depreciation to get funds from operations.

There appears to have been no increased use of the funds statement by the early 1940s, though various writers continued the mechanistic approach to explaining. One authority, Hiram Scovill of the University of Illinois, used the cash approach. Another, John N. Myer, used the working capital approach and used the figures on the income statement rather than "net profit from operations." He did not attempt a complete funds statement and bemoaned the confusion inherent in the term "funds." Maurice Moonitz, a professor of accounting at Stanford University, in 1943 presented a flexible approach, employing a "minimum-maximum viewpoint." He offered a "minimum" definition of funds as "cash on hand plus demand deposits," and a "maximum" definition as "cash, short-term receivables and highly marketable securities . . . less short-term payables." A.B. Carson, a professor of accounting at the University of California, Los Angeles, in 1949, while admitting that the funds statement was not a "primary" financial report, hypothesized that "the major purpose of the accounting process is (or should be) to keep records of working capital and its sources and dispositions." He excluded prepaid expenses from working capital and stressed the need for the funds statement for stewardship reporting. Writers during the 1950s continued to reexamine the concept and format of the funds statement. Charles T. Horngren, then at Marquette University, reported in 1956 the results of a survey of security analysts. Horngren found that analysts would draft a funds statement if none were included in the statements. Hence, he concluded that they were better served by the inclusion of the statement. Accounting reporting practices were little changed until the issuance of Accounting Research Study (ARS) No. 2 in 1961 and Accounting Principles Board (APB) Opinion No. 3 in 1963.

ARS No. 2, *Cash Flow Analysis and the Funds Statement,* written by Perry Mason, presented a selected bibliography that omitted the writings of Cole, Esquerré, Walton, and Finney. It focused primarily on the writings of the 1950s and very early 1960s and was concerned with the use of "cash flow from operations"—net income plus add-backs for noncash expenses. Mason stressed the dangers of the use of "cash flow" by financial analysts, much as Esquerré had. However, Mason kept the basic model of the funds statement advocated by Finney. Mason wanted the funds statement to be a major statement with a broad, "all financial resources" base. Mason desired the use of "funds provided from operations" and wanted no standard format for the statement. APB No. 3, issued in 1963, "The Statement of Source and Application of Funds," followed Mason's main points and recommended use of the Statement of Source and Application of Funds as a major statement. APB No. 19, "Reporting Changes in Financial Position," in 1971 required the statement as a major statement.

Although APB No. 3 and APB No. 19 brought the funds statement to the category of a major statement, support for that was soft—and it was all but killed in an attack by Loyd C. Heath of the University of Washington in a 1978 journal article titled "Let's Scrap the 'Funds Statement.'" Based on an AICPA monograph by Heath, titled *Financial Reporting and the Evaluation of Solvency* (1978) which provided a much richer historical reference than Mason had, the journal article contained many of the same criticisms that Esquerré had presented. Heath held that (1) there was confusion over objectives of the funds statement, (2) the "all resources" approach was undefined, (3) "funds from operations" under the indirect method was not understandable to laymen, and (4) working capital was not a good measure of solvency. He recommended three statements to replace the funds statement: (1) Cash Receipts and Payments Statement, (2) Statement of Financing Activities, and (3) Statement of Investing Activities. Heath's article brought many other comments to the debate, much like the debate of 1925. New formats for the statement were suggested. In 1987 the Financial Accounting Standards Board (FASB) issued FAS No. 95, "Statement of Cash Flows," which dropped the working capital approach in favor of cash, favored the indirect approach, dropped the "all resources" approach, and reformatted the funds statement. FAS No. 95, which was issued by the seven-member board after a narrow 4-to-3 vote, has received some criticisms.

After nearly a century of controversy, the funds statement and its replacement, the cash flow statement, still lack a conceptual base and format. If Esquerré were writing in the 1990s, he could write many of the same criticisms he did in 1925. Perhaps he and Heath were correct that too much has been attempted in these statements. The response to criticism has been to make mechanistic changes rather than philosophical ones.

Richard Vangermeersch

Bibliography

Block, Max. "The 'Funds' Statement: Should It be Scrapped, Retained or Revitalized," *Journal of Accountancy*, December 1979, p. 96.

Carson, A.B. "A 'Source and Application of Funds' Philosophy of Financial Accounting," *Accounting Review*, April 1949, pp. 159–170.

Esquerré, P.J. "Resources and Their Application," *Journal of Accountancy*, May 1925, pp. 424–430.

Finney, H.A. "The Statement of Application of Funds: A Reply to Mr. Esquerré," *Journal of Accountancy*, June 1925, pp. 497–511.

———. *Principles of Accounting*. New York: Prentice-Hall, 1923.

Heath, L.C. "Let's Scrap the 'Funds Statement,'" *Journal of Accountancy*, October 1978, pp. 94–103.

Horngren, C.T. "The Funds Statement and Its Use by Analysts," *Journal of Accountancy*, January 1956, pp. 55–59.

Kafer, K., and V.K. Zimmerman. "Notes on the Evolution of the Statement of Sources and Applications of Funds," *International Journal of Accounting*, Spring 1967, pp. 89–121.

Largay, J.A. "The 'Funds' Statement: Should It Be Scrapped, Retained or Revitalized," *Journal of Accountancy,* December 1979, pp. 88–93.

Mason, P. *Cash Flow Analysis and the Funds Statement*. Accounting Research Study No. 2. New York: AICPA, 1961.

Myer, J.N. "Statements Accounting for Balance Sheet Changes," *Accounting Review*, January 1944, pp. 31–38.

Moonitz, M. "Inventories and the Statement of Funds," *Accounting Review*, July 1943, pp. 262–266.

Most K.S. "FAS 95: The Great Mystery," *Accounting Enquiries*, February 1992, pp. 199–214.

Rosen, L.S., and D.T. DeCoster. "'Funds' Statements: A Historical Perspective," *Accounting Review*, January 1969, pp. 124–136.

Scovill, H.T. "Application of Funds Made Practical," *Accounting Review*, January 1944, pp. 20–38.

Swanson, E.P., and R. Vangermeersch. "A Statement of Financing and Investing Activities: A Revitalized Funds Statement," *CPA Journal*, November 1981, pp. 32–40.

———. "The 'Funds' Statement: Should It Be Scrapped, Retained or Revitalized," *Journal of Accountancy*, December 1979, pp. 93–96.

"The 'Funds' Statement: Should It Be Scrapped, Retained, or Revitalized?" *Journal of Accountancy*, December 1979, pp. 88–97.

Vangermeersch, R. *Financial Reporting Techniques in Twenty Industrial Companies since 1861*. Gainesville: University Presses of Florida, 1979.

See also ACCOUNTING RESEARCH STUDIES; CASH FLOW ACCOUNTING; "CHARGE AND DISCHARGE" STATEMENT; COLE, WILLIAM MORSE; HORNGREN, CHARLES T.; KOHLER, ERIC LOUIS; LIQUIDITY: ACCOUNTING MEASUREMENT; MOONITZ, MAURICE; UNITED STATES STEEL CORPORATION; ZIMMERMAN, VERNON K.

G

Gantt, Henry Laurence (1861–1919)
The American industrial engineer Henry Laurence Gantt made notable contributions to accounting analysis during its formative period. A colleague and disciple of Frederick Winslow Taylor, Gantt saw budgeting as a means of assigning responsibility and measuring performance, not just as a way of limiting expenditures. He pioneered the use of visual aids in planning and controlling operations. The Gantt Chart, a forerunner of Program Evaluations and Review Technique (PERT), was a graphic display that allowed managers to see how work was progressing and take corrective action to keep projects on time and within budgetary allowances. Not until Taylor, Gantt, and other efficiency experts had made time and motion studies and test runs of each plant operation could cost standards be computed scientifically.

In 1915 Gantt examined the cost accounting problems of idle time, overhead allocation, and standard cost setting. He popularized the idea that idle time represented a loss, not a legitimate production cost. Gantt favored ratable overhead cost allocations based on normal capacity and considered historical product costs irrelevant. He considered that accountants ought to calculate what an item "should cost if the proper manufacturing methods were used and the shop were run at full capacity. This might be called the ideal cost, and toward its attainment all effort should be directed."

Michael Chatfield

Bibliography

Alford, L.P. *Henry L. Gantt: Leader in Industry*. New York: Harper and Row, 1934.
Clark, Wallace. *The Gantt Chart: A Working Tool of Management*. New York: Ronald Press, 1922.
Gantt, H.L. *Work, Wages, and Profits*, 2nd ed. New York: Engineering Magazine Company, 1916.
———. "The Relation Between Production and Costs," *Transactions: American Society of Mechanical Engineers*, vol. 38 (1915).
Garner, S.P. *Evolution of Cost Accounting to 1925*. University, AL: University of Alabama Press, 1954.

See also BUDGETING; COMMON COSTS; COST AND/OR MANAGEMENT ACCOUNTING; ENGINEERING AND ACCOUNTING; STANDARD COSTING; TAYLOR, FREDERICK WINSLOW

Garcke and Fells
In 1887 Emile Garcke, an English electrical engineer, and John Manger Fells, an incorporated accountant, published *Factory Accounts: Their Principles and Practice*. This was the nineteenth century's best known and most influential work on cost accounting (it went through seven editions by 1922). Garcke and Fells' description of the routine by which prime costs were passed through a series of ledger accounts from raw materials to finished goods sounds familiar and in fact has hardly been improved on. Materials and labor costs were transferred from stores and wages accounts to a summary manufacturing (work in process) account in the general ledger, which also received debits from the cashbook for expenditures directly applicable to the production process. Periodically, the prime costs of goods completed were transferred from the manufacturing account to a stock (finished goods) account, leaving the

work in process in manufacturing and accumulating cost of goods manufactured in stock. Two entries were required when a sale was made. One credited stock and debited trading for the cost of goods sold; the other debited the customer for the selling price and credited trading. The balances of the stores, manufacturing, and stock accounts showed ending inventories. The trading account showed total cost of goods sold in opposition to total sales revenues; its balance was gross profit.

Garcke and Fells were among the first to insist that all cost accounts be kept in double entry form and be completely integrated with the financial accounting records. This integration was not to be sacrificed because a plant had many departments or numerous subsidiary ledgers; these only made coordination more imperative. Tying the two systems together facilitated accounting control over factory materials and labor. In theory at least, the stores account could at any time be reconciled with the stores ledger, the manufacturing account with the prime cost ledger, and the stock account with the stock ledger balances. The advantages of a perpetual inventory were added to those of a job order cost system.

Garcke and Fells showed a conceptual understanding of overhead cost. They distinguished between factory costs and administrative expenses, and realized that the former should be allocated to jobs while the latter should go directly to profit and loss. They were far ahead of their time in reasoning that, since fixed costs did not vary with changes in production volume, they were a hindrance to managerial analysis and should be excluded from overhead allocations. But Garcke and Fells confused the distinction between fixed and variable costs by inferring that all "shop expenses" were variable while nonfactory costs were mixed. Assuming that overhead cost was incurred to assist labor, they proposed to develop an allocation rate by dividing indirect costs by total direct labor hours. But this was to be done only after the year's expenses had been determined, and Garcke and Fells failed to specify how overhead costs would be passed through the inventory accounts.

Michael Chatfield

Bibliography

Garcke, E., and J.M. Fells. *Factory Accounts: Their Principles and Practice.* London: Crosby, Lockwood & Son, 1887. Reprint. New York: Arno Press, 1976.
Kitchen, J., and R.H. Parker. *Accounting Thought and Education: Six English Pioneers.* London: The Institute of Chartered Accountants in England and Wales, 1980, pp. 36–50. Reprint. New York: Garland, 1984.

See also ACTIVITY BASED COSTING; COMMON COSTS; COST AND/OR MANAGEMENT ACCOUNTING; DIRECT COSTING; LEWIS, J. SLATER; MANAGEMENT ACCOUNTING; PERPETUAL INVENTORY

Garner, S. Paul (1910–)

Noted accounting academic and administrator, S. Paul Garner has attained high stature in the fields of international accounting and the history of cost accounting.

Garner received his B.A. and M.A. in economics from Duke University in 1932 and in 1934. He received his Ph.D. in accounting from the University of Texas in 1940. His dissertation, written under the tutelage of Professor George H. Newlove, who was a highly-regarded writer in the field of cost accounting, served as the basis for one of the most notable contributions to the literature of cost accounting, *Evolution of Cost Accounting to 1925.* Published in 1956, it has received many honors and has been translated into Japanese and Chinese.

Garner has been active in many accounting associations. He was president of the American Accounting Association (AAA) in 1951–1952 and was instrumental in founding its International Section. He also was a founder in 1973 of the Academy of Accounting Historians. In 1990 the International Section and the academy jointly honored Garner for his 80th birthday at the AAA annual meeting in Toronto. The academy also prepared, under the editorship of O. Finley Graves, a monograph for the occasion, *The Costing Heritage: Studies in Honor of S. Paul Garner.*

Garner was instrumental in 1959 in the formation of the Academy of International Business, which had roughly 1,500 members worldwide in 1989. He was a long-time dean of the College of Commerce and Business Administration at the University of Alabama, retiring in 1971 to the emeritus status. Garner was president of the American Assembly of Collegiate Schools of Business (AACSB) in 1964–1965. In 1981 his past and continuing efforts led to the

AACSB requirement of business undergraduates having an exposure to international business.

Garner was named International Accounting Educator for 1990 by the AAA, and in 1993 he received the group's Outstanding Educator Award. He has touched the lives not only of his thousands of students but also of countless accounting and business academics and practitioners throughout the world. He is truly the U.S. Ambassador in Accounting to the World.

Richard Vangermeersch

Bibliography

"Celebration of Four Score Years," *Accounting Historians Notebook*, Fall 1990, pp. 24–25.

Garner, S.P. *Evolution of Cost Accounting to 1925*. University, AL: University of Alabama Press, 1954, 1976.

———. "Has Cost Accounting Come of Age?" *NACA Bulletin*, November 1951, pp. 287–292.

———. "Historical Development of Cost Accounting," *Accounting Review*, October 1947, pp. 385–389.

———. "Industrial Accounting Instruction and the National Defense Program, *Accounting Review*, April 1942, pp. 125–131.

———. "Some Impressions from the Seventh International Congress of Accountants, Amsterdam, Holland," *Accounting Review*, April 1958, pp. 228–229.

Gosselin, D. "S. Paul Garner." In *Biographies of Notable Accountants*, edited by Abdel M. Agami, 2nd ed. New York: Random House, 1989.

See also ACADEMY OF ACCOUNTING HISTORIANS; ACCOUNTING EDUCATION IN THE UNITED STATES; AMERICAN ACCOUNTING ASSOCIATION; CHURCH, ALEXANDER HAMILTON; COST AND/OR MANAGEMENT ACCOUNTING; CRONHELM, FREDERIC WILLIAM; STONE, WILLIARD E.

General Accounting Office, U.S.

The mission of the U.S. General Accounting Office (GAO) is to achieve honest, efficient management and full accountability throughout government. The GAO serves the public interest by providing members of Congress and others who make policy with accurate information, unbiased analysis, and objective recommendations on how best to use public resources in support of the security and well-being of the American people.

This mission reflects the historical evolution of the GAO, created by the Budget and Accounting Act of 1921 (P.L. 67–13, June 10, 1921). This law empowered the GAO to "investigate at the seat of government or elsewhere, all matters related to the receipt, disbursement, and application of public funds" and to "make such investigations and reports as shall be ordered by either House of the Congress or by any committee of either House having jurisdiction over revenue, appropriations, or expenditures."

The law provided the comptroller general, the head of the GAO, with clear statutory foundations for independence: a 15-year term and removal from office only because of permanent incapacity, neglect of duty, malfeasance in office, or conduct involving moral turpitude. Although still guided by this law, the modern GAO differs significantly from the agency that began operations in 1921. It has evolved into an organization deeply involved in the most important issues that the government faces.

During its first two decades, the GAO's most obvious activity was auditing financial actions of the executive branch through examination of millions of vouchers that emanated from departments and other agencies. J.R. McCarl, the first comptroller general, a lawyer, worked hard to establish the independence and integrity of the GAO after controversy developed, threatening the agency's continued existence. The executive branch believed that the GAO, in settling public accounts, was intruding on its prerogatives, thus violating the constitutional principle of separation of powers. Congress turned down several proposals to alter or abolish the GAO.

In the meantime, the GAO made its mark, through issuance of comptroller-general decisions and opinions on the use of appropriated funds, prescribing accounting systems for federal agencies, investigating fraud and abuse, handling government claims, and reporting on a variety of issues—some on its own initiative and some at the request of Congress. Although most of these early activities took place in its Washington offices, the GAO eventually developed extensive field operations, beginning with work on the New Deal agricultural support programs of the mid-1930s. By the 1950s, a formal regional-office structure existed along with overseas offices in Europe and the Far East.

During the term of Comptroller General Lindsay C. Warren (1940–1954), the GAO began a remarkable transformation. World War II proved that voucher auditing was not an efficient means for oversight of government operations; at war's end, there was a backlog of 35 million unchecked vouchers. Congress assigned new duties to the GAO, beginning with the Government Corporation Control Act of 1945, requiring commercial-type audits of more than 100 government corporations (P.L. 79–248, December 6, 1945). Based on experience with corporation audits, Warren developed the "comprehensive audit," which went beyond the routine examination of financial statements and accounts and looked at whether agencies were carrying out activities and programs as authorized by Congress and whether agency reports fully disclosed the nature and scope of activities and provided a sound basis for evaluation of operations.

Warren, a prominent Democratic member of Congress before becoming comptroller general, worked hard to improve the GAO's congressional relationships. He was instrumental in establishing a cooperative program with the Treasury Department and the Bureau of the Budget to improve federal financial management. Through this joint program, Warren moved the GAO away from the old emphasis on voucher checking and toward more substantive matters. Under his administration, the GAO shifted from doing most of its work at its Washington headquarters to locating some of its staff at agency sites where the work was being generated.

The Budget and Accounting Procedures Act of 1950 (P.L. 81–784, September 12, 1950) gave legislative sanction to the joint program and the comprehensive audit and clarified the comptroller general's role in prescribing accounting principles and standards and cooperating with government agencies in developing, reviewing, and improving systems. With the onset of the Cold War and the Korean conflict (1950–1953), the GAO became much more involved with military and foreign-policy issues. The modern GAO blue-cover report—reports that examine specific activities, such as military assistance or foreign-aid programs—originated in this era.

When he retired in 1954, Warren listed these GAO accomplishments during his term: financial leadership in the federal government; corporation audit reports containing recommendations for better management, enhanced financial control, and return on the government's investments; improved government accounting, budgeting, financial reporting, and auditing through the joint accounting program; and development of the comprehensive and other on-site audits.

Warren's successor was Joseph Campbell, a former member of the Atomic Energy Commission and the first accountant to become comptroller general. During his tenure, the GAO continued along the path of modernization and greater involvement in national issues, making it more visible, valued, and controversial.

After studying the GAO's operations, Campbell undertook a major reorganization, designed to eliminate competition among GAO divisions over responsibility for audits in specific executive agencies, to give more emphasis to defense audits, to improve the GAO's professional audit capabilities, and to establish a base for improved relations with Congress. In 1956 he strengthened the agency's recruitment and training programs, with emphasis on recruiting and training professional accountants. These efforts enhanced the GAO's ability to do the increasingly important work coming its way.

Campbell's biggest problem was defense-contract audits. During his term, they increased in number, bluntly criticized contractor and Defense Department practices, named persons allegedly involved in fraud, and recommended refunds from, and withholding of payments to, contractors. Eventually, in 1965, a U.S. House subcommittee headed by Congressman Chet Holifield held hearings during which both defense contractors and the Defense Department severely criticized the GAO audit approach, as did the committee in its report. Campbell, in ill health, resigned in 1965 before the hearings ended. Subsequently, the GAO modified its practices and somewhat de-emphasized its work on defense-contract audits. But the GAO's efforts in other defense areas, such as logistics, communications, personnel management, and major weapon systems, expanded after 1965.

By the time Campbell left office, the GAO's role in the government had expanded and, in spite of the Holifield hearings, its status had improved. Certainly the progress of professionalization in the GAO had been impressive, and the groundwork had been laid for the agency to move on to more sophisticated tasks.

Elmer B. Staats, deputy director of the Bureau of the Budget, became comptroller general in 1966. During his 15-year term, the GAO's transformation continued. The most striking change involved work on evaluation of government programs. The initial impetus came from 1967 legislation directing the comptroller general to evaluate the "poverty programs." The law required the GAO to examine the administrative efficiency of the programs and the extent to which they achieved stated objectives (P.L. 90–222, December 23, 1967). A large team of GAO auditors worked more than a year before issuing a major report in March 1969 and later more than 50 supplemental reports. The GAO noted that some of the programs had made progress, but pointed to administrative problems and insufficient results in others. The poverty-programs work was the most extensive job the GAO had done in response to a congressional request up to that time. It demonstrated the GAO's ability to do program evaluation, and it set the stage for the major thrust of GAO reporting in the 1970s and beyond.

Staats was greatly interested in improving the GAO's service to Congress. He reorganized the agency along functional lines and created new units, such as the Program Analysis Division and the Energy and Minerals Division. In 1975 the GAO adopted a "lead division" concept to establish focal points for planning and accomplishing work on particular jobs. Numerous "issue areas" were specified, including such subjects as automatic data processing, environmental protection, health, income security, military preparedness, and science and technology. Attention also went to the program-planning process, which became more extensive and formal than it had been in the past.

Like Campbell, Staats emphasized staff recruitment and training. The GAO began to hire college graduates and experienced specialists from a variety of disciplines, such as systems analysis, computer technology, actuarial science, economics, engineering, and the social sciences. In the expanded training area, through its own facilities and outside programs, the GAO combined formal instruction with on-the-job experience.

The results of these changes and new emphases could be seen in a variety of ways. The proportion of the GAO's work done at the direct request of Congress increased—reaching more than 40 percent by 1981. The GAO branched out into an ever-widening variety of report areas. For example, it maintained a field office in Saigon (1966–1973) to manage its oversight of U.S. military-support activities during the Vietnam War. In response to a legislative mandate, it established an Office of Federal Elections (1972–1974) to monitor U.S. presidential campaign expenditures. Examples of report areas during the 1970s, demonstrating the diversity of GAO work, included grain reserves, use of minicomputers in the federal government, the Federal Aviation Administration's airport-certification program, management of United Nations development-assistance activities, foreign oil-supply diversification, the metric system, the Law of the Sea Conference, and the multinational F-16 aircraft program. By the late 1970s, the GAO was issuing about 1,000 reports per year.

In October 1981, Charles A. Bowsher, a longtime partner in Arthur Andersen and Company, became comptroller general. Initially concerned with the quality of GAO service to Congress, Bowsher appointed a Task Force whose proposals on how GAO reports could best serve the agency's mission were a guide for change in the early years of his term. A major divisional reorganization assigned to four program divisions specific segments of government activity: human resources; national security and international affairs; resources, community, and economic development; and general government matters. Three other divisions were to provide technical support in the fields of accounting and financial management, program evaluation and methodology, and information management and technology. Bowsher also set up posts for new assistant comptrollers general for planning and reporting and for operations, positions that were mirrored in each of the seven divisions.

The Office of the General Counsel (OGC), which had played a key role in the GAO's operations since 1921, was reorganized to ensure that each GAO division had a corresponding OGC group to provide legal assistance. Bowsher also established under OGC an Office of Special Investigations to expand the GAO's ability to do investigative work.

Other innovations included creation of an Office of Quality Assurance and a Post Assignment Quality Review System (PAQRS) to do annual quality reviews of selected work areas. High-level daily meetings reviewed job starts and ongoing work in the divisions. The GAO's

G

product line expanded to include fact sheets, letter reports, and oral and written briefing reports as well as the traditional blue-cover chapter reports (in a new and more useful format) and testimony.

The scope and importance of the GAO's work continued to expand. The increased work load and productivity showed up in annual statistics on reports, congressional briefings, recommendations for improving the government's efficiency and effectiveness, and testimony. By the end of the 1980s, GAO staffers were testifying before congressional committees more than any other federal agency except the Defense Department—a total of 300 times during fiscal year 1990. By this time, more than 80 percent of the GAO's work was done at congressional request.

Behind these statistics lies the important fact that Congress called upon the GAO more and more to deal with the big issues. The Iran-Contra affair, health care, farm credit, major weapons systems, the 1987 stock market crash, AIDS, scandal in the Department of Housing and Urban Development, the savings and loan crisis, and the federal budget deficit were standard fare for GAO. Hardly a day went by without a major story about a GAO report or testimony appearing in the press. With no more staff resources than it had 20 years earlier, the GAO's role in the public-policy process had vastly expanded by the 1990s. It had become a key player on many of the most critical issues of the times.

This brief look at GAO's historical development makes clear that GAO has changed radically over the years, enabling it to respond to the central problems of the day, whether in the areas of foreign and defense policy or domestic programs, and that the GAO's service to the Congress has expanded tremendously. The modern GAO is a product of its environment—both an external environment molded by the nation's domestic and international challenges, and an internal environment, including increasing congressional dependence on the objective and independently derived, accurate, timely, and meaningful work that the GAO presents in a way most useful to responsible officials.

While continuing with traditional functions that date back to the 1920s, the GAO is constantly meeting new challenges, both on its own initiative and at congressional request. The GAO has built up an organization and professional staff designed to enable it to play an ever-increasing role of importance in national issues and to participate effectively in the policy debate accompanying these issues.

Roger R. Trask

Bibliography

Havens, H.S. *The Evolution of the General Accounting Office: From Voucher Audits to Program Evaluation.* Washington, DC: GAO, 1990.

Kloman, E.H., ed. *Cases in Accountability: The Work of the GAO.* Boulder, CO: Westview Press, 1979.

Mansfield, H.C. Jr. *The Comptroller General: A Study in the Law and Practice of Financial Administration.* New Haven, CT: Yale University Press, 1939.

Mosher, F.C. *The GAO: The Quest for Accountability in American Government.* Boulder, CO: Westview Press, 1979.

———. *A Tale of Two Agencies: A Comparative Analysis of the General Accounting Office and the Office of Management and Budget.* Baton Rouge: Louisiana State University Press, 1984.

Pois, J. *Watchdog on the Potomac: A Study of the Comptroller General of the United States.* Washington, DC: University Press of America, 1979.

Trask, R.R. *GAO History, 1921–1991.* Washington, DC: GAO, 1991.

See also CONGRESSIONAL VIEWS; COST ACCOUNTING STANDARDS BOARD; FEDERAL GOVERNMENT ACCOUNTING (U.S.); INTERNAL AUDITING; OPERATIONAL (VALUE-FOR-MONEY) AUDITING; TREADWAY COMMISSION

Generally Accepted Accounting Principles

"Generally accepted accounting principles" is a combination of two terms found in the 1970 edition of Eric Louis Kohler's *A Dictionary for Accountants.* "Generally accepted" means "given authoritative recognition." "Accounting principles" means "the body of doctrine associated with *accounting,* serving as an explanation of current practices and as a guide in the selection of conventions and procedures." While the term "generally accepted accounting principles" (GAAP) did not enter the suggested auditor's opinion until 1939, the notion of GAAP had been in vogue since the 1917 issuance of "Uniform Accounting."

That document was a joint effort of the Federal Trade Commission (FTC), the Federal Reserve Board (FRB), and the American Institute of Accountants (AIA). While the document stressed the audit steps necessary for a balance-sheet audit, there were many inclusions of what is now called GAAP. An example is this passage in the section on inventories: "The auditor should satisfy himself that inventories are stated at cost or market prices, whichever are the lower at the date of the balance sheet. No inventory must be passed which has been marked up to market prices and a profit assumed that is not and may never be realized. If the market is higher than cost, it is permissible to state that fact in a footnote on the balance sheet." The suggested auditor's certificate included "I certify that the above balance sheet and statement of profit and loss have been made in accordance with the plan suggested and advised by the Federal Reserve Board. . . . " The 1929 revision of the 1917 document contained the same quote on inventory accounting. The suggested auditor's certificate was curt: "I certify that the accompanying balance sheet and statement of profit and loss, in my opinion, set forth the financial condition of the company. . . ." In the 1936 revision, which was published by the AIA and entitled *Examination of Financial Statements by Independent Public Accountants*, the term "accounting principles" was used in the preface. The related quote on inventory was modified to exclude the footnote of higher value of inventory. A definition for "market price" was given, as well as a rule on the deduction of trade discounts. The auditor's report was changed to ". . . fairly present, in accordance with accepted principles of accounting. . . ."

What caused this change in the 1936 revision was a statement in 1932 by the AIA Special Committee on Cooperation with Stock Exchanges, chaired by George Oliver May and published in 1934 as the *Audits of Corporate Accounts* . . . The term "fairly general acceptance" was employed, and a list of five such broad principles was included in an exhibit. In retrospect, these principles were more like specific rules than broad principles. For instance, the fourth principle was: "While it is perhaps in some circumstances permissible to show stock of a corporation held in its own Treasury as an asset, if adequately disclosed, the dividends on stock so held should not be treated as a credit to the income account of the company."

The American Accounting Association (AAA) joined this quest for principles in 1936 with *A Tentative Statement of Accounting Principles Affecting Corporate Reports*. Granting that there already were standards of public accounting practice established for the treatment of numerous items, the AAA statement then presented 20 such principles of a, in retrospect, fairly broad nature. For instance, it strongly recommended the historical cost principle. "Present procedure is unsatisfactory in that it permits periodic revaluation of assets, up or down, in accordance with current price levels and expected business developments." In a follow-up monograph in 1940, two of the members of the committee that wrote the 1936 report, William Andrew Paton and A.C. Littleton, stressed the use of the term "standards" over the term "principles." They stated: "Principles would generally suggest a universality and degree of permanence which cannot exist in a human service institution such as accounting." However, the AAA in its 1941 revision of the 1936 statement favored the term "principles" and increased the number of such to 27. The 1948 revision returned to "standards"—listing 32 such—and "concepts" rather than "principles." There were eight supplementary statements subsequent to the 1948 revision, including the AAA Committee on Concepts and Standards Underlying Corporate Financial Statements. In 1957 another revision occurred. In it, "concepts" were discussed, very general captions were used, and there was no numbering of "standards." The subsequent revisions, by the AAA's *A Statement of Basic Accounting Theory* in 1966 and *Statement on Accounting Theory and Theory Acceptance* in 1977, continued with the broader outlook of the 1957 statement.

Back in 1937, to mark its 50th anniversary, the AIA sponsored an essay contest on this question: "To What Extent Can the Practice of Accounting be Reduced to Rules and Standards?" In his winning essay, published in the November 1937 issue of *Journal of Accountancy*, Gilbert Byrne, a public accounting practitioner, stressed the need to isolate "accounting principles" from what he labeled "accounting rules," "accounting conventions," and "accounting standards." Byrne wrote: "Accounting principles, then, are the fundamental concepts on which accountancy, as an organized body of knowledge, rests. Like the axioms of geometry, they are few in number and general in terms; . . ." He then listed eight very general principles—for example, his first one was: "Accounting is essentially the allocation of historical costs and revenues to the current and succeeding fiscal periods." Byrne felt it was from these principles that accounting rules, practices, and conventions would arise. Howard Greer, an accounting practitioner and frequent contributor to the accounting literature, wrote soon after that accounting practice allowed too much variation in Byrne's principles. Greer favored the more detailed approach taken in the AAA's 1936 statement.

Another look at accounting principles was published in 1938 by Thomas Henry Sanders from the Harvard University Graduate Business School, Henry Rand Hatfield from the University of California, and Underhill Moore from the School of Law at Yale University. Their study, which they undertook in 1935 for the Haskins and Sells Foundation, presented six general principles, six income-statement principles, eight balance-sheet principles, four consolidated-statement principles, and one comments-and-footnotes principle.

In 1939 the AIA's Committee on Accounting Procedure (CAP) issued Accounting Research Bulletin (ARB) No. 1, "General Introduction and Rules Formerly Adopted," which formally adopted the six rules or principles that the AIA had previously passed. These six principles were: (1) unrealized profit not taken to the income statement; (2) capital surplus not be used for items belonging on the income statement; (3) earned surplus of a subsidiary prior to acquisition does not result in a credit to the parent's earned surplus; (4) dividends on treasury stock are not income; (5) notes receivable from officers are reported separately from other receivables; and (6) the proceeds from the sale of donated treasury stock are not to be credited to surplus. The CAP considered the general acceptability of its pronouncements as of the highest importance and, therefore, required a two-thirds vote of its 21 members to secure passage of an ARB. At its annual meeting in September 1939, the AIA adopted a short form of Independent Certified Public Accountant's Report on Opinion, which included this passage: ". . . in conformity with generally accepted accounting principles applied or a basis consistent with that of the preceding year."

The CAP transferred its role to a committee of the American Institute of Certified Public Accountants (AICPA), the Accounting Prin-

ciples Board (APB), in 1959. The APB planned to leave the brushfire approach of the CAP by basing GAAP on a more conceptual basis. To that end, the AICPA published several research monographs on the issue. In 1961, Accounting Research Study (ARS) No. 1, *The Basic Postulates of Accounting*, by AICPA Research Director Maurice Moonitz, presented a total of 14 postulates about accounting which were arrived at deductively. In ARS No. 3, *A Tentative Set of Broad Accounting Principles for Business Enterprises*, Moonitz and Robert T. Sprouse presented a very general set of accounting principles based on the postulates of ARS No. 1. However, ARS No. 3, which was published in 1962, was subjected to great criticism, and the deductive approach for GAAP based on postulates was dealt a severe blow. So much so that the AICPA in 1965 published ARS No. 7, *Inventory of Generally Accepted Accounting Principles for Business Enterprises*. Written by Paul Grady, a leading practitioner and former AICPA research director, this ARS noted 32 principles in five groupings. It also was encyclopedic in its inclusion of much of the then-current GAAP. This refusal to base GAAP on a rigorously deductive system was a severe blow to those who were opposed to the brushfire approach to solving accounting problems, in which a quick solution was given to a pressing problem and then attention would be given to a new problem.

GAAP was even more formally placed in the hands of the APB in 1964, when the Council of the AICPA required that departures from APBs and ARBs be disclosed in footnotes or in the independent auditor's reports. This was further emphasized in 1972 when the AICPA passed Rule 203 of its restated Code of Professional Ethics. This rule stated: "A member shall not express an opinion that financial statements are presented in conformity with generally accepted accounting principles if such statements contain any departure from an Opinion of the Accounting Principles Board . . . unless the members can demonstrate that due to unusual circumstances the financial statements would otherwise have been misleading. . . ." By 1973, there was a notation to Rule 203 in APB No. 28, "Interim Financial Reporting."

The APB did make one last effort in 1970 at conceptualizing GAAP. In APB Statement No. 4, it defined GAAP as encompassing the conventions, rules, and procedures necessary to define accepted accounting practice at a particular time. The APB also classified principles into three groupings: pervasive, broad operating, and detailed.

The Financial Accounting Standards Board (FASB) replaced the APB in 1973, as a result of recommendations by the AICPA Study Group on Establishment of Accounting Principles. The Study Group, called the Wheat Committee after its chairman, Francis M. Wheat, was quite explicit as to why the FASB was not to be the FAPB (Financial Accounting Principles Board). It wrote: "This historical review shows that while the APB and its predecessor (CAP) have done much to raise the level of financial reporting, many of their opinions have had little to do with "principles" as that word is normally understood. We therefore recommend the use in the future of the term "financial accounting standards" as better describing the nature of the Board's pronouncements."

The Wheat Committee did not think the research staff of the FASB should be conducting a broad, fundamental research program dealing with basic concepts on an ongoing basis; it believed this type of research was best left in the hands of accounting academics. However, the FASB has issued six Statements of Financial Accounting Concepts (SFACs), and in FAS No. 96, "Accounting for Income Taxes" (1987), it ruled that the approach for deferred income taxes of APB No. 11, "Accounting for Income Taxes" (1966) was not in line with SFAC No. 6, "Elements of Financial Statements" (1985).

The Wheat Committee was appointed by the AICPA in March 1971. In April of that year, the AICPA appointed a nine-member Study Group on Objectives of Financial Statements. This committee was chaired by Robert Martin Trueblood (hence, its 1973 report is commonly known as the Trueblood Report). The Trueblood Report was very strongly user oriented and stressed the importance of cash flow to users—a view expressed in 1987 by the FASB in FAS No. 95, "Statement of Cash Flows." The report also stressed the qualitative characteristics of reporting, later reflected in the Statements on Financial Accounting Concepts issued by the FASB.

While the Wheat Committee favored the term "standards" over the term "principles," the phrase "generally accepted accounting principles" remains an important component of the auditor's report. Until that phrase is changed, GAAP will remain perhaps the chief focal point for discussion about financial accounting. The long-lasting ability of GAAP may be in its flexibility to meet the needs of a complex and ever-changing society.

Richard Vangermeersch

Bibliography

Accounting Principles Board. "Basic Concepts and Accounting Principles Underlying Financial Statements of Business Enterprises." APB Statement No. 4. New York: AICPA, 1970.

American Accounting Association. *Accounting and Reporting Standards for Corporate Financial Statements and Preceding Statements and Supplements.* Sarasota, FL: American Accounting Association, undated.

American Institute of Accountants. *Audits of Corporate Accounts: Correspondence between the Special Committee on Co-operation with Stock Exchanges of the American Institute of Accountants and the Committee on Stock List of the New York Stock Exchange, 1932–1934.* New York: AIA, 1934.

———. *Examination of Financial Statements by Independent Public Accountants.* New York: AIA, 1936.

American Institute of Certified Public Accountants. *Establishing Financial Accounting Standards.* Report of the Study Group on Establishment of Accounting Principles [the Wheat Report]. New York: AICPA, 1972.

———. *Objectives of Financial Statements.* Report of the Study Group on Objectives of Financial Statements [the Trueblood Report]. New York: AICPA, 1973.

Byrne, G.R. "To What Extent Can the Practice of Accounting Be Reduced to Rules and Standards?" *Journal of Accountancy*, November 1937, pp. 364–379.

Gerboth, D.L. "'Muddling Through' with the APB," *Journal of Accountancy*, May 1972, pp. 42–49.

Greer, H.C. "What Are Accepted Principles of Accounting?" *Accounting Review*, March 1938, pp. 25–31.

Paton, W.A., and A.C. Littleton. *An Introduction to Corporate Accounting Standards.* American Accounting Association Monograph No. 3. New York: American Accounting Association, 1940.

Sanders, T.H., H.R. Hatfield, and U. Moore.

A Statement of Accounting Principles.
New York: AIA, 1938.

"Uniform Accounting," *Journal of Accountancy*, June 1917, pp. 401–433.

U.S. Federal Reserve Board, "Verification of Financial Statements," *Journal of Accountancy*, May 1929, pp. 321–353.

Zeff, S.A. *Forging Accounting Principles in Five Countries: A History and an Analysis of Trends.* Champaign, IL: Stipes, 1972.

See also A STATEMENT OF BASIC ACCOUNTING THEORY; ACCOUNTING PRINCIPLES BOARD; ACCOUNTING RESEARCH BULLETINS; ACCOUNTING RESEARCH STUDIES; AMERICAN ACCOUNTING ASSOCIATION; AMERICAN INSTITUTE OF CERTIFIED PUBLIC ACCOUNTANTS; *AN INTRODUCTION TO CORPORATE ACCOUNTING STANDARDS;* AUDITOR'S REPORT; COMPARABILITY; CONCEPTUAL FRAMEWORK; ETHICS, PROFESSIONAL; FINANCIAL ACCOUNTING STANDARDS BOARD; GRADY, PAUL; HOXSEY, J.M.B.; KOHLER, ERIC LOUIS; LITTLETON, A.C.; MATCHING; MAY, GEORGE OLIVER; NEW YORK STOCK EXCHANGE; PATON, WILLIAM ANDREW; SANDERS, HATFIELD, AND MOORE; SECURITIES AND EXCHANGE COMMISSION; SOLOMONS, DAVID; SPACEK, LEONARD; STATE AND LOCAL GOVERNMENTS (U.S., 1901–1991); TREASURY STOCK; TRUEBLOOD, ROBERT MARTIN; *UNIFORM ACCOUNTING;* WHEAT COMMITTEE

Germany

There are four major aspects to the history of accounting and accounting thought in Germany: bookkeeping and financial accounting, inflation accounting and dynamic accounting, investment calculus, and standard costing and internal control.

Bookkeeping and Financial Accounting

Up to the eighteenth century, German accounting was strongly influenced by Italian bookkeeping. For instance, Matheus Schwartz, bookkeeper for the Fugger mining operations in the sixteenth century, underwent his professional training in Venice. In the seventeenth century, French scholars, especially Jacques Savary and M. de la Porte, dominated. However, Hinrich Magelsen, a German accounting practitioner, contributed the original idea of asset depreciation in 1772.

Common law prohibited profit distribution prior to the liquidation of a trading company. By contrast, Prussian law from 1794 later established the rule of annual profit distribution. In cases in which the company articles did not contain any disposition concerning income determination, profit had to be calculated on basis of the "lower of cost or market" principle. Prussian law also constituted the first regulations concerning depreciation.

Articles of stock companies, especially those of railway companies in Germany in the nineteenth century, emphasized the idea of ascertaining profit by a revenue-surplus calculation that ignored depreciation expense. In this period, corporations used double entry, as well as single entry bookkeeping in their balance sheets. Nineteen of 20 stock companies followed the "lower of cost or market" principle. Usually, unrealized profits were disclosed, and payments for a self-created goodwill could be found in balance sheets. Accounting standards were developed particularly after the abolition of the authorization procedure for the establishment of corporations in 1870. The most important statement about financial accounting was written by Herman Veit Simon in 1886. Since 1891 tax-ordained accounting has greatly influenced accounting standards.

Inflation Accounting and Dynamic Accounting

At the beginning of the inflationary period following World War I, practitioners and business economists developed proposals for inflation accounting. These proposals were most remarkable and, by international standards, original contributions to accounting theories. Walter Mahlberg and Eugen Schmalenbach, both leading German accounting theorists, in 1921 and 1925 developed price-level-adjusted accounting. They adjusted original costs by means of an index of the general level of prices or by a gold standard.

Fritz Schmidt, also a German accounting theorist, recommended appraising assets at their current values in his 1921 book, *Die Organische Tageswertbilanz.* In his theory, the difference between historical- and current-cost valuation is transferred to a tax-free reserve account. The problem of purchasing-power profits for debtors and such losses for creditors concerning nominal assets is eliminated by his premise of an equality of value of debt and credits.

In order to control efficiency, Schmalenbach confronted the accounting standards of the commercial law with his "dynamic accounting" theory in 1919. Schmalenbach tried to present profit as a measure to achieve allocative efficiency. Thus, in his first approach, he charged interest on equity and imputed entrepreneurial wages to expense and refuted the "lower of cost or market" principle. From 1925 on, Schmalenbach and his followers interpreted dynamic accounting theory as the concept underlying correctly understood law for financial and tax accounting. This concept prevailed to 1960 and has partly been accepted by court rulings in tax matters. The accounting thought of the last three decades adopted topics of the Anglo-Saxon literature.

Investment Calculus

After the first use of a discounting formula by the Dutch writer Simon Stevin in 1582, Gottfried Wilhelm Leibniz, the famous German mathematician, presented a juridical justification of the "net present value" method in 1682. He deduced it from three axioms derived for familiar legal principles: (1) In case that a loan is redeemed before it is due, the legal interest for the interim period up to maturity may be charged by the debtor; (2) every compensation is a kind of payment; and (3) creditor and debtor may agree on the premature repayment of a liability.

From these assumptions, he derived the following: If the debtor repays a ducat today, falling due after one year, the creditor would owe him the legal interest for the interim period (axiom 1). Because debtor and creditor agree on immediate payment (axiom 3), the debtor may ask the creditor to pay him his interest charges at once. This payment may be carried out by compensation (axiom 2), so that the legal interest is deducted from the initial amount of the liability. If the legal interest comes up to a 20th of the liability, the debtor has to repay 1/1–1/20 at once. But since the debtor obtains the 1/20 due after one year at once, he will have to grant interest to the creditor (axiom 1); in fact, a 20th of 1/20—that is, 1/400. This payment may be carried out by compensation (axiom 2) and so on. The total amount of this infinite geometrical series equals 20/21 resp. 1/1.05 of the liability, and thus the capitalization is deduced from the legal principles assumed above. By proving that the present value (as a kind of calculation with compound interest) can be derived from undisputed principles, Leibniz questioned one of the social dogmas of his time:

the prohibition against charging compound interest.

Objections to capitalized-value calculation with compound interest were still being raised at the beginning of the nineteentth century. In this context in 1829, Friedrich Löhmann, a lieutenant of the Saxon army and teacher of mathematics in Dresden, discussed the reinvestment implications in *Handbuch für Juridische und Staatswirthschaftliche Rechnungen*. The first managerial investment calculation was published in 1822 by the Prussian mining official Karl von Oeynhausen, who discussed the problems of data acquisition, estimated the "breakeven point," and stressed the importance of fixed costs and taxes.

Standard Costing and Internal Control

Cameralists were German writers of the 1600s and 1700s who were concerned with rationalizing the management of the many feudal states of the German Empire. These writers not only dealt with traditional governmental financing but also with such state enterprises as agriculture, mining, and manufacturing. An example of such writers is Johann Heinrich Gottlob von Justi, a professor as well as an administrator of public enterprises in Germany. Cameralists constructed, more or less systematically, budgets and accounted for the unspent appropriations. Reflections about the feasibility of accounting for the issue of budgeted amounts and actual amounts began when variances had to be explained. An application of modern-like standard-cost accounting was presented by Leopold Friedrich Fredersdorff in 1802 in his description of the management of a governmental ironwork in northern Germany.

Other reflections about accounting systems arose as part of a reconstruction of accounting in bureaucracies under the Enlightenment ideal during the reign of the Habsburg monarch Joseph II (1765–1790). Renewing the system of domainial accounting, between 1764 and 1774, Johann Matthias Puechberg discussed diverse accounting systems for different purposes. Later, the distinction between balance sheets to determine profits and losses and balance sheets to determine wealth was made by Johann Gottfried Brand, whose 1790 work anticipated Schmalenbach's "dynamic accounting." There was no significant cumulative development in the theory of management accounting for controlling problems.

Dieter Schneider

Bibliography

Berry, M. "Financial Accountability in West German Government," *Advances in International Accounting*, 1987, pp. 39–84.

Brand, J.G. *Grundsätze der Staatsrechnungswissenschaft.* Vienna: N.p., 1790.

Fredersdorff, L.F. *Praktische Anleitung zu einer guten Eisenhütten=Oeconomie, Verfertigung der Eisenhütten= Ertrags=Anschläge oder jährlichen Hütten=Etats und zur zweckmäßigen Einrichtung der Betriebs= und Handlungsrechnungen.* Bad Pyrmont: Pyrmont, 1802.

Leibniz, G.W. *Meditatio Juridico-mathematica de Interusurio Simplice.* N.p., 1682.

Magelsen, H. *Die ersten Gründe des Buchhaltens, sammt Anwendung derselben auf die gewöhnlichsten Vorfälle der Handlung und Wirthschaft.* Altona: N.p., 1772.

Puechberg, J.M. *Einleitung zu einem verbeßerten Cameral-Rechnungs=Fuße, auf die Verwaltung einer Herrschaft angewandt.* Vienna: J.T. Trattner, 1764.

———. *Grundsätze der Rechnungs=Wissenschaft auf das Privatvermögen angewendet, zum Gebrauche der öffentlichen Vorlesungen bey den K.K. Ritterakademien, und der Realschule allhier. Erster Theil.* Vienna: 1774.

Schmalenbach, E. *Dynamische Bilanz.* 3d ed. Leipzig: N.p., 1925.

Schmidt, F. *Die Organische Tageswertbilanz.* Wiesbaden: N.p., 1921.

Simon, H.V. *Die Bilanzen der Aktiengesellschaften und der Kommanditgesellschaften auf Aktien.* Berlin: N.p., 1886.

Small, A.W. *The Cameralists: The Pioneers of German Social Polity.* Chicago: University of Chicago Press, 1909. Reprint. Chicago: Burt Franklin, 1969.

von Justi, J.H.G. *System des Finanzwesens.* Halle: Renger, 1766. Reprint. Salem: Scientia-Zerl, 1969.

von Oeynhausen, K. "Ueber die Bestimmung der Kapitalwerthes von Steinkohlen-Zechen," in *Archiv für Bergbau und Huttenwesen*, vol. 5, edited by C.J.B. von Karsten, pp. 306–319. Berlin: G. Reimer, 1822.

See also AGRICULTURAL ACCOUNTING; BREAK-EVEN CHART; CHART OF ACCOUNTS; COMPOUND INTEREST; CONSERVATISM; FUGGER COST ACCOUNTS; GOODWILL; INFLATION ACCOUNTING; MICROECONOMICS IN GERMANY; PACIOLI, LUCA; SAVARY, JACQUES; SCHMALENBACH, EUGEN; SCHMIDT, JULIUS AUGUST FRITZ; SCHREIBER, HEINRICH; SCHWEICKER, WOLFGANG; SOMBART, WERNER; SPRAGUE, CHARLES EZRA; STANDARD COSTING; STEVIN, SIMON; SWEENEY, HENRY WHITCOMB; TAX-ORDAINED ACCOUNTING; TRANSFER PRICES; UNIFORMITY

Gilman, Stephen (1887–1959)

Stephen Gilman, a native of Illinois, graduated from the University of Wisconsin in 1910. He was a certified public accountant (CPA) who owned and operated the International Accountants Society, a correspondence school, and served as a member of the editorial board of *Accounting Review* from 1944 to 1946. He also was a member of the Committee on Accounting Procedure of the American Institute of Accountants from 1941 to 1944.

In his comprehensive book, *Accounting Concepts of Profit* (1939), Gilman provided a legacy of accounting ideas. He was one of the earliest writers to emphasize the income statement as opposed to the balance sheet and to discuss the uncertainties of accounting data in terms of the amounts and timing of income figures. Other issues he addressed in his work included: (1) the semantic problem of defining accounting terms and developing accounting postulates; (2) the problems in formulating generally accepted accounting principles; (3) the impact of law, economics, and statistics on accounting; (4) the nature of users of accounting data; (5) the problems in accounting under inflationary conditions; (6) the allocation problem in income measurement; (7) the proprietary and entity theories; and (8) the economic consequences of accounting.

A descriptive writer who dealt with inconsistencies in accounting practice, Gilman focused on a number of issues in his book that were later discussed in the accounting literature. He evaluated many misconceptions about accounting and focused on the limitations of accounting.

Gilman set forth the following taxonomy for accounting: "principles," "rules," "conventions," and "doctrines." He defined and illustrated each term. He considered principle to be a basic truth, but he found no such examples in accounting. A convention is arbitrary, based on consensus. Gilman emphasized the entity, valuation, and period conventions. Rules are formulated as guides to action, such as the "lower of cost or market" rule. According to Gilman, the conventions and rules are the sources of a multitude of problems in accounting. The problems he perceived in formulating accounting principles included: (1) the periodic-reporting and historical-cost conventions; (2) the attempt to fit the entity model to the complexity of business; (3) the various contradictions between principles; (4) the self-interest of different parties in formulating accounting principles; and (5) the difficulties in defining accounting terms.

An early opponent of conservatism, Gilman was highly critical of the "lower of cost or market rule," which he viewed as an inventory rule. This application of conservatism has a distortive effect on profit. Conservatism, Gilman observed, conflicts with consistency and full disclosure. Gilman argued that total revaluation of a firm's assets in terms of future replacement cost or realizable value is not feasible in view of the subjectivity of those values. Furthermore, he pointed out that such figures would generate unrealized gains and thus violate conservatism. While Gilman observed the importance of general price-level adjustments, he did not believe that it is the function of accounting to furnish such adjustments in the financial statements.

In his book, Gilman provided his own nontraditional views and, in so doing, furnished a synthesis of antecedent accounting thought. He was clearly ahead of his time in accounting thought, influencing many subsequent writers on the development of accounting. Gilman's book offers a blend of practice and theory, stemming from the shift in emphasis from the balance sheet to the income statement. In it can be found the roots of many long-term issues in financial reporting and management accounting.

The irony is that, while his book is highly regarded in universities in other countries such as Australia and Japan, where considerably greater emphasis is placed on accounting theory than in American schools, in the United States Gilman is virtually ignored in accounting education, even at the doctoral level. His book should be required reading for all graduate students in accounting.

Robert Bloom

Bibliography
Bloom, R., M. Collins, and A. Debessay. "Gilman's Contributions to Accounting Thought: A Golden Anniversary Retrospective," *Accounting History* (Australia), vol. 2, no. 2, 1990, pp. 107–123.
Gilman, S. *Accounting Concepts of Profit.* New York: Ronald Press, 1939.
Zeff, S.A. *American Accounting Association: Its First Fifty Years, 1916–1966.* Sarasota, FL: American Accounting Association, 1966.

See also CONCEPTUAL FRAMEWORK; CONSERVATISM; OBJECTIVITY

Goodwill

Goodwill is the differential ability of one firm, in comparison with another or an assumed average firm, to make a profit. A product of its environment, the commercial concept of goodwill did not take form until the institution of business enterprise began to develop. Goodwill's prerequisites are thus those of business enterprise, including the evolution and gradual acceptance of a concept of money, and valuing things as assets for ultimately making a profit instead of the older manorial concept of value in terms of a nonquantified goal of livelihood. The measurement of profit led to the development of a concept, however loosely defined, of a normal profit or return and, consequently, to recognition that some firms were more profitable than others. The advantaged firms were said to possess another element to account for the above-average profits, and the new asset was assigned the term "goodwill."

The asset was so named because it appears in its initial form to have resulted from the good feeling or good will of the customer toward the proprietor due to such factors as the proprietor's friendly treatment of patrons, reputation, and quality of goods and/or services. It could also have been due to the business being strategically located at a busy crossroads, for example.

In comparison to the evolution of other elements of commercial law, the legal protection of goodwill was relatively slow in developing. Particularly in the fifteenth and sixteenth centuries, the sale of goodwill ran afoul of then-existing "restraint of trade" doctrines. Opportunity for making a livelihood was so restricted during that time that it was considered bad public policy to allow a seller even voluntarily to give up or limit his ability to compete. From at least 1417 forward for more than 200 years, parties to a contract involving the transfer of goodwill could be subjected to fine and/or imprisonment under English law. A fundamental change in policy was indicated in 1620 when, for the first time, a "restraint of trade" agreement was upheld in the courts. An individual could finally sell his liberty as well as his property, and goodwill was at last accorded legal protection.

With the increase in size of businesses and the rise of the modern corporation, commercial and legal perceptions of goodwill began to change. While personal aspects traditionally associated with small businesses could still foster the asset, the concept of goodwill gradually expanded, both commercially and legally, to include any and every advantage that contributed to a greater-than-normal return. Particularly in larger concerns, goodwill could be due to a complex of inseparable and possibly numerous factors contributing to a firm's extraordinary profitability.

Various authorities over the years have attempted to describe the asset through an analysis of its characteristics, but even these characteristics are subject to reinterpretation as business enterprise (and thus goodwill) continues to evolve.

(1) *Intangibility* has always been associated with goodwill specifically and "intangibles" generally, but it is a description in need of clarification. Any item considered as an asset, whether it be plant and equipment, inventories, trademarks, or goodwill, is but a contemplation of its probable future cash flows—or, as could be stated, an asset is nothing but a hope grounded on a probability. Such contemplation and hope are simply thoughts concerning the future, and thus all assets may be regarded as intangible. Furthermore, bank accounts and accounts receivable are just as immaterial as goodwill but are generally not considered as intangibles. Ironically, the term "intangible" correctly applies only to the present molecular structure of goodwill, which has no bearing on its status as an asset. Intangibility thus may be viewed as a necessary but not a sufficient description of goodwill.

(2) *Attachment to the business* is a fundamental quality of goodwill, for goodwill represents the ability of a given business to succeed in comparison to its competitors. It is inconceivable that goodwill could be sold separate from a firm or some semiautonomous portion thereof.

(3) *Independence of cost* has long been associated with goodwill, since in its earliest development in relatively small businesses, the asset was thought to be an incidental by-product of such factors as a merchant's honesty and quality of wares. In the larger, perhaps global, firms of the twentieth century, this characteristic may be open to question. Some modern authorities contend that such huge businesses possess the ability through techniques such as advertising to create demand for their products. In this case, the development of goodwill may not be independent of expenditures made on its behalf.

(4) The *differential and monopolistic advantage* associated with goodwill is closely associated with its inseparability from a given firm. The asset confers a differential advantage in comparison with other businesses or an assumed average firm, and goodwill is monopolistic because it is enjoyed exclusively by the advantaged firm in comparison with all others. The advantage is both inseparable from, and exclusive to, the firm possessing it.

(5) *Instability of value* is a necessary but not exclusive characteristic associated with goodwill. All items in their dimension as assets may fluctuate in value, so the difference between goodwill and other assets in this regard is one of degree rather than kind. Furthermore, to the extent that businesses in the modern environment can plan their demand, goodwill becomes less unstable.

(6) *Technical nonserviceability* is a fundamental characteristic of intangible assets in general and of goodwill in particular. Goodwill makes no technical contribution to the production process because the asset represents a firm's ability to succeed in terms of profitability, not in terms of technical serviceability. Goodwill is a phenomenon of business enterprise instead of industry or industrial processes.

First mention of goodwill in the professional accounting literature appears to have been in the mid-1880s, wherein British authors discussed the asset's nature and treatment primarily from a proprietary and partnership perspective. In such firms, goodwill's transferability upon the retirement or death of a proprietor or partner presented major problems, and writers were concerned with the asset's appropriate valuation.

After 1900, accounting literature, particularly in the United States, was increasingly devoted to corporate matters, and transferability of goodwill ceased to be a major topic of discussion. Lump-sum write-off, permanent retention, and amortization of goodwill were treatments debated by many writers—a discussion that would continue uninterrupted until 1970 with the issuance of Accounting Principles Board Opinion No. 17.

Because of the generally optimistic economic outlook through 1929 and lack of authoritative pronouncements in the United States, different accounting treatments for goodwill at this time proliferated. Goodwill was recorded at cost, by capitalizing various advertising expenditures, or by merely writing it on the books. It then could be written up further, written down, written off, or amortized through the income statement, earned surplus, or capital surplus. It also could be permanently retained, or various of these treatments could be mixed, subject only to the wishes and imagination of the firm in question. Its financial-statement presentation was also a matter of some flexibility.

While goodwill's accounting treatment was left to future generations to delimit, goodwill's tax treatment was precisely defined by the end of the 1920s. Goodwill was to be recorded at cost, and after a 1930 U.S. Supreme Court ruling in *Clark v. Haberle Crystal Spring Brewery Company,* 280 U.S. 384 (1930), no deduction for its obsolescence was allowed.

With the onslaught of the Great Depression, emphasis shifted from putting goodwill on the books to taking it off. All treatments for the initial recording of goodwill except valuing the asset at cost disappeared by the mid-1930s, and immediate write-off was considered a sound practice even if substantial goodwill was known to exist.

The first authoritative pronouncement concerning goodwill was Accounting Research Bulletin (ARB) No. 24, "Accounting for Intangible Assets," promulgated in 1944. Generally speaking, equal weight was accorded to permanent retention and systematic amortization of the asset, and the discretionary write-offs permitted in the 1930s were discouraged. Write-offs of goodwill should only be made, according to the Committee on Accounting Procedure (CAP), on a basis beyond traditional conservatism.

In ARB No. 43, "Restatement and Revision of Accounting Research Bulletin," written in 1953, the CAP expressly disallowed discretionary write-offs of goodwill and furthermore indicated a preference for systematic amortization of the asset over permanent retention. This stance had a profound effect beyond the immediate treatment of intangibles, impacting business combinations generally and the employment of the "pooling of interest" treatment (see the "Pooling of Interests" entry).

From the mid-1950s through the 1960s, a bitter debate was joined concerning pooling of interests, the purchase method, and goodwill's treatment. The larger issue of business combinations was addressed in Accounting Principles Board (APB) Opinion No. 16, "Business Combinations," issued in 1970 (see "Pooling of Interests"). At the same time, the board issued APB No. 17, "Intangible Assets," in which goodwill basically was to be amortized mandatorily in the income statement over its useful life not to exceed 40 years.

The long history of accounting for goodwill involves about 40 years of creating various methods for recording the asset followed by another 40 years of gradually eliminating all but one of these alternatives. The future status and treatment of goodwill is uncertain, however. The slowly changing and always subjective nature of the asset, the broader issue of business combinations, the evolving goals of financial statements, and any changes in the tax status of the asset are just some of the important variables that might cause future reexamination of the accounting treatment of goodwill.

Hugh P. Hughes

Bibliography

Commons, J.R. *Legal Foundations of Capitalism.* New York: Macmillan, 1924.

Hughes, H.P. *Goodwill in Accounting: A History of the Issues and Problems.* Atlanta: Business Publishing Division, Georgia State University, 1982.

Miles, J.R. *The Treatment of Goodwill in Federal Income Taxation.* Lincoln: Extension Division, University of Nebraska, 1935.

Veblen, T. "On the Nature of Capital: Investment, Intangible Assets, and the Pecuniary Magnate," *Quarterly Journal of Economics,* November 1908, pp. 104–136.

———. "On the Nature of Capital: [The Productivity of Capital Goods]," *Quarterly Journal of Economics,* August 1908, pp. 517–542.

Yang, J.M. *Goodwill and Other Intangibles: Their Significance and Treatment in Accounts.* New York: Ronald Press, 1927.

G

Grady, Paul (1900–1984)

Paul Grady was born in Cereal Springs, Illinois, and entered the University of Illinois as a chemical engineering student at the age of 18. In 1920 he switched majors, focusing on commerce. In 1923 he began graduate work at Illinois. However, he passed the certified public accountant (CPA) exam and changed his career plans, leaving school and accepting a position at Arthur Andersen and Company in September 1923.

He spent his early years in the Chicago office, working mainly on the public utility staff. He was made a partner on July 1, 1932, and soon after was transferred to the New York office to head the public utility section there.

Between 1932 and 1934, Grady became involved in broad professional issues, as noted by Previts (1989). As a consultant to a committee of the Controllers Institute (which later became the Financial Executives Institute), he helped draft correspondence that promulgated two critical terminology changes: the switch from "accounting practices" to "accounting principles" and the coining of the term "substantial authoritative support." The purpose of both changes was "to give added strength to the reporting and accounting structure."

In 1937, Grady returned to the Chicago office of Arthur Andersen and Company as the firm's administrative partner, but he became frustrated in that position and did not feel he ". . . could function with the kind of 'harness'. . ." that the founder, Arthur Andersen, desired (Previts, 1989). In 1942, Grady took a leave of absence and accepted a position as executive assistant in the Cost Inspection Division of the U.S. Navy Department. His service there resulted in the issuance of a report in 1943, the "Grady Report" that led to a major reorganization in cost-reimbursement systems of the Navy.

As a result of his time at the Navy Department and frictions with Arthur Andersen, Grady was removed as an Andersen partner at the end of 1942. In 1943 he joined Price Waterhouse and Company as a technical partner, a position that he would hold until his retirement in 1960 and that afforded him a long professional association with George Oliver May, long-time managing partner at Price Waterhouse and a leading accounting theorist.

From 1944 to 1948, Grady chaired the Committee on Auditing Procedure. In that position he championed a study that resulted in the *Special Report on Internal Control*, issued in 1948. That report, which remains a worldwide accounting best-seller, highlighted the central importance and design of internal control systems in a broad sense that is still relevant today.

Grady served on a number of important committees. He chaired the Hoover Commission on Reorganization of the Executive Branch of Government in 1948. In 1957 he became a member of the Committee of Research Program of the American Institute of Certified Public Accountants (AICPA), which recommended in 1958 (Zeff) the dissolution of the Committee on Accounting Procedure and the chartering of the Accounting Principles Board. He was honored with the AICPA's Gold Medal in 1959 and admitted to the Accounting Hall of Fame at the Ohio State University in 1964.

After his retirement in 1960, Grady remained an active member of the profession. After May passed away in 1961, Grady collected and edited his papers and published them as the *Memoirs and Accounting Thought of George O. May* in 1962.

He also served as the AICPA's director of research from 1963 to 1964, a position from which he continued to influence the profession's development. While director, he recorded two outstanding achievements. He helped launch the Practice Review Section, which later developed into peer review. Grady also set out to construct an "inventory" of generally accepted accounting principles in the belief that such a document would provide a valuable resource and partial codification of accounting standards. The result of this work was Accounting Research Study No. 7, *Inventory of Generally Accepted Accounting Principles for Business Enterprises*. Published in 1965, it, too, became a best-seller.

In 1968 Grady relocated to Florida. He continued lecturing and speaking on professional issues until his death in 1984.

Stephen J. Young

Bibliography

Burns, T.J., and E.N. Coffman. *The Account-ing Hall of Fame: Profiles of Fifty Members*. Columbus: College of Business, Ohio State University, 1992.

Grady, P.F. "Navy Cost Inspection." In *War-time Accounting: Papers Presented at the Fifty-fifth Annual Meeting of the American Institute of Accountants*, pp. 25–28. New York: AIA, 1942.

Previts, G.J. "Remembering Paul F. Grady, Accountancy's Statesman, 1900–1984." Working paper no. 68 in *Working Paper Series Volume 4*, edited by R.H. Tondkar and E.N. Coffman, pp. 122–123. Richmond, VA: Academy of Accounting Historians, 1989.

Zeff, S.A. *Forging Accounting Principles in Five Countries: A History and an Analysis of Trends*. Champaign, IL: Stipes, 1972.

Zimmerman, V.K., ed. *Written Contributions of Selected Accounting Practitioners: Vol. No. 2, Paul Grady*. Champaign, IL: Center for International Education and Research in Accounting, University of Illinois at Urbana-Champaign, 1978.

See also ACCOUNTING HALL OF FAME; AC-COUNTING RESEARCH STUDIES; AMERICAN INSTITUTE OF CERTIFIED PUBLIC ACCOUN-TANTS; BIG EIGHT ACCOUNTING FIRMS; GEN-ERALLY ACCEPTED ACCOUNTING PRINCIPLES; HISTORICAL COST; INTERNAL CONTROL; MAY, GEORGE OLIVER

Graham, Willard J. (1897–1966)

Willard J. Graham liked to refer to himself as a "renegade accountant." He used this term to mean "one who rejects tradition," because he felt that tradition needed to be forsaken when to do so was in the best interests of the cause. Among his "renegade" ideas was the need for relevance in published financial statements, such as adjusting the information for price-level changes, and in management accounting reports, such as providing information useful for helping management solve its problems. He presented his views regarding relevance in financial reporting in articles published in 1949 and two in 1959 in *Accounting Review*; and his views regarding relevance in management reports, in an article in *Nation's Business* in 1958.

Graham published and/or presented more than 70 papers during his distinguished career. In addition, he edited more than 50 books on accounting. As accounting editor for Richard D. Irwin Publishing Company, Graham under-took the then-risky venture of recommending publication in 1956 of Robert Anthony's pio-neering text, *Management Accounting: Text and Cases*, which, as it turned out, was indeed a rare jewel awaiting discovery.

Graham was president of the American Accounting Association (AAA) in 1955. He also served from 1957 through 1959 on the American Institute of Certified Public Accountants (AICPA) Committee on Accounting Procedure (CAP), the initial accounting body to establish financial-reporting guidelines that preceded the Accounting Principles Board (APB) and the Financial Accounting Standards Board (FASB). In 1959 he testified at a congressional hearing in Washington, D.C., on the depreciation-deduction issues related to proposed changes in the federal income tax laws.

As early as the 1930s, Graham recognized the need for accountants to be broadly educated. In an article in *Accounting Review* in 1939, he recommended "a five-year program leading to a Master's degree," which would be built on a base of two years devoted to "cultural subjects." He also believed that the most detailed technical training should be received in the office of the employer after graduation. Many of his thoughts expressed in the 1930s and 1940s were entirely consistent with the AICPA Common Body of Knowledge study (1967) and the AICPA Beamer Committee report (1969), both of which stressed the importance of communication, logic, and ethics. The Beamer Committee recommended a five-year educational requirement to become a certified public accountant.

Graham would have been delighted with the white paper, "Perspectives on Education: Capabilities for Success in the Accounting Profession," issued by the Big Eight accounting firms in 1989. This paper recommended greater emphasis on the development of communication and analytical skills using unstructured learning tools, such as cases, role-playing, and other forms of oral presentation. That initiative and others that built on Graham's earlier position regarding the education of accountants contributed to the initiation in 1987 of the 150-hour education requirement by the AICPA. He also would have been gratified that the University of North Carolina, where he was employed as a faculty member and founder and director of the Executive Program from 1952 until his death in 1966, was in 1987 the first American university to adopt a required master's of accounting degree for students majoring in accounting.

While testifying before Congress in 1959, Graham wrote this note on his copy of the *Tax Revision Compendium:* "World We Have—World We Want." He believed that each person could help with a creative conversion to a better world. This upbeat attitude permeated the significant contributions he made to the business world and the accounting profession.

Harold Q. Langenderfer
Grover L. Porter

Bibliography

American Institute of Certified Public Accountants. *Report of the Committee on Education and Experience Requirements for CPAs.* New York: American Institute of Certified Public Accountants, 1969.

Arthur Andersen et al. *Perspective on Education: Capabilities for Success in the Accounting Profession.* Tempe, AZ: Accounting Education Change Commission, 1989.

Graham, W.J. "Accounting Economy by Machine Methods," *NACA Bulletin*, April 15, 1936, pp. 935–951.

———. "Accounting Education, Ethics and Training," *Accounting Review*, September 1939, pp. 258–262.

———. "Changing Price Levels and the Determination, Reporting, and Interpretation of Income," *Accounting Review*, January 1949, pp. 15–26.

———. "Choose Cost Figures for Better Decisions," *Nation's Business*, November 1958, pp. 100–106.

———. "Depreciation and Capital Replacement in an Inflationary Economy," *Accounting Review*, July 1959, pp. 367–375.

———. "Education for Management," *Federal Accountant*, September 1963, pp. 103–107.

———. "How Can Colleges Serve the Profession?" *Journal of Accountancy*, February 1956, pp. 45–50.

———. "Income Tax Allocation," *Accounting Review*, January 1959, pp. 14–27.

Langenderfer, H.Q., and G.L. Porter, eds. *Rational Accounting Concepts: The Writings of Willard J. Graham.* New York: Garland, 1988.

———. "Willard J. Graham: Price Level Advocate," *Accounting Historians Notebook*, Spring 1987, pp. 8–11.

Porter, G.L., and H.Q. Langenderfer. "Willard J. Graham: Renegade Accountant," *Accounting Historians Notebook*, Spring 1985, pp. 1, 20–25.

Roy, R.H., and J.H. MacNeill. *Horizons for a Profession: The Common Body of Knowledge for Certified Public Accountants.* New York: American Institute of Certified Public Accountants, 1967.

See also ACCOUNTING EDUCATION IN THE UNITED STATES; AMERICAN ACCOUNTING ASSOCIATION; BIG EIGHT ACCOUNTING FIRMS; INFLATION ACCOUNTING

Greece (750–31 B.C.)

Greece was a collection of city-states that became a nation when united by Philip of Macedonia in 338 B.C. and then a vast empire during the brief reign of Philip's son, Alexander the Great (336–323 B.C.). The empire soon dissolved after his death, and by 31 B.C. Greece was a part of the Roman Empire. However, while the empire of Alexander the Great was short lived, the Greek culture of that period has been quite long lived, especially in philosophy and politics. The names of Homer, Pythagoras, Solon, Socrates, Hippocrates, Pericles, Plato, Aristotle, and Demosthenes live on today.

The Greek colonizing movement occurred from 750–500 B.C. The various city-states established trading posts through the Mediterranean area. Local trade in Greece was primarily conducted by barter. There were many wars between the city-states of Sparta, Athens, and Thebes, with varying alliances with other city-states. From accounting and administrative viewpoints the focal point must be Athens, with its well-developed laws and governing bodies, its academy and lyceum. In fact, Aristotle became the tutor of Alexander when the future ruler was a boy of 13.

Most of the evidence of accounting in Greece in this period deals with administrative, both governmental and temple, matters. Williard E. Stone of the University of Florida, writing in 1969, said that slaves were preferred as accountants, since, unlike freemen, they could be tortured, and testimony given under torture was felt to be better evidence than the testimony of a freeman under oath. Pericles adopted the custom of requiring contractors of public buildings to report receipts and expenditures on tablets chiseled in stone on the walls of buildings, such as the Parthenon. This was consistent with the practices of ancient Egypt, where a similar inscription was found on the Pyramid of Cheops. The council governing the city-state of Athens had an elaborate public recording and reporting system. Aristotle, in his *Politics,* discussed the role of the government auditor, who received all accounts of expenditures and subjected them to audit, a duty so important that these officials handled no other business.

George J. Costouros (1978) from San Jose State University, described the writing of Aeschines, Athenian orator and politician at the beginning of the 4th century B.C., who stated, "In this city (Athens) so ancient and so great, no man who has held any public trust is free from audit." The official, once rendering his accounts for a successful audit, was then "crowned." Aristotle, in his *Constitution,* distinguished between three boards of accountants, each of 10 men: the Council Accountants; the Administrative Accountants, assisted by 10 assessors; and the Examiners, assisted by 20 assessors. The accounts and the related officials were subjected to public hearings where actual and budgeted amounts were compared, and the officials faced charges if discrepancies were found.

A rich historical source of accounting by a Greek are the third-century B.C. Zenon papyri, which were found in the Fayum area of Ptolemaic Egypt. Zenon, a Greek, was the chief executive for Apollonios, the chief financial minister of Ptolemy Philadelphus. Apollonios, in addition to his governmental duties, conducted a variety of business activities on his own account. H.P. Hain, from the University of Melbourne, Victoria, Australia, in 1966 described the use of responsibility accounting by Zenon, who kept detailed written documents. On the papyri, extensive auditing was evidenced by a sloping downstroke or a heavy dot in front of each figure. Among the documents were monthly, annual, and triennial summaries of accounting transactions. Together, the papyri illustrate a highly developed, centrally managed system of accounting, controls, and businesslike efficiency.

Richard Vangermeersch

Bibliography

Costouros, G.J. "Auditing in the Athenian State of The Golden Age, 500–300 B.C.," *Accounting Historians Journal*, Spring 1978, pp. 41–50.

———. "Development of Banking and Related Bookkeeping Techniques in Ancient Greece, 400–300 B.C.," *International Journal of Accounting*, Spring 1973, pp. 75–81.

De Ste. Croix, G.E.M. "Greek and Roman Accounting." In *Studies in the History of Accounting*, edited by A.C. Littleton and B.S. Yamey, pp. 14–74. Homewood, IL: Irwin, 1956.

Hain, H.P. "Accounting Control in the Zenon Papyri," *Accounting Review*, October 1966, pp. 699–703.

Smolinski, H.C., D.W. Chumley, and D.E. Bennett. "In Search of Ancient Auditors," *Accounting Historians Notebook*, Fall 1992, pp. 7–9, 26–28.

Stone, W.E. "Antecedents of the Accounting Profession," *Accounting Review*, April 1969, pp. 284–291.

See also ARITHMETIC AND ACCOUNTING; BARTER; EGYPT; EXTERNAL AUDITING; INTERNAL AUDITING; LEDGER; ROME (509 B.C.–A.D. 476); STEVIN, SIMON; STEWARDSHIP; TAX-ORDAINED ACCOUNTING

Green, Wilmer L.

Wilmer L. Green's *History and Survey of Accountancy* (1930) was an early attempt to write a general history of accounting. Green began with an extended survey of account keeping from Babylonian to modern times, emphasizing the development of double entry bookkeeping and accounting practice in various countries during the nineteenth and early twentieth centuries. He then discussed regulatory legislation and the origins of professional accounting associations on the same country-to-country basis.

In trying to cover so much factual detail in one volume, Green necessarily gave superficial treatment to the important topics discussed. However, his book has been reissued and remains a useful chronological discussion and source reference.

Michael Chatfield

Bibliography

Green, W.L. *History and Survey of Accountancy*. Brooklyn: Standard Text Press,

1930. Reprint. Osaka: Nihon Shoseki, 1974.

Gregory Case

In 1934, the Second Circuit Court of Appeals under the leadership of Chief Judge Learned Hand decided the case of *Helvering v. Gregory* (69 F. 2d 809). This opinion marked a turning point in tax history.

The *Gregory* tax case was the first of its kind to come before the courts and the first to be decided by the Supreme Court. The Supreme Court upheld the decision of the Second Circuit Court of Appeals [293 U.S. 465 (1935)]. The facts of the case involved a reorganization done solely for tax purposes. Mrs. Gregory had arranged a series of transactions that would allow her to receive appreciated property from her wholly owned corporation without its being taxed as a dividend. In this series of transactions, Mrs. Gregory caused her wholly owned corporation to transfer the appreciated property to a newly formed corporation that she also completely owned. A few days later, she liquidated the new corporation and received the property.

The Board of Tax Appeals ruled for Mrs. Gregory because she had literally complied with the reorganization statutes. However, the Second Circuit Court of Appeals reversed this lower court ruling. The ruling held that this was not a reorganization as intended by Congress, and thus Mrs. Gregory had received a taxable dividend.

The Second Circuit Court's opinion, written by Judge Hand, rejected the literal interpretation of the statutes. A liberal interpretation of the law would presuppose a continuation of business that did not exist in this case. Hand did not agree with the position of the Internal Revenue Service that the steps in the transactions and the corporation should be ignored as a sham. Instead Hand said that the steps and the corporation were real and could not be voided. Rather, the steps should be collapsed to analyze the result. This marked the introduction of the step-transaction doctrine.

Hand relied on unwritten requirements in the law in denying the reorganization. He looked at the intent of Congress and applied a business-purpose test for the first time. There must be a business purpose for the transactions other than the avoidance of taxes. However, Hand emphasized that this opinion was not based on the fact that this was a tax-avoidance scheme. This is reflected in Hand's often-quoted remarks from the *Gregory* case: "Any one may so arrange his affairs that his taxes shall be as low as possible. . ." and ". . . there is not even a patriotic duty to increase one's taxes."

The concepts introduced in the *Gregory* case include the business-purpose test, continuity of business, substance over form, the taxpayer's right to minimize tax liability, the taxpayer's burden of proof of substance and business purpose, the step-transaction doctrine and sham transactions. These principles remain a foundation of tax law.

The principles introduced by Hand in this case have been affirmed and have endured the test of time. Hand's views were followed by the Supreme Court in upholding the ruling. The terminology used in this case has been included in the regulations since 1934. The business-purpose test is still applied, even in areas other than reorganizations. Not only is this the primary case in the area of reorganizations, but it is also the origin of the concept that mere compliance with the form of the law is not sufficient. Tax practitioners can no longer rely on literal compliance with the law but must also adhere to the substance of the law.

Gregory remains a landmark tax case. It has been cited in well over 1,000 tax cases, including at least 19 Supreme Court opinions. In fact, its influence has increased over time in that it was cited more during the decade of the 1980s than in any other decade since the 1950s. *Gregory* concepts may still be found in the Internal Revenue Code, and, according to one court decision, the framework of the entire 1954 Code was based on the *Gregory* principle of substance over form. The *Gregory* principles remain among the strongest tax-enforcement weapons.

The *Gregory* case dramatically altered the course of tax practice and, in the process, made it a more interesting, exciting, and challenging field.

Tonya K. Flesher

Bibliography

Flesher, T.K. "An Analysis of the Tax Opinions of Judge Learned Hand and His Contributions to the Development of the Federal Tax System." Ph.D. diss., University of Mississippi, 1979.

———. "A Turning Point in Tax History," *Journal of Accountancy*, May 1987, pp. 193–194.

Holzman, R.S. "The *Gregory* Case," *Journal of Accountancy*, July 1955, pp. 54–58.
————. "Ten Years of the *Gregory* Case," *Journal of Accountancy*, March 1945, pp. 215–225.
————. "Thirty Years of the *Gregory* Case," *Journal of Accountancy*, May 1965, pp. 34–37.
————. "Forty Years of the *Gregory* Case," *Business Operations Tax Journal*, vol. 1, no. 2, 1976, pp. 143–152.

See also INCOME TAXATION IN THE UNITED STATES

Guo, Daoyang (1940–)

Daoyang Guo is a professor of accounting at Zhongnan University of Finance and Economics in Wuhan, People's Republic of China, and author of *Accounting History of China* (Volume 1, 1982, Volume 2, 1988), which was the first thorough treatment of the pattern of development of Chinese accounting.

Important developments Guo described in his book are: Chinese accounting originated in the late stage of the Old Stone Age; single entry bookkeeping was invented in the Shang Dynasty (1650–1100 B.C.); an internal-control system and auditing came into existence in the Zhou Dynasty (1100–770 B.C.); Chinese accounting flourished in the Tang Dynasty (A.D. 618–906), in which the "four-column accounting method" was first used; Chinese double entry bookkeeping (Longmen account) was established in the period between the late Ming Dynasty and the early Qing Dynasty (about A.D. 1600–1700); Western-style debit-credit bookkeeping was introduced into China in about A.D. 1905.

Guo has also researched and written about possible future developments in accounting. He has also published such articles as: "Basis of Accounting Control" (1989), which illustrated that modern accounting is an important tool to control economic relationships; "Modern Accounting and the Macroeconomic World" (1990), in which the basic mission of modern accounting was expanded to macroeconomics; and "Present Conditions and Trends in Modern Accounting" (1989), in which the world-wide reform of accounting was discussed in light of future reforms planned for accounting education.

Guo is a certified public accountant in China and is the vice-chairman of the executive committee of the Daxin Public Accounting firm in Hubei Province. He heads the Accounting Research Institute of the Zhongnan University of Finance and Economics. In addition, he is involved with the Accounting Society of China and the Internal Auditing Society of China.

Xiao Wei

Bibliography

Guo, Daoyang. "Confucius and Accounting," *Accounting Historians Notebook,* Spring 1988, pp. 8–10.
————. "The Historical Contributions of Chinese Accounting (or R-P=E-B)," *Accounting Historians Notebook*, Fall 1989, pp. 6–10.
Qiu Shui. "Professor Guo, Daoyang: A Famous Expert in Accounting History," *Wuhan Finance and Accounting*, April 1988, pp. 15–16.
Shi Yu. "Mr. Guo, Daoyang," *Communication in Finance and Accounting.* September 1990, inside front cover.

See also CHINA

H

Hamilton, Robert (1743–1829)

The industrial revolution made it essential that double entry bookkeeping be adapted to include manufacturing accounts. Robert Hamilton, Professor of natural philosophy and mathematics at Aberdeen University, devoted a few pages of *An Introduction to Merchandise* (1777–1779) to the accounts of "artificers and manufacturers." He described a system comprising work in process and finished goods accounts, and three subsidiary books. These included a book of materials for recording quantities of raw materials purchased and used, a book of wages, and a book of "work" in which quantities of materials delivered to outworkers, quantities of processed goods returned, and the value of materials, wages, and goods in process were entered in separate columns. A manufacturing account was debited at the end of each year for expenses and ending balances of materials, and credited for the value of goods manufactured. The balance in this account, after subtracting the value of work in process, was intended to show profit and loss.

Michael Chatfield

Bibliography

Bywater, M.F., and B.S. Yamey. *Historic Accounting Literature: A Companion Guide*. London: Scholar Press, 1982.

Hamilton, R. *An Introduction to Merchandise*. 2nd ed. Edinburgh: N.p., 1788. Reprint (parts 4 and 5). New York: Garland, 1988.

See also Cost and/or Management Accounting; Scotland: Early Writers in Double Entry Accounting

Harrison, G. Charter (1881–)

The idea that predetermined standard costs are more useful than actual costs became well established in the accounting literature between 1910 and 1920. During this period standard cost estimates were used in practice not only to control expenditures and eliminate waste, but also in budgeting and to predict new product costs.

In 1911 the Anglo-American management consultant G. Charter Harrison designed the earliest known complete standard cost system. He elaborated on this system in a series of articles, "Cost Accounting to Aid Production" (1918–1919). His descriptions of accounts, ledgers, and cost analysis sheets were detailed enough to be applied in cookbook fashion.

Harrison also wanted to use standard costs to simplify overhead allocations to departments and products. He criticized the "elaborate rituals" that occurred each month when overhead costs were recalculated and distributed. He proposed to make just one analysis of manufacturing overheads and from it develop predetermined application rates that could be used month after month until the production configuration changed. To be effective, such a system required routinized comparisons between standard and actual costs. In "Scientific Basis for Cost Accounting" (1920), Harrison published the first set of formulas for the analysis of cost variances.

Michael Chatfield

Bibliography

Harrison, G. Charter. "Cost Accounting to Aid Production," *Industrial Management* (October 1918–June 1919).

———. "Scientific Basis for Cost Accounting," *Industrial Management* (March 1920), pp. 237–242.

Solomons, D. "The Historical Development of Costing." In *Studies in Costing*, edited by D. Solomons, pp. 1–52. London: Sweet and Maxwell, 1952.

Sowell, E.M. *The Evolution of the Theories and Techniques of Standard Costs.* Champaign, IL: Center for International Education and Research in Accounting, University of Illinois, 1966.

See also BUDGETING; COMMON COSTS; COST AND/OR MANAGEMENT ACCOUNTING; MANAGEMENT ACCOUNTING; STANDARD COSTING; TAYLOR, FREDERICK WINSLOW

Haskins, Charles Waldo (1852–1903)

Charles Waldo Haskins was born in Brooklyn, New York, on January 11, 1852. He attended Brooklyn Polytechnic Institute with an interest in becoming an engineer. Upon graduation he found that engineering was not to his liking and he decided to enter the field of accountancy.

For five years, Haskins worked in the accounting department of a New York importing firm. He later spent two years in Paris studying art and touring Europe to learn about European business methods. Upon returning home, he worked in his father's brokerage office and later joined the accounting department of a construction company. In 1886 Haskins opened his own office in New York City as a public accountant.

In 1893 Haskins and Elijah Watt Sells, an auditor with various railroads, were appointed as expert accountants under the Joint Commission of the 53rd Congress to examine the accounting system for the entire country to determine if modifications could be made that would be more efficient and economical without hurting public service. Many of their recommendations were adopted. Upon completion of this assignment in 1895, Haskins and Sells formed the firm Haskins and Sells (now Deloitte and Touche) in New York City. The partnership was a continuation of the public accounting practice that Haskins had started in 1886.

Haskins was one of the important pioneers who laid the foundation of the accounting profession in the United States. He took an active interest in the passage of a law in New York in 1896 that established a commission to examine candidates desiring to become certified public accountants. This was the first legislation in the country to create the professional designation "certified public accountant."

Haskins was also instrumental in gaining acceptance of accountancy in university curricula. He took a leading role in the founding in 1900 of the School of Commerce, Accounts and Finance of New York University. He was the first dean of the school, and he served as professor of accounting history. His appointment as professor of accounting history was the first such appointment in the nation. To Haskins, history was always relevant in that an appreciation of the past enhances judgment and enables one to test the validity of new ideas in the light of the past experience.

Haskins was a convincing lecturer and writer. A selection of his essays and addresses was published in *Business Education and Accountancy* (1904), edited by Frederick Cleveland.

Edward N. Coffman

Bibliography

Coffman, E.N. "Charles Waldo Haskins, 1852–1903." In *Biographies of Notable Accountants*, edited by H.R. Givens, pp. 13–15. New York: Random House, 1987.

Foye, A.B. *Haskins and Sells: Our First Seventy-Five Years.* New York: Garland, 1984.

Haskins and Sells: The First Fifty Years, 1895–1945. Privately printed, 1947.

Haskins, C.W. *Business Education and Accountancy.* New York: Harper & Brothers, 1904. Reprint. New York: Arno Press, 1978.

Merino, B.D. "Charles Waldo Haskins, 1852–1903." In *A Report on a Seminar Presented by the Ross Institute: The Relevance of History to Contemporary Accounting Issues*, edited by B.D. Merino. New York: Vincent C. Ross Institute of Accounting Research, New York University, 1978.

"University Memorial for an Accountant," *Journal of Accountancy,* October 1910, pp. 463–464.

"University School Honors Accountant," *Journal of Accountancy,* January 1911, p. 220.

See also ACCOUNTING EDUCATION IN THE UNITED STATES; AMERICAN INSTITUTE OF CERTIFIED PUBLIC ACCOUNTANTS; BENTLEY,

Harry Clark; Big Eight Accounting Firms; Certified Public Accountant; Certified Public Accountant Examination: The Early Years (1896–1930); Federal Government Accounting (U.S.); Sells, Elijah Watt

Hatfield, Henry Rand (1866–1945)

Henry Rand Hatfield was born in Chicago on November 27, 1866. Prior to attending college, Hatfield worked in the municipal bond field from 1886 to 1890. In 1892 Hatfield received his bachelor's degree from Northwestern University; in 1897 he received his doctorate in political economy from the University of Chicago. Hatfield's teaching career began in 1894 at Washington University (St. Louis), where he taught political economics until 1898. In that year, he returned to the University of Chicago, where from 1898 to 1902 he served as an instructor. In 1902 he was promoted to assistant professor and appointed dean of the College of Commerce and Administration. Hatfield then accepted a position as an associate professor at the University of California at Berkeley in 1904. He was promoted to the rank of full professor in 1909 and remained at Berkeley until his death in 1945. While at Berkeley, he served as dean of the College of Commerce from 1909 until 1920, and again from 1927 until 1928. In addition, he served as the dean of faculties from 1917 to 1918 and 1920 to 1923.

Hatfield was the author or coauthor of four books and a number of articles. The books were *Modern Accounting* (1909), which was reissued as *Accounting* in 1927; *A Statement of Accounting Principles* (1938); and *Accounting Principles and Practices* (1940). This latter work was co-authored with Thomas Henry Sanders of Harvard and Underhill Moore of Yale. *Accounting Principles and Practices* was an early attempt to formulate the basic concepts upon which accounting functioned in the U.S. business community. Hatfield's most memorable article was probably "An Historical Defense of Bookkeeping," which traced the development of accounting. This article, which appeared in the *Journal of Accountancy* in 1924, was originally given as a speech before the American Association of University Instructors in Accounting (AAUIA) on December 29, 1923.

Hatfield had been instrumental in 1916 in organizing that national association, which eventually evolved into the American Accounting Association. Hatfield served as the AAUIA's first vice president and became its president in 1918. That year Hatfield also served as the vice president of the American Economics Association. The Internal Revenue Bureau (forerunner of the Internal Revenue Service) appointed Hatfield to its Tax Advisory Board in 1919. Among his other service activities, Hatfield was the U.S. representative to the International Congress on Commercial Education in Amsterdam in 1929.

In 1951 Hatfield was elected to the Accounting Hall of Fame for his contributions to the development of accounting. On this occasion, he was described as an inspiring teacher, a gifted author, and an individual whose keen insight and independent thinking were potent influences in the early development of accounting theory. This was evidenced by A.C. Littleton's, a professor of accounting at the University of Illinois, dedication of *Accounting Evolution to 1900* (1933) to Hatfield, saying his "An Historical Defense of Bookkeeping" served as an inspiration and model for the book. In addition, Maurice Moonitz, a professor of accounting at the University of California at Berkeley, and Littleton chose this article as one of the significant essays of the 1920s.

Early in Hatfield's career, there were no arbiters, such as the Financial Accounting Standards Board or the Securities and Exchange Commission, to establish correct accounting principles. Therefore, a variety of accounting treatments could be selected for use in a particular situation. In this environment, Hatfield opted to show in his books the existing variations in practice rather than formulate rigid rules. Since Hatfield recognized that accounting was still in its formative stage, he cited authorities and court cases in his ratings.

In the preface to *Accounting*, Hatfield observed that perhaps more serious study and writing about accounting had occurred in the 18 years between his two books than in the previous 400 years since Luca Pacioli, the author of the first printed treatise on accounting in 1494. Hatfield cited three major developments as necessitating this revised version of his book: (1) a growth in the size of corporations and the widening separation between the owners and management; (2) the growing influence of the Interstate Commerce Commission; and (3) the enactment of the federal income tax law in 1913. The notable additions to the 1927 edition of the book were a chapter on consolidated statements, a chapter on interpretation of the balance sheet using analytical techniques, and a discussion of no-par stock. While the income statement was not a new topic, Hatfield, in comparison to other authors of his day, placed increased emphasis on its importance.

Without a doubt, Hatfield was a pioneering scholar in accounting. His writings were a potent formative influence in the development of accounting theory, and, as a result of his contributions, accounting grew in professional status. Current accounting theory and practice owe him a sizable debt.

Robert M. Kozub

Bibliography

Cattell, J. McK., J. Cattell, and E.E. Ross. *Leaders in Education*. 2d ed. New York: Science Press, 1941.

Hatfield, H.R. "An Historical Defense of Bookkeeping," *Journal of Accountancy*, April 1924, pp. 241–253.

Kozub, R.M. "Henry Rand Hatfield." In *Biographies of Notable Accountants*, edited by H.R. Givens, pp. 16–17. New York: Random House, 1987.

Littleton, A.C. *Accounting Evolution to 1900*. New York: American Institute Publishing, 1933. Reprint. New York: Russell and Russell, 1966.

See also ACCOUNTING EDUCATION IN THE UNITED STATES; ACCOUNTING HALL OF FAME; AMERICAN ACCOUNTING ASSOCIATION; CAPITAL ACCOUNT; CAPITAL MAINTENANCE; CONCEPTUAL FRAMEWORK; CONSERVATISM; CONTINUITY; INCOME STATEMENT/INCOME ACCOUNT; JAPAN; MACNEAL, KENNETH; PROPRIETARY THEORY; SANDERS, HATFIELD, AND MOORE

Herzfeld v. Leventhol, Krekstein, Horwath and Horwath

On November 22, 1969, Firestone Group Limited bought a group of nursing homes from the Monterrey Company for $13,362,500; four days later, it sold them to Continental Recreation Company for $15,393,000. Firestone Group paid only $5,000 down to Monterrey and requested only a $25,000 down payment from Continental. Of the $2,030,500 difference between cost and sale price, $235,000 was recorded by Firestone Group as 1969 income, and $1,795,500 as unrealized gross profit. The $235,000 current income was apparently arrived at by adding the $25,000 down payment, another $25,000 payment due January 2, 1970, and $185,000 liquidated damages provided for nonperformance by the buyer. This was the largest transaction the Firestone Group had ever made, and including it in 1969 sales revenue converted an annual loss into a profit.

At a meeting of Firestone Group officials and Leventhol auditors, the Firestone Group objected to the tentative treatment of profits from the nursing home sale and asked that the entire gross profit of $2,030,500 appear as 1969 income. Under pressure from the Firestone Group, Leventhol voided the original 1969 financial statements and audit report and issued a second report in which the $1,795,500 "unrealized gross profit" was changed to "deferred gross profit." The footnote on the nursing home purchase and sale was revised to read: "Of the total gross profit of $2,030,500, $235,000 is included in the consolidated income Statement and the balance $1,795,500 will be considered realized when the January 30, 1970 payment is received. The latter amount is included in deferred income in the consolidated balance sheet."

The revised audit opinion included a qualification which stated that the Firestone Group's financial statements presented fairly the results of operations, "subject to collectability of the balance receivable on the contract of sale." Neither the purchase nor the sale of the nursing homes was ever completed, and just over a year later Firestone Group Limited filed a Chapter 11 bankruptcy petition.

Herzfeld, a Firestone Group investor, sued Leventhol under Section 10(b) of the Securities and Exchange Act of 1934, claiming that despite the footnote and qualified opinion, Firestone Group's 1969 annual report was materially misleading because certain facts known to Leventhol when it performed its audit were omitted or misstated. In 1974 the court ruled in Herzfeld's favor. Judge Lloyd F. MacMahan stated that full disclosure should have included the fact that Continental Recreation Company, which had assumed a debt of over 15 million dollars, had a net worth of only $100,000. The purchase and sale of the nursing homes was not recorded in Firestone Group's journal or minute book. Firestone Group never acquired title to the nursing homes and no deed, title search, or title insurance had been obtained. Above all, income had been recognized and recorded on a transaction that was never consummated and in which the earnings process was nowhere near complete.

The court rejected Laventhol's defense that it had limited its liability by qualifying its audit opinion. Such qualification did not excuse misrepresentation of facts in the financial statements, or Laventhol's failure to provide a clear explanation of the reasons for its qualification, as required by professional auditing standards. The *Herzfeld* decision suggests that auditors cannot associate themselves with misleading financial statements and then hope to extricate themselves by qualifying their opinion. If there are facts known to the auditor which cast doubt on the reliability of financial statements, a qualified opinion will not excuse auditors from liability unless they disclose the reasons for their qualification, including the facts that required the qualification in the first place.

Michael Chatfield

Bibliography

Causey, D.Y. "*Herzfeld* Revisited after *Hochfelder*: The 'Scienter' Standard Applied to the Reporting of Uncertainties," *American Business Law Journal*, Fall 1976, pp. 252–267.

Herzfeld v. Laventhol, Krekstein, Horwath and Horwath, 540 F. 2d 27 (2d Cir. 1976).

See also AUDITOR'S REPORT; LEGAL LIABILITY OF AUDITORS

Historical Cost

Historical cost is cost to the present owner at the time of acquisition. Perhaps the longest-lasting issue of twentieth-century accounting has been the issue of cost versus some other base of valuation in the balance sheet. Writing in 1943, George Oliver May, noted accounting practitioner and theoretician, seemed to imply that the valuation approach was popular in the United States until the 1930s: "In reading American accounting literature, it is surprising to find how generally accounting was described at one time as a process of valuation, up to how recent a date this view was maintained, and how pronounced and rapid the change has been. In a more mature economy, when greater capital resources and, also, perhaps changes in labor conditions tend to produce constantly increasing capital investment, business units become larger and enterprises more complex. Thus, the valuation approach becomes impracticable and resort to cost as the primary line of approach becomes almost inevitable."

May also believed that accounting was more balance sheet than income statement oriented. Since May's views tended to become fact by the weight of his stature, it is important to ascertain the correctness of his view.

Luca Pacioli started "Particularis de Computis et Scripturis," his treatise on accounting in *Summa de Arithmetica* (1494), with a comprehensive inventory of personal and real property owned by the businessman. Pacioli recommended using current prices for asset valuation at the beginning of the books. He presented a fairly well-developed profit and loss account, and he also recommended closing the books at the end of each year and opening up a new set of books for the new year.

Robert Colinson, a Scottish accounting writer, stated in his *Idea Rationaria* (1683) that beginning inventories should be entered at their costs. House and household furnishing were to be included, but no valuation base was given for them, though he did value the share of a ship at cost. Colinson, like Pacioli, had a well-developed profit and loss account. He closed his books twice a year, on June 30 and December 31, and transferred the open account balance to the new period. He avoided the inventory-valuation problem by either having all the inventory per item left or having it all sold. John Mair, also a Scottish accounting writer, in his *Book-Keeping Methodized* (1763) included a one-fourth ownership of a ship at cost, as well as ending-inventory valuation for partially sold inventory items at prime cost. Mair also had a well-developed profit and loss account and followed the same pattern of closing as Colinson. Depreciation was not a factor for any of these writers. An examination of some 19th-century bookkeeping and accounting books from the United States reveals similar procedures but far less detail.

Railroads were the first major companies to be confronted with the whole range of asset-valuation problems. Railroads had significant capital investments with different contributors. Records of the 1830s and 1840s show instances of revaluations (upward apparently more common than downward). By 1850, however, the revaluation approach lost favor as being outside the control of the company and not yielding any funds for replacement. While there were attempts to estimate depreciation reserves in excess of current renewals, by 1880 the dominant method was the retirement method, in which the expense due to exhaustion was recognized at the retirement of the unit of property. This practice was justified as long as there was adequate maintenance, and there was no decrease in the value of the capital asset.

The industrial mergers that occurred from the late 1880s through the early 1900s led to a practice of valuing capital assets by the par value of stock issued for the merger. Robert Hiester Montgomery, both a leading accounting practitioner and writer, in 1912 warned auditors to be cautious about this valuation, adding: "We are dealing with enterprises which are continuing in business, and of which a forced sale or liquidation is not contemplated, so that in attempting to fix the net value to a concern of its fixed assets, we may say that, as a general rule, the correct basis is cost, less adequate depreciation for wear and tear and obsolescence." Quoting from the regulations of the Treasury Department on the 1909 corporate income tax, he added "This estimate should be formed upon the assumed life of the property, its cost value, and its use. . . ."

The increased price levels in the United States during and immediately following World War I led to such concepts as base stock for inventories and allowances for excess costs of capital assets, but the sharp drop in the price level in 1920 and 1921 ended the practice of allowances for excess costs of capital assets. However, the great boom from 1922 through 1929 led to a significant literature about asset write-ups. In a paper published in 1977, Richard Vangermeersch, from the University of Rhode Island, reported the results of a review of the annual reports of 200 companies for the 1920s he conducted to ascertain the number of companies that wrote up the value of their tangible fixed assets. He found that 30 of these companies had written up tangible fixed assets, and that 21 of the 30 had just one write-up during this period, with the credit account almost always either earned surplus, property surplus, or Goodwill and Patents. Only two of the companies, both involved in minerals, had a policy of frequent revaluations. Vangermeersch concluded that he doubted that there were wholesale write-ups of assets in the 1920s. However, in a related study, which covered 1892 through 1953 and was limited to 20 of the 300 companies of the other study, he did note

significant problems with the original valuations of 12 of 20 companies, primarily dealing with valuations based on the par value of stock and with intangible assets.

The stock market crash of 1929 led to the institutionalizing of the historical cost concept and a strong revulsion to the valuation methods employed by management, especially for intangibles. In the related study described previously, Vangermeersch concluded that 12 of the 20 companies he reviewed probably had misinformed investors about the intangibles present in the original valuations of the companies. He also concluded that the write-downs of the 1930s were caused by original valuation of intangibles that were hidden in the original valuation of fixed assets. Dale L. Flesher and Tonya K. Flesher, both of the University of Mississippi, in a 1986 article, concluded that the giant pyramid scheme in the 1920s and early 1930s of Ivar Kreuger, the "Match King," was a significant reason for passage of the Securities Acts of 1933 and 1934, as the stocks and bonds of Kreuger and Toll, Inc., were then the most widely held securities in the United States. Kreuger controlled about 400 different corporations by owning Class A shares with full voting rights, and his balance sheets showed match monopoly rights as major assets. But many of these corporations were shells, and many of the assets, like $140 million for a match monopoly in Italy, did not exist. Another financier, Samuel Insull, was accused in the early 1930s of similar behavior in his Chicago-based electric utilities companies but was subsequently acquitted, even though he did participate in a few wash sales of assets between the companies he controlled in the last days of his empire. The excesses of the various boards of directors probably led to the 1936 U.S. Supreme Court ruling in *American Telephone and Telegraph et al v. United States et al*, 57 S.Ct. 170 (1936), that the Federal Communications Commission be allowed to use the "original cost" of the property first placed in public service for FCC accounting. The court was wary of intercompany transfers: "There is a widespread belief that transfers between affiliates or subsidiaries complicate the task of rate-making for regulatory commissions and impede the search for truth. Buyer and seller in such circumstances may not be dealing at arm's length, and the price agreed upon between them may be a poor criterion of value. . . ."

The first statement on accounting principles by the American Accounting Association (AAA) in 1936 reflected a strong bias toward historical cost. This statement was further elaborated by William Andrew Paton and A.C. Littleton in their 1940 classic, *An Introduction to Corporate Accounting Standards*. They wrote: "The basic subject matter of accounting is therefore the measured consideration involved in exchange activities, especially those which are related to services acquired (cost, expenses) and services ordered (revenue, income)." The AAA continued to focus on historical cost with its 1940 and 1948 statements.

The topic of historical cost remained a contentious issue in both accounting theory and practice into the 1960s, with a number of accounting theoreticians urging a break with the historical cost concept. Among them were leading accounting theoreticians as Edgar O. Edwards and Philip W. Bell, who developed replacement-cost accounting, R.J. Chambers, Robert R. Sterling, Robert T. Sprouse, and Maurice Moonitz. Perhaps the greatest single battleground of the controversy was over Sprouse and Moonitz's suggestion in 1962 in Accounting Research Study (ARS) No. 3, *A Tentative Set of Broad Accounting Principles*, that inventories be measured at either net realizable value or current cost and that plant and equipment "could be restated at periodic intervals, perhaps every five years." These comments were vigorously opposed in eight of the nine commentaries to the study by members of its advisory committees. Perhaps the most telling comment was that of a former chief accountant of the Securities and Exchange Commission (SEC), Carman G. Blough, who wrote "Shades of the 1920's!" as his objection to the proposal of restating the value of plant and equipment. Significant theoretical opposition was raised to other suggestions of Sprouse and Moonitz as well.

Yuji Ijiri then at Stanford University in 1965, and in his continuing work on accounting theory, stressed by use of the axiomatic method the usefulness of the historical cost approach. Also in 1965 Paul Grady, a leading practitioner in accounting, in ARS No. 7, *Inventory of Generally Accepted Accounting Principles for Business Enterprises*, which was written as a response to ARS No. 3, stated: "It should be understood that the financial position or balance sheet statements do not purport to show either present value of assets to the enterprise or values which might be realized in liquidation." Robert K. Mautz, another leading accounting academe who had just become a partner with a Big Eight accounting firm in 1973, spoke for the historical cost approach in a classic response to 10 oft-expressed criticisms.

There certainly have been full-blown practical attempts to depart from the historical cost system. The American Institute of Certified Public Accountants (AICPA) had long favored a price-level-adjusted approach, rather than a replacement-cost approach, as evidenced in Accounting Principles Board (APB) Statement No. 3, "Financial Statements Restated for General Price-Level Changes" (1969). (Whether price-level-adjusted statements are departures from the historical cost basis remains a contentious issue in accounting.) In a classic attack on the price-level approach in 1975, John C. Burton, then chief accountant of the SEC, labeled it "Pu Pu accounting." He favored the replacement-cost approach, which the SEC adopted the following year in Accounting Series Release No. 190, "Notice of Adoption of Amendments to Regulation S-X Requiring Disclosure of Certain Replacement Cost Data."

The most significant break from the historical cost approach was Financial Accounting Standards (FAS) No. 33, "Financial Reporting and Changing Prices," issued by the Financial Accounting Standards Board (FASB) in 1979. FAS No. 33 required large corporations to report on a supplementary basis the current cost amounts of inventory and property, plant, and equipment at the end of the fiscal year and also report increases or decreases in current cost amounts of inventory and property, plant, and equipment, net of the yearly increase in inflation. FAS No. 33 also required two supplementary computations of income from continuing operations (adjusted for the effects of general inflation and adjusted for current cost basis). The SEC then dropped No. 190. In 1984 in FAS No. 82, "Financial Reporting and Changing Prices: Elimination of Certain Disclosures," the FASB unanimously dropped the price-level requirements of FAS No. 33, as being less useful than the current cost approach. By 1986 in FAS No. 89, "Financial Reporting and Changing Prices," the FASB made FAS No. 33 voluntary. FAS No. 89 passed by a 4-to-3 vote, with strong objections written by the dissenters.

The historical cost approach of U.S. financial reporting has not been practiced in all countries. From 1951 to 1991 Philips Industries of the Netherlands has followed the current-value accounting approach promulgated in the 1920s by Theodore Limperg Jr., a Dutch accounting theorist. Brazil has long followed a price-level-adjusted approach. Great Britain has also permitted the use of write-ups of fixed assets to appraisal value, as recommended in the Sandilands Report from the Inflation Accounting Committee in 1975.

However, historical cost remains part of the common thread that has held accounting together for centuries. Such topics as objectivity, matching, time period, and realization all are woven with historical cost into the practice of accounting. May probably overstated the importance of accounting based on balance-sheet valuations. The history of historical costs seems to indicate that accountants are wary about leaving the concept, feeling a need to explain their departures from it, and often making those departures in a supplementary manner. Accountants seem to have a yearning for historical cost.

Richard Vangermeersch

Bibliography

American Accounting Association. *Accounting and Reporting Standards for Corporate Financial Statements and Preceding Statements and Supplements.* Iowa City: American Accounting Association, 1957.

Boockholdt, J.L. "Influence of Nineteenth and Early Twentieth Century Railroad Accounting on Development of Modern Accounting Theory," *Accounting Historians Journal*, Spring 1978, pp. 9–28.

Burton, J.C. "Financial Reporting in an Age of Inflation," *Journal of Accountancy*, February 1975, pp. 68–71.

"Court Decision on Uniform Accounts for Telephone Companies," *Journal of Accountancy*, January 1937, pp. 55–64.

Enthoven, A.J.H. *Current Value Accounting: Its Concepts and Practice at N.V. Phillips Industries, the Netherlands.* Dallas: Center for International Accounting Development, University of Texas at Dallas, 1982.

Financial Accounting Standards Board. "Financial Reporting and Changing Prices." Financial Accounting Standard No. 33. Stamford, CT: FASB, 1979.

Flesher, D.L., and T.K. Flesher. "Ivar Kreuger's Contribution to U.S. Financial Reporting," *Accounting Review*, July 1986, pp. 421–434.

Grady, P. *Inventory of Generally Accepted Accounting Principles for Business Enterprises.* Accounting Research Study No. 7. New York: AICPA, 1965.

Ijiri, Y. "Axioms and Structures of Conventional Accounting Measurement," *Accounting Review*, January 1965, pp. 36–53.

———. "A Defense for Historical Cost Accounting." In *Asset Valuation and Income Determination: A Consideration of the Alternates*, edited by R. Sterling, pp. 1–44. Lawrence, KS: Scholars Book, 1971.

———. *Historical Cost Accounting and Its Rationality.* Vancouver, BC: Canadian Certified General Accountants' Research Foundation, 1981.

Inflation Accounting Committee. *Inflation Accounting.* London: Her Majesty's Stationery Office, 1975.

Littleton, A.C. "Prestige for Historical Cost." In *Essays on Accountancy by A.C. Littleton*, edited by C.A. Moyer, pp. 338–340. Urbana, IL: University of Illinois Press, 1961.

Mautz, R.K. "A Few Words for Historical Cost," *Financial Executive*, January 1973, pp. 23–27, 60.

May, G.O. *Financial Accounting: A Distillation of Experience.* New York: Macmillan, 1943.

Montgomery, R.H. *Auditing: Theory and Practice.* New York: Ronald Press, 1912.

Paton, W.A., and A.C. Littleton. *An Introduction to Corporate Accounting Standards.* American Accounting Association Monograph No. 3. New York: American Accounting Association, 1940.

Schwarzbach, H., and R. Vangermeersch. "The Current Value Experiences of the Rouse Company, 1973–1989," *Accounting Horizons*, June 1991, pp. 45–54.

Sprouse, R.T., and M. Moonitz. *A Tentative Set of Broad Accounting Principles for Business Enterprises.* Accounting Research Study No. 3. New York: AICPA, 1962.

Vangermeersch, R. "Two Papers on the History of Valuation Theory." Working paper no. 15 in *Working Paper Series Volume 1*, edited by E.N. Coffman, pp. 230–245. Richmond, VA: Academy of Accounting Historians, 1979.

Zeff, S., ed. *Asset Appreciation, Business Income, and Price-Level Accounting, 1919–1935.* New York: Arno Press, 1976.

Hochfelder v. Ernst and Ernst

First Securities Company of Chicago, a small brokerage firm, retained Ernst and Ernst as its auditors from 1946 to 1967. Leston B. Nay was president of First Securities and owned 92 percent of its stock. Between 1962 and 1966, Nay induced customers of First Securities to invest in escrow accounts that he claimed would yield a high rate of return. In 1968 Nay committed suicide, leaving a note in which he described First Securities as bankrupt due to his embezzlement from the escrow accounts. Actually there were no escrow accounts. Investors wrote checks either to Nay or to a designated bank for his account. Nay then diverted the money for his own use. The transactions were never recorded, and investors never received records of their purchases or of their balances in the fictitious escrow accounts.

The defrauded investors sued Ernst and Ernst, claiming that Nay's scheme violated Section 10(b) of the Securities and Exchange Act of 1934 and that "inexcusable negligence" by the auditors had aided and abetted Nay's fraud. Specifically, they charged that Ernst and Ernst should have discovered Nay's "mail rule," which required that all mail addressed to him or to the company for his attention be opened only by him or held unopened during his absence. The investors alleged that this mail rule was the key to concealment of the fraud, and that Ernst and Ernst had a duty of inquiry to investigate this practice. They further contended that the mail rule constituted a weakness in internal control that the auditors should have detected and disclosed.

The question facing the court was whether the wording of Section 10(b) holds accountants liable only for fraudulent acts, or whether it also includes negligent conduct. The District Court ruled in favor of Ernst and Ernst. On appeal, a federal Court of Appeals reversed the decision and found for the investors. In 1976 the case was appealed to the U.S. Supreme Court, which dismissed the claim against Ernst and Ernst, ruling that auditors cannot be held liable under Section 10(b) without proof "of intent to deceive, manipulate, or defraud."

The *Hochfelder* decision is thought to have narrowed the scope of liability for auditors accused of filing false and misleading financial statements with the Securities and Exchange Commission. Because of the difficulty of proving intent to deceive, accountants also believed that this decision would reduce the number of lawsuits brought against them involving SEC disclosures. However, *Hochfelder*'s significance as a precedent remains unclear. Liability has been imposed on accountants in numerous cases under Section 10(b). If an accountant is judged to have been grossly negligent, courts may infer from his conduct that he had an intent to deceive.

Michael Chatfield

Bibliography

Hampton, J.J. "Accountants' Liability: The Significance of *Hochfelder*," *Journal of Accountancy*, December 1976, pp. 69–75.

Ernst and Ernst v. Hochfelder, 425 U.S. 185 (1976).

Miller, R.L., and G.P. Brady. *CPA Liability: Meeting the Challenge*. New York: John Wiley & Sons, 1986.

See also CONGRESSIONAL VIEWS; FRAUD AND AUDITING; INTERNAL CONTROL; LAW AND ACCOUNTING; LEGAL LIABILITY OF AUDITORS; REGULATION (FEDERAL U.S.) AND ACCOUNTING; SECURITIES AND EXCHANGE COMMISSION

Hopwood, Anthony G. (1944–)

Professor of accounting at the London School of Economics and Political Science, Anthony G. Hopwood has an international reputation because of his institutional commitments and involvements and his pioneering writings in the behavioral, organizational, and social aspects of accounting thought and practice.

Hopwood's institutional involvements have been varied and significant and have complemented his intellectual and educational interests. His policy work has included the recommendation and establishment of the European Accounting Advisory Forum in 1991. His involvement in accounting policy work has been premised on the assumption that there should not be a great divide between policy work and academic matters. This is reflected in his writings on the relationship of accounting research and practice and his concern to explore accounting in action. Hopwood's interest in European accounting was formalized in the 1970s. Since 1972 he has organized a program of accounting research seminars and workshops for the European Institute for Advanced Studies in Management in Brussels. This activity gave rise to the creation of the European Accounting Association (EAA) in which Hopwood served as the founding president (1977–1979) and as president again in 1987–1988.

This European accounting network of researchers brought Hopwood into contact with differing research traditions and theoretical understandings of accounting. For example, his understanding of accounting as an organizationally grounded practice was influenced, in part, by the Scandinavian tradition of accounting and management research. The idea of the interactive nature of accounting and organizations and the exploration of accounting in action was not new to Hopwood. Hopwood's Ph.D. studies at the University of Chicago

(M.B.A., 1967; Ph.D., 1971) were marked by an interest in the behavioral aspects of accounting systems and the organizational functioning of accounting. His field-research strategy and design were new for accounting at that time, and the resultant study was significant in focusing on the differing ways in which managers used the same accounting system, leadership styles and behavioral consequences of budgets in performance evaluation. This study spawned a significant number of studies on the behavioral effects of accounting. His subsequent appointments back in Great Britain broadened Hopwood's organizational understandings of accounting from the perspectives gained from studying in the United States, which were too narrowly focused in the social psychological literature and its resulting individualistic orientation. Hopwood was: a Lecturer in Management Accounting, Manchester Business School, 1970–1973; Senior Staff Member, Administrative Staff College, Henley-on-Thames, 1973–1976; Professor and Fellow, Oxford Centre of Management Studies, 1976–1978; and Institute of Chartered Accountants Professor of Accounting and Financial Reporting, London Business School, 1978–1985. This encouraged his increasingly European perspective of being interdisciplinary and of the need to study accounting in the context in which it operates.

Hopwood's text *Accounting and Human Behavior* (1974) gave him the opportunity to think through in more detail the organizational givenness of accounting. The text explored the behavioral effects of accounting on organizational issues such as budgeting, performance evaluation, cost control and decision making. It became a frequently quoted work in the field of behavioral accounting. Hopwood's most significant institutional contribution and some of his important intellectual contributions have been through the journal *Accounting, Organizations, and Society* (*AOS*). He has steered and influenced the journal as editor in chief since its founding in 1976. The journal has established itself as an important international forum for the dissemination and discussion of quality research on the behavioral, organizational, and social aspects of accounting. The emerging understandings of the organizational and social nature of accounting are in large part due to Hopwood's concern to publish substantive research that reflects an intellectual diversity that links accounting practice to important developments within the human sciences. Along with his concern to position accounting within the wider community of the human sciences, he is concerned with any kind of intellectual imperialism or epistemological claims that would delimit the understanding of accounting or the research agenda in accounting. His own work in *AOS* has probed the differing rationales and the multifaceted nature of accounting. He has emphasized both the reflective and constitutive aspects of accounting, has reflected on accounting change, and has always been interdisciplinary in his focus. Hopwood's contribution to accounting has been a questioning path of inquiry concerned with observing accounting rather than propagating it—a path that appreciates the actual consequences of accounting rather than its stated rationales and that explores its organizational and social bases rather than presuming a technical autonomy for accounting.

Ross E. Stewart

Bibliography

Hopwood, A.G. *Accounting and Human Behavior.* Englewood Cliffs, N.J.: Prentice-Hall, 1974.
———. "Accounting in its Social Context: Toward a History of Value Added in the United Kingdom," *Accounting, Organizations, and Society,* vol. 10, no. 4, pp. 381–413.
———. "On Trying to Study Accounting in the Contexts in Which It Operates," *Accounting, Organizations, and Society,* vol. 8, no. 2/3, 1983, pp. 287–305.
———. "The Archaeology of Accounting Systems," *Accounting, Organizations, and Society,* vol. 12, no. 3, 1987, pp. 207–234.
———, et al. "The Roles of Accounting in Organization and Society," *Accounting, Organizations, and Society,* vol. 5, no. 1, 1980, pp. 5–27.

See also BUDGETING; CONTROL: CLASSICAL MODEL; COST AND/OR MANAGEMENT ACCOUNTING; MANAGEMENT ACCOUNTING; NORMATIVE ACCOUNTING; SOCIAL RESPONSIBILITIES OF ACCOUNTANTS

Horngren, Charles T. (1926–)

Charles T. Horngren is generally regarded as the most influential cost and management accountant in the latter half of the twentieth century. Horngren authored or coauthored four influential accounting texts dating back to 1962, *Cost Accounting: A Managerial Emphasis, Introduction to Management Accounting, Introduction to Financial Accounting,* and *Accounting.* All continue to be among the leading textbooks in their respective fields.

The traditional focus of cost accounting was on accumulation of costs for the purposes of calculation of product costs and valuation of inventory. Through his book *Cost Accounting: A Managerial Emphasis,* Horngren was the dominant force in shifting the emphasis of cost accounting toward providing useful information for management decision making, planning, and control.

Horngren introduced the two key ideas that are widely taught and practiced today. First, "different costs for different purposes"—the idea, for example, that managers may choose one cost-allocation method for decision making but a different method to influence the behavior of subordinates. This notion of different costs for different purposes led Horngren to define and develop the concept of "relevant costs," which forms the basis of much of how cost and management accounting is taught today. Second, management-accounting systems are economic goods subject to the cost-benefit criterion. This is, when evaluating management-accounting systems, the costs of accounting information must be measured against the benefits of the better action choices that managers make as a result of the information. These ideas were pivotal in moving cost and management accounting thought from the search for "absolute truth" to an orientation that stressed the "economics of accounting information."

Horngren was valedictorian from Marquette University in 1949 and majored in accounting. He received an MBA degree in 1952 from Harvard University and a doctorate from the University of Chicago in 1955. He was a professor there from 1959 through 1966 when he joined the faculty at Stanford University where he still teaches. He was a member of the Accounting Principles Board (1968–1973), the Financial Accounting Standards Board (FASB) Advisory Council (1976–1980), and Financial Accounting Foundation (1984–1989). He was president of the American Accounting Association in 1976–1977 and a member of the Board of Regents of the Institute of Management Accounting. He became a member of the Accounting Hall of Fame in 1990.

Srikant M. Datar

Bibliography

Burns, T.J., and E.N. Coffman. *The Accounting Hall of Fame: Profiles of Fifty Members.* Columbus: College of Business, Ohio State University, 1991.

Horngren, C.T. "Accounting Discipline in 1999," *Accounting Review*, January 1971, pp. 1–11.

———. "Capacity Utilization and the Efficiency Variance," *Accounting Review*, January 1969, pp. 86–89.

———. "Cost and Management Accounting: Yesterday and Today," *Journal of Management Accounting Research*, Fall 1989, pp. 21–32.

———. "Depreciation, Flow of Funds and the Price Level," *Analysts Journal*, August 1957, pp. 45–47.

Williams, K. "Charles T. Horngren: Management Accounting's Renaissance Man," *Management Accounting*, January 1986, pp. 22–29.

See also ACCOUNTING HALL OF FAME; AMERICAN ACCOUNTING ASSOCIATION; COST AND/OR MANAGEMENT ACCOUNTING; DEMSKI, JOEL S.; DIRECT COSTING; FUNDS FLOW STATEMENT; MANAGEMENT ACCOUNTING; MCKINSEY, JAMES O.

Hoxsey, J.M.B.

During the 1920s, when the general public first began buying corporate securities, auditors faced the problem of certifying financial statements for distribution to investors who had little or no accounting knowledge. J.M.B. Hoxsey, executive assistant to the Committee on Stock List for the New York Stock Exchange, believed that overconservatism and other accounting practices which might have been excusable in an era of smaller firms and short-term bank borrowing had become misleading in reports to this less sophisticated group of readers. In his speech "Accounting for Investors" at the 1930 American Institute of Accountants (AIA) meeting, Hoxsey argued for improved corporate publicity, pointing out that many corporations kept sales figures secret, while others did not take depreciation or failed to distinguish between operating income and other gains and losses. Still others did not separate retained earnings from paid in capital, or reported stock dividends and consolidations inconsistently. Some chose not to disclose arbitrary asset revaluations. In conclusion, Hoxsey said the stock exchange would welcome the cooperation of an AIA committee in considering these problems. The result was the AIA's Committee on Cooperation with Stock Exchanges, chaired by George Oliver May, which proposed that businesses be free to choose their accounting methods within a framework of "accepted accounting principles," provided they disclosed such methods and used them consistently from year to year.

Michael Chatfield

Bibliography

Hoxsey, J.M.B. "Accounting for Investors," *Journal of Accountancy*, October 1930, pp. 251–284.

See also ACCOUNTING RESEARCH BULLETINS; AMERICAN INSTITUTE OF CERTIFIED PUBLIC ACCOUNTANTS; AUDITOR'S REPORT; GENERALLY ACCEPTED ACCOUNTING PRINCIPLES; MAY, GEORGE OLIVER; NEW YORK STOCK EXCHANGE; PAID IN CAPITAL

Hugli, Friedrich

During the nineteenth century, the proprietary theory of accounts largely replaced account personification, causing a shift in accounting emphasis from relationships among individuals to the statistical classification of data. Friedrich Hugli, a Swiss government accountant, became the leading European publicist for the proprietary viewpoint, summarizing and elaborating on the work of two earlier German authors, G.D. Augspurg (1852), and George Kurzbauer (1850). Kurzbauer had argued that account classifications should be derived from the two essential accounting purposes: profit finding and the inventorying of assets. These produce real and nominal accounts, in effect two opposed accounting systems in the same ledger. Double entry is the merger into one system of the "property bookkeeping" and the "results bookkeeping" of a business firm. Augspurg had also concluded that double entry bookkeeping requires simultaneously maintaining two sets of accounts—one presenting proprietor's net assets, the other individual assets. Liabilities are negative property; capital, representing investments as a whole, is reciprocal to the specific assets. The two groups of accounts are complementary and their reconciliation helps prove the ledger's correctness.

In *Buchhaltungs-systeme und Buchhaltungs-forme* (1887) and *Buchhaltungs-Studien* (1900), Hugli approached proprietary theory from a mathematical viewpoint, showing by means of algebraic symbols and equations how accounting equilibrium is maintained between the "two series of accounts" and how transactions ultimately affect capital. Hugli also argued that the firm owns business property and does not merely owe it to a proprietor in the sense that it owes debts to third parties.

Michael Chatfield

Bibliography
Kafer, K. *Theory of Accounts in Double-Entry Bookkeeping.* Urbana, IL: Center for International Education and Research in Accounting, University of Illinois, 1966.
Littleton, A.C. *Accounting Evolution to 1900.* New York: American Institute Publishing, 1933. Reprint. New York: Russell and Russell, 1966.

See also PROPRIETARY THEORY

Human Resource Accounting

Human Resource Accounting (HRA) has been defined by the American Accounting Association's Committee on Human Resource Accounting as "the process of identifying and measuring data about human resources and communicating this information to interested parties." It involves accounting for investments made in people by the organizations that employ them and the replacement cost of those people. It also involves accounting for the economic value of people as organizational resources.

The field of HRA has been developing since the 1960s. The field is an outgrowth of the convergence of several independent but closely related streams of thought as well as the fundamental metamorphosis of the U.S. from an industrial to a service economy. This has all led to the increasing recognition that human capital, or human assets, is the distinctive feature of today's economy. This qualitative transformation, which began around the end of World War II, has led to fundamental changes in the composition of the labor force not only in the sectors in which people are employed, but also in the nature of the types and levels of skills demanded.

In the 1990s, the economy has increasingly become a knowledge-based one, and the services provided are increasingly what may be described as high-technology services, which are the product of considerable amounts of training and experience. Thus, the economy is increasingly comprised of white-collar, technical, and professional personnel. The distinctive feature of the emerging economy is a growing emphasis upon human capital (the knowledge, skills, and experience of people) rather than physical capital. A related attribute is that the development of human capital is costly and requires significant investments both by individuals and the organizations which employ them.

Impetus for the Development of HRA
Under agricultural and industrial economic structures, where the extent of human capital was significantly less than it is today, the theories and methods of accounting did not treat either people, or investments in people, as assets (with the exception of slaves, who were viewed as property). However, with the increasing importance of human capital at the level not only of the individual firm but also of the economy as a whole, a great deal of research has been designed to develop concepts and methods of accounting for people as assets.

HRA is, at least in part, a recognition that people comprise human capital or human assets. This is the essence of the economic theory of human capital. It is based upon the concept that people possess skills, experience, and knowledge that are a form of capital, termed human capital. Thus, University of Chicago Professor of Economics Theodore W. Schultz, who received the Nobel Prize in Economics in 1980 for his work on the economic theory of human capital, has stated that "laborers have become capitalists not from a diffusion of the ownership of corporation stocks as folklore would have it, but from the acquisition of knowledge and skill that have economic value." In a review of the history of the development of the economic theory of human capital, B.F. Kiker indicated that the list of early economists who had recognized that human capital exists included the Scottish economist Adam Smith (1723–1790); the English economist Sir William Petty (1623–1687); the French economist Jean-Baptiste Say (1767–1832); the English political economist Nassau William Senior (1790–1864); the German political economist Friedrich List (1789–1846); the German economic theorist Johann Heinrich von Thünen (1783–1850); the German historical economist Wilhelm Georg Friedrich Roscher (1817–1894); the Frenchman Leon Walras (1834–1910); and the American economist Irving Fisher (1867–1947). The two methods used by economists to measure the amounts of human capital were based upon cost-of-production and capitalized-earnings procedures.

HRA has also developed from a parallel tradition in personnel management known as the "Human Resources School," which is based upon the premise that people are valuable organizational resources and, therefore, ought to be managed as such. Personnel theorists such as George S. Odiorne and organizational psychologists such as Rensis Likert have treated people as valuable organizational resources in their work. For example, in his 1967 book *The Human Organization: Its Management and Value*, Likert stated that "every aspect of a firm's activities is determined by the competence, motivation and general effectiveness of its human organization."

There is also support among some of the early accounting theorists for treating people as assets and accounting for their value, even before the nature of the economic structure changed and human capital increased in importance. For example, DR Scott, an accounting professor at the University of Missouri, noted in his 1925 book *Theory of Accounts* (Vol. 1) that "a trained force of technical operatives is always a valuable asset." Similarly, William Andrew Paton, a long-time professor of accounting at the University of Michigan, in his 1922 book *Accounting Theory* stated that "in a business enterprise a well organized and loyal personnel may be a much more important asset than a stock of merchandise."

In addition to academic theorists, practicing managers have for some time recognized the importance of human assets. For example, the 1966 annual report of Uniroyal stated "Our prime resource is people. (We are) essentially a collection of skills—the varied expertise of our 68,000 employees . . . Uniroyal has plants and has capital, but most of all, it has people."

Taken together, these various streams of thought all led to the conclusion that organizations possess a valuable asset in the people whom they employ, and that the people themselves are a form of capital, human capital. This recognition led, in turn, during the 1960s to both academic research and business development of concepts and methods of measuring the cost and value of people as organizational assets, or the field that is known as human resource accounting.

The Five Stages of Research in HRA

The first stage (1960 to 1966) was marked by interest in HRA and the derivation of basic HRA concepts from related bodies of theory (Flamholtz, 1985). One of the earliest approaches to measure and account for the value of human resources was developed by R.H. Hermanson, an academic accountant, as part of his Ph.D. dissertation, and later published as a monograph in 1964 under the title *Accounting for Human Assets*. Hermanson's principal concern was that conventional financial statements failed to reflect adequately the financial position of a firm because they did not include human assets. Hermanson developed a method to measure the value of human assets possessed by a firm and acquired through the normal course of operations by recruiting, training, and the like, but that had not been previously accounted for in connection with the acquisition of one firm by another.

The second stage (1967 to 1970) included a few exploratory experimental applications for HRA in actual organizations (Flamholtz 1985). In 1967, a group of researchers began a pioneering program of research on HRA at the University of Michigan. This team was comprised of: Rensis Likert, Director of the Institute for Social Research; R. Lee Brummet, professor of accounting; William C. Pyle, Assistant Project Director in the Institute of Social Research; and Eric G. Flamholtz, also an Assistant Project Director in the Institute of Social Research.

The third stage (1971–1976) was probably best highlighted by the group from the University of Michigan's work at R.G. Barry Corporation, which led to the publishing in the early 1970s of pro forma financial statements that included human assets based on their historical cost (Flamholtz, 1974). Another model, based on the present value of workers' remaining future earnings from employment, was developed by Baruch Lev from The Hebrew University of Jerusalem and Aba Schwartz from the University of Tel-Aviv.

The fourth stage (1977–1980) was marked by declining interest in HRA in both the academic and the corporate world. Flamholtz (1985) felt the relatively easy research had been done and that corporate interest was diverted to more pressing issues. The fifth stage (1981–mid-1990s) has involved the beginnings of a resurgence of interest in the theory and practice of HRA. One reason was a research project in HRA sponsored by the U.S. Office of Naval Research in the early 1980s. Another reason was the growing concern in the U.S. about increased productivity. Another reason was the growing success of the Japanese as major world-class competitors. One more reason was the metamorphosis of the U.S. economy from an industrial to a high-tech service economy in which human capital is the critical resource. Flamholtz (1985) detailed many of these studies, which were done for internal decision making purposes. A study by Flamholtz, Professor at the University of California, Los Angeles, D. Gerald Searfoss, Director of Accounting Standards at Touche Ross and Company, and Russell Coff, Doctoral student at the University of California, Los Angeles, described in 1988 an integrated system to measure both the replacement cost and economic value of human assets. Another study by Flamholtz in 1987 involved the valuation of human assets acquired in a corporate merger, in order to amortize human capital in measuring income for income tax reporting. In 1992, a comment in *Management Accounting* by Hermanson, Ivancevich, and Hermanson questioned whether massive downsizing of U.S. companies would have occurred if the HRA approach had been used rather than the traditional expense model. In 1994, an article in *Fortune* entitled "Your Company's Most Valuable Asset: Intellectual Capital," illustrated HRA remains a vital topic.

Eric G. Flamholtz

Bibliography

Brummet, R.L., E.G. Flamholtz, and W.C. Pyle. "Human Resource Measurement: A Challenge for Accountants," *Accounting Review*, April 1968, pp. 217–224.

Cook, J. "The Molting of America," *Forbes*, November 22, 1982, pp. 161–167.

Flamholtz, E.G. *Human Resource Accounting*. Encino, CA: Dickenson, 1974.

———. *Human Resource Accounting*. 2nd ed. San Francisco: Jossey-Bass, 1985.

———. *The Theory and Measurement of Individual's Value to an Organization*. Ph.D. diss., Ann Arbor: University of Michigan, 1969.

———. "Valuation of Human Assets in a Securities Brokerage Firm: An Empirical Study," *Accounting, Organizations, and Society*, vol. 12, no. 4, 1987, pp. 309–318.

———, D.G. Searfoss, and R. Coff. "Developing Human Resource Accounting as a Human Resource Decision Support System," *Accounting Horizons*, September 1988, pp. 1–9.

Hermanson, D., D.M. Ivancevich, and R.H. Hermanson. "Human Resource Accounting in Recessionary Times," *Management Accounting*, July 1992, p. 69.

Hermanson, R.H. *Accounting for Human Assets*. Occasional paper No. 14. East Lansing: Bureau of Business and Economic Research, Michigan State University, 1964.

Kiker, B.F. "The Historical Roots of the Concept of Human Capital," *Journal of Political Economy*, October 1966, pp. 481–499.

Lev, B., and A. Schwartz. "On the Use of the Economic Concept of Human Capital in Financial Statements," *Accounting Review*, January 1971, pp. 103–112.

Likert, R. *New Patterns of Management*. New York: McGraw-Hill, 1961.

Odiorne, G.S. *Personnel Policy: Issues and Practices*. Columbus, OH: Charles E. Merrill Books, 1963.

Pyle, W.C. "Accounting for Your People," *Innovation*, No. 10, 1970, pp. 46–54.

Sackmann, S.A., E.G. Flamholtz, and M.L. Bullen. "Human Resource Accounting: A State-of-the-Art Review," *Journal of Accounting Literature*, vol. 8, 1989, pp. 235–264.

Schultz, T. "Investment in Human Capital," *American Economic Review*, March 1961, pp. 1–17.

Stewart, T.A. "Your Company's Most Valuable Asset: Intellectual Capital," *Fortune*, October 3, 1994, pp. 68–72, 74.

See also MANAGEMENT ACCOUNTING; PATON, WILLIAM ANDREW; SCOTT, DR; SMITH, ADAM

I

Ijiri, Yuji (1935–)

Probably the simplest way to identify the scope and significance of Yuji Ijiri's contributions is to note that he has been inducted into Ohio State University's Accounting Hall of Fame (1989) and is the only Japanese citizen to have served as president of the American Accounting Association in 1983. Thus, he has received recognition for contributions to accounting both for his research and for his activities on behalf of the profession. This recognition is worldwide and goes back to the start in his 1963 doctoral thesis, *Management Goals and Accounting for Control,* which was published in 1965 by North Holland Press and then translated, successively, into Japanese, French, and Spanish.

The "spreadsheet" ideas of accounting used in that book had already made their way into articles coauthored by Ijiri in the literature of operations research and computer science, as well as accounting. This contribution has been paid the ultimate compliment: These ideas are so widely used in so many different forms that their sources in Ijiri's writings have been lost from view. The use of spreadsheets and related ideas on matrix representations are reviewed in Ijiri's *Momentum Accounting and Triple Entry Bookkeeping: Exploring the Dynamic Structure of Accounting Measurements.*

Yuji Ijiri was born in Kobe, Japan, in 1935 when the country was about to plunge into total war. To escape aerial bombardment he was evacuated, as a fourth-grader, to the countryside, where he whiled away his time by learning algebra from a math teacher who had similarly moved from the city. When Yuji was 14, his father, a no-nonsense man, put him in charge of accounting for their bakery-confec-

tionery business. Going to night school to learn more about the subject, Ijiri quickly passed the nation's qualifier exam, which, in Japan, is a prerequisite to sitting for the CPA unless one has a university degree. At 21—the youngest ever—he received his certificate shortly after graduating from Ritsumeikan University in Kyoto. He then went into public practice, first with a small firm and then with Price Waterhouse and Company in Tokyo.

Two men who exercised great influence on Ijiri's character and points of view were his father, Takejiro Ijiri, and his teacher, Taminosuke Nishimura (later to become his father-in-law). Complementing his father's pragmatic "so what can you do with it that's of any use to anybody?" attitude was the scholarly, philosophical bent of his teacher, who based his accounting seminar on Thomas Carlyle's *Sartor Resartus (Tailor Retailored)* and, in the course of this seminar, taught Ijiri the use of analogy as guides to beauty and how to unite, with elegance, seemingly separate fields of inquiry in previously unperceived ways.

By the time he was 24, Ijiri had saved $1,650, which he used to emigrate to America. He quickly earned a master's degree in 1960 at the University of Minnesota, then entered Carnegie Tech's (now Carnegie Mellon) new Graduate School of Industrial Administration.

At Carnegie, Ijiri joined in the excitement of a new, broad-based, analytically oriented curriculum that provided unusual opportunities for early participation in research with faculty that included Herbert Simon—who was subsequently to win the Distinguished Scientific Contribution Award from the American Psychological Association (cognitive processes), the A.M. Turing Award of the Association for Computing Machinery (artificial intelligence and computer science), the Nobel Prize (economics and econometrics), and the National Medal of Science from the U.S. government—as well as Richard Cyert and James March, then embarking on their now classic research in *Behavioral Theory of the Firm* (1963). Also there was W.W. Cooper, a sort of head factotum for "quantitative approaches" who was responsible for teaching accounting, econometrics, and operations research—and who was able to persuade Ijiri to write his dissertation in accounting.

As his Ph.D. degree drew near, Ijiri finally received Professor Nishimura's consent to marry his daughter, Tomo, and return with her to America. After receiving his degree in 1963, he spent four years at Stanford University where he taught a regular course load and, in addition, audited courses in physics, mathematical logic, and philosophy.

By this time, Ijiri was well launched in research, making contributions that have not been confined to accounting, but have extended to economics (including econometrics), statistics, operations research and organization theory, mathematics, logic, and beyond. This continued, and accelerated, after Ijiri rejoined Carnegie Mellon University in 1967, first as a full professor, then in 1975 as the Robert M. Trueblood Professor of Accounting and Economics, and since 1987 Robert M. Trueblood university professor of accounting and economics—the highest honor the university accords to any of its faculty. Those who liked the early 1900s accounting professor Henry Rand Hatfield's "An Historical Defense of Bookkeeping" in 1924 will love Ijiri's response as printed by Carnegie Mellon University under the title "The Accountant: Destined to be Free" on September 18, 1975.

Ijiri's contributions to accounting cover more than 100 articles and 20 books and include coeditorship of the sixth edition of the encyclopedic *Kohler's Dictionary for Accountants* (Prentice-Hall, 1983). He has been honored both in the United States and abroad for his work and is the only four-time winner of the American Institute of Certified Public Accountants (AICPA) Notable Contributions to the Accounting Literature Award. These are as follows:

1966 Award: "Reliability and Objectivity of Accounting Measurement," *Accounting Review*, July 1966. Coauthored with R.K. Jaedicke

1967 Award: *The Foundations of Accounting Measurement: A Mathematical, Economic, and Behavioral Inquiry* (Prentice-Hall, 1967)

1971 Award: "A Model for Integrating Sampling Objectives in Auditing," *Journal of Accounting Research*, Spring 1971. Coauthored with Robert S. Kaplan

1976 Award: *Theory of Accounting Measurement*. Studies in Accounting Research. American Accounting Association, 1975

Ijiri wrote in his fourth American Accounting Association monograph, *Momentum Accounting and Triple Entry Bookkeeping: Exploring the Dynamic Structure of Accounting Measurements*: "To know the past, one must first know the future." This quotation is from a book on chess by the mathematician Raymond Smullyan, but it might better be replaced by: "The past is even more meaningful if you can use it to influence the future in desired directions, as in Ijiri's triple-entry (momentum) accounting."

Ijiri avidly reads Smullyan, a philosopher as well as a mathematician, who wrote on the topic of ontology and creativity as follows:

> One dictionary defines ontology as the science of being; the branch of metaphysics that investigates the nature of being and the essence of things. . . Thus Willard van Orman Quine [the Harvard philosopher-logician] starts his famous essay *On What Is There* with the words "A curious thing about the ontological problem is its simplicity. It can be put in three Anglo Saxon monosyllables: "What is there?" It can be answered, moreover, in a word—"Everything."

A similar philosophy was expressed in Mandel's delightful book, *Chi Po and the Sorcerer: A Tale for Chinese Children*. In one scene, the boy Chi Po is taking painting lessons from the sorcerer Bu Fu. At one point Bu Fu says, "No, no! You have merely painted what is! Anyone can paint what is; the real secret is to paint what isn't!" Chi Po, quite puzzled, replies, "But what is there that isn't?"

Surely the answer to the boy's question is—"What can be created!"—and Ijiri provides the example. How did he create the ideas of triple entry bookkeeping? The basic connections between balance sheets and income statements had been noted by many others since Luca Pacioli first published his book on double entry bookkeeping some 500 years ago. If "it was there," why hadn't someone before him seen how to extend this principle to tie successive income statements together as well? The answer lies in Ijiri's creativity—his ability to bring into existence things that *weren't* there.

As a result, there is now one integrated system available in which balance sheets and *changes* in balance sheets, income statements and *changes* in income statements can all be tied together with supporting schedules such as funds-flows and *changes* in funds-flows. A whole array of new accounting statements with accompanying new uses of accounting have thus been brought into view—or *created*, if you will—and their full exploitation only awaits development of the computerization and experimentation that are required for their adoption and successful implementation.

This still leaves open the question of why it took nearly 500 years to go from Pacioli to Ijiri despite the attention of many fine minds. The answer lies in the depth to which Ijiri had previously probed in his studies on the foundations of accounting, which finally led to his demonstration that all of accounting, including its multidimensional extensions, can be derived from three simple axioms, which he refers to as the axioms of controls, of quantities, and of exchanges.

At a conference in Siena, Italy, celebrating the 500th year of Pacioli's publication of the first tract on double entry accounting, Ijiri offered an up-to-date portrayal of his invention of triple entry bookkeeping. His paper, "The Beauty of Double Entry Bookkeeping and Its Impact on the Nature of Accounting Information," is published in the 1993 issue of *Economic Notes*. Those who prefer a didactic approach can refer to Ijiri's recent computerized text: *The Evolution of Bookkeeping: From Single to Double to Triple Entry Systems— Interactive Courseware Written in Wing Z for the Macintosh in Color with Piano Accompaniment by T.W. McGuire.*

W.W. Cooper

Bibliography

Burns, T.J., and E.N. Coffman. *The Accounting Hall of Fame: Profiles of Fifty Members*. Columbus: College of Business, Ohio State University, 1991.

Ijiri, Y. *Momentum Accounting and Triple Entry Bookkeeping: Exploring the Dynamic Structure of Accounting Measurements*. American Accounting Association Monograph No. 31. Sarasota, FL: American Accounting Association, 1989.

———. *The Evolution of Bookkeeping: From Single to Double to Triple Entry Systems—Interactive Courseware Written in Wing Z for the Macintosh in Color with Piano Accompaniment by Timothy W. McGuire*. Pittsburgh: Carnegie Mellon University, 1990.

Smullyan, R. *5000 B.C. and Other Philosophical Phantasies*. New York: St. Martin's Press, 1983.

See also ACCOUNTING HALL OF FAME; AGENCY THEORY; AMERICAN ACCOUNTING ASSOCIATION; CASH FLOW ACCOUNTING; CONCEPTUAL FRAMEWORK; COOPER, WILLIAM WAGER; HISTORICAL COST; KOHLER, ERIC LOUIS; NORMATIVE ACCOUNTING; PACIOLI, LUCA

Imputed Interest on Capital

Imputed interest on capital refers to the attribution of an interest rate to capital, usually invested capital (owners' equity), and treatment of the amount as a product cost. Capital could also be defined as fixed capital (balance of fixed assets) or as fixed capital plus working capital. A journal entry may or may not be made for the result of this computation. It is probably fair to say that one key goal of the proponents of imputed interest has been to convince governmental regulators and others that private-sector firms should be allowed to include imputed interest in their "cost pool," as do public utility companies.

The issue of imputed interest has been hotly debated in accounting. In a 1911 article, Arthur Lowes Dickinson, a noted accounting practitioner and writer both in Great Britain and the United States, argued that while many engineers and a few accountants favored the inclusion of imputed interest as a product cost, such imputation was much too uncertain and theoretically flawed to be acceptable in accounting. In 1912, the editor of the *Journal of Accountancy* called for a debate on Dickinson's position, and the battle was on. Among those writing articles taking the "pro" position were William Morse Cole, a writer of accounting texts (April 1913), Alexander Hamilton Church, an industrial engineer (April 1913), and John Raymond Wildman, a practitioner and academic in accounting (June 1913). The "con" position was presented by, among others, W.B. Richards (April 1913), Joseph Edmund Sterrett, a noted accounting practitioner (April 1913), George Oliver May, a leading opinion-maker in accounting (June 1916), and William B. Castenholz, an accounting consultant (April 1918). In 1918, the issue was brought to the membership of the American Institute of Accountants (AIA), the predecessor of the American Institute of Certified Public Accountants (AICPA). The membership agreed with the "con" position taken by an AIA special committee on the topic, a position also taken by the Federal Trade Commission (FTC) in 1916.

The formation in 1919 of the National Association of Cost Accountants (NACA, now the Institute of Management Accountants) led to a new battleground for the proponents, led by Clinton H. Scovell and J. Lee Nicholson. Scovell, who articulated the "pro" position in articles, speeches, and a 1924 book, *Interest as a Cost,* led the battle for this position on the floor of the 1921 annual meeting of the NACA. Scovell had served on a special committee of the NACA that studied the topic. The committee conducted a detailed literature search in 1920 and 1921 and wrote briefs on both positions but made no conclusions. The decision was to be left to the membership. Speaking for the "pros" at the annual meeting, Scovell quoted economists who held that interest was a cost of getting capital from investors. Imputation of interest was necessary, for instance, to distinguish between kinds of business or lines of sales and for making uniform cost plans for associations. He argued for the use of the ordinary interest rate on reasonably secured long-term investment, in the locality in which the business is situated. He then skillfully anticipated the "con" arguments.

A "con" speech followed by Elmer E. Staub, an industrial accountant. He argued basically that (1) returns upon investments are profits, not costs; (2) the proper interest rate is impossible to determine; and (3) inventory would be overvalued. Dr. Francis Walker, chief economist of the Federal Trade Commission, next said that the FTC's "con" position was consistent with its predecessor, the U.S. Bureau of Corporations. There just was no agreement on the rate of interest or on the investment base on which to impute the interest. The NACA sent ballots to its members. Of the 2,106 ballots sent, 567 were returned, with 112 votes for the "pro" position and 455 against. The vote marked the beginning of the end of the imputation argument until it was revived by Robert Anthony in the mid-1970s.

Anthony, a professor at Harvard University and a management accountant, expressed the "pro" position in his book *Accounting for the Cost of Interest* (1975). Anthony had been assistant secretary of defense, comptroller, from 1965 to 1968 and a consultant to the Cost Accounting Standards Board (CASB). Acknowledging that he was re-creating the "pro" position of the early period, Anthony held that there was much merit in harmonizing management accounting, for which the imputation procedure was quite common, with financial accounting. He argued that the imputation was equitable and should be allowed by the Defense Department just as regulators allowed it for public utilities. Anthony favored an interest rate set by the Financial Accounting Standards Board (FASB) at a rate somewhat lower than the average cost of equity capital. He argued that financial accounting would be improved by the imputation procedure since net income would be more realistic. He also stressed that both Germany and Great Britain allowed this imputation.

The CASB in 1976 promulgated Standard No. 414, which allowed an imputation on an interest rate chosen by the secretary of the treasury for this purpose. Under this standard, the interest rate is multiplied by the book value of tangible and intangible capital assets in the relevant facility. The CASB felt that this process would serve to offset the inflation of that time.

The history of the imputed-interest debate provides a good example of how accountants and accounting bodies can effect significant societal changes. The failure of the proponents in the early part of the twentieth century was turned around in the mid-1970s. Has the time come for the recognition of cost of capital in the financial-accounting arena as well? Perhaps another full-scale debate is needed.

Richard Vangermeersch

Bibliography

Anthony, R.N. *Accounting for the Cost of Interest*. Lexington, MA: Lexington Books, 1975.

Bursal, N. "The Use of Interest as an Element of Cost in Germany in the Sixteenth and Seventeenth Centuries," *Accounting Historians Journal*, Spring 1986, pp. 63–70.

Castenholz, W.B. "Is Interest on Invested Capital a Cost?" *Journal of Accountancy*, April 1918, pp. 248–254.

Church, A.H. "On Inclusion of Interest in Manufacturing Costs," *Journal of Accountancy*, April 1913, pp. 236–240.

Cole, W.M. "Interest on Investment in Equipment," *Journal of Accountancy*, April 1913, pp. 232–236.

Cost Accounting Standards Board. "Cost of Money as an Element of the Cost of Facilities Capital." CASB Standard No. 414. *Federal Register*, March 5, 1976, pp. 9562–9563.

Dickinson, A.L. "The Fallacy of Including Interest and Rent as Part of Manufacturing Cost," *Journal of Accountancy*, December 1911, pp. 588–593.

"Differing Opinions Should Find Expression," *Journal of Accountancy*, April 1912, pp. 287–289.

May, G.O. "Reasons for Excluding Interest from Cost," *Journal of Accountancy*, June 1916, pp. 401–409.

Richards, W.B. "Interest Not a Charge Against Costs," *Journal of Accountancy*, April 1913, pp. 240–241.

Scovell, C.H. "Brief in Favor of Interest as a Cost," *NACA Yearbook 1921*, pp. 47–64.

———. *Interest as a Cost*. New York: Ronald Press, 1924.

Staub, E.E. "Digest of the Arguments against Inclusion of Interest as an Element of Cost," *NACA Yearbook 1921*, pp. 65–74.

Sterrett, J.E. "Interest Not a Part of the Cost of Production," *Journal of Accountancy*, April 1913, pp. 241–244.

Walker, F. "Attitude of the Federal Trade Commission Regarding Interest as an Element of Cost," *NACA Yearbook 1921*, pp. 75–78.

Wildman, J.R. "Interest on Owned Capital," *Journal of Accountancy*, June 1913, pp. 428–431.

Zeff, S.A. "Some Junctures in the Evolution of the Process of Establishing Accounting Principles in the U.S.A., 1917–1972," *Accounting Review*, July 1984, pp. 447–468.

See also CHURCH, ALEXANDER HAMILTON; COLE, WILLIAM MORSE; COST ACCOUNTING STANDARDS BOARD; DICKINSON, ARTHUR LOWES; INSTITUTE OF MANAGEMENT ACCOUNTANTS; MAY, GEORGE OLIVER; NICHOLSON, J. LEE; OPPORTUNITY COST; STERRETT, JOSEPH EDMUND; WILDMAN, JOHN RAYMOND

Income-Determination Theory

Income determination is a key objective of the financial-accounting process. The reasons for this can be found in the nature of business operations and the historical origins of financial accounting.

The system of double entry bookkeeping that forms the basis of modern financial accounting appeared in medieval and Renaissance Italy as the product of the economic, social, and political environment of the times. A key feature of this environment was the development of a sophisticated money economy with the widespread use in business operations, such as banking and trading, of private capital in the form of money for the purpose of generating profit (income) measured in terms of money.

The key characteristics of the double entry system are: (1) the keeping of accounting records based on monetary measurement; (2) distinguishing between capital and income in the analysis and classification of business transactions; and (3) the integrating role played by the capital account, the ultimate recipient of all gains and losses, and the inherent state of balance between assets (A) and claims on those assets, or liabilities (L), and proprietorship (P) reflected in the accounting equation

$$A - L = P$$

In a money economy, business operations through the investment of money for the purpose of earning income in the form of monetary return in excess of monetary outlay is best illustrated by the lending of money at interest, as in banking. However, most business operations, such as manufacturing and trading, involve an interim investment in nonmonetary (noncash) assets such as inventories, plant and machinery, and land and buildings, giving an operating cycle of

cash ————> noncash assets ————> cash

In the above context, the determination of income arising from completed cycles (business ventures) involves the matching of two monetary amounts: monetary revenue and monetary outlays associated with a cycle. This is the system of accounting for trading ventures employed by merchants in medieval and Renaissance Italy and described by Luca Pacioli in "Particularis de Computis et Scripturis," his historic treatise on double entry bookkeeping in *Summa de Arithmetica* (1494).

The matching of revenue and expense is still a key concept in the accounting measurement of income. The complex problems that are currently encountered in accounting for business income arise from the continuing nature of business operations and the need to prepare periodic reports on the results and state of affairs of business enterprises in a complex and dynamic economic, social, and political environment. These problems include: (1) The allocation of revenues and expenses to different accounting periods to ensure the "proper" matching of revenue and expense in the measurement of period income—a process that requires the assignment of value to nonmonetary (noncash) assets at balance date to be carried forward to be matched against the revenue of future periods; (2) the alternative methods and procedures that are available for dealing with accounting problems and issues; and (3) the lack of agreement on whether and how to account for, and report on, the effects of general and specific price changes.

These problem areas will be considered in turn.

Asset Valuation and Uncertainty

In accounting, as in general, "value" is a future-oriented concept. According to Edward Stamp, an accounting theorist from England, "if there were no tomorrow nothing in today's world would have any value." Accounting valuation, therefore, and the resulting allocations reflect expectations about an uncertain future and cannot be empirically tested whether they relate to inventory valuation, provision for doubtful debts, depreciation, or accounting for research and development expenditure.

Accounting Alternatives

In the absence of an internally consistent frame of reference for dealing with accounting issues, accounting methods and procedures have been developed to a large extent in an ad hoc manner, in response to the exigencies of practice rather than the strict dictates of logic. As a re-

sult, current accounting practice contains generally accepted alternatives for dealing with specific accounting problems and issues that give rise to inconsistencies in accounting measurement and difficulties in the interpretation of financial statements.

Price and Price-Level Changes

Current accounting measurement is largely based on the related principles of historical cost and realization. This model is still best described by William Andrew Paton, professor of accounting at the University of Michigan, and A.C. Littleton's, professor of accounting at the University of Illinois, 1940 classic, *An Introduction to Corporate Accounting Standards*. Current accounting practice, however, allows some significant departures from the principles of historical cost and realization, as in the case of inventory valuation at a "lower than cost or market" value, the recognition of profit on uncompleted contracts, and the revaluation of fixed assets in some countries.

The Effect of General Price-Level Changes

Underlying income measurement is the notion of capital maintenance. The nature of what is reported as business income, therefore, would depend on the nature of what is defined, explicitly or by implication, as business capital. In the preceding discussion, capital was defined in financial terms as monetary investment in business operations for the purpose of earning income measured as a monetary return in excess of monetary outlay.

The failure of current accounting practice to reflect the effects of general price-level changes means that capital is recorded and maintained in terms of the number of dollars invested rather than in terms of what is economically significant—that is, purchasing power. Similarly, the cost of nonmonetary assets introduced into the business operating cycle is recorded and recovered from revenue in terms of number of dollars and not in terms of purchasing power. Further, current accounting practice does not recognize purchasing-power gains and losses on monetary accounts, which, for example, in times of high inflation can be very significant.

Historical Cost, Specific Price Changes and the "Current Value" of Assets

In the measurement of income, the significance of the historical cost of assets is that it represents the monetary investment in the assets that must be recovered from revenue before income can be said to have been earned. A restatement of historical cost in dollars of constant purchasing power would allow the recovery from revenue of the purchasing power of investment as a precondition for determining income in "real" terms.

In some cases, historical cost (HC) may also be taken as affecting the current value of assets—as, for example, when tax-allowable depreciation is based on historical cost, or in the case of enterprises subject to price control based on historical cost, such as public utilities in the United States. In the business context, "current value" is a complex notion since it has no intrinsic meaning and has to be defined and interpreted in terms of specific attributes of business assets and their relevance to the determination and evaluation of results in a particular set of circumstances.

The following financial attributes may be used to determine the current value of business assets:

(1) *Present value (PV) of expected net receipts*. The present value of the expected net receipts associated with the use of assets in business operations plays a key role in determining the current value of business assets. PV is generally regarded as being too subjective to be used as a direct valuation basis in the accounting evaluation of operating results and state of affairs.

(2) *Replacement cost (RC)*. The replacement cost of assets represents the monetary outlay that would be necessary if the firm were to enter into its field of operations at current prices. Operating profit determined on the basis of RC gives a measure of the long-term viability of the firm's operations given current costs and prices.

(3) *Net realizable value (NRV)*. Net realizable value is a relevant basis for income measurement where a major objective of business operations is to earn income through increases in the market (realizable) value of assets, as in the case of investment companies. NRV also measures opportunity cost and may be regarded as a relevant basis for asset valuation in short-run operating situations, as in the case where returns are such that they do not justify the replacement of assets at current cost but provide an adequate rate of return on the NRV of assets.

Accounting for the Effects of Price and Price-Level Changes

Some proposals in the 1950s and early 1960s for dealing with the problem of price changes in the measurement of business income reflected the belief that the information value of conventional financial statements would be greatly enhanced if they were restated in dollars of constant purchasing power. Such restated financial statements, however, proved to be of limited value because while they attempted to deal with the effects of general price-level changes, they ignored the impact of specific price changes on the operations of business firms.

In the 1960s, a number of academics attempted to develop comprehensive theories for the measurement of business income in the face of price and price-level changes. One of the most important books on business income to come out in the period after World War II was Edgar O. Edwards, Hargrove Professor of Economics at Rice University, and Philip W. Bell's, professor of economics at Haverford College, *The Theory and Measurement of Business Income* (1961). According to Edwards and Bell, the principal function of accounting data was to serve as a fundamental tool in the evaluation of managerial decisions through comparisons of specified expectations with actual events. They attempted to reconcile the essentially subjective approach of economists to the measurement of income with the accountants' insistence on "objectivity and the measurement of actual, . . . often historic, events." The central concept of business income proposed by Edwards and Bell was that of "business profit" measured on the basis of replacement cost and consisting of (1) "current operating profit," represented by the excess of sales over the current-replacement cost of sales; and (2) "realizable cost savings" ("holding gains"), represented by the excess of current-replacement cost over the historical cost of assets acquired during the period or the replacement cost at the beginning of the period for assets already held.

R.S. Gynther, an Australian accounting academic, proposed income measurement based on replacement cost and the maintenance of the physical capital (operating capacity) of the firm. Under the proposal, the income of the firm is represented by operating profit measured by the difference between sales and replacement cost of sales and "holding gains" arising from changes in the replacement cost of assets being treated as restatements of capital rather than as components of business income.

R.J. Chambers, an accounting theorist from Australia, proposed net realizable value as a single measurement concept for all assets. The proposal is based on the argument that only like magnitudes may be properly added, subtracted, or related. The capital-maintenance concept employed is that of maintaining the general purchasing power of the shareholders' equity measured on the basis of the net realizable value of assets. Income for a period is then represented by increases in the shareholders' equity after restating the shareholders' equity at the beginning of the period for changes in the general purchasing power of money and adjusting the ending shareholders' equity for contributions to capital and distributions during the period.

Norton M. Bedford, a professor of accounting at the University of Illinois, in *Income Determination Theory: An Accounting Framework* (1965), provided an operational view of income measurement. He recognized that there are different concepts of income and that they change as society changes. However, he developed a model in which income is earned from four business operations: acquisition of service resources; holding service resources prior to use; recombining services to produce and deliver a product; and dispositon of services, from which comes revenue. Bedford's approach is an extremely broad one, including the communication of the model and the results of the model to users.

Value to the Owner
The value of assets to business operations depends on their expected use; this value may be formally quantified in terms of the present value (PV) of expected net receipts. Present value, however, is usually regarded as too subjective to be used as a direct basis of valuation in accounting. More objective measures of current value, therefore, have been sought in current market prices. The notion of "value to the owner," first introduced into the accounting literature in 1961 by David Solomons, professor of accounting at the Wharton School of the University of Pennsylvania, aims to provide a basis for making a choice between replacement cost (RC) and selling price (NRV) as relevant measures of current value (CV) when RC and NRV differ significantly.

Under "value to the owner," RC represents the upper limit of value on the ground that an asset is not worth to a business more than it would cost to acquire it at current prices. RC is a relevant basis for asset valuation where PV is greater than RC (that is, where the replacement of assets is a viable proposition in terms of ex-

pected returns). Along the same lines, NRV is regarded as the lower limit of value on the ground that an asset cannot be worth less to a business than the amount that would be received if the asset were sold. NRV is a relevant basis for asset valuation where RC is greater than PV (that is, where the asset is not worth replacing) and where NRV is greater than PV (that is, where the asset is not worth holding onto). The range of value between RC and NRV may be referred to as "value in use." Value in use is a relevant basis for asset valuation, presumably at PV, when PV is greater than NRV (that is, when the asset should be used rather than sold) and when RC is greater than PV (that is, when the asset should not be replaced at the end of its useful life). Valuation at value in use would indicate a short-run operation.

Summary
While the basic notion of business income as a monetary return on monetary investment is relatively simple, the measurement of income generated by business enterprises operating in a complex and dynamic economic environment creates some very complex problems. These problems include the need to value nonmonetary assets on the basis of expectations of future events, the lack of general agreement on how to deal with some important accounting issues including accounting for price changes, and the availability of alternative methods and procedures for dealing with problem areas of accounting measurement and reporting. As a result, accounting figures for income can be defined and interpreted only in terms of the specific accounting methods and procedures used to arrive at the income figure in each case; such income figures cannot be empirically tested.

The problems associated with income measurement have led to the questioning of the usefulness of the whole process. Some, like Solomons (1961), have predicted the demise of income measurement. Some have sought alternatives to income measurement in shifting emphasis to cash flows. Notwithstanding the problems discussed, income measurement continues to be the central issue in the financial-accounting process as income generation continues to be the central objective of business operations.

If one were to accept the subjective nature of income measurement as the unavoidable consequence of the nature of business operations in the contemporary environment, then improvement in income reporting and the uses of income data for decision making would require the exercise of responsible professional judgment by those preparing financial statements and those expressing an opinion on their fairness. There would have to be an adequate appreciation of the nature and limitations of accounting figures by decision makers.

Boris Popoff

Bibliography

Bedford, N.M. *Income Determination Theory: An Accounting Framework.* Reading, MA: Addison-Wesley, 1965.

Edwards, E.O., and P.W. Bell. *The Theory and Measurement of Business Income.* Berkeley: University of California Press, 1961.

Gynther, R.S. *Accounting for Price-Level Changes: Theory and Procedures.* Oxford: Pergamon, 1966.

Hicks, J.R. *Value and Capital.* 2d ed. Oxford: Clarendon, 1946.

Littleton, A.C. *Accounting Evolution to 1900.* New York: American Institute Publishing, 1933. Reprint. New York: Russell and Russell, 1966.

Moonitz, M. *Changing Prices and Financial Reporting.* Champaign, IL: Stipes, 1974.

Paton, W.A., and A.C. Littleton. *An Introduction to Corporate Accounting Standards.* American Accounting Association Monograph No. 3. New York: American Accounting Association, 1940.

Revsine, L. "Technological Changes and Replacement Costs: A Beginning," *Accounting Review*, April 1979, pp. 306–322.

Solomons, D. "Economic and Accounting Concepts of Income," *Accounting Review*, July 1961, pp. 374–383.

———. "The Twilight of Income Measurement: Twenty-five Years On," *Accounting Historians Journal*, Spring 1987, pp. 1–6.

Stamp, E. "Why Can Accounting Not Become a Science Like Physics?" *Abacus*, June 1981, pp. 13–27.

Sterling, R.R. "Relevant Financial Reporting in an Age of Price Changes," *Journal of Accountancy*, February 1975, pp. 42–51.

Sweeney, H.W. *Stabilized Accounting.* New York: Harper & Row, 1936.

See also AN INTRODUCTION TO CORPORATE ACCOUNTING STANDARDS; CAPITAL ACCOUNT; CHAMBERS, RAYMOND JOHN; COMPOUND INTEREST; CONTINUITY; EDWARDS AND BELL: REPLACEMENT-COST ACCOUNTING; HISTORICAL COST; INCOME STATEMENT/INCOME ACCOUNT; INFLATION ACCOUNTING; LITTLETON, A.C.; MATCHING; MAY, GEORGE OLIVER; MONEY; PACIOLI, LUCA; PERIODICITY; STUDY GROUP ON BUSINESS INCOME'S *FIVE MONOGRAPHS ON BUSINESS INCOME;* ZAPPA, GINO

Income Statement/Income Account

The income statement is a summary of the revenues and expenses of an accounting unit, or group of such units, for a specified period. The income statement did not become the formal report that it is now until the 1830s. However, it is clear that the income account was a vital part of management accounting in the early 1300s with the birth of double entry accounting. In his historic treatise on double entry, "Particularis de Computis et Scripturis," in *Summa de Arithmetica* (1494), Luca Pacioli described an income account that would be the repository of the profits and losses (really, gross profits) from different ventures, trips, inventory items, and miscellaneous income. For each of these items there would be a computation of gross profit or loss. To these amounts, expenses and extraordinary losses along with household expenses would be debited to the income account as a part of the closing process. The balancing figure was either net income or net loss and closed to the capital account. Others used and described this income account through the years, including Simon Stevin (1607), Robert Colinson from Scotland in 1683, and James Arlington Bennett from the United States in 1820. It is evident that the income account provided business owners much more information than the single entry approach, which measured net income as the difference between the beginning and ending balances of the capital account.

The income statement became a matter of public record in the 1830s with the beginning of the annual reports of railroads. It is interesting to note that the 1833 income statement of the Baltimore and Ohio Railroad was presented in the format of an income account. The securities of railroads were publicly traded and widely analyzed during the 1800s. Railroads were important investments for the cities on their lines. States were interested in information for regulatory purposes. Hence, analyses of railroad statements—those of business analyst Henry Varnum Poor are described by Alfred D.

Chandler (1988)—appeared in such sources as the *American Railroad Journal* and the *Manual of the Railroads of the United States*.

While income statements had long been included in the annual reports of railroads, the industrial trusts of the late 1800s and very early 1900s rarely included income statements. Net income was shown as a part of the earned surplus (retained-earnings account). However, there were important exceptions, such as United States Steel Corporation in 1901 and Westinghouse Corporation in 1911. In a study of 20 industrial companies, Richard Vangermeersch (1979) noted that it was not until 1930 that all 20 companies presented an income statement. This was despite repeated calls for such reports in editorials in the *Journal of Accountancy*.

There were definite signals that the accounting profession, the financial community, and governmental agencies favored the portrayal of a detailed income statement. In 1917, the Federal Reserve Board recommended in "Uniform Accounting" a format of a two-year comparative income statement with such captions as: net sales, cost of sales, gross profit on sales, selling expense, general expense, administrative expense, net profit on sales, other income, gross income, deductions from income, and net income. The statement continued with the inclusion of special credits, special charges, surplus beginning of period, dividends paid, and surplus ending of period. In 1929 in "Verification of Financial Statements," the Federal Reserve Board recommended the same format. In 1936 the American Institute of Accountants (AIA), in *Examination of Financial Statements by Independent Public Accountants*, dropped the computation of ending earned surplus in the income statement and combined other income with extraordinary income. The caption "other changes" involved interest, extraordinary charges, and provisions for income taxes. The Securities and Exchange Commission (SEC) in 1935 had recommended a similar format.

Three techniques that tended to equalize, or "smooth," earnings were once prevalent in accounting. The first of these was the use of "reserves" on the income statement for expenses anticipated for subsequent periods. This practice pretty much came to an end in 1947 with the publication of Accounting Research Bulletin (ARB) No. 31, "Inventory Reserves," following ARB No. 26 in 1946, "Accounting

for the Use of Special War Reserves," and ARB No. 28 in 1947, "Accounting Treatment of General Purpose Contingency Reserves." In the study cited above, Vangermeersch noted a total of 185 examples of such reserves for the 20 industrial companies he surveyed.

The second method to "smooth" earnings was the use of the earned-surplus account (now called retained earnings) for what were felt to be unusual credits and charges. There have been many official promulgations that have limited the use of such items. A prohibition of some of these credits and charges occurred in 1947 in ARB No. 32, "Income and Earned Surplus." A further narrowing of this technique occurred in 1966 in Accounting Principles Board (APB) Opinion No. 9, "Reporting the Results of Operations," and again in 1977 in Financial Accounting Standard (FAS) No. 16, "Prior Period Adjustments." Vangermeersch concluded that five of the 20 companies he analyzed could have been perceived as possible abusers of the earned-surplus account. Overall he found total charges of $1.71 billion compared to total credits of $1.54 billion. Hence, he did not issue a general castigation of management on this issue.

The third of the income "smoothing" techniques dealt with the use of extraordinary charges and credits to remove items from the calculation of operating income. ARB No. 32, "Income and Earned Surplus" (1947), when it removed some items from the earned-surplus account, probably caused more activity in the extraordinary classifications. Both the previously mentioned APB No. 9, issued in 1966, and APB No. 30, "Reporting the Results of Operations," in 1973 further limited the classification of extraordinary items. On this issue, Vangermeersch felt that eight of the 20 companies he reviewed were probably abusive of the extraordinary items. He noted 322 debits, totaling $596 million, and 93 credits, totaling $443 million, for the 20 companies. Since conservatism tends to encourage the writing down of assets, he was unwilling to make a general castigation of management.

A related income-statement topic is earnings per share, which has had a checkered history in accounting. In his study, Vangermeersch found that it was first used in 1925, and that by 1960 all 20 companies were reporting this figure. Information about earnings per share first appeared in the 1923 edition of *Poor's and Moody's Industrials* in the analysis of 1922 data. The term was not explained in that year but was by the 1925 publication of *Moody's Industrials.* Apparently, the first mention in the *Wall Street Journal* of earnings per share occurred in an April 14, 1915, article in which Charles M. Schwab, president of Bethlehem Steel, mentioned earnings per share for 1913 and 1914 in a news story entitled "Facts Versus Fancies in Bethlehem Steel Rise." In an August 4, 1915, article Schwab discussed projected earnings per share.

The first mention of the topic in the *Journal of Accountancy* appeared in an April 1930 article of a tutorial nature by Andreas Natvig on the computation of earnings per share. In May 1930, two editorials in the *Journal of Accountancy* were very critical of the concept and the portrayal of the figure. There were occasional debates in various journals until APB No. 9 in 1966 first officially recognized earnings per share as an accounting figure and APB No. 15, "Earnings Per Share" (1969), detailed computational rules for it. More than 50 years had gone by before earnings per share became anointed as generally accepted.

Another income-statement topic of historical note is the single-step format versus the multiple-step format. This controversy sprung from the desire in the late 1930s of corporate management, as expressed by the National Association of Manufacturers, to have the annual reports become simple so that the readers would be more supportive of the private-enterprise economy. The most articulate argument for the single-step income statement came from William Andrew Paton, from the University of Michigan, in 1943. There are different gradations of the format of the income statement, so it is at times too simplistic just to categorize a particular format as being either the single-step approach or the multiple-step approach. This is especially true in the light of the additions to the income statement mandated in such opinions as the previously mentioned APB No. 30, issued in 1973, and APB No. 20, "Accounting Changes" (1971).

To summarize, management has utilized the income account from the 1300s and has presented an income statement to the public since about the 1830s. It took about 100 more years to arrive at an income statement as we know it now for all companies in their public reports. Much attention in the later half of the twentieth century has been paid to the components of the income statement, an effort to minimize the attempts by management to "smooth" or manipulate earnings. The income account/income statement has been a vital tool for management since the 1300s. The income statement and the income-statement orientation of accountants is not just a function of the tightening of accounting rules and the increased disclosure that occurred during and after the Great Depression.

Richard Vangermeersch

Bibliography

American Institute of Accountants. *Examination of Financial Statements by Independent Public Accountants.* New York: AIA, 1936.

Bennett, J.A. *The American System of Practical Book-keeping.* Abm. Paul, 1820.

Brief, R.P. "Corporate Financial Reporting at the Turn of the Century," *Journal of Accountancy,* May 1987, pp. 142–157.

Brown, C.D. *The Emergence of Income Reporting: An Historical Study.* East Lansing: Michigan State University, 1971.

Chandler, A.D. "Henry Varnum Poor: Business Analyst." In *The Essential Alfred Chandler: Essays toward an Historical Theory of Big Business,* edited by T.K. McGraw, pp. 22–45. Boston: Harvard Business School Press, 1988.

Colinson, R. *Idea Rationaria.* Edinburgh: Lindsay, Kniblo, Van Solingen, and Colman, 1683.

"Earnings Not an Accurate Index," *Journal of Accountancy,* May 1930, pp. 324–325.

"Earnings per Share," *Journal of Accountancy,* May 1930, pp. 323–324.

McMickle, P.L., and R. Vangermeersch. *The Origins of a Great Profession.* Memphis: Academy of Accounting Historians, 1987.

Natvig, A.S. "Earnings per Share," *Journal of Accountancy,* April 1930, pp. 251–263.

Paton, W.A. "Adaptation of the Income Statement to Present Conditions," *Journal of Accountancy,* January 1943, pp. 8–15.

Salvage, J.P., and M.M. Lee. *Making the Annual Report Speak for Industry: Compiled by the National Association of Manufacturers.* New York: McGraw-Hill, 1938.

Stevin, Simon. *Vorstelicke Bouckhouding op de Italiaensche Wyse in Domeine en Finance Extraordinaire.* Leyden: Ian Bouwensz, 1607.

U.S. Federal Reserve Board. "Uniform Accounting," *Journal of Accountancy*, June 1917, pp. 401–433.

———. "Verification of Financial Statements," *Journal of Accountancy*, May 1929, pp. 321–353.

Vangermeersch, R. "Comments on Accounting Disclosures in the Baltimore and Ohio Annual Reports from 1828 through 1850." Working paper no. 38 in *Working Paper Series Volume 2*, edited by E.N. Coffman, pp. 318–337. Richmond, VA: Academy of Accounting Historians, 1979.

———. "Earnings per Share, the Multiple, and Book Value: A Look Back at U.S. Steel." In *Collected Papers of the Sixth World Congress of Accounting Historians*, vol. 3, pp. 1281–1308. Kyoto: Accounting History Association, 1992.

———. *Financial Reporting Techniques in Twenty Industrial Companies since 1861*. Gainesville: University Presses of Florida, 1979.

See also ACCOUNTING PRINCIPLES BOARD; ACCOUNTING RESEARCH BULLETINS; ACCRUAL ACCOUNTING; BALANCE SHEET; BALL AND BROWN'S "AN EMPIRICAL EVALUATION OF ACCOUNTING INCOME NUMBERS"; BRANCH ACCOUNTING; CAPITAL ACCOUNT; CREDIT; DE PAULA, FREDERIC RUDOLF MACKLEY; FINANCIAL-STATEMENT ANALYSIS; HATFIELD, HENRY RAND; INCOME-DETERMINATION THEORY; MANIPULATION OF INCOME; PACIOLI, LUCA; PATON, WILLIAM ANDREW; PROPRIETORSHIP; RAILROAD ACCOUNTING (U.S.); RETAINED EARNINGS; STEVIN, SIMON; *UNIFORM ACCOUNTING;* UNITED STATES STEEL CORPORATION

Income Taxation in the United States

Alexander Hamilton said in *The Federalist Papers* (No. 30) that "a complete power . . . to procure a regular and adequate supply of revenue . . . may be regarded as an indispensable ingredient in every constitution." The tariff provided most of this revenue for the first 100 years of the United States. Over 100 years later, the personal income tax has become the primary supplier of federal revenue.

The use of income taxes as a revenue source was generally motivated by the need to pay the expenses of war in the early history of the United States. The first proposal for an income tax was in answer to the revenue needs generated by the War of 1812. At the time, taxes were generally tariffs, excise taxes, property taxes (including slaves), and inheritance taxes.

The first federal income tax was imposed during the Civil War. Legislation enacted by Congress in 1861 seemed to leave no source of potential revenue untouched as it taxed income "derived from any kind of property, or from any profession, trade, employment, or vocation carried on in the United States or elsewhere, or from any other source whatever" (Act of August 5, 1861). The 1861 act generated some controversy concerning whether the intent of the law was to tax net or gross profits, since only property taxes were explicitly allowed as a deduction against income. The act allowed for a 3 percent tax on all income over $800. The first special provision in income tax law allowed a 1.5 percent tax rate on interest from government bonds.

However, the 1861 act was so poorly drafted that it never became operative, and in 1862 Congress replaced it with a more workable law. The 1862 act attempted to further define gains, profits, and income as net rather than gross. It also put forth the first progressive tax rate schedule. Income between $600 and $10,000 was taxed at 3 percent; income over $10,000, at 5 percent. Legislation enacted in 1864 further confirmed the net-income concept and explicitly stated several allowable deductions, including casualty losses, trade or business losses, and bad-debt losses. It also gradually increased the top marginal tax rate to 10 percent.

The constitutionality of the 1864 act was challenged, but the Civil War ended and the income tax statutes were repealed by the time the Supreme Court found in *Springer v. United States (1880)* 102 US 586, 598–599 (1880) that the Civil War income tax was an excise tax rather than a direct tax on the underlying property and was, therefore, constitutional.

The Reconstruction era generated additional demands on federal revenue. A federal income tax was enacted in 1870 to meet those needs, but it was repealed in 1872. The drive for an income tax was dormant until the late 1800s, when the Populists and many members of the Democratic Party pushed for the passage of a personal income tax. The Income Tax Act of 1894 was passed when the Democratic Party controlled both houses of Congress and the presidency, although the Supreme Court, with its control by Republican Party appointees, quickly ruled the act unconstitutional.

Support for the income tax varied by geographical region. The agricultural South had little income or wealth and preferred an income tax over tariffs, excise, and property taxes. The more industrial North preferred those taxes to an income tax. This stance was understandable; one-third of the tax revenue from the Civil War and Reconstruction-era income taxes was collected from New York residents alone.

In its last decision regarding the constitutionality of a personal income tax before the passage of the Sixteenth Amendment in 1913, the Supreme Court, by a 5-4 vote, found the Income Tax Act of 1894 unconstitutional in *Pollock v. Farmers' Loan and Trust Company (1895) 158 US 601 (1895)*. The court considered the 1894 levy on income from real and personal property to be an unapportioned direct tax and thus in violation of Article 1 of the Constitution. Although the Court found the entire act unconstitutional because of this legal flaw, the portion of the act imposing an income tax on wages would not have been unconstitutional if it had stood alone, because such a tax would not have been considered a direct tax on property.

In 1906, President Theodore Roosevelt proposed an income tax on both income and estates. In 1909 Republican Progressives in Congress, known as the Insurgents, and Democrats, led by William Jennings Bryan, began supporting a constitutional amendment allowing a personal income tax as a solution to the problem of high tariffs.

The 61st Congress proposed the Sixteenth Amendment in July 1909, and the amendment was adopted in February 1913. After the 1912 elections, when the Democrats controlled both the presidency and Congress, the Revenue Act of 1913 was passed. There were many subsequent attempts to declare the personal income tax unconstitutional, largely based on the idea that the ratification process of the Sixteenth Amendment was flawed. However, the Supreme Court has consistently upheld the validity of the Sixteenth Amendment and the constitutionality of an income tax.

With the constitutional problems of the early income taxes solved, the Revenue Act of 1913 was passed. The income tax imposed by the act was generally nominal, as it only im-posed a normal tax rate of 1 percent on all income over an allowed exemption amount. However, the act did provide for a progressive rate structure. Beginning at income levels of $20,000, surcharges up to 6 percent were added to the normal tax, making the top marginal tax rate 7 percent on incomes over $500,000. Every taxpayer received an exemption of at least $3,000, with married couples receiving a $4,000 exemption. All income was treated similarly—there was no distinction made between capital gains and other forms of income. However, not all taxpayers were treated alike. The current president and sitting judges were exempted from the income tax, as were state and local government employees. State and local bond interest was exempted from the federal income tax because of a contention that the federal taxation of this interest would violate the Constitution. The 1913 act excluded life-insurance proceeds, gifts, and inheritances from income and allowed deductions for all personal and business taxes and interest, business expenses, casualty losses, and dividends received from corporations subject to an income tax.

An increasing deficit and the onset of World War I created new revenue needs, and revenue acts were passed in rapid succession in 1917 and 1918. By the time the Revenue Act of 1918 passed, personal exemptions were lowered to $1,000 for single persons and $2,000 for married couples. Normal tax rates for individuals were 5 percent on incomes below $4,000 and 12 percent on incomes above $4,000, with surtaxes increased up to a 65 percent maximum rate. Thus, by 1918 the top individual tax rate grew to 77 percent from the 7 percent top rate contained in the 1913 act. Additionally, normal tax rates for corporations were increased from 2 percent to 4 percent, and an excess-profits tax was created with tax rates as high as 60 percent.

Under the 1913 act, only 2 percent of U.S. workers paid any income tax, and federal revenues were only moderately affected by the income tax. By the end of World War I, income tax revenue accounted for almost 60 percent of federal receipts, although most of this revenue was collected from corporations paying the excess-profits tax.

The first major movement to reduce income taxes followed close behind this rapid escalation of income tax burdens. In the 1920s, Andrew Mellon, the secretary of the treasury appointed by President Warren G. Harding, argued for lower taxes, using what became known 60 years later as supply-side economics. The 1920s did become a period of tax reduction, with individual rates falling from 77 to 24 percent and corporation rates also falling considerably. The legacy of the revenue acts of the 1920s was the introduction of differential taxation of capital gains and losses and earned versus unearned income along with the creation of a special federal tax court known as the Board of Tax Appeals.

The Great Depression reversed the tax-reduction trend of the 1920s, and the tax acts of the 1930s generally raised income taxes back to the level of the 1924 act. Revenue acts appeared annually from the mid-1930s through the end of World War II. The proliferation of revenue acts since 1913 resulted in their first codification in 1939, producing the Internal Revenue Code of 1939.

The tax changes of the Franklin D. Roosevelt years were substantial and influential. The income tax base was expanded considerably with a tripling of the number of individual taxpayers. Along with this expansion of the income tax burden to the middle class, and tax rates on some as high as 93 percent, many more special provisions were enacted, adding to the complexity of the income tax system. Most significantly, a pay-as-you-go withholding system was instituted.

After World War II, the general desire to reduce the income tax to prewar levels was met with resistance by President Harry S. Truman. He vetoed a 1947 tax-reduction bill three times and sustained a congressional attempt to overturn the vetoes. The New Deal policies of the previous decade and the lasting influence of the war spending lessened the desire of both Presidents Truman and Dwight D. Eisenhower to reduce taxes. A tax-reduction bill was eventually passed over Truman's veto, but the level of income taxation still greatly exceeded prewar tax levels.

Partly because of the costs of the Korean conflict, revenue acts between 1950 and 1952 again raised income taxes. However, many special tax provisions in current tax law were born in these acts. These include exclusions of gain from the sale of a personal residence, exclusion of foreign earned income, and the allowance of a deduction for medical expenses.

The major tax legislation during the Eisenhower administration was the first rewriting of the Internal Revenue Code. Although the numerous revenue acts since 1913 had been codified in 1939, and the Internal Revenue Code of 1939 had been updated for all the revenue-act changes since 1939, the Internal Revenue Code was woefully complicated, inconsistent, and confusing. The rewriting eventually produced the Internal Revenue Code of 1954, a document that stood almost unchanged until 1962. Although improved both substantively and administratively, the 1954 code continued the trend of increased complexity through its myriad of special exclusions, deductions, and credits. Special provisions were enacted dealing with issues such as child care and employer-provided health and retirement benefits. Increasingly complex organizational forms also produced greater specificity in the tax law.

The 1960s produced two major tax bills: the 1964 and 1969 tax acts. The major push of the Kennedy administration was to reduce tax rates for individuals and corporations and to close tax "loopholes." The Revenue Act of 1962 was generally modest, but it did first introduce the investment tax credit to the income tax system. This credit would remain controversial over the next three decades, with changes or repeal taking place every few years. The 1962 act also introduced for the first time a more comprehensive approach to the taxation of U.S.-owned companies in foreign countries. The 1962 act marked the end of the last period of extended tax-policy stability for the next 30 years. The Revenue Act of 1964 substantially lowered tax rates for both individuals and corporations and added several new provisions that further reduced tax burdens. The standard deduction was introduced, simplifying the tax-filing process for both taxpayers and tax administrators.

By the end of the 1960s, the increased deficits caused by the war in Vietnam led to calls for new tax revenues. This new demand for revenue occurred while the Treasury Department was examining the issue of tax reform. The Tax Reform Act of 1969 evolved from these two disparate objectives. The passage of the 1969 act heralded the modern age of tax legislation and income tax policy. Complexity wrought complexity as provisions to "reform" income tax laws added several new layers of detailed statutory language. For example, the so-called "maximum tax" provision introduced a top tax rate of 50 percent on earned income (compared to the 70 percent maximum tax rate on unearned income). The "minimum tax" also was created by the 1969 act in an attempt to close many of the tax "loopholes" that, ironically, were being concurrently handed out by Congress. The investment tax credit suffered a short-lived repeal.

The early 1970s was a period of tax reduction, with acts such as the Tax Reduction Act of 1971 and the Tax Reduction Act of 1975. The investment tax credit was reinstated during this period, and a new retirement provision, the Individual Retirement Account, was created.

Later in the decade, reform reared its head again and resulted in the Tax Reform Act of 1976. Calls for the integration of corporate and individual taxation were increasing, and work was being discussed that resulted in the important 1977 book *Blueprints for Basic Tax Reform* by the U.S. Treasury Tax Policy Staff. The 1976 act introduced many provisions against tax shelters to address the complaints that the wealthy were using "loopholes" to unfairly reduce their tax burden. Perhaps the most controversial provision of the 1976 act was its call for a "carryover" basis for assets received by inheritance. This tax-increasing provision was delayed and repealed before it became effective. On the other end of the income distribution, the 1976 act extended the earned-income credit and the general tax credit.

The 1970s ended with two additional tax-reduction acts. The most significant new provision to come out of the Tax Reduction and Simplification Act of 1977 was the jobs tax credit, a mechanism that allowed employers to significantly reduce the early years' costs of hiring certain employees. A tax-reduction law passed in 1978 repealed the general tax credit and extended the jobs credit. A twist on the "minimum tax," called the "alternative minimum tax," also was introduced.

The 1980s saw some of the most significant and frequent changes to income tax law in the post–World War II period. Tax reduction and simplification were the goals of the Reagan administration, and supply-side economics moved to the forefront in the debate over tax policy. The Economic Recovery Tax Act of 1981 substantially reduced taxes across the income distribution and introduced many of the "reform" provisions that had been debated during the previous decade. The top individual tax rate was reduced to 50 percent, Individual Retirement Account rules were expanded to cover more taxpayers, and depreciation rules were simplified and liberalized. The provision of the 1981 act that had the most impact was the introduction of the indexing of tax brackets, standard deductions, and exemption amounts. The liberalized depreciation rules, combined with other features of the 1981 act, increased tax-shelter activity and set the stage for the eventual 1986 reforms.

The quickly mounting deficits of the early 1980s led to an immediate move to counter the tax reduction of the 1981 act. The Tax Equity and Fiscal Responsibility Act of 1982 and the Deficit Reduction Act of 1984 scaled back the benefits of accelerated depreciation and the investment tax credit, although not to pre-1981 levels. These acts contained further attempts to reduce the benefits of tax shelters.

The combination of rising deficits and calls for tax simplification set the stage for the most significant base-broadening tax reform of the post–World War II period. The Tax Reform Act of 1986 attempted to reverse at least 40 years of tax policy, which had produced numerous special tax breaks. The intent of the 1986 act was to create a level playing field and reduce the tax-driven decisions of the 1970s and early 1980s. The 1986 act lowered marginal tax rates significantly and considerably expanded the tax base. The changes produced by the Tax Reform Act of 1986 were so substantial that the tax code was renamed the Internal Revenue Code of 1986, the first change since 1954.

The late 1980s and early 1990s was a period of relative stability in tax policy. Although several revenue acts were passed—generally for the purpose of increasing revenue—the reforms put in place by the 1986 act remained intact. Substantive changes in the 1990s were a return to slightly more progressive tax-rate schedules, but the small rate increases of the 1993 tax act left the rate schedule less progressive than pre-1986 rates.

The income tax began in the United States as an emergency measure, generally imposed only during times of war or drastic revenue needs. Its growth over the twentieth century was caused by a combination of increased federal revenue demands and an increased willingness to use the tax law as an instrument of economic and social change.

Gary A. McGill

Bibliography

Blakey, R.G., and G.C. Blakey. *The Federal Income Tax*. New York: Longmans, Green, 1940.

Hansen, S.B. *The Politics of Taxation*. New York: Praeger, 1983.

Paul, R.E. *Taxation in the United States*. Boston: Little, Brown & Co., 1954.

Roberts, M.L., and W.D. Samson. "Historical Survey of the Progressivity of the U.S. Income Tax," *Accounting Historians Notebook*, Spring 1989, pp. 11–13.

Steuerle, C.E. *The Tax Decade*. Washington, DC: Urban Institute Press, 1992.

Waltman, J.L. *Political Origins of the U.S. Income Tax*. Jackson, MS: University Press of Mississippi, 1985.

Witte, J.F. *The Politics and Development of the Federal Income Tax*. Madison, WI: University of Wisconsin Press, 1985.

See also BASE STOCK METHOD; *BRUSHABER V. UNION PACIFIC RAILROAD COMPANY;* DEPRECIATION; *DOYLE V. MITCHELL BROTHERS COMPANY; EISNER V. MACOMBER; FLINT V. STONE TRACY COMPANY;* GREGORY CASE; HISTORICAL COST; MONTGOMERY, ROBERT HIESTER; NATURAL BUSINESS YEAR; OBJECTIVITY; PERIODICITY; *POLLOCK V. FARMERS' LOAN AND TRUST COMPANY;* REALIZATION; SIXTEENTH AMENDMENT; *SPRINGER V. UNITED STATES;* TAX REFORM ACTS

Independence of External Auditors

Independence provides the accounting profession with a philosophical and historical foundation. At one time, independence was assumed to mean integrity, honesty, and objectivity. Another interpretation has referred to freedom from the control of those whose records are being reviewed. Independence has also been characterized as a state of mind and a matter of character.

Thus, independence is considered to be the cornerstone of the profession. The certified public accountant (CPA) must not subordinate his judgment to clients, bankers, or governmental agencies. In addition, the CPA must avoid relationships that would be likely to impair objectivity, permit personal bias, or affect professional judgment.

Concern in the United States regarding auditor independence grew slower than it did in England. The American Association of Public Accountants (AAPA) was established in 1887 and did not initially incorporate independence in its constitution or bylaws. By 1900 evidence of the development of the concept was beginning to appear in literature. In 1907 the bylaws of the AAPA were amended to recognize the importance of avoiding inconsistent or incompatible occupations.

An incident in 1915 is noteworthy since it anticipated the intense debates to occur years later on the subject of independence. A question arose regarding the propriety of a public accounting firm auditing statements in which a member of the firm was also the internal auditor. In 1926 the report of the American Institute of Accountants' (AIA) Committee on Professional Ethics posed the question of whether it is ethical for a CPA who is a director of a company to also certify the company's balance sheet. The question of an auditor who was also a stockholder came up two years later.

Although there had been a growing number of references to the independence of auditors in the professional literature, the word "independence" was still absent from the Rules of Professional Conduct. Although several rules already adopted were designed implicitly to strengthen independence, there was an absence of explicit discussions regarding relationships with clients that might tend to impair independence or appear to do so.

The Securities Act of 1933 required a public accountant or certified public accountant to express an opinion regarding the financial statements that accompany a registration statement. Additionally, there was concern for the independence of the auditors. A rule was adopted in 1933 by the Federal Trade Commission, the federal agency that administered the Securities Act of 1933 until the 1934 formation of the Securities and Exchange Commission, that said that any CPA or public accountant would not be recognized as independent if such an accountant was not, in fact, independent. Consequently, the concept of auditing independence was evolving from one of integrity and honesty with respect to fraud detection to one of fraud detection plus the objective application of accounting principles to describe the true economic and financial position and results of a firm.

While the Securities and Exchange Commission (SEC) rule prohibited any financial interest, the AIA passed a resolution in 1934 prohibiting a "substantial financial interest." In 1936 the SEC rule was amended to agree with the AIA position. Thereafter, disputes developed over the meaning of "substantial."

The SEC exerted leadership during the 1930s concerning the determination of what constituted independence. This was evidenced by its issuance of Accounting Series Release (ASR) No. 2, "Independence of Accountants: Relationship to Registrant" in 1937. This was the first release to describe specific cases in which accountants had been found to be not independent. The first release referred to a case in which an accountant was not independent because he owned stock in a client corporation, the value of which accounted for more than one percent of his personal fortune.

It was not until 1940 that the AIA adopted a rule of professional conduct regarding financial independence to replace its 1934 resolution. After modifications of this rule were made in 1942, independence was seen to be impaired if the auditor or his immediate family owned or was committed to buy a financial interest in an enterprise that was substantial in relation to its capital or to his own personal fortune.

At about this same time, the SEC was issuing ASRs regarding auditing independence. ASR No. 22, "Independence of Accountants: Indemnification by Registrant" (1941), contains an excellent summary of the SEC's attitude toward the general question of independence. It states that the main objective of total independence is to assure the impartiality and objectivity needed for fair consideration of problems arising in an audit. Any circumstances that might be likely to bias the mind of the auditor may be considered evidence of the lack of independence.

Then, in 1944, ASR No. 47, "Independence of Certifying Accountants: Summary of Past Releases of the Commission and a Compilation of Hitherto Unpublished Cases or Inquiries Arising Under Several of the Acts Administered by the Commission," listed and summarized 20 rulings on auditors' independence in specific cases. These ranged from fairly clear-cut situations to other situations in which it was not very clear that the relationships were likely to impair independence.

It was not until 1947 that a specific definition of independence was formulated by the AIA. The AIA defined independence in its "Tentative Statement of Auditing Standards" as a state of mind—an impartial attitude regarding the auditor's findings. The auditor should be able to render judgment unaffected by any self-interest that could influence his opinion. Key characteristics of the independence concept thus include honest disinterest, unbiased judgment, objective consideration of facts, and judicial

impartiality. Independence "in fact" is emphasized in this document.

The AIA also noted that rules of conduct only dealt with objective standards and, accordingly, could not assure independence. Since independence is a state of mind, its existence is at a much deeper level than the visible display of standards.

In 1950 the SEC amended its rule on independence by omitting the word "substantial" from the phrase "any substantial interest." This change was prompted because the SEC was tired of debates regarding the essence of a "substantial" financial interest. It was not until 1962 that the American Institute of Certified Public Accountants (AICPA) moved to disallow the direct financial interest or material indirect financial interest in a firm being audited by a member. Thus, during a 12-year period, a double standard existed. No direct financial interest was allowed for SEC engagements and no substantial direct financial interest was permitted for non-SEC engagements.

In 1960 the AICPA Committee on Professional Ethics proposed an amendment of the rules of conduct to prohibit any member from serving as an employee or director of a firm for which he was the auditor or from having any financial interest in such a firm. After a long and vigorous debate, the proposal was voted on and passed at the AICPA's 1961 annual meeting. In effect, the rule moved the AICPA closer to the SEC position.

In 1961, Robert K. Mautz, professor of accounting at the University of Illinois, and Hussein A. Sharaf, professor of accounting at the University of Cairo, published a monograph called *The Philosophy of Auditing*, which included a critical examination of the concept of independence. One important aspect of independence addressed was whether the rendering of management services to a client is likely to impair a CPA's independence in expressing an opinion on the financial statements.

Practitioners were disturbed to learn that the propriety of offering management services was being challenged. The AICPA Committee on Professional Ethics believed that an authoritative opinion on this question was needed to guide the membership. Therefore, in 1963 the committee issued its Opinion No. 12, "Independence." The opinion stated that there was no likelihood of a conflict of interest arising from the offering of management advisory services and tax services. It was, therefore, ethical to offer such services.

This statement did not satisfy the academic accountants. Several conducted surveys indicating that approximately half of those surveyed believed that the provision of management services tended to impair audit independence (Schulte, 1965).

In response, the AICPA appointed in 1966 a special ad hoc committee on independence to study the problem. The committee stated in 1969 in its final report that it had found no substantive evidence to indicate that the provision of management services had, in fact, impaired independence. However, it also found no empirical evidence to dispute findings linking management services with an "apparent" lack of independence. The committee suggested the use of the audit committee of the board of directors to determine questions relating to the appearance of independence and proposed management advisory services. In addition, the CPAs should report periodically to the audit committee regarding all services rendered.

In 1972, the SEC issued ASR No. 126, "Independence of Accountants: Guidelines and Examples of Situations Involving the Independence of Accountants," which covered several areas, including: (1) The provision of guidelines for determining the existence of independence; (2) a listing of example situations in which independence could be challenged; (3) a statement that the basic consideration in management-service activities was whether the client appears to be completely dependent upon the CPA's judgment and skill or is reliant only to the extent that is customary with respect to consultation advice; (4) a statement that systems design is a proper function of a public accountant and that computer programming is an aspect of systems design and does not constitute a bookkeeping service; (5) a statement that when unpaid fees to the accountant become material relative to the current audit fee, a question may arise regarding the accountant's independence; and (6) a statement that joint business ventures with clients, limited partnership agreements, investments in supplies or customer companies, and rental of blocks of computer time to a client would adversely affect independence.

In 1973 the AICPA adopted new rules of conduct (Rule 101), which required accountants to issue opinions about the fairness of presentation of financial statements only if they are independent both in fact and in appearance. Rule 101 was modified slightly in 1978. Neither the Commission on Auditor's Responsibility (also known as the Cohen Commission after its chairman, Manuel F. Cohen, former Commissioner of the SEC) in 1978 nor the Public Oversight Board of the SEC Practice Section of the AICPA in 1979 changed the status of MAS in relationship to independence (Goodwin and Younkins, 1990). This status continues through the mid-1990s.

Edward W. Younkins

Bibliography

Carey, J.L., and Doherty, W.O. "The Concept of Independence: Review and Restatement," *Journal of Accountancy*, January 1966, pp. 38–48.

DeVore, M.M. "Compatibility of Auditing and Management Services: A Viewpoint from within the Profession," *Journal of Accountancy*, December 1967, pp. 36–39.

"Final Report of Ad Hoc Committee on Independence," *Journal of Accountancy*, December 1969, pp. 51–56.

Goodwin, S., and E.W. Younkins. "How the Expanding Scope of CPA Services Threatens Accountants' Claim to Independence," *Practical Accountant*, September 1990, pp. 92–94, 96, 98–99.

Hurdman, F.H. "Independence of Auditors," *Journal of Accountancy*, January 1942, pp. 57–58.

"Independence and Services to Management" (editorial), *Journal of Accountancy*, November 1963, p. 44.

Littleton, A.C. "Auditor Independence," *Journal of Accountancy*, April 1935, pp. 286–291.

Mautz, R.K., and H.A. Sharaf. *The Philosophy of Auditing*. Sarasota, FL: American Accounting Association, 1961.

Previts, G.J. *The Scope of CPA Services: A Study of the Development of the Concept of Independence and the Profession's Role in Society*. New York: Wiley, 1985.

Schulte, A.A. Jr. "Compatibility of Management Consulting and Auditing," *Accounting Review*, October 1965, pp. 587–593.

See also AMERICAN INSTITUTE OF CERTIFIED PUBLIC ACCOUNTANTS; BIG EIGHT ACCOUNTING FIRMS; CHIEF ACCOUNTANTS OF THE SE-

CURITIES AND EXCHANGE COMMISSION; COHEN COMMISSION: COMMISSION ON AUDITORS' RESPONSIBILITIES; CONGRESSIONAL VIEWS; ETHICS, PROFESSIONAL; EXTERNAL AUDITING; FRAUD AND AUDITING; MANAGEMENT ADVISORY SERVICES BY CPAs; MAUTZ, ROBERT K.; SECURITIES AND EXCHANGE COMMISSION; TRUEBLOOD, ROBERT MARTIN

India (600 B.C.–A.D. 1856)

For many centuries, the subcontinent that includes the areas of present-day India, Pakistan, and Bangladesh was subject to provincial rule. Central rule was rare, although a strong province did sometimes dominate its own and other regions of this huge and populous area.

The first Indian Empire (325–150 B.C.) was ruled by the Mauryan dynasty. A book written during that time, the *Arthsastra*, described the political economy. The financial base for the imperial system was provided by the income from land revenue and, to a lesser extent, from trade. There appears to have been a large and recognizable body of administrators, and offices for a treasurer, who kept accounts, and a chief collector, who was responsible for revenue records. The emperor sent officers on inspection every five years for an additional audit and check on provincial administration. The village was the basic administrative unit.

This administrative pattern continued through the years in other dynasties, including the Guptas in northern India (A.D. 320–540), the Muslim Hegemony (A.D. 1200–1526), the Bahmani Dynasty (A.D. 1347–1527), the Vijayanagar Empire (A.D. 1336–1646) and the Mughal Empire (A.D. 1526–1761). The land tax appears to have been a constant as the most important source of revenue. By the mid-1700s, European influences became quite strong; by the late 1700s, the British dominated through the East India Company. British rule brought with it Western-type business records. By 1857 the British had complete political control of India.

As with ancient Greece and Rome, accounting scholars have examined surviving sources to detect the presence of a double entry system in India. In a 1986 article, B.M. Lall Nigam at the Delhi School of Economics (India) attempted to relate the accounting references in the *Arthsastra* and the *Manu Samhita* to double entry, though his efforts were disputed

the following year in an article by Christopher W. Nobes at the University of Reading (U.K.). In 1992, Michael E. Scorgie at La Trobe University (Australia) and Somendra Chandra Nandy, a historian from Calcutta (India) were unable to find documentary evidence of double entry but did present a close look at late-eighteenth-century accounting in India. Double entry aside, the Indian literature does give evidence of the importance of accounting and accountants in the administration of early governments.

Richard Vangermeersch

Bibliography

"India," *The New Encyclopaedia Britannica: Macropedia*. 15th ed, vol. 21. Chicago: Encyclopaedia Britannica, 1991.

Lall Nigam, B.M. "Bahi-Khata: The Pre-Pacioli Indian Double-Entry System of Bookkeeping," *Abacus*, September 1986, pp. 148–161.

Nobes, C.W. "The Pre-Pacioli Indian Double-Entry System of Bookkeeping: A Comment," *Abacus*, September 1987, pp. 182–184.

Scorgie, M.E., and S.C. Nandy. "Emerging Evidence of Early Indian Accounting," *Abacus*, March 1992, pp. 88–97.

See also GREECE; ROME (509 B.C.–A.D. 476)

Industrial Relations and Accounting

Industrial relations and accounting interface in a way not unlike the familiar financial/managerial distinction—that is, accounting information may be provided to labor leaders in the form of financial reports, or compiled for labor costs and used by management.

Labor leaders have consistently decried the inability of general-purpose financial statements to assist them in collective bargaining. They have often requested special financial statements that incorporate such items as changes in productivity data, competitor-related performance, explicit impact of inflation, and ability to absorb wage increases, but these data are rarely if ever provided by the accounting department. Papers by Brubaker (1948), O'Farrell (1965), and Pillsbury (1958) were early and clear enunciations of labor's information needs and continuing frustrations with the accounting profession. Craft (1981) identified important factors that impact the labor-management relationship and influence the extent that accounting information is disclosed voluntarily.

The collection of labor cost and productivity data is typically considered management's prerogative; however, there have been instances in which more accommodative endeavors have emerged. The nature of collective-bargaining structures and the level of interfirm competition are two key factors that have dictated the extent to which cost and productivity data have been mutually developed and shared in the United States textile industry. For example, in the men's clothing industry, data surrounding several pre-1920 collective-bargaining agreements indicate that production standards were jointly developed, mutually beneficial, and helped to stabilize sales prices and labor costs (Tyson, 1993). In the vast majority of industries, however, labor-management relations have been characterized by mistrust, antagonism, and conflict. In these industries, production standards were often imposed without labor's input, and labor-cost information was used exclusively by management, primarily for cost reduction and control purposes.

Since the early 1980s, a number of articles have appeared in *Accounting, Organizations, and Society* and *Critical Perspectives in Accounting*, among other journals, that underscore the adversarial relations and opposing interests that exist between capital and labor. Articles by Owen and Lloyd (1985) and Ogden and Bougen (1985) are notable among a genre that either contests the neutrality of accounting numbers, challenges the motives of those preparing financial reports, or questions the ability of financial information to serve labor's needs. The issues raised in these articles suggest a number of fruitful research opportunities. For example, survey research is needed to identify labor's specific information needs in different workplace settings and in varying labor-management relationships. In addition, empirical studies should help determine how accounting information is used in particular decision-making scenarios and whether this information has an impact on collective-bargaining activities, strategies, and outcomes.

A number of researchers in the 1990s have reexplored the origins of cost accounting in the United States and abroad. Several investigations of the early industrial-revolution era indicate that owners and key managers of large manufacturing firms in highly competitive environments clearly understood the correlation of costs and profit. Fleischman and Parker (1991) and Tyson (1992) examined business archives (company record books, letters and correspondence, business memoranda) in Great Britain and the United States, respectively. Their studies reveal that labor-cost data were regularly collected and purposefully used to establish piece rates, measure labor productivity, and facilitate make-or-buy decisions.

Notwithstanding, the motives underlying the development and implementation of cost-accounting data internally are continually being challenged. Whereas traditional business historians argue that labor-cost data, be it in actual- or standard-cost form, were primarily used to increase organizational efficiency, social theorists contend that the data were chiefly employed to dominate and control workers. In essence, the argument turns on whether one believes that economic or social forces predominate in the human actions and relationships within large organizations.

A growing number of authors have been applying the Foucauldian framework of power/knowledge to identify and explain key labor-costing activities. Hoskin and Macve (1988) produced a detailed analysis utilizing this framework in their interpretation of key events at the Springfield Armory in Massachusetts in the 1830s and 1840s. Their efforts are representative of the so-called "new" histories of accounting. In several of these studies, a particular social theory or philosophical interpretation appears to drive the search for historical episodes to confirm the underlying view.

Clearly, researchers will continue to explore the interplay of accounting and industrial relations from social or philosophical perspectives, in both contemporary and historical settings; however, they will need to carefully examine the role that labor-cost data actually played in fulfilling organizational constituents' particular needs and objectives. Studies that focus on single industries, encompass relatively narrow time frames, and utilize materials prepared and used by the principals directly involved offer the best chance of clarifying the complex interface that has existed between industrial relations and accounting.

Thomas N. Tyson

Bibliography

Brubaker, O. "Labor's Interest in Financial Information." Paper presented at the Michigan Accounting Conference, October 23, 1948.

Craft, J.A. "Information Disclosure and the Role of the Accountant in Collective Bargaining," *Accounting, Organizations, and Society*, vol. 6, no. 1, 1981, pp. 97–107.

Fleischman, R.K., and L.D. Parker. "British Entrepreneurs and Pre-Industrial Revolution Evidence of Cost Management," *Accounting Review*, April 1991, pp. 361–375.

Hoskin, K.W., and R.H. Macve. "The Genesis of Accountability: The West Point Connection," *Accounting, Organizations, and Society*, vol. 13, no. 1, 1988, pp. 37–73.

O'Farrell, P.J. "Accounting: A Labor Viewpoint." Paper presented at the Nineteenth Annual Conference of Accountants, University of Tulsa, Tulsa, Oklahoma, April 28–29, 1965.

Ogden, S., and P. Bougen. "A Radical Perspective on the Disclosure of Accounting Information to Trade Unions," *Accounting, Organizations, and Society*, vol. 10, no. 2, 1985, pp. 211–224.

Owen, D.L., and A.J. Lloyd. "The Use of Financial Information by Trade Union Negotiators in Plant Level Collective Bargaining," *Accounting, Organizations, and Society*, vol. 10, no. 3, 1985, pp. 329–350.

Pillsbury, W.F. "Organized Labor's Views of Corporate Financial Information," *Journal of Accountancy*, June 1958, pp. 46–56.

Tyson, T. "Letting the Data Speak: Exploring the Impact of Collective Bargaining and Continuous Arbitration on Piece Rates, Production Standards, and Standard Costs," a paper presented at the *Third Critical Perspectives on Accounting Symposium*, New York, April 16–18, 1993.

———. "The Nature and Environment of Cost Management Among Early Nineteenth Century U.S. Textile Manufacturers," *Accounting Historians Journal*, December 1992, pp. 1–24.

Inflation Accounting

Inflation refers to increases in the general level of prices. The prices of commodities change over time—some prices may increase, other prices may fall, some prices may fluctuate, other prices may remain relatively stable. In addition to individual price changes, a general trend in prices will also be observed. Over time, prices in general may increase or decrease or remain relatively stable. If during a period prices in general increase by, say, 10 percent, it is said that during the period there has been inflation of 10 percent. A fall in the general level of prices is referred to as deflation.

Price-level changes affect the general purchasing power of money. For example, in times of inflation, as prices in general increase, one can buy, in general, less with a given number of monetary units (dollars). If during a period 10 percent inflation takes place, then, at the end of the period, one would need 10 percent more in terms of number of dollars to buy goods and services than was the case at the beginning of the period. In terms of the purchasing power of money, it can be said that $1.00 at the beginning of the period had the general purchasing power of $1.10 at the end of the period, or that $1.00 at the end of the period was equivalent in general purchasing power to $0.909 at the beginning of the period (that is, 1.00/1.10). The effect of 10 percent inflation, therefore, is to decrease the general purchasing power of money by 9.1 percent (that is, 1.00–0.909/1.00).

Inflation affects accounting measurement and financial statements through its effect on the value of money—its general purchasing power. In a monetary economy, business operations involve the investment of money or money equivalent for the purpose of earning income in the form of monetary return in excess of monetary outlay. Money and monetary measurement, therefore, play a key role in the conduct of business operations and in the evaluation of results. In the final count, income is determined by matching two monetary amounts: revenue and the monetary outlay associated with earning the revenue.

From an accounting point of view, changes in the size of the monetary unit (its general purchasing power) is a problem that involves scales of measurement. To correct the effects of inflation on accounting, it is necessary to restate the accounting data so that all the figures are expressed in terms of a single scale of measurement: the general purchasing power of the monetary unit at a single point of time.

Current accounting practice ignores changes in the general purchasing power of money. As a result, in times of general price-level changes, business transactions are recorded, aggregated and interrelated in monetary units (dollars) of different purchasing power, monetary units that are not comparable in real terms. The failure to account for the effects of inflation causes distortions in financial statements the cumulative effects of which may be significant even in times of relatively mild inflation. The following may be noted in particular:

(1) Income measurement presupposes the maintenance of capital. In the context of business operations, capital is perceived as monetary investment for the purpose of earning income in the form of a monetary return on investment. Under current accounting practice, invested capital is maintained in terms of number of dollars and not in terms of what is economically significant—purchasing power.

(2) Current accounting practice ignores purchasing-power gains or losses on monetary accounts. In the context of accounting for inflation, monetary accounts are assets and liabilities, the amounts of which are fixed by contract or otherwise in terms of number of dollars regardless of changes in the general level of prices.

(3) Following from (2), in times of inflation, the reported cost of debt finance may bear little relation to the real cost.

Professional attitudes in the 1950s and 1960s tended to favor the restatement of financial statements for general price-level changes as a means of dealing with the financial accounting and reporting problems created by inflation. For example, Accounting Research Study (ARS) No. 6, *Reporting the Financial Effects of Price-Level Changes*, which was issued by the American Institute of Certified Public Accountants (AICPA) in 1963, claimed that financial data adjusted for price-level effects would provide a basis for "more intelligent, better informed allocation of resources" whether those resources were in the hands of individuals, of business entities or of government. Similarly, Statement No. 3 of the Accounting Principles Board (APB) of the AICPA, "Financial Statements Restated for General Price-Level Changes" (1969), held that financial statements adjusted for general price-level changes should prove useful to investors, creditors, management, employees, government officials and others who are concerned with the economic affairs of business enter-

prises. Similar interest in the general price-level adjustment was expressed by professional organizations in Great Britain.

The appeal the price-level restatement of financial statements had for the accounting profession was easy to understand. A price-level restatement, as such, does not require a departure from current accounting practice. It only requires the restatement of financial statements in dollars of constant purchasing power. The restatement is relatively easy to effect and can be done objectively on the basis of a specified price-level-adjustment model and an agreed general price-level index; further, the restatement is easily verifiable by the auditors.

Experiments with price-level adjustments, however, showed that restated financial statements were of limited usefulness. While the general price-level adjustment attempted to deal with the effects on accounting of changes in the purchasing power of money, what was ignored were the effects of specific price changes on the value of business assets and on the operations of business firms.

The restatement of financial statements for general price-level changes, whether applied on its own or in combination with some form of "current value" accounting, creates problems, some of which are discussed below.

A Price-Level-Adjustment Model

Strictly speaking, the restatement of financial statements in, say, end-of-period dollars would require the conversion of dollars at the time of each transaction into end-of-period dollars by the application of an appropriate general price-level index. Since such a restatement is, from a practical point of view, impossible (it would require the preparation of innumerable index numbers at every point of time), a price-level-restatement would have to be made on the basis of an assumed price-level-restatement model. For example, sales and expenses (other than depreciation) may be assumed to have been made/incurred in average dollars for a year, or quarter, or month; ending inventory may be assumed to have been acquired in average dollars for, say, the last quarter; in the calculation of purchasing-power gains and losses on monetary accounts, it may be assumed that changes in monetary accounts have occurred in average dollars for a year, or quarter, or month, and so on. While a price-level-restatement model would make it possible to carry out the restatement, it would also affect the accuracy of the restatement and would, therefore, limit its usefulness.

R.J. Chambers, an accounting theorist from Australia, proposed a "black box" adjustment to deal with the problem of reflecting the effects of inflation in financial statements restated for specific price changes. For example, if a set of financial statements has been expressed in terms of "current value" (in the case of Chambers's proposal, net realizable value), the total effect of general price-level changes, including gains and losses on monetary accounts, can be incorporated into the income calculation by restating the amount of shareholders' equity at the beginning of the period in end-of-period dollars, with a corresponding debit to the income statement (for a rising general level of prices) or credit to the income statement (for a falling general level of prices).

Purchasing Power Gains and Losses on Monetary Accounts

In times of inflation, the holder of money and monetary assets suffers a loss of an economic sense in that a given amount of money would buy progressively fewer goods and services in general. On the other hand, a debtor gains in time of inflation in that the real burden of debt in terms of purchasing power necessary for repayment diminishes. There are differences of opinion, however, regarding the nature of such gains and losses and the manner in which they should be reported in price-level-adjusted financial statements.

Henry Whitcomb Sweeney, a leading U.S. expert on inflation accounting, thought that the actual settlement of a debt or the use of cash was necessary before gains and losses on monetary accounts could be taken as realized. He advocated the reporting of a figure for "realized income" that would include realized gains and losses on monetary accounts. To this figure would be added the unrealized gains and losses on monetary accounts in order to arrive at a figure for "final net income for the period." R.C. Jones, a professor of economics at Yale University, supported realization as a criterion for including in income gains and losses on long-term monetary accounts but saw no objection on theoretical grounds for including it in the computation of income gains and losses on operating (short-term) monetary accounts. ARS No. 6 and APB No. 3 held the position that price-level gains and losses on monetary accounts arise from changes in the general level of prices, that they are not related to subsequent events such as a receipt or payment of money. Such gains and losses were to be recognized as part of the net income for the period and disclosed as a separate item in price-level-adjusted statements.

The Index Problem

Accounting for changes in the general level of prices involves the restatement of financial statements for changes in the general purchasing power of money. While goods and services can be valued in terms of money (their prices), money cannot be valued in terms of itself; it can only be valued in terms of the goods and services it can buy. The best available method for measuring changes in the purchasing power of money is by means of a general price-level index. This approach creates a number of problems regarding the type of index to use—for example, how general a general index should be; what prices (input prices or output prices) to use; input prices or output prices; the comparability of the prices used in the preparation of the index, in particular how to account for the effect of technological changes on the prices of the commodities used in the preparation of the index; and changes in available commodities over time.

Summary

Given the key role money plays in business operations, there are compelling theoretical grounds for recognizing the effects of general price-level changes in the determination of, and reporting on, the results and state of affairs of business enterprises. On its own, a general price-level restatement of financial statements is unlikely to produce satisfactory results except, perhaps, in cases of hyperinflation where the significance of differences between specific and general price-level changes may be materially diminished. A general price-level adjustment, however, may be applied as an integral part of a generally accepted model of asset valuation and income measurement in terms of "current value." A general price-level adjustment in such cases would be necessary for the realistic evaluation of results because income determined on the basis of the "current value" of assets and changes in this value (that is, specific price changes) will produce the same result regardless of the level of general inflation.

While it is generally recognized that general and specific price changes have a significant effect on the operations and state of affairs of business enterprises, as yet there is no general agreement on how to deal in a systematic manner with these effects in the preparation of financial statements. Notwithstanding the failure of current accounting practice to deal effectively with the problems created by general and specific price changes, some allowance should be made for these effects in the analysis and interpretation of reported results and state of affairs if financial statements are to be used effectively in the making of informed decisions.

Boris Popoff

Bibliography

Accounting Standards Steering Committee. *Accounting for Changes in the Purchasing Power of Money.* ED8. London: ASSC, 1973.

American Institute of Certified Public Accountants. *Reporting the Financial Effects of Price-Level Changes.* Accounting Research Study No. 6. New York: AICPA, 1963.

Chambers, R.J. *Accounting, Evaluation, and Economic Behavior.* Englewood Cliffs, NJ: Prentice-Hall, 1966.

Edwards, E.O., and P.W. Bell. *The Theory and Measurement of Business Income.* Berkeley: University of California Press, 1961.

Financial Accounting Standards Board. *Financial Reporting in Units of General Purchasing Power.* Stamford, CT: FASB, 1974.

Jones, R.C. *Effects of Price-Level Changes on Business Income, Capital, and Taxes.* Sarasota, FL: American Accounting Association, 1956.

Moonitz, M. *Changing Prices and Financial Reporting.* Champaign, IL: Stipes, 1974.

Sweeney, H.W. *Stabilized Accounting.* New York: Harper & Row, 1936.

See also ACCOUNTING PRINCIPLES BOARD; ACCOUNTING RESEARCH BULLETINS; ACCOUNTING RESEARCH STUDIES; ACCOUNTING SERIES RELEASE NO. 190; AMERICAN INSTITUTE OF CERTIFIED PUBLIC ACCOUNTANTS; BASE STOCK METHOD; BRAZIL: INFLATION ACCOUNTING; CAPITAL MAINTENANCE; CHAMBERS, RAYMOND JOHN; CHIEF ACCOUNTANTS OF THE SECURITIES AND EXCHANGE COMMISSION; EDWARDS AND BELL: REPLACEMENT-COST ACCOUNTING; GER- MANY; GRAHAM, WILLARD J.; HISTORICAL COST; INCOME-DETERMINATION THEORY; LAST IN, FIRST OUT (LIFO); LIMPERG, THEODORE, JR.; MONEY; MOONITZ, MAURICE; PATON, WILLIAM ANDREW; PHILIPS INDUSTRIES (N.V.); REALIZATION; SANDILANDS REPORT; SCHMALENBACH, EUGEN; SCHMIDT, JULIUS AUGUST FRITZ; SPACEK, LEONARD; STUDY GROUP ON BUSINESS INCOME'S *FIVE MONOGRAPHS ON BUSINESS INCOME;* SWEENEY, HENRY WHITCOMB; UNITED STATES STEEL CORPORATION

Institute of Chartered Accountants in England and Wales

This is the largest of the six major accountancy bodies in the British Isles, the others being: the Institute of Chartered Accountants of Scotland (ICAS); the Institute of Chartered Accountants in Ireland (ICAI); the Chartered Institute of Public Finance and Accountancy (CIPFA); the Chartered Association of Certified Accountants (ACCA); and the Chartered Institute of Management Accountants (CIMA).

The Institute of Chartered Accountants in England and Wales (ICAEW), the very first national body of chartered accountants, was incorporated by Royal Charter on May 11, 1880; a supplemental charter was granted in 1948. The ICAEW was founded by the amalgamation of five societies of accountants. These, together with their dates of formation, were: the Incorporated Society of Liverpool Accountants (1870); the Institute of Accountants (formerly the Institute of Accountants in London, 1870); the Manchester Institute of Accountants (1871); the Society of Accountants in England (1872); and the Sheffield Institute of Accountants (1877). Originally, all but the Society of Accountants in England, which had its headquarters in London, were local societies based in commercial and industrial centers in England. However, after representations from provincial practitioners, who did not wish to join the Society of Accountants in England, which had lower entry requirements, the Institute of Accountants in London changed its name and became a national body in 1872. Although there was rivalry between these two bodies, the desirability of a united profession was soon seen, and the ICAEW was formed.

New rivals emerged. Founded in 1885, the Society of Accountants and Auditors, which became the Society of Incorporated Accountants (SIA) in 1954, was open to those who were unable to qualify for membership of the ICAEW. Competition between these two bodies continued until 1957, when members of the SIA were absorbed into the ICAEW, the ICAS and the ICAI. Attempts have since been made at further unification. One scheme envisaged the six major bodies forming three national bodies of chartered accountants; in 1970 all parties, apart from the ICAEW, voted in favor of this proposal. A positive consequence of this failure was the setting up, in 1974, of the Consultative Committee of Accountancy Bodies (CCAB), a coordinating organization for the six bodies. Two attempts by the ICAEW to merge with just one of the other institutes have also failed: with the ICAS in 1989 and CIPFA in 1990.

At the time of formation, there were 599 members of the ICAEW; by 1890 this figure had nearly trebled to about 1,700; by 1930 membership had reached 9,000; and by 1970 it was almost 50,000. In 1991 membership approached 100,000, approximately the same as that of the other five bodies combined. Initially members were in, or employed in, public practice, but gradually they began to enter industry and commerce. By the early 1990s, only about 45 percent of members were in, or employed in, public practice.

For the first 40 years, the ICAEW was a male preserve, and it took a change in legislation, the Sex Disqualification (Removal) Act of 1919, before women were admitted. Mary Harris Smith, the first female member, was admitted in 1920, and in 1924 Ethel Watts became the first woman to qualify by examination. In 1991 female members formed only 12 percent of total membership, although of those newly admitted nearly a third were women.

There have always been two categories of members: associates and fellows, who may use the designatory letters ACA and FCA, respectively. To begin with, associates who had been in public practice continuously for five years could apply to become fellows. Additionally, from 1960, fellowship was granted automatically to all associates 10 years after admission. For all associates admitted after June 1978, a period of 10 years' continuing professional education (CPE) is required to be eligible for fellowship.

The ICAEW is governed by a Council, subject to the requirements of the Royal Charter and the bylaws, first adopted in 1882 and subsequently revised substantially. The Council was originally 45 in number but is now made up of 60 elected and not more than 20 co-opted members, from whom are chosen annually a president, a vice- president, and, since 1966, a deputy president. It was not until 1943 that the first nonpracticing member, F.R.M. de Paula, was elected to the Council, and not until 1979 that the first women were so elected.

The ICAEW's main purpose has always been to elevate the profession's standing by enforcing strict rules of conduct and by requiring a high standard of education and training. As a self-regulatory body, its supervisory status has increased since the mid-1980s with delegated statutory responsibility for members undertaking insolvency work, investment business, and auditing.

From the beginning, members were governed by, and were disciplined for any violations of, a code of ethics. The code has evolved over time, especially during the 1970s when emphasis was placed on the importance of professional independence. In 1980 a Joint Disciplinary Scheme (JDS) was introduced, in conjunction with the ICAS and the ACCA, to deal with "public interest" cases. Under the JDS, for the first time, firms as well as individuals could be disciplined.

At the start, admission to the ICAEW was open to those with suitable practical experience, but thereafter entry was largely restricted to those who additionally had passed internally administered examinations, first held in 1882.

A period of practical experience has always been required before admittance. This had to be gained in public practice until 1991, when, for the first time, training outside public practice was permitted. Potential members served articles of clerkship until 1973: since then they have entered into a training contract. The length of service required has depended on the level of education of the trainee. For graduates, some 90 percent of entrants, the period has always been three years. For nongraduates, articles were for five years until, with increasing standards of education generally, four-year articles were introduced in 1963 for certain candidates. Minimum entry standards were eventually raised so that by 1973 five-year articles were abolished. Members admitted after 1973 must complete a further two years of approved practical experience and, since June 1978, two years' CPE, before being eligible to engage in public practice.

Apart from a preliminary examination as a test of general education, last held in 1963, examinations have been on a two-stage basis: the intermediate, known as the foundation from 1974, and the final, which since 1965 has been divided into two parts. The latter was renamed the professional examination from 1975, but since the early 1990s the two parts have been known as the intermediate and the final. Students with a recognized accounting degree, first established in 1945, are exempt from the foundation stage. To reflect changes in accountants' work, the number of papers and the subjects examined have been revised from time to time.

The ICAEW has left the preparation for examinations to independent tutors, but it does provide post-qualification courses. The need to update members after the disruption of World War II led to the holding of refresher courses in 1945 and 1946, followed by the organization of annual summer courses from 1947 (renamed summer conferences in 1971). Additionally, since the mid-1960s, a program of courses has been developed, and this has subsequently expanded largely because of the introduction of CPE.

The ICAEW publishes two magazines: *Accountancy*, a monthly professional journal (first published in 1889 as the SIA's *Incorporated Accountants' Journal*, and retitled in 1938); and *Accounting and Business Research*, a quarterly academic journal. While the latter was first published in 1970, it was a revival of the SIA's *Accounting Research* (1948–1958), which was only the second academic accounting journal in English, the first being *Accounting Review*.

The Council had always been reluctant to issue guidance on technical matters, fearing resentment by, or embarrassment to, members, but, with the creation of the Taxation and Financial Relations Committee, the first in the series of Recommendations on Accounting Principles was issued in 1942. Following criticisms of financial reporting in the 1960s, the Accounting Standards Steering Committee was formed in 1970 (from 1976 the Accounting Standards Committee, ASC, constituted under the CCAB). The first in the series of Statements on Auditing was issued in 1961, and the Auditing Practices Committee (APC) was formed in 1973, but, following criticisms of auditors, it too was constituted under the CCAB in 1976. The ASC and APC issued, for the first time,

prescriptive standards, as well as other forms of guidance. In 1990 the ASC was replaced by the Accounting Standards Board, overseen by the new, independent Financial Reporting Council. In 1991 the APC was restructured and renamed the Auditing Practices Board.

Although slow, perhaps, in dealing with technical issues, the ICAEW has played an important role in influencing government legislation that impinges on members. This is especially true in the case of insolvency, company, and taxation law, and when gaining recognition within legislation, for example, to audit certain types of organizations.

Since the 1890s, the ICAEW has had its own purpose-built headquarters, Chartered Accountants' Hall. Two extensions to this building, one opened in 1931 and the other in 1970, have proved necessary, reflecting the growth in membership and activities of the ICAEW. The Hall houses a library, which has a fine collection of early and rare books on accounting, including the only perfect, or near-perfect, copy of James Peele's *Maner and Fourme* (1553), the earliest extant original work on bookkeeping in the English language. The collection contains some 3,000 items, encompassing books in most European languages published up to the early twentieth century.

Peter Boys

Bibliography

Boys, P. *Chartered Accountants' Hall: The First Hundred Years*. London: Institute of Chartered Accountants in England and Wales, 1990.

Harper, A.C. *The Institute of Chartered Accountants in England and Wales: A Short Sketch of Its Inception 11th May, 1880*. London: N.p., 1930.

Hopkins, L. *The Hundredth Year*. Plymouth: Macdonald and Evans, 1980.

Howitt, Sir H. *The History of the Institute of Chartered Accountants in England and Wales, 1880–1965, and of Its Founder Accountancy Bodies, 1870–1880: The Growth of a Profession and Its Influence on Legislation and Public Affairs*. London: William Heinemann, 1966.

Margerison, T. *The Making of a Profession*. London: Institute of Chartered Accountants in England and Wales, 1980.

Zeff, S.A. *Forging Accounting Principles in Five Countries: A History and Analysis of Trends*. Champaign, IL: Stipes, 1972.

See also ADVERTISING BY ACCOUNTANTS;
CERTIFIED PUBLIC ACCOUNTANT; CHARTERED
ACCOUNTANTS EXAMINATIONS IN ENGLAND
AND WALES; CONTINUING PROFESSIONAL
EDUCATION; DICKSEE, LAWRENCE; PEELE,
JAMES; SOLOMONS, DAVID; WOMEN IN AC-
COUNTING

Institute of Cost and Management Accountants
See CHARTERED INSTITUTE OF MANAGEMENT
ACCOUNTANTS

Institute of Internal Auditors

The Institute of Internal Auditors (IIA), the premiere professional organization for internal
auditors throughout the world, held its formal
organizational meeting on December 9, 1941.
This meeting was the fruition of work started
earlier in the year by Victor Z. Brink, Robert B.
Milne and John B. Thurston, who had served
as an organizing committee. Thurston was
named as the first president by the 24 charter
members of the organization. By its 50th anniversary in 1991, the IIA, headquartered in
Altamonte Springs, Florida, had become a dynamic international organization with 43,000
members.

There were two significant events in 1941:
the publication of the first major book on internal auditing and the founding of the IIA. The
latter event was related to the former. Brink's
doctoral dissertation, *Internal Auditing,* was
published in 1941 by Ronald Press. At the same
time, Thurston, internal auditor for the North
American Company (a utility holding company), had been contemplating an organization
for internal auditors. Thurston and Milne had
served together on an internal-auditing subcommittee formed jointly by the Edison Electric
Institute and the American Gas Association.
Both had decided that bringing internal auditing to its proper level of recognition would be
difficult in these two organizations, and that
what was needed instead was a national group
for internal auditors. When Brink's book came
to the attention of Thurston, the two men got
together and found they had a mutual interest
in furthering the role of internal auditing.

Membership grew quickly. The original 24
increased to 104 by the end of the first year, to
1,018 at the end of five years, and to 3,700 by
1957, with 20 percent of the members then located outside the United States. The new organization was quick to begin activities to further
the development of its members. A director of
research was approved in January 1942, the
first book *Internal Auditing: A New Management Technique* (1943) published under IIA
auspices was in March 1943, and a journal,
Internal Auditor, was begun in September 1944.
Membership was divided into local chapters
beginning in December 1942 when the New
York chapter was formed. The Detroit, Chicago, Los Angeles, and Philadelphia chapters
followed in 1943. In 1944 chapters were
formed in Dayton, Cleveland, and Toronto. By
the end of 1947, there were 19 chapters
throughout North America. Overseas chapters
were formed in London and Manila in 1948.

Initially the business of the group was
handled by the secretary, but as the organization grew larger, that became impossible. Thus,
in February 1947, the IIA hired its first paid
managing director, Bradford Cadmus. Cadmus
had been IIA secretary in 1944 while working
for Standard Brands and was familiar with the
business activities of the organization. Cadmus
served as the head of IIA's paid staff until 1962.
He was followed by Archie McGhee (1962–
1971), Louise E. Maloney (1971–1972), John
E. Harmon (1972–1978), Victor Brink (1978),
Robert L. Richmond (1979–1980), Stanley C.
Gross (1981–1985), G. Peter Wilson (1985–
1992), and William G. Bishop III (1992–).

In September 1947, the IIA issued *Statement of Responsibilities of the Internal Auditor,*
which established guidelines defining the role
and responsibilities of the internal-auditing
function within organizations. Revised in 1957
and again in 1971, 1976, and 1981, the original statement declared that the responsibilities
were primarily concerned with accounting and
financial matters. The 1957 revision expanded
that role, while the 1971 version gave equal
concern to every aspect of an organization's
operations, including efficiency, effectiveness,
and compliance. Recent changes have been
minor. In effect, the *Statement* serves as a foundation upon which to establish a charter for an
internal-auditing department.

The late 1960s and early 1970s witnessed
the adoption of a code of ethics and the establishment of a certification program. In 1978 the
IIA promulgated the *Standards for the Professional Practice of Internal Auditing*, which consisted of five general standards and 25 specific
standards.

The impetus for the growth of internal auditing has come from the IIA. Indeed, since 1941 the history of internal auditing has been synonymous with the history of the IIA. Brink and Thurston established an organization that could grow to meet a need.

One of the most far-reaching programs of the IIA has been its Certified Internal Auditor (CIA) program, developed under the direction of William S. Smith. Smith, 1966–1967 IIA chairman, championed the idea of a certification program throughout the decade of the 1960s, despite opposition from Bradford Cadmus and half of the IIA membership. The CIA exam was first given in 1974, but that first exam was the product of a decade of planning and development to create the essential components of a certification program, including a code of ethics for internal auditors and a common body of knowledge for the profession.

As complicated as the development stage was, the complexity of the implementation phase was even greater. IIA staff and committees had to define the areas in which candidates should demonstrate competence and then prepare the examinations. To assist members in passing the exam, review courses were implemented at the chapter level, and private authors such as Irvin Gleim from the University of Florida developed CIA review materials.

Today, an internal auditor can demonstrate his or her knowledge via an examination that tests what internal auditors do on a daily basis. Internal auditors benefit in the form of higher salaries, greater prestige, and enhanced self-worth. Aspects of certification, including the acronym itself, have been controversial over the years, but the CIA program has grown to the point where the controversies have been forgotten.

Dale L. Flesher

Bibliography

Brink, V.Z. *Foundations for Unlimited Horizons*. Altamonte Springs, FL: Institute of Internal Auditors, 1977.

———. *Internal Auditing*. New York: Ronald Press, 1941.

Flesher, D.L. *The Institute of Internal Auditors: Fifty Years of Progress through Sharing*. Altamonte Springs, FL: Institute of Internal Auditors, 1991.

Institute of Internal Auditors. *Statement of Responsibilities of the Internal Auditor*. Orlando, FL: Institute of Internal Auditors, 1957.

Internal Auditing. Studies in Business Policy No. 11. New York: National Industrial Conference Board, 1963.

Jones, R.H. "Audit of the Future," *Internal Auditor,* November-December 1969, pp. 65–72.

Survey of Internal Auditing. Orlando, FL: Institute of Internal Auditors, 1975.

See also AUDIT COMMITTEES; ETHICS, PROFESSIONAL; INTERNAL AUDITING; OPERATIONAL (VALUE-FOR-MONEY) AUDITING; TREADWAY COMMISSION

Institute of Management Accountants

The Institute of Management Accountants (IMA) is an organization consisting of professionals interested in management accounting. Headquartered in Montvale, New Jersey, as of 1992 it counted 314 chapters in the United States and 16 affiliates in other countries, and a membership of more than 90,000. The IMA started as the National Association of Cost Accountants (NACA) in 1919. Following changes in the nature and breadth of industrial accounting, the NACA renamed itself the National Association of Accountants (NAA) in 1957. Then, as the NAA had increasingly focused its efforts on management accounting, its leadership recommended a name change to the Institute of Management Accountants, and the membership approved that change in 1991.

The inadequacies of cost accounting in the United States became very apparent during World War I. On October 13, 1919, J. Lee Nicholson, both a consultant and a textbook writer, called a meeting in Buffalo to form an organization focused on cost accounting in manufacturing industries. This focus was significantly different from most of the members of the American Institute of Accountants that felt a new organization was needed. Among the 37 accountants at that meeting were William B. Castenholz, a practitioner and an accounting writer, Stephen Gilman, also a practitioner and an accounting writer, Harry Dudley Greeley, a tax expert, Edward P. Moxey Jr., a professor of accounting at the Wharton School of the University of Pennsylvania, and Clinton H. Scovell, a public accountant with expertise in cost accounting. The 97 charter members also included such well-known accountants as Arthur Andersen, Eric A. Camman, Frederick H.

Hurdman, William M. Lybrand, Robert Hiester Montgomery, C. Oliver Wellington, and John Raymond Wildman. The NACA hired Dr. Stuart C. McLeod, formerly a professor of statistics at New York University, as its first secretary, and he served in that post until his death in 1944.

From the beginning, the organization published a journal titled *Official Publications*, and a membership news publication *Bulletin Service*. They were issued monthly through June 1921, twice a month after that. On September 21, 1925, *Official Publications* became Section 1 of the *NACA Bulletin*, and *Bulletin Services* became Section 2. The two-section *NACA Bulletin* continued to be issued twice a month until September 1949, when it became a monthly publication. From 1919 through 1941, each issue was primarily devoted to one long and very detailed article. Beginning in 1942, articles in the issues became more numerous and much shorter. The *NACA Bulletin* became the *NAA Bulletin* in July 1957, containing both technical and news articles, and *Management Accounting*, in September 1965. From 1920 through 1951, the NACA published its conference proceedings annually in the *NACA Yearbook*. From 1952 through 1960, these proceedings were published as Section 3 of various *Bulletins*.

The variously named journals have been practical publications designed to provide useful information for members. The majority of articles, in the beginning, were in the area of cost measurement and control. As the circumstances within the business environment became more complex, the organization broadened the journal's focus. Among the influences that caused this expansion were the economic Depression of the 1930s, war, government regulations, changing technology, and increased global business competition.

The more than 6,000 journal articles provide insight into the historical development of management accounting since 1919. For example, the journal articles written during the Great Depression chronicled a shift in emphasis. Prior to the Depression, the primary focus of management accounting was on supporting the scientific-management effort to increase production. The high unemployment during the Depression created doubts concerning this earlier focus. In the June 1, 1931, *NACA Bulletin*, Arthur E. Andersen wrote an article titled, "The Major Problem Created by the Machine Age," in which he advocated a shift away from the emphasis on the cost of production toward keeping the greatest number of workers employed.

Each time period brought its own issues, and these are reflected in the journal articles. For example, World War II had a great influence on the journal. The war emergency tended to emphasize reimbursability of costs at the expense of cost control. During this period, the journal included articles on the cost-allocation procedures for government contracts. The end of the war brought renegotiation or termination of these cost-plus defense contracts, and the accountant's role in these negotiations was discussed. The end of the war also brought labor unrest, which the journal addressed. In addition, during the war, techniques for the application of mathematical models to decision-making situations were developed. After the war, the application of these techniques to business decision making became a major emphasis of the journal. In the 1990s, the major emphasis has been the changing manufacturing environment.

In addition to its journals, the organization has conducted and sponsored research in cost and management accounting. Among those who helped develop and direct the Research Department, studies, and staff in the early years were Professor Gould Harris of New York University, who had part-time responsibility for the Research Department from 1920 through 1924 and gave it a good start; his successor, Professor Roy B. Kester of Columbia University; NACA Research Committee directors such as J.P. Jordan, a writer of a leading textbook in cost accounting, Thomas Henry Sanders, a long-time professor at Harvard, Eric A. Camman, a noted practitioner and writer, I. Wayne Keller, an industrial accountant, and Dr. Raymond P. Marple, who became the staff member in charge of research in 1934.

The organization issued its first research publication, "Accounting for By-Products," in 1920 and has published by 1994 approximately 240 research studies. Many of the studies were reports on field surveys; others were vehicles for communicating better accounting practices to practitioners; and a few advanced new approaches and opened up new areas for investigation and discussion.

The majority of the research reports are written for the accounting practitioner. They supply an in-depth understanding of a subject to allow a practitioner to implement the con-

I

cepts and techniques. Often, the application of the techniques and concepts is illustrated by field studies showing the implementation by other companies. A three-part series, published in 1949–1950, that reported on a study of the variations of cost with volume, illustrates the practical nature of the organization's research studies. The first report in the series, "The Variation of Costs with Volume," published in the June 15, 1949, *NACA Bulletin*, reviewed the existing literature on this subject and reported on a limited field study. It endeavored to provide an understanding of the terms and concepts involved in the study of this topic. The next in the series, "The Analysis of Cost-Volume-Profit Relationships," published in the December 1949 *NACA Bulletin*, reported on a more extensive field study that described how cost-volume-profit analysis is used in actual practice. The third report in the series, "Volume Factor in Budgets in the Control of Costs," published in the June 1950 *NACA Bulletin*, summarized the prior two reports and applied the concepts and techniques to the process of development and utilization of a master budget.

Some concepts and techniques of the earlier studies are applicable to the topics being discussed in the 1990s. Research Series No. 19, "Assignment of Nonmanufacturing Costs for Managerial Decisions," published in the May 1951 *NACA Bulletin*, is a good example. The purpose of this study is to show practitioners how to determine profit margins by products, territories, customer classes, and similar lines of marketing activity through the proper allocation for costs. The issues and concepts of this research report are in the mainstream of the discussions in the "activity-based costing" (ABC) literature of the 1980s and 1990s.

Anyone doing research in cost and managerial accounting should carefully search for these research reports. They provide not only an excellent historical backdrop to today's problems but also, many times, a solution for these problems.

In 1969 the NAA created the Committee on Management Accounting Practices, its senior technical committee. Through this vehicle, NAA volunteer members began to identify and define the emerging discipline of management accounting. In 1981 the NAA promulgated, in Statement of Management Accounting (SMA) 1A, a widely accepted definition of management accounting. In 1983 it published SMA 1D, "Standards of Ethical Conduct for Man-

agement Accountants." SMAs are issued periodically by the IMA and are distributed through its yearly catalogue of publications.

In 1972 the NAA created the Certified Management Accountant (CMA) program. This program and the CMA exam have added a great deal to the professional status of management accountants.

Richard Vangermeersch
Robert Jordan

Bibliography

Bulloch, J. "The CMA Is Twenty Years Old," *Management Accounting*, April 1992, pp. 23–27.

"Fifty Years, 1919–1969," *Management Accounting*, August 1969, pp. 68–80.

"Institute of Management Accountants," *Management Accounting*, June 1991, p. 1.

McFarland, W.B. "Research in Management Accounting by NAA," *Management Accounting*, March 1970, pp. 31–34.

Meyers, G.U., and E.S. Koval. *Proud of the Past: 75 Years of Achievement, 1919–1994.* Montvale, NJ: Institute of Management Accountants, 1994.

"NAA: Through Forty Years of Growth," *NAA Bulletin*, April 1959, pp. 3–5; May 1959, pp. 3–4, 11; and June 1959, pp. 3–5. (All in Section 2).

Vangermeersch, R. "A Call to Share in NAA's History," *Association Leader*, May 15, 1989, pp. 3, 11.

See also ACTIVITY BASED COSTING; AMERICAN INSTITUTE OF CERTIFIED PUBLIC ACCOUNTANTS; ANDERSEN, ARTHUR E.; BREAK-EVEN CHART; CERTIFIED MANAGEMENT ACCOUNTANT (CMA) EXAMINATION; CHART OF ACCOUNTS; CHARTERED INSTITUTE OF MANAGEMENT ACCOUNTANTS; COST AND/OR MANAGEMENT ACCOUNTING; DIRECT COSTING; DISTRIBUTION COSTS; ETHICS, PROFESSIONAL; GILMAN, STEPHEN; IMPUTED INTEREST ON CAPITAL; MANAGEMENT ACCOUNTING; MONTGOMERY, ROBERT HIESTER; NICHOLSON, J. LEE; SANDERS, THOMAS HENRY; STANDARD COSTING; TREADWAY COMMISSION; WILDMAN, JOHN RAYMOND

Intangible Assets

"Intangible assets" is a term that has come to be used as a classification for these four assets: goodwill, patents, trademarks, and copyrights.

Three of these accounts, excluding trademarks, were well covered by Robert Hiester Montgomery in his 1912 book *Auditing: Theory and Practice*, but the term "intangible assets" was not used. While patents and copyrights were to be amortized to earnings, goodwill was not to be. However, goodwill could be written down if its viability was in question.

Neither the term "intangible assets" nor these four accounts appeared on the sample balance sheet in "Uniform Accounting." Since that 1917 publication of the Federal Reserve Board was orientated toward bankers, perhaps the absence of the classification and the accounts was due to the emphasis on tangible assets for pledges against loans. The 1929 revision of "Uniform Accounting" entitled "Verification of Financial Statements" did not change this nondisclosure. It was not until the 1936 revision, published by the American Institute of Accountants, that the caption "intangible assets" appeared on the sample balance sheet.

The first noted U.S. reference to intangible assets occurred in the *Journal of Accountancy* in 1916 in "Intangible Values in Balance Sheets." This editorial noted the progress made by about 100 companies in segregating the capitalized value of all intangible assets from tangible assets. Earl A. Saliers in the first edition of the *Accountant's Handbook* in 1923 did list "intangible" as one of the four classifications of assets. He listed goodwill, patents, trademarks, and copyrights. He also listed a classification of "deferred assets," with one of the accounts being "organization expenses."

Perhaps the best theoretical work on the topic was J.M. Yang's *Goodwill and Other Intangibles: Their Significance and Treatment in Accounts*, published in 1927, which included this about intangibles and bankers: "Intangibles are ordinarily looked upon with considerable disfavor, particularly by bankers, because they have been subject to manipulations of value to such a degree that they have become more or less of a nuisance and fail to possess any significance in the eyes of the ordinary reader."

Perhaps the most significant event for the classification of intangible assets was the stock market crash of 1929. Of 20 companies he studied, Richard Vangermeersch noted write-downs in the 1930s for patents and goodwill in seven of them. Another of the companies had a write-down in 1929, another in 1944, and one more in 1950. Hence, 10 of the 20 companies studied experienced write-downs of intangibles. Many of these companies first mentioned the intangibles as a break-off amount from tangible fixed assets valued from mergers. The catalyst for this was the Securities and Exchange Commission (SEC) requirement in 1936 that the value of intangibles be displayed in the balance sheet. Another spur by the SEC was the note in Accounting Series Release (ASR) No. 7, "Commonly Cited Deficiencies in Financial Statements Filed Under the Securities Act of 1933 and the Securities Exchange Act of 1934" in 1938. One of these deficiencies was for intangible assets not listed by major classes as required by instructions. Many firms chose to write down intangibles to $1.00 soon after.

In December 1944, in Accounting Research Bulletin (ARB) No. 24, "Accounting for Intangible Assets," the Committee on Accounting Procedure established Type a (limited life) and Type b (unlimited life) intangibles. Type a intangibles included patents, copyrights, leases, licenses and goodwill. Type b intangibles included goodwill, trade names, secret processes, subscription lists, perpetual franchises, and organization costs. Arbitrary write-downs were to be discouraged, especially if charged to capital surplus. It was not until Accounting Principles Board Opinion (APB) No. 17, "Intangible Assets," in 1970 that all intangibles were ruled to have a limited life, with a period of no more than 40 years. There was a strong dissent to APB No. 17 on the amortization of Type b intangibles. Four of the dissenters wrote that "whether amortization is appropriate depends on the particular circumstances of each case, including the evidence of increases or decreases in the value of such assets. In some cases, the facts may indicate maintenance or enhancement rather than elimination of value of its intangibles. In such cases, amortization is inappropriate." APB No. 17 is still enforced in 1994. APB No. 16, "Business Combinations," also in 1970, listed these intangible assets to be recognized separately in the case of a merger treated as a purchase: "contracts, patents, franchises, customer and supplier lists, and favorable leases, at appraisal values." Goodwill was to be debited for the amount of unidentifiable intangibles.

The practice of labeling research and development costs as intangible assets, which was sometimes done if the research was to yield a patent, was ended by Financial Accounting Standard No. 2, "Accounting for Research and Development Costs," in 1974.

With the passage of APB No. 16, the dollar amount of intangibles has greatly increased, which is significant in light of the large numbers of intangible assets, write-downs of intangible assets after the Crash of 1929. The last chapter on intangibles may not yet have been written.

Richard Vangermeersch

Bibliography

American Institute of Accountants. *Examination of Financial Statements by Independent Public Accountants*. New York: AIA, 1936.

Greidinger, B.B. *Accounting Requirements of the Securities and Exchange Commission for the Preparation of Financial Statements*. New York: Ronald Press, 1939.

"Intangible Values in Balance Sheets," *Journal of Accountancy*, 1916, pp. 122–125.

Montgomery, R.H. *Auditing: Theory and Practice*. New York: Ronald Press, 1912.

Saliers, E.A. *Accountants' Handbook*. New York: Ronald Press, 1923.

U.S. Federal Reserve Board. "Uniform Accounting," *Journal of Accountancy*, June 1917, pp. 401–433.

———. "Verification of Financial Statements," *Journal of Accountancy*, May 1929, pp. 321–353.

Vangermeersch, R. "An Historical Survey of Management Behavior on Original Valuation of Tangible and Intangible Fixed Assets." Working paper No. 15 in *Working Paper Series Volume 1*, ed. by Edward N. Coffman, pp. 230–241. Richmond, VA: Academy of Accounting Historians, 1979.

Yang, J.M. *Goodwill and Other Intangibles: Their Significance and Treatment in Accounts*. New York: Ronald Press, 1927.

See also ACCOUNTING PRINCIPLES BOARD; ACCOUNTING RESEARCH BULLETINS; GOODWILL; HISTORICAL COST; POOLING OF INTERESTS; SECURITIES AND EXCHANGE COMMISSION; *UNIFORM ACCOUNTING*

Internal Auditing

Internal auditing has become the growth profession of accounting in the last half of the twentieth century. The evaluation of internal controls and managerial efficiency and effectiveness by nonmanagerial personnel is known by such terms as internal auditing, operational auditing, and management auditing. At the heart of the development of internal auditing has been a professional group, the Institute of Internal Auditors (IIA).

Although the modern work of the internal auditor involves auditing for efficiency and effectiveness as much as for financial propriety, such activity has not always been among the auditor's duties. The profession of internal auditing has changed over the past half century. Prior to 1941, internal auditing was basically a clerical function with no organization nor standards of conduct. Because the record keeping at that time was performed manually, auditors were necessary to check accounting work after it was done to locate errors in postings and footings. Manual processing also made fraud easier. Combining the need for uncovering errors and the need to catch misappropriations resulted in the auditor being little more than a verifier and a policeman. Today the auditor is an integral part of the management team.

The concept of internal auditing is of more recent vintage than that of auditing by external accountants. Although a form of internal auditing existed among the manor houses of England as early as the Middle Ages, such internal audits are usually discounted by historians since the audits were performed by the lord of the manor who was trying to keep up with his own business. Early Greek and Roman writers such as Aristophanes and Cicero make mention of "accountants, auditors, and auditing of accounts and audit rooms." Similarly, the Zenon papyri record the application of internal audits on the Egyptian estate of the Greek ruler Ptolemy Philadelphus II as early as 2,500 years ago. These early audits were in many ways akin in their scope to that of the modern internal auditor in that they included both an examination of the correctness of accounting records and an evaluation of the propriety of activities reflected in the accounts. Emphasis was on improving management control. Such broad emphasis was not to reappear until after World War II.

In the United States, there was little need for internal auditing in the colonial period because there was little in the way of large industry. In fact, textbooks of the period never referred to internal auditing or internal control. In government, the need for an audit function was recognized. The first Congress in 1789 approved an act that included a provision for the appointment of an auditor. The auditor's job—basically a clerical function—was to receive public accounts, examine them, and certify the balances.

Railroads are usually credited with being the first modern employers of internal auditors. It was during the latter part of the nineteenth century that these first legitimate internal auditors became commonplace. The title applied to these employees was "traveling auditors"; their duty was to visit the railroads' ticket agents and determine that all monies were accounted for. Other early industries to employ internal auditors included the large Krupp Company in Germany. The Krupp Company apparently employed some type of internal audit staff at least as early as 1875 since there is a company audit manual dated that year.

Although the roots of internal auditing date back into the nineteenth century, the real growth did not occur until the early part of the twentieth century with the growth of the large corporate form of business. The major factor in the emergence of internal auditing was the extended span of control faced by management in firms employing thousands of people and conducting operations in many locations. Defalcations and improper records were major problems, and the growth in the volume of transactions resulted in a substantial bill for public accounting services for the organization that tried to maintain control by continuing the traditional form of audit by the public accountant.

The objectives of early internal auditors centered on the protection of company assets. The National Industrial Conference Board's 1963 study of internal auditing found that the protection of company assets and detection of fraud were the principal objectives of internal auditors. Thus, auditors concentrated most of their attention on examinations of financial records and on the verification of assets most easily misappropriated. Many management people a generation ago felt that the main purpose of an audit was to serve as a psychological deterrent against wrongdoing by other employees.

Events of the 1940s and 1950s
The year 1941 marked a turning point in the development of internal auditing as two major events occurred. One was the publication of the first major book on the subject, Victor Z. Brink's *Internal Auditing*. Also in 1941, 24 individuals joined together to form the IIA.

During the 1940s, internal auditors began to expand their audits to encompass more than the traditional financial audit. The shift to a war economy in the early 1940s was a major cause for the expansion of audit scope. Management became more concerned with production scheduling, shortages of materials and laborers, and compliance with government regulations. Simultaneously, cost finding became more important than external reporting. As a result, internal auditors began directing their efforts toward assisting management in whatever way possible. Following the war, the benefit of the auditor's assistance was so obvious to management that there was no consideration of reducing the auditor's scope to prewar levels. The term "operational" auditing was adopted to describe the expanded activity.

The growth in the internal auditor's scope of responsibility can be observed through a comparison of the 1947 *Statement of Responsibilities of the Internal Auditor*, promulgated by the IIA, and the 1957 revision of the same document. The 1947 version stated that internal auditing dealt primarily with accounting and financial matters but may also properly deal with matters of an operating nature. In other words, the emphasis was on accounting and financial matters, but other activities were also fair game for the auditor. That emphasis was to change in just a decade.

The IIA described the broad role of internal auditing with its 1957 *Statement of Responsibilities of the Internal Auditor*. According to that publication, the services the internal auditor provides to management include such activities as: (1) reviewing and appraising the soundness, adequacy, and application of accounting, financial, and operating controls; (2) ascertaining the extent of compliance with established policies, plans, and procedures; (3) ascertaining the extent to which assets are accounted for, and safeguarded from, losses of all kinds; (4) ascertaining the reliability of accounting and other data developed within the organization; and (5) appraising the quality of performance in carrying out assigned responsibilities.

Later Developments
In 1975, a study by the IIA entitled "Survey of Internal Auditing" found that 95 percent of all respondents conducted operational audits for purposes of judging efficiency, effectiveness, and economy. That study found that 51 percent of

the total audit time was spent on operational auditing.

In 1977 the internal-auditing environment changed when the U.S. Congress passed the Foreign Corrupt Practices Act (FCPA). Although the media emphasized that the purpose of the law was to eliminate payments by U.S. corporations to foreign officials, the secondary purpose of enhanced internal controls was more important to internal auditors. Congress was wise to include in the law a provision that companies should have sufficient controls so that illegal payments would be uncovered by the accounting system. Thus, if a firm were guilty of making an illegal payment, management could not escape conviction by claiming a lack of knowledge of those payments. If managers did lack knowledge, then they were guilty of having a system that could not uncover illegal payments. As a result, management began placing more emphasis on internal controls. The result was the hiring of more internal auditors by corporations with audit departments and the establishment of new audit departments by companies that did not already have them.

A similar change in the environment occurred in 1987 when the Treadway Commission report was issued. The Treadway Commission was officially known as the National Commission on Fraudulent Financial Reporting. It was organized by five accounting organizations, including the IIA, to study the cause of fraudulent reporting. The formation of the commission was a defensive response against possible action by Congress as a result of highly publicized corporate failures that had been caused by fraudulent reporting. Two of the main conclusions of the Treadway Commission were that (1) an internal audit function should exist in every public corporation, and (2) there should be a corporate audit committee composed of nonmanagement directors. These conclusions enhanced the image of the internal auditor and resulted in more emphasis being placed on the internal audit function.

Various government audit agencies have played a role in the movement toward the modernization of internal auditing. The U.S. General Accounting Office (GAO) has played a major part in broadening the role of the auditor. That organization's 1972 publication, *Standards for Audit of Governmental Organizations, Programs, Activities, and Functions* (commonly called the "Yellow Book" because of the color of its cover), explains the meta-

morphosis basically as a widening of audit scope.

Internal auditing has changed during the past half century. The antecedents of internal auditing go back many centuries, but the true development is a twentieth-century phenomenon. The main objective of internal auditing has moved from that of fraud detection to assisting management in making decisions. Whereas the job of internal auditing was once thought to be lackluster, the internal audit staff of today is considered the training ground for management personnel. The real impetus for the growth of internal auditing has come from the IIA. Indeed, much of the history of internal auditing has been synonymous with the history of the IIA.

Dale L. Flesher

Bibliography
Brink, V.Z. *Foundations for Unlimited Horizons*. Altamonte Springs, FL: Institute of Internal Auditors, 1977.
Flesher, D.L. *The Institute of Internal Auditors: Fifty Years of Progress through Sharing*. Altamonte Springs, FL: Institute of Internal Auditors, 1991.
Grier, E. *Accounting in the Zenon Papyri*. New York: Columbia University Press, 1934.
Internal Auditing. Studies in Business Policy No. 11. New York: National Industrial Conference Board, 1963.
Smith, C.A. *Internal Audit Control*. Austin, TX: University Cooperative Society, 1933.
U.S. General Accounting Office. *Standards for Audit of Governmental Organizations, Programs, Activities, and Functions*. Washington, DC: GPO, 1972.

See also AUDIT COMMITTEES; CONTROL ACCOUNTS; CONTROL: CLASSICAL MODEL; ETHICS, PROFESSIONAL; EXTERNAL AUDITING; FRAUD AND AUDITING; GENERAL ACCOUNTING OFFICE, U.S.; GREECE; INSTITUTE OF INTERNAL AUDITORS; INTERNAL CONTROL; MANORIAL ACCOUNTING; MEDICI ACCOUNTS; OPERATIONAL (VALUE-FOR-MONEY) AUDITING; RAILROAD ACCOUNTING (U.S.); TREADWAY COMMISSION

Internal Control

Some have written that there is concrete evidence that the concept of internal control existed in Mesopotamia as early as 3600 B.C.; similar assertions have been made with respect to pharaonic Egypt. Others have classified such claims as speculative, because little is known of the nature of business transactions among the ancients.

In early modern times, a standardized system of double entry bookkeeping was authored and promoted in Venice by Luca Pacioli in *Summa de Arithmetica* (1494). He and subsequent writers looked upon double entry bookkeeping as both a control device and a recording procedure. Pacioli wrote that his system would help merchants to control their business activities.

The concept of internal control, as applied and used by accountants and auditors, has been repeatedly reinterpreted. The profession's view has been relatively narrow. A broader definition appeared in a 1957 article by Paul Grady, a partner in Price Waterhouse, which summarized the views held by many then: Internal accounting control was seen to comprise the plan of organization and the coordinated procedures used within the business to (1) safeguard its assets from loss by fraud or unintentional errors, (2) check the accuracy and reliability of the accounting data that management uses in making decisions, and (3) promote operational efficiency and encourage adherence to adopted policies in those areas in which the accounting and financial departments have responsibility, directly or indirectly.

The accounting profession had implemented a narrower concept in the American Institute of Accountants' (AIA) Second Standard of Fieldwork (1947) and incorporated in 1972 in "Statement of Auditing Standards (SAS) No. 1, "Codification of Auditing Standards and Procedures": "There is to be a proper study and evaluation of the existing internal control as a basis for reliance thereon and for the determination of the resultant extent of the tests to which auditing procedures are to be restricted." Internal control was interpreted a little later as referring almost exclusively to internal accounting control.

Four comments can be made, each of which will be discussed in some detail. First, although internal control represents a technique to be installed, maintained, and utilized by management, the auditors' adaptation was based on their own perceived needs—that is, reliance on internal control to restrict substantive testing. Second, the concept proved to be difficult to work with due to the circular reasoning inherent in its design and application. Third, the narrow concentration on internal accounting controls created problems immediately recognized by some. Fourth, the auditors adopted a patently naive assumption of managerial integrity.

Applying a broader perspective, students of business organization have noted that every control is intended to change behavior or to prevent its change, but that the targets of, and means for, control can differ. Control can be viewed from individual, behavioral, ideological, and ecological perspectives, each of which has different objectives, control techniques, and targets. Seen in personal terms, the target can be: the total person, his or her behavior or actions, ideas and perceptions, or the person's immediate environment. In times of economic declines, it is possible that narrow definitions, such as those implemented by auditors, could cause managements to move from looser to tighter modes of control; the direction could be dysfunctional, when compared to the available reverse move toward looser control.

As noted, internal control has been used by auditors primarily to assist them in determining the nature, timing, and extent of substantive tests. This application embodies dangers of circular reasoning: The design of the scope of the examination involves two unknown quantities that react upon each other. On the one hand, the nature and extent of the sampling and testing to be made of recorded transactions must be determined, in part at least, in light of the system of internal check and control. On the other hand, the effectiveness of such a system must be judged, to a considerable extent, by the results of the audit tests.

Moreover, an arbitrary distinction was made by the profession between internal accounting controls and administrative/operational controls. Grady thought that this move represented serious retrogression. In 1977 the AICPA created a Special Advisory Committee on Internal Accounting Control to give guidance on internal accounting control to management. Its 1979 report did not succeed in clarifying the differences between internal accounting controls and administrative/operational controls. The auditors' control dichotomy did not enter the literature of other learned professions; it has been largely reversed by the accounting profession.

The principle of internal control was based upon the assumption that management was concerned with preventing fraud; therefore, controls were designed to bring fraud, should it be discovered, to management's attention. The assumption does not comprehend the existence of management fraud, the manipulation of controls to prevent its discovery, or management overrides of existing controls. When the assumption was adopted, it may have been idealistic; today it appears naive.

The history of internal control reflects its longstanding usage as a management technique. Indeed, in most of the world, developments had been influenced by a need for control and audit of government funds. Following the decline of the Holy Roman Empire, emphasis switched from safeguarding government funds to facilitating commercial activities; double entry bookkeeping became an important element of internal control.

The English Joint Stock Companies Act of 1844 included a short-lived requirement for the appointment of auditors, though such persons were not required to be independent. Generally, internal control was ignored at this period, despite Pacioli's earlier initiatives. Fraud detection continued as the primary audit objective; usually, audits were performed on a 100 percent basis.

In the United States, reporting requirements were spotty and audit requirements nonexistent. Accordingly, buyer needs influenced changes in the nature of audit services. From the turn of the century until the 1930s, U.S. audits were performed not for statutory purposes, but largely to guide credit grantors; accordingly, the "balance-sheet audit" concept evolved. The former detailed audit and the new balance-sheet audit were distinguished (1) by the objective of the detailed audit to uncover all defalcations discernible from the records and from transaction documents, and (2) by the fact that immaterial defalcations may not be of consequence when the interests of creditors predominate. A crucial fact was quickly established: The balance-sheet audit may not be effective in detecting fraud, or certain types of errors or omissions. The limitations of such an audit still may not be fully understood by either the public or the rulemakers.

In 1905 Robert Hiester Montgomery, an accounting practitioner in the United States, edited the American version of Lawrence Dicksee's, the English auditing writer, *Auditing*. The book recognized internal control as important in deciding on the amount of detailed verification. The concept of reliance on controls was echoed in the first set of auditing standards prepared and distributed by the AIA in 1917 under the title *Uniform Accounting*. The standard was reaffirmed in 1929, *Verification of Financial Statements*, and on subsequent occasions. In other words, management's internal-control concept was adapted to unwonted audit purposes by professional fiat.

The attraction offered by the ability to rely on internal control is obvious. The choice of internal control as a surrogate for detail tests may have been proper at the time it was made, especially given an emphasis on meeting creditor needs. Then such events as the identification of investors and creditors as primary users of financial statements, the incidence of massive management frauds, and the increased use of technology by auditors lay very much in the future.

Following the 1929 stock market crash, managers, investment bankers, corporate lawyers, stockbrokers, and certified public accountants were thought by some to be the agents of a massive conspiracy to defraud small private investors of what little they had been able to accumulate. The consequent establishment of the Securities and Exchange Commission (SEC) in 1934 led to a partnership of the profession and government designed to promote financial-statement disclosures thought to be useful to investment decisions. The arrangement represented an indirect boon to internal control. Also, 1934 marked the beginnings of the examination of external-audit evidence in quantity.

As pointed out, another important event bearing on internal control involved the splitting apart of internal accounting and operational/administrative controls in the 1950s. The "swing" toward financial controls could have been part of a worldwide trend away from operational and toward financial decision making.

The splintering of the internal-control concept resulted in the creation of the administrative/operational category of controls, which defied the formulation of a truly workable definition. However, the slightly less opaque category of internal accounting control was incorporated into the Foreign Corrupt Practices Act in 1977. Thus, accounting-control terminology was adapted to accomplish very different governmental objectives. Consequently, many auditors had to perform research to determine the degree of documentation (or redocumentation) of control systems to be undertaken by their clients.

The emergence of electronic data processing (EDP) systems temporarily buoyed the importance of internal-control evaluations to a cost-effective audit. However, it also became progressively more difficult to separate issues of attest significance from management control, and to define the relationship between many computer controls and the attest audit. To lessen the confusion, a key control concept evolved, clarifying the relationship between internal control and the reliance concept.

Statement on Auditing Standards No. 55, effective for periods beginning January 1, 1990, marked the reunification of the control structure and an affirmation that an auditor must look at any type of internal control that could have a bearing on his expression of opinion on the financial statements.

Mention should be made of the development of statistical sampling and its effect on internal control. The research performed in this connection set an important precedent, in that it drew on another discipline, a branch of mathematics. The advent of statistical sampling may have lessened the extent of auditor reliance on internal control, because a test-basis audit with no reliance on internal control could now be justified. However, it is probable that statistical sampling was never implemented by a majority of U.S. practitioners.

Major unresolved questions related to internal control are continuing. A proposal by the AICPA's Public Oversight Board (POB) would require public companies to assess the effectiveness of their internal-control structures and report the results to the public. The POB has also called in 1993 on external auditors to attest to that assessment made by the management of publicly-traded companies. The proposal is still pending in 1994.

The outmoded distinction between internal accounting and administrative/operational controls will continue to fade away. A comprehensive definition of internal control incorporating standards of proper business behavior will be developed and either adopted by or imposed on large corporations. A more comprehensive internal-control system will encompass all management levels in the corporate hierarchy by adding an executive or management control subsystem to the traditional employee-centered systems. An executive information system designed to meet the needs of a corporate audit committee, especially in regard to the control structure, represents a probable future development.

Traditionally, U.S. auditors have examined internal control as a basis to determining the extent to which substantive tests could be restricted, modified, or shifted in time. While this objective of the internal-control review may be changing, two attributes of internal control have gained importance. The first is attention to separation of duties; the second relates to the usefulness of internal control as a barometer of a client's sensitivity to corporate accountability.

Felix Pomeranz

Bibliography

American Institute of Accountants. *Tentative Statement of Auditing Standards: Their Generally Accepted Significance and Scope.* New York: American Institute of Accountants, 1947.

American Institute of Certified Public Accountants. *Report of the Internal Accounting Control Special Advisory Committee.* New York: American Institute of Certified Public Accountants, 1979.

Armstrong, P. "The Rise of Accounting Controls in British Capitalist Enterprises," *Accounting, Organizations, and Society,* 1987, vol. 12, no. 5, pp. 415–433.

Barrett, M.J. "Internal Auditing and Corporate Financial Information Systems," *Internal Auditor,* June 1980, pp. 26–33.

Czarniawska-Joerges, B. "Control Processes in Declining Organizations: The Polish Economy, 1971–1981," *Organizational Studies,* vol. 8, no. 2, 1987, pp. 149–168.

Dicksee, L.R. *Auditing,* edited by R.H. Montgomery. New York: Ronald Press, 1905.

Elliott, R.K., and P.D. Jacobson. "Audit Technology: A Heritage and a Promise," *Journal of Accountancy,* May 1987, pp. 199–217.

Grady, P. "The Broader Concept of Internal Control," *Journal of Accountancy,* May 1957, pp. 36–41.

Hackett, W., and S.C. Mobley. "An Auditing Perspective of the Historical Development of Internal Control," pp. 1–9. In *Touche Ross/University of Kansas Symposium on Auditing Problems.* Lawrence, KS: University of Kansas, College of Business, 1976.

Lee, T.A. "The Historical Development of Internal Control from the Earliest Times to the End of the Seventeenth Century," *Journal of Accounting Research*, Spring 1971, pp. 150–157.

Short, F.G. "Internal Control from the Viewpoint of the Auditor," *Journal of Accountancy*, September 1940, pp. 224–231.

Stempf, V.H. "Influence of Internal Control upon Audit Procedure," *Journal of Accountancy*, September 1936, pp. 170–173.

See also AMERICAN INSTITUTE OF CERTIFIED PUBLIC ACCOUNTANTS; AUDIT COMMITTEES; AUDITOR'S REPORT; COMPUTING TECHNOLOGY IN THE WEST: THE IMPACT ON THE PROFESSION OF ACCOUNTING; CONTROL: CLASSICAL MODEL; EGYPT; EXTERNAL AUDITING; FRAUD AND AUDITING; GRADY, PAUL; *HOCHFELDER V. ERNST AND ERNST;* INTERNAL AUDITING; MAUTZ, ROBERT K.; MEDIEVAL ACCOUNTING; MONTGOMERY, ROBERT HIESTER; PACIOLI, LUCA; SECURITIES AND EXCHANGE COMMISSION; STATISTICAL SAMPLING; TREADWAY COMMISSION; *UNIFORM ACCOUNTING*

International Accounting Standards Committee

The International Accounting Standards Committee (IASC) was formed in 1973, the result of a lengthy gestation period that culminated in a decision at the Tenth International Congress of Accountants in Sydney, Australia, in the autumn of 1972 to form such a body. Its origin can be traced back to an agreement among Canada, Great Britain, and the United States in 1966 to create a "study group" to organize a program of comparative studies of current trends in accounting thought and practice in the three countries. This led to the formation of the Accountants International Study Group (AISG) in 1967. It issued 20 authoritative papers prior to 1973, papers that began to shape international thinking in the profession. The principal motivator behind the creation of both the AISG and the IASC was Lord Henry Benson of Great Britain, who served as the first chairman of the IASC.

Initially the Board of IASC consisted of representatives of 16 professional bodies from nine countries: Australia, Canada, France, Germany, Great Britain, Japan, Mexico, the Netherlands, and the United States. Appointment of representatives was made by the respective na-

tional professional bodies. The objectives adopted, which remain in effect, are: (1) to formulate and publish in the public interest accounting standards to be observed in the presentation of financial statements and to promote their worldwide acceptance and observation; and (2) to work generally for the improvement and harmonization of regulations, accounting standards and procedures relating to the presentation of financial statements.

In 1994 the Board of IASC represented 106 professional bodies from 79 countries. It consisted of 14 voting members, with the IASC constitution providing for three additional appointments from other organizations having an interest in financial reporting. Members were: Australia, Canada, France, Germany, Great Britain, India, Italy, Japan, Jordan, the Netherlands, Norway (representing the Nordic countries), South Africa, the United States, and the International Association of Financial Analysts. In order to issue a standard, approval of 11 of the 14 voting members is required.

The Board of IASC generally meets three times a year, with one meeting often held in a non-Board country. It has a small Secretariat based in London. Much of the work of the board is effected through steering committees, generally of four or five representatives, appointed for each individual project undertaken. Occasionally, staff work is performed by professional bodies in individual countries. The result is that much of the work of the board is accomplished by volunteer assistance, which reduces the cost of the board's work and permits the Secretariat to operate more in a supervisory or coordinating role.

From time to time, the board considers possible issues for addition to its agenda. The staff of the Secretariat develops discussion papers on the issues, and the board decides whether to add a project to its agenda. Once a project is added to the agenda, a steering committee is appointed. Its first task is to develop a statement of principles, based upon the IASC conceptual framework, that it believes are appropriate for the board to use to resolve the issues. After discussion and approval by the board, the statement of principles is often issued to member organizations and their consultants for comments and suggestions. The steering committee then prepares an Exposure Draft, based upon the then-agreed statement of principles. This draft is discussed at one or more board meetings. When agreement is reached, the Exposure Draft is issued and broadly distributed for comment. Often the exposure period runs six to nine months, partly to permit translation into languages other than English. Exposure Draft responses are reviewed by board members and staff, staff analyses are prepared, and the steering committee prepares a new draft for board discussion and final approval. On occasion a revised Exposure Draft will be issued, which starts the exposure process again.

By 1994 the IASC had issued 31 standards, many characterized by the acceptance of alternative accounting practices. Given the voting requirements and the diversity in accounting concepts around the world, the acceptance of alternatives for dealing with a large number of issues is not surprising. Even so, the board recognized in the late 1980s that the time had come to attempt to eliminate as many alternative conclusions as possible. Work was started on what was styled as the "comparability" project, which then evolved to the "improvements" project. In this project, the board reconsidered about a dozen of its standards with a view to (1) eliminating as many alternatives as possible; (2) providing additional guidance in some areas based upon experience gained since the standard was issued; and (3) sharpening disclosure requirements with a view to the needs of creditors and investors.

The "improvements" project was, in part, motivated by the interest of the International Organization of Securities Commissions (IOSCO). With the rapid development of cross-border finance in the late 1980s, the IOSCO recognized the need for a more uniform set of definitive accounting standards and thus encouraged the IASC in its improvements project. An implicit expectation was that if the IASC met high standards of quality in its improvements project, the IOSCO would work to have the major capital-market countries move toward a requirement to accept only financial statements prepared in accordance with IASC standards when nondomestic companies wanted to raise capital in their markets.

The ultimate significance of the work of the IASC remains uncertain. While its objectives are sound and its performance to date impressive, many hurdles remain to successful completion of the improvements project and the ongoing efforts to reduce severely the number of acceptable accounting alternatives. Since the IASC has no power to enforce application of its standards on any jurisdiction, the complementary role of the IOSCO becomes quite significant. Optimism in this regard, however, is warranted if one considers the successful partnership in the United States between the government (Securities and Exchange Commission) and the private sector (the Financial Accounting Standards Board). The IASC-IOSCO relationship could evolve in a similar manner.

The need for capital formation is likely to become more pervasive. If so, international standards that focus on full and open disclosure and broad standards that are relatively simple and straightforward can provide significant impetus to successful and efficient capital formation. Such an end result would be a most rewarding consequence for those who had the vision to establish the IASC and those whose voluntary efforts have kept the process moving in such a positive direction.

Arthur R. Wyatt

Bibliography

Cairns, D. "IASC Prepares to Tighten Up Standards," *International Accounting Bulletin*, September 1987, p. 12.

———. "IASC's Blueprint for the Future," *Accountancy*, December 1989, pp. 89–82.

Choi, F.D.S., ed. *Handbook of International Accounting*. New York: John Wiley & Sons, 1991.

Choi, F.D.S., and V.B. Bavishi. "International Accounting Standards/Issues Needing Attention," *Journal of Accountancy*, March 1983, pp. 62–68.

Mason, A.K. "The Evolution of International Accounting Standards." In *Multinational Accounting: A Research Framework for the Eighties*, edited by F.D.S. Choi, pp. 155–170. Ann Arbor, MI: UMI Research Press, 1981.

Wallace, R.S.O. "Survival Strategies of a Global Organization: The Case of the International Accounting Standards Committee," *Accounting Horizons*, June 1990, pp. 1–22.

Wyatt, A.R. "International Accounting Standards: A New Perspective," *Accounting Horizons*, September 1989, pp. 105–108.

See also Congresses on Accounting, International; Italy, after Pacioli; Uniformity

Inventory Valuation

Inventory valuation is perhaps the most pervasive of all accounting topics. In ancient societies, inventories were recorded and controlled by quantities only and not by monetary valuations. Governments and religious orders received inventory items for taxes and for offerings and disbursed these items for designated purposes. Inventory records were audited by designated officials. This was true also for manorial accounting.

In "Particularis de Computis et Scripturis," his treatise on double entry accounting in *Summa de Arithmetica* (1494), Luca Pacioli, a professor of mathematics at various universities in Italy, included quantities, descriptions, and monetary valuations for each of the types of inventory on hand at the beginning of the business. An inventory account was kept for each item. When inventory items were transferred to a ship, for instance, for transfer to a foreign port, each item was transferred to that particular venture account. When inventory items were sold, the inventory accounts were credited for the proceeds. The same process was used for ventures of all sorts. Pacioli, like Robert Colinson from Scotland in *Idea Rationaria* (1683), avoided the problem of inventory valuation at the end of the period by having either all units of an item sold or all of them left. Both of these authors, like almost all others through the nineteenth century, transferred the credit or debit balance of each closed inventory account to profit and loss.

In his 1763 text, *Book-keeping Methodized,* John Mair from Scotland faced the problem of an inventory account in which some goods were sold. Mair credited the inventory account for the "prime cost" of the inventory remaining. "Prime cost" was the cost of the merchandise to the retailer. "Prime costs" for manufacturers were direct materials and direct labor. Manufacturing overhead was excluded until J. Slater Lewis, an industrial engineer from England, championed, in his *The Commercial Organization of Factories* (1896), a very general overhead-application system. Alexander Hamilton Church, an industrial engineer both in England and the United States, in the early 1900s designed and popularized a much more complex allocation system for manufacturing overhead based on an individual rate for each machine center in *The Proper Distribution of Expense Burden* (1908) and *Production Factors in Cost and Works Management* (1910). The perplexing question of inclusion of selling and administrative costs in inventory valuation was settled in the 1920s in the negative.

The topic of conservatism found its way into inventory valuation as auditors faced the problem of inventory valuations for statement purposes. Robert Hiester Montgomery, a practitioner and the writer of the leading textbook on auditing, in 1912 gave the classic rule for inventory value as "cost or market, whichever is the lower." He also noted the inconsistency of not writing up over cost but said that "the conservative course is to carry the items at cost and thus do away with the objectionable practice of anticipating a profit." In 1947, the Committee of Accounting Procedure (CAP) of the American Institute of Accountants issued Accounting Research Bulletin (ARB) No. 29, "Inventory Pricing," which limited the use of "market" by the concept of the "ceiling"—net realizable value—and the "floor"—net realizable value less normal profit margins. This seemed to be a moderating of the concept of conservatism. ARB No. 29 stated: "In applying the rule (cost or market, whichever is lower), however, judgement must always be exercised and no loss should be recognized unless the evidence indicates clearly that a loss has been sustained." This moderation was probably felt necessary in light of the practice of general reserves for inventory.

The increased economic activity during World War I and the resultant price increases brought the base stock inventory method into the forefront. In this method, basic raw materials are carried by some manufacturers at a certain level at fixed and, perhaps, arbitrary prices. The excess over the level was valued at current costs. While this method worked in World War I, there was subsequently strong opposition to it by the Bureau of Internal Revenue, which disallowed its use.

The topic of standard costs became the dominant topic for inventory valuation in the early and mid-1930s. The topic of last in, first out (LIFO) inventory valuation for basic commodities came to the forefront in the late 1930s. One of the leaders in the LIFO struggle was Maurice Peloubet, who was also in the leadership of those arguing for the base stock method, somewhat analogous to the LIFO approach. The 1950s marked the beginning of the use of the direct costing method of inventory valuation. While the method was first mentioned by Jonathan Harris in 1936, it remained relatively dormant during the Depression years and the "cost plus" days of World War II and the Korean conflict. While continuing in popularity in some circles, the concept of direct costing came under heavy fire in the 1980s and later from the proponents of activity-based costing.

In the late 1950s and in the 1960s, theorists developed current-value bases for inventory valuation. This interest was a part of overall valuation philosophies expressed by such writers as R.J. Chambers, Edgar O. Edwards and Philip W. Bell, and Robert R. Sterling. By 1979 the Financial Accounting Standards Board (FASB), in Financial Accounting Standard (FAS) No. 33, "Financial Reporting and Changing Prices," required large public enterprises to report current cost of inventory in a supplementary schedule. In 1986 FAS No. 89 dropped the requirement, although it encouraged such reporting on a voluntary basis.

There was a refocusing on manufacturing in the United States during the middle and late 1980s. With this refocusing came an inventory accounting response, activity-based costing (ABC). In the late 1980s, the just-in-time (JIT) philosophy tended to minimize the issues in inventory valuation with its emphasis on inventory reduction.

Inventory accounting has been and will remain a very complex topic. The topic seems to be an additive one, in that each iteration in inventory accounting adds complexity without a corresponding drop in the older methods. In fact, there appears to be recycling of ideas in the case of base stock/LIFO and JIT/ABC.

Richard Vangermeersch

Bibliography

Chambers, R.J. *Accounting, Finance and Management.* Sydney: Arthur Andersen and Co., 1969.

Edwards, E.O., and P.W. Bell. *The Theory and Measurement of Business Income.* Berkeley and Los Angeles: University of California Press, 1961.

Harris, J.N. "What Did We Earn Last Month?" *NACA Bulletin*, January 15, 1936, pp. 501–526.

Montgomery, R.H. *Auditing: Theory and Practice.* New York: Ronald Press, 1912.

Peloubet, M.E. "Valuation of Normal Stocks at Fixed Prices." In *Proceedings: International Congress on Accounting, New York City, 1929*, pp. 565–581. New York: International Congress of Accounting, 1930.

Sterling, R.R. *Theory of the Measurement of Enterprise Income.* Lawrence, KS: The University Press of Kansas, 1970.

See also ACCOUNTING RESEARCH BULLETINS; ACTIVITY BASED COSTING; BASE STOCK METHOD; CHAMBERS, RAYMOND JOHN; CHURCH, ALEXANDER HAMILTON; COMMON COSTS; CONSERVATISM; DIRECT COSTING; EDWARDS AND BELL: REPLACEMENT-COST ACCOUNTING; JUST-IN-TIME MANUFACTURING; LAST IN, FIRST OUT (LIFO); LEWIS, J. SLATER; MONTGOMERY, ROBERT HIESTER; PACIOLI, LUCA; STERLING, ROBERT R.

Italy, after Pacioli

During the first part of the sixteenth century, many books of accounting were printed in Venice: Giovanni Antonio Tagliente in *Luminario di Arithmetica* (1525), Gerolamo Cardano in *Practica Arithmeticae et Mensurandi Singularis* (1539), Domenico Manzoni (1540), Alvise Casanova (1558). Nearly 100 years after Luca Pacioli's *Summa de Arithmetica* (1494), Don Angelo Pietra, in *Indrizzo degli economi* (1586), first set forth the true function of a trial balance and recommended the use of financial statements. Ludovico Flori (1636) was first to recommend an allocation of income and expense to the specific accounting periods to which they might pertain and was one of the first adherents of the personification of accounts, a teaching device often used in Pacioli's *Summa* on double entry, considered one of the best up to the nineteenth century.

The oldest society of professional accountants, *Collegio dei Raxonati*, was founded in Venice in 1581. Requirements for membership were rigorous. By 1669 the college had become so powerful that no Venetian could do accounting work, in connection with either public administration or the law, unless he was a member.

The numerous works by seventeenth- and eighteenth-century Italian authors offered rules and norms for managing mercantile, banking, and insurance operations efficiently and for keeping double entry accounts of such operations in order to calculate their results. It was in the nineteenth century that works of a more scientific character began to appear.

Fundamental movements in the evolution of accounting studies in nineteenth-century Italy are represented by Ludovico Giuseppe Crippa

(1838) and Francesco Villa (1840–1841, 1850), the first authors to offer a core of accounting theories founded on impersonal accounts and who can be seen as forerunners of the contemporary entity theory of accounts. Other influential authors of the first half of the nineteenth century included Niccolo D'Anastasio in *La Scrittura Doppia Ridotta a Scienza* (1803), Giuseppe Bornaccini in *Idea Teoriche e Pratiche di Ragionateria e di Doppia Registrazione* (1818), and Antonio Tonzig (1857–1859), who addressed the issues in government accounting in *Trattato della Scienza dell'amministrazione e della Contabilita Privata e dello Stato*.

Until the end of the last century, the personalistic theory was dominant in Italy. The framework of Francesco Marchi's (1867) four-series-of-accounts view of double entry theory emphasized the distinction among proprietor accounts, administrator accounts, consignees accounts, and correspondents accounts. Marchi's theory was the starting point for Giuseppe Cerboni's logismography (1873, 1866/1894), a complex accounting model extended to a theory of both private firms and government administration and applying as well to state accounts: Starting from an agency concept that there are two parties in business management, the owner and the agency, there follows the principle that there are two fundamental accounts of logismography, the proprietor account and the agency account, which form the capital balance or economic balance.

One of Cerboni's followers, Giovanni Rossi, the philosopher of logismography (*Delle attinenzi Logismografiche, Studi sulle Teoriche Cerboniane*, 1878, *Trattato di Ragioneria Scientifica*, 1921), was the promoter of a special form of personalistic double entry theory, called juristic theory. Rossi also developed a mathematical theory of double entry (1889, *Teorio Matematica della Scrittura doppio Italiana*, 1901), a methodology in the form of *scacchiera* (chessboard), but a generalization of accounting method is perhaps already traceable in D'Anastasio (1803). Toward the end of the last century, Fabio Besta introduced a shift from personal accounts to impersonal accounts and formulated a materialistic theory in reaction to logismography. Another example of materialistic theory is in Pisani (1880).

Besta's insights are founded on a clearly outlined proprietorship theory. His three-volume *La Ragioneria* (1891–1916) is to date the best treatise on equity-based accounting. At the center of his discussion of accounting is the notion of proprietorship.

Besta defined accounting as a science of economic control, applicable to every sort of concern—(family) properties, firms' patrimonies, public utilities, and public properties. He included in economic control not only all of the calculations, estimates, conjectures, and final balance sheets that throw light upon the stewardship of management, but also "administrative compulsion," or those acts calculated to force managers, employees, and workmen to carry out their duties with care and precision.

He established a general business framework, outlining the organizational design as a premise to economic control, allowing management to make rational decisions and govern the business according to economic laws. Besta had many faithful disciples who developed and refined his ideas, but the most notable among them is Gino Zappa, a leader of the so-called Venetian school and the founder of concern economics.

Concern economics (*economia d'azienda*) is the core of modern Italian accounting theory. It is a comprehensive system covering all aspects of economic activity and including such different areas as decision theory, accounting and finance theory, and organization theory.

The main components of concern economics are: (1) premises of value; the institution, its environment and the concern; economic subject and economic object; (2) personnel organization; (3) capital; capital components for production and consumption; (4) taxation; (5) management and planning systems; (6) economic efficiency; (7) economic environment; markets and sectors of concerns and (8) concern information systems.

The special discipline of concern information systems yields theories for synthetic expression of the concern "system of values," a particular class of economic values. So the system of values, an economic system of interdependent evaluation principles used for each class of elements, is both a continuous, dynamic, general system as well as a composite of subsystems. It clarifies relevant aspects of the movements of market prices and brings to the study of these movements knowledge of every kind of concern that participated in production, consumption, and exchange; from this should follow a new structure of the "theory of value," of the "theory of money," and the units of measure.

In Italian doctrine, the valuation theory of financial statements, which constitute logical economic systems, has been scientifically elaborated according to well-defined hypotheses on information requirements of financial statements, the rationale of valuation, and the system of values that can best provide the information sought. The specific valuation principles of each element of a values-system for a given financial statement cannot be defined without reference to how the element functions in the system, the logical consistency among values within the system, and the function of the system itself.

The minimum standard of reporting in Italy is governed by the Civil Code. The institutional context of accounting at present is also characterized by the company law reform and tax law reform, passed in the 1970s. Legislation enacted in April 1974 established the National Commission for Companies and Stock Exchange—*Commissione Nazionale per le Società e la Borsa* (CONSOB)—to control quoted companies and stock-exchange activities.

The company law reform, initially enacted in June 1974 and integrated by numerous subsequent acts, presidential and ministry decrees, implemented by the Ministry of Finance, improved considerably the quantity and quality of information required in published financial statements, particularly those concerned with the income capacity of an enterprise. In Italy consolidated statements (still not the basis for dividends and taxes computation) had been reported on a voluntary basis together with separate statements of parent and subsidiary companies. The CONSOB is not allowed by law to indicate the criteria used to draw consolidated accounts, but can only request information on accounting principles adopted, consolidation criteria, changes in group structure, connections between holding company annual accounts and consolidated ones and so on.

Italy prescribes historic-cost accounting, and there are some companies that explicitly relate their annual report figures voluntarily to inflation accounting as a basis for their cost calculation and dividend policy. From the legalistic point of view, inflation accounting can hardly be applied since it undermines the certainty of rights which is supposedly assured by historical values when adjusted by general price-level restatement. The recent revaluations decided by the Ministry of Finance in act no.

576, 1975, act no. 72, 1983, act no. 408, 1990, and act no. 413, 1991 are a case in point. The last revaluation provision is a compulsory one.

Thus, for the correct portrayal of the "faithful picture" (EEC 4th Directive, article 22) referred to the situation of the closing financial year to the results of future financial years, the directors, upon recurrence of the circumstances which so require, with the consent of the Board of Auditors, must make a revaluation of the past values of fixed assets, in order to contribute to the correct determination of the profits of future financial years by means of depreciation computed on the revaluated assets.

The provisions in force in Italy, except for that which has been laid down by special provisions of the law, do not explicitly provide for the revaluation of past values. A notable constraint upon resort to revaluation is of a tax nature; but the compulsory revaluation provision of 1991 does not exempt the revaluation surplus from taxation.

It is not unusual in Italy to prepare two sets of financial statements at the end of each financial reporting period—one set for purposes of tax accounting and another for financial accounting and reporting. They are prepared on different premises and this very difference is responsible for their side-by-side appearance. In Italy massive legal requirements underly both tax accounting and financial accounting. The heavy emphasis on tax considerations is induced by the fact that Italian financial accounting strongly influences taxation and vice versa: valuation in the balance sheet prepared for tax authorities depends to a great extent on the valuation in the annual financial statement. In this way, financial accounting and tax computation are tied together, and, therefore, in Italy the tax consequences are the most important economic consequences. The debate about the implementation of the EEC 4th and 7th Directives into Italian law in 1991 can hardly be understood without references to its tax implications.

The implementation of these directives in Italy, without changing the basic structure of the accounting system, has not created an accounting revolution, taking into consideration the recent company law reform and tax law reform. The most recent accounting regulations have involved the observation of the principles elaborated by the National Council of Doctors of Commerce and the IASC principles.

Giuseppe Galassi

Bibliography

Amaduzzi, A. *L'azienda nel suo sistema e nei suoi principi*. Torino: UTET, 1992.

Amodeo, D. *Ragioneria generale delle imprese*. Napoli: Giannini, 1965.

Besta, F. *La Ragioneria*. 3 vols. Milano: Vallardi, 1891–1916.

Casanova, A. *Specchio lucidissimo nel quale si vedono essere diffinito tutti i modi, et ordini de scrittura, che si deve menare nelli negotiamenti della Mercantia, Cambii, Recambii, con li loro corrispondentie, disgarbugliando, et illuminando l'intelletto a negotianti, opera non più veduta*. Venezia: Comin Trino, 1558.

Cerboni, G. *La Ragioneria Scientifica e le Sue Relazioni con le Discipline Amminutrative e Sociali*, vols. 1, 2. Rome: Loescher, 1886, 1894.

———. *Primi saggi di logismografia*. Firenze: Minerva, 1873.

———. *Quadro di Contabilita per le Scritture in Paptita Doppia della Ragioneria Generale dello Stato*. Rome: Stamperia Reale, 1877.

Chatfield, M. *A History of Accounting Thought*. Hinsdale, IL: Dryden Press, 1974.

Crippa, L.G. *La Scienza dei Conti Ossia l'arte di Tenere i Registri e Compilare i Bilanci di ogni Azienda*. Milano: G.B. Bianchi, 1838.

Ferrero, G. *La valutazione del capitale di bilancio*. Milano: Giuffrè, 1988.

Flori, L. *Trattato del Modo di tenere il libro doppio domestico col suo esemplare*. Palermo: St. Decio Cirillo, 1636.

Galassi, G. *Misurazioni differenziali, misurazioni globali e decisioni d'azienda*. Milano: Giuffrè, 1974.

Manzoni, D. *Quaderno Doppio col suo Giornale Novamente composto et Diligentissimamente ordinato Secondo il costume di Venetia*. Venezia: Comin de Trino, 1540.

Marchi, F. *I cinquecontisti, ovvero la ingannevole teorica che viene insegnata negli Istituti Tecnici del Regno e fuori del Regno, intorno al sistema della scrittura a partita doppia, e nuovo saggio per la facile intelligenza e applicazione di quel sistema*. Prato: Giacchetti, 1867.

Pisani, E. *La statmografia applicata alle aziende private*. Modica: Piccilto e Antoci, 1880.

Rossi, G. *Lo scacchiere anglo-normanno e la scrittura in partita doppia a forma di scacchiera*. Roma: Botta, 1889.

Villa, F. *Elementi di amministrazione e contabilita*. Pavia: Bizzoni, 1850.

———. *La Contabilita Applicata alle Amministrazioni Private e Pubbliche*, vols. 1, 2. Milano: Angelo Monti, 1840–1841.

See also DIRECTIVES OF THE EUROPEAN COMMUNITY (UNION); FLORI, LUDOVICO; HISTORICAL COST; INTERNATIONAL ACCOUNTING STANDARDS COMMITTEE; MANZONI, DOMENICO; PACIOLI, LUCA; PIETRA, ANGELO; PROFESSIONAL ACCOUNTING BODIES; SOCIAL RESPONSIBILITIES OF ACCOUNTANTS; STEWARDSHIP; TAX-ORDAINED ACCOUNTING; UNIFORMITY; ZAPPA, GINO

J

Japan

Nara Period (710–794)

The earliest surviving accounting books in Japan date back to the eighth century. Among them are *Shouzei-cho*, accounting documents of the 730s that were saved and stored in the *Shousoin*, or Imperial Treasure House, in Nara. The *Shouzei-cho* were reports compiled by each province to report final accounts on tax to the Central Government in Nara. In the Nara Period (710–794), provinces were governed by the Law Code. It was mandatory for each province to report taxes to the Government.

The history of accounting in Japan was much in the dark for the next 800 years. It is likely that an accounting system was adopted by large Buddhist temples as well as at the central government; however, no clear evidence is available regarding the kind of system used and how it functioned in those years.

Around 1542, a group of Portuguese sailors drifted to the island of Tanegashima and introduced firearms for the first time into Japan. Western culture has continued to make its way into Japanese culture since that time. Most well-accepted theories in Japan's academic circles of accounting are that Japan's accounting system was not under Western influence until the nineteenth century.

Shiwake-chouzuke, "classification bookkeeping," prevailed in the late sixteenth century. It has much the same meaning as Italy's "Partia Doppia" or double entry bookkeeping and could be the adoption of an Italian-style system into Japanese bookkeeping in the late sixteenth century.

Edo Period (1600–1867)

The Tomiyama family's account book, known as "Ashikaga-cho," and used by merchants, is the oldest that still exists in Japan. The Tomiyama family's "Ashikaga-cho" accounting record contained calculation of its properties for a period of 25 years, from 1615 to 1640.

The second oldest merchant account book is the Konoike family's "Sanyo-cho" or "calculation note" in Osaka Province. The book covered accounting records in 1670 and kept track of final accounts. It was a notebook for account settlement based on a double entry bookkeeping method.

The most representative account books in the eighteenth century include the Mitsui family's "Oomotokata-kanjyo-mokuroku" ("Account Lists of H 28 1620 Head Office") dated in 1710 and the Nakai family's "Tanaoroshi-ki" ("Inventories Lists") in 1746. Both families were well established. The Mitsui family started in the Edo Period in Ise Province and still enjoys celebrity for its continuous prosperity up to the present, while the Nakai family started in Oomi Province, where many merchants became wealthy.

Also noteworthy are account books that were kept in 1753 and 1762 by the Honma family in Dewa Province. The "Kanjo-mokuroku" ("Account Lists") kept by the Tanabe family of Izumo Province from 1801 to 1804 became famous as the first account book on which academic analysis was performed on the basis of evidence, in 1936. All of these accounting books were double entry, and all were indigenous to Japan.

Meiji Era (1868 to 1911)

The end of the Edo Period marked the end of Japan's isolation and the beginning of its modernization. The landmark year falls in 1873, when Western-style bookkeeping was introduced and accounting based on modern schemes began to spread.

The first book on Western-style accounting—*Choai-no-ho*—was written and issued in Japan by Yukichi Fukuzawa (1834–1901). In December 1873, a manuscript written by Alexander Allan Shand (1844–1930) was translated and published as *Ginko-Boki-Seiho*, Japan's first book on the subject of double entry bookkeeping. Shand was born in Aberdeen, Scotland and came to Japan to enter the service of the Japanese government. In 1895, Naotaro Shimono (1866–1939) published the first work on bookkeeping based on the concept of Japan's own *Boki Seiri* (detailed method of bookkeeping). Since then, modern Western-style bookkeeping has been generally accepted.

Accounting by Ryozou Yoshida (1878–1943) was published in 1910 and is regarded as a rough translation of Henry Rand Hatfield's *Modern Accounting*. With its publication, a static theory of accounting began to penetrate Japan.

Meanwhile Michisuke Ueno (1888–1962) introduced Johann Friedrich Schär's theory into Japan. The theories addressed the calculation systems of Japan's Commercial Law and Tax System. In 1917, the Japan Society of Accounting was established by scholars and those good at handling practical business affairs, including Yoshida and Sekigoro Higashi (1865–1947), a foremost professional accountant in Japan.

1920s to World War II

It was Shimono who strongly proposed an accounting theory for Japan. He put forth outspoken criticism of static accounting theory which, at that time, constituted a traditional accounting thought, and asserted a dynamic thought of accounting as expressed in his theses, 1926 and 1929.

Shimono's accounting theory lacked a cost allocation doctrine. The shortcoming of his theory came to light and posed criticism that the concept of fixed assets and depreciation would not work in his theory.

Following Shimono's theory, Tetsuzo Ohta (1889–1970) corrected Shimono, acknowledged the cost allocation doctrine, and laid the foundation for a dynamic theory of accounting in Japan. With Yoshida's cooperation, Ohta drafted the "Rules for the Preparation of Finan-

cial Statements" in 1934. Along with the "Rules for Manufacturing Cost Accounting" established in 1937, the "Rules for the Preparation of Financial Statements" paved the way for organizing a new accounting system for Japanese corporations. In 1938, the Japan Accounting Association was founded by scholars including Yoshida, Ohta and Kiyoshi Kurosawa (1902–1990).

The Japanese Army compiled the "Guidelines for Cost Accounting for Military Supplies" to decide prices for procurement of goods. The guidelines were fixed in 1939 for the Ground Force (Army) and in 1940 for the Maritime Force (Navy). These two sets of guidelines were combined by the Planning Agency in 1935 under the leadership of Torao Nakanishi (1896–1975). As a result, they were incorporated in the "Essentials of Cost Accounting," enacted in 1942.

Post–World War II

The dismantling of the *Zaibatsu* (financial group alignment) was carried out after World War II. Since then, Japan's economy has undergone a revolutionary change. The improvements of various previously established systems including tax reform, amendment of the Commercial Code, and the Securities and Exchange Law led to the establishment of an entirely new accounting system. The Registered Public Accountants Law of 1927 was replaced with the Certified Public Accountants Law established in 1948.

In 1948, the Business Accounting Investigation Committee was set up within the government. Thus four divisions were established with Ueno as chairman and with chairmen for each individual division.

The activities by each division were promoted by Kurosawa's chairman in the first division, specializing in accounting standards for business, by Ueno in the second division for educational issues on accounting, by Iwao Iwata (1905–1955) in the third division for audit standards, and by Nakanishi in the fourth division for cost accounting standards.

The Business Accounting Investigation Committee disseminated the products of its activities: "Financial Accounting Principles (or Standard)" in 1949 and "Audit Standards" in 1950. Furthermore, the "Cost Accounting Standards" were made public in 1953 by the Business Accounting Deliberation Council, the reorganized and renamed former Business Accounting Investigation Committee.

Several amendments have been made to the "Financial Accounting Principles" and "Audit Standards," which contributed much to Japan's accounting system and contributed greatly to the high economic growth of postwar Japan.

There are two groups of professional accountants in Japan: the Japan Institute of Certified Public Accountants and the Japanese Federation of Tax Accountants' Associations. The former was established in 1949 as a voluntary association, became a corporate organization in 1953, and was reorganized as a special corporate organization in 1966. The Japanese Federation of Tax Accountants' Associations was founded after the existing federation was transformed with the enactment of the Certified Tax Accountant Law in 1951 and was reorganized again in 1956.

Kozo Iwanabe

Bibliography

Iwanabe, K. "Accounting in Japan: Some Aspects," *Chaire de science comptables*, Chaire No. 4, École des Hautes Études Commercials, Montreal, November 1990. Reprinted in *Assurances*, April 1991, pp. 95–113.

Someya, K. "Accounting Revolutions in Japan," *Accounting Historians Journal*, June 1989, pp. 75–86.

See also DOUBLE ENTRY BOOKKEEPING: ORIGINS; HATFIELD, HENRY RAND; KIMURA, WASABURO; KOJIMA, OSAMU; MEDIEVAL ACCOUNTING; PACKARD, SILAS SADLER

Johnson and Kaplan's *Relevance Lost: The Rise and Fall of Management Accounting*

The 1988 winner of the American Accounting Association/Deloitte Haskins and Sells Wildman Medal for excellence in accounting literature, *Relevance Lost* (1987) was the combined effort of H. Thomas Johnson, a noted accounting and business historian, and Robert S. Kaplan, Arthur Lowes Dickinson Professor of Accounting at the Harvard Business School and also professor of industrial administration at Carnegie Mellon University. *Relevance Lost* has been widely viewed as bringing the topics of cost accounting and management accounting out of the closet and to the attention of all levels of managers, accountants, and accounting academics.

It is a book that is both readable and worth reading, especially for those with no background in economic history and business history. *Relevance Lost* details the decline of management accounting in terms of decision making from a strong beginning in the nineteenth century to the first part of the twentieth century. The authors stress that modern computing capabilities allow the lost ideas of the past to be operable today. Johnson and Kaplan felt that management accounting started to stagnate in the 1920s, when financial accounting needs of inventory valuation and the cost of computing made obsolete the excellently designed cost systems established by such engineers as Alexander Hamilton Church.

The authors reviewed the history of a number of firms and industries for a single activity—such leaders as Andrew Carnegie in steel and Albert Fink in railroads, as well as Marshall Field in distribution.

Relevance Lost offers a review of the scientific management movement of the works of Frederick W. Taylor, Harrington Emerson, G. Charter Harrison, and Church. The authors give illustrations from DuPont Powder, a vertically integrated company, and from General Motors, a multidivisional organization. Much attention is given to the excellent management accounting techniques of F. Donaldson Brown, who was involved with both companies.

Relevance Lost concluded that American industrial companies had by 1925 developed virtually every management accounting procedure up to the 1980s. Diversity of products led to a muddling of financial information based on the allocation of overhead costs by direct labor methods. America was fortunate to be relatively isolated from world competition until about 1970, so that this misinformation was not disastrous. Johnson and Kaplan were very critical of cost accounting texts, which ignored the excellent work of the engineers from the scientific management movement and accounting academics in general.

Relevance Lost reviews the works of J.M. Clark on overhead; economists from the London School of Economics on opportunity costs; and William Vatter for a clear distinction between management accounting and financial accounting. The book delves into a typical cost system utilizing a direct cost allocation system. This system generates misinformation to and misdirection for operating managers by introducing unintended cross subsidies among products. Johnson and Kaplan stress that managers are rewarded in the short run by financial accounting for misbehaving in the long run in managerial accounting by exploiting accounting conventions, playing games in paper entrepreneurship, and reducing discretionary expenditures for such items as research and employee training costs.

The book offers an up-to-date overview of total quality control, just-in-time inventory systems, computer-integrated manufacturing systems, short product life cycles, and deregulation. Overhead costs, it concludes, are a much higher percent of total costs and need to be understood and controlled much more carefully than in the past. This is possible by modern technology for data management. Johnson and Kaplan present some general solutions for improvements in using management accounting systems to facilitate process control and to compute product costs. Cost control system designers must leave their offices and become involved on the production floor. The authors warn against various uses of information on short-term product cost. They call for a reversal in the thinking that led to the direct cost movement, and encourage the Japanese model for the reduction of set-up time. Marketing, distribution and service costs are covered with a call for the need to apply the same methods which control product costs. Johnson and Kaplan conclude with a reiteration of the need for nonfinancial indicators present in the management accounting of the 19th century.

Reviewers of *Relevance Lost*, while praising the work, raised some important questions. One of these deals with the Japanese culture towards control with emphasis on the group and unit outputs compared to the West with emphasis on individual control and accounting profits. All in all *Relevance Lost* is probably the most important book written in management accounting in the last fifty years.

Richard Vangermeersch

Bibliography

Ezzamel, M., K. Hoskin, and R. Macve. "Managing It All by Numbers: A Review of Johnson and Kaplan's *Relevance Lost*," *Accounting and Business Research*, Spring 1990, pp. 153–166.

Johnson, H.T., and R.S. Kaplan. *Relevance Lost: The Rise and Fall of Management Accounting*. Boston: Harvard Business School Press, 1987.

———. "The Rise and Fall of Management Accounting: Management Accounting Information Is Too Late, Too Aggregated, and Too Distorted to Be Relevant," *Management Accounting*, January 1987, pp. 22–29.

Kaplan, R.S. "The Evolution of Management Accounting," *Accounting Review*, July 1984, pp. 390–418.

———. "Managerial Manufacturing Performance: A New Challenge for Managerial Accounting Research," *Accounting Review*, October 1983, pp. 686–705.

Noreen, E. "H. Thomas Johnson and Robert S. Kaplan's *Relevance Lost: The Rise and Fall of Management Accounting*," *Accounting Horizons*, December 1987, pp. 110–116.

Staubus, G.J. "The Dark Ages of Cost Accounting: The Role of Miscues in the Literature," *Accounting Historians Journal*, Fall 1987, pp. 1–18.

See also ACTIVITY BASED COSTING; BROWN, F. DONALDSON; CHURCH, ALEXANDER HAMILTON; CLARK, JOHN MAURICE; COMMON COSTS; COMPUTING TECHNOLOGY IN THE WEST: THE IMPACT ON THE PROFESSION OF ACCOUNTING; COST AND/OR MANAGEMENT ACCOUNTING; DIRECT COSTING; EMERSON, HARRINGTON; ENGINEERING AND ACCOUNTING; JOHNSON, H. THOMAS; JUST-IN-TIME MANUFACTURING; MANAGEMENT ACCOUNTING; TAYLOR, FREDERICK WINSLOW; VATTER, WILLIAM JOSEPH

Johnson, H. Thomas (1938–)

H. Thomas Johnson is an accounting scholar well versed in economic and business history. He has a B.A. in economics from Harvard University, an M.B.A. in accounting from Rutgers University, a CPA, an M.A. in history, and a Ph.D. in history/economics from the University of Wisconsin. He holds the Retzlaff Chair in Quality Management at Portland State University. Johnson was awarded the Newcomer Award in Business History for the best article published in the *Business History Review* in 1978 and the Hourglass Award of the Academy of Accounting Historians in 1981. He was president of that organization in 1982 and 1983.

Johnson has focused on the history of management accounting, rather than on the more usual—perhaps because the data are more accessible—history of financial accounting. His efforts have broadened and deepened through the years as he has brought the visions of the business and economic historians Alfred D. Chandler Jr. and Oliver E. Williamson to the fields of accounting and accounting history. Johnson's trademark is digging deep into the archival records of companies. His first venture, into the archival records of the Lyman Mills, showed his scholarship and led to the finding that an integrated double entry cost accounting system existed long before prior researchers had thought. The management of Lyman Mills utilized its elaborate cost system to facilitate control of internal plant operations.

Johnson then focused on an organization of a much larger scale, DuPont, researching company records at the Eleutherian Mills Historical Library and stressing the importance of the centralized accounting system at DuPont for both planning and finance. Johnson continued his research by studying General Motors, focusing on the work of F. Donaldson Brown, who had transferred from DuPont to GM in the early 1920s.

Johnson offered the results of his research and his new interpretations of management-accounting history in a series of articles and books. He believes accounting historians can provide valuable insights into the relationship between the growth of productivity and innovation in the organization of big business. He also articulated in "Markets, Hierarchies, and the History of Management Accounting" the work of Williamson into management accounting by stressing his concepts of "bounded rationality" and "opportunism" to explain the organizational strategy of the firm. Johnson and Robert S. Kaplan used the theme of the historical method as the basis of their award-winning 1987 book, *Relevance Lost: The Rise and Fall of Management Accounting*. (This book is separately reviewed in the *Encyclopedia*.) More recently, in his quest to satisfy customer expectations, Johnson has focused his attentions on the importance of statistical control over process, rather than managerial control through traditional accounting measurements. He believes strongly that organizations need to empower their employees at all levels to meet the challenges in today's global environment. Once again, in *Relevance Regained* (1992), Johnson utilized his historical research to place his findings in an historical setting, both for business and business schools.

Richard Vangermeersch

Bibliography

Johnson, H.T. "Early Cost Accounting for Internal Management Control," *Business History Review*, Winter 1972, pp. 466–474.

———. "Management Accounting in an Early Integrated Industrial: E.I. duPont de Nemours Powder Company, 1903–1912," *Business History Review*, Summer 1975, pp. 184–204.

———. "Management Accounting in an Early Multidivisional Organization: General Motors in the 1920s," *Business History Review*, Winter 1978, pp. 490–517.

———. "Markets, Hierarchies, and the History of Management Accounting," originally presented at the Third International Congress of Accounting Historians, August, 1980. In *A New Approach To Management Accounting History*. New York: Garland, 1986.

———. *Relevance Regained: From Top-Down Control to Bottom-Up Empowerment*. New York: Free Press, 1992.

———. "The Role of Accounting History in the Study of Modern Business Enterprise," *Accounting Review*, July 1975, pp. 444–450.

See also ACADEMY OF ACCOUNTING HISTORIANS; ACTIVITY BASED COSTING; BROWN, F. DONALDSON; JOHNSON AND KAPLAN'S *RELEVANCE LOST: THE RISE AND FALL OF MANAGEMENT ACCOUNTING*

Jones, Edward Thomas (1767–1833)

Bristol accountant and author of *The English System of Bookkeeping by Single or Double Entry* (1796), Edward Thomas Jones patented a hybrid system that tried to combine the simplicity of single entry bookkeeping with the arithmetic checks on accuracy provided by a double entry system.

The English System included a daybook, a ledger, an alphabetical chart of accounts, and an optional journal. The daybook had three columns. Transactions were first entered in the center column to establish the correct monetary amounts, which were later posted as debits and credits to the left and right columns. Each month the debit and credit columns were to be totaled and reconciled to the center, or money, column.

Jones omitted all ledger accounts except cash, receivables, payables, and capital. Without a running balance of sales and purchases, income had to be found by side calculations. Because neither his daybook nor his ledger comprised a complete double entry record, Jones' claimed check on bookkeeping accuracy was incomplete.

Though his English System was never widely adopted, Jones was more than a failed critic of double entry bookkeeping. In his later writings he advocated the use of tabular account books, subsidiary ledgers, control accounts, and other labor saving devices that adapted Luca Pacioli's fifteenth-century system to the needs of nineteenth-century commerce.

Michael Chatfield

Bibliography

Strong, R. "Edward Thomas Jones." In *Biographies of Notable Accountants*, edited by H.R. Givens, pp. 18–19. New York: Random House, 1987.

Yamey, B.S. "Edward Jones and the Reform of Bookkeeping, 1795–1810." In *Studies in the History of Accounting*, edited by A.C. Littleton and B.S. Yamey, pp. 313–324. Homewood, IL: Irwin, 1956.

See also CHART OF ACCOUNTS; DAY BOOK; LEDGER; PACIOLI, LUCA; SUBSIDIARY LEDGER

Jones, Thomas (1804–1889)

Thomas Jones was an accountant and director of a business school in New York City. His *Principles and Practices of Bookkeeping* (1841) and *Bookkeeping and Accountship, Elementary and Practical* (1849) deserve to be called the first modern accounting textbooks.

Jones wrote at a time when there were few full-time public accountants and no national accounting firms, professional accounting organizations, or university accounting courses. Students had traditionally learned transaction analysis by memorizing debit and credit rules. Ledger classification was taught by account personification—that is, by treating ledger accounts either as living persons or as individuals separate from the business owner but responsible to him. In most textbooks, the final step

in the bookkeeping cycle was preparation of a trial balance to verify ledger accuracy.

Jones was among the first authors to depart from memorization and personification of accounts. He taught the bookkeeping cycle in reverse order: first introducing the financial statements, then the individual ledger accounts, and finally the rules of debit and credit. Jones believed that if bookkeeping and transaction analysis were taught in relation to financial statements, students would better understand the logic of bookkeeping, which would in turn provide a better understanding of the accounting process than could be achieved by memorizing arbitrary rules.

Jones also introduced proprietary theory into accounting instruction. His exposition was directly opposite to account personification and everything it implied. Accounting as he described it was mainly concerned with the statistical classification of data, and hardly at all with relationships among individuals. He viewed debits and credits as increases or decreases in account balances. He saw financial statements, not ledger balances, as the final step in the bookkeeping cycle. Accounts implied two statements of owners' affairs, the balance sheet and the income statement, each of which arrived independently at the same profit figure. Moreover, the interrelationship of real and nominal accounts suggested that both financial statements were equally important—that is, expenses and revenues are not mere modifications of capital, but produce an income figure which is valid in its own right because it includes far more detail than is revealed by asset revaluations and balance sheet changes in equities.

Jones' approach to accounting education was widely imitated, without acknowledgment, by later authors. Beginning in the mid-nineteenth century, journalization by rote and personification of ledger accounts gradually diminished in importance. Every modern financial accounting textbook owes something to Thomas Jones.

Michael Chatfield

Bibliography

Hughes, H.P. "The Contributions of Thomas Jones and Benjamin Franklin Foster," *Accounting Historians Journal,* Fall 1982, pp. 43–51.

Tondkar, R.H. "Thomas Jones." In *Bibliographies of Notable Accountants*, edited by H.R. Givens, pp. 20–21. New York: Random House, 1987.

See also ACCOUNTING EDUCATION IN THE UNITED STATES; DEBIT AND CREDIT; PERSONIFICATION OF ACCOUNTS; PROPRIETARY THEORY; TRIAL BALANCE

Journal

The journal is considered now to be any book of original entry. It is a chronological record of business events that are considered to be appropriate for accounting transactions.

The journal appears to have been a child of the fourteenth century in the city-states of Italy. The book of original entry before that period was the ledger. The earliest extant ledger of the period of the late Middle Ages consists of some fragments of the customers' ledger of an unidentified firm of bankers operating in Florence, Bologna, and Pisa in 1211. These accounts were kept in a narrative format, which wasted little space on the page, in contrast to a two-sided account.

Lee (1977) considered the earliest extant ledger of a double entry nature to be that of the Salon branch of the Florentine mercantile firm of Giovanni Farolfi and Company for 1299–1300. The accounts were also kept in a narrative format. De Roover (1956) found journals in the Genoese archives for the Lomellini Bank. In these journals, covering the years 1397 to 1431, albeit with numerous gaps, entries followed each other in chronological order. Starting in 1408, another bank in Genoa, the Bank of St. George, made use of journals. By 1460 the Medici Bank had a clerical staff of about 60 persons and had a wastebook, a journal, and a ledger. This was the basis of the accounting system described by Luca Pacioli in his treatise on double entry in *Summa de Arithmetica* (1494).

De Roover also noted two journals in the medieval account books from 1366 to 1369 of two Bruges money changers. In form and content, the journals resembled closely the journals of the Genoese bank. Entries were strictly in chronological order and were crossed out diagonally to indicate posting to the ledger. "Since checks were not in use, the journal served to record transfer orders as they came from the customer's lips."

Pacioli's treatise, titled "Particularis de Computis et Scripturis" (Particulars of Reckonings and Their Recordings), was the first printed piece on double entry accounting. In it, Pacioli placed much stress on the journal. He adopted the method of Venice with its three books—the memorandum book, also known as the scrapbook, wastebook, daybook, or blotter; the journal; and the ledger. In this method, as described by Pacioli, the journal starts with an inventory of the merchant. The memorandum book is used by the staff to note all transactions—in effect, this is a log of happenings in the business. A bookkeeper then transcribes each transaction into a journal. (Pacioli cautions that the journal must be carefully marked, as well as each page, not only for accurate record keeping but also so that the theft or other loss of a page will be noticed.) There is to be one currency used in the journal entry, which has to have a debit and a credit part. These entries are then posted to the ledger, and the pages of the relevant ledger accounts are noted in the journal for each entry. The closing of an old ledger calls for a detailed checking by two people of each journal entry to the ledger to determine the veracity of the ledger.

The legal importance of the journal was stressed by De Roover, who noted that the 1807 Napoleonic Code of Commerce considered the journal as the only official record and required that entries be made in strict chronological order without any blanks between them.

In *Accounting Evolution to 1900*, A.C. Littleton presented an excellent history of journal entries 1430 through 1900. In that 1933 book, Littleton said he thought the journal entry was not indispensable, and might conceivably disappear altogether from bookkeeping practice. He wrote: "Posting is made directly to the ledger from the column totals of various special books for most of the transaction of modern American business; only a minor portion of the ledger details comes through formal debit and credit journals." However, even today, with accounting systems using a database-management approach, there is still a need for journal entries.

Transactions that do not fit into the standard processing systems, such as cash receipts, cash disbursements, purchases, and the like, are recorded on journal vouchers. These basically represent a general journal. Additionally, many companies print out journals from their transaction files to assist auditors. The concept of the journal lives on.

Henry R. Schwarzbach
Richard Vangermeersch

Bibliography

De Roover, R. "The Development of Accounting prior to Luca Pacioli according to the Account Books of Medieval Merchants." In *Studies in the History of Accounting*, edited by A.C. Littleton and B.S. Yamey, pp. 114–174. Homewood, IL: Irwin, 1956.

Lee, G.A. "The Coming of Age of Double Entry: The Giovanni Farolfi Ledger of 1299–1300," *Accounting Historians Journal*, Fall 1977, pp. 79–96.

———. "The Florentine Bank Ledger Fragments of 1211: Some New Insights," *Journal of Accounting Research*, Spring 1973, pp. 47–61.

Littleton, A.C. *Accounting Evolution to 1900*. New York: American Institute Publishing, 1933. Reprint. New York: Russell and Russell, 1966.

Pacioli, L. "Particulars of Reckonings and Their Recordings." In J.B. Geijsbeek, *Ancient Double-Entry Bookkeeping. Luca Pacioli's Treatise*. Denver: Geijsbeek, 1914. Reprint. Houston: Scholars Book Company, 1974, and Osaka: Nihon Shoseki, 1975.

See also BARBARIGO, ANDREA; CLOSING ENTRIES AND PROCEDURES; COMPUTING TECHNOLOGY IN THE WEST: THE IMPACT ON THE PROFESSION OF ACCOUNTING; DEBIT AND CREDIT; DONALDO SORANZO AND BROTHERS; FAROLFI COMPANY LEDGER; LEDGER; LITTLETON, A.C.; MANZONI, DOMENICO; MEDICI ACCOUNTS; MEMORANDUM BOOK; PACIOLI, LUCA; STEPHENS, HUSTCRAFT

Just-in-Time Manufacturing

Most people think of Just-in-Time (JIT) manufacturing as a "new" concept born in the lean years of the Japanese post-World War II economy. It is true that the formal JIT model was developed by Taiichi Ohno at Toyota in the 1960s, but few people know that the basis for this revolutionary design of plant-floor operations grew from the writings of Henry Ford in 1926. In his landmark book, *Today and Tomorrow*, Ford laid out his thesis on the design and operation of manufacturing systems, the penultimate achievement being the River Rouge project that transformed iron ore to automobiles in under five days. He wrote: "Time waste differs from material waste in that there can be no salvage. The easiest of all wastes, and the hardest to correct, is this waste of time, because

wasted time does not litter the floor like wasted materials."

What were the keys to Ford's, and later Toyota's, success? Three basic concepts formed the basis for the JIT model: (1) learning from waste; (2) the importance of the human element (Ford doubled wages in his plants, resulting in massive increases in productivity); and (3) the central role played by time, systems thinking, and quality in the manufacturing process. Today, JIT models are being used to cut waste and improve the performance of companies in every major industry. On the plant floor, company after company is using JIT to organize workflows and manage inventories. Off the plant floor, banks are using JIT methods to manage the check-processing function. Far from being a fad, JIT is a tried and proven method for increasing the effectiveness of work processes.

JIT is one of the core techniques clustered under the philosophy of *continuous improvement* through the elimination of waste, whenever it occurs in the organization. JIT attempts to minimize the waste (time and materials) resulting from moving and queuing materials on the plant floor by grouping machines together in a cellular design that reflects the sequence of tasks necessary to complete a product. A cellular structure is a radical shift from the functional grouping of machines and activities that typifies Western businesses. The benefits of the cellular design are reduced work-in-process inventory, a balanced production process, smoother flows of materials through the plant, and greatly reduced cycle and throughput times.

JIT is more than a new way of arranging machines on the plant floor. By coordinating the delivery of raw materials with customer demand for finished goods, JIT transforms manufacturing from a "push" to a "demand pull" setting. Products are moved from one work station to the next based on demand; if there is no need for the output of a work center, production does not take place. Finally, JIT relies heavily on the expertise and skills of the workforce for its success. Line workers design, maintain, manage, and control the cell's activities. Without honest empowerment of the workforce, in fact, JIT implementations falter. Moving the authority to make decisions to the point of action is the key to the "stop and fix" mentality that pervades successful JIT systems.

JIT's impact on the accounting process starts with the development of the basic cost pools that are used to estimate product costs. Where traditional standard-costing systems focus on direct labor or direct materials as the primary elements of cost, JIT systems assign all of the costs caused by a manufacturing cell directly to it. These costs include the labor used in the cell (both direct and indirect), all machine costs (that is, depreciation, power, maintenance, and supplies), indirect materials, supervision, material handling and control, and, in some cases, even accounting support.

The costs accumulated in the cell are charged to products on a "cycle time" basis: Total costs in a cell are divided by good units produced. The tie to the financial-accounting system is achieved through "backflushing"; the accounting transactions needed to transfer inventory dollars from raw materials to finished goods are triggered by the completion of the manufacturing cycle. This change greatly simplifies the accounting process, removing time, effort, and transactions from the accounting system and freeing up financial managers to do their value-creating activities.

Companies are continuing to experiment with other accounting innovations in JIT settings, including the use of trended average historical costs as the basis for tracking continuous improvement efforts; "cost of quality" reporting to detail the costs of, and improvements in, the quality of products and services; activity-based costing for support activities; cycle time and velocity-based costing; and value chain analysis. In synchronizing the flow of materials through the manufacturing process, then, JIT is doing more than speeding the delivery of raw materials to the loading dock; it is redefining value-added manufacturing and the accounting that it entails.

C.J. McNair

Bibliography

Dertouzos, M., R.K. Lester, and R.M. Solow. *Made in America: Regaining the Productive Edge.* Cambridge: MIT Press, 1989.

Ford, H. *Today and Tomorrow.* Reprint. Cambridge, MA: Productivity Press, 1989.

Foster, G., and C. Horngren. "JIT: Cost Accounting and Cost Management Issues," *Management Accounting*, June 1987, pp. 19–25.

Hall, R. *Attaining Manufacturing Excellence.* Homewood, IL: Dow Jones-Irwin, 1987.

Hunt, R., L. Garrett, and C.M. Merz. "Direct Labor Cost Not Always Relevant at H-P," *Management Accounting*, February 1985, pp. 58–62.

McNair, C.J., W. Mosconi, and T. Norris. *Beyond the Bottom Line: Measuring World Class Performance.* Homewood, IL: Dow Jones-Irwin, 1989.

———. *Meeting the Technology Challenge: Cost Accounting in a JIT Environment.* Montvale, NJ: Institute of Management Accountants, 1986.

Stasey, R., and C.J. McNair. *Crossroads: A JIT Success Story.* Homewood, IL: Dow Jones-Irwin, 1990.

Suzaki, K. *The New Manufacturing Challenge: Techniques for Continuous Improvement.* New York: Free Press, 1987.

See also COMMON COSTS; INVENTORY VALUATION; JOHNSON AND KAPLAN'S *RELEVANCE LOST: THE RISE AND FALL OF MANAGEMENT ACCOUNTING;* STANDARD COSTING

J

K

Kempten, Valentin Mennher von (1521–1571)

In 1550 Valentin Mennher von Kempten, a German mathematics teacher, published *Practique brifue pour cyfrer et tenir livres de compte*, which grafted Italian double entry bookkeeping methods onto an older system of agency accounting. Kempten used the three traditional German account books: journal, goods book, and debts ledger. But his goods book only had columns for inventory *quantities* purchased and sold. The agent-bookkeeper accounted for his stewardship in a "master's account," which was credited for money received from the master or collected for him and debited for purchases, expenses, and remittances. The cash balance and remaining payables were transferred to this master's account at period end. Kempten demonstrated compound entries but made no profit calculations.

In *Practicque pour brievement apprendre a ciffrer et tenir livre de comptes* (Antwerp, 1565), Kempten described a more complete double entry system, including a profit and loss account. A journal and ledger replaced the three book system; the capital account became more important than the master's account. Money columns replaced the quantities columns for inventories received and sold. Inventory purchases were booked at acquisition costs, which were restated to current market values each time the accounts were closed.

Michael Chatfield

Bibliography

Bywater, M.F., and B.S. Yamey. *Historic Accounting Literature: A Companion Guide*. London: Scholar Press, 1982.

Littleton, A.C. *Accounting Evolution to 1900*. New York: American Institute Publishing, 1933. Reprint. New York: Russell and Russell, 1966.

See also CAPITAL ACCOUNT

Kimura, Wasaburo (1902–1973)

Wasaburo Kimura retired in 1965 as Emeritus Professor of Osaka City University. Kimura's achievements span the field of accounting, beginning with the historical development of bookkeeping and later extending to financial accounting, management accounting, and auditing. He was also an eminent economist, as illustrated by his economic analyses of the production and distribution of rice and coal, both of which were staple commodities in prewar Japan.

Kimura introduced in the 1930s the axiology of Marxist economics to accounting, liberating it from the mere technique of accounting that had been the prevailing view of the field. Indeed, he seemed to have intended to develop accounting as a social science. What distinguished his fresh and original contributions, affectionately termed Kimura Accounting, were (1) his use of the scientific method, characterized by historical study and economic analysis, to grasp accounting's true nature and develop theory; and (2) a critical spirit, based on this scientific method, which informed not only his theories but their practical application as well. His pioneering work introduced an intrinsic consistency among history, theory, and policy to the field of accounting.

Kimura's spirit and dedication to his study never waned, even after 1950 when he began to suffer from failing vision, generally considered professionally fatal to a researcher. Many were guided by the unwavering spirit of their mentor as he fostered numerous prominent accounting historians. The following are Kimura's main literary works, culled from his numerous research projects, publications, and editing accomplishments: *Theory of Bank Bookkeeping* (1935); *Distribution Cost of Rice* (1936); *General Theory of Bank Bookkeeping* (1938); *Coal Industry in North China* (1940); *Cost Accounting: A Historical Perspective* (1949); *Depreciation Theory* (1947–1965); *Introduction of Costing* (with Osamu Kojima) (1952); *Accounting Theory* (1954); *Introduction of Costing* (with Osamu Kojima) (1960); and *Accounting as a Science* (1972).

Atsuo Tsuji
Hiroshi Okano

See also JAPAN; KOJIMA, OSAMU

Kingston Cotton Mills Company

During the last third of the nineteenth century, a series of English court decisions helped clarify the scope of audit engagements and the responsibilities of auditors. In *Re Kingston Cotton Mills* (1896), the court ruled that an auditor, having no reason to suspect dishonesty, had no duty to verify inventory figures given him by a company official who himself certified to the amount of inventory on hand.

Michael Chatfield

Bibliography

Re Kingston Cotton Mills Co. (1896), 1, Ch. 331.

See also CAPITAL MAINTENANCE; CONSERVATISM; DIVIDENDS; LEGAL LIABILITY OF AUDITORS

Kohler, Eric Louis (1892–1976)

Paul Hoffman, an astute public-policy oriented businessman, was selected by President Truman and confirmed by the U.S. Senate in 1948 as administrator of the Marshall Plan. Asked why he chose Eric Louis Kohler to be his comptroller, Hoffman replied that Kohler was generally regarded as "the conscience of the American accounting profession." Wanting his program to be free of scandal, the case was clinched for Hoffman when he noted Kohler's wide experience in business, government, public (CPA) practice and academia. As documented in *Eric Louis Kohler: Accounting's Man of Principles*, Hoffman's judgment was not misplaced. The Marshall Plan disbursed more than $20 billion of U.S. government funds to thousands of business firms and governmental agencies over a period of years in many different countries and remained remarkably free of scandal.

Kohler was the only two-time president (1936, 1946) of the American Accounting Association (AAA) and editor of *Accounting Review* longer than any other person (1928–1942).

Through his actions and writings, he enormously impacted not only accounting thought and practice, but also its institutions, during the critically important 1930s and 1940s. During this period, his interest centered on the need for an authoritative statement of basic principles and standards of accounting undergirding corporate financial reports. His interest in this topic was given vigorous expression in his controversial 1934 *Accounting Review* editorial, "A Nervous Profession, Standards Must Come," in which Kohler expressed his lack of confidence in the American Institute of Accountants (AIA, now the American Institute of Certified Public Accountants, or AICPA) and called for the American Association of University Instructors in Accounting (now AAA) to take the lead in articulating such a body of principles and standards. Indeed, this editorial, together with Kohler's other actions, may well have provided the added momentum that led to the 1935 replacement of this instruction-oriented organization with the new AAA under a charter that (1) expanded the membership to include practitioners and (2) provided a new set of objectives that included an emphasis on research as a basis for informed progress in accounting practice as well as instruction.

Stephen A. Zeff reported the following as ranking high among the AAA's announced purposes: "to develop accounting principles and standards, and to seek their endorsement or adoption by business enterprises, public and private accountants and governmental bodies." As exemplified in the June 1936 *Accounting Review* publication of "Tentative Statement of Accounting Principles Affecting Corporate Reports," authored by the newly formed AAA Executive Committee, this development was to take the form of a unified (but compact) statement of accounting principles, in contrast to the separate (not necessarily connected) statements represented in subsequent actions of the Financial Accounting Standards Board (FASB) and its predecessors.

Kohler's monumental *Dictionary for Accountants* (sixth edition, 1983) was also conceived in this same standard-setting spirit. In fact, the origin of this book can be traced to Kohler's reaction when the report of the AIA Committee on the Definition of Earned Surplus on which he served with Arthur Andersen was rejected in 1931 by the AIA because it believed that the committee's attempt to define "earned surplus" would excise the indispensable element of judgment from an auditor's findings, as noted by Kohler in "In All My Years" (1975). Kohler's subsequent effort at definitions of accounting terms stretched over many years and came to be influenced by the torrent of scientific-technological-methodological developments that followed World War II. Thus the first publication of the results of his effort, in 1952, reflected a change in objectives from the original "A Dictionary of Accounting Terminology" to a newer "Dictionary for Accountants." In terms of the original objective, this work can be regarded as a peak reached from preceding developments in accounting. In its revised, dictionary-cum-encyclopedia form, it can be regarded as having provided a plateau from which further new developments could be launched in response to influences emanating from statistics, quality control, computers, operations research, and like disciplines. In any case, the effects of this effort have continued into the present, as witness, for instance, the extensive citations to this *Dictionary* as the source of the definitions used in Statement of Accounting Standards No. 1, "Financial Resources, Funded Liabilities, and Net Financial Resources of Federal Entities," released in November 1991 by the federal government's Accounting Standards Advisory Board.

A review of Kohler's writings shows that the ideas in his 1934 "A Nervous Profession . . ." editorial were presaged by earlier thoughts. This editorial is regarded as the start of his enormous impact on the profession, which was the result not only of the force with which Kohler expressed his ideas but also of the context in which he expressed them. These were the years of Franklin D. Roosevelt's New Deal and the Great Depression in an era that led to the formation of the Securities and Exchange Commission—all of which had enormous import for standards of accounting, and to which the profession was bound to respond. In this context, Kohler saw accounting and accounting disclosure as offering important possibilities for social (self) control. This led him to his emphasis on relatively simple, but comprehensive, and clearly expressed accounting terms and concepts, and to his emphasis on historical cost as the basis for accounting disclosures.

The focus here has been on the central driving forces in Kohler's thoughts and activities. Interested readers may use the collected writings of Eric Kohler to examine his many other thoughts on accounting, auditing, taxation, and finance. His ingenuity in uses of accounting and his creativity in practice are set forth in the chapters of *Eric Louis Kohler: Accounting's Man of Principles*, with an updating in G. Aiyathurai, W.W. Cooper, and K.K. Sinha in 1991.

W.W. Cooper

Bibliography

Aiyathurai, G., W.W. Cooper, and K.K. Sinha. "Note on Activity Accounting," *Accounting Horizons*, December 1991, pp. 60–68.

Burns, T.J., and E.N. Coffman. *The Accounting Hall of Fame: Profiles of Fifty Members*. Columbus: College of Business, Ohio State University, 1991.

Cooper, W.W., and Y. Ijiri, eds. *Eric Louis Kohler: Accounting's Man of Principles*. Reston, VA: Reston Publishing, 1979.

Cooper, W.W., Y. Ijiri, and G.J. Previts, eds. *Eric Louis Kohler: A Collection of His Writings, 1919–1975*. Monograph No. 5. Tuscaloosa, AL: Academy of Accounting Historians, 1980.

Kohler, E.L. "In All My Years," *Accounting Historians Journal 1974–1976*, vol. 2, 1975, pp. 27–30.

Zeff, S.A. *The American Accounting Association: Its First Fifty Years*. Sarasota, FL: American Accounting Association, 1966.

See also ACCOUNTING HALL OF FAME; ACTIVITY BASED COSTING; AMERICAN ACCOUNTING ASSOCIATION; AMERICAN INSTITUTE OF CERTIFIED PUBLIC ACCOUNTANTS; ANDERSEN, ARTHUR E.; COOPER, WILLIAM WAGER; COST AND/OR MANAGEMENT ACCOUNTING; EDWARDS, JAMES DON; GENERALLY ACCEPTED ACCOUNTING PRINCIPLES; IJIRI, YUJI; SECURITIES AND EXCHANGE COMMISSION; TREASURY STOCK; UNIFORMITY; ZEFF, STEPHEN A.

K

Kojima, Osamu (1912–1989)

Osamu Kojima was Emeritus Professor of Kwansei Gakuin University (Hyogo, Japan) and author of *An Introduction to Accounting History* (1987).

One of Kojima's major contributions was to examine accounting history in Europe by studying original materials and documents. His methodology was unique under the circumstances, as most research in Japan on the topic is based on the second-hand materials available in Japan.

Most historical studies of accounting have been based on investigation of bookkeeping in Italy, especially Luca Pacioli's theory of bookkeeping. Kojima, however, studied the influence of Italian bookkeeping in other countries, including England and Scotland, as a bridge to the history of modern accounting.

In addition, Kojima emphasized the socioeconomic background in his study of accounting. For example, he provided evidence to support the theory that the emergence of a bookkeeping procedure depends on socioeconomic conditions of the society. From his reading of secondary materials, he noted how merchants in early times managed their work.

Kojima also was interested in the development of bookkeeping systems. His academic belief was that the current structure of bookkeeping and its essential function cannot be explicitly understood without the thorough examination of the development of modern accounting and of the specialization and the generalization of journals and ledgers.

At the end of his life, Kojima's interest was accounting history in America in the nineteenth and twentieth centuries.

Yoshihiro Hirabayashi

See also Japan; Kimura, Wasaburo; Pacioli, Luca; Research Methods in Accounting History; Scotland: Early Writers in Double Entry Accounting

Kraayenhof, Jacob (1899–1982)

A Dutch auditor with a marked influence on modern financial reporting in the Netherlands, Jacob Kraayenhof played an important liaison role between the auditing profession, company managements, and the Dutch Legislature. In this position, he was able to convey the views on financial accounting held within the auditing profession to those who shaped contemporary Dutch accounting practice and accounting regulation. In transmitting these views, Kraayenhof added his distinctive imprint to the concepts he propagated.

The foundation for Kraayenhof's influence was laid by his auditing practice. Unlike some other prominent Dutch auditors, Kraayenhof never occupied a research or teaching position at a university. As a result, his published writings are few and far between and do not give an indication of his significance for the profession. Nevertheless, a proper understanding of the recent history of Dutch financial accounting is not possible without sufficient appreciation of his role.

Kraayenhof became a partner of the auditing firm of P. Klynveld in 1930. After the retirement of the founding partner in 1939, Kraayenhof presided over the growth of Klynveld, Kraayenhof and Company (currently affiliated with KPMG) to a dominant position among Dutch auditing firms. Among the clients of the firm were such large multinational companies as N.V. Philips Industries and Royal Dutch Petroleum/Shell. This professional record was acknowledged both within the auditing profession (in his chairmanship of the largest Dutch accountancy body, Nederlandsch Instituut van Accountants (NIvA), from 1944 to 1947) and by business circles and the government, which saw him as a valued adviser on accounting matters. His international reputation rested mainly on his professional work, but also on a few English-language publications and his chairmanship of the Seventh International Congress of Accountants in 1957.

During most of Kraayenhof's active life, the organized Dutch auditing profession, because of its strict adherence to the principle of impartiality, took a very reticent attitude in airing its views on financial reporting. It was up to individual auditors who were faced with deficient financial statements to persuade their clients to adopt more suitable practices.

In this context, it fell to the organizations of Dutch employers to take the initiative in the field of financial reporting. That they did so at all was based on an awareness, developing since World War II, of the usefulness of informative financial reporting as a tool for creating goodwill among investors, and for countering the growing pressure for more social accountability and control that arose during the 1950s. In 1955 and 1962, the combined Dutch employers' associations published two influential brochures in which they expounded their views on financial reporting. Kraayenhof played an important role as a draftsman on both occasions. That surprisingly progressive positions were taken in the two reports, especially concerning the still widespread practice of secret-reserve accounting, is to a great extent a reflection of his influence.

Kraayenhof was able to present his views in an even more authoritative fashion when he became involved in a major revision of Dutch company law in the 1960s. As the revision process centered on the sensitive issues of corporate control and labor participation in management, the politicians involved were happy to leave the relatively uncontroversial matter of financial reporting largely in the hands of Kraayenhof.

The resulting law, passed in 1970, contained the core of current Dutch legislation on financial reporting. Subsequent changes to reflect European Community directives on company law have not materially affected the major clauses of the original law. In this law, Kraayenhof managed to orient Dutch financial reporting firmly on the Anglo-American principle of "substance over form," and to turn it away from the Continental tradition of strict and formal disclosure rules and income determination according to tax principles. Kraayenhof's premise was that regulation should encourage progress rather than enforce rigid and deadening uniformity.

Besides containing a general clause comparable in its effects to the British "true and fair view" requirement, the law, at the suggestion of Kraayenhof, also mandated that valuation and income determination adhere to "norms that are considered acceptable in the social and economic climate." This phrase was originally devised to counter, yet again, secret-reserve accounting while avoiding the necessarily detailed rules on valuation that complete regulation of the subject by law would require. In the case of secret reserves, it was obvious from published profes-sional opinion that this practice could no longer be considered acceptable. But the broad nature of the clause made the law essentially open-ended, and requirements on many accounting issues could conceivably change to reflect shifts in knowledgeable opinion. In later years, it has, for instance, been argued that accounting on the basis of historical costs was no longer acceptable without at least supplementary information on the basis of current cost. But such debates on "acceptability" must remain inconclusive without a mechanism of arbitrage. In the Netherlands, such arbitrage is ultimately provided in a court of law. In order to provide the court with guidance on opinions held in the "economic and social climate," Kraayenhof made the suggestion, and saw it implemented, that an attempt to specify "acceptable" practice was to be made by a tripartite committee on which auditors, employers, and employees were represented. This uniquely Dutch institution has been issuing statements on financial accounting of an advisory nature since 1971.

Kees Camfferman

Bibliography
Kraayenhof, J. "International Challenges for Accounting," *Journal of Accountancy*, January 1960, pp. 34–38.
———. "The Profession in the Netherlands, Sixty Years of Growth and Development," *Accountant*, October 1, 1955, pp. 382–390.
Zeff, S.A., F. Van der Wel, and K. Camfferman. *Company Financial Reporting: A Historical and Comparative Study of the Dutch Regulatory Process.* Amsterdam: North Holland, 1992.

See also BIG EIGHT ACCOUNTING FIRMS; CONGRESSES ON ACCOUNTING, INTERNATIONAL; HISTORICAL COST; NETHERLANDS; PHILIPS INDUSTRIES (N.V.); SOCIAL RESPONSIBILITIES OF ACCOUNTANTS; UNIFORMITY

L

Ladelle, O.G. (1862–1890)

By the late nineteenth century, a variety of depreciation methods had become established in accounting practice. O.G. Ladelle began "The Calculation of Depreciation" (1890) by reviewing four such methods: (1) Take depreciation as the decrease in asset market value; or (2) divide asset cost by the number of years of expected life, and write off the same amount of depreciation each year; or (3) write off each year a constant portion of the outstanding asset balance; or (4) set aside each year a constant amount that, with accumulated interest, will be sufficient to replace the asset.

Using the example of a gasworks with a 20-year life, whose market value fell drastically after the 10th year, Ladelle concluded that "these rules are all defective." Instead of relying on rules, accountants needed a theory of depreciation. Recognizing the inherent arbitrariness of depreciation calculations, Ladelle regarded depreciation as part of the general problem of allocating joint costs—that is, as a system of cost allocation rather than asset valuation. He therefore viewed the cost of an asset as joint to the periods of its use, and suggested that the allocation of depreciation to each period should be based on the expected net benefit to be derived during that period, after adjusting for an agreed rate of interest on the unallocated portion of asset cost.

Michael Chatfield

Bibliography

Brief, R. "A Late Nineteenth Century Contribution to the Theory of Depreciation," *Journal of Accounting Research*, Spring 1967, pp. 27–38.

See also BRIEF, RICHARD P.; COMMON COSTS; DEPRECIATION; THOMAS'S *THE ALLOCATION PROBLEM IN FINANCIAL ACCOUNTING THEORY*

Last In, First Out (LIFO)

The development and initial application of the LIFO method can be characterized as a response to income taxes. Companies that were innovators in applying the last in, first out method operated in industries in which a nontrivial portion of inventory represented a relatively permanent investment in the business. Common characteristics of such businesses are the use of substantially uniform raw materials and a relatively long processing period or relatively slow turnover; classic examples are industries involved in the production and fabrication of nonferrous metals, tanning, textile manufacturing, and the refining and processing of petroleum. For companies in these industries, failure to maintain sufficient raw-material or finished-goods inventory reserves might result in losses due to lags in the production of goods and delays in filling customer orders.

Conventional inventory cost assumptions forced these entities to report and pay taxes on income that implicitly recognized profits or losses reflecting changes in prices on their fixed investment in inventory. These reporting entities viewed both base stock, a predecessor to LIFO, and LIFO as attractive inventory-costing methods because of their income-smoothing properties. By matching current costs with current revenues, these methods generate a more stable income stream than would be attained with the application of alternative inventory-costing methods such as FIFO (first in, first out) or weighted average.

Not surprisingly, companies initially encountered strong resistance in their attempts to apply for tax reporting purposes, first, the base stock method and, later, the LIFO cost-flow assumption. In 1919 the Treasury Department expressly prohibited the use of the base stock method for income tax purposes. The Supreme Court effectively closed the issue in 1930 by unanimously ruling against the application of the base stock method in *Lucas v. Kansas City Structural Steel*, 281 US 264, 1930. It was at this point that the LIFO cost-flow assumption was developed and promoted as an alternative to the base stock method.

The results obtained by applying LIFO are essentially equivalent to those produced under the base stock method. However, because application of the method is much less subjective, LIFO has a distinct advantage in terms of its acceptability to legislative bodies. While the base stock method requires management estimates of the amount and value of the base stock component, LIFO is applied by strict adherence to the last-in, first-out rule. Application of LIFO was thus not subject to the possibility of management manipulation for avoiding taxes.

The LIFO method appears to have been developed and named by the American Petroleum Institute's (API) Committee on Uniform Methods of Oil Accounting (Hoffman, 1962, pp. 146–152). In August 1934, the API received a report from that committee unanimously recommending the approval of LIFO for petroleum companies. The API then acted on that resolution by providing detailed guidance on the use of LIFO in its *Uniform System of Accounts for the Oil Industry* (1936) and by petitioning the tax authority for a ruling that would accept LIFO for tax purposes.

In 1936 the Special Committee on Inventories of the American Institute of Accountants (AIA), a predecessor of the American Institute of Certified Public Accountants, issued a joint report with the American Petroleum Institute. The report concluded that application of the LIFO method to oil inventories constituted an acceptable accounting principle and urged that LIFO be allowed for tax purposes, provided that certain conditions ensuring both the applicability of LIFO and the materiality of the inventory cost-flow assumption were met.

After holding hearings on LIFO in both 1936 and 1938, Congress sanctioned the use of LIFO on a limited basis by a select group of industries as part of the Revenue Act of 1938.

Specifically, the use of LIFO was allowed for certain raw materials of tanners and brass smelters and refiners. Ironically, the petroleum industry, which had "created" LIFO, was not included.

While the 1938 act represented a much-wanted breakthrough in the acceptance of LIFO, the legislation was not well received. Constituents complained about the provision restricting the LIFO method to certain specified industries and about the coherence of the legislation. In response to these criticisms, Congress appointed a committee to rewrite the tax law relating to LIFO. The committee's work resulted in the more general acceptance of LIFO in the Revenue Act of 1939.

The conformity rule incorporated in the 1939 act requires that companies electing to use LIFO for taxes must also use LIFO for financial reports. This rule, a unique feature in the tax laws, was one of the most important features of the act. The inclusion of this requirement suggests that Congress intended to rely on the accounting profession to ensure that LIFO was used only when appropriate—that is, in cases in which LIFO application resulted in reasonable financial-statement figures. If auditors refused to certify the financial statements of a company that used LIFO inappropriately, the company would not be permitted to apply LIFO for tax purposes.

Initially, Congress was justified in its belief that the profession would consider circumstances indicating whether or not LIFO application was appropriate. In 1947 Accounting Research Bulletin (ARB) No. 29, "Inventory Pricing," took the position that where sales prices are promptly influenced by changes in reproductive costs, the LIFO cost-flow assumption may be the more appropriate; where no such cost-price relationship exists, FIFO or an "average" method may be more properly utilized.

In 1953, however, the profession eliminated the above passage from ARB No. 29, effectively rejecting the premise that LIFO should be applied only under certain conditions.

The 1939 act expanded the acceptance of LIFO by permitting its use by all industries, even those not characterized by homogeneous inventories. However, universal LIFO application was only possible after the development of the LIFO-Retail and the Dollar-Value LIFO methods. Prior to the acceptance of LIFO-Retail, retailers had to operationalize the LIFO assumption by dividing their inventories into many small homogeneous groups, or "pools," and applying the LIFO rule to each pool. This procedure frustrated retailers in that it required extensive record keeping and involved some uncertainty about the definition of a qualified pool—complications that directly resulted from applying the method to situations for which it was not well suited.

LIFO-Retail eliminates the need for constructing inventory pools. The method treats the retailer's inventory as one basic inventory unit, which is measured in dollars rather than physical units. Inventory layers are priced at the base year price at which they were acquired, and the change in the dollar value of the inventory is determined at each valuation date. Dollar-Value LIFO is similar in concept, but it does not include a markup; it is used by wholesalers. LIFO-Retail became acceptable over the objections of the Internal Revenue Service (IRS) in a 1947 court decision (*Hutzler Brothers v. United States*, 8 Tax Court 14, 1947). Dollar-Value LIFO was approved by the courts in the following year (*Basse v. Commissioner*, 10 Tax Court 328, 1948).

Expansion of LIFO usage was again promoted when accountants argued that LIFO companies should be allowed to use "lower of cost or market" in conjunction with the LIFO cost assumption, thus removing one of the last economic drawbacks to the use of LIFO. These advocates maintained that to prohibit the write-down of inventory to market and, consequently, recognition of an associated tax deduction, was to discriminate against LIFO taxpayers. Ironically, this argument contradicts the basic rationale for the application of LIFO—namely, that changes in the value of the permanent inventory investment should not be recognized. Nevertheless, in 1952, in response to the passage of the Excess Profits Tax of 1950, the American Institute of Accountants' Committee on Federal Taxation recommended amending the tax law to permit LIFO companies to value their inventories at the lower of cost or market for a specified period of time. However, lower of cost or market has not been approved in conjunction with LIFO.

A second important, albeit temporary, development of LIFO relates to involuntary liquidations. During war time, shortages develop in many industries. LIFO companies suffer from involuntary liquidations that would subject them to tax on the difference between selling prices and LIFO cost. To alleviate this situation, Congress passed relief provisions for all involuntary liquidations occurring during World War II and the Korean conflict and in response to certain energy shortages. These congressional relief provisions are important because they allowed charging cost of goods sold with a replacement price rather than an actual price.

The final major development in LIFO application came about in 1981, when the IRS substantially modified the conformity rule. The new rule has a number of important features: (1) supplementary disclosure of income is permissible on any basis, as long as LIFO income is the primary income presentation; (2) in valuing the asset inventory on the balance sheet, any method may be used; (3) even primary income may be reported using any method if the income report is to be used for internal-management reports or for interim statements; and (4) the lower of LIFO cost or market may be used in calculating even primary LIFO income.

By allowing a broad range of disclosures while at the same time requiring that LIFO income should be the primary public-reporting method, the relaxation of the LIFO conformity rule may have played an important role in encouraging the widespread use of the LIFO cost-flow assumption by U.S. companies.

Harry Z. Davis
Joyce A. Strawser

Bibliography

American Institute of Accountants, Committee on Accounting Procedure. "Accounting Research Bulletin Number 29," *Journal of Accountancy*, September 1947, p. 198.

American Petroleum Institute, Committee on Uniform Methods of Oil Accounting. *Uniform System of Accounts for the Oil Industry*. New York: American Petroleum Institute, 1936.

Davis, H.Z. "History of LIFO," *Accounting Historians Journal*, Spring 1982, pp. 1–23.

Hoffman, R.A. *Inventories: A Guide to Their Control, Costing, and Effect Upon Income and Taxes*. New York: Ronald Press, 1962.

See also ACCOUNTING RESEARCH BULLETINS; AMERICAN INSTITUTE OF CERTIFIED PUBLIC ACCOUNTANTS; BASE STOCK METHOD; CAPITAL MAINTENANCE; INFLATION ACCOUNTING;

Law and Accounting

Considerable legal disparity exists among the several states regarding the liability of accountants and auditors to third parties in civil common law suits. Anglo-American contract law traditionally denied third parties (those not directly in "privity of contract") the right to bring legal action against principals (the parties to the contract) unless the third party was an intended beneficiary of the contract. Professionals, including accountants, thus were protected, subject to the intended-beneficiary exception, even when their negligence damaged third parties. This is known as the privity rule. It is the most protective for accountants since it is the most restrictive against bringing suit.

Although leading accountants in the early decades of the twentieth century asserted their ultimate responsibility to the public, they clung to the privity rule with respect to legal liability. Accelerating commercial and industrial activity, however, increased business and private demand for financial information. This development helped produce, in 1931, the first major breach in the privity rule in the landmark case of *Ultramares Corporation v. Touche, Niven and Company* (255 N.Y. 170). Plaintiff Ultramares, although without a contractual relation with Touche, brought action against them nevertheless, claiming that the defendant's negligence in preparing a balance sheet for the Fred Stern and Company had caused Ultramares monetary damages. A Touche junior accountant had negligently accepted as true, crude and fraudulent accounts-receivable entries placed in the ledger by a Stern executive. Ultramares subsequently purchased the bogus accounts receivable from Stern.

Justice Benjamin Cardozo's decision in *Ultramares* left the privity rule intact, but it created a new doctrine under which third parties could bring suit against accountants, namely, constructive fraud. The judge's reasoning was that when negligence was so extreme— that is, gross—that it was sure to bring loss to an innocent party, then the activity was less like simple negligence and more like fraud, for

which one could always bring suit. Under those circumstances, the absence of privity would not bar an action for damages. But the privity rule itself remained dominant with respect to accountants in state jurisdictions for more than 50 years.

Changes in tort law in the 1960s resulted in abandonment of the privity rule in most states. Continuing criticism of the rules and results of the law of negligence culminated in the substitution of the rule of strict liability in tort where defective products harmed innocent third parties. Originally limited to incidents of physical injury by mechanical or medical products, the doctrine soon encompassed defective-product cases where the injuries were financial only and the defective products included services. The expansion in tort recoveries under the strict liability theory impacted upon the accounting profession. A legal argument was made by some legal scholars that a financial product was as capable of doing monetary damage as a physical product, and that, therefore, the party responsible for putting it upon the market should bear the consequences of the damages caused. As a result, when the *Restatement (Second) of Torts* was issued in 1977, it contained in Section 552 a standard that extended an auditor's liability beyond the client to known or intended users of financial statements, as well as to unknown third-party members of a known class as identified by the client to the auditor.

The first major departure from *Ultramares* was by a New Jersey court in 1983 (*Rosenblum v. Adler*, 461 A.2d. 138) and it went beyond the *Restatement* rule. Noting that the privity requirement had been abandoned in product-liability cases based on negligence, the court concluded that there was no difference between negligent misrepresentation in written statements and an implied representation of a product's safety and suitability for use upon its sale. Negligence, however, still remained the cornerstone requirement for accountants' liability, whereas in product-liability cases all that was required was a showing that the product was defective.

Subsequent cases revealed that four different rules were being applied in different state jurisdictions with respect to an auditor's liability to third parties. Some states validated the *Ultramares* privity rule. Among them was New York, which in the case of *Credit Alliance Corporation v. Arthur Andersen and Company,*

N.E. 2d. 110 (N.Y. 1985), asserted that third-party recovery required that the accountant understood the plaintiff's reliance on specific reports. Other states eliminated or de-emphasized the privity requirement, and three legal variations on the product-liability rule emerged. The three rules, in increasing order of permissiveness, are the contact rule, the known-user rule, and the foreseeable-user rule.

Under the contact rule, negligent auditors can be sued by third parties when they have had some contact and the auditor had reason to believe that the third party would rely on the audit opinion. The known-user rule, in essence *Restatement* Section 552, covers auditor liability situations where the independent auditor knows its work product will be used by a third party. The foreseeable-user rule is both the most permissive and the majority view. Under that approach, a negligent independent auditor is liable to unknown persons reasonably anticipated to rely on the work product. In spite of the fact that no single legal theory has emerged to dominate the thinking behind including independent auditors' opinions within the defective-products category, the effect has been to create a solid body of legal precedent expanding accountant/auditors' liability. Given the predominant use of the partnership form of organization for accounting firms, recent large malpractice awards, sometimes involving joint and several liability, have injected considerable uncertainty among accountants about the advisability of continuing to use that legal form in the future.

Political and procedural steps have been taken by the profession to limit its expanding legal liabilities. State legislatures have been lobbied vigorously, and with some success, as in Illinois in 1986, and in Kansas and Arkansas in 1987, for example, to place statutory limits upon plaintiffs' negligence recoveries against accountants. The Treadway Commission report of 1987 was an attempt by the profession to deal with some of the fundamental reporting and internal-control issues that had led to major financial claims against accountants and auditors. The report stressed the need to improve internal-control systems within client firms, and for auditors to monitor those controls. The emphasis was upon process rather than law, but the motivation was to avoid legal liability in civil suits.

On a federal level, accountants are subject to civil liability under some of the provisions of the Securities Acts (see the "Regulation and Accounting" entry). Tangentially, the vulnerability of accountants is reflected in the tougher federal sentencing guidelines for white-collar criminals, which went into effect on November 1, 1991. Increased sanctions, including longer jail sentences and fines in the millions, were specified by the U.S. Sentencing Commission for those convicted of corporate lawbreaking. Since the doctrine of *respondeat superior* (holding the employer responsible for its agents' acts) applies throughout the corporation, it is prudent for corporations to install internal procedures designed to discourage lawbreaking. Corporate codes of conduct, recognized in the Treadway Report, may become important components of these procedures. The potential legal responsibility of the outside auditor to encourage the use of internal controls, as well as the responsibility for monitoring their presence and application, has not yet been tested, but may become an important future legal issue for accountants, since this area of activity will involve considerable interaction and exchange of communications. A related point worth noting is that the U.S. Supreme Court held in *United States v. Arthur Young* (465 U.S. 805, 1984) that accountant-client work papers are not privileged from disclosure because of "the significance of the accountant's role as a disinterested analyst charged with public obligations."

Robert Chatov

Bibliography
Chatov, R. "Auditors' Liability: States, Congress Mull Changing Standards," *Legal Times*, September 1987, pp. 28–30.
———. "Corporate Codes of Conduct: Economic Determinants and Legal Implications for Independent Auditors," *Journal of Accounting and Public Policy*, Spring 1993, pp. 3–35.
———. *Corporate Financial Reporting: Public or Private Control?* New York: Free Press, 1975.
National Commission on Fraudulent Financial Reporting. *Report of the National Commission on Fraudulent Financial Reporting* [the Treadway Report]. Washington, DC: National Commission on Fraudulent Financial Reporting, 1987.
Stone, C. "The Place of Enterprise Liability in the Control of Corporate Conduct," *Yale Law Journal*, November 1980, pp. 1–77.

See also Auditor's Report; Congressional Views; *Escott v. BarChris Construction Corporation;* Fraud and Auditing; *Hochfelder v. Ernst and Ernst;* Legal Liability of Auditors; Materiality; McKesson and Robbins Case; Regulation (Federal U.S.) and Accounting; *Rosenblum v. Adler;* Securities and Exchange Commission; Treadway Commission; *Ultramares Corporation v. Touche, Niven and Company; United States of America v. Carl Simon*

Ledger

A ledger is a book of accounts. Researchers in accounting history have found hints of a ledger in ancient Greece and Rome. Grier (1934) noted this in her research on the papers of a Greek recordkeeper in Egypt during the Ptolemaic period of about 257 B.C. While Grier did not find a ledger, she thought there might have been a permanent official record. Martinelli (1990) considered the Roman *tabulae* or *codex* probably to be a ledger.

The earliest extant ledger is the surprisingly sophisticated ledger of an unknown Florentine banking firm in 1211. Lee (1973) wrote that the 1211 fragments were confined, with one exception, to debtors' accounts and included such details as the borrower's name, amount advanced, rate of interest, witnesses, and sometimes guarantor(s), followed by particulars, in narrative form, of repayment of the principal. By 1299 the ledgers of Giovanni Farolfi and Company in Florence had the appearance of being kept in the double entry method. These ledgers served as a combined memorandum book (daybook), journal, and ledger. It appears that journals were developed during the fourteenth century in such cities as Genoa in Italy. Journals were used in France by the Bonis Brothers, merchants and bankers at Montauban in Languedoc, in the mid-1300s. Hence, it appears that for all of the thirteenth century and for a good part of the fourteenth century, the ledger was the book of original entry. The ledgers of the fourteenth century were all bound books and their pages were prenumbered to prevent fraud.

De Roover (1956) stressed the difference between Florence, a banking center, and Venice, a trading center: The latter would have had more day-to-day activities and joint ventures. Luca Pacioli's treatise on accounting in his *Summa de Arithmetica* (1494) was based on the methods employed in Venice. He clearly differentiated between the memorandum book, the journal, and the ledger. Pacioli's ledger had prenumbered pages and an alphabetical index, and he instructed that the debit account and the credit account be as close together as possible. The ledger was a private book, in contrast to the memorandum book, which was open to all employees who could write. Pacioli recommended the closing of the ledger either when it was filled or at year end; he favored a closing of books at year end. The ledger was to be balanced with this proviso: "But if one of the grand totals is bigger than the other, that would indicate a mistake in your ledger, which mistake you will have to look for diligently with the industry and the intelligence God gave you and with the help of what you have learned. This part of the work, as we said in the beginning, is highly necessary to a good merchant, for, if you are not a good bookkeeper in your business you will go on groping like a blind man and may meet great losses."

Pacioli, in effect, institutionalized the practice of a bound ledger, which had begun at least by the mid-1300s. Even as the concepts of control accounts and subsidiary ledgers began to take hold in the latter half of the 1800s, the necessity of a bound volume with prenumbered pages and an alphabetical index continued. Some authorities even urged having each ledger notarized for further control over fraud.

The major break with the tradition of the bound ledger took place in the 1890s in the United States, where trailblazing ideas in accounting were more likely to be tried than in Europe at that time. Patents were granted for innovations in the ledgers starting in 1880. By 1900 George Lisle, in a book published in Edinburgh and London, listed five significant advantages of the card, or loose-sheet, system of keeping a ledger, one of which was that the accounts could be arranged in any order and that the order could be altered at any time. By 1906 this movement was being called a "revolution." In order to keep the control feature of the bound ledger, binders were made with locks and patent keys, so that there were only certain employees who could remove a leaf. The new ledger led to speedier use, reduced labor, and greater compactness. Doyle (1907) lauded the loose-leaf system but presented a number of control steps and tools to prevent fraudulent removal of accounts. He felt that the loose-leaf, or perpetual, system of ledgers could be successful only when steps were taken to guard against fraud or discrepancy from loss of sheets.

The continued revolution in record keeping in the twentieth century from bookkeeping machines, to punched cards, to computers has led further and further from the bound volumes of Pacioli's day. Certainly, fraudulent use of accounting records has not diminished. Perhaps a certain carelessness, most likely caused by a feeling of helplessness, dominates current thought about the ledger.

Richard Vangermeersch

Bibliography

De Roover, R. "The Development of Accounting prior to Luca Pacioli according to the Account Books of Medieval Merchants." In *Studies in the History of Accounting*, edited by A.C. Littleton and B.S. Yamey, pp. 114–174. Homewood, IL: Irwin, 1956.

Doyle, N. "The Uses and Limitations of the Card, Loose-leaf Ledgers, and Slip Systems, in Relation to Matters of Account," *Accountant*, November 9, 1907, pp. 581–589.

Geijsbeek, J.B. *Ancient Double-Entry Bookkeeping: Lucas Pacioli's Treatise*. Denver: Geijsbeek, 1914.

Grier, E. *Accounting in the Zenon Papyri*. New York: Columbia University Press, 1934.

Lee, G.A. "The Development of Italian Bookkeeping, 1211–1300," *Abacus*, December 1973, pp. 137–155.

Lisle, G. *Accounting in Theory and Practice*. Edinburgh and London: William Green & Sons, 1900. Reprint. New York: Arno Press, 1976.

"The Loose-Leaf Revolution in Bookkeeping," *Worlds Work*, November 1906, pp. 8248–8249.

Martinelli, A. "Notes on the Origin and Evolution of the Ledger Account." Paper presented at the Northeast Region American Accounting Association Meeting, New York City, April 26–28, 1990.

See also Arithmetic and Accounting; Badoer, Jachomo; Balance Account; Balance Sheet; Barbarigo, Andrea; Barter; Cash Basis Accounting; Closing Entries and Procedures; Computing Technology in the West: The Impact on the Profession of Accounting; Donaldo Soranzo and Brothers; Farolfi Company Ledger; Fini, Rinerio; Fraud and Auditing; Greece; Jones, Edward Thomas; Journal; Manzoni, Domenico; Pacioli, Luca; Rome (509 b.c.–a.d. 476); Sprague, Charles Ezra; Stephens, Hustcraft; Subsidiary Ledger; Trial Balance

L

Lee v. Neuchatel Asphalte Company

The common law rule that dividend payments could not reduce capital below the amount paid in by stockholders was modified by *Lee v. Neuchatel Asphalte Company* (1889). An English Court of Appeals held that in calculating the profits from which dividends were to be paid, a company could ignore declines in the value of its depletable assets. Moreover, the court ruled, "It is not a subject for an Act of Parliament to say how accounts are to be kept; what is to be put into a capital account, what into an income account, is left to men of business." The wider implication of *Lee v. Neuchatel* was that the law preferred to leave the choice of accounting methods to company managers, even when such choices affected stockholders and the public. As Basil Yamey put it, "Business men were to be the judges on business matters."

Michael Chatfield

Bibliography

Lee v. Neuchatel Asphalte Company. In *The Late Nineteenth Century Debate Over Depreciation, Capital, and Income*, edited by R. Brief. New York: Arno Press, 1976.

Yamey, B.S. "The Case Law Relating to Company Dividends." In *Studies in Accounting Theory*, edited by W.T. Baxter and S. Davidson, pp. 428–442. Homewood, IL: Irwin, 1962.

See also Capital Maintenance; Conservatism; Dividends

Leeds Estate Building & Investment Company v. Shepard

The scope of audit engagements and responsibilities of auditors were clarified in a series of nineteenth-century English court decisions, among which was *Leeds Estate Building and Investment Company v. Shepard* (1887). Leeds's articles of association specified that the manager and directors were entitled to bonuses based on the amount of income available for dividends. To increase these bonuses, they inflated profits by overstating asset valuations. Without making a detailed examination, the auditor certified to the correctness of financial statements given him by the directors, and dividends were illegally paid out of capital. When Leeds went into liquidation, the auditor and directors were sued. The auditor, though he had been elected by the stockholders, maintained that he was merely a servant of management. The judge disagreed, saying it was the auditor's duty to inquire into the "substantial accuracy" of the balance sheet provided by management, not merely its arithmetic correctness. It followed that an auditor had to examine the records from which financial statements were taken and satisfy himself as to the existence and approximate value of company resources.

Michael Chatfield

Bibliography

Leeds Estate Building and Investment v. Shepard, 36 ch. D787 (1887).

See also DIVIDENDS; EXTERNAL AUDITING; LEGAL LIABILITY OF AUDITORS

Legal Liability of Auditors

Legal responsibilities have always comprised an important aspect of the public accounting profession. This is especially true for the attest function as both clients and outside parties rely on the auditor for a competent examination of financial statements or other documents.

Nineteenth-Century Precedents

While the beginnings of the attest function might be traced back for centuries, outside auditors began to flourish in the nineteenth century. The British Companies Acts established minimum auditing and reporting standards that fostered the use of outside auditors.

As shareholders and other parties began to rely on the reports of professional auditors, questions arose as to the duties of these accounting experts. To what degree of diligence could an auditor be held? Was his only duty to verify the mathematical accuracy of the financial statements, or should he determine whether the numbers were reasonably derived and presented? Several British court cases addressed those issues.

One of the earliest cases involving auditor negligence was *Leeds Estate Building and Investment Company v. Shepard,* 36 Ch.D. 787 (1887). The auditor was charged with failing to do his duty in determining whether the balance sheet was "fair" and "properly drawn up." The auditor maintained that his duty was to determine whether the balance sheet properly reflected the books of the company. However, the judge found a breach of duty since the auditor only verified the statement's arithmetic accuracy as opposed to its "substantial" accuracy.

Eight years later in *London and General Bank,* 2 Ch. 673 (C.A. 1895), the duty to audit with reasonable care and skill was imposed upon the auditor. The auditor had discovered problems regarding the firm's assets. While he discussed the problems with the board of directors, his audit report was silent on the matter except for a qualifying statement that the actual value of the assets depended on their ultimate realization. The judge concluded that this warning was inadequate and that the auditor's duty was to convey information and not merely arouse inquiry. The London case provided an early indication of the meaning of the phrase "reasonable care and skill."

The degree of skill to be exercised by an auditor was further refined in *re Kingston Cotton Mills,* 2 Ch. 279 (C.A. 1896). Here, the firm's inventories had been overstated, causing the payment of dividends from capital. The judge ruled in favor of the auditor, asserting that it was not the auditor's duty to count inventory for the client, and the auditor did not guarantee the accuracy of the balance sheet. The judge concluded that an auditor was not bound to approach his work with skepticism, and that while the auditor could be viewed as a "watchdog," he was not a "bloodhound."

Early Twentieth Century (1900–1930)

The "reasonable care and skill" question arose in the United States as the accounting profession began to develop in the late nineteenth century. The first United States answer came in *Smith v. London Assurance Corporation* 109 App. Div. 882, 96 N.Y.S. 820 (1905). A key holding in *Smith* was that a professional accountant was required to work with the same care and skill exercised by an average person in the profession.

As a defense against lawsuits, auditors hoped to prove that reasonable care and skill had been exercised. However, if the standard of due care was not met, an important issue was whether a client's contributory negligence could be used as a defense. This question in the United States was addressed in *Craig v. Anyon* 208 N.Y.S. 2d 259 (App. Div.) (1925). After finding that the audit client failed to maintain effective internal controls that could have detected an embezzlement scheme, the court reduced the auditor's damages to the amount of the audit fee.

Most of the early twentieth-century cases involved situations in which a client sued its auditor for breach of contract or perhaps a tort such as negligence. The issue of auditor responsibility to a third party first arose in an American court in *Landell v. Lybrand*, 264 Pa. 406, 107 Atl. 783 (1919). The case established an important precedent—namely, auditors were not liable to unnamed third parties unless there was an intent to deceive.

Early Regulatory Period (1931–1960)

Statutory Law. In 1933 Congress passed the Securities Act of 1933, which contained provisions that expanded auditor liability in certain security transactions. Section 11 provided that plaintiffs who have purchased part of an original security distribution need only prove that a loss was incurred and that the financial statements were misleading. Congress placed the burden of proof on the auditing experts, who must prove that they were not negligent or that the plaintiff's damages were not caused by reliance on the financial statements. Despite the potential liability, few Section 11 cases have involved auditors.

The Securities and Exchange Act of 1934 created the Securities and Exchange Commission (SEC) and gave it the authority to regulate both the purchase and sale of securities. Many 1934 act lawsuits have arisen, since auditors are potentially liable to both security sellers and purchasers.

Section 10(b), an antifraud section, forbade the use of any deceptive device in contravention of rules that the SEC might establish to protect the public. In 1942, the SEC released Rule 10b-5, which prohibited any act that would constitute a fraud or deceit upon any person in connection with the purchase or sale

of any security. This language has been expanded and subjected to various interpretations over the years, but before the 1960s, few auditor-related cases arose.

Common Law. In a landmark case, *Ultramares Corporation v. Touche, Niven and Company* [255 N.Y. 170 (1931)], Justice Benjamin Cardozo ruled that in cases of ordinary negligence an auditor should be liable to a primary beneficiary. However, liability should not extend to unknown third parties as this would expose auditors to an indeterminate amount of liability. Of course, auditors would be liable to other third parties in cases of fraud or gross negligence.

While *Ultramares* upheld auditor liability to third parties for gross negligence, the term was subject to different interpretations. In *O'Connor v. Ludlam,* 92 F.2d. 50 (2d Cir. 1937), the Federal Court of Appeals, 2d Cir., held that auditors should not be liable if they honestly believed the audit report was true, even if this belief was unreasonable. However, one year later, in *State Street Trust Co. v. Ernst,* 278 N.Y. 104, 15 N.E. 2d 416 (1938), the New York Court of Appeals ruled that auditors may be held liable for gross negligence that amounts to fraud even though there was no deliberate attempt to defraud anyone. *State Street* was important in that it helped delineate those actions that might constitute gross negligence.

Period of Expanded Liability (1961–Current)

Statutory Law. Entering the 1960s, several key issues were unresolved. The case of *Escott v. BarChris Construction Corporation* [283 F. Supp. 643 (S.D.N.Y. 1968)] focused attention on auditor responsibility for subsequent events. The auditors were sued under Section 11(b) of the 1933 Securities Act for allegedly failing to properly review subsequent events that affected the client's public registration of securities with the SEC. The court held that the audit program was adequate but had not been adequately followed.

BarChris is noteworthy because it was the first major case of importance to arise under Section 11. In addition, it caused the profession to reexamine its guidance in identifying and analyzing subsequent events.

While in *BarChris* the judge stated that auditors should not be held to a higher standard than that recognized by professional standards, this view did not prevail. In *United States of America v. Carl Simon,* 425 F.2d 796 (2d Cir.

1969), the court stripped auditors of the professional standard shield. The *Simon* case indicated that, in the final analysis, a court may use its own judgment in deciding whether a set of financial statements are fairly presented.

The *Fund of Funds, Ltd. v. Arthur Andersen and Company,* 545 F.Supp. (S.D.N.Y. 1982) case provided additional evidence that adhering to professional standards may not protect one from legal liability. The Federal District Court informed the jury that professional standards, while relevant, were not the determinative factors as to whether auditors had met the standards of care prescribed by the securities laws.

Finally, in the *Lincoln Savings and Loan Association v. Wall,* 743 F. Supp. 901, D.D.C. (1990), auditors were warned against blindly following professional standards while ignoring the economic reality of the client's transactions. Arthur Andersen and Company lost this case and was ordered to pay $80 million to the shareholders, up to then by far the biggest settlement. Auditors must closely examine the substance of the transactions and question whether they make sense from an economic standpoint.

Another unsettled question was whether defendants should be held liable for negligent omissions or misstatements under section 10(b) of the 1934 act. In 1976, the U.S. Supreme Court held in *Hochfelder v. Ernst and Ernst* [425 U.S. 185 (1976)] that the plaintiff must prove scienter—an intent to deceive—as opposed to ordinary negligence.

However, *Hochfelder* did not determine whether gross negligence or recklessness could be construed as the equivalent of scienter. In subsequent cases such as *Resnick v. Touche Ross and Company,* 470 F.Supp. 1020 (S.D.N.Y. 1979) and *IIT v. Cornfeld,* 619 F.2d 909, 926 (2d. Cir. 1980), reckless behavior has been viewed as equivalent to scienter.

Another aspect of the legal environment during the 1961–1990 period has been increased auditor exposure to criminal liability. Here, the plaintiff must show that the defendant acted in a willful manner. In *U.S. v. Benjamin,* 328 F.2d 854, 863 (2d. Cir. 1964), the Federal Court of Appeals held that in proving willfulness the plaintiff need only show that the defendant ignored facts that should have been considered. Moreover, an auditor's willful act could consist of recklessly stating an opinion when there was no underlying basis for the opinion.

Since Benjamin, several criminal cases have involved auditors. *U.S. v. Simon* (1969), *U.S. v. Natelli,* 527 F.2d 311, 319 (2d Cir. 1975), and *U.S. v. Weiner,* 578 F.2d 757 (9th Cir. 1978), were among the more famous cases. As a defense, auditors tried to show that they acted in good faith and without intent to mislead anyone. However, in all of the above cases, the "good faith" defense was unsuccessful.

In 1970 Congress passed the Racketeer Influenced and Corrupt Organization law (RICO). RICO provides for treble damages and maximum prison sentences of 20 years for individuals who engage in a pattern of racketeering crimes. Congress designed the law as a weapon to impede the efforts of organized crime to infiltrate legitimate business organizations; however, RICO has been used against auditors.

Common Law. The case of *Rusch Factors, Inc. v. Levin,* 284 F. Supp. 85, 87 (D.R.I. 1968), dealt a direct blow to auditors' limited responsibility to third parties. The Federal District Court of Rhode Island ruled that auditors were liable to foreseen, limited groups of third parties that relied on the auditor's report. After *Rusch Factors,* auditors could no longer feel confident in successfully defending a third-party negligence suit. In some districts, however, the older *Ultramares* precedent continued to be followed.

Cases since *Rusch Factors* have added to the confusion. In *Rosenblum v. Adler* 461 A.2d 138 (N.J. 1983), liability for ordinary negligence was expanded to include "reasonably foreseeable" third parties. This term includes virtually any potential user of financial statements.

In contrast to *Rosenblum,* the New York State Court of Appeals held in *Credit Alliance Corporation v. Arthur Andersen and Company,* N.E. 2d 110 (N.Y. 1985) that the auditors were liable to third parties for acts of ordinary negligence only when certain conditions were present such as knowing the particular purpose and user of the statements.

Rulings in several other states have followed the *Credit Alliance* precedent with the most recent being in California, where the state Supreme Court placed limits on auditor liability. Thus, in 1994, *Rosenblum* does not appear to be the precedent-setter that auditors had feared.

Conclusions

The courts have greatly expanded the auditor's legal liability in the 100 years that have elapsed since *Leeds Estate*. From the idea that auditors are only responsible for verifying the mathematical accuracy of the books to the concept of liability to foreseen third parties, the auditing profession has seen a drastic increase in auditor exposure to risk.

This higher exposure has made it difficult to obtain adequate insurance coverage, and many small CPA firms now refuse to perform audits. Some other CPA firms are only willing to audit small companies that are not under SEC jurisdiction, thus reducing their liability exposure. According to a 1992 survey, only 53 percent of California CPA firms are willing to accept any kind of audits, as reported by Arthur Andersen and Company.

Some CPA firms have been forced out of business due to insurmountable liability claims. One of these, Laventhol and Horwath in late 1990, was the seventh-largest public accounting firm in the United States. Even members of the Big Six accounting firms are not completely safe from potential bankruptcy. In 1991 the Big Six accounting firms spent $477 million on litigation costs.

Auditing firms have reacted by closely screening prospective clients. Some firms have refused to accept new engagements in high-risk industries.

Thus, while individuals who rely on financial statements may find it easier to seek redress in the courts, the process of raising capital may have suffered. Efficient capital markets require creditable financial information. To the extent that the auditing function has been oligopolized by driving thousands of small CPA firms from the auditing field, and thus increasing the price of audits, the capital-raising process has become more expensive. Moreover, some companies may find it difficult to get an audit by even the largest CPA firms. At some point, society must decide when to place restrictions on the amount of damages that can be assessed on auditors by the courts in order to maintain the supply of reasonably priced audits.

Jimmy W. Martin

Bibliography

Arthur Andersen & Co. et al. *The Liability Crisis in the United States: Impact on the Accounting Profession, a Statement of Position*. Chicago: Arthur Andersen and Company, 1992.

Reid, J.M. *Law and Accounting: Pre-1889 British Legal Cases*. New York: Garland, 1986.

Schmitt, R. "California Court Limits Liability of Auditors," *Wall Street Journal*, August 28, 1992, sec. B, pp. 1, 8.

"The Big Six Are in Big Trouble," *Business Week*, April 6, 1992, pp. 78–79.

"These White Shoes Are Splattered with Mud," *Business Week*, September 7, 1992, p. 32.

See also AMERICAN INSTITUTE OF CERTIFIED PUBLIC ACCOUNTANTS; BIG EIGHT ACCOUNTING FIRMS; CAPITAL MAINTENANCE; COMPANIES ACTS; CONGRESSIONAL VIEWS; CONSERVATISM; *CRAIG V. ANYON; ESCOTT V. BARCHRIS CONSTRUCTION CORPORATION;* EXTERNAL AUDITING; *FISCHER V. KLETZ;* FRAUD AND AUDITING; *HERZFELD V. LAVENTHOL, KREKSTEIN, HORWATH AND HORWATH; HOCHFELDER V. ERNST AND ERNST; KINGSTON COTTON MILLS COMPANY;* LAW AND ACCOUNTING; *LEEDS ESTATE BUILDING AND INVESTMENT COMPANY V. SHEPARD;* MATERIALITY; MCKESSON AND ROBBINS CASE; REGULATION (FEDERAL U.S.) AND ACCOUNTING; *REX V. KYLSANT; ROSENBLUM V. ADLER;* SECURITIES AND EXCHANGE COMMISSION; *ULTRAMARES CORPORATION V. TOUCHE, NIVEN AND COMPANY; UNITED STATES OF AMERICA V. CARL SIMON*

L

Leonardo of Pisa (Leonardo Pisano) (Fibonacci) (11??–12??)

Not much biographical information exists concerning Leonardo Fibonacci; he himself provides some of it in his *Liber Abaci* (*Book of the Abacus*), composed in 1202. It is known that he was a citizen of the seafaring Republic of Pisa, which in the twelfth and thirteenth centuries played a determining role in the first commercial revolution of Western Europe. This was the time of St. Francis, Saladin (Salah ad Din), and Richard the Lion Hearted. In the preceding centuries, improved agricultural techniques had contributed to the growth of population, with the consequent greater demand for goods and services, but the movement of goods overland posed many difficulties; it was faster and more economical to transport merchandise by sea. By the twelfth century, the Mediterranean Sea had become the road that united different territories representing diverse political entities, religions, and cultures.

The Islamic world had partially opened its markets to commerce with Christians, and by

the end of the twelfth century the seafaring re-
publics had constructed a dense network of
trading links with the Islamic states, especially
those on the coast, notwithstanding the Crusades and the piracy at the time. From the final
decade of the eleventh century, Pisa had built up
commercial relationships with the countries of
Northwest Africa. From the first half of the
following century, it had concluded regular
treaties of friendship with them, the documents
of which are preserved in the Archivio di Stato.
At the time of Leonardo Fibonacci, these commercial treaties granted special privileges to the
merchants and merchandise of the Pisan Republic; a large number of warehouses were put at
their disposal, particularly in the major Mediterranean ports of call in the Arab world: Ceuta,
Bougie (the present-day Bejaia, terminus of the
Algerian pipeline), Madhia, and Tunis. In the
markets, the merchants of Pisa sold fabrics,
dressed hides, iron weapons, timber, and other
goods, despite the prohibition of the Catholic
Church and the express proscriptions of the
laws. From these same markets, they took in,
among other things, woolen goods, rawhides,
wax, alum, coloring materials, and spices.

Leonardo, son of Bonaccio, was born into
this milieu of trade in the seventh or eighth decade of the twelfth century. His father was a
notary—that is, a member of that part of the
middle class connected through professional
bonds and common interests to the merchant
class. In fact, as Leonardo himself writes at the
beginning of his *Liber Abaci*, his father practiced his profession in the customs house at
Bougie on behalf of the Pisan merchants there.
His father had taken him there when Leonardo
was still a child. At Bougie, in contact with Arab
culture, Leonardo learned, along with algebra
and geometry, the Hindu art of numbers—the
"arte per novem figure indorum"—which, with
the "signo O quod arabice zephirum appel-
latur," allows the speedy resolution of any arithmetic operation. Indeed, the dissemination of
the practice of writing numbers composed of
numerals, instead of letters as in the Roman
fashion, began then, through his own work.
Subsequently, Leonardo perfected his mathematical knowledge, again thanks to the contacts he had with other scholars, Muslim
and Christian, during his voyages to Constantinople, Syria, Provence, and Sicily. Through his
commercial activity, he learned how arithmetic
could be applied in commercial operations and
practiced as a technique in commerce; in 1202

he wrote *Liber Abaci,* in which he imparted
elementary mathematical principles of accountancy—among them, the rules to be followed in
keeping the record of expenditures.

Liber Abaci, the most widely known of
Leonardo's works, is the first and unsurpassed
model of a compendium of mathematics and
commercial technique. Of the 15 chapters that
make it up, the first seven and the last three are
concerned primarily with arithmetic, algebra,
and numerous rules for mathematical speculation. It is in the third chapter of *Liber Abaci,*
titled "De additions integrorum," that
Leonardo formulates the rules of accountancy
that the treasurer and the scribe must follow for
the recording of expenditures relevant to the
operation of a merchant ship. The amounts
must be classified in the account ("tabula")
according to their characteristics. In Chapter 8
through Chapter 12, Leonardo demonstrates
how mathematics may be applied in concrete
commercial situations. With a great number of
practical problems as examples, he sets forth the
rules governing buying and selling, barters,
mercantile companies, and mintage quality and
exchange rates for existing currencies, and then
he gives the solution to various computational
and trading problems.

For the massive quantity of information
relating to the practices in the various markets,
Chapters 8 through 12 of *Liber Abaci* might be
likened to a "Manual of Trading Practices." In
fact, in the first part of Chapter 8, which discusses the buying and selling of goods ("De
emptione et venditione rerum venalium et
similium"), the author shows, through the solution of numerous problems, the methods to be
used in the calculation of the price of merchandise according to the quality (hides, woolen
fabrics, linens, spices, cheese, oil, wheat, barley,
and the like) and according to weight. He then
gives information regarding the actual money
with which business transactions were carried
out. Finally, he gives guidelines on the way to
do business in the various markets: Garb in
Northwest Africa, Syria, Alexandria, Provence,
and Constantinople.

In the second part of Chapter 8, in which
he discusses exchange rates ("De cambiis
monetarum"), Leonardo, through the solution
of numerous problems, gives instruction on the
method of calculating the values of the various
currencies in different markets. The third part
of the chapter describes the units of measurement used in the various markets for the sale of

merchandise. This part ends with the discussion of partnerships between individuals, and of the sharing of profits from business transactions, almost always using Constantinople as the place of reference. The fourth and final part of the chapter discusses the conversion of one unit of measurement to another.

In Chapter 12, Leonardo confronts and resolves the most varied problems of applied arithmetic and commercial technique, some of them already alluded to in the preceding chapters. Among the most original are: (1) the "questio nobis proposita a peritissimo magistro Musco constantinopolitano in Constantinopoli" (in the fifth part of Chapter 12), regarding the acquisition and running of a ship with the consequent sharing of the profits among the five partners; (2) the "De homine qui prestavit ad usuras sine noticias" (in the sixth part), where Leonardo explains the amortization of an onerous loan, which Federigo Melis, an expert in the history of Italian accounting, related in 1950 in his *Storia della Ragioneria* (*History of Accountancy*); and (3) the "Quot paria coniculorum in uno anno ex uno pario germinentur," from which is derived that famous recurring series of numbers (1, 2, 3, 5, 8, 13, 21, 34, 55, 89, 144, 233, 377) given by Leonardo in the margin of the text of the famous problem of the reproduction of rabbits. This sequence of numbers has the property that any number in the series is the sum of the preceding two, and the relationship between the following number and the one before is always constant. Such a relationship, known as "golden," was defined by Luca Pacioli three centuries later as "divina proportione."

Leonardo wrote other scientific and mathematical works, including *Pratica geometrie* (1220), *Liber quadratorum* (1225), and *Flos* (undated). He traveled widely, meeting and exchanging ideas with some of the most famous learned men of his time, including even the Emperor Frederick II himself, who took a great interest in his mathematical studies. In 1241, on returning to his homeland, he was charged by the government of the Republic of Pisa with reorganizing the public account-keeping system. This activity is attested to by a "provision" of the Senate of the Republic, in 1242, with which he was granted the sum of 20,000 "denarii" (the value of a large galley), for the magnificent work done as "revisor of the accounts" by "... Leonardo Bigolli sapienti viro magistro in abbaccandis estimnationibus et rationibus civitatis. . . ."

Tito Antoni

Bibliography

Antoni, T. "Leonardo Pisano, Called Fibonacci, Mathematician and Accountant." In *Congress Proceedings: Fourth International Congress of the History of Accountancy*. Pisa: University of Pisa, 1984.

Gies, J., and F. Gies. *Leonard of Pisa and the New Mathematics of the Middle Ages*. New York: Crowell Company, 1969.

See also ANTONI, TITO; ARABIC NUMERALS; COMPOUND INTEREST; MONEY; PACIOLI, LUCA; ROMAN NUMERALS

Lewis, J. Slater

Beginning about 1900, accountants started paying serious attention to the overhead element of manufacturing cost. It had become not only a problem in its own right, but one that blocked solutions to other problems. Earlier writers had been unable to agree on which expenses should be included in the overhead applied to products, or what basis of allocation should be used. In *Factory Accounts: Their Principles and Practice* (1887), Englishmen Emile Garcke and J.M. Fells had shown how to incorporate materials and labor costs into the double entry system. But no one had yet demonstrated a practical method for distributing overhead costs to work in process through the ledger accounts.

The English factory accountant J. Slater Lewis was an early advocate of integrating cost and financial accounts, but his preferred treatment of overhead costs was to bring them into contact with prime costs only at the end of an accounting period. In *The Commercial Organisation of Factories* (1896), Lewis proposed that accounts containing overhead items be closed to profit and loss like ordinary expenses. At the same time, work in process and finished goods would be debited with their respective shares of overhead cost, and a suspense account in the general ledger would be credited. At the start of the next period a reversing entry was to be made, debiting suspense and crediting profit and loss. Then suspense was again debited and finished goods and work in process were credited, bringing the inventory accounts back to a prime cost basis and leaving total overhead cost as a balance in suspense. During the accounting period this balance was to be absorbed gradually into cost of goods sold, though Lewis failed to specify exactly how this would be done. Although his system was complicated, its effect was orthodox. It allowed overhead costs to be handled as a group, avoided the problem of passing them through the inventory accounts, and made sure that overhead applied to products exactly equaled incurred overhead costs.

As if realizing that this solution skirted the essential difficulties, Lewis suggested an alternative. Certain overhead costs might be reduced to rates and absorbed directly into work in process. Overhead accounts would be debited to record actual expenditures, then credited for allocations to products according to the amounts of direct labor used to make each type of goods. Of course this is essentially the modern method, but having proposed it, Lewis did not feel safe with it. He thought that in most cases ratable overhead allocations were not worth the trouble. And there was always the danger of a wrong absorption rate, which would underapply actual overhead costs and "create a fictitious asset." Compared to this suspense account allocation method, Lewis was vague about procedure.

Michael Chatfield

Bibliography

Garner, S.P. *Evolution of Cost Accounting to 1925.* University, AL: University of Alabama Press, 1954.
Lewis, J.S. *The Commercial Organisation of Factories.* London: E. & F.N. Spon, 1896.

See also CHURCH, ALEXANDER HAMILTON; COMMON COSTS; COST AND/OR MANAGEMENT ACCOUNTING; DIRECT COSTING; ENGINEERING AND ACCOUNTING; GARCKE AND FELLS; INVENTORY VALUATION

Liabilities

The treatment of liabilities has undergone significant changes in U.S. accounting in the twentieth century. These changes have been more subtle than the changes in accounting for assets, which is perhaps why they seemed to have gained more solid support than the changes in accounting for assets.

The start of the twentieth century witnessed a balance sheet in which fixed assets were listed as first among the assets and fixed (long-term) liabilities were listed as first among the liabilities. The industrial companies of that time followed the balance sheet model long followed by the railroads. In a study of the financial-reporting techniques of 20 such companies, Vangermeersch (1979) found that the change to the format of listing current assets and current liabilities first occurred slowly during the first four decades of the twentieth century, as the focus of analysts turned more to the computation of working capital.

A major change in accounting took place when the Committee on Accounting Procedure (CAP) of American Institute of Accountants (AIA) issued Accounting Research Bulletin (ARB) No. 28, "Accounting Treatment of General Purpose Contingency Reserves" in 1948. This ARB prohibited the use of contingency reserves as expenses in determining net income. ARB No. 26, "Accounting for the Use of Special War Reserves" in 1946 dealt with the issue of special wartime reserves set up in accordance with ARB No. 13, "Accounting for Special Reserves Arising Out of the War" in 1942, which called for the termination of general contingency reserves. These reserves had been used to smooth earnings. In good years, they were established or increased in order to lower net income. In bad years, current expenses and losses were charged to these reserves. Vangermeersch found numerous (185) such noncurrent liability reserve accounts created in the 20 companies studied. While ARB No. 50, "Contingencies," in 1958 dealt more generally with the topic of contingencies, it was not until Financial Accounting Standard (FAS) No. 5, "Accounting for Contingencies," in 1975 that a more rigorous definition and rules were promulgated. FAS No. 105, "Disclosure of Information about Financial Instruments with Off-Balance-Sheet Risk on Financial Instruments with Concentration of Credit Risk" in 1990 appeared to broaden the disclosure of contingencies by the use of footnotes.

The issue of the balance sheet placements of bond discounts and bond premiums was long unsettled. While immediate write-offs were condemned by authorities like William Andrew Paton in 1934, these write-offs did occur. If they didn't, bond discounts were generally treated as a deferred charge, which Paton also condemned, arguing that bond discounts were not an asset in any sense. Bond premiums were correspondingly often treated as a deferred credit. There was continued opposition to such practices (Healy 1942), and the opposition grew more virulent. Wixon (1961) was especially stinging in his attack of deferred charges and credits, "since they defy logical explanation independent of bookkeeping techniques."

There has been a significant tightening of the guidelines for the placement of the current portion of long-term debt. ARB No. 30, "Current Assets and Current Liabilities—Working Capital" in 1947 stated that the current portion could not be classified with current liabilities if the liability was expected to be refunded. A much more rigorous test for such exclusion was developed in 1975 by FAS No. 6, "Classification of Short-Term Obligations Expected to be Refinanced." Another example of this tightening is that the offsetting of assets and liabilities permitted in 1942 by ARB No. 14, "Accounting for United States Treasury Tax Notes" for tax anticipation notes was not permitted by APB No. 10, in "Omnibus Opinion—1966."

This same steady march is noted in three most significant liabilities: leases, pensions and postretirement benefits, and deferred income taxes. ARB No. 38, "Disclosure of Long-Term Leases in Financial Statements of Lessees" in 1949 called for the capitalization of leases which were "in substance not more than an installment purchase of property." While APB No. 5, "Reporting of Leases in Financial Statements of Lessees," in 1964 rejected the "property rights" argument John H. Meyers made in 1962 in Accounting Research Study No. 4, *Reporting of Leases in Financial Statements*, it did redefine the installment purchase as "the creation of a material equity in the property." This concept was illustrated by four circumstances that could indicate a capitalization if the lease should occur. Further disclosure was required by APB No. 31, "Disclosure of Lease Commitments by Lessees," in 1973. FAS No. 13, "Accounting for Leases" in 1976 presented an even more rigorous definition of when a capital lease should be recorded.

In 1948 in ARB No. 36, "Pension Plans—Accounting for Annuity Costs Based on Past Services," the issue of pension plans focused on the accounting for past service cost. By 1956 the CAP, in ARB No. 47, "Accounting for Costs of Pension Plans," had rationalized the superiority of the accrual basis for pension plans but said that "the accounting for pension costs has not yet crystallized sufficiently to make it possible at this time to assure agreement on any one method." There was to be, at the minimum, a difference accrued between vested pension commitments and the pension trust fund assets or annuity contracts purchased. Further crystallization had occurred by 1966 in APB No. 8, "Accounting for the Cost of Pension Plans," which rejected the "pay-as-you-go" approach for the accrual basis within a fairly wide range of minimum and maximum amounts. By 1980 in FAS No. 36, "Disclosure of Pension Information," there was a requirement to disclose the amounts of trust fund assets and of the actuarial present value of accumulated plan benefits in an "off-the-ledger" manner. By 1985 in FAS No. 87, "Employers' Accounting for Pensions," that information became "on the ledger." A liability will occur if the amount of trust fund assets is lower than the present value of accumulated plan benefits. In FAS No. 87, the Financial Accounting Standards Board (FASB) again stressed the evolutionary nature of accounting for pensions, stating that while a comparison of trust fund assets to the projected benefit obligation was preferable, it was too great a change at that time. In FAS No. 106, "Employers' Accounting for Postretirement Benefits other than Pensions" in 1990, the FASB extended FAS No. 87 reporting to postretirement benefits other than pensions.

Nowhere was this evolutionary role more evident than the topic of accounting for deferred taxes. In ARB No. 23, "Accounting for Income Taxes" in 1944, income taxes were considered to be an expense to be allocated, "when necessary and practicable." In ARB No. 44, "Declining-Balance Depreciation" in 1954, the CAP stated that ordinarily the deferred income tax procedure did not apply to tax/book differences based on declining-balance depreciation. This statement was reversed in 1958 by ARB No. 44, "Declining-Balance Depreciation" (Revised), because of the practice of most companies to include the deferral of income taxes on depreciation differences as an income tax expense. This view, labeled the comprehensive approach, was reiterated in 1967 by APB No. 11, "Accounting for Income Taxes." The APB also adopted the deferred method over the liability method for determining the recorded amount of the liability. The deferred method was considered in 1985 to be outside the definition of a "liability" in FASB Concepts Statement No. 6, "Elements of Financial Statements." Hence, the liability method was to be followed. While FAS No. 96, "Accounting for Income Taxes," was postponed three times, and then was replaced in 1992 by FAS No. 109, "Accounting for Income Taxes," the liability method was still held to be the preferred method and, hence, finally replaced the deferred method of APB No. 11.

While it is all too easy to assume a "liability is a liability," this seems to be an unwarranted view. The scope of liabilities is ever-widening.

Richard Vangermeersch

Bibliography
Healy, R.E. "Treatment of Debt Discount and Premium upon Refunding," *Journal of Accountancy*, March 1942, pp. 199–212.
Lang, D.M., Jr. "Dissenting Viewpoint: Has It Played a Meaningful Role in the Development of Accounting Principles?" *Price Waterhouse Review*, Winter 1960, pp. 6–13.
Myers, J.H. "Summary and Conclusions from 'Reporting of Leases in Financial Statements,'"*Journal of Accountancy*, June 1962, pp. 63–66.
Paton, W.A. *Accountants' Handbook*. 2d ed. New York: Ronald Press, 1934.
Sprouse, R.T. "Accounting for What-You-May-Call-Its," *Journal of Accountancy*, October 1966, pp. 45–53.
Vangermeersch, R. *Financial Reporting Techniques in Twenty Industrial Companies since 1961*. Gainesville: University Presses of Florida, 1979.
Wixon, R. *Accountants' Handbook*. 4th ed. New York: Ronald Press, 1961.

See also ACCOUNTING RESEARCH BULLETINS; ACCOUNTING RESEARCH STUDIES; BALANCE SHEET; CONCEPTUAL FRAMEWORK; DEFERRED INCOME TAX ACCOUNTING; FINANCIAL ACCOUNTING STANDARDS BOARD; MANIPULATION OF INCOME; PATON, WILLIAM ANDREW

Limited Liability

The legal doctrines underlying modern corporations derive from three much older ideas: (1) that each such firm is an independent, property-owning entity in its own right; (2) that the individuals comprising it therefore have limited liability for corporate activities; and (3) that it has continuity of existence beyond the lives of its owners. Three leading institutions of the medieval world—the church, the town, and the craft guild—were treated as separate entities with perpetual existence. Monastery property was never considered to belong to individual monks or abbots, nor were they personally responsible for church obligations. Medieval municipalities were also viewed as entities apart from their inhabitants, and they often obtained articles of incorporation that recognized their separate status. Craft guilds offered mutual association for the protection of occupational groups. Like the church and town, they held property in their own names and created permanent offices through which many individuals passed.

In each case, the entity's independent existence provided the rationale for giving its members limited liability. If a business exists apart from its owners, its property cannot logically be made available to their personal creditors. Similarly, if a corporation is a separate entity with the power to contract and hold property, its creditors cannot expect to reach stockholders' personal assets to satisfy corporate debts.

Italian *commenda* partnerships were direct ancestors of the limited liability corporation. During the Renaissance, investors evaded church usury laws by entrusting their cash to overseas traders for a share in the profits of joint ventures. The partnership contract *en commendite* established the precedent that while trading partners were fully liable for partnership debts, an investing partner could share in profits while risking only the amount he had contributed.

Influenced by Italian practice, many European commercial codes made a distinction between the liability of active and silent partners, holding the latter responsible only to the extent of their investment. The French Code Savary of 1673 provided for limited partnerships in the Italian manner. Early in the seventeenth century, certain English corporations extended a type of limited liability to their investors as an inducement to buy stock. The "par value doctrine" did not protect the personal assets of investors from company creditors, but merely assured subscribers to fully paid shares that the corporation would not call on them for further capital contributions. But even before this, the British government had begun promoting limited liability corporations for reasons of its own.

The discovery of America and the opening of sea routes to China and India turned investors' attention to overseas trading. The earliest

British "Companies of Adventurers" formed to carry on this trade were partnerships, but as with the Italian *commendas*, certain partners wished to trade actively while others merely wanted to invest. In a high risk environment, some form of limited liability was needed if investor and adventurer were to collaborate effectively.

The first joint stock-companies were partnerships with a few corporate features. They generally had limited life and imposed unlimited liability for company debts, but in many cases they issued transferable shares. Their purposes ranged from trade to colonization and included military expenditures and voyages of discovery. Parliament preferred them to competitive businesses because they were easier to regulate and tax. They were granted monopoly rights partly as compensation for the large initial investments such ventures required. The Russia Company (lumber), the Virginia Company (tobacco), the East India Company (spices), and the Hudson's Bay Company (furs) were four of the best known. In chartering companies such as the Bank of England, whose activities touched vital national interests, the government allowed shareholders individual immunity from the bankruptcy laws if the firm failed. The effect was to make them liable for company debts only up to the amount unpaid on their shares.

There remained the problem of regulating these new companies. A corporation created by Crown Charter had virtually an unlimited scope of activities, whatever its original purpose. The South Sea Company was chartered in 1710, mainly to fund about 10 million pounds of floating national debt. For 10 years it tried without much success to develop an overseas trade. Then, during England's first great era of stock speculation, the company decided to take over the entire national debt and to pay for it by issuing large amounts of stock. The directors inflated share prices by selling stock on 10 percent margin, spreading rumors of dividends, and offering prospective buyers loans equal to half the stock's market value. In 1720, after wild speculation, South Sea Company stock prices collapsed, falling 85 percent from their highest level. Finally there was not enough money in the country to meet subscription installments as they came due or to buy the shares that were being thrown on the market. Though the company continued in business for another 130 years, millions of pounds of investor funds had been lost and the nation's commercial development was slowed for half a century.

The final result of this speculative frenzy was popularly known as the Bubble Act of 1720. It aimed to correct four evils: (1) excessive stock speculation, (2) formation of fraudulent joint-stock companies, (3) the use of corporate prerogatives by unincorporated firms, and (4) the use of corporate charters to conduct inappropriate types of businesses. This act not only denied limited liability status to all firms not incorporated by Crown or Parliament, but it was also used as a policy instrument to restrain the formation of new corporations. It inhibited the natural growth of limited liability companies for the next 100 years.

This prohibition came at the worst possible time, retarding at the start of the industrial revolution the type of enterprise most suitable for industrial expansion. Manufacturers were forced to establish partnerships in which every member, no matter how small his investment, was by law personally responsible for all the company's debts. Being unable to protect investors, such partnerships had very limited ability to raise capital. Often they consisted of a large, fluctuating body of individuals, and a person dealing with them might not be sure with whom he was contracting. A number of canals, railroads, and other public utilities were given limited liability status between 1720 and 1844, but most commercial and industrial firms were not. They could incorporate only by charter or by special act of Parliament, both cumbersome and very expensive processes.

Early in the nineteenth century, a series of court decisions undermined the Bubble Act. A statute of 1825 repealed it entirely and enabled the Crown to specify in company charters exactly what degree of liability or nonliability stockholders had for corporate debts. Beginning in 1837, the Crown was empowered to grant unincorporated firms letters of patent that in effect chartered them as joint-stock companies. The Companies Act of 1844 allowed nearly all businesses to incorporate by registration, though still with unlimited liability. An 1855 statute permitted firms registered under the 1844 act to get certificates of limited liability for their stockholders. The Companies Act of 1862 codified earlier rules for incorporating and regulating joint-stock companies, removing the last barriers to corporate dominance of England's basic industries.

It should be remembered that in the 1860s relatively few firms were incorporated and not many people realized how great a role the "limited" company was to play in British commercial life. As the importance of the corporate form rapidly increased, so did demands for more reliable accounting information, even if the price for incorporation with limited liability was compulsory disclosure and enforced uniformity of accounting methods.

Contributing to this change in public opinion was the spectacular failure in 1878 of the incorporated City of Glasgow Bank. By overvaluing assets, undervaluing liabilities, and misdescribing balance sheet items, the bank's directors had for years hidden its insolvency while continuing to pay dividends. The immediate response to this fraud was a clause in the Companies Act of 1879 requiring annual audits for all banks registered thereafter with limited liability. And despite its policy of noninterference with commercial corporations, Parliament had always been willing to regulate companies whose failure was apt to dislocate the economy. The Companies Acts of 1855–1856 had excluded banks and insurance companies from the privilege of limited liability, and when this right was granted them a few years later, it was on condition that they publish semiannual balance sheets and file copies of them with the Board of Trade. Compulsory accounting and audit requirements had never been abandoned for corporations chartered directly by Parliament, among them the railroads. The 1868 Regulation of Railways Act was a forerunner of similar laws prescribing accounting methods and audit for building societies, water works, gasworks, and electric light companies. By the 1880s, statutory regulation was an accepted fact of life for nearly all limited liability corporations.

Michael Chatfield

Bibliography
Littleton, A.C. *Accounting Evolution to 1900*. New York: American Institute Publishing, 1933. Reprint. New York: Russell and Russell, 1966.
Watzlaff, R.H. "The Bubble Act of 1720," *Abacus*, June 1971, pp. 8–28.

See also CAPITAL MAINTENANCE; CAPITAL STOCK; CITY OF GLASGOW BANK; COMMENDA CONTRACTS; COMPANIES ACTS; CONTINUITY; CORPORATIONS: EVOLUTION; DIVIDENDS; EAST INDIA COMPANY; FRANCE; PAR VALUE

DOCTRINE; PARTNERSHIP ACCOUNTING; REGULATION OF RAILWAYS ACT (BRITAIN, 1868); SAVARY, JACQUES; SEPARATE ENTITIES; SOUTH SEA BUBBLE

Limperg, Theodore Jr. (1879–1961)

Born in Amsterdam, the Netherlands, on December 19, 1879, Theodore Limperg Jr. attended the Commercial High School—a typical preparation for students intending to find employment or commence a career in private or corporate business—and graduated in 1897. He then began to study for the national examination in advanced bookkeeping (accounting); he earned the certificate qualifying him for teaching bookkeeping and related subjects in high schools.

It is noteworthy that Limperg did not enroll as an accounting student in a university; he never earned a college degree. In the early twentieth century, there was no business administration program available in the Dutch universities. The rapid progress and the amazing accomplishments of this young accountant resulted from his deep interest in the accounting profession and his strong dedication to the development of a theory of business economics and business administration. His lack of higher education was more than compensated by an iron will that maintained him in an exacting schedule of self-study, continuing until late in life.

In 1901, three years before he passed the public accountants examination and gained admission to the Netherlands Institute of Accountants, Limperg was accepted as a member of Volmer and Co., a partnership of certified public accountants in Amsterdam. At that time (January 1901), he had just turned 21. Only two years later, the title of the partnership was changed to include his name (Nijst, Bianchi and Limperg), notwithstanding the fact that only Jules Nijst could sign for the firm. It was not until 1904 that Nijst's co-partners would be admitted to the Institute of Accountants. After the resignation of Nijst from the firm in 1905, the partnership continued with the name of Bianchi and Limperg. Later, Limperg practiced as a partner in the firm of Th. and L. Limperg.

In the meantime, Limperg had also become active elsewhere. In 1903 a new professional magazine for Dutch accountants, *Accountancy*, began publication; Limperg was one of its founders and a member of the editorial staff.

Before long, Limperg became the editor-in-chief, a post he held for 20 years. Under his guidance, the periodical became a powerful factor in the development of the accounting profession and the Netherlands Institute of Accounting. His contribution to the success of the magazine could easily be recognized by the new, innovative, and scholarly articles that appeared, with or without his signature. In 1924 the name of the magazine was changed to *Monthly Journal of Accountancy and Business Administration*. It is currently published under the name of *Monthly Journal of Accountancy and Business Economics*.

Conflicts with the "old guard" of the Netherlands Institute of Accounting developed on matters concerning the development of accounting and the regulation of the profession. Limperg would be patient when discussing innovative proposals, but he had a propensity to make his new ideas prevail, and when principles were involved, he was firm in his refusals to compromise. In 1906 his decision to publish an uncomfortable letter to the editor resulted in revocation of his membership in the Institute. But on the same day, Limperg and about 20 supporters organized their own Netherlands Accountants Association, which would grow to be a powerful force in developing accountancy in the Netherlands. The new group organized an educational program and an examination committee (headed by Limperg) for professional degree candidates.

In 1918 the institute and the association agreed to merge, and Limperg's membership was reinstated. He became the chairman of the committee on examinations. All honors were bestowed on him. The Dutch accounting community had finally discovered his greatness.

The strong support Limperg had given to the teaching of accounting and business economics on the level of higher education contributed to the organization of a Department of Economics and Business Administration at the University of Amsterdam. Limperg accepted a professorship, teaching both undergraduate and graduate students in 1922. Accountancy, business economics, and business administration were studied within one comprehensive framework of social and business economics. He held that, essentially, the concepts and laws in all areas were identical; their scientific analysis should use deductive methods where appropriate. These ideas were in marked contrast to the pragmatic views of most accountants of the time, especially those held by the faculty of the Business Academy in Rotterdam.

Limperg's opposition to the applicability of nominalism and the original-cost doctrine became widely understood. As the principal debaters about methodology and specific issues in accounting theory and practice began to be identified as members of the Amsterdam and the Rotterdam "schools," the antagonism grew stronger. However, after the conclusion of World War II and after Limperg's death, most of the controversy on the basic issues had disappeared.

The famous Limpergian postulate of continuity and his replacement-value theory are topics found in the extensive theoretical and practical Dutch literature, especially after the giant N.V. Philips Industries adopted replacement-valuation principles in its management and financial accounting. Still, in the Dutch business sector, the replacement-value concept has never found significant adoption.

In 1947 the Netherlands School of Economics (now Erasmus University) awarded Limperg a doctoral degree, *honoris causa*. Limperg retired from the university in 1949 but remained active as president of the Conseil International de l'Organisation Scientifique (CIOS) and as advisory board member of the Netherlands Institute of Efficiency (NIVE). He died on December 5, 1961.

Along with the writings of Fritz Schmidt and Eugen Schmalenbach, two of the foremost scholars in Germany, Limperg's work marked the end of the predominance of nominalistic concepts among leading accounting theorists. The nominalist school of thought had held for many years that accounting data must be expressed in money units, measuring the transactions at the time of their origin; thus the maintenance of the original investment in terms of recorded money units was the accepted basis for determining income. Development of modern accounting theory in Europe and elsewhere has required the sophistication of talented and dedicated scholars to extend and refine the legacies of Limperg and his contemporaries. So far, the Dutch have done their share.

It is not clear why Limperg never wrote a book. His many articles and incidental presentations cover a diversity of topics; the writing is always strict and judicious, reflecting his extreme attention to detail and exactness, and often innovative and controversial. The "grand Limpergian theory," written between 1922 and

1929, is a closed, stringent structure in which external and internal organization, accounting, finance, auditing, and labor relations were placed as specialized fields according to their function. This material was presented to his students in lectures that were meticulously edited and often innovative and controversial. The Limperg Instituut in Amsterdam has sponsored the publication of assembled course notes and related material under the title *Bedriifs-economie, Verzameld Werk*. A revised edition was published (in part) in 1976.

After Limperg's death, his supporters continued to perfect and develop his theory. Several premises and conclusions have been questioned and a few are now abandoned. But the basic design has survived, and the great value of Limperg's contribution to methodology and principles of accounting is widely acknowledged.

A. van Seventer

Bibliography

Ashton, R.K. *The Use and Extent of Replacement Value Accounting in the Netherlands*. London: Institute of Chartered Accountants in England and Wales, 1981.

Clarke, F.L., and G.W. Dean. *Contributions of Limperg and Schmidt to the Replacement Cost Debate in the 1920s*. New York: Garland, 1990.

Limperg, T., Jr. "The Accountant's Certificate in Connection with the Accountant's Responsibility." In *Proceedings of the International Accountants' Congress 1926*, pp. 85–104. Amsterdam: J. Musses, Purmerend. 1926. Reprinted. New York: Arno Press, 1980.

———. [Limperg Instituut]. *Bedriifseconomie*. Verzameld Werk. Parts 1-7. Deventer, Netherlands: Kluwer, 1964. Rev. ed. 1976.

Mey, A. *On the Application of Business Economics and Replacement Value Accounting in the Netherlands*. International Business Series No. 8. Seattle: International Accounting Studies Institute and Graduate School of Business Administration, University of Washington, 1970.

———. "Theodore Limperg and His Theory of Value and Costs," *Abacus*, September 1966, pp. 3–23.

Muis, J.W. "Who Was Limperg? Outcast Who Blazed the CCA Trail," *Accountancy*, October 1980, p. 69.

Spinoza Cattela, R.C. "An Introduction into Current Value Accounting and its Application within Philips N.V." In *Current Value Accounting: Its Aspects and Impacts, Proceedings of April 1983 Conference*, pp. 35–46. International Accounting Research Study No. 4. Dallas: Center for International Accounting Development, University of Texas, 1983.

See also HISTORICAL COST; INFLATION ACCOUNTING; MOST, KENNETH S.; NETHERLANDS; PHILIPS INDUSTRIES (N.V.); SCHMALENBACH, EUGEN; SCHMIDT, JULIUS AUGUST FRITZ

Liquidity: Accounting Measurement

Liquidity represents both an important accounting topic and a difficult one to define. This definitional problem is one of the key reasons accountants have always gravitated toward issues of profitability rather than issues of liquidity. Loyd C. Heath, an accounting professor who has directed much needed attention to the topic, illustrated this definitional problem. He considered one of the two uses of "liquidity" to be to "describe some relationships between a company's liquid assets and its short-term liabilities." This he contrasted to "solvency," the ability of the firm to pay its debts when due. "The nature of a company's assets and the relationship between its assets and its short-term liabilities are relevant in evaluating solvency; but solvency does not depend solely, perhaps not even primarily, on a company's recorded assets and liabilities; it depends on its ability to raise cash by whatever means available to it in relation to its need for cash." Given that "solvency" is a topic of extremely broad depth, the focus of this entry is "liquidity." However, "solvency" must never be far from the minds of accountants.

"Cash" was stressed in the first paragraph of Chapter 1 of Luca Pacioli's 1494 treatise on the "Particulars of Reckonings and Their Recording": "For, as we know, there are three things needed by anyone who wishes to carry on business carefully. The most important of these is cash or any equivalent. . . . Without this, business can hardly be carried on." Pacioli, writing well before modern bankruptcy laws, recommended that a businessman report his six classes of personal assets first, with cash being the first one, and then nine classes of business and immovable assets: (1)-(4) inventory-type assets, (5) real estate, (6) agricultural land, (7) cash in banks, (8) debtors, and (9) creditors. This listing by Pacioli is a far cry from today's working capital—current assets minus current liabilities—which is commonly stressed for liquidity measurement.

Arthur Stone Dewing, the leading writer of finance texts in the 1920s, 1930s, and 1940s, noted a rough approximation of balance-sheet reporting in a "working capital versus other assets" format in 1564 in England. He also noted the confusion present in 1934 between accountants and economists on the topic of working capital. In his 1683 textbook, *Idea Rationaria*, Robert Colinson opened his sample problem with this listing: (1) cash, (2) merchandise, (3) ship, (4) house, (5) movables and house furnishing, (6) debtors, and (7) creditors. Adam Smith in his 1776 classic, *The Wealth of Nations*, stressed the difference between circulating capital—really, current assets—and fixed capital. However, in its October 1, 1840, balance sheet, the Baltimore and Ohio Railroad Company listed its assets (debit balances) in reverse order of liquidity with no groupings. The credit balances were listed with capital stock first, then a series of current liabilities, then long-term loans payable, and lastly a version of retained earnings. The U.S. Steel Corporation balance sheet of December 31, 1902, was a classified one, with "current assets" as the last caption heading for assets in an order of inverse liquidity. "Current liabilities" was the fifth of eight classifications on the liabilities side.

A focal point for the emphasis on the balance sheet audit and balance sheet presentation was the 1917 report, "Uniform Accounting," published by the Federal Reserve Board in conjunction with the Federal Trade Commission and the American Institute of Accountants. The focus group of the report was bankers performing their credit function by short-term loans. While the report stressed the audit steps needed during the opinion-rendering process, it did provide a sample balance sheet. Its format was in the "current assets first format" in the order of liquidity, except for marketable securities. It is interesting to note that prepaid expenses were classified in the deferred-charges section. Liabilities were listed with current liabilities first and long-term (fixed) liabilities following before net worth. The 1929 revision of the report,

"Verification of Financial Statements," did not change the suggested format.

Vangermeersch reviewed the annual reports of 20 industrial companies, starting from 1861 through 1912 and ending in 1969. It took until 1938 for all of these companies to list current assets in order of liquidity. It took until 1939 for all of the companies to list current assets first on their balance sheets. There was a brief period from 1945 through 1953 in which eight of these companies started their balance sheet with the current assets minus current liabilities format, but most of them eventually reverted back to their traditional format. Six of these twenty companies classified Prepaid Expenses in the Other Asset category. Another four companies classified it as a current asset but switched it to other assets. The other ten companies eventually adopted the current asset classification for prepaid expense starting in 1947 through 1961.

The 2:1 ratio of current assets to current liabilities remains even today a key ratio in the measurement of liquidity. In his *Financial Policy of Corporations* Dewing explains that the theory of 2:1 ratio ". . . . rests on the theory that in case of failure the current capital can be transformed into cash, liquidated as the banks call it, to an extent equal to the current debts, even though the forced sale of inventories and the forced collection of accounts receivable will involve a considerable shrinkage. The bank presumes that this shrinkage in cash sale values of inventories and accounts receivable will not exceed one-half under the pressure of immediate sale and payment. There is nothing magical in the ratio, and banks are gradually coming to recognize that it means very little."

In effect, the topic of working capital has been a closed matter since the 1940s. One practicing accountant, Anson Herrick, clearly dominated the discussion of the topic. Herrick, a long-term member of the AIA Committee on Accounting Procedure and Committee on Accounting Terminology, lobbied in 1944 for two basic changes in the topic of working capital. The time period for the determination of current assets was to change from one year after the balance sheet date to the end of the accounting cycle. The second change was the reclassification of prepaid expenses as a current asset. Herrick felt that these changes were necessary to reflect a lessening on the use by bankers of the "pounce value" of working capital. Herrick's views were mostly mirrored in 1947

L

when the Committee on Accounting Procedure passed ARB No. 30, "Current Assets and Current Liabilities: Working Capital." ARB No. 30 held that creditors relied more on an analysis of the proceeds of current operations for debt repayment than on the "pounce value" of working capital. Prepaid expenses were reclassified but the now classic "one year or the normal operating cycle, whichever is greater" rule was adopted as a compromise to achieve a unanimous vote.

While there were significant criticisms for the use of working capital as the basis for the funds statement, there was limited criticism of the topic itself. John W. Coughlan in 1960 criticized ARB No. 30 for not yielding anywhere as a good measurement of liquidity as a Statement of Receipts and Disbursements for an eight-year period. Broken down, these years were comprised of the last three years at actual, the next year by budgeted amounts for each quarter, and the subsequent four years by yearly budgeted amounts. Herrick responded to Coughlan by agreeing that the current portion of long-term debt should not have been included in current liabilities. However, in a comments section following Coughlan's article, Herrick thought Coughlan's suggested statement too undependable to be acceptable and useful in cases of a marginal application for short-term credit. Herrick expressed puzzlement because Coughlan did not discuss the effects of working capital of using LIFO.

Philip E. Fess, an accounting professor at the University of Illinois, questioned the effectiveness of working capital as a "buffer" for the creditor. Fess stressed the varying lengths of the normal operating period in different industries. He made a logically compelling case for the exclusion of prepaid expenses from current assets. He argued for the net realizable value basis for cash and claims to cash, including marketable securities and receivables. Inventories were classified separately as well as other short-lived resources.

William H. Beaver in 1968 questioned the efficacy of working capital and the working capital ratio as predictors of business failure. Beaver found that there was consistently superior performance of the nonliquid asset ratios of cash flow and net income to the liquid asset ratios like working capital. Within the liquid asset ratios he found that working capital predicted better than current assets. Quick assets (cash, marketable securities, and receivables) were better than current assets. Cash predicted better than both current assets and quick assets.

Two valiant efforts were made in 1978 to draw more attention to liquidity. Heath's *Financial Reporting and the Evaluation of Solvency* reached the high water mark of a theoretical study in accounting on liquidity. His balance sheet included a non-classified asset section in traditional order and accounting basis. He classified liabilities into operating liabilities (due within one year) and financing liabilities. Heath also recommended a revision of the funds statement into three statements: (1) statement of cash receipts and payments; (2) statement of financing activities; and (3) statement of investing activities. Heath's work was very instrumental in the changes to the cash approach versus the working capital approach in the revised statement of cash flows. A second monograph by Backer and Gosman, entitled *Financial Reporting and Business Liquidity*, provided a wealth of data and analysis to portray a very significant decline in liquidity of U.S. corporations.

There is no doubt that accountants have spent considerably more effort in the theory of income determination than in the theory of liquidity determination. As a matter of fact, the field of accounting has never offered more than lip service to the equality of liquidity determination to income determination. Only partial solutions have ever been offered on liquidity. Businesses and society would be better served if accountants devoted time to developing a number of holistic accounting solutions to liquidity determination.

Richard Vangermeersch

Bibliography

American Institute of Accountants, Committee on Accounting Procedure. "Current Assets and Current Liabilities: Working Capital." ARB No. 30. New York: AIA, 1947.

Backer, M., and M.L. Gosman. *Financial Reporting and Business Liquidity*. New York: National Association of Accountants, 1978.

Beaver, W.H. "Alternative Accounting Measures as Predictors of Failure," *Accounting Review*, January 1968, pp. 113–122.

Coughlan, J.W. "Working Capital and Credit Standing," *Journal of Accountancy*, November 1960, pp. 44–50, and "Comments by Anson Herrick," pp. 50–52.

Dewing, A.S. *The Financial Policy of Corpo-*

rations. 3d rev. ed. New York: Ronald Press, 1934.

Fess, P.E. "The Working Capital Concept," *Accounting Review*, April 1966, pp. 266–270.

Heath, L.C. *Financial Reporting and the Evaluation of Solvency*. Accounting Research Monograph No. 3. New York: AICPA, 1978.

Herrick, A. "Current Assets and Liabilities," *Journal of Accountancy*, January 1944, pp. 48–55.

Smith, A. *The Wealth of Nations*. Reprint. New York: Random House, 1937. Published originally London: W. Strahan and T. Cadell, 1776.

U.S. Federal Reserve Board. "Uniform Accounting," *Journal of Accountancy*, June 1917, pp. 401–433.

———. "Verification of Financial Statements," *Journal of Accountancy*, May 1929, pp. 321–353.

Vangermeersch, R. *Financial Reporting Techniques in Twenty Industrial Companies since 1861*. Gainesville: University Presses of Florida, 1979.

See also AMERICAN INSTITUTE OF CERTIFIED PUBLIC ACCOUNTANTS; BAD DEBTS; BALANCE SHEET; BEAVER, WILLIAM; CASH FLOW ACCOUNTING; COLE, WILLIAM MORSE; CONSERVATISM; FINANCIAL-STATEMENT ANALYSIS; FUNDS FLOW STATEMENT; PACIOLI, LUCA; SMITH, ADAM; *UNIFORM ACCOUNTING;* UNITED STATES STEEL CORPORATION

Littleton, A.C. (1886–1974)

A.C. Littleton left a position as a young railroad telegrapher to enter the field of accounting education, and went on to become one of the prime movers in the development of accounting and accounting education in the United States and internationally. Littleton graduated from the University of Illinois in 1912 with a degree in business administration with an emphasis in accounting. There was no accounting major at that time. After a short period as an auditor in Chicago with Deloitte, Plender, Griffiths and Company, Littleton returned to his former campus as an instructor of accountancy in 1915. He found his new experiences as a teacher to be stimulating. He was one of the pioneer professors of accounting in the United States from 1915 to 1952. His influence on accountancy

education is nowhere better demonstrated than in his pioneering and creative work in graduate accounting education. His influence there was clearly manifested in three special areas: course development and teaching assignments, thesis advising, and research.

Professor H.T. Scovill, the longtime head of the accounting program at the University of Illinois in the first half of the twentieth century, asked Professor Littleton to prepare a graduate accounting course, the first ever at the University of Illinois, in the 1920s. The course proved successful academically, and as the area of accounting activity grew so did the number of graduate accounting courses. The initial course in accounting theory was subsequently subdivided into separate theory and history courses; the process of division into new areas continued. Until his retirement in 1952, Professor Littleton's imprint on all graduate accounting courses at the University of Illinois was both apparent and real.

His own process of learning, both formal and informal, continued throughout his entire academic career. Littleton earned an M.A. in economics in 1918, at the University of Illinois, an unusual step at that time for a current faculty member. He continued that path of formal learning, which required personal and professional courage, by undertaking a doctoral program in economics, which he successfully completed in 1931, also at the University of Illinois. His thesis, *Accounting Evolution to 1900*, published in 1933, was widely acclaimed and remains one of the major works in accounting history.

Professor Littleton dominated the area of thesis advising at the University of Illinois. Of 225 graduate theses completed during his years there from 1913 to 1952, Professor Littleton supervised 76, or 34 percent of them. His domination in the Ph.D. thesis area was even more complete: he supervised 24 of the 26 theses completed during his time with the department. He also was perhaps the most important individual to devise and promote for academic acceptance the first Ph.D. program in accountancy in the world. The first graduate completed the program in 1938.

Littleton's own scholarly habits of wide reading and contemplative thought quite logically led to a heavy emphasis on publications for the field of accountancy, which had relatively few outlets at that time. He served as an editor for *Accounting Review* for several years and contributed many articles to that journal throughout his long and active career. Littleton authored or coauthored six books in the area of accounting theory. Several have won long-term recognition. For example, his previously mentioned *Accounting Evolution to 1900* was reissued in 1966. His well-known work with University of Michigan Professor William Andrew Paton, *An Introduction of Corporate Accounting Standards* (1940), is still an accounting bestseller and is recognized as perhaps the basic work in the expression of modern accounting theory. Littleton also wrote a monograph published in 1953 by the American Accounting Association (Monograph No. 5, *Structure of Accounting Theory*), which was widely read. In addition, he contributed more than 100 articles to accounting and business periodicals.

Throughout his long lifetime work as an accounting educator, Littleton had a number of ideas that he advocated and that he found to be increasingly essential for accounting to become a more perfect instrument of business. He advocated the historical cost concept, although this was not accepted by all. Because he personally experienced the booming 1920s and the depressing decade of the 1930s, he clearly saw, perhaps more than current accountants, the impact of inflation and deflation on an economy and on the published accounts of businesses. The historical cost concept is still basic to contemporary accounting for business transactions, although there have been a number of modifications and suggested expansions for what is thought by some to be a greater explanation of the impact of purchasing-power changes on accounting data. In addition, in his writings and his speeches, Littleton was a champion of the primary role of income determination in accounting theory. He also firmly believed in cost-allocation procedures. This led to his articulation, with Paton, of the concept of matching—the matching of costs with related revenues—which has remained a major concept in accounting. He also felt that the structure of accounting theory rested upon inductively derived principles rooted in experience and action, which, too, continues to be an important concept in accounting theory discussions.

The national and international awareness of the important role Littleton played in graduate accounting education and the body of important accounting literature existed even early in his career, but the awareness and respect continue to grow. This increasing recognition stems from two sources: (1) the unique contribution he made to accounting education in writing during his active academic life, and (2) a continuing flow of important academic writings even after he retired from the University of Illinois.

Perhaps the ultimate national recognition of any accountant, academician or practitioner, is election to the Accounting Hall of Fame. Littleton was one of the first individuals accorded this honor. Evidence of the international respect and recognition of Littleton's great contributions to accounting theory may also be gathered from the numerous translations of his books and articles and the continued citing of his views. Few individuals contributed more to the field of accounting education.

Vernon K. Zimmerman

Bibliography

Burns, T.J., and E.N. Coffman. *The Accounting Hall of Fame: Profiles of Fifty Members*. Columbus: College of Business, Ohio State University, 1991.

Current, K.T. "A Study of Littleton's Contributions to Selected Areas of the Theory of Accountancy." Ph.D. diss., University of Alabama, 1971.

Littleton, A.C., and B.S. Yamey, eds. *Studies in the History of Accounting*. Homewood, IL: Irwin, 1956.

Moyer, C.A., ed. *Essays on Accountancy by A.C. Littleton*. Urbana: University of Illinois Press, 1961.

Zeff, S.A. "Leaders of the Accounting Profession: 14 Who Made a Difference," *Journal of Accountancy*, May 1987, pp. 46–71.

Zimmerman, V.K. "The Long Shadow of a Scholar," *International Journal of Accounting*, Spring 1967, pp. 1–20.

See also ACCOUNTING EDUCATION IN THE UNITED STATES; ACCOUNTING HALL OF FAME; ACCOUNTING RESEARCH BULLETINS; ACCRUAL ACCOUNTING; AMERICAN ACCOUNTING ASSOCIATION; *AN INTRODUCTION TO CORPORATE ACCOUNTING STANDARDS;* CREDIT; DEBIT AND CREDIT; DEFINITIONS OF ACCOUNTING; EDWARDS, JAMES DON; GENERALLY ACCEPTED ACCOUNTING PRINCIPLES; HISTORICAL COST; INCOME-DETERMINATION THEORY; JOURNAL; MANORIAL ACCOUNTING; MATCHING; MONEY; NATURAL BUSINESS YEAR; PATON, WILLIAM ANDREW; PROPRIETORSHIP; ROME (509 B.C.–A.D. 476); SCHRADER, WILLIAM JOSEPH; SINGLE ENTRY BOOKKEEPING; STEWARDSHIP; ZEFF, STEPHEN A.; ZIMMERMAN, VERNON K.

M

MacNeal, Kenneth (1895–1972)

Kenneth MacNeal, the author of *Truth in Accounting* (1939), was a critic of accounting based on historical cost and of the accounting profession in the 1930s. MacNeal attended three colleges without obtaining a degree and seemed more enamored with economics than accounting. However, he received the Gold Medal in Illinois for the highest score on the CPA exam in 1919. He started his career with Price Waterhouse and Company in 1916. After service in World War I, he was involved with an investment trust and had various real estate holdings. He resumed the practice of public accounting in 1944. MacNeal's background does much to explain the tone and the positions he took in his classic book.

MacNeal's theme was that the closer accounting got to the reporting of the market value of assets (truth), the better informed the small, uninformed, and temporary investor was. MacNeal felt that accountants had adopted the expedient of historical cost over the truth of market value. He illustrated this in three accounting fables: (1) the fable of the two factories, (2) the fable of the two flour mills, and (3) the fable of the two investment trusts. The first fable illustrated the superiority of the replacement cost of a building over its historical cost. The second fable illustrated the superiority of the market value of a commodity, wheat, over its historical cost. The third fable illustrated the superiority of the current market value of marketable securities over their historical cost. MacNeal distrusted the reliance of accountants upon footnotes and upon disclosure in general as being informative to the investor. He was fearful of the manipulation of accounting information by insiders.

Accountants, however, were on the whole not dishonest. MacNeal much preferred the word "truth" to the term "fairly represent" adopted by the profession in the mid-1930s. He developed the traditional rationales for conservative inventory valuations, for the realization principle, and for the reluctance to write down longer-term assets. In so doing, he quoted accounting writers of the turn of the century such as Henry Rand Hatfield, Arthur Lowes Dickinson, Robert Hiester Montgomery, and Paul-Joseph Esquerré. MacNeal wanted accounting, like economics, to have wealth shown on the balance sheet and have changes in wealth shown on the income statement. He developed a tripartite system of values: (1) market value, (2) replacement cost, and (3) historical cost for items like patents, copyrights, and mines. Market value was to be used in both booms and in depressions. MacNeal's model income statement separated operating gains from capital gains. He felt that stockholders could be trained not to confuse unrealized profits with cash proceeds. He deplored the recognition of goodwill and favored the valuation of liabilities at their legal value.

MacNeal's book received a number of reviews, none of them favorable. Norman J. Lenhart ridiculed the three fables and the notion that the CPA was the "big bad wolf." J. Hugh Jackson thought the book was dangerous. John Bennett Canning wrote that "truth may be both expensive and useless." William Andrew Paton, while sympathetic, commented on the pre-Depression usage of estimated market values and criticized the wild attacks on the accounting profession. Pearson Hunt used terms like "pamphleteer," "naive," and "too light" to describe MacNeal and his book.

Controversy for MacNeal was to continue. Shortly after the issuance of his book, he was commissioned by *Fortune* to write an article on the McKesson and Robbins fraud. The editors of *Fortune* rejected the piece, and it was subsequently published in the *Nation* in two parts. MacNeal felt that Price Waterhouse had pressured *Fortune* into canceling the piece, in which MacNeal concluded that Price Waterhouse could have prevented the fraud if it had followed the accounting precepts recommended in his book.

While the effect of MacNeal's works on accounting practice is problematic, his book has had a substantial readership among accounting graduate students. *Truth in Accounting* is timeless and highly readable. It makes the reader think and question. Its polemical nature, however, may not be the most efficient way to initiate change in accounting.

Richard Vangermeersch

Bibliography

Canning, J.B. "A Review of *Truth in Accounting*," *Journal of the American Statistical Association*, December 1939, pp. 757–758.

Hodgins, E., and R.W. Davenport. "Zounds!" *Nation*, August 5, 1939, p. 157.

Hunt, P. "A Review of *Truth in Accounting*," *Yale Law Journal*, November 1939, pp. 167–170.

"In the Wind," *Nation*, May 20, 1939, p. 588.

Jackson, J.H. "A Review of *Truth in Accounting*," *American Economic Review*, December 1939, pp. 853–855.

Lenhart, N.J. "A Review of *Truth in Accounting*," *Journal of Accountancy*, June 1939, pp. 395–396.

MacNeal, K. "What's Wrong with Accounting?" *Nation*, October 7, 1939, pp. 370–372, and October 14, 1939, pp. 409–412.

———. "You Cur," *Nation*, August 5, 1939, pp. 157–158.

Paton, W.A. "A Review of *Truth in Accounting*," *Journal of Political Economy*, April 1940, pp. 296–298.

Zeff, S.A. "*Truth in Accounting*: The Ordeal of Kenneth MacNeal," *Accounting Review*, July 1982, pp. 528–553.

See also CANNING, JOHN BENNETT; CONSERVATISM; DICKINSON, ARTHUR LOWES; HATFIELD, HENRY RAND; HISTORICAL COST; MCKESSON AND ROBBINS CASE; MONTGOMERY, ROBERT HIESTER; PATON, WILLIAM ANDREW; REALIZATION; ZEFF, STEPHEN A.

Management Accounting

Management accounting is the measurement and reporting of economic information for managerial decision making. It provides information to identify, measure, and report on the performance of various segments of the organization for better internal decisions.

As businesses grew in size, complexity, and geographical diversity in the nineteenth century, managers needed improved systems to provide the information that was necessary for various management decisions, including performance evaluation, planning, and control. The field of study and practice now called "management accounting" was developed to produce those systems and provide the information for improved managerial decision making.

The industrial revolution changed the nature of business. The mass production of steel aided in the establishment of the railroads and the construction of factories. The building of the railroads throughout the United States provided American business with a distribution system for increased factory production. The marriage of mass production and mass distribution aided the growth of big business. Factories grew with demand for increased productivity and uniformity of products. Businesses not only grew in size, but they also became geographically decentralized. They needed new methods of management and control.

Early contributions to the field were made in England in 1887 by Emile Garcke and J.M. Fells, whose *Factory Accounts: Their Principles and Practice* was an effort to calculate the actual cost of production, including overhead and the allocation of factory burden. In the United States, Henry Metcalfe, in *The Cost of Manufacturing and the Administration of Workshops* in 1885, attempted to develop an accurate system of determining actual costs and centralize these for the government arsenal where he worked.

The scientific-management movement of the late nineteenth and early twentieth century offered new ideas and approaches for management and control that were focused on efficiency. In order for the engineers and managers to operate factories more efficiently and profitably, they needed precise production costs.

They began by concentrating on the wage problem, with continuing debates on whether the best way to pay workers was on a piece-rate system or on an hourly basis. Frederick Winslow Taylor, the father of scientific management, promoted a standard wage system along with standards for all forms of work and costs in factories. Taylor sought to standardize all elements of the workplace, including wages and the costs of production. He broke down the work process into minute detail and developed standards based on time-and-motion studies.

The need for management-accounting information grew during the height of the scientific-management movement (1900–1920) and was focused on controlling the costs of manufacturing. Harrington Emerson, an engineer, wrote about standard costs in a series of articles for *Engineering Magazine* in 1909 titled "Efficiency as a Basis for Operations and Wages." Alexander Hamilton Church, an industrial engineer in England and the United States, wrote about the allocation of overhead costs, the cost of capital, and depreciation. He referred to these costs as "establishment charges." An associate of Emerson, G. Charter Harrison, elaborated on standard costs and included cost variances. He developed formulas for variance analysis and sought to include predetermined standards in the budgeting process. An academic, John Maurice Clark, wrote a now classic work about overhead costs, *Studies in the Economics of Overhead Cost,* in 1923. He pointed out that there were different kinds of costs that were useful for various managerial decisions.

As corporations grew into large industrial complexes, corporate managers required more control over their operations. The role of the accountant grew as the corporations grew in size and complexity. Dupont, General Motors, Standard Oil, and others grew substantially during the early part of the twentieth century and strove for vertical integration and divisional decentralization. They looked to analyze and control their operations through the use of return on investment (ROI), flexible budgets, and transfer pricing. As the demand for accounting information increased, the role of the accountant expanded. The management accountant was asked to prepare budgets, assist in pricing, and work on the internal control of operations.

By the mid-twentieth century, management-accounting practices were well established and continued to expand. In the 1950s, Joel Dean, a managerial economist, introduced the capital-budgeting concept and promoted the use of the "discounted cash flow" method of analysis. But as the economy, societal needs, and management trends changed, so did the need for management-accounting information.

In the 1950s and 1960s, behavioral considerations became more important to management theorists and business executives. They turned to the management accountants to examine the impact of accounting information on employee behavior. Argyris (1952), Becker and Green (1962), Hofstede (1968), Stedry (1960) and others focused on the impact of budgets on employees. Robert Anthony's classic 1965 book, *Planning and Control Systems: A Framework for Analysis,* was central to the discussions of the use of accounting information by managers to improve decision making. David Solomons' 1965 classic, *Divisional Performance Measurement and Control,* examined the difficulties in developing performance-evaluation systems that motivate improved performance by divisional managers. Another major development was the publication of Charles T. Horngren's college text, *Cost Accounting,* in 1962. Still popular, it has gone through numerous editions and has likely influenced more students of management accounting than any other book. The 1960s and 1970s also brought a focus on the applicability of management science, operations research, statistics, and other quantitative models for management accounting practice, as noted by Kaplan (1982, 1984) and Bierman and Dyckman (1971).

Starting in the late 1960s and continuing through the 1970s and 1980s, Eric G. Flamholtz from the University of California, Los Angeles, and others like R. Lee Brummet from the University of Michigan examined the cost and value of the human resource to the organization. Social accounting, as developed in works by Mark J. Epstein at the University of California, Los Angeles, Ralph Estes at the University of Texas at Arlington, Lee J. Seidler, a Ph.D. and CPA with Bear, Sterns, and Company, and others in the 1970s, used management-accounting frameworks to look at the impact of the corporation on society, including effects on employees, the environment, and the community. In each of these new developments, management accountants attempted to respond to managers' needs for information to better manage the enterprise.

M

In the 1980s and 1990s, management needs have turned to improved operations management and global competitiveness. Johnson and Kaplan's important book *Relevance Lost* (1987) examined the evolution of management-accounting practice and the obsolescence of cost systems that had their foundations in the works of Taylor. It looked at industry and its need for "relevant" management-accounting information to aid in decision making. Other writings by Kaplan, Robin Cooper, a professor at the Harvard Business School, and others, like H. Thomas Johnson, from Portland State University, have further changed the direction of management accounting, focused new concerns on the measurement of both product quality and management performance, and continued to develop better methods for the design of cost-management systems, activity-based costing, and customer-oriented performance-measurement techniques.

Researchers and practitioners alike have teamed up to try to improve the effectiveness of the management of organizations by improving the quality of information used for decision making. The importance of management accountants has grown substantially in organizations, and their role is likely to continue to grow to respond to the changing informational needs of organizations in response to the continuous changes in the regulatory environment, management philosophy, operations, and society. Management accounting originally developed to respond to needs for information to improve operations, and those informational needs continue to grow.

Marc J. Epstein

Bibliography

Anthony, R.N. *Planning and Control Systems: A Framework for Analysis.* Cambridge: Harvard University Press, 1965.

Argyris, C. *The Impact of Budgets on People.* Ithaca, NY: Controllership Foundation, 1952.

Becker, S., and D. Green Jr. "Budgeting and Employee Behavior," *Journal of Business*, vol. 35, 1962, pp. 392–402.

Bierman, H. Jr., and T.R. Dyckman. *Managerial Cost Accounting.* New York: Macmillan, 1971.

Brummet, R.L., E.G. Flamholtz, and W.C. Pyle. "Human Resource Measurement: A Challenge for Accountants," *Accounting Review*, April 1968, pp. 217–224.

Church, A.H. "The Proper Distribution of Establishment Charges," *Engineering Magazine*, July 1901, pp. 508–517.

Clark, J.M. *Studies in the Economics of Overhead Cost.* Chicago: University of Chicago Press, 1923.

Cooper R., and R.S. Kaplan. "Profit Priorities from Activity-based Costing," *Harvard Business Review*, May–June 1991, pp. 130–135.

Dean, Joel. *Managerial Economics.* Englewood Cliffs, NJ: Prentice-Hall, 1951.

Epstein, M.J., E. Flamholtz, and John J. McDonough. "Corporate Social Reporting in the United States of America: State of the Art and Future Prospects," *Accounting, Organizations, and Society*, vol. 1, no. 1, 1976, pp. 23–42.

Estes, R. *Corporate Social Accounting.* New York: Wiley, 1976.

Flamholtz, E. *Human Resource Accounting.* Encino, CA: Dickenson, 1974.

Hofstede, G.H. *The Game of Budget Control.* London: Tavistock, 1968.

Johnson H.T. *Relevance Regained: From Top-Down Control to Bottom-Up Empowerment.* New York: Free Press, 1992.

Johnson, H.T., and R.S. Kaplan. *Relevance Lost: The Decline and Fall of Management Accounting.* Boston: Harvard Business School Press, 1987.

Kaplan, R.S. *Advanced Management Accounting.* Englewood Cliffs, NJ: Prentice-Hall, 1982, 1989.

———. "The Evolution of Management Accounting," *Accounting Review*, July 1984, pp. 400–414.

Seidler, L.J., and L.L. Seidler. *Social Accounting: Theory, Issues and Cases.* Los Angeles: Melville, 1975.

Solomons, D. *Divisional Performance Measurement and Control.* Homewood, IL: Irwin, 1965.

Stedry, A.C. *Budget Control and Cost Behavior.* Englewood Cliffs, NJ: Prentice-Hall, 1960.

See also BREAK-EVEN CHART; BROWN, F. DONALDSON; BUDGETING; CHURCH, ALEXANDER HAMILTON; CLARK, JOHN MAURICE; COMMON COSTS; CONTROL: CLASSICAL MODEL; COST AND/OR MANAGEMENT ACCOUNTING; DISCOUNTED CASH FLOW; EMERSON, HARRINGTON; ENGINEERING AND

ACCOUNTING; GARCKE AND FELLS;
HARRISON, G. CHARTER; HORNGREN,
CHARLES T.; HUMAN RESOURCE ACCOUNT-
ING; JOHNSON AND KAPLAN'S *RELEVANCE
LOST: THE RISE AND FALL OF MANAGEMENT
ACCOUNTING;* McKINSEY, JAMES O.;
METCALFE, HENRY; RETURN ON INVESTMENT;
SOLOMONS, DAVID; STANDARD COSTING; TAY-
LOR, FREDERICK WINSLOW; VATTER, WILLIAM
JOSEPH

Management Advisory Services by CPAs

In a sense, CPA firms have engaged in management advisory services (MAS) from the time the
first audit client convinced its accountant to
provide advice on a company problem. Many
small CPA firms continue to provide informal
consulting as part of their client service. Ernst
and Ernst was probably the first major firm to
realize that it could charge fees for consulting
services. As early as 1908, this firm had set up
a separate management-consulting function,
focusing primarily on how to improve internal
financial controls. CPA firms determined that
since they were confirming the soundness of a
particular firm's accounting system in an audit,
it was but one more step to help the firm improve its internal accounting system.

It was not until after World War II that
MAS by CPAs began reaching significant levels.
Firms switching from a wartime footing wished
to reassess their former product lines and frequently turned to their auditors.

It was the introduction of the computer
during the 1950s and its subsequent widespread
use during the 1960s, however, that really accelerated the expansion of MAS. Exploring the
business applications of computers, CPA firms
soon understood that they would facilitate decision making as well as control. CPA firms also
realized that this knowledge would place them
in an excellent position to help management
take full advantage of the computer's potential.
Where factors affecting the operations of a firm
could be expressed mathematically, the computer could be used to affirm the heretofore
intuitive judgments of the manager by enabling
him to test present situations against past data.
Clients soon began asking their auditors for
advice on the relative merits of the various systems available. Consequently, many CPAs
found themselves transformed into management consultants. Further impetus was given by
requirements such as systems integration, com-

puter-integrated manufacturing, and the establishment of more complex links between what
a company purchases and produces.

Other factors driving the growth of MAS
include regulatory changes, the need for greater
competitiveness, and globalization. During the
last 20 years, the explosion of the number, variety, and complexity of laws affecting business
operations, particularly in the areas of health
care and the environment, has fueled the demand for the in-depth knowledge provided by
consultants. As firms have come under greater
pressure from imports, each other, and adverse
economic factors, the need to lower costs has
resulted in increased use of consultants. Awareness of the opportunities posed by increased
international trade, whether in the form of the
opening of Eastern Europe, the European Common Market, or the liberalization of trade rules
affecting Latin America, has provided a new
base for MAS growth. Indeed, all Big Six accounting firms are represented internationally
and in some cases have even aided in the restructuring of the economies of Eastern Europe
by serving as advisers to particular governments.

The growth of MAS by CPAs is reflected
in the percentage of revenues it contributes to
overall CPA firm earnings. Revenue from MAS
in 1978 accounted for an average of 8 percent
of total firm revenues. By 1990, the percentage
of Big Six revenues accounted for by MAS
ranged from a high of 44 percent (Arthur
Andersen and Company SC) to a low of 20
percent (Deloitte and Touche, and KPMG Peat
Marwick). The remaining three had MAS percentage revenues of 25 percent (Coopers and
Lybrand), 24 percent (Price Waterhouse), and
22 percent (Ernst and Young).

The growth of MAS within CPA firms has
resulted in two organizational developments for
MAS: industry specialization and a trend toward greater autonomy. As industries restructure, facing their own unique set of problems,
specialized industry-specific knowledge has
become critical in gaining clients. Consultants
can no longer be all things to all people; an
MAS function must possess orchestrated spe-
cialties with technical specialists commanding
complex process skills.

The trend toward greater autonomy of
MAS practice reached its culmination with the
creation of Andersen Consulting in 1989. MAS
growth during the early 1980s was so rapid that
it ceased being merely an adjunct to accounting.

Consulting partners at Andersen believed that their compensation and ability to make independent business decisions were not commensurate with the revenues generated by MAS. Following much internal dissension, it was decided to create a separate consulting business unit, with its own strategy, mission statement, and almost complete financial autonomy. While none of the other Big Six have followed this route by 1994, greater autonomy of the MAS function is likely as CPA firms evolve into wide-ranging professional services firms.

With the growth of MAS, the issue of independence from auditing arose. The debate was between those who believed that a CPA cannot be independent in auditing a system that his firm may have created, and those who believed that the CPA's expertise makes him uniquely qualified to offer management advice.

Several bodies studied the issues of the debate over MAS. As early as 1957, the American Institute of Certified Public Accountants (AICPA) was distributing materials offering advice on MAS ethical issues. In April of 1961, the Council of the AICPA passed a nonbinding resolution stating that service should be based upon competence to perform rather than on lack of their relationship to accounting (Briloff, 1966). This allowed for broad services decided upon by each provider and set the tone going into the 1960s. But by the late 1960s the Big Eight had become a target for government investigation and reform. The most dunning venue for this investigation was the Senate Subcommittee on Reports, Accounting and Management of the Senate Committee on Government Operations. The Subcommittee, chaired by Senator Lee Metcalf (D-Montana), issued in 1977 *The Accounting Establishment: A Staff Study*, which proclaimed that MAS created an interest which was inconsistent with the auditor's responsibility to remain independent in fact and appearance. This same belief led in 1979 to issuance by the Securities and Exchange Commission of Accounting Series Release No. 264, "Scope of Services by Independent Accountants," which warned CPA firms away from too much MAS involvement.

To counter these governmental threats, the AICPA took a number of steps. In 1966, it formed an Ad Hoc Committee on Independence. This committee reported in 1969 that there was no substantive evidence that the rendering of MAS had impaired the independence of CPAs in fact. However, the Committee believed "that as long as a significant minority of users of financial statements were concerned about MAS and independence, the profession should be sensitive to those concerns." The committee also noted and approved of the first three statements of the MAS committee of the AICPA: (1) "Tentative Description of the Nature of Management Advisory Services by Independent Accounting Firms" (1969); (2) "Competence in Management Advisory Services" (1969); and (3) "Role in Advisory Management Services" (1969). In 1973 the AICPA began the MASBOKE (MAS Body of Knowledge and Examination) study, which determined that creation of an MAS certification exam would be possible. That study was published in 1976 (Summers and Knight). At the same time, the AICPA initiated an annual MAS conference to discuss ethical issues. Finally, in order to curtail encroaching government regulators, it issued its first binding MAS guideline in 1982. This Statement on Standards for *Management Advisory Services* stopped short of setting strict limits, yet it signaled that the industry intended to self-regulate.

In the 1990s, as in the past, CPA firms maintain that doing consulting work for their audit clients does not impair their independence since audit and consulting functions are kept separate from each other. Current SEC rules allow CPA firms to provide their clients with management advisory services as long as no direct or materially indirect business relationship exists between an auditor and its clients.

Roger R. Nelson

Bibliography

Briloff, A.J. "Old Myths and New Realities in Accountancy," *Accounting Review*, July 1966, pp. 484–495.

Carmichael, D.R., and R.J. Swieringa. "The Compatibility of Auditing Independence and Management Services: An Identification of Issues," *Accounting Review*, October 1968, pp. 697–705.

"Final Report of Ad Hoc Committee on Independence," *Journal of Accountancy*, December 1969, pp. 51–56.

Mednick, R., and G.J. Previts. "The Scope of CPA Services: A View of the Future from the Perspective of a Century of Progress," *Journal of Accountancy*, May 1987, pp. 220–238.

Metzger, R.O. *Profitable Consulting: Guiding*

America's Managers into the Next Century. Reading, MA: Addison-Wesley, 1989.

Previts, G.J. *The Scope of CPA Services: A Study of the Development of the Concept of Independence and the Profession's Role in Society*. New York: Wiley, 1985.

Stevens, M. *The Big Eight*. New York: Macmillan, 1981.

———. *The Big Six: The Selling Out of America's Top Accounting Firms*. New York: Simon & Schuster, 1991.

Summers, E.L., and K.E. Knight. *Management Advisory Services by CPAs: A Study of Required Knowledge*. New York: American Institute of Certified Public Accountants, 1976.

Titard, P.L. "Independence and MAS—Opinions of Financial Statement Users," *Journal of Accountancy*, July 1971, pp. 47–52.

See also AMERICAN INSTITUTE OF CERTIFIED PUBLIC ACCOUNTANTS; ANDERSEN, ARTHUR E.; BIG EIGHT ACCOUNTING FIRMS; CHIEF ACCOUNTANTS OF THE SECURITIES AND EXCHANGE COMMISSION; COMPUTING TECHNOLOGY IN THE WEST: THE IMPACT ON THE PROFESSION OF ACCOUNTING; CONGRESSIONAL VIEWS; ETHICS, PROFESSIONAL; INDEPENDENCE OF EXTERNAL AUDITORS; SECURITIES AND EXCHANGE COMMISSION; SPACEK, LEONARD; TRUEBLOOD, ROBERT MARTIN

Manipulation of Income

Income manipulation—or the more precise modern term, earnings management—refers to any management action within the rules of accounting taken to increase or decrease reported accounting income or to smooth accounting income. "Income smoothing" is management action intended to reduce the volatility of the accounting income time-series. At times, management may make accounting choices with the dual objective of both increasing or decreasing reported income and smoothing income.

The first era (late nineteenth century to about 1965) was characterized by publications describing the effect of various accounting methods on accounting income or prescribing certain methods for achieving specific earnings-management goals. There were a number of assumed motivations for earnings management, including reducing income taxes, dampening business cycles, and increasing stock prices. The

second era (1966–1977) is most notable for the several empirical tests of income smoothing that represent the early use of hypothesis testing in academic accounting research. Authors of these studies generally relied upon the assumption that statement users can be fooled by earnings-management techniques to justify management's attempts to smooth income. Earnings-management studies entered the mainstream again after 1977 (modern era) when Watts and Zimmerman (1978) used agency theory to construct a theory of earnings management. Agency theory continues to provide the underlying theoretical construct for earnings-management studies.

Comments on earnings management probably appeared as soon as there was a literature and separation of ownership and management started becoming a common phenomenon. "Secret reserves" was a hot topic in accounting literature in the last decade of the nineteenth century and the first two decades of the twentieth century. A secret reserve is created by overstating expenses or understating revenues. Then a less prosperous future period is relieved of the expenses that were overstated, or the unreported revenues of the previous period are reported in the less prosperous period.

Even though many companies did not prepare an income statement for stockholders, accounting income was considered important since many stockholders expected the entire amount of accounting income to be distributed as dividends. Management created "secret reserves" to avoid disastrous payouts that would disrupt operations and to make "fat years pay for lean." Varying depreciation with income and intangible-asset write-offs were two common techniques for creating these reserves. Advocates of LIFO (last in, first out) emphasized its income-smoothing properties. Some maintained that LIFO would result in dampened business cycles and better production decisions, but the underlying motivation for the promotion of LIFO was its impact on taxable income. Buckmaster (1992) reviewed this literature on income-smoothing up to 1954.

Academic accountants were identifying more with other academics than with accounting practitioners by the mid-1960s. Technology and institutional pressures combined to push academic accountants toward empirical studies. Gordon (1964) provided the best available theoretical construct for empirical research in accounting. Gordon argued that stockholders

M

prefer less volatile income time-series because of the effect on security prices. Others, like Ronald M. Copeland (1968) and Barry E. Cushing (1969) had commented on this over the years, but Gordon's argument was more completely and carefully developed. Income smoothing seemed perfectly suited for empirical testing, and tests of the hypothesis proliferated in the literature from 1966 through 1973. Then such studies became infrequent in the next few years. One factor accounting for the reduction in published income-smoothing studies was the acceptance of the efficient-markets hypothesis, which seemed to make income-smoothing researchers' reliance on assuming management tried to fool investors with accounting techniques invalid.

The big-bath phenomenon was also recognized during this period. A big bath occurs when management seeks to eliminate charges against future income. Large-scale write-offs of assets and disposition of costly subsidiaries are common methods for taking a big bath. The rationale for big-bath behavior is that there are some situations in which management perceives little additional disutility from reporting additional accounting losses. Then management will engage in wholesale activity that will eliminate charges against future accounting income. Asset write-offs and disposition of unprofitable segments are two common examples of such management action.

The best known income-smoothing study, *Smoothing Income Numbers* (Ronen and Sadan 1981), was a transitional study. Ronen and Sadan did not adopt Watts and Zimmerman's (1978) rationale for smoothing, nor did they rely upon a "naive investor" rationale. Rather they used signaling theory from the field of finance to justify their income-smoothing hypothesis. In addition, they introduced the concept of classificatory smoothing—that is, they hypothesized that management used the classification of "extraordinary gains and losses" to smooth the important operating-income series. Watts and Zimmerman borrowed agency theory from the field of economics to legitimize their argument that the choice of accounting methods affects the wealth of management and the firm. Consequently, management chooses accounting methods that maximize its welfare. Three hypotheses of earnings-management behavior were tested: (1) the management-bonus hypothesis that managers will select accounting methods that increase accounting income in order to increase their incentive bonuses based

on accounting income; (2) the political-cost hypothesis that very large firms will select income-decreasing methods in order to minimize political costs; and (3) the bond-covenant hypothesis that firms will select accounting methods that help avoid violation of accounting-based bond covenants. The Watts and Zimmerman theory and hypotheses (positive-accounting theory) spawned a large volume of studies of accounting-method choice over the next few years, like Dan S. Dhaliwal (1982) and Lauren Kelly (1983).

Dale A. Buckmaster

Bibliography

Buckmaster, D.A. "Income Smoothing in Accounting and Business Literature Prior to 1954," *Accounting Historians Journal*, December 1992, pp. 147–173.

Copeland, R.M. "Income Smoothing," *Empirical Research in Accounting: Selected Studies, 1968*, Supplement to the *Journal of Accounting Research*, 1968, pp. 101–116.

Copeland, R.M., and M.L. Moore. "The Financial Bath: Is it Common?" *MSU Business Topics*, Autumn 1972, pp. 63–69.

Cushing, B.E. "An Empirical Study of Changes in Accounting Policy," *Journal of Accounting Research*, Autumn 1969, pp. 196–203.

Dhaliwal, D.S. "Some Economic Determinants of Management Lobbying for Alternative Methods of Accounting: Evidence from the Accounting for Interest Cost Issue," *Journal of Business Finance and Accounting* (Eng.), Summer 1982, pp. 255–265.

Gordon, M.J. "Postulates, Principles, and Research in Accounting," *Accounting Review*, April 1964, pp. 251–263.

Hepworth, S. "Smoothing Periodic Income," *Accounting Review*, January 1953, pp. 32–39.

Johnson, J.F., and E.S. Meade. "Editorial: Maintenance Expenses and Concealment of Earnings," *Journal of Accountancy*, March 1906, pp. 410–412.

Joplin, J.P. "Secret Reserves," *Journal of Accountancy*, December 1914, pp. 407–417.

Kelly, L. "The Development of a Positive Theory of Corporate Management's Role in External Financial Reporting," *Jour-*

nal of Accounting Literature, Spring
1983, pp. 111–150.

Ronen, J., and S. Sadan. *Smoothing Income
Numbers: Objectives, Means, and Implications*. Reading, MA: Addison-Wesley,
1981.

Warshaw, H.T. "Inventory Valuation and the
Business Cycle," *Harvard Business Review*, October 1924, pp. 27–34.

Watts, R.L., and J.L. Zimmerman. "Towards
a Positive Theory of the Determination
of Accounting Standards," *Accounting
Review*, January 1978, pp. 112–134.

See also ACCOUNTING RESEARCH BULLETINS;
AGENCY THEORY; BASE STOCK METHOD;
CAPITAL MAINTENANCE; CONSERVATISM;
DIVIDENDS; EFFICIENT MARKET HYPOTHESIS;
INCOME STATEMENT/INCOME ACCOUNT; LAST
IN, FIRST OUT (LIFO); LIABILITIES; POSITIVE
ACCOUNTING; RETAINED EARNINGS APPRO-
PRIATIONS

Manorial Accounting

Manorial accounting is associated with the
management and control system of the landlord
(lord of the manor) over the people who lived
in his domain (manor). The lord of the manor
could either farm his own land or rent it to tenants. A thirteenth-century writer counseled that
the ideal lord of the manor should ". . . command and ordain that the accounts be heard
every year, not in one place but on all the manors, for so can one quickly know everything,
and understand the profit and loss. He ought to
ask for his auditors and rolls of account" (Hone
1906).

The manorial system was a complex political, economic, and social system in which the
peasants (*villeins*) of medieval Europe were rendered dependent on their land and on their lord.
While the most frequently studied manorial
system is that of England, this system can be
found in the Roman Empire, Russia, and Japan,
as well as on the Continent of Europe. Important persons in the manorial system included the
steward, who had, as one of his functions, to
control the assets of the manor. The bailiff had,
as one of his tasks, the keeping of account rolls
(*compoti*). Auditors heard the report of the
bailiff and, in a sense, were witnesses to the
events recorded by the bailiff. In those days,
very few people could read or write. The account rolls were written in Latin with an occa-

sional English word. They were kept in narrative form under various headings such as rents,
works sold, sales of grain, expenses, and the
like. The figures were not in columnar form.
Receipts were compared to expenses, and the
net amount was reported to, and perhaps
settled with, the lord. The yearly reporting took
place at Michaelmas, which was just after the
main harvest. This was the church feast of the
archangel Michael and was celebrated on September 29th.

Littleton (1933) classified manorial accounting outside the scope of double entry accounting. The basic reporting format was that
of the "charge and discharge" account, especially toward the latter period of feudalism in
the seventeenth century.

Manorial accounting was a much more
inclusive system than the ledger system of early
double entry reporting. It was, in effect, a managerial accounting system or, even more, a management data base for control purposes. In the
parlance of today, it included much off-the-ledger information.

Richard Vangermeersch

Bibliography

Hone, N.J. *The Manor and Manorial
Records*. London: Methuen, 1906. Re-
print. Port Washington, NY: Kennikat
Press, 1971.

Littleton, A.C. *Accounting Evolution to
1900*. New York: American Institute
Publishing, 1933. Reprint. New York:
Russell and Russell, 1966.

See also AGRICULTURAL ACCOUNTING; CASH
BASIS ACCOUNTING; "CHARGE AND DIS-
CHARGE" STATEMENT; COMPANIES ACTS;
DOMESDAY BOOK; EXTERNAL AUDITING;
INTERNAL AUDITING; LITTLETON, A.C.; ME-
DIEVAL ACCOUNTING; PERSONIFICATION OF
ACCOUNTS; PIPE ROLL; PROFFER SYSTEM;
SCOTLAND: EARLY WRITERS IN DOUBLE
ENTRY ACCOUNTING; SPAIN; STEWARDSHIP;
TRUSTEE ACCOUNTS

Manzoni, Domenico

The first important work on double entry bookkeeping after Luca Pacioli's was *Quaderno
doppio col suo giornale secundo il costume di
Venetia* (1540) by Domenico Manzoni, a Venetian teacher of arithmetic and bookkeeping.
Manzoni has been called a popularizer and il-

lustrator of the accounting methods described by Pacioli. Many of his chapters were transcribed from Pacioli's "Particularis de Computis et Scripturis" (1494). But whereas Pacioli's text included only a few sample entries, Manzoni's contained 300 sequentially numbered journal entries keyed to an index in which various types of transactions were listed, grouped into categories, and referenced to ledger accounts. The right margin of Manzoni's journal included a descriptive side heading for each entry. This indexed and annotated journal gave bookkeepers a ready reference for transaction analysis if a particular business event fitted one of Manzoni's 300 sample entries.

Manzoni made the earliest attempt to formulate general rules for transaction analysis, writing that the four most important things about transactions are the one who gives, the thing given, the one who receives, and the thing received.

Manzoni's other innovations included subordinating the daybook to the journal and ledger, describing specialized books of original entry, classifying ledger accounts, introducing ledger posting references to journal entries, and journalizing transfers of nominal accounts to profit and loss. Unlike Pacioli, Manzoni added money amounts to all inventory items.

Manzoni specified that the ledger should be balanced annually or at regular intervals. He totaled ledger debits and credits and tested their equality as a proof of bookkeeping accuracy. In closing his ledger, Manzoni transferred asset, liability, and capital balances directly from the old ledger to the new one, without preparing a balance account or trial balance.

Manzoni's book went through seven editions. He directly influenced later texts by the Dutchman Jan Ympyn (1543), the German Wolfgang Schweicker (1549), and the Englishman John Carpenter (1632).

Michael Chatfield

Bibliography

Brown, R., ed. *A History of Accounting and Accountants*. London: T.C. & E.C. Jack, 1905. Reprint. New York: B. Franklin, 1966.

Bywater, M.F., and B.S. Yamey. *Historic Accounting Literature: A Companion Guide*. London: Scholar Press, 1982.

See also CAPITAL ACCOUNT; CLOSING ENTRIES AND PROCEDURES; DEBIT AND CREDIT; ITALY, AFTER PACIOLI; JOURNAL; LEDGER; MEMORANDUM BOOK; PACIOLI, LUCA; PEELE, JAMES; SCHWEICKER, WOLFGANG; YMPYN, JAN

Massari Commune Ledgers

The *Massari* accounts of the city of Genoa (1340) are the oldest surviving accounting records definitely having all the characteristics of double entry bookkeeping. The city accounted for its finances in two ledgers, one kept by two *Massari* (city treasury officials), and a duplicate ledger kept by two *Magistri Racionali*, whose job it was to check on the *massari's* work.

The *Massari* accounts reflect a fully developed double entry format, indicating that the system must have been in use for a number of years before 1340. Probably it dates back at least to 1327, when because of "many frauds" it was decreed that the city's ledgers were to be kept "after the manner of banks." The surviving ledger contains 478 pages. All entries are recorded twice, with debits and credits placed side by side on the left and right sides of each open folio. The date, nature of each transaction, parties involved, the amount, and a cross-reference to other affected ledger accounts are contained in one narrative paragraph.

Though it cannot be called typical business bookkeeping, the *Massari* ledger also includes inventory accounts similar to those of merchants. To raise money, the city government speculated in pepper, salt, silk, and wax, which it bought on credit and sold immediately at a lower price.

Michael Chatfield

Bibliography

Martinelli, A. *The Origination and Evolution of Double Entry Bookkeeping to 1440*. Ph.D. diss., North Texas State University, 1974. Ann Arbor, MI: University Microfilms.

Peragallo, E. *Origin and Evolution of Double Entry Bookkeeping: A Study of Italian Practice from the Fourteenth Century*. New York: American Institute Publishing, 1939. Reprint. Osaka: Nihon Shoseki, 1974.

See also DOUBLE ENTRY BOOKKEEPING: ORIGINS

Matching

Matching is the principle of accruing related revenues and expenses in the same accounting period. While William Andrew Paton and A.C. Littleton wrote their classic American Accounting Association (AAA) monograph, *An Introduction to Corporate Accounting Standards*, in 1940, it remains the most significant work in terms of the topic of matching. According to Paton and Littleton, costs attach to assets and then expire as revenue is realized from them in the accounting period. "Costs are considered as measuring effort, revenues as measuring accomplishments."

Two passages from this monograph remain as the basis for generally accepted accounting principles in the United States. The first, which deals with the "costs-attach theory," states: "Since specific costs express significant parts of the total effort expended in producing and selling a commodity or service, they may be assembled by operating divisions, product parts, or time intervals as if they had the power, like their physical counterparts, of cohesing in groups." This vivid description of the costs-attach theory continues to be used in accounting pedagogy and likely has helped keep this theory alive.

The second passage is a representation of the "meter theory" of accounting: "With acquisition and disposition prices measuring both the efforts to produce results and the results produced, the principal concern of accounting is the periodic matching of costs and revenues as a test-reading by which to gauge the effect of the efforts expended." The vividness of this passage, which has captivated accounting teachers and students for over 50 years, explains perhaps why this qualifying comment from the monograph has long been forgotten: "Not all costs attach in a discernible manner, and this fact forces the accountant to fall back upon a time period as the unit for associating certain expenses with certain revenues. Time periods are a convenience, a substitute, but the fundamental concept is unchanged. The ideal is to match costs incurred with the effects attributable to or significantly related to such costs."

The matching principle remained a focal point for the AAA in the 1941 revision, included in the 1957 revision, of its 1936 *A Tentative Statement of Accounting Principles Underlying Corporate Financial Statements*. The 1948 AAA revision, included in the 1957 revision, no longer stressed the matching principle.

It said: "The income of an enterprise is the increase in its net assets (assets less liabilities) measured by the excess of revenue and expense." These expenses were classified as (1) directly associated with revenue, (2) indirectly associated with revenues, or (3) "a measurable expiration of asset costs even though not associated with the production of revenue for the current period. . ." The 1957 AAA revision did not list the matching principle as an underlying concept. This was also true of the 1966 "A Statement of Basic Accounting Theory" and 1977 "Statement on Accounting Theory and Theory Acceptance" statements.

The matching principle was not included as a postulate of accounting in Accounting Research Study (ARS) No. 1 in 1961 by Maurice Moonitz. The wealth of a company, as measured in its assets, was stressed as opposed to the stress on the income statement in the Paton and Littleton monograph. Robert T. Sprouse and Moonitz's attempt in ARS No. 3 in 1962 to adopt a current-cost concept was ill-received by the members of the advisory committees for ARS No. 1 and No. 3. There have been a number of other theoretical attempts to leave the income-statement orientation of the matching principle, by such writers as Edgar O. Edwards and Philip W. Bell in *The Theory and Measurement of Business Income* (1961), Robert R. Sterling in *Theory of the Measurement of Enterprise Income* (1970), and R.J. Chambers in *Accounting Finance and Management* (1969).

Another attack on the matching principle came in 1969 by Arthur L. Thomas. He made a compelling case for the ultimate arbitrariness of the cost-allocation period. Thomas wrote ". . . [T]he profession will probably continue to follow the conventional matching approach—at least until allocation theory is improved to a point where better allocations become possible at the present level of data aggregation."

In 1970 in Accounting Principles Board (APB) Statement No. 4—in paragraphs 154–168 on expenses—the APB recognized the difficulties with the matching principle. Three types of expenses for a period were listed: (1) costs directly associated with the revenue of the period, (2) costs associated with the period on some basis other than a direct relationship with revenue, and (3) costs that cannot, as a practical manner, be associated with any other period. Even in its explanation for the first classification, the APB skirted the use of "matching." Instead, it used the term "associating cause and

M

effect." This was explained as: "Some costs are recognized as expenses on the basis of a presumed direct association with specific revenue." By 1980 the Financial Accounting Standards Board (FASB), in its Statement of Financial Accounting Concepts No. 3, "Elements of Financial Statements of Business Enterprises," adopted a substantially different definition for expenses: "Expenses are outflows or other using up of assets or incurrences of liabilities (or a combination of both during a period . . .)."

The matching principle, at least witnessed from accounting literature, appears to be a phenomenon of the period of the Great Depression. Yet it also appears to be alive and well in terms of the explanation of accounting to students. Hence it lives on in practice today. Does it live on because of the vividness and the simplicity of the Paton and Littleton monograph? Or is it because the matching principle offers a much more certain answer than methods offered to change it or other explanations for expenses? Is it still around because of the unwillingness of accountants and accounting bodies to drop the historical cost principle, or because the income statement is really still the most important statement in accounting, or because the balance-sheet approaches to measure wealth have failed? Perhaps it is time to determine why the matching principle is still in vogue and then decide whether it should be.

Richard Vangermeersch

Bibliography

American Accounting Association. *Accounting and Reporting Standards for Corporate Financial Statements and Preceding Statements and Supplements.* Sarasota, FL: American Accounting Association, 1957.

American Institute of Certified Public Accountants, Accounting Principles Board. "Basic Concepts and Accounting Principles Underlying Financial Statements of Business Enterprises." APB Statement No. 4. New York: AICPA, 1970.

Financial Accounting Standards Board. *Accounting Standards: Statements of Financial Accounting Concepts 1–4.* Stamford, CT: FASB, 1983.

Moonitz, M. *The Basic Postulates of Accounting.* Accounting Research Study No. 1. New York: AICPA, 1961.

Paton, W.A., and A.C. Littleton. *An Introduction to Corporate Accounting Standards.* American Accounting Association Monograph No. 3. Sarasota, FL: American Accounting Association, 1940.

Sprouse, R.T., and M. Moonitz. *A Tentative Set of Broad Accounting Principles for Business Enterprises.* Accounting Research Study No. 3. New York: AICPA, 1962.

Taggart, H.F., ed. *Paton on Accounting: Selected Writings by William A. Paton.* Ann Arbor, MI: Bureau of Business Research, Graduate School of Business Administration, University of Michigan, 1964. See "The Significance and Treatment of Appreciation in the Accounts," 1918; and "Measuring Profits Under Inflation Conditions: A Serious Problem for Accountants," 1950.

Thomas, A.L. *The Allocation Problem in Financial Accounting Theory.* Studies in Accounting Research No. 3. Sarasota, FL: American Accounting Association, 1969.

See also ACCOUNTING PRINCIPLES BOARD; ACCOUNTING RESEARCH STUDIES; ACCRUAL ACCOUNTING; AMERICAN ACCOUNTING ASSOCIATION; *AN INTRODUCTION TO CORPORATE ACCOUNTING STANDARDS;* BASE STOCK METHOD; CHAMBERS, RAYMOND JOHN; CONCEPTUAL FRAMEWORK; CONSERVATISM; DEFERRED INCOME TAX ACCOUNTING; DEFINITIONS OF ACCOUNTING; DICKSEE, LAWRENCE; EDWARDS AND BELL: REPLACEMENT-COST ACCOUNTING; FINANCIAL ACCOUNTING STANDARDS BOARD; FIXED ASSETS; GENERALLY ACCEPTED ACCOUNTING PRINCIPLES; INCOME-DETERMINATION THEORY; LITTLETON, A.C.; OBJECTIVITY; PATON, WILLIAM ANDREW; PERIODICITY; POSTULATES OF ACCOUNTING; REALIZATION; STERLING, ROBERT R.; THOMAS'S *THE ALLOCATION PROBLEM IN FINANCIAL ACCOUNTING THEORY;* TRANSFER PRICES

Materiality

A subjective concept that addresses the influence and/or importance of qualitative and quantitative items on the users of financial-statement information, materiality determination has been a problem for both the accounting profession and the courts.

Accountants have recognized that the profession would benefit if a general definition of materiality could be developed. In 1973, the issue of materiality was one of the original items considered by the newly formed Financial Accounting Standards Board (FASB). The board's conclusions on materiality criteria were issued in the 1980 Statement of Financial Accounting Concepts (SFAC) No. 2, "Qualitative Characteristics of Accounting Information." The board announced that it would not attempt to codify basic rules for materiality, because the formulation of such general standards could not embody all considerations of experienced judgment. The board instead issued this general definition of materiality: "The magnitude of an omission or misstatement of accounting information that, in the light of surrounding circumstances, makes it probable that the judgment of a reasonable person relying on the information would have been changed or influenced by the omission or misstatement."

Lacking substantive guidance from the FASB's definition, accountants tend to quantify the complexities of materiality. Although authoritative accounting pronouncements with quantitative guidelines concerning materiality are rare, SFAC No. 2 notes that materiality judgments are primarily quantitative. Decisions with regard to materiality are made in terms of the comparative magnitude of the information: Pattillo (1976) established that most accountants view materiality criterion in terms of 5 to 10 percent of net income.

Reliance upon the courts and definition from the Securities and Exchange Commission (SEC) is becoming increasingly important for the accounting profession. Vulnerability of accountants to a judicial determination of materiality exists when subjective definition and lack of standards are perceived by the courts and the SEC as demonstrably unresponsive. It is vital that accountants stay current on overall judicial trends, since they may be compelled to adopt the courts' definition of materiality, one that may not always agree with the FASB's conceptual accounting framework.

The application of a legal standard of materiality to accountants is drawn from the common law of torts. Accountants have been sued for supplying misleading information under the common-law remedies for misrepresentation and fraud. An item is material under the *Restatement of Torts 2d* (1958) if "a reasonable man would have regarded the fact misrepresented to be important in determining his course of action."

The Securities Acts of 1933 and 1934 created criminal and civil liability for certain actions and omissions. Although the acts use "material" to describe the offenses involving misleading information, the term is never defined. Securities regulations [17 C.F.R. S230.405 (1) and 240.12b-2 (1984)] provide some guidance by emphasizing that a material information requirement is one that allows an average prudent investor to be reasonably informed before purchasing the security registered.

Accountants may be unsettled by what appears to be a lack of uniformity in the courts when defining materiality. Major variations of the materiality standard in the courts can be traced primarily to the facts of each case and the particular statute or regulation involved. However, trends have been developing since the early 1960s in court-derived materiality standards with respect to (1) information influence versus importance, (2) error or omission effects on average investors versus reasonable laymen, and (3) error or omission effects on prudent investors versus speculative investors.

The first trend of the courts focuses on influence versus importance and reveals a movement away from the standard that information must influence the decision of a recipient of information in order to be material. Examples of these cases include *Kardon v. National Gypsum Company* [73 F.Supp. 798 (E.D.Pa. 1947)], *Kohler v. Kohler Company* [319 F.2d 634, 642 (Cir. 7, 1963)], *List v. Fashion Park* [340 F.2d 457 (Cir. 2, 1965), cert. den. 382 U.S. 811], and *Crane Company v. Westinghouse Air Brake Company* [419 F.2d 787 (Cir. 2, 1969)]. Instead, more recent decisions require that any important information under securities laws be considered material and this places a higher burden of disclosure on accountants. Examples of these cases include *United States Securities and Exchange Commission v. Texas Gulf Sulphur* [401 F.2d 833 (Cir. 2, 1967), cert. den. 394 U.S. 976], *Affiliated Ute Citizens of Utah v. United States* [406 U.S. 89 (1972)], *Mills v. Electric Auto-Lite* [396 U.S. 375 (1970)], and *TSC Industries v. Northway* [426 U.S. 438 (1976)].

The second trend relates to the materiality of financial information as it impacts a layman versus an investor. The focus is on whether the users of financial information are hypothetical "reasonable men," as adopted under common law or "average prudent investors," as developed under the securities laws. The distinction of whether the "investor" (who is assumed to have some basic knowledge of investment activities) is held to a higher or lower standard than the "reasonable man" is specific to case facts. In some situations, a layman might require a more thorough explanation of the activities of a company. An example of the court adopted definition of materiality for whether a "reasonable man" would attach importance to misrepresented financial information was stated in *Smallwood v. Pearl Brewing Company* [489 F.2d 579, 604 (Cir. 5 , 1974) cert. den. 419 U.S. 873]. At other times, a knowledgeable investor might demand that more information be disseminated, as indicated in such cases as *Escott v. BarChris Construction Corporation* [283 F.Supp. 643 (S.D.N.Y. 1968)], *Osofsky v. Zipf*, [645 F.2d 107 (2d Cir. 1981)], and *Flamm v. Eberstadt* [814 F.2d 1169 (7th Cir.), cert. denied, 484 U.S. 853 (1987)]. The emerging trend of more current materiality cases show greater application of the securities laws' standard of the "average prudent investor."

A third trend focuses on average prudent investments versus speculative investment activities and indicates movement toward an even higher standard of materiality that is applied in special cases. This distinction focuses on the reliance placed on securities by a speculative investor, who has different needs and risks than the average prudent investor in balancing both the probability that an event will occur and the anticipated magnitude of the event in the totality of company activity for decisions of buying, selling, and holding stocks. Examples of this unusual but important definition of materiality applied by the courts are presented in *United States Securities and Exchange Commission v. Texas Gulf Sulphur Company*, supra, and *Basic, Inc. v. Levinson*, 108 S. Ct. 978, 983 (1988).

All judicial trends indicate an application of qualitative standards and an examination of the use of the information by the readers of financial statements. For the courts, the magnitude of an item may be one factor to consider in determining materiality, but not the controlling factor.

Despite the accounting profession's development of its own view of materiality, the judicial definition cannot be ignored. Trends and variations of the courts present the best judicial test for accountants as: would the average reasonable (or speculative) investor (or layman) consider information to be important (or be influenced by this information)? If an accountant's judgment is questioned, today's litigious society demands the ultimate determination be made by the courts. Avoiding legal liability will require accountants to comply with the evolving common-law definition of materiality, where the courts do not consider application of generally accepted accounting principles and the FASB conceptual framework to be full and fair disclosure.

LuAnn G. Bean
Deborah W. Thomas

Bibliography
Financial Accounting Standards Board. "Qualitative Characteristics of Accounting Information." Statement of Financial Accounting Concepts No. 2. Stamford, CT: FASB, 1980.

Pattillo, J.W. *The Concept of Materiality in Financial Reporting*. Financial Executives Research Foundation, 1976.

Reckers, P.M.J., D.C. Kneer, and M.M. Jennings. "Concepts of Materiality and Disclosure," *CPA Journal*, December 1984, pp. 20, 22–24, 27–28, 30.

See also CONCEPTUAL FRAMEWORK; CONSERVATISM; FINANCIAL ACCOUNTING STANDARDS BOARD; LAW AND ACCOUNTING; LEGAL LIABILITY OF AUDITORS; SECURITIES AND EXCHANGE COMMISSION; STATISTICAL SAMPLING

Mattessich, Richard V. (1922–)

The contributions of Richard V. Mattessich to the discipline and practice of accounting are varied and fundamental. Among others, the formalization of basic accounting conventions, the heralding of computer spreadsheets, the consideration of the representational significance of financial statements, the categorization and critique of modern accounting research, and the inquiries into early Sumerian recording techniques are of important consequence. In all such efforts, Mattessich insists on the need to examine accounting in its full economic and social aspects. As a consequence of the need for this, he brings to his work an enormous knowledge of the related disciplines and skills of the humanities and the social and physical sciences.

Richard V. Mattessich was born in 1922 in Trieste (Italy). He grew up and was educated in Vienna where he received degrees in Mechanical Engineering, Business Administration and a doctorate in Economic Sciences. After several years of practical experience as an engineer and accountant, he became a fellow of the Austrian Institute of Economic Research and subsequently an instructor at the Rosenberg College in Switzerland. After emigration to Canada, he was active with the Prudential Assurance Co. and as an instructor at McGill University. In 1953 he became head of the Commerce Dept. at Mount Allison University in New Brunswick.

In 1958 he joined the Faculty at the University of California at Berkeley. In 1966 he obtained (simultaneous with his position at Berkeley) an academic chair at the Ruhr University in Bochum, Germany, and a year later accepted a Professorship at the University of British Columbia, Canada, where he received in 1980 the distinguished Arthur Andersen and Company Alumni Chair. He has simultaneously held a Chair at the University of Technology in Vienna. He is a dual citizen of Canada and Austria. He retired in 1988 from the University of British Columbia where he remains the Arthur Andersen and Company Professor Emeritus. He continues his research work in retirement. His 1995 book, *Critique of Accounting,* pleads for a more purpose-oriented approach to the discipline.

The early work of Mattessich in *Accounting and Analytical Methods* (1964) is concerned with the need to generalize and conceptually clarify basic accounting assumptions and definitions. To those ends, the disciplines of logic and mathematics—particularly set theory and matrix algebra—together with decision theory and micro- and macroeconomics are brought to bear on the fundamental accounting issues of measurement, definition, methodology and domain. *Accounting and Analytical Methods* also presages much of Mattessich's subsequent work, in which he probes in much greater depth the issues raised there. *Simulation of the Firm through a Budget Computer Program* (1964) foreshadows the basic principles behind today's computer spreadsheets: the use of matrices, (budget) simulation, and, most important, the calculations that support each matrix cell. Similarly, *Instrumental Reasoning and Systems Methodology* (1978) is a wide-ranging general philosophic work that provides the conceptual foundations for his belief that accounting, engineering, administration, and similar disciplines are applied sciences. After examining the major problems in the philosophy of science, he derives a counterpart methodology for the applied sciences in terms of their purpose-orientation (instrumentalism) and their integrative aspects (systems theory).

Of enormous general academic interest are Mattessich's imaginative insights into recent archaeological findings in Mesopotamia (1987). Clay tokens and receptacles are seen as a counterpart form of our existing double entry system in which variously shaped tokens were placed in hollow clay envelopes (the debit), and their image impressed (the credit) on the envelope or onto flat clay tablets. With cuneiform symbols later evolving to replace these impressions, credence can be given to the interpretation that accounting was the precursor to writing as well as abstract counting—and not the other way around.

Subsequent work in "Social Reality and the Measurement of Its Phenomena" (1991) addresses the important problem of financial-statement representation. Mattessich carefully distinguishes those representations and finds their counterparts in existing physical realities (for example, inventories) or social realities (property rights).

Of significant importance are his detailed reviews of accounting research in *Accounting Research in the 1980s and Its Future Relevance* (1991), which both categorize and evaluate recent research from philosophic and practical viewpoints. While praising the breadth of recent accounting inquiry, he laments the rigid boundaries of certain schools of inquiry (positive accounting) and, more generally, the displacement of normative accounting and the too-frequent absence of holistic and foundational philosophic approaches to the discipline and its research.

George J. Murphy

Bibliography

Mattessich, R.V. *Accounting and Analytical Methods: Measurement and Projection of Income and Wealth in the Micro- and Macro-Economy.* Homewood, IL: Irwin, 1964. Reprint. Houston: Scholars Book, 1977.

———. "Conditional-Normative Accounting Methodology: Incorporating Value Judgments and Means-End Relations of an Applied Discipline," *Accounting Organizations and Society,* vol. 20, no. 4, 1995a, pp. 259–284.

———. *Critique of Accounting: Examination of the Foundations and Normative Structure of an Applied Discipline.* Westport,

CT: Quorum Books, 1995b.

———. "Editorial Commentary: A Decade of Growth, Sophistication, and Impending Crisis." In *Accounting Research in the 1980s and Its Future Relevance*, pp. 1–72. Vancouver, BC: Canadian Certified General Accountants' Research Foundation, 1991.

———. *Foundational Research in Accounting: Professional Memoirs and Beyond.* Tokyo: Chuo University Press, 1995.

———. *Instrumental Reasoning and Systems Methodology: An Epistemology of the Applied and Social Sciences.* Dordrecht and Boston: D. Reidel, 1978.

———. "On the History of Normative Accounting Theory: Paradigm Lost, Paradigm Regained?" *Accounting Business and Financial History*, vol. 2, no. 2, 1992, pp. 180–198.

———. "Prehistoric Accounting and the Problem of Representation: On Archaeological Evidence of the Middle East from 8000 B.C. to 3000 B.C.," *Accounting Historians Journal*, Fall 1987, pp. 71–91.

———. *Simulation of the Firm through a Budget Computer Program.* Homewood, IL: Irwin, 1964.

———. "Social Reality and the Measurement of Its Phenomena," *Advances in Accounting*, 1991, pp. 3–17.

See also CONCEPTUAL FRAMEWORK; NORMATIVE ACCOUNTING; POSITIVE ACCOUNTING

Mautz, Robert K. (1915–)

Robert K. Mautz has contributed significantly to accounting education and to the development of an increased interaction of accounting education with the auditing profession. Mautz received his B.A. from the University of North Dakota in 1937 and his M.A. and Ph.D. in accountancy from the University of Illinois in 1938 and 1942, respectively. The university's accounting doctoral program had only recently been established and was the first such program in the world. Professor Mautz added much to its reputation by his own study as a candidate in the program and his leadership role in subsequent years in course instruction and dissertation supervision.

Mautz was a member of the Chicago office of Haskins and Sells both before and after military service. He had two additional years of auditing experience with Alexander Grant and Company in Chicago. In 1948 he accepted an invitation to return to the University of Illinois Department of Accountancy. He remained there until 1972, retiring as the Weldon Powell Professor of Accountancy. From 1972 until 1978, he was a partner with Ernst and Ernst. In 1979 he became director of the Paton Accounting Center and professor of accounting at the University of Michigan until his retirement in 1985.

Throughout his highly productive career, Mautz continued to maintain and develop his contacts with the auditing profession. He was very active in professional accounting associations, including the American Institute of Certified Public Accountants (AICPA), the Financial Executive Institute, and the U.S. General Accounting Office. He was selected by his colleagues to be the editor of *Accounting Review* from 1958 to 1961. He also served on a number of significant commissions and committees for academic and professional organizations, including the Board of Directors of the AICPA, the Cost Accounting Standards Board, the Financial Accounting Standards Advisory Committee, and the SEC Practice Section of the Public Oversight Board.

Mautz has made numerous contributions to the accounting literature, particularly in the areas of financial accounting and auditing. His writings have ranged from a search for accounting postulates and principles (1965), to diversified reporting (1968). One of his pioneering works, with Hussein A. Sharaf, from the University of Cairo, was a monograph, published in 1961 by the American Accounting Association, *The Philosophy of Auditing*, which is recognized as one of the major philosophical examinations of the field. Other of his leading works covered such topics as corporate audit committees, *Corporate Audit Committees* (1970) and internal control, *Internal Control in U.S. Corporations: The State of the Art* (1980). His writings are characterized by clarity and economy of expression. Those who have been privileged to know him and to work with him have always been impressed by his industry, his candor, and his readiness to help younger colleagues, particularly in their beginning research experiences.

For his many contributions to accounting education and the accounting profession, Mautz received many of the top recognitions available to him, such as the AICPA Gold

Medal for Service to the Profession in 1979, admission to the Accounting Hall of Fame in 1978, and president of the American Accounting Association in 1965.

Though retired from formal teaching, Mautz continues to remain actively interested in the current development of accounting.

Vernon K. Zimmerman

Bibliography

Burns, T.J., and E.N. Coffman. *The Accounting Hall of Fame: Profiles of Fifty Members.* Columbus, OH: College of Business, Ohio State University, 1991.

Mautz, R.K. "A Few Words for Historical Cost," *Financial Executive*, January 1973, pp. 23–27, 60.

———. *Effect of Circumstances on the Application of Accounting Principles.* New York: Financial Executives Research Foundation, 1972.

———. *Financial Reporting in Diversified Companies.* New York: Financial Executives Research Foundation, 1968.

———. "Place of Postulates in Accounting," *Journal of Accountancy*, January 1965, pp. 46–49.

——— and F.L. Neumann. *Corporate Audit Committees.* Urbana, IL: Bureau of Economic and Business Research, University of Illinois, 1970.

——— and Others. *Internal Control in U.S. Corporations: The State of the Art.* New York: Financial Executives Research Foundation, 1980.

——— and H.A. Sharaf. *The Philosophy of Auditing.* Sarasota, FL: American Accounting Association, 1961.

See also ACCOUNTING HALL OF FAME; AMERICAN ACCOUNTING ASSOCIATION; AMERICAN INSTITUTE OF CERTIFIED PUBLIC ACCOUNTANTS; AUDIT COMMITTEES; BIG EIGHT ACCOUNTING FIRMS; CASH FLOW ACCOUNTING; COST ACCOUNTING STANDARDS BOARD; EXTERNAL AUDITING; HISTORICAL COST; INDEPENDENCE OF EXTERNAL AUDITORS; INTERNAL CONTROL; PUBLIC OVERSIGHT BOARD; UNIFORMITY

May, George Oliver (1875–1961)

George Oliver May was born May 22, 1875, at Teignmouth, Devonshire, England. He joined the London office of Price Waterhouse in 1897 and later that year came to the United States and joined the staff of Jones, Caesar and Company, which was an affiliate firm of Price Waterhouse in the United States. He was admitted to the partnership of Price Waterhouse in 1902, was named senior partner in 1911, and continued in that capacity until 1927 when he stepped down from active practice in order to devote his energies to professional matters, primarily through the American Institute of Accountants. He retired from Price Waterhouse in 1940 but continued to be active in the profession almost until the time of his death on May 25, 1961. His most significant contributions to the development of accounting thought came after he stepped down from active practice in 1927. This coincided with what was probably the most significant period in the development of accounting—the 1930s. May was an intellectual and was interested in a wide variety of areas in addition to accounting, including economics, taxation, law, and philosophy.

Probably because of his British background, May was a pragmatist. His pragmatic influence can be clearly seen in the work of the Special Committee on Cooperation with Stock Exchanges (1932–1934), which was chaired by May. It is also reflected in the output of the Committee on Accounting Procedure, of which May was the active head for the first four years from its inception in 1936 and on which he remained as a member until 1944.

May considered his service on the Special Committee on Cooperation with Stock Exchanges to be his greatest contribution to the profession. The correspondence between this committee and the Committee on Stock List of the New York Stock Exchange clearly reflects his views. May believed that it was important that the public be educated as to both the significance and the limitations of financial statements. He reasoned that financial statements reflect events that occur in a world of uncertainty and cannot reflect a greater degree of certainty than do those events. May stressed the conventional nature of accounting, and he believed that corporations should choose their own methods of accounting, should disclose these methods, and should apply them consistently. He believed that accounting is largely conventional, should serve a useful social purpose and should change with changes in economic conditions and social policies.

May's pragmatic influence was felt in the approach taken by the Committee on Accounting Procedure in the development of accounting principles. One school of thought wanted to publish nothing until a body of doctrine could be accumulated. May, on the other hand, took the position that the committee should deal with individual matters until a reasonable body of doctrine could be obtained. It was the latter approach that the committee took. He was opposed to any attempt to promulgate uniform rules of accounting. He believed that uniform standards necessarily meant low standards, and he was convinced that uniform accounting would lead to the creation of bureaucracies to enforce it, which would be detrimental both to the public interest and the accounting profession. In his judgment, what was appropriate was to develop new methods of analysis and presentation that would result in more meaningful financial statements, and to modify accounting practice to serve the needs of three classes of corporations. He classified them as the small corporation, the large publicly held corporation, and the regulated ones. May believed that there would be no particular advantage to applying uniform standards to the small corporations and, since the large corporations were constantly growing and changing, any attempt at sustained uniformity was futile. Further, he reasoned that any attempt at uniformity would end progress in the development of the profession and would emphasize form at the expense of substance. In his judgment, there was a danger in creating a belief in a degree of uniformity and comparability that could not be achieved.

Throughout his professional life, May maintained an interest in income determination, and he devoted considerable thought to the subject. In 1947 he was instrumental in organizing the Study Group on Business Income, and he served as research consultant to the group until it published its final report in 1952. May stressed the need for an interdisciplinary approach in defining income, and he believed that the role of the accountant was to advise and cooperate with members of related disciplines in arriving at a definition and to implement an accepted concept. It was the role of the accountant to make clear to others the significance of the income measured. May was primarily interested in the concept of business income and believed that it consisted of two components—one generated by the operations of the business, and a second by profits and losses resulting from changes in the price level. He noted that the LIFO (last in, first out) method of inventory valuation essentially accomplished the reporting of income in current dollars. He believed that depreciation should be handled in the same manner—a departure from the historical cost principle. Because it was so closely allied to income determination, May took a keen interest in taxation, and he believed that taxes should be disclosed as a separate item in the income statement. It was his opinion that the primary value of income statements lay in the light they threw on future earning capacity. Income statements should point out significant trends, and increased taxation was a significant trend in the 1930s and 1940s.

George Oliver May was a guiding light to the profession.

Henry Francis Stabler

Bibliography

American Institute of Accountants. *Audits of Corporate Accounts: Correspondence between the Special Committee on Cooperation with Stock Exchanges of the American Institute of Accountants and the Committee on Stock List of the New York Stock Exchange, 1932–1934.* New York: AIA, 1934.

Grady, P., ed. *Memoirs and Accounting Thought of George O. May.* New York: Ronald Press, 1962.

May, G.O. *Business Income and Price Levels: An Accounting Study.* New York: Study Group on Business Income, 1949.

———. *Financial Accounting: A Distillation of Experience.* New York: Macmillan, 1943.

———. "Improvement in Financial Accounts." In *Dickinson Lectures in Accounting.* Cambridge: Harvard University Press, 1943.

———. "Truth and Usefulness in Accounting," *Journal of Accountancy,* May 1950, p. 387.

———. "Uniformity in Accounting," *Harvard Business Review,* Autumn 1938, pp. 1–8.

Stabler, H.F. *George O. May: A Study of Selected Contributions to Accounting Thought.* Research Monograph No. 61. Atlanta: Publishing Services Division, College of Business Administration, Georgia State University, 1977.

Storey, R.K. *The Search for Accounting Principles: Today's Problems in Perspective.* New York: AICPA, 1964.

McKesson & Robbins Case

Early in 1938, Julian Thompson, a creditor of
McKesson & Robbins drug company, noticed
that while the firm's crude drug division was its
most profitable operation, these profits were
immediately reinvested and no cash ever accumulated. It was also curious that crude drug
inventories shown on the books were very much
underinsured. The company's directors had
voted previously to reduce inventory balances
and now asked President Philip Coster to do so.
Instead, by the end of 1938 inventories had increased by $1 million. Becoming suspicious,
Thompson refused to sign $3 million in deben-
tures until management furnished proof that the
crude drug inventories actually existed. A Securities and Exchange Commission investigation
followed.

SEC examiners found that Philip Coster
was an ex-convict living under a false name,
assisted by his three brothers, also using false
names and occupying strategic executive positions in the company. McKesson & Robbins's
domestic drug business was legitimate; its foreign crude drug operation existed only on paper. Using company funds, Coster pretended to
buy crude drugs from five Canadian suppliers,
who held the nonexistent merchandise at warehouses for the account of McKesson &
Robbins. Coster then made imaginary sales to
foreign dealers and collected "payments" of fictitious accounts receivable from imaginary
debtors. The fraud was concealed by an elaborate facade of false documents: invoices, purchase orders, receiving tickets, shipping notices,
bills of lading, debit and credit memos, inventory tally sheets and signed summaries, statements from bankers, confirmations from outside suppliers, forged contracts and guarantees,
even forged credit ratings. Over 12 years,
Coster and his brothers had stolen about $2.9
million from McKesson & Robbins.

In January 1939, the SEC opened public
hearings on the case in New York City. Expert
witnesses testified that in auditing McKesson &
Robbins, Price Waterhouse and Company had
conformed to generally accepted procedures as
described in the American Institute of Accountants' "Examination of Financial Statements"
(1936). During audits made before 1935, the
auditors had been given inventory sheets signed
or initialed by company employees. After 1934
they had obtained written confirmations of inventory quantities held by the Canadian "suppliers" and had test-checked them to purchase
orders. Each year, two or more McKesson &
Robbins officials formally certified to the condition and quantity of inventories shown on the
balance sheet. Though receivables were not
confirmed by mail, credits to subsidiary accounts receivable were compared with entries
in the cash receipts book, and crude drug
sales records were test-checked to perpetual inventories and to copies of customers' invoices
and shipping advices (all were forgeries).
Price Waterhouse's defense was that it had ad-
hered to prevailing professional standards.
Frauds involving managerial collusion were notoriously elusive, and the usual audit of the
company's books could not be expected to reveal
them. More extensive audit tests would simply
have encountered additional expertly forged
documents.

The SEC committee agreed, but with res-
ervations. Every required procedure had been
followed in annual examinations for 12 years
by the largest accounting firm in the United
States. It seemed reasonable that even an audit
program not geared to fraud detection should
have found *something* wrong with a consolidated balance sheet that included $9 million in
fictitious receivables and $10 million in ficti-
tious inventories. The SEC committee concluded that existing audit standards were inadequate and that the type of audit being
performed by American CPAs was not serving
even its ostensible purposes. Auditors should
extend verification outside the accounting

M

records to establish the actual existence of the assets and debts shown on the balance sheet. If the auditors had inspected McKesson & Robbins's inventories, the fraud would have been discovered. Direct mail confirmation of receivables and observation of inventory counts, including physical tests if necessary, should become mandatory audit procedures. When inventories were located abroad, corespondent firms could make such observations. The committee also recommended changes in the form of the auditor's report, proposed that the audit opinion be addressed directly to stockholders, and even suggested that auditors be elected by the stockholders.

The McKesson & Robbins fraud forced a long overdue appraisal of audit priorities. In 50 years, American accountants had gone from one extreme to the other. Detailed stewardship audits had been tried and rejected as being too costly and unsuited to local conditions. Then for a generation most American audits had been dangerously superficial credit investigations. Now the profession confronted a problem of finesse: to make an examination comprehensive enough to inform the public and protect the accountant, yet economical enough to justify its cost to the client. The voluntary refund by Price Waterhouse of more than $500,000 in audit fees to McKesson & Robbins indicated the scale of liability faced by auditors who failed to detect fraud. The result was a final break with the older British tradition of auditing the accounts instead of the business. The new tendency to seek physical contact with company affairs was part of a general expansion of audit responsibility to include long-term as well as current assets, the income statement equally with the balance sheet.

On January 30, 1939, just three weeks after the first SEC hearings on McKesson & Robbins, the American Institute of Accountants formed a Special Committee on Auditing Procedure. Its report, *Extension of Auditing Procedure*, recommended the physical observation of inventory counts and the direct confirmation of receivables; if either of these tests was omitted, an exception must be noted in the auditor's report. The committee also recommended that the auditor's opinion be reworded to emphasize that the extent of audit testing depended on the auditor's review of his client's internal control system.

In 1941, as a final result of its McKesson & Robbins investigation, the SEC issued Ac-

counting Series Release No. 21, amending Regulation S-X to include the following: "The accountant's certificate . . . shall state whether the audit was made in accordance with generally accepted auditing standards applicable in the circumstances."

Michael Chatfield

Bibliography

Carey, J.L. *The Rise of the Accounting Profession*, vol. 2, *To Responsibility and Authority, 1937–1969*. New York: AICPA, 1970, pp. 22–41.

Edwards, J.D. *History of Public Accounting in the United States*. East Lansing: Bureau of Business and Economic Research, Michigan State University, 1960. Reprint. University, AL: University of Alabama Press, 1978, pp. 163–170.

See also AMERICAN INSTITUTE OF CERTIFIED PUBLIC ACCOUNTANTS; AUDITOR'S REPORT; BIG EIGHT ACCOUNTING FIRMS; CHIEF ACCOUNTANTS OF THE SECURITIES AND EXCHANGE COMMISSION; EXTERNAL AUDITING; FRAUD AND AUDITING; LAW AND ACCOUNTING; LEGAL LIABILITY OF AUDITORS; MACNEAL, KENNETH; NATURAL BUSINESS YEAR; SECURITIES AND EXCHANGE COMMISSION; WILDMAN, JOHN RAYMOND

McKinsey, James O. (1889–1937)

James Oscar McKinsey is remembered as the founder of the management consulting firm of McKinsey and Company, but it was management accounting that first intrigued the man. The first textbook on management accounting and the first book on business budgeting were both written by McKinsey. Before McKinsey, internal users of accounting information were largely neglected by educators. Only through years of experience could an accountant master the knowledge needed to use accounting information.

In 1912 McKinsey received a bachelor's degree from the State College at Warrensburg, Missouri; a year later he received a law degree from the University of Arkansas. His accounting career began in 1914 at St. Louis University, where he studied and taught bookkeeping. He later earned both bachelor's and master's degrees in commerce from the University of Chicago. He received his master's degree in 1919, the same year that he passed the CPA examination. Before he had finished his degree at Chicago, he was asked to join the accounting faculty and remained there through 1935. McKinsey became president of the American Association of University Instructors in Accounting (now the American Accounting Association) in 1924. He was instrumental in that organization starting an accounting research journal, the *Accounting Review*.

The publication of McKinsey's *Budgetary Control* in 1922 provided impetus for the spreading of industrial budgeting. World War I and the resultant emphasis on efficiency provided stimulus for acceptance of McKinsey's work, which summarized all experimentation to date into a complete budgetary program. McKinsey's book was the first book on budgeting and the first attempt to cover the entire budgetary program. Before McKinsey's book, budgeting was not considered applicable to business operations, only governmental units. In 1945 *Budgetary Control* was included on a list of the 12 most indispensable books in the field of management.

McKinsey believed that accounting was something that should serve as a basis for functional control in a business. In the preface of his 1924 text, *Managerial Accounting*, he stated that it was time to organize the business curriculum into one coherent whole. McKinsey pioneered the emphasis on teaching students how to use accounting data. The problems at the end of the text's chapters could not be answered by memorizing the text material, but instead required application of the text material to new situations.

McKinsey's influence on managerial accounting did not end with this text; his legacy can be traced to later authors. William Joseph Vatter has stated that he visited with McKinsey in 1935 and that he was influenced by McKinsey's book. Vatter published his own *Managerial Accounting* in 1950 in a preliminary edition that was reissued about a dozen times throughout the decade. Vatter's work served as an inspiration to Charles T. Horngren, who has dedicated each edition of his book, *Cost Accounting: A Managerial Emphasis*, to Vatter, to whom he assigns his primary obligation in the preface. The Horngren book has been the standard for managerial- and cost-accounting education, and its seeds can be traced through Vatter to McKinsey. McKinsey also authored the first edition of the successful accounting principles textbook published by South-Western Publishing Company.

In 1925, McKinsey started his own accounting and consulting firm, McKinsey and Company, which was to become the largest management consulting firm in the world. Still teaching as well, he would have his chauffeur drive him to class and carry his briefcase into the classroom. Following class, the chauffeur would reappear, erase the blackboard, and take his employer downtown to his office.

In 1935 McKinsey was hired to conduct a study of Marshall Field and Company, the Chicago department store. The directors were so impressed with his work that they offered McKinsey the position of chairman of the board. He soon turned Marshall Field's red ink into profit, but he may have done so at the cost of his health. He died of pneumonia on November 30, 1937.

Dale L. Flesher
Tonya K. Flesher

Bibliography

Flesher, T.K., and D.L. Flesher. "James O. McKinsey." In *Biographies of Notable Accountants*, edited by H.R. Givens, pp. 25–28. New York: Random House, 1987.

McKinsey, J.O. *Bookkeeping and Accounting*. Cincinnati: South-Western, 1920.

See also AMERICAN ACCOUNTING ASSOCIATION; BUDGETING; CONTROL: CLASSICAL MODEL; COST AND/OR MANAGEMENT ACCOUNTING; HORNGREN, CHARLES T.; MANAGEMENT ACCOUNTING; VATTER, WILLIAM JOSEPH

Medici Accounts

The Medici Bank was founded in 1397 and lasted nearly 100 years, though it operated only in Western Europe and never grew as large as the Bardi or the Peruzzi banking houses. The Medici used double entry accounts for credit evaluation, management and control, audit, even income tax calculation. Every year on March 24, books of the branch banks were closed and copies of their balance sheets were sent to the home office in Florence. These balance sheets listed separately the amount owed by each customer, with the result that statements sometimes contained more than 200 line items. Because bad debts were the chief threat to a medieval banker's solvency, audit by the general manager and his assistants involved examining each debtor's account to see that excess credit had not been granted and to pick out doubtful or past-due accounts. A thorough audit also required the presence of branch managers. They were called to Florence once a year if they resided in Italy and at least once every other year if they lived abroad. The weakness of this internal audit system was that branches were not regularly visited by traveling auditors. The bank incurred huge losses because of uncontrolled and insubordinate branch managers and a general lack of coordination. Even its power as papal banker to obtain the excommunication of anyone who failed to pay church revenues could not save the Medici Bank, and it failed in 1494.

Industrial cost accounting, like double entry bookkeeping, originated in Renaissance Italy. During the fifteenth and sixteenth centuries, Medici industrial partnerships controlled two woolen shops and a silk factory in Florence. The Medici textile manufacturers purchased raw wool and sold finished cloth that had been produced by craftsmen in their own homes. Because every phase of production was performed by a different guild, each step in the conversion process had to be accounted for in a separate memorandum book that showed the quantity of cloth turned in by each worker and wages paid or due. A clearing account, "cloth manufactured and sold," matched the cost of each batch of material with the revenue from its sale, showing on balance the profit from all the cloth sold during an operating period. Since manufacturing was done by outworkers who owned their own tools, overhead cost was ignored in calculating selling prices. The Italian putting-out merchants may not have been the first to use cost accounting to rationalize production, but in their time they had no peers. They could, for example, import raw wool from England, manufacture it, and ship back the finished textiles to sell in England below English prices.

Michael Chatfield

Bibliography

De Roover, R. *The Rise and Decline of the Medici Bank, 1397–1494.* Cambridge: Harvard University Press, 1963. Reprint. New York: W.W. Norton, 1966.

Garner, S.P. *Evolution of Cost Accounting to 1925.* University, AL: University of Alabama Press, 1954.

See also BAD DEBTS; BALANCE SHEET; BARDI; BRANCH ACCOUNTING; CONTROL ACCOUNTS; COST AND/OR MANAGEMENT ACCOUNTING; DOUBLE ENTRY BOOKKEEPING: ORIGINS; INTERNAL AUDITING; JOURNAL; PERUZZI

Medieval Accounting

Bookkeeping during the Middle Ages evolved in several distinct directions. The development in northern Italy of venture partnerships and overseas trading led to the double entry system used today, and it is tempting to make accounting history the history of double entry record keeping by passing quickly over the thousand years between the fall of Rome and the publication of Luca Pacioli's *Summa de Arithmetica* in 1494. Being out of the mainstream of events leading to double entry bookkeeping, the details of medieval practice outside Italy tend to be neglected or allowed a merely historical interest.

In contrast to the codified accounting procedures of the Roman Empire, medieval record keeping tended to be localized and centered around a number of specialized institutions. While it is difficult to isolate Roman influences, in both periods accounts were kept mainly because employers needed to monitor subordinates who were acting as their agents. The closest parallel to Roman bookkeeping method is found in the receipt and disbursement accounting of the Catholic Church, which for hundreds of years levied and collected taxes throughout Europe. As early as the sixth century, deacons were appointed to administer church properties and report on their revenues. Agents of the papal treasury were located in the provinces and were responsible for forwarding receipts to Rome.

The value of accounting as an aid to systematic estate management was recognized early. In the ninth century, Charlemagne produced the *Capitulare di Villis,* a series of detailed instructions to his steward on supervision of the royal lands and reporting to the sovereign. Though methods of calculation were primitive and accounting periods irregular, Jack (1966) noted that "Charlemagne stressed the need for orderliness, for gathering together like topics under a single heading and going through the probable sources of revenue in order." An annual inventory was taken of the royal estates and chattels. Payments and receipts were recorded in separate books, with any balance remitted to the king.

In pre-Norman England, literacy was so rare, even among the nobility, that a written system of accounts would hardly have justified its cost. Until the eleventh century, financial data were nearly always communicated and verified orally, written documents being merely supplementary to the more important spoken word. At that time, introduction of the abacus and other improvements in arithmetic technique roughly coincided with a rebirth of interest in the written language. A system of written records gradually formalized an earlier, essentially oral accounting tradition.

Medieval English accounting methods deserve attention for several reasons. Early government tax rolls and manorial account books are among the oldest surviving documents in the English language, and the approaches that were made to problems in these areas find obvious parallels in modern practice. Medieval agency accounting laid the foundations for the modern doctrines of stewardship and conservatism. It helped create the conditions for the rapid advance in accounting technology that occurred during the Renaissance. Beyond this, the pervasiveness and durability of these systems suggest that double entry bookkeeping is not a uniquely efficient way to organize financial data—that in many cases, simpler methods can yield equally useful results.

Feudal society is often pictured as a multilayered pyramid, with individuals at each lower level guaranteed certain rights in exchange for certain duties. Such a system required many delegations of authority and the transfer of land rights from nominal owners to actual possessors and users. The characteristic accounting problem was one of vertical communication and verification between principal and agent. In English royal finance this led to the proffer system of recording and verifying tax collections, while in estate accounting it gave rise to the charge and discharge statement made on behalf of a manorial steward for his lord.

Until the late Middle Ages, human labor was the most dynamic productive factor, and feudal social systems were designed to keep labor on the land. Manors—the estates of the nobility—were the farms and workshops of medieval Britain. English manorial accounting described the receipts and payments of a self-contained economic entity; the results of its dealings with outsiders were designated "foreign" in the accounts. Another characteristic of manorial life was administration by proxy. The manorial duke or earl often depended for his living on the productivity of large land holdings and the efforts of hundreds of people whom he could not personally supervise. Day-to-day management was normally left to a hierarchy of officials and department heads. The lord's incentive for keeping accounts arose from his need to check on the integrity and reliability of these stewards, to prevent loss and theft, and generally to encourage efficiency. From the steward's viewpoint, accounting records provided evidence that he had discharged his duties honestly and well.

Manorial self-sufficiency and the agency relationship are keys to understanding differences between estate accounts and those of today. Economic independence and the absence of reports to outsiders meant that little of what we call financial accounting was needed. Credit sales were rare. Assets were inventoried, but balance sheets were seldom made. The lord's implements might be counted together with the personal property of his tenants, and cash values were sometimes combined with physical quantities of goods in statements of manorial assets. No clear distinction was made between capital and revenue expenditures, the cost of a horse being recorded in much the same way as the cost of the hay it consumed. Expenses might be allocated to various activities in detail, to show the results of each, but overall profit and loss was normally of little interest. Sometimes an account narrative was interrupted to make room for estimates of what might have been earned if a different course of action had been taken.

Manorial officers kept accounts not for the sake of the business entity, as they would today, but for their own protection. On large estates, a "surveyor" assembled a book of land rentals and fees due, which was used by the receiver-general who actually collected these revenues and recorded them by sources. Still other officials paid and kept account of wages and expenses. Auditors periodically examined and summarized all of these accounts, which were essentially the records of the individuals involved, not of the manor. Since their purpose was only to show that duties had been properly performed, there was a natural tendency for each steward to record just those items for which he was responsible and to show each type of receipt in opposition to payments.

Even more diversity could be expected in medieval bookkeeping than was the case. The modern reasons for accounting consistency and comparability hardly existed. But it does seem that the feudal environment, like any other, favored particular techniques. City governments, monastic and lay estates, households, and craft guilds, or "worshipful companies," shared a tradition of charge and discharge bookkeeping and accountability audits. Accounts of all types were synchronized with the farming seasons, Michaelmas signaling the harvest and the end of their natural business year. Single entry bookkeeping in feudal Japan followed a similar pattern of decentralized record keeping, visual numeration by abacus, emphasis on control, and the personal discharge of accounting officers.

The manor's self-sufficiency placed limits on its development as an institution. England had been cut off geographically from the Near East trade of the Renaissance, but following the discovery of America, it found itself in a more favorable position. During the seventeenth century, towns began to replace manors as centers of economic life, and independent manufacturers came into competition with closely regulated guild tradesmen. Expanding overseas trade created new markets and sources of supply. Emphasis shifted from stewardship of manorial assets to protection of corporate investors and problems of income finding and dividend payment. Agency accounting remained, but it began to assume the sophisticated form it had taken centuries earlier in northern Italy, where the accumulation of capital and the distances over which trading was carried on lent themselves to branch operations, credit arrangements, and consignment transactions.

Manorial accountants can hardly be blamed for failing to produce data they did not need. The typical medieval executive did practically no writing and very little reading. Exchequer and manorial accounts were normally kept on the assumptions that king or baron would never look at them. Accounting therefore tended to cease at the point where a department head had enough information for his own use.

Such men were unlikely to develop an accounting method that opposed assets and equities, because they had no real concept of capital. The manor was their capital. Land was seldom bought and sold; they could only value it in terms of some multiple of annual net produce. With production so interwoven with con-

sumption, there was little incentive for determining total income. Nor was systematic cost accounting necessary, because most manors had a repetitive and not easily altered pattern of receipts and expenditures.

But in the areas of internal control and audit, manorial practice was far ahead of Pacioli's "Method of Venice." It demonstrated how accounts kept mainly to strike an annual balance could be adapted to help management run a business from day to day. The doctrine of conservatism was a form of self-protection for a manorial steward facing audit; the same tendency to underestimate is central to modern corporate accounting. Executors and trustees continue to use the charge and discharge statement in accounting for their management of assets held in trust. Even the modern system of weights and measures, with all of its faults, comes from that era when a yard was the distance from the king's nose to the end of his outstretched arm. If many things have changed, enough similarities remain to make our accounting heritage from the Middle Ages rich in forms, techniques, and ideas.

Michael Chatfield

Bibliography

Chatfield, M. "English Medieval Bookkeeping: Exchequer and Manor." In *Contemporary Studies in the Evolution of Accounting Thought*, edited by M. Chatfield, pp. 30–38. Belmont, CA: Dickenson, 1968.

Jack, S.M. "An Historical Defence of Single Entry Bookkeeping," *Abacus*, December 1966, pp. 137–158.

Littleton, A.C. "Old and New in Management and Accounting," *Accounting Review*, April 1954, pp. 196–200.

Most, K.S. "New Light on Medieval Manorial Accounts," *Accountant*, January 1969, pp. 119–121.

See also AGRICULTURAL ACCOUNTING; ARITHMETIC AND ACCOUNTING; BRANCH ACCOUNTING; CASH BASIS ACCOUNTING; "CHARGE AND DISCHARGE" STATEMENT; CONSERVATISM; DOMESDAY BOOK; EXTERNAL AUDITING; INTERNAL CONTROL; JAPAN; MANORIAL ACCOUNTING; NATURAL BUSINESS YEAR; PACIOLI, LUCA; PIPE ROLL; PROFFER SYSTEM; ROME (509 B.C.–A.D. 476); SINGLE ENTRY BOOKKEEPING; SPAIN; STEWARDSHIP; TALLY STICK

Memorandum Book

The memorandum book—also called, through the years, the daybook, the blotter, or the waste book—was the first of the three accounting books recommended by Luca Pacioli in 1494, along with the journal and the ledger. This book became necessary because of the great increase in business transactions conducted by merchants during the 1300s and 1400s. It listed the kinds of money employed for every transaction, for instance. In the absence of the owner, the daybook (as it became generally known) was held by his servants for safekeeping. The book-keeper made journal entries based on the data in the memorandum book, which was generally bound with numbered pages. Missing pages were duly noted.

There was strong opposition to the redundant nature of the daybook by the early 1800s. Thomas Turner in *An Epitome of Bookkeeping by Double Entry* (1804) considered it as "inutile" to its learner. . . . James Arlington Bennett in *The American System of Practical Bookkeeping* (1820) recommended incorporating the daybook and the journal. As it was, each journal entry was listed opposite to the daybook entry. This, by Bennett's calculations, reduced the labor of writing in the journal by 19 in 20 parts. J.C. Colt in *The Science of Double Entry Bookkeeping* (1844) followed Bennett's approach, proposing a plan of uniting the two into one entry with details noted in the entry. However, Bryant, Stratton, and Packard in *Bryant and Stratton's Countinghouse Book-Keeping* (1863) felt quite strongly that the daybook provided important evidential matter. J.H. Goodwin in *Goodwin's Improved Book-Keeping and Business Manual* (1889) recommended dropping the journal altogether with postings made directly from the daybook. He furthermore suggested that the name "journal" be used rather than "daybook," as there was a customary preference for "journal." By 1901, the editors of *The American Business and Accounting Encyclopedia* had relegated the daybook to a record of orders received.

Richard Vangermeersch

See also JOURNAL; MANZONI, DOMENICO; PACIOLI, LUCA; PACKARD, SILAS SADLER

Mercantilism

Mercantilism was a set of economic theories and also a political policy based on developing business strength and increasing national wealth by trading. It affected accounting development because of its dominance between the sixteenth and eighteenth centuries when the corporate form of business was maturing. Like Adam Smith, the mercantilists saw business profits as a source of both personal and public good. But mercantilist doctrine held that the state should encourage trade and industry by granting monopoly patents to inventors and by chartering corporations with exclusive franchises to perform certain services or to exploit particular overseas areas. In emphasizing foreign trade, the nation should also be sure exports exceeded imports, creating a favorable trade balance that would enrich the national treasury through an influx of gold and silver. Because the imports tended to be raw materials and the exports manufactured products, this policy led naturally to the more sophisticated one of exporting surplus goods and acquiring needed foreign commodities in exchange.

Commerce in Elizabethan England typically took the form of desultory joint venture trading. In this environment, incorporation promoted business continuity—it was at first a privilege conferred only by Royal Charter and always for monopoly purposes. Trade guilds interested in dominating areas of commercial life had begun incorporation as early as 1394. Soon there were municipal corporations for activities such as firefighting and banking, and for almost 200 years these "livery companies" monopolized various public services.

Michael Chatfield

Bibliography

Littleton, A.C. *Accounting Evolution to 1900.* New York: American Institute Publishing, 1933. Reprint. New York: Russell and Russell, 1966.

See also CORPORATIONS: EVOLUTION; SMITH, ADAM.

Metcalfe, Henry (1847–1927)

The first modern book on cost accounting was Captain Henry Metcalfe's *The Cost of Manufactures and the Administration of Workshops* (1885). Metcalfe was an American Army ordinance officer, and his experience with arsenal production and discussions with commercial foremen convinced him that there should be a better way to assign material and labor costs to jobs. Since the usual production records were informal memorandum books carried by shop foremen, only the most cursory data were kept on job orders, which were often verbally authorized and were sometimes lost track of entirely. Neither the foremen's jottings nor the formal shop ledger seemed a proper mechanism for on-the-spot recording of shop-floor events.

Metcalfe proposed that each material requisition or transfer be recorded on a separate "shop order card," which included spaces for pricing the article and for the job number to which it was charged. To assign labor costs, each workman was given a book of cards, and as he moved from job to job, he noted the time spent on each to the nearest quarter day. In this way, a written record of costs literally followed the work through every factory department. Each day the cards were collected and a cost sheet was compiled, showing the material and labor costs applied to particular jobs. Until a job order was completed, the cards were filed by job numbers. Afterward, the cards for that job were summarized and entered in the shop order book. Metcalfe's system provided an ingenious and effective solution to the problem of collecting prime costs, and there is evidence that it was widely used.

In 1885 overhead cost was not the problem it later became, and Metcalfe gave it relatively less attention. He demonstrated four overhead allocation methods: an arbitrary charge, a percentage of gross cost, a percentage of labor cost, and a charge that varied in relation to production time. He preferred the last, a forerunner of the direct labor hours allocation method, on the grounds that indirect expenses were incurred mainly to increase labor's effectiveness. Pointing out that overhead costs were never precisely known until the year ended, he suggested dividing the total overhead charge for the preceding year (or the average of the past several years) by the total hours of shop work done during that period, to get a predetermined overhead rate that could be applied to jobs in process through his card system. But he never explained exactly how this was to be done or how estimated overhead applied to jobs was to be reconciled with actual overhead costs.

Metcalfe's attempt to tie cost accounts into the financial accounting system was an admitted failure. He was able partially to reconcile prime costs with the general ledger balances, but integrating overhead costs seemed to him impossible,

or at least so difficult as not to be worth the trouble. "Substantial truth," he felt, would be "neglected for the sake of striking a balance."

Though his book was intended for general use, Metcalfe's direct experience seems to have been limited to military production in an Army arsenal. His working environment was in effect a large machine shop that required expensive capital equipment, specialized labor, and complicated production techniques involving a high probability of waste. His writing implies a continuous need to evaluate different complex situations. But he never had to worry about selling finished products or earning a profit on invested capital. Most private businesses of the time operated in a simpler cost environment, but with a wider range of problems. Had Metcalfe shared their circumstances, his book might have been different in scope and emphasis.

Michael Chatfield

Bibliography

Garner, S.P. *Evolution of Cost Accounting to 1925.* University, AL: University of Alabama Press, 1954.

McMickle, P.L., and R.G. Vangermeersch. *The Origins of a Great Profession.* Memphis: Academy of Accounting Historians, 1987.

Metcalfe, H. *The Cost of Manufactures and the Administration of Workshops.* New York: John Wiley & Sons, 1885.

See also Common Costs; Cost and/or Management Accounting; Direct Costing; Management Accounting; Perpetual Inventory; Standard Costing

Microeconomics in Germany

Starting from Northern Italy since the times of Luca Pacioli, accounting was widely used in Germany, but it was recognized as an independent field of inquiry only during the second half of the nineteenth century. It became an academic subject with the foundation of the Handelshochschule in Leipzig in 1898. Its theoretical structure as an explanatory model was strongly influenced by microeconomics; Stackelberg with his 1931 book substantially influenced this direction. Specifically, cost accounting was approached not only as a field that consisted of procedural rules, but also as an analytic model (e.g., Bücher, Schär,

Fig. 1   TRADITIONAL COST MODEL AS DESCRIBED BY MELLEROWICZ

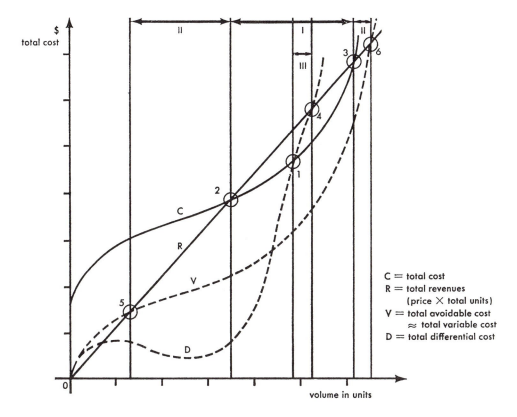

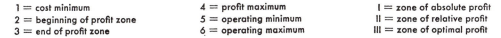

C = total cost
R = total revenues (price × total units)
V = total avoidable cost ≈ total variable cost
D = total differential cost

1 = cost minimum
2 = beginning of profit zone
3 = end of profit zone
4 = profit maximum
5 = operating minimum
6 = operating maximum
I = zone of absolute profit
II = zone of relative profit
III = zone of optimal profit

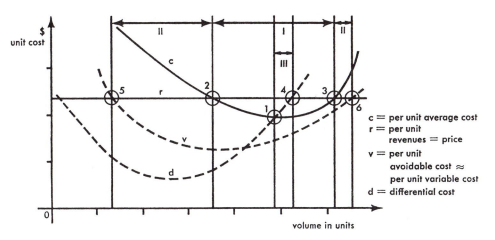

c = per unit average cost
r = per unit revenues = price
v = per unit avoidable cost ≈ per unit variable cost
d = differential cost

Schmalenbach, Nicklisch and other scholars) that outlined cost behavior and permitted establishing guidelines for policy.

Conceptual models initially used were based on macro- and microeconomics; thus the existence of an S-shaped cost curve was gener-

Fig. 2   COST DEVELOPMENT IN CASE OF UTILIZATION INTENSITY ADAPTATION

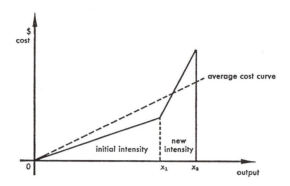

COST RESULTS OF ADJUSTMENT OF OPERATING TIME

COST DEVELOPMENT IN CASE OF A SELECTIVE ADAPTATION

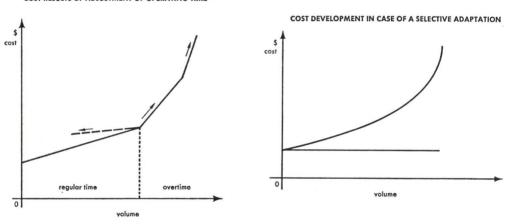

COST DEVELOPMENT IN CASE OF QUANTITATIVE (CAPACITY) ADAPTATION

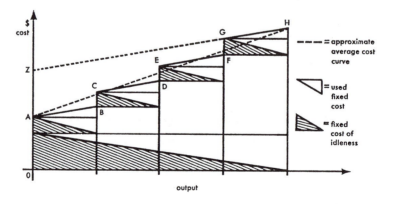

ally accepted. Initially applied by Schmalenbach to disaggregate fixed and variable cost (*mathematische Kostenauflösung*), the writings of several decades were summarized by Mellerowickz, who compiled a set of critical points and cost behavior zones for enterprise policy as shown in Fig. 1 (page 417).

These ideas prevailed until after World War II in spite of the fact that the validity of the law of diminishing returns was never empirically proven for manufacturing processes—nor was it ever falsified. It was Schmalenbach, in particular, who developed from it his cost-related pricing rules: in general, cost should be

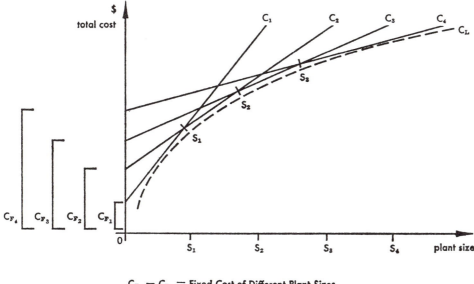

$C_{F_1} - C_{F_4}$ = Fixed Cost of Different Plant Sizes
$S_1 - S_3$ = Critical Points of Size Change
$C_1 - C_4$ = Short-Run Cost Curves
C_L = Long-Run Cost Curve

used at its optimal level. Different rules applied when volume could not be held at the output optimum, e.g., pricing should be based on variable cost, marginal cost or shadow prices, depending on the actual capacity utilization level; he called these solutions *optimale Geltungszahlen*.

It should also be noted that cost was regarded as the monetary expression of the underlying physical resource consumption (and not as financial accounting expenses). This led to the conclusion that cost curves reflected more independent variables than output alone—even if the cost-volume analysis (*Analyse des toten Punktes*, Schär) could be utilized as an approximation for short-term projections.

A logical extension of these ideas emerged from Gutenberg's writings. Observing that in manufacturing production factors often could not be substituted—and rarely in infinitesimal increments—the law of diminishing returns lacked universal applicability. He, therefore, regarded it a special case and called it production function of type A. He also pointed out that only by combining physical production functions with cost values will it become possible to explain cost behavior. Subsequently, he formulated his hypotheses of limitational production factors—called production function of type B. This represents a logical extension of microeconomic theory into a modern production environment. It is also a major change, because cost is regarded as largely capacity driven, that is input dependent. Volume is only a capacity utilization determinant.

If limitational production factors (machinery and equipment; that is, input factors permitting only limited output ranges determined by technology) are dominant, then these exert a (if not *the*) major influence over the real production function of any operation and thus determine its cost. Even under these circumstances, management has options to adjust operations to varying output demands by using (at least) four adaptation patterns: (1) intensity utilization adaptation (speed up of process), (2) time adaptation (adding overtime or additional shifts), (3) quantitative adaptation (adjusting capacity), and (4) selective adaptation (utilizing higher quality inputs). Cost behavior patterns emerging from this approach are summarized in Fig. 2 (page 418).

Adaptations to differing volumes provide management some limited flexibility, but never result in continuous "cost curves"—only in specific cost points, which are determined by the combination of measures selected. It also follows that cost is mainly determined by input decision (capacity and technology choices) and only indirectly influenced by later output decisions.

It is also obvious that the quantitative adaptation occurring with each capital expenditure decision change existing capacities (which tend to be somewhat disharmonious with other disharmonies), because capacity harmonization cannot be fully accomplished due to technological constraints. Nevertheless, it can be shown empirically that this development gradually results in a flattening of cost development over time (see Fig 3, page 419).

Manufacturers will always be left with quantitative and qualitative capacity disharmonies (to be absorbed as idle capacity cost).

In all other respects the impact of microeconomics on accounting and business administration is similar to the U.S. developments.

Hanns Martin Schoenfeld

Bibliography

Gutenberg, E. *Grundlagen der Betriebswirtschaftslehre,* Band 1, *Die Produktion.* 14th ed. Berlin: J. Springer Verlag, 1968 (1st ed., 1951).

Mellerowicz, K. *Kosten und Kostenrechnung: Theorie der Kosten, Bd. I.* Berlin: Walter DeGruyter, 1963.

Schmalenbach, E. *Pretiale Wirtschaftslenkung,* vol. 1, *Die Optimale Geltungszahl.* Bremen: Horn, 1947.

Schoenfeld, H.M. *Cost Terminology and Cost Theory: A Study of Its Development and Present State in Central Europe.* Urbana, IL: Center for International Education and Research in Accounting, University of Illinois, 1974.

Stackelberg, H. von. *Grundlagen einer reinen Kostentheorie.* Vienna: J. Springer Verlag, 1931.

See also COST AND/OR MANAGEMENT ACCOUNTING; GERMANY; MOST, KENNETH S.; SCHMALENBACH, EUGEN; TRANSFER PRICES

Money

Ederer (1964) defined money as "anything which is in general use in a given community as medium of exchange and/or a unit of reckoning." He considered money to have evolved through four stages: (1) barter exchanges; (2) exchange based on commodity money (for instance, wampum utilized by American Indians); (3) exchange based on state-issued money (starting with metals in about the eighth century B.C. in Lydia and with paper in China as early as the ninth century A.D.); and (4) exchange based on bank-issued money (starting in the seventeenth century with the Bank of Amsterdam). Ederer also noted that in times of great stress, societies sometimes revert to an earlier money stage—as in post-World War II Germany when cigarettes became a currency.

The first coin was the "stater" of Lydia, made from electrum. The first international currency was the "drachma" of Athens. It remained more favored than the Roman "denarius." When the Roman Empire ended, the currency of the Byzantine Empire—the "bezart" or "gold solidus"—became the international currency. Hence, the currencies of the various Italian city-states were well positioned to become international currencies.

A.C. Littleton included money as one of his six antecedents of double entry. In his treatise on double entry in *Summa de Arithmetica* (1494), Luca Pacioli discussed the importance of the currency in which the books were kept, "advising the businessman who would use his bookkeeping method: . . . Afterwards the bookkeeper, when he transfers the entry to the Journal and Ledger, will reduce that money to the standard money that you have adopted." If the receivable or payable were settled in the other currency, a transaction gain or loss would ensue. Pacioli also included a section on "money and exchange" illustrating the importance of foreign exchange in the late 1400s.

There has yet to be written a treatise on "money and accounting," although the topic of "money and economics" has been well covered. The transaction issues of Pacioli's time have become far more complicated today by such issues as (1) accounting for the translation of the statements of foreign subsidiaries to the given currency of the parent, (2) accounting during prolonged periods of inflation, and (3) accounting for the present value of future cash streams. Some countries, like Brazil, have clearly dropped the stable monetary assumption in law as well as accounting. Some accountants, like Henry Whitcomb Sweeney, in *Stabilized Accounting* (1936) have proposed reporting solutions for the situation of an unstable currency. The demise in the mid-1980s by the Financial Accounting Standards Board of its requirements for price-level adjusted inflation accounting of Financial Accounting Standard No. 33, "Financial Reporting and Changing Prices" (1979), has left a void in the study of empirical uses of this inflation data in accounting. All in all, money is not a simple topic in accounting.

Richard Vangermeersch

Bibliography

Ederer, R.J. *The Evolution of Money.* Washington, DC: Public Affairs Press, 1964.
Littleton, A.C. "Ingredients of Accounting." In *Essays on Accountancy by A.C. Littleton,* edited by C.A. Moyer, pp. 4–6. Urbana: University of Illinois Press, 1961.
Taylor, R.E. *No Royal Road: Luca Pacioli and His Times.* Chapel Hill: University of North Carolina Press, 1942.

See also BABYLONIA; BARTER; BRAZIL: INFLATION ACCOUNTING; COLONIAL AMERICA, ACCOUNTING IN; COMPOUND INTEREST; CREDIT; INCOME-DETERMINATION THEORY; INFLATION ACCOUNTING; LEONARDO OF PISA; LITTLETON, A.C.; PACIOLI, LUCA

Monteage, Stephen (1623–1687)

Stephen Monteage was an English accountant and auditor who tried to popularize double entry bookkeeping. Claiming in *Debtor and Creditor Made Easie* (1675) that most bookkeeping texts were written for "men of deep capacities," he demonstrated a simplified double entry system that omitted the journal and was based solely on a daybook and ledger. He included a glossary of technical terms. Monteage offered the familiar arguments for double entry: It is more comprehensive, organized, and accessible than other methods; the profit and loss account facilitates income finding; and, above all, a double entry system automatically registers wealth changes. He then provided illustrative accounts for people in a variety of occupations, including a simple set of household accounts for "the women and maidens of London."

Monteage's text went through three editions and was reprinted in 1708. According to the *Dictionary of National Biography,* Stephen Monteage "did much towards bringing into general use the method of keeping accounts by double entry."

Michael Chatfield

Bibliography

Bywater, M.F., and B.S. Yamey. *Historic Accounting Literature: A Companion Guide.* London: Scholar Press, 1982.
Yamey, B.S. "Stephen Monteage, A Seventeenth Century Accountant," *Accountancy,* November 1959, pp. 594–595. Reprinted in B.S. Yamey, *Essays on the History of Accounting.* New York: Arno Press, 1978.

See also CONSERVATISM; DEPRECIATION; FIXED ASSETS; SINGLE ACCOUNT METHOD

Montgomery, Robert Hiester (1872–1953)

Robert Hiester Montgomery was cofounder of an international CPA firm, author, lawyer, and educator, and a major figure in the development of professional accountancy in the United States. The son of a Methodist minister, he had little formal education and, at age 16, became an office boy in a Philadelphia public accounting firm. In six years he became a partner in the firm and, in 1898, he and three other partners formed Lybrand, Ross Brothers and Montgomery, which later became Coopers and Lybrand.

In 1905 Montgomery adapted the United Kingdom's most respected book on auditing—Lawrence Dicksee's *Auditing*—for conditions in the United States and published the "American" edition at his own expense. Montgomery's *Auditing Theory and Practice* was first published in 1912. Immediately it became the authority on accepted accounting and auditing practice and was widely used by auditors seeking guidance in unsettled areas. In subsequent editions, it remained the authoritative source of "good" practice. Although now written by others, *Montgomery's Auditing* is still published.

Montgomery passed the Philadelphia Bar examination in 1902 and was admitted to the New York Bar in 1904. However, his interest in the practice of law was not stimulated until 1909 when the Payne-Aldrich tariff bill was enacted. It included a provision that corporations would be taxed on income over $5,000. While most felt that the law would be declared unconstitutional, the rules required cash accounting and reporting on a calendar-year basis. This had obvious accounting implications.

Montgomery wrote many articles and testified before congressional committees to permit accrual accounting and fiscal-year reporting for tax purposes.

The Sixteenth Amendment to the U.S. Constitution in 1913 permitted the imposition of a general income tax. However, the rates were so low that there was little resistance to the law. Some of the leading lawyers openly admitted that income tax was ". . . a job for accountants." That, said Montgomery, ". . . is where the lawyers lost the trick." In the 1915 edition of *Auditing Theory and Practice* he devoted 94 pages to income taxes and warned: "The income tax has come to stay. Its importance . . . [for] the professional auditor cannot be overestimated." Montgomery's first book on taxes was *Income Tax Procedure 1917*. The book was revised annually until 1929 and was a major authoritative source for tax preparation. It also contained advice on how to keep the tax burden to a minimum within the requirements of the law. However, his underlying guides were: The laws should be kept as simple as possible, "relatively no one should pay more than another, and none should pay less than his just share." For more than 30 years, Montgomery wrote books on taxation and pointed out weaknesses and inequities in the laws. He had a significant impact in indicating the way for the accounting profession to become a major provider of tax services.

In the early part of the century, business subjects were not taught as part of the university curriculum. Montgomery and several members of the Pennsylvania Institute of Certified Public Accountants made arrangements with the University of Pennsylvania to permit them to teach accounting subjects in the evening school. This program, along with others being taught in New York, helped gain acceptance for business-related subjects in colleges and universities.

As a professor at Columbia University, from 1912 to 1931, Montgomery helped attract competent faculty and develop a recognized program for the study of accountancy. While there, he established an accounting laboratory in which were kept the accounting records of bankrupt companies. Students were required to "audit" the books and to write recommendations. This type of education continued, in one form or another, in most accounting programs well into the 1950s. In 1926 he donated his collection of historical accounting books to Columbia.

Professional accounting organizations have evolved as the public representatives of accountants. The American Institute of Certified Public Accountants (AICPA) had its start with the American Association of Public Accountants formed in 1887. This was the first serious attempt to form accountants and bookkeepers into a professional organization in the United States.

Montgomery was very active with professional accounting, taxation, and business organizations over most of his career. He spent much of his time and effort developing and participating in activities that would further the status of the accounting profession. He was a charter member of the Pennsylvania Institute of Certified Public Accountants, president of the New York State Society of Certified Public Accountants, twice president of the American Institute of Accountants (now the AICPA), and the organizer of the Third International Congress of Accountants (1929) in New York. In addition, he helped finance and organize the *Journal of Accountancy* in 1905.

Montgomery was a highly respected leader of the profession of accountancy for over 60 years. His influence is still felt in the areas of auditing theory and practice, federal income taxation, professional accounting organizations, and accounting education.

Alfred R. Roberts

Bibliography

Burns, T.J., and E.N. Coffman. *The Accounting Hall of Fame: Profiles of Fifty Members*. Columbus: College of Business, Ohio State University, 1991.

Krzystofik, A. "Robert Hiester Montgomery (1872–1953)," *Accounting Historians Journal*, 1974–1976, vol. 2 (1975), pp. 68–70.

Montgomery, R.H. *Fifty Years of Accountancy*. New York: Ronald Press, 1939.

Roberts, A.R. *Robert H. Montgomery: A Pioneer Leader of American Accounting*. Atlanta: Business Publishing Division, Georgia State University, 1975.

Zeff, S.A. "Leaders of the Accounting Profession: Fourteen Who Made a Difference," *Journal of Accountancy*, May 1987, pp. 46–71.

See also ACCOUNTING EDUCATION IN THE UNITED STATES; ACCOUNTING HALL OF FAME; ADVERTISING BY ACCOUNTANTS; AMERICAN

INSTITUTE OF CERTIFIED PUBLIC ACCOUNTANTS; ARCHIVES AND SPECIAL COLLECTIONS IN ACCOUNTING; BIG EIGHT ACCOUNTING FIRMS; CONGRESSES ON ACCOUNTING, INTERNATIONAL; DICKSEE, LAWRENCE; EXTERNAL AUDITING; HISTORICAL COST; INCOME TAXATION IN THE UNITED STATES; MACNEAL, KENNETH; NATURAL BUSINESS YEAR; SIXTEENTH AMENDMENT; STOCK DIVIDENDS; TREASURY STOCK

Moonitz, Maurice (1910–)

After a public school education that emphasized music, followed by two years at the University of Cincinnati, Maurice Moonitz was driven by the economic circumstances of 1929 to Sacramento, California, where he found work as a bank bookkeeper. By 1931 he had commenced his lifelong, intermittent association with the University of California at Berkeley, where he received his B.S. in 1933, M.A. in 1936, Ph.D. in 1941, tenure as associate professor in 1947, and retirement to emeritus status in 1978.

Moonitz's intellect, temperament, interests, and training led to a lifetime of scholarship. His success as a scholar has been recognized by several national honorary societies as well as by the California Society of Certified Public Accountants, which named him Distinguished Professor in 1976, and the American Accounting Association, which presented him with its Outstanding Educator Award in 1985. He is a member of the Accounting Hall of Fame. In the American Accounting Association, he was prominent on theory and standards committees, served as vice president in 1958 and as president in 1978.

Moonitz's success as an accounting scholar was based on the firm foundation of experience in several fields of accounting practice. His work as a bookkeeper and as an auditor spanned eight years. Three years on the Accounting Principles Board which was the American standards-setting body in the 1960s, together with years as an officer in the local CPA society, also kept him in touch with practitioners.

Moonitz's contributions to accounting thought have been varied. His first widely recognized work, *The Entity Theory of Consolidated Statements*, was published in 1944. There he introduced a coherent conceptual approach to consolidated statements, based on the objective of treating a group of closely allied corporations as a distinct economic and accounting entity. That view requires that all assets and liabilities, including goodwill, reflect 100 percent of their values as indicated by transactions, rather than only the majority interest percentage. Another early contribution was a two-volume textbook—*Accounting: An Analysis of Its Problems*, with Charles Staehling—that included a comprehensive, two-chapter example in which all elements of financial statements were measured at present value, including net income.

In 1960, Moonitz was appointed the first director of accounting research for the American Institute of Certified Public Accountants (AICPA). His *The Basic Postulates of Accounting* (1961) and, with Robert T. Sprouse, *A Tentative Set of Broad Accounting Principles for Business Enterprises* (1962) were published in the director's series of Accounting Research Studies as Nos. 1 and 3. The first monograph seemed to be exactly what the Institute Committee ordered: "a study of the basic postulates underlying accounting principles generally." But because the normative approach taken in the *Principles* study led to current-value accounting, the accounting establishment wanted nothing to do with it. In 1962 the Accounting Principles Board stated: ". . . while these studies are a valuable contribution to accounting thinking, they are too radically different from present generally accepted accounting principles for acceptance at this time." That view certainly fit the tenor of the times in professional accounting circles, but every conceptual study sponsored by the profession since then has reached conclusions much more closely allied with the Moonitz and Sprouse works than with the views of the 1962 Accounting Principles Board.

Moonitz also wrote in the area of inflation accounting, contributing refinements and explications that solidified the general price-level approach that is now generally accepted by scholars in the field; and authored analysis of the standards-setting process in America. Those works, like all of Moonitz's publications, were characterized by a uniformly high standard of scholarship. That scholarship works primarily through other academics to leave its mark on the field of accounting.

George J. Staubus

Bibliography

Moonitz, M. *The Basic Postulates of Accounting*. Accounting Research Study No. 1. New York: AICPA, 1961.

M

———. *The Entity Theory of Consolidated Statements.* Sarasota, FL: American Accounting Association, 1944.

———, and R.T. Sprouse. *A Tentative Set of Broad Accounting Principles for Business Enterprises.* Accounting Research Study No. 3. New York: AICPA, 1962.

Moonitz, M., and C.C. Staehling. *Accounting: An Analysis of Its Problems.* 2 vols. New York: Foundation Press, 1952.

See also ACCOUNTING HALL OF FAME; ACCOUNTING PRINCIPLES BOARD; ACCOUNTING RESEARCH STUDIES; AMERICAN ACCOUNTING ASSOCIATION; AMERICAN INSTITUTE OF CERTIFIED PUBLIC ACCOUNTANTS; CONCEPTUAL FRAMEWORK; CONSOLIDATED FINANCIAL STATEMENTS; FUNDS FLOW STATEMENT; HISTORICAL COST; INFLATION ACCOUNTING; NORMATIVE ACCOUNTING; POSTULATES OF ACCOUNTING

Most, Kenneth S. (1924–)

An articled apprentice who became an accomplished translator and writer of accounting history and accounting thought of much merit, Kenneth S. Most received a Bachelor of Laws from the University of London in 1955, an M.A. in accounting in 1968, and a Ph.D. in economics in 1970, both from the University of Florida. Most was in 1989 chairman of the Internal Accounting Section of the American Accounting Association and editor from 1984 through 1986 of *Accounting Historians Journal.* Since 1975 he has been a professor in accounting at Florida International University.

Most made a fairly complete translation of the German political economist Werner Sombart's *Der Moderne Kapitalismus* and then responded to interpretations of that text by Basil S. Yamey, who tended to downplay Sombart's thesis of the importance of double entry bookkeeping to the development of capitalism. Most praised Sombart's holistic writing and urged a planning and control interpretation of his thesis.

Most showed his linguistic ability, international training, innovative mind, historical interest, and his opinions on accounting in *Accounting Theory*, second edition. In this second edition, Most questioned, for instance, the cash-flow emphasis, à la the Trueblood Report, of the FASB. Most feels microeconomics is not an approach that is amenable for use in accounting. He uses his German-language ability in a

review of Schmalenbach's work as well as in a review of the management viewpoint of the great Dutch accounting theorist, Limperg. Most published a reflective work on his long experience, *The Future of the Accounting Profession: A Verbal Perspective*, 1993.

He has brought the viewpoints of a modern-day "Renaissance Man" to accounting.

Richard Vangermeersch

Bibliography
Most, K.S. *Accounting Theory.* 2d ed. Columbus, OH: Grid, 1982.

———. "The Accounts of Ancient Rome." Working paper no. 3 in *Working Paper Series Volume 1*, edited by E.N. Coffman, pp. 22–31. Richmond, VA: Academy of Accounting Historians, 1979.

———. *The Future of the Accounting Profession: A Global Perspective.* Westport, CT: Greenwood, 1993.

———. "How Bad are European Accounts?" *Accountancy*, January 1964, pp. 9–15.

———. "The Planning Hypothesis as a Basis for Accounting Theory," *Abacus*, December 1973, pp. 127–136.

———. "Sombart's Propositions Revisited," *Accounting Review*, October 1972, pp. 722–734.

Yamey, B.S. "Accounting and the Rise of Capitalism: Further Notes on a Theme by Sombart," *Journal of Accounting Research*, Autumn 1964, pp. 117–136.

———. "Scientific Bookkeeping and the Rise of Capitalism," *Economic History Review*, second series, vol. I (1949), pp. 99–113, reprinted in W.T. Baxter, ed. *Studies in Accounting.* London: Sweet and Maxwell, 1950, pp. 13–30.

See also CONCEPTUAL FRAMEWORK; LIMPERG, THEODORE, JR.; MICROECONOMICS IN GERMANY; ROME (509 B.C.–A.D. 476); SCHMALENBACH, EUGEN; SINGLE ENTRY BOOKKEEPING; SOMBART, WERNER; TRUEBLOOD, ROBERT MARTIN

Municipal Accounting Reform (1890–1920)

The need for municipal accounting reform grew with the population of American cities during the late 1800s and early 1900s. Before the industrial revolution, the population of the United States consisted largely of farmers clustered around rural villages. After the industrial revolution, urban areas grew at a rate three times that of rural populations. Political corruption was rampant, and city services broke down completely.

During the three decades from 1890 to 1920, a period known as the Progressive Era, municipal activists reshaped American cities through political and administrative reforms. The political remedies are known to any civics student: increased popular participation, direct democracy (initiative, recall, referendum), home rule, charter reforms (city manager and commission forms of city government), and the return of "honest men" to government. Alone, however, such remedies were inadequate to cope with the everyday problems of providing nutrition, education, public safety, and basic sanitation services to overcrowded cities.

The "municipal research movement" added better systems of accounting and control to the list of political solutions. This type of municipal reform became an integral part of a national "efficiency movement" that followed the work of Frederick Winslow Taylor and his theories of scientific management. These "scientific" reformers had come to understand that while an efficient accounting system could not guarantee good government, good government was virtually impossible without one.

Most reforms were carried out under the aegis of various civic organizations. The first (and possibly most important) was the National Municipal League (NML) founded in 1894. The NML worked strenuously toward the goal of a uniform municipal chart of accounts. Reformers sought uniformity to facilitate local control and statistical comparison between cities. By 1908, half of the large cities in the country had adopted the NML's uniform accounts. Combined with the long-established system of fund accounting, standardized accounts offered the potential for providing detailed information on city financial activities.

An equally important agent of municipal reform was the New York Bureau of Municipal Research (NYB). In response to the inefficiency and corruption of Tammany Hall, a group of young social workers, engineers, and accountants joined together to implement efficient business and accounting techniques designed specifically for city administration. Three of these reformers, William H. Allen, Henry Bruere, and Frederick Cleveland, founded the NYB in 1906. Sponsored by such wealthy citizens as John D. Rockefeller, Robert Fulton Cutting, Andrew Carnegie, J. Pierpont Morgan, and Mrs. E.H. Harriman, the bureau spent nearly $1 million in privately contributed funds during its first eight years of operation.

Reformers from the NYB conducted research on accounting procedures in cities all across the country, helping many to establish research bureaus of their own. In 1911 the NYB founded the Training School for Public Service, which opened to students in 1912. By 1914 graduates had been placed in municipal departments, chambers of commerce, and research bureaus throughout the country.

Of all the systems introduced by the NYB, none was more important or more pervasive than the introduction of the budget. Well established in Europe, but virtually unknown in the United States, the idea of budgeting quickly took hold. While expensive to install, most cities quickly learned that budgets saved more than they cost.

Imposition of budgeting largely eliminated the worst examples of graft and corruption. Budgets also helped to end the political arithmetic of multiplying jobs immediately preceding elections. Many such abuses did not represent theft *per se*, but they were nevertheless an intolerable waste of public resources.

With honesty reasonably assured, efficiency became the new goal of urban reform, and the principles of cost accounting received increasing attention. To municipal reformers, the budget represented the synthesis of accounting and the scientific method. With budgeting came concepts of "unit cost," output measurement, time-and-motion studies, and intercity cost comparisons. Efficiency had been joined by effectiveness.

Progressive reformers believed that the success of their movement depended upon citizen awareness and constant vigilance. Reformers exercised imagination in creating tools to keep the activities of municipal officials clearly in the public eye. Among these tools was the municipal reference library. With support from the NML, Baltimore established the first library in January 1907; by 1912 similar libraries existed in many of America's leading cities.

The NYB created a technique for public education in the form of the "budget exhibit," first held in New York in 1908. The budget exhibit used billboards and posters to show the public how its money was being spent. The city sponsored a second exhibit in 1910. More than a million citizens attended and millions more read of the events in their daily papers. The bud-

M

get exhibit spread to over 20 American cities, touching practically every section of the country.

The era of Progressive reform ended quietly after America's entry into World War I. Many historians have sought to explain why Progressive reform did not resume after the war was over. The original causes of the Progressive movement remained. The cities continued to grow, immigration continued unabated, and the early hopes Progressives held for direct democracy measures had been misplaced. City managers and commissions often resulted in administrations as inefficient and expensive as those of the bosses. What these historians fail to consider are the positive aspects of the municipal-reform movement. Accounting and auditing systems had largely ended widespread corruption and inefficiency. By the time of the war, hundreds of American cities had uniform systems of account classifications. By the early 1920s, 44 of the states had legislation passed or pending establishing budgetary systems. It was no longer necessary for reformers to maintain a constant vigil over honesty in public office. There were systems of accounting and auditing controls in place to do it for them.

R. Penny Marquette
Richard K. Fleischman

Bibliography

Bruere, H. *The New City Government*. New York: D. Appleton, 1920.

Cleveland, F.A., and A.E. Buck. *The Budget and Responsible Government*. New York: Macmillan, 1920.

Dahlberg, J.S. *The New York Bureau of Municipal Research*. New York: New York University Press, 1966.

Fleischman, R.K., and R.P. Marquette. "The Origins of Public Budgeting: Municipal Reformers during the Progressive Era," *Public Budgeting and Finance*, Spring 1986, pp. 71–77.

National Municipal League. *Proceedings of the Annual Meeting* (1895–1911), and *National Municipal Review* (1912–1929). Philadelphia: National Municipal League.

Potts, J.H. "The Evolution of Municipal Accounting in the United States, 1900–1935," *Business History Review*, Winter 1978, pp. 518–536.

See also BUDGETING; SOCIAL RESPONSIBILITIES OF ACCOUNTANTS; TAYLOR, FREDERICK WINSLOW; UNIFORMITY

N

National Association of Accountants
See INSTITUTE OF MANAGEMENT ACCOUN-
TANTS

National Association of State Boards of Accountancy
See STATE REGULATION OF THE ACCOUN-
TANCY PROFESSION (U.S.)

National Income Accounting

Although national-income measurement has had a long and honorable history that has been chronicled by Paul Studenski and others, national accounting is a relatively recent development. In 1940 Ragnar Frisch, a Norwegian econometrician, wrote about constructing national accounts for the purposes of macro-economic analysis in his *National Accounting* (in Norwegian), and Jan Tinbergen, an econometrician from the Netherlands, had used national-accounting concepts in his development of econometric models of the late 1930s and early 1940s (Studenski, 1958). In England, Richard Stone and James Meade, both national income economists, under the guidance of John Maynard Keynes, developed for the United Kingdom Treasury an analysis of national income and expenditure that put into operational form the concepts laid out in Keynes's *General Theory* (1936). Their analysis was published in a White Paper in April 1941 as an attachment to the Budget (Stone and Stone, 1962).

In a report published in 1947 by the United Nations, *The Measurement of National Income and the Construction of Social Accounts*, Stone advocated setting up a system of accounts to record the money flows and related bookkeep-

ing transactions between different sectors in the economy. Although by now these basic principles of national accounting are well recognized, back then they were a major innovation and were not easily accepted. Simon Kuznets, an American economist, for example, writing in 1941, viewed national accounting as "a dubious addition to the theoretical equipment by aid of which we define national income and reckon its distribution."

Nevertheless, immediately after World War II, the U.S. Economic Cooperation Administration and the Organization for European Economic Cooperation agreed that national-income accounts should be used as the framework for planning and monitoring European Economic Recovery. Stone was called on to set up a national-accounts research unit and to develop a system of national-income accounts. The resulting five-account System of National Accounts (SNA), published by the United Nations in 1952, was far simpler than the system outlined in the 1947 United Nations report and bears a striking resemblance to the present five-account system used by the United States. It consisted of a "national income and product" account, income and outlay accounts for the government and household sectors, a "saving and investment" account and a "rest of the world" account.

As the national-income accounts were being developed, there were also developments in related fields of economic accounting. Wassily Leontief, an economics professor at Harvard University, had been working on input-output analysis since the 1930s. By analyzing interindustry requirements and the destination of industry outputs, Leontief was able to show how the industrial structure of the economic system could be expected to change with changes in the final demand for goods and services. In the period after World War II, many countries undertook the construction of input-output tables, and in some countries, including Norway, Denmark, and the Netherlands, input-output tables were integrated with their national accounts.

During this period also, work was being done on flow of funds, national wealth and balance sheets. Morris Copeland, an American economist later a professor of economics at Cornell University, at the National Bureau of Economic Research developed "sources and uses of funds" accounts for recording money flows in his effort to estimate the component "T" in Irving Fisher's, long-time professor of economics at Yale University, quantity theory equation MV = PT. Despite his main concern with deriving the aggregate value of all transactions, he did erect a "sources and uses" accounting framework into which all transactions could be fitted.

At about the same time, Raymond Goldsmith, a professor of economics at Yale University, was estimating national wealth and national balance sheets using a perpetual-inventory method. This involved cumulating the capital-formation data in the national-income accounts over long periods to obtain estimates of the stocks of tangible assets. These were then combined with financial-transactions data in the flow of funds to obtain balance sheets.

It gradually became apparent that all of these economic accounting systems should be integrated into a single framework, and that the 1952 United Nations five-account SNA was not sufficiently comprehensive in its scope to serve as such a framework. In the early 1960s, as a consequence, Stone was again called on to head an effort to create such an integrated system. Although the development of the revised SNA involved the cooperation of statisticians from many national statistical offices, the basic SNA Blue Book, the official guidebook for national income accounting, was primarily the product of Stone working with Abraham Aidenoff, the director of the United Nations National Accounts Office.

The revised SNA was completed in 1968 and, as intended, it provided a comprehensive and detailed framework for recording the stocks and flows in the economy. It brought together in an articulated, coherent system data ranging in degree of aggregation from the con-solidated accounts of the old SNA to detailed input-output and flow-of-funds tables.

In the late 1960s, almost before the ink was dry on the new SNA, the values implicit in the traditional measures of economic progress began to be questioned. Specifically, it was argued that national-income accounting measures did not adequately reflect the deterioration of the environment, the using up of resources, and the disamenities of modern society. Some viewed GNP as standing for gross national pollution, and urged that small was beautiful and that happiness was learning to do without. Even those who did not take such extreme positions were forced to recognize that the data reported in the national accounts did not adequately measure the quality of life. Furthermore, there was an increasing concern with the distribution of well-being; it was argued that an increase in aggregate output might be accompanied by a worsening in the distribution of that output.

Perhaps the greatest blow to the use of national-income accounting as a basis for analyzing the behavior of the economy came from the stagflation that developed in the 1970s. Keynesian economists held the view that inflation and recession could not occur simultaneously. With the fuel crisis of 1973 and subsequent double-digit inflation and recession, this view was largely discredited. Those advocating supply-side or monetarist economic policies felt that income-determination models based on the national accounts were largely irrelevant.

The inflationary process of the 1970s, of course, involved changes in relative prices, and revaluations of assets and liabilities that produced both capital gains and capital losses. Although the revised SNA did in principle make provision for balance sheets and even proposed revaluation accounts, these were not implemented in detail in the 1968 Blue Book. As in the case of income-distribution statistics, provisional guidelines for balance sheets and reconciliation accounts were not published until almost a decade later.

Since 1980 the United Nations System of National Accounts (SNA) has been undergoing extensive revision. The major framework of the 1968 SNA was retained, but it was extended to provide fuller sets of accounts for institutional sectors. Much more attention was directed to accounting for the financial transactions and revaluations that take place in the economy.

Particular emphasis was placed on the harmonization of definitions and classifications used by international statistical agencies such as the International Monetary Fund and the World Bank and national statistical offices. Specifically, balance-of-payment statistics and government financial statistics were integrated with the corresponding information contained in the national accounts. In 1993, the Commission of the European Communities issued *System of National Accounts 1993*. The revision was prepared under the auspices of the Inter-Secretariat Working Group on National Accounts, Commission of the European Communities-Eurostat, the International Monetary Fund, Organization for Economic Co-operation and Development, the United Nations, and the World Bank. The Organization for Economic Co-operation reprinted the 1993 SNA in 1994. It is too soon to judge whether the revision of the SNA will clarify and simplify the national accounts, or whether the linkages between macro economic accounting and micro business and household accounting will be made more complex and difficult.

Richard Ruggles

Bibliography

Copeland, M. *A Study of Moneyflows in the United States*. New York: National Bureau of Economic Research, 1952.

Goldsmith, R. *The National Wealth of the United States in the Postwar Period*. Princeton: National Bureau of Economic Research. Princeton University Press, 1961.

Keynes, J.M. *The General Theory of Employment, Interest, and Money*. New York: Harcourt Brace, 1936.

Kuznets, S. *National Income and its Composition, 1919–1938*. New York: National Bureau of Economic Research, 1941.

Leontief, W. *The Structure of the American Economy, 1919–1929*. Cambridge: Harvard University Press, 1941.

Stone, R. "Definition and Measurement of the National Income and Related Totals." Appendix to *Measurement of National Income and the Construction of Social Accounts*. Studies and Reports on Statistical Methods, no. 7. Geneva: United Nations, 1947.

——— and G. Stone. *National Income and Expenditure*. 6th ed. Chicago: Quadrangle Books, 1962.

Studenski, P. *The Income of Nations*. New York: New York University Press, 1958.

United Nations. *A System of National Accounts and Supporting Tables*. New York: United Nations, 1952.

United Nations. *A System of National Accounts and Supporting Tables*, Studies in Methods, series F, no. 2. New York: United Nations, July 1953.

United Nations. *A System of National Accounts*. Studies in Methods, series F, no. 2, Revision 3. New York: United Nations, 1968.

Yu, S.C. "A Flow-of-Resources Statement for Business Enterprises," *Accounting Review*, July 1969, pp. 571–582.

See also FISHER, IRVING; NETHERLANDS

Natural Business Year

The natural business year (NBY) is a fiscal year ending with the annual low point of business activity or at the conclusion of a season. The NBY has had a tumultuous history.

The 1909 Excise Tax Law, which pertained only to corporations, did not permit them to choose a fiscal year—that is, a year different from the calendar year. By 1913, because of vigorous protest by accountants through the American Association of Public Accountants (AAPA)—forerunner to the American Institute of Accountants (AIA) and the American Institute of Certified Public Accountants (AICPA)—corporations were allowed to choose a fiscal year. However, nonincorporated taxpayers were prohibited from that choice by the Tax Act of 1913. This act was the result of the Sixteenth Amendment to the U.S. Constitution, which permitted the federal government to have an income tax.

The two tasks of convincing incorporated businesses to utilize the NBY and to get Congress to allow nonincorporated business to be able to choose a fiscal year were accepted by the AAPA Special Committee on Distribution of Work. This committee was chaired by Robert Hiester Montgomery. His committee report reflected the dilemma facing accountants of being proactive on a topic for which they had a special interest—in this case, a better spreading of their workload. The committee's solution was to recommend that accountants lobby each of the great industries to change its accounting period to reflect better its NBY. This point was reemphasized by an editorial, Perennial Pressure, in the April 1916 *Journal of Accountancy.* The Tax Act of 1918 permitted nonincorporated entities to choose the NBY. Again, the lobbying of the AIA was apparently successful.

Another leader, Elijah Watt Sells of the firm Haskins and Sells, stepped forth for the NBY in 1921. The AIA increased its editorials on the topic. The definitive research project on the NBY was Bulletin 11, *The Natural Business Year,* published in 1926 by the Bureau of Business Research of the University of Illinois. A.C. Littleton was the leader of this project. The advantages to management for adopting an NBY would be: (1) seasonal activity would be completed; (2) low stock of goods would remain at closing; (3) new contracts would be discussed between seasons; (4) more time would be available for the firm's auditors; and (5) statistical data would be collected for a natural period. The advantages to accountants would be: (1) more permanent and experienced staff would be possible; (2) long hours at high pressure would be avoided; (3) verification would be easier because of low inventories; (4) clients' statements would be less delayed; and (5) more time would be had for consultation with the client. Spurred by Bulletin 11, the AIA formed the Special Committee on NBY in 1928. The committee continued the education process for businessmen about the NBY.

In 1933 the issue of the one-time lump sum tax savings for adopters of the NBY entered the literature. In 1935 the NBY Council was formed and was administered by the AIA. It included representatives from the AIA, the *Wall Street Journal,* the American Management Association, the National Association of Cost Accountants, the New York Credit Men's Association, and the National Association of Credit Men. The NBY Council formed local committees in 32 cities. Dun and Bradstreet conducted studies on the NBY of selected industries. Another leader sprung forth in 1937. Ralph S. Johns, whose thesis had been the basis for Bulletin 11, became chairman of the NBY Committee of the American Institute of Accountants and in 1938 published his classic article on it. Support for the NBY was forthcoming in 1939 in the testimony of expert witnesses at the Securities and Exchange Commission (SEC) hearings on the McKesson and Robbins fraud. William W. Werntz, chief accountant for the SEC, endorsed the NBY in Accounting Series Release No. 17, "Use of Natural Business Year as Basis for Corporate Reporting" (1940).

The Revenue Act of 1940 required Internal Revenue Service (IRS) approval for a change in a fiscal year. The AIA continued its editorial pressure in the 1940s for the NBY, although the NBY Council had begun to wane and died in about 1947. The IRS appeared in the early 1950s to become increasingly concerned that the overriding reason businesses were changing to an NBY was to minimize taxes. By 1958 about one-half of U.S. corporations were filing on a fiscal-year basis, as reported by the chair of the NBY Committee of the AICPA. Perhaps this achievement may have been the goal of that committee, which was allowed to die in 1962.

Tax reasons, not business reasons, for adopting an NBY appeared to be the principal concern of taxable entities. Tax reasons became the reason exclusively mentioned in a number of articles in the 1960s, 1970s, and 1980s. There seemed to be more of a reactive attitude by accountants toward IRS pronouncements than the previous proactive behavior of getting entities to adopt the NBY. In an effort to moderate entities from enjoying tax benefits without valid business reasons, the IRS in the late 1960s and early 1970s issued a series of Revenue Procedures and rulings that carefully delineated the facts and circumstances under which a taxpayer could change taxable years.

In the 1980s, the IRS continued its efforts to reduce the number of taxpayers that could defer income as a result of their interest in "flow through" entities—partnerships and S corporations—with a different taxable year. Revenue Procedure 83–25, 1983–1, required S corporations, even those that had a substantial business purpose (that is, NBY), to meet mathematical tests in order to have a taxable year other than December 31. Section 806 of the Tax Reform Act of 1986 required all S corporations, partnerships, and personal-service corporations to use a calendar year. This section was passed without debate or hearings. Legislation in 1987, strongly supported by the AICPA, allowed individuals and "flow through" entities to maintain a fiscal year provided they prepaid the taxes that resulted from not having a calendar year.

Where did the NBY stand in the mid-1990s? Ironically, it was back to where it was 80 years ago. While Congress and the Treasury Department were successful in stripping away the tax advantages associated with having a fiscal year for proprietorships, partnerships, and "flow through" entities, the financial/managerial advantages still remained. The advantages of adopting the NBY, while not as instantaneous or permanent as the tax deferral, could, over time, result in a substantial savings to businesses in terms of efficiency and productivity.

Richard Vangermeersch
Mark Higgins

Bibliography

Bureau of Business Research, University of Illinois. *The Natural Business Year*. Bulletin No. 11. Urbana, IL: Bureau of Business Research, 1926.

Chatfield, M. "The Natural Business Year and Accounting Theory," *U.S. Army Audit Agency Bulletin*, September 1964, pp. 11–23.

Holzman, R.S. "Calendar v. Fiscal Year: Factors to Be Considered in Selecting a Corporate Accounting Period," *Taxes—The Tax Magazine*, April 1942, pp. 211–213, 249.

Johns, R.S. "Natural Business Year," *Certified Public Accountant*, January 1938, pp. 11–15.

Montgomery, R.H. "The Natural Business Year," *NACA Bulletin*, November 15, 1936, pp. 305–323.

Preinreich, G.A.D. "Taxation and The Natural Business Year," *Accounting Review*, December 1933, pp. 317–322.

Reiss, H.F. Jr. "Trend Continues to Natural Business Year," *Journal of Accountancy*, August 1960, pp. 25–26.

Vangermeersch, R., and M. Higgins. "The Natural Business Year: A Shift from Proactive to Reactive Behavior by Accountants," *Accounting Historians Journal*, December 1990, pp. 37–56.

See also AMERICAN INSTITUTE OF CERTIFIED PUBLIC ACCOUNTANTS; BIG EIGHT ACCOUNTING FIRMS; CONTINUITY; INCOME TAXATION IN THE UNITED STATES; LITTLETON, A.C.; MCKESSON AND ROBBINS CASE; MEDIEVAL ACCOUNTING; MONTGOMERY, ROBERT HIESTER; PERIODICITY; SAVARY, JACQUES; SECURITIES AND EXCHANGE COMMISSION; SELLS, ELIJAH WATT; TAX REFORM ACTS

Netherlands

The development of accounting and accounting thought in the Netherlands is generally presented as being fairly closely related to overall economic developments. And although this link is tenuous or absent in many instances, it provides useful guidance in an initial orientation.

A recognizable political entity roughly comprising the present-day Netherlands and Belgium did not begin to emerge until the beginning of the sixteenth century. During the three preceding centuries, the southern part of this area, mainly Flanders, led the way in economic development. Through extensive trade links, its commercial practices, including accounting, were much influenced by the Italian example. The northern half of the Dutch area generally followed more primitive Hanseatic practices.

Fittingly, the most well-known among the earliest Dutch authors on bookkeeping, Jan Ympyn and Simon Stevin, were of Flemish extraction. Their work is thought to have been of great importance for the propagation of Italian double entry bookkeeping in the northern Netherlands.

At the end of the sixteenth century, the northern Netherlands, newly established as an independent republic, embarked on a course of spectacular economic expansion, eclipsing its declining southern neighbor. During most of the seventeenth century, the Dutch republic played a major role in worldwide sea-borne commerce. Accounting practices were adapted to fit the needs of large chartered companies. But the effectiveness of accounting controls in the East and West India Companies in controlling their far-flung activities in colonial trade is open to serious doubt. Accounting techniques were also developed, apparently with more success, to cope with the growing importance of Amsterdam as a market for securities, foreign funds, and insurance.

Resting on a solid agricultural base, colonial trade and international finance remained the most conspicuous features of the Dutch economy during an extended period of economic languor lasting from the early eighteenth to the middle nineteenth century. When neighboring countries were caught up in the industrial revolution, the Netherlands was slow to follow suit. As a mirror image, development in accounting practice seems to have come to a halt. Until the later part of the nineteenth century, accounting followed the traditional mercatorial practices of the seventeenth century, occasionally even on the basis of seventeenth-century textbooks.

Modern industrial enterprises came into existence in significant number or size only after 1870. But the pace of industrialization quickened considerably during the period 1890–1910. By World War I, the Dutch economy boasted a large and reinvigorated trading and financial sector, and a sizeable and growing modern industrial sector.

This renewed vigor in the economy was reflected in accounting practice and thought. Reflection on current practice and possible improvements was stimulated by the need to adapt old practices to new circumstances. This movement, carried on chiefly in circles of qualified accounting instructors, resulted in the start of some technical journals, the production of numerous books dealing with accounting practices in specific industries, the founding, in 1895, of the first Dutch organization of auditors (*Nederlandsch Instituut van Accountants* or NIvA), and, finally, the founding of chairs in accounting and related branches of knowledge in a number of Dutch universities in the first decades of the twentieth century.

The chief characteristic of accounting thought in this period is the search for rational explanations underlying traditional practices, and, in the absence of such reasons, attempts to weed out inconsistent or obsolete practices. But the period also saw the development of new ideas, such as theories of depreciation and, in the sphere of financial accounting, the development of the idea that the balance sheet is not a mere extract from a ledger for the benefit of owners, but a statement of information for the benefit of more or less anonymous investors in large limited liability companies.

It is insufficient to point merely to economic developments in order to explain the outbreak of activity around the turn of the century. It was due in no inconsiderable degree to the talent and energies of a few individuals with sufficient vision to guide the transition from bookkeeping to a science of accounting and business administration. Among these individuals, J.G.Ch. Volmer and Theodore Limperg Jr. take a prominent place.

Unquestionably, the development of accounting thought during most of the twentieth century has been marked by the need to come to terms, either in acceptance or rejection, with the normative-deductive theories expounded with great persuasive power by Limperg. These ideas, among which the theory of current cost (or replacement-value) accounting is only the most well-known, gained widespread acceptance in circles of auditors and accountants through a unified professional examination system. Nevertheless, Limperg's views met with opposition as well, notably from professors N.J. Polak and O. Bakker. Polak represented an alternative, practice-oriented tradition, traceable to Volmer. Bakker is known for his theory of price-level, as opposed to current cost, accounting.

But during the 1950s and 1960s, the theoretical validity of the normative current cost theory was widely accepted. On the basis of Limperg's thinking, it was fully incorporated in cost accounting by the work of H.J. van der Schroeff. Current cost theory was to a certain extent espoused in business circles as well, apparently in the hope that income determination on the basis of current cost might become acceptable for tax purposes. Actual adoption of current cost accounting in financial statements has, however, been limited to a minority of listed companies, including, though, some highly visible multinationals such as Philips Industries.

Roughly since the middle 1970s current cost accounting began to lose its status as a cherished doctrine in Dutch accounting circles. This development is probably due to a number of factors, such as a lower rate of inflation, the awareness of theoretical flaws in Limpergian current cost theory, and more extensive exposure to foreign accounting practices largely devoid of current cost influences, both in European Community (EC) countries and in the United States.

Legal or other regulatory influences on accounting have, until quite recently, been negligible. Before World War II, this may be ascribed to a rather widespread belief in, on the one hand, the impropriety of government interference in business affairs and, on the other, the capability of shareholders to take care of their own interests. The first modern company law of 1928–1929 was, as far as financial reporting was concerned, restricted to requiring publication of financial statements by large limited liability companies, but did hardly specify their contents.

After World War II, regulation of business practice in general became more acceptable, but regulation of external financial reporting was, and is, only supported to a limited extent. The argument commonly employed both by business and auditors for not regulating financial reporting in any detail has been that detailed regulation would, of necessity, lead to a formal-ization of the reporting process. By strict confor-mity with the law, the circumstances of the indi-vidual firm would not be properly reflected in the accounts, and further development of account-ing practice would be inhibited by rigidity.

In keeping with this idea, the first law to regulate the contents of financial statements (1970) gave pride of place to the principle of "substance over form" and allowed numerous alternative practices. Since 1983, though, re-porting requirements have been influenced by attempts at harmonization under the auspices of the European Community, which has led to a rather stronger emphasis on formal disclosure rules.

Since 1971 a private-sector body (the Tri-partite Accounting Standards Committee), in which auditors, employers, employees, and other users of financial statements are repre-sented, has been issuing statements of an advi-sory nature, in which the requirements of the law are elaborated. The advisory nature of the statements again reflects the consensus that has generally prevailed in the postwar era on the undesirability of detailed, binding requirements. Completing the regulatory framework set up in the early 1970s, the Netherlands also has an Enterprise Chamber, which hears complaints about incorrect financial statements.

The influence of tax law on financial ac-counting has been minimal. Until 1940, corpo-rate taxes were not levied on profits but on divi-dends, allowing leeway for the development of a tradition that external financial statements and tax returns ought to be independent from each other. The subsequent introduction of a tax on corporate income has not affected this tradition.

Concerning foreign influences on modern accounting thought, the twentieth century has witnessed a shift of emphasis away from Ger-man toward Anglo-American influence. Aware-ness of French practice and thought has ever been limited and consequently of little impact. In early modern literature, references to Ger-man authors and legislation are frequent and often of a complimentary nature. Later on, the works of Eugen Schmalenbach and Fritz Schmidt offered ample opportunities for denun-ciation to Limperg and his disciples. But, since World War II, this has changed to an almost exclusive orientation toward the United King-dom and the United States. Combined with the influence of the European Community Direc-tives, this has, to a certain extent, resulted in the loss of a recognizably distinct Dutch account-ing culture.

Kees Camfferman

Bibliography

De Vries, J. *Lion Markus en de comptabiliteit in Nederland omstreeks 1900*. N.p.: Koninklijke Nederlandse Akademie van Wetenschappen, 1983.

De Waal, P.G.A. *De leer van het boekhouden in de Nederlanden tijdens de zestiende eeuw*. Roermond: Romen, 1927.

Klaassen, J. "An Accounting Court: The Im-pact of the Enterprise Chamber on Fi-nancial Reporting in the Netherlands," *Accounting Review*, April 1990, pp. 327–341.

Schoonderbeek, J.W. *Council for Annual Re-porting—Setting Accounting Standards in the Netherlands*. Amsterdam: Raad voor de Jaarverslaggeving, 1985.

Ten Have, O. *De leer van het boekhouden in de Nederlanden tijdens de zeventiende en achttiende eeuw*. Delft: N.p., 1933.

Zeff, S.A., F. Van der Wel, and K. Camfferman. *Company Financial Re-porting: A Historical and Comparative Study of the Dutch Regulatory Process*. Amsterdam: North Holland, 1992.

See also DIRECTIVES OF THE EUROPEAN COM-MUNITY (UNION); KRAAYENHOF, JACOB; LIMPERG, THEODORE, JR.; NATIONAL-INCOME ACCOUNTING; PACIOLI, LUCA; PHILIPS INDUS-TRIES (N.V.); STEVIN, SIMON; UNIFORMITY; YMPYN, JAN

New York Stock Exchange

The New York Stock Exchange apparently started informally about March 1792 on Wall Street. On May 17, 1792, 24 signatories founded the New York Stock and Exchanges Board. It became the New York Stock Exchange (NYSE) on January 29, 1863. The early years of the NYSE, like that of the economy of the early years of the United States, were dominated by Alexander Hamilton and his economic poli-cies, such as the National Bank; the redemption of the federal scrip; the assumption of the fed-eral government of the debts of the states; and the formation of the Society of Useful Manufac-turers. When the Society of Useful Manufactur-ers started operations in Paterson, New Jersey, it was in 1791 the first industrial organization to sell stock to the general public.

The NYSE has reflected the happenings of the U.S. and, to a lesser extent, foreign economies. While the first railroad stock was traded in 1830, the bulk of the trading was for banks and for national securities. Railroads dominated from the 1850s through the 1880s. The trust movements of the 1890s through early 1900s brought industrial companies to the forefront.

The term "panic" was used to reflect the rapid and significant fall of prices on the NYSE for about a hundred years. These panics and their very generalized root causes were: 1819, banking; 1837, land and banking; 1857, banking; 1873, railroads; 1893, industrials; and 1907, financial. Severe downturns also took place in such years as 1869 and 1903. There was a sharp fall during the period following World War I. The Crash of 1929 signaled the beginning of the Great Depression. Another momentous price crash occurred on October 19, 1987. The NYSE was the base for the exploits of such men as Daniel Drew, Jay Gould, Jim Fisk, Cornelius Vanderbilt, John D. Rockefeller, Andrew Carnegie, J.P. Morgan, William Durant, and Joseph P. Kennedy.

In 1869 the NYSE adopted a committee structure along with a Governing Committee of 28 members. One of the committees was the Committee on Stock List (CSL). Its duties, described by Haskell (1936) were: "considering and recommending new listing applications, formulating listing requirements and determining the time and conditions to indicate action for the delisting of listed issues." In 1895 the committee recommended that listed companies publish annual reports at least 15 days in advance of their annual meetings. In 1900 the CSL sought to obtain this by agreements with the listed companies; in 1909 it did the same for annual financial reports to stockholders. In 1921 it required consolidated financial statements or separate statements of the company and each of its subsidiaries. From 1925 through 1931, the CSL tightened its requirements on consolidated statements, profits on sale of intercompany stockholdings, depreciation, equity in earnings of subsidiaries, accepted accounting principles, and stock dividends. In 1932, the CSL required audited statements bearing the certificate of qualified accountants.

J.M.B. Hoxsey, executive assistant of the CSL, started a dialogue with the American Institute of Accountants (AIA)—forerunner of the American Institute of Certified Public Accountants (AICPA)—in 1930 at the AIA's annual meeting. Hoxsey's speech was based on his belief that there were "improvements upon certain commonly accepted practices which can be definitely and strongly recommended." This dialogue led in 1932 to the formation of the AIA Special Committee on Cooperation with Stock Exchanges, chaired by George Oliver May from Price Waterhouse and Company. The correspondence between this Special Committee and the CSL from 1932 through 1934 led to the first statement of "generally accepted accounting principles," and a model audit report. The CSL began to assist listed companies in their dealings with the Securities and Exchange Commission (SEC), formed in 1934. Some other examples reported in a letter to the author in 1969 of initiatives of the NYSE later on include encouraging quarterly reporting and the publication of the Statement of Sources and Uses of Funds in annual reports. In 1973 the NYSE issued a White Paper entitled "Recommendations and Comments on Financial Reporting to Shareholders and Related Matters." It included 17 recommendations, most of which have become matters disclosed in corporate annual reports. The NYSE has been a positive force in improving disclosure of accounting information to investors of listed corporations. Other than the spurt of activity from about 1925 through 1934, it has not been a major player in the standardization of accounting principles. However, the initiatives shown by the CSL of the NYSE during that period needs to be known by accountants and others so they can make a judgment about private-sector versus public-sector control of financial accounting. A related issue is to what extent the alleged excesses in financial accounting during the first three decades of the 1900s, detailed by Ripley (1927), were a major cause of the Crash of 1929.

Richard Vangermeersch

Bibliography

American Institute of Accountants. *Audits of Corporate Accountants: Correspondence between the Special Committee on Cooperation with Stock Exchanges of the American Institute of Accountants and the Committee on Stock List of the New York Stock Exchange, 1932–1934."* New York: AIA, 1934.

Benjamin, J.J., and V.C. Brenner. "Reaction

to NYSE White Paper's Call for Disclosure," *Management Accounting*, May 1975, pp. 13–18, 23.

Dillon, G.J. *The Role of Accounting in the Stock Market Crash of 1929.* Research Monograph No. 96. Atlanta: Georgia State University, 1984.

Haskell, J. "Objectives and Activities of the Committee on Stock List of the NYSE under Present Conditions," *Journal of Accountancy*, October 1936, pp. 271–281.

Hoxsey, J.M.B. "Accounting and the Stock Exchange," *Bulletin, NY State Society of CPAs*, April 1931, pp. 9–30.

———. "Accounting for Investors," *Journal of Accountancy*, October 1930, pp. 251–292.

Kline, M., ed. *Alexander Hamilton: A Biography in His Own Words.* New York: Newsweek, 1973.

New York Stock Exchange. *Historical Account of Relationship of NYSE with Listed Companies as It Affects Accountants.* April 8, 1938. Privately published by the New York Stock Exchange. Sent to author in 1969.

Ripley, W.Z. *Main Street and Wall Street.* Boston: Little, Brown & Co., 1927.

Satterfield, W.R., Assistant Director, Department of Stock List, NYSE. "Letter to Richard Vangermeersch, May 27, 1969."

Sobel, R. *The Big Board: A History of the New York Stock Market.* New York: Free Press, 1965.

Stedman, E.C. *The New York Stock Exchange.* New York: New York Stock Exchange Historical Co., 1905. Reprint. Westport, CT: Greenwood, 1969.

Warshow, R.I. *The Story of Wall Street.* New York: Greenberg, 1929.

See also ACCOUNTING RESEARCH BULLETINS; AMERICAN INSTITUTE OF CERTIFIED PUBLIC ACCOUNTANTS; AUDIT COMMITTEES; AUDITOR'S REPORT; BIG EIGHT ACCOUNTING FIRMS; COMPARABILITY; CONGRESSIONAL VIEWS; CONSOLIDATED FINANCIAL STATEMENTS; DEPRECIATION; EXTERNAL AUDITING; GENERALLY ACCEPTED ACCOUNTING PRINCIPLES; HOXSEY, J.M.B.; MAY, GEORGE OLIVER; OBJECTIVITY; PAID IN CAPITAL; RAILROAD ACCOUNTING (U.S.); REALIZATION; RIPLEY, WILLIAM Z.; SECURITIES AND EXCHANGE COMMISSION; STOCK DIVIDENDS; TREASURY STOCK

Nicholson, J. Lee (1863–1924)

J. Lee Nicholson, cost accountant, industrial consultant, and university lecturer, is of interest today for several reasons. First, because he refined and disseminated new knowledge about cost accounting, which had recently undergone revolutionary changes. Second, as one of the earliest American cost accountants to teach the subject at the university level, he helped standardize practice and facilitate the interaction of ideas between academics and practitioners. He organized the National Association of Cost Accountants (now the Institute of Management Accountants) and was its first president. Finally, his textbooks and periodical articles not only demonstrated the best practice of his time but anticipated future developments.

Nicholson began writing about cost accounting at a critical point in its evolution. After hundreds of years of painfully slow progress, cost accounting took off during the 1880s. Between 1885 and 1920, the essentials of modern cost technique were formulated and to some extent standardized in practice. Workable overhead allocation methods were devised, procedures were developed for integrating cost and financial accounts, and standard costing became routinized. In all of this, Nicholson was less an innovator than a synthesizer. His main contribution was to organize, improve, and propagate this new knowledge as it spread from a tiny minority of pioneering firms to the vast majority of manufacturers who still had no formal cost accounting systems at the beginning of the twentieth century.

Nicholson's *Factory Organization and Costs* (1909) was a how-to-do-it book that summarized and suggested improvements in current cost accounting practices. For instance, he not only described job order and process costing procedures, but also the circumstances in which each method was appropriate. He was one of the first writers to explain how departmental costs might be accumulated and transferred through successive stages of factory processing. He also proposed a summary of materials requisitions to facilitate posting to stores' ledgers and work in process accounts, originated several methods of accounting for scrap, and suggested an improved perpetual inventory system.

The problem of allocating overhead costs to products had baffled accountants for more than a century. Nicholson demonstrated seven overhead allocation methods. He argued that selling and administrative expenses added nothing to the value of manufactured goods and should be excluded from overhead distributions. He proposed a "new machine rate" whereby labor and overhead costs were to be collected by departments and then divided among output units according to the amount of machine processing time spent on each product.

Nicholson's second book, *Cost Accounting—Theory and Practice* (1913), drew on his teaching experiences at Columbia and at New York University. He showed how factory costs could be integrated into the general ledger through the use of reciprocal accounts. He distinguished between overhead allocations to manufacturing and service departments, and proposed a method for collecting overhead costs in control accounts before charging them to products. He also recommended a procedure for estimating cost of goods sold at current prices that foreshadowed the last in, first out method.

Nicholson's later writings anticipated post-1920 developments in the use of cost figures for decision making and in the psychology of cost control. His experiences as head of a management consulting firm focused his attention on the relationship between cost accounting and industrial efficiency. He emphasized that cost accounting is a service function whose value depends on its usefulness to other departments. As a staff man negotiating with foremen and executives, the cost accountant must be diplomatic, yet forceful enough to take full advantage of the discipline that costing makes possible. Nicholson stressed the importance of supplying cost figures that are appropriate for each executive level, and the need to educate foremen and department heads about overhead costs as a first step toward controlling such costs. Cost accountants should give department managers comparative costs of materials, labor, overhead, production quantities, and inventories. Each production department should in turn inform the sales department how all these amounts are likely to vary in relation to changes in sales volume.

Michael Chatfield

Bibliography

Chatfield, M. *A History of Accounting Thought.* Rev. ed. Huntington, NY: Krieger, 1977.

Garner, S.P. *Evolution of Cost Accounting to 1925.* University, AL: University of Alabama Press, 1954.

Hein, L.W. "J. Lee Nicholson: Pioneer Cost Accountant," *Accounting Review*, January 1959, pp. 106–111.

See also COMMON COSTS; CONTROL ACCOUNTS; COST AND/OR MANAGEMENT ACCOUNTING; DIRECT COSTING; IMPUTED INTEREST ON CAPITAL; INSTITUTE OF MANAGEMENT ACCOUNTANTS

Normative Accounting

The purpose of normative accounting is to recommend or prescribe accounting procedures, in contrast to positive accounting, which primarily aims at describing the economic behavior of producers and users of financial statements. The ultimate task of accounting practice is to represent—to approximate conceptually—a segment of financial reality, and thus it might be thought to be positive. Yet this representation is not scientific but pragmatic, and thus is subject to cost-benefit constraints requiring many value judgments (e.g., selecting one of many alternatives, ranging from simple to highly sophisticated systems). However, value judgments are introduced not only by specific purpose-orientation, but also by the macroprocess of choosing accounting standards (which often is biased toward a specific segment of society). Thus, accounting practice is bound to be normative.

Historical Perspectives

The earliest research in normative accounting goes back to Johann F. Schär (1846–1924) and Heinrich Nicklisch (1876–1946). The theories of Schär (1911/1923, 1914/1932) and particularly Nicklisch (1912, 1929/1932) were—in contrast to later normative theories, with the possible exception of the "British Critical Perspective School" as represented by Anthony G. Hopwood (1988) and others—motivated by an explicitly formulated "business ethics," according to which accounting (and business administration in general) ought to aim at maximizing efficiency and performance, rather than maximizing short-run profit (ethical-normative theory).

Normative accounting theory is often incorrectly identified with the deductive approach (actually, deductive and inductive inferences are required for normative as well as positive accounting). But the "golden age in the history of *a priori* research in accounting"—as Carl L.

Nelson, a noted accounting theorist, called it—did indeed coincide with the climax of pragmatic-normative accounting theory in the 1960s. Hendriksen (1982), in his chapter on normative accounting theory, lists in this connection mainly the works of Paton (1922/1972), Moonitz (1961), Mattessich (1964/1977), Chambers (1966/1975), Ijiri (1967/1978), and Sterling (1970/1975). While in the early 1980s a theory text like Hendriksen's could still devote a lengthy chapter to "The Normative Deductive Approach," by the late 1980s this research field had been so much discredited that the theory text by Wolk et al. (1992) does not even contain the expression "normative accounting (theory)" in its Subject Index (though the book does provide about two pages on "Normative and Descriptive Theories").

Since the end of the 1970s, the adherents of positive accounting theory—see Watts and Zimmerman (1986)—have been trying to banish value judgments from accounting and have branded normative accounting theory as unscientific. Normative accounting theorists themselves may be partly to blame for this unfavorable reputation. The theoretical frameworks of most of them concentrated on narrow objectives without any provision for a broad range of teleological interpretations. This is best illustrated by the theories of Chambers and Sterling in which, for example, current (exit) prices are the only acceptable or even the only "true" valuation basis.

In Mattessich (1964/1979, 1972, 1995a, 1995b) and Balzer and Mattessich (1991), on the other hand, there is a clear distinction between the general framework and the specific, purpose-oriented interpretations and specifications. Such a theoretical frame can, in accordance with different information objectives, accommodate a wide range of values (from historical cost to current entry values to discounted net revenues) and other variables. It may also provide an explicit statement of the value judgments involved. The resulting theory is then no longer geared toward a narrow objective but offers great flexibility. This approach may be called "conditional-normative" because it emphasizes the means-end relations ("if-then statements" in the form of instrumental hypotheses); it closely resembles the normative methods of operations research, auditing, and systems methodology (Mattessich 1978/1980). It is based on the presumption that academic accounting, like any other applied science, must provide a range of tools for practitioners to choose from, depending on their specific information requirements. Opposed to this is positive accounting theory, which implies that practitioners ought to provide their own framework for connecting the results of positive research with "external" goals and value judgments. This may have contributed in the 1980s to the increasing gap between accounting scholars and practitioners, alienating the two groups from each other.

Future Prospects

Mounting criticism of positive accounting theory (which must not be confused with the mere promotion of empirical research), and the growing insight that accounting requires a conditional-normative approach, seem to have awakened new interest in normative accounting theory. This by no means implies that empirical research can be dispensed with; on the contrary, the latter (particularly factual research into efficient means-end relations) is an indispensable component and ought to be reinforced. While empirical accounting research created new insights during the last two decades, positive accounting theory could not provide a satisfactory theoretical foundation for most of this research. Conditional-normative accounting theory aims at filling this gap. By searching for better standards and other accounting tools, this theory can shed more light on the actual goals an accounting body or a firm is pursuing. Above all, it explains why the present tools, such as historical costing, are employed to attain those objectives.

Of course, to develop a rigorous conditional-normative accounting theory, further foundational research is required. In a way, all applied sciences face the same basic problem of providing instrumental hypotheses that connect efficient means with desired ends. Some groundwork for such an analysis (in the epistemology of applied sciences) was laid in Mattessich (1978/1980). But, apart from finding an appropriate optimization calculus, the question arises whether deontology (the logic of normative and imperative sentences) is required. This kind of logic is more complex and less familiar to accountants than declarative logic (used in positive research). Perhaps the alternative approach of supplementing traditional logic with simple "conversion rules" instead of using a highly formalized normative logic, as proposed by the Nobel laureate

Herbert Simon (1966), might be a more practicable way for inferring satisfactory (or even optimal) means from the ends that are to be attained. For further details on normative accounting theory and its history, see Mattessich (1992, 1995a, 1995b).

Richard V. Mattessich

Bibliography

Balzer, W., and R. Mattessich. "An Axiomatic Basis of Accounting: A Structuralist Reconstruction," *Theory and Decision*, vol. 30, 1991, pp. 213–243.

Chambers, R.J. *Accounting, Evaluation, and Economic Behavior*. Englewood Cliffs, NJ: Prentice-Hall, 1966. Reprint. Houston: Scholars Book, 1975.

Hendriksen, E.S. *Accounting Theory*. 4th edition. Homewood, IL: Irwin, 1982.

Hopwood, A.G. *Accounting from the Outside: The Collected Papers by Anthony G. Hopwood*. New York: Garland, 1988.

Ijiri, Y. *The Foundations of Accounting Measurement*. Englewood Cliffs, NJ: Prentice-Hall, 1967. Reprint. Houston: Scholars Book, 1978.

Mattessich, R. *Accounting and Analytical Methods: Measurement and Projection of Income and Wealth in the Micro- and Macro-Economy*. Homewood, IL: Irwin, 1964. Reprint. Houston: Scholars Book, 1977.

———. "Conditional-Normative Accounting Methodology: Incorporating Value Judgments and Means-End Relations of an Applied Discipline," *Accounting Organizations and Society*, vol. 20, no. 4, 1995a, pp. 259–284.

———. *Critique of Accounting: Examination of the Foundations and Normative Structure of an Applied Discipline*. Westport, CT: Quorum Books, 1995b.

———. *Instrumental Reasoning and Systems Methodology: An Epistemology of the Applied and Social Sciences*. Dordrecht and Boston: D. Reidel, 1978. Reprint. Boston: D. Reidel, 1980.

———. "Methodological Preconditions and Problems of a General Theory of Accounting," *Accounting Review*, July 1972, pp. 469–487.

———. "On the History of Normative Accounting Theory: Paradigm Lost, Paradigm Regained?" In *Proceedings of the Sixth International Congress of Accounting Historians*, ed. by Atsuo Tsuji, pp. 937–974. vol. 3. Kyoto Accounting History Association (Japan) 1992; and *Accounting, Business, and Financial History*, September 1992, pp. 181–198.

Moonitz, M. *The Basic Postulates of Accounting*. Accounting Research Study No. 1. New York: AICPA, 1961.

Nelson, C.L. "A Priori Research in Accounting," pp. 3–19 in N. Dopuch and L. Revsine, eds. *Accounting Research 1960–1970: A Critical Evaluation*. Champaign: Center for International Education and Research in Accounting, University of Illinois, 1973.

Nicklisch, H. *Allgemeine kaufmännische Betriebslehre als Privatwirtschaftslehre des Handels*. Leipzig: C.E. Poeschel, 1912.

———. *Die Betriebswirtschaft*. 3 vols. Stuttgart: C.E. Poeschel, 1929–1932.

Paton, W.A. *Accounting Theory: With Special Reference to the Corporate Enterprise*. New York: Ronald Press, 1922. Reprint. Lawrence, KS: Scholars Book, 1972.

Schär, J.F. *Allgemeine Handelsbetriebslehre*. Basel: N.p., 1911; 5th ed. Leipzig: G.A. Gloeckner, 1923.

———. *Buchhaltung und Bilanz auf wirtschaftlicher, rechtlicher und mathematischer Grundlage*. Basel: N.p., 1914; 6th ed. (edited by W. Prion), Berlin: Springer, 1932.

Simon, H.A. "The Logic of Heuristic Decision Making." In *The Logic of Decision and Action*, edited by N. Rescher, pp. 1–20. Pittsburgh: University of Pittsburgh, 1966.

Sterling, R.R. *Theory of the Measurement of Enterprise Income*. Lawrence, KS: University of Kansas Press, 1970. Reprint. Houston: Scholars Book, 1975.

Watts, R.L., and J.L. Zimmerman. *Positive Accounting Theory*. Englewood Cliffs, NJ: Prentice-Hall, 1986.

Wolk, H.I., J.R. Francis, and M.G. Tearney. *Accounting Theory: A Conceptual and Institutional Approach*. 3rd ed. Boston: Kent, 1992.

See also CASH BASIS ACCOUNTING; CHAMBERS, RAYMOND JOHN; CONCEPTUAL FRAMEWORK; DEFINITIONS OF ACCOUNTING; HOPWOOD, ANTHONY G.; IJIRI, YUJI; MATTESSICH, RICHARD; MOONITZ, MAURICE; PATON, WILLIAM ANDREW; POSITIVE ACCOUNTING; STERLING, ROBERT R.

Objectivity

During the nineteenth century a series of court decisions, reinforced by statutes in England and America, specified that dividends could only be declared from current and retained earnings. But the emerging accounting profession was weak, with limited power to regulate its clients' behavior, and was generally unable to counter managerial pressures. Within wide limits each business was left to measure income in its own way. Naturally the methods used were designed to protect management as well as investor interests. As a result, according to George O. May, "accounting varied in its general character from industry to industry, from corporation to corporation, and even from place to place." In using their freedom to choose accounting methods some managements were ultraconservative, others were overbold. The majority of both factions showed a preference for smoothing reported income and equalizing dividend payments.

In 1900 most companies still used the single account or inventory method of asset valuation, which priced fixed assets as if they were unsold merchandise. Assets were appraised or at least revalued at the end of each accounting period, and for most firms using this method, profit was the increase in value of net assets from all causes. No distinction was made between capital and revenue expenditures, between current and fixed assets, between depreciation and appreciation, or between real income and inflationary increases. The variety of valuation methods in use prevented real adherence to the principles of objectivity, consistency, or comparability of data. From Adam Smith and other classical economists had come the idea that profit could only arise from actual exchanges of goods. But realization was not yet an accounting principle, nor was there a well understood notion of matching costs with related revenues, or even of converting asset values to expense.

The accounting concept of profit as an increase in net assets was undermined by income tax laws. For tax purposes there had to be an objective, legally authorized way to determine a year's income. The tax was on income, not wealth, and it was simply not feasible to make tax assessments on the basis of annual balance sheet revaluations. By defining taxable income as the excess of cash receipts over cash payments, early tax laws made it necessary to measure income separately from the capital that generated it. So from the first, a realization rule was an integral part of the tax code. Any increase in wealth had to be confirmed by some objectively measurable event or transaction, normally the receipt of money, before profit came into existence.

During the 1920s, it was the income tax laws that helped to systematize accounting practice. Standardized depreciation calculations, bad debt allowances, the wide use of historical cost valuations, and the matching principle owed much more to passage of the Sixteenth Amendment than to the progress of accounting theory. In particular, the realization rule promoted objectivity by providing a theoretical justification for valuing current as well as fixed assets at acquisition cost, since any higher valuation would create unrealized income.

After the 1929 stock market crash, attempts were made to codify accounting theory and to reconcile theory with the methods actually used by accountants. As a result, accounting procedures were further standardized. Despite downward price fluctuations during the 1930s, the first attempts to codify accounting principles stressed objectivity, consistency, comparability of data, the matching concept, and historical cost valuation as a stable base for income measurement. The first authoritative use of the word "realization" seems to have occurred in the 1932 correspondence between the American Institute of Accountants' (AIA) Special Committee on Cooperation with Stock Exchanges, and the Committee on Stock List of the New York Stock Exchange. The AIA committee supported the realization test of income and rejected asset appraisal methods on the grounds that in any large company the real value of assets is collective and depends mainly on the firm's earning power.

With the transition from "increased net worth" to realization at sale, it became common to speak of income finding as a process of matching related costs and revenues. This approach was actively promoted by the AIA and the Securities and Exchange Commission during the 1930s because its results were objective and verifiable. At that stage in accounting development, uniformity was considered more important than precision. The profession's bad experiences with appraisal writeups during the preceding decades gave an air of reform to techniques that minimized the possibility of manipulation. In realization and matching, the AIA offered CPAs the legal protection of easily standardized methods that were also explicable to the investing public. Both principles conformed to a tradition of accrual accounting, objectivity, and conservatism and were flexible enough to allow for such exceptions as cost or market writedowns and deferred realization on installment sales. Widespread acceptance of the income statement as an expression of the matching process closely followed a corporate shift from debt to equity financing and coincided with the advent of progressive taxation. It soon became common for theoretical and practical improvements to be promoted as attempts to refine income measurement. Even innovations such as last in, first out, accelerated depreciation, interperiod tax allocations, and the percentage of completion method were justified on the grounds that they improved cost and revenue matching.

Theorists might object that the realization rule actually frustrated matching by deferring recognition of holding gains until years after the costs of producing them had been recorded. But income finding now depended on a series of interlocking assumptions that included historical cost, objectivity, continuity, conservatism, and periodicity as well as matching and realization. These were made compatible by the ascendancy which income measurement had attained over asset valuation and by the fairly stable prewar price structure. It would prove very difficult to alter any of them without changing their conglomerate effect. After World War II, inflation would create an environment in which most of these conventions would be challenged and in which the classical notions of realization and matching, though continuing to prevail in practice, would become theoretically disreputable.

Michael Chatfield

Bibliography

Arnett, H.E. "What Does 'Objectivity' Mean to Accountants?" *Journal of Accountancy*, May 1961, pp. 63–68.

Grady, P., ed. *Memoirs and Accounting Thought of George O. May*. New York: Ronald Press, 1962.

Litherland, D.A. "Fixed Asset Replacement a Half Century Ago," *Accounting Review*, October 1951, pp. 475–480.

Storey, R.K. "Revenue Realization, Going Concern, and Measurement of Income," *Accounting Review*, April 1959, pp. 233–238.

See also ACCRUAL ACCOUNTING; AMERICAN INSTITUTE OF CERTIFIED PUBLIC ACCOUNTANTS; CASH FLOW ACCOUNTING; COMPARABILITY; CONSERVATISM; CONTINUITY; DEFERRED INCOME TAX ACCOUNTING; DICKSEE, LAWRENCE; DIVIDENDS; *EISNER V. MACOMBER;* FIXED ASSETS; GILMAN, STEPHEN; HISTORICAL COST; INCOME TAXATION IN THE UNITED STATES; LAST IN, FIRST OUT (LIFO); MATCHING; MAY, GEORGE OLIVER; NEW YORK STOCK EXCHANGE; POSTULATES OF ACCOUNTING; REALIZATION; SANDILANDS REPORT; SECURITIES AND EXCHANGE COMMISSION; SINGLE ACCOUNT METHOD; SIXTEENTH AMENDMENT; SMITH, ADAM; STUDY GROUP ON BUSINESS INCOME'S *FIVE MONOGRAPHS ON BUSINESS INCOME;* UNIFORMITY; VATTER, WILLIAM JOSEPH

Oldcastle, Hugh

The first English bookkeeping text was *A Profitable Treatyce* (1543) by Hugh Oldcastle, a London draper and teacher of bookkeeping and arithmetic. No copy survives, and Oldcastle's book is known only through the 1588 reprint *A briefe instruction and maner how to keepe bookes of Accompts after the order of Debitor and Creditor* by John Mellis, who acknowledged derivation from Oldcastle's work. Both books were almost literal translations of Luca Pacioli's 1494 bookkeeping treatise, "Particularis de Computis et Scripturis," with a few added examples of little value. Mellis omitted eleven chapters of "de Computis," including those relating to bank accounting, since no bank had yet been established in England.

Michael Chatfield

Bibliography

Coomber, R.R. "Hugh Oldcastle and John Mellis." In *Studies in the History of Accounting,* edited by A.C. Littleton and B.S. Yamey, pp. 206–214. Homewood, IL: Irwin, 1956.

Sutherland, P. "Hugh Oldcastle and the 'Profitable Treatyce' of 1543," *Accountant*, March 23, 1940, pp. 334–336.

See also PACIOLI, LUCA; PERSONIFICATION OF ACCOUNTS; TRIAL BALANCE

Operational (Value-for-Money) Auditing

The periodic evaluation of managerial efficiency and effectiveness by nonmanagerial personnel is known today by such interchangeable terms as operational auditing, management auditing, performance auditing, and (in the former British Empire) value-for-money auditing. An operational audit is a systematic, nonfinancial evaluation of an entity's operations and an organized search for ways to improve managerial efficiency and effectiveness. Typically, internal auditors have been associated with this type of audit, but public accountants and management consultants are also active in the field. The roots of operational auditing go in at least three directions. Besides internal auditors, the management profession and government accountants have played major roles in the development of the concept as it is practiced today.

Role of the Internal Auditor

Although internal auditors are the most typical performers of operational audits, such activity has not always been among the internal auditor's duties. The profession of internal auditing has changed considerably over the past half century.

During the 1940s, internal auditors began to expand their audits to encompass much more than the traditional financial audit. The first article published in *Internal Auditor* that described the expanded-scope audit was Arthur H. Kent's "Audits of Operations," in the March 1948 issue. Earlier authors had discussed the subject, but they had referred to "nonaccounting matters" instead of "operational subjects." The first paper to use the phrase "operational auditing" in the title was written by Frederic E. Mints and published in *Internal Auditor* in June 1954 and entitled "Operational Auditing." Mints later recalled that the term "operational" evolved in a 1953 brainstorming session with Kent. The two men considered several labels and finally decided "operational" had the most ear appeal.

Role of the GAO

The U.S. General Accounting Office (GAO) has played a major part in broadening the role of the auditor. That organization's publication, *Standards for Audit of Governmental Organizations, Programs, Activities, and Functions* (commonly called the "Yellow Book" because of the color of its cover) states that governmental audits should go a step beyond those standards and procedures that are applicable to audits of financial statements. The scope of a governmental audit is composed of three elements: (1) financial and compliance, (2) economy and efficiency, and (3) program results.

Congress played a role in getting the GAO involved in operational auditing by passing, in 1945, the Government Corporation Control Act, which provided the initial steps toward the modernization of GAO auditing as it is known today. Comptroller General Lindsay C. Warren had been a supporter of the audit legislation and quickly moved to establish the Corporation Audits Division in July 1945. Warren called upon the American Institute of Accountants (AIA) to recommend personnel who had extensive experience in public accounting in the private sector. John Carey, then executive secretary of the AIA, recommended T. Coleman Andrews, the senior partner of the Richmond, Virginia, CPA firm that bore his name.

From the beginning, Andrews conceived of the division's audits in broader terms than was typical for audits of private business. This was attributable to the specific requirements of the Corporation Control Act, which called for not only examination of financial statements and controls, but also reports to Congress on financial condition, impairments of capital, recommendations for the return of government capital or payment of dividends, and the effectiveness with which corporations were carrying out their objectives. The act and the manner in which it was carried out presaged the emphasis given in the early 1950s to program evaluation and comprehensive audits.

The audit reports issued by the Corporation Audits Division were similar to the reports issued by modern internal auditors, but at the time such reports were unique. In fact, Andrews bragged on the feature of having the report begin with a summary of the highlights of the auditors' findings. This was done to conserve the time of members of Congress.

In 1947, after having been on the job two years, Andrews left the GAO to head up the accounting and auditing study group of the Commission on Organization of the Executive Branch of the Government (the Hoover Commission). Andrews had accomplished the task of establishing an audit division in the federal government. His accomplishments did not go unnoticed; he received the AIA's Gold Medal Award for distinguished service to the profession.

Not only was the GAO innovative in the scope of its audits, but it was successful in meeting the objectives for which the broadened scope was intended. The successes of the GAO were reported in newspapers and in journals such as *Internal Auditor*. As a result, internal auditors in industry took steps to broaden the scope of their own audits.

Recognition by the AICPA

The work of the GAO led the American Institute of Certified Public Accountants (AICPA) to get more actively involved in the area of operational auditing. In fact, the AICPA published a small book entitled *Guidelines for CPA Participation in Government Audit Engagements to Evaluate Economy, Efficiency, and Program Results* (1977).

The AICPA formed a special committee in 1978 on operational auditing. The committee's charge was to research the subject and develop appropriate information for AICPA members. The committee's report was published in 1982 under the title *Operational Audit Engagements*. The conclusion reached was that an operational-audit engagement, when conducted by a CPA in public practice, is a management advisory service (MAS) that has some of the characteristics of a financial-audit engagement. Thus, CPAs seeking the standards applicable to operational audits should refer to the standards for MAS practice issued by the AICPA's MAS Division. Of most significance, this publication recognized that public accountants were important performers of operational audits—an activity traditionally associated with internal and government auditors.

Developments in the Management Profession

At the same time that internal auditors were developing the concept of operational auditing, a similar activity called management auditing was being developed by the management profession. The first book on the subject, *The Management Audit,* authored by T.G. Rose, was published in 1932 in London. That book recommended a questionnaire interview designed to analyze departmental activities.

In 1940 the Metropolitan Life Insurance Company published a similar guide entitled *Outline for a Management Audit.* The Metropolitan publication expanded upon the work of Rose but was not nearly as sophisticated as Howard G. Benedict's *Yardsticks of Management,* which was published in 1948. Benedict's questionnaire attempted to evaluate management with factorial analysis. These works were the earliest attempts at developing an interview type of management audit, but none of them generated much interest among management professionals.

In 1950 Jackson Martindell, president of the American Institute of Management, published *The Scientific Appraisal of Management,* which was a study of the business practices of what he considered well-managed companies. That book was the precursor of the American Institute of Management's work in the field of management auditing. Martindell's management auditing evolved from a study he conducted of companies that survived the Great Depression. The study identified the common factors of the surviving companies. By the early 1960s, the fields of management auditing and operational auditing began to merge as internal auditors saw the benefits of the management literature. Today the two terms are considered synonymous.

One of the first individuals to merge the work of the two fields was William Leonard in his 1962 book, *The Management Audit*. Although Leonard called himself a "consulting management engineer," his sources included a number of articles from both management and internal auditing publications. Leonard departed from the reliance on questionnaires recommended by his management predecessors. He placed more emphasis on development of audit programs and use of working papers—a decidedly internal-audit orientation.

Development in Other English-Speaking Nations

Outside of the United States, the concept of operational auditing is better known as value-for-money (VFM) or comprehensive auditing. VFM is a rather new phenomenon in most countries. It has been the public sector in other nations that has been responsible for the development of VFM. Canada was the first English-speaking nation other than the United States to experiment with VFM. J.J. Macdonell, a partner in a large firm of management consultants, was appointed as auditor general of Canada in 1972. In 1980, under the leadership of Macdonell, the Canadian Comprehensive Auditing Foundation (CCAF) was established. CCAF's objective is to serve as a center for disseminating comprehensive auditing experience.

Value-for-money auditing has even a shorter history in the United Kingdom. In fact, little has been accomplished in the private sector. The public sector has provided some impetus toward VFM audits. A 1977 Scottish report, of the Layfield Committee of enquiry into local government finance, recommended the inclusion of efficiency auditing in the government audit function. However, it was not until the election to power of a Conservative government in 1979 that efficiency audits received major attention. Finally, in 1981, it was announced that the Monopolies and Mergers Commission would carry out efficiency audits of nationalized industries. This was followed in 1982 by the Local Government Finance Act, which required local government auditors to conduct audits of efficiency, effectiveness, and economy.

Although the Institute of Internal Auditors (IIA) may not have been the originator of the concept, it can be credited with keeping the concept alive and supporting its growth. As the IIA has grown in stature, so too has the concept of operational auditing.

Dale L. Flesher

Bibliography
Flesher, D.L. *The Institute of Internal Auditors: Fifty Years of Progress through Sharing*. Altamonte Springs, FL: Institute of Internal Auditors, 1991.

Glynn, J.J. *Value-for-Money Auditing in the Public Sector*. London: Prentice-Hall International, 1985.

Mints, F.E. "Operational Auditing," *Internal Auditor*, June 1954, pp. 32–45.

Parker, L.D. *Value-For-Money Auditing: Conceptual, Development, and Operational Issues*. Caulfield, Victoria: Australian Accounting Research Foundation, 1986.

U.S. General Accounting Office. *Standards for Audit of Governmental Organizations, Programs, Activities, and Functions*. Washington, DC: GPO, 1972.

See also AMERICAN INSTITUTE OF CERTIFIED ACCOUNTANTS; CANADA; GENERAL ACCOUNTING OFFICE, U.S.; INSTITUTE OF INTERNAL AUDITORS; INTERNAL AUDITING

Opportunity Cost

The relevant costs for decision making are those that will be different depending on whether or not a particular action is taken. It is natural for businessmen to think in these terms, and early authors calculated the effect on profits of sowing different kinds of grain and of using different kinds of factory lighting. The first formal analyses of differential costs were made by neoclassical economists late in the nineteenth century. Pointing out that "In commerce, bygones are forever bygones," English economist W.S. Jevons in 1871 maintained that asset values depend on future utility rather than historical cost. The Austrian economist Friedrich von Wieser in 1876 first expressed the idea that the cost of any article is the value of productive forces that could have been employed elsewhere but instead were bound up in it. In 1894 the American economist D.I. Green reasoned that because the number of good opportunities is usually limited and since choosing one usually means forgoing others, the cost of these forgoings in effect becomes the cost of the opportunity chosen.

Economic theorists were not writing for, and were rarely read by practicing accountants and businessmen, and neither training nor experience fitted most accountants to think in terms of future alternative costs. The opportunity cost concept was seldom mentioned in American cost accounting literature before the 1950s. It became "generally accepted" by financial accountants only in the 1970s.

Michael Chatfield

Bibliography

Gould, J.F. "Opportunity Cost: The London Tradition." In *Debits, Credits, Finance, and Profits,* edited by H. Edey and B.S. Yamey, pp. 91–107. London: Sweet and Maxwell, 1974.

Parker, R.H. *Management Accounting: An Historical Perspective.* New York: Augustus M. Kelley, 1969.

See also IMPUTED INTEREST ON CAPITAL

P

Pacioli, Luca (c. 1445–c. 1517)

The first published work describing the double entry accounting system and giving us insight into the logic behind the accounting entries is the *Summa de Arithmetica, Geometria, Proportioni et Proportionalità*. Accounting is treated in Part 1, Section 9, Treatise 11, under the title of "Particularis de Computis et Scripturis" ("Particulars of Reckonings and Their Recordings"). The *Summa* was published in Venice by Luca Pacioli in 1494. Pacioli's *Summa* is commonly accepted as the foundation of modern accounting practices. But it should be noted that the first known treatise on bookkeeping appears to be that of Benedetto Cotrugli (*Della mercatura et del mercante perfetto, libri quattro scritti già più di anni CX ed hora dati in luce*), completed in Naples in 1458 but not published until 1573 in Venice, by the publisher all'Elefante. It is significant that Pacioli's *Summa* was printed only some 25 years after the first printing press with movable metal type was set up in Venice.

The name of the author of *Summa* does not appear next to the title of the work, but one reads "Frater Luca de Burgo Sancti Sepulcri" at carta 1(verso), 3(recto), 4(recto) and in the last carta 76(recto) of the treatise on geometry. In other books that he authored, he used the Latin name Patiolus, which most biographers translate to the Italian name Pacioli, while Luca is the Italian for the Latin Lucas. So there is some disagreement about the spelling of his name. The Tuscan usage is Luca Pacioli, while, if the first name is omitted, one can read "il Paciolo."

Pacioli is not only the first significant writer on double entry, he is also the most important one of this period. While Pacioli was not the originator of double entry bookkeeping, his book, primarily a treatise on mathematics, did much to spread the use of double entry bookkeeping beyond the boundaries of Italy throughout all of Europe and the world (partly by translations, partly through being transplanted to other countries by Venetian traders and clerks) and caused it to be known as the Venetian method or the Italian method. All of the accounting books published during the sixteenth century in other European countries, particularly in Germany, the Netherlands, and England, presented descriptions of bookkeeping similar to that one by Pacioli.

Repeatedly Pacioli stated that he described a system of bookkeeping that had been in use in Venice for more than 200 years, with the purpose of acquainting the merchants of his time with the method for keeping in good order their accounting books (chap. 1). Thus he did not mention things that were common practice a long time before 1494, as his treatise was a text for the untutored. Hence, Pacioli omitted most of the refinements common in practice of that day.

Pacioli was born at Borgo San Sepolcro, Tuscany. He was a Franciscan friar who devoted most of his life to teaching and scholarship, studying mainly mathematics and theology and becoming prominent in both fields, which he taught in many Italian cities and five universities (Florence, Milan, Perugia, Naples, and Rome).

Along with his peers, Piero della Francesca, Leon Battista Alberti, Federico the Duke of Urbino, Ludovico Sforza, Leonardo da Vinci, Leonardo da Pisa, Raphael, Michelangelo, Pope Sixtus V, and Pope Julius II, Pacioli represented the "all purpose" man of the Renaissance, eager to absorb and disseminate new ideas. This reputation was due to the *Summa*; *De Divina Proportione*, his second major book, published in 1509; and to other writings. He believed particularly in those disciplines exhibiting a natural harmony and balance, with the ideas of perspective, proportion, and symmetry, and continually stressed the duality, integrating tendencies, and balancing features of double entry methodology.

Pacioli never claimed to have invented double entry bookkeeping. He refers from time to time to Leonardo of Pisa (Fibonacci), who wrote in 1202 the famous *Liber Abaci*, and states that his own book is not original; it is a synthesis of several handwritten books. Fabio Besta considers it to be a reworked version of a fifteenth-century bookkeeping manuscript by Troilo de' Cancellaris.

"Particularis de Computis et Scripturis" is written in 36 chapters, from carta 197(verso) to 210(verso). It is divided into two principal arguments: inventory and disposition. The contents of the treatise can be summarized in the following main points: (1) things necessary to the merchant; (2) inventory; (3) three mercantile books: memorial, journal, and ledger; (4) authentication of accounting books; (5) the memorial; (6) the journal; (7) the ledger; (8) entries of facts related to purchases of goods, to barters, to companies; (9) entries connected to relations with public concerns; (10) expenses accounts; (11) the inventory account; (12) the profit and loss account; (13) correction of mistakes; (14) the closing of accounts; (15) filing the correspondence; (16) peculiarities about the "merchants book."

The general ledger stands in the center of Pacioli's system. The journal is the instrument for the correct posting on the general ledger accounts. It is the function of the memorial to record everything that has to do with the mercantile enterprise. The memorial is the source of the data that lead to the debiting and crediting of accounts and the drafting of journal entries for the transactions.

The method of double entry begins with an explanation of the "inventario," inventory statement (chaps. 2, 3). This is a list of all the assets and liabilities, which the owner should prepare before he starts business; it is a statement of his financial position. This inventory, to be completed in one day, is to be recorded in the journal at current market prices (chap. 12).

The crucial point in Pacioli's argument is that all items ought to be posted in *debito* and in *credito*. In that way, an equilibrium is created. Every transaction must be entered in the memorial with full explanation and in the particular monetary unit in which it was concluded. Everything that is entered in the journal must first be entered in the memorial (chap. 10). The exception is the inventory statement and all the mutations therein; these items are directly entered into the journal. In journalizing, all foreign monetary units are reduced to Venetian money (chap. 12).

For the closing procedure of the old books and the opening of the ones for the new period, Pacioli organizes the accounts in two groups. The first consists of the accounts that the businessman must have again in the new book, such as cash, capital, the merchandise account, claims and debts. The balances that the businessman does not want to bring forward to the new general ledger, such as expenses and revenues, are transferred to the profit and loss account, which in turn is balanced and carried to the capital account. The final entry closes the capital account, and its balance is transferred to a new account in the new general ledger (chap. 34).

Pacioli did not grasp the full meaning of the trial balance, or he would have drawn it up first instead of checking all journal entries against the ledger to prove its correctness. Pacioli says nothing about a balance-sheet account in his system of accounts. There is no connection between the closing and reopening of the books and the preparation of the balance sheet. Therefore, the balance sheet in Pacioli's system is not the financial statement in the modern sense—that is, the capital account—but merely the trial balance, which presents, however, only the sums of the accounts' values, *summa summarium*, without the balances of the accounts.

Pacioli was concerned also with internal controls. He recommended that the three books be numbered and dated and that their pages be prenumbered, that transaction documents be complete in detail and permanently filed, and that the books be audited for internal check.

Pacioli stated that the major objective of accounting was to provide without delay information for the owner about his assets and liabilities. It also provided a means for reporting on stewardship and a basis for the granting of credit. As a result, the accounts were to be held in secrecy and there was no external pressure for accuracy or uniform standards of reporting.

The reporting covered all of the personal and business affairs of a proprietor. Pacioli stated that the inventory should include cash, valuables, clothes, household goods, and other properties of the owner. However, there is some evidence to support that the business was a separate entity from the personal affairs of the owner. Moreover, he recommended that a partner's contribution of cash, property, or credits should be debited for their value and the partner's capital account should be credited for the same value. Pacioli made no mention of accruing and deferring revenues and expenses; that was not necessary because most business undertakings were ventures with short, definable lifespans.

Most financial information was taken directly from the ledger accounts. Statements were normally prepared only at the end of a major project, such as a trading voyage or after all the pages in a ledger had been filled. In Pacioli's view, the final results of the bookkeeping cycle consisted of operating totals summarized in proprietary capital and income accounts. Though Pacioli never mentions financial statements or periodic income determination, he recommended annual balancing for the main purpose of detecting the errors.

The basic framework for the double entry process and most of the accounting methodology detailed by Pacioli have remained unchanged for 500 years. Apart from the electronic equipment performing the accounting process, the entire structure governing these processes is the same as it was when Pacioli outlined it in 1494.

The theory underlying Pacioli's treatise (accounting is viewed as a mathematical problem, and it serves to create order in the mass of data) is even more contemporary. In making explicit the mathematical logic underlying double entry, he went to the roots of modern accounting theory.

Giuseppe Galassi

Bibliography

Besta, F. *La ragioneria*. 3 vols. Milano: Vallardi, 1891–1916.
Crivelli, P. *An Original Translation of the Treatise on Double-Entry Bookkeeping by Frater Lucas Pacioli*. London: N.p., 1924.
Geijsbeek, J.B. *Ancient Double Entry Bookkeeping: Lucas Pacioli's Treatise*. Denver: Geijsbeek, 1914. Reprint. Houston: Scholars Book, 1974.
Melis, F. *Storia della ragioneria. Contributo alla conoscenza e interpretazione delle fonti più significative della storia economica*. Bologna: Zuffi, 1950.
Peragallo, E. *Origin and Evolution of Double Entry Bookkeeping: A Study of Italian Practice from the Fourteenth Century*. New York: American Institute Publishing, 1938. Reprint. Osaka: Nihon Shoseki, 1974.
Weis, W.L., D.E. Tinius, and C. Burke. *Luca Pacioli: Unsung Hero of the Renaissance*. Cincinnati: South-Western, 1990, videocassette.

See also BALANCE SHEET; BARBARIGO, ANDREA; BARTER; CASH BASIS ACCOUNTING; CLOSING ENTRIES AND PROCEDURES; CONSERVATISM; COTRUGLI, BENEDETTO; DEBIT AND CREDIT; DOUBLE ENTRY BOOKKEEPING: ORIGINS; GERMANY; HISTORICAL COST; IJIRI, YUJI; INCOME-DETERMINATION THEORY; INCOME STATEMENT/INCOME ACCOUNT; INTERNAL CONTROL; INVENTORY VALUATION; ITALY, AFTER PACIOLI; JONES, EDWARD THOMAS; JOURNAL; KOJIMA, OSAMU; LEDGER; LEONARDO OF PISA; LIQUIDITY: ACCOUNTING MEASUREMENT; MANZONI, DOMENICO; MEDIEVAL ACCOUNTING; MEMORANDUM BOOK; MONEY; NETHERLANDS; OLDCASTLE, HUGH; PEELE, JAMES; PERIODICITY; PERSONIFICATION OF ACCOUNTS; PRINTING PRESS; PROPRIETORSHIP; SMITH, ADAM; STEVELINCK, ERNEST JEAN LEON; STEVIN, SIMON; SUBSIDIARY LEDGER; *SUMMA SUMMARIUM;* TRANSFER PRICES; TRIAL BALANCE; YMPYN, JAN

Packard, Silas Sadler (1826–1898)

Silas Sadler Parker was a leader in the reform of business education during the second half of the nineteenth century. He was an educator, an accountant, a proprietor of a commercial school in New York, and a leading author of textbooks on the subject of accounts and bookkeeping. He was the president of the Institute of Accounts, the first professional accounting organization in the United States, when the first CPA legislation in the country was enacted in New York State in April 1896. Packard was recognized as a good speaker, writer, and organizational leader.

Born in Cummington, Massachusetts, he was the fourth son of Chester and Eunice Packard. In 1833 when Silas was 7 years old, the Packards moved to Ohio, traveling the entire distance from Troy, New York, by water for a month. He spent his childhood and adolescent years growing up in an old log cabin until around 1840. Packard attended the district school and then the nearby Granville Academy. He enjoyed grammar and mathematics and was considered the best penman, showing a talent for writing at an early age.

At the age of 16, he began his career in education, which he pursued successfully throughout his life, by teaching penmanship classes at country schools. In 1845 he went to Kentucky, where he remained over two years as a teacher and a master of a school while also taking up the avocation of painting portraits. He moved to Cincinnati in 1848 to teach penmanship at Bartlett's Commercial College, and then bookkeeping, the field in which he excelled during the rest of his professional career. In the fall of 1851 he moved to Lockport, New York, to teach writing, bookkeeping, and drawing at a union school; in 1853 he moved to Buffalo, where he established a weekly newspaper, the *Niagara River Pilot*. He managed this publication successfully until he became associated with H.B. Bryant and H.D. Stratton, the owners of a chain of commercial colleges.

In his early years with Bryant and Stratton, Packard helped manage the Buffalo branch of the chain and was also involved in promoting the chain in Chicago and Albany. In 1858 Packard bought out the Bryant and Stratton school in New York and established it as Packard's Business College. It proved to be very successful and became a model for other business schools not only in the United States, but also in France and Belgium.

Packard was a leader in the movement to modernize business education in the latter half of the nineteenth century. He was recognized as one of the first business college proprietors to sense the importance of furnishing students with the social philosophy of business education. He molded the characters of his students toward high ideals, cleanness of conduct, and morality in business and trade. Packard fostered the education of women and was one of the leaders in persuading the business world that accuracy, punctuality, and capability were not questions of sex, but of training. His "Friday Morning Talks" were well remembered by former students of Packard's Business College, who were always proud to be called "Packard Boys" or "Packard Girls."

At the Chicago World's Fair in 1893, Packard organized a highly successful and well-attended exhibit that further served to spread his business education philosophy and methods.

His association with Bryant and Stratton involved him in compiling Bryant and Stratton's National Bookkeeping, a series of textbooks first published in 1860. In 1863, the premier textbook he authored for the chain, *Counting House Book-Keeping*, was published and soon became a standard text, not only in commercial schools in America but also abroad. A second text, published in 1868, *Manual of Theoretical Training in the Science of Accounts*, gained popularity in Japan during the revolution of accounting in that country in the last decades of the 1800s. In 1878 *The New Bryant and Stratton Counting House Book-Keeping* was published. A revision of the 1863 text, it covered not only the practical aspects of maintaining business records, but also some attempts to delineate the truthful theories behind intelligent business records. The first three chapters developed an important discussion regarding the acquisition of wealth and the problems of measurement as well as the process of producing value. There were also materials describing how to account for transactions of commission merchant and banking business. There were examples of the settlement of a completed partnership and of interest calculations. He also published *Packard's Monthly of Bookkeeping* for almost two years until March 1870.

Packard believed in the essentially scientific nature of accounting and the useful role it could play in addressing contemporary social problems. He believed that accounting is not merely a collection of rules: A true accountant thinks out with mathematical accuracy the activities of business and the state of its financial condition to represent *causes* and *effects* of business activities. According to Packard, accounting is both a practical and a serious matter. Behind accounting records, there lie philosophical facts that illustrate satisfactorily many fundamental truths addressed in the domain of economics. Therefore, the duty of a good accountant is not only to keep the books, but to tell what they mean. He expressed his views about the philosophical dimension of accounting on several occasions to the Institute of Accountants and Bookkeepers (later renamed the Institute of Accounts). "The Unlearned Profession," a speech he delivered at the institute's meetings, and his article, "Philosophy in Book-Keeping," in the semimonthly *The Book-Keeper*, December 6, 1881, summarized his feeling about accounting and its education. Packard often said, "The only office I ever want is that of school master, the most sacred and important office of all."

Packard was the first president of the Business Educators Association of America, which was organized in 1878, and the first president of Commercial Teachers Federation, founded in 1896. He participated in the organizations of the National Educational Association and the New York Commercial Teachers Association.

Friends held a complimentary banquet on April 28, 1896, at Delmonico's in New York City to celebrate Packard's 70th birthday. More than 200 guests, from all over the United States and from Canada, attended. Numerous speakers, including the mayor of New York, praised Packard, who was presented with a special award acknowledging his contributions to society. The banquet was held only a few days after the Governor of New York signed into law a bill establishing licensing for CPAs, the first such legislation in the country. Charles Ezra Sprague acknowledged in his speech at the banquet Packard's instrumental role in passage of the legislation for the benefit of accountants in the state.

Hekinus Manao

Bibliography

Packard, S.S. "Philosophy in Book-Keeping," *The Book-Keeper*, December 6, 1881, pp. 131–132.

———. *The New Bryant and Stratton Counting House Book-Keeping*. New York: Ivison, Blakeman, Taylor, 1878.

Previts, G.J., and B.D. Merino. *A History of Accounting in America: An Historical Interpretation of the Cultural Significance of Accounting*. New York: John Wiley & Sons, 1979.

Testimonial Banquet to S.S.Packard. Privately printed, 1896.

See also ACCOUNTING EDUCATION IN THE UNITED STATES; CERTIFIED PUBLIC ACCOUNTANT; JAPAN; MEMORANDUM BOOK; SPRAGUE, CHARLES EZRA

Paid In Capital

Paid in capital is the total market value of assets and services invested in a corporation by its stockholders. A corporation cannot rationally claim to be a going concern with indefinite life while dissipating its invested capital. To make sure that contributed capital was maintained intact, a series of nineteenth-century court decisions, reinforced by statutes in Britain and the United States, mandated that dividends could be declared only from current and retained earnings.

This capital maintenance doctrine required that the flow of wealth from investors (paid in capital) be accounted for separately from the flow of wealth from customers (retained earnings). But in the absence of specific accounting rules, corporate managements found it easy to blur the distinction between contributed capital and earned income. In a 1930 article, J.M.B. Hoxsey of the New York Stock Exchange criticized American corporations for paying dividends from capital. In *A Tentative Statement of Accounting Principles Underlying Corporate Financial Statements* (1936), the American Accounting Association finally made the first precise distinctions between the contents of the paid in capital and the retained earnings accounts.

Michael Chatfield

Bibliography

Hoxsey, J.M.B. "Accounting for Investors," *Journal of Accountancy*, 1930, pp. 251–284.

Littleton, A.C. *Accounting Evolution to 1900*. New York: American Institute Publishing, 1933. Reprint. New York: Russell and Russell, 1966.

See also AMERICAN ACCOUNTING ASSOCIATION; CAPITAL MAINTENANCE; DIVIDENDS; HOXSEY, J.M.B.; NEW YORK STOCK EXCHANGE; RETAINED EARNINGS

Par Value Doctrine

Italian *commenda* partnerships were direct ancestors of the limited liability corporation. During the Renaissance, investors evaded church usury laws, which held that money was barren, by entrusting their cash to overseas traders for a share in the profits of joint ventures. Besides combining venture capital and trading ability, the partnership contract *en commendite* established the precedent that while trading partners were fully liable for partnership debits, a nonparticipating investor might get a share of profits while risking only the amount of his investment.

Influenced by Italian practice, many European commercial codes made a distinction between the liability of active and silent partners, holding the latter responsible only to the extent of their contribution. The French Code Savary of 1673 provided specifically for limited partnerships in the Italian manner. But in England, the concept of partnership rested on the agency relationship, in which each partner could bind the others and all were jointly and severally liable for debts. This made corporations hard to establish in the nation that first required them on a large scale. Early in the seventeenth century, several English corporations extended a type of limited liability to their investors as an inducement to buy stock. The par value doctrine did not protect stockholders' personal assets from company creditors, but merely guaranteed subscribers to fully paid shares that the corporation would not call on them for further capital contributions.

Today's par value shares are issued with a nominal price printed on each stock certificate. This par value may have no relationship to the stock's original sale price or subsequent market value. Its purpose is to establish the contingent liability of stockholders if the corporation becomes insolvent or bankrupt. If stock is issued at or above par value and the corporation later incurs liabilities it cannot repay, stockholders may lose their entire investment but cannot lose more. But if stock is issued below par value and the corporation cannot subsequently repay its debts, the creditors can force original purchasers of the stock to pay into the corporation the amount of discount on their shares. In that case, stockholders may lose their original investment plus an amount equal to the discount at which they purchased the stock. This contingent liability is due to the corporation's creditors, not to the corporation. It becomes an actual liability only if the amount of the discount is needed to pay creditors when the corporation is liquidated.

Michael Chatfield

Bibliography

Littleton, A.C. *Accounting Evolution to 1900*. New York: American Institute Publishing, 1933. Reprint. New York: Russell and Russell, 1966.

See also CAPITAL STOCK; COMMENDA CONTRACTS; CORPORATIONS: EVOLUTION; FRANCE; LIMITED LIABILITY

Parker, Robert Henry (1932–)

A British academic of world renown in the areas of accounting history and comparative accounting, Robert Henry Parker was born and educated in Norfolk and, as a pastime, has traced his family's long roots there. Like many accounting academics of his generation, he studied economics at the University of London. After graduation he qualified in 1958 as a chartered accountant in London. Soon after, he went to Nigeria for a year or so, with a firm that later joined Peat Marwick, and then to Adelaide briefly as a lecturer and Perth until 1966 as a senior lecturer. So began a distinguished academic career and a lifelong association with Australia. His earliest book (Bennett, Grant, and Parker 1964) was published there; the next (Parker and Harcourt 1969), with another Adelaide colleague, is a classic.

His return to Europe saw Parker at the London School of Economics; at Manchester Business School as a reader in management accounting; at the Institut Européen d'Administration des Affaires (INSEAD); at Dundee, where, in addition to teaching, he served as dean of the law faculty; and finally since 1976 at Exeter. Meanwhile, there have been frequent stays in, or trips to, Australasia, particularly Sydney.

Books and papers have continued to flood from Parker's pen, unstemmed by increasing rank, age, or administrative pressures. His papers can be found in most of the world's leading accounting journals, including even the *Journal of Accounting Research* in the days when his topics would be considered for such a journal. Parker is keen on things classical but prefers to keep Greek out of accounting articles. He has written many serious, clear articles in the professional press that are of great value to enquiring practitioners and students. His books range from somewhat obscure, scholarly accounting history (Parker and Pryce-Jones 1974, or Kitchen and Parker 1980), to a major collection of his papers on history (Parker 1984), to a standard textbook (Nobes and Parker 1981), to "popular" work (Parker 1972). Perhaps his most obvious specialisms have been nineteenth-century Anglo-Saxon accountancy and international aspects of consolidation, but no one could usefully accuse Parker of having narrow interests, and new researchers in many fields often find an old Parker paper that addressed many of the problems years ago.

In many ways, Parker is one of the Grand Old Men of academic accounting in the close-knit enclave of the United Kingdom and Australia. For some years now, a large proportion of senior accounting scholars have either worked with him, written with him, been appointed to chairs by a committee containing him or advised by him, used him as a personal referee, or been examined for a Ph.D. by him. He was an *eminence grise* in the formation of what is now the British Accounting Association and founded the predecessor to the *British Accounting Review*. He edited one of the United Kingdom's major academic journals (*Accounting and Business Research*) from 1975, has sat on several editorial boards, and has served on research-oriented committees of professional accountancy bodies. Since 1991 a Professorial Fellow of the Scottish Institute, he has long been a prominent contributor to international conferences. Parker has also brought to accounting his irreverence, lack of conservatism, and general irrepressibility. Together with his scholarship and service, they have contributed to his success in launching, fostering, or molding the careers of many now successful academics, which will be perhaps his most influential achievement.

Christopher Nobes

Bibliography

Bennett, J.W., J. McB. Grant, and R.H. Parker. *Topics in Business Finance and Accounting.* Melbourne: Cheshire, 1964.

Kitchen, J., and R.H. Parker. *Accounting Thought and Education: Six English Pioneers.* London: Institute of Chartered Accountants in England and Wales, 1980.

Nobes, C.W., and R.H. Parker. *Comparative International Accounting.* Oxford: Philip Allan, 1981, 1985; London: Prentice-Hall International, 1991.

Parker, R.H. *Papers on Accounting History.* New York: Garland, 1984.

———. *Understanding Company Financial Statements.* Harmondsworth: Penguin, 1972, 1982, 1988.

Parker, R.H., and G. Harcourt. *Readings in the Concept and Measurement of Income.* Cambridge: Cambridge University Press, 1969, 1985.

Parker, R.H., and J. Pryce-Jones. *Accounting in Scotland: A Historical Bibliography.* Edinburgh: Institute of Chartered Accountants of Scotland, 1974, 1976.

See also CAPITAL MAINTENANCE; PIXLEY, FRANCIS WILLIAM; SCOTLAND: EARLY WRITERS IN DOUBLE ENTRY ACCOUNTING; SOLOMONS, DAVID; ZEFF, STEPHEN A.

Partnership Accounting

The partnership form was an important factor in the emergence of double entry bookkeeping. As their operations expanded, Renaissance businessmen found that accounting methods which worked well in a small proprietorship broke down when a merchant began trading through a network of factors and international partnerships. Unsystematic accounting records limited the size of such businesses and, beyond a certain point of growth and dispersion, caused so much disorder that owners lost control of distant operations.

During the Renaissance most large firms were partnerships. To divide profits fairly, they needed an accounting system in which all transactions were recorded. A proprietorship might mix business and personal assets, but a partnership had to strictly segregate them. The formation of long-lasting partnerships led to the recognition that such businesses were entities in their own right and that capital and income represented claims of the owners. An accounting system which produced automatic capital and profit balances had obvious attractions for them.

From the earliest Florentine *bilancio* in the fourteenth century, partnership income had been calculated as the difference between the net assets of two successive accounting periods. The admission or withdrawal of partners legally dissolved such businesses and required a fresh calculation of capital balances. Merely closing partnership books might not suffice, because then only the bookkeeping partner would preserve a record of the situation at that moment. The need for asset revaluations at the time of ownership changes also called for a separate schedule of resources and debts—in effect, a balance sheet.

The essential problem of the partnership form was that certain partners wished to trade actively while others merely wanted to invest. During the Renaissance investors evaded the church usury laws, which held that money was barren, by entrusting their cash to overseas traders for a share in the profits of joint ventures. Besides nicely combining capital with trading ability, these *commenda* contracts established the precedent that while trading partners were fully liable for partnership debts, a nonparticipating investor might get a share of profits while risking only the amount of his investment.

Influenced by Italian practice, European commercial codes made a distinction between the liability of active and silent partners, holding the latter responsible only to the extent of their investment. The French Code Savary of 1673 provided specifically for limited liability partnerships in the Italian manner. But in England, the concept of partnership rested on the agency relationship, in which each partner could legally bind the others and all were jointly and severally liable for company debts. This made limited liability corporations especially hard to establish in the nation that first required them on a large scale.

The earliest English joint-stock companies were partnerships with a few corporate features. They generally had limited life and imposed unlimited liability for company debts, but they also in many cases issued transferable shares. In chartering companies such as the Bank of England, whose activities touched vital national interests, the government allowed shareholders individual immunity from the bankruptcy laws if the firm failed. The effect was to make stockholders liable for company debts only up to the amount unpaid on their shares.

The South Sea Company was the most spectacular joint-stock company, and the one with major accounting implications. It was chartered in 1710, mainly to fund about 10 million pounds of floating national debt. Then, during England's first great era of stock speculation, the company decided to take over the entire national debt and pay for it by issuing large amounts of new stock. The directors inflated share prices by selling stock on 10 percent margin, spreading rumors of dividends, and offering prospective investors loans equal to half the stock's market value. In 1720, after wild speculation, stock prices fell to 15 percent of their highest level. Finally, there was not enough money in the country to meet subscription installments as they came due or to buy the shares that were being thrown on the market. Though the company continued in business for another 130 years, millions of pounds of investor funds had been lost, and the nation's com-

mercial development was slowed for half a century. A secret parliamentary committee, appointed to investigate, found that the company's accounts had been altered. A director was imprisoned in the Tower of London and the estates of others were confiscated.

The final result of this speculative frenzy was popularly known as the Bubble Act of 1720. This act denied limited liability to all firms not incorporated by Crown Charter or special act of Parliament, both cumbersome and very expensive processes. The Bubble Act was also used as a policy instrument to restrain the formation of new corporations. Its effect was to inhibit the growth of limited liability companies between 1720 and 1844.

This prohibition came at the worst possible time, retarding at the start of the industrial revolution the type of enterprise most suitable for rapid industrial expansion. Eighteenth-century manufacturers were forced to establish partnerships in which every partner, no matter how small his investment, was by law personally responsible for all the company's debts. Being unable to protect their investors, such partnerships had very limited ability to raise capital. They often consisted of a large, fluctuating group of individuals, and a person dealing with the partnership might not be sure with whom he was contracting.

A final penalty for failing to incorporate was that most eighteenth-century businessmen had no clear concept of capital as "wealth for profit" seeking a maximum return. Their accountants did not calculate return on investment in the modern sense. Worse, they failed to see that capital produced income. The profit of large industrial partnerships was commonly understood to be the surplus remaining after interest was paid to partners on their invested capital. This residual income was considered the businessman's reward for risk taking, ingenuity, or sheer luck, not for investing *per se*. Thus, capital in such partnerships was peripheral, not central to accounting measurements. It was simply a factor of production paid for by interest at the market rate.

Michael Chatfield

Bibliography
Carswell, J. *The South Sea Bubble.* Palo Alto, CA: Stanford University Press, 1960.
De Roover, F.E. "Partnership Accounts in Twelfth Century Genoa." In *Studies in the History of Accounting,* edited by

A.C. Littleton and B.S. Yamey, pp. 86–90. Homewood, IL: Irwin, 1956.

De Roover, R. "The Development of Accounting prior to Luca Pacioli according to the Account-books of Medieval Merchants." In *Studies in the History of Accounting*, edited by A.C. Littleton and B.S. Yamey, pp. 114–174. Homewood, IL: Irwin, 1956.

Littleton, A.C. *Accounting Evolution to 1900*. New York: American Institute Publishing, 1933. Reprint. New York: Russell and Russell, 1966.

Pollard, S. *The Genesis of Modern Management: A Study of the Industrial Revolution in Great Britain*. London: Edward Arnold, 1965.

Watzlaff, R.H. "The Bubble Act of 1720," *Abacus*, June 1971, pp. 8–28.

See also ALBERTI DEL GIUDICE; CAPITAL STOCK; *COMMENDA* CONTRACTS; CORPORATIONS: EVOLUTION; DOUBLE ENTRY BOOKKEEPING: ORIGINS; FRANCE; LIMITED LIABILITY; PROPRIETORSHIP; SEPARATE ENTITIES; SOUTH SEA BUBBLE

Paton, William Andrew (1889–1991)

William Andrew Paton was a distinguished financial accounting theorist and a prolific author who spent most of his career at the University of Michigan as a professor of accounting and economics. With A.C. Littleton, he coauthored the accounting classic *An Introduction to Corporate Accounting Standards* (1940). Paton also wrote *Accounting Theory: With Special Reference to the Corporate Enterprise* (1922) (essentially his 1917 Ph.D. dissertation in economics), several textbooks ranging from introductory through advanced accounting, other books, and over 100 articles. He received many honors, including the American Institute of Certified Public Accountants' Accounting Educator of the Century and Gold Medal Award (the first academic so honored) in 1944, and membership in the Accounting Hall of Fame (also the first academic so honored). He helped start and was the first editor in 1926 of *Accounting Review*. He also served on the Committee on Accounting Procedure from 1939 through 1950. While an undergraduate at the University of Michigan (where he also earned his masters and doctoral degrees), Paton was stimulated to further study accounting by books written by Charles Ezra Sprague and Henry Rand Hatfield, both early accounting theorists in the United States ranging from 1880 to the early 1900s for Sprague and the early to mid-1900s for Hatfield.

Paton addressed a number of issues in his career. He advocated the importance of earning power, replacement costs, matching, single-step income statements, the entity theory, and, more generally, capitalism and clear thinking. With respect to the latter, Paton analyzed issues as completely as possible, neither omitting nor downplaying opposing points of view but rather confronting them head-on.

Paton believed that the "outstanding business fact" is earning power. While this can be expressed in different ways, he favored the relationship of net income plus interest expense to total assets. To make this relationship meaningful, Paton emphasized the importance of taking into account changing prices. This was especially important following World War II when inflation was relatively high. Paton argued that corporate profitability was exaggerated. He felt that this resulted not only in unfair criticism of corporations, but, more significantly, in the confiscation of capital through U.S. income tax laws.

Paton, however, was not in favor of abandoning historical costs. He generally advocated that changing-price data be provided as supplementary information to historical cost financial statements. Further, if changing-price information is incorporated into the primary financial statements, historical costs should also be clearly disclosed. He also felt that quasi-reorganization procedures may be an effective means of incorporating replacement costs into the financial statements.

Paton thought replacement costs were superior to historical costs adjusted for the change in general price level. He argued that managers and investors needed to know the cost of replacement, which he considered the effective actual cost, to make sound economic decisions. However, Paton was concerned about the difficulty of obtaining reliable replacement costs of plant and equipment and other long-term assets.

During Paton's career, there was a change in emphasis by the accounting community from the importance of the balance sheet to the importance of the income statement. Given his belief in earning power, Paton thought that, while both are necessary, the income statement probably had the greater practical significance of the two.

With respect to the income statement, two notable themes in Paton's writings are matching and the single-step income statement. Paton and Littleton's 1940 monograph is known for its emphasis on matching cost and revenue as "the critical phase of accounting." However, the idea of matching is evident in his writings as early as 1920: ". . . expense . . . is the cost . . . of producing the particular quantum of revenue." In this regard, Paton felt that practicing accountants did not go far enough in matching since distribution (i.e., selling) costs not related to an immediate sale should also be allocated to inventory (e.g., advertising and traveling salespersons costs).

Paton became an advocate of the single-step income statement, disapproving of such subtotals as gross profit and income before depreciation. He felt that such disclosures are misleading since they imply that expenses are recovered in a certain order and that some expenses are more important than others. He pointed out that economically there are no priorities for all necessary costs. He also advocated, consistent with the entity theory, showing on the income statement interest and dividends as distributions of income, ending with the addition to capital surplus, if any. Such a procedure would also disclose all losses in a single statement rather than directly adjusting capital accounts, consistent with the all-inclusive approach to income determination.

Paton had his suggestions for the balance sheet as well. When Paton started writing, the entire right-hand side of the balance sheet was typically referred to as liabilities. He felt that a better word is equities, reflecting the entity theory, noting that the distinction between outside obligations and proprietorship ". . . is not fundamental." He believed convertible bonds demonstrated this lack of clear distinction.

Paton wrote, spoke, and testified on many other financial-accounting topics as well as issues related to tax, public utilities and accounting education. His economic writings show his staunch support of capitalism, his ardent opposition to socialism, and his belief that productivity should be rewarded. His writings also transcend accounting and economics. A popular article, written in 1962, discusses building underground, not just houses but whole cities. Another (1971) provides a negative view of the student protestors of the 1960s and early 1970s. At age 95, he published *WORDS! Combining Fun and Learning* (1984), a compilation of word games

which he enjoyed with his friends and family over the years. For Paton, using his mind was not just his profession, but his way of life.

Joel E. Thompson

Bibliography

Paton, W.A. *Accounting Theory: With Special Reference to the Corporate Enterprise.* New York: Ronald Press, 1922. Reprint. Chicago: Accounting Studies Press, 1962.

———. "On Going Underground," *Michigan Quarterly Review*, January 1962, pp. 19–26.

———. *Shirtsleeve Economics: A Common Sense Survey.* New York: Appleton-Century-Crofts, 1952.

———. "Some Current Valuation Accounts," *Journal of Accountancy*, May 1920, pp. 335–350.

———. "The Protestors," *Freeman*, January 1971, pp. 51–59.

———. *WORDS! Combining Fun and Learning.* Ann Arbor, MI: University of Michigan, 1984.

———, and A.C. Littleton. *An Introduction to Corporate Accounting Standards.* American Accounting Association Monograph No. 3. New York: American Accounting Association, 1940.

Taggart, H.F., ed. *Paton on Accounting: Selected Writings of W.A. Paton.* Ann Arbor, MI: University of Michigan, 1964.

See also ACCOUNTING EDUCATION IN THE UNITED STATES; ACCOUNTING HALL OF FAME; ACCOUNTING RESEARCH BULLETINS; AMERICAN ACCOUNTING ASSOCIATION; *AN INTRODUCTION TO CORPORATE ACCOUNTING STANDARDS;* CAPITAL MAINTENANCE; CONSERVATISM; DAVIDSON, SIDNEY; DEFINITIONS OF ACCOUNTING; DEVINE, CARL; DISTRIBUTION COSTS; EDWARDS, JAMES DON; ENTITY THEORY; GENERALLY ACCEPTED ACCOUNTING PRINCIPLES; HATFIELD, HENRY RAND; HISTORICAL COST; HUMAN RESOURCE ACCOUNTING; INCOME STATEMENT/INCOME ACCOUNT; INFLATION ACCOUNTING; LIABILITIES; LITTLETON, A.C.; MACNEAL, KENNETH; MATCHING; NORMATIVE ACCOUNTING; RESIDUAL EQUITY THEORY; SCHRADER, WILLIAM JOSEPH; SPRAGUE, CHARLES EZRA; SWEENEY, HENRY WHITCOMB; TREASURY STOCK; ZEFF, STEPHEN A.

Payen, Anselme (1795–1871)

The first comprehensive description of factory accounting systems was given by the French manufacturer Anselme Payen in *Essai sur la tenus Livres d'un Manufactures* (1817). Payen illustrated cost accounts for a carriage maker, a glue factory, and a manufacturer of two main products and a by-product.

In his carriage making example, Payen set up a job cost system, using a journal and ledger in money for transactions with outsiders, and a journal and ledger in quantities for internal transactions. His external ledger accumulated material and labor costs for each of three carriages and compared the total cost of each carriage to its selling price, leaving profit or loss as a final balance.

Payen's glue factory example illustrated process costing. Again, money values and quantities were accounted for in different books, but total processing costs, including interest and depreciation, were collected in the equivalent of a work in process account.

Payen's third and most complex example showed in detail the division of manufacturing costs between two main products (no costs were distributed to the by-product). Significantly, the costs allocated to the main products included not only expenditures for materials and factory wages, but rent, interest, wear of tools, and depreciation of furnaces.

In all three examples, Payen's attempts to compare total costs with cost of goods sold or sales prices brought him nearer than any of his predecessors to an integration of cost and financial accounts. Paul Garner suggested that the only missing link was a journal entry tying the ledger-in-kind inventory to the manufacturing account in the ledger-in-money. As A.C. Littleton said, Payen "succeeded in bringing manufacturing accounts under the control of double-entry bookkeeping."

Michael Chatfield

Bibliography

Edwards, R.S. "A Survey of French Contributions to the Study of Cost Accounting During the Nineteenth Century," *Accountant*, May 1937, pp. 1–36. Reprinted in *The Historical Development of Accounting*, edited by B.S. Yamey. New York: Arno Press, 1978.

Garner, S.P. *Evolution of Cost Accounting to 1925*. University, AL: University of Alabama Press, 1954.

Littleton, A.C. *Accounting Evolution to 1900*. New York: American Institute Publishing, 1933. Reprint. New York: Russell and Russell, 1966.

See also COST AND/OR MANAGEMENT ACCOUNTING; CRONHELM, FREDERIC WILLIAM; DEPRECIATION; FRANCE; GARNER, S. PAUL; LITTLETON, A.C.

Peele, James (d. 1585)

Double entry bookkeeping was introduced into England by Hugh Oldcastle, whose *A Profitable Treatyce* (1543) was apparently a translation of Luca Pacioli's 1494 text, "Particularis de Computis et Scripturis." Ten years later James Peele, teacher and clerk at Christ's Hospital in London, published the second bookkeeping textbook in the English language, and the oldest that survives. In *The Maner and Fourme how to kepe a Perfecte Reconyng* (1553), Peele borrowed from Pacioli, Domenico Manzoni, and Jan Ympyn, but also made important innovations. Pacioli discussed each accounting topic separately. His text offers no general rules and no comprehensive examples. In contrast, the entries in Peele's journal are numbered, the nature of each entry is described, and the relevant text discussion is keyed to the entries. Peele also offered a "general rule" to facilitate transaction analysis:

> To make the thinges Receivyd, or the receiver,
> Debter to the thinges delivered, or to the deliverer.

Other novelties in *Maner and Fourme* include showing the beginning inventory balance as a single total amount, demonstrating the techniques for transferring ledger balances from old to new account books, and advising how merchants might keep capital and other sensitive accounts secret from their employees.

Peele's second book, *The Pathe Waye to Perfectness* (1569), includes major departures from the Italian tradition of double entry bookkeeping. It takes the form of two Socratic dialogues, the first between a teacher and a merchant who approaches him with an accounting problem, and the second between the teacher and the merchant's apprentice, who seeks accounting instruction. Where *Maner and Fourme* included 94 journal entries, *Pathe Waye* illustrates 287 numbered transactions. Peele was the first author to recommend the segregation of bad debts. *Pathe Waye* included detailed instructions for balancing and closing the ledger. Borrowing from Ympyn, Peele described the treatment of barter transactions. Borrowing from Weddington, he demonstrated compound journal entries and the use of inventory quantity columns alongside the money columns in the ledger, creating a perpetual inventory record.

John Mellis drew heavily on Peele's works in his *Briefe Instruction* (1588), as did John Carpenter in *A Most Excellent Instruction* (1632). John Weddington's *A Breffe Instruction* (1567) and Richard Dafforne's *The Merchant's Mirrour* (1636) show that they had read Peele's *Maner and Fourme*. Apart from this, and despite Peele's originality and expository skill, his two books seem to have had little influence on later publications.

Michael Chatfield

Bibliography

Solomons, D. "The Maner and Fourme how to kepe a Perfecte Reconyng," *Lloyd's Bank Review*, no. 43, 1957, pp. 34–46.
Yamey, B.S. "Oldcastle, Peele, and Mellis: A Case of Plagiarism in the Sixteenth Century." In *Further Essays on the History of Accounting*. New York and London: Garland, 1982.
———. "Peele's Two Treatises in Context." In *Further Essays on the History of Accounting*. New York and London: Garland, 1982.

See also BAD DEBTS; BARTER; CAPITAL ACCOUNT; CLOSING ENTRIES AND PROCEDURES; COMPOUND INTEREST; DAFFORNE, RICHARD; DEBIT AND CREDIT; INSTITUTE OF CHARTERED ACCOUNTANTS IN ENGLAND AND WALES; MANZONI, DOMENICO; PACIOLI, LUCA; PERPETUAL INVENTORY; YMPYN, JAN

Periodicity

Far from being fixed and unvarying, accounting period concepts have for hundreds of years been adapted to changing business and legal conditions. In "Particularis de Computis et Scripturis" (1494), Luca Pacioli made no provision for financial statements and no serious attempt to determine the profits earned during any given period of time. Since business in his day was typically a series of disconnected ventures, there was little interest in unfinished operations and few of the modern reasons for assigning costs and revenues to specific years. Owners were usually in personal contact with their affairs, operations could easily be observed, and profits were not hard to estimate. Most financial information was taken directly from the ledger accounts. Financial statements were normally prepared only at the end of a major project, such as a trading voyage or after all the pages in a ledger had been filled. Accounting periods were usually unnecessary. The pace of operations guided the accounting process.

The commercial life of Tudor England was much like that of Renaissance Venice, and the British were fortunate that the Venetian style of double entry, with its venture accounts and irregular balancing, set the pattern for Italian bookkeeping throughout Europe. Most English businesses were small, trading tended to be sporadic, and profits were calculated separately for individual voyages or commodities. The striking difference between seventeenth-century and modern bookkeeping technique was the failure to balance and close the books regularly. The closing process was tied to random events: the end of a voyage, the filling of a ledger, the sale of a business, the dissolving of a partnership, a merchant's bankruptcy or death. There was no concept of periodic reckoning. Many early textbooks recommended closing ledgers only when they were full, and eighteenth-century authors who demonstrated annual balancing implied that it was optional.

Overseas trade posed different problems. The East India Company, chartered by Queen Elizabeth in 1600, evolved in just 60 years from a series of speculative voyages with terminable stocks to a continuing corporation with permanently invested capital. Between 1600 and 1617, the company sponsored 113 voyages, each supplied with newly subscribed capital and treated as a separate venture. This made liquidation necessary after each voyage so that those who wished to drop out might do so and new "adventurers" might be admitted. At that time, assets as well as earnings were subject to "divisions" among the shareholders. Profit was easily measured by the individual investor: He gained to the extent that he got back more than he had paid in.

But ships, trading posts and other long-lived assets carried over from one venture to the next, until finally the company's accounts became a jumble of successive voyages. As unliquidated balances of earlier voyages were merged with later ones, it became necessary to juggle assets and profits of many distinct ventures in various stages of completion. Also, during the seventeenth century trading abroad had developed into a fairly continuous process requiring permanent capital. It now became more useful to view the business as a going concern.

Continuity of operations radically changed accounting technique. Whereas bookkeeping for a completed venture was entirely historical, for a going concern it became a problem of viewing segments in a stream of continuous activity. Not only were results much more tentative, but the whole emphasis of record keeping shifted toward the future.

When a firm's life lasted through many ventures, it was no longer practical to wait until liquidation before preparing financial statements. Regular mercantile trading produced a demand for accounting reports at intermediate points in operations. Periodicity in turn created or affected other accounting concepts. To make the continuity principle technically feasible, events of different accounting periods had to be sharply distinguished. The idea of estimating periodic income by matching costs and related revenues followed naturally. Profit estimates were refined by a system of accruals and deferrals that allowed the effects of transactions to be split between periods.

Moreover, when revenues and expenses were related to a firm's performance during a particular accounting interval, net worth and periodic income began to be calculated quite apart from cash receipts and disbursements. It was now the use of goods, not merely their purchase, that created expense, and sales rather than cash collections which signaled that income had been earned. Recognition of periodicity brought accounting practice nearer reality in more subtle ways. For example, bookkeepers began to realize that interest ran day by day and that a certain amount would be earned by a given date even if the money was not received by then.

But the transition from venture to going concern made record keeping more subjective and left a wide area of accounting discretion to management. In apportioning costs between periods, accountants had to make estimates, the accuracy of which depended on the course of future events. Honest differences of opinion about inventory pricing and asset life spans could lead to large variations in reported profits. Or industrial managers could deliberately blur periodic results by shifting income from one period to another, overdepreciating assets, and charging capital goods to expense. There was also a considerable time lag between adoption of the period notion and acceptance of comparability, consistency, and other doctrines needed to answer questions it had raised.

And from the beginning there was a contradiction between the continuity assumption and the periodicity assumption that it made necessary. The one tells us to look at operations as a continuous flow; the other says we must break that flow into comparable time segments. The root of the period problem is that in assigning revenues and expenses to time intervals, the accountant is doing something that is absolutely necessary but is at the same time quite arbitrary and artificial.

The emergence of large corporations during the seventeenth century gave legal validity to the idea of continuity and tended to shorten and regularize accounting periods. The life of a business now eclipsed not only specific ventures but even the lifespans of its owners. Periodic accounting reports were helpful in pricing company shares. They were sometimes required by legal and tax authorities. The calculation of profits for a particular time interval became a major determinant of dividend payments. Often stockholders were absentee owners who had little direct contact with company affairs. The periodic income figure became an index of managerial effectiveness in the minds of many who lacked the time to study operations in detail.

The calendar year proved to be a convenient corporate reporting period. It was usually long enough to encompass one or more complete cycles of business activity, yet short enough to give investors fairly current information. Useful comparisons could be made when statements covered the same time span and appeared on the same date each year. As record keeping became more standardized, there was a tendency for corporations to prepare statements at progressively shorter intervals until they arrived at an annual reporting basis. A fiscal year ending at the low point in annual operations—a natural business year—was used as early as the 1770s, and reappeared at various times and places during the nineteenth century.

P

But by 1800, in England at least, the usual practice was to close the books either at year end or on the anniversary of the firm's inception.

Though certain cost finding techniques are as old as double entry bookkeeping, systematic cost accounting hardly existed at the start of the industrial revolution. Yet to find operating income, factory accountants had to calculate the value not only of finished products, but also of goods in various stages of completion. So at the same time that financial accountants were assigning costs to time periods, industrial accountants were given the task of somehow synchronizing the flows of costs and production. So urgent was this need for internal data that, according to A.C. Littleton, during the nineteenth century "corporate costs attached to the product, only secondarily to the period."

Yet account regularity was one aspect of a new sense of timeliness that emerged from the industrial revolution. The adoption of periodic routines enabled industrial managers to handle masses of detail and to regulate operations too extensive to be supervised directly. Periodic reports also helped solve the problem of management from a distance, when a company's factories were located at different places, or when an entrepreneur was traveling as a salesman or buyer. Reporting convenience dictated the use of calendar intervals: many expense items, such as wages, were paid weekly or monthly, and others, such as interest, had an annual connotation. Ironically, the regularizing of accounting periods forced the natural rhythm of work into uniform reporting segments just when machine techniques made operational time more important than ever before.

American tax laws favored the calendar year over more flexible time concepts. Many American companies had adopted the natural business year, but the Corporation Excise Tax Act of 1909, by requiring corporations to report on the calendar year, tended to establish it as a norm. The Revenue Act of 1913 permitted fiscal year reporting, but most corporations now had their accounting systems set up on a calendar year basis and were reluctant to change. Moreover, provisions of the next eight revenue acts (1923–1934) all became effective as of January 1, meaning that corporations not on a calendar year basis often had to file returns under two different tax laws.

By this time many of the economic activities that give rise to accounting were organized on a yearly basis. Annual income reporting had developed into a normal business procedure. The year was specified as an accounting period by the stock exchanges, the Securities and Exchange Commission, and often by corporate bylaws. It had become the basis for making interest accruals, pension calculations, and executive bonus payments. Many fixed costs, such as insurance and property taxes, have an annual connotation, and others, such as rent, are negotiated on an annual basis.

But accrual and realization techniques that developed around a tradition of annual reporting became less reliable when applied to shorter or longer periods. Eric Louis Kohler defined seasonal variations as "changes within a year, tending to follow the same pattern from one year to another." Because of their annual rhythm and recurrence, seasonal highs and lows are combined and "washed out" over the year, but not over shorter intervals. The more extreme the seasonal activity changes, the harder it becomes to match interim costs with related revenues. This is especially true when sales volume fluctuates widely while fixed costs are assigned ratably or proportionately to each month or quarter. In his classic article, "What Did We Earn Last Month?" (1936), Jonathan Harris proposed direct costing as a solution to the distorting effects of seasonal bias on monthly income statements.

Before World War II the common view was that seasonal fluctuations made quarterly income statements too unreliable to be published. Investor demands for financial data at shorter intervals soon made this position untenable. The SEC now requires certain corporations to file Form 10Q, in which they must disclose quarterly information similar to that disclosed in the annual 10K report. It also requires these companies to include selected quarterly data in the notes to their annual financial statements. In 1973 Accounting Principles Board Opinion No. 28, "Interim Financial Reporting," took the position that interim reports should not only reflect interim activity, but should anticipate and forecast annual operating results. But it also specified that the accounting methods used in annual reporting should be used for interim reports. In practice this usually means prorating fixed expenses to interim periods, on the grounds that such expenses are period costs, incurred to maintain capacity rather than to support particular activity levels. Often this is factually true, but identifying fixed expenses with short periods of time tends to make income a function of sales volume and thereby to magnify the effects of seasonal variations. A firm's peak selling season may show very high profits, while its slack periods apparently produce large losses. The fact that all such quarterly income statements are unaudited further diminishes their credibility.

Michael Chatfield

Bibliography
Gilman, S. *Accounting Concepts of Profit.* New York: Ronald Press, 1939.
Harris, J.N. "What Did We Earn Last Month?" *N.A.A. Bulletin*, vol. 18, January 15, 1936, pp. 501–527.
Littleton, A.C. *Accounting Evolution to 1900.* New York: American Institute Publishing, 1933. Reprint. New York: Russell and Russell, 1966.
Peragallo, E. *Origin and Evolution of Double Entry Bookkeeping: A Study of Italian Practice from the Fourteenth Century.* New York: American Institute Publishing, 1938. Reprint. Osaka: Nihon Shoseki, 1974.
Shillinglaw, G. "Concepts Underlying Interim Financial Statements," *Accounting Review*, April 1961, pp. 222–231.
Yamey, B.S. "Some Topics in the History of Financial Accounting in England, 1500–1900." In *Studies in Accounting Theory*, edited by W.T. Baxter and S. Davidson, pp. 14–43. Homewood, IL: Irwin, 1962.

See also ACCRUAL ACCOUNTING; CLOSING ENTRIES AND PROCEDURES; CONTINUITY; CORPORATIONS: EVOLUTION; COST AND/OR MANAGEMENT ACCOUNTING; DIRECT COSTING; DOUBLE ENTRY BOOKKEEPING: ORIGINS; EAST INDIA COMPANY; FLORI, LUDOVICO; INCOME TAXATION IN THE UNITED STATES; MATCHING; NATURAL BUSINESS YEAR; PACIOLI, LUCA; POSTULATES OF ACCOUNTING; REALIZATION; SECURITIES AND EXCHANGE COMMISSION

Perpetual Inventory

Double entry bookkeeping was originally promoted as an aid to memory. For 400 years the main purpose of asset accounting was the maintenance of comprehensive records for owners' reference. The merchant could review his financial affairs simply by scanning his ledger accounts. In doing so, he relied more on descriptions of assets than on their valuations. In inventory accounting the intention was not to make the correct transfer to cost of goods sold, but to segregate the results of trading in various commodities. Both textbooks and surviving accounting records show separate inventory accounts for different types of goods, and often these had quantity columns next to the money columns. Perpetual inventory records were maintained by recording purchases and sales directly into the inventory accounts. Not until the nineteenth century did it become common for a ledger to contain only a single inventory account.

Michael Chatfield

Bibliography
Yamey, B.S. "Scientific Bookkeeping and the Rise of Capitalism." In *Studies in Accounting*, edited by W.T. Baxter, pp. 13–30. London: Sweet and Maxwell, 1950. Reprinted in B.S. Yamey, *Essays on the History of Accounting*. New York: Arno Press, 1978.

See also ACCRUAL ACCOUNTING; CONTROL ACCOUNTS; COST AND/OR MANAGEMENT ACCOUNTING; CRONHELM, FREDERIC WILLIAM; GARCKE AND FELLS; METCALFE, HENRY; PEELE, JAMES; PLANTIN, CHRISTOPHER

Personification of Accounts

In "Particularis de Computis et Scripturis" (1494), Luca Pacioli gave no rules for teaching bookkeeping and used few illustrations of the kind needed to make the subject part of a school curriculum. Most early writers on double entry were intent on disseminating the new system to accounting practitioners. They did not theorize much or demonstrate how to analyze transactions. A majority of later textbook authors were teachers of bookkeeping. Though their writings are our main source of information about the development of accounting methods, they tended to imitate each other, and only a few of them tried to explain the logic underlying accounting procedures.

Both the desire to rationalize bookkeeping instruction and the search for general rules of debit and credit caused textbook writers to attribute human qualities to ledger accounts. Account personification had many precedents. The oldest organized ledgers described nothing but debtor-creditor relationships between individuals. Early ledger entries were always written from the viewpoint of an owner or owners dealing with persons outside the business. Manorial accounts were kept by a steward who charged himself with property and receipts entrusted to him and credited himself with expenditures made on his master's behalf. Later, the double entry system simply extended the use of the terms "debtor" and "creditor," first to impersonal accounts such as cash and inventory, then to abstract expense accounts. Pacioli resorted to personification in describing a merchant's relationship to his capital. And while the words of accountability in fifteenth century Italian journals often implied a statistical tabulation of items, personification can be traced to very early writings on double entry bookkeeping, with their conscious inclusion of an imaginary proprietor (shall have, shall give) in each transaction.

Personification was strengthened when Italian textbooks were translated into English. Lacking precisely corresponding terms, British writers rendered the Italian *debito* and *credito* as the more personal "oweth" and "trusts." In *A Profitable Treatyce* (1543), Hugh Oldcastle translated Pacioli's *cassa* (cash) as "chest" or strongbox which received and paid cash. In Oldcastle's translation, Pacioli's "per Cash, a Capital" became "Money Oweth to Thomas Lee." This connotation of inanimate objects possessing human qualities may have helped accounting students understand relationships among impersonal accounts. For example, plant assets are more easily explained as part of the owner's wealth than as an undivided portion of total assets. The artificiality of this approach was not apparent to those employing it. For 300 years, from the seventeenth to the early twentieth centuries, account personification remained the accepted way to teach general rules of bookkeeping.

Personification took three forms, which developed simultaneously and were sometimes found together in the same textbook. In the first, ledger accounts were treated as living persons ("Mr. Chest" and "Mr. Box"). In a second variant, accounts were considered an extension of the owner's personality. Frenchman Edmond Degrange Sr. based his Five Account System (1795) on the idea that cash, merchandise, receivables, payables, and profit and loss all function as subsidiary accounts to capital, and that by debiting and crediting these accounts the merchant was in effect debiting and crediting himself.

The most sophisticated type of personification occurred when ledger accounts were regarded as individuals separate from the owner but responsible to him. In 1831 the English mathematician Augustus De Morgan spoke of accounts being represented by "an array of clerks" who received and gave up value on behalf of the proprietor. De Morgan repeated this notion in an appendix to the fifth edition of his *Arithmetic* (1846), which Jackson (1956) called "in its effect on the teaching of bookkeeping, probably the most influential piece of writing to be found during the nineteenth century." Other textbook authors quickly appropriated De Morgan's concept of accounting transactions as a series of asset and liability movements between clerks.

Account personification resulted from contemporary attitudes toward education and from the absence of accounting theory during the seventeenth and eighteenth centuries. Both factors made it hard to explain impersonal accounts as abstractions, so they were discussed more concretely. Viewed as part of the revolt against rote learning that occurred after 1850, personification deserves some respect. It permitted transaction analysis without resort to memorized rules, provided a strategic view of account interactions, and helped shift instructional emphasis from the journal to the ledger. But in actual use personification was a sterile technique based on artificial reasoning. It failed to explain the true purposes of accounts or the real effect of transactions. As a result, the technical improvement of accounting was left mainly to practitioners, who had the advantage of describing actual business events and were at least compelled to deal with reality. As Jackson put it, the type of bookkeeping taught and the methods of instruction finally "satisfied none but the teachers."

Michael Chatfield

Bibliography

Jackson, J.G.C. "The History of Methods of Exposition of Double Entry Bookkeeping in England." In *Studies in the History of Accounting*, edited by A.C. Littleton and B.S. Yamey, pp. 295–302. Homewood, IL: Irwin, 1956.

Littleton, A.C. *Accounting Evolution to 1900.* New York: American Institute Publishing, 1933. Reprint. New York: Russell and Russell, 1966.

See also ACCOUNTING EDUCATION IN THE
UNITED STATES; DEBIT AND CREDIT; JONES,
THOMAS; MANORIAL ACCOUNTING;
OLDCASTLE, HUGH; PACIOLI, LUCA

Peru

The knotted cord may be the world's oldest
accounting device. Lyle Jacobsen described its
use in prehistoric Hawaii, the Marquesas Islands, and in ancient China, where the use of
knotted strings for record keeping apparently
predated the appearance of a written language
about 3300 B.C.

The best documented use of knotted cord
numeration occurred in Peru. The *quipu* was
used by the Incas from about A.D. 1200 as a
counting and recording device. It consisted of
a cotton or wool cord varying in length from a
few inches to more than a yard, to which one
or more knotted strings were attached. The
colors of these strings often indicated the types
of items being counted, while the size of each
knot and its distance from the main cord signi-
fied particular numbers, based on a decimal
system. A single knot at the bottom of the string
represented one; two knots in the same position
indicated two; a single knot closer to the main
cord represented ten; a knot still closer to the
main cord represented a hundred, and so on.
Quipus have been discovered with knots enumerating hundreds of thousands of items.

Men skilled in preparing and reading quipus
were called *quipucamayocs*. They combined the
functions of scribes, accountants, statisticians,
and historians. Like modern census takers, they
counted heads in each village, recorded births
and deaths, and specified the number of men
available for military service. They also helped
allocate resources within the empire, by recording taxes due, government revenues, storehouse
inventories, and even the quantities of raw materials distributed to weavers and the amounts of
cloth produced. All this information was recorded on quipus and forwarded by messenger
to the capital, Cuzco. The Incan empire was a
paradox: a highly centralized, planned economy
that functioned without a written language or
coined money. The *quipu* and the *quipucamayocs* were central to its administration.

Michael Chatfield

Bibliography
Jacobsen, L.E. "Use of Knotted String Accounting Records in Old Hawaii and

Ancient China," *Accounting Historians
Journal*, Fall 1983, pp. 53–61.
Keister, O.R. "The Incan Quipu," *Accounting
Review*, April 1964, pp. 414–416.
Yeakel, J.A. "The Accountant-Historians of
the Incas," *Accounting Historians Jour-
nal*, Fall 1983, pp. 39–51.

See also CHINA; SCRIBES

Peruzzi
Between 1300 and 1345, the most powerful
Florentine merchant-banking houses were the
Bardi, the Peruzzi, and the Acciaiuoli. In 1336
the Peruzzi, second largest of these "pillars of
Christendom," had 15 branches in Western Europe, North Africa, and the Levant. The Peruzzi
accounts stand partway between single and
double entry bookkeeping. They included many
independently kept and poorly integrated journals. Each ledger entry was cross referenced, but
the two sides of each account were not yet placed
next to each other. Instead, debits were entered
in the front half of the ledger and credits in the
rear half. Though revenue and expense accounts
were used, no arithmetic proof of equality was
attempted, and profits were determined, not by
closing the ledger, but by inventorying assets and
deducting them from total liabilities and capital.

Michael Chatfield

Bibliography
Martinelli, A. *The Origination and Evolution
of Double Entry Bookkeeping to 1440.*
Ph.D. diss., North Texas State University,
1974. Ann Arbor, MI: University Micro-
films.
Peragallo, E. *Origin and Evolution of Double
Entry Bookkeeping: A Study of Italian
Practice from the Fourteenth Century.*
New York: American Institute Publish-
ing, 1938. Reprint. Osaka: Nihon
Shoseki, 1974.

See also ALBERTI DEL GIUDICE; BARDI;
BRANCH ACCOUNTING; MEDICI ACCOUNTS

Philips Industries (N.V.)
Philips Industries started as a family partnership
in 1891 in the Netherlands and became incorporated in 1912. This international "giant" has
been renowned in accounting for its leadership
in the use of current value accounting from

1951 through 1991 and for its detailed and informative annual reports. Philips Industries dropped its reporting of current value accounting in 1992 for reasons of simplicity and of getting itself closer to United States generally accepted accounting principles.

Before it adopted current value reporting in 1951, Philips Industries had a varied history of accounting for tangible fixed assets and depreciation. From 1912 through 1929, Philips maintained its machinery, factory, and factory land at a nominal valuation of Fl 1. The amount of expenditures for these assets was deducted from net income. In 1930 and 1931, at the beginning of the worldwide depression, capital expenditures were charged to the Reserve for Extension account. In 1931 there was a write-down to that account for inventory in accordance with the "lower of cost or market" policy, mentioned for the first time. In that year, there was a footnote reference to the valuation of factory buildings and machinery for fire insurance purposes. From 1932 through 1938, Philips reclassified capital expenditures as a component of net income. Philips made no public reports during World War II. After the war, it adopted a base stock approach which values the minimum inventory at a constant amount through the year. From 1945 through 1950, Philips began to capitalize the expenditures for tangible fixed assets. Depreciation was increased, somewhat, on the increased replacement value.

In 1951 Philips made a major break with its past reporting tradition by including the replacement value of fixed assets and of inventories in its statements. Philips stated in its 1951 annual report: "It is our constant practice to revalue the fixed assets in accordance with changes in the price level, in order to make their book value correspond with replacement cost. In the Consolidated Statement they are shown at that value, and depreciation on the basis of replacement cost is deducted. Any increase in value has been taken to revaluation reserve." Inventories were handled the same way as long as they were not obsolete. This current (replacement) value approach adopted by Philips was developed in the Netherlands by Theodore Limperg Jr. in the 1920s and subsequently refined and updated by many Dutch authors. In 1990 H.J. van der Schroeff, Limperg's prime successor, stressed the importance of variations and deviations to a "consistent, forced-normative theory" as noted by Enthoven (1982).

There are three excellent descriptions in English of the application of replacement-value theory at Philips. The first was written in 1960 by A. Goudeket, the chief internal auditor of Philips. He stressed the importance of "sound business practice" in the development of accounting principles in the Netherlands. Goudeket stated that Philips had the same accounting system for fixed assets and inventory for both internal and external reports, utilized specific price levels for each group of assets and included an estimated tax procedure to reduce the credit balance of the Reserve for Appreciation accounts. Goudeket wrote: "The replacement value theory contends that, in order to assure the continuity of the enterprise, all costs incurred must be included in the income statement at their replacement values and not at the prices which actually may have been paid." He stressed the importance of this accounting theory for both dividend policy and for pricing when competition has yet to be felt and said Philips followed this external-reporting practice even though it made Philips' statements less favorable.

In 1982 Adolf J.H. Enthoven reported on the accounting policies of Philips. These policies had become very significant as a trailblazer in the light of the United Kingdom and United States efforts in the mid- and late 1970s to reflect the effects of inflation. Such efforts included Accounting Series Release No. 190, "Notice of Adoption of Amendments to Regulation S-X Requiring Disclosure of Certain Replacement Cost Data" (1976), of the Securities and Exchange Commission, Financial Accounting Standard No. 33, "Financial Reporting and Changing Prices" by the Financial Accounting Standards Board in 1979, and the Sandilands Report of the Inflation Accounting Committee of the United Kingdom and Ireland in 1975. Enthoven's research study provides an excellent theoretical and practical deepening of Goudeket's work. In 1983, Robert C. Spinosa Cattela, managing director and chief financial officer of Philips, explained its 1981 decision to include a "Gearing Adjustment" in its financial reporting system. This adjustment increased the value (revaluation) of those fixed assets and inventories, which were not financed with stockholders' interests, hence, was added back again to the profit and loss account.

Starting in 1971, Philips adopted a section in its annual report entitled "Calculation of Net Income Based on American Accounting Principles." In its 1991 annual report, Philips noted it was reappraising its accounting policies and procedures under an overall revitalization plan. Particular emphasis was to be placed on the concepts of current cost accounting including gearing and on the treatment of accounts in countries with excessively high inflation. In its 1992 annual report, Philips announced the end of its 40-year policy of current value accounting with historical cost basis accounting in the name of simplicity to improve communication with shareholders. Only one difference with U.S. generally accepted accounting principles (GAAP) was reported in 1992, and that was using accelerated, rather than straight-line, amortization of goodwill.

The annual reports of Philips Industries provide a panoramic view of many of the major accounting issues of the twentieth century. Its dropping in 1992 of the replacement-cost approach should be a well-studied event.

Richard Vangermeersch

Bibliography

Enthoven, A.J.H. *Current Value Accounting: Its Concept and Practice at N.V. Philips Industries, the Netherlands.* International Accounting Research Study No. 3. Richardson, TX: Center for International Accounting Development, University of Texas at Dallas, 1982.

———. "Replacement-Value Accounting: Wave of the Future?" *Harvard Business Review*, January-February 1976, pp. 6–8.

Goudeket, A. "An Application of Replacement Value Theory," *Journal of Accountancy*, July 1960, pp. 37–47.

Spinosa Cattela, R.C. "An Introduction into Current Value Accounting and Its Application within Philips N.V." In *Current Value Accounting: Its Aspects and Impacts, Proceedings of April 1983 Conference,* pp. 35–46. International Accounting Research Study No. 4. Richardson, TX: Center for International Accounting Development, University of Texas at Dallas, 1983.

Vangermeersch, R. "An Historical Analysis of the Financial Reporting Practices of Philips Industries of the Netherlands for Tangible Fixed Assets and Inventory, 1915–1981." Working paper no. 57 in *Working Paper Series Volume 3,* edited by A.C. Bishop and D.R. Richards, pp.
228–245. Richmond, VA: Academy of Accounting Historians, 1984.

See also ACCOUNTING SERIES RELEASE NO. 190; DEPRECIATION; HISTORICAL COST; INFLATION ACCOUNTING; KRAAYENHOF, JACOB; LIMPERG, THEODORE, JR.; NETHERLANDS; SANDILANDS REPORT

Pietra, Angelo (d. 1590)

In 1586 Don Angelo Pietra, a Benedictine monk, published *Indrizzo degli Economi*, the first printed book on nonbusiness accounting. Pietra adapted commercial double entry bookkeeping to the economic activities of a monastery. His model journal and ledger recorded monastery operations for a year, including purchases, production, sales, and consumption of various kinds of produce. He valued growing crops and calculated expenditures on seeds and manure for the next year's harvest. He correctly determined the earnings of a monastery farm.

At year end, Pietra made a trial balance and a balance account. Nominal accounts were closed into an income and expenditures account. Profits from monastery produce were calculated, and the produce accounts were closed. The excess of total income over expenditures was then transferred to a capital account.

Pietra thought monastery accounts could best be reviewed by examining detached financial statements. Though such statements had been used in commercial practice since the fourteenth century, this was the first time an author had mentioned them. Pietra was also the first writer to consider an enterprise as being separate and distinct from its owners, and his advocacy of a balance sheet, income statement, and detailed statement of monastery capital resulted from his desire to account for all changes in the entity's financial status, not just changes in owner's equity.

Michael Chatfield

Bibliography

Bywater, M.F., and B.S. Yamey. *Historic Accounting Literature: A Companion Guide.* London: Scholar Press, 1982.

Peragallo, E. *Origin and Evolution of Double Entry Bookkeeping: A Study of Italian Practice from the Fourteenth Century.* New York: American Institute Publishing, 1938. Reprint. Osaka: Nihon Shoseki, 1974.

Pipe Roll

The oldest surviving accounting record in English is the Pipe Roll, or "Great Roll of the Exchequer," compiled annually from valuations in the Domesday Book and from statements of account by sheriffs and others bringing payments to the Treasury. Beginning in A.D. 1130, the Pipe Roll provides a 700-year narrative description of rents, fines, taxes, and other fixed levies due the king, together with a summary of payments made on these debts and expenses incurred in collecting them.

In its feudal context the Exchequer was more than a department of state charged with responsibility for royal revenues. Its legitimacy resulted from a delegation of Crown authority. The essential relationship was still between the king and his subjects and depended on his power to tax and on their obligation to pay. Interactions between the Court of Exchequer's two divisions further illustrate this agency aspect of medieval accounting. The Treasurer's Department, or Lower Exchequer, received money and payments in kind and assayed coins to see that they were "of the prescribed goodness." The Pipe Roll was the record of the Upper Exchequer, or King's Council, which also had authority to audit the lower council, authorize allowances, settle legal questions arising from the accounts, and give the tax collectors their quittance.

Michael Chatfield

Bibliography

Stenton, D.M., ed. *The Great Roll of the Pipe for the Second Year of the Reign of King Richard the First*. Publications of the Pipe Roll Society, vol. 39, Introduction. London: Pipe Roll Society, 1925.

Pixley, Francis William (1852–1933)

An English chartered accountant and one of the founders of the British auditing profession, Francis William Pixley was also an attorney who regarded knowledge of the law as part of a practicing accountant's education.

The first modern auditing text was Pixley's *Auditors: Their Duties and Responsibilities*, which went through 12 editions between 1881 and 1922. It was less a textbook for students than a reference work for professional accountants. About half of the first edition consisted of excerpts from 18 acts of Parliament, particularly the 1862–1880 companies acts. The first edition also described bookkeeping and the form of accounts, financial statement categories, the nature of an audit, and of course the duties and responsibilities of auditors. Later editions added chapters on profits available for dividends and professional certification.

Kitchen and Parker (1980) have identified five recurring themes in Pixley's writings: (1) a strong sense of professional identity among chartered accountants; (2) a belief that auditing is the principal accounting task; (3) an emphasis on the legal framework of accounting; (4) a practical approach to solving accounting problems; and (5) advocacy of financial prudence and the going concern concept.

Pixley believed that an auditor's responsibility was to the audited company as an institution, not to its stockholders. Accordingly, he placed great emphasis on fiscal conservatism and business continuity. It was the duty of corporate directors to keep the company's capital intact and to do their best to make it a permanent institution. Pixley argued that accountants should permit the accumulation of secret reserves when needed to ensure the continuing existence of a company in difficult times. He regarded income as an indicator of the amount available to pay cash dividends, which also depended on fluctuations in monetary assets. While current assets should normally be written down to net realizable value, the going concern value of fixed assets "has no relation whatever to current market value." Changes in fixed asset values could be ignored because there was no intention to sell such assets.

Pixley was a pioneer who helped build a new profession and raise its educational standards and community standing. It is likely that men such as Pixley, Lawrence Dicksee, and Arthur Lowes Dickinson have influenced modern accounting thought more than almost anyone alive today. They came on the scene just at the time when accounting practice required codification, and they seized a unique opportunity to set standards for future generations of accountants.

Michael Chatfield

Bibliography

Kitchen, J., and R.H. Parker. *Accounting Thought and Education: Six English Pioneers.* London: Institute of Chartered Accountants in England and Wales, 1980.

Pixley, F.W. *Auditors: Their Duties and Responsibilities under the Joint-stock Companies Acts and the Friendly Societies and Industrial and Provident Societies Acts.* London: Good, 1881. Reprint. New York: Arno Press, 1976.

See also BAD DEBTS; CAPITAL MAINTENANCE; COMPANIES ACTS; CONSERVATISM; CONTINUITY; DICKINSON, ARTHUR LOWES; DICKSEE, LAWRENCE; DIVIDENDS; EXTERNAL AUDITING; PARKER, ROBERT HENRY

Plantin, Christopher (1514–1589)

Sophisticated cost accounting systems existed centuries before the industrial revolution. Cost methods that are today considered modern have been reinvented many times during the last 500 years.

Christopher Plantin, a sixteenth-century Antwerp printer and publisher, between 1563 and 1567 maintained what amounted to a job order cost system, with a separate ledger account for each book he published. In each such account he accumulated costs of paper used, wages paid, and other printing expenses identifiable with a particular book. Plantin's double entry and cost accounts were coordinated; after a book had been printed, an entry was made transferring the account balance to a finished goods account called "Books in Stock." Here quantities of books on hand were recorded together with costs, creating a perpetual inventory record.

Michael Chatfield

Bibliography

De Roover, F.E. "Cost Accounting in the Sixteenth Century," *Accounting Review,* September 1937, pp. 226–237.

Garner, S.P. *Evolution of Cost Accounting to 1925.* University, AL: University of Alabama Press, 1954.

See also COST AND/OR MANAGEMENT ACCOUNTING; PERPETUAL INVENTORY

Poland

The oldest accounting records found and preserved in Poland include single entry books and accounts of the city of Cracow from 1300–1400, a ledger of Gdańsk merchant Jan Pis from 1421–1454, and registers from the salt mines in Bochnia from 1394–1421. Accounting—commercial, agricultural, governmental, and municipal—developed in the period from the fifteenth to the eighteenth century.

The development of merchant bookkeeping accompanied the development of trade and growth of big cities, such as Gdańsk, Toruń, and Cracow. In those cities, especially in Gdańsk, were many merchants of German origin, so single entry bookkeeping, being a general commercial practice in Germany, was also applied here.

In the sixteenth century, the first double entry bookkeeping manuals appeared. In Gdańsk by the eighteenth century six books on mercantile double entry bookkeeping had been published, authored by: Erhart von Ellenbogen (1538), Sebastian Gamersfelder (1570), Wolffgang Sartorius de Sada (1592), Ambrosius Lerice (1606), Paul Hermling (1685), and Johan Gotfried Martzen (1713). The book with the greatest teaching value until the nineteenth century was the handbook by Gamersfelder, *Buchhalten durch zwei Bücher nach Italianischer Art und Weise* (1570).

Agricultural accounting had been employed in large landed estates since the fifteenth century in the central and southern part of Poland. Inventories and records of cash and agricultural goods were kept in Polish. Manuals of bookkeeping were also published in Polish. Recommendations for record keeping were included in the first publication on agricultural economics, Anzelm Gostomski's *Gospodarstwo (Farm Management)* (1588). The first Polish manual of agricultural accounting was written by Jakub Kazimierz Haur in the form of nine Modelleusze arythmetyczne (. . .) *(Arithmetical Models (. . .),* which was an appendix to his *Oekonomika ziemiańska generalna (General Agricultural Economics)* (1675), which had six later editions. Haur's Modelleusze are an example of using folio accounts to keep manorial farm records. The next handbook, by Duchess Anna Jabłnowska, appeared in 1786 after a century's stagnation which resulted from economic and cultural decline in Poland.

Governmental and municipal accounting comprised mainly receipts and expenditures, and sometimes inventory. Preserved registers of the Royal Treasury evidence the fact that public money was conscientiously accounted. Accounts from royal salt mines in Bochnia (1394–1421) and Wieliczka (1497–1594), as well as merchant books of the city of Cracow (1300–1400) and many other towns (Wojciechowski 1964) show that the form and content of governmental bookkeeping was also improved.

Initially, bookkeeping was taught only practically in merchant firms by accounting experts on the basis of available manuals. Commercial education including accountancy appeared at the end of the eighteenth century. The first School of Commerce in Poland was set up in Grodno around 1775 by Antoni Tyzenhauz, an aristocrat and entrepreneur.

From 1795, when Poland lost independence due to the Third Partitioning of Poland, until 1918 accounting was governed by the legislation of annexing countries: the German Commercial Code of 1861 in the Prussian Partition, the Austrian Code in the Austrian Partition (Galicia), and Russian regulations in the Russian Partition, whereas in the Duchy of Warsaw the Napoleonic Code of Commerce was used from 1808.

In the first half of the nineteenth century, legal requirements for accountancy were introduced, and the development of professional education and literature occurred. In the second half of the nineteenth century, professional organizations were established, and there was a significant increase in the number of publications on cost accounting in industry and on accounting theory. A whole series of books published in Polish was initiated by Stanisław Budny's *Buchalterya ułatwiona (. . .) podług metody Edmond Degrange Sr. (Bookkeeping Facilitated [. . .] after the Method of Edmond Degrange Sr.)* (1826). The first orginal work was a three-volume handbook by Antoni Barciński, *O rachunkowości kupieckiej (Merchant Accounting)* (1833, 1834, 1835), presenting double entry accounting for commerce, banking, factories, and farms.

Double entry bookkeeping was explained through the personification theory. A comprehensive explanation of accounting based on the ownership theory was presented by Erazm Nowicki in *Nauka buchalteryi teoretycznie wyłożona (Theoretical Basis of Accountancy Teaching)* (1876).

At the same time, the development of factories on Polish territories gave rise to rapid improvement in accounting techniques, as well as cost accounting theory and practice, which was reflected in books by Adolf Szumlański (1865), Erzam Nowicki (1876), Jan Danielewicz (1886), Ludwik E. Veltze (1895), and Bolesław Sobieski (1895). Double entry bookkeeping became prevalent in agricultural accounting owing to numerous publications by Barciński, Szumlański, Konstanty Sękowski (1889) and others.

Two leading theorists of this period were January F.K. Walicki, whose 1877 book is an interesting study of application of accounting principles to macroeconomic recording, and Paweł Ciompa, who elaborated an original econometric theory applied to the accounts theory in his publications of 1909 and 1910.

After regaining independence in 1918, till 1934, legal norms concerning accounting were the consequence of: (1) the legislation of the partitioning powers; (2) a number of legal acts, e.g. on joint-stock companies and cooperatives; and (3) the Napoleonic Code. In 1934 the Polish Commercial Code was proclaimed. The Code embraced accounting by individual merchants, stock and private companies, cooperatives, banks, and legal persons.

In this period, both a full system of bookkeeping by double entry in large public and private firms and a simplified single entry system for small business and budgetary institutions were applied. The form of the balance sheet and profit and loss account was optional. After 1934 the content of financial reports was regulated. Shareholders were protected by mandatory audit of financial standing upon establishment of joint stock companies, presentation of reports to registered courts, and obligatory publication of annual financial statements in journals.

At the end of the 1930s, the accounting system was improved both in form and content owing to the influence of fiscal legislation and the development of the auditing profession. The main function of financial accounting was stewardship, while its relevance for decision making was ignored.

In this period, the number of accountants and auditors was 100,000 (of a population in Poland of 35,000,000). Most accountants were trained at bookkeeping courses, though accounting was taught in secondary commercial schools and in four higher schools of commerce, the most important being the Central School of Commerce, founded in 1924. All teaching activities were of a strictly practical character, because accounting was treated as a skill (Skrzywan 1967). There were only several professors of accounting, and a few doctoral dissertations were written from the Department of Economics. The first dissertation in accounting was done in 1938 by Hanna Paszkiewicz, who used mathematical proofs for explaining many accounting questions. Books published mainly in the form of manuals played an important role in teaching bookkeeping. The leading authors of this period were Andrzej Bieniek, Witold Byszewski, Witold Góra, prof. Tomasz Lulek, Witold Skalski, Marcel Scheffs, and Stanisław Skrzywan. Foreign accounting literature (French, German, and Anglo-American) was also available in Poland. The level of sophistication and issues covered in articles published in accountancy journals edited by existing professional bodies was comparable to other European journals.

The major professional organization was the Bookkeepers Association in Poland, successor in 1926 to the Association of Bookkeepers in Warsaw, established in 1907. The organization delivered extension courses, worked to integrate the profession, and passed resolutions vital for the development of accountancy. It continues its activities today under the name of Accountants Association in Poland (AAP).

After World War II, a uniform chart of accounts based on German systems from the German occupation was introduced. Owing to the introduction of the command, centrally planned economy, with the dominance of state ownership, and the resulting adoption of Soviet financing and planning systems, in 1951–1953 the Soviet accounting plan was introduced. Successive reforms of this plan were carried out in 1959, 1976, and 1985.

Accountancy was no longer used for assessing economic performance but was reduced to the role of bookkeeping, and an instrument of state control over enterprises, as well as a means of protecting firms' property. Due to "unreal" prices of the regulated economy, financial reports contained limited information serving only macroeconomic needs. The significance of accounting information grew after 1982 owing to the decentralization of economic management.

At the end of the 1980s, a general restructuring of accountancy and financial reporting occurred as a result of the rapid transition to a market economy. The reforms aimed at updating and simplifying accountancy and reducing its legal regulation. Accounting principles for all types of economic entities were unified. Poland has returned to its former legal and institutional forms. This must be achieved in the context of the globalization of the world economy. Apart from the Commercial Code of 1934, which is still operative with slight amendments, accountancy is regulated by a 1991 order of the Minister of Finance on accounting principles, incorporating legal provisions of the European Community's Fourth Directive, and by a 1991 act on auditing and publication of financial reports by public accounting firms. The process of reform will continue.

Since 1945, accountancy in Poland has developed as an independent discipline, and contacts have been established with many foreign educational institutions, resulting in the improvement of teaching programs and methods.

Initially accounting research focused on determining "true cost," accounting history, cost behavior for planning and decision making, cost and cost accounting systems modeling (often computer aided), responsibility and inflation accounting. There has been a shift since the late 1980s from accounting regulations interpretation ("de lege lata") toward concepts and recommendations ("de lege ferenda").

The empirical direction in accountancy was initiated by Professor S. Skrzywan, an outstanding figure in this field. Professor Tadeusz Peche developed in 1963 the deductive trend within a general theory of accounting in his *Zarys ogólnej teorii rachunkowości (An Outline of General Accounting Theory)*. The normative theory, initiated by Professor Edward Wojciechowski (1962) was elaborated in the 1980s by a research team from the Accounting Department of the Łódź University, which is continuing to conduct comparative research on an international scale in 1994.

Alicia Jaruga
Anna Szychta

Bibliography

Jaruga, A.A. "Poland." In *The European Accounting Guide*, edited by D. Alexander and S. Archer. London: Academic Press, 1992.

Lagiewski, C. *Dzieje rachunkowości w Polsce*. Warsaw: N.p. 1934.

Scheffs, M. *Z historii księgowości*. Wydawnictwa Związku Księgowych w Polsce. Poznań, N.p., 1939.

Skrzywan, S. "Rachunkowość w Polsce Ludowej," *w: Rachunkowość polska*. Warsaw, 1967, pp. 7–40.

Szychta, A. *Bibliograficzne calendarium rachunkowości w Polsce od XVI do XIX wieku*. Warsaw: N.p., 1989.

Wojciechowski, E. *Rachunkowość przedsiebiorstw w Polsce powojennej w świetle praktyki i przepisów normatywnych (Accounting for Enterprises in Postwar Poland: Regulatory Framework and Practice)*. Lodz: Zeszyty Naukowe Uniwersytetu Ludzkiego, 1962.

Wojciechowski, E. *Zarys rozwoju rachunkowości w Dawnej Polsce*. Warsaw: N.p., 1964.

See also AGRICULTURAL ACCOUNTING; SINGLE ENTRY BOOKKEEPING; UNIFORMITY

Pollock v. Farmers' Loan and Trust Company

Grover Cleveland's election as president in 1892 on a platform of lower tariffs meant that other sources of federal funding were needed, and in 1894 Congress passed a personal and corporate income tax law. Charles Pollock, a stockholder in Farmers' Loan and Trust Company of New York, sued the company in 1895, claiming that the income tax law was unconstitutional and the company's willingness to pay the tax was therefore an illegal distribution of income.

The Constitution gave Congress power to levy taxes but, to prevent imposing an unfair tax burden on sparsely settled farm states, required that direct taxes be assessed in proportion to each state's population. No one knew exactly what a direct tax was, but all the legal precedents favored the new income tax. However, in *Pollock v. Farmers' Loan and Trust* (1895), the Supreme Court declared parts of the act unconstitutional because (1) the federal government lacked the power to tax income from municipal bonds, and (2) a tax on income was in effect a tax on the source of that income; thus a tax on rents was a direct tax on the land from which rents were received, and it was invalid unless assessed proportionally among the states on the basis of population. At the rehearing asked for by Pollock, the Court concluded that the invalid parts of the act were so important as to void the entire law. This meant that no federal personal income tax could be levied until the Supreme Court reversed its decision or the Constitution was amended.

Michael Chatfield

Bibliography

Pollock v. Farmers' Loan and Trust, 157 U.S. 429 (1895) 158 U.S. 601 (1895).

See also INCOME TAXATION IN THE UNITED STATES; SIXTEENTH AMENDMENT

Pooling of Interests

Pooling of interests is a term that has been used both in business generally and in accounting specifically. Prior to 1950, the term was used in a number of ways—at one time describing a type of transaction rather than a particular accounting treatment. Since that date, however, it has been defined in an accounting context through official pronouncements of the Committee on Accounting Procedure (CAP) and the Accounting Principles Board (APB). The criteria for a pooling have changed over the years, but the concept has remained the same: a continuance of substantially all of the common-stock ownership of the combining businesses regardless of the ultimate form of the transaction. Whether one of the combining entities survives or a new legal entity is formed, which supersedes the old ones is unimportant; a fusion of risks and benefits hitherto separate has been deemed to occur, and no one of the combining companies is deemed to have acquired any of the others. As a result, the term "corporate marriage" has been used to describe the pooling concept.

As no acquisition has taken place, no new cost basis for the combining assets is deemed to arise. Continuity of ownership furthermore implies continuity of all recorded elements of the combining entities; all assets, liabilities, and owner's equity amounts should be combined unchanged to the extent practicable. Application of this procedure means retained earnings of the pooling entities should be combined and no goodwill should be recorded.

Implementation of the pooling treatment is dependent upon application of certain criteria, and these criteria were initially defined in only the most general terms. Between 1950 and 1970, the subjectively stated criteria were liberally construed to the point of uselessness. As a result, the accounting profession was severely criticized for allowing and even aiding in their demise, and the APB was criticized for not taking prompt and effective action.

The first authoritative mention of poolings was the CAP's Accounting Research Bulletin (ARB) No. 40, "Business Combinations," issued in 1950. The primary criterion was continuance of most, if not all, of the equity interests of the pooling companies, supported by such factors as relative size of the firms, continuity of management and similar or complementary business activities. These factors were important primarily by their cumulative presence or absence, and the accounting treatment of a pooling was specified. If the combination did not meet the criteria for a pooling, then it was deemed to be a purchase of one of the firms by another, with recognition of purchased assets at fair value and the possibility of goodwill.

Initially, the distinction between poolings and purchases was not important. The then-current standard concerning goodwill, ARB No. 24, "Intangible Assets," permitted, even if it discouraged, immediate write-off of goodwill to earned surplus (then styled). In a purchase, assets of the acquired firm could be left at their old book values (within the latitude then allowed in actual practice), and any resulting goodwill would then immediately be written off to the purchasing firm's earned surplus. With the notable exception of the absence of the acquired firm's earned surplus, much the same result of a pooling had been achieved in a purchase setting.

Important changes occurred, however, when ARB No. 24 and ARB No. 40 were incorporated in the committee's ARB No. 43, "Restatement and Revision of Accounting Research Bulletins," in 1953. "Business Combinations" was incorporated virtually intact as Chapter 7, Section C of the new bulletin, but "Intangible Assets" was modified significantly as Chapter 5 of that pronouncement. Immediate, discretionary write-offs of goodwill to earned surplus and capital surplus were expressly disallowed,

and a preference for amortization of goodwill (over permanent retention of the asset) was expressed. Very different results were now produced by election of pooling or purchase accounting for a business combination.

The amortization of goodwill was a particularly unfavorable consequence associated with employment of the purchase method. First of all, net income was lower in comparison to the pooling treatment because of such amortization. Furthermore, no tax benefit occurred to "cushion" the charge because no deduction for goodwill was allowed for federal income tax purposes. Pressure thus developed to employ the pooling treatment and to avoid the purchase method where possible.

Circumvention of the subjectively defined pooling criteria and/or related factors proved to be an easy task. "Continuity of management" was sufficiently ambiguous to permit great leeway from the outset, and "similar or complementary business activities" ceased to have any meaning in an era of increasing business diversity. "Continuance of equity interests" was stretched to include not only common stock for common-stock transactions, but also common stock for preferred stock. "Relative size" had never appeared logical to some individuals, and progressively disproportionate poolings were permitted, which eroded whatever applicability this criterion/factor might have had.

The CAP made its last pronouncement concerning poolings in 1957 in ARB No. 48, "Business Combinations," which superseded Chapter 7, Section C of ARB No. 43. "Similar or complementary activities" was no longer mentioned, and the "relative size" criterion was so de-emphasized as to be useless. While an attempt appears to have been made through ARB No. 48 to improve the clarity of "continuance of equity interests," no benefit in actual practice seems to have occurred.

In fact, several abusive practices associated with poolings arose in the 1950s and 1960s—two of the more notorious being part-purchase, part-pooling and retroactive pooling. In a part-purchase, part-pooling, the business combination would be consummated with both payment of cash and issuance of common stock by the acquiring company. The transaction would be treated as a pooling to the extent that stock was issued, thus minimizing the recording of goodwill to the "purchase" portion of the combination. Retroactive poolings occurred because of the issuance of ARB No. 48. In weak-

P

ening yet further the already eroding criteria of ARB No. 43, the new pronouncement would have permitted some earlier combinations recorded as purchases to have been recorded as poolings. Some businesses then altered their accounts and financial statements involving a purchase made several years previous to reflect a pooling of interests; a pooling was thus retroactively recorded.

The APB assumed the responsibility of promulgating accounting standards from the CAP in 1959, and one of its earliest priorities was the business combinations/goodwill issue. Before acting in this area, it awaited the completion of, among other things, two research studies on business combinations and goodwill, respectively. Neither of these studies produced acceptable alternatives, and the goodwill study was not completed until 1968. In the intervening 11 years since ARB No. 48, the aforementioned abuses as well as others flourished, and the accounting profession was severely criticized for taking no action during the greatest merger movement in history to that time. Following a warning by the Securities and Exchange Commission (SEC) that it would have to set rules in this area if the profession did not, the APB held meetings and issued Exposure Drafts in 1969 and 1970, culminating in APB No. 16, "Business Combinations," and APB No. 17, "Intangible Assets," both issued in August 1970. During its meetings, the board originally concluded that pooling of interests should be abolished but changed its stance to allow both the pooling and purchase methods, though not as alternatives. Along with 12 other criteria for a pooling, the board included a size test whereby one of the pooling firms had to be at least one-third the size of the other, then relaxed this to one-ninth in a later Exposure Draft, and finally dropped it completely when Opinion No. 16 was issued. The board was again criticized for first proposing to do away with the pooling treatment and then relenting through three successively weakened positions.

If the 12 criteria are met, the business combination must be accounted for as a pooling. Otherwise, the transaction is deemed to be a purchase with subsequent possible recognition of goodwill.

The 12 criteria for a pooling, viewed in historical context, are all associated directly or indirectly with some facet of continuity of ownership interest of the combining firms. For the first time in the troubled history of pooling of interests, this continuity is defined in explicit detail, and certain abuses are eliminated through application of the criteria. Notwithstanding the possibility of some interpretation in certain of these guidelines, the criteria are notable for their specificity.

The pooling controversy was, in microcosm, indicative of many of the weaknesses besetting the APB. Resolution of the issue took far too long by a part-time organization viewed by some as insufficiently independent of clients and too sensitive to other outside pressures. Not coincidentally, a commission was formed shortly after APB Nos. 16 and 17 were written to find a better way to promulgate accounting standards, ultimately resulting in the formation, in 1973, of the Financial Accounting Standards Board (FASB).

The entire concept of pooling of interests rests upon theoretically troubled ground. Many unresolved issues and the constantly changing economic environment contribute to continued unrest and possible reexamination of the pooling issue at some future point. Inflation and resulting differences between market and book values of assets, the nature and significance of owners' equity classifications, the very nature of business combinations, the accounting and tax treatment of goodwill, and periodic merger movements are all factors that can contribute to the continuance, demise, or even subsequent reemergence of the "pooling of interests" concept.

Hugh P. Hughes

Bibliography

Briloff, A.J. "Dirty Pooling," *Accounting Review*, July 1967, pp. 489–496.

Gunther, S.P. "Part Purchase-Part Pooling: The Infusion of Confusion into Fusion," *New York Certified Public Accountant*, April 1968, pp. 241–249.

———. "Poolings, Purchases, Goodwill," *New York Certified Public Accountant*, January 1971, pp. 25–37.

Hughes, H.P. *Goodwill in Accounting: A History of the Issues and Problems*. Atlanta: Business Publishing Division, Georgia State University, 1982.

Mosich, A.N. "Retroactive Poolings in Corporate Mergers," *Journal of Business*, July 1968, pp. 352–362.

Rayburn, F.F., and O.S. Powers. "A History of Pooling of Interests Accounting for Business Combinations in the United States," *Accounting Historians Journal*,

December 1991, pp. 155–192.

Wyatt, A.R. *A Critical Study of Accounting for Business Combinations*. Accounting Research Study No. 5. New York: AICPA, 1963.

See also ACCOUNTING PRINCIPLES BOARD; ACCOUNTING RESEARCH BULLETINS; ACCOUNTING RESEARCH STUDIES; *CARPENTER V. HALL;* CONSOLIDATED FINANCIAL STATEMENTS; EUROPEAN COMMUNITY (UNION) ACCOUNTING: FOURTH AND SEVENTH ACCOUNTING DIRECTIVES; FINANCIAL ACCOUNTING STANDARDS BOARD; GOODWILL; INTANGIBLE ASSETS; SECURITIES AND EXCHANGE COMMISSION

Positive Accounting

In contrast to a normative theory, which relies on prescriptive pronouncements of what should be, a positive theory relies on prediction and explanation of an observed relationship. Positive research is based on scientific principles that require the researcher to be objective, logical, and neutral. Positive theories are based on inductive reasoning whereby general rules and principles are based on consistent observed behavior. In accounting, the positivist approach was most prominently popularized by R.L. Watts and J.L. Zimmerman in their two seminal articles in 1978 and 1979 and their subsequent book in 1986, so much so the positive-accounting theorists have been labeled the Rochester School after the university affiliation of Watts and Zimmerman.

The positive school owes much to the work of the French philosopher Auguste Comte, who developed his sociology in the early nineteenth century. His approach was value neutral in that knowledge was acquired through careful observation and empirical verification of the external world. He saw positivism as part of man's progression from religious theorist to scientific discoverer. Part of this discovery, however, was a realization that man is limited in his potential for understanding all that goes on around him.

John Neville Keynes, a British economic theorist in the 1890s and early 1900s and the father of the more famous economist, John Maynard Keynes, brought logical positivism into the realm of economics in the late nineteenth century by clearly distinguishing between positive science and normative science and proposing the positive approach as the only appropriate way of studying political economy. Logi-cal positivism was quite popular among behavioral scientists during the first half of the twentieth century, including such noted authorities as United States Nobel laureate Herbert Simon, who supported the approach to the study of administrative behavior. In fact, researchers in accounting, economics, and administration have used the positivist approach to varying degrees for much of the twentieth century. It has only been since the late 1970s, however, that accounting has acknowledged positive theory as a major paradigm in the field.

Positive accounting theory as developed by its proponents, while having many similarities to logical positivism, is not logical positivism. Positive accounting theory is an attempt to explain and predict accounting behavior based on the contracting costs between different stakeholders in an organization. These costs may consist of any combination of transaction costs, agency costs, information costs, negotiation costs, and bankruptcy costs. It is the relative magnitudes of each of these contracting costs that influences accounting choices. Based on assumed wealth-maximizing behavior of the parties involved, hypotheses can be developed and tested to predict accounting method choices. These hypotheses can be generally broken down into three categories: bonus plans, debt covenants, and political process.

The bonus-plan hypothesis states that managers will use accounting methods to adjust reported income so as to maximize their personal wealth. Many tests of this hypothesis have been conducted with Healy (1985) being the most cited. He found that managers increased reported income through the use of accounting accruals if it served to increase their bonuses. If a bonus would not be forthcoming because income was outside the bonus range, Healy found income-decreasing behavior that would lead to higher expected profits and bonuses in future years, all other things being constant.

The debt-covenant hypothesis predicts that managers are more likely to choose income-increasing accounting methods the closer they are to any restrictive covenant in their debt agreements. This behavior will help to avoid additional debt-contracting and possible bankruptcy costs. Due to the rather crude proxies that have been used to test this hypothesis, such as the overall corporate debt/equity ratio, only weak support is generally found. For instance, Hand, Hughes, and Sefcik (1990), in a study of insubstance defeasance behavior, conclude that their evidence "suggests that some firms may have had private information that they were likely to experience drastically worse future earnings, and thereby defeased when they did in order to avoid some of the effects on their bond covenants."

The political-cost hypothesis predicts that prominent firms will choose income-decreasing accounting methods, or income-smoothing methods, to avoid calling attention to themselves and to avoid political costs of investigation, regulation, and lobbying. In most studies, corporate size is used as a proxy for political sensitivity. The strongest support for this hypothesis deals with the oil and gas industry, particularly during the 1970s as evidenced by Zimmerman (1983). Additionally, some evidence to support the political-cost hypothesis was found by Cahan (1992) when he examined the accounting-accrual behavior of firms under monopoly-related antitrust investigations. These firms were more likely to report income-decreasing accruals in the years of investigation than in prior years or when compared to a matched sample of firms not under investigation.

The positive accounting school has gathered some criticism from those who perhaps can be classified as followers of the normative accounting school of thought. Such criticism has tended to sharpen the thinking of all involved in this debate between the two schools of thought. Some of the critics are Charles Christenson, Robert R. Sterling, and L.A. Boland and I.M. Gordon. Christenson (1983) stated that the positive accounting school (or, as he stressed, the Rochester School) confuses the phenomenal domains of accounting entities and accountants. He felt that the positive school of thought in science had long ago been considered to be obsolete. Christenson questioned the explanatory nature of the theories of the Rochester School. Lastly, he felt that the school had not rigorously attempted to falsify its theories.

Sterling (1990) attacked the school for its notion that science can be value free and for its underwhelming conclusions, especially in the light of the onerous amount of detail given about the tests to demonstrate how utility is being maximized. Boland and Gordon (1992), after discussing some of the other critics of the positive accounting school, questioned the neoclassical model of the positive accounting school. They questioned the equilibrium assumption of that model, in light of disequilibrium.

While some accounting researchers had used a positivist approach prior to 1978, it was Watts and Zimmerman who codified and strongly supported this new wave of research. Their influence on accounting thought, hypotheses for accounting choice behavior, and the methodology for testing the resulting predictions has been significant. They founded the *Journal of Accounting and Economics* in 1979 to publish economics-based accounting research, including positive theory research, and under their co-editorship it has become the most widely cited journal in accounting. The controversies that have occurred over the precepts and findings of positive accounting show that accounting thought has reached maturity as a discipline.

Jeffrey W. Power
Richard Vangermeersch

Bibliography

Boland, L.A., and I.M. Gordon. "Criticizing Positive Accounting Theory," *Contemporary Accounting Research*, Fall 1992, pp. 142–170.

Cahan, S.F. "The Effect of Antitrust Investigations on Discretionary Accruals: A Refined Test of the Political-Cost Hypothesis," *Accounting Review*, January 1992, pp. 77–95.

Christenson, C. "The Methodology of Positive Accounting," *Accounting Review*, January 1983, pp. 1–22.

Hand, J.R.M., P.J. Hughes, and S.E. Sefcik. "Insubstance Defeasances: Security Price Reactions and Motivation," *Journal of Accounting and Economics* (Netherlands), May 1990, pp. 47–89.

Healy, P. "The Impact of Bonus Schemes on the Selection of Accounting Principles," *Journal of Accounting and Economics*, April 1985, pp. 85–107.

Sterling, R.R. "Positive Accounting: An Assessment," *Abacus*, September 1990, pp. 97–135.

Watts, R.L., and J.L. Zimmerman. "The Demand for and Supply of Accounting Theories: The Market for Excuses," *Accounting Review*, April 1979, pp. 273–305.

———. *Positive Accounting Theory.* Englewood Cliffs, NJ: Prentice-Hall, 1986.

———. "Towards a Positive Theory of the Determination of Accounting Standards," *Accounting Review*, January

1978, pp. 112–134.

Zimmerman, J.L. "Taxes and Firm Size," *Journal of Accounting and Economics*, August 1983, pp. 119–149.

See also ACCRUAL ACCOUNTING; AGENCY THEORY; BALL AND BROWN'S "AN EMPIRICAL EVALUATION OF ACCOUNTING INCOME NUMBERS"; BEAVER, WILLIAM; MANIPULATION OF INCOME; MATTESSICH, RICHARD; MATCHING; STERLING, ROBERT R.

Postulates of Accounting

Postulates of accounting generally refers to Accounting Research Study No. 1, *The Basic Postulates of Accounting* by Maurice Moonitz, issued in 1961 by the American Institute of Certified Public Accountants (AICPA). In this study, the term postulate denotes "those basic propositions of accounting which describe the accountant's understanding of the world in which he lives and acts." Thus, the term "postulate" is similar to the economic term "assumption."

Moonitz's basic postulates of accounting are "self-evident propositions" extracted from the economic and political environment in which accounting functions, by both deductive and inductive approaches. Deductive inferences come out of the environment in which accounting functions. Inductive leads are pursued from the business, economic, and political realm in which accounting operates.

In defining the necessity for postulates, Moonitz explained that the postulates serve as a foundation for accounting principles. To be "fruitful," the postulates must relate principles to the existing world. Thus, if a postulate is "a fiction," then the principles and rules derived therefrom will relate to a "fictional" world (Moonitz 1963).

The first five postulates refer to the economic environment. These postulates have been generally accepted as statements about the environment. Dissenters generally feel that the postulates are "obvious truths" and/or "trivial," not requiring statement. These five postulates are:

A-1. Quantification. Quantitative data are helpful in making rational economic decisions—that is, in making choices among alternatives so that actions are correctly related to consequences.

A-2. Exchange. Most of the goods and services that are produced are distributed through exchange and are not directly consumed by the producers.

A-3. Entities (including identification of the entity). Economic activity is carried on through specific units or entities. Any report on the activity must identify clearly the particular unit or entity involved.

A-4. Time Period. Economic activity is carried on during specifiable periods of time. Any report on that activity must identify clearly the period of time involved.

A-5. Unit of Measure. Money is the common denominator in terms of which goods and services, including labor, natural resources, and capital are measured. Any report must clearly indicate which money is being used.

The following group of four accounting-specific postulates given by Moonitz also finds a wide acceptance in comments to the AICPA. Once again, dissenters indicate that they primarily find the set to be simple descriptions of current accounting practice. This group is:

B-1. Financial Statements. (Related to A-1). The results of the accounting process are expressed in a set of fundamentally related financial statements that articulate with each other since they are based upon the same underlying data.

B-2. Market Prices. (Related to A-2). Accounting data are based on prices generated by past, present, or future exchanges that have actually taken place or are expected to.

B-3. Entities. (Related to A-3). The results of the accounting process are expressed in terms of specific units or entities.

B-4. Tentativeness. (Related to A-4). The results of operations for relatively short periods of time are tentative whenever allocations between past, present, and future periods are required.

A third set of postulates relates to accounting "imperatives." This group is more controversial because the postulates stress "what ought to be goals, objectives, and standards" of accounting. Of this set, the first two postulates are generally accepted by respondents to the AICPA. However, many respondents do not believe that the latter three deserve to be classified as basic assumptions. Of this group, the postulate accepting a stable monetary unit creates the most controversy. Those dissatisfied point out that the purchasing power of the monetary unit should be considered—thus, the postulate should refer to a "constant monetary unit." The last group of postulates is:

C-1. Continuity (including the correlative concept of limited life). In the absence of evidence to the contrary, the entity should be viewed as remaining in operation indefinitely. In the presence of evidence that the entity has a limited life, it should not be viewed as remaining in operation indefinitely.

C-2. Objectivity. Changes in assets and liabilities, and the related effects (if any) on revenues, expenses, retained earnings, and the like, should not be given formal recognition in the accounts earlier than the point of time at which they can be measured in objective terms.

C-3. Consistency. The procedures used in accounting for a given entity should be appropriate for the measurement of its position and its activities and should be followed consistently from period to period.

C-4. Stable Unit. Accounting reports should be based on a stable measuring unit.

C-5. Disclosure. Accounting reports should disclose that which is necessary to make them not misleading.

To relate the postulates to accounting, *The Basic Postulates of Accounting* defined the term "accounting" as a function that (1) measures the resources held by specific entities; (2) reflects the claims against and interests in those entities; (3) measures the changes in those resources, claims, and interests; (4) assigns the changes to specifiable periods of time; and (5) expresses the foregoing in terms of money as a common denominator. The term "cost" is given a specific definition with respect to cash, as the price established in an exchange, suggesting that noncash acquisitions use terms such as "fair value" or "appraised value" to replace "cost." Lastly, the study attempts to distinguish between earnings and profit and restrict use of the term "income" to natural persons. The discussion of earnings, profits, income, and comprehensive income continues in accounting literature.

Leonard Spacek is a long-time managing partner of Arthur Andersen and Company, and the author of "Comments." Considerable attention is given to "Comments" at the conclusion of *The Basic Postulates of Accounting,* in which "fairness" is viewed as the "one basic accounting postulate underlying accounting principles." Three proponents of "fairness" as the sole accounting postulate point out in "Comments on the Basic Postulates of Accounting" (1963) that the sole objective of accounting is its "usefulness" to society as a whole. Some of the six opponents of "fairness" point out that it "is at best an ethical concept related to the existing sociological environment and at all times is a subjective judgment."

Moonitz's postulates of accounting are not incorporated into the conceptual framework of the Financial Accounting Standards Board (FASB). The conceptual framework chooses to follow the proponents of "fairness" or "usefulness" in establishment of the objectives of financial reporting in Concept Statement No. 1, Objectives of Financial Reporting by Business Enterprises (1978). The FASB's viewpoint follows the users approach proposed by the AICPA's 1973 Trueblood Report, "Objectives of Financial Statements." The postulates of accounting chosen by Moonitz (1963) instead "denote those basic propositions of accounting which describe the accountant's understanding of the world in which he lives and acts."

The first reference to "accounting postulates" occurs in *Changing Concepts of Business Income,* the 1952 report of the Study Group on

Business Income of the American Institute of Accountants (AIA). George Oliver May, long-time managing partner of Price Waterhouse and Company, was responsible for the Study Group's report, which states that "income accounting necessarily rests on a framework of postulates and assumptions; these are accepted and acceptable as being useful, not as demonstrable truths; their usefulness is always open to reconsideration."

The first of the three accounting postulates given by May arises from the Study Group's discussion of whether "income" in any given year from "manufacture" or "trading" is influenced by changes in the value of the monetary unit during the period. In literature prior to the 1913 enactment of a federal income tax, the word "profits" meant the realized increment in value of the whole amount invested in an undertaking. Reflecting the accounting, legal, and economic literature subsequent to 1913, the Study Group chose to accept the stable-currency concept. In choosing a stable currency, May cites American economist W.C. Mitchell, stating that "insight into the role of money in economic life should heighten our awareness of the danger that confronts us." The first postulate thus adheres to the 1940 statement by William Andrew Paton of the University of Michigan and A.C. Littleton of the University of Illinois that the "recorded dollar continues to represent actual cost."

> 1. The monetary postulate. . . . Fluctuations in value of the monetary unit, which is the accounting symbol, may properly be ignored.

The second postulate is outside of the discussion on "income." May states that it is adopted for "convenience" from Paton and Littleton's discussion of the "going concern," or continuity, concept.

> 2. The permanence postulate. . . . In the absence of actual evidence to the contrary, the prospective life of the enterprise may be deemed to be indefinitely long.

In the third postulate the Study Group emphasizes that unrealized appreciation is not an element in the "income from operations" following the works of Robert Hiester Montgomery, the noted accounting practitioner and

long-time writer of textbooks in auditing, and Alfred Marshall, a noted English economist of the late 1800s and early 1900s.

> 3. The realization postulate. . . . The entire income from sale arises at the moment when realization is deemed to take place.

In summarizing the need for postulates of accounting, Moonitz stated that "no set of accounting postulates and principles will ever solve all accounting problems, any more than the Ten Commandments can answer all questions of right and wrong. . . . Formulation of postulates and principles will give accounting the frame of reference, the integrating structure it needs to give more than a passing meaning to its specific procedures."

Adrianne E. Slaymaker

Bibliography

American Institute of Accountants. *Changing Concepts of Business Income*. Report of the Study Group on Business Income. New York: Macmillan, 1952.

American Institute of Certified Public Accountants. *Objectives of Financial Statements: Report of the Study Group on the Objectives of Financial Statements*. New York: American Institute of Certified Public Accountants, 1973.

———. "Comments on *The Basic Postulates of Accounting*," *Journal of Accountancy*, January 1963, pp. 44–55.

Littleton, A.C. *Structure of Accounting Theory*. Sarasota, FL: American Accounting Association, 1953.

Marshall, A. *Principles of Economics*. New York: Macmillan, 1890.

May, G.O. *Financial Accounting: A Distillation of Experience*. New York: Macmillan, 1943.

Mitchell, W.C. *The Backward Art of Spending Money*. New York: McGraw-Hill, 1937.

Montgomery, R.H. *Auditing Theory and Practice*. 4th ed. New York: Ronald Press, 1927.

Moonitz, M. *The Basic Postulates of Accounting*. Accounting Research Study No. 1. New York: AICPA, 1961.

———. "Basic Postulates of Accounting," *Journal of Accountancy*, November 1961, pp. 71–72.

———. "Why Do We Need 'Postulates' and 'Principles'?" *Journal of Accountancy*, December 1963, pp. 42–46.

Most, K.S., and A.L. Winters. "Focus on Standard Setting: From Trueblood to the FASB," *Journal of Accountancy*, February 1977, pp. 67–75.

Paton, W.A. *Accounting Theory: With Special Reference to the Corporate Enterprise.* New York: Ronald Press, 1922.

———, and A.C. Littleton. *An Introduction to Corporate Accounting Standards.* American Accounting Association Monograph No. 3. New York: American Accounting Association, 1940.

Scott, DR. "The Basics for Accounting Principles," *Accounting Review*, December 1941, pp. 341–349.

See also Accounting Research Studies; *An Introduction to Corporate Accounting Standards;* Comparability; Conceptual Framework; Continuity; Entity Theory; Matching; May, George Oliver; Moonitz, Maurice; Objectivity; Periodicity; Realization; Spacek, Leonard; Study Group on Business Income's *Five Monographs on Business Income;* Trueblood, Robert Martin

Present Value
See Discounted Cash Flow

Previts, Gary John (1942–)
Gary John Previts was one of the founders and first president (1973–1975) of the Academy of Accounting Historians. He received its Hourglass Award in 1980. Previts has served as the editor of *Accounting Historians Journal* (1987–1989), *Research in Accounting Regulation* (1987–), the Modern Accounting Perspectives and Practices Series (1978–), and the Accounting History Classic Series (1988–). He has served on the American Institute of Certified Public Accountants (AICPA) SEC Regulations Committee (1988–) and twice on the Governing Council of the AICPA. He received his Ph.D. from the University of Florida in 1972.

Previts and Barbara D. Merino (1979) placed American accounting into economic, institutional, political and social perspectives from the early European settlement of the U.S.

to the present. Robert Mednick and Previts (1987) traced the scope of CPA service, in an article in the AICPA Centennial Issue of the *Journal of Accountancy*. In an interesting passage they contrasted the cautious views of George Oliver May with the more expansive position of Arthur Andersen. Mark Moran and Previts (1984) traced the generally complementary, but occasionally troubled, relationship between the accounting profession and the Securities and Exchange Commission (SEC). Previts, Parker, and Coffman (1990) stressed the "was-is-ought" perspectives of accounting history in "Accounting History: Definition and Relevance." They later (1990) developed further their thoughts on the subject matter and methodology of research in accounting history in "An Accounting Historiography? Subject Matter and Methodology."

Previts is surely regarded as an "action type" accounting historian.

Richard Vangermeersch

Bibliography
Mednick, R., and G.J. Previts. "The Scope of CPA Services: A View of the Future from the Perspective of a Century of Progress," *Journal of Accountancy*, May 1987, pp. 220–238.

Moran, M., and G.J. Previts. "The SEC and the Profession, 1934–84: The Realities of Self-Regulation," *Journal of Accountancy*, July 1984, pp. 68–80.

Previts, G.J., and B.D. Merino. *A History of Accounting in America: An Historical Interpretation of the Cultural Significance of Accounting.* New York: John Wiley & Sons, 1979.

———, L.D. Parker, and E.N. Coffman. "Accounting History: Definition and Relevance," *Abacus*, March 1990, pp. 1–16.

———. "An Accounting Historiography? Subject Matter and Methodology," *Abacus*, September 1990, pp. 136–158.

See also Academy of Accounting Historians; American Accounting Association; American Institute of Certified Public Accountants; Andersen, Arthur E.; Research Methods in Accounting History; Securities and Exchange Commission; Stone, Williard E.; *Uniform Accounting*

Printing Press

The invention of Johannes Gutenberg in Germany in the 1440s, the printing press was instrumental in spreading the "Method of Venice," the double entry accounting system popularized by Luca Pacioli in his 1494 book, throughout Europe.

The printing press came about a few hundred years after the founding of the universities in Europe and the introduction of paper, a much cheaper printing medium than the vellum it replaced. Students provided a market for the books, as did the Catholic Church. Bookshops were established and flourished in the first half of the fifteenth century to match the new learning spreading through Europe.

By the 1480s, the art of printing had spread throughout Europe. The printers of that day still held the idea that books should resemble, as closely as possible, the hand-copied manuscripts of the scribes of prior times, which explains the unique beauty of the early printed books in accounting. One of the hotbeds of printing was Venice. Pacioli's treatise on bookkeeping was a small part of his encyclopedic work on mathematics, *Summa de Arithmetica, Geometria, Proportioni et Proportionalita*, published in Venice in 1494 by Paganino de Paganini. Within a century, the treatise had been translated into five languages. The invention and the spread of the printing press helped make the "Method of Venice" (or the "Italian Method") common knowledge throughout Europe.

Richard Vangermeersch

Bibliography

Chatfield, M. *A History of Accounting Thought.* Hinsdale, IL: Dryden Press, 1974.

Clair, C. *A History of European Printing.* London: Academic Press, 1976.

See also PACIOLI, LUCA

Professional Accounting Bodies

Professional accounting bodies have become a worldwide phenomenon by the end of the twentieth century, including a wide range of organizations besides those with the traditional public-accounting orientation.

The first association of accountants noted by Edward Boyd in Richard Brown's *A History of Accounting and Accountants* was the *Collegio dei Raxonati* founded in Venice in 1581. By 1669 it had become so influential that only members of the college could exercise the functions of an accountant in connection with either public administration or the law. Both an apprenticeship program and an examination process were established. Milan established a college and adopted a statute in 1744 that established rules for admission. "These required a knowledge of economics, commerce, and public affairs; a complete knowledge of Latin and arithmetic; a five years' apprenticeship, the attainment of 25 years of age, and an examination in the science of accounting." The college in Milan was a private, not a city, institution like Venice's, and had a turbulent history. The later unification of Italy led to the founding of colleges, or guilds, of accountants in each province.

The first professional accounting body in the English-speaking countries was founded in Edinburgh, Scotland, on January 17, 1853, under the leadership of Alexander Weir Robertson. The Society of Accountants in Edinburgh was granted a Royal Charter on October 23, 1854. It was followed on March 15, 1855 by the Institute of Accountants and Actuaries in Glasgow. The Edinburgh society quickly established the professional designation of chartered accountant (CA). By 1870, bodies were formed in Liverpool and London, then later in other cities in England. On May 11, 1880, the Institute of Chartered Accountants in England and Wales was granted a Royal Charter. On May 14, 1888, the Institute of Chartered Accountants in Ireland received its Royal Charter. Accounting bodies were founded before 1900 in these British colonies: the Association of Accountants in Montreal in 1880; the Institute of Chartered Accountants of Ontario in 1883; the Chartered Accountants Association of Manitoba in 1886; the Institute of Accountants in South Australia in 1885; the Incorporated Institute of Accountants of Victoria in 1886; the Queensland Institute of Accountants in 1891; the Sydney Institute of Public Accountants in 1894; the Incorporated Institute of Accountants of New Zealand in 1894; the Institute of Accountants in Natal in 1895; and the Institute of Accountants and Auditors in the South African Republic in 1894.

In the United States, the American Association of Public Accountants was founded in 1887. It cooperated with the Institute of Accounts, formed in 1882 and consisting of both public and other accountants, to attain the nation's first certified public accountant (CPA) exam, in New York in 1896. Pennsylvania soon followed.

Besides those in Italy, professional accounting bodies founded before 1900 in Continental Europe included the Netherlands Institute of Accountants in 1895 and the Swedish Society of Auditors in 1899. Professional accounting bodies were formed very early in South America, in Uruguay in 1825 and Argentina in 1836.

One way of showing the take-off of professional accounting organizations throughout the world in the twentieth century is to list the countries that are members of the International Federation of Accountants (IFAC), the worldwide organization of national professional accounting bodies. It has the broad objective of developing and enhancing a coordinated worldwide accounting profession with harmonized standards. These bodies represent approximately a million accountants in practice, industry and commerce, education, and government service. The countries in the IFAC in 1993 were: Australia, Austria, Bahamas, Bahrain, Bangladesh, Barbados, Belgium, Bolivia, Botswana, Brazil, Canada, Chile, Colombia, Cyprus, Denmark, Dominican Republic, Egypt, Fiji, Finland, France, Germany, Ghana, Greece, Hong Kong, Hungary, Iceland, Indonesia, Iraq, Republic of Ireland, India, Israel, Italy, Jamaica, Japan, Jordan, Kenya, Korea, Kuwait, Lebanon, Lesotho, Liberia, Libya, Luxembourg, Malawi, Malaysia, Malta, Mexico, Netherlands, New Zealand, Nigeria, Norway, Pakistan, Panama, Paraguay, Peru, Philippines, Poland, Portugal, Singapore, South Africa, Spain, Sri Lanka, Sweden, Swaziland, Switzerland, Syria, Taiwan, Tanzania, Trinidad and Tobago, Thailand, Tunisia, Turkey, the United Kingdom, the United States, Uruguay, Yugoslavia, Zambia, and Zimbabwe. To illustrate the fact that professional accounting bodies are not only public-accounting oriented, the following bodies in the English-speaking world were members in 1993 of the IFAC: the Australian Society of Certified Practicing Accountants; the Institute of Cost and Management Accountants of Bangladesh; the Certified General Accountants Association of Canada; the Institute of Cost and Works Accountants of India; the Institute of Cost and Management Accountants of Pakistan; the Chartered Institute of Management Accountants; the Chartered Institute of Public Finance and Accounting; the Institute of Management Accountants (U.S.); the Institute of Internal Auditors (U.S.); and the National Association of State Boards of Accountancy (U.S.).

The twentieth century marked the take-off period for professional accounting organizations throughout the world. The twenty-first century should see the continuation of this trend and also a consolidation of these bodies.

Richard Vangermeersch

Bibliography
Brown, R., ed. *A History of Accounting and Accountants*. Edinburgh: T.C. & E.C. Jack, 1905. Reprint. New York: B. Franklin, 1966.

See also ACCOUNTING AND THE ACCOUNTANT: PORTRAYALS; AMERICAN INSTITUTE OF CERTIFIED PUBLIC ACCOUNTANTS; CERTIFIED PUBLIC ACCOUNTANT; CHARTERED INSTITUTE OF MANAGEMENT ACCOUNTANTS; INSTITUTE OF CHARTERED ACCOUNTANTS IN ENGLAND AND WALES; INSTITUTE OF INTERNAL AUDITORS; INSTITUTE OF MANAGEMENT ACCOUNTANTS; ITALY, AFTER PACIOLI; SCOTLAND: EARLY WRITERS IN DOUBLE ENTRY ACCOUNTING; STATE REGULATION OF THE ACCOUNTANCY PROFESSION (U.S.)

Proffer System

The proffer system was a tax collection procedure in medieval England. While certain taxes could be paid directly to the treasury, in most cases an intermediary was needed between Crown and subjects. The sheriff was the king's representative in both civil and military affairs and usually occupied the principal castle in the county. He was collector of the king's revenues and bailiff of his country estates, which were farmed out for a fixed rent. He administered justice in the county court, collected rents for the use of roads, forests, and fields, collected import and export duties, tributes from the towns, fines, penalties, and other taxes. He was accountable for tax payments to the Exchequer.

Twice yearly, at Easter and Michaelmas (September 29), the sheriff of each county was summoned to attend the Exchequer sessions at Westminster. At Easter he brought with him and paid into the Lower Exchequer about half the annual assessments for which his county was liable. Any collections of arrears from prior years were checked against the Pipe Roll, which listed rents, fines, taxes, and other fixed levies due the king, but no entries were made for deposits of current year tax collections. Instead, the treasurer, having accepted the sheriff's proffer, or payment on account, ordered a wooden tally to be cut. This was the sheriff's receipt for payments rendered.

At Michaelmas the sheriff returned, deposited the rest of the Crown revenues, and submitted to audit. This was his final accounting. Though he had paid half his county's debt at Easter, the Michaelmas summons was not for the balance, but for the whole year's revenues, and the Receipt Roll was compiled. The treasurer began by formally asking the sheriff if he was ready to account. If so, the treasurer read the amounts due from his copy of the Pipe Roll. He asked if the sheriff's customary expenses were the same as in the previous year. The sheriff had to produce writs warranting any extraordinary expenditures. These were read aloud and checked against duplicates from the Exchequer, then recorded in the Pipe Roll. Expenses such as repairs to castles were vouched both by writ and by two of the king's surveyors who certified the performance and the cost of the work. There followed a list of accounts, which included any arrears of "farm" rents, "conventiones" or voluntary payments to gain the king's favor, murder fines imposed on the county when the murderers could not be found, aids and "gifts" of cities and boroughs, and the goods of felons and fugitives.

Final settlement took place across a table laid with the checkered cloth after which the Exchequer was named. On one side was the sheriff with his collections, his tally, and his disbursement vouchers. The treasurer read from the Exactory Roll on which the current year "farms" of all the counties were written. Across the table from the sheriff, an official called the calculator set out on the checkered squares counters representing the whole year's payments due the Crown. The total being agreed to by both parties, the calculator laid out another row of counters showing the amount paid by the sheriff at Easter. The Exchequer's tally stock and the sheriff's foil were fitted together to verify that the notches and cuttings corresponded. As the treasurer called the amounts due, the sheriff's Michaelmas collections were placed in the squares on his side of the calculating board and "blanched" by the accountant, who had assayed the coin and now subtracted the necessary number of pence in the pound. A new tally was later made for the adjusted amount. Crown vouchers for the sheriff's allowances were placed on the board as further deductions from the amount due. When all the Crown's vouchers were balanced by payments, tallies, and allowance vouchers, the sheriff was quit. He swore to the marshal of the Exchequer that he had made his lawful account according to his conscience, and was dismissed.

The modern relevance of this essentially visual and oral system is that accounting functions may be performed efficiently with very limited means. Paper was a novelty in England before the sixteenth century, yet without printed schedules or forms, taxes were routinely collected and delivered intact to the treasury. The notched stock or its equivalent was a necessary part of taxation in a society where most taxpayers were illiterates to whom a parchment receipt meant nothing. Protection against fraud was always central to feudal accounting, and the proffer system proved an ingenious way to assist and control revenue collectors who often had to count with the help of their fingers.

Michael Chatfield

Bibliography

Baxter, W.T. "Early Accounting: The Tally and Checkerboard," *Accounting Historians Journal*, December 1989, pp. 43–83.

Chatfield, M. *A History of Accounting Thought.* Rev. ed. Huntington, NY: Krieger, 1977.

See also EXTERNAL AUDITING; MANORIAL ACCOUNTING; MEDIEVAL ACCOUNTING; PIPE ROLL; TALLY STICK

Proprietary Theory

Luca Pacioli's transaction analysis in *Summa de Arithmetica* (1494) focused on proprietorship. Three hundred years later his interest in the motivation behind double entry bookkeeping was revived, under different conditions and for different reasons. The British classical economists, who were contemporary with the first accounting theorists, emphasized the distinction between a stock of wealth (capital) and its flow (income). At this same time, corporate accountants were given the tasks of calculating the amount of retained earnings available for dividends and of making sure that invested capital was maintained intact while fixed asset balances were converted to expense. For these and other reasons, "capital" became associated with ownership rather than being simply a residual balance. The accounting equation was rediscovered, and a more strategic view was taken of the bookkeeping process, giving less importance to the exchange of values between accounts and more to the purpose of the firm, the nature of capital, and especially to the meaning of accounts from an owner's viewpoint.

In *A New Treatise of Arithmetic and Bookkeeping* (Edinburgh, 1718) Alexander Malcolm touched on the essence of proprietary theory when he distinguished between the totality of a merchant's capital and its constituent parts. Malcolm also saw that profits constituted an increase in proprietorship, and that while some transactions only shifted assets and liabilities from one account to another, others raised or lowered total capital, changing the proprietor's wealth at the same time that they altered the balance of net assets. Hustcraft Stephens in *Italian Book-keeping Reduced into an Art* (London, 1735) made a similar distinction between the whole of a proprietor's capital and the individual assets that comprised it. As he saw it, the aim of bookkeeping was to find the "Condition and Extent of a Man's Estate."

In *British-Indian Book-keeping* (London, 1800), James Fulton, a bookkeeper with the Board of Revenue in Bengal, India, published a more readable attempt to explain the internal equilibrium of double entry bookkeeping. Noting how difficult it was to quickly determine a company's equity position, Fulton tried to develop methods that showed the effects of all transactions on capital. In taking this approach he grasped one basic aspect of proprietary theory. Owner's equity is the collective expression of all other accounts, which "form merely the particulars of it: and the grand aim of double entry is, to ascertain the true state of the stock [capital] account." He also saw that the balance of capital is not only the difference between assets and liabilities but is also the original investment plus and minus operating changes since a company's inception. To illustrate this, Fulton prepared a forerunner retained earnings statement showing the effect of all transactions on capital and reconciling the capital balance with net changes in asset and liability accounts.

The exposition of proprietary theory was completed by Frederic William Cronhelm in *Double Entry by Single* (London, 1818). Taking Fulton's book as a point of departure,

Cronhelm emphasized the equivalence between total capital and its constituent parts and argued that the purpose of bookkeeping "is to show the owner at all times the value of his total capital, and of every part of it." In his algebraic approach to transaction analysis, the capital account became a mathematical equilibrating device, by inference a credit item opposite to assets. Transactions affected the accounting equation by increasing or decreasing assets, liabilities, or capital. Cronhelm envisioned a series of asset conversions during a firm's operating cycle, with income entering the capital account as a net increase in proprietorship. Expense and revenue accounts, including profit and loss, were created to avoid the inconvenience of recording every change in wealth directly to capital. Cronhelm treated them as branches of owner's equity.

The proprietary theory was refined by a New York accountant and teacher, Thomas Jones, whose *Principles and Practices of Bookkeeping* (1841) has been called the first modern accounting textbook. Jones saw financial statements rather than ledger balances as the final step in the bookkeeping cycle. Accounts implied two statements of owner's affairs, the balance sheet and income statement, each of which arrived independently at the same profit figure. Moreover, the interrelationship of real and nominal accounts suggested that both financial statements should have equal status. That is, expenses and revenues are not mere modifications of capital but produce an income figure that is valid in its own right because it includes far more detail than is revealed by asset revaluations and balance sheet changes in equities. Accounting as described by Jones was mainly concerned with the statistical classification of data and hardly at all with relationships among individuals.

This same thread of ideology appeared independently in Continental Europe during the mid-nineteenth century. As in England, it resulted from attempts to rationalize bookkeeping practice, the accounting equation, and concepts of capital. A text by Franz Hautschl (Vienna, 1840) mentioned the integration of profits and losses with original investments in the capital account and described profit and loss as a temporary resting place for additions and subtractions from owner's equity, which otherwise would be overburdened with detail. Friedrich Hugli, a Swiss government accountant, became a leading advocate of the proprietary viewpoint, summarizing and elaborating on the work of two earlier authors, G.D. Augspurg (Bremen, 1852) and George Kurzbauer (Vienna, 1850). Kurzbauer had argued that account classifications should be derived from the two essential purposes of bookkeeping: profit finding, and the inventorying of assets. These two purposes produce real and nominal accounts, in effect two independent accounting systems side by side. Double entry is the merger into one system of the "property bookkeeping" and the "results bookkeeping" of a business firm. Augspurg had also concluded that double entry bookkeeping includes two sets of accounts—one summarizing a proprietor's net assets, the other cataloging his individual assets. Capital, representing investments as a whole, is reciprocal to the array of assets. The two systems are complementary and their equality helps prove the arithmetic correctness of the ledger. Hugli and Johann Friedrich Schär (1889) approached proprietary theory from a mathematical viewpoint, showing by the use of equations and algebraic symbols how accounting equilibrium is maintained and how transactions affect capital. Hugli went further, arguing that a firm owns business property and does not merely owe it to a proprietor in the sense that it owes debts to third parties.

Considering accounting a branch of mathematics, Charles Ezra Sprague in a series of 1880 articles visualized operating results in terms of an algebraic equation ("assets equal liabilities plus proprietorship") which must always be kept in balance. The proprietary theory was presented in complete form by Sprague in *The Philosophy of Accounts* (New York, 1907) and also in Henry Rand Hatfield's *Modern Accounting* (New York, 1909). Neither of them added anything to the system described by earlier writers. But they expressed a doctrine whose time had finally come and whose underlying assumptions quickly dominated American textbook presentations. The proprietor is the center of accounting interest. Accounting records are kept and statements are prepared from his viewpoint, and are intended to measure and analyze his net worth. Assets represent things owned by the proprietor or benefits accruing to him. Liabilities are his debts. Capital shows the firm's value to its owner. Revenues immediately increase capital; expenses decrease it. All types of income can be treated very much alike, because all go directly to the owner and increase his wealth.

For the same reason little distinction need be made between expenses and losses. Taxes and interest are expenses. Dividends represent a withdrawal of capital. Realistic in the economic context in which it originated, far superior to the methodologies it replaced, the proprietary theory was already obsolete at the time of its first widespread acceptance.

Michael Chatfield

Bibliography

Cronhelm, F.W. *Double Entry by Single*. London: Longman, Hurst, Rees, Orne, and Brown, 1818. Reprint. New York: Arno Press, 1978.

Hatfield, H.R. *Modern Accounting*. New York: D. Appleton and Company, 1909.

Littleton, A.C. *Accounting Evolution to 1900*. New York: American Institute Publishing, 1933. Reprint. New York: Russell and Russell, 1966.

Sprague, C.E. *The Philosophy of Accounts*. New York: 1907. Reprint. Lawrence, KS: Scholars Book, 1972.

See also CAPITAL ACCOUNT; CRONHELM, FREDERIC WILLIAM; ENTITY THEORY; HATFIELD, HENRY RAND; HUGLI, FRIEDRICH; JONES, THOMAS; SPRAGUE, CHARLES EZRA; STEPHENS, HUSTCRAFT; VATTER, WILLIAM JOSEPH

Proprietorship

A.C. Littleton, a noted accounting historian and theorist from the University of Illinois, considered proprietorship to be the vital factor that, when added to equilibrium and duality, led to double entry bookkeeping. In 1933 he wrote: "The full performance of bookkeeping is not called for until it undertakes to serve the enterprises."

The concept of the proprietor or owner of a business has been present for many centuries. The decline in economic activity in Europe from the fall of the Western Roman Empire in A.D. 476 through the Early Middle Ages (or Dark Ages) ended about A.D. 1000 with a revival that ushered in the 200-year period known as the Later Middle Ages. The Renaissance, which started in the Italian city-states at the beginning of the thirteenth century, brought other factors that made the concept of proprietorship much more crucial to bookkeeping. These factors were partnerships and profits.

Partnerships were necessary to raise the capital needed to conduct the expanding businesses of the Later Middle Ages. The numerous Crusades between 1095 and 1290 played a significant part in stimulating business opportunities both locally and internationally of various scope. Since the assets brought to a business by a new partner were to be noted by a debit entry in the firm, it is very natural to have the partner's contribution be noted by a credit entry to his capital account. In "Particularis de Computis et Scripturis," his treatise on double entry accounting in 1494, Luca Pacioli wrote about the importance of bookkeeping to a partnership: "But it is always good to close the books each year, especially if you are in partnership with others. The proverb says: Frequent accounting makes for long friendship."

Profits were very important to the more complex business organizations of the Later Middle Ages. While a locally based craftsman, likely to be controlled by a guild, was very limited in his economic opportunities, a businessman of the Later Middle Ages had alternative uses of his capital. These profits were computed for every inventory item, for separate ventures, and for each trip. These profits (or losses) were closed to the profit-and-loss account along with expenses (ordinary and extraordinary, as well as household) and miscellaneous gains. Then the profit-and-loss account was closed to the partner's accounts in the predetermined ratio for distribution of profit.

Proprietorship became an important ingredient of double entry bookkeeping only when partnerships and profits became vital components of business. Before that, simplicity of transactions called for relatively simple responses. The increased complexities of commerce in the Later Middle Ages called for the more complex response of double entry bookkeeping.

Richard Vangermeersch

Bibliography

De Roover, R. "The Development of Accounting prior to Luca Pacioli according to the Account Books of Medieval Merchants." In *Studies in the History of Accounting*, edited by A.C. Littleton and B.S. Yamey, pp. 114–174. Homewood, IL: Irwin, 1956.

Littleton, A.C. *Accounting Evolution to 1900*. New York: American Institute Publishing, 1933. Reprint. New York: Russell and Russell, 1966.

Pacioli, L. "Particularis de Computis et Scripturis." In *Ancient Double-Entry Bookkeeping: Luca Pacioli's Treatise*, translated by J.B. Geijsbeek. Denver: Geijsbeek, 1914.

See also CAPITAL ACCOUNT; DOUBLE ENTRY BOOKKEEPING: ORIGINS; INCOME STATEMENT/INCOME ACCOUNT; LITTLETON, A.C.; PACIOLI, LUCA; PARTNERSHIP ACCOUNTING; ROME (509 B.C.–A.D. 476)

Public Oversight Board

The Public Oversight Board (POB) of the SEC Practice Section of the American Institute of Certified Public Accountants (AICPA) is best understood as one element of the AICPA's self-regulatory program. Wallace E. Olson, former president of the AICPA, describes that program as a response both to threats of legislation from members of Congress and others during the 1970s and recognition by the profession's leadership that improvements in audit quality control were needed. The threat of professional regulation grew out of serious corporate excesses and some highly publicized audits widely considered to have been failures.

Because the AICPA was an organization of individuals rather than of firms, it had no way to reach the accounting firms in whose names audit reports were signed. To provide that authority, the AICPA in 1977 established a Division of Firms including two sections: an SEC Practice Section (SECPS) for firms auditing enterprises required to register with the Securities and Exchange Commission (SEC), and a Private Companies Practice Section (PCPS) for firms not concerned with SEC registrants. Any auditing firm could join both sections, and some did so. Each section was charged with the responsibility of strengthening, monitoring, and maintaining the audit quality of its members.

The major mechanism for achieving audit quality control was and is peer review. Among other requirements, membership rules for each section call for peer reviews at least triennially. From previous experience with multioffice internal inspections and with both voluntary and disciplinary peer reviews, the Peer Review Committee of each section was able to establish standards and procedures and get the review process underway promptly.

Peer review involves an independent, rigorous evaluation of a firm's quality-control system for its accounting and auditing practice and its compliance with that system. The peer review process encompasses the following: (1) evaluating a firm's quality-control system in light of its accounting and auditing practice; (2) testing compliance with a firm's quality-control procedures at each organizational or functional level within the firm; (3) reviewing reports, financial statements, and relevant working papers for a representative sample of accounting and auditing engagements; (4) testing adherence to SECPS membership requirements; and (5) issuing a written opinion and a letter of comments, if applicable, on the firm's quality-control system and its compliance with that system, as well as on compliance with section membership requirements.

Critics of the profession were quick to point out, and the SEC Practice Section early recognized, that regulation completely within the profession was not what Congress had in mind. An independent body to represent the public interest and to oversee the entire self-regulatory program was, therefore, part of the total plan.

The POB, founded in 1978, is an autonomous body consisting of five members with a broad spectrum of business, professional, regulatory, and legislative experience. Its primary responsibility is to assure that the public interest is carefully considered when (1) the SECPS sets, revises, and enforces standards, membership requirements, rules, and procedures, and (2) the section's committees consider the results of individual peer reviews and the possible implications of litigation alleging audit failure. To preserve its independence and objectivity, the POB appoints its own members, chairman, and staff, and establishes its own compensation and operating procedures.

Shortly after the POB was formed, its oversight duties were expanded. Concerned that triennial peer reviews performed on a test basis might not be sufficient to maintain adequate quality control, a question was raised by Congressional critics of the profession about the necessity for investigating any and all litigation against members of the section if that litigation charged failure in either the application of generally accepted accounting principles or of generally accepted auditing standards. Out of the ensuing discussion came the Special Investigations Committee in 1979, later renamed the Quality Control Inquiry Committee (QCIC). Member firms are now required to report to the section all litigation alleging an accounting or

audit failure. The QCIC does not duplicate the work of the courts, the SEC, or other regulatory agencies. These bodies determine whether the auditing firm or individual auditors were at fault and impose punishment. The QCIC determines whether deficiencies exist in the defendant firm's quality-control system and, if so, recommends corrective actions. If a firm refuses to cooperate with the QCIC, the QCIC can recommend to the SECPS Executive Committee that the firm be sanctioned.

The POB neither has nor desires line authority. Performance of its oversight role provides adequate opportunity to formulate and express its views and to influence the SECPS's regulatory program in the public interest. Meetings of the SECPS Executive and other committees are always attended by one or more staff members accompanied by a POB member. Both staff and board members are accorded the courtesy of the floor at all times, and their views are invited. Much of the work of the QCIC is performed by committee members meeting with representatives of the defendant firm and/or their peer reviewers. Representatives of the POB (staff and/or members) are always present at such meetings and participate in the questioning and discussions.

Oversight of the peer review process by the POB staff includes three levels of review. (1) *Visitation observation review* consists of an examination of work papers and reports prepared by the reviewers and of visits to one or more offices of the reviewed firm during the performance of the review, with emphasis on attendance at the exit conference between reviewers and reviewed firm personnel. These visits are made by POB staff members with selective attendance by POB members. The reviewed firm's written response to any letter of comments is also reviewed. (2) The *work-paper review* program consists of an examination of work papers, a report and letter prepared by the reviewers, and the reviewed firm's response. (3) *Report-review* consists of a reading of the report, letter of comments, and the reviewed firm's response.

The visitation/observation program is applied to all member firms with five or more SEC clients. All member firms with one to four SEC clients receive either the visitation/observation or the report-review programs. Ten percent of the firms with no SEC clients receive the visitation/observation review, 20 percent receive the work-paper review, and 70 percent receive the report-review.

The POB is itself subject to an oversight process. The SEC staff annually reviews the POB's peer review oversight work papers and closed-case summaries of QCIC cases, all of which have audit firm and client names removed for this purpose. In January 1990, AICPA members adopted a bylaw change mandating SECPS membership for all firms auditing SEC clients. This more than doubled SECPS membership and greatly increased the POB's influence within the profession. The board has established the John J. McCloy Award for Outstanding Contributions to Audit Excellence. The award is presented annually and consists of an 18-inch bronze statuette of McCloy—the senior partner at Mibank, Tweed, Hadley and McCloy, an outstanding public servant, and the first chairman of the POB—and a framed citation.

A.A. Sommer
Robert K. Mautz

Bibliography

American Institute of Certified Public Accountants, Division of Firms, SEC Practice Section. *SECPS Manual.* Rev. ed. New York: AICPA, 1986.

Mautz, R.K., and C.J. Evers. *Evolution of the Quality Control Inquiry Committee of the SEC Practice Section of the American Institute of CPAs.* New York: Public Oversight Board, 1991.

Olson, W.E. *The Accounting Profession: Years of Trial, 1969–1980.* New York: AICPA, 1982.

See also AMERICAN INSTITUTE OF CERTIFIED PUBLIC ACCOUNTANTS; CONGRESSIONAL VIEWS; EXTERNAL AUDITING; MAUTZ, ROBERT K.; SECURITIES AND EXCHANGE COMMISSION

Quasi-Reorganization

During the 1930s many corporations incurred successive annual losses that reduced their retained earnings accounts to deficit balances. In most states a retained earnings deficit restricted the ability to pay dividends, which in turn caused stock prices to fall and made it difficult for businesses to raise capital by issuing additional shares. In states where the law permitted it, and with stockholder approval, corporations sometimes eliminated their deficits by charging them off to paid in capital accounts. This act of creative accounting, known as a quasi-reorganization, offered the business a "fresh start" by establishing a zero retained earnings balance, which made current and future income immediately available for dividend distributions.

The quasi-reorganization took two forms. The simpler method, known as a "deficit reclassification," involved writing off a retained earnings deficit against paid in capital without revaluing assets or liabilities. The more complex procedure, called an "accounting reorganization," was accounted for as if the company's stockholders and creditors had purchased the business and its net assets in exchange for their claims. Assets were restated to fair market values, and liabilities to present values, with the net amount of these adjustments added to or deducted from the retained earnings deficit. The retained earnings balance was then closed to the paid in capital accounts, and retained earnings on the balance sheet was dated for a period of 10 years to disclose elimination of the deficit.

The quasi-reorganization was considered an expedient to overcome temporary legal, not financial difficulties. It was never intended to allow companies to conceal losses or permanently violate the doctrine of capital maintenance. Nor was the procedure meant to be used by a corporation with a history of operating losses, unless that firm seemed likely to be profitable in the future. Obviously, quasi-reorganization procedures could easily be abused. But accounting authorities never specified the circumstances in which a deficit elimination allowed under law was permissible in accounting practice. The basis for most textbook discussions of quasi-reorganization is still Securities and Exchange Commission (SEC) Accounting Series Release (ASR) No. 15 (1940) and ASR No. 16 (1940), and AIA's Accounting Research Bulletin (ARB) No. 43 (1953) and ARB No. 46 (1956). These bulletins simply described quasi-reorganization procedures, particularly asset revaluation, the closing of the retained earnings deficit, and the dating of the new retained earnings balance.

However, the quasi-reorganization is no mere artifact of the Great Depression. Since the 1960s, Lockheed and other major corporations have used it to relieve themselves of financial inconvenience. Recently the SEC and the AICPA have attempted to tighten its procedural requirements. In Staff Accounting Bulletin (SAB) No. 78, *Quasi-Reorganization* (1988), the SEC forbade net asset writeups arising from a quasi-reorganization, including income resulting from cumulative changes in accounting methods. SAB No. 78 also stated that elimination of a deficit is not permitted by publicly held companies unless asset revaluations and the other actions involved in a quasi-reorganization are also taken. In 1988 an AICPA Accounting Standards Division Task Force published a 75-page paper that identified 46 issues that need to be resolved regarding accounting and reporting for quasi-reorganizations.

Michael Chatfield

Bibliography

American Institute of Accountants. "Restatement and Revision of Accounting Research Bulletins." Accounting Research Bulletin No. 43. New York: AIA, 1953. Chapters 1A, 2, and 7A.

Fiflis, T.J., and H. Kripke. *Accounting for Business Lawyers*. St. Paul: West, 1971.

Issues Paper 88-1, American Institute of Certified Public Accountants, "Quasi-Reorganization." New York: AICPA, 1988.

Kieso, D.D., and J.R. Weygandt. *Intermediate Accounting*. 7th ed. New York: John Wiley & Sons, 1992.

See also AMERICAN INSTITUTE OF CERTIFIED PUBLIC ACCOUNTANTS; RETAINED EARNINGS; SECURITIES AND EXCHANGE COMMISSION

R

Railroad Accounting (U.S.)

The development of a railroad-accounting model responded to the information requirements of three groups whose influence on this process has varied since the mid-nineteenth century depending on changing business and political circumstances. The first group was railroad managers, who desired more precise cost and operating data for assuring the profitable coordination and control of their companies' activities. Second, investors who had committed vast sums to this capital-intensive industry wanted comprehensive financial reporting as a means both for evaluating their securities and for reducing some of the informational asymmetry separating them from corporate managements. Lastly, state and federal regulators wanted accounting information to control rates and to promote probity in railroad finance.

The initial focus in extending the railroad-accounting model combined the cost and financial objectives. A key development was the use of standardized operating statements and the definition of the "ton-mile" as a standard measure for operational analysis. This had been first developed at mid-century by Albert Fink, who had served as a senior executive for both the Louisville and Nashville Railroad and the Eastern Trunk Line Association. Fink's schedule of accounts arranged line operations under four broad cost headings: maintenance of roadway and general superintendence, station operation, train movements, and interest. Besides serving as components in the accumulation of total line-operating costs, this data also provided a basis for calculating analytical ratios expressed in ton-miles that could be used in making intersegment or interline comparisons. But though Fink's innovation provided useful operational insights, it was incapable of being disaggregated to determine precise costs of hauling particular freight items. The difficulty lay in the ability to establish methods for apportioning the joint costs of railroad operations in ways that were not arbitrary and distortive. Thus, they had limitations in assisting railroad managers in pricing decisions. Consequently, pricing was not based on the cost of service but on the value of service—that is, rates were set in proportion to the value of the articles transported. Low-unit-value agricultural and fuel commodities generally were granted the lowest rates, while high-unit-value manufactures and passengers were charged the highest tariffs.

The rapid expansion of the railroads during the latter half of the nineteenth century led to new demands for regulation of the industry, which also affected its accounting practices. Public concerns about the economic power of the early railroad monopolies induced some states to pass regulatory legislation. Two problems were foremost. First, there were concerns about rate equity and discriminatory tariffs that unfairly favored particular shippers as well as illegal rebating by particular lines to build traffic volume. Second, others worried about the need for adequate disclosure about railroad finance for investors.

Two patterns of regulation soon evolved. The first was best exemplified by the 1869 Massachusetts legislature, which sought to address the problems of rate equity and financial probity by requiring periodic disclosure of railroad operating and financial data. Reformers such as Charles Francis Adams Jr. thought that the broad dissemination of information about railroad affairs to the public would serve as a strong deterrent to abusive practices. Moreover, the emphasis on disclosure was doubtless favored by Boston's banking community, which had pioneered the financing of railroads in the 1840s as a means for overcoming the city's lack of navigable waterways into interior markets. Although the Massachusetts commission communicated the data it collected through its annual report, there were serious limitations to this process. The financial exhibits were generally limited to highly summarized balance sheets of local companies. Although Adams's annual essays on railroad affairs were often brilliantly composed, his primary concern was local regulatory cases and issues. Those students of railroad affairs who sought broader geographic coverage and more timely reporting were compelled to rely on specialized periodicals such as Henry Varnum Poor's *American Railroad Journal*.

The second state regulatory pattern most evident in the West and the South was exemplified by Illinois legislation of 1873, which primarily sought to regulate rates. In these regions, farmers and shippers were deeply concerned about railroad rates because they exerted a material and direct effect on their economic well-being. The Supreme Court decision in the *Munn* case (1876) affirmed the State of Illinois's right to regulate the railroads in the public interest because of the industry's monopolistic character. But like Massachusetts, the Illinois approach eventually encountered serious obstacles that diminished its effectiveness. The local state bureaucracy had insufficient resources to collect and analyze the mass of statistical and accounting data necessary for well-informed rate regulation. Moreover, the difficulties of a single state trying to regulate what was essentially an interstate business became evident in the Supreme Court's *Wabash* decision in 1886. In that case, the Court rebuffed Illinois's attempt to extend its authority over out-of-state rate policies that affected the economic interests of local residents.

The desire to overcome the shortcomings of state regulation led to the formation of a new federal agency, the Interstate Commerce Commission (ICC) through the passage of the Act to Regulate Commerce in 1887. The new national body, it was believed, could provide more comprehensive and efficient accounting compilations to further the regulatory process. A key feature of the new federal regime was the standardization of financial reporting for all railroads engaged in interstate commerce. This

work was initially directed by Professor Henry C. Adams of the University of Michigan, who served as chief of the ICC's Bureau of Accounts and Statistics from its founding until 1911. Lacking a large staff of experienced accountants and eager to minimize administrative costs, Adams during most of his tenure relied heavily on the voluntary efforts of industry accountants represented by the American Association of Railway Accounting Officers. Thus, the forms and classifications for balance sheet and operating statements initially adopted by the federal government in the *Annual Report of the Statistics of Railways of the United States* closely resembled many of those invented earlier by Albert Fink. Adams and his staff also sought to encourage state regulatory bodies to develop the local accounting models that complemented the federal one through his participation in the affairs of the National Association of State Railway Commissioners.

The embrace of the industry's accounting model had important implications for the administration of rate regulation. By accepting the limitations inherent in the model, the ICC inevitably was drawn to accept value of service as an appropriate standard for evaluating rate equity. Nevertheless, this system incorporated features that were consistent with the broader purposes of federal regulation. By establishing rates on food and fuel staples, the rate system helped to raise incomes in the underdeveloped Western, Southern and Midwestern states while at the same time subsidizing the growing needs of industrial workers in the nation's burgeoning Northern cities. Moreover, higher rates could be more effectively borne by higher-unit-value manufactures. This cross-subsidization did not materially distort natural economic efficiency. At the time, there was no more efficient alternative overland transportation modalities that were adversely affected by the government's rate policies. At seaports and junction points between competing railway lines, on the other hand, rates were not regulated and market forces prevailed. Although particular groups enjoyed subsidies, on an overall national economic basis the effects of this regulation on the efficient allocation of resources were negligible. In spreading the costs of rail transportation, one group of consumer's gain was offset by another's loss of equal magnitude.

The initial federal effort to use accounting to advance railroad regulation, however, was only marginally successful during the ICC's first two decades. A major barrier to effective regulation stemmed from the ICC's inability to prescribe uniform accounting methodologies. Although the reporting forms were the same, the ways that individual companies accounted for particular transactions varied greatly, thus undermining the comparability of reported data. Most problematic was the issue of capital asset costing. Some companies regularly calculated periodic depreciation, others wrote off the entire cost of acquisition in a single period, while still others made no provision at all for the diminishment of value of these assets. A second shortcoming of federal accounting-based regulation was the failure of Congress to extend the ICC's authority to industries ancillary to railroading that could serve as conduits for illegal transactions. Unregulated subsidiary enterprises specializing in such activities as equipment leasing, construction, and express service, for example, could serve as "blind pockets" for conveying illegal rebates. Additionally, the ICC's authority to intervene to control affairs in the industry was sharply curtailed during the 1890s by a series of adverse court decisions that reduced its powers to virtually the mere collection of statistics and accounting information. The courts further complicated regulatory matters when the Supreme Court established in 1898 in a Nebraska case, *Smyth v. Ames*, the requirement that rates should be set so as to assure investors of a "fair return" on their investments without explaining precisely how these returns should be measured.

However, accounting-based regulation revived strongly during the Progressive Era. The administration of President Theodore Roosevelt, through the Hepburn Act of 1906, empowered the ICC to mandate uniform accounting methodologies and regulate many ancillary businesses and increased its powers for establishing maximum rates. Subsequently, in the administration of President William Howard Taft, the Mann-Elkins Act of 1911 increased the ICC's power over establishing minimum rates, prohibited discrimination between long-hauls and short-hauls, and authorized the formation of the ill-fated Commerce Court for adjudicating railroad cases. Lastly, President Woodrow Wilson's administration, through the Valuation Act of 1913, authorized a massive valuation of all railroad assets nationwide in order to establish a reliable investment base for fair-return determinations in rate cases. This task, which sought to provide estimates of both historical and replacement costs of line assets, was also expected to be effective in revealing the true amount of "water," or inflation, that was long suspected as existing in railroad capital structures.

But not all Progressives were happy with the directions followed in accounting-based regulation, as was evident in the debate in the Advance Rate Case of 1911. Attorney and future Supreme Court Associate Justice Louis D. Brandeis attacked the traditional value-of-service tariff structures as failing to satisfy the rate-equity standard in the 1887 Act to Regulate Commerce. Brandeis's criticism reflected the views of his clients—small manufacturers and retailers—whose less-than-carload shipments incurred the highest shipping charges. Moreover, Brandeis, a strong critic of economic concentration, argued that regulatory accounting might be better structured to expose conflicts of interest that he suspected existed between particular railroad and banking interests.

In alliance with such pioneers in the scientific-management movement as Frederick Winslow Taylor, Harrington Emerson and Morris L. Cooke, Brandeis proposed reforms for regulatory accounting. First, persuaded by his allies in the scientific-management movement that more-useful cost data could be developed, Brandeis argued that the basis for rate evaluation should be shifted away from the value of service to the cost of service. Second, Brandeis accepted his allies' contention that major cost categories could be standardized as in manufacturing and applied by the ICC to make comparisons with actual performance to better inform the public about railroad efficiency. Lastly, influenced by his earlier experience in Massachusetts's public utility regulation, he further concluded that the ICC's approach in evaluating rate fairness was misguided. The ICC's staff sought historic- and replacement-cost data through the survey authorized by the Valuation Act, believing that both were necessary to satisfy the criteria established in *Smyth v. Ames*. Brandeis, however, objected because he thought the subjective character of replacement-cost estimates could be manipulated to justify overly burdensome rate increases. In Brandeis's view, the appropriate rate base was not the replacement value of the enterprise's asset pool. Instead, he thought the liability and equity side of the balance sheet offered a better guide. The fairness of rates, he argued, should be based on the returns earned by investors on the original costs of their bond and equity purchases adjusted for current market rates for investment capital.

The alternatives raised by Brandeis and his cohorts, however, did not have much immediate effect on regulatory accounting. The Wilson administration accorded railroad reform a low priority, concentrating its main efforts instead on banking and on antitrust-regulation reform and the imperatives associated with America's entry into World War I. Moreover, the economic pressures felt by many of Brandeis's clients also abated because of the advent of cheaper transportation for short hauls of relatively small freights made possible by the rise of the trucking industry. The only palpable result was the ICC's authorization of special studies conducted by one of its staff economists, Max Otto Lorenz, to attempt to solve the difficult problem of estimating the marginal costs of railroad service in different regions of the United States.

After World War I, the focus of accounting-based regulation was actually extended through the National Transportation Act (NTA) of 1920 in ways that Brandeis had opposed. Although a primary purpose of this legislation was to promote economic efficiency by consolidating redundant lines and by creating great regional rail networks, the act affirmed the central role of replacement-cost information in assessing fair return and rate equity. Although it was applauded by many in the industry, consumer groups, most notably farmers, argued as Brandeis had earlier that this form of measurement led to unconscionably high rates. Subsequently, farm interests in Congress sponsored the passage in 1925 of the Hoch-Smith Resolution, which instructed the ICC to consider agriculture as a special case free from the fair-return standard of the NTA in rate setting.

The decade-long economic Depression beginning in 1929 created economic circumstances that eventually led to a revision of accounting-based regulation along lines that Brandeis had earlier advocated. A key mover in revising regulatory accounting was Joseph B. Eastman, a Brandeis protégé who served as an ICC commissioner. Central to the new regulation was the intention to use managerial cost analysis as a means for apportioning the depressed demand for transportation services between the previously competitive railroad, river barge, and interstate trucking industries. Eastman and his ICC associates achieved this by persuading Congress to broaden the scope of

the ICC's regulatory authority. The Transportation Act of 1935 extended the ICC's control over interstate trucking; the Transportation Act of 1940, over inland water transport.

This new strategy, however, sacrificed economic efficiency for social-equity objectives. Rates on low-value food and fuel for the highly efficient barge operators were set at levels thought equivalent to the marginal cost of service for the less efficient railroads. Rates for higher-value merchandise for the efficient trucking industry, on the other hand, were set at levels that would have been fully compensatory to the less efficient railroads. In this way, a broad utilization of all classes of transportation was sought at a cost of lower overall economic efficiency. Unlike the circumstances that prevailed prior to World War I, the new cross subsidies inherent in the New Deal's rate regulation overly burdened the most efficient service providers and, thus, contributed to a suboptimal usage of the nation's transportation resources.

The focus of accounting regulation introduced during the waning years of the Great Depression continued in operation until 1980. Although critics for years had pointed out its deleterious economic consequences, it was a regulatory framework many in Congress long favored because their districts benefited from its inherent subsidies. Eventually, however, the desire to perpetuate this type of regulation waned. Rural regions that had been beneficiaries of subsidized rates eventually became less enamored of this system as their local economies later diversified away from their heavy dependence on agriculture. National economic policymakers also were critical of these practices, which placed a heavy economic drag on the United States as it faced growing competition in world markets. In the Staggers Transportation Act of 1980, rate regulation of railroads, inland water transportation and interstate trucking was finally abandoned. So, too, was the ICC's responsibility for defining industry accounting. From that date, the railroad industry looked to the Financial Accounting Standards Board to promulgate what was generally accepted in accounting for its activities.

Paul J. Miranti Jr.
Leonard Goodman

Bibliography
Brief, R. "The Evolution of Asset Accounting," *Business History Review*, Spring 1966, pp. 1–23.

———. "Nineteenth Century Accounting Error," *Journal of Accounting Research*, Spring 1966, pp. 1–30.

Churchman, J.H. "Federal Regulation of Railroad Rates, 1880–1898," Ph.D. diss., University of Wisconsin, 1976.

Dorfman, J., ed. *Relation of the State to Industrial Action and Economics and Jurisprudence: Two Essays by Henry Carter Adams*. New York: Columbia University Press, 1954.

Hoogenboom, A., and O. Hoogenboom. *A History of the ICC: From Panacea to Palliative*. New York: W.W. Norton, 1976.

McCraw, T.K. *Prophets of Regulation: Charles Francis Adams, Louis D. Brandeis, James M. Landis and Alfred E. Kahn*. Cambridge: Harvard University Press, 1984.

Martin, A. *Enterprise Denied: Origin of the Decline of American Railroads*. New York: Columbia University Press, 1971.

———. "The Mind's Eye of Reform: The ICC's Bureau of Statistics and Accounts and a Vision of Regulation, 1887–1940," *Business History Review*, Autumn 1989, pp. 469–509.

Miranti, P.J. Jr. "Measurement and Organizational Effectiveness: The ICC and Accounting-Based Regulation, 1887–1940," *Business and Economic History: Paper Presented at the Thirty-Sixth Annual Meeting of the Business History Conference, March 23–25, 1990*, pp. 183–192.

Ripley, W.Z. *Railroads: Rates and Regulation*. New York: Longmans, Green, 1914.

Sharfman, I.L. *The Interstate Commerce Commission: A Study of Administrative Law and Practice*, 4 vols. New York: Commonwealth Fund, 1931–1937.

Smykay, E.K. "The National Association of Railroad and Utility Commissioners as Originators and Promoters of Public Policy for the Public Utilities." Ph.D. diss., University of Wisconsin, 1955.

Thompson, G.L. "The Consequences of Misused Product Costing in the American Railroad Industry: The Case of the Southern Pacific during the Interwar Period," *Business History Review*, Autumn 1989, pp. 510–554.

Williams, E.W., Jr. *The Regulation of Rail- Motor Carrier Rate Competition*. New York: Harper, 1957.

See also BRIEF, RICHARD P.; CAPITAL MAINTENANCE; CHART OF ACCOUNTS; CONSERVATISM; COST AND/OR MANAGEMENT ACCOUNTING; DEPRECIATION; DOUBLE ACCOUNT METHOD; EMERSON, HARRINGTON; FINANCIAL-STATEMENT ANALYSIS; HISTORICAL COST; INCOME STATEMENT/INCOME ACCOUNT; INTERNAL AUDITING; NEW YORK STOCK EXCHANGE; RETURN ON INVESTMENT; RIPLEY, WILLIAM Z.; *SMYTH V. AMES;* SPACEK, LEONARD; TAYLOR, FREDERICK WINSLOW; UNIFORM ACCOUNTING SYSTEMS; UNIFORMITY; UNITED STATES STEEL CORPORATION

R

Realization

When corporations became the dominant business organizations, periodic income finding became the accountant's most important task. During the nineteenth century a series of court decisions, reinforced by statutes in England and the United States, required that dividends could be declared only from current and retained earnings. To make the necessary distinction between capital and income, industrial corporations developed sophisticated asset valuation and depreciation methods. Yet income measurement was nearly always subordinate to asset valuation. Assets were appraised, or at least revalued, at the end of each accounting period, and for most firms using this "inventory" method, profit was the change in value of net assets from all causes. Appraisal valuations are hard to standardize, and in 1900 there was still very little precision or consistency in profit calculations.

The accounting concept of profit as an increase in net assets was undermined by English and American income tax laws. For tax purposes there had to be an objective, legally authorized way to determine when income was earned. The tax was on income, not wealth, and it was simply not feasible to make tax assessments on the basis of annual balance sheet revaluations. By defining taxable income as the excess of cash receipts over cash payments, these early tax laws made it necessary to measure income separately from the capital that generated it. So from the first a realization rule was an integral part of the tax code. Any increase in wealth had to be confirmed by some event or transaction, normally the receipt of money, before taxable income came into existence. This principle of realization through cash receipt prevailed throughout the administration of the Civil War tax laws (1862–1873) and was probably strengthened by the fact that the 1909 corporate income tax was enacted in the guise of an excise tax.

The revenue acts that followed passage of the Sixteenth Amendment to the U.S. Constitution in 1913 began a process of convergence between tax and financial accounting income, in which each had an immediate and permanent influence on the other. Many if not most of the rules used today by accountants in determining business income emerged from tax cases decided between 1913 and 1922. Treasury Decision 2005 in 1914 ruled that receipt of "cash or its equivalent" sufficed to meet the realization test. Treasury Decision 2090 in 1913 stated that a sale and the existence of a valid account receivable were sufficient tests of realization. In *Doyle v. Mitchell Brothers Company* (1918), the Supreme Court ruled that only the gain from sales is income, and that the cost of goods sold and operating expenses needed to produce revenues may be deducted without express statutory permission. Tax court decisions supported the idea that assets should be carried at historical cost until realized. The courts held that the right to receive money might be equivalent to actual receipt in measuring earned income, and that the government could tax profits that had not yet been collected in cash.

Asked to define income as the term was used in the Sixteenth Amendment, the Supreme Court identified its sources and emphasized that it was entirely different and distinct from capital. In later decisions, the courts ruled that gains resulting from the sale of capital assets were taxable as income. A more critical question concerned the taxability of holding gains. In *Towne v. Eisner* (1918) and *Eisner v. Macomber* (1920), the Supreme Court ruled that receipt of common stock dividends did not constitute effective realization and was therefore not taxable income to the recipient, because such dividends took nothing from the property of the corporation and added nothing to that of the investor. In his opinion on the latter case, Justice Charles Evans Hughes stressed that income could not arise without (1) an effective addition to the wealth of the recipient, and (2) a "severance" of gain from capital. A man may grow rich from owning assets that increase in value, but he incurs no tax liability until he sells them.

The *Eisner v. Macomber* thesis that income requires a separation from capital by way of an exchange transaction remains the general rule in law and accounting. But tax decisions since 1920 have gradually extended the scope of realization to include events other than the receipt of cash or the creation of a receivable. Taxable income may now be realized when a change occurs in the legal status of property. Realization may also coincide with the "final enjoyment of income," whatever form this may take. In certain cases, the intent of the parties is considered decisive in determining whether or not income has been earned. The courts then amended *Eisner v. Macomber* by ruling that leasehold income can arise without a separation of the gain from capital. However, the legal view of realization is still that income comes into existence only when certain conditions have been met in connection with an asset value increase. The gain or increase must be objectively measurable, it must be definite and irrevocable, and it must be confirmed by some transaction or event such as the receipt of money or property, relief from liability, or a change in the nature of legal rights.

There were points of contact between the emerging legal concept of realization and accounting theory. By a different line of reasoning, Lawrence Dicksee (1864–1932) and other early theorists had reached similar conclusions. Dicksee's assumption of indefinite life for the corporation ruled out the use of liquidation prices in its balance sheet, just as the need for objectivity ruled out their use in tax reporting. Dicksee believed that if a business must maintain its fixed assets permanently, it was illogical to determine profits by annual appraisals based on current resale values. There being no intention to sell such assets, fluctuations in their market prices could not be considered gains or losses. Long-term assets should be booked at historical cost; income is realized on them only when production is completed, and trading income only at the time of sale.

The logic of business continuity required that current assets be priced at net realizable value, with holding gains as well as losses transferred to profit and loss. This conflicted with tax regulations and accounting conservatism. It is probable that the realization rule was superimposed on the going concern concept because the latter was too radical and subjective in its implications for current asset writeups above cost. Reed Storey concluded that "the failure to carry the going concern assumption to its logical conclusion left a gap in accounting theory which was filled by the realization convention." The realization rule provided a theoretical justification for valuing current as well as fixed assets at cost, since any higher valuation would create unrealized income. But its popularization meant that "asset valuation and income measurement were based on an incomplete application of the going concern convention tempered by conservatism."

George Oliver May stated that before World War I the notion that value equals cost was virtually unquestioned, the continuity principle was gaining acceptance, and the realization rule was not accepted at all. The first authoritative use of the word realization seems to have occurred in the 1932 correspondence between the American Institute of Accountants (AIA) Special Committee on Cooperation with Stock Exchanges and the Committee on Stock List of the New York Stock Exchange. The AIA committee supported the realization test of income and rejected asset appraisal methods, on the grounds that in any large company the real value of assets is collective and depends mainly on the firm's earning power.

With the transition from "increased net worth" to realization at sale, it became common to speak of income finding as a process of matching related costs and revenues. This approach was actively promoted by the AIA and the Securities and Exchange Commission (SEC) during the 1930s because its results were objective and verifiable. At that stage in accounting development, uniformity was considered more important than precision. The profession's bad experiences with appraisal writeups during the preceding decades gave an air of reform to techniques that minimized the possibility of manipulation. In realization and matching, the AIA offered CPAs legal protection in the form of easily standardized procedures that were also explicable to the investing public. Both methods conformed to a tradition of accrual accounting, objectivity, and conservatism and were flexible enough to allow for exceptions such as cost or market writedowns and deferred realization on installment sales. Widespread acceptance of the income statement as an expression of the matching process closely followed a corporate shift from debt to equity financing and coincided with the advent of progressive taxation.

While admitting the need for methods that reduced income finding to a routine, account-ing theorists of the interwar period were highly critical of realization-matching. They attacked the very constricted view realization offered of operating results, and the fact that accounting income measurement now depended on a series of arbitrary rules rather than a coherent theory. By focusing attention entirely on the *current* realization of assets while excluding or ignoring all other value changes, the realization rule produced at best a partial picture of operating results and managerial effectiveness. By making revenue recognition so dependent on decisions to take or not take particular actions, it permitted and encouraged the manipulation of periodic profit figures. The "events test" of income recognition left investors and financial analysts to make the subjective interpretations that accountants had avoided.

But such criticisms did not affect practice. The AIA's revamping of accounting during the 1930s had concentrated on matching and realization, and by 1940 the latter rule was almost universally applied. Without being quite sure what realization was, accountants understood perfectly what it did. Realization occurs when income has become definite and measurable enough to deserve recognition in the accounts. This is nearly always at the time of sale, when the earning process is almost complete, current assets and working capital increase, title passes, and there has been an objective, verifiable transaction with outsiders. The consequences of realization were equally well understood. Costs accrue as time passes, but income from sales appears all at once. Unrealized gains are irrelevant and can be ignored, but losses must be anticipated by means of asset writedowns. Accounting is essentially a process of matching related costs and revenues. Once these are known in total, the problem is to apportion them between present and future accounting periods. Expenses assigned to the present period are closed to income summary; the rest, and all assets generally, are simply the deferred costs of producing future revenues. Because it synchronized this matching process, Reed Storey considered that the realization test had become "the most important convention in the determination of income and the valuation of assets."

Theorists might object that the realization rule actually frustrated matching by deferring recognition of holding gains until years after the costs of producing them had been recorded. But profit finding now depended on a series of interlocking assumptions that included historical cost, continuity, conservatism, and periodicity as well as matching and realization. These were made compatible by the ascendancy that income measurement had attained over asset valuation, and by the fairly stable prewar price structure. It would prove very difficult to alter any of them without changing their conglomerate effect. After World War II, inflation would create an environment in which most of these conventions would be challenged and in which the classical notions of realization and matching, though continuing to prevail in practice, would become theoretically disreputable.

Michael Chatfield

Bibliography

American Accounting Association 1964 Concepts and Standards Research Study Committee—the Realization Concept. "The Realization Concept," *Accounting Review*, April 1965, pp. 312–322.

American Institute of Accountants. *Changing Concepts of Business Income*. Report of the Study Group on Business Income. New York: Macmillan, 1952. Reprint. Houston: Scholars Book, 1975.

Arnett, H.E. "Recognition as a Function of Measurement in the Realization Concept," *Accounting Review*, October 1963, pp. 733–741.

Brown, C.D. *The Emergence of Income Reporting: An Historical Study*. East Lansing: Michigan State University Business Studies, 1971.

Gilman, S. *Accounting Concepts of Profit*. New York: Ronald Press, 1939.

Horngren, C.T. "How Should We Interpret the Realization Concept?" *Accounting Review*, April 1965, pp. 323–333.

Sprouse, R.T. "Observations Concerning the Realization Concept," *Accounting Review*, July 1965, pp. 522–526.

Sterling, R.R. *Theory of the Measurement of Enterprise Income*. Lawrence, KS: University Press of Kansas, 1970.

Storey, R.K. "Revenue Realization, Going Concern, and Measurement of Income," *Accounting Review*, April 1959, pp. 232–238.

Thomas, A.L. *Revenue Recognition*. Ann Arbor, MI: University of Michigan Press, 1966.

Windal, F. "The Accounting Concept of Realization," *Accounting Review*, April 1961, pp. 249–258.

See also ACCRETION CONCEPT OF INCOME; ACCRUAL ACCOUNTING; AMERICAN INSTITUTE OF CERTIFIED PUBLIC ACCOUNTANTS; CASH BASIS ACCOUNTING; CONSERVATISM; CONTINUITY; CRITICAL-EVENT THEORY; DEPRECIATION; DICKSEE, LAWRENCE; DIVIDENDS; *EISNER V. MACOMBER*; FIXED ASSETS; HISTORICAL COST; INCOME TAXATION IN THE UNITED STATES; INFLATION ACCOUNTING; MACNEAL, KENNETH; MATCHING; MAY, GEORGE OLIVER; NEW YORK STOCK EXCHANGE; OBJECTIVITY; PERIODICITY; POSTULATES OF ACCOUNTING; SECURITIES AND EXCHANGE COMMISSION; SIXTEENTH AMENDMENT; SMITH, ADAM

Regulation (Federal U.S.) and Accounting

Federal regulation affecting accountants and auditors places direct, affirmative responsibilities upon them; failure to meet these federal standards may result in civil and/or criminal penalties.

Civil liabilities for accountants—that is, their vulnerability to suits for monetary damages—are present in the Securities Acts under specific conditions. Section 11(a) of the Securities Act of 1933 covers liabilities involved for failures of experts, including accountants, pertaining to registration statements for new issues. Misstatements of material facts, or their omission in a registration statement, or failure to find such misstatements or omissions are the criteria for liability. If accountants commit such errors in financial materials that are used in either a prospectus or a registration statement, they may be held liable on either fraud or negligence grounds. Plaintiffs need not prove that they relied on the erroneous materials. As compared to traditional common-law doctrine, privity of contract is not an issue under the 1933 Securities Act. Accountants may assert the due diligence defense in cases alleging Section 11(a) violations. The requirement for a successful due diligence defense is that the expert (accountant) conducted a reasonable investigation, had reasonable grounds to believe, and did believe at the time the registration statement became effective that there were no material facts omitted and that those facts stated were true. The landmark case in this area is *Escott v. BarChris Construction Corporation* [283 F. Supp. 643 S.U.N.Y. (1968)].

Civil liabilities can be imposed upon accountants for violating Section 10(b) of the 1934 Securities and Exchange Act or for violating Rule 10b-5 as issued by the Securities and Exchange Commission. Section 10(b) forbids manipulative or deceptive practices related to security purchases or sales. Rule 10b-5 forbids means of defrauding, misstatements or omissions of material facts, or activities involving fraud or deceit upon persons in the sale of securities. The actual imposition of civil liabilities under 10(b) and 10b-5 is relatively restrictive, however, since it requires a showing that the defendant acted with guilty intent (*scienter*), following the decision by the U.S. Supreme Court in *Ernst and Ernst v. Hochfelder* [425 U.S. 185 (1976)]. Thus under 10(b) and 10b-5, negligence by itself is insufficient to render accountants liable to harmed security purchasers.

Criminal liability may be directed toward accountants under several federal laws. The 1933 Securities Act's Section 24 makes a criminal offense of willfully making untrue statements of material facts in SEC submissions, of omitting material facts necessary to ensure that registration statements are not misleading, or of willfully violating provisions of the act or rules adopted under its provisions. A similar provision is included in the 1934 act under Section 32(a), which makes it a crime to make false or misleading statements in any SEC filings or under any rules adopted pursuant to the 1934 act. Penalties against convicted individuals are heavy—up to 10 years in prison, provided that the individual had full knowledge of the violated regulation or rule, and/or a fine of up to $1 million.

The 1970 Racketeer Influenced and Corrupt Organizations Act (RICO) was frequently used as a basis for suing accountants and other professionals, given its civil and criminal penalties, particularly since securities fraud under the act is considered racketeering. Treble damages are available against the defendant in a private action. The employment of RICO in civil cases not involving organized crime was widespread, although its original intent was that it be directed against organized crime. The broad wording of the act, however, made it applicable to a wide array of situations. This has led to a judicial reaction in which the application of the statute in private cases has become more difficult to pursue. In 1993 the Supreme Court held that in *Reves v Ernst and Young and Company* 113 S.Ct.1163 (1993) one must participate in the operation or management of the enterprise itself to be subject to RICO Sec. 1962(c) liability under RICO, 18 U.S.C. Sec. 1962(c), somewhat similar to the scienter requirement under Section 10(b) and Rule 10b-5.

The Foreign Corrupt Practices Act (FCPA) of 1977 was intended to put a halt to the practice of making bribes in international business transactions. In addition to making it illegal for employees of SEC-listed companies to pay bribes, the act required installing internal accounting systems that would assure that all payments were legal. The 1988 amendment of the FCPA, as part of the Omnibus Trade and Competitiveness Act, eased the liability standards for individuals. Most important for accountants was that technical accounting errors were eliminated from coverage under the act, and criminal liability was imposed only when failure to keep proper accounting records is intentional, and when the payments of bribes are done knowingly.

All of the acts mentioned above have several consistent themes concerning regulation of accountants. For one, the acts all deal with vital aspects of information dissemination and control within the U.S. business system. Secondly, imposition of civil liability upon accountants, where permitted under these acts, requires intent to violate the applicable statute. Finally, when there are intentional violations of these laws, the penalties are not trivial under the 1991 *Federal Sentencing Guidelines.*

Robert Chatov

Bibliography

Chatov, R. "Auditors' Liability: States, Congress Mull Changing Standards," *Legal Times*, 10(17), September 1987, pp. 28–30.

———. *Corporate Financial Reporting: Public or Private Control?* New York: Free Press, 1975.

United States Sentencing Commission. *Federal Sentencing Guidelines Manual.* Effective November 1, 1987, including November 1 and 27, 1991, amendments. St. Paul: West, 1992.

See also Escott v. BarChris Construction Corporation; Hochfelder v. Ernst and Ernst; Law and Accounting; Legal Liability of Auditors; Securities and Exchange Commission

Regulation of Railways Act (Britain, 1868)

About 75 percent of Britain's railroad track mileage was built between 1830 and 1870. Near the end of this Railway Age, the Regulation of Railways Act of 1868 attempted for the first time to standardize and improve railway accounting and reporting methods.

The 1868 act required railroad companies to adopt the double account method, under which original investments in fixed assets were capitalized, while asset replacement and maintenance costs were expensed. English law had not previously tried to specify which expenditures belonged to capital and which to revenue. During the construction boom of the 1840s, many railroads had paid large dividends out of capital, creating a windfall for short term speculators at the expense of creditors and long term investors. Stockholders were misled about actual income, future earnings potential, and managerial efficiency.

The Companies Act of 1862 recommended that assets be placed on the right side of the balance sheet and liabilities and capital on the left side. The 1868 act made this arrangement mandatory for railroads and also required a horizontal division of balance sheet data in terms of related opposites. The upper left quadrant of the balance sheet reported capital stock and mortgage debt; the upper right quadrant showed the long-term assets financed by these debts and equities. The lower left quadrant reported current liabilities and profits available for dividends; the lower right quadrant showed current assets available to pay dividends and liabilities.

The 1868 act, which remained in force until 1911, was a forerunner of similar laws that prescribed accounting and auditing methods for building societies, waterworks, gasworks, and electric light companies. By the 1880s, statutory regulation was a fact of life for nearly all British public service corporations.

Michael Chatfield

Bibliography

Littleton, A.C. *Accounting Evolution to 1900*. New York: American Institute Publishing, 1933. Reprint. New York: Russell and Russell, 1966.

Pollins, H. "Aspects of Railway Accounting before 1868." In *Studies in the History of Accounting*, edited by A.C. Littleton and B.S. Yamey, pp. 332–355. Homewood, IL: Irwin, 1956.

See also COMPANIES ACTS; DIVIDENDS; DOUBLE ACCOUNT METHOD; LIMITED LIABILITY

Research Methods in Accounting History

This entry looks at research methods used in the history of accounting. A more practical, rather than a theoretical, approach will be used to help researchers actually on projects. Researchers must refer to previous scholars because it is indispensable to be aware of the results of their studies. Modern researchers must compare their findings with those of other authors, unless the subject is an entirely new one.

Once this ethical point has been dealt with, accounting history researchers have three hurdles to cross: (1) to decide on an aim, (2) to choose an in-depth option compatible with that aim, and (3) to use appropriate tools for the chosen aim and option.

Deciding an Aim

Lucius Annaeus Seneca (Seneca "the Younger," B.C. 4–A.D. 65) said that there is no good wind for a person who doesn't know where he's going. Flesher and Samson (1990) have shown how some accounting historians find the answers and the documents before even asking the right questions. They also demonstrated that there are five possible goals in historical accounting research: (1) describing phenomena, (2) exploring the relationship between several phenomena, (3) explaining these phenomena, (4) predicting future events that make it possible to confirm the validity of the theory, and (5) influencing future events.

The researcher's role is to make sense out of the chaos represented by a diverse multitude of conflicting documents of varying importance, while at the same time making a statement different from previous authors on the subject. Accounting historians have the advantage of working in a technical field, where the choice of subjects is relatively limited, and things change fairly slowly. They must, however, avoid a number of traps in connection with achieving their objectives. The first trap is the researcher's own personality, which has been influenced by modern culture and today's environment. Over the past century, accounting, auditing, and management control have all made great strides, especially since computerization. This must be borne in mind when considering old documents.

Neither should a historian make the mistake of seeking to prove his point at all costs. It is not enough to retain only those facts that support the historian's point of view out of the many that are available to him. When in doubt, it is wise to base studies on a method using a hypothesis, facts, and critical analysis of the facts, leading to a conclusion. Nor should the historian take too superficial a view of his subject. The best way to avoid this error is to have an in-depth knowledge of accounting. It is much easier if the aim is just to describe a phenomenon. This, however, is only really the case in very unusual circumstances where a truly original discovery has been made. The first step is then to make a simple description.

The second-level aim may be to work out the relationship between several phenomena. In this case, one should start with a scientific approach, involving a hypothesis, subsequent testing of the hypothesis, and a conclusion. Often these sorts of subjects are connected with the relationship between the history of accounting and economics. Once a relationship has been discovered, it should be explained by going from a statistical demonstration to deeper analysis. These three basic elements should be the objective standard of reference for accounting historians. In some cases, the model that has been developed may be used to make predictions to provide further confirmation. The final objective may be to influence the course of current events. This last objective is operational in many cases in which there are organizations and commissions. Historians should also be ambitious as far as the scientific content of the objectives, the period of history studied, and the length of time allowed for the work are concerned. Once the aims have been selected, an accounting historian has to make another fundamental decision: how to deal with the subject.

Deciding on a Basic Option

There are at least three types of accounting history, and historians have to decide with which one they are going to deal. This will define the type of tools to be used and the breadth of the results achieved.

The first, and easiest, option is to study the history of authors on accounting and their doctrines. This is the history of thought on accounting, as evidenced by books, articles, and published works by well-known authors such as Luca Pacioli. If one goes back still farther in time, one can look at other evidence: tokens, clay tablets, papyrus, and carved stones. From this angle, accounting practices (entries, audits, customs) are not the primary object of the study, but rather secondary considerations, the reflec-

tion of an author's ideas. Prior to 1960, most historical research was of this type. It has the disadvantage of concentrating on the double entry system, and it makes reference mainly to learned books rather than taking reality into account, thus isolating accounting from its context. This approach is useful for writing biographies or for showing the respective contributions of various authors on a subject, but it is rarely sufficient on its own.

The second possibility is to explore the influences of the various people involved in accounting. This approach deals more specifically with systems. This was the viewpoint chosen by Chatfield (1977), for example. In his opinion, accounting is the product of a set of technological, social, and institutional influences. Professors of accounting are by no means the only people involved. Accountants and public authorities also make a contribution. The discipline of accounting brings together science and social studies, and it is impossible to discuss it without mentioning law, taxation, economics, organizations, and labor relations.

Finally, the third possible approach is to look at the social history of accounting and its consequences. In this rather ambitious type of research, one takes into account not only the interdisciplinary aspects of accounting but also its interaction with economic systems. Accounting becomes a social object that has an influence on society. Werner Sombart, a German economic historian, was the first to state this point of view. He considered that the double entry system was indispensable to capitalism. A number of authors, such as Basil S. Yamey, an English expert on the history of accounting, who have analyzed accounting theory and social practices, have contradicted Sombart's thesis. The double entry accounting system gained ground in the world much more slowly than capitalist firms. Nineteenth-century accounts show that a firm's property was not distinguished from that belonging to the firm's owners, and the distinction between capital and income was far from systematic. In the 1990s, several English authors (Miller, Hopper, and Laughlin), led by Anthony Hopwood, the English editor of *Accounting, Organizations, and Society,* have adopted this general method, attempting to show how accounting systems can play a part in setting up societies.

In summation, it is possible to write a one-dimensional, isolated history of accounting writers; a systematic, correlated history of people involved in accounting; or, finally, a multifaceted, varied history of accounting from a social point of view. Some of the same tools are used for all three approaches; others are specific to each one.

Using the Appropriate Tools

It is not possible to write accounting history without documents. Documents are historical markers. During the classical periods, documents were always in the form of written matter—accounts books, letters, reports, files, plans, flow charts. Documents in ancient times were more varied—tokens, sticks, tablets, coins, walls of buildings. In dealing with the contemporary period, which will very soon be history too, one will have to get used to using various media—photographs, punched cards, tape recordings, compact disks, electronic chips, and software printouts. Documents are the basic materials, but they are as closely linked to the tools as bricks are to a bricklayer's trowel. Each one has to be examined. Paper documents are read, and other types of documents are consulted in various ways. Historians cannot always include a whole document in the work they are writing, so they have to use a few classical tools to sort the information.

Cards are the simplest. Every historian has his own habits, but, even in this age of portable computers, it is difficult to manage without cards, which serve as primary analytical tools. Cards of various sizes may be used—to note discoveries, to comment on them, to preserve specific extracts, and, above all, to list names, key words, figures, and references. Syntheses, methods, and directions can also be noted on cards. A coherent set of cards constitutes a card index, and a set of card indexes makes up a file. Photocopies are a useful addition to cards. If standard cards are used, photocopies may be used in the same way. They must, however, be clearly identified, giving page numbers and document references. Photocopies should not be simply stored, but must also be correctly analyzed, annotated, and important passages underlined.

Portable computers with large-capacity RAMs and diskettes are becoming more widely used to replace cards. Bibliographical data banks provide direct access, either to references or to texts themselves. Computers make it possible to enter details into the file when working in the field—in libraries or private archives, for example. Computers will be of even greater use

to historians in the future. As more organizations store their data on computer disks, it will be possible to extract information from their archives in the same way as accounting information is sampled today, so as to audit computerized accounts.

The historian very quickly finds himself surrounded by a multitude of documents, both primary and secondary sources. He makes direct use of primary sources (reads and examines them) and may make use of secondary sources to add nuances to his opinion. When vast amounts of data and documents are available, he has several options for dealing with them, depending on his objectives and approach. In the simplest case, he may describe a situation by referring to histories by other authors, so careful study of his cards and his own good sense will suffice. If he is more ambitious, if his aim is to describe phenomena, to explore the relationships between them, then explain his findings, he will need to refer not only to primary sources, but also to secondary sources, using simple descriptive statistical techniques (curves on a graph) or more elaborate ones (breakdown into major components). Finally, if he has decided to make an in-depth study of social history, he will need to analyze, first, primary sources, then secondary sources, then an enormous amount of direct and indirect environmental data. This will require a more sophisticated statistical approach (canonical correlations), rather than a limited, two-dimensional analysis.

To obtain optimum results, historical researchers have to combine a set of objectives, a set of options, and a set of methods. The art of historical research consists of defining fundamental questions, selecting realistic options, and skillfully using various methods of synthesis and representation, because a detailed, well-reasoned study of factors is at least as important as the production of qualitative data.

Jean-Guy Degos

Bibliography

Barzun, J., and H.R. Graff. *The Modern Researcher*. 3d ed. Chicago: Harcourt Brace Jovanovich, 1977.

Bricker, R.J. "The Importance of History for Accounting Research," *Abacus*, March 1991, pp. 72–77.

Chatfield, M. *A History of Accounting Thought*. Hinsdale, IL: Dryden Press, 1977.

Costouros, G.J., and A. van Seventer. *Contemporary Accounting Issues*. Palo Alto, CA: Bays Books, 1979.

Degos, J.-G. "Les grands précurseurs de la comptabilité," *Revue Française de Comptabilité*, October 1985, pp. 34–41.

Edwards, J.R. *A History of Financial Accounting*. London: Routledge, 1989.

Fishlow, A. "The New Economic History Revisited," *Journal of European Economic History*, Fall 1974, pp. 453–467.

Flesher, D.L., and W.D. Samson. "What is Publishable Accounting History Research: An Editorial View," *Accounting Historians Journal*, June 1990, pp. 1–4.

Gaffikin M.J.R. "Legacy of the Golden Age: Recent Developments in the Methodology of Accounting," *Abacus*, March 1988, pp. 16–36.

———. "Methodology for Historical Accounting Research." In *Collected Papers of the Third World Congress of Accounting Historians*. London: London School of Economics, 1980.

———. "The Methodology of Early Accounting Theorists," *Abacus*, March 1987, pp. 17–30.

Miller, P., P. Hopper, and R. Laughlin. "The New Accounting History: An Introduction." *Accounting, Organizations, and Society*, vol. 16, no. 5/6, 1991, pp. 395–403.

Parker, L.D., and O.F. Graves. *Methodology and Methods in History: A Bibliography*. New York: Garland, 1990.

Previts, G.J., L.D. Parker, and E.N. Coffman. "Accounting History: Definition and Relevance," *Abacus*, March 1990, pp. 1–16.

See also ARCHIVES AND SPECIAL COLLECTIONS IN ACCOUNTING; KOJIMA, OSAMU; PREVITS, GARY JOHN; SOMBART, WERNER

Residual Equity Theory

In 1922 William Andrew Paton referred to common stockholders as residual equity holders, recipients of residual rewards and bearers of residual risk, whose claims to retained earnings were preceded by the claims of bondholders and preferred stockholders, and whose financial position was affected by every change in corporate equity and by every change in the relative interests of other equity holders. Paton concluded: "A clear-cut showing of the residual balancing equity in the financial statement is a practice to be commended."

The residual equity theory, developed by George J. Staubus, makes common stockholders the center of accounting attention. In a going concern, the market value of common stock depends largely on future profit and dividend expectations. If the common stockholder's portion of assets, income, cash flows, and retained earnings can be identified and isolated, financial statements can disclose more about the prospective selling prices of common stock. Information about the residual equity may also be useful in predicting the size of common stock dividends. Accordingly, Staubus suggested that the balance sheet equity of common stockholders should be presented separately from the equities of preferred stockholders and others. The cash flow statement should segregate funds available for payment of common stock dividends. The income statement should show earnings available to common stockholders after all prior claims are satisfied—not only interest payments due to bondholders, but dividend payments due to preferred stockholders. Accounting Principles Board Opinion No. 15, "Earnings per Share" (1969) took a residual equity position in its specifications for calculating fully diluted earnings per share.

Michael Chatfield

Bibliography
Paton, W.A. *Accounting Theory*. New York: Ronald Press, 1922. Reprint. Chicago: Accounting Studies Press, 1962, and Lawrence, KS: Scholars Book, 1973.

Staubus, G.J. *A Theory of Accounting to Investors*. Berkeley and Los Angeles: University of California Press, 1961. Reprint. Houston: Scholars Book, 1975.

See also PATON, WILLIAM ANDREW

Retained Earnings

"Retained Earnings" is the replacement term for "earned surplus," which was dropped from acceptable usage by the American Institute of Accountants (AIA)—forerunner of the American Institute of Certified Public Accountants (AICPA)—in 1949. However, the term "earned surplus" stayed around in balance sheets until about the mid-1960s.

Apparently, the terms "surplus" and "earned surplus" were used by the industrial corporations that became publicly traded during the trust periods of the late 1880s through the very early 1900s. Railroads did not utilize these terms. What is today labeled "retained earnings" was labeled "profit and loss" in the balance sheets of railroads. Common stock with a low par value would have generated a surplus figure for industrial corporations, and it appears that some companies included that "excess over par value" amount together with the balance of historical earnings minus dividends. For instance, the 1901 edition of the *American Business and Accounting Encyclopedia* defined the "surplus account" as "an account representing undistributed profits and the excess of assets over liabilities not included in any other account." However, the first full-year annual report of U.S Steel Corporation in 1902 did separate "capital surplus" from "surplus accumulated by all companies since organization of U.S. Steel Corporation."

The mingling of both capital and earned surplus, under the generic title "surplus," continued during the 1920s in some companies, despite being considered undesirable by accounting experts. However, the Special Committee on Accounting Terminology of the AIA did not help in 1922 by reporting the common meaning of "surplus" as measuring the excess of assets over liabilities and capital and by giving four examples of accumulating surplus: (1) normal operations, (2) capital transactions, (3) reappraisal of assets, and (4) treasury stock transactions.

The AIA took another look at the term later in the 1920s. In 1929 the AIA Special Committee on Definition of Earned Surplus reported the following definition: "Earned surplus is the balance of net profits, income and gains of a corporation . . . after deducting losses and after deducting distributions to stockholders and transfers to capital-stock accounts when made out of such surplus" (Heckert, 1930). The use of unqualified term for "surplus" and "capital surplus" was discouraged as it was inadequate for use on balance sheets (Heckert, 1930).

In 1938, William Cranstoun, who was a partner in the respected public accounting firm of Hurdman and Cranstoun and edited the "Commentator" column in the *Journal of Accountancy*, started the campaign to eliminate "surplus" from the vocabulary of accountants and received support from influential accountants. However, in 1941 in Accounting Research Bulletin (ARB) No. 9, "Report of the Committee on Terminology," the AIA hesitated to change the term even though the term "earned surplus" had "brought no increase in accuracy or lucidity but rather the reverse." Later in 1941 in ARB No. 12, "Report of the Committee on Terminology," it recommended a study of the feasibility of the general discontinuance of the word "surplus." The AIA Subcommittee on Surplus recommended in 1942 that "surplus" be dropped because it was an unsatisfactory designation sometimes thought to imply the existence of excess cash resources that might be distributed. In October 1949 in ARB No. 39, "Discontinuance of the Use of the Term 'Surplus,'" the AIA declared that the generic word "surplus" and the specific term "earned surplus" were unacceptable and were to be replaced by one of these terms: (1) "retained income," (2) "retained earnings," (3) "accumulated earnings," or (4) "earnings retained for use in the business." This slow, and unsteady, process of change leaves in doubt the accounting profession's ability to meet the challenge of correcting poor terminology.

Richard Vangermeersch

Bibliography

Cranstoun, W.D. "Some General Observations on Surplus," *Journal of Accountancy*, January 1938, pp. 68–70.

Heckert, J.B. "Comments on the Definition of Earned Surplus," *Accounting Review*, June 1923, pp. 168–174.

"Is It Desirable to Distinguish between Various Kinds of Surplus?: A Symposium," *Journal of Accountancy*, April 1938, pp. 281–284.

Kohler, E.L. "The Concept of Earned Surplus," *Accounting Review*, September 1931, pp. 206–217.

Littleton, A.C. "Capital and Surplus," *Accounting Review*, December 1932, pp. 290–293.

"Should the Term 'Surplus' Be Eliminated?" *Journal of Accountancy*, May 1942, pp. 451–457.

Special Committee on Accounting Terminology of the American Institute of Accountants. "Terminology Department," *Journal of Accountancy*, October 1922, pp. 311–315.

Vangermeersch, R. *Financial Reporting Tech-*

niques in *Twenty Industrial Companies since 1861*. Gainesville: University Presses of Florida, 1979.

See also ACCOUNTING RESEARCH BULLETINS; AMERICAN INSTITUTE OF CERTIFIED PUBLIC ACCOUNTANTS; INCOME STATEMENT/INCOME ACCOUNT; PAID IN CAPITAL; QUASI-REORGANIZATION; TREASURY STOCK; UNITED STATES STEEL CORPORATION

Retained Earnings Appropriations

The practice of segregating that portion of income which is not available for distribution is as old as profit finding. It was done by Italian bookkeepers in Luca Pacioli's time. The British Companies Act of 1855–1856 included a model balance sheet whose authors thought it natural to divide retained earnings into "Reserve for Contingencies" and "Profit Available for Dividends."

There were other reasons for not distributing retained earnings besides the need to finance growth and plant expansion. Nineteenth-century British courts ruled that provision must be made for future operations before stockholders were entitled to dividends, and specifically that income calculation should include bad debt writeoffs and depreciation charges. But most businessmen of the time regarded depreciation as a means of financing asset replacements. Their main concern was that funds be provided to replace assets before distributable profits were recognized. The result of this sinking fund view of asset deterioration was that accumulated depreciation came to be seen as a kind of equity reserve, a segregation of income for future asset purchases. As an alternative to taking depreciation, some companies actually established funds or retained earnings appropriations to finance asset replacements.

The creation of equity reserves to provide for future contingencies became common only after conservatism was recognized as a principle of corporate accounting. In a cyclical economy, at a time when managers had wide discretion to manipulate income and control dividend policy, it was considered prudent to keep back part of earnings in prosperous years to finance dividend payments during recessions.

After World War II, the use of retained earnings appropriations to disclose dividend restrictions became less important. *Accounting Trends and Techniques*, the American Institute of Certified Public Accountants' annual survey of 600 companies, noted about a hundred such appropriations in 1950. A similar survey in 1971 found only 10, and in 1975 the AICPA stopped tabulating retained earnings appropriations because of their infrequency.

Michael Chatfield

Bibliography
Green, D. *Accounting for Corporate Retained Earnings*. New York: Arno Press, 1980.

See also BAD DEBTS; CAPITAL MAINTENANCE; COMPANIES ACTS; CONSERVATISM; DEPRECIATION; DIVIDENDS; MANIPULATION OF INCOME

Return on Investment

Return on investment is a seemingly simple concept but capable of many different approaches in its calculation. As such, caution needs to be applied any time the term is not rigorously defined. Some of the traditional approaches are: return on equity, return on tangible equity, return on assets, and return on tangible assets. The calculation can be made for common stockholders or for the firm for its total investment or for a proposed new investment. The calculation can be based on nominal dollars or on the present value of those nominal dollars. The veritable explosion of more advanced mathematical techniques for financial analysis since the 1970s has made this topic even more complex.

Adam Smith, in his 1776 classic *The Wealth of Nations,* described the return on capital as a function of the interest rate. He felt that double interest was a good, moderate, and reasonable profit. Since Smith did not include liabilities in his simple model of the firm, return on assets and equity would be the same. By 1920, the neoclassical economist Alfred Marshall, the noted British economist, had further developed the return on investment theory to include the present-value approach.

For a concept so well enunciated by Smith, it was surprising that a computation of such a return was not made by railroads early on. For instance, Dionysius Lardner, in his 1850 classic *Railway Economy,* was quite detailed in his analysis but did not include a computation for return on investment. Such a computation was done by Charles Francis Adams Jr., then a member of the Massachusetts Board of Railroad

Commissioners, when in 1875 he noted that Illinois Railways earned 4.8 percent. Because Adams was concerned about the overvaluation of assets, he made some adjustments to the capital of railroad stock in Kansas—considered along with Illinois, Iowa, Minnesota, and Wisconsin to be the five states most affected by the Granger movement of the 1870s—and estimated a return on capital of 6 percent. Adams was concerned about the railroad policies of these states. By 1885, A.M. Wellington, a railway engineer, showed considerable concern about present value in terms of justifying a capital expenditure. John H. Van Deventer, an engineer, in 1915 further expounded on the present-value approach for judging investments well before the modern classic in 1951 by Joel Dean, a managerial economist, *Capital Budgeting*, as noted by George A. Wing (1965). The classic description of the return on investment on a nominal basis was done by General Motors executive F. Donaldson Brown in the 1920s (Johnson, 1978). The two components of this computation were income as a percentage of sales multiplied by the sales over net assets. In 1991, a review of the Return on Investment heading in *Accountants' Index* found 90 references, with a wide range of methods of computing return on investment.

Richard Vangermeersch

Bibliography

Adams, C.F. Jr. "The Granger Movement," *North American Review*, April 1875, pp. 394–424.

Johnson, H.T. "Management Accounting in an Early Multidivisional Organization: General Motors in the 1920s," *Business History Review*, Winter 1978, pp. 490–517.

Marshall, A. *Principles of Economics*. 8th ed. London: Macmillan, 1920.

Scorgie, M.B. "Rate of Return," *Abacus*, September 1965, pp. 85–91.

Smith, A. *The Wealth of Nations*. 1776. Reprint. New York: Random House, 1937.

Wing, G.A. "Capital Budgeting, Circa 1915," *Journal of Finance*, September 1965, pp. 472–479.

See also BROWN, F. DONALDSON; DISCOUNTED CASH FLOW; FISHER, IRVING; MANAGEMENT ACCOUNTING; RAILROAD ACCOUNTING (U.S.); RIPLEY, WILLIAM Z.; SMITH, ADAM; *SMYTH V. AMES*

Rex v. Kylsant

An English court decision in *Rex v. Kylsant* (1931) placed limits on financial understatement. The auditor of the Royal Mail Steam Packet Company was accused of aiding and abetting in the publication of false annual reports. The company had placed 2 million pounds earned during World War I into a funded taxation reserve, and during the 1920s it turned operating losses into apparent profits by transferring portions of this reserve to its current income account. The auditor's defense was that management had a right to smooth profits over the business cycle; that in fact such practices were needed to stabilize dividend payments and promote investor confidence. The only explanation given in the Royal Mail's annual report was the phrase "including adjustment of taxation reserves," and the case turned on whether these words gave statement readers sufficient warning. The auditor was acquitted of intent to deceive, but the court made it clear that conservatism was no longer a substitute for accounting disclosure.

Michael Chatfield

Bibliography

Davies, P.M., and A.M. Bourn. "Lord Kylsant and the Royal Mail," *Business History*, July 1972, pp. 102–123.

Hastings, P. "The Case of the Royal Mail." In *Studies in Accounting Theory*, edited by W.T. Baxter and S. Davidson, pp. 452–461. Homewood, IL: Irwin, 1962.

See also CONSERVATISM; LEGAL LIABILITY OF AUDITORS

Ripley, William Z. (1867–1941)

William Zebina Ripley earned a bachelor's degree in civil engineering at Massachusetts Institute of Technology in 1890. Later, in 1893, he earned a doctorate in political economy at Columbia University, submitting a dissertation titled "The Financial History of Virginia, 1607–1776." Although he began his teaching career at Columbia, he soon gravitated to the Economics Department at Harvard University, which thereafter remained his academic home. At Harvard he eventually occupied the Ropes Chair in economics.

Ripley's thinking about accounting institutions was conditioned by his perceptions about the forces that had begun to transform American society during the last quarter of the nineteenth century. During his lifetime, he witnessed how the processes of industrialization, urbanization, and immigration radically reordered what had once been an agrarian-rural society. A more complex and interdependent polity had emerged that was rapidly displacing the simplicity and self-sufficiency characteristic of the receding frontier environment.

Like many of his contemporaries, Ripley possessed a sensitivity to the ambiguity of modernism. This, in turn, fostered a belief that the attainment of moral improvement was contingent on the establishment of robust and vibrant institutions. Three features within a broader canvas of social change became the main focuses of Ripley's scholarship: (1) the composition of the new immigration and its implications for sustaining cultural traditions; (2) the governance of the railroad industry, which had provided the basis for the rise of the nation's urban-industrial economy; and (3) the problems associated with the regulation of the financial markets, which had expanded dramatically after World War I.

One implication of one of Ripley's earliest works, which was in sociology rather than in accounting or economics, was that strong institutions were crucial in preventing the subversion of the democratic, libertarian values that had long vitalized American civilization. In *The Races of Europe: A Sociological Study* (1899), Ripley contended that moral qualities were ascribable to particular racial backgrounds. What was most worrisome about this analysis was Ripley's contention that, unlike physiological features, behavioral characteristics could not be affected by changing environmental circumstances. In his view, these latter attributes were determined by racial origins. Thus, the rising multiculturalism resulting from massive immigration seemed threatening because it brought into America new peoples that Ripley's research suggested were inimical to the core values on which the nation had been constituted.

There was yet another implication about cultural diversity that carried over to Ripley's writings about economic and accounting institutions. Within a heterogeneous context, it was especially critical that social action be guided by explicit rules and regulations. Informal practices common in homogeneous nations were less reliable in achieving cohesion in societies where outlooks varied sharply because of differences in such factors as racial, religious, or regional backgrounds. Nowhere were these considerations more relevant than in the realm of economic affairs, where relationships were often competitive and materially affected individual status and wealth.

In economic affairs, the impetus toward the formalization of institutional relationships emanating from the pressures of cultural diversity also combined with the recognition of a need for standardization because of the increasing complexity of the modern business enterprise. The emergence of industrial organizations of enormous scale and scope of operations brought with it a need to define new types of social contracts, such as that between professional managers and an amorphous body of external investors. In these cases, institution-building took the form of the definition of legal rights and obligations of the corporation, its agents, and its owners. This also involved the creation of new lines for transmitting information, particularly relating to finances, that could be relied upon by external groups in evaluating corporate affairs.

Among Ripley's first works dealing with economic institutions were several studies that focused on the railroads, the nation's first big business. In 1907 he edited a collection of essays titled *Railway Problems*. This was followed by the authorship of two exhaustive studies titled *Railroads: Rates and Regulation* (1912) and *Railroads: Finance and Organization* (1915). In these works, Ripley generally applauded the efforts by the federal government, particularly during the administration of President Theodore Roosevelt, to strengthen the regulatory power of the Interstate Commerce Commission (ICC). The basic objective of governmental oversight in this industry, where many enterprises were essentially natural monopolies, was to assure rate equity for shippers and to assure financial probity for investors. To Ripley and other Progressives, state intervention was imperative to avoid the abusive exercise of private economic power that he attributed to the regimes of such controversial railroad magnates as Jay Gould and E.H. Harriman.

Although his railroad studies were wide-ranging, Ripley recognized that accounting and statistical measures were the lifeblood of the regulatory process. A capacity to measure was an essential prerequisite for controlling any phenomenon. This he illustrated through the analysis of two episodes. The first was the Hepburn Act of 1906, which among other matters empowered the ICC to prescribe uniform accounting methodologies. Previously, the agency had only been authorized to standardize accounting-report formats. The mandating of methodological uniformity diminished investor uncertainty about the results of railroad operations and facilitated the ICC's monitoring by assuring that its analyses would be based on comparative data. The second reform in which accounting played an important role was the passage of the Valuation Act of 1913. This law called for a national inventory of all railroad assets. Accurate information about these values was critical in satisfying the standard set forth in the *Smyth v. Ames* case 171 U.S. 361 (1898), which required that regulated industries be allowed to earn a fair return on the fair value of their property. But this proved to be hard to achieve in practice. At many railroad lines, information about the original cost of assets was incomplete because of either poor bookkeeping practices during their early days or the loss of records at the time of subsequent mergers. Some critics also believed railroad accounts had been grossly inflated through the issuance of watered stock. For these and other purposes, the national inventory of railroad property to estimate original costs and current replacement costs was initiated. This project continued through the 1930s.

During the 1920s, Ripley turned his attention to the problems associated with the growing markets for corporate equity securities and, in this case, functioned more as an advocate for reform rather than as an apologist for existing regulatory structures. The contemporary interest in equity investing represented a deviation from earlier conditions. Bonds had previously been the preferred investment vehicle. Trading in common stock had largely been left to speculators. But this attitude changed radically after World War I as many investors sought to capitalize on the nation's growing prosperity through share ownership, particularly in leading industrial and public utility enterprises.

Ripley first documented his concerns about the institutional framework supporting the equity markets in 1926, in a series of essays that appeared in the *Atlantic Monthly*. These essays were collected and issued in book form the following year under the title *Main Street and Wall Street*. Some of his criticisms had to do with the limited legal rights of shareholders, such as the common practice of issuing nonvoting shares.

Other criticisms seemed to reflect a penchant for thinking about equity as though this form of investment possessed qualities similar to those of bonds. He argued, for example, that no-par stock, which had first been introduced in New York prior to World War I, served to obscure the true value of a shareholder's equity. But the major thrust of his attack was on the deficiencies in financial reporting. His essays detailed many inadequacies in the disclosure of leading public companies that made it difficult for investors to make informed decisions about the value of their shares. In other instances, he believed that current accounting failed to measure adequately the results of enterprise operations, such as the practice of many public utility holding companies to magnify their earnings through pyramiding.

The public stir caused by the publication of *Main Street and Wall Street* induced the Social Science Research Council to form in 1927 a special committee to study the problem of the modern corporation. Ripley served as chairman of this body until he sustained serious injuries that same year in a taxi accident in New York City en route to one of its meetings. The chairmanship then passed to George Oliver May, a retired partner of Price Waterhouse and Company, who had earlier taken strong exception to some of the criticisms laid out in Ripley's book.

The committee's most important achievement was the support it provided for the research and publication of Adolf A. Berle Jr. and Gardiner C. Means's book, *The Modern Corporation and Private Property* (1932). This study analyzed the distribution of wealth in America and its relationship to the increased holding of corporate investment securities. It also recognized the problem of informational asymmetry that arose in modern corporate finance because of the separation of ownership by outsiders from the control exercised by professional managers. The remedy for this latter problem, the authors argued, lay in the mandating of fuller financial-disclosure rules by major stock exchanges and the more extensive reliance in corporate governance on the auditing services provided by public accountants. These measures represented a logical extension of the law of trusts, which had sought to protect principals by imposing fiduciary responsibilities on their agents. In the context of corporate finance, certified accounting reports were now beginning to be viewed as being crucial to external investors as a means of evaluating management's stewardship over enterprise resources. It was this same notion of accounting as a mechanism for judging the efficacy of a trustee relationship that eventually shaped key provisions of the Securities Acts of 1933 and 1934 enacted during the administration of President Franklin D. Roosevelt to better order the nation's financial markets.

Paul J. Miranti Jr.

Bibliography

Higham, J. *Strangers in the Land: Patterns of American Nativism, 1860–1925.* New York: Atheneum, 1963.

Miranti, P.J. Jr. *Accountancy Comes of Age: The Development of an American Profession, 1886–1940.* Chapel Hill: University of North Carolina Press, 1990.

See also AMERICAN INSTITUTE OF CERTIFIED PUBLIC ACCOUNTANTS; BERLE AND MEANS; HISTORICAL COST; MAY, GEORGE OLIVER; NEW YORK STOCK EXCHANGE; RAILROAD ACCOUNTING (U.S.); RETURN ON INVESTMENT; SECURITIES AND EXCHANGE COMMISSION; *SMYTH V. AMES;* UNIFORMITY

Roman Numerals

A basic reason for the backwardness of Roman accounting can be found in the Latin system of numerical notation. This was inferior because the Romans never learned to express a number's value merely by the position of each of its digits in relation to the others. This lack of position value made arithmetic cumbersome and errors hard to find. It also meant that there was little incentive to arrange numbers in columns, since they could not be added down, digit by digit, to arrive at a total. The use of Roman numerals helped perpetuate a narrative form of account in which no attempt was made to tabulate figures or even to bring receipts and expenditures face to face in parallel columns.

The Roman accounting legacy to the Middle Ages was tenacious but of doubtful value. The preference for Roman numerals continued among bookkeepers until the sixteenth century, hundreds of years after the introduction of Arabic numbers. Roman numerals were considered the proper form for official or public documents. They were also judged to be less subject to fraudulent alternation. A 1299 statute of the *Arte del Cambio* (guild of moneychangers) prohibited Florentine bankers from using Arabic numbers in their account books. As late as 1510 the municipality of Freiburg refused to accept accounting entries as legal proof of debt unless they used Roman numerals or had amounts written out in words.

Michael Chatfield

Bibliography

De Ste. Croix, G.E.M. "Greek and Roman Accounting." In *Studies in the History of Accounting*, edited by A.C. Littleton and B.S. Yamey, pp. 14–74. Homewood, IL: Irwin, 1956.

See also ARABIC NUMERALS; ARITHMETIC AND ACCOUNTING; LEONARDO OF PISA; ROME (509 B.C.–A.D. 476)

Rome (509 B.C.–A.D. 476)

The city of Rome was the center of the Republic of Rome (509–27 B.C.) and the Roman Empire (27 B.C.–A.D. 476). After defeating and destroying Carthage in 146 B.C., the Republic of Rome gained control of the Mediterranean from North Africa, to Syria, to Macedonia, to Greece, to Egypt. Notable figures during the period of the Republic were Marius, Sulla, Pompey, Cicero, and Julius Caesar. The first emperor was Caesar Augustus in 27 B.C.; noted emperors for the first 200 years included Trajan, Hadrian, Antonius Pius, and Marcus Aurelius. By the end of the second century, the Roman Empire extended over areas of the Rhine, the Danube, Asia Minor, Syria, Palestine, Egypt, Africa, Spain, France, and Britain. There were 43 provinces to administer, connected by a complex road system. Aqueducts provided water and still stand today. Christianity became the official religion of the empire in 313 under Constantine I. In 395 the empire was split into an Eastern part, ruled in Constantinople, and a Western part, ruled in Rome. In 410 Rome was sacked, and by 476 the German chieftain Odoacer removed the last Western Roman emperor. The Eastern Roman Empire continued until 1453, when Constantinople fell.

Rome had a highly developed and versatile language, Latin, and its people wrote in script on papyrus. Rome also had an excellent legal system. It utilized the currency of Greece as its international coin. Roman peace ruled for many years.

The well-developed commerce of Rome was described by Herbermann (1880). Bankers were regarded with great respect and had correspondents in various parts of the empire. Companies were formed to collect the public revenues. Money lending at high interest rates was quite common. Roman bankers were under state control; the law required them to keep books for the purpose of legal evidence in court and mandated that the books were open to inspection by city officials.

Littleton (1933) considered that there were seven factors that were necessary for double entry bookkeeping: (1) private property, (2) capital, (3) commerce, (4) credit, (5) writing, (6) money, and (7) arithmetic. Littleton, a noted accounting historian and theorist from the University of Illinois, felt that the complexities of arithmetic, not helped by the use of Roman numerals, and the lack of the notion of productive capital meant that it was unlikely double entry bookkeeping existed in Rome. The records of the Roman family were little more than a record of receipts and disbursements. Littleton wrote that equilibrium and duality must be added to the element of commercial proprietorship before double entry bookkeeping can be implemented. Because trade was regarded beneath the dignity of a Roman patrician and held negative implications for his political rights as a Roman citizen, it was likely that only educated slaves maintained the business and the records through the use of a charge-discharge form of accounts. The well-developed state of Roman law and banking certainly played a significant role in record keeping. Littleton was of the opinion that the well-developed Roman banks may have led naturally to the self-contained scheme of dual entries in bilateral accounts. It is problematical whether such knowledge survived in banking during the long Dark Ages (A.D. 476–A.D. 1000) preceding the revival of commerce in the Italian city-states.

The fascination with double entry bookkeeping and ancient record keeping affected other accounting scholars besides Littleton. Kats (1929, 1930), who had the advantage of fluency in different languages, worked with the writings of Fabio Besta (in Italian), Rudolph Beigel (in German), and Raymond de Roover (in French). In a 1930 article, Kats wrote that he did not find any money values associated with the record keeping for commodities in Rome, but that money values were kept for cash, receivables and payables. He also noted these following records of a wealthy Roman family: *adversaria* (waste book); *codex accepti et expensi* (cashbook); *codex rationum mortalium* (a ledger containing personal accounts); and *codex rationum domesticarum* (accounts for quantities only). In a 1929 article, Kats concluded that double entry accounting arose due to the slave/master relationship of the Roman economy: "Double entry accounting began when for the first time the claims of the master and the borrower's obligations were balanced against each other in the books of a Roman slave."

Peragallo (1938) stressed the continuity of the Roman culture throughout the Dark Ages, arguing that since private property did not disappear, the Roman bookkeeping system remained. Peragallo felt that double entry bookkeeping may have been present in embryonic form in the Roman bookkeeping system.

However, de Ste. Croix (1956) was quite emphatic that the Romans did not use double entry bookkeeping. He felt that the Roman economic system had not developed to the point that double entry bookkeeping was needed and that Roman numerals were awkward for this purpose and were not put in columnar form. De Ste. Croix considered that accounting existed in ancient times to expose losses due to fraud or inefficiency on the part of the proprietor's servants and others. He did report the anomaly of the bilateral form in the account from Karanis in A.D. 191–192 in which journal entries in the present double entry formats seem to have occurred.

De Ste. Croix did give an example of the use by Columella, an author of a 12 book treatise on farming, *De Re Rustic*, in A.D. 60 of making a conservative estimate of profits to be derived from vine-growing. De Ste. Croix also wrote that the noted Roman orator and lawyer, Cicero, referred to the household accounts of a wealthy Roman in a court case. Marcus Porcius Cato (234–149 B.C.), in his treatise on agriculture, *De Agri Cultura*, advised the Roman landowner to review cash accounts and various inventories each time he visited his farm and to check frequently the account of his slave steward, as also noted by de Ste. Croix.

Most (1979) challenged some of the assumptions of de Ste. Croix. Most considered the Roman economic system well-advanced, for example, and argued that the lack of the use of columns for figures does not make double entry bookkeeping impossible. He also referenced a German work by B.G. Niebuhr, who had studied fragments of Cicero's oration *pro Fonteio* at the Vatican Library and concluded that they implied the existence of double entry bookkeeping.

The double entry controversy should not obscure the point that different versions of accounting documentation, controls, and information were important components of Roman civilizations. Manuals for husbandry, laws, recorded legal arguments, and government records all show this importance.

Richard Vangermeersch

Bibliography

Barrow, R.H. *The Romans*. 2d ed. Chicago: Aldine Publishing, 1964.

De Ste. Croix, G.E.M. "Greek and Roman Accounting." In *Studies in the History of Accounting*, edited by A.C. Littleton and B.S. Yamey, pp. 14–74. Homewood, IL: Irwin, 1956.

Herbermann, C.G. *Business Life in Ancient Rome*. New York: Harper & Brothers, 1880.

Kats, P. "Early History of Bookkeeping by Double Entry," *Journal of Accountancy*, March and April 1929, pp. 203–210 and pp. 275–290.

———. "A Surmise Regarding the Origin of Bookkeeping by Double-Entry," *Accounting Review*, October 1930, p. 311–316.

Littleton, A.C. *Accounting Evolution to 1900*. New York: American Institute Publishing, 1933. Reprint. New York: Russell and Russell, 1966.

Most, K.S. "The Accounts of Ancient Rome." Working paper no. 3, in *Working Paper Series Volume 1*, edited by E.N. Coffman, pp. 22–41. Richmond, VA: Academy of Accounting Historians, 1979.

Peragallo, E. *Origins and Evolution of Double Entry Bookkeeping: A Study of Italian Practice from the Fourteenth Century*. New York: American Institute Publishing, 1938. Reprint. Osaka: Nihon Shoseki, 1974.

See also ARITHMETIC AND ACCOUNTING; DOUBLE ENTRY BOOKKEEPING: ORIGINS; GREECE; LEDGER; LITTLETON, A.C.; MEDIEVAL ACCOUNTING; MOST, KENNETH S.; PROPRIETORSHIP; ROMAN NUMERALS; SINGLE ENTRY BOOKKEEPING; STEVIN, SIMON; STEWARDSHIP; TAX-ORDAINED ACCOUNTING; TRUSTEE ACCOUNTS; VITRUVIUS

R

Rosenblum v. Adler

In 1972 Harry and Barry Rosenblum approved a merger agreement under which they received common stock of Giant Stores Corporation in exchange for their business. Touche Ross and Company, the auditor of Giant Stores, had failed to discover during its 1971 and 1972 audits that Giant Stores had falsified its accounts by booking assets it did not own and by omitting accounts payable. Early in 1973 the fraud was revealed, and Giant Stores Corporation filed a bankruptcy petition in September 1973. The Giant Stores common stock received by the Rosenblums became worthless.

The Rosenblums sued Touche Ross and Company, claiming that Touche had negligently conducted its audits of Giant Stores, and that because the Rosenblums had relied on Giant Stores's audited financial statements, Touche's negligence was a cause of their loss.

In 1983 the New Jersey Supreme Court agreed, rejecting Touche's defense that it could not be foreseen that the Rosenblums would rely on Giant Stores's audited financial statements. The court noted that (1) when an auditor issues an opinion on a company's financial statements, it has a duty of care to anyone who is reasonably foreseen as a recipient of those statements, and (2) the situation in which the Rosenblums used and relied on the financial statements was reasonably foreseeable.

The *Rosenblum* decision is considered to have diminished the auditor's privity defense under common law. *Rosenblum* indicated that auditors may be held liable for ordinary negligence to third parties who are not primary beneficiaries of the audit, particularly if those third parties and their reliance on the auditor's opinion are reasonably foreseeable.

Michael Chatfield

Bibliography

Miller, R.L., and G.P. Brady. *CPA Liability: Meeting the Challenge*. New York: John Wiley & Sons, 1986.

Rosenblum v. Adler, 261 A. 2d 138 (New Jersey Supreme Court, 1983).

See also LAW AND ACCOUNTING; LEGAL LIABILITY OF AUDITORS

Royal Mail Case

See REX V. KYLSANT

Russia

Accounting in Russia has been marked by seven periods of development: (1) 862–1240, Byzantine influence; (2) 1240–1480, Tatar influence; (3) 1480–1700, First Russian School; (4) 1700–1861, European double entry accounting; (5) 1861–1917, Second Russian School; (6) 1917–1985, Marxism; and (7) 1985–, International Accounting Standards.

The formation of Russia in 862 led to primitive accounting methods connected with the collection of tributes to each principality. Early in its history, Russia was dominated by the state ownership of property. With the adoption of Christianity, many multifaceted monasteries were formed. The controls within monastery walls were so tight that missing inventory resulted in severe forms of punishment, including death sentences.

In the second period, the epoch of the "Tatar Yoke," the dominating theme was the attempt to enforce a poll tax. Each person was responsible for payment of this tax regardless of age or status. The entire amount of the tax was to be paid by the village, and if a person couldn't pay his share, it was to be paid by the other members of the community.

The period from 1480–1700 marked the strengthening of the Russian State—the so-called "Moscow Period of Russian History." During the second half of the seventeenth century, a system of formal state control was instituted in Russia. A special Department of Accountancy became responsible for the theory and practice of this system. This department conducted an audit function for all state entities and could revise their accounts in Moscow. All accounting ledgers were delivered to Moscow from throughout the country, and inspectors were sent from Moscow to its entities.

The next epoch (1700–1861) brought with it the influence of Western accounting thought which caused the transformation of Russian accounting to the double entry system. Regulations were promulgated that required European accounting—the "Regulations of Admiralty and Shipyard Management" in 1722 and the "Statute about Bankruptcy" in 1740. The founders of the double entry system in Russia were M. Tchoulkov, K. Arnold, I. Akhmatov, and E. Moudrov, all of whom were heavily influenced by the German accounting tradition.

The year 1861 saw some remarkable changes in Russia. First, serfdom was abolished. Second, the institutions of local government and of the jury trial were established in accordance with the European experience. Third, the national economy began to develop along the lines of capitalism. At first, the writings of Italian, French, and German accountants guided practice in Russia. However, an indigenous crop of accounting writers soon developed. F. Ezersky stressed the importance of a perpetual-inventory system, which allowed for profit determination at various time intervals during the year. S. Ivanov focused on prime costs for his "Cost of Basic Production." I. Valitsky designed the methodology of both a national and a firm's balance sheet along the lines of current and noncurrent classifications. E. Feldhausen introduced standard costs. L. Gomberg created his own original theory of "economology," which placed theoretical accounting concepts into a system. By 1888 there was a professional accounting journal, and from 1783 to 1917 there were 1,356 accounting books published in Russia. Professional accounting groups also were formed.

The Russian Revolution in 1917 led to significant changes in accounting, although the former traditions continued to develop in the 1920s with work done by A. Roudanovsky and A. Galagan. However, starting in the 1930s, the traditional accounting system was significantly changed: (1) such business elements as promissory notes, stocks, bonds, and dividends vanished under communism; (2) there was no need for accounting methodology to determine liquidity and financial leverage, for instance; (3) and theoretical research was limited to scholastic disputes about the limits of accounting and the classification of accounts.

In the first years of the establishment of Soviet power, there was an attempt to liquidate traditional accounting, and ancient control devices were reinstituted by the governments. For instance, under a special accounting system, called Extraordinary Accounting, all material values had to be registered with a municipality, not the enterprise. No one except representatives of the Soviet could spend a penny or use a nail. Monetary measurement was expelled from accounting. The double entry system was declared "bourgeois" and was liquidated.

By 1921 the economic disaster of such a view of accounting became evident. Traditional accounting was restored and the traditional European version of double entry accounting again occupied its proper place in the economic life of Russia.

On August 9, 1928, the Council of People's Commissars, the main executive power of Russia, issued a crucial document, "Regulations on Chief Accountants." It mandated that a chief accountant was responsible to both the director of the enterprise for administrative matters and to the head accountant of that industry for accounting methodology. It also specified that it was the duty of the chief accountant to keep an eye on possible illegal actions of the management of the enterprise and to report them to the authorities in that industry.

Since October 1, 1929, there has been a compulsory monthly calculation of prime cost of production for all enterprise. On July 29, 1936, the document "Regulation on Accounting Statements and Balance Sheets" declared that only prime cost can be used for valuation of production.

Since 1930, a special accounting system of perpetual inventory cards became the dominant system, following the German system of "Definitiv Kontroll-buchhaltung." At that time the first attempts of mechanized accounting procedures were made and much attention was given to standard costing. The state professional journal *Accounting* began its monthly publication in 1937; in 1992 it had a circulation of 315,132.

One of the merits of the Soviet period of accounting was the establishment of university education for accountants. About 170 universities have five-year graduate programs in accounting.

The advent of great changes in accounting were marshalled in with Mikhail Gorbachev's 1985 policy of *perestroika*. The National Association of Accountants was created in Russia in 1990, with Professor A. Sheremet as chairman. Now there are new accounts for intangibles, stocks, and leases, for instance. A new chart of accounts was issued on December 19, 1991, prepared by specialists from the Russian Ministry of Economics and Finance and consultants from the United Nations Center on Transnational Corporations. The new set of financial statements are quite similar to Western financial statements.

The history of accounting and accounting thought in Russia shows how closely the field of accounting is tied to economic and social policy.

Jaroslav. V. Sokolov
Valery V. Kovalev

Bibliography

Bailey, D.T. "Accounting in Russia: The European Connection," *International Journal of Accounting*, Fall 1982, pp. 1–36.

———. "Accounting in the Shadow of Stalinism," *Accounting, Organizations, and Society*, vol. 15, no. 6, 1990, pp. 513–525.

Mazdorov, V.A. *History of Accounting Evolution in USSR, 1917–1972.* Moscow: Finance Publishers, 1972. (Published in Russian).

Motyka, W. *Annotated Bibliography of Russian Language Publications on Accounting.* New York: Garland, 1993.

———. "The Impact of Western Europe on Accounting Development in Tzarist Russia Prior to 1880," *Abacus*, March 1990, pp. 36–62.

See also CHART OF ACCOUNTS

S

Sanders, Hatfield, and Moore

In 1935 the Haskins and Sells Foundation invited three academics, Thomas Henry Sanders (Harvard), Henry Rand Hatfield (Berkeley), and Underhill Moore (Yale Law School) "to formulate a code of accounting principles which would be useful in the clarification and improvement of corporate accounting and of financial reports issued to the public." In compiling *A Statement of Accounting Principles* (1938), Sanders, Hatfield, and Moore interviewed both preparers and users of accounting data, reviewed the periodic literature, and studied laws, court decisions, and corporate annual reports.

Their method of analysis had the effect of a public opinion survey, producing a catalog of generalizations from current practice. This placed its authors in a trap: Their principles were derived almost entirely from the methods they sought to improve. And by condoning most bad practices so long as they were widely used, the authors left accountants in an essentially passive role. At a time when the profession was seeking recognition of its independent status, Sanders, Hatfield, and Moore assumed it was management's responsibility to decide what information should be included in financial statements and how that information should be presented. However, Storey (1964) called this study "the first relatively complete statement of accounting principles." As such, it influenced the formats of later principles codifications.

Michael Chatfield

Bibliography

Sanders, T.H., H.R. Hatfield, and U. Moore. *A Statement of Accounting Principles.* New York: AIA, 1938. Reprint. Columbus, OH: American Accounting Association, 1959.

Storey, R.K. *The Search for Accounting Principles.* New York: AICPA, 1964.

See also ACCOUNTING RESEARCH STUDIES; GENERALLY ACCEPTED ACCOUNTING PRINCIPLES; HATFIELD, HENRY RAND; SANDERS, THOMAS HENRY

Sanders, Thomas Henry (1885–1953)

An educator and a scholar, Thomas Henry Sanders was one of the leading American accountants of the twentieth century. He was born in Staffordshire, England, and received his bachelor's (1905) and master's (1914) degrees from the University of Birmingham in England and a doctorate from Harvard University in 1921. From 1905 to 1910, he was with Rudge-Whitworth in Coventry, England, and from 1911 to 1917, he taught commercial practice at the Higher Commercial School in Yamaguichi, Japan.

He came to the United States in 1917 and joined the University of Minnesota as assistant professor (1918–1920). He received his doctorate from Harvard University in 1921 and served there as assistant professor (1921–1924), associate professor (1924–1927), and professor (1927–1952) until his retirement. During the academic year 1948–1949, he was Dickinson Lecturer at Harvard. This was a title established in 1929 by Price Waterhouse and Company in recognition of an outstanding member of the profession, Sir Arthur Lowes Dickinson.

Professor Sanders was also active in professional organizations and public service. He served as vice president (1923–1924) and president (1924–1925) of the Boston chapter of the National Association of Cost Accountants (NACA)—forerunner of the National Association of Accountants (NAA) and the Institute of Management Accounting (IMA). Subsequently, he was vice president and director of publications (1930–1931) of the NACA, its president (1931–1932), and a member of its board of directors. He was also involved with the NACA as director of education (1927–1929), and research (1929–1930; 1933–1934), and as chairman of the Committee on Research (1945–1946).

As research director in 1934 for the Committee on Statistical Reporting and Uniform Accounting for Industry, which reported to the Business Advisory and Planning Council of the U.S. Commerce Department, he was instrumental in the Council's successful efforts at more clear specification of the nature of corporate reports to stockholders. He emphasized in "Reports to Stockholders" (1934) uniformity in basic accounting and reporting practices while at the same time recognizing that "there are important differences in the nature and scope of the operations of companies in different industrial or business groups and of companies within the same industrial group." He also held the view that "while from many viewpoints the income statement is of fundamental importance, income reporting has been less satisfactory than balance sheet reporting."

Sanders was consultant to the Securities and Exchange Commission (SEC) (1934–1935) at a critical point in its history. He considered the role of the SEC vital in providing more definition to accounting principles and aided it in drafting its forms and regulations. While there was general concern that the SEC was using the "stick" approach in defining accounting principles, Sanders claimed that these principles would, in effect, be liberating—that the SEC would not insist only on rigid rules but would provide flexible guidelines. He felt that the success of the SEC as a regulatory body would depend largely on the development of a generally accepted body of principles on which it could rely. He looked in 1936 at SEC regulations as a positive move designed to "strengthen the hands of all who are concerned with good accounting."

Sanders also contributed to the profession in the area of cost accounting, with *Cost Accounting for Control* (1934). Reflecting on the tremendous growth in mechanization in industry and the consequent increase in the proportion of fixed costs, he stressed the importance of cost accounting and the problem of allocating fixed costs. This book is a good reference for early case studies in cost accounting.

Sanders is probably most widely recognized for his efforts on the Haskins and Sells Foundation-sponsored *A Statement of Accounting Principles*, which he coauthored with Professors Henry Rand Hatfield and Underhill Moore. In the Foreword to the original 1938 edition, the American Institute of Accountants, which published the book, stated that the report constituted a "highly valuable contribution to the discussion of accounting principles." The work was based on the premise that effective distinction between capital and income "are the ultimate objectives which determine the activities of accountants and the functions of accounting." The authors believed that there did exist a coherent body of accounting principles that was generally accepted and endeavored to portray these principles.

Sanders's contributions in the development of accounting principles is also evidenced by his many publications in this area. He authored a number of books, including *Problems in Industrial Accounting* (1923), *Bookkeeping and Business Knowledge* with J.H. Jackson and A.H. Sproul (1926), *Accounting Principles and Practices* with Hatfield and N.L. Burton (1940), *Company Annual Reports* (1949), and *Effects of Taxation on Executives* (1951). In addition, he published many articles in academic journals, particularly *Accounting Review*. In recognition of his academic and public service achievements, he was inducted into the Accounting Hall of Fame in Columbus, Ohio in 1954.

Nadine Chandar

Bibliography
Burns, T.J., and E.N. Coffman. *The Accounting Hall of Fame: Profiles of Fifty Members*. Columbus: College of Business, Ohio State University, 1991.
Sanders, T.H. *Cost Accounting for Control*. 2d ed. New York: McGraw-Hill, 1934.
———. "Influence of the Securities and Exchange Commission upon Accounting Principles," *Accounting Review*, March 1936, pp. 66–74.
———. "Overhead in Economics and Accounting," *NACA Bulletin*, April 15, 1926, pp. 583–591.
———. "Reports to Stockholders," *Accounting Review*, September 1934, pp. 201–219.

See also ACCOUNTING HALL OF FAME; AC-
COUNTING RESEARCH BULLETINS; AMERICAN
INSTITUTE OF CERTIFIED PUBLIC ACCOUN-
TANTS; COMMON COSTS; DICKINSON,
ARTHUR LOWES; HATFIELD, HENRY RAND;
INSTITUTE OF MANAGEMENT ACCOUNTANTS;
SANDERS, HATFIELD, AND MOORE; SECURI-
TIES AND EXCHANGE COMMISSION

Sandilands Report

The Sandilands Report is the unofficial name of
Inflation Accounting, the report of the Inflation
Accounting Committee of the United Kingdom
and Ireland. It was presented to Parliament by
the Chancellor of the Exchequer and the Secretary of State for Trade by Command of Her
Majesty in September 1975. The report drew its
name from the chairman of the committee,
F.E.P. Sandilands, the chairman of the board of
Commercial Union Assurance Company. The
committee was formed on January 21, 1974,
during the worst period of inflation in the history of the United Kingdom. It was composed
of 12 members, three of whom were chartered
accountants, and issued its unanimous report
on June 25, 1975. Its conclusions were that
"current purchasing power" and "replacement
cost" accounting are not alternatives to each
other, and that the usefulness of historical cost
accounting is sharply reduced in times of rising
costs and prices. The committee recommended
that a current cost accounting system be developed, while the net book value of assets and
yearly depreciation on a historical cost basis be
shown as notes to the accounts.

The Sandilands Report is an extremely
well-written and well-reasoned document. It
presented an excellent discussion of inflation,
expertly placed inflation accounting within the
"true and fair view" of reporting, and reviewed
the Accounting Standards Steering Committee
(ASSC), founded in 1969, in light of its Statements of Standard Accounting Practice (SSAP)
and its Exposure Drafts. The Sandilands Committee compared and contrasted five concepts
of profit for the year, after determining three
general bases of value: (1) current purchase
price, (2) net realizable value, and (3) the "economic" value (discounted present value). It also
discussed these qualitative requirements for an
accounting system: (1) objectivity, (2) realism,
(3) prudence, (4) comparability, (5) consistency,
(6) intelligibility, and (7) ease and economy in
preparation.

Historical cost accounting was reviewed,
especially in light of the Companies Act of
1967, which permitted revaluation upwards
for fixed assets. The Sandilands Committee
closely studied and then rejected the last in,
first out (LIFO) method of inventory valuation, as well as the base stock method. The report also rejected the "current purchasing
power" method of accounting for inflation,
recommended by SSAP No. 7, "Accounting for
Changes in the Purchasing Power of Money"
(1974), as supplementary information.
"Gains" on net monetary liabilities were felt
to be particularly misleading.

The Sandilands Committee recommended
that current-cost accounting be approximated by
the measure of the "value to the business" of an
asset equated to the amount of loss suffered by
the company concerned if the asset is lost or
destroyed. This approach was recommended for
quick adoption by companies even before formal
standards were issued. Taxation and other social
implications were carefully discussed. The report
then separately listed its 199 principal conclusions and recommendations.

The report of the Sandilands Committee
is the reference point for how an accounting
research study should be conducted and
drafted. The report is in contrast to the U.S.
and the U.K. accounting rules bodies tendencies to favor the purchasing-power approach
for inflation accounting. The "value to the
business" standard is surely a useful one for
internal reporting purposes, though its use for
external reporting has some severe objectivity
problems. The Sandilands Report should be
carefully restudied during the next round of
inflation.

Richard Vangermeersch

Bibliography

"A Brief Guide to Sandilands," *Management
Accounting* (England), October 1975,
pp. 312–313.
Fisher, J. "Value to the Business: Some Practi-
cal Problems," *Management Accounting*,
July 1976, pp. 213–232, 237.
Inflation Accounting Committee of the
United Kingdom and Ireland. *Inflation
Accounting* [The Sandilands Report].
London: Her Majesty's Stationery Office,
1975.
Wollstadt, R.D. "The Challenge of the
Sandilands Report," *Management Ac-
counting*, July 1976, pp. 15–22.

See also ACCOUNTING SERIES RELEASE NO.
190; BASE STOCK METHOD; DISCOUNTED
CASH FLOW; HISTORICAL COST; INFLATION
ACCOUNTING; LAST IN, FIRST OUT (LIFO);
OBJECTIVITY; PHILIPS INDUSTRIES (N.V.);
SOLOMONS, DAVID

Savary, Jacques (1622–1690)

Jacques Savary was the principal author of a 1673 French government ordinance that required every merchant and banker to keep written records of his transactions in a book signed by a public official, and to prepare semiannual inventories "of all their fixed and movable properties and of all their debts receivable and payable." The Code Savary was meant to reveal a merchant's ability to pay his debts from his existing assets in case he went bankrupt, and thereby to facilitate a fair sharing of his resources among creditors. If a merchant did not keep authenticated records, his bankruptcy was considered fraudulent and he was subject to the death penalty. The Code Savary also authorized limited liability partnerships similar to the Italian *commendas*. The bankruptcy provisions of this 1673 ordinance were incorporated into the Napoleonic Code of 1807.

In 1675 Savary published *Le Parfait Negociant* (The Perfect Merchant), in which he commented on the Code Savary and presented examples of bookkeeping technique from the retail textile trade where he had made his fortune. He now favored preparation of annual rather than semiannual inventories, and recommended closing the books during "a month of the least activity in order to have more time to value your merchandise." The sixth edition of *Le Parfait Negociant* (1712) advocated current market price valuations of inventory, unless it had begun to deteriorate or go out of style, in which case its carrying value should be reduced. Carrying value should also be reduced if replacement cost fell below acquisition price. Vance (1943) considered Savary the person most responsible for promoting the lower of cost or market rule.

Michael Chatfield

Bibliography

Howard, S.E. "Business Partnership in France before 1807," *Accounting Review*, December 1932, pp. 242–257.
———. "Public Rules for Private Accounting in France, 1673 and 1807," *Accounting Review*, June 1932, pp. 91–102.
Littleton, A.C. *Accounting Evolution to 1900*. New York: American Institute Publishing, 1933. Reprint. New York: Russell and Russell, 1966.
Parker, R.H. "A Note on Savary's *Le Parfait Negociant*," *Journal of Accounting Research*, Autumn 1966, pp. 260–261.
Vance, L. "The Authority of History in Inventory Valuation," *Accounting Review*, 1943, pp. 219–227.

See also CAPITAL STOCK; CHART OF ACCOUNTS; CLOSING ENTRIES AND PROCEDURES; COMMENDA CONTRACTS; CONSERVATISM; FRANCE; GERMANY; LIMITED LIABILITY; NATURAL BUSINESS YEAR; TRANSFER PRICES

Schmalenbach, Eugen (1873–1955)

Eugen Schmalenbach is regarded as one of the most influential scholars for teaching, research, and accounting practice in Germany and Continental Europe. His ancestors were Westfalian farmers; his father operated a small hinge- and lock-making business where—after high school graduation and completion of practical training in engineering—Schmalenbach worked for four years. In 1898 he began his studies of business economics at the newly founded Handelshochschule (Commercial College) in Leipzig; he graduated among the first group of students in 1900 and stayed on as a personal assistant to Professor Karl Buecher, who combined interests in economics, anthropology, and history. After completion of advanced degrees, Schmalenbach moved to the Handelshochschule in Cologne and was appointed full professor in 1906. The Handelshochschule became the University of Cologne in 1919 and, due to Schmalenbach's efforts, one of the leading business schools in Germany.

Schmalenbach continued teaching until 1933, when he was forced to take early retirement because his wife was Jewish. He remained active in his field through writing and consulting until the end of World War II. In 1945 he resumed his famous seminars, which he continued to conduct almost to the time he died. Schmalenbach received many honorary doctorates for his contributions to accounting and business theory from German and foreign universities, in spite of the fact that he never taught abroad.

Schmalenbach, a member of the first generation of German business professors, is regarded as one of the founding fathers of academic business administration and accounting. His major contributions were made in the areas of (1) accounting and income measurement (*Bilantheorie*) by developing the concept of dynamic accounting, (2) the uniform chart of accounts, and (3) managerial accounting and pricing. Schmalenbach was a pragmatist; he strongly believed that in an applied field, theories without a direct impact on business operations were useless. As a result, he was active in consulting, and many of his writings dealt with practical problems. He also contributed to advances in organization theory, auditing, finance, and marketing.

Following the German microeconomic tradition, Schmalenbach viewed an enterprise as an entity, which converts cash into other resources for economic utilization; eventually, all resources will be turned back into cash. His balance sheet, therefore, measured assets at various intermediate stages of this conversion; it represented a record of unconsumed resources, or, in his words, different classes of accruals or prepayments. Some of these were essential for operations (*betriebsnotwendig*), and others were held for speculative purposes. The major emphasis for income and performance measurement, consequently, had to be placed on the income statement, which was similar to views held by American A.C. Littleton and other contemporaries.

His "dynamic" view represented a drastic departure from the prevailing legalistic (so-called static) view of financial statements, which regarded assets only as a record of available values. Before him, few attempts had been made to interpret economic meaning and content of financial statements, and hardly anyone had tried to justify existing valuation rules. Because of the transitional nature of balance-sheet values and their function as support for income-statement data, he rejected market-adjusted inflation-accounting valuation and, reluctantly, conceded only a need for indexed supplementary statements during the rampant inflation of the 1920s.

Schmalenbach's most lasting contribution, with the strongest international impact, derived from his uniform chart of accounts. His system consisted of 10 classes of accounts (0 = inactive accounts containing noncurrent assets and liabilities; 1 = financial accounts; 2 = adjustment accounts separating financial and managerial data; 3 = general cost; 4 = raw materials and wages; 5 = free for internal accounting use; 6 = service cost centers; 7 = production cost centers; 8 = work in process and finished goods; 9 = selling cost, sales revenues, monthly annual, etc., results). The uniform chart systematized accounts, using flow-through principle classifications, and attempted to trace resource consumption.

Schmalenbach considered cost an accounting expression of resource quantities consumed and measured in monetary units only for purposes of additivity. To accomplish jointly the collection of conventional financial-accounting data and the measurement of true resource consumption, including those assets that are either not recorded (e.g., donated assets) or not measured appropriately for decision-making purposes (e.g., changed prices), his system permitted the simultaneous utilization of several different values (needed as a consequence of price changes, inflation, more accurate depreciation patterns, inclusion of interest to reflect accurately total capital utilization rather than borrowing cost only) by using imputed cost items (*kalkulatorische Kosten*) for managerial purposes. To operationalize the system, he introduced cost, that is resource consumption-accounts, as a separate set of accounts in class 2. These accounts were automatically eliminated at the end of each period in the summary accounts of class 9, thus retaining traditional expense measurements within the financial-accounting cycle. Financial and managerial accounts were either operated jointly within (monistic system) or separately from the traditional accounting system (dualistic or separate statistical system). To increase the information content of his accounting system, he distinguished clearly between: (1) cash expenditures and cash inflow (for cash-flow measurement); (2) expenses and revenues (for traditional income measurement); and (3) cost and performance results (for managerial measurements with emphasis on efficiency).

Each measurement can be taken by using data from separate account classes. In 1939 during World War II, this uniform chart of accounts was made mandatory in Germany with slight modifications (special charts for various industries with regrouped account classes); but no credit was given to Schmalenbach. Later the system was enforced in all occupied countries; in some, it remained mandatory with modifications even after the war . A modified system is presently used by most German businesses and their foreign subsidiaries. Though ideological changes have occurred, the closest resemblance to the original chart of accounts could be found in the former USSR and Eastern European countries until the early 1990s. This demonstrates that Schmalenbach's system is usable for different economic systems. In addition, it has also been demonstrated that uniform systems have substantially speeded up computerization and communication among subsidiaries.

In later years Schmalenbach concentrated on the development of accounting-based decision-making values that facilitate market-oriented and profit-maximizing management behavior, since different values (prices) can be used within his accounting system. He already mentioned and later published in 1947 and 1948 his suggestion for conditions under which a business should use full cost (acquisition or replacement cost), marginal or direct cost (capacity underutilization), or some other values (called optimal guidance values, later were shown to be shadow prices) for capacity overutilization to improve its profitability. Through these efforts he created the foundations for a decision-oriented accounting-based information system as required in today's competitive environment. In rereading Schmalenbach, it is always a surprise to find how modern his views appear—even many years after their first publication.

Hanns Martin Schoenfeld

Bibliography

Cordes, W., ed. *Eugen Schmalenbach: Der Mann, sein Werk, die Wirkung.* Stuttgart: Schaeffer Verlag, 1984.

Forrester, D.A.R. *Schmalenbach and After.* Glasgow: Strathclyde Convergencies, 1977.

Most, K.S. *Uniform Cost Accounting and the Classification and Coding of Accounts.* London: N.p., 1962.

Most, K.S., and G.W. Murphy. *Dynamic Accounting* (translation of *Dynamische Bilanzen*). London: N.p., 1959.

Schoenfeld, H.M. *Cost Terminology and Cost Theory: A Study of Its Development and Present State in Central Europe.* Urbana, IL: Center for International Education and Research in Accounting, University of Illinois, 1974.

Schmalenbach, E. *Der Kontenrahmen.* 6th ed. Leipzig: G.A. Glöckner Verlagsbuchhandlung, 1939. (first edition, 1929)

———. *Die Beteiligungsfinanzierung.* 7th ed. Köln and Opladen: Westdeutscher Verlag, 1949. (first edition, 1915)

———. *Dynamische Bilanz.* 11th ed. Köln and Opladen: Westdeutscher Verlag, 1953. (first edition, 1919, as *Dynamische Bilanzlehre*)

———. *Pretiale Wirtschaftslenkung.* 2 vols. Bremen Horn: Industrie und Handelsverlag Walter Dorn, 1947–1948.

———. *Selbstkostenrechnung und Preispolitik.* 8th ed. Köln and Opladen: Westdeutscher Verlag, 1963. (first edition, 1924)

———. *Über die Dienststellengliederung im Grossbetrieb.* Köln and Opladen: Westdeutscher Verlag, 1959.

Schweitzer, M. "Eugen Schmalenbach as the Founder of Cost Accounting in the German-speaking World." In *Collected Papers of the Sixth World Congress of Accounting Historians,* edited by A. Tsuji. vol. 2, pp. 1–24. Osaka: Accounting History Association, 1992.

See also CHART OF ACCOUNTS; GERMANY; INFLATION ACCOUNTING; LIMPERG, THEODORE, JR.; MICROECONOMICS IN GERMANY; MOST, KENNETH S.; SINGLE ENTRY BOOKKEEPING; SWEENEY, HENRY WHITCOMB; TRANSFER PRICES; UNIFORMITY

Schmidt, Julius August Fritz (1882–1950)

Fritz Schmidt's published contributions are large in number and substantial in content. He published 16 books, the best known in accounting being his magnum opus, *Die Organische Tageswertbilanz* (1929), and over 120 articles on topics encompassing stock-exchange, foreign-exchange and banking practices, organic current-value accounting, costs and pricing, theory of trade cycles, trusts and taxation theory, and matters to do with education and the economics profession.

Karl Schwantag, a student of Schmidt, suggests that one of Schmidt's greatest contributions was to view things systematically, to look for general propositions from observed day-to-day particulars. His publications cover three stages: (1) 1907–1918 books and articles in which he recorded observations of stock exchange and banking practices resulting in the recording and classification of business forms and methods, (2) 1918–1936 works aimed at deriving theoretical breakthroughs with respect to accounting and business economics from observed particulars, and (3) works thereafter in which he consolidated the efforts of the second stage, seeking a consistent theory of business administration. Schmidt's works on accounting occurred in the early decades of the twentieth century during a shift in European business administration thought from static, balance sheet-oriented theories to more dynamic, income-oriented theories.

Schmidt, along with the Dutch academic Theodore Limperg Jr., has been recognized in the Anglo-American literature as providing the theoretical antecedents of modern-day versions of replacement-cost accounting. While there is dispute as to primacy, it has been argued that Schmidt had the earliest and greatest impact on those developments. Schmidt's *organic* current-value accounting calculates the turnover result on the basis of current revenues minus current costs of factor inputs. Thus, expenditures on materials, labor, and even overhead items such as depreciation are all valued at replacement costs at the respective sales dates, and assets of the balance sheet are to be shown at their then-replacement costs. Any changes in the replacement values of nonmonetary assets were not regarded as income (or loss), but as changes in capital. They are recorded separately in Schmidt's system in a capital-adjustment account (*Wertberichtigungskonto*). Schmidt claimed that the same input data could be used to prepare an income statement and a balance sheet. Hence he was described as a dualist, in contrast to some other monist *Betriebswirtschaftslehre*, who suggested it was impossible to use the same data for both purposes.

Schmidt's system was premised on maintaining relative physical values in the economy. Schwantag noted another aspect in which relative was to apply: The value of capital employed automatically would be adjusted relative to the extent to which customers' needs were satisfied. Schmidt's organic accounting system was claimed to have a further benefit of mitigating the cyclical nature of economic activity. This aspect was relied upon by the Australian, Gottfried von Haberler, a leading pre–World War II authority on trade cycles. Innovative and pragmatic indexation mechanisms, such as *Indexbuchführung* and *Goldmarkbilanz*, so prevalent in Germany in the early 1920s, were regarded by Schmidt as partial solutions. They failed to analyze firms and their related accounting in the context of the market economy, particularly in its depressed postwar state. In this respect, they lacked an organic, relative perspective. Clearly, Schmidt perceived accounting as an integral facet of any theory of economic equilibrium, placing the theory of the firm, and accounting for a firm, in the context of a dynamic economy. And it is clear that his theory tries to accommodate the practical experience of the effects of inflation and the fall in productivity resulting from the World War I and postwar period, which had led to the disruption of the currency, wear and tear of the stock of fixed assets, and the unprecedented weakening of physical and productive working capacities. The fundamental organic nature of Schmidt's accounting theory is well captured by Schwantag, who also suggests that another positive and lasting feature of Schmidt's work is the recognition that the money unit is "flexible in reality and that this flexibility had to be taken into account when measuring." It has been suggested by the Dutch followers of Limperg's ideas that Schmidt's system was overly concerned with the war and inflation problems—that it was too incident specific and hence did not provide a general theory of accounting or business administration. This view is disputed in Clarke and Dean (1990).

Schmidt's insights concerning the functions of accounting are important. The link with economic action and measurement were essential in developing his accounting theory. While recognizing that the unit of measure is variable, Schmidt did not incorporate general price-level changes into the accounts. In contrast, he directed managers physically to match an entity's monetary assets and liabilities. This was known as his "identity of values principle," and it was widely criticized by the German accounting theorists Eugen Schmalenbach and Walter Mahlberg at the time as being consistent with his totalitarian views. Arguably, this managerial policy of matching monetary assets and liabilities was the antecedent of the solution to which the gearing adjustments in the United Kingdom's mid-1970s' proposals concerning current cost accounting were directed.

Schmidt's early professional life is instructive. He was a professor of business administration at Frankfurt University, having had previously nine years of practical experience in the retail business, wholesale, manufacturing, book selling, insurance, and overseas import and export; and then formally studied and taught economics at several German universities. Since he was a trained economist and an observer of stock-exchange and foreign-currency activities, it is not unexpected that his writings drew upon current economic thought, particularly price theory, marginalism, and Irving Fisher's, a noted American economist, work on indexation. Nor unexpected was his acknowledged indebtedness to the classical economists, the English David Ricardo (1772–1823), and the American Henry Charles Carey (1793–1879). The latter two authors had proposed that the replacement costs of factor inputs were relevant for businessmen contemplating action. As Schwantag notes, this did not mean that Schmidt uncritically accepted the current economic ideas. His organic accounting proposals extended and systematized the selling-price-based ideas of Pawel Ciompa (1910), and the replacement-cost-based ideas of Ilmari Kovero (1912) and Emil Fäs (1913). Schmidt's works gained an international recognition. They appeared not only in German, but also in Dutch (1923), in English (1929), and a Japanese translation of *Die organische Tageswertbilanz* (1929) was published in 1934. His ideas gained further exposure at the Second International Accountants Congress in Amsterdam in 1926, and at the Third International Congress in New York in 1929. Schmidt's ideas are recognized to have had an impact on American accountant Henry Whitcomb Sweeney when he was developing his stabilized-accounting mechanism. The established linkage between Sweeney's *Stabilized Accounting* (1936, 1964) and the post–World War II proposals concerning current cost accounting ensures Schmidt's continued influence on the contemporary development of accounting thought and practice.

Frank L. Clarke
Graeme W. Dean

Bibliography

Ciompa, P. *Grundriss einer Ökonometrie und die auf der Nationalökonomie aufgebaute natürliche Theorie der Buchhaltung.* Lemberg: C.E. Pöschel, 1910.

Clarke, F.L., and G.W. Dean. *Contributions of Limperg and Schmidt to the Replacement Cost Debate in the 1920s.* New York: Garland, 1990.

Fäs, E. *Die Berücksichtigung der Wertverminderung des stehenden Kapitals in den Jahresbilanzen der Erwerbswirtschaften.* Tübingen: H. Laupp, 1913.

Graves, O.F. "Fritz Schmidt, Henry Sweeney and Stabilised Accounting," *Accounting and Business Research*, Spring 1991, pp. 119–124.

Kovero, I. *Die Bewertung der Vermögensgegenstände in den Jahresbilanzen der privaten Unternehmungen mit besonderer Berücksichtigung der nicht realisierten Verluste und Gewinne.* Berlin: C. Heymann, 1912.

Shwantag, K. "F. Schmidt's wissenschaftliches Werk" (Academic Work of Fritz Schmidt), *Abacus,* September 1986, pp. 90–99 (translation of original, which appeared in *Zeitschrift für Betriebswirtschaft*, January 1951, pp. 1–14).

Voigtlaender, D. "Bibliographie: Das wissenschaftliche Werk von F. Schmidt" (Bibliography: Fritz Schmidt's Academic Work), *Abacus,* September 1986, pp. 99–102 (translation of original, which appeared in *Zeitschrift für Betriebswirtschaft*, January 1952, pp. 182–185).

See also CONGRESSES ON ACCOUNTING, INTERNATIONAL; FISHER, IRVING; GERMANY; INFLATION ACCOUNTING; LIMPERG, THEODORE, JR.; SWEENEY, HENRY WHITCOMB

Schrader, William Joseph (1929–)

William Joseph Schrader is an American accounting academician and theorist. Schrader received a Ph.D. from the University of Washington in 1959. He was on the faculty of Pennsylvania State University from 1954 until 1992 (Emeritus). In "An Inductive Approach to Accounting Theory" (1962), he offered a profound explanation of transaction-based accounting, circa 1960, that just may have reached accounting bedrock.

Schrader based his observations on generalizations about the data base with which accountants work. He examined accounting records reflecting the entire life of an entity and then derived conclusions, the foremost being that accounting is based on the equation: cost + net income = revenues. Thus, the income statement, and not the balance sheet, is the basic accounting statement.

Other findings included that debits are "values received in exchanges," credits are values given, "costs" are nonfinancial values received, and revenues are services (and/or products) given in an exchange. Entities exist to provide outputs; this they do by utilizing inputs.

In Schrader's view, transactions are the basic concern of accounting. These are the "facts" of accounting; financial statements are "interpretations" of those facts. These assertions stand in direct lineage to *An Introduction to Corporate Accounting Standards* (1940) by William Andrew Paton and A.C. Littleton.

Schrader's theory was incorporated and extended by John J. Willingham in 1964 in a theory of accounting based on social organization and interaction.

Carl W. Brewer

Bibliography

Paton, W.A., and A.C. Littleton. *An Introduction to Corporate Accounting Standards*. American Accounting Association Monograph No. 3. New York: American Accounting Association, 1940.

Schrader, W.L. "An Inductive Approach to Accounting Theory," *Accounting Review*, October 1962, pp. 645–649.

———. "Business Combinations," *Accounting Review*, January 1958, pp. 72–75.

———, and R.E. Malcom. "A Note on Accounting Theory Construction and Verification," *Abacus*, June 1973, pp. 93–98.

———, R.E. Malcom, and J.J. Willingham. *Financial Accounting: An Input/Output Approach*. Homewood, IL: Irwin, 1970.

———, R.E. Malcom, and J.J. Willingham. "Partitioned Events View of Financial Reporting," *Accounting Horizons,* December 1988, pp. 10–20.

Willingham, J.J. "The Accounting Entity: A Conceptual Model," *Accounting Review*, July 1964, pp. 543–552.

See also AN INTRODUCTION TO CORPORATE ACCOUNTING STANDARDS; CONCEPTUAL FRAMEWORK; DEFINITIONS OF ACCOUNTING; LITTLETON, A.C.; PATON, WILLIAM ANDREW

Schreiber, Heinrich (c. 1496–1525)

The second published text on double entry bookkeeping was written by a German mathematician and arithmetic teacher, Heinrich Schreiber, also called Henricus Grammateus. Schreiber's *Ayn neu Kunstlich Buech* (Nuremberg, 1518) included chapters on algebra, commercial arithmetic, music, and bookkeeping. Schreiber's text was revised and reprinted several times after his death; it was plagiarized twice during the sixteenth century.

Schreiber did not imitate Luca Pacioli's *Summa de Arithmetica* (1494); he seems to have derived his double entry system from German commercial practice. He used three account books: a journal, a goods ledger, and a debts ledger. Purchases were entered on the left side of the inventory accounts in the goods ledger, and sales were entered on the right side. In the debts ledger, which contained receivables, payables, and a cash account, debts were recorded on the right side, and payments to creditors on the left side. Accounts receivable were entered on the right, and receipts on the left. Thus there was no fixed positioning of debit and credit entries. Nor were the balances due from and owed to individual debtors and creditors compiled separately in the debts ledger.

Schreiber offered 10 rules for recording purchases and sales and described the treatment of expenses. Profit or loss on each type of inventory could be found by subtracting purchases from sales. He compiled these individual profits and losses at the end of his journal. He concluded with a crude test of bookkeeping accuracy: "Add together the receipts, what is owed to you, and then the remaining goods; and from the whole sum subtract the payments, that you still owe, and if the balance left over is equal to the profit, then it is correct." This calculation, equating profits with net assets, worked only because Schreiber's illustrative accounts contained no beginning asset or liability balances.

Michael Chatfield

Bibliography

Bywater, M.F., and B.S. Yamey. *Historic Accounting Literature: A Companion Guide*. London: Scholar Press, 1982.

See also COMPOUND ENTRIES; GERMANY

Schweicker, Wolfgang

Wolfgang Schweicker's *Zwifach Buchhalten* (Nuremberg, 1549) introduced Italian double entry bookkeeping into Germany. Most of Schweicker's text was freely translated from Domenico Manzoni's *Quaderno doppio col suo giornale* (Venice, 1540). Schweicker was also influenced by Johann Gottlieb's *Ein teutsch verstendig Buchhalten* (Nuremberg, 1531). But Schweicker was more than a transcriber of Venetian bookkeeping techniques. He condensed, simplified, and sometimes improved Manzoni's text. Schweicker introduced a ledger account for bills of exchange payable and receivable and added a chapter that demonstrated how to index the ledger, a topic not illustrated in Manzoni's first edition. Unlike Manzoni, Schweicker collected all outstanding accounts receivable and payable into summary accounts before balancing and closing the ledger.

Michael Chatfield

Bibliography
Bywater, M.F., and B.S. Yamey. *Historic Accounting Literature: A Companion Guide*. London: Scholar Press, 1982.

See also GERMANY; MANZONI, DOMENICO

Scotland: Early Writers in Double Entry Accounting

In 1974, the then President of the Institute of Chartered Accountants of Scotland, J. Crawford, wrote: "The first Scottish book on accounting was published in 1683. That book heralded a century during which Scotland established its reputation as a land of accountants: a steady stream of textbooks, including some which ran to so many editions that they could be called classics, appeared from Scottish presses" (Mepham). In his *Accounting in Eighteenth Century Scotland*, Michael J. Mepham, a professor of accounting and a noted expert on Scottish accounting history, considered five writers of these Scottish classics in accounting for detailed review—Robert Colinson, Alexander Malcolm, John Mair, William Gordon, and Robert Hamilton.

The first treatise on bookkeeping/accounting in Scotland was Robert Colinson's *Idea Rationaria* (1683). Colinson dedicated his book to the Honorable James Kennedy, the Lord Conservator of the privileges of the Scottish nation in the 17 provinces of the Netherlands (McMickle and Vangermeersch). At the time, Scotland's trading relationship with the Netherlands was vital to Scotland. Colinson considered bookkeeping to be useful not only in commerce but also to any businessman, from prince to pauper. Colinson considered bookkeeping to be an instrument of economic development: "And it is obvious to all considering persons that this honorable and profitable science of bookkeeping is the only help that encourages many to join their small stock together and, by so doing often from a small foundation erect a most admirable trade." Colinson utilized the question/answer method of teaching in his book and had a total of 242 of these question/answer sets. In a subsequent study of Colinson's book, 40 topics in the book were analyzed (Vangermeersch). One of these was the two poems in the introductory section of Colinson's book, both of which stressed the importance of bookkeeping to the nation.

Alexander Malcolm (1685–1763) in 1718 wrote *A New Treatise of Arithmetick and Book-keeping*. Like Colinson, Malcolm stressed the importance of bookkeeping to the nation (Mepham). Malcolm, a teacher of mathematics and bookkeeping in 1731, wrote *A treatise of book-keeping*. In it, he stressed the overriding importance of the capital (or stock) account: ". . . The Stock-Account. . . may be considered as a Root or Truck to which all the other Accounts in the Ledger-Book, do, in some Sense, belong as Branches. . ."

John Mair (1702/3–1769) was also a teacher of mathematics and bookkeeping and in 1736 published his first edition of *Book-keeping Methodiz'd*. This book went through a ninth edition in 1772. After Mair's death, *Book-keeping Moderniz'd* was published under his name from 1773 to 1808 in a total of nine editions. Mepham considered Mair to be the most influential of the Scottish writers of this period, because of the wide usage of his texts, not only in Great Britain but also in the United States. The users included George Washington, who had a copy of *Book-keeping Moderniz'd* in his private library at his plantation at Mount Vernon, Virginia. Mair had added a section of the appendix on commerce with the tobacco colonies in Mair's third edition. In the seventh edition, another section of the appendix was added for commerce of the sugar colonies. Mair had this interesting passage in the appendix section on commerce of the tobacco colonies in his seventh edition (1762):

This shows the usefulness of these colonies to their mother company, especially if it be considered, that all tobacco from these colonies is imported in British vessels, which creates employment, and gives bread to several thousand sailors; and that three-fourths of all tobacco brought home is imported by private merchants, or companies residing in Britain, and purchased in exchange for European and India goods sent out, a great part of which are British manufacturers. . .

William Gordon (1720/1–1793) was, like Malcolm and Mair, a teacher of bookkeeping (Mepham). His two-volume work *The Universal Accountant and Complete Merchant*, first published in 1763 (Vol. 1) and 1765 (Vol. 2), went through six editions, ending in 1796. *The General Counting-House and Man of Business'* was published in 1766 and a second edition in 1770. Thomas Jefferson, the third president of the United States and, like Washington, a plantation owner, had a copy of *The General Counting-House and Man of Business'* in his library at his mansion, Monticello. Gordon, in vol. 2 of his *The Universal Accountant and Complete Merchant*, stressed not only the importance of profit maximization but also of integrity and honor.

Robert Hamilton (1743–1829) replaced John Mair as the rector of the Perth Academy and later was appointed in 1779 to the Chair of Natural Philosophy at Marischal College at the University of Aberdeen. He taught mathematics classes there and in 1817 he was transferred to the chair of Mathematics (Mepham). His *An Introduction to Merchandise* had five editions from 1777 to 1820. Mepham considered Hamilton to have written the most important accounting text of the 18th century, as it was a forerunner of texts in cost accounting.

Mepham also gave brief coverage to these following Scottish writers: (1) W. Newall in *The Merchant's Companion* (1715); (2) John Drummond in *The Accomptant's Pocket-Companion* (1718); (3) Robert Lundin in *The Reason of Accompting by Debitor and Creditor* (1718); Alexander Macghie in *The Principles of Book-keeping Explained* (1718); Alexander Brodie in *A New and Easy Method of Book-keeping* (1722); William Stevenson in *A General Discourse Showing the Usefulness of the Italian Method of Book-keeping* (1732); William Hamilton in *Bookkeeping New Mod-*elled (1735); William Webster in *Essays on Book-keeping* (1758); William Perry in *The Man of Business and Gentleman's Assistant* (1774); James Scruton in *The Practical Counting House* (1777); David Young in *The Farmers Account-Book*; and Colin Buchanan in *The Writingmaster and Accountant's Assistant* (1798).

These early books probably gave Scotland a competitive advantage in accounting. The Institute of Accountants in Edinburgh occurred in 1853, soon followed by the Institute of Accountants and Actuaries in Glasgow (Brown). The designation of "Chartered Accountant" (CA) was quickly adopted by the Institute of Accountants in Edinburgh. Scotland was almost three decades ahead of the forming of chartered accountants by Royal Charter in England and Ireland. Two of the former "Big Eight" international accounting firms were founded by Scottish immigrants to the United States. Arthur Young, the founder of Arthur Young and Company, emigrated from Scotland to the United States in 1890. James Marwick emigrated from Scotland to the United States in 1894 and Simpson Roger Mitchell also emigrated to the United States from Scotland. Marwick and Mitchell became partners in 1897 in Marwick, Mitchell and Company. In 1911 James Marwick met William Peat from London and agreed to create the American firm of Marwick, Mitchell, Peat and Company.

The Scottish pride in accounting can be witnessed by Richard Brown's *A History of Accounting and Accountants* (1905) which he wrote "for the Chartered Accountants of Scotland." This interest in history seems to have continued. In 1988 Mepham's book was ". . . published on behalf of the Scottish Committee on Accounting History of the Institute of Chartered Accountants of Scotland." In 1994 (as noted in the introduction to this book), the Institute of Chartered Accountants of Scotland hosted a major celebration in Edinburgh in honor of the 500th anniversary of Luca Pacioli's first printed treatise on accounting.

David A.R. Forrester
Richard Vangermeersch

Bibliography
Brown, R. *A History of Accounting and Accountants*. Edinburgh: T.C. and E.C. Jack, 1905.
Colinson, Robert. *Idea Rationaria*.

Edinburgh: Lindsay, Kniblo, van Solingen and Colmar., 1683.

Hamilton, R. *An Introduction to Merchandise: Part IV: Italian Book-keeping and Part V: Practical Book-keeping, with Note by B.S. Yamey.* New York: Garland, 1982.

Higgins, T.G. "Arthur Young 1863–1948," *Arthur Young Journal*, 75th Anniversary Edition, Spring-Summer 1969, pp. 20–23.

Mair, J. *Book-keeping Methodiz'd*, 7th ed. Edinburgh: Sands, Murray, and Cochran, 1763.

McMickle, P.L., and R. Vangermeersch. *The Origins of a Great Profession.* Memphis, TN: Memphis State University, 1987.

Mepham, M.J. *Accounting in Eighteenth Century Scotland.* New York: Garland, 1988.

Vangermeersch, R. "Colinson's Idea Rationaria," in A.T. Craswell, ed. Paper No. 214, *Collected Papers of the Fifth World Congress of Accounting Historians.* Sydney: Accounting and Finance Foundation within the University of Sydney, 1988.

Wise, T.A. *Peat, Marwick, Mitchell & Co. 85 Years.* New York: Peat, Marwick, Mitchell and Company, 1982.

See also ARCHIVES AND SPECIAL COLLECTIONS IN ACCOUNTING; BIG EIGHT ACCOUNTING FIRMS; "CHARGE AND DISCHARGE" STATEMENT; CITY OF GLASGOW BANK; COMPANIES ACTS; HAMILTON, ROBERT; KOJIMA, OSAMU; MANORIAL ACCOUNTING; PARKER, ROBERT HENRY; TAX-ORDAINED ACCOUNTING; TRUSTEE ACCOUNTS

Scott, DR (1887–1954)

DR Scott was an early proponent of the idea that accounting is constantly in the process of development, changing to meet new demands of economic organization and society. His historical perspective and identification with the institutionalist philosophy led Scott to observe that institutions and social order change from one period to the next, often at different rates. Likewise, social values, governments, and economic systems are in a constant state of evolution. Thus, Scott viewed change as a normal condition and thought a student was best served to approach accounting primarily on a theoretical

basis, first learning its social significance and its place in the field of economic affairs.

In his 1925 introductory accounting text, *Theory of Accounts*, Scott paid particular attention to the historical evolution of accounting within the context of economic development and to how accounting has enabled modern business enterprise to grow. Yet the book also looked to the future, recognizing, for example, that the judgment of accountants would play an increasingly important role in the preparation of financial statements and that market value could sometimes offer advantages over cost-based accounting.

Scott stressed the importance of related disciplines, particularly statistics, to the development and application of accounting. He believed that the use of selected statistical methodologies in accounting would give greater validity to accounting reports and to the recommendations of accountants for the solution of economic problems and the management of business enterprises.

Scott's broad views were perhaps the result of two principal causes:

(1) Although he was associated for many years with the Department of Accounting and Statistics at the University of Missouri at Columbia, both as chairman and as professor, Scott began his academic career in economics and earned a Ph.D. in economics from Harvard in 1930.

(2) Scott's thinking was heavily influenced by another Missouri faculty member, notable economist Thorstein Veblen, perhaps best known for his work, *Theory of the Leisure Class: An Economic Study of the Evolution of Institutions* (1899).

Veblen's influence is apparent in Scott's 1931 (and probably best known) work, *The Cultural Significance of Accounts*, which observed that contemporary economic theory had not at that time adjusted to changes in the market. As a result, government regulation assumed responsibility for certain economic activities, adding impetus to the development of accounting as regulators asked for additional information and advice. Scott viewed accounting as a young field that could eventually help reshape economic institutions and support objective insights into economic realities. His thoughts foreshadowed the growth of government regulation and of business in the United States and the consequent emphasis on accounting and accountants as a major information-providing and stabilizing force in the American economy.

Perhaps as much a philosopher and historian as an accountant or economist, Scott saw accounting in the context of what justly could be termed the "Big Picture." He viewed developments in twentieth-century accounting as a continuation of changes necessitated by commerce in fourteenth-century Italy, where double entry accounting originated, and saw these as part of a continuing cycle of change stretching back through history. He foretold the mutually beneficial growth of business and of accounting principles and methodologies. And he predicted a much greater role for accounting, to the extent it was willing to grow and change, in economics and government of the future. DR Scott was a man of vision, truly one of the thinkers of modern accounting history.

Joseph R. Oliver

Bibliography

Benninger, L.J. "Accounting Related to Social Institutions: The Theoretical Formulations of DR Scott," *Accounting Research*, January 1958, pp. 17–30.

Elam, R. "The Cultural Significance of Accounts: The Philosophy of DR Scott," *Accounting Historians Journal*, Fall 1981, pp. 51–59.

———. "DR Scott." In *Biographies of Notable Accountants*, edited by H.R. Givens, pp. 42–44. New York: Random House, 1987.

Kvam, R.L., ed. *Collected Writings of DR Scott.* Columbia, MO: Lucas Brothers, 1964.

Scott, DR. *The Cultural Significance of Accounts.* New York: Henry Holt, 1931.

———. *Theory of Accounts.* New York: Henry Holt, 1925.

See also CONTROL: CLASSICAL MODEL; HUMAN RESOURCE ACCOUNTING; SOCIAL RESPONSIBILITIES OF ACCOUNTANTS; ZEFF, STEPHEN A.

Scribes

The Babylonian scribe has been called the predecessor of today's accountant, and his functions were similar, but even more extensive. It was his duty not only to put business transactions in writing but to see that legal provisions were complied with in drawing up commercial agreements. Such a "public" scribe might be found sitting near the city gates. The contracting parties would arrive, reach an understanding, and explain to him the nature of their transaction. Using as pencil a wooden rod with a blunt, triangular end, the scribe then recorded their agreement on a small lump of moist clay, enumerating the names of the parties, the items paid or received, promises made, and any other pertinent details. The inconvenience of mass illiteracy was circumvented by having each man carry his signature around his neck in the form of a stone amulet engraved with its owner's mark (and buried with him when he died). Each party to the transaction, and any witnesses, affixed their signatures by impressing these seals into the clay tablet, and the scribe completed the record by writing out their names. The more important commercial tablets were kiln-dried; the others were allowed to dry in the sunlight.

After an agreement had been written and signed, the scribe sometimes took in hand a new piece of clay and, flattening it to the thickness of a piecrust, wrapped it completely around the original tablet. Like a modern envelope, this outer covering might merely be inscribed with the names and seal impressions of the contracting parties, to identify the inner contents and ensure their privacy. But if the scribe's purpose was to prevent alteration of a tablet, the whole transaction would be rewritten and signed again on this outer surface, providing in effect a carbon copy. Since the inner and outer messages were supposed to be identical, any tampering with this envelope could immediately be detected by comparing it to the original inscription. Nor could anyone alter the original tablet without first cracking off and destroying the outer shell. Effective forgery would require a complete rewriting and rewitnessing of both tablet and envelope.

The temples and the central and provincial governments of Babylonia employed hundreds of scribes as administrators. Surviving temple accounts on "a great mass of tablets" describe a variety of receipts and disbursements, wage payments, rental income, interest on loans, and real estate transactions. Both the temples and the royal treasury sent scribes to distant parts of the empire as collectors of sacrifices and taxes. These men incurred traveling expenses for which they were later reimbursed, and the allowance tablets that were prepared are equivalent to modern expense accounts. Tithes and property taxes were normally paid in kind.

Cereals, cattle, and other farm commodities were received daily at storehouses throughout the country. If not quickly disposed of, they would have overloaded the facilities and caused spoilage losses. Scribes recorded the types and quantities of goods as they arrived and supervised their segregation for sale, use, or accumulation. Periodically they prepared inventories of assets on hand and summaries of a charge and discharge type for commodities received and paid out. There are evidences of royal examination and audit.

Michael Chatfield

Bibliography

Chiera, E. *They Wrote on Clay.* Chicago: University of Chicago Press, 1938.

Keister, O.R. "Commercial Record-Keeping in Ancient Mesopotamia," *Accounting Review*, April 1963, pp. 371–376.

See also ACCOUNTING AND THE ACCOUNTANT: PORTRAYALS; BABYLONIA; "CHARGE AND DISCHARGE" STATEMENT

Securities and Exchange Commission

The Securities and Exchange Commission (SEC) has been the central focus of the American national system for regulating investment securities markets since its formation during the midst of the Great Depression. Two legislative acts defined this agency's mission. First, the Securities Act of 1933 (Truth in Securities Act) authorized the extension of federal regulation over the public issuance of new securities, initially vesting the authority for these matters in the National Securities Department of the Federal Trade Commission (FTC). The subsequent Securities and Exchange Act of 1934, besides authorizing the establishment of an independent SEC, mandated that all publicly traded companies provide continuous disclosure of their financial position and results of operation. What soon emerged was a system of market governance that was dependent upon the honest and competent service of many professional groups.

Background of Federal Securities-Market Regulation

Prior to the securities acts, the federal government's involvement with corporate finance and the securities market had been haphazard. One early intervention involving the Interstate Commerce Commission (ICC) had prescribed uniform accounting formats (1887) and later uniform accounting methodologies (1906) to assist regulators in evaluating the fairness of transportation rates and to assist investors in evaluating the worth of financial securities for America's first "big business," the railroads. Later, in 1920, through the authority provided by the National Transportation Act, the ICC formed a Bureau of Finance that was empowered to review prospectively railroad-financing plans—particularly those relating to the impending formation of great regional networks through the consolidation of smaller independent lines. Another initiative mounted by the Federal Reserve Board (1917) in cooperation with the American Institute of Accountants (AIA)—forerunner of the American Institute of Certified Public Accountants (AICPA)—sought to standardize both financial-statement formats and auditor's reports that were submitted in support of commercial paper discounted by member institutions at the central bank. The newly organized FTC unsuccessfully sought the power in 1916 to formulate uniform accounting for commercial and industrial corporations, which, besides informing investors, might also assist regulators in monitoring for infractions of antitrust statutes.

State governments had also tried to regulate corporate finance. Some followed the example of Massachusetts, which, beginning in 1869, first required local railroads and then later other public utilities to file periodic financial statements. In addition, many states passed "blue sky" laws, which prohibited fraudulent dealing in investment securities. Both these approaches, however, were generally ineffective because the states typically failed to support these regulatory efforts with sufficient administrative resources.

Overseas in Great Britain, on the other hand, a more elaborate regulatory model had gradually been evolving since the 1840s. By 1900, British corporate enterprises were required to submit annually audited financial statements with the registrar of companies in the Board of Trade. Under this system, a key monitor was the profession of independent public accountants, which exercised considerable leverage in assuring probity in financial reporting through its ability to withhold required certifying reports. Moreover, British investors, like their American counterparts, also had the right to sue for losses incurred through financial fraud. In Britain, however, this course of action was rarely implemented. One drawback was the threat of countersuits for character defamation in fraud cases brought against unsuccessful plaintiffs. Moreover, in a more ascriptive society like Britain, the public was more likely to defer to the judgments of trusted and respected classes of experts in deciding questions about the adequacy of financial disclosure.

During the early decades of the twentieth century, several prominent American accounting, legal, and economics scholars began to militate for securities-market reform. Three milestones in this continuing dialogue are noteworthy. Attorney and future Supreme Court jurist Louis D. Brandeis, for example, authored *Other Peoples' Money and How the Bankers Use It* (1913) in support of the congressional Pujo Committee's investigation of the so-called "money trust." Arsène P. Pujo (D, La.) chaired the subcommittee on the Money Trust Investigation of the Committee on Banking and Currency of the United States House of Representatives in 1913. Besides attacking the control implied by the interlocking directorates that bound industries to particular banking groups, Brandeis advocated federally mandated uniform financial reporting as had been required earlier of the nation's railroads. A second critic, accounting educator Eric Louis Kohler, beginning in the 1920s complained through editorials in *Accounting Review*, the official organ of the American Association of Instructors of Accounting (predecessor to the American Accounting Association), that the public was not being well served by the reluctance of the accounting profession to standardize financial accounting. A third commentator, William Z. Ripley, a professor of economics at Harvard University, detailed in a series of essays first published in 1926 in the *Atlantic Monthly* (reissued the following year as a book titled *Wall Street and Main Street*), many shortcomings in contemporary corporate financial disclosure. Later, Ripley served as chairman of a committee at the Social Science Research Council that sponsored the publication of Adolf A. Berle Jr. and Gardiner C. Means's classic *The Modern Corporation and Private Property* (1932). This latter work argued compellingly that the asymmetric distribution of information between managers and investors in the modern business corporation created new needs for regular and reliable flows of financial information to support the operation of the nation's burgeoning markets for investment securities. Berle and Means called on the New York Stock Exchange (NYSE) to cooperate with the AIA in defining accounting rules that proscribed manipulative reporting practices.

The judiciary also took cognizance of the problems of corporate governance. Under the common law, investors had long been prevented from suing accountants who had certified inaccurate financial statements for negligence because they lacked "privity of contract"—that is, investors' rights were limited because they had not contracted directly with accountants but merely tangentially benefited from their professional services. In these circumstances, third parties could only sue professional accountants for fraud, a charge often difficult to prove. This began to change in 1931 however. A new precedent was established in the New York State Court of Appeals in the *Ultramares Corporation v. Touche, Niven and Company* 255 N.Y. 170 (1931), which extended the potential liability of accountants to third parties for negligence. Judge Benjamin Cardozo ruled that third parties identified in a contract for audit services as primary beneficiaries were entitled to sue professional accountants whose work was performed negligently. In addition, other third-party beneficiaries who had placed reliance on false or misleading financial statements might also sue in cases where the practitioners attestation services were "grossly negligent"—that is, so great that the effects were constructively equivalent to fraud.

The public accounting profession also began to address the problems of financial disclosure in conjunction with the NYSE after the Great Crash of 1929. The NYSE's Committee on Stock List, for example, chose to follow the Berle and Means recommendations for accounting standardization. A key facilitator in this process was George Oliver May, a retired Price Waterhouse and Company partner, who, besides serving on Professor Ripley's committee at the Social Science Research Council, also served as a liaison between the NYSE and the AIA. The principal outcome of this interaction was the NYSE's adoption of six accounting principles defined in the 1934 AIA publication, *Audits of Corporate Accounts*.

Defining a New Regulatory Structure

The extension of federal authority over the issuance of new securities through the passage of the Securities Act of 1933 was a cornerstone of the first 100 days of the New Deal administration of President Franklin D. Roosevelt. It was drafted by three former students of Harvard Law School Professor Felix Frankfurter: James M. Landis, Benjamin Cohen and Thomas G. Corcoran. They were enlisted to this task after earlier separate drafts prepared by Samuel Untermyer, a former counsel to the 1913 Pujo Committee, and Huston Thompson, a former FTC official, encountered insurmountable congressional opposition. Central to the legislation crafted by these attorneys was the recognition of how dependent effective market ordering was on the competent and honest functioning of many classes of experts such as accountants, bankers, lawyers, appraisers, and engineers. Thus, in their view, public policy was best served through the creation of new regulations that held all market participants responsible for their actions.

The new law sought to achieve one of its fundamental purposes of protecting investors against losses from false or misleading information by redefining the legal responsibilities of the various professional groups serving these markets. The new federal statutes extended significantly the powers of third-party beneficiaries to sue in order to recover losses due to the incompetent or dishonest performance of securities-market professionals such as underwriters or accountants. In these cases, plaintiffs merely had to prove that they incurred losses from the purchase of a new issue and that there was a material false or misleading statement or omission of a material fact in the associated SEC registration statement. The defendant professional, on the other hand, was confronted with the daunting problem of either proving that his work had not been negligent (due diligence defense) or that the plaintiff's loss had resulted from circumstances other than inadequate disclosure.

Although the subsequent Securities Act of 1934 established a continuous-disclosure requirement for publicly traded securities, the legal vulnerability of experts was generally lower than in the case of the 1933 act. Under this second law, plaintiffs had to be either purchasers or sellers of securities who had experienced losses that resulted from placing reliance on incomplete, false, or misleading information in SEC filings. Two sections of the 1934 act further defined the circumstances necessary for a plaintiff to initiate suit. Under Section 10 the plaintiff must prove that the expert acted fraudulently, while under Section 18 no proof of fraud is required. The independent expert, on the other hand, could deflect an adverse finding by either proving that he had acted in good faith or, alternatively, that he was unaware of any false statements.

One testimony to the soundness of the regulatory framework established by the securities acts has been the fact that these laws remain essentially unchanged since their inception over a half-century ago. Although innumerable cases have more sharply defined the precise meaning of their various provisions, the laws have remained essentially intact and continue to define the responsibilities of professional groups who serve the nation's financial markets.

Most of the cases litigated with respect to federal securities-market governance have been under the provisions of the Securities and Exchange Act of 1934. Two cases, however, highlight important dimensions of this law. The case of the *United States of America v. Carl Simon* 425 F.2d 796 (2d Cir. 1969) illustrated the possibility of successful criminal prosecution of accountants who knowingly certified financial statements that contained material misstated. Moreover, the Circuit Court in this case rejected the defense that the financial statements were not in violation of generally accepted accounting principles (GAAP). Instead, it concluded that the defendants' most fundamental responsibility was in determining whether the statements were fairly stated in all material respects. A Supreme Court case, *Hochfelder v. Ernst and Ernst* 96 S.Ct. 1375 (1976), involved the negligent failure of accountants to discover fraud in an engagement and their liability under Rule 10b-5 of the Securities and Exchange Commission. This provision prohibits all types of fraud in sales of seasoned securities. But the Court ruled that the accountants could not in this case be held liable for simple negligence. This decision has raised doubts about whether Rule 10b-5 can successfully be applied in negligence suits—a question that subsequent litigation will, doubtless, continue to refine. A primary shortcoming of the plaintiff's suit was the failure to prove *scienter*—that is, the accountants' knowledge of the fraud and their intent to deceive.

Besides the securities acts, the SEC's authority has been extended by subsequent legislation that has only tangentially affected the roles of accountants. Among other provisions the Public Utilities Holding Act of 1935, for example, mandated guidelines for simplifying the capital structures of companies in this industry and prohibited the pyramiding of earnings through multilayer consolidations of operating results. Additionally, accountants have been called upon to certify disclosures under other legislation such as the Trust Indenture Act of 1939, the Investment Company Act of 1940, the Investment Advisers Act of 1940, and the Securities Act of 1970.

More recently, the Foreign Corrupt Practices Act of 1977 extended the requirements of the Securities and Exchange Act of 1934 by prohibiting registrants from making illegal payments to promote their business overseas. It also required that public companies maintain accounting systems capable of both producing reliable and accurate financial reports and providing reasonable assurance that only properly authorized transactions would be processed.

SEC's Relationship to the Accounting Profession

The process of standardizing and monitoring the quality of information provided to investors was influenced both by the SEC and the public accounting profession. The line of demarcation separating the spheres of authority between these contenders for leadership in this field was flexible. Ultimately, the borders were set by the force of public opinion communicated through congressional action. Although the SEC possessed substantial administrative powers during periods of stable market conditions, it was inclined to defer to the agendas for self-regulation propounded by professional groups. In a nation with deep historical commitments to free-market solutions, the independent efforts of professional groups generally garnered much public support. During crises, on the other hand, when expert groups seemed incapable of adequately protecting the public interest, pressures mounted for more vigorous intervention by regulatory agencies.

The competition between public and private agencies for primacy in ordering the financial markets was reflected in the ongoing debates about professional standards in accounting and auditing. Although Congress had empowered the SEC to promulgate professional standards, the agency has since the 1940s generally deferred to the initiatives taken in these matters by professional associations. Criticisms of the quality of reports submitted to the SEC during the mid-1930s, for example, had initially motivated the agency's chief accountant, Carman G. Blough, to call upon the AIA to establish a standard-setting body for financial accounting. Later, the adverse findings of the McKesson and Robbins case in 1939 led to a call for the standardization of audit practice. The McKesson and Robbins case involved a massive inventory fraud and embroiled its auditors, Price Waterhouse, in the most noted legal liability case up to that time. The AIA successfully responded to both these challenges. In 1936 it formed the Committee on Accounting Procedure, which issued Accounting Research Bulletins (ARBs), a source recognized by the SEC as authoritative in providing guidance in financial accounting. This responsibility passed first, in 1959, to the Accounting Principles Board (APB) and later, in 1973, to the Financial Accounting Standards Board (FASB). The first focus for the standardization of auditing, on the other hand, was the Committee on Auditing Procedure, whose *Extensions of Auditing Procedure* (1939) formed the nucleus of its subsequent Statements on Auditing Procedure (SAPs). Later, in 1972, the responsibility for standardizing auditing passed to the Auditing Standards Board of the AICPA, which issued Statements on Auditing Standards (SASs).

The form and content of financial statements filed with the SEC were basically defined in Regulation S-X. This regulation was codified in 1940 and is regularly updated. Together with regulation S-K, it delineates the main body of financial and non-financial data required to be filed with the SEC. In addition, during the period 1937–1982, the SEC issued its Accounting Series Releases (ASRs) both to identify its unique financial-reporting requirements and to explain how accounting and auditing matters had affected its enforcement activities. In 1982 those ASRs dealing with general financial-reporting matters that had not previously been rescinded were codified in Financial Reporting Release No. 1. This series has been subsequently amplified to reflect the SEC's views on both accounting and auditing issues that relate to financial reporting regulation. A companion series, Accounting and Auditing Enforcement Releases, codified those ASRs that dealt with accounting and auditing matters in an enforcement context. In addition, the SEC since 1975 has circulated Staff Accounting Bulletins (SABs) "to inform the financial community of the [SEC] staff's views on accounting and disclosure issues."

Although the SEC has generally accepted the standards promulgated by authoritative professional bodies, it has reserved its right to establish its own reporting requirements when it deemed that GAAP were insufficient in measuring particular business activities. The differences in practice that have arisen between the SEC requirements and GAAP have generally been minor. Some examples include such matters as the measurement of petroleum exploration and production costs, the reporting of discretionary expenses, and adjustments of valuation allowances. Although there were a few sharp disagreements with the profession, as in the 1962 controversy relating to APB Statement No. 2, "Accounting for the 'Investment Credit'" (1962), dealing with the proper accounting for the investment tax credit, the general pattern has been one of mutual supportiveness.

More recently, the continued cooperation of private and public regulatory institutions has been evidenced by the SEC's acceptance of the peer review programs established by the AICPA in 1977. This step had been taken in response to the criticisms of public practice raised during the 1970s by congressional committees chaired by Representative John Moss and Senator Lee Metcalf. Although some political leaders had favored aggressive federal intervention, what ultimately emerged was a dual structure of governance. The primary responsibility for monitoring practice became centered in new regulatory institutions sponsored by professional groups. The credibility and authority of these efforts, however, were contingent on the active support of government.

A key element in this reform was the adoption by the AICPA of peer review requirements along the lines that the SEC had begun to initiate with firms that had experienced serious audit failures. The AICPA peer reviews, however, were directed at all practice units. These examinations sought to determine whether professional firms were adequately adhering to newly promulgated standards of practice quality-control. To encourage compliance, continued membership in good standing in either the SEC Practice Section or the Private Companies Practice Section—both of the AICPA's Division of Firms formed in 1977—was made contingent on successful completion of periodic reviews. Moreover, the AICPA also established the Public Oversight Board in 1977, whose membership consisted of five distinguished public fig-

ures with responsibility for monitoring the effectiveness of the peer review process. In this and other ways, the SEC and professional groups were able to protect the public interest in the nation's financial markets with a minimum degree of federal intervention.

The effective interaction of the SEC and professional groups in accounting and other aspects of corporate governance has helped to contain the costs of governmental regulation of the securities markets. The SEC's staff, for example, grew only modestly from the levels of the 1930s. During its existence, the maximum staffing level has only been about 2,000. The total value of annual security issues grew from about $5 billion in 1937 to $1.7 trillion in 1990. This great increase in value of securities registrations was accommodated largely by the enormous growth in the ranks of the professional groups on which the financial markets' self-regulatory system depended. In 1929, the total cumulative number of CPA licenses issued in the United States barely exceeded 13,000. By 1991, however, the total membership of the AICPA exceeded 300,000. Similarly, the numbers of attorneys rose during this same period from 161,000 to 744,000.

Besides the low cost of governmental monitoring, the SEC's regulation of financial reporting has been beneficial in two additional ways. First, by helping to assure greater reliability and accuracy in financial reporting, it has helped to reduce the informational asymmetry that separates investors from corporate managements. This has bolstered public confidence and, thus, has contributed to greater market efficiency. Second, the proliferation of information mandated under the disclosure process has increased the opportunities for profitable transacting. The expanding core of information about corporate affairs heightened the potential for raising the overall level of national wealth by providing market participants with greater economic insights that were capable of being profitably exploited.

The professional relationships embodied in the securities acts were designed to revive and preserve valued institutions under pressure during the Great Depression. This structure has proven over the course of subsequent decades its durability and worth. The major achievement of the reformers of the New Deal era was the establishment of a strong and flexible institutional foundation to support an enormous modern expansion of financial-market activity in America. It is a model that may serve as a useful guide for foreign nations that wish to create vibrant financial markets capable of fostering strong economic growth.

Paul J. Miranti Jr.
Leonard Goodman

Bibliography

Carey, J.L. *The Rise of the Accounting Profession.* 2 vols. New York: AICPA, 1969–1970.

Chatov, R. *Corporate Financial Reporting: Public or Private Control?* New York: Free Press, 1975.

Coffey, W.J. "Government Regulations and Professional Pronouncements: A Study of the Securities and Exchange Commission and the American Institute of Certified Public Accountants from 1934 through 1974." Ph.D. diss., New York University, 1976.

Douglas, W.O. *Democracy and Finance.* New Haven: Yale University Press, 1940.

Edwards, J.D. *History of Public Accounting in the United States.* East Lansing: Bureau of Business and Economic Research, Michigan State University, 1960.

Loss, L. *Securities Regulation.* 2d ed. Boston: Little, Brown & Co., 1961.

McCraw, T.K. *Prophets of Regulation: Charles Francis Adams, Louis D. Brandeis, James M. Landis, Alfred E. Kahn.* Cambridge: Harvard University Press, 1984.

————. "With the Consent of the Governed: The SEC's Formative Years," *Journal of Policy Analysis and Management*, Spring 1982, pp. 346–370.

Parrish, M.E. *Securities Regulations and the New Deal.* New Haven, CT: Yale University Press, 1970.

Previts, G.J., ed. *The Development of SEC Accounting.* Reading, MA: Addison-Wesley, 1981.

Previts, G.J., and B.D. Merino. *A History of Accounting in America: An Historical Interpretation of the Cultural Significance of Accounting.* New York: John Wiley & Sons, 1979.

Ritchie, D.A. *James M. Landis: Dean of the Regulators.* Cambridge: Harvard University Press, 1980.

Seligman, J. *The SEC and the Future of Finance.* New York: Praeger, 1985.

————. *The Transformation of Wall Street: A History of the Securities and Exchange Commission and Modern Corporate Finance.* Boston: Houghton Mifflin, 1982.

Skousen, F.K. *An Introduction to the SEC.* 5th ed. Cincinnati: South-Western, 1991.

See also ACCOUNTING RESEARCH BULLETINS; ACCOUNTING SERIES RELEASE NO. 190; AMERICAN ACCOUNTING ASSOCIATION; AMERICAN INSTITUTE OF CERTIFIED PUBLIC ACCOUNTANTS; AUDIT COMMITTEES; AUDITOR'S REPORT; BERLE AND MEANS; BIG EIGHT ACCOUNTING FIRMS; CAPITAL MAINTENANCE; CHIEF ACCOUNTANTS OF THE SECURITIES AND EXCHANGE COMMISSION; COMPARABILITY; CONGRESSIONAL VIEWS; *ESCOTT v. BARCHRIS CONSTRUCTION CORPORATION;* EXTERNAL AUDITING; *FISCHER v. KLETZ;* FRAUD AND AUDITING; GENERALLY ACCEPTED ACCOUNTING PRINCIPLES; *HOCHFELDER v. ERNST AND ERNST;* INDEPENDENCE OF EXTERNAL AUDITORS; INTANGIBLE ASSETS; INTERNAL CONTROL; KOHLER, ERIC LOUIS; LAW AND ACCOUNTING; LEGAL LIABILITY OF AUDITORS; MANAGEMENT ADVISORY SERVICES BY CPAS; MATERIALITY; MAY, GEORGE OLIVER; MCKESSON AND ROBBINS CASE; NATURAL BUSINESS YEAR; NEW YORK STOCK EXCHANGE; OBJECTIVITY; PERIODICITY; POOLING OF INTERESTS; PREVITS, GARY JOHN; PUBLIC OVERSIGHT BOARD; QUASI-REORGANIZATION; REALIZATION; REGULATION (FEDERAL U.S.) AND ACCOUNTING; RIPLEY, WILLIAM Z.; SANDERS, THOMAS HENRY; TREADWAY COMMISSION; *ULTRAMARES CORPORATION v. TOUCHE, NIVEN AND COMPANY; UNIFORM ACCOUNTING;* UNIFORMITY; *UNITED STATES OF AMERICA v. CARL SIMON;* UNITED STATES STEEL CORPORATION; WHEAT COMMITTEE

Sells, Elijah Watt (1858–1924)

Elijah Watt Sells was cofounder of the international CPA firm Haskins and Sells (now Deloitte and Touche). Sells's father was active in governmental affairs in Iowa and in Washington, D.C., serving as auditor of the Treasury Department under President Abraham Lincoln. Sells attended Baker University in Kansas but never received his degree. From 1874 through 1893, he had a long run of successful positions in accounting for railroads, the last being chief clerk for the general auditor of the Atchison,

Topeka and Santa Fe Railroad. The turning point of his life came when he and Charles Waldo Haskins were appointed in 1893 by the Joint Commission on Congress to Inquire into the Status of the Laws Organizing the Executive Departments (The Dockery Commission) as two of its three accounting experts.

This bipartisan committee recommended vast changes in the administration of federal financial management; its goal was to bring the business techniques of railroads, banks, and factories into the federal government. In the course of a debate on the bill arising from the Dockery Commission's recommendations in the U.S. Senate, Senator Cockrell of Missouri reported that the then Secretary of the Treasury Charles Foster had insisted on ". . .three experts, able men, disinterested, in no manner connected with the Government." In the same debate, Senator Proctor of Vermont reported on his impression of the experts, with whom he had spent a great deal of time. He said, "These experts are men thoroughly competent, experienced, and skillful, and have been extremely careful and conservative in their methods."

After this service, Haskins and Sells opened an accounting firm on March 4, 1895. A significant part of the firm's practice was in governmental accounting, including the city of Chicago. In 1901 the firm opened an office in London. Sells helped his partner, Haskins, in establishing the School of Commerce, Accounts, and Finance at New York University in 1900. When Haskins died in 1903, Sells became the senior administrator of the firm.

Like Haskins, Sells left a written legacy of his thoughts and deliberations. John R. Wildman selected, edited, and commented on Sells's writings in *The Natural Business Year and Thirteen Other Themes* (1924). The writings show Sells's wide-ranging interests and concerns through the years. In 1921, for example, he called for the increased use of the natural business year by American businesses, and also stressed the role played by accountants in keeping businesses in a state of financial health. In 1915, he pushed for the selection of public auditors by stockholders, and urged accountants to run for public office so they could bring their expertise to public administration. In 1909 Sells, like many of the accounting pioneers, urged the adoption of an up-to-date costing system by manufacturers. The collected writings also show that in 1917 he advocated federal recognition and regulation of the ac-

counting profession, in 1914 he spoke out for certified quarterly statements to offset the effect on investors of the "muck-rakers," and in 1908 he compared public administrators very unfavorably to business executives in terms of job performance. In 1912 he presented a call for tax reform, and in 1915 he endorsed an international peace plan to end the Great War.

Sells became a CPA in 1896; in 1906 and 1907 he was president of the American Association of Public Accountants—forerunner of the American Institute of Certified Public Accountants (AICPA)—and through the years performed many other services in that organization. In 1908 he investigated the financial system of the Philippine Islands. The AICPA continues to honor him through the Elijah Watt Sells Award, which is given to those with superior grades on the CPA exam. The best summation of his life is contained in the citation for his honorary doctorate in 1916 from New York University: "Elijah Watt Sells—for preeminence in a department of human effort in which the prime essentials are accuracy and truth; for the prevision which prompted you to secure for accountancy academic recognition; for distinguished service rendered to local governments, and especially to the Government of the United States, both at home and abroad. . . ."

Richard Vangermeersch

Bibliography

Burns, T.J., and E.N. Coffman. *The Accounting Hall of Fame: Profiles of Fifty Members*. Columbus: College of Business, Ohio State University, 1991.

Congressional Record, May 2, 1894, pp. 5196–5206.

Congressional Record, July 15, 1894, pp. 8864–8881.

"Elijah Watt Sells," *Journal of Accountancy*, May 1924, pp. 357–358.

Wildman, J.R., ed. *The Natural Business Year and Thirteen Other Themes*. Chicago and New York: A.W. Shaw, 1924.

See also ACCOUNTING EDUCATION IN THE UNITED STATES; ACCOUNTING HALL OF FAME; AMERICAN ACCOUNTING ASSOCIATION; AMERICAN INSTITUTE OF CERTIFIED PUBLIC ACCOUNTANTS; BIG EIGHT ACCOUNTING FIRMS; FEDERAL GOVERNMENT ACCOUNTING (U.S.); HASKINS, CHARLES WALDO; NATURAL BUSINESS YEAR; WILDMAN, JOHN RAYMOND

Separate Entities

The legal doctrines underlying modern corporations derived from three much older ideas: (1) that each such firm is an independent, property-owning entity in its own right, (2) that therefore the individuals comprising it have limited liability for corporate activities, and (3) that it has continuity of existence apart from the lives of its owners. Three leading institutions of the medieval world—the church, the town, and the craft guild—all were treated as separate entities with perpetual existence. Monastery property was never considered as belonging to individual monks or abbots, nor were they personally responsible for church obligations. Medieval municipalities were also viewed as entities apart from their inhabitants, and they often obtained articles of incorporation that legally recognized their separate status. Craft guilds offered mutual association for the protection of an occupational group. Like the church and town, they held property in their own names and created permanent offices through which many individuals passed.

In each case, the entity's independent existence provided the rationale for giving its members limited liability. If a business exists apart from its owners, its property cannot logically be made available to their personal creditors. Similarly, if a corporation is a separate entity with the power to contract and hold property, its creditors cannot expect to reach stockholders' personal assets to satisfy corporate debts.

Public acceptance of the idea that certain institutions had existence apart from their owners also created an obligation to preserve invested capital by limiting dividend payments to the amount of accumulated profits, both to protect creditors and to preserve enterprise continuity. Restricting dividends in this way required systematic profit measurement, including a precise distinction between assets and expenses.

Proprietorship was a central feature in the development of double entry bookkeeping. The concept of capital helped bridge the gap between the reasoning involved in simple personal debt records and the Method of Venice with its integrated real and nominal accounts. Double entry also promoted the idea that a business firm was a separate entity whose purpose was profit maximization.

In 1586 Don Angelo Pietra, a Benedictine monk, published *Indrizzo Degli Economi,* the first printed book on accounting for nonprofit organizations. Pietra thought monastery accounts could best be reviewed by examination of detailed financial statements. Though statements had been used in practice since the fourteenth century, this was the first time an author had mentioned them. Pietra was also the first writer to consider an enterprise as being separate and distinct from its owners, and his advocacy of a balance sheet, income statement, and detailed statement of monastery capital resulted from his desire to account for all changes in the entity's financial status, not just changes in owner's equity.

The partnership and agency aspects of Italian commerce also encouraged the development of separate entities doctrine. Most large firms were partnerships. To divide profits fairly, they needed an accounting system in which all transactions were recorded. A system that produced automatic profit and capital balances had obvious attractions for them. The formation of long-lasting partnerships led to a recognition that such businesses were entities in their own right and that capital and income represented claims of the owners.

But the accounting practices of smaller firms were typically much more primitive. Most kept single entry records that amounted to little more than lists of payments and receipts. Even double entry systems could be quite crude. Many were hybrids, using some dual entries but without profit and loss or capital accounts. The typical sixteenth-century ledger was a single book containing all a firm's accounts, with little attempt at classification. Even a hundred years later many ledgers included only receivables and payables, and the same customer's account might handle both. Well into the industrial revolution, business and personal assets were mixed together in double entry accounts. With no responsibility to outsiders, merchants could please themselves.

The lack of accrual accounting and periodic balancing, and the mixing of personal and business affairs in the ledger, are evidences of a disinterest in calculating total income. Company profit was usually thought of as the change in value of all a merchant's possessions from all causes between two balancing dates, or "rests." Its determination was not a task in itself, but a byproduct of closing the books. In these circumstances, the profit and loss account tended to become simply a clearing mechanism. Business and personal items, realized and unrealized income and losses, capital and revenue expenditures, capital contributions and drawings, asset revaluations—all were cleared through, or entered directly to, the profit and loss account.

Before the industrial revolution, the size of manufacturing firms was limited by their owners' inability to cope with the management problems involved in large scale operations. After 1750, developments in technology and marketing made it essential that progressive companies should grow beyond the size where a small group of partners could directly oversee operations. Such firms often needed outside capital, and became accountable to investors and creditors. Profit finding became integral, not incidental, to their accounting calculations.

In *Der Moderne Kapitalismus* (1919), the German historian Werner Sombart advanced three arguments for the importance of "scientific" bookkeeping: (1) *rationalization*: The balancing features and mathematical logic inherent in double entry bookkeeping, together with manufacturing capitalism, helped quantify, systematize, and control business affairs and gave a new rationality to resource allocation. (2) *abstraction*: By reducing assets and equities to numerical abstractions and by expressing the total results of operations as profit and loss, double entry bookkeeping clarified the aim of business as the "rationalistic pursuit of unlimited profits." (3) *depersonalization*: By substituting an abstract concept of capital for the idea of personal ownership, double entry bookkeeping facilitated the separation of business firms from their owners and thereby permitted the growth of large corporations.

So for Sombart accounting had far-reaching economic implications. It defined the entrepreneur's goals, rationalized his activities, and summarized for judgment the results of his operations. It might be added that all three of these benefits resulted from specifying the business firm, not its owners, as the accounting area of attention.

Michael Chatfield

Bibliography

Littleton, A.C. *Accounting Evolution to 1900*. New York: American Institute Publishing, 1933. Reprint. New York: Russell and Russell, 1966.

Peragallo, E. "A Commentary on Vigano's Historical Development of Ledger Balancing Procedures, Adjustments and Financial Statements During the Fifteenth, Sixteenth, and Seventeenth Centuries," *Accounting Review*, July 1971, pp. 531–534.

Sombart, W. *Der Moderne Kapitalismus.* Munich: Dunker and Humblot, 1919.

Winjum, J. "Accounting in its Age of Stagnation," *Accounting Review*, October 1970, pp. 743–771.

See also CONTINUITY; CORPORATIONS: EVOLUTION; DIVIDENDS; LIMITED LIABILITY; PARTNERSHIP ACCOUNTING; PIETRA, ANGELO; SOMBART, WERNER

Single Account Method

Most nineteenth-century manufacturers accounted for depreciable assets as if they were unsold merchandise. The single account or "inventory" technique was a traditional method of valuing long-term assets. John Mellis described it in his *Briefe Instruction* (1588), as did Stephen Monteage in *Debtor and Creditor Made Easie* (1683), and John Mair in the fifth edition of *Bookkeeping Methodiz'd* (1757). Although the single account method had many variations in practice, the procedure was similar to today's periodic inventory method. Plant assets were supposed to be appraised, or at least revalued, at the end of each accounting period. Typically, the new balance was debited and the old one credited directly to the asset account, allowing the asset's current appraisal to remain in the account while any reduction in value was charged to profit and loss. Depreciation in these terms was a valuation concept, and for the majority of firms using the single account method, profit was the change in value of net assets between two successive accounting periods.

Valuation methods of depreciation have always been difficult to standardize. The single account method had innumerable variations. There was no agreed on set of best practices, nor was there a definitive answer to the question: What is value? Long-term asset values included cost, lower of cost or market, and other valuations used in inventory accounting. Asset appreciation between balance sheet dates tended to be ignored, while asset decreases were generally written down. Nonrecurring changes were often not recorded. Moreover, revaluing assets at the end of each accounting period was awkward and expensive compared to the use of a depreciation rate. Some firms compromised by ratably depreciating plant assets each year, then making appraisals or asset revaluations at longer intervals.

The larger fault of a method that adjusted for every kind of value change—even those caused by inflation and business cycle fluctuations—was that many of these changed market values were independent of the asset's use and were determined by factors that the company could not control and which therefore did not reflect management's efficiency in using the assets. Systematic depreciation implies that long-term assets contribute directly to a product's value and thus, like materials and labor expense, should be allocated to its cost. The emergence of corporations with large investments in plant assets made it essential for accountants to deal directly with the problem of capital consumption, because in a setting of increasing manufacturing competition, product costs had to be calculated as precisely as possible. The single account method sidestepped the real issues of asset valuation, particularly the need to distinguish between capital and revenue expenditures.

Michael Chatfield

Bibliography

Brief, R. "The Origin and Evolution of Nineteenth Century Asset Accounting," *Business History Review*, Spring 1966, pp. 1–22.

Litherland, D.A. "Fixed Asset Replacement a Half Century Ago," *Accounting Review*, October 1951, pp. 475–480.

See also DEPRECIATION; DICKSEE, LAWRENCE; DOUBLE ACCOUNT METHOD; FIXED ASSETS; MONTEAGE, STEPHEN; OBJECTIVITY

Single Entry Bookkeeping

Single entry bookkeeping is generally associated with accounting books containing only cash and personal (people and organizations) accounts, which are kept in a systematic manner. These accounts in the ledger are periodically balanced and may be included with other accounting data for a formal report. Kohler considered single entry bookkeeping to be " . . . always incomplete 'double entry,' varying with circumstances. There is usually no detailed record of gains or losses; a statement of financial position is prepared from whatever data are available from the records or by inspection or count. . . ." Meservey (1882) advised that single entry should be learned before double entry because of its simplicity, common usage, and practicality, especially for those such as mechanics, farmers, and others who were not doing extensive business. However, Meservey insisted that all businessmen keep a cash account—a double entry recording for cash receipts from debtors and for cash payments to creditors. Writing almost 40 years before Meservey, Colt (1844) dismissed single entry accounting as not worthy for discussion: "It is a sort of 'get-along-way,' adopted only by the inexperienced, and approved of only by those who do not understand the science."

In his search for the origins of double entry bookkeeping, Yamey (1947) suggested it was more likely that single entry as a system developed from double entry. He referred to such sources as Jager, Schmalenbach, and Flugel to support his argument. Littleton (1933), however, indicated that certain transactions for profit and loss and owner's capital may have eventually led to a complete double entry system. Most (1979) showed what looked like a set of journal entries in double entry format from records from ancient Rome. Peragallo (1938) concluded: "From the information now available, there seems to have been no use of double entry, as we know it, during the Roman period, though it may have been present in embryonic form in the Roman bookkeeping system." Peragallo thought it likely that the Roman bookkeeping system did not disappear during the Dark Ages following the fall of Rome.

Like the founding of double entry accounting, the derivation of single entry accounting remains a mystery. The importance of a cash account certainly makes the case for the probability of a duality of entries for receipts from debtors and payments of creditors. This duality probably would have been present in bank accounting records, as well as the exchange of drafts, and could have been present in ancient societies. Whatever one's opinions are as to the origin of single entry bookkeeping, for a more extensive business it certainly requires a much more complex network of records than does the double entry approach.

Richard Vangermeersch

Bibliography

Colt, J.C. *The Science of Double Entry Bookkeeping: Simplified, Arranged, and Methodized.* . . . 10th ed. New York: Nafis and Cornish, 1844.

S

Kohler, E.L. *A Dictionary for Accountants.* 4th ed. Englewood Cliffs, NJ: Prentice-Hall, 1970.

Littleton, A.C. *Accounting Evolution to 1900.* New York: American Institute Publishing, 1933. Reprint. New York: Russell and Russell, 1966.

Meservey, A.B. *Meservey's Book-keeping: Single Entry, for Grammar Schools.* Boston: Thompson, Brown, 1882.

Most, K.S. "The Accounts of Ancient Rome." Working paper no. 3 in *Working Paper Series Volume 1,* edited by E.N. Coffman, pp. 22–41. Richmond, VA: Academy of Accounting Historians, 1979.

Peragallo, E. *Origins and Evolution of Double Entry Bookkeeping: A Study of Italian Practice from the Fourteenth Century.* New York: American Institute Publishing, 1938.

Yamey, B.S. "Notes on the Origin of Double-Entry Bookkeeping," *Accounting Review,* December 1947, pp. 263–272.

See also BARTER; CAPITAL ACCOUNT; CASH BASIS ACCOUNTING; "CHARGE AND DISCHARGE" STATEMENT; COLONIAL AMERICA, ACCOUNTING IN; DATINI, FRANCESCO DE MARCO; DOUBLE ENTRY BOOKKEEPING: ORIGINS; LITTLETON, A.C.; MEDIEVAL ACCOUNTING; MOST, KENNETH S.; POLAND; ROME (509 B.C.–A.D. 476); SCHMALENBACH, EUGEN; WILDMAN, JOHN RAYMOND; YAMEY, BASIL SELIG

Sixteenth Amendment (1913)

The Sixteenth Amendment to the U.S. Constitution granted Congress the power "to lay and collect taxes on incomes, from whatever source derived, without apportionment among the several States, and without regard to any census or enumeration." This amendment did not define income or set forth any particular framework within which income might be taxed. However, and more important, the adoption of the Sixteenth Amendment put an end to the long-standing debate over the constitutionality of an income tax and set the stage for the development of what is now called the Internal Revenue Code.

Income taxes had been imposed on individuals in the United States at various times beginning with the Civil War, but never for an extended period. The tax provisions were either never put in effect, repealed after their purpose had passed (e.g., the "war" taxes), or found unconstitutional. The constitutional problems associated with early attempts to tax income arose from Article 1 of the Constitution, which requires that a direct tax on property be apportioned according to the state populations.

Defining a direct tax proved to be difficult because of the conceptual nature of property and the income it produces. Taxation of the *income* from property was not always considered a direct tax on the *property*. A tax on a property's income was often considered an excise tax on the right to use the property or engage in the underlying activity, thus removing such an income tax from the definition of a direct tax under Article 1.

In *Hylton v. United States* 3 U.S. 171 (1796), the Supreme Court found that a tax on carriages was a tax on the right to use the carriage rather than a direct tax on the property itself. With regard to an income tax, in *Springer v. United States* 102 U.S. 586, 598–599 (1880), the Supreme Court found that the Civil War income tax was an excise tax rather than a direct tax on the underlying property.

In its last decision regarding the constitutionality of a personal income tax before the passage of the Sixteenth Amendment, the Supreme Court, in a 5-to-4 vote, found the Income Tax Act of 1894 unconstitutional in *Pollock v. Farmers' Loan and Trust Company* (1895). The Court considered the 1894 levy on income from real and personal property to be an unapportioned direct tax and thus in violation of Article 1 of the Constitution. Although the Court found the entire act unconstitutional because of this legal flaw, the portion of the act imposing an income tax on wages would not have been unconstitutional if it had stood alone because such a tax would not have been considered a direct tax on property.

In the late 1800s, the Populists and many members of the Democratic Party pushed for the passage of a personal income tax. The Income Tax Act of 1894 was passed when the Democratic Party controlled both houses of Congress and the presidency, although the Supreme Court, with its control by Republican Party appointees, quickly ruled the act unconstitutional. In 1906 Theodore Roosevelt proposed an income tax on both income and estates. In 1909 Republican Progressives in Congress, known as the Insurgents, and Democrats, led by William Jennings Bryan, began supporting a constitutional amendment allowing a personal income tax as a solution to the problem of high tariffs.

The 61st Congress proposed the Sixteenth Amendment in July 1909, and the amendment was adopted in February 1913. After the 1912 elections, when the Democrats controlled both the presidency and Congress, the Revenue Act of 1913 was passed, setting the stage for the development of income tax law later codified as the Internal Revenue Codes of 1939, 1954, and 1986. There were numerous subsequent attempts to declare the personal income tax unconstitutional, largely based on the idea that the ratification process of the Sixteenth Amendment was flawed. However, the Supreme Court has consistently upheld the validity of the amendment and the constitutionality of an income tax.

Gary A. McGill

Bibliography

Blakey, R.G., and G.C. Blakey. *The Federal Income Tax*. New York: Longmans, Green, 1940.

Hansen, S.B. *The Politics of Taxation*. New York: Praeger, 1983.

Paul, R.E. *Taxation in the United States*. Boston: Little, Brown & Co., 1954.

Witte, J.F. *The Politics and Development of the Federal Income Tax*. Madison, WI: University of Wisconsin Press, 1985.

See also BAD DEBTS; BIG EIGHT ACCOUNTING FIRMS; *BRUSHABER V. UNION PACIFIC RAILROAD COMPANY; FLINT V. STONE TRACY COMPANY;* INCOME TAXATION IN THE UNITED STATES; MONTGOMERY, ROBERT HIESTER; QUASI-REORGANIZATION; *POLLOCK V. FARMERS' LOAN AND TRUST COMPANY;* REALIZATION; *SPRINGER V. UNITED STATES;* TAX REFORM ACTS

Smith, Adam (1723–1790)

Adam Smith was the author of *The Wealth of Nations*, the 1776 classic that brought a laissez-faire and market-driven economy into prominence over the previous school of mercantilism, in which each country strove to control its economy to maximize the flow of wealth to it. Smith stressed the importance of individual initiatives to achieve the highest degree of satisfaction and, hence, to lead to a maximizing of wealth for the country.

Smith was educated at the University of Glasgow (1737–1740) and at Oxford University (1740–1746). Before becoming a professor of logic and then moral philosophy at the University of Glasgow in 1751, he spent two years at home in Kirkcaldy, Scotland, and three years giving lectures in Edinburgh. During his 12 years at the University of Glasgow, Smith was very involved in administrative and financial matters. He then became a tutor for two years to the stepson of Charles Townshend, the author of the colonial taxes that led to the American Revolution. Smith traveled throughout Europe in that period and became well acquainted with French economists. With the very generous lifetime pension awarded to him by Townshend, Smith was able to devote nine years to the writing of *The Wealth of Nations*, which was published in 1776. His subsequent appointments as a commissioner of customs for Scotland and as a commissioner for the salt duties for Scotland allowed him to publish four more editions of *The Wealth of Nations* before his death in 1790.

Smith did not write about the field of accounting specifically, although it was well developed in Scotland by such writers as Robert Colinson in *Idea Rationaria* (1683) and John Mair in *Bookkeeping Methodiz'd* (1736 and later editions). However, Smith did write about the general stock of a country, which was the sum of the stock of its inhabitants. He listed three classifications of stock. The *first* was the unconsumed food, clothes, and household furniture held by individuals. The *second* was fixed capital, which was composed of (1) machines and instruments of trade, (2) buildings used in trade, (3) land improvements, and (4) the acquired and useful abilities of all the inhabitants of the society. The *third* was circulating capital consisting of money and inventories.

It is interesting to compare Smith's notion of stock with that held by such accounting writers as Luca Pacioli, Colinson, and Mair. For the latter three, stock meant assets minus liabilities. In his treatise on accounting in *Summa de Arithmetica* (1494), Pacioli stressed the detailed listing of: (1) personal assets of the merchant—money, jewels, household furnishings, (2) inventories of goods, (3) real estate, (4) land, (5) bank deposits, (6) receivables, and (7) payables. Colinson included: (1) money, (2) merchandise, (3) ships, (4) house, (5) rents, (6) movables and house furnishings, (7) receivables, and (8) payables. Mair listed: (1) money, (2) inventories, (3) ships, (4) receivables, and (5) payables. Mair was far less inclusive than Pacioli and Colinson; Smith did not include residential houses or receivables as assets and ignored liabilities. He favored the recognition of profit only when cash had been collected for the sale of inventory. "The goods of the merchant," he wrote, "yield no revenue or profit till he sells them for money, and the money yields him as little till it is again exchanged for goods." The latter part sounds like the classic argument for LIFO (last in, first out) inventory as a part of the purchase-sale-purchase cycle for recognizing profit.

In a review of the contents of Smith's library by Mizuta (1967), the only accounting book found to be owned by Smith was Mair's (no edition noted by Mizuta). While one can give Smith possible credit for fixed and circulating capital, he apparently did not develop his ideas with accounting writers in mind. However, Smith can clearly be listed as a proponent of the human resource accounting approach that developed much later, in the twentieth century, and that includes the notion of human capital as an asset.

Smith is significant in the field of accounting for his exposition of the doctrine of the division of labor and his classic discussion of the "pin factory." Smith described the benefits to the manufacturer of laborers performing repetitive functions rather than each laborer trying to make a complete pin from start to finish. Furthermore he rationalized "profits" and their importance. Profits, by his definition, were the return to the owner of the stock for the functions of inspection and direction performed by the owner. Profits fluctuate greatly and are affected by countless factors. Profits and interest rise and fall together. Smith felt that profit should be double that of interest on borrowed money and that competition tended to lower profits.

Adam Smith's *The Wealth of Nations* remains a cornerstone of the capitalistic form of economics. Because of this, students in accounting should be familiar with it.

Richard Vangermeersch

Bibliography

Mizuta, H. *Adam Smith's Library: A Supplement to Bomar's Catalogue with a Checklist of the Whole Library*. Cambridge, England: University Printing House, 1967.

Rae, J. *Life of Adam Smith*. London: Macmillan, 1895. Reprint. New York: Augustus M. Kelley, 1965.

Smith, A. *An Inquiry into the Nature and Causes of The Wealth of Nations*, ed. by E. Connan. The Modern Library. New York: Random House, 1937.

See also BABBAGE, CHARLES; CONCEPTUAL FRAMEWORK; HUMAN RESOURCE ACCOUNTING; LAST IN, FIRST OUT (LIFO); LIQUIDITY: ACCOUNTING MEASUREMENT; MERCANTILISM; OBJECTIVITY; PACIOLI, LUCA; REALIZATION; RETURN ON INVESTMENT

Smyth v. Ames

In America the first debates over historical cost versus replacement cost occurred not among accounting theorists, but between the railroads and the Interstate Commerce Commission (ICC). The ICC's task was to set public utility rates just high enough so that a reasonable return could be earned on the regulated company's investment in plant assets. The commission was responsible for developing a rate base, which was then multiplied by a percentage to determine the total return that a railroad was entitled to earn. The question arose: Should this rate base be developed from the original costs or the replacement costs of assets?

This choice presented problems because so many railroads had been built just after the Civil War, at the beginning of a long period of price declines, with the result that by 1900 the historical costs of their assets far exceeded the replacement prices. In an effort to get higher rates, the railroads argued that acquisition costs should be their rate base. The ICC, as the agency responsible for protecting the public from excessive railroad charges, countered that replacement costs were a more appropriate rate base. Considering this question, the Supreme Court in *Smyth v. Ames* (1898) ruled that fair market values of railroad properties as well as acquisition costs should be considered in establishing the rate base.

After 1900, with price levels moving upward, the conflict between the ICC and the railroads continued, but the disputants exchanged arguments. Prices soon increased enough so that the railroads could obtain higher rates based on current replacement costs. The commissioners likewise had a change of heart, becoming advocates of the now more conservative historical costs.

Michael Chatfield

Bibliography

Boer, G. "Replacement Cost: A Historical Look," *Accounting Review*, January 1966, pp. 92–97.

Smyth v. Ames, 16 U.S. 466 (1898).

See also HISTORICAL COST; RAILROAD AC-COUNTING (U.S.); RETURN ON INVESTMENT; RIPLEY, WILLIAM Z.

Snell, Charles (1670–1730)

Like the 1929 stock market crash, the collapse of the South Sea Bubble in 1720 led to demands for audit verification. Following large declines in South Sea Company stock prices, the company's banker, the Sword Blade Company, became insolvent in September 1720. In January 1721, a House of Commons Committee of Secrecy was appointed to investigate, and discovered "false and fictitious entries" in the South Sea Company's books. This was not surprising. To be sure of getting legislative approval for its plan to take over part of the national debt, the South Sea Company had paid more than a million pounds in bribes to members of Parliament. Charles Stanhope, Secretary to the Treasury, had profited £250,000 from issuances of South Sea Company stock that were recorded as sales on the company's books but were never received or paid for by him. The company later resold this stock at a higher price and he got the difference.

Charles Snell, writing master and accountant, was employed by officials of the Sword Blade bank to examine the records of Sawbridge and Company, a failed subsidiary of the South Sea Company, and specifically to report on the book entries relating to Charles Stanhope. Snell thus became the first independent accountant engaged to audit the records of a public corporation, and the first to conduct what we would call a fraud investigation.

In his audit report, *Observations made upon examining the books of Sawbridge and Company* (1721), Snell showed that the entries affecting Charles Stanhope canceled each other out, and concluded: "It does not appear to me, by their books, that the said £250,000, or any profit, was made on the said account of stock." Stanhope was eventually acquitted of accepting bribes.

Michael Chatfield

Bibliography

Bywater, M.F., and B.S. Yamey. *Historic Accounting Literature: A Companion Guide.* London: Scholar Press, 1982.

Carswell, J. *The South Sea Bubble.* Palo Alto, CA: Stanford University Press, 1960.

See also EXTERNAL AUDITING; SOUTH SEA BUBBLE

Social Responsibilities of Accountants

The social responsibilities of accountants, whether employed in public practice, industry, or government, come from accounting's status as a practice that is generally regarded to be among the "professions." This professional status imposes responsibilities on accountants in two ways. The first is through the general responsibilities associated with all practices that are considered to be professions; the other is through the uniqueness of accounting practice.

Members of professions enjoy status and privileges that are denied to most people. A functionalist interpretation of the professional's status and privilege attributes them to the essential social function that the professional performs. Medicine, law, the clergy, or accounting all represent essential social functions that impose on their practitioners the responsibility for public service; their responsibilities have a distinctly public character.

Because of the public character of professional service, according to Kultgen (1988), all professions share certain common responsibilities. One of these is the responsibility of competence. Since all professions rely on some theoretical knowledge base, the practitioner must be knowledgeable and well trained in that base. Society expects skillfullness from those to whom it gives professional status.

A second responsibility of a professional is that of integrity. The public must be able to expect the practitioner of a profession to conform to norms of behavior that assure trustworthiness. Virtually all professions (including accountants employed in most fields of the profession) have written codes of conduct; integrity, as a minimum, means adherence to a code of conduct.

The third responsibility of a professional is that for the welfare of others. Self-interestedness is not the paramount consideration of professionals in performing their services. For the professional, an obligation exists to perform certain activities even if those activities are not in that professional's interests. As a minimum, the professional is obliged to do no harm.

However, the practice of accounting has a rather unique characteristic that imposes some responsibilities on accountants that are of particular importance. Professions are client centered; professionals perform their services for individuals who seek them and, when able, pay for those services. Physicians tend to the health of their individual patients. If the physician does this well, she can claim to have fulfilled her social responsibilities as a physician. Likewise, an attorney relies upon the adversarial nature of the legal system to provide him with the assurance that by concerning himself only with the welfare of his client he has fulfilled his responsibilities as an attorney.

An accountant, no matter where or by whom employed, does not have that employer as his or her sole client. Thus, an accountant, unlike an attorney or physician, does not serve society merely by serving an individual client. This is because accountants are involved in a rather complex communicative process. The services of accountants constitute a primary medium through which enterprises (public and private) give an economic accounting of themselves to the community. This imposes on accountants a larger duty than just to serve the client.

Everyone directly or indirectly affected by accounting reports is a client. For example, public accountants typically refer to their client as the management of the firm they are expected to audit. However, unlike a physician, attending only to the interests of this client is an abrogation of social responsibility, not a fulfillment of it. Accountants are relied upon by society to provide it with information it uses to make decisions that have significant effects on various persons or groups of persons within the society. Because these effects generally involve the distribution of income or wealth, two social responsibilities of accountants are particularly acute.

The first is the responsibility of honesty. Francis (1990), for example, rates honesty as the paramount internal good of the practice of accounting. If individual accountants are not fastidious in being as truthful as they can be, then public trust will be diminished. And any loss of public trust erodes the professional status of any group of practitioners. The accountant's responsibility of honesty is institutionalized through the requirement to be "independent." Independence requires accountants to be objective in making judgments, which means not letting self-interest influence them.

The second crucial responsibility of accountants is a concern for fairness. Accounting practice revolves around the development and application of the rules, assumptions, conventions, and procedures that, when applied to economic activity, result in the accounting reports that represent "accounting information." Economic activity results in both the creation of wealth *and* its distribution. Thus, accounting practice is deeply implicated in the relative economic welfare of members of society. Judgments of fairness are inescapable when devising and applying accounting rules and techniques since they represent and, thus, affect the distribution of economic goods. The professional accountant has a responsibility to reflect upon the distributive effects of what he or she does; the professional accountant must strive to assure the effects of his or her practice are fair.

In recent years, some accountants and social scientists have advocated a more expansive social role for accountants. Rather than limiting accounting to a "financial-performance measurement" function, they have argued that it should be extended to encompass reporting on the social performance of large business organizations (see Bauer 1966, Bauer and Fenn 1977, Belkaoui 1984, and Gambling 1974). These organizations affect the world in numerous and complex ways, and the traditional financial-reporting system is inadequate for fully capturing and communicating all the significant effects.

To satisfy this greater social responsibility, accountants would need a commitment to developing methods of representing and reporting the behavior of corporations as it pertains to effects on the environment, employment opportunity, worker health and safety, product safety, and similar areas. Thus far, the profession has been reluctant to accept this greater social responsibility, although some accounting scholars as Christine Cooper (1992), Rob Gray (1992), and Ruth Hines (1991) are continuing to work on developing the enabling knowledge necessary for the profession to accept such responsibility.

Paul F. Williams

Bibliography

Bauer, R.A., ed. *Social Indicators*. Cambridge: MIT Press, 1966.

Bauer, R.A., and D.H. Fenn Jr. *The Corporate Social Audit*. New York: Russell Sage Foundation, 1972.

Belkaoui, A. *Socio-Economic Accounting.* Westport, CT: Greenwood, 1984.

Cooper, C. "The Non and Nom of Accounting for (M)other Nature," *Accounting, Auditing, and Accountability,* vol. 5, no. 3, 1992, pp. 16–39.

Devine, C.T. "Ethics: General and Professional Dimensions." In *Essays in Accounting Theory, vol. 5,* pp. 63–78. Sarasota, FL: American Accounting Association, 1985.

Flores, A. "Introduction: What Kind of Person Should a Professional Be?" In *Professional Ideals.* Belmont, CA: Wadsworth, 1988.

Francis, J.R. "After Virtue? Accounting as a Moral and Discursive Practice," *Accounting, Auditing, and Accountability,* vol. 3, no. 3, 1990, pp. 5–17.

Gambling, T. *Societal Accounting.* London: Allen & Unwin, 1974.

Gray, R. "Accounting and Environmentalism: An Exploration of the Challenge of Gently Accounting for Accountability, Transparency, and Sustainability," *Accounting, Organizations, and Society,* vol. 17, no. 5, 1992, pp. 399–425.

Hines, R. "On Valuing Nature," *Accounting, Auditing, and Accountability*, Special Issue on the Environment, 1991, pp. 27–29.

Kultgen, J. *Ethics and Professionalism.* Philadelphia: University of Pennsylvania Press, 1988.

Linowes, D.F. "An Approach to Socio-Economic Accounting," *Conference Board Record,* November 1978, pp. 58–61.

Williams, P.F. "The Legitimate Concern with Fairness," *Accounting, Organizations, and Society,* 1987, vol. 12, no. 2, pp. 169–189.

See also ACCOUNTING AND THE ACCOUNTANT: PORTRAYALS; BIG EIGHT ACCOUNTING FIRMS; BRILOFF, ABRAHAM J.; CLARK, JOHN MAURICE; DEVINE, CARL; ENTERPRISE THEORY; ETHICS, PROFESSIONAL; HOPWOOD, ANTHONY G.; ITALY, AFTER PACIOLI; KRAAYENHOF, JACOB; MUNICIPAL ACCOUNTING REFORM; SCOTT, DR; TRUEBLOOD, ROBERT MARTIN; ZAPPA, GINO

Societas Maris
See COMMENDA CONTRACTS

Solomons, David (1912–1995)

S

David Solomons is an author of important articles and books on accounting theory, standard-setting, management accounting, and accounting education, who has been a sought-after consultant to professional accountancy institutes and standard-setting bodies. Solomons is perhaps best known for writing the first major exposition of the "value to the owner" construct of current value accounting, for predicting the demise of the income concept in accounting determinations, for serving as the principal draftsman of the Wheat Report that led to the establishment of the Financial Accounting Standards Board (FASB) and for drafting the FASB's second concepts statement on qualitative characteristics, and for defending neutrality as an indispensable attribute of responsible standard setting.

Solomons received a bachelor of commerce degree from the University of London in 1932, having taken his studies at the London School of Economics (LSE). He became a chartered accountant in 1936 and practiced in a London firm until 1939, when, upon the outbreak of war, he enlisted as a private in the Royal Army and was commissioned the following year. During the war, he was interned for almost three years in Italian and German prison camps, where he taught accounting to his fellow prisoners. In 1946 he became an accounting lecturer at the LSE. There he was much influenced by Ronald S. Edwards, an industrial economist who had written several important articles on costing history and accounting theory in the journal *Accountant* during the 1930s. In 1955 Solomons became the foundation professor of accounting at the University of Bristol, and in 1959 he crossed the Atlantic to take up a professorship in the Wharton School of the University of Pennsylvania. He received a doctor of science degree from the University of London in 1966, and in 1974 he was named the first Arthur Young Professor at the Wharton School. He retired from the university in 1983.

Solomons has headed academic accounting associations in two countries: in 1958 he was chairman of the Association of University Teachers of Accounting (later renamed the British Accounting Association), and in 1977–1978 he was president of the American Accounting Association (AAA). In 1980 the AAA selected Solomons as an Outstanding Accounting Educator, and in 1989 the Institute of Chartered Accountants in England and Wales (English

Institute) gave him its International Award. In 1992 he was inducted into the Accounting Hall of Fame.

Solomons's first major article, in 1952, dealt with costing history. He undertook a revision of Sidney Alexander's, a professor of economics at Harvard, famous 1950 essay, "Income Measurement in a Dynamic Economy," following which Solomons concluded, ruefully, in 1961, in "Economic and Accounting Concepts of Income," that it was not operationally feasible to isolate changes in expectations from Alexander's "economic income," thus diminishing its usefulness as a satisfactory measure of enterprise performance. It was in this 1961 article that he made his famous prediction that "so far as the history of accounting is concerned, the next twenty-five years may subsequently be seen to have been the twilight of income measurement." In 1987, he acknowledged that his prediction had not been fulfilled, and that perhaps his forte was not as a seer.

In 1966, Solomons published a major essay, "Economic and Accounting Concepts of Cost and Value," on James C. Bonbright's, a professor of Finance at Columbia University, "value to the owner" formulation for valuing property, and gave it impetus in the debates over current-value accounting by expressing it in an inequality notation. Directly or indirectly, this paper influenced the Sandilands Committee in the United Kingdom and the FASB in the United States on their deliberations on accounting for inflation.

In 1965, he wrote his first book, *Divisional Performance: Measurement and Control*, in which he reported on a survey of 25 major companies and presented recommendations on how best to evaluate and control decentralized operations. It was a path-breaking study, and it earned him the American Institute of Certified Public Accountants (AICPA) Notable Contribution to the Literature Award in 1969.

Solomons chaired a committee formed in 1970 by the AAA to propose a more effective process for establishing "generally accepted accounting principles," in the wake of widespread disillusionment with the performance of the Accounting Principles Board. Following publication in 1971 of the committee's report, he was named to the AICPA's Wheat Study, whose 1972 recommendations led, in 1973, to the founding of the FASB. Solomons wrote the first draft of the report.

He drafted the FASB's concepts statement of qualitative characteristics (1980), and he advised a special AICPA committee on the structure and authority of what was to become the Auditing Standards Board. In 1989, at the request of the Research Board of the English Institute, he drafted a concise conceptual framework for consideration by the United Kingdom's Accounting Standards Committee, which published the *Guidelines for Financial Reporting Standards* in that year.

In 1986 he synthesized his ideas on standard-setting and the conceptual framework in a book titled *Making Accounting Policy: The Quest for Credibility in Financial Reporting*, which is a model of thoroughness, careful scholarship, and persuasive writing. In accounting education, Solomons was invited by the six accountancy bodies in the British Isles to undertake a major long-range study of accounting education and training, which he completed in 1974 under the title, *Prospectus for a Profession*.

Solomons has left an important and salutary mark on the accounting literature as well as on the policy deliberations of professional accountancy institutes and standard-setting bodies.

Stephen A. Zeff

Bibliography

Alexander, S.S. "Income Measurement in a Dynamic Economy." In the Study Group on Business Incomes, *Five Monographs on Business Income*. New York: American Institute of Accountants, 1950. Reprint. Lawrence, KS: Scholars, 1973.

Alexander, S.S. (revised by D. Solomons). "Income Measurement in a Dynamic Economy." In *Studies in Accounting Theory*, edited by W.T. Baxter and S. Davidson, pp. 126–200.

American Institute of Certified Public Accountants. *Establishing Financial Accounting Standards*. Report of the Study Group on Establishment of Accounting Principles [The Wheat Report]. New York: AICPA, 1972.

Financial Accounting Standards Board. "Qualitative Characteristics of Accounting Information." Statement of Financial Accounting Concepts No. 2. Stamford, CT: FASB, 1980.

"Report of the Committee on Establishment of an Accounting Commission," *Accounting Review*, July 1971, pp. 609–616.

Solomons, D. *Collected Papers on Accounting and Accounting Education*. New York: Garland, 1984 (especially the Introductions: vol. 1, pp. xiii–xx; vol. 2, pp. xiii–xvi).

———. *Divisional Performance: Measurement and Control*. New York: Financial Executives Research Foundation, 1965.

———. "Economic and Accounting Concepts of Cost and Value." In *Modern Accounting Theory*, edited by M. Backer, pp. 117–140. Englewood Cliffs, NJ: Prentice-Hall, 1966.

———. "Economic and Accounting Concepts of Income," *Accounting Review*, July 1961, pp. 374–383.

———. *Guidelines for Financial Reporting Standards*. London: Institute of Chartered Accountants in England and Wales, 1989.

———. "The Historical Development of Costing." In *Studies in Costing*, edited by D. Solomons, pp. 1–52. London: Sweet and Maxwell, 1952.

———. *Making Accounting Policy: The Quest for Credibility in Financial Reporting*. New York: Oxford University Press, 1986.

———. "The Twilight of Income Measurement: Twenty-Five Years On," *Accounting Historians Journal*, Spring 1987, pp. 1–6.

Solomons, D., and T.M. Berridge. *Prospectus for a Profession: The Report of the Long Range Enquiry into Education and Training for the Accounting Profession*. London: Advisory Board of Accountancy Education, 1974.

See also ACCOUNTING HALL OF FAME; AMERICAN ACCOUNTING ASSOCIATION; CERTIFIED MANAGEMENT ACCOUNTANT (CMA) EXAMINATION; CHARTERED ACCOUNTANTS EXAMINATIONS IN ENGLAND AND WALES; CONCEPTUAL FRAMEWORK; FINANCIAL ACCOUNTING STANDARDS BOARD; GENERALLY ACCEPTED ACCOUNTING PRINCIPLES; INSTITUTE OF CHARTERED ACCOUNTANTS IN ENGLAND AND WALES; MANAGEMENT ACCOUNTING; SANDILANDS REPORT; WHEAT COMMITTEE

Sombart, Werner (1863–1941)

Werner Sombart, influential political economist, was born and died in Germany. He studied law, economics, history, and philosophy at the Universities of Berlin, Rome, and Pisa, and eventually became a professor of economics in Berlin. He was a student of the so-called *Katheder* Socialists (Schmoller and Wagner) in Berlin, and as a young man became a Marxist. However, he was probably too bright to be a Marxist for long and eventually turned anti-Marxist; in fact, his *Der Moderne Kapitalismus* (Modern Capitalism), published in 1919, is really a book in praise of capitalism, in which he predicted that capitalism would reach its zenith in the twentieth century. Late in life he became an apologist for the National Socialists, but the Nazis did not accept him in this role primarily because his observations on the role of Jews in the Middle Ages conflicted with their own theories.

In terms of sheer volume of publications and translations of his publications, Sombart must be reckoned as one of the more successful economists of his time, but he failed to form a school or produce disciples for his views, and must be regarded as a historical curiosity at the present time. This is probably because he combined the social and historical origins of his economic thought into an exciting but rather unstable mixture, in a manner that subsequent generations have come to view as unscientific.

These so-called "Sombart Propositions" have received considerable attention in accounting literature. Yamey (1950, 1964) reviewed them critically in two articles, Winjum (1972) identified "substantial academic support for the Sombart thesis," and Most (1972) found some merit in them. The propositions relate to the role of accounting in the development of capitalism. Sombart went so far as to state that the introduction of accounting was of the highest importance for the development of capitalism, and clearly, such perception deserves special study.

Sombart took as his point of departure a precapitalistic feudal Europe in which the goal of every man was a sufficiency for existence. He then observed that, at some point, the profit motive replaced satisfaction of personal wants as the driving force in society. He posed the question: By what means did this take place? What turned the precapitalistic artisan or craftsman into the capitalistic manufacturer? His answer was that man developed two faculties: to calculate and to save, and the significance of accounting was that it combined these two skills into a powerful management tool: the capitalistic firm viewed as an accounting entity.

Shortly stated, Sombart saw the invention of double entry bookkeeping as a device for rendering objective the concept of capital. He wrote that "the representation of the firm in terms of accounts, particularly the representation of the ownership interests, in the form of the capital accounts, renders objective the idea of wealth, and dissociates it from the human persons who are engaged in the enterprise." The idea of capital was divorced from all want-satisfying objectives or motivations of the people who took part in the development of the firm, and this led directly to the formulation of economic rationalism. By this means, production and distribution were reduced to calculations, which meant that the tools of mathematics could be used to plan saving and investment and to further the growth of capitalism.

In a striking passage, Sombart quoted the words that Goethe put into the mouth of Wilhelm Meister's brother-in-law: "Double entry bookkeeping is one of the most beautiful discoveries of the human spirit." He went on to explain that: "If the significance is to be correctly understood, it must be compared to the knowledge which scientists have built up since the sixteenth century concerning relationships in the physical world. Double entry bookkeeping came from the same spirit which produced the systems of Galileo and Newton and the subject matter of modern physics and chemistry. By the same means, it organizes perceptions into a system, and one can characterize it as the first Cosmos constructed purely on the basis of mechanistic thought. Double entry bookkeeping captures for us the essence of an economic or capitalistic world by the same means that later the great scientists used to construct the solar system, and the corpuscles of the blood. Without too much difficulty, we can recognize in double entry bookkeeping the ideas of gravitation, of the circulation of the blood, and of the conservation of matter. And even on a purely aesthetic plan we cannot regard double entry bookkeeping without wonder and astonishment at one of the most artistic representations of the fantastic spiritual richness of European man."

Kenneth S. Most

Bibliography

Most, K.S. "Sombart's Propositions Revisited," *Accounting Review*, October 1972, pp. 722–734.

Winjum, J.O. *The Role of Accounting in the Economic Development of England, 1500–1750*. Champaign, IL: Center for International Education and Research in Accounting, 1972.

Yamey, B.S. "Accounting and Rise of Capitalism: Further-the-Notes on a Theme by Sombart," *Journal of Accounting Research*, Autumn 1964, pp. 117–136.

———. "Scientific Bookkeeping and the Rise of Capitalism." In *Studies in Accounting*, edited by W.T. Baxter. London: Sweet and Maxwell, 1950.

See also ACCOUNTING AND THE ACCOUNTANT: PORTRAYALS; CAPITAL ACCOUNT; DOUBLE ENTRY BOOKKEEPING: ORIGINS; GERMANY; MOST, KENNETH S.; RESEARCH METHODS IN ACCOUNTING HISTORY; SEPARATE ENTITIES; YAMEY, BASIL SELIG

Soranzo Brothers

See DONALDO SORANZO AND BROTHERS

Soulé, George (1834–1926)

A pioneer in business education in the South and author of several successful business textbooks, George Soulé was born in New York. At an early age, however, his parents moved to Illinois, where young Soulé received his early schooling. He later pursued studies in law and medicine but finally resolved to become a teacher of commercial subjects. In 1856 he graduated from Jones Commercial College in St. Louis.

Upon graduation he moved to New Orleans, where he founded the Soulé Commercial College and Literary Institute. The school, which started in a single room, soon prospered, and in 1861 it was chartered by the legislature of Louisiana with authority to confer degrees and grant diplomas. Although the primary objective of the institution was to meet the needs of those who wished to be trained in the management of business affairs, Soulé did not fail to perceive the rising need for a broader education. As a result, he expanded the range of programs to include a variety of academic courses.

Dissatisfied with the textbooks of his time, Soulé wrote and published several texts in practical mathematics, bookkeeping, and accounting. One of his more well-known works was *Soulé's New Science and Practice of Accounts* (1881). The seventh edition of this book (1903)

was reprinted by Arno Press in 1976. Other textbooks he authored were: *Soulé's Analytic and Philosophic Commercial and Exchange Calculator* (1872); *Soulé's Intermediate Philosophic Arithmetic* (1874); *Soulé's Introductory Arithmetical Drill Problems* (1882); *Soulé's Philosophic Practical Mathematics* (1895); and *Soulé's Manual of Auditing* (6th ed., 1905).

Soulé was a member of many learned societies and was very active in the Business Educators Association of America. In recognition of his eminent attainments, Tulane University of Louisiana conferred upon him the honorary degree of doctor of laws.

Vahé Baladouni

Bibliography

Baladouni, V. "George Soulé," *Accounting Historians Journal, 1974–1976*, vol. 3, 1976, pp. 72–74.
"Soulé, George." *Dictionary of American Biography*, vol. 17. New York: Scribner's, 1935, pp. 403–404.

See also ACCOUNTING EDUCATION IN THE UNITED STATES.

South Sea Bubble

The South Sea Bubble of 1720 was the largest and most infamous financial collapse until 1929. In 1710 Queen Anne's chief minister, Robert Harley, had two major problems. There were no funds for the £9 million of Great Britain's national debt due for redemption, and he lacked a power base, not having the support of either the large Whig trading companies or the great Tory landowners. He solved both by creating "The Governor and Company of Merchants of Great Britain trading to the South Sea and other parts of America and for encouraging the Fishery" (the South Sea Company), which had a capital greater than the total of the Bank of England, the East India Company, and the Royal African Company. The huge capital was provided through a charter allowing the South Sea Company to allot shares in exchange for £9.4 million of the government debt. The inducement for debt holders to exchange was the government paying the equivalent of 6 percent interest to the company plus granting it a monopoly for trade between Britain and Spanish South America. This trade was never profitable and in 1718 ceased.

Unwilling to maintain their company as a mere disburser of government interest, the South Sea directors in 1719 persuaded Parliament to permit the conversion of annuities payable to the winners of the 1710 government lottery into South Sea shares. This proved so lucrative the directors in November 1719 successfully tendered for the right to convert the remaining £30 million of national debt, half of which was in the form of annuities, with the right to increase the authorized capital by one £100 share for every £100 of debt converted. For example, a £100 long annuity was valued at £2,000, which meant the company was permitted to increase its authorized capital by 20 shares for every long annuity converted. As South Sea stock was currently selling at £114, an annuitant prepared to accept 18 shares each would make a gain of £52 while the company would be free to sell the other two shares for £228. John Blunt, the dominant director who initiated the scheme, regarded the full cash receipt, not just the share premium, as profit available for dividend; furthermore, the higher the market price of a South Sea share, the fewer would need to be allocated to the annuitants and so the greater the profit for the company. This so appealed to investors that when in April 20,000 new South Sea shares were offered on terms of £300 each, 20 percent payable on application, the issue was fully sold within hours. A few weeks later, a further issue of 10,000 shares, this time at £400 each, 20 percent payable on applications, was oversubscribed. These new shares were not authorized since they were issued before annuitants had converted—a practice described at the time as "selling the bear's skin" before they had killed the bear.

During 1720 Blunt took further steps to raise the market price and so make the conversion offer even more attractive to annuitants. The company bought £2 million of its own shares and lent the subscription monies received from the sale of the 20,000 new shares to shareholders so that they could purchase yet more South Sea shares. In May 1720, the annuitants were each offered terms of £500 in South Sea bonds and cash plus seven South Sea shares currently selling for £400, an offer so attractive most annuitants accepted and the stock rose to £800. The company offered a further 50,000 shares at £1,000 each, only 10 percent payable on subscription, which sold within two days. The £5 million when received was also lent to shareholders, advancing the stock on June 24 to £1,050.

But this spectacular success had encouraged imitators since 1719, promoters who, unaware that South Sea directors were rigging the stock, reasoned the factors in the South Sea success were: a company with very large capital, an impressive though vague purpose, promises of large profits, and, lastly, a small proportion of the par value payable on subscription. About 190 so called "Bubble" companies were floated, all with outrageously large capitals and grand objectives but a small initial payment per share. For example, the company For Improving the Royal Fishery, capitalized at £10 million, was fully subscribed in two days. In comparison, the Bank of England's capital was only £5.5 million. One promotion was even for "a Company for carrying on an undertaking of Great Advantage but no one to know what it is."

Companies could be created only by Royal Charter or act of Parliament; since most of the Bubble companies had neither, they were illegal. A concerned government in 1719 passed the famous Bubble Act, to operate from June 1720, which made it clear that unchartered joint stock companies had no legal existence. In August 1720, the South Sea directors, worried that these competitors were syphoning off funds needed for their new issues, persuaded the government to enforce the Bubble Act against the companies it considered to be its main competitors for investors' money. This certainly caused the collapse of the Bubbles, but, since many investors had purchased shares on margin in a number of companies, all share prices plummeted, including South Sea stock. Widespread financial distress followed, for which the outraged public blamed South Sea directors. This led to a parliamentary investigation of the company.

The subsequent inquest revealed that to gain support for the right to convert government debt, the company had paid bribes exceeding £1.25 million to 122 members of the House of Lords and 62 members of Parliament. The bribes were distributed through a special book kept by the company in which were recorded sales of stock to members. No money was ever received, and the stock was never actually delivered. The company merely waited until the market price had risen sufficiently and then paid out as a bribe the difference in the price the parliamentarian had supposedly paid and the current price. Included among the bribe takers were four leading members of the government, including the Chancellor of the Exchequer. Both the South Sea directors and those bribed were punished by having major portions of their estates confiscated. The parliamentary investigation produced the first British audit report, written by Charles Snell.

After the crash, the belief that a company could create economic wealth with no more than a very large capital and a worthy object was replaced by a distrust of joint-stock companies in general, so it became difficult to form a new company in Britain until the Bubble Act was repealed in 1825. The South Sea Company continued, still not trading, until 1854, when it was liquidated by converting its capital into government stock.

J. Bruce Tabb

Bibliography

An Act to Restrain the Extravagant and Unwarrantable Practices of Raising Money by Voluntary Subscriptions for Carrying on Projects Dangerous to the Trade and Subjects of the Kingdom [The Bubble Act of 1720]. 6 George I, c. 18.

Carswell, J. *The South Sea Bubble.* London: The Cresset Press, 1960.

Cowles, V. *The Great Swindle: The Story of the South Sea Bubble.* New York: Harper & Brothers, 1960.

Dubois, A.B. *The English Business Company after the Bubble Act 1720–1800.* New York: The Commonwealth Fund, 1938.

Scott, W.R. *The Constitution and Finance of English, Scottish, and Irish Joint-Stock Companies to 1720.* Vols. 1, 3. Cambridge: Cambridge University Press, 1912.

Worthington, B. *Professional Accountants.* New York: Arno Press, 1978.

See also BALANCE SHEET; CORPORATIONS: EVOLUTION; LIMITED LIABILITY; PARTNERSHIP ACCOUNTING; SNELL, CHARLES

Spacek, Leonard (1907–)

An accounting practitioner, relentless and forthright in challenging tradition, Leonard Spacek became managing partner of Arthur Andersen and Company in 1947, after the unexpected death of Arthur Andersen. In fact, the surviving partners had voted to dissolve the firm. There were philosophical differences between partners in Chicago and New York. Andersen's son was not acceptable to the partners as a successor to the founder. And there was the problem of finding a way to purchase Arthur Andersen's 50 percent interest in the firm from his estate. That alone would require more than $1.7 million at a time when the firm's total capital was less than $1.5 million.

Spacek was equal to the challenge. In the process of rescuing and reviving Arthur Andersen and Company, he also institutionalized, and significantly changed, the firm. One of Spacek's earliest contributions to remolding Arthur Andersen and Company was his attention to what was first called the Administrative Services Division—accountants who helped their clients improve their business systems. In those days, primitive mechanized information systems depended largely on punched-card equipment. It was Spacek who insisted, over the objections of the nation's leading computer manufacturers, that electronic computers could be adapted for economical business use. He personally recruited men who had learned about computers during World War II, and he challenged them to apply computers to business use. Spacek also allocated one-third of the partners' profits to personnel development and training.

Another contribution was his spearheading the firm's expansion into Europe, Latin America, and, eventually, the rest of the world, creating a new organizational structure in the process. Other firms—primarily those that had originated in England and Scotland—had created international networks of national firms that agreed to serve local operations of companies headquartered elsewhere. Spacek saw such networks as nothing more than "franchises" and rejected that organizational concept. He insisted that the only way he could control the quality of the work his firm's clients received outside the United States was to control the firms that provided the service. So he rejected loose alliances with various non-U.S. firms and set up Arthur Andersen and Company offices wherever needed to serve the firm's U.S. clients. To this day, other large international firms operate worldwide networks of loosely affiliated firms, while the Arthur Andersen Worldwide Organization comprises fully integrated member firms throughout the world. By the time he retired in 1973, the firm had grown from 20th in size among U.S. professional firms to ranking with the Big Eight, the giants of the accounting establishment.

To Spacek's way of thinking, quality service to clients demanded the application of ac-counting principles, applied across the board, and based on the fundamental principle of fairness to all parties: labor, management, consumers, investors, and the public at large. In 1957 he visualized an Accounting Court as the appropriate forum for discussion as to whether or not an accounting principle met the fairness test, with decisions handed down by a judge. This idea had been germinating since the mid-1930s, when he first started testifying in the utility field. Worried at that time that his lack of a college education might adversely affect his courtroom performance, he bought an entire set, some 200 volumes, of U.S. Supreme Court decisions and started working his way through them. He thus became convinced that accounting principles could be laid down through the same reasoning process that lawyers followed from case precedent.

Spacek promoted accounting reforms, mainly through speeches, which attracted the attention of the press by their language and the use of metaphor. Among the various issues he took on were railroad accounting, price-level adjustments, and off-balance sheet financing. In 1957 his severe criticism of the Interstate Commerce Commission's (ICC) unwillingness to allow railroads to record track depreciation and deferred taxes, and allegations that the Committee on Accounting Procedure (CAP) had yielded to ICC pressure, set him seriously at odds with the American Institute of Certified Public Accountants (AICPA). Five years passed before the ICC, in 1962, permitted the railroads to use generally accepted accounting principles (GAAP) in financial reporting, but by this time the poor financial condition of many of them, which could have been disclosed earlier, was largely beyond salvaging. Spacek's proposal for price-level-adjusted financial reporting to draw attention to phantom profits, as he put it, and the need to identify and eliminate inflation, filed in a petition to the Securities and Exchange Commission, was rejected in 1954. The Financial Accounting Standards Board (FASB) finally acted on this topic in 1979 when it issued Statement No. 33, "Financial Reporting and Changing Prices." Spacek had more success with his arguments for reporting on the balance sheet the true financial significance of some sale and leaseback transactions. In 1964, when he was a member of the Accounting Principles Board (APB), the standard-setting body adopted Opinion No. 5, "Financial Reporting of Leases in Financial Statements of

Lessees" (1964), the first of a number of lease-related standards.

Spacek's background is an Horatio Alger story. Born to a poor family, he completed his high school degree through night classes and subsequently studied accounting by correspondence while working at a second job as a switchboard operator. He held an accounting position with the Iowa Electric Light and Power Company, his employer in both jobs. He then joined the auditors of that company, Arthur Andersen and Company, in 1928 as a utilities specialist. Spacek was a member of the APB from 1960 to 1965. In 1986 he was awarded the Hourglass Award of the Academy of Accounting Historians for his book and videotape titled *The Growth of Arthur Andersen & Co. 1928–73, an Oral History.*

While much has changed since Spacek's days, notably a general reluctance to take sides on debatable issues, Spacek's integrity, and the vigor with which he pursued what he thought to be right for the profession and the public it serves, should provide a role model for the new generation of professionals today.

Maureen Berry
John A. Ruane

Bibliography

Arthur Andersen & Co. *The First Sixty Years, 1913–1973.* Chicago: Arthur Andersen & Co., 1974.
———. *A Search for Fairness in Financial Reporting to the Public.* Chicago: Arthur Andersen & Co., 1969.
Arthur Andersen Worldwide Organization. *Vision of Grandeur.* Chicago: Arthur Andersen & Co., 1988.
Berry, M.H. "Leonard Paul Spacek." In *Biographies of Notable Accountants.* 2d ed., edited by A.M. Agami, pp. 37–40. New York: Random House, 1989.
Hall, W.D. *Accounting and Auditing: Thoughts on Forty Years in Practice and Education.* Chicago: Arthur Andersen & Co., 1987.
Zeff, S.A. "Leaders of the Accounting Profession: Fourteen Who Made a Difference," *Journal of Accountancy,* May 1987, pp. 46–71.

See also ACADEMY OF ACCOUNTING HISTORIANS; ACCOUNTING HALL OF FAME; ACCOUNTING PRINCIPLES BOARD; ACCOUNTING RESEARCH BULLETINS; AMERICAN INSTITUTE OF CERTIFIED PUBLIC ACCOUNTANTS; ANDERSEN, ARTHUR E.; BIG EIGHT ACCOUNTING FIRMS; COMPUTING TECHNOLOGY IN THE WEST: THE IMPACT ON THE PROFESSION OF ACCOUNTING; FINANCIAL ACCOUNTING STANDARDS BOARD; GENERALLY ACCEPTED ACCOUNTING PRINCIPLES; INFLATION ACCOUNTING; MANAGEMENT ADVISORY SERVICES BY CPAS; POSTULATES OF ACCOUNTING; RAILROAD ACCOUNTING (U.S.); ZEFF, STEPHEN A.

Spain

There are five stages in the evolution of accounting in Spain: (1) the premodern stage, before the introduction of the double entry system, up to the end of the fifteenth century; (2) the introduction and diffusion of double entry bookkeeping, fifteenth and sixteenth centuries; (3) the silent period, in which the ancient Castilian tradition of double entry bookkeeping appears to have been forgotten, from the middle of the seventeenth century till the middle of the eighteenth century; (4) the reappearance of references to the double entry system as a novelty imported from France, adopting the French terms and models, from the middle of the eighteenth century till the end of the nineteenth century; and (5) the contemporary period, twentieth century.

Before Double Entry

Before the fifteenth century, account books are known to have existed in Spain, together with some legal provisions referring to various aspects thereof, including some imposing the obligation to keep books. However, there are no known treatises or doctrinal works dealing with accounts or accounting systems. Unfortunately, only very few of the known books of accounts have been studied in detail, and there is a considerable amount of work remaining to be done. Furthermore, there is no evidence that these books were kept by the double entry system; in fact, apparently quite the contrary. The first references to accounting systems and account books in Spain relate to public accounting and to the Kingdom of Aragon, specifically to Catalonia in 1275 and Majorca in 1304, as well as to the Kingdom of Navarre in 1339.

There are regulatory references to private books of accounts. The first of these is possibly contained in the *Código de las Siete Partidas,* promulgated by King Alfonso X the Wise in 1265. The *Cuaderno de Alcabalas,* issued by the Catholic Monarchs in 1484, imposed on traders and shopkeepers the express obligation to keep a book of accounts of their transactions so that the tax agents could verify that the taxes had been correctly calculated. The accounting system to be used in keeping such books was not specified, however. This regulation was transcribed, almost word for word, in the 1491 *Cuaderno de Alcabalas*.

Introduction and Diffusion of the Double Entry System

The fifteenth and sixteenth centuries witnessed the most brilliant moments in the history of accounting in Spain, since it saw the promulgation of the world's oldest legislation obliging merchants, businessmen, and bankers operating in the Kingdom of Castile to keep accounts using the double entry system. This system was also introduced to keep the central accounts of the Castilian Royal Treasury, which was the first case in history of the use of double entry in the public accounting of a large state. Spain's role in spreading double entry must also have been important, although the suggestion by several authors in the past that Spain was the cradle of this system has been discarded. This theory was based on the idea that Spain must have known the Arabic numerals before any other European country, and those commentators considered Arabic numerals to be indispensable for keeping accounts by double entry, but this has no basis in fact.

This period of accounting history in Spain is rich in legal regulations and related aspects. The first important event was the promulgation of two laws, the Pragmatic Sanction of Cigales, dated December 4, 1549, and the Pragmatic Sanction of Madrid, dated March 11, 1552, making it obligatory for all merchants, businessmen, and bankers operating in the Kingdom of Castile to keep books using precisely the double entry system. This is the earliest known legislation of its type that expressly mentions double entry. Evidently, it was not promulgated for the benefit of the merchant class, but to better prevent misappropriation and pursue the extraction of precious metals, given the reliability of the accounting entries using this system.

Many private account books from this period are known, although as with the previous period the vast majority have yet to be studied in depth. The *Real Hacienda* (Royal Treasury) itself also used double entry accounting from an early date. The most impor-

tant event in this context took place in 1580, with the decision to introduce double entry for the central accounts of the Castilian *Real Hacienda*. While this initiative failed, due to the fact that the king was occupied with the incorporation of Portugal into his realm, a second edict was issued and implemented in 1592, and the new *Contaduría del Libro de Caja* (Double Entry Accounting Department) was established. Spain thus became the first great nation to introduce double entry as the central accounting system for its Royal Treasury. Although it did not produce the expected results, this *Contaduría del Libro de Caja* persisted until Felipe IV abolished it on his accession to the throne in 1621.

The *Libro de Caxa y Manual de cuentas de Mercaderes y otras personas, con la declaracion dellos*, by Bartolomé Salvador de Solórzano, printed in Madrid in 1590, was the first and only work on double entry accounting by a Spaniard in this period. It appeared considerably later than other works on the subject in such countries as Italy, Germany, the Netherlands, England, and France, but it is comparable with the best of them.

The Period of Silence

The times of splendor and prestige revealed by the sparse research to date were suddenly eclipsed toward 1640, when a period of silence in accounting matters began. Undoubtedly the lack of knowledge on this period of accounting history is mainly due to the lack of research, since merchants and bankers almost certainly continued with their business and recorded their transactions in their books. A systematic search in archives would probably reveal texts and treatises referring to public and private accounting matters. The long and fruitful Castilian accounting tradition had surprisingly been forgotten, and the double entry system, including the related terminology, was accepted as a novelty imported from France— a curious case of collective cultural amnesia. However, this tradition was not forgotten by the Sephardic Jews who had long been living in the Netherlands, after passing through Portugal. They wrote two books in Spanish about double entry: Jacob de Metz, *Sendero Mercantil* (1697) and Gabriel de Souzo Brito, *Norte Mercantil y Crisol de Cuentas* (1706). These books had no impact on Spanish accounting, as they were generally unknown in Spain.

The Reappearance of References to Double Entry

The period of silence ended with the promulgation in 1737 of the *Ordenanzas* of the *Casa de Contratación de Bilbao* by King Philip V. Chapter 9 of these *Ordenanzas*, which deals with accounting, made it obligatory for all "merchants, traders and wholesalers" to keep at least four books of account: "a *Borrador o Manual* (Journal), a Ledger, a book for charges or invoices, and a book with copies of correspondence." It also stated that these books could be kept by "single or double entry." This was the first time that the term *partida doble* (double entry) was used in Spain instead of the traditional Castilian term for this accounting system: method of *debe y haber* or method of the *libro de Caxa* (Ledger) with its *Manual* (Journal).

The French accounting authors who had great influence on Spanish accounting in the eighteenth and nineteenth centuries were: Matthieu de la Porte, *Le Guide des Negociants & Teneurs de Livres* (1685); Edmond Degrange, Sr., *Le Tenue des Livres Rendue Facile* (1795); J.J. Jaclot, *La Tenue de Livres* (1826); and J.G. Courcelle-Seneuil, *Cours de Comptabilité* (1867) and *Traite Elementaire de Comptabilité* (1869).

The most important authors of this period were: Luis de Luque y Leyva, *Arte de partida doble ilustrado* (1783); Sebastián Jocano y Madaria, *Disertación critica y apologética del arte de llevar cuenta y razón* (1793); José María Brost, *Curso completo de Teneduria de libros, o modo de llevarlos por partida doble* (1825); and Manuel Victor Christantes y Cañedo, *Tratado de cuenta y razón* (1838).

Contemporary Period

Although all periods of Spanish accounting history are lacking in broad and systematic research efforts, the twentieth century is the least studied of all. However, the late 1980s saw the awakening of a vigorous interest in accounting history in academic and professional circles in Spain. An early sign of this interest was the First Seminar on Spanish Accounting History, organized by the University of Seville in May 1990. The inaugural lecture of the Fourth Conference of Accounting Professors, organized by the University of Cantabria in Santander in May 1991, also dealt with a historical subject. The Workshop on the Writing of an Accounting History in Spain was held in the Autonomous University of Madrid in September 1992. The exposition and discussion of papers on this subject were aimed at the Committee for the Study of Accounting History founded within the Spanish Association for Accounting and Business Administration (AECA).

Esteban Hernández-Esteve

Bibliograhy

Gonzalez Ferrando, J.M. "Panorama histórico de las fuentes de la historia de la contabilidad en España, siglos XII (España cristiana) al XVIII." Paper presented at the workshop En Torno a la Elaboración de una Historia de la Contabilidad en España, Miraflores de la Sierra (Madrid), September 24–26, 1992.

Hernández-Esteve, E. *Contribución al estudio de la historiografía contable en España*. Madrid: Banco de España, Servicio de Estudios, 1981.

———. "Origins and Development of Accounting in Spain (from the Thirteenth to the Nineteenth Century)." In *Accounting in Spain 1992*, edited by J.A. Gonzalo. Book prepared for the 15th Annual Congress of the European Accounting Association (EAA). Madrid: Asociación Española de Contabilidad y Administración de Empresas (AECA), 1992.

Mills, P.A., translator. *The Legal Literature of Accounting: "On Accounts" by Diego del Castillo*. New York: Garland, 1988.

Vlaemminck, J.H. *Historia y doctrinas de la contabilidad*, translated, amended, and enlarged by J.M. González Ferrando. Madrid: N.p., 1961.

See also ARABIC NUMERALS; MANORIAL ACCOUNTING; MEDIEVAL ACCOUNTING

Sprague, Charles Ezra (1842–1912)

An accountant, banker, educator, and author, Charles Ezra Sprague had a great deal of influence upon the initial development of the accountancy profession in the United States. He was a multifaceted, multitalented man who had interests in cultures and languages. This influenced his view of accounting. Sprague was the son of a Methodist minister. By the end of his life, Sprague was fluent in 16 languages.

He graduated Phi Beta Kappa from Union College in 1860. Subsequently, he earned a master's degree in 1862 and received an honorary doctorate in 1896 from the same institution. He served with the Union Army in the American Civil War, but left following an injury sustained in the battle of Gettysburg. In 1870 Sprague took a job at the Union Dime Savings Bank in New York City as a clerk. His knowledge of languages was a major reason that he was hired for this job. Thus, his education in accounting began through his interest in languages. He rose through the ranks at the bank; in 1877 he was elected secretary of the bank. During this time, he became a very skilled accountant.

In 1892 he was elected president of the Union Dime Savings Bank and continued in this post until his death. During his career at the bank, he introduced many innovations. Small bank passbooks, small checkbooks, loose-leaf ledgers and a ledger entry posting machine were some of his innovations, and many continue to be used today in some form by the banking industry.

He made frequent trips to Europe to learn more about languages. During these trips, he learned about the practice of accounting in other countries. He was especially impressed with the English system, from which he learned the importance of having procedures in place to recognize accounting professionals. He introduced the system of a board of examiners for public accountants and became one of the first certified public accountants in the state of New York. He served as chairman of the New York Board of Examiners from 1896 until 1898. His frequent trips to Germany during this same time also introduced Sprague to German approaches to accounting, which influenced his later writings in the field.

Sprague was also very concerned about the education of businesspeople. He exerted his influence to establish the New York University School of Commerce, Accounts, and Finance in 1900, and he taught at the school from 1900 until his death in 1912. During this time, he wrote *The Accountancy of Investment* (1904), *Extended Bond Tables* (1905), *Problems and Studies in the Accountancy of Investment* (1906), *Tables of Compound Interest* (1907), *Amortization* (1908), *The Philosophy of Accounts* (1908), and *Logarithms to 12 Places* (1910). Prior to this time, he became involved in the publication of *The Bookkeeper*. He wrote extensively for this publication and was associate editor from 1880–1883.

Although Sprague had great influence on the banking industry, his most important contribution was to the accounting profession. His most important book, *The Philosophy of Accounts*, had a large impact upon the practice of accounting; it went through five editions in less than 15 years. Prior to this book, most of the books on bookkeeping were practice manuals, providing the reader with examples and exercises in bookkeeping. Sprague attempted to explain the "why" rather than just the "how" of accounting. This was a departure from the traditional American or English approach, resembling instead the approach used in Germany.

At this time, the conventional teaching was that each account was treated separately, and there was a debtor and creditor associated with each account. "Debit all that comes in and credit all that goes out" was a familiar phrase. Attempting to follow this single rule, which had no apparent justification, was a confusing process. Sprague emphasized that debit could mean addition in one class of accounts and subtraction in another class of accounts. Debits still equaled credits. However, this relationship did not exist because of some principle. It existed as a means to check for accuracy. In *The Philosophy of Accounts*, Sprague also argued for a new classification of accounts. Prior to his book, accounts were divided into personal and impersonal accounts. Sprague made a simple division: One group included the assets and liabilities, and the second group included the capital and profit-and-loss accounts. A concept first introduced by Sprague in *The Bookkeeper*, assets equal liabilities plus proprietorship (A = L + P), was used to show algebraically the theory of accounts. Thus, Sprague provided the basic organization and theory for bookkeeping.

Sprague made major contributions to accountancy, banking, and education. His influence and work have had a lasting impact on the profession of accountancy. He was recognized posthumously with election to Ohio State University's Accounting Hall of Fame in 1953.

Rodney K. Rogers

Bibliography

Burns, T.J., and E.N. Coffman. *The Accounting Hall of Fame: Profiles of Fifty Members*. Columbus: College of Business, Ohio State University, 1991.

Graves, O.F. "Charles Ezra Sprague, 1842–1912." In *Biographies of Notable Ac-*

countants. 2d ed., edited by A.M. Agami, pp. 41–43. New York: Random House, 1989.

Zeff, S.A. "Leaders of the Accounting Profession: Fourteen Who Made a Difference," *Journal of Accountancy*, May 1987, pp. 68–70.

See also ACCOUNTING EDUCATION IN THE UNITED STATES; ACCOUNTING HALL OF FAME; BENTLEY, HARRY CLARK; CAPITAL ACCOUNT; CERTIFIED PUBLIC ACCOUNTANT; CERTIFIED PUBLIC ACCOUNTANT EXAMINATION: THE EARLY YEARS (1896–1930); COMPOUND INTEREST; CONCEPTUAL FRAMEWORK; DEBIT AND CREDIT; DISCOUNTED CASH FLOW; GERMANY; LEDGER; PACKARD, SILAS SADLER; PROPRIETARY THEORY; SUBSIDIARY LEDGER; WILDMAN, JOHN RAYMOND; ZEFF, STEPHEN A.

Springer v. United States

America's first federal income tax was a war measure passed in 1861. It was so badly drafted that it never became operative, and in 1862 Congress replaced it with a more workable law. Despite lack of adequate enforcement machinery, the tax was financially successful, producing $347 million in 11 years, including one-fifth of all federal internal revenues during the Civil War. The Supreme Court upheld the constitutionality of this Civil War income tax in *Collector v. Hubbard* (1870) and *Springer v. United States* (1881).

Michael Chatfield

Bibliography
Collector v. Hubbard, 12 Wall. 1 (1870).
Springer v. United States, 102 U.S. 586 (1881).

See also INCOME TAXATION IN THE UNITED STATES; SIXTEENTH AMENDMENT

Standard Costing

Standard costing is defined by Eric Louis Kohler in his *A Dictionary for Accountants* (1970) as "a forecast or predetermination of what actual costs should be under projected conditions, serving as a basis of cost control and as a measure of productive efficiency (or standard of comparison) when ultimately aligned against actual cost." While definitely a child of the twentieth century, standard cost-ing had its roots in the preceding century and is at a crossroads as the twenty-first century nears.

Frederic William Cronhelm, an English accounting writer, in 1818 in *Double Entry by Single,* stressed a system of control of inventories that would enable an estimation of material cost. Charles Babbage, an English engineer, economist, and the "father of computers," in 1832 in *On the Economy of Machinery and Manufacturers,* recognized the importance of time study to establish an estimate of direct-labor costs for a job. The American Captain Henry Metcalfe in 1885 in *The Cost of Manufactures and Administration of Workshops, Public and Private,* developed a job-order cost system. G.P. Norton, an Englishman, in 1889 in *Textile Manufacturers' Bookkeeping*, developed a process-cost system, while in 1887, Emile Garcke and J.M. Fells, both from England, called for the complete integration of costs accounts and the financial records in their *Factory Accounts.* Alexander Hamilton Church, then in England and subsequently in the United States, in 1901 developed a system for overhead-burden accounting and, with it, a concept of idle-time accounting for machinery in a series of articles in the *Engineering Magazine.* Frederick Winslow Taylor, an American industrial engineer, in 1903 published in the *Transactions of the American Society of Mechanical Engineers* a long paper, "Shop Management," that summarized his long-time work on standardization in manufacturing. John Whitmore, an American accountant and a disciple of Church, in 1908 published an article describing the mechanics—the difference between standard and actual costs—in a general journal of variances. The last key player in this early era was Harrington Emerson, an efficiency engineer and early popularizer of scientific management. In *The Twelve Principles of Efficiency* (1912), the last of his principles, efficiency reward, stressed the development of, and continuous changes in, time standards and wage rates. Emerson relegated accounting to a minor role, record keeping, in his quest for efficiency. This quest was centered on standardization to eliminate waste.

The stage was set for the "father of standard costing," G. Charter Harrison. He was an English chartered accountant who came to the United States in 1907 and had significant manufacturing experience. Harrison was clearly a disciple of Emerson and wanted to place accounting into the efficiency movement by the use of standard costing. Harrison in 1921 wrote his classic book, *Cost Accounting to Aid Production: A Practical Study of Scientific Cost Accounting*. His goal was to revolutionize cost accounting by bringing to it the broad concept of scientific management so as to go from retrospective behavior based on the records of the past to prospective behavior based on predictions of the future. Harrison felt this task should be done by an accountant, not an engineer, as an engineer in accounting is about as useful as an accountant in engineering. Harrison called for the daily reporting of both payroll and machine data. The "principle of exceptions" was expressed as "the concentration of attention to the abnormal and unfavorable condition and the spending of no more time on the normal than is necessary to establish the fact of its being normal." Harrison believed that standard costing could be simplified from complex conditions. He was interested in determining the causes of inefficiencies. Accountants were to be in control of the actual design of the cost system and its forms, as well as the keeping of records. However, the accounting department was not to set operating standards. Harrison developed operating guidelines for a sample standard-costing system, including revised standards for the determination of operating efficiencies to bring them into line with current operating standards. Harrison envisaged a coordination between the scientific planning and dispatching of work with the standard-costing system.

Another champion of standard costing was Eric A. Camman from Peat, Marwick, Mitchell and Company. He was more interested in the debits/credits of the topic than was Harrison. Camman wrote about an age-old dilemma of standard costing: Does one change standards to reflect current operating conditions or does one keep the standard at the former operating conditions so as to draw comparison with times past? If the production process is changed, however, the standards must be changed.

Both Harrison and Camman wrote more explicit texts on standard costing in the early 1930s, as did Cecil Merle Gillespie, a professor of accounting at Northwestern University, in 1935. Standard costing became a component of books on cost accounting during that time. Stanley B. Henrici, an American expert in standard costing, published the first edition of his book on standard costing, *Standard Costs for Manufacturing*, in 1947. The NACA (National Association of Cost Accountants, now Institute of Management Accountants) published five research monographs on standard costing in 1948 and one in 1952, all subsequently reprinted in one publication, *Standard Costs and Variance Analysis*. The NACA was an early supporter and promulgator of articles and papers on standard costing from its inception in 1919. The reprint illustrates how timeless the issues concerning standard costs are. Furthermore, these issues need to be continually placed before anyone studying the topic. The first issue is that any important decision made without a predetermination of costs is gambling and not managing. The second is that controllability of indirect cost calls for a flexible budget. The third is the level of "tightness" of the standard—ideal, attainable, average, and normal. The NACA team recommended "that the type of standard most effective in control of costs is one which represents an attainable level of good performance." The fourth issue is revision of standards with the trade-off of clerical cost versus up-to-date information. The fifth is the use of standard costs for inventory valuation. The sixth is the relationship, if any, between standards and budgets; the seventh, between standards and prices. The eighth is the number of overhead variances. The ninth is the difficulties present when there are many small orders in process; and the tenth how to determine and report the causes of the variances.

The topic of standard costing came under review in a much more probabilistic or statistical sense in accounting literature in the 1960s and 1970s. Zannetos (1964) placed variance analysis into a probabilistic framework utilizing a statistical procedure used in quality-control analysis. An excellent review of such literature was done by Kaplan (1975), who also provided an action plan for various time intervals. Miller and O'Leary (1987) placed the standard-costing process into a power perspective with the organizational goal of furthering the control of employees. By the end of the 1980s, standard costing was under attack as the United States was coming to grips with its inability to compete with Japan. Standard costing in Japan tends to be utilized more for financial accounting purposes than for control purposes, as reported by Sakurai and Huang (1989). This is especially true as there are fewer and fewer direct laborers. Target costing seemed to motivate managers to achieve cost

S

reduction. The proposed selling price minus profit per unit becomes the target cost figure to be attained by new efficiencies. Another 1989 survey of five U.S. manufacturers by McNair, Mosconi, and Norris indicated a dissatisfaction with standard costing in a JIT (Just-in-Time) environment. The JIT goal of continuous improvement is felt to be achieved better by the rolling average of job costs than by an inefficient and inflexible standard-cost system. This is especially true as indirect costs, which were formerly allocated, are traded to cost drivers. As companies move from a material-control system based on a storeroom, material-usage variances cannot be assigned at point of issue. Such companies are much closer to a process-cost environment than a job-order environment.

It is all too easy to forget the importance of a sound engineering estimate of what a unit, given a meaningful economic lot size, should cost. The standard-cost card appears to have been somewhat forgotten as a holistic control device in accounting. As indirect costs (overhead) become more associated with cost drivers, the standardization process, which includes standard costing, becomes even more crucial. What is needed for the topic of standard costing is a champion to bring it from the early 1950s into the year 2000. Writers like Harrison, Camman, and Henrici are needed again to analyze the less than ideal world of many different small jobs in a plant in which management has the intention of getting good information at a low clerical cost through the use of computers. Standard costing should also be studied behaviorally. If standard costing does not get this rebirth, it may wither away, which would be an unfortunate event for accounting and for the economy.

Richard Vangermeersch

Bibliography

Camman, E.A. "Standard Costs: Installation and Procedure." In *International Congress of Accounting 1929*. New York: 1930.

Emerson, H. *The Twelve Principles of Efficiency*. New York: Engineering Magazine, 1912.

Gillespie, C.M. *Accounting Procedure for Standard Costs*. New York: Ronald Press, 1935.

Harrison, G.C. "Fundamentals of Standard Costs." In *International Congress of Accounting 1929*. New York: 1930.

Henrici, S.B. *Standard Costs for Manufacturing*. New York: McGraw-Hill, 1947.

Kaplan, R.S. "The Significance and Investigation of Cost Variances: Survey and Extensions," *Journal of Accounting Research*, Autumn 1975, pp. 311–337.

Kranowiski, N. "The Historical Development of Standard Costing Systems until 1920." Working paper No. 32 in *Working Paper Series Volume 2*, edited by E.N. Coffman. Richmond, VA: Academy of Accounting Historians, 1979.

McNair, C.J., W. Mosconi, and T. Norris. *Beyond the Bottom Line: Measuring World Class Performance*. The Coopers & Lybrand Performance Solutions Series. In conjunction with the National Association of Accountants. Homewood, IL: Dow Jones-Irwin, 1989.

Miller, P., and T. O'Leary. "Accounting and the Construction of the Governable Person," *Accounting, Organizations, and Society*, vol. 12, no. 3, 1987, pp. 235–265.

National Association of Accountants. *Standard Costs and Variance Analysis*. An NAA Classic. Montvale, NJ: National Association of Accountants, undated.

Sakurai, M., and P.Y. Huang. "A Japanese Survey of Factory Automation and Its Impact on Management Control Systems." In *Japanese Management Accounting: A World Class Approach to Profit Management*, edited by Y. Monden and M. Sakurai. Cambridge, MA: Productivity Press, 1989.

Sowell, E.M. *The Evolution of the Theories and Techniques of Standard Costs*. University, AL: The University of Alabama Press, 1973.

Whitmore, J. "Shoe Factory Costs," *Journal of Accountancy*, May 1908, pp. 12–25.

Zannetos, Z.S. "Standard Costs as a First Step to Probabilistic Control: A Theoretical Justification and Extension and Implications," *Accounting Review*, April 1964, pp. 296–304.

See also ACTIVITY BASED COSTING; BABBAGE, CHARLES; BIG EIGHT ACCOUNTING FIRMS; BROWN, F. DONALDSON; BUDGETING; CHURCH, ALEXANDER HAMILTON; COMMON COSTS; CONTROL: CLASSICAL MODEL; COST AND/OR MANAGEMENT ACCOUNTING;

CRONHELM, FREDERIC WILLIAM; EMERSON, HARRINGTON; ENGINEERING AND ACCOUNTING; GANTT, HENRY LAURENCE; GARCKE AND FELLS; GERMANY; HARRISON, G. CHARTER; INSTITUTE OF MANAGEMENT ACCOUNTANTS; JUST-IN-TIME MANUFACTURING; MANAGEMENT ACCOUNTING; METCALFE, HENRY; TAYLOR, FREDERICK WINSLOW; WHITMORE, JOHN

State and Local Governments (U.S., 1901–1991)

There appears to be no record of any organized effort to develop and publicize accounting and financial-reporting standards for local governments in the United States until 1901 when the National Municipal League formed a Committee on Uniform Municipal Accounting and Statistics. Efforts of the National Municipal League are said to have contributed to the enactment by the state of New York in 1904 of legislation requiring uniform reporting by cities within the state.

The first truly national organization dedicated to developing principles and standards of municipal accounting, to developing standard classifications and terminology for municipal reports, and to promoting the recognition and use of those standards was called the National Committee on Municipal Accounting (NCMA). The NCMA, formed in 1934, was a committee made up of the chairmen of committees of organizations of governmental finance officers, public administrators, independent auditors, and accounting professors. The objective of the NCMA was to develop an integrated accounting and reporting system to serve the needs of internal users as well as external users. Consequently, the NCMA's pronouncements dealt with interim reports as well as year-end reports, and with information considered useful for reporting to citizens.

The leadership of the NCMA believed that general acceptance of its pronouncements would be promoted if it followed what is now called a "due process procedure." Preliminary drafts of all publications were first prepared by the committee staff, then submitted for public exposure to the entire committee, to members of the advisory committees of sponsoring organizations, and to other public officials, accountants, and interested citizens. Thus, the final draft of the committee's publications reflected the coordinated ideas of individuals and groups with varied interests and experiences. Although

the due process procedure was time-consuming, NCMA Bulletin No. 1, "Principles of Municipal Accounting," was published in 1934.

The first two principles listed in NCMA Bulletin No. 1 were (1) the Organization Principle: "the accounts should be centralized under the direction of one officer . . . who should be responsible for preparing all financial reports"; and (2) the General Ledger Principle: "the general accounting system should be on a double entry basis, with a general ledger in which all financial transactions are recorded in detail or in summary. Additional subsidiary records should be kept where necessary." In the 1942 edition of Lloyd Morey and Robert P. Hackett's *Fundamentals of Governmental Accounting*, Morey, initial vice chairman of the NCMA, commented: "In the present stage of the advancement of accounting, it would hardly seem necessary to state that the double entry basis is essential. However, doubtless because of the incompleteness and primitive character of the records of many governmental bodies, particularly the smaller units, this basic stipulation has been included by the committee."

The NCMA became inactive during World War II; after the war it was reactivated, and its membership was broadened to include representatives of organizations interested in improving accounting and financial reporting for state governments. Its name was changed in 1948 to the National Committee on Governmental Accounting (NCGA).

The NCGA held annual meetings in conjunction with the Municipal Finance Officers Association (MFOA) annual meetings. In order to increase participation in the standards-setting process, the NCGA's annual meetings were open to anyone who wanted to attend. The NCGA operated under an Executive Committee and, for major projects, employed consultants. The executive director of the MFOA served as secretary to the National Committee. This organization of volunteers, all doing NCGA work as an overload on top of their full-time jobs, and all representing other organizations that had to ratify tentative decisions made by the Committee before pronouncements became final, was amazingly productive. Between 1949 and 1968, it published 18 pronouncements, culminating in the 1968 *Governmental Accounting, Auditing, and Financial Reporting* (GAAFR), which was accepted by independent CPAs as an authoritative statement of generally accepted accounting principles (GAAP) for state and local governments.

The NCGA continued to be concerned with managerial uses of financial information and the reporting to the general public, but it gave more explicit attention to the needs of legislative and governing bodies of the reporting entity and of superior jurisdictions. The 1968 GAAFR does not mention the "Organization Principle" nor the "General Ledger Principle." It placed demonstration of legal compliance ahead of conformity with GAAP in its statement of "Basic Principles."

In 1973 the National Committee was replaced by the National Council (still the same initials: NCGA) of 21 members elected as individuals experienced as governmental finance officers, independent auditors, academicians, and as serious users of governmental financial reports. The National Council's first official pronouncement was its Statement No. 1, "Governmental Accounting and Financial Reporting Principles" in 1979, which was intended to be a "modest revision to update, clarify, amplify, and reorder" the principles set forth in 1968 GAAFR to incorporate "pertinent aspects" of the American Institute of Certified Public Accountants' (AICPA) 1974 *Audits of State and Local Governmental Units* (ASLGU).

NCGA Statement No. 1, and the other six statements issued between 1979 and early 1984, were heavily influenced by the practicing CPAs who, in turn, were influenced by the activities of the Financial Accounting Standards Board (FASB). Accordingly, the National Council's pronouncements emphasized general-purpose external financial reporting and the need for general-purpose financial statements to conform with GAAP. Legal-compliance reporting was admitted to be essential, but financial statements "prepared to reflect legal provisions or other criteria different from GAAP" were considered to be "special reports," as defined in AICPA auditing standards. Thus, the emphasis of the National Council was the reverse of that of the National Committee.

The 1968 GAAFR illustrated combined financial statements but stressed the importance of individual fund and account group financial statements. Accordingly, the examples of independent auditor's reports illustrated in the 1974 ASLGU related the auditor's opinion to the financial statements of the various funds and account groups. NCGA Statement No. 1 changed the reporting focus to the general-purpose financial statements (GPFS), and the AICPA consequently amended the independent auditor's reports examples in the 1974 ASLGU to show that the auditor's opinion related to the GPFS. Subsequent editions of *ASLGU*, and related Statements of Position (SOP), continue to stress that the reporting focus is on the general-purpose financial statements.

Although the pronouncements of the NCGA were generally accepted as authoritative by CPA firms, the Council of the AICPA had not required that members of the AICPA consider NCGA statements and interpretations as statements of generally accepted accounting principles. In order to place GAAP for state and local governments on a par with Financial Accounting Standards Board (FASB) statements for business organizations, the Governmental Accounting Standards Board (GASB) was formed in 1984; the NCGA became inactive at that time. GASB Statement No. 1, "Authoritative Status of NCGA Pronouncements and AICPA Industry Audit Guides," was issued in 1984 to affirm the authoritative status of NCGA pronouncements and the AICPA *Audits of State and Local Governmental Units* until amended or superseded by subsequent GASB pronouncements.

The mission statement of the GASB emphasizes that financial reporting by state and local governments plays a major role in fulfilling government's duty to be accountable to citizens, legislative and oversight bodies, and those who participate in the process of financing governments. The GASB mission statement also emphasizes that governmental financial reports should provide information needed by users to make social and political decisions, as well as economic decisions. Financial-reporting standards promulgated by the GASB are intended to be consistent with the broad concept of financial reporting embodied in the GASB mission statement.

Leon E. Hay

Bibliography

Figlewicz, R.E., D.T. Anderson, and C.D. Strupek. "The Evolution and Current State of Financial Accounting Concepts and Standards in the Nonbusiness Sector," *Accounting Historians Journal*, Spring 1985, pp. 73–98.

Hackett, R.P. "Recent Developments in Governmental and Institutional Accounting," *Accounting Review*, June 1933, pp. 122–127.

Morey, L. "Principles of Municipal Accounting," *Accounting Review*, December 1934, pp. 319–325.

———. "Trends in Governmental Accounting," *Accounting Review*, July 1948, pp. 227–234.

Potts, J.H. "The Evolution of Municipal Accounting in the United States, 1900–1935," *Business History Review*, Winter 1978, pp. 518–536.

Remis, J.S. "Governmental Accounting Standards—A Historical Perspective." In A.R. Drebin, J.L. Chan, and L.C. Ferguson, *Objectives of Accounting and Financial Reporting for Governmental Units: A Research Study*, vol. 2, pp. 1–1 to 1–22. Chicago: National Council on Governmental Accounting, 1981.

See also GENERALLY ACCEPTED ACCOUNTING PRINCIPLES; UNIFORMITY

State Regulation of the Accountancy Profession (U.S.)

With the passage of the first certified public accountant law in New York State in 1896, the accountancy profession began a process that led to the enactment of licensing laws in each state, granting statutory recognition to CPAs. These laws have established boards of accountancy in 54 jurisdictions. The boards are commonly called state boards of accountancy. All accountancy statutes provide that the membership of the board of accountancy includes certified public accountants. The statutes of most states provide also for board membership by other licensed accountants and public or consumer representatives. Board members are appointed by the governor for terms varying in length from about three years to six years.

The function of a state board of accountancy is to protect the public interest by regulating the practice of public accountancy within the borders of the state. Toward this end, states have found it useful to limit the expression of an opinion on financial statements (sometimes called the attest function) to those persons whom the states regulate. The state board issues a CPA certificate to candidates who have passed the CPA examination, who have met certain educational requirements, and who, in most states, have met the board's requirements for practical experience.

State accountancy laws provide for endorsement of certificates issued by other states. This action is frequently referred to by such terms as reciprocal recognition or reciprocity.

Typically, the law provides for the issuance of a certificate to a holder of a certificate of another state upon a demonstration that the qualifications for the other state's certificate were comparable to those of the state where the certificate is to be issued.

The state board is authorized to set standards of professional conduct of its licensees and to take disciplinary action for violations of the public accountancy laws and regulations. In most states, the board is also authorized to take legal action against those who improperly hold themselves out as licensees.

A state board also has a responsibility to provide assurance to the public that all of its licensees maintain minimum standards of competence. In recent years, toward accomplishment of this objective, almost all state boards have required each licensee to complete a program of continuing professional education as a condition for renewal of his or her license. The *Uniform Accountancy Act*, a model statute published in 1992 that states are urged to adopt, would enable a state board to require a public accounting firm, as a condition for renewal of its permit to practice, to undergo periodic quality reviews—that is, independent reviews of the firm's professional work. Some state boards already mandate participation in such programs. The *Uniform Accountancy Act* would allow a firm to comply with the requirement by showing that it has undergone a quality review that is a satisfactory equivalent to the quality review required under the act. The act would require that the equivalent quality review be subject to oversight by a body established or sanctioned by the board. Thus, many firms may be able to comply with the state board's requirements by participating in the quality-review program of a professional association.

A number of professional accounting associations have undertaken programs for purposes of self-regulation of their members. The most prominent of these associations are the American Institute of Certified Public Accountants (AICPA) and the state societies of CPAs. Important characteristics of self-regulation are that members of the association complete a continuing professional education requirement and that individuals in public practice be associated with firms that participate in programs that review the quality of their professional practice. These requirements are established in the public interest so as to provide for standards of competence on the part of the members of the association. Of course, only the members of the association are subject to these requirements.

The National Association of State Boards of Accountancy (NASBA) is the national voluntary organization of the 54 boards of accountancy. The NASBA's mission is to enhance the effectiveness of state boards in meeting their regulatory responsibilities. The NASBA's principal functions are to seek to clarify issues facing state boards of accountancy, build consensus among state boards on selective issues affecting the regulation of public accountancy, and be a proponent of specific positions on major issues affecting state boards of accountancy.

The NASBA was established in October 1908 as the National Association of CPA Examiners. The association recognized early the need for uniformity among states and began to deal with the emerging problems of the interstate nature of public accountancy. Although each state board has statutory responsibility for the conduct of an examination of candidates for the CPA certificate, in 1917 the association encouraged state boards to use the membership examination of the American Institute of Accountants, now the AICPA, as their licensing examination. Since 1962 all state boards have used the Uniform CPA Examination and Advisory Grading Service of the AICPA.

In 1978 the NASBA established the CPA Examination Review Board, through which it conducts an annual review of the Uniform CPA Examination on behalf of NASBA member state boards. The program is designed to help ensure the integrity and credibility of the CPA examination process and to assist the state boards in fulfilling their statutory responsibilities for the examination. Each year the CPA Examination Review Board, appointed by the NASBA's Board of Directors, reports to the state boards on the appropriateness of the construction, grading, administration, and security of the Uniform CPA Examination.

Another means by which the NASBA provides assistance to the state boards is the publication of model accountancy legislation. In November 1984, the NASBA and the AICPA jointly published a *Model Public Accountancy Bill*. As stated in the introductory comments of the bill, the need for interstate mobility and maintenance of high minimum standards of competence in the public interest requires uniform licensing qualifications, insofar as possible, among the states. The model bill was offered toward the fulfillment of this need.

A revised edition of the model bill was approved in 1992 by the boards of directors of the NASBA and the AICPA. The 1984 model bill has been renamed the *Uniform Accountancy Act* (UAA). It updates the 1984 model bill to reflect current standards of education and experience and to address other current issues such as tort reform. The UAA is designed to advance the goal of uniformity, protect the public interest, and promote high professional standards. As stated in the introductory comments, uniformity in accountancy regulation will become even more essential in the future as international agreements such as the U.S.-Canada Free Trade Agreement and the European Mutual Recognition Directive continue to be adopted, causing the accounting profession to adopt a global focus.

Wilbert H. Schwotzer
James E. Thomashower

Bibliography

CPA Candidate Performance on the Uniform CPA Examination. An Annual Publication. New York: NASBA.

Digest of State Accountancy Laws and State Board Regulations. New York: AICPA and NASBA, 1992.

Information for CPA Candidates. 10th ed. New York: AICPA, 1991.

Model Public Accountancy Bill. New York: AICPA and NASBA, 1984.

NASBA: A Review of the History, Organization, Accomplishments, Policies and Other Activities of the National Association of State Boards of Accountancy. New York: NASBA, 1973.

Olson, W.E. *The Accounting Profession: The Years of Trial, 1969–1980.* New York: AICPA, 1982.

Rimerman, T.W., and J.P. Solomon. "Uniformity of Regulation: The Time is Now," *Journal of Accountancy,* April 1991, pp. 69–72.

The State Board Report, a Digest of Current Developments Affecting State Accountancy Regulation. A Monthly Newsletter. New York: NASBA.

Uniform Accountancy Act, Designed to Update the 1984 Model Public Accountancy Bill. New York: AICPA and NASBA, 1992.

Van Rensselaer, W.H. "State Boards of Accountancy: The Guardians of Self-Regulation," *CPA Journal,* May 1986, pp. 12, 14.

See also AMERICAN INSTITUTE OF CERTIFIED PUBLIC ACCOUNTANTS; CERTIFIED PUBLIC ACCOUNTANT; CERTIFIED PUBLIC ACCOUNTANT EXAMINATION: THE EARLY YEARS (1896–1930); ETHICS, PROFESSIONAL

Statistical Sampling

The Development of Probability Proportional to Size Sampling and the Audit-Risk Model: A Focus on Kenneth W. Stringer

In 1957 the accounting firm of Haskins and Sells assigned Kenneth W. Stringer to its executive office to assist in the research efforts of the firm. Stringer was dissatisfied with the lack of authoritative auditing guidelines concerning the extent of testing and the selection process. He believed that in similar audit situations there existed an unjustifiably wide variation in the extent of testing prescribed by various auditors.

Stringer first reviewed existing methods of statistical sampling, which included acceptance sampling, discovery sampling, and estimation sampling. He concluded that each of these methods had significant limitations when applied in the typical audit situation. Professor Frederick Stephan of Princeton University concurred with Stringer's observations and agreed to assist him in the development of a statistical sampling plan (hereafter "the Plan") that was more suited to the auditor's objectives. The development of the Plan required two closely integrated, but conceptually autonomous, developments: (1) a new mathematical approach to avoid certain limitations of the sampling techniques available at that time, and (2) an interface or model for integrating statistical measurements with auditing concepts.

In developing the Plan, Stringer grappled with a number of other issues that he perceived to be problems arising from the application of statistical sampling and evaluation techniques to audit practice, some of which were unique to auditing. The first problem was relating the two parameters or dimensions of the Plan (precision and reliability) to the audit process.

At an early stage, he decided that it was logical to link precision with materiality. The auditor ultimately needs assurance that a material level of error does not exist. Stringer felt that the upper precision limit should be the level of error that is less than, or equal to, materiality. He believed that the linkage of the auditing concept of materiality to the statistical concept of precision limits would enable the auditor to quantitatively express his judgment concerning various audit objectives. In addition, he felt that having to identify specifically the level of precision would force a more cogent focus upon materiality. Concerning the second parameter of the Plan, reliability, Stringer believed that this measure was directly related to the overall risk that the auditor might issue an inappropriate opinion—namely, audit risk.

Stringer then began to compare and contrast the (1) relationship of the level of reliability of sample results to the overall level of audit risk in an audit application, and (2) the relationship of the level of reliability of sample results to the final inference concerning a population in a nonaudit application (e.g., a natural or social science application). Stringer realized that, unlike various scientific applications of statistical sampling, the auditor usually gathers more evidence to draw conclusions regarding the reasonableness of account balances than simply the sample results of substantive tests of details. As Stringer developed the Plan, he began to analyze the nature of the interrelationships of the various testing procedures to each other and to the overall level of audit risk; this was the genesis of what is now referred to as the audit-risk model.

As the first step in developing the risk model, Stringer decided to establish an overall level of audit risk that would be acceptable as a matter of Firm policy. Stringer decided that a 95 percent reliability level was reasonable in the context of clients' expectations, public responsibility, and litigation; consequently, this level was adopted for use in the Plan.

Having determined an acceptable overall level of audit risk, Stringer next addressed the more difficult task of finding a way to quantitatively relate the degree of reliance that could be placed on internal control (based on the evaluation of the internal control) to the extent of substantive testing under the Plan, and, in turn, to quantitatively relate the integration of these two audit tests to overall audit risk. Ideally, Stringer desired an objective method to evaluate the effectiveness of internal control and an objective method to determine the effect of the evaluation of internal control on the extent of substantive tests.

Convinced that there would be significant benefits from finding a way to quantitatively relate the extent of various audit procedures to overall audit risk, Stringer first divided audit procedures into three groups: (1) tests of the system of internal control, (2) substantive tests of details, and (3) the category of substantive tests referred to as analytical review. Since the Plan already provided a quantitative evaluation technique for substantive tests of details, he focused his efforts on developing a quantitative measure of the effectiveness of internal control and analytical review.

The great amount of his time and effort consumed in developing the other facets of the Plan forced him to defer to the future any effort to quantitatively measure the effectiveness of analytical review and the related degree of reliance. Stringer decided to direct his efforts toward constructing a quantitative measure of reliance on internal control, by developing various scenarios. In the first scenario, he assumed that the auditor's evaluation of the system of internal control indicates that no significant reliance can be placed on it and that the only auditing procedures to be performed are substantive tests of details. In such a situation, he determined that the level of audit risk must be the same as the level of sampling risk associated with the substantive tests, since there is no other evidence upon which the auditor can base an opinion.

In the second scenario, Stringer assumed that maximum reliance could be placed on internal control. The problem here was to determine how much reliance could be placed on internal control in the best circumstances. Stringer felt strongly that there were inherent limitations in any system of internal control and that in no circumstance should the auditor rely 100 percent on internal control to the preclusion of substantive testing. Since there was no explicit guidance in the auditing standards at that time regarding the extent of reliance on internal control, he searched for some way to resolve this issue. After a rather extended search, he found two studies of irregularities that had been conducted by insurance companies that provide fidelity insurance.

The studies found that approximately 10 percent of the claims had been the result of collusion, forgery, and other types of irregularities not expected to be detected by internal control. Based on the data of the two studies, Stringer then calculated a plus or minus $2^{1}/_2$ percent precision limit using an estimation sampling approach. This gave him an upper precision limit of $12^{1}/_2$ percent concerning the portion of claims resulting from collusion, forgery, etc. With these results, he concluded that even in the best internal-control situations, the reliance on internal control should not exceed $87^{1}/_2$ percent; that is, in the best situations, there exists an internal control risk of $12^{1}/_2$ percent. Stringer described this effort, as noted by Tucker (1989), as, "The best I could do in an area where there really wasn't much to turn to—an admittedly inexact approach, but the only way I could address the problem."

Stringer then deduced that the probability of a material error occurring and not being detected (audit risk) by either the system of internal control or the substantive test of details could be calculated by the multiplicative rule of probabilities, since these two risks are statistically independent. In equation form it appears as follows:

Audit Risk = Internal Control Risk x Sampling Risk

Using the overall audit risk level of 5 percent and maximum reliance on internal control of $87^{1}/_2$ percent (risk of $12^{1}/_2$ percent as discussed above), the acceptable sampling risk and desired reliability level in these circumstances are calculated as follows:

Sampling Risk = Audit Risk / Internal Control Risk = .05 / .125

Sampling Risk = .40

Reliability Level = 1 − .40 = .60

With slight modifications relating to the precision of compliance tests and the convenience of manual computations in designing samples, this equation became the risk model that was incorporated into the Plan for use where maximum reliance on internal control was considered appropriate.

Stringer also believed that the final reliance on internal control should be a combination of (1) the preliminary evaluation of the system as prescribed, and (2) the degree of compliance with the prescribed system as indicated by audit tests for that purpose. To assist in the application of these concepts, the Plan included a table of reliability factors (*Table 1—Reliability Factors*) to be used in determining sample size and in evaluating sample results. The table provides three levels relating to the results of the preliminary evaluation of prescribed control procedures ("Good," "Mixed," and "Bad").

The statistical sampling plan developed by Stringer and Stephan was completed by the fall of 1959, although efforts to improve and refine various aspects of the Plan are ongoing. Within the firm, the Plan was first referred to as the "Haskins and Sells Audit Sampling Plan" and is sometimes referred to as "CMA Sampling" (Cumulative Monetary Amount Sampling), which relates to an aspect of the selection process. Literature on statistical sampling provided by the American Institute of Certified Public Accountants (AICPA) refers to sampling approaches that are a derivation of the Plan as "probability proportional to size" sampling. In textbooks, journal articles, and other publications, these approaches are widely referred to as Dollar Unit Sampling (DUS). In 1981 Stringer became the first recipient of the Distinguished Service in Auditing Award, which is sponsored by the Auditing Section of the American Accounting Association.

Evolution of Auditing Standards for Statistical Sampling and Audit-Risk Evaluation

By November 1956, the accounting profession's interest in statistical sampling had progressed to the point that a special AICPA committee, the Committee on Statistical Sampling (AICPA-CSS), was formed to research the issue. Although this committee reported to the Committee on Auditing Procedure (a predecessor of the Auditing Standards Board), it did not have the authority to establish standards. Early reports issued by the AICPA-CSS were published only in the *Journal of Accountancy*. During this period, Stringer, a partner at Haskins and Sells, was heavily involved in the development of these standards.

In the February 1962 issue of the *Journal of Accountancy*, the AICPA-CSS issued its first special report, titled "Statistical Sampling and the Independent Auditor." In 1963, the Committee on Auditing Procedure issued Statement of Auditing Procedure (SAP) No. 33, "Auditing Standards and Procedures," which stated that when determining the extent of a particular audit test and the method of selecting items to be examined, the auditor might consider using statistical sampling techniques that have been found to be advantageous in certain instances. The statement also stated that the use of statistical sampling does not reduce the use of judgment by the auditor but provides certain statistical measurements as to the results of audit tests that otherwise may not be available.

Stringer served as a member of the AICPA-CSS for 1961–1962 and as its chairman for the next three years. Stringer viewed the 1962 report of the AICPA-CSS and SAP No. 33 (1963) as gradual forward steps in the profession's effort to comprehensively address the numerous issues concerning the use of statistical sampling. While chairman of the AICPA-CSS, he was the principal draftsman of a committee report that focused upon what he believed to be the next logical issues to be addressed concerning statistical sampling. Titled "Relationship of Statistical Sampling to Generally Accepted Auditing Standards," the report (hereafter referred to as the "1964 CSS Report") was approved by the AICPA-CSS and published in the *Journal of Accountancy* in July 1964.

The 1964 CSS Report is based on a number of concepts which Stringer had developed earlier while constructing the Haskins and Sells Statistical Sampling Plan. The first was the linkage of the statistical concepts of precision and reliability to materiality and audit risk, respectively. To provide guidance concerning the integration of the various sources of audit evidence and their relation to audit risk, Stringer next described the components of the audit-risk model (ARM) and explained the interrelationship of its various components. The report describes nearly all of the variables contained in the ARMs of subsequent pronouncements: Statement on Auditing Standards (SAS) No. 39, "Audit Sampling," in 1981; and SAS No. 47, "Audit Risk and Materiality in Conducting an Audit," in 1983.

Another key issue addressed in the 1964 CSS Report was the selection of the appropriate level of reliability for testing. Stringer had observed that statistical sampling applications in the natural and social sciences often used a reliability level of 90 percent to 99 percent in the sample design. Usually, the only source of evidence in these applications is the data collected from the sample. Stringer feared that this might be interpreted by auditors, clients, and other users of financial statements to mean that to achieve a certain level of audit risk, all individual tests (e.g., tests of internal control and substantive tests of details) must be performed at the same risk level as the level selected for overall audit risk. For example, if the auditor desired to achieve an audit risk level of 5 percent, he might assume erroneously that all audit tests need be performed at the 5 percent risk level. In this scenario, if tests of both internal control and substantive tests of details are performed at the 5 percent risk level, the following would result:

Audit Risk = Internal Control Risk x Sampling Risk

$$.0025 = .05 \ x \ .05$$

Here, an audit risk level of 1/4 of 1 percent is achieved rather than 5 percent. Since the auditor usually has multiple sources of evidence, Stringer believed that it was important to emphasize this distinction, as well as the related consequences, for the determination of reliability levels for the various individual audit tests. Within the framework of the audit-risk model, the overall confidence level is a function of the confidence levels of the underlying tests, which individually may have lower confidence levels than the overall level of confidence. Stringer's observation concerning the auditor's access to multiple sources of evidence echoes in SAS No. 39 (p. 7).

In 1967 Stringer was appointed to the Committee on Auditing Procedure (CAP), the authoritative standard-setting body, on which he served for the five fiscal years 1967–1968 to 1971–1972. During this period, a CAP subcommittee was formed, with Stringer as chairman, to examine an issue concerning internal control. Stringer recounted, as noted by Tucker (1989), the events that provided the impetus for the formation of the subcommittee: "At that time, several of the larger banks had published reports on internal control by their auditors. There was concern among many people that the auditor's report on internal control was essentially being used for advertising purposes and that there existed very little in the way of standards to determine the appropriate actions by the auditor in this area. It was viewed by some as possibly misleading or at least not a constructive form of reporting." The result of the subcommittee's activity was the issuance of SAP No. 49, "Reports on Internal Control," in 1971 and a subsequent follow-up, SAP No. 52, "Reports on Internal Control Based on Criteria Established by Governmental Agencies," in 1972. Stringer was the principal draftsman of both.

The issuance of SAP Nos. 49 and 52 completed the initial assignment of the CAP's subcommittee on internal control. However, Stringer believed there were a number of important issues related to internal control that had not yet been addressed, and he was able to broaden the scope of the subcommittee's assignment to include those issues. The result of the subcommittee's additional work was the issuance in November 1972 of SAP No. 54, "The Auditor's Study and Evaluation of Internal Control," of which Stringer was the primary author. Stringer believed that any comprehensive analysis of the nature of the auditor's study and evaluation of internal control necessarily included a discussion of the relationship of evidence gathered concerning internal control to the other sources of audit evidence and to audit risk. He believed it would be beneficial to incorporate a number of concepts and guidelines regarding the ARM and statistical sampling into the study.

Stringer attempted to incorporate the 1964 CSS Report into the main text of SAP No. 54, as well as an elaboration on the concepts contained in the report, since he considered the report to have had relatively limited exposure. However, during this era, the use of statistical sampling, and especially the ARM, were relatively new and controversial issues. Stringer's efforts to include the 1964 CSS Report in the main text of the pronouncement met significant resistance. As a compromise, the 1964 CSS Report was reproduced verbatim as Appendix A of SAP No. 54, and the elaboration of concepts and further guidance on statistical sampling applications were included in Appendix B. Other issues involved in the compromise included the wording of various terms in the appendices. (SAP No. 54 was codified soon thereafter in 1973 as Section 320 of Statement on Auditing Standards No. 1, "Codification of Auditing Standards and Procedures.")

Appendix B was titled "Precision and Reliability for Statistical Sampling in Auditing," and it contained the first authoritative publication of the ARM in the form of an equation (p. 276). In addition, paragraphs 35 and 36 provided an example to illustrate the application of the ARM. The illustration contained two concepts resulting from Stringer's earlier work in developing the Haskins and Sells Statistical Sampling Plan: first, the use of an overall reliability level of 95 percent; and second, the use of 90 percent for maximum reliance on internal control. The example does not provide for 100 percent reliance on internal control; the main text of SAP No. 54 explicitly stated that there are inherent limitations in the potential effectiveness of any system of accounting control.

Lastly, Appendix B contained the first explicit definition and reference to "inherent risk" and stated that "it has been treated implicitly and conservatively as being 100%. . . ." This treatment of inherent risk is mirrored in SAS

No. 39 (p. 17) and is further elaborated upon in paragraphs 20–22 of SAS No. 47.

In 1981 the Auditing Standards Board (ASB) issued SAS No. 39, which superseded Appendices A and B of SAP No. 54. Although Stringer had no role in the issuance of SAS No. 39, he viewed it as a conceptually congruent extension of the concepts embodied in Appendices A and B, as well as a more authoritative recognition of these concepts. He also noted that considerable conceptual continuity between the two pronouncements was provided, as noted by Tucker (1989), by Robert K. Elliott, who was chairman of the subcommittee that drafted SAS No. 39. Earlier, in 1972, Elliott provided important support for Appendices A and B of SAP No. 54; at that time, Elliott was a member of the AICPA-CSS and Thomas L. Holton was the Chairman of the Committee on Auditing Procedure, both of whom were partners of Peat, Marwick, Mitchell and Company.

In 1983 the ASB issued SAS No. 47, and the ASB's statistical sampling subcommittee issued an audit and accounting guide titled *Audit Sampling*, both of which include concepts and illustrative material that is traceable to the appendices of SAP No. 54.

James J. Tucker III

Bibliography

American Institute of Certified Public Accountants. "Audit Risk and Materiality in Conducting an Audit." Statement on Auditing Standards No. 47. New York: AICPA, 1983.
———. "Audit Sampling." Statement on Auditing Standards No. 39. New York: AICPA, 1981.
———. *Auditing Sampling, Audit and Accounting Guide.* New York: AICPA, 1983.
———. "Auditing Standards and Procedures." Statement on Auditing Procedures No. 33. New York: AICPA, 1963.
———. "The Auditor's Study and Evaluation of Internal Control." Statement on Auditing Procedures No. 54. New York: AICPA, 1972.
———. *Codification of Auditing Standards Numbers 1 to 49.* New York: Commerce Clearing House, 1986.
———. Committee on Statistical Sampling, "Relationship of Statistical Sampling to Generally Accepted Auditing Standards," *Journal of Accountancy,* July 1964, pp. 56–58.
———. "Statistical Sampling and the Independent Auditor," *Journal of Accountancy,* February 1962, pp. 60–62.
Elliott, R.K. "Relating Statistical Sampling to Audit Objectives," *Journal of Accountancy,* July 1972, pp. 46–55.
Haskins & Sells. *Statistical Sampling Instructions.* New York: 1962.
Kinney, W.R., ed. *Fifty Years of Statistical Sampling.* New York: Garland, 1986.
Stringer, K.W. "Practical Aspects of Statistical Sampling in Auditing." Paper presented at the 1963 Annual Meeting of the American Statistical Association.
———. "Some Basic Concepts of Statistical Sampling in Auditing," *Journal of Accountancy,* November 1961, pp. 63–69.
———. "A Statistical Technique for Analytical Review." In *Studies on Statistical Methodology in Auditing* (supplement to *Journal of Accounting Research,* 1975), pp. 1–9.
Stringer, K.W., and T.R. Stewart. *Statistical Techniques for Analytical Review in Auditing.* New York: John Wiley & Sons, 1986.
Tucker, J. "An Early Contribution of Kenneth W. Stringer: Development and Dissemination of the Audit Risk Model," *Accounting Horizons,* June 1989, pp. 28–37.

See also AMERICAN INSTITUTE OF CERTIFIED PUBLIC ACCOUNTANTS; EXTERNAL AUDITING; INTERNAL CONTROL; MATERIALITY; TRUEBLOOD, ROBERT MARTIN

Stephens, Hustcraft

During the eighteenth century, a few textbook authors saw the limitations of bookkeeping instruction based on memorized rules, and tried instead to teach the logic of accounting procedures. Their reasoning about the fundamental nature of double entry bookkeeping marked the beginnings of accounting theory. It was a theory centered on the purpose of the firm, the nature of capital, and especially on the meaning of accounts to a business owner.

The English accountant Hustcraft Stephens began *Italian Book-Keeping Reduced into an Art* (1735) by distinguishing between the whole of a proprietor's capital and the individual assets that comprised it. Stephens believed that the purpose of bookkeeping was to find the "present condition and Extent of a Man's Estate." He was among the first to discard traditional teaching methods, being determined "to offer no Rules, until he had shown them to be the Consequences of conclusions, plainly drawn from Self-evident Principles." Shifting attention from the journal to the ledger, Stephens explained how to record assets, liabilities, and equity interests without remembering all possible journal entries or drilling on debits and credits. Treating ledger accounts as statistical sorting devices, he classified transactions into three categories, depending on whether they affected only assets, only liabilities, or both assets and liabilities. This abstract approach to accounting instruction was a complete departure from the usual textbook explanations in terms of account personification. Though Stephens's book had little direct influence on later advocates of proprietary theory, his teaching method, in its freedom from rote learning, was a hundred years ahead of its time.

Michael Chatfield

Bibliography

Bywater, M.F., and B.S. Yamey. *Historic Accounting Literature: A Companion Guide*. London: Scholar Press, 1982.

Jackson, J.G.C. "The History of Methods of Exposition of Double Entry Bookkeeping in England." In *Studies in the History of Accounting*, edited by A.C. Littleton and B.S. Yamey, pp. 288–312. Homewood, IL: Irwin, 1956.

See also JOURNAL; LEDGER; PROPRIETARY THEORY

Sterling, Robert R. (1931–)

American professor of accounting and accounting theorist, Robert R. Sterling is one of the prominent theorists whose work resulted in the title "Golden Age of Accounting Theory" for the decades of the 1960s and 1970s. During this period, Sterling and his contemporaries addressed the problems of traditional accounting based on historic costs, allocations, and forecasts. Sterling's principal contributions in the effort to reform accounting practice through the development of sound accounting theory include *Theory of the Measurement of Enterprise Income* (1970) and *Toward a Science of Accounting* (1979).

In *Enterprise Income*, Sterling rigorously evaluates alternative methods of asset valuation and income measurement, including the traditional accounting approach. Applying the criteria of relevance (i.e., to economic-decision models) and verity (i.e., conformance with reality, reliability) to the output of the alternatives, Sterling concludes that a market-valuation method using exit prices or values is superior.

Enterprise Income is not only the foundation of Sterling's works, but the source of his most egregious error as well—namely, the belief that verity as a requirement for information is clear and obvious to everyone. Much of his subsequent career has been spent trying to correct that error.

Toward a Science is a carefully developed treatise on the selection of an attribute of assets and liabilities to use in accounting for, and reporting on, the same in financial statements. Based on the criteria of relevance and empirical testability (the verity criterion restated), Sterling concludes that accountants should use exit values as the basis for financial accounting and reporting.

As a result of these and other works, Sterling has become widely known as a leading proponent of exit-value accounting. Indeed, many accountants, academics and practitioners alike, think of Sterling solely in terms of exit values. Such a perception is unfortunate, as exit values are not the true focus of his work.

Labeled a normative theorist, Sterling is also a common-sense empiricist with intellectual roots in economics and the philosophy of science. His use of exit values is not an unexamined premise that he defends with his theories, but an inescapable conclusion that follows from the application of scientific principles to the discipline of accounting. It is not the use of exit values *per se* that is important to Sterling, but the use of an attribute of assets and liabilities that has an empirical referent and is relevant to economic decisions.

Robert R. Sterling has a BS in Economics (1956) and an MBA (1958) from the University of Denver. He earned a PhD in Economics from the University of Florida (1965) and was a postdoctoral fellow in Philosophy of Science at Yale University (1966–67). In addition to teaching during his degree and postdoctoral programs, Sterling has been an accounting professor at the University of Kansas (1967–1974), Rice University (1974–1980), the University of Alberta (1980–1981), and the University of

Utah (1983–1992). He also served as senior fellow in the research division of the Financial Accounting Standards Board (1981–1983).

Kevin H. McBeth

Bibliography

Sterling, R.R. "Accounting Research, Education and Practice," *Journal of Accountancy*, September 1973, pp. 44–52.

———. "Confessions of a Failed Empiricist," *Advances in Accounting,* Spring 1988, pp. 3–35.

———. "A Glimpse of the Forest," *Accountant's Magazine*, November 1968, pp. 589–594.

———. "The Going Concern," *Accounting Review*, July 1968, pp. 481–502.

———. "On Theory Construction and Verification," *Accounting Review*, July 1970, pp. 444–457.

———. "Positive Accounting: An Assessment," *Abacus*, Fall 1990, pp. 97–135.

———. "Relevant Financial Reporting in an Age of Price Changes," *Journal of Accountancy*, February 1975, pp. 42–51.

———. *Theory of the Measurement of Enterprise Income*. Lawrence, KS: University Press of Kansas, 1970. Reprint. Houston: Scholars Book, 1979.

———. *Toward a Science of Accounting.* Houston: Scholars Book, 1979.

See also AUSTRALIA; BALL AND BROWN'S "AN EMPIRICAL EVALUATION OF ACCOUNTING INCOME NUMBERS"; CONCEPTUAL FRAMEWORK; HISTORICAL COST; INVENTORY VALUATION; MATCHING; NORMATIVE ACCOUNTING; POSITIVE ACCOUNTING; THOMAS'S *THE ALLOCATION PROBLEM IN FINANCIAL ACCOUNTING THEORY*

Sterrett, Joseph Edmund (1870–1934)

The first American-born partner of Price Waterhouse, Joseph Edmund Sterrett brought a broad social vision to accounting at a time when the profession was at a nascent stage. His innovative leadership in the areas of education and ethics were central to accountants' efforts to gain professional recognition. His organizing ability, combined with his ability to join strong men in cooperative efforts, made him a natural leader. Sterrett's leadership was recognized by his colleagues as he served as president of the Pennsylvania Society of CPAs from 1904–1906

and of the American Association of Public Accountants (AAPA) from 1908–1910, but it was not in these official roles that he made his greatest contributions to the profession. It was his work behind the scenes, as chair of many important committees and as a member of the AAPA, and later the American Institute of Accountants (AIA) Council and/or Executive Committee for over 20 years, that enabled Sterrett to have a profound influence on the profession during its formative years.

Born in Brockwayville, Pennsylvania, in 1870, the son of a minister, as were so many of the early leaders of the profession, Sterrett joined the staff of John Francis in Philadelphia at the age of 21. Two years later, in 1893, he became a partner in the firm. He and Francis led the drive to organize Pennsylvania's accountants. Sterrett's ability to bring together a diverse group of independent men demonstrated not only his organizational skills, but also his unique leadership ability. In 1897, due primarily to Sterrett's relentless efforts, the Pennsylvania Society of CPAs was formed. He served as secretary of the organization during its first four years and as president from 1904 through 1906. It was through his work as chair of the Committee on Education that Sterrett may have made his most lasting contribution. While his success in developing effective evening programs was important, it was his vision in outlining a broad educational base that set him apart from many of his colleagues. He urged young men to dig deep and get a broad foundation, arguing that technical knowledge could best be handled through practical experience in a preceptor-student relationship.

Sterrett also provided consistent and powerful leadership to the profession in the area of ethical conduct. He vigorously resisted all efforts to reduce fundamental concepts, such as independence, to a series of rules. The *Minutes* of the AAPA and later the AIA show the constancy of his position. Rules could only ensure minimal conduct, and minimal conduct simply was not acceptable with respect to concepts such as independence. In these cases, he argued, no deviation could be tolerated and to codify rules would be to trivialize fundamental norms. His classic speech on "Professional Ethics," delivered to the annual meeting of the AAPA in 1907, clearly reflected his strong belief that abstract concepts, such as truth, justice, and honor, if internalized by all accountants, would provide the strongest base to ensure ethical conduct within the profession.

S

Sterrett's abilities and high visibility within the accounting profession brought him national attention and frequent calls to Washington, D.C. He served as one of four members on the Board of Consulting Accountants to the President's Commission on Economy and Efficiency in 1911, as adviser to the Treasury on administration of the Excess Profits Tax during World War I, and as an adviser to the Capital Issues Committee also during World War I. His work after World War I would bring him international recognition. In 1920 he set up the administration of the Repatriation Commission in France. In 1924 he was called back to Europe, where he spent two years as the American member of the Transfer Committee that managed reparation payments under the Dawes Plan. He received decorations from four countries, Belgium, France, Germany, and Italy, for his work on this committee. After a brief respite in the United States, a group of bankers in Mexico requested that he examine the financial condition of that country. He responded with his usual thoroughness, coauthoring a 274-page report at the culmination of his examination. In 1929 he was off again, this time to Germany, where he conducted a study of the management and administration of the German railroads. In 1953 Sterrett's contributions to the profession were recognized by his election to the Accounting Hall of Fame.

Due to the whims of chance, much of Sterrett's legacy has been lost. Like his partner at Price Waterhouse, George Oliver May, Sterrett had a great sense of history and had accumulated in his basement a comprehensive library documenting his lifetime's work. In 1932 a fire destroyed his home and shattered his dream. According to colleagues and friends, this loss crushed Sterrett's spirit; they indicated that he never fully recovered from this devastating blow. He died in 1934 at the age of 64; his personal achievements have been recognized, but what he hoped would be a permanent legacy to the profession went up in smoke.

Barbara D. Merino

Bibliography

Sterrett, J.E. "Chairman's Address." In *Congress of Accountants World Fair, St. Louis, September 26–28th, 1904*, pp. 23–33. Reprinted in Richard P. Brief, ed., *Development of Contemporary Accounting Thought Series*. New York: Arno Press, 1978.

———. "Education and Training of a Certified Public Accountant," *Journal of Accountancy*, November 1905, pp. 1–15.

———. "Legislation for the Control of Corporations," *Journal of Accountancy*, February 1910, pp. 241–247.

———. "Present Position and Probable Development of Accountancy as a Profession." In *Proceedings of the Annual Meeting of the American Economic Association, 1908*, pp. 85–96. Princeton, NJ: American Economic Association, 1909.

———. "The Profession of Accountancy," *Annals of the American Academy of Political and Social Science*, July 1906, pp. 16–27.

———. "Professional Ethics," *Journal of Accountancy*, October 1907, pp. 407–431.

See also ACCOUNTING EDUCATION IN THE UNITED STATES; ACCOUNTING HALL OF FAME; AMERICAN INSTITUTE OF CERTIFIED PUBLIC ACCOUNTANTS; BIG EIGHT ACCOUNTING FIRMS; ETHICS, PROFESSIONAL; FEDERAL GOVERNMENT ACCOUNTING (U.S.); IMPUTED INTEREST ON CAPITAL; MAY, GEORGE OLIVER

Stevelinck, Ernest Jean Leon (1905–)

Ernest Stevelinck is a Belgian professional accountant, author, and editor who wrote extensively, in French, on the history of accounting in Europe. In particular, he researched the life and works of Luca Pacioli in great depth. Stevelinck and Robert Haulotte are the authors of *Luca Pacioli: Sa vie Son oeuvre* (1975). It is the first translation into French (from Latin) of what is generally recognized as the first complete treatise on double entry bookkeeping— "Particularis de Computis et Scripturis," contained in Pacioli's *Summa de Arithmetica, Geometria, Proportioni et Proportionalita* (1494). Stevelinck's knowledge of art, history, and languages enabled him to research extensively the interaction of Pacioli with the other intellectuals of his time, such as Leonardo da Vinci, Leon Battista Alberti, and Piero della Francesca.

Also, Stevelinck spent three decades in searching for the true image of Pacioli. This effort culminated in a 1986 article, "The Many Faces of Luca Pacioli: Iconographic Research over Thirty Years."

In addition to his interest in Pacioli and double entry accounting, Stevelinck was an organizer of several professional societies in Belgium and France and was the editor of several professional journals. His numerous articles on the history of accounting were published in these journals. In 1970 he organized and conducted the first Symposium of Accounting Historians in Brussels. Subsequent Congresses of Accounting Historians have been held in Atlanta, London, Pisa, Sydney, and Kyoto.

Alfred R. Roberts

Bibliography

Brown, R.G., and K.S. Johnson. *Pacioli on Accounting*. New York: McGraw-Hill, 1963.

Stevelinck, E. "The Many Faces of Luca Pacioli: Iconographic Research over Thirty Years," *Accounting Historians Journal*, Fall 1986, pp. 1–18.

Stevelinck, E., and R. Haulotte. *Luca Pacioli: Sa vie Son oeuvre*. Vesoul, France: Pragnos Vesoul, 1975.

Taylor, R.E. *No Royal Road: Luca Pacioli and His Times*. Chapel Hill: University of North Carolina Press, 1942.

See also PACIOLI, LUCA

Stevin, Simon (1548–1620)

It is not possible to give a complete bibliography of Simon Stevin's publications, because he wrote on a variety of topics. Stevin was deeply influenced by the Founding Father of Accounting, the most celebrated mathematician and scholar Luca Pacioli. Like Pacioli, Stevin was interested in the practical application of sciences (especially mathematics): arithmetic, geometry, perspective, military science, navigation, architecture, music. Here the focus is on Stevin's contributions to accounting.

Simon Stevin was born in 1548 in Bruges, an important commercial harbor then, and worked, like Pacioli, for a rich merchant (in Antwerp). As such, Stevin had to learn the practices of bookkeeping and commercial arithmetic. The latter resulted in his first book in 1582, *Tafelen van Interest* (Tables of Interest), in which he set out the rules of single and compound interest and, as a help, gave tables for the computation of discounts and annuities (important for the bill of exchange). There were, for example, 16 tables from 1 percent to 16 percent and for 1–30 years with three columns: present value, compound interest, and the annuities. The idea of tables was not new. Pacioli had published some in his *Summa de Arithmetica* (1494), entitled "Tariffa." In Italy bankers had already been using tables for two centuries, but often the tables were kept secret as tools of trade.

Like Pacioli, Stevin stressed that the native language, not Latin or Greek, was the best tool for communication. This point of view turned out to be not so successful and even significant, because it limited the circulation of his books and the reputation of the author.

Stevin was one of the first authors to compose a treatise on governmental accounting. He did this in *Vorstelicke Bouckhouding op de Italiaensche Wyse* in 1604 (Flesher). This book included four parts: Commercial Bookkeeping; Bookkeeping for Domains; Bookkeeping for Royal Expenditures; and Bookkeeping for War and Other Extraordinary Finances. The book was written for Stevin's patron and friend, Prince Maurice of Nassau. Stevin stressed that the application of double entry for municipalities and governments was very much needed because supervision in municipalities and governments was weaker there than in businesses. Governmental treasurers often became rich, and the government poor on account because of the lack of a strong double entry control system. It is likely that Stevin also had an impact in Sweden as well as in the Netherlands. The Swedish government reorganized its accounting system and introduced double entry for its government in 1623. O. Ten Have (1956), head of the Department of Social and Economic Statistics, Netherlands Central Bureau of Statistics, traced Stevin's effect through the Dutch merchant, Abraham Cabeljau, who headed the Swedish efforts on double entry accounting.

Stevin's works were collected in a massive two-volume set entitled *Wisconstighe Ghedachtenissen* (vol. 1, 1608 and vol. 2 in 1605) which was a collection of the manuscripts of the lessons given from Stevin to Prince Maurice. Stevin's bookkeeping text was included in the set. It is important to note for accounting education that Stevin used the form of a dialogue between himself and Prince Maurice for setting a systematic rationale for bookkeeping practices.

The basis of bookkeeping, according to Stevin, is the beginning and the end of "property rights." This idea is a current topic, and

S

there is rich "property rights" literature with emphasis on rights established by contracts. Stevin was one of the first accounting historians, and he made investigations into the antiquity of bookkeeping. Double entry accounting, he stated, has many roots in Roman (or even Greek) times. The importance of accounting history for the development of a sound and realistic accounting theory and a deeper understanding of the accounting heritage by accountants has recently been recognized. The accounting profession has evolved over many centuries. Stevin recognized, too, that bookkeeping is first of all a way of sorting financial information, and his balance sheet compilation (*staet proef*) is carried out to ascertain mathematically the profit of the year. Stevin is considered to be the inventor of the income statement. "Stevin developed the income statement as proof of the accuracy of the change in owners' equity on the balance sheet" (Flesher).

There is a great difference between Pacioli and Stevin, too. While Pacioli, for example, began the inventory: "In the name of God, November 8th, 1493, Venice," Stevin omitted all religious notations at the tops of pages or at the beginning of books. This is a fundamental point indeed. Perhaps this is one of the reasons that when in 1645 a proposal was made to erect a statue to this otherwise so illustrious native in Stevin's birthplace Bruges, there was much opposition from the local clergy to the plan (Flesher).

Frans Volmer

Bibliography

Bywater, M.F., and B.S. Yamey. *Historic Accounting Literature: A Companion Guide*. London: Scholar Press, 1982.

Flesher, D.L. "Simon Stevin of Bruges." In *Biographies of Notable Accountants*. 2d ed., edited by A.M. Agami, pp. 45–47. New York: Random House, 1989.

Geijsbeek, J.B. *Ancient Double Entry Bookkeeping*. Denver: Geijsbeek, 1914. Reprint. Houston: Scholars Book, 1974.

McMickle, P.L., and R. Vangermeersch. *The Origins of a Great Profession*. Memphis: Academy of Accounting Historians, 1987.

Ten Have, O. "Simon Stevin of Bruges." In *Studies in the History of Accounting*, edited by A.C. Littleton and B.S. Yamey, pp. 236–246. Homewood, IL: Irwin, 1956.

See also ARITHMETIC AND ACCOUNTING; BALANCE SHEET; CLOSING ENTRIES AND PROCEDURES; COMPOUND ENTRIES; COMPOUND INTEREST; DAFFORNE, RICHARD; DISCOUNTED CASH FLOW; GERMANY; GREECE; INCOME STATEMENT/INCOME ACCOUNT; NETHERLANDS; PACIOLI, LUCA; ROME (509 B.C.–A.D. 476)

Stewardship

Stewardship refers to the functions performed by a steward, who was in English feudal law an officer on a lord's estate having general control of its affairs. However, the concept was present in even more ancient times. There are two biblical sources related to this topic. In the 41st chapter of Genesis, Joseph interpreted the Pharaoh's dream of seven fat cows eaten by seven lean cows. The interpretation led to a storing of one-fifth of the crops of the seven boom years so that there would be food to distribute in the seven years of famine. The second source comes from the New Testament, Mark 25:15–30, and is known as the parable of the talents. The master gave five, two and one talents, respectively, to three servants. The first two servants used their talents wisely and presented the master with ten and four talents respectively. The third servant hid his talent and presented it to the master, who then condemned the servant for not, at the least, investing the talent with money exchangers. It is not surprising then that Chatfield (1974) makes references to the stewardship concept in such ancient societies as Babylonia, Assyria, Greece, and Rome.

Perhaps George Oliver May (1943) brought the most attention to stewardship by listing it as the first of the ten major uses of accounts. The first five were felt to be older than the last five. For the older five, May felt that there was no attempt to use the past as a measure of the future, nor was there any great stress in assigning past achievement to particular years. May's ten major uses were: (1) as a report of stewardship; (2) as a basis for fiscal policy; (3) to determine the legality of dividends; (4) as a guide to wise dividend action; (5) as a basis for granting credit; (6) as information for prospective investors in an enterprise; (7) as a guide to the value of investments already made; (8) as an aid for government supervision; (9) as a basis for price or rate regulation; and (10) as a basis for taxation.

A most detailed coverage of the relationship of accounting to stewardship is found in

A.C. Littleton's *Structure of Accounting Theory* (1953). Littleton believed the charge-discharge nature of stewardship reporting in a medieval English manor, in which the steward was charged with certain assets and then was required to report on the discharge of them, has been replaced by the income statement. Perhaps stewardship is best expressed as Littleton's use of the "moral scope of accounting."

> . . . When we think of the limited liability corporations of today with hired managers and large numbers of absentee stockholders, it becomes evident that the moral scope of accounting has been vastly expanded. Many people, wholly out of touch with the physical aspects of enterprise operation, depend upon figure representations of managerial actions, of results of actions, and of potentialities for future actions. As the size of enterprises increases and the distance between owner-lenders and operating managers grows wider, the opportunities expand for the practice of deceit by people of authority (Littleton, 1953).

The concept of stewardship in accounting has great meaning for internal auditors, operating accountants, and chief financial officers. Certainly, chief executive officers and chairmen of boards of directors should be aware of this concept. However, if the concept is to be an important one for external reporting of financial-accounting reports, much work has to be done to fit accounting statements and disclosures into a stewardship framework.

Richard Vangermeersch

Bibliography

Chatfield, M. *A History of Accounting Thought.* Hindsdale, IL: Dryden Press, 1974.

Littleton, A.C. "Stewardship or Proprietorship." In *Essays on Accountancy by A.C. Littleton,* edited by C.A. Moyer, pp. 36–40. Urbana: University of Illinois Press, 1961.

———. *Structure of Accounting Theory.* Monograph No. 5. Sarasota, FL: American Accounting Association, 1953.

May, G.O. *Financial Accounting: A Distillation of Experience.* New York: Macmillan, 1943.

See also AGENCY THEORY; BABYLONIA; BANKRUPTCY ACTS; CAPITAL MAINTENANCE; CASH FLOW ACCOUNTING; "CHARGE AND DISCHARGE" STATEMENT; COMMANDER THEORY; CONSERVATISM; DEFINITIONS OF ACCOUNTING; DEVINE, CARL; GREECE; ITALY, AFTER PACIOLI; LITTLETON, A.C.; MANORIAL ACCOUNTING; MAY, GEORGE OLIVER; MEDIEVAL ACCOUNTING; ROME (509 B.C.–A.D. 476); TRUSTEE ACCOUNTS

Stock Dividends

Stock dividends have been a controversial issue for over 100 years though they date back to at least 1690, when the English Hudson's Bay Company declared "that the stock should be trebled—each interestent shall (according to his stock) have his credit trebled in the company's books. . . ." The controversy surrounding stock dividends resulted from disagreement concerning the economic substance of stock dividends: Does a stock dividend constitute income to the shareholder (analogous to a cash dividend) or, is a stock dividend simply the splitting of shares into smaller pieces (analogous to a stock split)?

Since England was first to experiment extensively with the corporate form of organization, it was first to grapple with the economic-substance issue. Prior to 1800, English court decisions were often conflicting. However, early in the nineteenth century, the Court of Chancery and the House of Lords determined that stock dividends did not constitute income but, rather, were analogous to stock splits. Although the English courts finally agreed on this issue, the same could not be said for their American counterparts.

Securities fraud is associated with the early American corporate experience, especially in the railroad industry. The disagreement in America concerning the economic substance of stock dividends led many to believe that these distributions were a form of securities fraud known as stock watering. Consequently, many states outlawed the use of stock dividends in the late 1800s. However, the courts eventually re-established their legality.

On three separate occasions (1890, 1918, 1920), the U.S. Supreme Court attempted to determine if stock dividends constitute income to the recipient or a mere splitting of the evidences of ownership into smaller pieces. In all three cases, the Supreme Court ruled that stock dividends did not constitute income. However, in the last case, *Eisner v. Macomber*, U.S. Supreme Ct., 252, 1920, of the nine-member Court, four justices dissented. The persistent conceptual confusion concerning the economic substance of stock dividends is illustrated clearly in the dissenting opinion in *Eisner v. Macomber* and by subsequent legislative and regulatory efforts to tax stock dividends as well as investigate the use of these distributions.

Reflecting concern by reporting authorities, in 1928 Robert Hiester Montgomery and Herbert C. Freeman, both public accounting practitioners and active writers in accounting theory, complained that "the unsophisticated stockholder" was "not to be blamed" for assuming that periodic stock dividends are a distribution of earnings equal to the "cash value of the quarterly dividends." He further stated that regular stock dividends were an important concern for auditors and predicted that if retained earnings were reduced by the market value of the shares distributed, the use of stock dividends would "come to an abrupt end."

Concerned about misconceptions related to the use and reporting of stock dividends, the New York Stock Exchange (NYSE) formed in 1929 a Special Committee on Stock Dividends. In 1930 the Governing Committee of the NYSE adopted a statement of accounting policy regarding stock dividends based on the Special Committee's recommendations. The statement observed that periodic stock dividends with little or no charge to retained earnings were likely to mislead stockholders and were "not regarded as good practice." The statement recommended that the minimum amount of retained earnings to be capitalized should be the "per share amount of capital and capital surplus" (paid in capital). The statement also noted that such accounting treatment was not required for "an occasional large stock-split, made for convenience in the form of a stock dividend."

George Oliver May was vice-chairman of the Committee on Accounting Procedure (CAP) when the committee issued Accounting Research Bulletin (ARB) No. 11, "Corporate Accounting for Ordinary Stock Dividends" in 1941, which was the first authoritative pronouncement regarding stock dividends and splits. A letter in 1941 written by May to J.S. Seidman (also a member of the CAP) just six weeks prior to the issue of ARB No. 11 lends insight into the committee's objectives:

I think those present generally were of the opinion that periodic stock dividends were objectionable and I believe this view is shared by the Listing Committee of the Stock Exchange. Neither the Institute nor the Exchange can say that they are not permissible as long as the law allows them. . . . the conclusions reached were that in general, the effort should be to restrict the possibilities of declaring stock dividends in such a way as to create false impressions in the minds of stockholders. . . . This, I think, would have a very discouraging effect on those corporations which continue to pay stock dividends.

The requirements of ARB No. 11 appear to have reflected directly the sentiments expressed by May and Montgomery and were considerably more restrictive than current requirements. They included: (1) the capitalization of retained earnings for all stock dividends (regardless of size) using market value per share when market value is significantly above the amount per share of paid in capital, (2) the restriction of stock dividends to current income, and (3) notification to each shareholder "as to the percentage by which the interest which he had in the corporation before the issuance of the stock dividend will be reduced if he should decide to dispose of his dividend shares."

The writings of May and Montgomery suggest that the actual motive underlying ARB No. 11 was to restrict or eliminate the use of stock dividends. The clear identification of this motive or reporting objective provides an unofficial alternative to the official justification of the accounting treatment of stock dividends.

In 1952, ARB No. 11 was revised and reissued as ARB No. 11 (Revised). The complete text of ARB No. 11 (Revised) was subsumed verbatim under ARB No. 43, "Restatement and Revision of Accounting Research Bulletins" (1953), Chapter 7B, and has not been revised since its original issue in 1952; consequently, the text of ARB No. 11 (Revised) (1952) constitutes the current reporting requirements for stock dividends and splits with the well-known "big" and "small" distinction. There was only one dissenter from the 20 members of the CAP. Edward B. Wilcox questioned the consistency of the bulletin, its arbitrary decisions, and its information content. ARB No. 11 (Revised) apparently was tackled by the CAP without any public controversy. It appears that the current pronouncement is a retreat by the CAP from its first effort in 1941, to the less aggressive position that had been taken earlier, in 1930, by the NYSE.

Accounting policy decisions are often heavily influenced, and sometimes constrained, by legal, political, and societal forces. The issue of stock dividends reveals the extent to which these forces may impact the construction of reporting requirements as well as the ethical issues that may arise when policymakers attempt to determine the most appropriate reporting requirements for controversial, unusual, or questionable financial practices.

James J. Tucker III

Bibliography

May, G.O. Letter to J.S. Seidman, dated July 14, 1941. National Office Library of Price Waterhouse and Company, New York.

Montgomery, R.H., and H.C. Freeman. "The North American Company's Dividend," *Journal of Accountancy,* July 1928, pp. 42–47.

Sussman, M.R. *The Stock Dividend.* Ann Arbor, MI: University of Michigan, Bureau of Business Research, 1963.

Tucker, J.J., III. "The Role of Stock Dividends in Defining Income, Developing Capital Market Research and Exploring the Economic Consequences of Accounting Policy Decisions," *Accounting Historians Journal,* Fall 1985, pp. 73–94.

Wilcox, E.B. "Accounting for Stock Dividends: A Dissent from Current Recommended Practice," *Journal of Accountancy,* August 1953, pp. 176–181.

See also ACCOUNTING RESEARCH BULLETINS; *EISNER V. MACOMBER;* MAY, GEORGE OLIVER; MONTGOMERY, ROBERT HIESTER; NEW YORK STOCK EXCHANGE

Stone, Williard E. (1910–)

Williard E. Stone rose through the ranks in accounting academics the old-fashioned way—through hard work over a long period of time. A mathematics graduate of Penn State in 1933, he joined the accounting field as an auditor for the commonwealth of Pennsylvania in that year. He was a principal auditor with the U.S. General Accounting Office in 1943. Stone received the CPA certificate in 1945. In 1947 he became a partner in Stone and Fisher, CPAs, in Philadelphia and started his teaching career with the Wharton School, from which he also received his M.A. in finance in 1950 and a Ph.D. in management and economics in 1957. From 1950 to 1952, he also was assistant to the president and controller for Rollie Manufacturing Company. In 1960 Stone became chairman of the Accounting Department at the University of Florida. He chaired that department for 14 years and retired from the University of Florida in 1980. He held visiting posts in such schools as the University of New South Wales, the University of Virginia, the University of Port Elizabeth in South Africa, the University of Kentucky, and Deaken University in Australia.

Stone, along with Gary John Previts and Paul Garner, founded the Academy of Accounting Historians in 1973. He was manuscript editor of *Accounting Historians Journal* from 1973 to 1980. While he was a frequent contributor to the accounting literature from 1956, it was only in April 1969 that he started to publish historical works, with "Antecedents of the Accounting Profession" in *Accounting Review.* With the start of the academy, Stone also began to produce a prolific stream of historical pieces. An example of these is "Accounting Records Reveal History: the Virginia Cobbler" in the July 1976 *Journal of Accountancy.* In 1982 he and Previts served as editors of the Yushodo American Historic Accounting Literature, a series of Yushodo Booksellers Ltd. of Japan. Stone also conveyed in 1981 his personal library of over a thousand books to the Osaka Genkins Stone Library at the University of Osaka. Many of his books were autographed. He continues to be an active contributor to the literature of accounting. He was recently ranked, by Jean Louis Heck, Robert E. Jensen, and Philip L. Cooley (1990), as the eighth most prolific writer in accounting, as measured by an examination of 24 academic accounting journals.

Stone helped to make historical research in accounting an acceptable academic endeavor. Those who were not present in the 1960s and early 1970s probably fail to realize the struggle it was to publish pieces in accounting history then.

Richard Vangermeersch

Bibliography

Coleman, A.R., W.G. Shenkir, and W.E. Stone. "Accounting in Colonial Virginia:

A Case Study," *Journal of Accountancy*,
July 1974, pp. 32–43.

Goldberg, L., and W.E. Stone. "John
Caldwell Colt: A Notorious Accoun-
tant," *Accounting Historians Journal*,
Spring 1985, pp. 121–130.

Heck, J.L., R.E. Jensen, and P.L. Cooley. "An
Analysis of Contributors to Accounting
Journals: Part 1, The Aggregate Performance," *International Journal of Accounting*, vol. 25, no. 3, 1990, pp. 202–
217.

Stone, W.E. "Abacists versus Algorists," *Journal of Accounting Research*, Autumn
1972, pp. 345–350.

———. "Barter: Developing of Accounting
Practice and Theory," *Accounting Historians Journal*, Fall 1985, pp. 95–108.

———. "Early English Cotton Mill Cost Accounting System: Charlton Mills, 1810–
1889," *Accounting and Business Research* (Eng.), Winter 1973, pp. 71–78.

———. "Managerial Accounting on the U.S.
1758 Frontier," *Accounting Historians
Journal*, Spring 1977, pp. 107–111.

See also ACADEMY OF ACCOUNTING HISTORI-
ANS; COLONIAL AMERICA, ACCOUNTING IN;
GARNER, S. PAUL; PREVITS, GARY JOHN

Study Group on Business Income's *Five Monographs on Business Income*

Five Monographs on Business Income is a book
published in 1950 by a group of economists and
accountants established by the American Institute of Accountants and the Rockefeller Foundation. This group was chaired by Percival F.
Brundage, then senior partner in Price Waterhouse and Company. The group was founded
in 1947 to (1) see if the LIFO (last in, first out)
inventory method could be replicated for capital assets during the post–World War II price
rise, and (2) counter the notion in utilities accounting that the cost of capital assets should
be that paid by the original owner of the item.
The group had a prestigious membership of 46,
including two of the authors in the 1950
report—Solomon Fabricant and Clark Warburton. In 1952, the study group published its
final report, *Changing Concepts of Business
Income*. This 1952 report suffered significantly
from an attempt to include different viewpoints
and, hence, was unclear as a guide for action.
It is, though, an important historical document.

The first monograph in the 1950 book was
written by Sidney Alexander, then with the
International Monetary Fund. Alexander espoused the view that there was no unique, well-
defined ideal concept of income, and that
different concepts should be judged against the
different purposes for the measurement of income. He stressed the importance of dispelling
the money illusion of an assumption of a stable
dollar, and also made an interesting comparison
of different conceptual methods that could
be employed in measuring income. Martin
Bronfenbrenner, then a professor of economics
at the University of Wisconsin, presented a historical perspective of inflation, and he predicted
a continuation of a long-term, but not necessarily stable, price increase. He thought this particularly likely due to the national goal of full
employment.

Solomon Fabricant, a professor of economics at New York University, wrote two brief
monographs. The first described the inventory-
valuation adjustment to business income done
by the U.S. Commerce Department to get its
calculation of national income. He noted that
while the predecessor to the Commerce Department did attempt to adjust depreciation for
price-level changes, the Commerce Department
didn't. Fabricant's second monograph dealt
with his opinion that inflation had very different effects among industry groupings. Clark
Warburton, an economist with the Federal De-
posit Insurance Corporation, disagreed in the
fifth monograph with some of the historical
analysis done by Bronfenbrenner in the second
monograph and offered hope that a wise federal
monetary policy could result in a stable price
level.

The book then presented a transcript of a
discussion group of economists, accountants,
and business scholars on these monographs.
Much of the discussion dealt with the impossibility of the present value of future cash streams
espoused by Alexander. However, the discussion group seemed to focus on the need to measure capital gains that have occurred but were
not recognized in accounting because of its concern with objectivity and conservatism. The
book ended with a legal-type brief given by
George Oliver May on why the traditional depreciation method should be maintained. May
went so far as to recommend the dropping of
the LIFO inventory method so that a congruent
treatment of fixed and inventory assets would
occur.

Five Monographs on Business Income is a very readable treatise on a still-open subject, the theory of business income. It is especially useful because of the transcription of the discussion meeting on the five monographs.

Richard Vangermeersch

Bibliography
Alexander, S.S., et al. *Five Monographs on Business Income*. New York: Macmillan, 1950. Reprint (edited by Robert R. Sterling). Accounting Classic Series. Lawrence, KS: Scholars Book, 1973.
American Institute of Accountants. *Changing Concepts of Business Income*. Report of Study Group on Business Income. New York: Macmillan, 1952.
Brundage, P.F. "Study Group on Business Income Published Its Conclusions after Three Years of Work," *Journal of Accountancy*, February 1952, pp. 190–198.
———. "Three Year Study of Business Income, Its Concepts and Terminology, Started by Institute," *Journal of Accountancy*, August 1947, pp. 116–117.
"What is Business Income?" *Journal of Accountancy*, Editorial, January 1949, pp. 3–4.

See also AMERICAN INSTITUTE OF CERTIFIED PUBLIC ACCOUNTANTS; CONCEPTUAL FRAMEWORK; CONSERVATISM; DEPRECIATION; DISCOUNTED CASH FLOW; HISTORICAL COST; INCOME-DETERMINATION THEORY; INFLATION ACCOUNTING; LAST IN, FIRST OUT (LIFO); MAY, GEORGE OLIVER; OBJECTIVITY; POSTULATES OF ACCOUNTING

Subsidiary Ledger

The subsidiary ledger is a concept that took centuries to develop after Luca Pacioli's treatise on accounting in *Summa de Arithmetica* (1494). Eric L. Kohler defined a subsidiary ledger as "a supporting ledger consisting of a group of accounts the total of which is in agreement with a control account." The writer considered to be the first to take a step toward this concept was Benjamin Booth of London, by way of New York as he apparently was a loyalist and relocated in London during the Revolutionary War, in 1789. Booth presented a much more efficient system of bookkeeping than was current at that time. In his system, there was to be minimal use made of the memorandum (waste) book, since the cashbook was also the waste book for all cash transactions. The various journals were to be posted monthly, so that the ledger would be prevented from swelling to an enormous size. Booth recommended one account for Merchandise rather than a multitude of accounts for each type of good. Information on each sale could be garnered from an examination of the sales book. Booth was concerned with the minutia of such information in the ledger from what is today called "information overload." He recommended daily posting to "running accounts" for account receivables and payables. He tried to keep accounts of one class in one section of the ledger.

While Booth presented his case plainly, the English accountant Edward T. Jones fumed at the inadequacies of double entry. In 1796 he designed his own system of bookkeeping in *Jones' English System of Bookkeeping by Single or Double Entry*. Jones was scornful of the claim that double entry accounting prevented fraud if the debit balances equaled the credit balances. He relied on an elaborate proof of the total debits in the journal to the total debits in the ledger (and the same for the credits). Jones designed a tabular (multicolumned) type journal to minimize postings to the ledger.

The arrival of subsidiary ledgers apparently took place in the practice of accounting in about the 1860s. It was written about in 1882 in a series of articles in the *Bookkeeper*, either by Charles Ezra Sprague (most likely) or Selden R. Hopkins, who were coeditors of the journal. In the system described, a column in the journal for Dealers' Ledger Account was utilized as the control account, and a separate entry was made in an additional (subsidiary) ledger. The author went on to describe the considerable time and ledger space saved in this system. Another important step in this evolution took place around the turn of the twentieth century when subsidiary ledgers were kept in a looseleaf or a card manner. Certainly the movement toward efficiency and simplification of recording has continued throughout the century.

Richard Vangermeersch

Bibliography
Booth, B. *A Complete System of Book-keeping by an Improved Mode of Double-Entry*. London: Welles, Grosvenor, Chater, Cornhill, and Johnson, 1789.
"Jones's English Bookkeeping: A Curiosity of History," *Bookkeeper*, September 12,

September 26, and October 10, 1892. Reprint. New York: Garland, 1989. Vol. 2, pp. 285–286, 302–304, and 317–318.

Kohler, E.L. *A Dictionary for Accountants.* 4th ed. Englewood Cliffs, NJ: Prentice-Hall, 1970.

"Small Economies in Bookkeeping by a Business-Manager, III, IV, and VI," *Bookkeeper*, September 6 and October 24, 1882, and May 8, 1883. Reprint. New York: Garland. Vol. 2, pp. 301–302, 333–334, and 144–147.

Staub, W.A. "Controlling Accounts," *Journal of Accountancy*, November 1909, pp 29–35.

See also JONES, EDWARD THOMAS; LEDGER; PACIOLI, LUCA; SPRAGUE, CHARLES EZRA

Summa Summarium

The earliest writers on double entry bookkeeping emphasized that it provided an automatic check on the correctness and completeness of ledger postings. But while Luca Pacioli understood the purpose and construction of a trial balance, neither of the summarizing statements he recommended in *Summa de Arithmetica* (1494) were trial balances in the modern sense. The *Bilancio del libro* (balance of the ledger) was to be compiled first, after revenue and expense accounts had been closed to capital. Like a post–closing trial balance, it simply verified the debit-credit equality of remaining asset, liability, and capital balances.

The *summa summarium* (sum of sums) was prepared as a final test of closed accounts whose balances had been closed to a new ledger. The sums of all debit entries in each account from the *old* ledger were listed on the left side of a sheet of paper, and the sums of all credit entries in each account were listed on the right side. The proof was their equality. Edward Peragallo calls this a futile procedure, which "proved" only that all the ledger accounts had been closed. The old ledger was sure to balance even if it contained errors, because both sides of each account had been equalized when their balancing figure was entered before transfer to the new ledger. The trial balance, which tested the equality of all ledger account balances, was in general use by the end of the fifteenth century, but the *summa summarium* had a short life and may never have been widely adopted.

Michael Chatfield

Bibliography

DeRoover, R. "Andrea Barbarigo's Trial Balance," *Accounting Review,* January, 1946, pp. 98–99.

Peragallo, Edward. "Origin of the Trial Balance." In *Studies in the History of Accounting*, edited by A.C. Littleton and B.S. Yamey. Homewood, IL: Irwin, 1956, pp. 215–222.

See also CLOSING ENTRIES AND PROCEDURES; PACIOLI, LUCA; TRIAL BALANCE

Sweeney, Henry Whitcomb (1898–1967)

A certified public accountant and an attorney with a variety of professional experiences including educator, public accountant, federal government administrator, and attorney specializing in income taxation and government contracts, Henry Whitcomb Sweeney authored or coauthored four books on accounting and income taxes as well as numerous articles on stabilized accounting, income taxation, and government contracts. He was preparing a book on government contracts at the time of his death. Sweeney's doctoral dissertation at Columbia University, published in 1936 as *Stabilized Accounting*, is his best-known work.

Stabilized Accounting was the first book in the United States containing a comprehensive inflation-accounting model. In the 1964 reprint of *Stabilized Accounting*, Sweeney acknowledged the influence of post–World War I German and French inflation-accounting writings on his ideas (Julius August Fritz Schmidt, Walter Mahlberg, and Eugen Schmalenbach in Germany; Fernand Leger, Georges Valois, and Gabriel Faure in France), as well as the influence of the writings of Livingston Middleditch and William Andrew Paton. In the years prior to the original publication of the book, Sweeney sought to foster professional interest in inflation accounting by publishing several articles in *Accounting Review* from the developing manuscript. Unfortunately, the book itself appeared during a period of economic depression and stable prices: It met with little response on the part of the profession.

In *Stabilized Accounting*, Sweeney stated three objections to existing historical cost systems. First, historical cost accounting yielded no information about the effects of changing prices. As a result, capital-maintenance assumptions based thereon (understood as purchasing-power capital maintenance) were unreliable. Second, historical cost accounting combined dollar amounts that were not homogeneous (dollar amounts that did not recognize the changing value of money over time), which violated basic mathematical principles. Third, the data of historical cost accounting were incomplete—and thus incorrect—because they did not recognize gains and losses caused by fluctuations in the value of money. Sweeney's stabilized-accounting model sought to overcome these deficiencies.

Stabilized Accounting actually contains two stabilization models. The model Sweeney considered the more practicable, and thus the more likely to be adopted in practice (in formulating his models, Sweeney considered practicality and cost effectiveness overriding principles), used a forward indexation method (restatement to period-end dollars using a general index) to provide information supplemental to historical cost statements. The model employed the general price index as an expression of the average purchasing power of a dollar and thus of one's command over economic commodities and services in general. Sweeney illustrated two procedural approaches: One could stabilize each entry during an accounting period or stabilize the balance sheet accounts at the end of the period. He preferred the latter approach because it allowed for quicker, more cost-effective production of financial statements. To stabilize the balance sheet, Sweeney first classified assets and liabilities as "money-value" items or "real-value" items and restated real-value items to the value of money at the end of the period. Preparation of the stabilized income statement followed stabilization of the balance sheet and included monetary gains and losses as well as operating gains and losses.

Sweeney's second model involved stabilization on the basis of replacement costs and incorporated his concept of "appreciation," which apparently is the earliest conceptualization of a holding gain/net of inflation in the literature. Sweeney contended that "appreciation" resulted when the specific price index of an asset rose at a faster rate than the general price index. He considered "appreciation" a gain and included both unrealized and realized appreciation in income. Sweeney considered replacement-cost stabilization superior to general price-level stabilization since it more accurately measured purchasing-power capital mainte-nance. He did not, however, consider it practical or cost-effective.

Although *Stabilized Accounting* made a strong impression on academic accountants at the time of its publication, it was nearly three decades before practitioners showed interest in Sweeney's work. Above-average inflation in the 1960s and rapid inflation in the 1970s focused professional attention on stabilizing price-level fluctuations. In 1963 the basic elements of Sweeney's "general price-level adjustment" model were incorporated in Accounting Research Study No. 6, *Reporting the Financial Effects of Price-Level Changes*. These elements also appeared in Accounting Principles Board (APB) Statement No. 3, "Financial Statements Restated for General Price-Level Changes" (1969), and the Financial Accounting Standards Board's 1974 Exposure Draft, "Financial Reporting in Units of General Purchasing Power."

Perhaps of even greater significance is the fact that Sweeney's stabilization model based on replacement cost, which is the earliest current cost/constant dollar model in the literature, antedates Edgar O. Edwards and Philip W. Bell's *Theory and Measurement of Business Income* (1961) by a quarter of a century. Furthermore, it antedates calls for the disclosure of replacement-cost information by the Securities and Exchange Commission (in Accounting Series Release No. 190, "Disclosure of Certain Replacement Cost Data," of 1976) and the Financial Accounting Standards Board (in Statement of Financial Accounting Standards No. 33, "Financial Reporting and Changing Prices," of 1979) by 40 years. Thus, although Sweeney's name is most often associated with general price-level accounting and indexation, he also pioneered the concept of replacement-cost stabilization (current cost/constant dollar accounting), including the idea of a holding gain/net of inflation.

Laurie Henry
O. Finley Graves

Bibliography

Clarke, F.L. "A Closer Look at Sweeney's Stabilized Accounting Proposals," *Accounting and Business Research*, Autumn 1976, pp. 264–275.

Fesmire, W.E. "Henry Sweeney." In *Biographies of Notable Accountants*, 2d ed., edited by A.M. Agami, pp. 48–51. New York: Random House, 1989.

Graves, O.F. "Accounting for Inflation: Henry Sweeney and the German Gold-

Mark Model," *Accounting Historians Journal,* Spring 1987, pp. 33–56.

———. "Fritz Schmidt, Henry Sweeney and Stabilized Accounting," *Accounting and Business Research*, Spring 1991, pp. 119–124.

Nasso, C., ed. *Contemporary Authors: Permanent Series.* vol. 2, p. 504. Detroit: Gale, 1978.

Sweeney, H.W. *Stabilized Accounting.* New York: Harper & Row, 1936. Reprint. New York: Holt, Rinehart and Winston, 1964.

———. "Maintenance of Capital," *Accounting Review*, December 1930, pp. 277–287.

———. "Capital," *Accounting Review*, September 1933, pp. 185–199.

———. "How Inflation Affects the Balance Sheets," *Accounting Review,* December 1934, pp. 277–299.

See also ACCOUNTING RESEARCH STUDIES; ACCOUNTING SERIES RELEASE NO. 190; CAPITAL MAINTENANCE; EDWARDS AND BELL: REPLACEMENT-COST ACCOUNTING; FINANCIAL ACCOUNTING STANDARDS BOARD; HISTORICAL COST; INFLATION ACCOUNTING; PATON, WILLIAM ANDREW; SCHMALENBACH, EUGEN; SCHMIDT, JULIUS AUGUST FRITZ

T

Tally Stick

The notched stick and the knotted cord are probably the world's oldest accounting devices. The tally stick was a receipt for tax payments in medieval England. In the twelfth century, it was usually a narrow hazelwood stick, eight or nine inches long, notched to indicate the amount received. An incision the width of a man's palm represented a thousand pounds; a hundred pounds was a thumb's-width cut; twenty pounds the width of a little finger; a pound "the thickness of a grain of ripe barley"; a shilling just a notch; a penny a simple cut with no wood removed; and a half penny a punched hole. After the amount paid had been carved, a diagonal crosscut was made an inch or two from the thicker end of the tally, and the whole stick was split down the middle into two identically notched parts of equal length. The flat sides of both pieces were inscribed in Latin to show that they related to the same debt, and as additional protection, the crosscuts were made at various angles on different tally sticks so that no "foil" or shorter piece could be matched to any "stock" but its own.

While continuing to serve as receipts, tallies in later years were also used as notes payable, tax-anticipation warrants, postdated checks, and bills of exchange. A private debt might be acknowledged by a tally cut for the amount owed and given to the creditor, who at the proper time presented it for payment. Resorting to deficit financing, the Plantagenet and Tudor kings first occasionally and then routinely raised money on the security of tallies, which gave their recipients the right to receive future tax revenues or even, in the Roman fashion, to collect certain taxes themselves. Still later, government tallies circulated as negotiable instruments, reducing the inflow and outflow of coined money at the Exchequer and complicating the recording of the Receipt Roll. As the volume of Exchequer tally transactions increased, they came to be regarded as a speculative government security and were discounted by the Goldsmith Bankers. During the eighteenth century they were gradually replaced by Exchequer bills, and were finally abolished in 1826.

Michael Chatfield

Bibliography

Baxter, W.T. "Early Accounting: The Tally and Checkerboard," *Accounting Historians Journal*, December 1989, pp. 43–83.

Robert, R. "A Short History of Tallies." In *Studies in the History of Accounting,* edited by A.C. Littleton and B.S. Yamey, pp. 75–85. Homewood, IL: Irwin, 1956.

Stone, W.E. "The Tally: An Ancient Accounting Instrument," *Abacus*, June 1975, pp. 49–57.

See also AGRICULTURAL ACCOUNTING; MEDIEVAL ACCOUNTING; PROFFER SYSTEM

Tax-Ordained Accounting

In ancient Greece, people believed that a tax on wealth was fair. They invented different means of control because a verifiable accounting system was unknown. If someone believed a neighbor unfairly paid less tax than he should have, he could publicly challenge the neighbor. If the challenger proved that there was an evasion of tax, he received three-quarters of that undeclared asset as a reward and subsequently had to pay a tax on the reward. If he were beaten in the lawsuit, the informer had to pay a fine of 1,000 drachmas. One drachma corresponded to the day's pay of a construction worker. In addition, he would lose his right to publicly act as plaintiff for another case.

Until the conquest of Macedonia (167 B.C.), which brought great bounties into the Roman treasury, Roman citizens had to pay tributes (direct taxes) to the Roman treasury (Coffield). Roman citizens had to register their net wealth in lists under oath. Therefore these lists were the first examples of rendering an accounting for purposes of taxation. Guidelines for this Roman taxation of wealth had been the rule adapted from Roman civil law, that a tax is a burden on fruits. One consequence is that taxes paid on the dowry of a wife did not reduce the assets that would be repaid to her by her former husband after a divorce.

Attempts at tax-ordained accounting could be found in governmental budgets in which government officials had to calculate the amount of tax revenue needed to make public expenditures. In about 1086 William the Conqueror set up a register of land estates in England. Based on this Domesday Book and other records, the Chancellor of the Exchequer deduced the Crown's claims against its subjects. This occurred first in a Pipe Roll about 1130. The Pipe Roll provided a narrative description of rents, taxes, and other fixed levies due to the king, together with a summary of payments made on these debts and expenses incurred in collecting them.

In the Middle Ages, sovereigns requested the lower classes to pay new taxes. Wealth taxes were imposed, particularly in cities. Citizens had to make a self-assessment of their wealth and take an oath swearing its veracity in the presence of tax commissions. There was no general control of tax evasion, but punishment for false statements was severe. In Basle, Augsburg, and other cities, for instance, if a citizen lied, the members of the commission had the right to purchase the assets for the underrated price.

Common practice was to state the fair market value of one's assets. Merchandise was exempted, because according to Roman law it did not belong to the fruit-bearing assets. This was because the sale of inventory, rather than its use, was fruitful. Generally merchandise did not become a taxable asset until the seventeenth century. Therefore, no generally accepted valuation rule had been adopted for tax-ordained accounting.

In 1443 the consultants of Cosimo di Medici in Florence invented a progressive tax on estimated receipts and called it *la graziosa*. Competitors of the Medici had to present books and closing accounts to the tax authority. Above all these documents served as a means to verify inventories of foreign deposits and claims. They did not serve for profit determination or as a statement of wealth.

The proposal by Marshal Sébastien Le Prestre de Vauban in a tract in 1707 for tax reform during the time of Louis XIV in France, as well as the various income taxes introduced in Great Britain during the Napoleonic Wars and in the nineteenth century, did not impose tax-ordained accounting. For example, the British income taxes in the nineteenth century were mainly taxes on gross revenue. Mining companies, commerce, and small businesses had to pay taxes on self-declared average profit of the last five years. Whereas estate owners and tenant farmers could not avoid the taxation of their gross revenues, merchants were privileged, because their records were not inspected. If a merchant did not agree with the result of the tax official, the merchant could appeal against it under the conditions that he would have to reply to questions and to allow examinations into books and records. Since the introduction of the income tax in 1842 by Sir Robert Peel until 1885, only 38 judgments on tax disputes were pronounced. That is the reason why only a few people were irritated about the dubious contents of special tax regulations, e.g., that it was not until 1878 that depreciation on assets were allowed to reduce the taxable income.

The idea to apply commercial balance sheets for income taxation had been realized first in 1874 in the Kingdom of Saxony, in the town of Bremen, and 1891 in Prussia. The reason was the convenience of preparing only one balance sheet for capital markets and tax authorities. The different content between profit determination by accretion accounting for commercial law and by cash-based accounting for tax purposes, as was the practice at that time, was hardly recognized.

The income determination for tax purposes had been originated in the "fruit" or income from sources concept in Roman law. One consequence is that the supreme expert in tax matters in Prussia, Bernhard Fuisting, in 1907 explained it would be foolish to deduct losses from taxable profit that was caused by fire or new inventions.

Following the principle in Prussian law that the commercial accounts should be identical with the tax accounts, depreciation was seen as an entry that served to put aside revenues for replacement of the assets. For that reason, the Prussian law accepted only depreciation shortened by compound interest. In 1895 the tax official B. von Wilmowski criticized that the annual depreciation charge for a building with a useful economic life of 50 years and 4 percent interest per annum is only 0.63 percent of original cost. Therefore, less than a third of the original cost reduced taxable profit. On the strength of this argument, the tax law was changed to allow the periodic allocation of original cost. The financial courts in Prussia and Saxony elaborated in detail the German accounting standards for tax-ordained accounting.

In 1896 income taxation based on accrual accounting was developed by Georg Schanz, an economist in Wuerzburg. His article in the *Finanz Archiv* was the main source of the Haig-Simons income concept. The origin of this income concept may also be traced to a book of the Bavarian economist Friederick Benedikt Wilhelm von Hermann in 1832, who recognized the need to adjust for the changing purchasing power of money in contrast to Schanz, whose knowledge of accounting standards was limited. The Haig-Simons concept of income tax was a comprehensive one. The concept was promoted by Henry C. Simons, an economist at the University of Chicago in 1938, and was based on the writings of Robert Murray Haig, a professor at Columbia University. The Haig-Simons concept was "that the income tax should be levied on the most comprehensive measure of income with no personal deductions" (Feldstein). Simons was in favor of a progressive income tax system so as to moderate economic inequality.

In the 20th century, taxation of corporate profits became generally accepted and led to a vast number of special regulations concerning tax-ordained accounting in every country. The development of tax-ordained accounting has differed to such a degree in these countries that nobody can in 1994 provide valid international comparisons of effective tax rates for the profit of firms and the income of persons.

Dieter Schneider

Bibliography

Coffield, J. *A Popular History of Taxation: From Ancient to Modern Times.* London: Longman, 1970.

Feldstein, M. "A Contribution to the Theory of Tax Expenditures: The Case of Charitable Giving." In *The Economics of Taxation*, edited by H.J. Aaron and M.J. Boskin, pp. 99–122. Washington: Brookings, 1980.

Fuisting, B. *Die Preussischen direkten Steuren.* 1. Bd. 7th ed. Berlin: C. Heymann, 1907.

Hermann, F.B.W. von. *Staatswissenschaftliche untersuchungen über Vermögen.* Munich: A. Weber, 1832.

Schanz, G. "Der Einkommenbegriff und die Einkommensteuergesetze," *Finanz Archiv*, vol. 13, 1896, pp. 1–87.

Schneider, D. *Allgemeine Betriebswirtschaftslehre.* 3d ed. Munich and Vienna: Oldenbourg, 1987.

Simons, H.C. *Personal Income Taxation: The Definition of Income as a Problem of Fiscal Policy.* Chicago: University of Chicago Press, 1938.

Vauban, S.L.P. de. *Projet d'une Dixme Royale.* Paris: N.p., 1707.

Wilmowski, B. "Die Abschreibungen für Abnutzung von Gebäuden, Maschinen, Betriebsgeräthschaften . . ." *Verwaltungsarchiv.* vol. 3, 1895, pp. 366–383.

See also BRAZIL: INFLATION ACCOUNTING; CONSERVATISM; DOMESDAY BOOK; FRANCE; GERMANY; GREECE; ITALY, AFTER PACIOLI; PIPE ROLL; ROME (509 B.C.–A.D. 476); SCOTLAND: EARLY WRITERS IN DOUBLE ENTRY ACCOUNTING; TRANSFER PRICES

Tax Reform Acts

Tax reform in the United States followed closely behind the permanent introduction of the income tax in 1913. Attempts to reform the income tax laws began in the early 1930s and continued for the rest of the twentieth century. Most major reforms consisted of attempts either to reduce the abuses of the tax laws or to improve the efficiency and effectiveness of the income tax structure.

The first tax act that could be considered a reform bill was the Revenue Act of 1934. The income tax burden had increased considerably between 1913 and 1930 and had become an important component of federal revenues. Furthermore, many more people were affected by the income tax, increasing the political pressure for a simple, equitable tax system. Revenue acts appeared annually from the mid-1930s through the end of World War II. This proliferation of revenue acts resulted in their first codification in 1939, producing the Internal Revenue Code of 1939.

The post–World War II period saw the first major rewriting of Internal Revenue Code. By the early 1950s, the Internal Revenue Code of 1939 was woefully complicated, inconsistent, and confusing. The rewriting eventually produced the Internal Revenue Code of 1954, a document that stood almost unchanged until 1962. Although improved both substantively and administratively, the 1954 Code continued the trend of increased complexity through its myriad of special exclusions, deductions, and credits.

By the end of the 1960s, the increased deficits caused by the war in Vietnam led to calls for new tax revenues. This demand for revenue occurred while the Treasury Department was examining the issue of tax reform. The Tax Reform Act of 1969 evolved from these two disparate objectives. The passage of the 1969 act heralded the modern age of tax legislation and income tax policy. The Tax Reform Act of 1969 began as an attempt to improve the fairness of the income tax structure, particularly as it affected low- and middle-income taxpayers. Although in the end the act increased rather than decreased the number of special provisions in the tax law, it did increase the progressivity of the income tax system.

The early 1970s was a period of tax reduction and the introduction of new incentives in the tax code, but calls for tax reform continued. During this period, the Treasury Department tax policy staff prepared a seminal work on tax reform. In this work, eventually published as *Blueprints for Basic Tax Reform* (1977), a great deal of attention was paid to the idea of broadening the tax base and integrating the taxation of corporations and individuals.

The Tax Reform Act of 1976 was produced after a major political battle between the liberal Democrats and the conservative Democrats and Republicans. Very few of the *Blueprint* study's reform recommendations found their way into the 1976 act. In the end, the act left most lawmakers unsatisfied, and its changes added considerably to the complexity of the tax code. However, the 1976 act did introduce many anti-tax shelter provisions to address the complaints that the wealthy were using "loopholes" to un-

fairly reduce their tax burden. The act also helped the working poor by extending the earned income credit and the general tax credit.

The 1980s saw some of the most significant and frequent changes to income tax law in the post–World War II period. Tax reduction and simplification were the goals of the Reagan administration, and supply-side economics moved to the forefront in the debate over tax policy. The Economic Recovery Tax Act of 1981 substantially reduced taxes across the income distribution and introduced many of the "reform" provisions that had been debated during the previous decade. The top individual tax rate was reduced to 50 percent, Individual Retirement Account rules were expanded to cover more taxpayers, and depreciation rules were simplified and liberalized. A major recommendation of the 1977 *Blueprints* study was finally enacted when the 1981 act introduced the indexing of tax brackets, standard deductions, and exemption amounts.

The liberalized depreciation rules, combined with other features of the 1981 act, increased tax-shelter activity and set the stage for the eventual 1986 reforms. The quickly mounting deficits of the early 1980s led to an immediate move to counter the tax reduction of the 1981 act. The Tax Equity and Fiscal Responsibility Act of 1982 and the Deficit Reduction Act of 1984 scaled back the benefits of accelerated depreciation and the investment tax credit, although not to pre-1981 levels. These acts contained further attempts to reduce the benefits of tax shelters.

The combination of rising deficits and calls for tax simplification set the stage for the most significant base-broadening tax reform of the post–World War II period. The Tax Reform Act of 1986 attempted to reverse at least 40 years of tax policy, which had produced many special tax breaks. The intent of the 1986 act was to create a level playing field and reduce the tax-driven decisions of the 1970s and early 1980s. The 1986 act lowered marginal tax rates significantly and considerably expanded the tax base. The changes produced by the Tax Reform Act of 1986 were so substantial that the tax code was renamed the Internal Revenue Code of 1986, the first change since 1954.

The Tax Reform Act of 1986 was almost a surprise. Tax reform had not been a major issue during the 1984 presidential election campaign, and few lawmakers wanted to tackle the daunting task of removing 40 years' worth of special tax benefits. Somehow, the right people were at the right places and the 1986 act happened. The detailed story of this political and economic feat was set forth in *Showdown at Gucci Gulch: Lawmakers, Lobbyists, and the Unlikely Triumph of Tax Reform* (1987) by Jeffrey Birnbaum and Alan Murray.

The tax reform put in place by the 1986 act was still virtually intact by 1994. Several tax acts in the late 1980s and early 1990s produced minor changes in income tax law, but the base-broadening of the 1986 act remained in place.

Tax reform will remain an important economic and social issue, given the importance of the income tax to federal revenues and the increasing complexity of the Internal Revenue Code. Past tax reform efforts have demonstrated amply the difficulties in achieving "good" tax policy.

Gary A. McGill

Bibliography

Birnbaum, J.H., and A.S. Murray. *Showdown at Gucci Gulch: Lawmakers, Lobbyists, and the Unlikely Triumph of Tax Reform.* New York: Vintage Book, 1987.

Bradford, D.F., and the U.S. Treasury Tax Policy Staff. *Blueprints for Basic Tax Reform.* 2d ed. Arlington, VA: Tax Analysts, 1984.

Steuerle, C.E. *The Tax Decade.* Washington, DC: Urban Institute Press, 1992.

Witte, J.F. *The Politics and Development of the Federal Income Tax.* Madison, WI: University of Wisconsin Press, 1985.

See also INCOME TAXATION IN THE UNITED STATES; LAST IN, FIRST OUT (LIFO); NATURAL BUSINESS YEAR; SIXTEENTH AMENDMENT

Taylor, Frederick Winslow (1856–1915)
An American mechanical engineer considered the father of scientific management, Frederick Winslow Taylor implemented scientific management in various factories in the United States. Taylor was born in Philadelphia and studied engineering at the Stevens Institute of Technology in Hoboken, New Jersey. He worked in various factories, including the Midvale Steel Company where he first introduced his shop-order system of control. He later became a consultant to factories installing his system. He died in 1915 at the height of the efficiency movement in the United States.

Among Taylor's most influential writings was "Principles and Methods of Scientific Management," published in the *Journal of Accountancy* in June and July 1911. He also wrote several books, including *The Principles of Scientific Management* and *Shop Management,* which were both published in 1911.

Scientific management was a system that attempted to increase worker efficiency by setting standards for the worker, the quality of equipment, and the method of doing work. Also referred to as the "Taylor system," it was an attempt to systematize, organize, and standardize all methods of operations in manufacturing concerns. The basis for achieving these standards was elementary time study, which breaks down each element of work so that a basis may be established for the development of standards. He implemented scientific management into numerous factories, including the Midvale Steel Company, Tabor Manufacturing Company, Bethlehem Steel Company, Link Belt Company, H.H. Franklin Company and the Manufacturing Investment Company. Link Belt and Tabor were the only companies that installed the Taylor system throughout their factories.

The American Society of Mechanical Engineers (ASME) from 1880 to 1912 was the center of the discussions regarding wage-incentive systems for factory workers and for the scientific management movement. Taylor wrote about a new wage-payment method, "A Piece Rate System" (1895), that was the foundation of his later studies. These concepts were debated in the society among its members, including Henry Laurence Gantt, H.R. Towne and F.A. Halsey, who also had wage-payment systems. Taylor's wage system required time-and-motion studies to determine how long it should take to do each piece of work. The wage-rate scheme was based on the setting of realistic production standards and their implementation in the factory process. All factory operations, from equipment and supply maintenance to office procedures, were standardized.

Taylor's system determined standards for work output. The accounting systems in these factories were seen as means of informing management and others of the costs of production. In order to set prices for a bid contract, the management needed to be able to predetermine or estimate costs. Therefore, accounting also fell under the principle of standardization. His public involvement in cost accounting started in 1886 with his comments at the annual meeting of the American Society of Mechanical Engineers. Taylor was president of the ASME in 1906, and his presidential address, "The Art of Cutting Metals," provided a summary of his 26 years spent fostering scientific management.

Scientific management was popularized by the Eastern Rate Case of 1910–1911. In the last quarter of the nineteenth century, the railroads were among the largest corporate enterprises. The railroads helped to transform the United States from an agrarian economy to an industrial economy. As the railroads grew in size, they also needed to better control their costs, which was an integral element of scientific management. Louis D. Brandeis, who later became a U.S. Supreme Court justice, was the attorney representing Eastern railroad shippers in rate hearings before the Interstate Commerce Commission. He argued that operating costs could be decreased by the application of the principles of Taylor's scientific management. Gantt, Harrington Emerson, and Frank Gilbreth, all noted industrial engineers, also testified at these public hearings, which were effective in making scientific management a household word. The discussions of "efficiency" became widespread in the popular press during 1910–1920. Conferences were held and numerous articles were written dealing with efficiency in all aspects of life.

Scientific management required that work procedures be broken down into minute time periods and cost structures. Thus, each element of work—the cost of labor, for example—necessary to make a steel beam was broken down into minutes, seconds, and dollars. Costs of materials were defined and calculated precisely. Engineers and accountants needed to work together to develop a system that could provide management with the information it needed to make decisions for more effective planning and control.

The development of scientific management created a need for new accounting systems that could break down production costs into their various component parts and estimate the costs of future production. It needed an accounting system that could determine actual costs and compare those costs with the predetermined standards that the engineers had calculated. It needed an accounting system that could attach costs to the predetermined standards of performance. Standard cost accounting was that system. It was developed as a direct result of the work of Taylor and the scientific management movement.

Though after Taylor's death the scientific management movement lost its strength, accountants such as Alexander Hamilton Church, G. Charter Harrison, Harrington Emerson, and John Whitmore continued to develop and refine the methodology for developing standard cost accounting. But Taylor's work can be directly seen as at the foundation of modern cost accounting.

Marc J. Epstein

Bibliography

Copley, F.B. *Frederick W. Taylor: Father of Scientific Management*. New York: Harper & Brothers, 1923.

Drury, H.B. *Scientific Management: A History and Criticism*. New York: Drury, 1915.

Epstein, M.J. *The Effect of Scientific Management on the Development of the Standard Cost System*. New York: Arno Press, 1978.

Taylor, F.W. "On the Art of Cutting Metals," *Transactions of the American Society of Mechanical Engineers*, vol. 28, 1907, pp. 31–350.

———. *The Principles of Scientific Management*. New York: Harper & Brothers, 1911.

———. "A Piece Rate System," *Transactions of the American Society of Mechanical Engineers*, vol. 16, 1895, pp. 856–883.

———. "Comments on Henry Metcalfe's 'The Shop-Order System of Accounts'," *Transactions of the American Society of Mechanical Engineers*, vol. 7, 1886, pp. 475–476.

See also BUDGETING; CHURCH, ALEXANDER HAMILTON; COMMON COSTS; CONTROL: CLASSICAL MODEL; COST AND/OR MANAGEMENT ACCOUNTING; EMERSON, HARRINGTON; ENGINEERING AND ACCOUNTING; GANTT, HENRY LAURENCE; HARRISON, G. CHARTER; JOHNSON AND KAPLAN'S *RELEVANCE LOST: THE RISE AND FALL OF MANAGEMENT ACCOUNTING;* MANAGEMENT ACCOUNTING; MUNICIPAL ACCOUNTING REFORM; RAILROAD ACCOUNTING (U.S.); STANDARD COSTING; WHITMORE, JOHN

Thomas's *The Allocation Problem in Financial Accounting Theory*

An American Accounting Association Study in Accounting Research (No. 3), this 1969 book has become a classic. In it, Arthur L. Thomas strove to prove the arbitrariness of the decision to allocate the cost of nonmonetary assets. Because his conclusions concerning the arbitrary nature of cost allocations have gained wide support and his work is often quoted by accounting scholars, his magnum opus should be carefully read. While it challenges much of what is done by accountants, it is not challenging reading and is quite logical in format.

Thomas sought to find theoretical justification for an allocation method that (1) should be unambiguous, (2) should be possible to defend, and (3) should divide up what is available to be allocated. Thomas selected depreciation as his example for the study. He quickly rejected the standard formula approach and spent much time with the "net-revenue contribution" approach for depreciation. Could this approach isolate a depreciation amount equal to the present value of the incremental gain associated with a machine? Thomas decided it couldn't because of the fact that revenues are a joint product of all the inputs of a firm. It is not possible to decompose the present value of nonmonetary inputs into specific items.

Thomas examined some solutions to this problem but could not find a clear-cut one. He felt the "continuously contemporary accounting" approach of R.J. Chambers, an Australian accounting theorist, and the current-valuation measurements of Robert R. Sterling, a United States accounting theorist, to be promising but not yet a solution. Thomas felt that another solution would be to substitute the funds statement for the measurement of income. This also was promising but, again, not yet a solution. While Thomas grudgingly admitted the safety of the matching approach, he made this prediction: "*Arbitrary* variety cannot persist forever; eventually, standardization is inevitable."

Thomas included an appendix in which he asked readers to attempt to disprove his deductive reasoning. He offered nine examples of possible rebuttals to the study. One key question raised in the examples is: "How arbitrary can accounting be without losing effectiveness as a model?" That question should be asked and answered each time an accountant is making a cost-allocation decision.

Arthur Thomas received his B.S. from Cornell in 1952, an MBA from Cornell in 1956, and his Ph.D. from the University of Michigan in 1963. In 1980, he was appointed the second Arthur Young Distinguished Professor of Accounting at the University of Kansas School of Business. He retired from that position in 1987. Just prior to his appointment at the University of Kansas, he had been the Harmon Whittington Professor at Rice University's Graduate School of Administration from 1977. He has also taught at McMaster University in Ontario (1969–1977) and at the University of Oregon (1963–1969). His other books were *Revenue Recognition* (1966), *Financial Accounting—The Main Ideas* (1972), and *The Allocation Problem: Part Two* (1974).

Richard Vangermeersch

Bibliography

Staubus, G. "The Dark Ages of Cost Accounting: The Role of Miscues in the Literature," *Accounting Historians Journal*, Fall 1987, pp. 1–18.

Thomas, A.L. *Financial Accounting: The Main Ideas*. Belmont, CA: Wadsworth, 1972.

———. *Revenue Recognition*. Michigan Business Reports No. 49. Ann Arbor, MI: Bureau of Business Research, Graduate School of Business Administration, University of Michigan, 1966.

———. *The Allocation Problem in Financial Accounting Theory*. Study in Accounting Research No. 3. Sarasota, FL: American Accounting Association, 1969.

———. *The Allocation Problem: Part Two*. Studies in Accounting Research No. 9. Sarasota, FL: American Accounting Association, 1974.

See also AMERICAN ACCOUNTING ASSOCIATION; CHAMBERS, RAYMOND JOHN; COMMON COSTS; DEPRECIATION; LADELLE, O.G.; MATCHING; STERLING, ROBERT R.

Towne v. Eisner

See EISNER V. MACOMBER

Transfer Prices

In a broad sense, all valuations in accounting that differ from former or present market prices may be called transfer prices. Such valuations are necessary to account for matching purposes (e.g., depreciation of fixed assets, if it should not coincide with the reduction of the used assets' market prices) or for unfinished and not yet marketable products. In a narrow sense, transfer prices are all those valuations that are used for the following four reasons. The first reason concerns special taxation purposes, as in the transfer price employed in the international taxation of affiliated companies as a result of the failure to deal at arm's length.

The second reason is for the elimination of the fluctuations of the prices for factors of production in order to make planning and controlling easier. This accounted for the first time transfer prices were used in the history of accounting.

In his *Indrizzo degli Economi* (1586), Don Angelo Pietra, a Benedictine friar from Genoa, recorded his inventory at lower transfer prices to ensure it would not be sold at a loss. Today it would be considered unethical for a manager to determine profits based on arbitrarily reduced values. Similar arguments can be found in Luca Pacioli's 1494 treatise on accounting in *Summa de Arithmetica*—"Increase the value of your merchandise in order to make it easier for you to show a profit"—as well as in Frenchman Jacques Savary's *Le Parfait Negociant* (1675): "Preparing one's inventory there is enough time to consider the values carefully and there is no need to sell at this price later." It appears that these much-praised early authors in bookkeeping did not intend to deceive the recipients of balance sheets. They rather followed the thinking of their time and took symbols (figures) for facts, following a concept of profit that seems to be absurd today. In 1636 Ludovico Flori in his *Trattato del Modo di Tenere il Libro Doppio Domestico* also called for transfer prices as a means to simplify accounting.

Simon Peter Gasser demanded in 1729 the use of long-term average prices for the valuation of agricultural products in planning and budgeting in *Einleitung zu den Œconomischen Politischen und Cameral-Wissenschaften*. He was the first professor at a chair for business economics in the University of Halle in Prussia in 1729. Gasser's example was followed in Berlin by Albrecht Daniel Thaer, who was an important teacher in agricultural economics and in 1809 wrote *Grundsätze der rationellen Landwirthschaft*. The first time that the difficulties of joint-production costing were discussed was by Johann Freyherr von Puteani and concerned the slightly "smelly" question of how to account for a dunghill in his 1818 book *Grundsätze des allgemeinen Rechnungswesens*.

Leopold Friedrich Fredersdorff used transfer prices to eliminate price fluctuation for the ironworks industry in 1802 in *Praktische Anleitung zu einer guten Eisenhütten-Œconomie*.

The third reason many writers in accounting have employed the concept of transfer prices is to work out a meaningful concept of profit. Thus, the author of one of the important Cameralistic publications (Johann Mathias Puechberg, 1774, head accountant at the Austrian Treasury) stressed the importance of fixed transfer prices for opening and closing stock in *Grundsätze der Rechnunges-Wissenschaft auf das Privatvermögen angewendet*.

The fourth reason concerns the modern emphasis on transfer prices as a means to approximate efficient allocation within a firm that produces numerous goods at various stages of production. Eugen Schmalenbach was the first to make use of the cost theory of the marginal utility school in his article "uber Verrechnungspreise" in *Zeitschrift für handelswissenschaftliche Forschung*, vol. 3 (1908/1909). He particularly employed the imputation theory of Friedrich von Wieser, who had developed in *Über den Ursprung und die Hauptgesetze des Wirtschaftlichen Werther* (1884) the concept of opportunity costs. Because Schmalenbach did not know the mathematical technique of linear programming, he could take into account only one scarce factor. The fact that in the case of unimpeded procurement, marginal costs represent the correct transfer prices was mathematically proved for the first time by Heinrich von Stackelberg, a mathematical economist in Germany, in 1934. Today shadow prices as a by-product from mathematical programming form the generalization of the marginal utility school's transfer prices.

To achieve an optimal allocation using transfer prices, a central planning authority must know all possible actions and all capacities at hand. Therefore, transfer prices can only make sense in a centrally planned economy where the planning authority needs to have nearly universal knowledge. The socialist Abba P. Lerner for example went to see Leon Trotsky in exile in Mexico. Trotsky was Vladimir Lenin's second in command during the early years of the USSR and later was purged by Josef Stalin. Lerner tried to convince Trotsky that if prices were set at marginal costs, a communist economy would run smoothly.

The theory of allocating efficient transfer prices played a major role in the "accounting in socialism" debate from 1920 to 1940 with such theorists as Fred M. Taylor from the University of Michigan, and Oskar Lange, a Polish economist and also a lecturer at the University of Michigan and the University of Chicago. In 1947 Schmalenbach recognized that transfer prices as shadow prices contradicted a decentralized organization. He had to accept that his price-related allocation, also, was the same as that being done in a centrally planned economy.

The main objections against that social order had been put forward already in 1920 by Ludwig von Mises, a German economist, and in 1935 by Fredrich A. von Hayek, an Austrian and then American economist: How is a central planning authority supposed to acquire that level of knowledge that is incompletely and unevenly spread among the members of an economic organization? What is the motivation of centrally controlled socialist and capitalist managers in socialist economies or large-scale enterprises to pursue the interest of their enterprises? And what attitude will they show toward risk? These problems have marked the discussion about allocational transfer prices during the last decades. It started in 1956 with the University of Chicago business economist Jack Hirshleifer's propositions for the determination of transfer prices and the works of Andrew Whinston, Professor of Economics and Industrial Management at Purdue University (1964), and William Baumol and Tibor Fabian, both mathematical economists (1964), which were more concerned with the shadow prices of programming. Mises's and von Hayek's questions have been adopted by authors of recent works in agency theory.

But there remain unsolved problems for coordination problems by transfer prices within the firm. The signaling function of market prices in a competitive environment distributes the knowledge about scarcity and surplus among individually operating "economic entities" that coordinate their economic plans only by the help of market prices as exchange-rate indicators. To rely on unadjusted observed market prices in multistage production is only possible in a few cases. The adjustment to an approximation of market prices increases information costs and opens up a scope of discretion that will definitely have a distorting effect.

Empirical studies such as Robert G. Eccles of the Harvard University Graduate School of Business Administration (1985) show a diverse bundle of transfer prices, often based on cost plus basis and partly negotiated among components of a company. Transfer prices based on direct costs are scarcely ever found in practice.

Dieter Schneider

Bibliography

Baumol, W., and T. Fabian. "Decomposition, Pricing for Decentralization and External Economies," *Management Science*, September 1964, pp. 1–32.

Eccles, R.G. *The Transfer Pricing Problem*. Lexington, MA: Lexington Books, 1985.

Hirshleifer, J. "On the Economies of Transfer Pricing," *Journal of Business*, July 1956, pp. 172–184.

Lange, O. "On the Economic Theory of Socialism," *Review of Economic Studies*, October 1936 and February 1937, pp. 53–71 and pp. 123–142. Reprint, with additions. O. Lange and F.M. Taylor, *On the Economic Theory of Socialism*. Minneapolis: University of Minnesota Press, 1938.

Mises, L. von. "Economic Calculation in the Socialist Society." In *Collectivist Economic Planning,* edited by F.A. von Hayek, pp. 87–130. London: G. Routledge, 1935. The article published in 1920 as "Die Wirtschaftsrechnung im sozialistlichen Gemeinwesen" in *Archiv für Sozialwissenschaften*, vol. 47.

Schneider, D. *Allgemeine Betriebswirtschaftslehre*. 3d ed., Munich and Vienna: Oldenbourg, 1987.

Stackelberg, H. von. *Marktform und Gleichgewicht*. Wien und Berlin: J. Springer, 1934.

Whinston, A. "Price Guides in Decentralized Organizations." In *New Perspectives in Organization Research,* edited by W.W. Cooper, H.J. Leavitt, and M.W. Shelly II, pp. 405–448. New York: Wiley, 1964.

See also BROWN, F. DONALDSON; FLORI, LUDOVICO; GERMANY; MATCHING; MICROECONOMICS IN GERMANY; PACIOLI, LUCA; PIETRA, ANGELO; SAVARY, JACQUES; SCHMALENBACH, EUGEN; TAX-ORDAINED ACCOUNTING

Treadway Commission

In October 1985, five of the most prominent private-sector accounting associations undertook the formidable task of identifying the factors that promote fraudulent financial reporting, as well as offering recommendations to mitigate these factors. Over the next two years, the American Institute of Certified Public Accountants (AICPA), the American Accounting Association, the Financial Executives Institute, the Institute of Internal Auditors, and the National Association of Accountants sponsored and funded an independent National Commission on Fraudulent Financial Reporting. Ultimately, the Commission took on the name of its chairman, James C. Treadway, who had been a former commissioner of the Securities and Exchange Commission (SEC).

The Treadway Commission was charged with three major objectives: (1) to investigate the impact of fraud on the integrity of the entire financial-reporting system, (2) to examine the external auditor's degree of responsibility in detecting fraudulent practices, and (3) to highlight those attributes of corporate structure that facilitate or fail to detect fraud. Its final report, dated September 1987, included numerous conclusions and recommendations across four constituent groups that represent the divergent influences on the reporting process: the public company, the independent public accountants, the SEC and other regulatory/legal bodies, and accounting educators.

Initially, the commission reached several fundamental conclusions that were utilized to shape and guide its myriad recommendations. Specifically, it noted that organizations that acquire funds from the public markets assume an obligation of public trust and must be held accountable for full and fair disclosure of financial information to all interested users. The independent auditors, in turn, assume a public responsibility to examine and evaluate the reasonableness of these disclosures. Moreover, although the commission members acknowledged the exceptional quality of the American financial-reporting system, they concluded that there was still a need for improvement. As a result, the commission identified other relevant factors to guide its conclusions, including the material impact of fraudulent financial reporting, the risk of its occurrence and likely causes, and the realistic potential for reducing this risk via a multidimensional strategy directed toward each participant group.

The final report first presented an integrated description of the financial-reporting system for public companies, followed by a discussion of the causes of fraudulent reporting, the perpetrators and their means, the implica-

tions of fraud, and the evolutionary nature of fraudulent financial reporting. In essence, the committee observed that all companies, to some degree, have environmental, institutional, or individual forces and opportunities that permit individuals and companies to engage in fraudulent practices. Inevitably, these forces and opportunities are influenced by societal changes, which necessitate continued study and revision.

Clearly, however, the Treadway Commission devoted the major part of its report to recommendations for the four key participant groups. Foremost in the financial-reporting process, the public company is responsible for the preparation and content of published financial information, and, accordingly, the commission stressed the need for top management to set the tone for the overall organization. This would entail identifying and assessing the factors that can lead to fraudulent financial reporting and, in turn, establishing adequate systems of internal control and developing written codes of conduct. The commission strongly urged that organizations establish an informed, vigilant, and effective audit committee to oversee the financial-reporting process and scrutinize the nature and scope of audit activities.

While independent public accountants do not take responsibility for the content of reported financial information, they do assume a crucial role in the reporting process. Consequently, the Treadway membership urged the accounting profession to work more diligently to uncover fraudulent practices and to improve the detection capabilities of the independent audit (e.g., analytic procedures). Several recommendations were also offered for improving audit quality through peer and concurring reviews, and for more effective communication of the independent auditor's roles and responsibilities in the reporting process. In its closing section, the commission urged the accounting community to reorganize the Auditing Standards Board (ASB) and the audit standard-setting process. Of particular note was the suggestion that the overall process be opened to more knowledgeable individuals who are concerned about the direction and content of auditing standards but who are not practicing CPAs.

The recommendations to the SEC and other oversight bodies focused on the benefits of reforming the regulatory and legal environment. The commission advocated expansion of SEC sanctions and greater criminal prosecutions in order to enforce the law, and as a means of mitigating the temptation to more effectively commit fraud. Notwithstanding the effectiveness of increased legal jurisdiction, the SEC was also charged with taking a more visible role in encouraging a substantive self-regulation program by public accountants. The commission also urged parties involved in tort reform initiatives to consider the impact of the liability crisis on external auditors, and it encouraged the SEC to reevaluate its policy that restricts liability indemnification of corporate officers and directors.

Accounting educators were recognized as playing a key role in the development of aspiring accountants. Accordingly, the commission endorsed a business and accounting curriculum that would foster understanding of fraudulent financial reporting and the nature of internal control, and knowledge of regulation and law-enforcement policies designed to protect the financial-reporting system. These curriculum changes must be balanced with an emphasis on developing the student's requisite skills to be a competent accountant, integrating and encouraging the understanding and acceptance of ethical values in the context of the accounting profession, and continued faculty development to improve classroom content.

A tangible measure of any authoritative commission is its subsequent impact on effecting change. Retrospectively, the Treadway Commission appears to have had a direct and far-reaching influence on the manner in which fraudulent practices are regulated, as well as increasing the awareness of key participants in the detection and prevention of fraudulent financial practices. As an example, the call for a more concerted effort to identify and resolve compelling issues and problems in the area of internal control was addressed by the Committee of Sponsoring Organizations of the Treadway Commission (COSO). Under the auspices of the five private-sector accounting associations, Coopers and Lybrand conducted a comprehensive study of internal control, collecting insights from hundreds of individuals with expertise in various aspects of internal control. In March 1991, COSO issued its first draft of *Internal Control: Integrated Framework,* which offered perhaps the most comprehensive and logically ordered depiction of the control networks that support the reporting system. The manuscript represents a state-of-the-art look at the nature, components, and role of internal control in contemporary organizations. Ultimately, as the title suggests, COSO attempts to develop a theoretically sound and practically usable framework of internal control.

Soon after the issuance of the Treadway Commission's report, Congress also took an interest in the status and influence of this consortium. Representative John Dingell, chairman of the Subcommittee on Oversight and Investigation, charged the General Accounting Office (GAO) with monitoring the implementation of the commission's recommendations for one year, beginning December 1987. Since 1985, Dingell's subcommittee had been involved in a sweeping examination of the adequacy of external auditing and the financial-reporting system, as well as addressing the expectations gap (the difference between CPAs' perception of their role in financial reporting and the public's expectation).

Since the issuance of the Treadway Commission report, the role and status of audit committees and internal auditors have been elevated substantially within the financial community. The internal-audit function, in contrast, seems to have benefited the most from the Treadway Commission report. Internal auditors, in a number of surveys, have indicated greater exposure within their companies, increased responsibility in monitoring control, and a perceived improvement in their status from top management due to the impact of the Treadway Commission's recommendations.

Edmund J. Boyle
Marshall A. Geiger

Bibliography

Bull, I. "Board of Directors Acceptance of Treadway Responsibilities," *Journal of Accountancy*, February 1991, pp. 67–74.

Committee of Sponsoring Organizations of the Treadway Commission. *Internal Control: Integrated Framework.* New York: Committee of Sponsoring Organizations, 1991.

National Commission on Fraudulent Financial Reporting. *Report of the National Commission on Fraudulent Financial Reporting* [The Treadway Report]. Washington, DC: National Commission on Fraudulent Financial Reporting, 1987.

U.S. General Accounting Office. *CPA Audit Quality: Status of Actions Taken to Improve Auditing and Financial Reporting of Public Companies.* Washington, DC: GAO, 1989.

See also AMERICAN ACCOUNTING ASSOCIA-
TION; AMERICAN INSTITUTE OF CERTIFIED
PUBLIC ACCOUNTANTS; AUDIT COMMITTEES;
BIG EIGHT ACCOUNTING FIRMS; CHIEF AC-
COUNTANTS OF THE SECURITIES AND EX-
CHANGE COMMISSION; CONGRESSIONAL
VIEWS; EXTERNAL AUDITING; FRAUD AND
AUDITING; GENERAL ACCOUNTING OFFICE,
U.S.; INSTITUTE OF INTERNAL AUDITORS; IN-
TERNAL AUDITING; INTERNAL CONTROL; LAW
AND ACCOUNTING; SECURITIES AND EX-
CHANGE COMMISSION

Treasury Stock

Treasury stock has been a controversial topic
during the twentieth century. The most important of the many controversies about treasury
stock have been: donations; asset versus contra-
equity; cost versus par valuation; and paid in
versus earned surplus.

It was a common practice in the United
States for stockholders of such publicly traded
companies as mining firms to donate stock back
to the company for later sale to raise working
capital. The stock had been issued at par value
for assets such as a mine or a patent. Since the
original purchaser of the stock would have been
liable for the discount under the par value of the
stock, the reissue avoided that liability. Harry
Clark Bentley in 1911 warned against the valuation of such donated stock at its par value and
a credit of such amount to donation. He felt the
entry should be for the amount that the corporate authorities thought would be received from
the resale. If not, the gain on donated stock
would be usually fictitious and misleading and,
hence, not conservative. Robert Hiester Montgomery, however, in his *Auditing: Theory and
Practice* (1913) held that the best authorities
sanctioned the use of par value in such a case
for the valuation amount, although the surplus
account should be clearly differentiated from
the surplus arising from profits and, hence, available for dividends. Seymour Walton, the editor
of the Students' Department of the *Journal of
Accountancy*, agreed in 1915 with Montgomery,
as did Paul-Joseph Esquerré in 1917 in *The Applied Theory of Accounts*. Sir Arthur Lowes
Dickinson in 1922 urged that this donation practice be illegal as a part of the disallowing of corporations owning their own stock. He also noted
the *Trevor v. Whitworth* case (1887) in which the
House of Lords in England ruled that a corporation could not acquire its own stock.

Perhaps the most contentious issue remains
the assets versus contra-equity placement of
treasury stock. Both Bentley in 1911 and Montgomery through the years favored the asset
approach. The classical argument for the
contra-equity viewpoint was made by W.T.
Sunley Jr. in 1915. After stating the reasons why
treasury stock was purchased—enhance the
value of remaining stock, buy out a dissatisfied
investor, and the expectation of realizing a
profit—he argued logically that treasury stock
cannot be an asset of the corporation. Sunley
also classified the donation of treasury stock to
be an admission of the overstatement of the
value of the investment as originally stated.
William Andrew Paton in 1919 in "Some
Phases of Capital Stock" and again in 1969 in
"Postscript on 'Treasury' Shares," agreed with
Sunley, as did Eric Louis Kohler in 1933 in an
editorial, "Treasury Stock." However, by then,
more and more corporations had started to
purchase treasury stock, in light of the "bargain
purchase" attraction caused by the Great Depression. This practice reoccurred during the
1950s and became significant in the 1960s—so
much so that a movement back to the asset
approach was attempted by B. Horwitz and A.
Young in the early 1970s. Young wrote later, in
1978, that he felt that the reasons for purchasing treasury stock had changed, as the intent of
management had changed from defensive repur-
chasing to a careful plan to attain a valuable
corporate resource for use in (1) stock option
or purchase agreements, (2) convertible corporate securities, (3) warrants, (4) mergers, and (5)
share distributions. He concluded that, in those
cases, treasury stock should be classified as an
asset.

As noted from the discussion of the do-
nated-stock controversy, the cost versus par
value amount was evident from the turn of the
twentieth century. Dickinson invoked the
"lower of cost or market" rule for treasury
stock classified as an asset. Young favored the
"cost or market" approach if the treasury stock
were classified as a current asset, depending on
the intent of management.

Montgomery in 1913 wrote that the sale of
treasury stock at a profit resulted in an increase
of earned surplus. He still held this view in
1938. Sunley in 1915 stated that dividends on
treasury stock could not logically be income.
The Committee on Stock List of the New York
Stock Exchange took the same view as Sunley
in 1933, as noted in Zeff and Moonitz. In Ac-

counting Research Bulletin No. 1, "General Introduction and Rules Formerly Adopted," in 1939, the Committee on Accounting Procedure ruled that, except for unmaterial transactions, the gains and losses on the sale of treasury stock should not be brought to earned surplus (retained earnings). Young, however, argued in 1978 for a separate portrayal of gains and losses on treasury stock on the income statement, for treasury stock classified as an asset.

Terry K. Sheldahl in his 1982 review of the topic of treasury stock concluded that treasury-stock accounting was an area more intriguing than the volume of scholarly attention directed to it might have suggested. He is correct. There is a lot more than meets the eye on this topic from a historical viewpoint.

Richard Vangermeersch

Bibliography

Bentley, H.C. *Corporate Finance and Accounting*. New York: Ronald Press, 1911.

Dickinson, A.L. *Accounting Practice and Procedure*. New York: Ronald Press, 1922.

Horwitz, B., and A. Young. "The Case for Asset Disclosure of Treasury Stock," *CPA Journal*, March 1975, pp. 31–33.

May, G.O. "Recent Opinions on Dealings in Treasury Stock," *Journal of Accountancy*, July 1939, pp. 17–22.

Montgomery, R.H. "Dealings in Treasury Stock: We Call It Capital, The Courts Call It Income," *Journal of Accountancy*, April 1938, pp. 466–479.

Musselman, D.P. "On the Nature of the Gain on Treasury Stock," *Journal of Accountancy*, August 1940, pp. 104–116.

Paton, W.A. "Postscript on 'Treasury' Shares," *Accounting Review*, April 1969, pp. 276–283.

Sheldahl, T.K. "Reporting Treasury Stock as an Asset: Law, Logic, and Economic Substance," *Accounting Historians Journal*, Fall 1982, pp. 1–23.

Sunley, W.T. Jr. "Treasury Stock," *Journal of Accountancy*, December 1915, pp. 424–429.

Walton, S. "Stock Issued for Property—Treasury Stock," *Journal of Accountancy*, March 1915, pp. 235–238.

Young, A.E. "Accounting for Treasury Stock," *Journal of Accounting, Auditing, and Finance*, Spring 1978, pp. 217–230.

Zeff, S.A., and M. Moonitz, eds. *Sourcebook on Accounting Principles and Auditing Procedures 1917–1953*: Volume 1. New York: Garland, 1984.

See also ACCOUNTING RESEARCH BULLETINS; BENTLEY, HARRY CLARK; DICKINSON, ARTHUR LOWES; GENERALLY ACCEPTED ACCOUNTING PRINCIPLES; KOHLER, ERIC LOUIS; MONTGOMERY, ROBERT HIESTER; NEW YORK STOCK EXCHANGE; PATON, WILLIAM ANDREW; RETAINED EARNINGS

Trial Balance

Trial balance is a process that has served, to varying degrees of importance over time and situations, as (1) a test of the correctness of the postings from the journal, (2) a part of the closing process, and (3) a basis from which to prepare the financial statements.

In "Particularis de Computis et Scripturis," the first printed treatise on bookkeeping and accounting, published in Venice in 1494, Luca Pacioli developed a very elaborate process to achieve these goals. He described, mostly, a process that arrived at what is today called a post–closing trial balance. Pacioli believed strongly in the closing of the books each year. He recommended that the owner of the business and a helper "tick off" each entry from the journal to the ledger. Asset and liability accounts were each balanced to get a closing amount transferred to the new ledger. After this, the nominal accounts were balanced and closed to profit and loss, which was then closed to capital. Then the capital account was balanced and brought to the new ledger. Then what was, in effect, a post–closing trial balance was taken. Pacioli also seemed to prepare a trial balance by his recommended procedure for closing a filled ledger during the year to a new ledger.

Peragallo (1956) noted that in 1543, both Hugh Oldcastle in England in his *Profitable Treatyce* and Jan Ympyn in Antwerp in his *Niewe Instructie* published works that followed Pacioli's formats for the post–closing trial balance at year end and for a full ledger. Ympyn was the first author to use the balance account as an account in the ledger. In his 1586 book, *Indrizzo degli Economi*, Don Angelo Pietra, as noted by Peragallo (1941) prepared two trial balances, one for nominal accounts closed to profit and loss, and the other for all open (or real) accounts. He then added the debit and credit balances for each sheet and, if they agreed, the ledger was correct.

It appears that the financial-statement function of the trial balance became the dominant function between about 1890 to 1910. Saliers (1923) stated that businesses were bigger and more complex than before and that costs of business were becoming analyzed more in the interest of "efficiency." The use of sales and "cost of goods sold" accounts had begun to replace the ages-old merchandise account, to which costs were debited and sales and ending inventory credited. The Interstate Commerce Commission had issued a uniform classification of railroad accounts. Loose-leaf ledgers were in use and allowed more flexibility than the bound ledger book. This allowed for the beginning of a classified ledger rather than the former bound ledger with its alphabetized index. Hence, the trial balance of the twentieth century, especially the last half of it, is quite different in appearance and importance than in the period from the end of the fifteenth century to the end of the nineteenth century.

Richard Vangermeersch

Bibliography

Gordon, C. "The First English Books on Book-keeping." In *Studies in the History of Accounting*, edited by A.C. Littleton and B.S. Yamey, pp. 202–205. Homewood, IL: Irwin, 1956.

Hernández-Esteve, E. "Comments on Some Obscure or Ambiguous Points of the Treatise 'De Computis et Scripturis' by Luca Pacioli." Paper presented at the Sixteenth Annual Congress of the European Accounting Association, Turku, Finland, April 28–30, 1993.

More, R.H. "Trial Balance." In *The American Business and Accounting Encyclopedia*, edited by E.H. Beach, W.W. Thorne, and A.E. Rouch, pp. 1039–1048. 3d ed. Detroit: Book-keeper Publishing, 1901. Reprint. Yushodo Booksellers, 1982.

Peragallo, E. "Origin of the Trial Balance," *Journal of Accountancy*, 1941, pp. 448–454.

———. "Origins of the Trial Balance." In *Studies in the History of Accounting*, edited by A.C. Littleton and B.S. Yamey, pp. 215–222. Homewood, IL: Irwin, 1956.

Saliers, E.A. *Accountants' Handbook*. New York: Ronald Press, 1923.

See also Balance Account; Balance Sheet; Barbarigo, Andrea; Capital Account; Closing Entries and Procedures; Jones, Thomas; Ledger; Oldcastle, Hugh; Pacioli, Luca; Pietra, Angelo; *Summa Summarium*; Ympyn, Jan

Trueblood, Robert Martin (1916–1974)

As chairman of the Study Group on the Objectives of Financial Statements, Robert M. Trueblood is best known for the 1973 American Institute of Certified Public Accountants (AICPA) publication, *Objectives of Financial Statements*, appropriately called the Trueblood Report. Prior to his service as chairman of the Study Group, Trueblood provided the profession with significant contributions on numerous AICPA committees, the Accounting Principles Board (APB), and as president of the AICPA. He also took a leadership role in advancing the application of statistical methods, the future of accounting education, the focus of the CPA profession, and the objectives and definition of financial reporting.

Born in North Dakota, Trueblood received his bachelor's degree in Business Administration, with an accounting concentration, with distinction from the University of Minnesota in 1937. Embarking on a career in public accounting with Baumann, Finney and Company in Chicago, Trueblood recognized the importance of continuing his formal education by pursuing postgraduate education at Northwestern and Loyola universities. In 1941 he received the Elijah Watt Sells Award and Gold Medal from the Illinois Society of CPAs, before entering the Navy as a lieutenant commander.

Following World War II, Trueblood returned to the profession as a partner of Touche, Ross, Bailey and Smart. Continuing his association with higher education, Trueblood worked closely with the faculty of Carnegie Mellon University in a broad study of the application of statistical techniques to accounting and auditing. Following the process of academic inquiry, he first reviewed the statistical literature, publishing a bibliography in 1954. Supplying "live data," Trueblood assisted many case studies applying statistical techniques to various areas of accounting and auditing in 1954. "Research and Practice in Statistical Applications to Accounting, Auditing, and Management Control" (1955) summarizes the objectives and results of these case studies through 1954. "Statistical Sampling" (1960) provides an excellent discussion of sampling methods, sampling accuracy, statistical precision, and reliability, and suggests applications to accounting and auditing situations.

Leading the introduction of statistical techniques was reflective of Trueblood's leadership role within the community and profession. Trueblood served as a city councilman and member of President Johnson's Commission on Budget Concepts. Professionally, he served as president of the Pennsylvania Institute of CPAs and president of its Pittsburgh chapter. Within the AICPA, he was chairman of the Committee on Statistical Sampling, member of the Committee on Long-Range Objectives, and member of the governing Council. After a brief term on the APB, he was elected president of the AICPA, 1965–1966. He then served as chairman of the Accountants International Study Group and member of the Common Body of Knowledge Commission.

The dynamics of Trueblood's leadership role within the profession corresponded with his vastly expanding area of academic inquiry. Throughout the remainder of his life, he authored numerous presentations and articles on the future of accounting education and the public accounting profession, and the objectives and definition of financial accounting.

Experience within the profession and as Ford Distinguished Research Professor at Carnegie Mellon University led Trueblood to embrace the recommendations of the "Perry Report" issued in 1956 by the Commission on Standards of Education and Experience for CPAs and reviewed in an editorial in August of that year in the *Journal of Accountancy*. Trueblood advocated a broadened liberal-arts curriculum in an era when only 17 states required a baccalaureate degree; proposing in a 1962 article in *Illinois CPA* that undergraduate accounting courses be pared to the "promulgation of basic principles," with one to two years of postgraduate education providing technical training. He strongly believed that the future is dependent on "preparing the student for the professional requirements which he will face during the forty or more years of his career."

Most of Trueblood's papers and articles relate to advancing the practice of public accounting and the objectives of financial statements. In a 1960 article in the *Journal of Accountancy* defining the practice of public accounting as one with all the characteristics of a profession, he forecast the impact of the emergence of electric data processing and manage-ment advisory services, believing in the absolute necessity for strict adherence to "an independent point of view." Observing the transitions occurring in the economy and society, he advocated that the accounting profession expand its research activity to prepare for the future.

Editing William W. Werntz's papers and working with the Long-Range Planning Committee, Trueblood pondered the question: "Whose balance sheet is it?" in a 1968 article, "Accountant Considers his Profession." Reflective of his reaction to societal transitions that emphasized the individual, he believed that "accounting principles should be framed with primary concern for the general public" and guided by their "value to those who use them for all the different categories of users, a common core of information is necessary; but for none of them is a common core sufficient." Thus, the accountant needs to "extend his traditional skills in measuring and reporting . . . take on new responsibilities and more importantly, new attitudes."

Trueblood's Accounting Objectives Study Group reflected his concern with the users of financial information. Departing from the more technical APB Statement No. 4, the group's *Objectives of Financial Statements* spent the first nine chapters discussing the goals of financial statements and their relationship to the goals of business and governmental enterprises and society, devoting only the final chapter to the technical, qualitative characteristics of reporting. This focus has been incorporated into the conceptual-framework statements published by the Financial Accounting Standards Board.

Thus, Trueblood's leadership in expansion of the horizons of the profession to encompass societal concerns, exemplified in the Trueblood Report, has had a profound influence on the profession. Likewise, his advocacy of innovative techniques and influence on accounting education have assisted the certified public accountant to expand and meet the long-range requirements of the profession.

Adrianne E. Slaymaker

Bibliography

American Institute of Certified Public Accountants, Accounting Principles Board. "Basic Concepts and Accounting Principles Underlying Financial Statements of Business Enterprises." APB Statement No. 4. New York: AICPA, 1970.

American Institute of Certified Public Accountants. *Objectives of Financial Statements. Report of the Study Group on Objectives of Financial Statements* [The Trueblood Report]. New York: AICPA, 1973.

Commission on Standards of Education and Experience for Certified Public Accountants. *Standards of Education and Experience for CPAs.* Ann Arbor, MI: University of Michigan, 1956.

"Education and Experience for CPAs," *Journal of Accountancy*, August 1956, pp. 26–26.

"The Education and Experience of Donald Perry," *Journal of Accountancy*, August 1956, p. 8.

Trueblood, R.M. "Accountant Considers his Profession," *California CPA Quarterly*, June 1968, pp. 10–14.

———. "Education for a Changing Profession," *Journal of Accounting Research*, Spring 1963, pp. 86–94.

———. "Future of Accounting Education," *Illinois CPA*, Spring 1962, pp. 1–15.

———. "Information for Proprietors and Others," *Accountant*, October 26, 1972, pp. 517–518.

———. "Professional and Technical Practitioners in Accounting," *Journal of Accountancy*, September 1960, pp. 57–62.

———. "Report of the President's Commission on Budget Concepts," *Federal Accountant*, June 1968, pp. 4–15.

Trueblood, R.M., and W.W. Cooper. "Research and Practice in Statistical Applications to Accounting, Auditing, and Management Control," *Accounting Review*, April 1955, pp. 221–229.

Trueblood, R.M., and R.M. Cyert. "Statistical Sampling Applied to Aging of Accounts Receivables," *Journal of Accountancy*, March 1954, pp. 293–298.

Trueblood, R.M., and H.J. Davidson. "Statistical Sampling," *Retail Control*, November 1960, pp. 15–19.

Trueblood, R.M., and R.J. Monteverde. "Bibliography on the Application of Statistical Methods to Accounting and Auditing," *Accounting Review*, April 1954, pp. 251–254.

Trueblood, R.M., and G.H. Sorter. *William W. Werntz: His Accounting Thought.* New York: AICPA, 1968.

See also ACCOUNTING EDUCATION IN THE UNITED STATES; ACCOUNTING HALL OF FAME; AMERICAN INSTITUTE OF CERTIFIED PUBLIC ACCOUNTANTS; BIG EIGHT ACCOUNTING FIRMS; COMPUTING TECHNOLOGY IN THE WEST: THE IMPACT ON THE PROFESSION OF ACCOUNTING; CONCEPTUAL FRAMEWORK; COOPER, WILLIAM WAGER; GENERALLY ACCEPTED ACCOUNTING PRINCIPLES; INDEPENDENCE OF EXTERNAL AUDITORS; MANAGEMENT ADVISORY SERVICES BY CPAs; MOST, KENNETH S.; POSTULATES OF ACCOUNTING; SOCIAL RESPONSIBILITIES OF ACCOUNTANTS; STATISTICAL SAMPLING; WHEAT COMMITTEE

Trustee Accounts

Trust accounts and reports have usually been meticulously prepared, because the trustee's motive for accounting was to justify his stewardship of assets placed in his care.

Wealthy Romans appointed managers to invest their surplus funds, and special account books were kept by these *curators calendarii*, who were often educated slaves. Kats (1930) suggested that the duty of rendering account for stewardship in such cases led naturally to a system of bookkeeping that would allow the owner to see at a glance how his affairs stood and to check their agreement with a summary "master's account." On receiving money for investment, the curator would make a debit entry in the cashbook and credit the master's account. When he loaned money at interest, he debited the borrower's account in the *liber calendarii* and credited cash in the *codex expensi*. When a loan was repaid, these entries were reversed. Cash would be credited and the master's account debited for any payments made to the owner. Thus, a running balance of stewardship could be achieved by means of books in which the master's account was the reciprocal and summary of all the others, rather like a modern trustee's account.

Manors—the estates of the nobility—were the farms and workshops of medieval Britain. The manorial duke or earl often depended for his living on the productivity of large landholdings and the efforts of hundreds of people whom he could not personally supervise. Day-to-day management was normally left to a hierarchy of officials and department heads. The lord's incentive for keeping accounts arose from his need to check on the integrity and reliability of these stewards, to prevent loss and theft, and generally to encourage efficiency. He wished to protect his property by controlling his servants. From the steward's viewpoint, accounting records provided evidence that he had performed his duties honestly and well.

Manorial officers kept accounts not for the sake of the business entity, as they would today, but for their own protection. On large estates, a "surveyor" assembled a book of land rentals and fees due, which was used by the receiver-general who actually collected these revenues and recorded them by sources. Still other officials paid and kept account of wages and expenses. Auditors periodically examined and summarized all these accounts, which were essentially records for the individuals involved, not of the manor. Since their purpose was only to show that duties had been properly performed, there was a natural tendency for each steward to record just the items for which he was responsible and to show each type of receipt in opposition to payments.

The charge and discharge statement is often incorrectly assumed to have originated in executory accounting. In fact it was developed in fifteenth-century Scotland by government accountants, adopted by English manorial stewards, and not widely used by executors until 300 years later. The statement itself was the report of an agent on the assumption and discharge of his responsibilities. It was typically headed with the name of the manor and included the names of the stewards, sometimes those of the auditors, the place and date of the audit, and the period under review. It often contained a money account, with rents and other receipts subdivided by types, and a corn and stock account, with separate categories for grains, cattle, and various types of produce. Beginning balances for each item were shown, then the steward "charged" himself for receipts and natural increases in flocks, and "discharged" himself by deducting his cash payments, losses, and other uses of these resources. Today's executors and trustees continue to use the charge and discharge statement in accounting for their management of assets held in trust.

Trusts were created by English common law to break the feudal system of land tenure. Trust agreements distinguished between the corpus, or property that the trust acquired from the trustor, and the trust income derived from use of that property. Unless otherwise specified, the corpus was to be preserved intact, while the income could be distributed.

The feudal stipulation was that the lord must suffer no loss from fraud, negligence, or bad judgment by his stewards. In contrast, the common law differentiated between three kinds of waste: permissive, voluntary, and equitable. The trustee was not legally liable for permissive waste—the natural deterioration of trust property—nor did such depreciation have to be charged against trust income. Neither was the trustee liable for voluntary waste, even if his own acts inadvertently caused damage to the property. The courts would punish only inequitable actions by the trustee—that is, acts which purposely reduced the value of trust capital.

In framing the companies acts, beginning in 1844, Parliament was strongly influenced by this English tradition of responsibility accounting. Promoters and company officials were considered trustees placed in charge of investors' capital. Incorporation was granted as a privilege, in return for which managers were required to publicize their handling of corporate affairs. The British balance sheet evolved as a formal report of management's stewardship of assets held in trust. Annual audits were seen as an instrument of stockholder control over the performance of duties that they had delegated to management.

Michael Chatfield

Bibliography

Hay, L.E. "Executorship Reporting—Some Historical Notes," *Accounting Review*, January 1961, pp. 100–104.

Jack, S.M. "An Historical Defence of Single Entry Book-keeping," *Abacus*, December 1966, pp. 137–158.

Kats, P. "A Surmise Regarding the Origin of Bookkeeping by Double Entry," *Accounting Review*, December 1930, pp. 311–316.

Most, K.S. "New Light on Medieval Manorial Accounts," *Accountant*, January 25, 1969, pp. 119–121.

See also "CHARGE AND DISCHARGE" STATEMENT; COMPANIES ACTS; EXTERNAL AUDITING; MANORIAL ACCOUNTING; ROME (509 B.C.–A.D. 476); SCOTLAND: EARLY WRITERS IN DOUBLE ENTRY ACCOUNTING; STEWARDSHIP

U

Ultramares Corporation v. Touche, Niven & Company

Until the case of *Ultramares Corporation v. Touche, Niven & Company* (1931), auditors admitted no liability for negligence affecting third parties. The common law rule was that a negligent professional man could normally be sued only by his clients. Having no contract with outsiders, he had no responsibility to them unless he committed fraud.

In 1924 Touche Niven gave an unqualified audit certificate to a rubber importer, Fred Stern and Company, failing to discover that management had falsified entries in order to overstate accounts receivable. The auditors supplied Stern with 32 numbered copies of the certified balance sheet, knowing the company would use them in applying for credit. Ultramares Corporation, a factor, made loans to Stern and Company on the basis of these certified balance sheets. When Stern declared bankruptcy in 1925, Ultramares sued the auditors for the amount of Stern's debt on the grounds that a careful audit examination would have showed that Stern was insolvent on the balance sheet date. The auditors were acquitted on a fraud charge but were found guilty of negligence. But the trial judge set even this aside, applying the doctrine of privity, which protected auditors from third party negligence suits. An intermediate appellate court affirmed dismissal of the fraud count but reinstated the negligence verdict. The case then went to the New York Court of Appeals.

Judge Benjamin Cardozo agreed that third parties could not hold an auditor responsible for ordinary negligence, only for fraud. But he then argued that courts could infer fraud from grossly negligent actions and, in so doing, could subject the auditor to liability from any injured party who relied on the auditor's report, whether or not the auditor knew that the third party was doing so. In short, the greater the negligence, the more widespread the legal recourse. Even an honest mistake or oversight so gross as to support the inference that an auditor did not believe his own opinion might justify a fraud verdict and open the door to indefinite third party liability.

In *Ultramares* the substantive question was whether the audit had been so grossly negligent as to constitute constructive fraud. Deciding that it had been, Judge Cardozo ordered a new trial. Before it could be held, the suit was settled out of court. But the precedent established has been reiterated in similar cases ever since, until today the auditor's liability to the public at large is nearly as extensive as to his clients.

The *Ultramares* decision caused changes in the short form audit report. The court had criticized Touche Niven for not clearly indicating the scope of its examination, and particularly for failing to distinguish its statement of the audit's scope from its statement of opinion. As a result, the word "certify" was dropped from the audit report. The American Institute of Accountants emphasized that the auditor's certificate was an opinion, not a guarantee. Moreover, it was an opinion of the client's actions, not the auditor's. His examination of the books was not intended to prove anything, but simply to put his mind in contact with the company's affairs. His knowledge and his skill in applying audit techniques then allowed him to express a professional opinion of management's financial statements.

Michael Chatfield

Bibliography

Carey, J.L. *The Rise of the Accounting Profession*, vol. 1, *From Technician to Professional, 1896–1936*. New York: AICPA, 1969, pp. 255–259.

Edwards, J.D. *History of Public Accounting in the United States*. East Lansing: Michigan State University, 1961, pp. 141–145.

Ultramares Corporation v. Touche, Niven & Company, 255 N.Y. 170, 174 N.E. 441 (1931).

See also AMERICAN INSTITUTE OF CERTIFIED PUBLIC ACCOUNTANTS; AUDITOR'S REPORT; *ESCOTT V. BARCHRIS CONSTRUCTION CORPORATION;* FRAUD AND AUDITING; LAW AND ACCOUNTING; LEGAL LIABILITY OF AUDITORS; SECURITIES AND EXCHANGE COMMISSION

Uniform Accounting

Government regulation of the accounting profession is often associated with the creation of the Securities and Exchange Commission (SEC) in the early 1930s. However, one of the earliest interventions of government into the practice of auditing and financial reporting occurred on April 1, 1917, when the Federal Reserve Board (FRB) issued the bulletin *Uniform Accounting*. Regarding the initiation of the document, the Federal Trade Commission (FTC) had been concerned with the lack of uniformity and enlisted the aid of the American Institute of Accountants (AIA) to help remedy the situation. Consequently, the AIA—predecessor of the American Institute of Certified Public Accountants (AICPA)—prepared and approved a memorandum that was an adaptation of an internal-control program prepared by J. Scobie for Price Waterhouse. The memorandum was submitted to the FTC and the FRB, accepted with only minor changes, and published in the *Federal Reserve Bulletin* of April 1, 1917. Zeff (1972) has noted that this was the first such comprehensive statement in the English-speaking world that carried the approval of a body of public accountants.

This regulatory effort reflected an emerging philosophy that viewed uniform accounting standards as a quick remedy to reporting problems. This movement was especially prevalent in regulated industries and municipalities. The bulletin advocated an extension of the philosophy of "uniformity" to manufacturing and merchandising industries and noted that it was an "initial step which may easily be succeeded by future developments tending to establish uniformity . . . [in] the field of financial statements."

Though titled *Uniform Accounting*, the bulletin was concerned primarily with "uniformity as to the extent of verification" of accounts—that is, the audit process. The bulletin presented a step-by-step approach to auditing each balance sheet account. Prepared in narrative form, it specifically describes each procedure. For some accounts, the audit procedures are sequentially numbered and strongly resemble today's audit programs. For example, the inventory section consists of an introduction followed by 27 specific audit procedures covering everything from testing "original stock sheets" to analytical review procedures such as analyses of turnover rates and gross profit percentages. Also, the FRB recommended a standard report-opinion that included the statement: "I certify that the above . . . have been made in accordance with the plan suggested and advised by the Federal Reserve Board and in my opinion. . . ."

Concerning accounting methods, the FRB recommended that securities and inventories be stated at the "lower of cost or market," the latter of which proved controversial. Also, a fully illustrated balance sheet and income statement were presented.

Although the bulletin was primarily a government effort to increase uniformity, ironically, it granted an extraordinary amount of discretion to the auditor in the selection and extent of tests. Most notably, the bulletin did not require the taking of a physical inventory, especially in the case of large companies where personal supervision of inventories is "arduous and perhaps impracticable." In addition, the bulletin describes the need to confirm accounts and notes receivable as "optional . . . if time permits and the client does not object."

Since the AIA had been very influential in preparing the bulletin, it is not surprising that the selection and extent of even the most crucial audit procedures are reserved for the judgment of the auditor rather than required. However, if the AIA had designed its original memorandum to enhance the amount of auditors' discretion, this strategy may have inadvertently backfired. As Previts and Merino (1979) note, "Management now had an 'authoritative' source to prohibit such procedures as too costly and they fell into disuse in the twenties."

The bulletin initially received only little support from practitioners, but its influence increased steadily during the 1920s. The AIA revised the bulletin, which was reissued in 1929 by the FRB as *Verification of Financial Statements*. In 1936 the AIA again revised and published the pronouncement as *Examination of Financial Statements by Independent Public Accountants*. By 1939, its usage had become so widespread that it was referred to as the "accountant's bible."

In retrospect, it appears that this early government regulatory effort did indeed have a significant impact on the practice of accounting and auditing. Also significant is the working relationship that developed between the accounting profession (AIA) and regulators (FRB and FTC). In many respects, *Uniform Accounting* brought the profession a glimpse of the shape of things to come.

James J. Tucker III

Bibliography

Previts, G.J., and B.D. Merino. *A History of Accounting in America: An Historical Interpretation of the Cultural Significance of Accounting.* New York: John Wiley & Sons, 1979.

U.S. Federal Reserve Board. "Uniform Accounting," *Journal of Accountancy*, June 1917, pp. 401–433.

———. "Verification of Financial Statements," *Journal of Accountancy*, May 1929, pp. 321–353.

Zeff, Stephen A. *Forging Accounting Principle in Five Countries: A History and an Analysis of Trends.* Champaign, IL: Stipes, 1972.

See also ACCOUNTING RESEARCH BULLETINS; AMERICAN INSTITUTE OF CERTIFIED PUBLIC ACCOUNTANTS; AUDITOR'S REPORT; BIG EIGHT ACCOUNTING FIRMS; COMPARABILITY; DICKINSON, ARTHUR LOWES; EXTERNAL AUDITING; GENERALLY ACCEPTED ACCOUNTING PRINCIPLES; INCOME STATEMENT/INCOME ACCOUNT; INTERNAL CONTROL; LIQUIDITY: ACCOUNTING MEASUREMENT; PREVITS, GARY JOHN; SECURITIES AND EXCHANGE COMMISSION; UNIFORMITY

Uniform Accounting Systems

Uniform accounting systems were defined by Eric Louis Kohler in his 1952 edition of *A Dictionary for Accountants* as a system of accounts common to similar organizations, such as those developed or promoted by trade associations, and those promulgated by federal and state regulatory bodies such as public utility commissions. The latter systems have often been established with social, political, and economic motivations dominating accounting considerations. In the United States, the least-credible system, many accountants say, was the railroad accounting system promulgated by the Interstate Commerce Commission (ICC) starting in 1906. The 1972 Wheat Report, which laid the groundwork for the Financial Accounting Standards Board (FASB), was extremely critical of the accounting efforts of the ICC.

The importance of cost accounting to industry was highlighted in the United States during the World War I effort. The federal government and industry groups noted that much development was needed in cost accounting to help establish pricing policies for governmental contracts. With this problem in view, trade associations began to develop standard forms for collecting costs. These forms were voluntarily sent to the trade associations for the development of industry statistics to be distributed to its membership. The accounting systems, as noted by Bentley and Leonard (1935) in the second volume of their bibliography, were widespread by the late 1920s.

The Great Depression brought the best example in the United States of a federal government attempt to establish accounting systems for different industry groupings. The National Industrial Recovery Act was a "New Deal" attempt in 1933 to allow companies in an industry to work together with the National Recovery Administration (NRA) to write and enforce industrial codes designed to shorten work hours, raise wages, and end unfair and irrational business practices. The practice that most involved accounting was the practice of selling "below cost." However, the complexities of cost accounting caused the NRA numerous difficulties. Charles F. Roos, who was an official at the NRA, concluded that the NRA code provisions prohibiting sales below cost were completely unenforceable. Roos (1937) also wrote: "As a member of the NRA staff once remarked, 'If the NRA had only adopted price fixing through cost formulas in all codes, all the unemployed would have been needed to check compliance.'" The NRA ended in 1935 when the U.S. Supreme Court ruled it was unconstitutional.

A "general cost finding" system administered by trade associations is a valuable tool for its membership. There is enough freedom within this system to allow for differences in operations, structures, and member needs to avoid the rigidity of complete uniformity. The U.S. experiences in the NRA and with the ICC illustrate the difficulties with rigidity.

Richard Vangermeersch

Bibliography

Bentley, H.C., and R.S. Leonard. *Bibliography of Works on Accounting by American Authors*, vol. 2, *1901–1934*. Boston: Harry C. Bentley, 1935.

Kellogg, R.S. "The Use of Cost Data by Trade Associations." In the *NACA Yearbook: 1923*. Reprinted in *Relevance Rediscovered: An Anthology of 25 Significant Articles from the NACA Bulletins and Yearbooks, 1919–1929*, edited by R. Vangermeersch, pp. 169–184. Montvale, NJ: Institute of Management Accountants, 1990.

Roos, C.F. *NRA Economic Planning*. Bloomington, IN: Principia Press, 1937. Reprint. New York: Da Capo Press, 1971.

See also BENTLEY, HARRY CLARK; CHART OF ACCOUNTS; COMPARABILITY; COST AND/OR MANAGEMENT ACCOUNTING; RAILROAD ACCOUNTING (U.S.); UNIFORMITY; WHEAT COMMITTEE

Uniformity

Uniformity is a long-lasting issue in accounting, especially important recently in the light of the globalization of business. The definition for uniformity in *Webster's* that is most applicable for accounting is: "Of the same form with others; conforming to one rule or mode; consonant." However, while agreement may be found on the definition of uniformity, much disagreement is found when it is attempted to be applied in accounting.

It is necessary to distinguish between uniformity in accounting terminology and uniformity in accounting principles and rules. Eric Louis Kohler pioneered in the domain of uniformity in accounting terminology in his classic 1952 edition of *A Dictionary for Accountants*. He had stressed in 1935 the necessity for a common language in accounting, and in 1936 he chaired the American Institute of Accountants' Committee on Terminology, which updated a 1931 publication, *Accounting Terminology*. Examples of uniformity of terminology and its importance include Accounting Research Bulletins No. 30, "Current Assets and Current Liabilities: Working Capital" in 1947; No. 34, "Use of the Term 'Reserve' in 1948, and No. 39, "Discontinuance of the Use of the Term 'Surplus'" in 1949. Another example of rigor in accounting definitions is Financial Accounting Standards (FAS) No. 2, "Accounting for Research and Development Costs," in which these two terms were defined in 1974 by the Financial Accounting Standards Board. All in all, accounting has achieved significant improvement in uniformity of its terminology, leading to much clearer communication.

However, the issue of uniformity of accounting principles and rules is much more controversial. A major reason is the issue of the scope of the application of uniform accounting principles and rules. For instance, one could consider these six areas for accounting uniformity: (1) a plant in a division, (2) a division in a company, (3) all divisions in a company, (4) all companies in a country, (5) all countries in an economic block, and (6) all countries in the world. There is a declining enthusiasm by accountants for uniformity as one goes from (1) through (6).

Another frame of reference for this topic is the classification format mentioned by Merino and Coe (1978). They found four levels of uniformity: (1) strong form, (2) moderate-strong form, (3) moderate-weak form, and (4) weak form. When one combines these four classifications with the previously mentioned six classifications, one can appreciate the intensity level of debates about this controversial issue.

In the United States, the alleged role that uniform railroad accounting played in the failure of railroads is a frequently used example against uniformity at the strong level in an industry. The Hepburn Act of 1906 allowed the Interstate Commerce Commission (ICC) to establish an inflexible form of accounts with the alleged goal of understating depreciation, so as to achieve lower rates. Merino and Coe found that "with the low return on investment afforded by the ICC policy, it had become difficult to attract new capital or to maintain existing capital." Since many hold that uniformity in principles and rules will be achieved by federal government action, the railroad example is commonly used by those opposing federal government-enforced uniformity.

While the railroad example focused on federal government actions, another example of a more positive nature was the setting of uniform accounting for municipalities at the turn of the twentieth century. Here, CPAs, led by Harvey Chase, worked with the National Municipal League to get adoption of a uniform accounting system. Obviously, there is a third classification for uniformity, that (1) set by the federal government, or (2) set by professional groups. Much heat has been generated in the United States and other countries by the issue of what body has the power to set the principles and rules.

Edward N. Hurley, chairman of the U.S. Federal Trade Commission in 1916, was the chief proponent for uniform cost-accounting systems for different industries. He felt this system would lead to better pricing decisions and to less destructive cutthroat competition. Countless industries, through their trade associations, established uniform charts of accounts but did not establish comprehensive accounting principles and rules.

The American Institute of Accountants (AIA) adopted a similar approach in 1917 in *Uniform Accounting,* which, in 1918, was reprinted with the more accurate table of "Approved Methods for the Preparation of Balance Sheet Statements: A Tentative Proposal." *Uniform Accounting* was approved and published by the Federal Reserve Board. While there were illustrative forms for the comparative statement of profit and loss and for the balance sheet, the publication was much more concerned with auditing steps than uniform accounting principles and rules. This was also true for the 1929 and 1936 revisions, titled respectively, *Verification of Financial Statements* and *Examination of Financial Statements by Independent Public Accountants.*

The Great Depression of the 1930s was instrumental in bringing the issue of uniformity in accounting to the forefront of public debate in the United States. The leader of the forces that favored consistency and disclosure of accounting methods over uniformity established by the federal government through its Securities and Exchange Commission (SEC) was George Oliver May of Price Waterhouse and Company. May felt that complete uniformity was unobtainable and that different groups could work out an acceptable modicum of behavior. May

(1938), like others, warned, "There is, no doubt, a desire for uniformity in accounting which is a part of a vague, general yearning for rules which will eliminate (or at least obscure) the complexities and uncertainties of life." May's approach has been generally followed by the SEC and, in the United States, accounting remains subject to a weak form of uniformity established by a private-sector body, the Financial Accounting Standards Board.

Robert K. Mautz, a longtime academic and researcher and then a partner in an international accounting firm, took over from May as the leading proponent of flexibility over uniformity. With a research grant from the Financial Executives Research Foundation of the Financial Executives Institute (FEI), Mautz (1972) sought to document cases that illustrated why companies had "sets of circumstances, conditions, or transactions which were sufficiently unusual to lead to departures from the treatment they otherwise have applied." Mautz then tested the selected cases in five seminars that included financial analysts, independent CPAs, and corporate financial executives. One of the conclusions he drew was that detailed rule making does not hold promise for great improvement in corporate financial reporting. However, he also concluded that "the present extent of freedom to choose any one of a number of generally accepted accounting methods is undesirable." Mautz proposed a corporate audit committee to reduce the abuses of this number of methods and recommended other steps along the lines of peer evaluation and peer sanctions to limit abuses, rather than uniformity. Mautz articulated well his basic conclusion (his emphasis): *"There is no inherent rightness in any given accounting method apart from the circumstances in which it is applied."*

During times of business downturns and failures and of negative attitudes toward business, like the Vietnam and Watergate periods, uniformity becomes a significant issue. For instance, the staff report *The Accounting Establishment* (1977) of Senator Lee Metcalf's subcommittee concluded that "the Federal Government should directly establish financial accounting standards for publicly-owned corporations." The Metcalf Committee investigated in 1975 and 1976 the Federal Government's role in establishing accounting principles in light of " . . . continual revelations of previously unreported wrongdoing by major corporations, as well as a series of corporate failures. . . ." There can be no doubt that the strong grain of populism in the United States has, as one of its tenets, uniformity in accounting.

Uniformity in accounting varies from country to country. For example, Nobes (1984) classed countries into a micro-based (Business Economics and Business Practice) and macro-uniform (Continental and Government Economics). Only the Netherlands was classified as in the Business Economics class. Within the Business Practice class are U.K.- and U.S.-influenced countries. Within the Continental class are tax-based (Italy, France, Belgium, and Spain) and law-based (Germany and Japan) countries. The accounting Directives of the European Community (Union) must be broad enough, for instance, to encompass the principles of the Netherlands and those of Germany, a broad area indeed.

As one might expect from the increased emphasis on globalization of the world economy and on privatization of state enterprises, worldwide accounting uniformity has gained increased emphasis in recent years. The International Accounting Standards Committee (IASC) was founded in 1973 and, as of 1991, was composed of 106 professional bodies from 79 countries. It has an ongoing goal of comparability of accounting principles throughout the world, as a part of a worldwide financial market.

The topic of uniformity in accounting will not go away. The questions of scope, strength, structure, and sanctions remain open. The overriding fear of rigidity of the bureaucratic structure for establishing uniformity remains a worrisome concern to many. The strongly negative feelings about the effects that ICC accounting regulations had on U.S. railroads remains ingrained in U.S. accountants' thinking about uniformity. However, uniformity in accounting retains its attractions for many.

Richard Vangermeersch

Bibliography

International Accounting Standards Committee. "Comparability: A Critical Stage," *IASC Insight*, July 1992, p. 1, pp. 9–22.

Kohler, E.L. *A Dictionary for Accountants*. New York: Prentice-Hall, 1952.

———. "Some Principles for Terminologists," *Accounting Review*, March 1935, pp. 31–33.

Mautz, R.K. *Effect of Circumstances on the Application of Accounting Principles*. New York: Financial Executives Research Foundation, 1972.

———. "Uniformity or Flexibility in Accounting," *Financial Executive*, August 1973, pp. 26–30.

May, G.O. "The Choice Before Us," *Journal of Accountancy*, March 1950, pp. 206–210.

———. "Uniformity in Accounting," *Harvard Business Review*, Autumn 1938, pp. 1–8.

Merino, B.D., and T. L. Coe. "Uniformity in Accounting: A Historical Perspective," *Journal of Accountancy*, August 1978, pp. 62–69.

Moonitz, M. "Three Contributions to the Development of Accounting Principles Prior to 1930," *Journal of Accounting Research*, Spring 1970, pp. 145–155.

Nobes, C. *International Classification of Financial Reporting*. London and Sydney: Croom Helm, 1984.

U.S. Congress. Senate Committee on Government Operations. Subcommittee on Reports, Accounting, and Management. 95th Cong., 1st sess., 1977. *The Accounting Establishment: A Staff Study*. Washington, DC: GPO, 1977.

See also ACCOUNTING RESEARCH BULLETINS; AMERICAN INSTITUTE OF CERTIFIED PUBLIC ACCOUNTANTS; BENTLEY, HARRY CLARK; CHART OF ACCOUNTS; COMPARABILITY; CONGRESSIONAL VIEWS; CONSERVATISM; COST ACCOUNTING STANDARDS BOARD; COST AND/OR MANAGEMENT ACCOUNTING; EFFICIENT MARKET HYPOTHESIS; FINANCIAL ACCOUNTING STANDARDS BOARD; FRANCE; GERMANY; INTERNATIONAL ACCOUNTING STANDARDS COMMITTEE; ITALY, AFTER PACIOLI; KOHLER, ERIC LOUIS; KRAAYENHOF, JACOB; MAUTZ, ROBERT K.; MAY, GEORGE OLIVER; MUNICIPAL ACCOUNTING REFORM; NETHERLANDS; OBJECTIVITY; POLAND; RAILROAD ACCOUNTING (U.S.); RIPLEY, WILLIAM Z.; SCHMALENBACH, EUGEN; SECURITIES AND EXCHANGE COMMISSION; STATE AND LOCAL GOVERNMENTS (U.S., 1901–1991); *UNIFORM ACCOUNTING;* UNIFORM ACCOUNTING SYSTEMS

U.S. Industrial Commission

The U.S. Industrial Commission (1898–1902) was established by Congress to investigate and to report on questions relating to immigration, labor, agriculture, manufacturing, and business. The commission included five U.S. senators, five members of the U.S. House of Representatives, and nine public members from different industries appointed by the president with the consent of the Senate. The nineteen volumes published by the commission between 1900 and 1902 provide a rich source of information about business practices and customs at the turn of the century. Experts were employed in each field, and it probably was a reflection of the status of accountants in 1898 that none were engaged. But the commission's *Preliminary Report on Trusts and Industrial Combinations*, issued in 1900, made it clear that the public outrage against those who controlled the nation's trusts demanded some form of corporate oversight; this provided accountants with a golden opportunity to join the mainstream of the reform movement. Both businessmen and government officials appeared to prefer that control be left in the private sector. One of the conclusions reached in that preliminary report was that an independent public accounting profession ought to be established if corporate abuses such as stock watering and overcapitalization were to be curtailed effectively.

Many of the businessmen who testified before the commission advocated corporate publicity as the preferred means of reducing various corporate abuses. A.S. White, president of National Salt Company, and Charles M. Schwab, then president of United States Steel Corporation, were among the many prominent businessmen who acknowledged that management could mislead investors through dividend policies, and who advocated publication of annual reports. Not all agreed. Henry O. Havemeyer, president of American Sugar Refining, railed against any form of corporate control, maintaining that the doctrine of *caveat emptor* must apply to the investor as well as the consumer. But his testimony appeared to undermine the testimony of those opposed to publicity. Opponents of publication of financial data claimed it was unnecessary because payment of dividends provided sufficient information for investors to make informed decisions. Havemeyer, when asked how he could pay dividends while losing money, replied that was simple, he could borrow the money. When asked how long this could go on, he replied, well that is a puzzle; if we knew we would either buy or sell our stock. His testimony signaled the demise of the dividend alternative.

In its preliminary report, the commission stated that its prime objective would be "to prevent the organizers of corporations or industrial combinations from deceiving investors and the public, either through suppression of material facts or by making misleading statements." The final report, issued in 1902, concluded: "The larger corporations—the so-called trusts—would be required to publish annually a properly audited report, showing in reasonable detail their assets and liabilities, with profit and loss; such a report and audit under oath to be subject to government regulation." A minority report, rejected by the commission, advocated that a bureau be established in the Treasury Department to register all state corporations engaged in interstate commerce and to secure from each an adequate financial report, to make inspections and examinations of corporate account, and to collate and publish information regarding such combinations.

The only argument presented in opposition to the reporting of financial data, which the commissioners conceded was a convincing one, was that no independent group of technically qualified professionals was available to perform the necessary audits. The lack of an organized accounting profession appeared to preclude reliance on the private sector for more adequate, accurate, and reliable information. The conclusions of the Industrial Commission established the need for independent public accountants. After 1902, accountants could also count on the support of businessmen, who may have preferred corporate secrecy, but for whom, when faced with the real threat of direct government intervention in corporate affairs, the alternative—independent audits by established professional accountants—became more attractive.

The functions of the commission were absorbed by the U.S. Bureau of Corporations, established in February 1903 as a division of the Department of Commerce and Labor. The U.S. Bureau of Corporations was absorbed by the Federal Trade Commission in 1914.

Barbara D. Merino

Bibliography

Henderson, G.C. *The Federal Trade Commission.* New Haven, CT: Yale University Press, 1924.

Pure Oil Trust vs. Standard Oil Company, Being the Report of an Investigation by

U

the *U.S. Industrial Commission: Compiled from Private and Official Sources by the Oil City Derrick, 1899–1900.* Oil City, PA: Derrick Publishing, 1901.

U.S. Congress. House. *Final Report of the Industrial Commission.* 57th Cong., 2d sess., 1902. H. Doc. 380.

————. *Preliminary Report on Trusts and Industrial Combinations.* 56th Cong., 1st sess., 1900. H. Doc. 476.

————. *Report of the Industrial Commission on Transportation.* 57th Cong., 1st sess., 1901. H. Doc. 178.

————. *Report of the Industrial Commission on Transportation and Trusts.* 57th Cong., 1st sess., 1901. H. Doc. 182.

See also CONGRESSIONAL VIEWS; DIVIDENDS; EXTERNAL AUDITING; UNITED STATES STEEL CORPORATION

United States of America v. Carl Simon

Harold Roth, president of Continental Vending Machine Corporation, financed his personal stock market dealings between 1958 and 1962 by having Continental loan money to an affiliate, Valley Commercial Corporation, whose funds he then borrowed. During the 1962 audit of Continental by Lybrand, Ross Bros. & Montgomery, Roth informed the auditors that Valley was unable to repay Continental because he was unable to repay Valley. He agreed to post collateral for Valley's $3.5 million debt to Continental, and the auditors decided that if this were done there was no need for them to examine Valley's books, which were audited by another accounting firm. The loan to Valley was footnoted on Continental's balance sheet, but the footnote failed to disclose that 80 percent of the collateral used to secure Valley's debt consisted of Continental's own securities, which were worth only $2.9 million when the auditors issued their opinion. The footnote merely stated that the amount due from Valley Commercial Corporation was backed by securities with a market value greater than the *net amount* owed by Valley to Continental. This was technically correct, since Continental also owed Valley about a million dollars on the balance sheet date. However, Continental had created most of this million dollar debt by issuing notes to Valley, which then discounted the notes and returned the proceeds to Continental. Shortly after the auditors approved its financial statements, Continental Vending Machine Corporation filed a bankruptcy petition.

The auditors of Continental were sued by the federal government for conspiring to file false statements and use the mails to defraud. Their defense, supported by eight expert witnesses, was that they had followed generally accepted accounting principles and auditing standards, which included no specific obligation to disclose the nature of loan collateral or examine the accounts of affiliates that had other auditors. The prosecution argued that they should have inquired into the affairs of Valley Commercial Corporation and that failure to do so gave them a reason to falsify Continental's 1962 balance sheet. The government did not dispute that they had followed professional standards but argued that this was not sufficient. Circuit Court Judge Henry J. Friendly agreed: "Generally accepted accounting principles instruct an accountant what to do in the usual case when he has no reason to doubt that the affairs of the corporation are being honestly conducted. Once he has reason to believe that this basic assumption is false, an entirely different situation confronts him."

In June 1968, after an earlier trial had ended in a hung jury, an audit manager and two partners of Lybrand, Ross Brothers & Montgomery were found guilty. The convictions were upheld on appeal, and the Supreme Court declined to review the case. The accountants later received a presidential pardon and Lybrand settled a civil suit out of court. The fact remained that this was the first criminal conviction in 70 years involving partners in a major American public accounting firm.

The Continental Vending decision created immediate pressure to expand the scope of audit investigations. In effect this decision indicted the accounting profession for failing to adapt its rules to meet changing public needs. It also sent the message that courts could hold auditors to higher standards than those set by the accounting profession.

Michael Chatfield

Bibliography
Memorandum of the American Institute of Certified Public Accountants, *Amicus Curiae,* in *USA v. Simon, et al.,* August 23, 1968. Reprinted in *Journal of Accountancy,* November 1968, pp. 54–64.

Reiling, H.B., and R.A. Taussig. "Recent Liability Cases: Implications for Accountants," *Journal of Accountancy*, September 1970, pp. 39–53.

The United States of America v. Carl Simon, et. al., U.S. District Court, S.D.N.Y., Docket No. 66, Crim 831. 1968.

See also BIG EIGHT ACCOUNTING FIRMS; LAW AND ACCOUNTING; LEGAL LIABILITY OF AUDITORS; SECURITIES AND EXCHANGE COMMISSION

United States Steel Corporation

United States Steel Corporation (1901–1986) was perhaps the most heralded U.S. corporation of the twentieth century. The importance of U.S. Steel (hereafter USS) to the economy and its detailed annual reports have been widely studied. A review of those annual reports and the literature about them is a very good way of getting an overview of U.S. financial accounting.

Founded on April 1, 1901, USS was the first "Billion Dollar Trust," the result of the merger of eight steel companies, with four others joining later in that year. Its founders included such famous financiers and industrialists as J.P. Morgan, Charles Schwab, and Judge Elbert Gary. One of the key companies was owned by Andrew Carnegie.

The first full-year annual report of 1902 remains a "classic" of industrial reporting. The 1902 report started with the income account and the undivided-surplus account. Detailed information was given for production, inventories, long-term debt, the property account, acquisitions, employees, stockholders, orders on hand, comparative monthly earnings, and photos of plants. There were detailed financial statements for the balance sheet, profit-and-loss account, and a "funds" statement, as well as the certificate of chartered accountants.

Key issues in the 1902 report were: (1) "watered stock," (2) consolidated statements, and (3) the bond sinking fund. A significant part of USS's original capital was "water." Stock watering was the issuance of nominally fully paid stock in an amount that exceeded the value of the assets against which the stock was issued. The water for USS was, at the minimum, all the $508 million par value of its $100 par common stock. The board of directors held the power to value the assets of the new company.

USS's public accounting firm for all its history, Price Waterhouse and Company, through its managing partner, Arthur Lowes Dickinson, insisted on consolidated statements for USS so that shareholders could acquire a more accurate presentation of their company. Dickinson was also instrumental in having USS adopt the conservative approach of deducting the contribution to the bond sinking fund as an expense.

USS continued its conservative practices in inventory valuations. It also adopted a policy of "de-watering" its original valuation by charging $185 million to the income account for the Appropriation for Property Expenditures from 1905–1913 and by "excessive depreciation." The turbulent times of World War I led USS to adopt a base stock procedure and an inflation procedure for depreciating new construction. Both approaches lowered net income and were used to justify wartime prices. The inventory reserves were partly reduced in the deflationary years of 1921 and 1922. In 1929 this reserve was transferred to "surplus" as a part of a major cleansing of accounts.

The Great Depression from 1930 through 1939 brought many accounting adjustments to USS. It reclassified $270 million from "appreciated surplus invested in capital expenditures" to "depreciation reserves." In 1936, $260.6 million of intangible assets were first shown as a component of fixed assets. In 1938, the intangible account was written down to $1, as a part of reduction of the $100 par common stock to $75. The 1939 annual report was completely revised to reflect a more "reader friendly approach." There were new sections titled "the corporation and the nation," and "how the corporation earned its living" in 1939. The balance sheet was presented in order of liquidity for the first time.

The U.S. entry into World War II led to a series of accounting policies at USS reminiscent of those during World War I. LIFO (last in, first out), a variant of the base stock approach, was adopted. Numerous wartime reserves were established. Amortization of the cost of emergency facilities appeared in the income statement. Detailed notes to accounts were added in 1942. In 1945, the end of the war, about $36 million of emergency facilities were written off. In 1946, $27.6 million of wartime reserves were used to absorb the cost of a prolonged strike.

The rapid price movement following the end of World War II led USS to adopt a version of "inflation depreciation" in 1947. It did so against the opposition of Price Waterhouse and Company, the Securities and Exchange Commission (SEC), the American Institute of Accountants (now AICPA), and labor leaders. However, this opposition was undoubtedly instrumental in USS's adoption of accelerated depreciation in 1948. Depreciation policy remained a matter of controversy through the years as USS felt that its depreciation expense was not realistic for pricing, income determination, capital replacement, and income taxation.

While USS had a few positive spurts from 1950 on, its remaining years were ones of decline, and its financial accounting practices seemingly mirrored this decline. In 1958, USS radically revised its accounting for pension costs to stop funding and, hence, expensing for past service cost and to reduce current expense by credit for past overcontributions. The annual report became a pulpit for "profits." In 1968, USS adopted the straight-line depreciation method, dropping its accelerated method. It also revised its policy on accounting for the investment credit, so as to reduce income tax expense in the current year.

Diversification into other lines of business, especially oil and gas, caused significant accounting issues for USS and, ultimately, its "death" when it became USX in 1986. USS's segmental reporting practices to reflect this diversification were inconsistent and, hence, unclear. The pulpit-like nature of the annual report continued on such topics as comparative wages, low profits, environmental legislation, and imports. Major shutdowns in its steel plants started in 1979 and caused huge write-offs of assets and major restructuring charges, often labeled "Big-Bath Accounting." Financial Accounting Standard (FAS) No. 33, "Financial Reporting and Changing Prices" (1979) on inflation accounting led to the reporting of the very bad news of increased amounts of depreciation in a supplementary section in the annual report.

The annual reports of companies represent accounting and business historical documents that are being utilized more and more for analysis and study. This is true both on one company through the years and for companies on a comparative basis, both on an industry and international level. The many studies of the annual reports of USS offer examples of this type of historical research.

USS probably adopted its exemplary reporting practices in its early years because of the controversy surrounding the trust movement and watered stock. It was not until 1916 that the year-end price of USS common stock was $100, its par value. USS certainly was a trailblazer in financial reporting for its first 50 years, as exemplified by its consolidated reporting, detailed annual reports, and the depreciation controversies of 1947 and 1948. However, as the economic situation worsened, it became less than an exemplary model.

Richard Vangermeersch

Bibliography

Clair, R.S. "Evolution of Corporate Reports: Observations on the Annual Reports of United States Steel Corporation," *Journal of Accountancy*, January 1945, pp. 39–51.

Reed, S.A. "A Historical Analysis of Depreciation in Accounting: The United States Steel Experience," *Accounting Historians Journal*, December 1989, pp. 119–153.

Schiff, A. "Annual Reports in the United States: A Historical Perspective," *Accounting and Business Research*, Autumn 1978, pp. 279–284.

Vangermeersch, R. "The Capitalization of Fixed Assets in the Birth, Life, and Death of U.S. Steel, 1901–1986." Working paper no. 76 in *Working Paper Series Volume 4,* edited by R.H. Tondkar and E.N. Coffman, pp. 264–293. Richmond, VA: Academy of Accounting Historians, 1989.

———. *Financial Accounting Milestones in the Annual Reports of United States Steel Corporation: The First Seven Decades.* New York: Garland, 1986.

———. "A Historical Overview of Depreciation: U.S. Steel, 1902–1970," *Mississippi Valley Journal of Business and Economics*, Winter 1971–1972, pp. 56–74.

Younkins, E., D.L. Flesher, and T.K. Flesher. "The Financial Statements of U.S. Steel, 1902–1951: A Half Century of Leadership in Reporting." Working paper no. 58 in *Working Paper Series Volume 3,* edited by A.C. Bishop and D.R. Richards, pp. 246–59. Richmond, VA: Academy of Accounting Historians, 1984.

See also AMERICAN INSTITUTE OF CERTIFIED PUBLIC ACCOUNTANTS; ARCHIVES AND SPECIAL COLLECTIONS IN ACCOUNTING; BASE

STOCK METHOD; BIG EIGHT ACCOUNTING FIRMS; CAPITAL MAINTENANCE; COMPARABILITY; CONSOLIDATED FINANCIAL STATEMENTS; DEPRECIATION; DICKINSON, ARTHUR LOWES; DIVERSIFIED REPORTING; FUNDS FLOW STATEMENT; INCOME STATEMENT/INCOME ACCOUNT; INFLATION ACCOUNTING; LAST IN, FIRST OUT (LIFO); LIQUIDITY: ACCOUNTING MEASUREMENT; RAILROAD ACCOUNTING (U.S.); RETAINED EARNINGS; SECURITIES AND EXCHANGE COMMISSION; U.S. INDUSTRIAL COMMISSION

U

V

Vatter, William Joseph (1905–1990)

A professor at the University of Chicago and the University of California at Berkeley and author of *The Fund Theory of Accounting and Its Implications for Financial Reports* (1947), William Joseph Vatter developed a theory to indicate the underlying logic of modern accounting. He found both proprietary and entity theories wanting because they personalize the unit for which accounts are kept. As one result, those theories are not conducive to the objectivity toward which all quantitative analysis should be aimed. Objectivity is particularly important to management, who must continually make choices between alternative courses of action. It is in the realm of managerial accounting, then, that the shortcomings of traditional accounting are most evident.

In his theory, the concept of a "fund" is the central idea that Vatter employed to attain objectivity. A "fund" is an area of operations, a center of interest, or a center of attention. In an illustrative example, he presented six sets of statements: a cash and banks fund, a general operating fund, an investment fund, two sinking funds (one for current items, the other for investments), and a capital fund. For each fund he presented a balance sheet, conventional in form, and a statement of fund operations. Each operating statement included (1) revenues and expenses, as ordinarily defined; (2) financing transactions, such as classified cash movements, issue and retirement of securities, and donations or retirements of fixed assets; and (3) effects of market forces, such as inventory appreciation and declination.

Vatter's theory is equally applicable to governmental and private-sector entities; to profit and not-for-profit entities; to departments, divisions, or branches, as well as to combined or consolidated entities. One consequence is that the concept and measurement of income was not an essential ingredient of his accounting. No net profit appeared in his reports, although one can be calculated from the data presented. Another consequence is that he employed a loose definition of "equities" (i.e., liabilities and owners' equity), identifying them merely as "restrictions" upon the assets of the fund. His "restrictions" may be legal, equitable, economic, or even those based on managerial considerations. Since "valuation" is not exclusively an accounting matter, he omitted any systematic treatment of this subject.

Vatter's direct influence is most clearly seen in the textbooks published in the 20 years after his own *Managerial Accounting* appeared in 1950. His influence on financial accounting is less clear, but his penetrating criticism of extant theory and practice foreshadowed such developments as segmented financial statements, criticisms of the reports issued by conglomerates, and the interest of the Financial Accounting Standards Board in the need for "disaggregation of data" in consolidated financial statements.

Maurice Moonitz

Bibliography

Gaffikin, M., and M. Aitken, eds. *The Development of Accounting Theory: Significant Contributions to Accounting Thought in the Twentieth Century.* New York: Garland, 1982.

Horngren, C.T. "William J. Vatter: Notable Contributor to Management Accounting," *Journal of Management Accounting Research,* Fall 1991, pp. 233–235.

Moonitz, M. "Memorial, William Joseph Vatter (1905–1990)," *Accounting Review*, October 1991, pp. 862–865.

Vatter, W.J. "A Fund Theory Approach to Price Level Adjustment," *Accounting Review*, April 1962, pp. 189–207.

———. *The Fund Theory of Accounting and Its Implications for Financial Reports.* Chicago: University of Chicago Press, 1947.

———. "A Fund Theory View of Accounting for Depreciable Assets." In *Betriebswirtschaftliche Forschung in Internationaler Sicht: Festschrift für Erich Kosiol*, edited by H. Kloidt, pp. 313–326. Berlin: Dunker and Humblot, 1969.

———. *Managerial Accounting.* Englewood Cliffs, NJ: Prentice-Hall, 1950.

See also COMMANDER THEORY; COST AND/OR MANAGEMENT ACCOUNTING; DEMSKI, JOEL S.; DIVERSIFIED REPORTING; ENTITY THEORY; JOHNSON AND KAPLAN'S *RELEVANCE LOST: THE RISE AND FALL OF MANAGEMENT ACCOUNTING;* MANAGEMENT ACCOUNTING; MCKINSEY, JAMES O.; OBJECTIVITY; PROPRIETARY THEORY

Vitruvius

Probably the oldest concept of depreciation is that of falling price—the idea that taking possession of an asset reduces it to second hand, lowering its value, though not always its usefulness. This concept of falling price depreciation was expressed in the first century B.C. by Vitruvius, the Roman writer on architecture. Describing annual depreciation as "the price of the passing of each year," Vitruvius suggested that in valuing a masonry wall with an 80-year life expectancy, one-eightieth of its cost should be deducted for each year it had stood. Depreciation in these terms was a reduction in the price to be paid for a limited life asset. Vitruvius was merely trying to make an asset valuation in connection with a legal settlement. He was concerned with the durability of materials and with the future replacement cost of a particular kind of wall, not with the use or depreciation of productive business assets.

Michael Chatfield

Bibliography

Goldberg, L. "Concepts of Depreciation." In *Studies in Accounting Theory*, edited by W.T. Baxter and S. Davidson, pp. 240–241. Homewood, IL: Irwin, 1962.

Vitruvius. *On Architecture*, translated by F. Granger, vol. 2, chap. 8, pp. 8–9. London: William Heinemann, 1931.

See also DEPRECIATION; ROME (509 B.C.–A.D. 476)

W

Waste Book
See MEMORANDUM BOOK

Wells, Murray Charles (1936–)
A native of Christchurch, New Zealand,
Murray C. Wells completed his early education
at Christ College and the University of Canterbury. He obtained his professional experience
in auditing and accounting in Christchurch and
obtained his first academic appointment at the
University of Canterbury in 1966. While he
established his research interest in management
accounting at Canterbury, it was not until he
was appointed lecturer at the University of
Sydney and came under the influence of R.J.
Chambers that his research interests expanded
and intensified. He was appointed professor at
Sydney in 1975 and dean of the Faculty of Economics in 1988. He has been director of the
Graduate School of Business since 1987.

Wells's major contribution to the accounting literature is his early identification of activity accounting as a preferred method of cost
accounting. This development arose from his
research into the early works of Alexander
Hamilton Church and others of the scientific
management movement. This work was published in 1978 by the University of Illinois as
Accounting for Common Costs, for which he
was awarded the Hourglass Award of the Academy of Accounting Historians in 1979. As
councilor and president of the New South Wales
Division of the Australian Society of CPAs and
chairman of the National Education Committee, Wells has also made a major contribution
to accounting education. From 1987 to 1992,
he was president of the International Association for Accounting Education and Research. In

1986, he was the American Accounting Association (AAA) International Distinguished Visiting Lecturer. He has been editor of *Abacus*
since 1974. In addition to his 1978 book, his
major publications include "Costing for Activities," "A Revolution in Accounting Theory?"
and "What is Wrong with Accounting Education?"

Allen T. Craswell

Bibliography
Wells, M.C. *Accounting for Common Costs.*
   Urbana: University of Illinois, 1978.
———. "Costing for Activities," *Manage-
   ment Accounting* (U.S.), May 1976, pp.
   31–37.
———. "A Revolution in Accounting
   Theory?" *Accounting Review*, July 1976,
   pp. 471–482.
———. "What is Wrong with Accounting
   Education?" *Hokkaigakuen University
   Journal of Economics*, October 1987,
   pp. 17–28.

See also ACADEMY OF ACCOUNTING HISTORI-
ANS; AMERICAN ACCOUNTING ASSOCIATION;
AUSTRALIA; CHAMBERS, RAYMOND JOHN;
COMMON COSTS; DOMESDAY BOOK; ENGI-
NEERING AND ACCOUNTING

Westec Case
See CARPENTER V. HALL

Wheat Committee
The Wheat Committee is the informal name
given to the American Institute of Certified
Public Accountants (AICPA) Study (Group) on

Establishment of Accounting Principles. This seven-member committee was formed in 1971 to study the establishment of accounting principles and to make recommendations for improving that process. The chairman was Francis M. Wheat, who was the commissioner of the Securities and Exchange Commission, 1964–1969. He was joined by senior partners from three international and large national CPA firms, an investment banker, a vice president of General Motors, and a leading accounting academic, David Solomons. The Wheat Committee was made necessary by the stress placed on the Accounting Principles Board (APB) during the latter part of the 1960s and early 1970s, best illustrated by the turmoil about accounting for mergers in 1970. The APB was unable to pass an opinion on accounting for combinations that was in accord with its exposure draft in 1970 on the matter. The APB then weakened its position taken in the exposure draft and ultimately passed APB No. 16, "Business Combinations" (1970) by a 12 to 6 vote, the minimum passing vote, and APB No. 17, "Intangible Assets" (1970) by a vote of 13 to 5. Stephen A. Zeff felt that those two opinions seemed "to have been responsible for a movement to undertake a comprehensive review of the procedure for establishing accounting principles."

The Wheat Committee strove to be independent from the AICPA. This independence, and especially the appearance of independence, was an important recommendation so that the general public would have greater faith in the standards. The committee met on numerous occasions and held a two-day public hearing. It encouraged position papers and strove to make its proceedings a public record. From the outset, it dropped the term "principles" and substituted the term "standards," because it was more descriptive of the work of the APB and its predecessor, the Committee on Accounting Procedure (CAP). The Wheat Committee recommended the formation of a new rules body that would focus not only on items requiring immediate attention but focus on accounting concepts. Concurrently the AICPA had established at about the same time another committee to focus on a more conceptual approach. The Study Group on the Objectives of Financial Statements was chaired by Robert M. Trueblood, and its report in 1973 was entitled *Objectives of Financial Statements* (also known as the Trueblood Report).

The Wheat Committee presented a strong case for the new accounting rules body to remain in the private sector. In its 1972 report, it recommended a full-time, seven-member board with a five-vote minimum needed to pass a standard. Four of the members were to be CPAs from public accounting. The other three did not need to be CPAs but had to have extensive experience in the financial-reporting field. The new body also was to have full-time research staff support. The committee recommended the formation of a Financial Accounting Foundation and a Financial Accounting Standards Advisory Council, and a broad base of support, both financial and other, for the new rules body. That body, the Financial Accounting Standards Board (FASB), was established the following year, 1973, replacing the APB.

The Wheat Committee was very successful in achieving its goals and recommendations. Its report should be studied, first, as a model of the successful attainment of its goals for a financial accounting rules body, and second, as a good history of the CAP and, especially, the APB. Since the topic of "What Sector Sets the Standards—Private or Public?" seems never to go away, this report will always be a significant one.

Richard Vangermeersch

Bibliography

"AICPA Adopts Wheat Report on Accounting Standards Board," *Journal of Accountancy*, June 1972, pp. 10, 12–16.

American Institute of Certified Public Accountants. *Establishing Financial Accounting Standards*. Report of the Study (Group) on Establishment of Accounting Principles [The Wheat Report]. New York: AICPA, 1972.

"Recommendations of the Study on Establishment of Accounting Principles," *Journal of Accountancy*, May 1972, pp. 66–71.

Zeff, S.A. *Forging Accounting Principles in Five Countries: A History and an Analysis of Trends*. Champaign, IL: Stipes, 1972.

See also Accounting Principles Board; American Institute of Certified Public Accountants; Financial Accounting Standards Board; Generally Accepted Accounting Principles; Securities and Exchange Commission; Solomons, David;

preferred to collect only "probable costs" in
the financial accounting records.

Michael Chatfield

Whitmore, John

The first detailed description of a standard cost
system was made by an American accountant,
John Whitmore. A disciple of Alexander
Hamilton Church, Whitmore in 1906 wrote a
series of articles in which he provided the ledgers, accounts, and entries needed to make
Church's system operative in a factory. While
accepting Church's scientific machine rate as a
basis for overhead allocation, he disapproved of
Church's treatment of idle capacity costs.
Whitmore viewed such costs as waste, not as
"proper costs" of production, and criticized
Church's supplementary rate, which charged
them to work in process. Whitmore was am-
bivalent as to whether idle capacity costs should
be written off as period expenses, but he urged
that they be segregated from normal production
costs in a ledger account called Factory Capacity Idle.

In a 1908 lecture, Whitmore elaborated
on his idea that true manufacturing cost need
not include every expenditure made to produce an item. If idle capacity expense was not
part of a product's cost, might there not be
other costs resulting from waste or accident
that should also be excluded? Whitmore considered it feasible to determine what product
costs ought to be *before production began*,
and then analyze the differences between
these predetermined costs and actual expenditures. He knew of industries in which
manufacturing orders were so numerous that
it was impossible to set up a separate cost
account for each order, but quite simple to
calculate a standard product cost for each
type of goods. Using as his example a shoe
factory, Whitmore showed how each grade of
leather could be costed at a "proper" price,
and how variances would automatically result if the actual prices paid or quantities used
were different from the standard amounts. He
also explained how direct labor cost could be
charged to work in process at standard rates.
Though admitting that he had not calculated
or applied standard overhead costs,
Whitmore believed it could be done. However, he did not propose the use of scientifically developed cost standards. While not
ruling out the use of engineered standard
costs for internal accounting purposes, he

Bibliography

Sowell, E.M. *The Evolution of the Theories
and Techniques of Standard Costs.* University, AL: University of Alabama Press,
1973.

Whitmore, J. "Factory Accounting as Applied to Machine Shops," *Journal of
Accountancy,* August 1906–January
1907.

———. "Shoe Factory Cost Accounts," *Journal of Accountancy,* May 1908, pp. 12–
25.

See also CHURCH, ALEXANDER HAMILTON;
COST AND/OR MANAGEMENT ACCOUNTING;
STANDARD COSTING; TAYLOR, FREDERICK
WINSLOW

Wildman, John Raymond (1878–1938)

John Raymond Wildman was an early leader of
the U.S. accounting profession whose works
and ideas influenced the development of professional organizations, research for accounting
practice, and accounting education. Wildman
entered Yale University but left school early to
enter public service during the Spanish-Ameri-
can War. He was assigned to Puerto Rico and
served as a hospital steward in the Army Hospital Corps from 1898 to 1900; as a government disbursing officer in Puerto Rico from
1900 to 1905; and as the general manager of
the Puerto Rican Teachers Expedition to the
United States in 1904.

Wildman returned to New York in 1905
and enrolled in New York University in 1906 at
night. He was also on the staff of Haskins and
Sells from 1905–1909. He graduated in 1909
with a degree in accounting. He also passed the
CPA examination early that year and received
a master's degree from the same school in 1911.
Wildman began his teaching career as an accounting faculty member at his alma mater in
1909; he left his post at the university in 1923.
As a teacher Wildman was respected for his
masterly use of written and spoken words. He
also had the ability to judge and develop the
talents of those whom he provided formal training in accounting subjects.

Wildman wrote several textbooks on such
topics as financial accounting, cost accounting,

and auditing. Through his lectures and writings he introduced in *Principles of Accounting* (1913) a modified accounting equation: "Assets = Liabilities + Accountabilities," which amended the equation developed by Charles Ezra Sprague, who also taught at NYU. Wildman's modification from "Proprietorship" to "Accountabilities" was due to his important recognition of the increasing separation between owners and managers of corporations. However, like Sprague, Wildman ignored the "entity" fiction and noted that financial-statement orientation was not to the corporate entity but to the individual owner/proprietor/capitalist.

Wildman always stressed to his students the necessity of linking theory and practice, as noted by G.J. Previts and R.F. Taylor (1978), both experts on the history of accounting in the United States. He stated that experience shows that something more than the study of theory is necessary for proper and satisfactory execution of work in the field. The implementation of a laboratory approach in his teaching reflected an actualization of his teaching philosophy. Wildman used the same approach in his writings. However, he did not use his writings to merely provide theoretical support for existing practice. Instead, he often used them to criticize common accounting practices such as the widespread use of single entry bookkeeping and the inclusion of interest on owned capital in selling expenses. He argued that such practices lacked theoretical support.

His writings also reflected progressive ideas. He was among the early authors who supported depreciation of fixed assets. Yet, he also recognized that asset values might appreciate. He proposed that value appreciation be classified as "unrealized appreciation" in the capital accounts when asset "value in use" increased in his 1928 article "Appreciation from the Point of View of the Public Accountant." He was also credited for original thinking about issues related to the development of standard costing.

Wildman's proposal for preparing students to master theory and practice was forged not only by his background as an active practitioner-educator but also by his contact with company executives. He taught a course, "Accounting for Business Men," in which George Merck, who was later president of Merck and Company, was one of the students.

Wildman's influence in accounting education and thought went far beyond NYU. He was one of the founders of the predecessor organization of the American Accounting Association—the American Association of University Instructors in Accounting (AAUIA). He proposed a constitution for the organization and served as its first president in 1916. In 1926, when he was the chair of a research committee, Wildman wrote a report on research needs in accounting and submitted a plan for a research program for the association. In his report, he asserted that the purpose of accounting research is to produce data that will make for more scientific and more satisfactory accounting. Basically this is what accounting researchers are now still trying to achieve.

He remained a faculty member at NYU until 1923, although he returned to Haskins and Sells in 1918 as head of the Department of Professional Training. Later that year, he was admitted as a partner. Under Wildman's direction, Haskins and Sells research and training unit pioneered technical research and practice innovations applicable to auditing. This unit initiated, among other things, the establishment of audit programs for the evaluation of internal control, tests of transaction, and cash-auditing procedures. In addition, his knowledge of the academic community based on his professorship at New York University enabled Wildman to recruit some of the best college graduates for the firm. Among those who were recruited by Wildman and who later played important roles in the development of accounting practice were Arthur Foye, John W. Queenan, Weldon Powell, and Ralph S. Johns.

Wildman's involvement in accounting practice was not limited to activities inside Haskins and Sells. He also served as an active member and leader of the American Institute of Accountants (AIA)—predecessor of the American Institute of Certified Public Accountants (AICPA)—and the NACA (now the Institute of Management Accountants). He became Director of Education of the NAA and chaired several committees of the AICPA.

Wildman proposed the idea that accounting engagement services be classified specifically and clearly referred to in any engagement of CPAs in 1928 in "Classification of Accountancy Services." He argued that such specification gives both clients and CPAs a clear understanding of what the firm of CPAs was expected to do and its responsibility. Lack of such complete understanding, he observed, made difficult the fixing of responsibility in cases where errors of one kind or another come to light.

Wildman also insisted that the observation of physical inventories and confirmation of receivables be included in audit procedures (Previts and Taylor). This view was opposite to the traditional British view commonly held then that auditors could rely on management representation to determine the value of inventories and the balance of receivables. The subsequent audit failure related to the 1938 McKesson and Robbins case made clear the importance of Wildman's idea. Shortly after his death in 1938, the extension of auditing procedures adopted by the AICPA in May 1939 followed along these lines.

Wildman also was heavily involved in defending Haskins and Sells in a lawsuit brought against the firm by shareholders of G.W. Miller and Company in October 1928 in *O'Connor v. Ludlam*. The firm was sued for audit malpractice, as to a certification of the balance sheet of G.W. Miller and Company dated August 31, 1925, that, the plaintiffs asserted, was fraudulently false and misleading. The initial verdict delivered on May 18, 1934, was in favor of the firm. Later, on August 16, 1937, the Second Circuit Court of Appeals upheld the 1934 jury's verdict. However, this long litigation process put a great strain on Wildman and took its toll on his health. This, coupled with the death of his first wife on October 18, 1932, led him to request retirement from practice on June 1, 1936.

John Raymond Wildman was a role model for professionals. He contributed to accounting education, accounting thought, and accounting practice. He was dedicated and had a great influence on shaping the accounting profession. In recognition and tribute to John Raymond Wildman, the American Accounting Association annually selects an applied-research paper or project to receive the Wildman Medal, awarded since 1979.

Sudarwan

Bibliography

Previts, G.J., and R.F. Taylor. *John Raymond Wildman*. Monograph No. 2. University, AL: Academy of Accounting Historians, 1978.
Wildman, J.R. "A Research Program," *Accounting Review*, March 1926, pp. 43–60.
———. "Appreciation from the Point of View of the Public Accountant," *Accounting Review*, December 1928, pp. 396–406.
———. "Classification of Accountancy Services," *Accounting Review*, June 1928, pp. 124–130.
———. *Principles of Accounting*. New York: William G. Hewitt, 1913.
———. *Principles of Auditing*. New York: William G. Hewitt, 1916.
———. *Principles of Cost Accounting*. New York: William G. Hewitt, 1914.

See also ACCOUNTING EDUCATION IN THE UNITED STATES; AMERICAN ACCOUNTING ASSOCIATION; BIG EIGHT ACCOUNTING FIRMS; IMPUTED INTEREST ON CAPITAL; MCKESSON AND ROBBINS CASE; SELLS, ELIJAH WATT; SINGLE ENTRY BOOKKEEPING; SPRAGUE, CHARLES EZRA

Women in Accounting

The participation of women in accounting-related activities was documented as early as the 1700s, specifically in Benjamin Franklin's autobiography. More recent reference to women in accounting can be found in census data from the late 1800s and early 1900s. For example, census data for 1910 listed the number of women who worked within the employment category of bookkeepers, accountants, and cashiers as 190,000.

The number of women who became CPAs was very limited throughout most of the 1900s. Ried, Acken, and Jancura state in a May 1987 *Journal of Accountancy* article that 90 percent of the CPA certificates then held by women had been earned since 1970. The primary difficulty women had in becoming certified was obtaining the necessary experience to qualify them to sit for the CPA examination. Women were not hired in large numbers until the 1970s, and the reasons consistently stated were: the extensive hours and travel required, difficulties expected from women working and traveling with male colleagues, and client resistance to women. A respite from the cultural and business-community resistance to female accountants occurred during World War II when significant numbers of women accountants were hired to replace men supporting the war effort. The soldiers' return produced an oversupply of accountants, and many positions held by women during the war years reverted to men.

The post–World War II culture instigated the change that resulted in many college-educated women entering the accounting profession in the 1970s. The newly accepted middle-class norm of educating both sons and daughters produced the first real numbers of women trained for accounting and expecting to be hired. The beginning wave of this phenomenon, those women graduating from college in the 1960s, encountered greater resistance and difficulty in finding entry-level accounting jobs than those graduating 10 years later. Despite contradictory research findings, a common perception was that women were not well suited to accounting because of its demands. Women were not expected to stay in accounting for the long term because of the rigors of the job and its incompatibility with family responsibilities. Consequently, women were not given assignments that developed their professional competencies. The result was that women left, often because of lack of career opportunity. However, the departures seemed to confirm the common perception that women resign early.

Supreme Court cases in the 1980s resulted in precedents that should be favorable for women's upward mobility into public accounting partnerships. In *Hishon v. King and Spaulding* 104 S.Ct. 2229, 1984, the Supreme Court ruled that firms making decisions to admit individuals to a partnership (with 15 or more employees) cannot discriminate based on race, color, religion, sex, or national origin. In *Price Waterhouse v. Hopkins* 490 U.S. 228 (1989) the Supreme Court ruled that stereotypes are unlawful decision criteria for partnership admissions.

Women's involvement in professional organizations has evolved along with their employment roles. The American Woman's Society of CPAs, founded in 1933, and the American Society of Women Accountants, chartered in 1938, were the first organizations with large numbers of female members. Since that time, women have played major roles in all professional accounting organizations, including the American Institute of Certified Public Accountants (AICPA), state societies, state boards of accountancy, the Institute of Management Accountants, and the American Accounting Association. Participation in these organizations is still growing as evidenced by the formation in 1989 of a Gender Issues special-interest section in the American Accounting Association.

Gender issues have become of interest to many accounting researchers, and articles addressing varied topics have been published in numerous journals. *The Woman CPA* traditionally published many articles on topics involving women accountants, including many reports of survey research. By the mid-1980s journals as varied as the *Journal of Accountancy* (see, for example, Shirley J. Dahl and Karen L. Hooks, 1984) and *Accounting, Organizations, and Society* (see, for example, Anthony M. Tinker and Marilyn Neimark, 1987) had published gender-related articles. Topics that have been studied range from the more typical (motivation, job satisfaction, turnover, college performance, recruiting) to feminist-inspired subjects such as the use of language, the framing of recorded history, and discrimination. *Issues in Accounting Education* has published numerous gender-related articles on education topics. For publications on feminist-related topics, see *Accounting, Organizations, and Society*; *Advances in Public Interest Accounting*; *Critical Perspectives on Accounting*.

Controversial issues remain central to the topic of women in accounting. Most are driven by the fact that 50 percent of accounting graduates since the 1980s are women, yet very few women have achieved top management status either in public accounting firms or industry. Limiting turnover and facilitating career progression are proposed as major challenges facing employers of female accountants in the 1990s. Flexible work schedules, child-care assistance, and personal and career growth enhancement through mentoring are often identified as likely avenues for improvement. Supporting programs have been implemented by many companies and public accounting firms.

Karen L. Hooks

Bibliography

American Institute of Certified Public Accountants. *Upward Mobility of Women Special Committee Report to the AICPA Board of Directors*. New York: AICPA, 1988.

Ciancanelli, P., S. Gallhofer, C. Humphrey, and L. Kirkham. "Gender and Accountancy: Some Evidence from the UK," *Critical Perspectives on Accounting*, June 1990, pp. 117–144.

Dahl, S.J., and K.L. Hooks. "Women Accountants in a Changing Profession,"

Journal of Accountancy, December 1984, pp. 108–116.

Lehman, C. "The Importance of Being Ernest: Gender Conflicts in Accounting," *Advances in Public Interest Accounting*, 1990, pp. 137–157.

Pillsbury, C.M., L. Capozzoli, and A. Ciampa. "A Synthesis of Research Studies regarding the Upward Mobility of Women in Public Accounting," *Accounting Horizons*, March 1989, pp. 63–70.

Tinker, A.M., and M. Niemark. "The Role of Annual Reports in Gender and Class Contradictions at General Motors, 1917–1976," *Accounting, Organizations, and Society*, vol. 12, no. 1, 1987, 71–88.

See also Big Eight Accounting Firms; Institute of Chartered Accountants in England and Wales

W

Y

Yale Express Case
See Fischer v. Kletz

Yamey, Basil Selig (1919–)

A distinguished economist and educator, Professor Basil Selig Yamey, now emeritus, is also known for his invaluable contribution to accounting history. Yamey's interest in accounting history began when he was working on his doctoral dissertation at the London School of Economics in 1939–1940. Although his dissertation was never to be completed due to World War II, Yamey's interest in accounting history had already kindled, and from that time on he was to devote a portion of his academic life to the study of early accounting treatises and of surviving accounting records—beginning with the nineteenth century and reaching all the way back to the Middle Ages.

Born and raised in South Africa, Yamey served in the South African Air Force during the war years. After the war, with ideas of obtaining a Ph.D. abandoned, Yamey started on a full-time career as a university professor in economics. He lectured at a number of European and North American universities but spent most of his teaching career at the London School of Economics (1947–1949 and 1950–1984).

Yamey's works in the history of accounting can be classified into three groups: (1) studies in the early literature of accounting, 1543–1800, designed to trace the influences of one author or treatise on another and to throw light on accounting practices of the times; (2) studies of extant account books of English merchants, mostly from the seventeenth and eighteenth centuries, designed to examine variations in practice and to test how far the best accounting treatises differed from practice; and (3) examination and analysis of German historian and political economist Werner Sombart's thesis on the relationship between double entry bookkeeping and the rise of capitalism in Western Europe.

Alongside his scholarship in applied economics and accounting history, Yamey has pursued an active interest in Western art, 1400–1800. This interest led him in 1986 to publish a collection of art works, *Arte e Contabilita* (in Italian), which included representations of account books and countinghouse activities. A revised English version of the book, *Art and Accounting,* was published by Yale University Press in 1989.

Yamey is an honorary life member of the Academy of Accounting Historians and the recipient of the academy's 1976 Hourglass Award. For his public service, Yamey was appointed Commander of the Order of the British Empire (CBE) in 1972, and for his scholarship he was elected Fellow of the British Academy (FBA) in 1977.

Vahé Baladouni

Bibliography

Baladouni, V. "Basil Selig Yamey." In *Biographies of Notable Accountants*, 2d ed., edited by A.M. Agami, pp. 52–55. New York: Random House, 1989.

Parker, R.H., ed. *Bibliographies for Accounting Historians*. New York: Arno Press, 1980.

Yamey, B.S. "Accounting and the Rise of Capitalism: Further Notes on a Theme by Sombart," *Journal of Accounting Research*, Autumn 1964, pp. 117–136.

———. "Scientific Book-keeping and the Rise of Capitalism." In *Studies in Accounting*, ed. by W.T. Baxter, pp. 13–30. London: Sweet and Maxwell, 1950.

———. "Some Topics in the History of Financial Accounting in England 1500–1900." In *Studies in Accounting Theory*, edited by W.T. Baxter and S. Davidson, pp. 14–43. London: Sweet and Maxwell, 1962.

———, H.C. Edey, and H.W. Thomson. *Accounting in England and Scotland: 1543–1800*. London: Sweet and Maxwell, 1963.

———, and A. von Gebsattel. *Luca Pacioli's Exposition of Double Entry Bookkeeping: Venice 1494*. Venice: Albrizzi Editor, 1994.

See also COMPOUND ENTRIES; SINGLE ENTRY BOOKKEEPING; SOMBART, WERNER

Ympyn, Jan (1485–1540)

Jan Ympyn was a Flemish merchant who traveled widely, lived 12 years in Venice, and finally settled in Antwerp. His *Nieuwe Instructie* (1543), the first Dutch treatise on double entry bookkeeping, was translated into French in 1543 and English in 1547. Though largely derived from Luca Pacioli's treatise "Particularis de Computis et Scripturis" (1494), Ympyn's text contained several important innovations. Pacioli considered each accounting topic separately; Ympyn drew his discussion together with a set of illustrative accounts. Ympyn's procedures for ledger balancing and closing were superior to Pacioli's. Ympyn was the first author to incorporate a balance account into the ledger and the first to show the new ledger with its opening entries. Ympyn began the ledger closing process by transferring the ending balances to the balance account, closing the ledger. The balance account was reopened in the new ledger and then immediately closed by carrying the individual account balances to the various reopened accounts.

Beginning with Alvise Casanova (1558), James Peele (1569), and Angelo Pietra (1586), later textbook authors adopted Ympyn's balance account, and his ledger closing procedures became standard practice.

Michael Chatfield

Bibliography

Bywater, M.F., and B.S. Yamey. *Historic Accounting Literature: A Companion Guide*. London: Scholar Press, 1982.

Yamey, B.S. "The Authorship and Sources of the *Nieuwe Instructie*." In *Essays on the History of Accounting*. New York: Arno Press, 1978.

Ympyn, Jan. *A Notable and Very Excellente Worke*, edited by O. Kojima and B.S. Yamey. Kyoto: Diagakudo Shoten, 1975.

See also BALANCE ACCOUNT; CLOSING ENTRIES AND PROCEDURES; CONSERVATISM; MANZONI, DOMENICO; NETHERLANDS; PACIOLI, LUCA; PEELE, JAMES; PIETRA, ANGELO; TRIAL BALANCE

Z

Zappa, Gino (1879–1960)

Gino Zappa has been one of the accounting and economy giants of the twentieth century for the influence he had on the scientific world and on the profession. The central theme of business accounting in Zappa's view is income determination. This basic phenomenon is the foundation of all explanations of the accounting process and its elements, specifically for accounting theories of the balance sheet and income statement.

Zappa recognized the dynamic aspect of accounting by emphasizing the role of the income statement. The balance sheet thereby becomes an instrument of income determination. This accounting theory, emphasizing income determination, is a four-series-accounts theory. In adherence to present-day practice, it distinguishes two series of status accounts (accounts for assets, on the one hand, and liabilities and net equities, on the other) and two series of achievements accounts (expense and revenue accounts). The inclusion of different series of accounts for expense and revenue in accounting theory enables the recognition of all transactions and processes in all kinds of entities, the continuous inflow and internal formation of goods and services, the subsequent consumption of such resources, and the final output of products.

Zappa developed the dynamic aspect of accounting and business economics that is still predominant in Italy. Profit-and-loss accounts clarify the general correlation between positive and negative income components attributable to a definite time period. The balance sheet shows a system of values (a fund of values), referred to the end of the time period, for future income determination. Income components are basically determined from monetary exchanges.

In order to give expression in one comprehensive measure to the size of these components, they are best considered as amounts of exchange values. Thus, income is regarded as a concept of value. Income is, in essence, a fact of value and, therefore, of distribution because it is determined only in the exchange and for the exchange.

Zappa saw the balance sheet as a reflection of the future. Basic to Zappa's thinking is that values depend on future incomes. His concept of the balance sheet has, simultaneously, the character of both budgeting and valuation—future events have to be discounted to present-day values. It is to the credit of the Zappa school of accounting thought that it has seen the effect of future activities on both sides of the balance sheet—and this at a time when the balance sheet was commonly interpreted as a reflection of past events.

Zappa was the founder of concern economics (*economia d'azienda*), which is an overall theory regarding concerns as complex wholes: It consists of specific but interconnected branches and aims at investigating the concern's whole complexity. Zappa expressed his view as follows: ". . . if it is felt that which is organically a whole can be safely split up, if it is felt that the even greater range of phenomena under investigation requires a high degree of specialization, then we can accept the scientific autonomy of the three disciplines of management, organization and information system. However, we must not forget the many bands, both obvious and hidden, that join the three disciplines; an order of knowledge cannot be developed, or worse, given credence, isolating it from the knowledge which constitutes its natural substratum and logical complement."

The earnestness, the originality, and the reality of his scientific thoughts, rooted in experience and in an unusual power of observation of economic phenomena, gave rise to many disciples who distinguished themselves in accounting and concern-economics studies. Accounting studies in Italy after Zappa were almost identical to those in business administration, and the methodology continually moved in the direction of concern-economic events, a direction more and more widespread. The real object of accounting studies is the economy of the concern—concerns of all kinds—expressed in terms of quantities mainly elaborated with accounting methods and developed in the concern in response to its information and control needs.

Giuseppe Galassi

Bibliography
Academia Italiana di Economia Aziendale. *Gino Zappa: Founder of Concern Economics* (economia d'azienda). Papers for the hundredth anniversary of his birth. Bologna: AIDEA, 1980.

See also INCOME-DETERMINATION THEORY; ITALY, AFTER PACIOLI; SOCIAL RESPONSIBILITIES OF ACCOUNTANTS

Zeff, Stephen A. (1933–)
Stephen A. Zeff is a highly respected accounting academic who has undertaken leadership roles in developing the fields of accounting history, international accounting, accounting education, and accounting professionalism. His works have spanned five decades. Zeff, who received his Ph.D. from the University of Michigan in 1962, is the Herbert S. Autrey Professor of Accounting at Rice University. He has extensive teaching and research experience throughout the world and has been the recipient of many teaching awards, as well as the Hourglass Award from the Academy of Accounting Historians. He was editor of *Accounting Review* for 1977–1982 and president of the American Accounting Association (AAA) for 1985–1986. He has been the public member of the planning committee of the Auditing Standards Board of the American Institute of Certified Public Accountants (AICPA) since 1989.

Zeff and Thomas F. Keller edited in 1964 a book of readings for use in intermediate and other accounting theory classes. The purpose of the book was to show students that their chosen field is not free of debate or disagreement. The editors included an introduction to each section, a bibliography at the end of each section, and a brief biography of the author of each entry. The selected readings included such accounting controversies as income tax allocation and the investment credit and such noted writers as DR Scott, George Oliver May, and William Andrew Paton. The book remains a magnificent source for accounting classics.

Zeff chaired the AAA Committee on Accounting History in 1970 and was the principal draftsman of its report, which stressed both the intellectual and utilitarian ends of accounting history. The report called for collaborative research with business and economic historians. The committee noted the lack in accounting history of preliminary research into the reasons for actions taken, bemoaned the "ex cathedra" teaching of current rules without any historical background, and called for different venues for discussions of accounting history.

Zeff in 1972 wrote a comparative study of accounting rules-making in five countries: (1) England, (2) Scotland, (3) Mexico, (4) the United States, and (5) Canada. He showed what has become the trademark of his research: an immersion into data and people on site. In his book, Zeff stressed that inevitable environmental and philosophical differences among nations affect their accounting. He also said that accounting did not have a research tradition and needed a long-term plan for this. This book remains an excellent source for the accounting history of these countries and a comparison of them.

Zeff again illustrated his investigatory-type research in the 1982 article he wrote on Kenneth MacNeal, the author of *Truth in Accounting* (1939) (see also the "MacNeal, Kenneth" entry in the encyclopedia). Zeff gained access to MacNeal's scrapbook and corresponded with him. He also reviewed the Hatfield Papers at the University of California at Berkeley, as Hatfield had corresponded with MacNeal. Zeff interviewed W.W. Cooper, a compatriot of Eric Louis Kohler, long-term editor of the *Accounting Review,* to ascertain why MacNeal's book was not reviewed in *Accounting Review.* This is the type of basic research discussed in the report of the Committee on Accounting History.

Zeff continued on with the more personal side of accounting historical research in an article presenting brief biographies of 14 accounting leaders in the May 1987 AICPA Centennial Issue of the *Journal of Accountancy*. Zeff placed each of the 14 into the accounting milieu of his times so that the reader could understand both the individual and his role in accounting. The coverage and time span range from Charles Ezra Sprague of the 1880s to Leonard Spacek of the early 1970s.

Zeff has long been an advocate of moving the CPA exam to late July or early August so there will be less emphasis on that exam in the accounting curriculum. While this has not happened, he was successful as a leader in the move against an all-objective CPA exam. Zeff in 1989 reiterated his call for accounting educators to adopt a historical perspective in their field, so that students will be better able to determine the adequacy of current practice. He remains critical of authors of accounting textbooks as followers not leaders.

Given the breadth and depth of his contributions, Zeff will be mentioned in the same breath as A.C. Littleton by the year 2000.

Richard Vangermeersch

Bibliography

"Committee on Accounting History," *Accounting Review*, 1970 Supplement, 1970, pp. 52–64.

Zeff, S.A. "Does Accounting Belong in the University Curriculum?" *Issues in Accounting Education*, Spring 1989, pp. 203–210.

———. "Does the CPA Belong to a Profession?" *Accounting Horizons*, June 1987, pp. 65–68.

———. *Forging Accounting Principles in Five Countries: A History and an Analysis of Trends*. Champaign, IL: Stipes, 1972.

———. "Leaders of the Accounting Profession: Fourteen Who Made a Difference," *Journal of Accountancy*, May 1987, pp. 46–71.

———. "Truth in Accounting: The Ordeal of Kenneth MacNeal," *Accounting Review*, July 1982, pp. 528–553.

Zeff, S.A., and T.F. Keller, eds. *Financial Accounting Theory: Issues and Controversies*. New York: McGraw-Hill, 1964.

See also AMERICAN ACCOUNTING ASSOCIATION; CERTIFIED PUBLIC ACCOUNTANT EXAMINATION: THE EARLY YEARS (1896–1930); COOPER, WILLIAM WAGER; KOHLER, ERIC LOUIS; LITTLETON, A.C.; MACNEAL, KEN-NETH; MAY, GEORGE OLIVER; PATON, WILLIAM ANDREW; SCOTT, DR; SPACEK, LEONARD; SPRAGUE, CHARLES EZRA

Z

Zimmerman, Vernon K. (1928–)

An American accountant and recipient of many professional awards, Vernon K. Zimmerman was educated at the University of Illinois, where he received his B.S. in 1949, M.S. in 1951, and Ph.D. in 1954. He was a student of A.C. Littleton, specializing initially in accounting history and later in international accounting. He has served as director of the International Center for Accounting Education and Research at the University of Illinois at Urbana-Champaign since 1963. He was dean of the College of Commerce and Business Administration at the University from 1967 to 1985 and was subsequently appointed to the Distinguished Service Chair in Accounting. While dean of the college, he was elected vice-president (1978–1979) and president (1979–1980) of the American Assembly of Collegiate Schools of Business.

Zimmerman has lectured in many countries, including Germany, Austria, and Sweden, and has served as a consultant for the Peace Corps, the Agency for International Development, the World Bank, and the International Labor Office, and as associate director (1969–1971) of the Office of International Programs and Studies at the University of Illinois.

In addition to facilitating the early development of international accounting in the United States, Zimmerman has made substantial academic contributions by editing 18 monographs and contributing many articles in this field in the United States and abroad. His primary contribution to accounting history was made as coauthor of *Accounting Theory: Continuity and Change* (1962) with A.C. Littleton, in which accounting developments in the United States and abroad are examined in their historical context and with respect to their economic importance and impact.

Hanns Martin Schoenfeld

Bibliography

Kafer, K., and V.K. Zimmerman. "Notes on the Evolution of the Statement of Sources and Applications of Funds," *International Journal of Accounting Education and Research*, Spring 1967, pp. 89–121.

Littleton, A.C., and V.K. Zimmerman. *Accounting Theory: Continuity and Change.* Englewood Cliffs, NJ: Prentice-Hall, 1962.

Zimmerman, V.K. "Long Shadow of a Scholar," *International Journal of Accounting Education and Research,* Spring 1967, pp. 1–20.

See also CENTER FOR INTERNATIONAL EDUCATION AND RESEARCH IN ACCOUNTING; FUNDS FLOW STATEMENT; LITTLETON, A.C.

Index

Page references to encyclopedia entries appear in boldface.

Accounting Research Bulletins, **15–18**, 39
    ARB No. 1, 15, 276, 586–87
    ARB No. 3, 15
    ARB No. 4, 15, 17, 257
    ARB No. 5, 15, 17
    ARB No. 9, 500
    ARB No. 11, 18, 568
    ARB No. 12, 500
    ARB No. 13, 380
    ARB No. 14, 381
    ARB No. 23, 18, 381
    ARB No. 24, 18, 283, 337, 469
    ARB No. 26, 316, 380
    ARB No. 28, 17, 316, 380
    ARB No. 29, 15, 346, 368–69
    ARB No. 30, 15–16, 381, 388, 596
    ARB No. 31, 316
    ARB No. 32, 17, 316
    ARB No. 33, 17
    ARB No. 34, 17, 596
    ARB No. 36, 18, 381
    ARB No. 37, 18
    ARB No. 38, 18, 381
    ARB No. 39, 17–18, 500, 596
    ARB No. 40, 18, 469
    ARB No. 43, 17, 258, 283, 469–70, 485, 568–69
    ARB No. 44, 381
    ARB No. 46, 485
    ARB No. 47, 18, 381
    ARB No. 48, 469–70
    ARB No. 49, 18
    ARB No. 50, 18, 380
    ARB No. 51, 17, 168
Accounting Review, 9, 32, 406, 411, 453
Accounting Series Releases, 527–28
    ASR No. 2, 323
    ASR No. 4, 15
    ASR No. 7, 337
    ASR No. 11, 257
    ASR No. 15, 485
    ASR No. 16, 485
    ASR No. 17, 430
    ASR No. 21, 52, 410
    ASR No. 22, 323
    ASR No. 47, 323
    ASR No. 126, 324
    ASR No. 150, 121
    ASR No. 190, **22–23**, 121, 142–43, 297, 462, 573
    ASR No. 250, 158
    ASR No. 253, 142–43
    See also Securities and Exchange Commission
Accounting Terminology Bulletins, 18
accounts receivable, 58–59, 128, 160, 594, 611
accreditation, 6–9
accretion concept of income, **23**
accrual accounting, **23–24**, 102, 129, 172, 256, 440, 457, 531
activity based costing, **24–26**, 80–81, 136, 182, 347, 354, 394

Adams, A., 31
Adams, Charles Francis, Jr., 43, 487–88, 501–2
Adams, Henry C., 488
Adelberg, Arthur H., 240
Adhikari, Ajay, 235–37
advertising by accountants, **26–27**, 42, 74, 233–35
agency bookkeeping, 413–14, 450, 531
agency theory, **27–29**, 397–98, 583
agricultural accounting, 23, **29–31**, 111–113, 133–34, 180, 399, 412–14, 463, 465–66, 506
Aidenoff, Abraham, 428
Aitkin, Michael J., 605
Aiyathurai, G., 25
Alberti del Giudice, **31–32**, 76
Alderson, Wroe, 211
Alexander, Sidney S., 570–71
Alford, L.P., 124, 269
all inclusive income statement, 17, 121, 139, 454
Allan, J.N., 92
Allen, William H., 425
Altman, Edward, 252
Amaduzzi, A., 350
Ameiss, Albert P., 106
American Accounting Association, **32–34**
    committee reports, 8, 153, 177, 584, 618
    educational reform efforts, 6–7, 9
    founded by academic accountants, 6–7, 32, 37, 293
    promoted codified accounting principles, 16, 32, 194–95, 275–77
    publications, 3, 32, 275–76, 297
    research program, 8, 32, 177
    theory formulation, 3, 194–95, 275–77
    See also A Statement of Basic Accounting Theory; An Introduction to Corporate Accounting Standards
American Assembly of Collegiate Schools of Business, 7–8, 619
American Association of Public Accountants, 26, 34–37, 106, 107, 154, 156–57, 233, 322, 422, 429, 477–78, 530
American Association of University Instructors in Accounting, 6–7, 32, 37, 293, 362, 411, 610
American Bar Association, 49
American Institute of Accountants, 37–40
    Audits of Corporate Accounts, 51, 115, 275, 525
    Certified Public Accountant (CPA) exam, 37–38, 108
    codified accounting principles, 15, 493–94, 525
    Committee on Accounting Procedure, 11–12, 15, 39–40, 158, 246–47, 276, 284, 407, 453, 568
    Committee on Auditing Procedure, 39, 52, 410, 527, 560–61
    Committee on Cooperation with Stock Exchanges, 51, 115, 142, 275, 302, 407–8, 434, 440, 493
    Committee on Professional Ethics, 26, 322–24

255, 439, **532–33**
"replacement" or double account method, 204–5, **216–17**, 255–56, 496
in England, 101, 160, 162–63, 171, 204–5, 255–56, 295–96, 492
in the United States, 17, 44, 68, 92–93, 439–40
assets, concepts of, 92–93, 109–11, 198–201, 214–15, 230–31, 312–13
Association of Certified Fraud Examiners, 264
Assyria, 57–58, 566
audit committees, **48–50**, 406–7, 585, 597
auditing: external, **237–40**
    in the ancient world, 123, 237, 240, 287
    in medieval England, 237, 399, 590–91
    in Renaissance Italy, 76–77, 400
    in modern England, 62–63, 125, 137, 238, 342, 373–74, 384, 464–65, 537
    in the United States, 140, 234, 238
        balance sheet audit, 51, 163, 238, 342, 410, 594–95
        detailed audit, 238, 409–10, 421, 594–95
        modern audit programs, 28–29, 130, 142–43, 238–40, 341–44, 375–77, 406–7, 557–61, 583–85, 593–94
        operational auditing, 339, **441–43**
        statistical sampling, 343, **557–61**, 588–90
    See also internal auditing; internal control; legal liability of auditors
Auditing Standards Board, 41, 584
auditor's report, **50–54**, 138, 140–43, 234, 238, 275–76, 295, 399, 410, 537, 593, 594
Augspurg, G.D., 302–3, 481
Australia, 31, 47, **54–55**, 109–11, 134–35, 607
Austrian, Geoffrey D., 146, 149

Babbage, Charles, **57**, 124, 180, 550
Babylonia, **57–58**, 145, 184, 226, 237, 523–24, 313–14, 566
Backer, Morton, 214, 388
backlog, 143
bad debts, 24, **58–59**, 76–77, 114, 138, 160, 163, 171, 318, 411–12, 439, 456, 501
Badoer, Jachomo, **59–60**, 144
Bahnson, Paul R., 250
Bailey, Derek T., 509
Bailey, George D., 10
Baiman, Stanley, 27–29
Bakker, O., 432
Baladouni, Vahé, 4–5, 47, 221–23, 542–43, 615–16
balance account, **60**, 61, 63, 128, 241, 257, 400, 463, 587, 616
balance sheet, **60–64**
    in Australia, 134
    in England, 62–63, 66, 114, 137–39, 160, 187, 198, 216, 222–23, 387, 413, 492, 496, 591
    in Northern Europe, 62, 128, 279, 508, 515, 566, 576, 617
    in Renaissance Italy, 60–61, 76, 173–74, 187–

88, 411–12, 451, 463
    in the United States, 63–64, 97, 163–64, 230, 337, 387–89, 453–54, 480, 573, 588, 601
balance sheet audit, 51, 163, 238, 342, 410, 594–95
Ball and Brown's *An Empirical Evaluation of Accounting Income Numbers*, 54, **64–65**, 252
Ball, Raymond J., 54, 64–65, 69, 252
Balzer, Wolfgang, 437–38
Bank of England, 99, 383, 452, 543
banking and accounting, 14, 57, 58, 60–61, 63, 67, 72, 76, 122, 125, 141–42, 160, 163, 184, 251, 311, 357, 372, 411–12, 441, 506, 549
bankruptcy, 73, 89, 99, 113, 138, 162, 237–38, 252–53, 514
Bankruptcy Acts, 61, **65–66**, 238, 383
Barbarigo, Andrea, 60, **66–67**, 127
BarChris Case, 231–32, 375, 404, 494
Barcinski, Antoni, 466
Barden, Horace G., 13, 21
Bardi, 31, **67**, 76, 145, 411, 461
Barker, P., 236–37
Barnes, Paul, 251–53
Barr, Andrew, 10, 121, 144
Barrett, Gene R., 156
Barrett, Michael J., 343
Barrow, R.H., 507
Barrow, Wade, Guthrie and Company, 74, 106, 183
barter, 60, **67–68**, 133–34, 184, 286, 420–21, 456, 570
Barth, Mary, 69
Barton, Allan D., 79–81
Barzun, Jacques, 498
base stock method, **68–69**, 296, 346, 367–68, 513, 601
Bashe, C.J., 149
Basse v. Commissioner, 369
Bates v. the State Bar of Arizona, 26
Battersby, T., 136
Bauer, R.A., 538
Baumol, William, 583
Bavishi, Vinod B., 345
Baxter, William T., 68, 113, 188–89, 201, 479
Beamer Committee, 42, 169, 285
Beamer, Elmer G., 42, 169–70
Bean, Lu Ann G., 402–4
Bear, James A. Jr., 134
Beard, Victoria, 5, 6–9, 47
Beatty, S.G., 91
Beaver, William, **69–70**, 195, 252, 388
Becker, Edward A., 240
Becker, S., 393–94
Becker, Selwyn W., 86–87
Bedford Committee, 9
Bedford, Norton M., 10, 314–15
behavioral effects, 86–87, 300–1, 307–8, 393

Cutting, Robert Fulton, 425
Cyert, Richard M., 308
Czarniawska-Joerges, B., 343

Dafforne, Richard, 62, **187**, 190, 456
Dahl, Shirley J., 612
Dahlberg, J.S., 426
D'anastasio, Nicolo, 348
Dartmouth College v. Woodward, 6
Datar, Srikant M., 301–2
Datini, Francesco de Marco, 46, 76–77, 160, **187–88**
Davenport, R.W., 392
Davey Committee, 138
Davidson, E.E., 132–33
Davidson, H. Justin, 590
Davidson, Sidney, 10, 14, 20, 65, **188–89**
Davies, J.J., 254
Davies, P.M., 502
Davis, Harry Z., 68, 367–69
Davis, J.J., 232
Davis, J.P., 178
Dawes Plan, 564
Day, Clarence M., 181
daybook, 356–57, 372, 400, 415. *See* blotter, memorandum, and wastebook
Dean, Graeme W., 64–65, 109–11, 386, 516–18
Dean, Joel, 81, 209, 393–94, 502
Debessay, Araya, 281
debit and credit, 46, 48, 60, 66–67, **189–90**, 356, 446, 460, 482, 549
debtors, 65–66, 460
De Coster, Don T., 265, 267
Defense Production Act of 1950, 178–80
deferred charges and credits, 24, 101, 380–81, 387
deferred income tax accounting, **190–93**
deficiency statement, 66
definitions of accounting, 3, 11–14, **193–96**, 518–19
Defliese, Philip L., 10, 264
Defoe, Daniel, 4, 6
Degos, Jean-Guy, 496–99
de Graef, Abraham, 113–14
Degrange, Edmond Sr., 114, 259–60, 460, 548
DeLany, Clarence M., 73
De la Porte, Matthew, 259, 278, 548
Deloitte and Company, 75
Deloitte and Touche, 72–75, 105, 292, 395, 529
Deloitte Haskins and Sells, 72–75
Deloitte, Plender, Griffiths, 36, 389
Deloitte, William Welch, 72
Deming, W. Edwards, 176
De Mond, C.W., 75
De Morgan, Augustus, 460
Demski, Joel S., 28–29, 69, 196–97
Denmark, 428
Department of Defense, 85, 178–79
De Paula, F.C., 198
De Paula, Frederic Rudolf Mackley, 116, 118, **197–98**, 331

depreciation, **198–201**
  ancient and medieval, 160, 198, 591, 606
  in Northern Europe, 114, 161, 198–99, 278, 576–77
  in Renaissance Italy, 198
  in the United States and England, 14, 57, 59, 81–82, 95–98, 138, 141, 160–64, 171–73, 209, 367, 439–40, 491, 532–33, 576–77, 580–81
    accelerated vs. straight line, 97–98, 166, 200–1, 440, 570, 578, 602
    and accounting error, 59, 81–82, 95–98, 161–63, 216–17
    and capital maintenance, 95–98, 171, 532–33
    concepts of, 199–200, 204–5, 255–56, 367, 580–81, 606
    and railroad accounting, 216–17, 255–56
    on replacement cost, 17, 97, 203, 408, 462, 577, 601–2
    and tax regulations, 200–1, 439, 576–77
depressions and accounting development, 63, 66, 71, 73, 96, 162, 217, 252, 283, 320, 335, 337, 434, 452, 485, 489–90, 501, 527, 586, 595, 597, 601–2. *See also* business cycles
De Roover, Florence Edler, 135
De Roover, Raymond, 32, 64, 67, 77, 218, 372, 412, 465, 506, 572
Derrida, Jacques, 175
Dertouzos, M., 359
DeSte. Croix, G.E.M., 46, 506
Devine, Carl T., 68–69, 166, **202–3**, 539
Devore, Malcolm M., 324
De Vries, J., 433
De Waal, P.G.A., 433
Dewey, John, 8, 202–3
Dewey, Melvil, 36
Dewhirst, John F., 166
Dewing, Arthur Stone, 387–89
Dhaliwal, Dan S., 398
Diacont, George H., 122
Dickinson, Arthur Lowes, 10, 36, 97, **203–4**, 309–11, 391, 464, 511, 586–87, 601
Dicksee, Lawrence, 172–73, **204–5**, 238, 255–56, 342–43, 421, 464, 492
Diemer, Hugo, 228–29
Dillon, Gadis J., 435
Dingell Committee, 158–59, 585
Dingell, John D., 158, 249, 585
direct costing, 136, 181–82, **205–8**, 346–47, 353, 458
Directives of the European Community (Union), **235–37**, 260, 349, 433, 467, 598
Dirlam, Joel B., 212–14
disclosure:
  in Australia, 54
  in England, 62–63, 114, 125, 136–39, 140, 222–23, 384, 502, 567, 591
  in France and Germany, 114

Ernst, Alwin C., 73
Ernst and Ernst, 21, 73, 75, 122, 299–300, 395
Ernst and Ernst v. United States, 101
Ernst and Whinney, 72–75
Ernst and Young, 72–75, 395
Ernst, Theodore C., 73
Escott v. BarChris Construction Company, **231–**
    32, 375, 404, 494
Eskow, Benjamin, 253
Esquerré, Paul-Joseph, 265–67, 391, 586
estate accounting, 29, 111–13, 160, 237, 338, 346,
    351, 399, 413–14, 460, 567, 590
Estes, Ralph, 393–94
ethics, professional, 26–27, 38, 41–42, 74, 106,
    233–35, 276, 322–24, 331, 334, 336,
    396, 537–39, 563–64. *See also* advertis-
    ing by accountants, and independence of
    external auditors
European Accounting Association, 300
European Community (Union) accounting: Fourth
    and Seventh Accounting Directives, **235–**
    37, 260, 349, 433, 467, 598
European Economic Community, 235–37, 260
Evans, A.H., 229
Evans, Holden A., 135, 228
Evans, S.J., 28–29
Evers, Charles J., 484
Examination of Financial Statements by Indepen-
    dent Public Accountants (1936), 143,
    275, 316, 401, 594–95, 597
exchequer, 111, 464, 478–79, 575
executorship reporting, 413–14, 591
expenses, 76, 94, 231, 253, 356
extractive industries, 21
extraordinary gains and losses, 13, 316, 398
Ezersky, F., 508
Ezzamel, Mahmoud A., 354

FDIC Improvement Act of 1991, 49–50
Fabian, Tibor, 583
Fabricant, Solomon, 570
Fairness Doctrine, 165, 474, 538–39, 545–46
Falk, Haim, 240
Fama, Eugene F., 69
farm accounting. *See* agricultural accounting
Farolfi Company ledger, **241**, 357–58, 372
Fas, Emil, 518
Faure, Gabriel, 572
Fayol, Henri, 174
Federal Communications Commission (FCC), 296
Federal Energy Act, 121
federal government accounting (US), 133–34, **241–**
    46, 271–74. *See also* budgeting, General
    Accounting Office, US, Securities and
    Exchange Commission
Federal Reserve Board, 16, 51, 141, 157, 316, 524,
    594–95
Federal Trade Commission, 15, 37, 51, 141, 157,
    234, 310, 524, 594–95, 597, 599
Federal Trade Commission Act, 157

Feldhausen, E., 508
Feldstein, Martin, 577
Fells, John Manger, 135, 181, 206–7, 269–70
Felt, Dorr E., 145
Feltham, Gerald A., 28–29, 197
Fenn, D.H. Jr., 538
Ferrara, William L., 79–81
Ferrero, G., 350
Fesmire, Walker E., 573
Fess, Philip E., 388–89
feudalism, 111–13, 123, 399, 412–14, 591. *See*
    also manorial accounting, medieval ac-
    counting
Fibonacci, Leonardo, 45–46, 48, 145, 377–79, 446
Field, Marshall, 353
Field, Robert E., 13, 20
Fields, Kent T., 106–9
Fiflis, Ted, 101
Figlewicz, Raymond E., 554
Filios, Vassilios P., 113, 240
Financial Accounting Foundation, 40–41, 246–47,
    608
Financial Accounting Standards Advisory Council,
    247, 608
Financial Accounting Standards Board (FASB), 8,
    14, 40–41, 102, 121, 131–32, 142, 152–
    53, 158, 179, 194–95, 213, **246–50**,
    345, 470, 539–40, 595, 597, 607–8
  Conceptual Framework Project, 152–53
  Emerging Issues Task Force, 247–48
  Statements of Financial Accounting Concepts,
    14, 152
    SFAC No. 1, 152–53, 194–95, 474
    SFAC No. 2, 153, 403–4, 539–40
    SFAC No. 3, 153, 402
    SFAC No. 4, 153
    SFAC No. 6, 153, 191, 381–82
  Statements on Financial Accounting Standards,
    246–50
    SFAS No. 1, 258
    SFAS No. 2, 337, 596
    SFAS No. 5, 380
    SFAS No. 6, 381
    SFAS No. 8, 259
    SFAS No. 13, 381
    SFAS No. 14, 214
    SFAS No. 16, 316
    SFAS No. 19, 249
    SFAS No. 25, 249
    SFAS No. 32, 41, 132
    SFAS No. 33, 20, 98, 224, 297, 347, 421,
      462, 545, 573, 602
    SFAS No. 35, 20
    SFAS No. 36, 20, 381
    SFAS No. 52, 259
    SFAS No. 82, 297
    SFAS No. 87, 20, 381
    SFAS No. 89, 297, 347
    SFAS No. 93, 132, 249
    SFAS No. 95, 266–67, 277

General Accounting Office, US (GAO), 158, 176, 179, 244, **271–74**, 340, 441–43, 585

General Electric Corporation, 24

General Motors Corporation, 83–84, 353, 355, 502, 613

generally accepted accounting principles (GAAP), 3, 15, 20, 40, 43–44, 115, 139–44, 234, 274–78, 280–81, 302, 362–63, 401–2, 405, 407–8, 434, 511, 526, 528, 540, 545, 553–54, 589, 598, 600, 608. *See also* citations to individual principles

generally accepted auditing standards (GAAS), 234, 600

Genoa, 76, 135, 167, 180, 184, 217–18, 357, 372, 400, 452

Gerboth, Dale L., 277

Gerhardt, Paul, 32

German Commercial Code of 1897, 161

Germany, 47, 61, 114, 140, 144, 161, 178, 264–65, **278–80**, 361, 419–20, 514–16, 517–18, 519–20, 542, 564, 572, 576–77, 582, 598

Gerstenberg, Richard C., 20

Gerth, H.H., 175

Gibson, Robert W., 54–55

Gies, F., 379

Gies, J., 379

Gilbreth, Frank, 580

Gillespie, Cecil M., 551–52

Gilman, Stephen, 164, **280–81**, 334

Giovanni Farolfi and Company, **241**, 357–58, 372

Girshick, M.A., 197

Givens, Horace R., 6

Gleeson, Robert, 176–77

Gleim, Irvin N., 334

Glynn, John J., 443

Godefroid, H., 114

Goethe, Johann von, 4, 542

Goetz, Billy, 182

going concern concept. *See* continuity

Goldberg, Louis, 47, 134–35, 570, 606

Goldfarb v. Virginia State Bar, 234

Goldratt, Eliyahu, 80

Goldsmith bankers, 575

Goldsmith, Raymond, 428–29

Gomberg, Leon, 230, 508

Gonzalez Ferrando, J.M., 548

Goodman, Leonard, 42, 487–91, 524–29

Gorbachev, Mikhail, 509

goodwill, 14, 18, 20–21, 70, 104, 138, 163, 168, 204, 278, **281–84**, 336–38, 463, 469–70

Goodwin, J.H., 415

Goodwin, S., 324

Gordon, Cosmo, 588

Gordon, Irene M., 472

Gordon, Myron J., 397–98

Gordon, Paul N., 87

Gordon, Robert A., 8–9

Gore, Al, 246

Gosselin, David J., 271

Gossman, Martin L., 388

Gostomski, Anzelm, 465

Gottlieb, Johann, 61, 520

Goudeket, A., 462–63

Gould, J.F., 444

Gould, Jay, 434, 503

government accounting, 131–33, 241–46, 271–74, 286–87, 325, 348, 400, 424–26, 441–43, 464, 466, 546–47, 575–77, 597, 605. *See also* federal government accounting (US)

Government Corporation Control Act of 1945, 441–42

Government Finance Officers Association, 234

government regulatory bodies, 40, 125, 140, 143–44, 156–59, 241–46, 349, 352, 364–65, 441–43. *See also* companies acts, Federal Reserve Board, Federal Trade Commission, Securities and Exchange Commission, and Treasury Department

Governmental Accounting Standards Board (GASB), 41, 131–32, 247

Govindarajan, Vijay, 86–87

Grady, Paul, 10, 13, 20, 276, **284–85**, 297–98, 341, 343, 408

Graff, H.R., 498

Graham, Willard J., **285–86**

Grammateus, Henricus, 144, 519

Grant, Julia, 120–22

Grant, McB., 450–51

Graves, O. Finley, 270, 499, 518, 549–50, 572–74

Gray, Dahli, 259

Gray, Rob, 538–39

Greece, 48, 67, 114, 237, **286–87**, 338, 372, 420, 505, 566, 575–76

Greeley, Harry Dudley, 334

Green, D.I., 443

Green, David O., 86–87, 188–89, 393–94, 501

Green, Wilmer L., **287–88**

Greer, Howard, 181, 210–11, 276–77

Gregory case, **288–89**

Greidinger, B. Bernard, 338

Grier, Elizabeth, 340, 372–73

Groebner, David F., 235

Gross, Stanley C., 333

Gruchy, A.G., 127

Guilbault, Adolphe, 260

guilds, 170, 177, 180, 382

Gunther, Samuel P., 470

Guo, Daoyang, 122–23, **289**

Gupta, A.K., 87

Gutenberg, E., 419–20

Gutenberg, Johannes, 477

Guthrie, Edwin, 34, 106

Gutierrez-Hidalgo, Fernando, 47

Gynther, Reginald S., 98, 313, 315

Haberler, Gottfried von, 517

Habermas, Jurgen, 175

Hackett, Robert P., 553–54

Margerison, T., 332
marginal costs, 582
marine insurance, 60, 184
Marple, Raymond P., 207, 335
Marquette, R. Penny, 233–35, 424–26
Marshall, Alfred, 150, 208, 475, 501
Marshall Plan, 176, 362
Martin, A., 491
Martin, Jimmy W., 374–77
Martindell, Jackson, 442
Martinelli, Alvaro, 60, 218, 372–73
Martins, A., 79
Marwick, 73, 521
Marwick, Mitchell and Company, 521
Marwick, Mitchell, Peat and Company, 73, 521
Maslow, Abraham, 174
Mason, Alister K., 345
Mason, Perry E., 10, 13, 19, 266–67
Massari Commune ledgers, 218, **400**
matching concept, 23, 44, 68, 95, 101, 109, 129,
163–65, 172, 193, 197, 205, 256, 312,
347, 390, **401–2**, 439–40, 454, 457,
493–94, 581
materiality concept, 165, **402–4**, 557–61
mathematics and accounting, 145, 377–79, 480–81
Mattessich, Richard V., 151, 153, **404–5**, 436–38
Mauchly, John, 147
Mautz and Sharaf, *The Philosophy of Auditing*,
323–24, 406–7
Mautz, Robert K., 10, 48, 50, 234–35, 297–98,
323, **406–7**, 482–84, 597–98
May, George Oliver, 10, 15, 38–39, 51, 115, 161–
62, 164, 217, 224–25, 238–39, 275,
284, 295, 298, 302, 310–11, **407–8**,
434, 439, 475, 476, 493, 504, 525, 564,
566–67, 568–69, 570, 587, 597–98, 618
Maycock, R., 246
Mazdorov, V.A., 509
McBeth, Kevin H., 562–63
McCallum, David, 156
McCarl, J.R., 271
McCloy, John J., 42, 484
McCraw, T.K., 43
McCullers, Levis D., 201
McDonough, John J., 394
McFarland, Walter B., 214, 336
McGhee, Archie, 333
McGill, Gary A., 318–22, 534–35, 577–79
McGregor, Douglas, 174
McKesson and Robbins case, 39, 52, 121, 392,
409-10, 430, 527, 611
McKinsey, James O., 86–87, 174, 182, **410–11**
McLaren, N., 144
McLean, Judge Edward, 232
McLeod, Stuart C., 335
McMickle, Peter L., 134, 145–50, 520, 522
McMurray, K., 31
McNair, Carol J., 358–59
McNair Committee, 117, 119
McNair, Malcolm P., 175

McNall, P., 31
Mead, Edward Sherwood, 70, 398
Meade, James, 427
Means, Gardiner C., 39, 71–72
Means, Kathryn M., 193
Meckling, William H., 28–29
Medici Bank, 58, 76–77, 173–74, 357, **411–12**
Medici, Cosimo di, 576
Medici cost accounts, 180, **412**
Medici tax accounts, 576
medieval accounting, 101, 111–13, 160, 338, 346,
412–14, 464, 479, 506, 531, 546–48,
567, 575
Mednick, Robert, 396, 476
Melcher, Beatrice, 13, 21
Melis, Federigo, 144, 218, 257, 379
Mellerowicz, K., 417–18, 420
Mellis, John, 255, 441, 456, 532
Mellon, Andrew, 319–20
Melumad, Nahum D., 28–29
memorandum book, 128, 357, 372, 400, **415**, 571
Mepham, Michael J., 520–22
mercantilism, **415**
Merck, George, 610
mergers, 13–14, 17–18, 20, 156, 167–68, 212–14,
222, 239, 296, 468–71, 586, 608
Merino, Barbara D., 9, 82, 292, 476, 563–64, 594,
596, 598–99
Merz, C. Mike, 235, 359
Meservey, A.B., 533–34
Mesopotamia, 57–58, 340–41, 405–6
Metcalf, Lee, 158, 249, 396, 528
Metcalf Subcommittee, 158, 250, 396, 597–98
Metcalfe, Henry, 180–81, 206, 208, 392, **415–16**,
550, 580
Metropolis, N., 149
Metz, Jacob de, 547
Metz, M.S., 50
Metzger, R.O., 396–97
Mexico, 154, 564, 618
Mey, Abram, 386
Meyers, G.U., 336
microeconomics in Germany, **416–20**, 424, 466,
515–16, 582–83
Microsoft, 148–49
middle ages, 160, 412–14, 481–82, 515–16, 533.
See also manorial accounting, and medi-
eval accounting
Middleditch, Livingston, 572
Milan, 477
Miles, Edward V., 132–33
Miles, J.R., 283
Miller, Herbert E., 10, 32
Miller, Hermann C., 10
Miller, Merton H., 69
Miller, Paul B.W., 250
Miller, Peter, 261, 497, 499, 551–52
Miller, R., 91
Miller, Richard L., 232
Mills, C. Wright, 175

Pryce-Jones, J., 450–51
Ptolemy Philadelphus II, 287, 338
Public Oversight Board, 42, 343, **482–84**, 527
Public Utilities Holding Act of 1935, 526–27
Puechberg, Johann Matthias, 279–80, 582
Pujo, Arsene P., 525–26
purchase method of consolidation, 20
Puteani, Johann Freyherr von, 582
putting out manufacturers, 412
Pyhrr, P.A., 87
Pyle, William C., 304–5, 394

Quality Control Inquiry Committee, 483–84
quality review, 42, 555
quantifiability, 3, 19
quasi-reorganization, 15, 453, **485–86**
Queenan, John W., 10, 610
quipu, 461

R.G. Barry Corporation, 304
Rabito, George A., 169–70
Racketeer Influenced and Corrupt Organizations
        Act (RICO), 376, 495
Radford, Jack, 31
Rae, J., 536
railroad accounting, 35, 37, 63–64, 81, 95, 115,
        135, 141, 145, 156, 161–62, 180, 183,
        199–200, 204, 208, 216–17, 227, 229,
        255, 265, 295–96, 298, 315–16, 318,
        339, 380, 383–84, 387, 392, 434, **487–
        91**, 495–96, 500–504, 524, 536, 545,
        580, 588, 595–96, 596–98
Randolph, L.S., 228–29
ratio analysis, 69, 250–53, 387–88, 487, 501–2.
        See also current ratio, financial state-
        ment analysis, liquidity, and price-earn-
        ings ratio
Rayburn, Frank R., 178–80, 193, 470
Rayburn, L. Gayle, 211
Raymond, I.W., 185
Reagan, Ronald, 321, 578
realization concept, 14, 23–24, 93, 140, 164–65,
        173, 185, 205, 226, 256, 439–40, 458,
        475, **491–94**, 536
Reckers, Philip M.J., 404
Redding, Rodney J., 250
Reed, Sarah A., 602
regulation (Federal US) and accounting, 71–72,
        374–77, **494–95**, 503–4. See also Cost
        Accounting Standards Board, Federal
        Reserve Board, Federal Trade Commis-
        sion, Securities and Exchange Commis-
        sion, and Treasury Department
Regulation of Railways Act of 1868, 63, 217, 384,
        495–96
Reichelstein, Stefan, 28–29
Reid, Jean Margo, 377
Reiling, Henry B., 601
Reiss, H.F. Jr., 431
Reitell, Charles, 181, 210, 212

relevance concept, 3, 285, 562
religion and accounting, 170, 177, 412, 505, 508,
        566
Remington Rand, 147
Remis, J.S., 555
Renaissance, 23, 445–46, 481
Renold, Hans, 124
research and development costs, 14, 21, 337
research methods in accounting history, 46–47,
        364, **496–99**
reserve-recognition accounting, 121
residual equity theory, **499**
Resnick v. Touche Ross and Company, 376
resource allocation, 62, 582
responsibility accounting, 62
retained earnings, 14, 17, 94, 114, 138, 316, 363,
        439, 449, 485, **499–500**
retained earnings appropriations, 17–18, 63, 114,
        138, 160, 163, 171, 316, **501**
return on investment, 83, 208–9, 393, 452, 487–
        90, **501–2**, 536
revenues, 94, 231, 356
Reves v. Ernst and Young and Company, 495
Revsine, Lawrence, 224, 315
Rex v. Kylsant, **502**
Ricardo, David, 518
Richard, Thomas, 112
Richards, W.B., 310–11
Richardson, A.P., 109
Richardson, Alan J., 89–92
Richmond, Robert L., 333
Rickover, Admiral Hyman G., 178–79
Riggs, J.B., 47
Rimerman, Thomas W., 556
Ripley, William Z., 38–39, 43, 434–35, 491, **502–
        5**, 525
Ritchie, D.A., 529
Ritty, James, 145
Robert Morris Associates, 251
Robert, Rudolph, 575
Roberts, Alfred R., 3, 33, 421–22, 564–65
Roberts, D., 31
Roberts, Elizabeth, 84–87
Roberts, Michael L., 322
Robertson, Alexander Weir, 477
Robinson, H.W., 66
Rockefeller, John D., 6, 167, 425, 434
Rogers, Rodney K., 548–50
Rogers, Wade, 261
Roland, Henry, 228–29
Roll, Richard, 69
Roman numerals, 46, 48, **505–6**
Rome, 48, 177, 286, 338, 372, 412, 420, 424, 481,
        505–7, 533–34, 566, 575–76, 590, 606
Ronen, Joshua, 398–99
Roos, Charles F., 595–96
Roosevelt, Franklin D., 39, 142, 157, 320, 363,
        505, 526
Roosevelt, Theodore, 36–37, 157, 243, 319, 489,
        503, 534

and audit committees, 48–49
and auditor independence, 322–23
and auditors' reports, 52
chief accountants of, **120–22**
and McKesson and Robbins case, 51–52, 409–10, 527
Securities Act of 1933, 39, 71, 142, 157, 193, 232, 238–39, 296, 322, 375, 494–95, 505, 524, 525–26
Securities and Exchange Commission Act of 1934, 39, 71, 142, 157, 193, 294, 296, 299, 375, 494–95, 505, 524–25, 527
Securities Act of 1970, 527
Staff Accounting Bulletin (SAB) 78, 485
See also Accounting Series Releases
Sefcik, Stephen E., 471–72
segment reporting, 211–14, 393, 602
Seidler, L.L., 394
Seidler, Lee J., 393–94
Seidman, Jack S., 568–69
Seligman, B.B., 127
Seligman, J., 529
Sells, Elijah Watt, 10, 73, 243, 292, 430, **529–30**
Senior, Nassau William, 304
separate entities concept, 61, 128–29, 382, 447, 451, 463, 473, 531–32
Serra, Luigi, 47
shadow prices, 419, 582–83
Shand, Alexander Allan, 352
Shannon, H.A., 66
Sharaf, Hussein A., 234–35, 323–24, 406–7
Sharfman, I.L., 491
Shaw, R.W., 86–87
Sheldahl, Terry K., 71, 587
Shenkir, William G., 134, 569–70
Sheremet, A., 509
Shillinglaw, Gordon, 459
Shimono, Naotaro, 352
Short, F.G., 344
Shriver, Keith A., 224
Shui, Qiu, 289
Siers, H.L., 106
Simon, Herbert A., 174, 307–8, 437–38, 471
Simon, Hermann Veit, 278, 280
Simons, Henry C., 577
single account method, 204–5, 255, 439, **532–33**
single entry bookkeeping, 101, 111–13, 128, 187, 355, 413, 513, 531, **533–34**, 610
Sinha, K.K., 25
sinking fund, 601
Sixteenth Amendment, 59, 73, 84, 256, 319, 422, 429, 439, 468, 492, **534–35**
Skinner, Ross M., 91–92
Skousen, K. Fred, 214, 529
Skrzywan, S., 467–68
Slater, R., 150
Slaymaker, Adrianne E., 150–54, 473–76, 588–90
Sloan, A.P., 84
Smails, R.G.H., 91
Small, A.W., 280

Smith, Adam, 57, 71, 150, 303, 387, 415, 439, 501, **535–36**
Smith, C.A., 340
Smith, J. David, 209
Smith, L.M., 6
Smith, Mary Harris, 331
Smith, Oberlin, 228
Smith, Raymond F., 252–53
Smith v. London Assurance Corporation, 374–75
Smith, William Robert, 93
Smith, William S., 334
Smolinski, H. Carl, 287
Smullyan, Raymond, 308–9
Smykay, E.K., 491
Smyth v. Ames, 489, 504, **536–37**
Snell, Charles, **537**, 544
Sobel, R., 435
social audit, 538
social responsibilities of accountants, 4–5, 82–83, 126, 233–35, 393–94, 424–26, 522–23, **537–39**
Social Science Research Council, 39
socialism, 581–83
Societas Maris, 135
Society of Accountants in Edinburgh, 477
Society of Incorporated Accountants, 330–31
Sokolov, Jaroslav, 508–9
Solomon, Jerome P., 556
Solomons, David, 105, 118–19, 129, 227, 314–15, 393–94, **539–41**, 608
Solorzano, Bartolome Salvador de, 547
Solow, R.M., 359
solvency, 166, 386, 389
Sombart, Werner, 4, 6, 94, 218, 424, 497, 532, **541–42**, 615
Someya, Kyojiro, 353
Sommer, A.A., Jr., 482–84
Soranzo Brothers, 93, 216
Sorter, George H., 207, 590
Soulé, George, 6, **542–43**
Souzo Brito, Gabriel de, 547
South Sea Bubble, 62, 178, 383, 452, 537, **543–44**
Sowell, Ellis Mast, 292
Spacek, Leonard, 10–11, 18, 474, **544–46**, 619
Spain, 46–47, 48, **546–48**
specialized journals, 400
Sperry, John B., 197–98, 237
Spicer, E.E., 119
Spinoza Cattela, Robert C., 386, 462–63
Sprague, Charles Ezra, 10, 70, 94, 150, 153, 190, 230, 453, 481, **548–50**, 571, 610, 619
Springer, Durand, 38
Springer v. United States, 318, 534, **550**
Sproul, A.H., 512
Sprouse, Robert T., 13, 19, 22, 276, 382, 423–24, 494
Staats, Elmer B., 10, 179, 273
Stabler, Henry Francis, 407–8
Stackelberg, H. von, 416, 420, 582
Staehling, Charles, 423–24

Sylvestre, Anne Jeannette, 26–27
Szychta, Anna, 465–68

Tabb, J. Bruce, 543–44
Taft, William Howard, 243, 246, 489
Taggart, Herbert F., 402, 454
Tagliente, Giovanni Antonio, 347
Takatera, Sadao, 64
tally stick, 479, **575**
Tammany Hall, 425
Tanner, E.L., 116, 119
target costing, 81, 551–52
Taussig, Russell A., 601
tax ordained accounting, 216, 286–87, 367–69, 439–40, 464, 478–79, 481, 491, 550, **575–77**. *See also* income taxes
tax reform acts, **577–79**
tax shelters, 578
Taylor, Fred M., 583
Taylor, Frederick Winslow, 124, 135–36, 174–75, 181, 227–29, 269, 353, 393–94, 425, 489, 550, **579–80**
Taylor, R. Emmett, 421
Taylor, R.F., 610–11
Tearney, Michael G., 438
Ten Have, O., 433, 565–66
Tennessee Valley Authority, 24–25, 175–76, 181, 183
tentativeness concept, 17, 19, 474
terminology, 15, 18, 363, 596, 598
Thaer, Albrecht Daniel, 582
theory of constraints, 80–81
third party responsibility, 538
Thomas, Arthur L., 200–1, 401–2, 494, 580–81
Thomas, Deborah W., 402–4
Thomas, Wade, and Guthrie, 34
Thomashower, James E., 555–56
Thomas's *The Allocation Problem in Financial Accounting Theory*, **580–81**
Thompson, Huston, 526
Thompson, Joel E., 453–54
Thompson, Julian, 409
Thomson, H.W., 24
Thorndike, Edward L., 8
Thunen, Johann Heinrich von, 304
Thurston, John B., 333
Tierney, C.E., 246
Tierney, Cecelia V., 22
Tinbergen, Jan, 427
Tinius, David E., 447
Tinker, Anthony Maxwell, 82–83, 612–13
Titard, Pierre L., 397
Tondkar, Rasoul H., 235–37, 356
Tonge, Stanley D., 239–40
Tonzig, Antonio, 348
total quality control, 354
Touche, George A., 73
Touche, Niven and Company, 73–74, 370, 593
Touche, Niven, Bailey and Smart, 74
Touche Ross and Company, 41, 72–75, 91, 105, 507

Touche Ross Foundation, 48
Towne, H.R., 135, 228–29, 579
Towne v. Eisner, 226, 492, 567–68
Townshend, Charles, 535
trademarks, 138, 336–38
transaction analysis, 400
transfer prices, 83–84, 393, **581–83**
Transportation Act of 1935, 490
Transportation Act of 1940, 490
Trask, Roger R., 271–74
Treadway Commission, 49–50, 122, 158–59, 234–35, 340, 371, **583–85**
Treadway, James C. Jr., 49, 159, 584
Treasury Department, 68, 85, 157, 242–44, 272, 296, 577–79, 599
treasury stock, 16, 275–76, **586–87**
Trenchant, Jan, 145, 208
Trevor v. Whitworth, 586
trial balance, 61–62, 67, 127–29, 183, 187, 347, 356, 446, 463, 572, **587–88**
Trotter, Alexander, 29
Trueblood Committee, 41, 152, 224, 424, 474, 476, 608
Trueblood, Robert Martin, 10, 41, 176, 277, **588–90**
Truman, Harry S., 320, 362
Trust Indenture Act of 1939, 527
trustee accounts, 111–13, 412–14, **590–91**
trusts, 167, 178, 599-600, 601–2
Tsuji, Atsuo, 361–62
Tucker, James J. III, 557–61, 567–69, 594–95
Turck, J.A.V., 145, 150
Turkey, 114
Turner, Deborah H., 193
Turner, Thomas, 6, 415
Tweed Ring, 36
Tyler, Judge Harold R., 254
Tyson, Thomas N., 325–27
Tyzenhauz, Antoni, 466

Ueno, Michisuke, 352
Ultramares Corporation v. Touche, Niven & Company, 232, 370, 375, 525, **593–94**
uncertainty, 165–66
Uniform Accountancy Act of 1992, 555–56
Uniform Accounting (1917), 15, 51, 141–42, 144, 203–4, 274–75, 278, 316, 318, 337, 342, 387, **594–95**, 597
uniform accounting systems, 113–15, 178–80, 180–81, 259–62, 344–45, 408, 425–26, 427–29, 446, 467, 488, 504, 509, 512, 515–16, 524, 553, 555–56, 588, **595–96**, 597–98
uniformity, 38, 70, 113–15, 139–44, 178–80, 204, 259–62, 408, 493, **596–98**
U.S. Industrial Commission, **598–600**
U.S. v. Benjamin, 376
U.S. v. Natelli, 376
U.S. v. Weiner, 376
United States v. Arthur Young, 371